A BIBLIOGRAPHY OF
LATIN AMERICAN BIBLIOGRAPHIES

Compiled by

Arthur E. Gropp, Librarian

An updating of the Second Edition
(1942) compiled by C. K. Jones in
the Hispanic Foundation of the
Library of Congress

The Scarecrow Press, Inc.
Metuchen, N.J.   1968

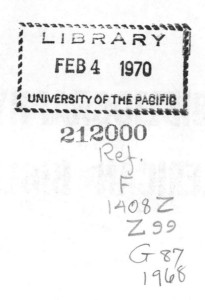
Copyright 1968, by Pan American Union
Library of Congress Card No. 68-9330

Table of Contents

INTRODUCTION

The compiling of bibliographies of bibliographies began, historically with the contribution of Antoine Teissier (1) Catalogus Auctorum Qui Librorum Catalogos, published
in Geneva in 1686. Later, outstanding works of the 19th Century are: Bibliotheca Bibliographica (Leipzig, 1866) by Julius Petzholdt; Bibliographie des Bibliographies
(Paris, part 1, author arrangement, 1883; part 2, subject arrangement, 1887) by León
Vallée; and Manuel de Bibliographie Générale (Paris, 1897) by Henri Stein. These compilations reflected the need of the times in an attempt to keep pace with the extraordinary increase in publishing as the 19th Century drew to a close.

Bibliographers and librarians, confronted with the ever increasing volume of publication have been hard-pressed to maintain an up-to-date record of production, and at the
same time comply with demands for the dissemination of bibliographic information.
Fremont Rider (2) already in 1944, felt that American research libraries which try to
collect everything on a given subject would double their size every 16 years. Otto
Frank in 1961 (3) avers that if a chemist fluent in 30 languages "started on January
1st to read all the papers in his particular field for 40 hours a week ... by December
31st he would have read not more than one-thenth of all the material published during
that year". Frank affirms, further, that in this situation the chemist would have no
remaining time to apply the knowledge gained.

It is in this setting that bibliographers, librarians and documentalists undertake to
define and resolve the problem of presenting in the briefest time possible, a record of
what has been published and what is being published. Those who are engaged in Latin
American studies are intensely aware that the sources of information, generally speak-
ing, are not thus far organized so as to constitute a comprehensive dissemination of
bibliographic information. It is estimated that more than 20,000 publications in monographic form and an equal number of periodical titles are published annually throughout Latin America. When Libros en Venta (4) was published by the R. R. Bowker Company
in 1964, and its Suplemento (5) in 1967, a greater body of bibliographic information
about Latin American publications was made accesible. Nevertheless, the research
worker still needs additional information to bibliographic sources on Latin America.

Among the most rewarding "aids to information" covetted by the student and investiga-
tor is the bibliography of bibliographies. With respect to Latin America, the first
bibliography of bibliographies was the compilation by Cecil Knight Jones (1872-1945)
published in 1922. Earlier bibliographers who list bibliographies useful in Latin
American research, are: James Jackson, who included 137 references to America in his
Liste Provisoire des Bibliographies Geographiques (2a. ed. Paris, 1881); John Boynton
Kaiser, who included only South America in his work, The National Bibliographies of the
South American Republics (Boston, 1913. Bulletin of Bibliography Pamphlets, no. 21);
Ramón A. Laval, who referred to bibliographies concerning Chile in his Bibliografía de

1) Besterman, Theodore. World Bibliography of Bibliographies; 4th ed. 1965-1966.
    v.1, col. 17-18.
2) Quotation from Otto Frank, Modern Documentation and Information Practices (The
    Hague, FID Publication 334, 1961. p. 11) citing F. Rider, The Scholar and the Fu-
    ture of the Research Library (New York, 1944).
3) Frank, Otto. Op. cit., p.12.
4) Libros en Venta en Hispanoamérica y España. New York, 1964. 1891 p. Contains
    over 87,000 items.
5) Ib. Suplemento. Buenos Aires, 1967. 683 p. Contains 30,000 items.

Bibliografías Chilenas (6) (Santiago de Chile, 1915); and Narciso Binayán, who compiled a list of bibliographies concerning Argentina in his Bibliografía de Bibliografías Argentinas (7) (Buenos Aires, 1919). Subsequently, in 1922, Binayán compiled a similar work with reference to Paraguay, Bibliografía de Bibliografías Paraguayas (8).

In 1922 Cecil Knight Jones emerged as the pioneer figure with respect to bibliography concerning Latin America as a whole. Jones was on the staff of the Library of Congress from 1900 until the time of his death in 1945. In 1920 he joined the George Washington University faculty as instructor in Spanish American literature. It was during his teaching career that Jones began the compilation of needed bibliographic information as an aid to his course. Simultaneously he published his findings in the Hispanic American Historical Review, 1920-1921. Then in 1922 he published a cumulated edition under the title, Hispanic American Bibliographies, citing references to 1,281 publications. Jones followed with seven supplements from 1927-1938, all published in the Hispanic American Historical Review.

The Hispanic Foundation of the Library of Congress suggested to Jones that he prepare a second edition of his bibliography. The completed compilation was published by the Library of Congress in 1942 with a new title, Bibliography of Latin American Bibliographies. The new edition contained 3,016 numbered and approximately 500 inserted items, totaling references to nearly 3,500 publications: monographs, indexes, catalogs, articles from periodicals, general books containing bibliographies, and some reference and miscellaneous works.

The present compilation is an effort to bring the Jones second edition up-to-date. It was undertaken as a result of repeated recommendations in various conferences, meetings, and seminars, principally the Seminar on the Acquisition of Latin American Library Materials, held annually under the auspices of the Pan American Union, now in its 13th year. Work began in 1963 with a close scrutiny of the second edition for the purpose of including as many as possible of the items cited by Jones. Approximately 2,900 were accepted. These are identified in the bibliography by a reference to the item number in the second edition. The exclusions are principally items obviously not bibliographic in nature, such as diplomatic lists, directories of personnel, most genealogies, and many works of a general nature. When possible, a doubtful item was examined, and if the publication referred to contained bibliographic information, the item cited by Jones was retained for the present edition.

Jones included many references to articles in periodicals and to books of a general nature that contained bibliographies. However, it was soon recognized that an examination of this voluminous literature for bibliographic content was not possible in this edition. Consequently, the present compilation comprises the items retained, some 2,900, from the Jones 1942 edition, and the more than 4,000 new references to publications of a monographic nature, attaining a total of 7,210 numbered plus a considerable number of inserted items, all with imprint dates before January 1, 1965.

Jones organized his Bibliography by country, whereas, in the present compilation the arrangement is by subject (see list of subjects which follows), an apprach which was chosen in the firm belief that it offers the specialist definite advantages. However, within the subject groups, the usual arrangement is geographical by country. Subject subdivisions are occasionally used in order to bring together under a single heading,

---

6) Also included in Emilio Vaïsse, Bibliografía General de Chile (Santiago de Chile, 1915. p. i-lxii).
7) Reprinted from Revista de la Universidad de Buenos Aires, t.43, p. 114-49.
8) Reprinted from Humanidades, Buenos Aires, v.3.

specific topics such as the Common Market under Economics, Coffee and Cacao under Agriculture, names of languages under Language, names of religious orders under Religion, and the name of the biographee under Biography (Individual).

The Bibliography is accompanied by a detailed index to names of persons, corporate bodies, government offices, titles of series and subject entries. Also included in the index are the main subject groups and the subdivisions under each. The main subject groups are identified by an asterisk (*).

The usefulness of any bibliography, to a large degree, is enhanced by the availability of the works cited. In this bibliography when the entry does not indicate the source, the reader may assume it to be obtainable in the Columbus Memorial Library and/or in the Library of Congress. Otherwise, an alternate source for bibliographic information is noted. These sources are listed below, accompanied by the item number if included in the Bibliography.

The compiler gratefully acknowledges the help received from many persons who provided useful information leading to the addition of numerous items to the bibliography. He is especially indebted to the staff of the Columbus Memorial Library who were on the watch for new acquisitions that otherwise might have been overlooked. Special thanks go to Mrs. María E. Olivera de Gowland for the task of preparing draft copy, and to Mrs. Sylvia Gajardo de Poblete for the many hours of dedicated work in preparing copy for the publisher.

Arthur E. Gropp, Librarian
Columbus Memorial Library

Washington, D.C.
September 1968

ABREVIATIONS

COLBAV	Colegio de Bibliotecónomos y Archivistas de Venezuela
DPU	Pan American Union. Columbus Memorial Library
HLAS	Handbook of Latin American Studies
LC	Library of Congress
PAIGH	Pan American Institute of Geography and History
OAS	Organization of American States
US	United States of America
UN	United Nations
UNESCO	United Nations Educational, Scientific and Cultural Organization

SOURCES CITED

ADAMS, Eleanor Burnham. A bio-bibliography of Franciscan authors in colonial Central America. Washington, D.C., 1953. xxi, 97 p. (Publ. of the Academy of American Franciscan History, Bibliographical ser., v.2)   (6941

ANUARIO bibliográfico colombiano, 1951/1956- . Bogotá, 1958- .   (1001

ANUARIO bibliográfico costarricense, 1956- . San José, 1958- .   (1016

ANUARIO bibliográfico cubano, see Bibliografía cubana.

ANUARIO bibliográfico peruano, 1943- . Lima, 1945- .   (1131
    Cited in some cases as Bib. peruana.

ANUARIO bibliográfico salvadoreño, 1952. San Salvador, 1954. 39 p. (Anexo de "Ana-
    queles", ép 5, no.4, 1954)   (1047

ANUARIO bibliográfico venezolano, 1942- . Caracas, 1944- .   (1154
    Cited in some cases as An. Venez.

ARCHILA, Ricardo. Bibliografía médica venezolana; 2a. ed. Caracas, 1955.
    1041 p.   (5635a

ARGENTINA. Biblioteca Nacional. La Biblioteca Nacional en 1945-46. Buenos Aires,
    1947. 155 p.

-----. Ministerio de Agricultura y Ganadería. Departamento de Bibliotecas. Exposi-
    ción internacional del libro cooperativo. Buenos Aires, 1959. 63 p. (Circular bi-
    bliográfica, no. 9)   (3194
    Cited as Circular bibliográfica.

AYALA ECHAVARRI, Rafael. Bibliografía histórica y geográfica de Querétaro. México,
    D.F., 1949. 387 p. (Monografías bibliográficas mexicanas, 2a. ser., no.2)   (3567

BAYITCH, S. A. Latin America; a bibliographical guide to economy, history, law, poli-
    tics and society. Coral Gables, Fla., 1961. 335 p. (Interamerican legal studies,
    no. 6)   (25

BIBLIOGRAFIA argentina de artes y letras, no.1- , en./mar. 1959- . Buenos
    Aires.   (5753

BIBLIOGRAFIA brasileira, 1938/1939- . Rio de Janeiro, 1941- .   (971

BIBLIOGRAFIA brasileira de ciências sociais, v.1, no.1- , 1954- .   (7066

BIBLIOGRAFIA brasileira de documentação, v.1: 1811/1960. Rio de Janeiro, 1960.
    237 p.   (877

BIBLIOGRAFIA cubana, 1937- . Habana, 1938- .   (1020

BINAYAN, Narciso. Bibliografía de bibliografías argentinas. Buenos Aires, 1919.
    39 p.   (905

BISSAINTHE, Max. Dictionnaire de bibliographie haitienne. Washington, D.C., 1951.
1052 p. (1067

BOLETIM bibliográfico, Biblioteca Nacional, n.s., v.1- , 1951- . Rio de Janeiro. (5880

BOLETIN de adquisiciones, no.1- , oct. 1959- . Medellín. (5981

BOLETIN de la Biblioteca Nacional, 2a. ép., t.1- , en./mar. 1950- . Mexico, D.F. (6094

BRAZIL. Arquivo Nacional. Elenco das publicações e dos documentos. Rio de Janeiro,
1941. 736 p. (515

BRISEÑO, Ramón. Estadística bibliográfica de la literatura chilena. Santiago,
1862-1879. 2 v. (989

BRYANT, Shasta M. A selective bibliography of bibliographies of Hispanic American
literature. Washington, D.C., 1966. 48 p. (Pan American Union. Division of
Philosophy and Letters. Basic bibliographies, 3)

BUENOS AIRES. Universidad. Instituto bibliotecológico. Catálogo de la Biblioteca;
obras. Buenos Aires [1964] 146 p. (2500

CARREÑO, Alberto María. Semblanzas. Mexico, D.F., 1936-1939. 3 v. (Colección de
obras diversas, 2, 5, 8)

CHAVES, Alfredo. Fuentes principales de la bibliografía ecuatoriana. Quito, 1958.
24 p. (Asociación de Bibliotecarios del Ecuador. Grupo Bibliográfico Nacional,
Publ., no. 1) (921

CURRENT Caribbean bibliography, v.1- , June 1951- . Port-of-Spain, Caribbean
Commission. (67

DE NOIA, John. Brazil. Washington, D.C., 1948. 223 p. (Library of Congress; Latin
American ser., no. 35) (3751
Vol. 3 of A guide to the official publications of the other American republics.

DORIA, Irene de Menezes. The situation of bibliography in Brazil. Washington, D.C.,
1964. 21, 18 p. (IX Seminar on the Acquisition of Latin American Library Materials,
St. Louis, 1964. Working paper no. 7) (909

FLOREN LOZANO, Luis. Bibliografía bibliotecológica colombiana, 1953/1955- . Bogotá,
1956- . (Manuales de bibliografía y documentación colombiana, 1) (5031
Cited in some cases as Florén, 1961-1962.

-----. Bibliografía de la bibliografía dominicana. Ciudad Trujillo, 1948.
66 p. (920

FLORIDA. University. Libraries. Caribbean acquisitions, 1957/1958- . Gainesville,
1959- . (85
Cited as Caribbean acquisitions.

GEOGHEGAN, Abel Rodolfo. Obras de referencia de América Latina. Buenos Aires [1965]
280 p.

GIRALDO JARAMILLO, Gabriel. Bibliografía de bibliografías colombianas; 2a. ed. corr. y puesta al día por Rubén Pérez Ortiz. Bogotá, 1960. xvi, 204 p. (Instituto Caro y Cuervo. Publ.; ser. bibliográfica, 1)   (916

GONZALEZ Y GONZALEZ, Luis. Fuentes de la historia contemporánea de México. Libros y folletos, I . Mexico, D.F., 1961. lxxxii, 527 p.   (4041

GROPP, Arthur Eric. Guide to libraries and archives in Central America and the West Indies, Panama, Bermuda, and British Guiana. New Orleans, La., 1941. 721 p. (Publ. of the Middle American Research Institute, no. 10)   (426

-----. Bibliografía sobre las bibliotecas nacionales de los países latinoamericanos y sus publicaciones. Washington, D.C., 1960. 58 p. (Columbus Memorial Library. Bibliographic ser., no. 50)   (5040

GUIDE to microforms in print, 1961- . Washington, D.C., Microcard Editions.

HANDBOOK of Latin American studies, 1935- . Cambridge, Mass.; Gainesville, Fla., 1936- .   (97

HILL, Roscoe R. National archives of Latin America. Cambridge, Mass., 1945. 169 p.   (431

IGLESIAS, Dolores. Bibliografia e índice da geologia do Brasil, 1641-1940. Rio de Janeiro, 1943. 323 p. (Brazil. Depto. Nacional da Produção Mineral. Divisão de Geologia e Mineralogia, Boletim 111)   (3679

IGUINIZ, Juan Bautista. Algunas bibliografías mexicanas. (El Libro y el pueblo., México, D.F., t.11, p. 300-05, 338-43, 416-21, 456-63, 1933)   (939

INSTITUTE of Jamaica. West India Reference Library. A list of books on West Indian Federation; 2d ed. compiled by Anne Benewick. Kingston, 1962. 47 p.   (6833

INTER-AMERICAN review of bibliography, v.1, no.1- , Jan./Mar. 1951- . Washington, D.C.   (6186

JONES, Cecil Knight. A bibliography of Latin American bibliographies; 2d. ed. Washington, D.C., 1942. 307 p. (Library of Congress; Latin American ser., 2)   (924

KER, Annita Melville. Mexican government publications. Washington, D.C., 1940. 333 p.   (3793

LA PLATA. Universidad Nacional. Facultad de Ciencias Jurídicas y Sociales. Biblioteca. Catálogo general de obras y autores. La Plata, 1939. 1105 p.   (2529

LAVAL, Ramón A. Bibliografía de bibliografías chilenas. Santiago de Chile, 1915. 71 p.   (912

MARTINEZ, Angelina, and JAMES, C. Noel. Café. Turrialba, C.R., 1960. 637 p. (Instituto Interamericano de Ciencias Agrícolas. Biblioteca. Lista bibliográfica, no.1, rev.)   (266

MEXICO, Universidad Nacional. Instituto de Geología. Publicaciones editadas desde su fundación (1895) hasta el mes de julio de 1957. México, D.F., 1957. 26 p.   (4430

MILLARES CARLO, Agustín, and MANTECON, José Ignacio. Ensayo de una bibliografía de
bibliografías mexicanas. México, D.F., 1943. xvi, 224 p.   (941
   Cited as Millares.

-----. Registro bibliográfico, 1940-1941. México, D.F., 1941. 2 v.   (138

MUSSO AMBROSI, Luis Alberto. Bibliografía de bibliografías uruguayas. Montevideo,
1964. vii, 102 p.   (947

-----. Bibliografía del Poder Legislativo desde sus comienzos hasta el año 1965.
Montevideo, 1967. 236.

OCHSENIUS, Hermina Elgueta de. Suplemento y adiciones a la Bibliografía de bibliografías chilenas que publicó en 1915 Ramón A. Laval. Santiago, 1930. 71 p.   (913

PAN AMERICAN Institute of Geography and History. Catálogo de la Biblioteca. Tacubaya,
D.F., México, 1940. 412 p. (Publ. 47)   (2826

-----. -----. México, D.F., 1945. 2v. (Publ. 79)   (2827

PAN AMERICAN UNION. Columbus Memorial Library. Bibliographies pertaining to Latin
America in the Library of the Pan American Union. Washington, D.C., 1928.
34 p.   (928
   Cited as PAU Bibliographies

PAULUS, Wolfgang. Lateinamerika. 2. völlig neubearbeitete auflage. Freiburg, 1964.
278 p. (Materialien des Arnold-Bergstraesser-Instituts für kulturwissenschaftliche
forschung)   (183

PERAZA SARAUSA, Fermín. Bibliografías corrientes de la América Latina, 1962- . Medellín, Col. [etc.] 1962- . (Biblioteca del bibliotecario, 65)   (933

-----. Fichas para el anuario bibliográfico colombiano, t.1- . Medellín, Col.;
Gainesville, Fla, 1961- . (Biblioteca del bibliotecario, 61-2, 67-8, 71-2)   (1012

REIS, Antonio Simões dos. Bibliografia das bibliografias brasileiras. Rio de Janeiro,
1942. 186 p. (Instituto Nacional do Livro. Coleção B 1; Bibliografia 1)   (911

REVISTA do livro, ano 1, no.1- , jun. 1956. Rio de Janeiro.   (5928

RICHARDSON, Ivan L. Bibliografia brasileira de administração pública e assuntos corre-
latos. Rio de Janeiro, 1964. xxii, 840 p.   (6849

SABOR, Josefa Emilia. Manual de fuentes de información. Buenos Aires, 1957. 335 p.
(Contribuciones bibliotecológicas, 2)   (5086

SANTIAGO, Chile. Universidad Católica. Biblioteca Central. Bibliografía eclesiástica
chilena. Santiago, 1959. xxx, 358 p.   (6894
   Cited by title.

SÃO PAULO. Universidade. Biblioteca Central. Indice bibliográfico das publicações da
Universidade de São Paulo. São Paulo, 1951- .   (4436

SCHAIBLE, Carl H. Bibliografía de José Toribio Medina. Santiago de Chile, 1952. xviii,
251 p.   (1829

SOCIEDAD ARGENTINA de Bibliotecarios de Instituciones Sociales, Científicas, Artísticas y Técnicas, Buenos Aires. Catálogo colectivo de publicaciones periódicas existentes en bibliotecas científicas y técnicas argentinas; 2a. ed. Buenos Aires,
1962. 1726 p.   (6387

TORO, Alfonso. El dr. dn. Agustín Rivera y San Román. México, D.F., 1917.
86 p.   (1971
    "Bibliografía" by Juan B. Iguíniz.

TORRES QUINTERO, Rafael. Bibliografía de Rufino José Cuervo. Bogotá, 1951. 104 p.
(Publ. del Instituto Caro y Cuervo, Ser. minor, 2)   (1563

UNION LIST of serials in libraries of the United States and Canada; 3d. ed. edited
by Edna Brown Titus. New York, 1965. 5 v.

URUGUAY. Ministerio de Agricultura y Ganadería. Biblioteca Central. Bibliografía
agrícola del Uruguay, 1962/1963- . Montevideo.   (305

VALLE, Rafael Heliodoro. Bibliografía mexicana (1937-1938) (Hispanic American historical review, Durham, N.C., v.20, p. 294-334, 686-746, May, Nov. 1940; v.21 p. 143-
81, Feb. 1941)   (1117

VENEZUELA. Biblioteca Nacional. Catálogo de la sección de bibliografía nacional.
Caracas, 1921. 66 p.   (2885

-----. -----. Cuarto catálogo de la biblioteca circulante. Caracas, 1930.
148 p.   (2887

-----. Dirección de Planificación Agropecuaria. Catálogo de las publicaciones efectuadas durante el año 1960. Caracas, 1961. 16 p.   (3814

YANG, Winston L. Non-Western resources in American libraries; a bibliographical guide.
1966.
    MS. in preparation.

CONTENTS WITH DISTRIBUTION OF ITEMS IN SUBJECT GROUPS (9)

---

9) Inserted items not included in the totals

ACADEMIA Colombiana, Bogotá. Anuario. Bogotá, 1874-1957. 12 v. (1
Includes many papers on Colombian men of letters. Volume 10: contains an analytical index. Jones, item 1665a, begins Vol. 1 with 1938, whereas Pérez Ortíz, p. 126, gives the present imprint. Neither mentions the repinted edition of Vol. 1, 1874-1910: "Reimpresión con adiciones" Published in 1935. The Academia suspended publication, 1875-1910, 1912-1913, and 1915-1936.

ACCION Católica Chilena. Libros de ayer y de hoy, síntesis de mil volúmenes clasificados, Vol. I. [Santiago de Chile] Secretariado de Moralidad de la Acción Católica, 1949. 196 p. (2

ADLER, Betty. Latin America; books for North American readers. Chicago, American Library Association [1940] p. 49-61. (The Booklist, v. 37, no. 2, pt. 2) (3
Classified and annotated.---Jones 2

ALBANELL, Norah, MANGO, Nancy, and others. Cuba, Dominican Republic, Haiti and Puerto Rico; a selected bibliography on the Caribbean area, including only islands which are members of the Organization of American States. Gainesville, Fla., School of Inter-American Studies, Univ. of Florida, 1956. 35 1. Mimeogr. (4
Prepared for the Seventh Annual Conference on the Caribbean, Dec. 6-8, 1956.

ALCEDO, Antonio de. Bibliotheca americana; catálogo de los autores que han escrito de la América en diferentes idiomas y noticia de su vida, patria, años en que florecieron y obras que dejaron escritas. (Boletín de la Academia Nacional de Historia, Quito, v. 2, p. 71-93, 1921) (5
An extract from the inedited manuscript giving the authors related to Ecuador; prepared by Gonzalo Zaldumbide.---Jones 1942.

-----. Introducción de Jorge A. Garcés. Quito, Ayuntamiento de Quito. 1964. v. 1 (Publ. del Museo Municipal de Arte e Historia, 32) (5a

ALDERSON, Donald J. Spain, Portugal and the Latin American Republics, an introductory bibliography. [Baltimore] (6
Reprinted from Hispania, v. 40 (3): 395-402, Sept. 1957.

AMERICAN Association of University Women. Washington Society. Pan American policies and problems; a study course and bibliography by Esther Caukin Brunauer. Washington, D.C., 1933. 13 1. Mimeogr. (7

AMERICAN Library Association. Committee on Library Cooperation with Latin America. Books of Latin American interest in public libraries of the United States. Chicago, 1942. 26 p. (Studies of the A.L.A. Committee on Library Cooperation with Latin America, no. 4) (8
Compilers: William C. Haygood, George Finney, Manuel Sánchez, and Mary E. Brindley.

AMERICAN Universities Field Staff. A select bibliography: Asia, Africa, Eastern Europe, Latin America. N.Y., [1960] 534 p. (9

-----. Supplement, 1961. N.Y., [1961] 75 p. (10
Compiled by Teg C. Grondahl and T. D. Long.

-----. Supplement, 1963. N.Y., [1963] 66 p. (11
Compiled by Teg C. Grondahl.

AMO, Julián, and, SHELBY, Charmion. La obra impresa de los intelectuales españoles en América, 1936-1945; bibliografía. Prólogo de Alfonso Reyes. Stanford, Stanford Univ. Pr. [1950] xiii, 145 p. (12
Prefatory matter in English and Spanish.

ANDREWS, David H. Latin America; a bibliography of paperback books, compiled by David H. Andrews. Edited by T. J. Hillmon. Washington, Hispanic Foundation, Reference Dept., Library of Congress, 1964. 38 p. (Hispanic Foundation bibliographical series, no. 9) (13

ANGLO-SOUTH American handbook for 1921 (incorporating Mexico and Central America) Ed. by W. H. Koebel. London, Federation of British Industries, 1921. 929 p. (14
Bibliography of works on South America from 1870: p. 891-907.---Jones 16.

ANTONIO, Nicolás. Bibliotheca hispana; sive, Hispanorvm, qvi vsqvam vnqvamve sive latina sive populari sive alia quavis lingua scripto aliquid consignaverunt notitia, his qvae praecesservnt locvpletior et certior brevia elogia, editorum atque ineditorum operum catalogum dvabvs partibvs continens, qvarvm haec ordine qvidem rei posterior, conceptu verò prior duobus tomis de his agit, qvi post annvm secvlarem MD. usque ad praesentem diem floruere. Romae, Ex officina N. A. Tinassii, 1672. 2 v. (15
First edition of the part published in the new ed., 1788, under the title, Bibliotheca hispana nova; the first edition of the other part, Bibliotheca hispana vetus, was not published until 1696.
A fundamental work of value for early Americana.---Jones 19.

ANTONIO, Nicolás. Bibliotheca hispana nova;
sive, Hispanorum scriptorum qui ab anno MD.
ad MDCLXXXIV. floruere notitia...nunc primum
prodit recognita emendata aucta ab ipso
auctore. Matriti, J. de Ibarra, 1788.
2 v.   (16
    Title page of v. 1 is erroneously dated
1783.
    The 2d ed., edited by T. A. Sánchez, J. A.
Pellicer and R. Casalbón.---Jones 20.
    Now available in microprint.

-----. Bibliotheca hispana vetus, sive, His-
pani scriptores qui ab Octaviani Augusti
aevo ad annum Christi MD. floruerunt.
Auctore D. Nicolao Antonio Hispalensi...
Curante Francisco Perezio Bayerio ... qui et
prologum, & auctoris vitae epitomen, & no-
tulas adiecit. Matriti, apud viduam et heredes D. J. Ibarrae, 1788. 2 v.   (17
    The 2d edition.---Jones 21.
    Now available in microprint.

ANUARIO español e hispano-americano del libro
y de las artes gráficas con el Catálogo mundial del libro impreso en lengua española,
v. 1, 1945- . Madrid, Editores del Anuario
Marítimo Español.   (18
    Last volume received DPU: v.10, 1956/1957.
Editors: Javier Lasso de la Vega Jiménez-
Placer and Francisco Cervera Jiménez-Alfaro,
the latter only through v.6.

ARGENTINA. Congreso. Biblioteca. Información bibliográfica; publicaciones, no.1- ,
1949- . Buenos Aires   (19
    DPU has no. 1, 7, 9-10, 13. Contents:-
1. Derecho constitucional y derecho público
provincial. - 2. Prostitución. Enfermedades
venéreas y problemas conexos. - 3. Locación
urbana. Legislación de emergencia. - 4. Vivienda. - 5. Tobaco. - 6. Accidentes del
trabajo. Enfermedades profesionales. Higiene del trabajo. - 7. Bibliografía de San
Martín. - 8. Servicios públicos. - 9. Propiedad intelectual. - 10. Derecho municipal.
- 11. Arquitectura y urbanismo. - 12. Bibliografía general de Chile. - 13. Derecho
constitucional y derecho público provincial.

AVELLINO, F. Ivor D. A Latin American read-
ing list for the general reader. N.Y., New
York Public Library, 1942. 7 p.   (20
    Reprinted from Bulletin of the New York
Public Library, Nov. 1942.

BARD, Harry Erwin. South America; brief outline of study suggestions with bibliography.
Boston, New York [etc.] D. C. Heath & Co.,
1916. 68 p.   (21
    Bibliography: p. 27-68.---Jones 41.

BARRET, P. Bibliographie américaniste.
(Journal de la Société des Américanistes de
Paris. Paris, 1933- . v. 25- .)   (22

BARRET, P. (Cont.)
    A comprehensive classified list issued
annually; previous issues compiled by P.
Rivet and others were published in volumes 11 to 24 of the Journal.---Jones 43a.

BARROS ARANA, Diego. Notas para una bibliografía de obras anónimas i seudónimas sobre
la historia, la jeografía i la literatura
de América. Santiago de Chile, Impr. Nacional, 1882. 171 p.   (23
    Jones 44.

-----. Obras completas. Santiago de Chile,
Impr. Cervantes, 1908-14. 16 v.   (24
    "Estudios histórico-bibliográficos": v.
6, 8-11.---Jones 45.

BAYITCH, S. A. Latin America; a bibliographical guide to economy, history, law, politics, and society. Coral Gables, Fla., University of Miami Pr.; distributed by Oceana
Publications, New York, 1961. 335 p. (Interamerican legal studies, no. 6)   (25

BELTRAN, Francisco. Biblioteca biobibliográfica. Catálogo de una importante colección
de libros y folletos españoles y extranjeros referentes a bibliografía, biografía,
bibliofilia, la imprenta y sus artes auxiliares. Madrid, 1927. 498 p.   (26
    Jones 50.

BERISTAIN DE SOUZA, José Mariano. Biblioteca
hispano-americana septentrional; o, Catálogo o noticia de los literatos, que o nacidos,
o educados, o florecientes en la América
Septentrional española, han dado a luz algún
escrito, o lo han dexado preparado para la
prensa. México, 1816-21. 3 v.   (27
    A fundamental work for Mexican bibliogra-
phy.---Jones 2073.

-----. 2. ed. publícala el presbítero br.
Fortino Hipólito Vera. Amecameca, Tip. del
Colegio Católico, 1883. 3 v.   (28
    Jones 2073a.
    Now available in microprint.

-----. -----. Tomo IV; comprende los anónimos que dejó escritos el autor, las adiciones del dr. Osores y otras añadidas poste-
riormente por las personas que se expresan.
José Toribio Medina publícalo ahora con una
introducción bio-bibliográfica. Santiago
de Chile, Impr. Elzeviriana, 1897.
198 p.   (29
    Jones 2073b.
    Now available in microprint.

-----. -----. Adiciones y correcciones que
a su fallecimiento dejó manuscritas el sr.
lic. d. José Fernando Ramírez, y son las
que cita con el nombre de "Suplemento"; o,
"Adición" en las apostillas que pasó a su

BERISTAIN DE SOUZA,.. (Cont.)
ejemplar de la Biblioteca hispano-americana
del dr. d. Mariano de Beristain y Souza.
Publícanlas por vez primera el lic. Victoriano Agüeros y el dr. N. León. México,
Impr. de el Tiempo, 1898. XLVII, 662 p. (30
"D., José Fernando Ramírez (Datos bio-bibliográficos)", signed, Luis González Obregón: p. v-xlvii.---Jones 2074.
Now available in microprint.

-----. 3a. ed. México, D.F., Edit. Fuente
Cultural, [1947] 5 v. in 2 v. (Colección
Daniel) (31

BERLINER, J. J. & Staff, N.Y. Bibliography of
Latin America, 1936-1944/1948. N.Y. 1936-
1948. 6 v. (32
DPU collection lacks 1941-1943.
Near-print reproduction.

BEYHAUT, Gustavo. Sociedad y cultura latinoamericanas en la realidad internacional.
[Montevideo] Consejo Interuniversitario Regional [1959] 81 p. (33
Cited in Musso 498, noting that the work
is a bibliographical guide prepared for the
summer courses in Santiago, Buenos Aires and
Montevideo, 1960.

BIBLIOGRAFIA americanista española, 1935-1963.
Sevilla, Comité Organizador del XXXVI Congreso Internacional de Americanistas, 1964.
565 p. (34
Edited by Jose Alcina Franch.

BIBLIOGRAFIA de Centroamérica y del Caribe,
1956-1959. Habana, Agrupación Bibliográfica
Cubana José Toribio Medina, 1958-1961.
4 v. (35
Printing directed by the Dirección General
de Archivos y Bibliotecas de España in Ma-
drid at the Talleres Gráficos "Victoria".
Title of 1961 Volume: Bibliografía de Centro
America y del Caribe, Argentina y Venezuela.
No more published.

BIBLIOGRAFIA general española e hispanoamericana, año 1- , en./abr. 1923- . Madrid-Bar-
celona, Cámaras Oficiales del Libro,
1925- . (36
Jones 56. Last issue received at DPU: año
8, dic. 1930. Includes references to some
Latin American publications.

BIBLIOGRAFIA general sobre México; selección
preliminar. n.p., 1959. 11 p.
Mimeogr. (37

BIBLIOGRAPHIE hispanique, 1905-15. New York,
The Hispanic Society of America [1909-15]
11 v. (38
Compiled by Foulché-Delbosc.
"La ... bibliographie est consacrée aux
langues, aux littératures et à l'histoire

BIBLIOGRAPHIE ... (Cont.)
des pays castillans, catalans et portugais,
en Europe et hors d'Europe... Non seulement
les livres et brochures, mais aussi les articles de revues ont été répertoriés."---
Jones 59.

BIBLIOTECA Artigas-Washington, Montevideo.
Catálogo de obras norteamericanas en tra-
ducción española preparado por Elvira A.
Lerena Martínez y Ermelinda Acerenza.
Montevideo, 1947. 53 p. (39
Contains 1017 items.

-----. Suplemento 1-3. Montevideo, 1947-
1949. (40
Reprinted from Biblioteca Artigas-Washington, sept. 1947, p. 111-115; sept./dic.
1948, p. 116-131; dic. 1949, p. 121-131.
Contains items, 1018-1563.

-----. Suplemento 4. Montevideo, 1952.
unpaged. (41
Contains items, 1564-1979.

BIBLIOTECA Benjamín Franklin, México.
United States books on Mexico, 1935-1949.
México, 1949. 38 p. (42

BIBLIOTECA mexicana. Sammlung des Baron
Kaska. I. Mexikanische u. spanische
handschriften; II. Bücher über geschich-
te, sprachwissenschaft, naturgeschichte
u. s. w. Mexikos; III. Varia. Berlin,
J. A. Stargardt, 1911. 54 p. (43
The second section contains 632 titles.
Jones 2082.

BOLETIN informativo de obras en francés e
italiano. [Bogotá, 1963] [16] p. (44
Cited in Peraza, Fichas, 4/6, item 511.

BON, Antoine. Livres français parus en
Amérique, 1940 à 1944. Rio de Janeiro,
Institut Franco Brésilien de Haute Culture,
1944. 62 p. (Documents bibliographiques,
no. 1) (45
Cited in Bibliogr. bras., 1942-1945,
v. 1.

-----. Livres français hors d'Amérique, 1940
à 1944, 1e. partie. Rio de Janeiro, Atlân-
tica Editora, 1945. 80 p. (Documents bibliographiques, no. 2) (46
Cited in Bibliogr. bras., 1942-1945,
v. 1.

BRASSEUR DE BOURBOURG, Charles Etienne.
Bibliothèque mexico-guatémalienne, précédée
d'un coup d'oeil sur les études américaines
dans leurs rapports avec les études classi-
ques et suivie du tableau par ordre alphabétique des ouvrages de linguistique américaine contenus dans le même volume; rédigée
et mise en ordre d'après les documents de

BRASSEUR DE BOURBOURG, ... (Cont.)
sa collection américaine par M. Brasseur de
Bourbourg. Paris, Maisonneuve, 1871.
183 p.   (47
    Acquired by A. L. Pinart, of whose collec-
tion a sale catalogue was issued in 1883.---
Jones 2102.

BRAZIL. Biblioteca Nacional. Anais, v. 1)
1876- . Rio de Janeiro.   (48
    Published as Annaes, v. 1-50, 1876-1928;
as Anais, v. 51- , 1929- . Indexes:
v. 1-20, 1876-1898 in v. 20; v. 1-69 in
v. 70.
    In the "Annaes" are numerous valuable bib-
liographical contributions. Of these the
following are illustrative: Catálogo dos
manuscriptos da Bibliotheca Nacional: pte.
1. Manuscriptos relativos ao Brasil; Bibliographia da lingua tupí, por A. do Valle Cabral; Catálogo da exposição de historia do
Brasil; Catálogo da exposição permanente dos
cimelios; Catálogo das Biblias; Subsidios
existentes na Bibliotheca Nacional para o
estudo da questão de limites do Brasil pelo
Oyapoch, coordenados pelo dr. Teixeira de
Mello; Garrettiana da Bibliotheca Nacional,
por J. A. Teixeira de Mello; Estampas grava-
das por Debrie, catálogo organisado pelo dr.
J. Z. de Menezes Brum; Catálogo da colleção
Cervantina com que a Bibliotheca Nacional
concorreu á exposição commemorativa do 3.o
centenario do d. Quixote, organisado por A.
Jansen do Paço; Inventario dos documentos
relativos ao Brasil existentes no Archivo
de Marinha e Ultramar, organisado por E.
Castro e Almeida: 1-5 Bahia, 1613-1807. 6-
Rio de Janeiro, 1616- ; A Nova gazeta da
terra do Brasil (Newen zeytung auss Presillg
landt) e sua origem mais provavel por Rodolpho R. Schuller; Historisch-geographi-
scher katalog für Brasilien (1500-1908) von
J. Scherrer; Catálogo da exposição biblio-
iconographica organisada pela Bibliotheca
Nacional ... e commemorativa do sexto centenario de Dante; Nobiliarchia pernambucana, por Antonio José Victoriano Borges da
Fonseca.---Jones 1161.

-----. Ministério das Relações Exteriores.
Biblioteca. Traduções de autores brasileiros e livros sôbre o Brasil escritos em
idioma estrangeiro. [Rio de Janeiro]
Serviço de Documentação. [1960] 92 1.   (49

BROMLEY, J. S., and GOODWIN, Albert. A select
list of works on Europe and Europe overseas,
1715-1815. Oxford, Clarendon Pr., 1956.
132 p.   (50
    Contains sections on French, Spanish and
Portuguese possessions.

BROOKLYN. Public Library. A list of books
on the West Indies and the Bermuda islands
in the Brooklyn Public Library. Brooklyn,

BROOKLYN. Public Library... (Cont.)
1904. 12 p.   (51
Jones 2984.

BROWN, Ann Duncan. British possessions in the
Caribbean area, a selected list of references.
Washington, D.C., Library of Congress, 1943.
2, 192 p.   (52

BROWN, Lyle C. Latin America, a bibliography.
Kingsville, Texas College of Arts and Industries, 1962. 80 p.   (53

BRUNER PRIETO, Fernando. La bibliografía española e hispano-americana. Palma de Mallorca, Francisco Soler, 1923. 65 p.   (54
    Cited in Ochsenius, item 41.

CALDERON, Alba Rosa, and BENDFELDT ROJAS,
Lourdes. Registro bibliografico de publi-
caciones de catedraticos de la Facultad de
Humanidades. [Guatemala] Universidad de
San Carlos, 1962. 77 p.   (55
    Colophon dated 30 abril 1963. Contains
952 entries, and an Addenda of 142 entries.
Also "Tesario (1945-1962)"; "Indice analí-
tico de temas"; and "Fuentes".

CATALOGO general de la librería española e
hispanoamericana, años 1901-1930. Autores.
[Madrid y Barcelona] Cámaras Oficiales del
Libro, 1932-1951. 5 v.   (56
    Jones 90.

-----. [Suplemento] 1931-1950. Madrid.
Instituto Nacional del Libro Español,
1957- .   (57

CANSTATT, Oskar. Kritisches repertorium der
deutsch-brasilianischen literatur. Berlin,
D. Reimer (E. Vohsen) 1902. 124 p.   (58
    Jones 1011.

-----. Nachtrag zum Kritischen repertorium.
Berlin, D. Reimer, 1906. 64 p.   (59
    Jones 1011.

CHICAGO. Public Library. Books of the
Americas in Spanish and Portuguese. [Chi-
cago] 1943. 19 p.   (60

CLAREMONT Colleges. American hemispheric
solidarity; library resources. Claremont,
Calif., 1943. 49 p. Mimeogr.   (61
    Compilers: Wendell W. Greenlee and
Janet E. Turner.

COLOMBIA. Biblioteca Nacional. Catálogo de
la biblioteca española obsequiada por el
Ministerio de Estado de esa República a la
Biblioteca Nacional de Bogotá. Bogotá,
Edit. "El Gráfico", 1935. 156 p.   (62

-----. Directorio intelectual de la ciudad,
mayo 1934. Bogotá, Edit. Minerva, 1934.

COLOMBIA. Biblioteca Nacional... (Cont.)
78 p.   (63
 Jones 1690.
 Lista de los periódicos y revistas que
actualmente se publican en Bogotá, p. 39-78.

CUENCA BENET, Francisco. Biblioteca de autores andaluces. Habana, Tip. Moderna, 1921-
1925. 2 v. (Biblioteca de divulgación de
cultura contemporánea, v. 1, 3)   (64

CUMMINS, Alice. Pan Americanism; a bibliography of the books in the library of the University of Florida, relating to the countries of South America, Central America,
Mexico, and the West Indies. Gainesville,
Fla., University of Florida, 1930. 15 l.
(Supplement of the Library bulletin, v. 6,
no. 1, Sept./Oct. 1930)   (65

CUNDALL, Frank. Bibliography of the West
Indies (excluding Jamaica) Kingston, Insti-
tute of Jamaica, 1909. 179 p.   (66
 Contains also sections on Florida,
Honduras, Nicaragua, Costa Rica, Panama,
Colombia, Venezuela, the Guianas, etc.---
Jones 2986.

CURRENT Caribbean bibliography, v. 1- , June
1951- . Port-of-Spain, Caribbean Commission.   (67
 Last issue received at DPU: v. 9/10,
1959/1961, part 1.

DEUTSCHES Ausland-Institut, Stuttgart.
Bibliographisches handbuch des ausland
deutschtums. Stuttgart, Ausland und
Heimatverlag, a.-g., 1932-33. 7 pts.   (68
 Pt. 7, Ibero-Amerika (56 p.)
 A classified list by countries and subdi-
visions under countries.---Jones 123.

-----. Wichtige bücher über ausland-deutsch-
tum (1919-1927) Stuttgart, Ausland und
Heimatverlag, a.-g., 1928. 39 p.   (69
 Jones 124.

DICCIONARIO enciclopédico hispanoamericano de
literatura hispanoamericano, ciencias y artes. Barcelona, Montaner y Simón, 1887-
1898. 23 v.   (70
 Jones 127.

-----. Apéndice. 1898-1899. 2 v.   (71
 Jones 127.

-----. Apéndice segundo. 1907-1910. 3v. (72
 Jones 127.

-----. Barcelona, New York, 1938. 23v. (73
 Jones 127a.

-----. Estos últimos años, suplemento...
1939. 2 v.   (74
 Jones 127a.

DICCIONARIO SALVAT; enciclopédico popular ilustrado . . . comprende, además de todos los
vocablos que se hallan en la última edición
del Diccionario de la Real Academia Española,
las voces técnicas de ciencias, artes y oficios; las más corrientes en los países de
América y las extranjeras adoptadas por el
uso; frases, modismos y refranes más conocidos; artículos y notas geográficas, historicas, de ciencias físicas y naturales, literatura, bellas artes, deportes, etc. Barcelona, Salvat. [1907?-13?] 9 v.   (75
 Jones 128.

-----. Apéndice. Barcelona, Salvat. [1914]
1059 p.   (76
 Jones 128.

DILLON, Dorothy Rita. Latin America, 1935-
1949, a selected bibliography. N. Y., United
Nations, 1952. unpaged. (Bibliographical
series, no. 2)   (77
 Contains 4,837 entries prepared by Dorothy
Dillon of the Hispanic Foundation, Library
of Congress. UN publication, ST/LIB/Ser.B/2.

EBERHARDT, Fritz. Amerikaliteratur. Die wichtigsten seit 1900 in deutscher sprache erschienenen werke über Amerika. Leipzig,
Koehler und Volckmar, 1926. 335 p.   (78
 A classified list of 1635 items, with descriptive notes and author and subject indexes.---Jones 133.

EÇA, Raúl d'. Some recent Brazilian and Portuguese publications. [Washington, D.C.] (79
 Reprinted from the Hispanic American historical review, v. 18, no. 3, p. 426-32, Aug.
1938.

ENCICLOPEDIA universal ilustrada europea americana. Barcelona, J. Espasa [1907?-1930]
70 v. in 71 v.   (80
 An indispensable work; the general article
on bibliography and the special bibliographies that accompany the articles are valuable.---Jones 139.

-----. Apéndice. Madrid, Espasa-Calpe.
[1930-33] 10 v.   (81
 Jones 139.

-----. Suplemento anual, 1934- . Madrid,
Espasa-Calpe, 1935- .   (82
 Jones 139.

ENCYCLOPEDIA e diccionario internacional; organizado e redigido de distinctos homens de
sciencia e de lettras brasileiros e portugueses. Rio de Janeiro, Nova York [1933?]
20 v.   (83
 Edited by W. M. Jackson; a standard general encyclopedia in Portuguese.---Jones 140.

FALCIONELLI, Alberto. Tentativa de bibliografía razonada de la Rusia contemporánea.
Mendoza, República Argentina [1961] 125 p.
(Mendoza, Argentina. Universidad Nacional
de Cuyo. Biblioteca Central. Cuadernos,
1)   (84
     Contains 1,732 entries.

FLORIDA. University, Gainesville. Libraries.
Caribbean acquisitions, 1957/1958- .
Gainesville, 1959- .   (85
     Latest received in DPU: 1963.

FONSECA, Martinho Augusto Ferreira da. Adita-
mentos ao Dicionario bibliografico portugues
de Inocencio Francisco da Silva. Coimbra,
Imprensa da Universidade, 1927. 377 p. (86
     Part of the material was published in the
     Boletim da Sociedade de Bibliophilos Barbosa
     Machado, v. 3-4, 1915-17, and also as a
     separate. cf. Pref.---Jones 1195.

FOREIGN Policy Association-World Affairs
Center. Selected readings: Latin America.
N. Y. [1960] [12] p.   (87
     Contents: --General readings. -- U.S. re-
     lations with Latin America. -- The economic
     situation. -- The communist threat. -- Some
     country studies. -- The role of internation-
     al organizations.

FORERO NOGUES, Marian. Books in English on
Latin America published in 1948. [Washing-
ton, D.C., Pan American Union] n.d.
[4] p.   (88

FOULCHE-DELBOSC, Raymond, and BARRAU-DIHIGO,
Louis. Manuel de l'hispanisant. New York,
G. P. Putnam's sons, 1920-1925. 2 v. (89
     Contents - t. 1: 1. Généralités. 2. Typo-
     bibliographies. 3. Biographies et bio-
     bibliographies. 4. Bibliographies mono-
     graphiques. 5. Archives, bibliothèques et
     musées. 6. Collections dispersées.
     Additions (p. 413-501) - t.2: Collections.
     ---Jones 154.

GALVAN, Sarah M. Background readings on Latin
America. N. Y., 1942. 61 p.   (90

GALVAO, Benjamin Franklin Ramiz. Notas bibliographicas. Addições a Barbosa e Innocencio da Silva. (Annaes da Bibliotheca Nacional. Rio de Janeiro, 1876-1877. v. 1, p.
150-57, 363-72; v. 3, p. 210-23)   (91
     Jones 1152.

GIRALDO JARAMILLO, Gabriel. Apuntes para una
bibliografía colombo-cubana. La Habana,
Seoane, Fernández y Cía., 1953.   (92
     Reprint from Revista de la Biblioteca Na-
     cional, La Habana, p. 109-52, en./mar. 1953.

GOLDSMITH, Peter H. A brief bibliography of
books in English, Spanish and Portuguese,
relating to the republics commonly called
Latin American, with comments. New York,
The Macmillan Co., 1915. 107 p.   (93
     Jones 168.

GRANDE enciclopedia portuguesa e brasileira.
Lisboa, Rio de Janeiro, Edit. Enciclopedia,
1935-1958. 37 v.   (94
     Began publication in 1935, issued in month-
     ly parts; it promises to be the most impor-
     tant reference work in its field.---Jones
     1051a.
     Apéndice starts in v. 37.

-----. Apendice. Lisboa, Rio de Janeiro,
[1958- . v. 37 (p. [425]-922)-]   (94a
     Volumes through 40 have appeared.

GRIFFIN, Appleton Prentiss Clark. A list of
books (with references to periodicals) on
the Danish West Indies. Washington, D.C.,
Govt. Print. Off., 1901. 18 p. (56th Cong.,
2d sess. Senate Doc., 223)   (95

GURIN, Ruth Melamed. Our neighbors to the
south, an informal list of books on Latin
America for diverse insterests and tastes.
Chicago, 1942.   (96
     Reprinted from the Booklist, v. 39, no. 4,
     pt. 2, p. 81-93.
     Cited in HLAS, 8, item 38.

HANDBOOK of Latin American studies, a guide to
the material published in 1935- , by a number of scholars. Cambridge, Mass., Harvard
University Pr., 1936- .   (97
     This indispensable tool for Latin American
     studies consists of selective bibliographies,
     with critical and informative commentary,
     prepared by specialists in the various fields
     covered by the Handbook.
     In publishing the volume for 1944, the
     editor announced that the Editorial Office
     had become an integral part of the Hispanic
     Foundation of the Library of Congress. In
     no. 19, a departure of policy was announced
     from that of including only items published
     in the year of coverage by the Handbook to
     the policy of including all important publi-
     cations seen for the first time by the Edi-
     torial Office or by the contributing editors
     during the year since the preparation of the
     last volume, regardless of imprint date.
     Editors of volumes 1935-1939, Lewis Hanke;
     1940-1945, Miron Burgin; 1946 (no. 12)-no.
     20, Francisco Aguilera; no. 21-23, Nathan A.
     Haverstock; no. 23- , Earl J. Pariseau.
     Imprint varies: 1935-1947 (no. 1-13),
     Cambridge, Mass., Harvard University Pr.;
     no. 14- , Gainesville, Fla., Florida Univer-
     sity Pr.

HANDBOOK of Latin American studies...(Cont.)
Provisional cumulative author index. Washington, D.C., Library of Congress, 1959.
2 v. (97a
Covers volumes 1-20.

HARRISSE, Henry. Bibliotheca americana vetustissima; a description of works relating to
America, published between 1492 and 1551.
New York, G. P. Philes, 1866. 519 p. (98
304 titles, arranged chronologically;
transcribed line for line, with exact colla-
tions, historical notes, references to authorities and libraries, etc.---Jones 188.
Now available in microprint.

-----. -----. Additions. Paris, Tross, 1872.
199 p. (99
186 titles.---Jones 189.

-----. Madrid, Librería General V. Suárez.
1958. [2] p., reprint: liv., 519 p. (100
Reproduction of the 1866 edition, prepared
by Carlos Sánz López.

-----. -----. Additions. Madrid, Librería General V. Suárez, 1958. [2] p., reprint:
xl, 199 p. (101
Reproduction of the 1872 edition, prepared
by Carlos Sánz López.

HIDALGO, Dionisio. Diccionario general de bi-
bliografía española. Madrid, Impr. de las
Escuelas Pías, 1862-1881. 7 v. (102
Jones 203.

HILTON, Ronald. Los estudios hispánicos en
los Estados Unidos. Versión y adaptación
española de Lino Gómez Canedo. Madrid, Ediciones Cultura Hispánica, 1957.
xii, 493 p. (103

-----. Handbook of Hispanic source materials
and research organizations in the United
States. Toronto, The University of Toronto
Pr., 1942. 441 p. (104

-----. -----. 2d ed. Stanford, Calif., Stanford Univ. Pr., 1956. xiv, 448 p. (105

HISPANIC and Luso-Brazilian Councils. Latin
America; an introduction to the basic books
in English concerning the countries of Latin
America. London, 1960. 30 p. (105a

HUMPHREYS, Robert Arthur. Latin America,
London, The Royal Institute of Internation-
al Affairs; N.Y., Oxford Univ. Pr., [1941]
36 p. (Chatham House bibliographies) (106
Reprinted in 1942; also with additions in
July 1942.

-----. [1949] 63 p. (107
Lists approximately 900 titles.

IBERO-AMERIKANISCHE bibliographie . . .
Auswahl-verzeichnis der deutschsprachigen
literatur. Bearbeitet von dr. Hans Praesent.
Berlin und Bonn, F. Dümmler, 1930- .
1- . (108
Beilage su Ibero-Amerikanisches archiv,
v. 4, no. 2- .---Jones 211.

INDEX translationum, n.s. v. 1- , 1948- .
Paris, Unesco, 1949- . (109
Latest volume received at DPU v. 16, 1963.
Continues the series published by the International Institute of Intellectual Cooperation 1932-1940. The older series included
mainly European countries, whereas the new
series generously includes also the American
nations. For example volume 10 included 14
Latin American countries for a total of
1,122 translations.

INDICE de ediciones francesas (de 1939 a 1946)
[Montevideo, Surcos] n.d. [40] p. (Docu-
mento, no. 31) (110
Cited in Musso 65.

INTER-AMERICAN book exchange. Index to Latin-
American books, 1938. Washington, D.C.,
1940. 484 p. mimeogr. (111
Compiled by Raul d'Eça.---Jones 215b.

JACOB, Ernest Gerhard. Literaturbericht aus
der ibero-amerikanischen kulturwelt.
(Archiv für kulturgeschichte. Leipzig,
v. 25, p. 231-50, 1934) (112
A review of some European and American
books recently published on Hispanic culture.---Jones 221.

JACQUET, Constant H. Our neighbors to the
South; a selected and annotated bibliography of English titles on the Republics of
Central America and the Caribbean, including the colonies, territories, and possessions of the United Kingdom, France, the
Netherlands and the United States. N.Y.,
Missionary Research Library, 1954.
41 p. (113

JONES, Cecil Knight. The Archer M. Huntington
fund for the purchase of Hispanic books in
the Library of Congress. Durham, N.C., Duke
University Pr., 1929. p. 545-50. (114
From Hispanic-American historical review,
v. 9.---Jones 224.

KISER, Margaret. Some references on Latin
America suggested for the general reader.
Washington, D.C., Division of Intellectual
Cooperation, Pan American Union, 1947.
12 p. (115

KLEINER literarischer wegweiser zum studium
des ibero-amerikanischen auslandes. Hrsg.
vom Ibero-Amerikanischen Institut. Hamburg,
Hanseatische Verlagsanstalt Aktiengesell-

KLEINER literarischer... (Cont.)
schaft, 1924. 29 p.   (116
   Reprinted from _Iberica_, zeitschrift für
spanische und portugieische auslandskunde,
bd. 1, 1924.---Jones 238.

KLOOSTERBOER, Willemina. Bibliografie van
Nederlandse publikaties over Portugal en
zijn overzeese gebiedsdelen. Utrecht, 1957.
231 p. (Uitgave von de Bibliotheek der
Rijksuniversiteit te Utrecht)   (116a

LAGRANGE, Mario J. Latin America; an anno-
tated bibliography. Indianapolis, Ind.,
Indiana State Library, 1940.
Various pagings.   (117

LEMOS, Maximiano Augusto d'Oliveira. Encyclopedia portugueza illustrada; diccionario
universal, pub. sob. a direcção de Maximiano
Lemos. Porto, Lemos & Ca., successor
[19-?] 11 v.   (118
   Jones 1076.

LEON PINELO, Antonio Rodríguez de. Epítome
de la biblioteca oriental i occidental,
náutica i geográfica. Madrid, I. González,
1629. 186 p.   (119
   Titles translated into Spanish.---Jones
256.

-----. Epítome de la bibliotheca oriental y
occidental, náutica y geográfica ... aña-
dido, y enmendado nuevamente, en que se con-
tienen los escritores de las Indias orien-
tales y occidentales y reinos convecinos,
China, Tartaria, Japón, Persia, Armenia,
Etiopía y otras partes. Madrid, F. Martínez
Abad, 1737-1738. 3 v.   (120
   Enlarged and annotated by A. González de
Barcia.
   Titles in Spanish. Includes indexes of
authors by forenames and family names and
titles.---Jones 257.

-----. Con prólogo de Diego Luis Molinari, y
reimpreso por Juan Roldán. Buenos Aires,
Edición Bibliófilos Argentinos. [1919]
xxxiii, 46 l. facsims., 186, xij p.,
1 l.   (121
   Facsimile reprint of the 1629 edition.

-----. Washington, D.C., Unión Panamericana,
1958. xlii, 46 l. facsims., 186, xij p.,
1 l.   (122
   Facsimile reprint of the 1629 edition.

LEUBEL, Alfredo G. El Perú en 1860 o sea
Anuario nacional, política, comercio, esta-
dística, literatura, industria, agricultura.
Lima, Impr. de Comercio, 1861. 306 p. (123
   Cf. _Bib. peruana_, v. 1, no. 1271.---Jones
2676.

LIBRARY of International Relations, Chicago.
Titles chosen as representative of the
collection on Central and South America.
Chicago, [1943] 35 p.   (124
   This is the 4th of the quarterly annotated
bibliographies and includes the preceeding
3 quarters.

LIBROS en venta en Hispanoamérica y España.
Un servicio informativo preparado bajo la
dirección de Mary C. Turner. New York,
Bowker, 1964. 1891 p.   (125
   Includes references to approximately
87,750 titles.

LICHTENSTEIN, Walter. Report to the presi-
dent of Northwestern University on the
results of a trip to South America.
Evanston and Chicago, Northwestern University Pr., 1915. 43 p. (Northwestern University bulletin, v. 16, no. 1. Sept. 3,
1915)   (126
   Jones 259.

-----. 2d ed. Evanston and Chicago, Northwestern University Pr., 1915. 43 p.
(Northwestern University bulletin, v. 16,
no. 1. Sept. 3, 1915)   (127
   Jones 260.

LOS ANGELES County Public Library, Los Angeles.
Republics of the Western Hemisphere; a reading list designed to help Americans gain
insight into the history, politics, resources,
and customs of the countries of Latin America and on understanding of the problems of
hemisphere defense. [Los Angeles] 1942.
14 p.   (128
   Issued in commemoration of the 400th anniversary of the landing of Cabrillo in California.

LOWELL, Mass. City Library. Mexico, Central
and South America. Lowell, Mass., 1911.
29 p.   (129

McDONALD, James Grover. Latin America. Chicago, American Library Association, 1931.
38 p. (Reading with a purpose,
no. 65)   (130
   Books recommended in this course: p. 35.
Jones 269.

MEDINA, José Toribio. Biblioteca hispano-americana (1493-1810) Santiago de Chile, Impreso en casa del autor, 1898-1907.
7 v.   (131
   Includes: "Primero: Libros publicados por
americanos o españoles que vivieron en América y que no tratan de una manera directa
de las cosas de nuestro continente ... Segundo: Libros escritos en castellano o en
latín e impresos en España o fuera de ella
por españoles o americanos, o publicados en
la península por individuos de cualquier

MEDINA, José Toribio ... (Cont.)
nacionalidad, en alguno de aquellos idiomas".
Transcribes line for line, 8,481 titles,
with bio-bibliographical notes, and frequent
references to authorities and to libraries
containing copies of the works described.
The "Prólogo" (t. 6, p. ix-cxxx) contains
(1) a historical sketch of the press law and
liberty of the press in Spanish America;
(2) a notice of the life and works of Antonio León Pinelo (the titles of his published
works numbered 7,702-7,737); and (3) notices
of earlier bibliographies relating to Spanish America.
Contents. - t. 1, 1493-1600 (449 titles) -
t. 2, 1601-1650 (no. 450-1, 152) - t. 3,
1651-1700 (no. 1,153-2,023) - t. 4, 1701-
1767 (no. 2,024-4,284) - t. 5, 1768-1810
(no. 4,285-6, 151) - t. 6, Prólogo. Sin fecha determinada, siglo XVII-XIX (no. 6,152-
7,737) Adiciones. Ampliaciones. Dudosos.
Manuscritos. - t. 7, Algo más de León Pinelo.
Nuevas adiciones. Sin fecha determinada.
Ultimas adiciones. Ampliaciones. Notas biográficas (no. 7,738-8,481)---Jones 300.
Now available in microprint.

-----. Ed. facsimilar. Santiago de Chile,
Fondo Histórico y Bibliográfico José Toribio
Medina, 1958-1962. 7 v.   (132

-----. Catálogo de libros españoles cuya des-
cripción solicita José Toribio Medina.
Sevilla, Impr. de E. Rasco, 1893. 90 p. (133
Jones 1537.

METFORD, J. C. J. British contributions to
Spanish and Spanish-American studies. N.Y.,
Longmans, Green for the British Council,
1950. 86 p.   (134

MEUSEL, Johann Georg. Bibliotheca historica
instructa a B. Burcardo Gotthelf Struvio,
aucta a B. Christi. Gottlieb Budero, nunc
vero a Ioanne Georgio Meuselio ita digesta,
amplificata et emendata, ut paene novum
opus videri possit. Lipsiae, apud Heredes
Weidmanni et Reichium, 1782-1804. 11 v. (135
Vol. 3 contains a valuable bibliography
of works relating to the New world.---Jones
315.

MEXICO. Departamento de Bibliotecas. Libros
sobre las Américas. Contribución de la Sección de Biblioteconomía al Tercer Congreso
Nacional de Bibliotecarios y Primero de Archiveros. Mexico, D.F., 1944. 49 p.
mimeogr.   (136
Over 500 references.

MIAMI University, Oxford, Ohio. Romanic Dept.
A selective elementary bibliography for
Spanish teachers. Ithaca, N.Y., Thrift Pr.,
n.d. 24 p. mimeogr.   (137
Section XVIII: Hispanic American life

MIAMI University,... (Cont.)
and customs.

MILLARES CARLO, Agustín. Registro bibliográfico, 1940-1941. México, D.F., 1941.
2 v.   (138
Published by the Facultad de Filosofía y
Letras of the Universidad Nacional Autónoma
de México, suplementos de la revista Filosofía y letras, t. 1-2.

MONTEVIDEO. Intendencia Municipal. Sección
Biblioteca. [Lista de libros] Montevideo,
Tip. Moderna, 1917. 47 p.   (139

MOSCOW. Akademiia Nauk SSSR. Instiut
Latinskoi Ameriki. Latinskaia Amerika
v sovetskoi pechati; bibliografiia. Moscow,
1964. [132] p.   (140
Contains over 1,900 entries.

-----. Publichnaia Biblioteka. Nauchno-
metodicheskii otdel bibliotkovedeniia i
bibliografiia. Strany Latin-Ameriki.
Moscow, 1962. 117 p.   (141
Cited in HLAS 26 item 64b. Recommended
reading on Latin American countries.

-----. Vsesoiuznaia Gosudarstvennaia Biblioteka Inostrannoi Literatury. Kuba v sovetskoi pechati: bibliografiia ... 1959-1963.
Moscow, 1963. 75 p.   (142
Compiler E. V. Braginskaia, listing
approximately 700 entries. Cited in HLAS
26 item 64c.

MUGGLESTONE, Ethel Annie. Anglo-Hispanic
bibliography for 1930. Leicester, The
Minerva Co., 1931. 16 p.   (143
Books published in Great Britain.---Jones
323.

NATIONAL Education Association. Research Division. Latin American backgrounds; a bibliography of 497 references. Washington, D.C.,
1940. 74 p. mimeogr.   (144

-----. [1941] 48 p.   (145
Contains 714 references.

NATIONAL Recreation Association. Our neighbors
to the South. A bibliography listing references including dances, music, plays, pag-
eants, festivals, customs, games, party
plans, and other sources of program material
from Central and South America. [N.Y.,
1944?] 11 p. mimeogr.   (146

NEW ENGLAND Institute of Inter-American Affairs,
Boston. An informal list of books on Latin
America for the general reader and a directo-
ry of Latin American collections in New
England libraries. [Boston, Silver Burdett,
1943] 16 p.   (147

NEW JERSEY. State College, Trenton. Roscoe
L. West Library. Latin America today; a
bibliography, compiled by Joyce H. Brodowski,
with the cooperation of Parker Worley.
Trenton, 1961. 27 p.   (148
   Based on a similar bibliography prepared
by Doris M. Perry and Mary Jane Getlen in
1958.

NEW YORK. Public Library. Latin America.
1962. p. 27-34. (Branch Library book news,
v. 39, no. 3, Feb. 1962)   (149

-----. List of works relating to the West
Indies. New York, 1912. 392 p.   (150
   Reprinted at the New York Public Library,
from the Bulletin, Jan.-Aug., 1912.---Jones
3004.

O'HALLORAN, T. P. A bibliography of South
America. Buenos Aires, Mackern; London,
T. F. Unwin, 1912. 55 p.   (151
   Jones 342.

OKINSHEVICH, Leo, and GOROKHOFF, Cecilia J.
Latin America in Soviet writings, 1945-1958;
a bibliography, edited by Nathan A. Haver-
stock. Washington, D.C., Library of Congress, 1959. 257 p. (Hispanic Foundation
bibliographical ser., no. 5)   (152

1800 books about Latin America; libros sobre
la América Latina. N.Y., R. R. Bowker,
1959. 86 p.   (153
   Compiled from the last edition of Subject
guide to Books in print in the USA.

OSPINA, Joaquín. Bibliografía universal.
Bogotá, Edit. Aguila, 1941.
xxi, 602 p.   (154

PALAU Y DULCET, Antonio. Manual del librero
hispano-americano; inventario bibliográfico
de la producción científica y literaria de
España y de la América Latina desde la invención de la imprenta hasta nuestros días,
con el valor comercial de todos los artículos descritos. Barcelona, Librería Anticuaria, 1923-1927. 7 v.   (155
   Jones 348.

-----. 2a. ed. corr. y aum. por el autor.
Barcelona, 1948- .   (156
   Last volume received at DPU: v. 17
(Rierra-Rossi)

PAN AMERICAN UNION. Lista de publicaciones
en español. Washington, D.C., 1944.
5 p.   (157

-----. A selected list of books prepared for
the imaginary "Good Neighbor" tour of the
General Federation of Women's Clubs. Washington, D.C., 1939. 17 p. mimeogr. (158

PAN AMERICAN UNION. Columbus Memorial Library.
Additions to the Columbus Memorial Library,
library series, no. 1-12, Jul./Dec. 1900-Jan.
/June 1906. Washington, D.C., Govt. Print.
Off., 1901-1906.   (159

-----. -----. Duplicate books offered in exchange. Wshington, D.C., 1939. 42 p. (160

-----. -----. 1940. 50 p.   (161

-----. -----. 1942. 59 p.   (162

-----. -----. List of books for reading
courses on Latin American subjects. Washington, D.C., [1915] [10] p.   (163

-----. -----. Selected list of recent books
(in English) on Latin America. Washington,
D.C., 1930. 21 p. (Bibliographic ser., no.
4) mimeogr.   (164
   This is a second edition of Recent books
in English on description and travel of
Latin America issued in 1929.

-----. -----. 3d ed., rev. and enl. 1933.
27 p. (Bibliographic ser. no. 4)
mimeogr.   (165
   This is the third edition of Recent books
in English on description and travel of
Latin America issued in 1929. Jones 362.

-----. -----. 4th ed., rev. and enl. 1935.
34 p. (Bibliographic ser., no. 4)
mimeogr.   (166

-----. -----. 5th ed., rev. and enl. 1939.
55 p. (Bibliographic ser., no. 4)
mimeogr.   (167
   Second printing with additions.

-----. -----. 6th ed., rev. and enl. 1942.
69 p. (Bibliographic ser., no. 4)
mimeogr.   (168

-----. -----. 7th ed., rev. and enl. 1945.
86 p. (Bibliographic ser., no. 4)
mimeogr.   (169

-----. -----. Sources of information for
books on Latin America, containing book
reviews, library and book trade journals,
selected list of book dealers; 2d ed. rev.
Washington, D.C., 1930. 18 p. (Bibliographic ser., no. 2)   (170
   First ed. 1929. The part relative to book-
dealers and publishers appeared with revi-
sions in the Bibliographic series, no. 2,
pt. 3, published in 1941, 1945, and 1958.

-----. -----. part 2, rev., Latin American
booktrade and library journals in the
Columbus Memorial Library. Washington, D.C.,
1941. 14 p. (Bibliographic ser.,
no. 2, pt. 2)   (171

PAN AMERICAN UNION. Division of Intellectual
Cooperation. Latin America in recent articles published by the Pan American Union.
Washington, D.C., [1936] 14 p.
mimeogr.   (172

-----. -----. Latin America in 300 articles
published in the Bulletin of the Pan American Union. Washington, D.C., [1941]
34 p.   (173

-----. -----. Latin America in 351 articles
published in the Bulletin of the Pan American Union. Washington, D.C., [1941]
39 p.   (174

-----. -----. Latin American culture in articles published in the Bulletin of the Pan
American Union (1923-1939) Washington, D.C.
[1939] 4 p.   (175

-----. -----. Recently published textbooks
and supplementary materials for the study
of Latin America in elementary and secondary schools. [Washington, D.C., 1948]
8 p.   (176

-----. -----. Some inexpensive references on
Latin America for the general reader.
[Washington, D.C., 1943] 3 p.
mimeogr.   (177

-----. Division of Sales and Promotion.
Quarterly list of publications released by
the Pan American Union. Lista trimestral
de publicaciones en circulación de la Unión
Panamericana, v. 1, no. 1-3/4; v.2, no. 1/2,
[1962-1963] Washington, D.C., [1962-
1963]   (178
No more issued.

PANE, Remigio Ugo. English translations from
the Spanish, 1484-1943, a bibliography.
New Brunswick, Rutgers Univ. Pr., 1944.
218 p. (Rutgers university studies in Spanish, no. 2)   (179
Includes many items of Latin American
works.

-----. Two hundred Latin American books in
English translation; a bibliography.
1943.   (180
From the Modern language journal, v. 27,
no. 8, p. 593-604, Dec. 1943.

PARIS. Bibliothèque Nationale. Catalogue de
l'histoire de l'Amérique, par George A.
Barringer. Paris, 1903-1911. 5 v. (181
Jones 364

PATCH, Richard Wilbur. Bibliography of the
Andean countries. N.Y., American Universities Field Staff [1958] 23 p.   (182
References to selected current works
relating to Peru, Bolivia, and Ecuador.

PAULUS, Wolfgang. Lateinamerika; bibliographie zum studium lateinamerikanischer
entwicklungsprobleme; 2. völlig neubearbeitete auflage. Freiburg, 1964. 278 p.
(Materialien des Arnold-Bergstraesser-
Instituts für kulturwissenschaftliche
Forschung)   (183

QUELLE, Otto. Literaturbericht. (Ibero-
amerikanisches archiv, Berlin-Bonn, v. 8,
p. 297-338, 381-417; v. 9, p. 50-89, 131-50,
1934-1936)   (184
Covers comprehensively German works on the
Hispanic countries.---Jones 384a.

-----. Neue bibliographien aus den ibero-
amerikanischen ländern. (Ibero-amerikanischen archiv, Bonn-Berlin, v. 1, p. 151-54,
1924)   (185
Jones 385.

-----. Das romanische Amerika, 1913-1925.
(Geographisches jahrbuch, Gotha, J. Perthes,
v. 41, p. 360-424, 1926)   (186
A valuable critical review of the geograph-
ical literature, in three sections, General,
South America and Central America, the West
Indies and Mexico, with various sub-sec-
tions.---Jones 385a.

-----. Verzeichnis wissenschaftlicher
einrichtungen, zeitschriften und bibliographien der ibero-amerikanischen kulturwelt.
Stuttgart und Berlin, Druck der Deutschen
Verlags-Anstalt, 1916. 67 p. (Veröffentlichungen des Deutsch-Südamerikanischen
und Iberischen Instituts, no. 3)   (187
Jones 386.

-----. -----. 1. Nachtrag. (Mitteilungen
des Deutsch Südamerikanischen und Iberischen
Instituts, Stuttgart und Berlin, 7. bd.,
p. 47-71, 1919)   (188
Jones 386.

QUESADA, Ernesto. L'imprimerie et les livres
dans l'Amérique espagnole au XVIe, XVIIe et
XVIIIe siècle. Discours prononcé au Congrès
International des Américanistes (3me session)
Séance du 24 septembre 1879. Bruxelles, X.
Havermans, 1879. 30 p.   (189
Jones 387.

QUESADA, Vicente Gregorio. La vida intelectual en la América española durante los Siglos XVI, XVII, XVIII con una introducción
de Horacio Ramos Mejía. B.A., 1917. 326 p.
(La Cultura argentina)   (190

RAEDERS, Georges. Bibliographie franco-brésil-
ienne, 1551-1957, avec la collaboration de
Edson Nery da Fonseca. Rio de Janeiro, Ministério da Educação e Cultura, Instituto Nacional do Livro. Coleção, B 1. Bibliografia,
11)   (191

REID, Dorcas Worsley, and REID, John T.   An
annotated bibliography of books on Spanish
South America and the West Indies. (Hispania, Stanford University, v. 20, p. 313-26,
1937)   (192
    Lists books of general character published
in the United States after 1920.---Jones
390b.

RIBADENEIRA, Carlos A. Guía moral de lecturas,
50.000 obras de los principales autores del
mundo juzgados a la luz de la fe y de la moral y recopilados sintéticamente. México,
Buena Prensa. n.d. 399 p.   (193

RICH, Obadiah. Bibliotheca americana nova; or,
A catalogue of books in various languages
relating to America, printed since the year
1700. Compiled principally from the works
themselves. London, O. Rich; New York,
Harper and Brothers, 1835. 424 p.   (194
    Half-title: Bibliotheca americana nova,
part 1, 1701-1800.---Jones 402.

-----. Supplement to the Bibliotheca americana nova, part 1. Additions and corrections, 1701-1800. London, Rich, 1841.
p. 425-517.   (195
    Jones 402.

-----. Vol. 2, 1801-1844. London, Rich and
Sons, 1844-1846. 2 pts.   (196
    Jones 402.

-----. Another edition. London, Rich and
Sons, 1846. 2 v.   (197
    Vol. 1 is a reissue of the Bibliotheca
americana nova published as an independent
work in 1835 (with half-title Pt. 1: 1701-
1800) and its Supplement, first pub. in
1841.
    Vol. 2 is a reissue of two parts, issued
in 1844 and 1846, covering literature of
1801-1830 and 1831-1844 respectively.
    The period 1500-1700 is covered by Rich's
Catalogue of books relating principally to
America, London, 1832. A proposed "Bibliotheca americana vetus" was completed but
never published, owing to loss of the manuscript.---Jones 403.

-----. A catalogue of books, relating principally to America, arranged under the years
in which they were printed. London, O. Rich,
1832. 129 p.   (198
    Contents.-pt. 1. Books printed between
1500 and 1600.-pt. 2. Books printed between 1600 and 1700.---Jones 401.

RIPON COLLEGE, Ripon, Wisc. Works in English
of a relatively contemporary nature...
suitable for small liberal arts colleges of-
fering courses in the Latin American area.
Ripon, Wisc. 1964. 26 p.   (199

RIVET, Paul. Bibliographie américainiste.
(Journal de la Société des Américanistes de
Paris, Nouv. sér., t. 11-24, 1919-1932) (200
    Vol. 20, by P. Rivet and H. Vosy-Bourbon;
21, by Rivet and P. Lester; 22, by Rivet
and M. A. Maurer; 23-24, by Rivet and P.
Barret. Continued by P. Barret in the
Journal, v. 25 (1933)- . ---Jones 410.

SABIN, Joseph. Bibliotheca americana. A
dictionary of books relating to America,
from its discovery to the present time.
Begun by Joseph Sabin, continued by Wilberforce Eames and completed by R.W.G. Vail for
the Bibliographical Society of America...
New York, 1868-1936. 29 v.   (201
    Editors: v. 1-19, and v. 20, pt. 1-2,
Joseph Sabin. - v. 20, pt. 3-6 and v. 21,
pt. 1, Wilberforce Eames for the Bibliographical Society of America. - v. 21, pt. 2-6
and v. 22-29, R. W. G. Vail.
    Publication was suspended from 1892 to
1927, when it was resumed with the parts
numbered continuously with the last issued
in 1892. Suspended with pt. 115/116 (v. 20,
pt. 1/2) 1892; resumed with pt. 117 (v. 20,
pt. 3) 1927.
    "Bibliographia americana 1866 and 1936":
v. 29, p. xiii-xxi.---Jones 425.
    Now available in microprint.

-----. Amsterdam, N. Israel, 1962. 7 v.
in 4 v.   (201a

SANZ, Carlos. Bibliotheca americana vetustissima. Madrid, Librería General Victoriano Suárez, 1960. 2 v.   (202
    v. 1, to 1507: p. 1-629; v. 2, to 1551:
p. 645-1407.

-----. Bibliotheca americana vetustissima;
comentario crítico e índice general cronológico de los seis volúmenes que componen
la obra. Madrid, Librería General Victoriano Suárez, 1960. 79 p.   (203

SÃO PAULO. Universidade. Facultade de Filosofia, Ciências e Letras. Retrospectiva de
publicações. São Paulo, 1961. 325 p. (204
    Listing of publications of faculty mem-
bers, 1945-1961.

SEMINARIO de Problemas Hispanoamericanos, Madrid. Hispanoamérica en España, 1948; Índice de libros, artículos y conferencias,
sobre Hispano-américa, producidos en España
en 1948. Madrid, 1949. 122 p. (Santo y
seña, 3)   (205

SEVILLANO COLOM, Francisco. List of micro-
filmed materials at the Barbados Public Library. Barbados, W.I., 1960. 23 p.   (206

-----. Lista de materiales microfilmados en
la Biblioteca Nacional y en el Archivo Na-

SEVILLANO COLOM, ... (Cont.)
cional de Santiago de Chile, con una noticia histórica de estas instituciones. Santiago, Misión de la Unesco en Chile, 1961.
25 p.   (206a

-----. Materiales microfilmados en la Biblioteca Nacional de Panamá, en el Archivo Nacional de Panamá y en la Biblioteca de la
Universidad. Panamá, [1958] 53 p. (207

SILVA, Innocencio Francisco da. Diccionario
bibliographico portuguez. Estudos de Innocencio Francisco da Silva, aplicaveis a
Portugal e ao Brasil. Lisboa, na Imprensa
Nacional, 1858-1919. 22 v.   (208
Vols. 10- . Continuados e ampliados por
Brito Aranha (v. 21, com amplo estudo crítico acerca da obra monumental de Alexandre
Herculano, por J. J. Gomes de Brito. - v.
22, Revistas por Gomes de Brito e Alvaro
Neves)
"Resenha das obras nacionaes e estrangei-
ras ... que foram ... consultadas:" t. 1,
p.xxv-liii, t. 8, p. xxvii-xxxi.---Jones
1194.

SMITH, John Russell. Bibliotheca americana.
A catalogue of a valuable collection of
books, pamphlets, manuscripts, maps, engravings, and engraved portraits, illus-
trating the history and geography of North
and South America, and the West Indies.
London, 1845.   (209
Cited in Giraldo Jaramillo, p. 56.

SOJUSZ dla Postepu: wykaz wybranych dokumen-
tów i literatury za okres 1961-1962.
Opracowal: Andrzej Abraszewski. Warszawa,
1963. 44 p. mimeogr.   (210
HLAS 26, item 77 noted that Publication
was by the Polish Institute of International
Affairs.

THE SOUTH AMERICAN handbook, 1935; South and
Central America, Mexico, Cuba. London,
Trade & Travel Publications, 1935.
628 p.   (211
Books recommended: p. 553-563.
Other issues.---Jones 453.

THE SOUTH AMERICAN year book and directory.
(Incorporating the South American railway
year book, South American annual, and South
American blue book) Containing general
information relating to the ten republics of
the continent of South America, British,
Dutch, and French Guiana, the Panama Canal
and the Falkland Islands. Comp. and ed. by
C. S. Vesey Brown. London, The Louis
Cassier Co., 1913-1916. 2 v.   (212
Include bibliographies.---Jones 454.

SPELL, Lota M. Research materials for the
study of Latin America at the University of

SPELL, Lota M. ... (Cont.)
Texas. Austin, University of Texas Pr.,
1954. 107 p. (Latin American studies,
14)   (213

STEVENS, Henry. Catalogue of the American
books in the library of the British Museum
at Christmas MDCCCLVI. London, Printed by
C. Whittingham at the Chiswick Pr., 1866.
4 pt. in 1 v.   (214
Part 3: Catalogue of the Mexican and
other Spanish American & West Indian books,
62 p.---Jones 462.

STURGIS, Cony. A suggestive bibliography for
teachers of Spanish.   (215
Reprinted from Hispania, v. 13, no. 1,
p. 35-54, Feb. 1930. List is mainly of
books in English, with a section devoted to
Hispanic America.

TERMER, Franz. Deutsche und nordamerikanische
auslandsforschung in den iberoamerikanischen
ländern. Hamburg, Friederichsen de Gruyter,
1936. 21 p.   (216
Jones 471.

TERNAUX-COMPANS, Henri. Bibliothèque américaine; ou, Catalogue des ouvrages relatifs
à l'Amérique qui ont paru depuis sa découverte jusqu'à l'an 1700. Paris. Arthus-
Bertrand, 1837. 191 p.   (217
1153 titles.---Jones 472.

TE VELDE, Johan C. Modern Latin America: a
popular bibliography. Chicago, The Pan American Forum, Central Y.M.C.A. College, 1939.
31 p. (The good neigbor series; Ernest
Schwartz, editor, no. 1)   (218
Jones 474.

TRÜBNER'S American and Oriental literary
record. A register of the most important
works published in North and South America,
in India, China, and the British colonies;
with occasional notes on German, Dutch,
Danish, French, Italian, Spanish, Portuguese,
and Russian books. v. [1]-12, Mar. 1865-Dec.
1879; new ser. v. 1-9, Jan. 1880-Dec. 1888;
3d ser. v. 1, Mar. 1889-Feb. 1890. London,
Trübner & co., 1865-1890. 22 v.   (219
Replaced in part by Luzac's Oriental
list.---Jones 494.

UNITED NATIONS Educational, Scientific and
Cultural Organization. Guía de centros nacionales de información bibliográfica; 2a.
ed. La Habana, Centro Regional de la Unesco
en el Hemisferio Occidental, 1962.
67 p.   (220
Includes centers in Latin American
countries, listing publications issued by
each.

UNITED NATIONS Educational, Scientific and
Cultural Organization. Guide des centres
nationaux d'information bibliographique.
2. ed. Paris, UNESCO, 1962. 72 p.   (221
   Includes centers in Latin American countries, listing publications issued by each.

UNITED Presbyterian Church in the U.S.A. Commission on Ecumenical Mission and Relations.
Bibliography for Latin American studies. N.Y.
1963. 19 p. (Bulletin, Office for Research, v. 3, no. 2, Dec. 5, 1963)   (222

U.S. Air Force. Caribbean Air Command. Historical Division. Bibliography for Latin
America. Albrook Air Force Base, Canal Zone
[1959] 106   (223

-----. Air University. Library. Latin America: selected references. Maxwell Air Force
Base, Alabama, 1962-1963. 2 v. (Special
bibliography, 166, Suppl. 1-2)   (224
   Cited in HLAS 26, item 87.

-----. Department of State. External Research Division. American republics; a
listing of recently completed studies. Washington, D.C.,1954- . (External research
list, 12.5-)   (224a
   The series began as an annual in 1952 listing unpublished research. The "complete
studies" was initiated in October 1954 as
an annual. The unpublished compilation
appears in the Spring issues.

-----. Department of the Army. Latin America:
hemispheric partner; a bibliographic survey.
Washington, D.C., 1964. 128 p. 3 maps in
pocket. (DA pamphlet 550-1, Headquarters
Department of the Army)   (225

-----. Military Assistance Institute. Library. Suggested reading list on Central America and the Caribbean; revised. Arlington,
Va., 1962. 26 p.   (226

-----. -----. Suggested reading list on Latin
America; revised. Arlington, Va., 1962.
42 p.   (227

-----. -----. 2d revision. Arlington, Va.,

U.S. Military Assistance ... (Cont.)
1963. 32 p.   (227a
   Cited in HLAS 26, item 90.

URQUIZA GARCIA, Rosina. Ensayo de una bibliografía para bibliotecas de centros secunda-
rios. La Habana, Ucar, García, 1959.
338 p.   (228
   First published in the Boletín de la Asociación Cubana de Bibliotecarios, June 1954-
Mar. 1957.

UTRECHT. Rijksuniversiteit. Bibliotheek.
España e Hispanoamérica. Catálogo de libros
españoles y publicaciones extranjeras sobre
España e Hispanoamérica. Utrecht, 1948.
360 p.   (229

-----. Suplemento, I-VIII, Utrecht, 1949-
1963.   (230

-----. Portugal e o Brasil: Catalogo de
livros portugueses e publicações estrangei-
ras sôbre Portugal e o Brasil, in samen-
werking met de Stichting "Het Spaans, Por-
tugees en Iber-Amerikaans Institut".
Utrecht, 1959-1962. 2 v.   (231
   Cited in HLAS 26, item 73a.

WEAVER, Agnes Rice. Bibliography on Latin
America. Los Angeles, Office of the County
Superintendent of Schools, 1940.
20 p.   (232

WEBER, Friedrich. Beiträge zur charakteristik
der älteren geschichtsschreiber über
Spanisch-Amerika, eine biographischbiblio-
graphische skizze. Leipzig, R. Voigtländer,
1911. 338 p. (Beiträge zur kultur- und
universalgeschichte; hrsg. von K. Lamprecht,
14. hft.)   (233
   A historical and critical review of the
literature.---Jones 526.

WILGUS, Alva Curtis. Source material and
special collections dealing with Latin
America in libraries of the United States.
Washington, D.C., 1934. 22, [1] p.
(Congress and conference series, no.
14)   (233a
   Prepared for the Inter-American Conference
on bibliography, Havana, 1934.

AGRICULTURE

GENERAL

ANTON RAMIREZ, Braulio. Diccionario de bibliografía agronómica y de toda clase de escritos relacionados con la agricultura, seguido de un índice de autores y traductores, con algunos apuntes biográficos. Madrid, M. Rivadeneyra, 1865. 1015 p. (234
    Jones 18.

BARNES, Helen Virginia, and ALLEN, Jessie May. A bibliography of plant pathology in the tropics and in Latin America [1937-1949] Washington, D.C., Govt. Print. Off., 1951. 78 p. (U.S. Department of Agriculture. Bibliographical bulletin, no. 14) (234a

DIAZ BORDENAVE, Juan E. Folletos en extensión agrícola. Turrialba, C.R., Instituto Interamericano de Ciencias Agrícolas, 1958. 11 p. mimeogr. (235

GRAVENHORST, Hans. Documentación bibliográfica en el campo de la agronomía y medicina veterinaria. Clase correspondiente al ciclo "Bibliografías especiales" del Curso de capacitación para documentalistas organizado por el Instituto Bibliotecológico. Buenos Aires, Instituto Bibliotecológico, 1953. 16 p. mimeogr. (236
    Cited in Catálogo, Inst. Bibliotecológico, Buenos Aires, 1964, item 712.

HERNANDEZ DE CALDAS, Angela. Cerca de dos mil publicaciones agropecuarias o de ciencias afines que se pueden consultar en Colombia. Pasto, Universidad de Nariño, Instituto Tecnológico Agrícola, 1962. 37 p. mimeogr. (237
    Cited in Florén, Bibliogr. bibliot., 1961/62, item 203.

INTER-AMERICAN Committee for Agricultural Development. Inventario de la información básica para la programación del desarrollo agrícola en la América Latina; selección bibliográfica. Washington, D.C., Unión Panamericana [1964] 187 p. (238

-----. English language edition. Washington, D.C., Pan American Union, [1964] 187 p. (239

INTER-AMERICAN Conference on Agriculture, Caracas, 3d, 1945. Handbook for the use of the delegates, v. 2. Washington, D.C., Pan American Union, [1945] 2 pts. (240
    Pt. 1: Foodstuffs and raw materials (136 p.).-pt. 2: Animal industry. Both parts contain a large body of bibliographical information relative to the various countries of Latin America.

PAN AMERICAN UNION. Division of Agricultural Cooperation. Lista seleccionada de publicações sôbre agricultura tropical, preparada para a Conferencia Inter-americana sôbre Agricultura, Silvicultura, e Indústria Animal, setembro 8-20, 1930. Washington, D.C., União Pan-Americana, 1930. 90 p. mimeogr. (241

-----. Lista selecta de publicaciones sobre agricultura tropical, compilada para la Conferencia Interamericana de Agricultura, Selvicultura e Industria Animal, 8-20 de setiembre de 1930. Washington, D.C., Unión Panamericana, 1930. 90 p. mimeogr. (242

-----. Selected list of publications on tropical agriculture. Prepared for the Inter-American Conference on Agriculture, Forestry and Animal Industry, September 8-20, 1930. Washington, D.C., Pan American Union, 1930. 90 p. mimeogr. (243

REUNION Técnica de Bibliotecas Agrícolas de Colombia, Medellín, 1962. Informe. Suplemento, libros básicos sobre agricultura. Medellín, Escuela Inter-americana de Bibliotecología, 1962. 41 p. (244

SHAW, Ralph Robert, and others. Facilidades de intercomunicación científica agrícola en América Latina, por Ralph R. Shaw, Armando Samper, Arthur E. Gropp. Turrialba, C.R., 1953. 71 p. (Inter-American Institute of Agricultural Sciences, Turrialba, C.R., Publ. miscelánea, no. 3) (245

U.S. Office of Foreign Agricultural Relations. Published information on foreign agriculture, January 1937-December 1946. Washington, D.C., 1947. 56 p. (246
    Includes Latin American countries.

-----. -----. Jan. 1937-Dec. 1947. Washington, D.C., 1948. 64 p. (247

URUGUAY. Poder Legislativo. Biblioteca. Alimentos (Material existente en la Biblioteca) ... Montevideo, 1948. various pagings. (Referencia, 2) (248

-----. Universidad. Facultad de Agronomía. Nómina de publicaciones de la cátedra de industrias agrícolas y Estación Experimental del Frío (1927-1935) Montevideo, Augusta, 1936. 8 p. (249
    Contains 67 items.---Musso, item 46.

VIVAS BERTHIER, Gastón. Contribución bibliográfica a las investigaciones en ciencias agrícolas y biológicas y otras relacionadas con ellas. Caracas, Edit. Crisol, 1946.

VIVAS BERTHIER, Gastón... (Cont.)
  353 p. (Conferencia Interamericana de Agricultura, Caracas, 3a., 1945, Cuadernos ver-
  des, no. 59)   (250

CACAO

GARCIA PAYON, José. Amaxocoatl, o Libro del
  chocolate. Toluca, Méx., Tip. Escuela de
  Artes, 1936. 116, vi p.   (251
    "Apéndice. El chocolate en la literatura
  española del siglo XVII. Por Julio Monreal"
  (p. 105-116) reprinted from an article in
  Ilustración artística, 1885, entitled: El
  chocolate.
    Bibliografía: vi p.---Jones 159a

MARTINEZ, Angelina, and JAMES, C. Noel.
  Cacao: bibliografía de las publicaciones que
  se encuentran en la Biblioteca del Instituto.
  Turrialba, C.R., Instituto Interamericano de
  Ciencias Agrícolas, 1954. 258 p. mimeogr.
  (Lista bibliográfica, no. 2)   (252

-----. Supplement. 1958. 132 p.   (253

MARTINEZ, Angelina. Fuentes de información
  sobre literatura de cacao. Turrialba, C.R.,
  Instituto Interamericano de Ciencias Agrícolas, 1958. 11 p. mimeogr.   (254

MUELLER, Wolf. Bibliographie des Kakao.
  Hamburg, M. Rieck, 1951. 120 p.   (255
    Lists approximately 3,500 titles. Gener-
  al in character, but includes a large number of references to cacao in the Americas.

COFFEE

AGUIRRE B., Francisco. Café; utilización industrial del grano y los subproductos. Guatemala, Instituto Centroamericano de Investigación y Tecnología Industrial (ICAITI)
  1959? 40 p.   (256
    A review of the literature.

FIGUEROA, Carlos A. Bibliografía preliminar
  sobre el cultivo del café. Washington,
  Unión Panamericana, Oficina de Cooperación
  Agrícola, 1933. 17 p.   (257

HOUK, William G. Nomenclatura dos cafeeiros;
  lista de referencias e bibliografia. São
  Paulo, Instituto Agronômico de Campinas.
  1939. 49 p. (Boletín técnico, no.
  63)   (258
    Cited in Martínez, Café, p. 2.

INSTITUTO AGRONOMICO do Estado de São Paulo,
  Campinas, Brazil. Trabalhos sôbre o ca-
  feeiro publicados por técnicos do Instituto
  Agronômico de Campinas a partir de 1930.
  São Paulo, 1951. 28 p.   (259
    Contains 238 references. Cited in
  Martínez, Café, p. 2.

INSTITUTO AGRONOMICO do Estado de São Paulo,
  Campinas, Brazil. São Paulo, 1954. 27 p.
  (Boletim no. 52)   (260
    Cited in Martínez, Café, p. 2.

INSTITUTO Centroamericano de Investigación y
  Tecnología Industrial, Guatemala. Café;
  bibliografía preliminar compilada con especial énfasis sobre la utilización industrial
  del grano de café y sus subproductos. Guatemala, 1958. 90 p.   (261
    Cited in Martínez, Café, p. 2.

LOCKHART, Ernest E., and BLOOMHARDT, Fred B.
  A survey of world literature on coffee,
  1953. New York, Coffee Brewing Institute,
  1956. 23 p. (Publ. no. 7)   (262

-----. 1954. New York, Coffee Brewing Institute, 1956. 35 p. Publ. no. 13)   (263

-----. 1955. New York, Coffee Brewing Institute, 1957. 32 p. (Publ. no. 23)   (264

MARTINEZ, Angelina, and JAMES, C. Noel. Café;
  bibliografía de las publicaciones que se encuentran en la Biblioteca del Instituto.
  Turrialba, C.R., Instituto Interamericano
  de Ciencias Agrícolas, 1953. 226 p. (Lista
  bibliográfica, no. 1)   (265
    Contains 1,840 entries.

-----. 2d ed. Turrialba, C.R., Instituto Interamericano de Ciencias Agrícolas, 1960.
  637 p. (Lista bibliográfica, no. 1,
  rev.)   (266
    Contains 5,227 entries. Title-page also
  in English.

-----. -----. Suplemento no. 1, compilado por
  Ghislaine P. de Montoya. Turrialba, C.R.,
  1963. 181 p.   (267
    Contains 1,587 entries.

MARTINEZ, Angelina. Fuentes de información
  sobre literatura de café. Turrialba, C.R.,
  Instituto Interamericano de Ciencias Agrícolas, 1956. 6 p. mimeogr.   (268

PEREZ DE LA RIVA, Francisco. Bibliografía
  cafetalera cubana. La Habana, Banco de Fomento Agrícola e Industrial de Cuba, 1953.
  228 p. (Publ. del Banco de Fomento Agrícola e Industrial de Cuba, 6)   (269

CORN (Maize)

INTER-AMERICAN Institute of Agricultural Sciences. Maíz; bibliografía de las publicaciones
  que se encuentran en la Biblioteca Conmemorativa Ortón. Turrialba, C.R., 1964. 188 p.
  (Bibliografías, no. 3, suppl. no. 1)   (270

MARTINEZ, Angelina, and JAMES, C. Noel. Maíz;
bibliografía de las publicaciones que se encuentran en la Biblioteca del Instituto.
Turrialba, C.R., Instituto Interamericano
de Ciencias Agrícolas, 1960. 2 v. (Lista
bibliográfica, no. 3)   (271
   Contains 10,734 entries.

PERGAMINO, Argentina. Estación Experimental
Agropecuaria. Bibliografía sobre maíz exis-
tente en la Estación Agropecuaria Pergamino.
Dirigió: Eduardo Ferreira Sobral. [Perga-
mino] Instituto Nacional de Tecnología
Agropecuaria [1964] 198 p. (Serie biblio-
gráfica, t. 15)   (271a
   Added t.-p. in English.

U.S. Department of Agriculture. Library.
Corn in the development of the civilization
of the Americas; selected and annotated bibliography. Washington, D.C., 1940. 195 p.
(Agricultural economic bibliographies,
87)   (271b

FORESTS AND FOREST PRODUCTS

AHERN, George Patrick, and NEWTON, Helen K.
A bibliography of woods of the world exclusive of the temperate region and with emphasis on tropical woods. New York. The
American Society of Mechanical Engineers,
1928. 77 p. (Tropical Plant Research
Foundation. Scientific contributions,
no. 10)   (271c
   Includes tropical America: Mexico and
Central America, Colombia and Venezuela,
the Guianas, Argentina, Brazil, Chile, and
other South American countries.

FLICK, Frances Josephine. The forest of continental Latin America, including European
possessions; a bibliography of selected literature, 1920-1950. Washington, D.C. Govt.
Print. Off., 1952. 193 p. (U.S. Dept. of
Agriculture, Bibliographical bull.,
no. 18)   (272

PAN AMERICAN UNION. Bibliography on forests
and forestry. Books and magazine articles.
[Washington, D.C., [n.d.] 17 p.   (273
   Cited in PAU Bibliographies, p. 28.

-----. Division of Agricultural Cooperation.
Partial bibliography on rubber. Washington,
D.C., 1946. 5 p. mimeogr.   (274

RECORD, Samuel J. Bibliography of the woods
of the world ... 2d ed., rev. and enl. New
Haven, Conn., 1923. 40 p. mimeogr.   (275
   Tropical America: p. 6-20.

TOBACCO

ARGENTINA. Instituto Nacional del Tabaco.
Bibliografía sobre fitotecnia del tabaco.
[Buenos Aires] Ministerio de Agricultura de
la Nación [1942] 34 p. mimeogr.   (275a
   Compiler: José Llorca.

-----. -----. Ensayo de una bibliografía
argentina del tabaco. [Buenos Aires] Ministerio de Agricultura de la Nación [1943]
84 p. mimeogr.   (275b
   Compiler: José Llorca.

-----. Another ed. 1945. 79 p.   (275c

CARNER, Wightman Wells. Bibliografía selecta
sobre el tabaco, Washington, D.C., Unión
Panamericana, Oficina de Cooperación Agrícola, 1933. 25 p. mimeogr.   (275d
   Published also in English.

VEGETABLES

BOSWELL, Víctor Rickman. Bibliografía selecta sobre hortalizas. Washington, D.C.,
Unión Panamericana, 1933. 81 p. (Columbus
Memorial Library, Bibliographic ser.,
no. 11)   (276

HERNANDEZ DE CALDES, Angela, and DIAZ, Carolina. Literatura sobre enfermedades de la
papa. Bogotá, Centro Nacional de Investigaciones Agrícolas Tibaitatá, 1956. 39 p.
(Ser. bibliográfica, no. 1)   (277
   Cited in Giraldo Jaramillo, p. 82.

LA MOLINA, Perú. Estación Experimental Agrícola. Biblioteca. Publicaciones sobre
papa catalogadas en la Biblioteca. Lima,
1956. 49 p. (Ser. bibliográfica,
no. 1)   (278
   Introduction signed: Amalia Cavero.

MARTINEZ, Angelina, and JAMES, C. Noel. Lista de referencias sobre horticultura en el
idioma español; incluyendo además una lista
de textos y otras publicaciones importantes
en inglés. Turrialba, C.R., Instituto Interamericano de Ciencias Agrícolas, Biblioteca Conmemorativa Ortón, 1954. 23 p.
mimeogr.   (279

OTHER PRODUCTS

ARGENTINA. Ministerio de Agricultura y Ganadería. Departamento de Bibliotecas. Arroz;
bibliografía seleccionada. Buenos Aires,
1959. 12 p. (Circular bibliográfica,
no. 8)   (280
   Cited in Circular bibliográfica, no. 9.

ANTHROPOLOGY

GENERAL

BARROSO, Gustavo. Aquem da Atlantida. São Paulo, Companhia Editora Nacional, 1931. 288 p. (311
"Fontes bibliograficas" at end of each chapter.---Jones 971.

COMAS, Juan. Historia y bibliografía de los congresos internacionales de ciencias antropológicas, 1865-1954. México, D.F., Dirección General de Publicaciones, 1956. 490 p. (Universidad Nacional Autónoma de México, Instituto de Historia, Publ. 1, ser. 37) (312

-----. Recopilación bibliográfica de antropología prehistórica; Homo Neanderthalensis. México, D.F., 1941. 8 p. (313
Cited in Millares, Registro, 1941, p. 1.

INTERNATIONAL bibliography of social and cultural anthropology, v. 1- . 1955- . [Paris, London] Unesco. (314
Includes references to articles in Latin American periodicals.

MASON, Gregory. Columbus came late. New York, London, The Century Co., 1931. 341 p. (315
Bibliography: p. 329-34.---Jones 292.

PERICOT GARCIA, Luis. América indígena. Barcelona, Salvat Editores, 1936- . v. 1- . (316
Bibliographical notes at end of chapters. ---Jones 370.

POSNANSKY, Arthur. Antropología y sociología de las razas interandinas y de las regiones adyacentes; 2. ed. Instituto "Tihuanacu" de Antropología, Etnografía y Prehistoria. La Paz, Edit. "Renacimiento", 1938. 150, iv, [5] p. (317
"Cuadro sióptico-cronológico de cronistas, historiadores e investigadores que se ocuparon de los urus, chipayas, puquinas, changos, kunzas y otros aruwakes": iv p.
"Trabajos del prof. ing. Arthur Posnansky": 5 p. at end.---Jones 931.

RUYSCH, W. A., and MAIER, Carlos G. Bibliografía sistemática de antropología; a systematic bibliography of anthropology. Buenos Aires, Ediciones Keiron, 1953. 16 p. (Archivos ethnos; ser. D, no. 1) (318

STEWART, Thomas Dale. A bibliography of physical anthropology in Latin America: 1937-1948. N. Y., Wennes-Gren Foundation for Anthropological Research [1952] 59 p. (319

VALLE, Rafael Heliodoro. Bibliografía antropológica americana (1938-1940) (Boletín bibliográfico de antropología americana, México, D.F., v. 4, no. 2, p. 165-215, mayo/ag. 1940) (320
Contains "Noticias" and "Hemerobibliografía".---Jones 507a.

VERRILL, Alpheus Hyatt. Old civilizations of the New World. Indianapolis, The Bobbs-Merrill Co., 1929. 393 p. (321
Bibliography: p. 357-77.---Jones 512.

BRAZIL

FARIA, L. de Castro. Pesquisas de antropologia física no Brasil; história, bibliografia. Rio de Janeiro, 1952. 106 p. (Boletim do Museu Nacional, nova série; antropologia, 13) (322
Bibliography and index to bibliography: p. 63-106.

MATTOS. Prehistoria brasileira; varios estudos. São Paulo [etc.] Comp. Editora Nacional, 1938. 324 p. (Biblioteca pedagogica brasileira, ser. 5: Brasiliana, v. 137) (323
Bibliographia: p. 311-20.---Jones 1096a.

CHILE

LATCHAM, Ricardo Eduardo. Bibliografía chilena de las ciencias antropológicas, 1.-2. serie. (Revista de bibliografía chilena y extranjera, Santiago, año 3, no. 6, p. 148-85; no. 7, p. 229-61, 1915) (324
625 and 547 items cited.---Jones 1505.

-----. La prehistoria chilena. Santiago, Soc., Impr. y Lit. Universo, 1928. 243 p. (325
Bibliography at the end of each chapter.---Jones 1506.

MONTANE M., Julio C. Bibliografía selectiva de antropología chilena: primera parte, Araucanos - Pehuenches - Chiloé y territorios adyacentes. La Serena, 1963. 34 p. (La Serena. Museo. Contribuciones arqueológicas, no. 2) (326

PORTER, Carlos Emilio. Bibliografía chilena de antropología y etnología. Buenos Aires, Coni, Hnos., 1910. 24 p. (327
Reprinted from Anales del Museo Nacional, Buenos Aires.

-----. -----. Trabajo presentado al 4. Congreso Científico (1. Pan-Americano) con un

PORTER, Carlos Emilio... (Cont.)
prólogo de Ricardo E. Latcham. Ed. del autor.
Buenos Aires, Impr. "Juan A. Alsina", 1910.
44 p. (328
From Anales del Museo Nacional de Buenos
Aires, t. 20, ser. 3, t. 13.
Continued by Latcham in Revista de bibliografía chilena y extranjera, t. 2, p. 49-52.
Cf. Laval (Bib. de bib. chilenas, no. 258-74)
for a list of Porter's bibliographical contributions.---Jones 1570.

-----. Bibliografía chilena de ciencias antropológicas. Santiago, Impr. "Santiago",
1912. 62 p. (329
Jones 1571.

-----. Les études anthropologiques au Chili.
Macon, Protat Frères, 1910. 19 p. (330
Extract from Journal of the Société des
Américanistes de Paris, n.s., t. 7, p. 203-
19, 1910.
Cited in Laval, item 269.

-----. Literatura antropológica y etnológica
de Chile. Santiago, 1906. 36 p. (331
Jones 1577.

COSTA RICA

LINES, Jorge A. Bibliografía antropológica
aborigen de Costa Rica; incluye especialmente: arqueología, cartografía, etnología, geografía, historia y lingüística. San José,
Costa Rica, 1943. 263 p. (332

GAUTEMALA

ANNALS of the Cakchiquels. Memorial de Tecpán-
Atitlán (Anales de los cakchiqueles) por
Francisco Hernández Arana Xajilá y Francisco
Díaz Gebutá Quej; texto y traducción revisa-
dos con notas y estudios sobre lingüística
guatemalteca, por J. Antonio Villacorta C.
Guatemala, Tip. Nacional, 1934. 383 p (333
"Bibliografía de los mayances guatemaltecos": p. 65-86. See also Villacorta's "Bibliografía de la lengua maya y de los mayances guatemaltecos" in Primer centenario de
la Sociedad Mexicana de Geografía y Estadística, 1833-1933. (México, 1933), v.1, p. 74-
104.---Jones 1283a.

EWALD, Robert Harold. Bibliografía comentada
sobre antropología social guatemalteca, 1900-
1955. Guatemala, Seminario de Integración
Social Guatemalteca, 1956. 132 p. (334

MEXICO

BEAUVOIS, Eugène. Les publications relatives
à l'ancien Mexique depuis une trentaine

BEAUVOIS, Eugène... (Cont.)
d'années. Paris, Au Siège de la Société,
1899. 23 p. (335
Congrès Bibliographique International
tenu à Paris du 13 au 16 avril 1898, sous
les auspices de la Société Bibliographique.
Extrait du Compte rendu des travaux, t. 1,
p. 475-97.---Jones 2072.

CASTILLO TEJERO, Noemí, and MIRAMBELL SILVA,
Lorena E. Bibliografía antropológica; trabajos publicados en México, 1955-1962, editada bajo la dirección de Lauro José Zavala.
México, 1962. 172 p. (335a

COMAS, Juan. La antropología física de México
y Centro América. Estadísticas, bibliografía y mapas de distribución de caracteres
somáticos. México, Edit. Stylo, 1943. 131 p.
(Publ. del Instituto Panamericano de
Geografía e Historia, no. 68) (336
Bibliografía: p. 81-129.

COMAS, Juan, and GENOVES TARAGAZA, Santiago.
La antropología física en México, 1943-1959;
inventario y programa de investigaciones.
México, Universidad Nacional Autónoma de México, 1960. 66 p. (Cuadernos del Instituto
de Historia; serie antropológica, no.
10) (337
Universidad Nacional Autónoma de México.
Publ. del Instituto de Historia, la. ser.,
no. 59)

COMAS, Juan. Bosquejo histórico de la antropología en México. México, 1950. p. 97-
[192]. (338
Reprinted from Revista mexicana de estudios antropológicos, t. 11.

GENOVES TARAGAZA, Santiago, and COMAS, Juan,
La antropología física en México, 1943-1964;
inventario bibliografico. México, Universi-
dad Nacional, 1964. 55 p. (Cuadernos del
Instituto de Investigaciones Históricas;
serie antropológica, 17) (339
Also issued as la serie, no. 91 of the
Instituto de Investigaciones Históricas.

HRDLICKA, Ales. Physiological and medical
observations among the Indians of south-
western United States and northern Mexico.
Washington, D.C., Govt. Print. Off., 1908.
460 p. (Smithsonian Institution. Bureau
of American Ethnology. Bulletin 34) (340
Bibliography: p. 407-25.---Jones 2248.

LEON, Nicolás. La antropología física y la
antropometría en México. Notas históricas
(seguido de) Bibliografía antro-somatológica
mexicana. México, 1922. (341
Jones 2283.

-----. Apuntes para una bibliografía antropológica de México (Somatología). México,

LEON, Nicolás... (Cont.)
  Impr. del Museo Nacional, 1901. 18 p. (342
    Jones 2285.

PARRA, Manuel Germán, and JIMENEZ MORENO,
  Wigberto. Bibliografía indigenista de México y Centroamérica (1850-1950) México, Instituto Nacional Indigenista, 1954. ci,
  342 p. (Memorias del Instituto Nacional Indigenista, v. 4)   (343

SAHAGUN, Bernardino de. A history of ancient
  Mexico, translated by Fanny R. Bandelier
  from the Spanish version of Carlos María de
  Bustamante. Nashville, Fisk Univ. Pr.,
  1932- . (Fisk University social science
  series)   (344
    Bibliography of Fray Bernardino de
  Sahagún's writings": v. 1, p. 251-305.---
  Jones 2480.

VAILLANT, George Clapp. Early cultures of the
  valley of Mexico. New York, The American
  Museum of Natural History, 1935. p. 281-328.
  (Anthropological papers of the American Museum of Natural History, v. 35, pt. 3) (345
    Bibliography; p. 305-28.---Jones 2541.

WILLIAMS, George Dee. Maya-Spanish crosses
  in Yucatan, Cambridge, Mass., 1931. 256 p.
  (Papers of the Peabody Museum of American
  Archaeology and Ethnology, v. 13, no.
  1)   (346
    Bibliography: p. 251-56.---Jones 2584.

PERU

DORSEY, George Amos. A bibliography of the
  anthropology of Peru. Chicago, 1898.
  p. 55-206. (Field Columbian Museum, Publ.
  23; Anthropological ser., v. 2,
  no. 2)   (347
    Jones 2653.

SCHWAB, Federico. Bibliografía de antropología
  peruana, 1936 a 1937. Lima, Compañía de Impresiones y Publicidad, 1938. 40 p. (348
    Reprinted from Boletín bibliográfico, Bi-
  blioteca Central, Universidad Mayor de San
  Marcos, v. 8, no. 1.

TELLO, Luis C. Bibliografía antropológica del
  Perú. (Boletín bibliográfico, Universidad
  Mayor de San Marcos, Lima, v. 3, p. 31-6,
  1927)   (349
    Jones 2757.

PUERTO RICO

MORALES CABRERA, Pablo. Puerto Rico indígena;
  prehistoria y protohistoria de Puerto Rico;
  descripción de los usos, costumbres, lenguaje, religión, gobierno, agricultura, industrias del pueblo taino de Boriquén, según
  los cronistas de Indias en la época del descubrimiento de América. [San Juan, Puerto
  Rico, "Impr. Venezuela", 1932?]
  381 p.   (350
    Bibliografía: p. 304-06.---Jones 2798.

SOUTH AMERICA

COMAS, Juan. Bibliografía morfológica humana
  de América del Sur. México, Ediciones del
  Instituto Indigenista Interamericano, 1948.
  2 v.   (351
    Contents: v. 1 (208 p.): 2,971 entries.
  v. 2: 8 maps.

MEANS, Philip Ainsworth. Ancient civilizations
  of the Andes. New York, C. Scribner's Sons,
  1931. 586 p.   (352
    Bibliography: p. 545-73.---Jones 2687.

MISSION scientifique du Cap Horn: t. 7,
  Anthropologie, ethnographie, par P. Hyades
  et J. Deniker. Paris, Gauthier-Villars,
  1891.   (353
    Bibliography: p. 393-402.---Jones 1549.

URUGUAY

FIGUEIRA, José Joaquín. Contribución al estudio de la bibliografía de los aborígenes
  del Uruguay: "Los charrúas" de Pedro Stag-
  nero y "Cerro de las cuentas" por Mario
  Isola. Montevideo [Gaceta Comercial] 1957.
  40 p. (Notas antropológicas, 2)   (354

ARCHAEOLOGY

GENERAL

ALCINA FRANCH, José. Bibliografía básica de arqueología americana. Sevilla, Universidad de Sevilla, Facultad de Filosofía y Letras, 1960. 124 p. (Publ. del Seminario de Antropología Americana, 1)   (355

AVELEYRA ARROYO DE ANDA, Luis. Antigüedad del hombre en México y Centroamérica; catálogo razonado de localidades y bibliografía selecta, 1867-1961. Contribución al XXXV Congreso Internacional de Americanistas, Ciudad México, agosto de 1962. México, Universidad Nacional Autónoma de México, 1962. 72 p. (Publ. del Instituto de Historia, la. ser., no. 70. Cuadernos: Serie antropológica, no. 14)   (355a

BANDELIER, Adolph Francis Alphonse. Note on the bibliography of Yucatan and Central America; comprising Yucatan, Chiapas, Guatemala (The ruins of Palenque, Ocosingo, and Copan), and Oaxaca (ruins of Mitla). A list of some of the writers on this subject from the sixteenth century to the present time. Worcester, Press of C. Hamilton, 1881. 39 p.   (356
From Proceedings of the American Antiquarian Society, Oct. 21, 1880.---Jones 1229.

BENNETT, Wendell C., and others. Publications on Latin American archaeology and ethnology in 1937. Cambridge, Mass., 1938. p. 9-50.   (357
Reprinted from Handbook of Latin American Studies, 1937.

BRINTON, Daniel Garrison. The missing authorities on Mayan antiquities. Washington, D. C., Judd & Detweiler, 1897. p. 183-91.   (358
Reprinted from American anthropologist, June, 1897.---Jones 2103.

FEWKES, Jesse Walter. Catálogo de los objetos etnológicos y arqueológicos exhibidos por la Expedición Hemenway. Madrid, Jaramillo, 1892. 115 p.   (359
Jones 2167.

-----. Commemoration of the fourth centenary of the discovery of America. Columbian Historical Exposition, Madrid. Catalogue of the Hemenway collection in the Historico-American Exposition of Madrid. From the report of the Madrid Commission, 1892. Washington, D.C., Govt. Print. Off., 1895. p. 279-327.   (360
Contents: Catalogue of the Hemenway collection in the Historico-American Exposition of Madrid.-The Bandelier collection of copies of documents relative to the his-

FEWKES, Jesse Walter... (Cont.) tory of New Mexico and Arizona. (From the Archives of the Hemenway expedition)-Exhibit of the Peabody Museum.---Jones 2168.

JOYCE, Thomas Athol. Central American and West Indian archaeology. London, P. L. Warner, 1916. 270 p.   (361
Bibliographical appendix: p. 258-63.---Jones 1235.

LAVACHERY, Henri A. Les arts anciens d'Amérique au Musée Archéologique de Madrid. Anvers, Editions "De Sikkel" [1929] 128 p.   (362
Includes bibliographies.---Jones 250.

MASON, Gregory. South of yesterday. New York, H. Holt and Co., 1940. 401 p.   (363
Maya bibliography: p. 351-77. Tairona bibliography: p. 378-85.---Jones 2321a.

POLLOCK, Harry Evelyn Dorr. Round structures of aboriginal Middle America. Washington, D.C., Carnegie Institution of Washington, 1936. 182 p. (Carnegie Institution of Washington, Publ., no. 471)   (364
References: p. 174-82.---Jones 1246.

VAILLANT, George Clapp. Some resemblances in the ceramics of Central and North America, English version of Semejanzas del material de cultura en la América Central y la del Norte. [Globe, Ariz., Priv. print. for the Medallion, 1932] 50 p.   (365
Delivered at the Second Scientific Congress of the Sociedad Científica Antonio Alzate in Mexico city, September, 1930.
Works consulted: p. 39-50.---Jones 1259.

WAUCHOPE, Robert. Ten years of Middle American archaeology; annotated bibliography and news summary, 1948-1957. [Margaret A. L. Harrison, editor. New Orleans] 1961. 106 p.   (366
Reprinted from publication 28, Middle American Research Institute, Tulane University, New Orleans, 1961.

WINSOR, Justin. Mexico and Central America [with a critical essay on the sources of information and notes] (Narrative and critical history of America. Boston and New York, 1884-89. v. 1, p. 133-207)   (367
Jones 2587.

ARGENTINA

BOMAN, Eric, and GRESLEBIN, Héctor. Alfarería de estilo draconiano de la región Diaguita (República Argentina) Buenos Aires,

BOMAN, Eric, and GRESLEBIN,... (Cont.)
  Impr. Ferrari Hnos., 1923. 62 p.   (368
    Literatura: p. 44-8.---Jones 607.

BOMAN, Eric. Antiquités de la région andine
  de la République Argentine et du désert
  d'Atacama. Paris, H. La Soudier, 1908.
  2 v.   (369
    "Auteurs cités": v. 2, p. 879-904.---
  Jones 606.

BREGANTE, Odilla. Ensayo de clasificación de
  la cerámica del noroeste argentino. Buenos
  Aires, A. Estrada y Cía., 1926.
  321 p.   (370
    Bibliography: p. 317-21.---Jones 609.

TORRES, Luis María. Los primitivos habitantes del delta del Paraná. Buenos Aires,
  Impr. de Coni Hermanos, 1913.
  616 p.   (371
    "Autores consultados": p. 579-91.---
  Jones 868g.

-----. Los tiempos prehistóricos y protohis-
  tóricos en la República Argentina; 2. ed.
  corr., y actualizada. Buenos Aires, A.
  Kapelusz y Cía. [1935?] 185 p.   (372
    Bibliography at the end of each chap-
  ter.---Jones 868h.

VIGNATI, Miciádes Alejo. Los cráneos, trofeo
  de las sepulturas indígenas de la quebrada
  de Humahuaca (provincia de Jujuy) Buenos
  Aires, 1930. 165 p. (Archivos del Museo
  Etnográfico, no. 1)   (373
    Bibliografía: p. 159-65.---Jones 553.

BOLIVIA

BALLIVIAN, Manuel Vicente. Monumentos prehistóricos de Tiahuanacu. Homenaje al XVIIo
  Congreso de los americanistas. La Paz, J.
  M. Gamarra, 1910. 2 v.   (374
    "Anotaciones bibliográficas": v. 1,
  p. 79-120.---Jones 899.

BRAZIL

COSTA, João Angyone. Introdução á arqueologia
  brasileira, etnografia e historia. São
  Paulo, Companhia Editora Nacional, 1934.
  384 p. (Biblioteca pedagogica brasileira,
  ser. 5, v. 34)   (375
    Bibliografia: p. 326-38.---Jones 956.

-----. Migrações e cultura indigena; ensaios
  de arqueologia e etnologia do Brasil. São
  Paulo, Companhia Editora Nacional, 1939.
  273 p. (Biblioteca pedagogica brasileira,
  ser. 5: Brasiliana, v. 139)   (376
    Bibliography at end of each chapter.---
  Jones 956a.

CHILE

LATCHAM, Ricardo Eduardo. La alfarería indígena chilena. Santiago, Soc. Impr. y Lit.
  Universo, 1928. 232 p.   (377
    Bibliografía: p. 227-32.---Jones 1504.

COSTA RICA

LOTHROP, Samuel Kirkland. Pottery of Costa
  Rica and Nicaragua. New York, Museum of
  the American Indian, 1926. 2 v.   (378
    Bibliography, v.2, p. 468-87.---Jones
  1272a.

CUBA

ORTIZ FERNANDEZ, Fernando. Historia de la
  arqueología indocubana. Habana, Impr. "El
  Siglo XX", 1922. 107 p.   (379
    From Cuba contemporánea, Sept. and Oct.,
  1922.---Jones 1879.

ECUADOR

BARRERA, Jaime. Bibliografía para el estudio
  de la prehistoria ecuatoriana. (Anales de
  la Universidad Central del Ecuador, Quito,
  v. 58, p. 99-140, 1937)   (380
    "Translation of the bibliography in Louis
  Baudin's L'empire socialiste des Inka
  (Paris, 1928)" -HLAS, 3, p. 32.---Jones
  1960.

CONTRIBUTIONS to South American archaeology;
  the George G. Heye Expedition. New York,
  1907-1910. 2 v.   (381
    "Bibliography of the anthropology of Ecua-
  dor": v. 1, p. 121-35.---Jones 1968a.

GUATEMALA

MERWIN, Raymond Edwin, and VAILLANT, George
  Clapp. The ruins of Holmul, Guatemala.
  Cambridge, 1932. 106 p. (Memoirs of the
  Peabody Museum of American Archaeology and
  Ethnology, Harvard University, v. 3,
  no. 2)   (382
    Bibliography: p. 97-103.---Jones 1303.

MORLEY, Sylvanus Griswold. The inscriptions
  of Peten. Washington, D.C., 1938. 5 v.
  (Carnegie Institution of Washington, Publ.
  437)   (383
    "La bibliografía...tomo 1... vale como uno
  de los más completos recuentos bibliográficos sobre la especialidad de los estudios
  mayistas".-Review in Boletín de la Biblioteca Nacional, Guatemala, 1939, año 8, no. 3,
  p. 108. See also the extensive review by
  Mario Mariscal in Boletín bibliográfico de

MORLEY, Sylvanus Griswold... (Cont.)
   antropología americana, v. 3 (1939) no. 3,
   p. 237-47.---Jones 1304.

SAVILLE, Marshall Howard. Bibliographic notes
   on Quiriguá, Guatemala. New York, Museum
   of the American Indian, Heye Foundation,
   1919. 22 p. (Indian notes and monographs,
   v. 6, no. 1)   (384
   Jones 1310.

HONDURAS

IDE, Jens. An archaeological reconnaissance
   of northwestern Honduras. A report of the
   work of the Tulane University-Danish National Museum Expedition to Central America,
   1935. Copenhagen, 1938. 101 p.   (385
   Includes bibliography. Reprint of Acta
   archaeologica, v. 9.---Jones 1331.

MEXICO

BERNAL, Ignacio. Bibliografía de arqueología
   y etnografía. Mesoamérica y Norte de México, 1514-1960. México, D.F., Instituto Nacional de Antropología e Historia, 1962.
   634 p. (Memorias, 7)   (386
   Commemorative edition on the occasion of
   the 35th International Congress of Americanists, Mexico, 1962. Contains 13,990 entries.

BEYER, Hermann. Sucinta bibliografía sistemática de etnografía y arqueología mejica-
   nas. México, Secretaria de Educación Pública, 1923. 40 p.   (387
   Jones 2076a.

GARCIA, Rubén. Bibliografía razonada del calendario azteca. México, 1934. p. 113-48.
   (Publ. del Museo Nacional de México)   (388
   Reprint of t. 1, ép. 5, no. 1, of Anales
   del Museo Nacional de México.---Jones 2185.

GARCIA PAYON, José. Bibliografía arqueológica de Veracruz. [Xalapa, Veracruz] Universidad Veracruzana, 1963. 120 p. (Cuadernos del Instituto de Antropología,
   1)   (389

-----. La zona arqueológica de Tecaxic-Calix-
   tlahuaca y los matlatzincas. México, Tall.
   Graf. de la Nación, 1936- . v. 1- .   (390
   Bibliografía de las obras del idioma mat-
   latzinca, v. 1, p. 223-36. Bibliografía:
   v. 1, p. 239-51.---Jones 2204.

JONES, Julie. Bibliography for Olmec sculp-
   ture. New York, Library, Museum of Primitive Art, 1963. 8 p. (Primitive art bibliographies, no. 2)   (391
   Bibliography, in the main, compiled for

JONES, Julie... (Cont.)
   master's thesis, for the Institute of Fine
   Arts, New York University, 1962.

LEHMANN, Walter. The history of ancient Mexi-
   can art; an essay in outline. New York,
   Brentano, 1922. 28 p.   (392
   Bibliography: p. 2-22.
   For a bibliography of Lehmann, see Boletín
   bibliográfico de antropología americana,
   México, 1939, v. 3, p. 86-9.---Jones 2280.

-----. Methods and results in Mexican research;
   tr. by Seymour de Ricci. Paris, 1909.
   127 p.   (393
   Contains bibliographical information. The
   original, Ergebnisse und aufgaben der mexi-
   kanistischen forschung, was published in
   Archiv für anthropologie, Braunschweig,
   1907, n.f., bd. 6, p. 113-68.---Jones 2281.

LEJEAL, León. Les antiquités mexicaines (Mexique, Yucatan, Amérique Centrale) Paris,
   A. Picard et Fils, 1902. 78 p. (Bibliothèque de bibliographies critiques, publiée par
   la Société des Etudes Historiques, 19) (394
   A classified list of 388 titles.---Jones
   2282.

LINNE, Sigvald. Archaeological researches at
   Teotihuacan, Mexico. Stockholm, V. Petter-
   son, 1934. 236 p. (The Ethnographical Museum of Sweden. Riksmuseets etnografiska
   avdelning, new series, Publ. no. 1)   (395
   Works consulted: p. 221-33.---Jones 2308.

NADAL MORA, Vicente. Compendio de historia
   del arte precolombino de México y Yucatán.
   Buenos Aires, Compañía Impresora Argentina,
   1933. 253 p.   (396
   Indice bibliográfico: p. 19-21.---Jones
   2374.

NOGUERA, Eduardo. Ruinas arqueológicas del
   norte de México. Casas Grandes (Chihuahua),
   La Quemada, Chalchihuites (Zacatecas) México, D.F., Tall. Gráf. de la Nación, 1930.
   107 p. (Publ. de la Secretaría de Educación
   Pública)   (397
   Includes bibliographies.---Jones 2379.

PALACIOS, Enrique Juan. La ciudad arqueológica del Tajín; sus revelaciones. México, La
   Impresora, 1932. 74 p. (Biblioteca de estudios historicos y arqueológicos mexicanos;
   directores, v. 1)   (398
   Bibliografía comentada: p. 57-74.---Jones
   2400.

SAVILLE, Marshall Howard. Bibliographic notes
   on Palenque, Chiapas. New York, Museum of
   the American Indian, 1928. p. 119-80. (Indian notes and monographs, v. 6,
   no. 5)   (399
   Jones 2489.

SAVILLE, Marshall Howard. Bibliographic notes
  on Uxmal, Yucatan. New York, Museum of the
  American Indian, 1921. p. 55-131. (Indian
  notes and monographs, v. 9, no. 2)   (400
    Jones 2490.

-----. Bibliographic notes on Xochicalco,
  Mexico. New York, Museum of the American
  Indian, 1928. p. 185-207. (Indian notes
  and monographs, v. 6, no. 6)   (401
    Jones 2491.

-----. Torquois mosaic art in ancient Mexico.
  New York, Museum of the American Indian,
  1922. 110 p. (Contributions from the Museum of the American Indian, Heye Foundation)   (402
    List of works: p. 103-10.---Jones 2493.

-----. The wood-carver's art in ancient Mexico. New York, Museum of the American
  Indian, 1925. 120 p. (Contributions from
  the Museum of the American Indian, Heye
  Foundation, v. 9)   (403
    Works consulted: p. 107-20.---Jones 2494.

SAYLES, Edwin Booth. An archaeological survey of Chihuahua, Mexico. Globe, Ariz.,
  Priv. print. for the Medallion, 1936.
  119 p. (Medallion papers, no. 22)   (404
    Bibliography: p. 109-13.---Jones 2495.

NORTH AMERICA

BANCROFT, Hubert Howe. The native races of
  the Pacific states of North America. San
  Francisco, A. L. Bancroft & Co., 1874-1875.
  5 v.   (405
    "Authorities quoted": v. 1, p. XVII-
  XLIX.---Jones 2066a.

PANAMA

ARSANDAUX, H., and RIVET, P. L'orfévrerie
  du Chiriquí et de Colombie. (Journal de la
  Société des Américanistes de Paris, n.s.,
  v. 15, p. 169-213, 1923)   (406
    Index bibliographique: p. 207-13.---
  Jones 1678.

PERU

HORKHEIMER, Hans. Guía bibliográfica de los
  principales sitios arqueológicos del Perú.
  Lima, Tall. Gráf. de la Edit. Lumen, 1950.
  p. 181-234.   (407
    Reprinted from Boletín bibliográfico,
  Lima, año 23, v. 20, no. 3-4, dic. 1950.

LEHMANN, Walter. The art of old Peru...
  assisted by Heinrich Doering ... London, E.
  Benn, 1924. 67 p.   (408

LEHMANN, Walter... (Cont.)
    "List of recent and important publications":
  p. 66-8.---Jones 2674.

-----. Historia del arte del antiguo Perú ...
  con la colaboración del dr. Heinrich Doering,
  Barcelona, G. Gili, 1926. 67 p.   (409
    "Indice de la última literatura": p. 66-8.
  Jones 2675.

-----. Kunstgeschichte des alten Peru,
  erläutertdurch ausgewählte werke aus ton und
  stein, gewebe und kleinode ... unter mitarbeit
  von dr. Heinrich Doering. Berlin, E . Wasmuth,
  1924. 67 p.   (410
    "Neuere literatur in auswahl": 66-8.---
  Jones 2673.

LEHMANN-SITSCHE, Robert. Arqueología peruana;
  Coricancha, el templo del sol en el Cuzco y
  las imágenes de su altar mayor. Buenos Aires, "Coni", 1928. 260 p.   (411
    "De la Revista del Museo de La Plata", t.
  31, p. 1-260.
    Includes (p. 1-20) a critical review of
  the bibliography.---Jones 2675a.

MARKHAM, Clements Robert. The Inca civilization in Peru [with a critical essay on the
  sources of information and notes] (Winsor,
  Justin, ed. Narrative and critical history
  of America. Boston and New York, 1884-1889.
  v. 1. (1889) p. 209-82)   (412
    Jones 2684.

SCHWAB, Federico. Contribución a la bibliografía de arqueología peruana. (Boletín bibliográfico, Universidad Mayor de San Marcos,
  Lima, v. 8, no. 3, 1935)   (413
    Jones 2751.

SOUTH AMERICA

BENNETT, Wendell C. Archaeological work in
  South America. (American antiquarian, New
  York, v. 2, p. 248-59, 1937)   (414
    A review of the literature, 1934-1936.---
  Jones 51a.

LATCHAM, Ricardo Eduardo. Breve bibliografía
  de los petroglifos sudamericanos. (Revista
  de bibliografía chilena, Santiago, 1. trim.
  p. 42-9, 1927)   (415
    Jones 246.

LINNE, Sigvald. The technique of South American ceramics. Göteborg, Elanders-Boktryck-
  eri Aktiebolag. 1925. 199 p. (Göteborgs
  kungl. vetenskapsoch vitterhets-samhälles
  handlingar. 4 följden, bd. 29, no. 5) (416
    Bibliography: p. 179-99.---Jones 262.

LOTHROP, Samuel Kirkland. Inca treasure as
  depicted by Spanish historians. Los Angeles

LOTHROP, Samuel Kirkland... (Cont.)
[The Southwest Museum] 1938. 75 p. (Publ.

of the Frederick Webb Hodge Anniversary
Publication Fund, v. 2)   (417
    Bibliography: p. 69-75.---Jones 266.

ARCHITECTURE

DEHLKE, Hedda. Nationalismus in der baukunst
Südamerika. (Ibero-amerikanisches archiv,
Berlin, v. 8, p. 350-60, 1935)   (418
    Contains bibliography.---Jones 120.

GARCIA GRANADOS, Rafael, and MacGREGOR, Luis.
Huejotzingo, la ciudad y el convento franciscano. México, Tall. Gráf. de la Nación,
1934. 375 p.   (419
    "Noticia bibliográfica acerca de algunos
pintores que tienen obras en Huejotzingo":
p. 301-05. - "Principales obras y documentos consultados": p. 353-57.---Jones 2189.

NOEL, Martín S. Teoría histórica de la arquitectura virreinal. Buenos Aires, Peuser,

1932- , pt. 1- .   (420
    Bibliografía: p. 57-63.---Jones 794.

SÃO PAULO. Universidade. Facultade de Arquitetura e Urbanismo. Biblioteca. Indice
urbanístico. São Paulo, 1959. 32 p.
mimeogr.   (421
    Cited in Richardson, item 7291.

SMITH, Robert Chester. The colonial architecture of Minas Gerais in Brazil. Chicago,
College Art Association of America, 1931.
p. 110-59.   (422
    Reprinted from The Art bulletin, v. 21,
1939. Contains foot-note references to
sources.---Jones 1200.

ARCHIVAL AND MANUSCRIPT COLLECTION

GENERAL

AZAROLA GIL, Luis Enrique. Fondos documentales relativos a la historia del Uruguay
obrantes en los archivos extranjeros. Madrid, Gráficas Reunidas, 1930. 28 p. (423
    Jones 2817.

CASTELO DE ZAVALA, María. Noticias sobre algunos archivos hispanoamericanos. México,
D.F., Tall. Gráf. de la Edit. Stylo, 1947.
p. 373-419.   (424
    Reprinted from Anales del Instituto Nacio-
nal de Antropología e Historia, v. 2. Archives mentioned are: Argentina, Paraguay,
Chile, Peru, Ecuador, Colombia, Costa Rica
and Guatemala.

GOMEZ CANEDO, Lino. Los archivos de la historia de América, período colonial español.
México, D.F., 1961. 2 v. (Publ. del Instituto Panamericano de Geografía e Historia, no. 225)   (425
    Issued also as publication of the Comisión
de Historia, no. 87.

GROPP, Arthur Eric. Guide to libraries and
archives in Central America and the West
Indies, Panama, Bermuda, and British Guiana.
New Orleans, La., Tulane University of Louisiana, 1941. 721 p. (Publ. of the Middle
American Research Institute,
no. 10)   (426

GRUBBS, Henry A. A tentative guide to manuscript material in Latin American libraries.
(Handbook of Latin American studies, 1935.
Cambridge, Mass., Harvard Univ. Pr., 1936.
p. 219-30)   (427
    Jones 180a.

HILL, Roscoe R. Los archivos nacionales de
la América Latina. Habana, 1945 [cover
1948] 166 p. (Publ. del Archivo Nacional
de Cuba, 19)   (428

-----. Latin American archives in 1938.
Cambridge, Mass., Harvard Univ. Pr., 1939.
p. 45-52.   (429
    Reprinted from Handbook of Latin American
studies, 1938.

-----. Latin American archivology, 1949-1950,
1950-1951. [Durham, N.C.] 1951-1952.   (430
    Reprinted from Hispanic American histori-
cal review, 31(1): 152-76, Feb. 1951; 32
(3): 458-82, Aug. 1952.

-----. National archives of Latin America.
Cambridge, Mass., 1945. 169 p. (Joint
Committee on Latin American Studies, Natio-
nal Research Council, American Council of
Learned Societies, Social Science Research
Council, Miscellaneous publ., no. 3) (431

-----. -----. (Handbook of Latin American
studies for 1936. Cambridge, Mass., 1937.
p. 433-42)   (432

HILL, Roscoe R. .... (Cont.)
    A valuable guide by a recognized special-
ist. See also his "Impressions of Hispanic
American archives" in the Hispanic American
historical review, v. 17, p. 538-45.---Jones
203a.

MENDOZA L., Gunnar. Situación actual de los
    archivos latinoamericanos; manual de infor-
    mación básica. Washington, D.C., Reunión
    Interamericana sobre Archivos, 1961.
    xxxvii, 96 p.   (432a
    Arrangement geographical by country,
    citing publications of archives and describ-
    ing sources of information.

MILLARES CARLO, Agustín. Los archivos muni-
    cipales de Latinoamérica; libros de actas
    y colecciones documentales. Apuntes biblio-
    gráficos. Maracaibo, 1961. 220 p.   (433
    Contribution to the Sesquicentenario de
    la Independencia de Venezuela.

-----. Notas bibliográficas acerca de archi-
    vos municipales, ediciones de libros de
    acuerdo y colecciones de documentos conce-
    jiles. Madrid, Dirección Servicio de Pu-
    blicaciones del Ministerio de Educación
    Nacional, 1952. 172 p. (Bibliografías de
    archivos y bibliotecas)   (434
    Also published in Contribuciones a la
    historia municipal de América, publication
    no. 100 of the Pan American Institute of
    Geography and History, and in Revista de
    la historia de América, México, 35/36:
    175-208, en./dic., 1953.

-----. Repertorio bibliográfico de los archi-
    vos mexicanos y de los europeos y norteameri-
    canos de interés para la historia de México.
    México, D.F., 1959. xxiv, 366 p. (Institu-
    to Bibliográfico Mexicano, Publ. 1)   (435

PAN AMERICAN Institute of Geography and His-
    tory, México, D.F. Contribuciones a la
    historia municipal de América. México, D.F.,
    1951. 298 p. (Publ. del Instituto Paname-
    ricano de Geografía e Historia,
    no. 100)   (436
    Issued also as publication of the Comisión
    de Historia, no. 14, and as v. 2 of the se-
    ries: Estudios de Historia. Contains: Plan
    y documentación de la historia de las muni-
    cipalidades en las Indias españolas (siglos
    XVI-XVIII), por Rafael Altamira y Crevea.-
    Las actas municipales fuente de la historia
    de México, por Manuel Carrera Stampa.-Fun-
    ciones económicas del cabildo colonial his-
    panoamericano, por Francisco Domínguez y
    Compañy.-Notas bibliográficas acerca de ar-
    chivos municipales, ediciones de libros de
    acuerdos y colecciones de documentos conce-
    jiles, por Agustín Millares Carlo.-Los orígenes
    del urbanismo imperial en América, por Erwin
    Walter Palm.

PAN AMERICAN Institute of Geography and His-
    tory. Comisión de Historia. Guía de los
    documentos microfotografiados por la unidad
    móvil de microfilm de la Unesco. México,
    D.F., 1963. 317 p. (Publicación, 225 [i.e.,
    269]) mimeogr.   (437
    Issued also as Publication of the Comisión
    de Historia, no. 112, and Fuentes documenta-
    les para la historia de América, Guías, 1.
    Publication was edited with the financial
    assistance of Unesco under the auspices of
    the Consejo Internacional de la Filosofía y
    de las Ciencias Humanas, and of the Comité
    Consultivo Internacional de Bibliografía,
    Documentación y Terminología.

TESSIN, Georg. Das archivwesen Ibero-Amerikas.
    München, T. Ackermann, 1939.
    p. 239-89.   (438
    "Sonderabdruck aus Archivalische zeit-
    schrift".---Jones 473

VARGAS UGARTE, Rubén. Manuscritos peruanos.
    Lima, 1935-1947. 5 v. (Biblioteca peruana,
    v. 1-5)   (439
    Includes manuscripts in libraries and
    archives in and outside of Peru. Vol. 5 is
    a supplementary volume. Vols. 4-5 published
    in Buenos Aires. Supplement published in
    1961 (See item 440).---Jones, item 2771,
    2772.

-----. Suplemento a la Biblioteca peruana.
    Lima, [Universidad Nacional Mayor de San
    Marcos] 1961. 75 p.   (440
    Supplement divided into 2 parts: pt. 1,
    Manuscritos; pt. 2, Impresos.

GENERAL - Private collections

GARCIA ICAZBALCETA, Joaquín. Catálogo de la
    colección de manuscritos relativos a la his-
    toria de América formada por Joaquín García
    Icazbalceta; anotado y adicionado por Fede-
    rico Gómez de Orozco. México, D.F., 1927.
    287 p. (Monografías bibliográficas mexica-
    nas, no. 9)   (441
    Jones 2196.

-----. Catálogo de libros y manuscritos del
    sr. d. Joaquín García Icazbalceta. 160
    numb. 1.   (442
    From a type-written copy in the Genaro
    García collection of the Library of the
    University of Texas.
    Contents.- América en general. - México. -
    Lenguas indígenas y libros escogidos. -
    España. - Bibliografía, historia de la im-
    prenta. - Gramáticas, diccionarios, etc. -
    Biblias, clásicos. - Literatura extranjera,
    varios. - Manuscritos. - Manuscritos en
    lenguas indígenas.---Jones 2197.

GATES, William Edmond. The William Gates collection. Manuscripts, documents, printed literature relating to Mexico and Central America. New York, 1924. 93 p. (443
Auction catalogue.---Jones 2206.

-----. The Gates collection. [Baltimore, n.d.] 6 v. in 1 v. (444
Sec. A: Middle American literature. - B: General works, special studies, history, geography, archaeology, anthropology, economics, botany, medicine. - C: Publications and material in preparation for publication. - D: Old and rare books. - E: Miscellany of documents. - F: Art and archaeology, codices, maps, facsimiles of mural decoration. - G: A library of bibliographies.

-----. The William Gates collection. N.Y., American Art Association, Inc. [1924] [186] p. (445
To have been sold at auction April 9-11, 1924. Materials offered related to Mexico and Central America, purchased by Tulane University of Louisiana.

KRAUS, H. P., firm, booksellers, N.Y. Choice manuscripts, books, maps and globes, important for the history of European civilization and discovery of America. Illuminated codices, early drawings, incunabula and illustrated books, remarkable maps from Prince Liechtenstein collection and globes from a private library. N.Y., [1951] 94 p. (Catalog 56) (446

PATTERSON, Jerry E., and STANTON, William R. The Ephraim George Squier manuscripts in the Library of Congress: a checklist. [N.Y.] Bibliographical Society of America, 1959. p. 309-26. (446a
Separate from the Papers of the Society, v. 53, 4th quarter, 1959.

PINART, Alphonse Louis. Catalogue de livres rares et précieux, manuscrits et imprimés, principalement sur l'Amérique et sur les langues du monde entier, composant la bibliothèque de M. Alph. L. Pinart et comprenant en totalité la bibliothèque mexico-guatémalienne de M. l'abbé Brasseur de Bourbourg. Paris, Vve. A Labitte, 1883. 248 p. (447
1,440 entries.---Jones 2431.

RAMIREZ, José Fernando. Bibliotheca mexicana; or, A catalogue of the library of rare books and important manuscripts relating to Mexico and other parts of Spanish America, formed by the late señor don José Fernando Ramírez. Sold by Puttick and Simpson. London [G, Norman and Son] 1880. 165 p. (448
Jones 2442.

RICH, Obadiah. Catalogue of a collection of manuscripts principally in Spanish, relating to America. London, Printed by W. Bowden [1845?] 44, [4] p. (449
Original autograph letters: [4] p.---Jones 400.

STUDART, Guilherme, barão de. Relação dos manuscriptos, originaes e copias sôbre a história do Ceará, que constituem a colleção dr. Guilherme Studart. Lisboa, Typ. do "Recreio", 1892-1896. 2 v. (450
Jones 1212.

VICUÑA MACKENNA, Benjamín. Catálogo de la biblioteca y manuscritos de d. Benjamín Vicuña Mackenna. Santiago de Chile, Impr. Cervantes, 1886. 281 p. (451
Prepared by Carlos Castro Ruiz. The collection was acquired by the Biblioteca Nacional in 1887.---Jones 1656.

GENERAL - Codices, Pre-Columbian

ARPEE, Levon Harris. A catalogue of Maya and Mexican codices and papers relating to them. Chicago, 1937. 12 p. (452
Photoprinted.---Jones 2062a

BARLAND, Cottie A. The Selden Roll, an ancient Mexican picture manuscript in the Bodleian Library at Oxford, with a bibliography compiled by Gerdt Kutscher. Berlin, Verlag Gebr. Mann, 1955. 50 p. (Monuments americana, 2) (453

CRUZ, Martín de la. The Badianus manuscript (Codex Barberini, Latin 241) Vatican Library, and Aztec herbal of 1552, introduction, translation and annotations by Emily Walcott Emmart. Baltimore, The Johns Hopkins Pr., 1940. 341 p. (454
Bibliography, p. 339-41.---Jones 2137b.

GALINDO Y VILLA, Jesus. Las pinturas y los manuscritos jeroglíficos mexicanos. Nota bibliográfica sobre los más conocidos e importantes. (Anales del Museo Nacional de México, México, D.F., 2. ép., t. 2, p. 25-56, 1905) (455
Contains 1, Colección de Boturini; 2, Publicaciones del barón Humboldt; 3, Colección de Lord Kingsborough; 4, Antigua colección Aubin.---Jones 2176.

LEON PORTILLA, Miguel, and MATEOS HIGUERA, Salvador. Catálogo de los códices indígenas del México antiguo. México, 1957. 53 p. (Suplemento del Boletín bibliográfico de la Secretaría de Hacienda, año 3, no. 111, jun. 1957) (456

NOGUERA, Eduardo. Bibliografía de los códices precolombinos y documentos indígenas poste-

NOGUERA, Eduardo... (Cont.)
   riores a la conquista. México, 1933. (Publicaciones del Museo Nacional de Arqueología, Historia y Etnografía)   (457
      Cited in Millares, item 1083. Published
   in Anales del Museo Nacional de Arqueología,
   Historia y Etnografía, ép. 4a., t. 8, no. 4
   (t. 25 de la colección), p. 583-602, oct./
   dic. 1933)

RAMIREZ, José Fernando. Códices mexicanos de
   fr. Bernardino de Sahagún. (Boletín de la
   Real Academia de la Historia, Madrid, t. 6,
   p. 85-124, 1885)   (458
      Jones 2443.

-----. Another ed. (Anales del Museo Nacional de México, 2. ép. t. 1, p. 1-34,
   1903)   (459
      Jones 2444.

THOMAS, Cyrus. Notes on certain Maya and
   Mexican manuscripts. (Bureau of American
   Ethnology, Third annual report, 1881-1882.
   Washington, 1884. p. 3-65)   (460
      Jones 2527.

-----. A study of the manuscript Troano,
   with introduction by D. Brinton. Washington,
   D.C., Govt. Print. Off., 1882, xxxvii, 237 p.
   (Contributions to North American ethnology,
   v. 5 [pt. 3])   (461

GENERAL - Other manuscript materials

CATALOGO dos documentos mandados copiar pelo
   senhor d. Pedro II. (Revista do Instituto
   Histórico e Geographico Brasileiro, Rio de
   Janeiro, t. 67, pt. 1, p. 1-187,
   1906)   (462
      Jones 1020.

DESDEVISES DU DEZERT, Georges Nicolas. Les
   sources manuscrites de l'histoire de l'Amérique Latine à la fin du xviiie siècle
   (1760-1807) (Nouvelles archives des missions scientifiques et littéraires. Paris,
   1914. Nouv. sér., 12)   (463
      Jones 121.

DOMINGUEZ BORDONA, Jesús. Manuscritos de
   América. Madrid, 1935. 250 p. (Catálogo
   de la Biblioteca de Palacio, t. 9)   (464
      Jones 130.

OTHMER, Cayo. Noticia de algunos manuscritos
   jesuíticos en la lengua de los indios chi-
   quitanos de Bolivia (Siglo XVIII) (Archivum
   Historicum Societatis Jesu, Roma, v. 7,
   p. 220-39, 1938)   (465
      Jones 926.

SILVA, Serafím da. Textos medievais portuguê-
   ses e seus problemas. [Rio de Janeiro] Mi-

SILVA, Serafím da... (Cont.)
   nistério da Educação e Cultura, Casa de Rui
   Barbosa, 1956. 125 p. (Coleção de estudos
   filológicos, 2)   (466

ARGENTINA

ANGELIS, Pedro de. Colección de obras impresas y manuscritas, que tratan principalmente
   del Río de la Plata. Buenos Aires, 1853.
   232 p.   (467
      "Obras periódicas, publicadas en las Pro-
   vincias argentinas, y en el Estado Oriental
   del Uruguay, por orden cronológico": p. 90-
   100.
      "Catálogo metódico de la segunda bibliote-
   ca americana (después de la del doctor Segu-
   rola) formada en el Río de la Plata, y el
   primero publicado en él. Tiene su interés
   histórico por los libros raros e importantes documentos originales que registra...
   La mayor parte de esta colección fue vendida al Brasil... donde... existe en la Biblioteca Pública". Museo Mitre, Catálogo razonado de la Sección Lenguas Americanas, v. 1,
   p. 7.---Jones 557.

ARCHIVO histórico y administrativo de Entre
   Ríos. (Boletín del Instituto de Investigaciones Históricas, Buenos Aires, t. 18,
   p. 813-16, 1933-1934)   (468
      Jones 808b

ARGENTINA. Archivo General. Indice de Gobierno, correspondiente a los años 1810 a 1812.
   (Boletín del Instituto de Investigaciones
   Históricas, Buenos Aires, t. 3-4,
   1924-1926)   (469
      Jones 568a.

-----. -----. Indice de decretos, órdenes,
   reglamentos, 1813-1821. (Boletín del Instituto de Investigaciones Históricas, Buenos
   Aires, t. 7-18, 1928-1935)   (470
      Jones 568b.

-----. -----. Inventarios parciales. (Boletín del Instituto de Investigaciones Históricas, Buenos Aires, 1924. t. 2,
   1924)   (471
      Jones 568c.

-----. -----. Tomas de razón de despachos
   militares, cédulas de premio, retiros, em-
   leos civiles y eclesiásticos, donativos,
   etc., 1740 a 1821. Buenos Aires, G. Kraft,
   1925. 976 p.   (472
      Jones 568d.

-----. Biblioteca Nacional. Catálogo cronológico de reales cédulas, órdenes, decretos,
   provisiones, etc., referentes a América,
   1508-1810. Seguido de un índice alfabético
   de nombres de personas y otro auxiliar de

ARGENTINA. Biblioteca Nacional ... (Cont.)
lugares, instituciones, órdenes religiosas,
pueblos indígenas, mitos, animales y cosas.
Buenos Aires, 1938. 302 p.   (473
  Jones 609b.

-----. -----. Suplemento, Buenos Aires, 1940.
70 p.   (473a
  Contains "Indice general de personas citadas en el cuerpo de los documentos del
mismo suplemento".

-----. Biblioteca Nacional. Catálogo de manuscritos, papeles de Gregorio Funes; índice
del Plan de estudios para la Universidad
Mayor de Córdoba. Buenos Aires, 1940.
53 p.   (474

-----. -----. Catálogo de manuscritos, papeles de Gregorio Funes, Simón Bolívar, Antonio José de Sucre (1823-1828), Buenos Aires,
1939. 95 p. [i.e. 99], 5 l.   (475

-----. -----. Catálogo de manuscritos, papeles de Miguel de Azcuénaga, Saturnino Segu-
rola, Juan Moreno (1748-1851) sobre empedra-
do de Buenos Aires. Introducción de la va-
cuna. Cartas al jefe de policía de Rosas.
Buenos Aires, Impr. de la Biblioteca Nacional, 1937. 54 p.   (476
  Jones 612.

-----. -----. Catálogo por orden cronológico
de los manuscritos relativos a América existentes en la Biblioteca Nacional de Buenos
Aires. Buenos Aires, Impr. de la Biblioteca Nacional, 1905. 386 p.   (477
  Jones 613a.

-----. -----. Catálogo... de los manuscritos
relativos a América y Europa... Segunda
parte. Buenos Aires, Impr. de la Biblioteca Nacional, 1906. 97 p.   (478
  Jones 614.

-----. -----. Segundo catálogo de manuscritos.
Buenos Aires, 1944. xv, 1016 p.   (479

-----. Comisión Nacional Ejecutiva del 150o
Aniversario de la Revolución de Mayo. Indice del Archivo de Gobierno de Buenos Aires;
v. 1, en./abr. 1810. Buenos Aires, Dirección General del Boletín Oficial e Imprentas, 1961. 515 p.   (479a
  Contains 3,338 references.

-----. Ministerio de Relaciones Exteriores
y Culto. Catálogo de la Biblioteca, Mapoteca y Archivo. Buenos Aires. Tall. Tip.
de la Penitenciaría Nacional, 1902.
403 p.   (480
  Jones 584.

-----. -----. Buenos Aires, Tall. Gráf. de la
Penitenciaría Nacional, 1905. 555 p.   (481

ARGENTINA. Ministerio de Relaciones...(Cont.)
Jones 585.

-----. -----. 3. ed. Apéndice: Servicios
prestados en la carrera diplomática y administrativa, 1810-1910. Buenos Aires, Impr.
y Casa Editora "Juan A. Alsina", 1910.
1053 p.   (482
  Jones 586.

-----. Museo Histórico Nacional. Catálogo
de documentos. Buenos Aires, 1952.
3 v.   (483
  Contents: t. 1: 1605-1869; t. 2: 1870-
1879; t. 3: 1880-1889 and undated documents,
and "Indice diccionario" p. 219-428.

BUENOS AIRES. Museo Mitre. Documentos de su
archivo colonial, 1514-1810. Buenos Aires,
1909. 294 p.   (484
  Jones 621.

BUENOS AIRES (Province) Archivo General. Indice del Archivo del Gobierno de Buenos Aires, correspondiente al año de 1810. Buenos
Aires, Impr. de la Tribuna, 1860.
559 p.   (485
  Editor: Manuel Ricardo Trelles.---Jones 637.

CORDOBA, Arg. Universidad Nacional. Archivo
General. Catálogo de documentos. Córdoba,
Impr. de la Universidad, 1944-1945.
2 v.   (486
  Compilation by Juan Vélez and Héctor Gui-
llermo Vélez of documents in the General
Archive of the Universidad Nacional de Cór-
doba; v.1, 1611-1891; v. 2, 1892-1900.

FERNANDEZ OLGUIN, Eduardo. Los archivos de la
ciudad de Corrientes. Buenos Aires, 1921.
23 p.   (487
  See also his "Indice documental parcial
del Archivo de la provincia de Corrientes"
in Boletín del Instituto de Investigaciones
Históricas, v. 9, p. 74-9, 1929, and "La documentación relativa a Artigas en los archivos de Santa Fe" in the same review, v. 1
p. 324-35, 1923.---Jones 688.

-----. Los archivos de Salta y Jujuy. Buenos
Aires, 1927. 92 p.   (488
  Jones 689.

-----. Los archivos de San Luis, Mendoza y
San Juan. Buenos Aires, 1926. 62 p. (Universidad de Buenos Aires. Instituto de Investigaciones Históricas, Publ. 33)   (489
  Jones 690.

FIGUEROA, Andrés A. Los archivos de la ciudad
de Santiago del Estero. Buenos Aires, 1921.
31 p. (Universidad de Buenos Aires. Instituto de Investigaciones Históricas,
Publ. 11)   (490
  Jones 693.

FURLONG CARDIFF, Guillermo. Cartografía histórica argentina; mapas, planos y diseños
que se conservan en el Archivo General de
la Nación. Buenos Aires, 1963. 391 p. (490a
   Prepared under the sponsorship of the Comisión Nacional Ejecutiva de Homenaje al 150o
Aniversario de la Revolución de Mayo.

IRIBARREN, Alfredo A. Los archivos históricos
de Mercedes. La Plata, Tall. de Impresiones
Oficiales, 1943. 50 p. (Archivo Historico
de la Provincia de Buenos Aires; Los archivos históricos de la Provincia de Buenos
Aires, Publ. 4)   (490b
   Cited in Geoghegan 2538.

LARROUY, Antonio. Los archivos de Córdoba y
Tucumán. Buenos Aires, 1909. 61 p.   (491
   Jones 746.

-----. Los archivos de La Rioja y Catamarca.
Buenos Aires, 1921. 44 p.   (492
   Jones 746a.

-----. Los archivos de Parana y Santa Fe.
Buenos Aires, 1908. 24 p. (Universidad
de Buenos Aires. Instituto de Investigaciones Históricas, Publ. 1-2, 12)   (493
   Jones 746b.

-----. Documentos del archivo general de Tucumán. Invasiones inglesas y revolución.
t. 1, 1806-1807, 1810-1812. Buenos Aires,
Impr. y Casa Edit. "Juan A. Alsina", 1910.
560 p.   (494
   Catalog of letters and papers with notes.

MASINI, José Luis. Los archivos históricos
de Mendoza; historia, organización, contenido. Mendoza [Tall. Gráf. D'Accurzio,
1959] 44 p.   (494a

MONJARDIN, Federico F. Los archivos históricos de Luján. La Plata, 1938. 91 p.   (495
   Jones 785a.

MORALES GUIÑAZU, Fernando. El Archivo Histórico de Mendoza. (11. Congreso Internacional de Historia de América. Buenos Aires,
1938. v. 5, p. 240-49)   (496
   Published also in Revista de la Junta de
Estudios Históricos, Mendoza, 1938, t. 11,
p. 65-78.---Jones 787.

OUTES, Félix Faustino. Cartas y planos inéditos de los siglos XVII y XVIII y del primer
decenio del siglo XIX conservados en el archivo de la Dirección de Geodesia, Catastro
y Mapa de la provincia de Buenos Aires.
Buenos Aires, Tall. Casa J. Peuser, 1930.
45 p. (Instituto de Investigaciones Geográficas, ser. B, Publ. 3)   (497
   Jones 66.

SARAVI, Guillermo. El Archivo Histórico de
Entre Ríos. (11. Congreso Internacional de
Historia de América. Buenos Aires, 1938.
v. 5, p. 302-30)   (498
   Jones 837.

TORRE REVELLO, José. El Archivo General de
Nación Argentina. (Revista de historia de
América, México, D.F., no. 1, p. 41-52,
1938)   (499
   Jones 862b.

-----. El Archivo Histórico de la provincia
de Buenos Aires. (Revista de historia de
América, México, D.F., no. 5, p. 55-68,
1939)   (500
   Jones 862c

------. -----. La Plata, Tall. de Impresiones Oficiales, 1941. 28 p. (Publ. del Archivo Histórico; los Archivos historicos de
la Provincia de Buenos Aires, 3)   (501

-----. Los archivos de la República Argentina.
Sevilla, Tip. Zarzuela, 1925. 32 p.   (502
   Jones 863.

ZINGONI, Carmelo V. El Archivo Histórico de
la Provincia de Buenos Aires. La Plata,
1938. 37 p.   (503
   Jones 890a.

BOLIVIA

RENE MORENO, Gabriel. Los archivos historicos
de la capital de Bolivia. (Revista chilena,
Santiago, v. 4, 1876)   (504
   Jones 932a.

-----. Biblioteca boliviana. Catálogo del
archivo de Mojos y Chiquitos. Santiago de
Chile, Impr. Gutenberg, 1888. 627 p.   (505
   A collection of mss. made by René-Moreno
and presented by him to the Bolivian government.---Jones 935.

SOCIEDAD Geografica y de Historia "Potosí".
Indice analítico. Archivo de Documentos de
la Casa Real de Moneda, Potosí. Buenos Aires, Plantié, Tall. Gráf., 1944. 41 p (506
   Catalog of documents, 1619-1695.

VARGAS UGARTE, Rubén. Los archivos de la antigua Chuquisaca. (Boletín del Instituto de
Investigaciones Históricas, Buenos Aires,
t. 9, p. 298-315 oct./dic, 1929)   (507
   "Gran parte de los papeles ... se han dis-
persado o han desaparecido y los que se conservan --- hoy se guardan en el Archivo General de la Nación, en la Biblioteca Nacional, en el Archivo del Cabildo Eclesiástico
y en las librerías pertenecientes a sociedades o personas particulares".---Jones 943a.

BRAZIL

BRANCHE, Henri Boullier de. Inventário sumá-
rio dos documentos da Secretaria de Estado
da Marinha. Rio de Janeiro, Arquivo Nacional, 1960. 56 p. ([Publ.] Arquivo Nacional,
v. 43)   (508
    Cited in Richardson, item 7217.

BRAZIL. Arquivo Nacional. Catalogo da Secção
Histórica do Arquivo do Estado de São Paulo.
Indice alfabético de documentos relativos a
Sesmarias. - Congresso do Mundo Português
(1940) - Lista das publicações. Rio de Janeiro, 1939. xvii, 405 p. (Publ.,
v. 36)   (509
    Preface by E. Vilhena de Moraes. Cited
in Hill, p. 30.

─────. ─────. Catalogo das cartas régias,
provisões, alvarás, avisos, portarias, etc.
de 1662 a 1821, existentes no Arquivo Nacional; 2a. ed. Rio de Janeiro, 1922.
xlvi, 804 p. (Publ., v. 1)   (510
    Revision by Armando Esteves. Cited in
Hill, p. 26.

─────. ─────. Catalogo de cartas, provisões,
alvarás, avisos, portarias, etc., de 1662 a
1821, salvo expressas indicações em contrá-
rio. Rio de Janeiro, 1886. (Publ.,
v. 1)   (511
    Cited in Brazil, Arq. Nac., Elenco, p. 721

─────. ─────. Catalogo de Memorias e outros
documentos contidos em 19 volumes conservados na Secção Histórica. Rio de Janeiro,
Off. Graphicas do Arquivo Nacional, 1928.
54 p.   (512
    Compiler Antônio Carlos Chichorro da Gama.
Cited in Reis, item 376. Published also in
v. 26 of the Publicações of the Arquivo Nacional.

─────. ─────. Catalogo de plantas e mapas da
cidade do Rio de Janeiro, 1750-1962. Rio de
Janeiro, 1962. 82 p. (Publ., v. 51)   (513

─────. ─────. Catalogo dos livros da Secção
histórica. Rio de Janeiro, 1913-1915. 2 v.
(Publ., v. 13, 16)   (514
    Cited in Brazil, Arq. Nac., Elenco, p. 721

─────. ─────. Elenco das publicações e dos
documentos ... parte do seu programa de colaboração com a Comissão Brasileira dos Cen-
tenários de Portugal. Rio de Janeiro, Impr.
Nacional, 1951. 736 p.   (515

─────. ─────. Indice alfabetico das leys,
alvarás, cartas régias, decretos e mais
ordens que ha no Arquivo da Provedoria da
Fazenda Real. Rio de Janeiro, 1923. 354 p.
(Publ., v. 21)   (516

BRAZIL. Arquivo Nacional ... (Cont.)
    Editor: Alexandre Max Kitzinger. Cited
in Hill, p. 28.

─────. ─────. Indice da collecção, alvarás,
cartas e provisões - 1753 a 1808. Rio de
Janeiro, 1912. 308 p. (Pub., v. 12) (517
    Cited in Hill, p. 27.

─────. ─────. Indice da collecção "Correspondencia dos governadores do Rio de Janeiro.
Rio de Janeiro, 1911. 275 p.
(Publ., v. 11)   (518
    Editor: Armando Esteves. Period covered:
1680-1719. Cited in Hill, p. 27.

─────. ─────. Indice da collecção "Ordens
Régias", abrangendo o periodo de 1719 a
1807. Rio de Janeiro, 1906. 212 p.
(Publ., v. 5)   (519
    Editor: Armando Esteves. Cited in Hill,
p. 27.

─────. ─────. Indice da correspondencia da
Côrte de Portugal com os Vice-Reis, no Rio
de Janeiro, de 1763 a 1807. Rio de Janeiro,
1901. 204 p. (Publ., v. 3)   (520
    Editors: José de Lacerda and Eduardo
Marquês Peixoto. Cited in Hill, p. 26-27.

─────. ─────. Indice da correspondencia dos
governadores do Rio de Janeiro com diversas
autoridades - 1718 a 1736. Rio de Janeiro,
1908. 334 p. (Publ., v. 8)   (521
    Editor: Armando Esteves. Cited in Hill,
p. 27.

─────. ─────. Indice das publicações do
Arquivo Nacional. Rio de Janeiro, Cia. Brasileira de Artes Gráficas, 1944. 22 p. (522
    A complete list since 1886.

─────. ─────. Indice dos documentos que
compõem a correspondencia activa e passiva
do Vice-Rei Luiz de Vasconcellos e Souza
com os governadores das capitanias de Santa
Catharina, Rio Grande do Sul, e com os Vice-
Reis do Rio da Prata e Commissarios hespan-
hoes em Buenos Ayres, no decennio de 1779
a 1789. Rio de Janeiro, 1907. 410 p.
(Publ., v. 6)   (523
    Cited in Hill, p. 27.

─────. ─────. Indice dos officios dirigidos á
Côrte de Portugal pelos Vice-Reis do Brasil,
no Rio de Janeiro, de 1763 a 1808. Rio de
Janeiro, 1889. xxiv, 362 p.
(Publ., v. 2)   (524
    Cited in Hill, p. 26.

─────. ─────. Registro de estrangeiros. Rio
de Janeiro, 19 -1962. 3 v. (Publ., 1a.
ser. 46, 49-50)   (525
    v. 1, covers 1808-1822; v. 2, 1823-1830;
and v. 3, 1831-1839.

BRAZIL. Arquivo Publico do Imperio. Publicações. Rio de Janeiro, Impr. Nacional, 1888. (526
  Cited in Reis, item 128.

-----. -----. Rio de Janeiro, Impr. Nacional, 1889. (527
  Cited in Reis, item 135.

-----. Biblioteca Nacional. Catalogo da coleção Visconde do Rio-Branco. [Rio de Janeiro] Ministério das Relações Exteriores, Instituto Rio-Branco [1950] 2 v. (528
  Lists 5,122 items.

-----. -----. Catalogo dos manuscriptos da Biblioteca Nacional. Rio de Janeiro, Typ. G. Leuzinger, 1878-1904. 5 v. (529
  Published also in Annaes of the Biblioteca Nacional, v. 4-5, 10, 15 (fasc. 1: 286 p.), 18 (p. 3-332), 23 (p. 69-586), 1877/1878-1901.

-----. Ministério das Relações Exteriores. Mapoteca. Mapas e planos manuscritos relativos ao Brasil colonial conservados no Ministério das Relações Exteriores e descritos por Isa Adonias para as comemorações do quinto centenário da morte do Infante dom Henrique. [Rio de Janeiro] Ministério das Relações Exteriores, Serviço de Documentação, 1960. 2 v. (530
  Contents: v. 1, Texto; v. 2, Mapas.

CATALOGO dos livros manuscritos dos tempos coloniaes, do Imperio e dos livros impressos existentes na sua bibliotheca. São Paulo, 1908. (531
  Cited in Reis, item 232.

INSTITUTO Archeologico e Geographico Alagoano, Maceió. Catalogo da Secção de documentos, organisado por Craveiro Costa. Maceió, Casa Ramalho, 1926. 144 p. (532
  Lists 823 documents, with some supplementary items at end of sections. Lists also about 185 autographs.

INSTITUTO Archeologico e Geographico Pernambucano, Recife. Indice contendo todos os livros e papeis impressos e manuscriptos existentes no Archivo. Recife, Typ. do Jornal de Recife, 1870. 24 p. (533
  Cited in Reis, item 54.

INSTITUTO Archeologico, Historico e Geraphico, Recife. Os nossos manuscriptos. (Revista do Instituto, Pernambuco, v. 27, p. 109-327, 1926) (534
  Jones 1141.

INSTITUTO Histórico e Geográfico Brasileiro, Rio de Janeiro. Catalogo dos documentos sôbre São Paulo existentes no Arquivo do Instituto Histórico e Geográfico Brasileiro

INSTITUTO Histórico e Geográfico... (Cont.) e do Instituto Histórico e Geográfico de São Paulo para as comemorações de IV Centenário da Fundação de São Paulo. São Paulo, 1954. 354 p. (535

-----. Catalogo dos manuscriptos do Instituto Historico e Geographico Brasileiro existentes em 31 de dezembro de 1883. Organisado por ordem alphabetica e dividido em quatro partes: 1a., Biographias. 2.a, Documentos. 3.a, Memorias, 4.a, Poesias. Rio de Janeiro, Typ. Perseverança, 1884. 153 p. (536
  Organisado por Tristão de Alencar Araripe. Also issued in 1889.---Jones 1065.

PARA (State) Arquivo Pùblico. Catálogo chronológico da Secção de Manuscriptos; organizado sob a direcção de Arthur Vianna. Fasciculo primeiro. Belem, Typ. do Diario Off., 1901. 127 p. (537

-----. Bibliotheca Pública. Catalogo das plantas, mappas e desenhos manuscriptos existentes na primeira secção de manuscriptos. (Annaes da Bibliotheca e Arquivo Público, Pará, t. 4, p. 119-54, 1905) (538
  Jones 1131.

SANTOS, Francisco Agenor de Noronha. Indice da revista "Archivo do Districto Federal" cum extracto alphabetico de assumtos. Rio de Janeiro, Typ. do Jornal do Commércio, 1919. 169 p. (539
  "Contains an alphabetical index of all documents since the 16th century relating to the Brazilian capital and published in the records of the municipality". cf. Dr. Oliveira Lima's note in Hispanic American historical review, May 1921, p. 361.---Jones 1112.

-----. Resenha analítica de livros e documentos do Archivo Geral da Prefeitura. Rio de Janeiro, Secretaria Geral de Educação e Cultura, Departamento de Historia e Documentação, 1949. 26 p. (540

SAO PAULO (State). Archivo Publico. Historico do Archivo Publico de São Paulo; acompanhado da relação dos cidadãos que governaram a provincia e o estado no periodo republicano, do catalogo dos livros manuscriptos dos tempos coloniaes, do Imperio e dos libros impressos existentes ma sua biblioteca. São Paulo, Duprat & C., 1908. 267 p. (541

CHILE

CHILE. Archivo Nacional. Catálogo; fondos varios. Santiago, Dirección General de Prisiones, Impr., 1952. 378 p. (542

CHILE. Archivo Nacional. Catálogo de la colección de manuscritos de d. José Ignacio Víctor Eyzaguirre. Santiago, Dirección General de Prisiones, 1944. 188 p. (543

-----. -----. Catálogo del Archivo de la Real Audiencia de Santiago. Santiago, Impr. Barcelona, 1898-1942. v. 1-4. (544
Jones 1423a, 1592.

-----. -----. Guía para facilitar la consulta del archivo de escribanos. Santiago, Dirección General de Tall. Fiscales de Prisiones, Impr., 1914-1930. 3 v. (545
v. 1: Archivo de escribanos que se custodia en la Biblioteca Nacional; v. 2: 1696-1760; v. 3: 1761-1800.

-----. -----. Indice de los protocolos notariales de Valdivia, La Unión, Osorno y Calbuco y alcabalas de Chiloé, 1774-1848. Santiago, 1929. 188 p. (546
Jones 1424a.

-----. -----. Indice del Archivo Hidrográfico "Vidal Gormaz". Santiago, Impr. Universitaria, 1938. 37 p. (547
Contains 155 entries.

-----. Biblioteca Nacional. Catálogo de los manuscritos relativos a los antiguos Jesuítas de Chile que se custodian en la Biblioteca Nacional. Santiago, Impr. Ercilla, 1891. 543 p. (548
Compiled by José Manuel Frontaura y Arana; 2,752 items.---Jones 1603.

INDICE razonado del Archivo del Cabildo de San Felipe. Santiago, Impr. Cervantes, 1900. 83 p. (549
Published in Anales de la Universidad, t. 107. Cited in Laval, item 139.

MEDINA, José Toribio. Indice de los documentos existentes en el Archivo del Ministerio de lo Interior. Santiago, Impr. de la República de J. Núñez, 1884. 899 p. (550
"Un copioso y detallado índice de 1,300 volúmenes con 18,216 documentos".
"Libro sumamente raro, a causa de haber sido vendida la edición para papel de envolver". Chiappa, no. 16.---Jones 1547.

THAYER OJEDA, Tomás. La sección de manuscritos de la Biblioteca Nacional de Chile. (Hispanic American historical review, Baltimore, v. 4, p. 156-97, 1921) (551
With English translation.---Jones 1642.

VALPARAISO, Chile. Municipalidad. Indice del Archivo de la Alcaldía correspondiente al año 1894. Valparaíso, Tip. Gutenberg, 1895. 157 p. (552
Cited in Laval, item 49. Compiler: Fidel Barra.

VALPARAISO, Chile. Municipalidad. Indice general del Archivo. Valparaíso, Impr. de "La Patria", 1896. 2 v. (553
v. 1 (1130 p.) Actas municipales, 1791-30 de junio de 1895. - v. 2, (1057 p.) Documentos, 1779 - 30 de junio de 1895.
Cited in Laval, item 236-37.

COLOMBIA

AMAYA SIERRA, Juan M. Compilación de los índices de 221 volúmenes del Archivo de la Corte Suprema de Justicia que comprende desde el año 1822 hasta 1871. Bogotá, Impr. Nacional, 1927. t. 1: 280 p. (554
Cited in Giraldo Jaramillo, p. 89.

ANTIOQUIA, Col., Archivo Histórico. Indice del Archivo Colonial. Medellín, Impr. Departamental de Antioquia [1961] v. 1 (298 p.) (555
The first volume includes references to 3,105 entries in 108 volumes of the Archives, 1603-ca. 1825. The collection contains 12,774 entries in 813 volumes.

COLOMBIA. Archivo Nacional. Indice del Archivo Colonial. Bogotá, Impr. Nacional (v. 1-2); Edit. Antena, 1936-1946. 4 v. (Publ. del Archivo Histórico Nacional) (556
Contents: v. 1, Tierras. - v. 2, Capellanías, egidos, fincas, minas, poblaciones, Real Audiencia y Resguardos. - v. 3, Abastos, aduanas, alcabalas, archivos, colegios, competencias, consulados, correos, cruzadas, y genealogías. - v. 4, Caciques e indios, curas y obispos, lazaretos, y obras pías. Editors of v. 1-2: Carlos Gil S. and Manuel María Herrera.

-----. -----. Archivos nacionales, índice analítico, metódico y descriptivo, 1544-1819. Bogotá, 1913- . v. 1 (468 p.) (558
Compiler: Francisco Xavier Vergara y Velasco. Hill, p. 54, notes that this is the first of 8 v. planned, but remains as the only one published.---Jones 1775a.

-----. Congreso. Archivo. Indice alfabético, 1819 a 1935 ... leyes, proyectos, rehabilitaciones, memoriales, telegramas, etc. ... Bogotá, Impr. Nacional, 1936-1937. 2 v. (559
v. 1: A-D; v. 2: E-Z.---Jones 1700a.

-----. Ejército. Archivo. Catálogos e índices de la parte que se halla arreglado. Bogotá, Impr. Nacional, 1923. 184 p. (560
Index of 1,757 volumes of documents, military history of Colombia. Cited in Giraldo Jaramillo, p. 68.

CORTES, Vicenta. Mapoteca colombiana: catálogo de los mapas y planos manuscritos del

CORTES, Vicenta... (Cont.)
Archivo Nacional, 1556-1907. [Bogotá, 1960?]
312, 36 p.   (560a
National Union catalog cites photocopy
negative of "original typescript".

-----. La sección de la Colonia del Archivo
Nacional de Colombia. Bogotá, 195?, p. 184-
218.   (560b

FUNDACION John Boulton, Caracas. Sección venezolana del Archivo de la Gran COLOMBIA:
índice suscinto. Caracas, 1960.
148 p.   (561

QUEVEDO, Francisco. Manuscritos teológico-fi-
losóficos coloniales santafereños. Bogotá,
1952. 106 p.   (562
Cited in An. bibliogr. col., 1951-1956,
p. 6.

COSTA RICA

COSTA RICA. Archivos Nacionales. Indice alfabético y chronológico de los protocolos
del Archivo Nacional, San José, 1891.
23 v.   (563
Compilers: Gerardo Lara and Diego Cha-
morro. Index covers the periods 1851 to
1888. Cited in Hill, p. 62-3.

-----. Indice de los protocolos de Alajuela,
1793-1850. San José, 1908. 511 p.   (564
Cited in Hill, p. 62.

-----. Indice de los protocolos de Cartago.
San José, 1909-1930. 6 v.   (565
Contents: v. 1, 1607-1700 (474 p.), -
v. 2, 1700-1725 (569 p.). - v. 3, 1726-1750
(469 p.). - v. 4, 1751-1784 (451 p.). -
v. 5, 1785-1817 (497 p.). - v. 6, 1818-1850
(610 p.)

-----. Indice de los protocolos de Guanacaste,
1756-1850. San José, 1909. 368 p.   (566

-----. Indice de los protocolos de Heredia,
1721-1851. San José, 1904. 724 p.   (567

-----. Indice de los protocolos de San José.
San José, 1905. 2 v.   (568
Contents: v. 1, 1721-1836 (576 p.). -
v. 2, 1837-1850 (559 p.)

-----. Indice general de los documentos del
Archivo de Cartago anteriores al año de 1850
inclusive, arreglado bajo la dirección de
León Fernández. San José, 1883-1898.
4 v. in 3 v.   (569
Contents: t. 1, Protocolos, 1602-1850. -
t. 2, Mortuales, 1639-1850. - t. 3, Civiles.
t. 4, Criminales. Jones 1270, cites collection as "anteriores al año 1840" in 5 v.

COSTA RICA. Archivos Nacionales. Mortuarios
de Alajuela y Heredia anteriores al año 1851.
San José, 1898. 63 p.   (570
Hill, p. 62, notes that this is v. 5 pos-
sibly to connect it with Indice general de
los documentos del Archivo de Cartago.
Compiler: Anastasio Alfaro.

CUBA

CUBA. Archivo Nacional. Catálogo de los fondos de la Comisión Militar Ejecutiva y Permanente de la Isla de Cuba. Habana, 1945.
xiv, 147 p. (Publ., 8)   (571

-----. -----. Catálogo de los fondos de la
Junta Superior de Sanidad de la Isla de
Cuba. La Habana, 1947. 256 p.
(Publ., 13)   (572

-----. -----. Catálogo de los fondos de las
Floridas. La Habana, 1944. xcix, 323 p.
(Publ., 3)   (573
For title in English see Official list of
documentary funds of the Florida (item 578,
586)

-----. -----. Catálogo de los fondos del Consejo de Administración de la Isla de Cuba.
La Habana, 1948-1950. 3 v. (Publ., 20,
25, 28)   (574

-----. -----. Catálogo de los fondos del Li-
ceo Artístico y Literario de La Habana.
La Habana, 1944. 73 p. (Publ., 5)   (575

-----. -----. Catálogo de los fondos del Real
Consulado de Agricultura, Industria y Comercio de la Junta de Fomento. La Habana, 1943.
655 p. (Publ., 1)   (576

-----. -----. Catálogo de los mapas, planos,
croquis y árboles genealógicos existentes
en el Archivo Nacional de Cuba. La Habana,
1951-1956. v. 1-4. (Publ., 31, 34, 38,
45)   (577
v. 1-4 contains entries A through O.

-----. -----. Official list of documentary
funds of the Floridas, now territories of
the States of Louisiana, Alabama, Missis-
sippi, Georgia and Florida, kept in the
National Archives. Habana, 1945.
316 p.   (578
The Official list is the same as the Catálogo de los fondos de las Floridas, (item
573) but with a short introduction in English and an omission of illustrative matter.
It is also the same as item 586.

-----. Biblioteca Nacional. Indice de docu-
mentos existentes en el Archivo de Antonio
Bachiller y Morales que se conservan en la
Biblioteca Nacional. Habana Tip. Villegas,

CUBA. Biblioteca Nacional... (Cont.)
1950. 45 p. (Cuaderno no. 1)   (579
    Compiled by Rodolfo Tró and Lilia Castro.

LLAVERIAS Y MARTINEZ, Joaquín. Historia de los
    archivos de Cuba. Prólogo de F. de P. Coro-
    nado. Habana, Impr. de Ruiz y Comp., 1912,
    382 p.   (580
    Jones 1866.

-----. 2a. ed. La Habana, 1949. 429 p.
    (Publ. del Archivo Nacional de Cuba,
    24)   (581

PARTIDO revolucionario cubano. Inventario ge-
    neral del archivo de la delegación del Par-
    tido Revolucionario Cubano en Nueva York
    (1892-1898) Habana, Impr. "El Siglo XX",
    1921. v. 1.   (582
    Jones 1881.

-----. Another edition. La Habana, 1955.
    2 v. (Cuba. Archivo Nacional, Publ., 42,
    44)   (583
    Lists 17,910 entries of correspondence,
    documents and publications.

PEREZ, Luis Marino. Guide to the materials
    for American history in Cuban archives.
    Washington, 1907. 142 p. (Carnegie Insti-
    tution of Washington, Publ. no. 83)   (584
    Jones 1890.

ROJAS, María Teresa de. Indice y extractos
    del Archivo de Protocolos de la Habana.
    Habana, Impr. Ucar García, 1947-1950.
    2 v.   (585
    v. 1: 468 p. (1578-1585); v. 2: 503 p.
    (1586-1587)

SOCIEDAD Colombista Panamericana. Documents
    pertaining to the Floridas which are kept
    in different archives of Cuba; Appendix num-
    ber 1: Official list of documentary funds of
    the Floridas - now territories of the states
    of Louisiana, Alabama, Mississippi, Georgia
    and Florida - kept in the National Archives.
    Havana [For sale by the Sociedad Colombista
    Panamericana] 1945. 316 p.   (586
    Same as item 578.

ZAPATA CASANOVA, Felipe. Catálogo sumario de
    los fondos existentes en el Archivo Nacio-
    nal, 1958. 85 p. (Publ. del Comité de Ar-
    chivos, Instituto Panamericano de Geogra-
    fía e Historia)   (587

DOMINICAN REPUBLIC

SEVILLANO COLOM, Francisco. El Archivo Gene-
    ral de la Nación y el servicio de microfilm
    de la Unesco. Ciudad Trujillo, Edit. Mon-
    talvo, 1960. 26 p.   (588

ECUADOR

SANCHEZ ASTUDILLO, Miguel. Textos de catedrá-
    ticos jesuítas en Quito colonial; estudio y
    bibliografía. Quito, Casa de la Cultura
    Ecuatoriana, 1959. 146 p. (Archivo Nacio-
    nal de Historia)   (589

EUROPE

CALDERON QUIJANO, José Antonio, and NAVARRO
    GARCIA, Luis. Guía de los documentos, mapas
    y planos sobre historia de América y España
    moderna en la Biblioteca Nacional de Paris,
    Museo Británico y Public Record Office de
    Londres. Sevilla, 1962. 70 p. (Publ. de
    la Escuela de Estudios Hispano-Americanos
    [Univ. de Sevilla] no. general 142)   (590

CARRERA STAMPA, Manuel. Misiones mexicanas en
    archivos europeos. México, D.F., 1949.
    120 p. (Publ. del Instituto Panamericano de
    Geografía e Historia no. 93)   (591
    Issued also as publication of the Comisión
    de Historia, no. 8, and as first of the se-
    ries: Misiones americanas en los archivos
    europeos, 1.

CORRA, Virgilio, filho. Missões brasileiras
    nos arquivos europeus. México, F.F., 1952.
    158 p. (Publ. del Instituto Panamericano de
    Geografía e Historia, no. 119)   (592
    Issued also publication of the Comisión de
    Historia, no. 32, and as v. 4 of the series,
    Misiones americanas en los archivos europeos.

DONOSO, Ricardo. Fuentes documentales para la
    historia de la independencia de América.
    Misión de investigación en los archivos eu-
    ropeos. México, D.F., 1960. xii, 301 p.
    (Publ. del Instituto Panamericano de Geogra-
    fía e Historia, no. 233)   (593
    Issued also as publication of la Comisión
    de Historia, no. 99)

ESPEJO, Juan Luis. Indice de documentos rela-
    tivos a Chile existentes en el Public Record
    Office de Londres, Archivo de las Ordenes Mi-
    litares de Madrid y Archivo General de Indias
    de Sevilla. Santiago, 1915. 71 p.   (594
    Jones 1468.

GABALDON MARQUEZ, Joaquín. Misiones venezola-
    nas en los archivos europeos. México, D.F.,
    1954. 230 p. (Publ. del Instituto Panameri-
    cano de Geografía e Historia, no. 181) (595
    Issued also as publication of la Comisión
    de Historia, no. 73, and as v. 8 of the se-
    ries, Misiones americanas en los archivos eu-
    ropeos.

HILL, Roscoe R. American missions in European
    archives. México, D.F., 1951. 134 p. (Publ.
    del Instituto Panamericano de Geografía e

HILL, Roscoe R... (Cont.)
  Historia, no. 108)   (596
    Issued also as publication of the Comisión
  de Historia, no. 22, and as v. 2 of the series, Misiones americanas en los archivos
  europeos.

MOLINA, Raúl Alejandro. Misiones argentinas
  en los archivos europeos. México, D.F.,
  1955. 745 p. (Publ. del Instituto Panamericano de Geografía e Historia, no.
  167)   (597
    Issued also as Publication of the Comisión
  de Historia, no. 65, and as v. 7 of the series, Misiones americanas en los archivos
  europeos.

MOLINA ARGÜELLO, Carlos. Misiones nicaragüen-
  ses en archivos europeos. México, D. F.,
  1957. 163 p. (Publ. del Instituto Panamericano de Geografía e Historia, no.
  223)   (598
    Issued also as publication of the Comisión
  de Historia, no. 85 and as v. 12, of the series, Misiones americanas en los archivos
  europeos.

MORENO FRAGINALS, Manuel. Misiones cubanas en
  archivos europeos. México, D.F., 1951.
  124 p. (Publ. del Instituto Panamericano de
  Geografía e Historia, no. 115)   (599
    Issued also as publication of the Comisión
  de Historia, no. 28, and as v. 3 of the series, Misiones americanas en los archivos
  europeos.

ORTEGA RICAURTE, Enrique. Misiones colombianas en los archivos europeos. México, D.F.,
  1951. 158 p. (Publ. del Instituto Panamericano de Geografía e Historia, no.
  120)   (600
    Issued also as publication of the Comisión
  de Historia, no. 33, and v. 5 of the series,
  Misiones americanas en los archivos europeos.

RUBIO MAÑE, J. I. Fuentes documentales para
  la historia de la independencia de América,
  Misión de investigación en los archivos europeos. México, D.F. (Publ. del Instituto
  Panamericanos de Geografía e Historia, no.
  236)   (601
    In press.

SOTO CARDENAS, Alejandro. Misiones chilenas
  en archivos europeos. México, D. F., 1953.
  295 p. (Publ. del Instituto Panamericano
  de Geografía e Historia, no. 149)   (602
    Issued also as publication of the Comisión
  de Historia, no. 47, and as v. 6 of the series, Misiones americanas en los archivos
  europeos.

VARGAS, José María. Misiones ecuatorianas en
  archivos europeos. México, D.F., 1956.
  192 p. (Publ. del Instituto Panamericano

VARGAS, José María... (Cont.)
  de Geografía e Historia, no. 188)   (603
    Issued also as publication of the Comisión
  de Historia, no. 80, and as v. 9 of the series, Misiones americanas en los archivos
  europeos.

FRANCE

MOREL-FATIO, Alfred. Catalogue des manuscrits
  espagnols et des manuscrits portugais. Paris, Impr. Nationale, 1892. 422 p.   (604
    Collection in the Departement des Manus-
  crits, Bibliothèque Nationale.---Jones 321.

OCHOA, Eugenio de. Catálogo razonado de los
  manuscritos españoles existentes en la Biblioteca Real de París, seguido de un suplemento que contiene los de las otras tres
  bibliotecas (del Arsenal, de Sta. Genoveva
  y Mazarina) París, Impr. Real, 1844.
  703 p.   (606

PARIS. Bibliothèque Nationale. Catalogue des
  manuscrits mexicains. Paris, E. Bouillon,
  1899. 64 p.   (607
    "Extrait de la Revue des bibliothèques,
  1898 et 1899".
    385 of the manuscripts described formed
  the Goupil-Aubin collection acquired by the
  Bibliothèque Nationale in 1898. A complete
  catalogue of this collection will be found
  in Eugène Boban's Documents pour servir à
  l'histoire du Mexique. (See item 4028)
  Jones 2404.

RAGATZ, Lowell Joseph. Early French West
  Indian records in the Archives Nacionales.
  Washington, D.C. P. Pearlman [1941] 151-
  90 p.   (608

-----. 2a ed. Washington, D.C., Educational
  Research Bureau, 1949. 40 p.   (609

RANGEL, Alberto, and CALOGERAS, Miguel. Inventario dos inestimaveis documentos históricos da Casa Imperial do Brasil, no Castello d'Eu em França. Rio de Janeiro, 1939.
  2 v. (Anais da Biblioteca Nacional,
  v. 54-55)   (610
    The Imperial archives were sent to France
  after the exile of Dom Pedro II in 1889.---
  Jones 1154a.

GREAT BRITAIN

FIGANIÈRE, Frederico Francisco Stuart de, visconde de la Figanière. Catalogo dos manuscriptos portuguezes existentes no Museu
  Britannico. Lisboa, Imprensa Nacional, 1853.
  415 p.   (611
    Considered the standard source on the sub-
  ject. Supplementing this catalogue is F. A.

FIGANIÈRE, Frederico... (Cont.)
de Varnhagen's Succinta indicação de alguns
manuscriptos importantes ... no Museo Britannico ... Habana, 1863. 15 p.---Jones
1037a.

GAYANGOS, Pascual de. Catalogue of the manuscripts in the Spanish language in the British Museum. London, The Trustees, 1875-
1893. 4 v.   (612
    Class 5 (v. 2, 4): Spanish settlements
in America.---Jones 161.

LIMA, Manuel de Oliveira. Relação dos manuscriptos portuguezes e estrangeiros, de interesse para o Brazil, existentes no Museo
Britannico de Londres. Rio de Janeiro, Companhia Typ. do Brazil, 1903. 138 p. (613
    From Revista do Instituto Historico e
Geographico Brasileiro, t. 65, pt. 2,
p. 5-138.

RAGATZ, Lowell Joseph. A guide to the official correspondence of the governors of
the British West India colonies with the
Secretary of State, 1763-1833. London,
Edwards [1923] 79 p.   (614

VARNHAGEN, Francisco Adolpho de. Succinta
indicação de alguns manuscriptos importantes, respectivos ao Brazil e a Portugal,
existentes no Museo Britannico em Londres,
e não compreendidos no Catalogo Figanière,
publicado em Lisboa em 1853; o simples
additamento ao dito Catalogo. Habana, Impr.
de Antilla, 1863. 15 p.   (614a

GUATEMALA

CHAMBERLAIN, Robert S. A report on colonial
materials in the governmental archives of
Guatemala city. (Handbook of Latin American
studies, 1936. Cambridge, Mass., 1937.
p. 387-432)   (615
    Jones 1287.

GUATEMALA. Archivo General del Gobierno. Indice de los documentos existentes en el Archivo General del Gobierno. [Guatemala,
1937] v. 1 (524 p.)   (616
    Issued also as a supplement to the Bole-
tín del Archivo General del Gobierno, año
1, no. 2, en. 1936-año 9, no. 1, mar. 1944.
Continued, v. 2 (p. 1-38), in Boletín, año
9, no. 2-año 10, no. 4 dic. 1945. Prepared
by J. Joaquín Pardo. These installments
were issued in bound form: Guatemala, 1945.
521 p.

-----. Corte Suprema de Justicia. Archivo
General de Protocolos. Catálogo ... de los
protocolos existentes y que proceden de notarios y juzgados de la instancia y munici-
pios. Guatemala, Tip. Nacional, 1903.

GUATEMALA. Corte Suprema de... (Cont.)
47 p.   (617
    Cited in Gropp Guide, p. 443.

-----. Escribanía del Gobierno. Inventario
de los expedientes existentes en la Escribanía del Gobierno. Guatemala, 1924.
354 p.   (618
    Cited in Gropp Guide, p. 441.

PARDO, J. Joaquín. Prontuario de reales cédulas, 1529-1599. Guatemala, Unión Tip., 1941.
171 p.   (619
    "Cédulas" in the Archivo General del Go-
bierno de Guatemala.

HONDURAS

HONDURAS. Archivo y Biblioteca Nacionales.
Indice de los documentos y expedientes que
se custodian en el Archivo Nacional creados
desde 1580 al 30 julio 1927; 3a ed. Coma-
yagüela, Impr. "El Sol", 1927.
291, 4 p.   (620
    Cited in Gropp Guide, p. 503.

-----. -----. Indice de tierras; 3a ed. Co-
mayagüela, 1927.   (621
    Compiler: Abraham Gúnera. Cited in Hill,
p 109.

-----. -----. Indice del Archivo de Tierras.
Tegucigalpa, 1884.   (622
    Cited in Gropp Guide, p. 503.

-----. -----. Lista de materiales microfilmados, redactada por Francisco Sevillano
Colom. Tegucigalpa, 1958. 45 p.
mimeogr.   (623

-----. -----. Nuevo Indice del Archivo de
Tierras custodiado en el Archivo Nacional.
Comprende los expedientes creados desde 1580
a 1901; 2a. ed. Tegucigalpa, Tip. Nacional,
1901. 347 p.   (624

MEXICO

BOLTON, Herbert Eugene. Guide to materials
for the history of the United States in the
principal archives of Mexico. Washington,
D.C., 1913. 553 p. (Carnegie Institution
of Washington. Publ. no. 163)   (625
    Jones 2095.

CAMPECHE, México. Museo Arqueológico, Etnográfico e Histórico. Catálogo de documentos
(manuscritos e impresos) Campeche, Gobierno
del Estado, 1941. 78 p. (Cuaderno, no.
1)   (626
    Cited in Millares, item 1368.

CARRERA STAMPA, Manuel. Archivalia mexicana.
México, D.F., 1952. xvii, 276 p. (Publ.
del Instituto de Historia, 1, ser. no.
27)   (627
    Survey and guide to archives in the capi-
    tal and in the states of Mexico.

-----. Guía del archivo del antiguo ayuntamiento de la ciudad de México. Prefacio de
Emeterio S. Santovenia. Habana, 1949. 53 p.
(Publ. del Archivo Nacional de Cuba,
23)   (628
    Lists 4,326 volumes of records, and Actas
    of the Cabildo beginning with 1524.

CHAVEZ OROZCO, Luis. Indice del ramo de indios del Archivo General de la Nación.
México, D.F., 1951-1953. 2 v. (Ediciones
especiales del Instituto Indigenista Interamericano en Colaboración con el Archivo General de la Nación, 4)   (629

DURANGO. Ayuntamiento. Inventario general
de los libros y papeles del Excmo. Ayuntamiento de Durango. México, D.F., Academia
Mexicana de Historia, 1948. [74] p. (Biblioteca de la Academia Mexicana de Histo-
ria, t. 4)   (630
    Contains listing of 850 items.

GLASS, John B. Catálogo de la colección de
códices [del Museo Nacional de Antropología]
México, Museo Nacional de Antropología, Instituto Nacional de Antropología e Historia,
1964. 237 p.   (631

INVENTARIO del Archivo del Hospital de Jesús.
(Boletín del Archivo General de la Nación.
México, v. 9, p. 273-300, 437-59, 600-18,
1936)   (632
    "In 1929 the archives were moved to the
    National Archives ... The immensely impor-
    tant index to this material is now being
    printed". (A. S. Aiton).---Jones 2261.

MARISCAL, Mario. Reseña histórica del Archivo General de la Nación, 1550-1946. México,
D.F., Secretaría de Gobernación, 1946.
245 p.   (633

MEXICO. Archivo General de la Nación. Documentos para la historia de la cultura en
México, una biblioteca del siglo XVII; catálogo de libros expurgados a los jesuítas en
el siglo XVIII. México, D.F., Impr. Universitaria, 1947. xiii, 187 p. (Publicaciones en cooperación con la Universidad Nacio-
nal Autónoma de México, no. 3)   (634

-----. -----. [Catálogo de civil] n.d. (635
Microfilm CD-3.

-----. -----. [Catálogo de historia]
n.d.   (636
Microfilm CD-4.

MEXICO. Archivo General de la Nación [Catá-
logo de indios] n.d.   (637
Microfilm CD-5. 5 reels.

-----. -----. [Catálogo de infidencias]
n.d.   (638
Microfilm CD-2.

-----. -----. [Catálogo de Inquisición]
n.d.   (639
Microfilm CD-6. 3 reels.

-----. -----. [Catálogo de Mercedes]
n.d.   (640
Microfilm CD-7.

-----. -----. [Catálogo de reales cédulas]
n.d.   (641
Microfilm CD-10. 5 reels. duplicados.

-----. -----. [Catálogo de reales cédulas]
n.d.   (642
Microfilm CD-10. 10 reels.

-----. -----. [Indice del archivo de cartas
de bienes nacionales, preparado por el Dr.
Rubio Mañé] n.d.   (643
Microfilm CD-8. 7 reels.

-----. Biblioteca Nacional. Indice geográfico
de manuscritos que se conservan en la Biblioteca Nacional. (Investigaciones históricas,
México, D.F., I, p. 97-120, 211-40, 1938-
1939)   (644
Jones 2349a.

-----. Comisión de Historia Militar. Guía de
los documentos más importantes sobre el plan
y la revolución de Ayutla. México, D.F., Tall.
Autográfico, 1954. 134 p.   (645
Cited in Caribbean acquisitions, 1959. p. 5.

-----. Dirección de Archivo Militar. Guía del
Archivo Histórico Militar de México. México,
D.F., 1948. (Archivo histórico militar me-
xicano, no. 4)   (646

-----. Museo Nacional de Historia. Catálogo
de los fondos del Centro de Documentación en
el Castillo de Chapultepec. México, 1952.
62 p.   (647
Cataloger: Bertha Ulloa Ortiz. Published
in Anales del Instituto Nacional de Antropología e Historia, v. 4, p. 289-322, 1952, and
in Memorias de la Academia Mexicana de la Historia, 11(2): 173-230, abr./jun. 1952.

-----. Secretaría de Hacienda y Crédito Públi-
co. Guía del Archivo Histórico de Hacienda.
México, D.F., 1940.   (648
Separately paged by subject divisions.

MILLARES CARLO, Agustín, and MANTECON, José
Ignacio. Indice y extractos de los protocolos del Archivo de Notarías de México. México, D.F., Impr. Nuevo Mundo, 1945-1946.
2 v. (Publ. del Centro de Estudios Históricos, Colegio de México)   (649
v. 1: 1524-1528 (470 p.) v. 2: 1536-1538,
1551-1553.

-----. Repertorio bibliográfico de los archivos mexicanos y de las colecciones diplomáticas fundamentales para la historia de México. México, D.F., Impr. Aldina, 1948.
186 p. (Publ. del Instituto de Historia,
1a. ser., no. 6)   (650

PARRAL, México. Archivo. Index to the Archivo de Hidalgo del Parral, 1631-1821. [Tuc-
son, Arizona Silhouettes, 1961]
484 p.   (651

RIOS, Eduardo Enrique. Indice geográfico de
manuscritos que se conservan en la Biblioteca Nacional. (Investigaciones históricas,
México, D.F., v. 1, p. 97-120, 211-40,
349-60, 1938)   (652
Jones 2459a.

SAN LUIS POTOSI, México (City). Universidad.
Biblioteca. Catálogo de los manuscritos de
la Biblioteca Pública de la Universidad Autónoma de San Luis Potosí. Compilación, introducción y notas de Rafael Montejano y
Aguiñaga. [San Luis Potosí] 1958.
66 p.   (653

NICARAGUA

GAMEZ, José Dolores. Archivo Histórico de la
República de Nicaragua. Managua, 1896. t. 1
(373 p.)   (654
No more published? t. 1: 1821-1826.

NICARAGUA. Archivo Nacional. Indice de los
documentos que comprende la Sección de
Tierras y que existen en depósito en el Archivo Nacional. Managua, 1900-1916.
2 v.   (655
Cited in Gropp Guide, p. 526. v.1:1600-
1900, v. 2: 1744-1913.

PARAGUAY

DIAZ PEREZ, Vidriato. Documentos de 1534 a
1600 que se conservan en el Archivo Nacional. Primer ensayo de índice. Asunción,
1909. 22 p.   (656
From Revista del Instituto Paraguayo,
v. 10, p. 985-1000, 1909.---Jones 2605.

-----. Obras y manuscritos referentes al Paraguay que se encuentran en algunas bibliotecas españolas. (Revista del Instituto

DIAZ PEREZ, Viriato.. (Cont.)
Paraguayo, Asunción, v. 8, 235-44,
1906)   (657
Jones 2606.

PARAGUAY. Archivo Nacional. Catálogo de documentos de la Sección Histórica de los años
1534 a 1871 del Archivo Nacional. Asunción,
1935. 46 p.   (658
Hill notes, p. 135, that this catalog is
typewritten. DPU has copy.

-----. -----. Catálogo de testamentos y codicilos del Archivo Nacional. Asunción, 1936,
71 p.   (659
Compiler: José Doroteo Bareiro.

PEREZ, Juan Francisco. Los archivos de la
Asunción del Paraguay. Buenos Aires, 1923.
42 p. (Publ. del Instituto de Investigaciones Históricas, no. 15)   (660
The National Archive has published Catálogo; documentos de 1534 a 1600 (Asunción,
1909); Catálogo de testamentos y codicilos
(1936); Catálogo de la sección histórica de
los años 1534 a 1871 (1935). (R.R. Hill).
Jones 2619.

PERU

BARRA, Felipe de la. Historiografía general
y militar peruana y archivos; introducción
al catálogo del Archivo Histórico-Militar
del Perú. Lima, Impr. Diet, 1962.
93 p.   (661
Reprinted from v. 1 of the Catálogo (item
662)

PERU. Archivo Histórico-Militar. Catálogo
del Archivo Histórico-Militar del Perú.
Lima, [1962-] v. 1- .   (662

-----. Archivo Nacional. Breve inventario de
expedientes. Publicado por Luis Antonio
Eguiguren. Lima, Impr. Torres Aguirre, 1949,
v. 1 (403 p.)   (663
Caption, p. 9: Catálogo del Archivo Nacional del Perú.

-----. -----. Indice de notarios de Lima y
Callao, cuyos protocolos se hallan en el
Archivo Nacional del Perú (siglos XVI, XVII,
XVIII, XIX y XX) Lima, Gil, 1928.
76 p.   (664
Jones 2717a.

-----. Ministerio de Hacienda. Archivo Histórico. Catálogo de la Sección Colonial del
Archivo Histórico. Lima, Impr. Torres
Aguirre, 1944. 215 p.   (665
Covers 1,274 volumes and 55 legajos, 1548-
1820. Compilation by Federico Schwab assisted by Luis Felipe Muro Arias, Helena Gamarra V. and Julia Incháustegui Z.

PERU. Ministerio de Hacienda. Archivo Histórico. Catálogo de la Sección Republicana.
Lima, 1945-1946. 2 v.   (666
   Compiled by Federico Schwab. v. 1, 1821-
1822; v. 2, 1823-1825.

-----. -----. El índice del Archivo del Tribunal del Consulado de Lima, con un estudio
de esta institución por Robert Sidney Smith,
Lima, 1948. lix, 227 p.   (667

-----. -----. Reales cédulas, reales órdenes,
decretos, autos y bandos que se guardan en
el Archivo Histórico. Lima, 1947.
666 p.   (668

-----. Universidad Mayor de San Marcos. Catálogo del Archivo Central Domingo Angulo.
Introducción y noticia histórica por Daniel
Valcárcel. Lima, 1949. v. 1.
(108 p.)   (669
   v. 1 refers to the materials located in
"Sala I". Lists 696 volumes of records,
1577-1948.

VALDERRAMA, Lucila. Squier manuscripts in the
Biblioteca Nacional del Perú. [Durham,
N.C.], 1956. p. 338-41.   (670
   Reprinted from the Hispanic American his-
torical review, v. 36, no, 3, Aug. 1956.

PORTUGAL

ALMEIDA, Eduardo de Castro e. Inventario dos
documentos relativos ao Brasil existentes
no Archivo de Marinha e Ultramar, organisado para a Bibliotheca Nacional do Rio de Janeiro. Rio de Janeiro, 1913-1921.
6 v.   (671
   Published also in Annaes of the Biblioteca
Nacional, v. 31-32, 34, 36-37, 39, 1909-
1917.---Jones 1019.

BASTO, Arthur de Magalhães. Catalogo dos manuscriptos ultramarinos da Bibliotheca Municipal do Porto. Lisboa, 1938.
307 p.   (672
   Pages 101-304 relate to Brazil.---Jones
1090.

BRAZIL. Biblioteca Nacional. Inventario dos
documentos relativos ao Brasil existentes na
Biblioteca Nacional de Lisboa. Rio de Janeiro, [1957] 358 p. (Anais, v. 75) (673

EVORA, Portugal. Biblioteca Publica. Catalogo dos manuscriptos da Bibliotheca Publica eborense, ordenada pelo bibliothecario
Joaquim Heliodoro da Cunha Rivara. Lisboa,
Impr. Nacional, 1850-1871. 4 v.   (674
   Title of v. 2-4: Catalogo ... ordenado
com as descripções e notas do bibliothecario ... e com outras proprias por Joaquim
Antonio de Sousa Telles de Mattos.

EVORA, Portugal. Biblioteca ... (Cont.)
   t. 1, Codices e papeis relativos ás cousas
da America, Africa e Asia. - t. 2, Litteratura. - t. 3, Historia. - t. 4, pte. 1.
Sciencias, artes e polygraphia.---Jones 1037.

PORTUGAL. Arquivo Histórico Ultramarino. Catalogo de documentos sôbre a história de S.
Paulo existentes no Arquivo Histórico Ultramarino de Lisboa. [Rio de Janeiro, Depto.
de Impr. Nacional] 1956- . (Revista do
Instituto Histórico e Geográfico Brasileiro,
tomo especial, 1956)   (675

-----. Biblioteca Nacional. A secção ultramarina da Biblioteca Nacional: inventarios: 1, Codices do extincto Conselho Ultramarino, estudo e notas, por M. A. Hedwig
Fitzler; 2, Codices vindos de Moçambique por
iniciativa de Antonio Ennes; 3, Codices do
Arquivo da Marinha, publicados, anotados e
prefaciados por Ernesto Ennes. Lisboa, Biblioteca Nacional, 1928. 333 p. (Publ. da
Biblioteca Nacional)   (677
Jones 1080.

PUERTO RICO

GOMEZ CANEDO, Lino. Los archivos históricos
de Puerto Rico. San Juan, Instituto de Cultura Puertorriqueña, 1964. x, 154 p. (Publ.
del Archivo General de Puerto Rico,
2)   (678
   Cited in Revista interamericana de bibliografía, no. 33, p. 109.

GUIA DEL ARCHIVO General de Puerto Rico. San
Juan, Instituto de Cultura Puertorriqueña,
1964. 174 p. (Publ. del Archivo General de
Puerto Rico, 1)   (679

SPAIN

AITON, Arthur S., and MECHAM, J. Lloyd. The
Archivo General de Indias. (Hispanic American historical review, Baltimore, v. 4,
p. 553-67, 1921)   (680
Jones 3.

ARGENTINA. Biblioteca Nacional. Catálogo de
los documentos del Archivo de Indias relativos al Río de la Plata que se hallan publicados en la colección de documentos inéditos, con referencia al Catálogo formado por
el Ministerio de Relaciones Exteriores de
la República Argentina. Buenos Aires,1904.
12 p.   (681

-----. -----. Repertorio cronológico y alfabético del catalogo de documentos del Archivo de Indias referentes al Río de la Plata;
2a ed. completada. Buenos Aires, 1911.
136 p.   (682

ARGENTINA. Congreso. Biblioteca. Repertorio de los documentos históricos procedentes del Archivo de Indias, editados en los
años 1918-1919- 1920-1921, bajo la dirección de d. Roberto Levillier. Madrid, Rivadeneyra, 1921. 142 p.   (683
    Forms an index to the Colección de publi-
caciones históricas de la Biblioteca del
Congreso argentino.
    Papeles de los gobernantes del Perú, t.
1-3. - Organización de la iglesia en el Vto.
del Perú,1.-2. pte. - Papeles de oidores
de la Audiencia de Charcas, t. 1. - Papeles
de gobernadores de Tucumán, t. 1. - Correspondencia de los cabildos de Tucumán en el
siglo XVI. - Probanzas de méritos y servicios de los conquistadores de Tucumán, t.
1.-2. - Correspondencia de la ciudad de Buenos Aires, t. 1-3.---Jones 573.

-----. 1922-1926. Madrid, J. Pueyo, 1926.
150 p.   (684
    Jones 573.

-----. Ministerio de Relaciones Exteriores
y Culto. Catálogo de documentos del Archivo de Indias en Sevilla referentes a la historia de la República Argentina, 1514-1810.
Buenos Aires, Tall. Tip. de la Penitenciaría Nacional, 1901-1910. 3 v.   (685
    Contents. - v. 1-2, 1514-1810. - v. 3,
1778-1820.

CHAPMAN, Charles Edward. Catalogue of materials in the Archivo de Indias for the history of the Pacific Coast and the American
Southwest. Berkeley, Univ. of California
Pr., 1919. 755 p. (University of California publications in history, v. 8)   (686
    Jones 2125.

ESPINOSA Y QUESADA, P. Lenguas de América.
Catálogo bibliográfico de XXI ms. existen-
tes en la Biblioteca del Rey de España.
Madrid, V. Suárez, 1914. 36 p.   (687
    Cited in Millares, item 154.

GOMEZ RAMIREZ, José Joaquín. Indice de documentos existentes en el Archivo General de
Indias en Sevilla, y relativos a la guerra
de independencia en México. (Boletín del
Museo Nacional de Arqueología, Historia y
Etnografía. México, D.F., t. 2, ép. 4,
p. 63-4, 100, 136-40, 142-47, 1923)   (688
    Jones 2209.

GUILLEN Y TATO, Julio Fernando. Repertorio
de los mss., cartas, planos y dibujos relativos a las Californias existentes en este
museo. Madrid, 1932. 127 p. (Publ. del
Museo Naval)   (689
    Jones 2227.

INSTITUTO Hispano-Cubano de Historia de América, Sevilla. El Instituto Hispano-Cubano
de Historia de América (Sevilla) Madrid
[etc.] Compañía Ibero-Americana de Publicaciones [1931?] 46 p.   (690
    Apéndice 1-[3] Indice general del t.
1-[3] del Catálogo de los fondos americanos
del Archivo de Protocolos de Sevilla, siglo
XVI: p. 37-46.---Jones 215.

LARRABURE Y UNANUE, Eugenio. Les Archives des
Indes et la Bibliothèque Colombine de Séville;
renseignements sur leurs richesses bibliographiques et sur l'exposition d'anciens documents relatifs a l'Amérique. [Paris, Impr.
Hemmerlé, 1914] 88 p.   (691
    Jones 245.

-----. El Archivo de Indias y la Biblioteca
Colombina de Sevilla. Barcelona, A. Bosch
[1914] 54 p.   (692
    Jones 244.

LATORRE, Germán. Relaciones geográficas de Indias contenidas en el Archivo General de Indias de Sevilla. La Hispano-América del siglo XVI: Colombia, Venezuela, Puerto Rico,
República Argentina, Virreinato de Nueva
España. Sevilla, Tip. Zarzuela, 19.9-1920.
2 v.   (693
    Jones 249.

LLORENS Y ASENCIO, Vicente. Archivo ... de Indias. Catálogo de la Sección 1a.: Real patronato. (Boletín del Centro de Estudios Americanistas, Sevilla, v. 11, no. 82-4, p. 1-40;
no. 85-7, p. 1-103; no, 88-90, p. 49-71,
1924)   (694
    Jones 263.

MADRID. Museo Naval. Indice de la colección
de documentos de Fernández de Navarrete que
posee el Museo Naval, con prólogo de Julio F.
Guillén Tato. Madrid, Instituto Histórico de
Marina, 1946. xxxii, 363, xl p.   (695
    Includes 32 "legajos" with 2,521 entries.
Compiler: V. Vicente Vela.

MORALES PADRON, Francisco, and LLAVADOR MIRA, J.
Mapas, planos y dibujos sobre Venezuela existentes en el Archivo General de Indias. [Ma-
drid, 1964-1965] 2 v. (Publ. de la Escuela
de Estudios Hispano-Americanos, 156,
163)   (696

PAZ, Julián. Catálogo de los mapas que se conservan en el Archivo General de Simancas,
sección de "Límites de América". (Revista
de archivos, bibliotecas y museos, Madrid,
3a. ép. t. 3, p. 524-48, 1899)   (697
    Jones 366.

PEÑA CAMARA, José María de la. A list of Spanish residencias in the Archives of the Indies,
1516-1775; administrative judicial reviews of

PEÑA CAMARA, José María de la... (Cont.)
colonial officials in the American Indies,
Philippines and Canary Islands. Compiled
for the Library of Congress. Washington,
D.C., Library of Congress, 1955.
x, 109 p.   (698

PEREIRA, Ricardo S. Documentos sobre límites
de los Estados Unidos de Colombia, copiados
de los originales que se encuentran en el
Archivo de Indias de Sevilla y acompañados
de breves consideraciones sobre el verdade-
ro Uti possidetis juris de 1810. 1. serie:
Límites entre el antiguo virreinato de la
Nueva-Granada y las capitanías generales de
Venezuela y Tamayo, 1883. 167 p.   (699
   "Apéndice bibliográfico": p. 157-61.
Jones 1756.

RESTREPO TIRADO, Ernesto. Documentos del Archivo de Indias. Lista de los encomenderos
del partido de Santa Fe en 1595. (Boletín
de historia y antigüedades, Bogotá, v. 23,
p. 116-127, 1936)   (700
   Jones 1766.

RODRIGUEZ MOÑINO, Antonio R. Catálogo de los
manuscritos de América existentes en la "Colección de Jesuítas", de la Academia de la
Historia. Badajoz, 1935. 90 p.   (701
   Jones 419.

-----. Catálogo de los documentos de América
existentes en la colección de jesuítas en
la Academia de la Historia. [Badajoz, Impr.
de la Excma. Diputación Provincial] 1949.
249 p.   (702

-----. Catálogo de memoriales presentados al
Real Consejo de Indias (1626-1630). Descripción bibliográfica de más de cuatrocien-
tos rarísimos impresos y manuscritos. Madrid, Impr. y Edit. Maestre, 1953.
291 p.   (703
   Description of 430 "memoriales".

RUBIO MORENO, Luis. Inventario general de
registros cedularios del Archivo General de
Indias de Sevilla, presentado por el autor
en el Congreso de historia y geografía celebrado en 1921. Madrid, Compañia Ibero-Americana de Publicaciones, [1928?] 454 p.
(Colección de documentos inéditos para la
historia de Hispano-América, t. 5)   (704
   Jones 421.

-----. Inventarios del Archivo General de
Indias. Madrid, Tip. de la "Rev. de Arch.,
Bibl. y Museos", 1924- . v. 1- .   (705
   Jones 422.

-----. Pasajeros a Indias; catálogo metodo-
lógico de las informaciones y licencias de
los que allí pasaron, existentes en el Archivo General de Indias. Siglo primero de

RUBIO MORENO, Luis... (Cont.)
la colonización de América, 1492-1592. Trabajo presentado en el Congreso de la Asociación Española para el Progreso de las Ciencias, celebrado en Sevilla en 1917. Madrid,
Compañía Ibero-Americana de Publicaciones,
[1930?] v. 1- . (Colección de documentos
inéditos para la historia de Hispano-América, t. 8 [i.e. 9], 13-)   (706
   Jones 423.

SCHONS, Dorothy. Notes from Spanish archives.
Austin, Texas, 1946. 40 p. (New World
studies, book 1)   (707
   Notes are about the Archivo General de In-
dias, Archivo General de Simancas, Archivo
Nacional, and Academia de la Historia.

SEVILLA. Archivo de Protocolos, Sevilla. Catálogo de los fondos americanos del Archivo
de Protocolos de Sevilla. Madrid, Buenos
Aires [etc.] Compañía Ibero-Americana de
Publicaciones, 1930-1937. 5 v. (v. 1-3:
Colección de documentos inéditos para la historia de Hispano-América, t. 8 [i.e., 10]
11, 14)   (708
   "Publicaciones del Instituto Hispano-Cubano de Historia de América, Sevilla, v. 4-5.
v. 4 published with title: Documentos americanos del Archivo de Protocolos de Sevilla,
as an official document of the 26th International Congress of Americanists.---Jones
455.

-----. Catalogue of the library of Ferdinand
Columbus. Reproduced in facsimile from the
unique manuscript in the Columbine Library
of Seville, by Archer M. Huntington. New
York, 1905. 260 p.   (709
   Jones 447a.

SOUTO MAIOR, Pedro. Nos archives de Hespanha,
relação dos manuscriptos que interesam ao
Brasil. (Revista do Instituto Historico e
Geographico Brasileiro, Rio de Janeiro,
v. 81, p. 7-208, 1918)   (710
   Jones 1202a.

SPAIN. Archivo General de Indias, Sevilla.
Archivo General de Indias de Sevilla; guía
del visitante, por José María de la Peña y
Cámara. [Madrid] Dirección General de Archivos y Bibliotecas, 1958. 206 p. (Ediciones conmemorativas del centenario del
cuerpo facultativo, 1858-1958, 13)   (711

-----. -----. Catálogo, cuadro general de la
documentación [del Archivo General de Indias]
Sevilla, Tip. Zarzuela, 1918. 165 p. (Publ.
del Centro Oficial de Estudios Americanistas
de Sevilla. Biblioteca colonial americana,
t. 1)   (712
   Compilers: Pedro Torres Lanzas and German
Latorre.---Jones 490.

SPAIN. Archivo General de Indias, Sevilla.
Catálogo de la sección 1.: Real patronato
... redactado por Vicente Lloréns Asensio.
Sevilla, Tip. Zarzuela, 1924. 167 p. (Publ.
del Centro Oficial de Estudios Americanistas
de Sevilla. Biblioteca colonial americana,
t. xii)   (713

-----. -----. Catálogo de legajos del Archivo
General de Indias, secciones 1 y 2: Patro-
nato y contaduría de Indias. Sevilla, Tip.
Zarzuela, 1919. 203 p. (Publ. del Centro
Oficial de Estudios Americanistas de Sevilla.
Biblioteca colonial americana, t. 2)   (714
   Compiler: Pedro Torres Lanzas.---Jones
484.

-----. -----. Catálogo de legajos del Archivo
General de Indias. Sección tercera: Casa
de la Contratación de Indias. Sevilla, Tip.
Zarzuela, 1921-1922. 4 v. (Publ. del Centro Oficial de Estudios Americanistas de Sevilla. Biblioteca colonial americana.
t. 6, 8)   (715
   Covers the years 1492-1795. Compiler: Pedro Torres Lanzas.----Jones 485.

-----. -----. Catálogo de los documentos de
la Sección Novena. t. 1: 1724-1834, Santo
Domingo, Cuba, Puerto Rico, Luisiana, y Florida. Sevilla, Impr. de la Gavidia, 1945.
285 p.   (716
   Contains v. 1, 1724-1834.
   Compiler: Cristóbal Bermúdez Plata.

-----. -----. -----. Sevilla, 1949. v. 1
(822 p.) (Publ. de la Escuela de Estudios
Hispano-Americanos de Sevilla, no. 51 (no.
gen.); Serie 6: Colección de documentos,
no. 1)   (716a
   Contents: Ser. 1, Santo Domingo, Cuba,
Puerto Rico, Luisiana y Florida.- Ser. 2,
México.

-----. -----. Catálogo de los fondos cubanos
del Archivo General de Indias. Madrid, Compañía Iberoamericana de Publicaciones,
[1929]-1935. 2 v. in 3 v. (Colección de
documentos inéditos para la historia de Hispano-América, t. 7, 12)   (717
   Preparation by José María de la Peña y Cámara and issued as Publicaciones del Instituto Hispano-Cubano de Historia de América.
Tomo 2, i.e., the final volume of the Catálogo was published in Sevilla as continuation
of the compilation but not in the series.
   Jones 1799, 1909.

-----. -----. Catálogo de pasajeros a Indias
durante los siglos XVI, XVII y XVIII, Madrid, Impr. Espasa Calpe, 1930- . v. 1- .
(Ministerio de Trabajo y Previsión. Publ.
de la Inspección General de Emigración.
Serie D. - Estudios históricos)   (718
   Jones 456.

SPAIN. Archivo General de Indias, Sevilla.
Catálogo de pasajeros a Indias durante los
siglos XVI, XVII y XVIII. Sevilla, Impr.
Edit. de la Gavidia, 1940-1946. 3 v. (719
   Publication under direction of: Consejo
Superior de Investigaciones Científicas.
Instituto "Gonzalo Fernández de Oviedo".
   Contents: v. 1, 1509-1534.- v. 2, 1535-
1538.- v. 3, 1539-1559.

-----. -----. Extracto del catálogo de los
documentos del Consejo de Indias conservados en la Sección de Consejos del Archivo
Histórico Nacional. Madrid, Tip, de la Revista de Archivos, Bibliotecas y Museos,
1920. 41 p.   (720
   Also published in Revista de archivos, bibliotecas y museos, Madrid, ép. 32, t. 41,
p. 417-48.---Jones 172

-----. -----. Independencia de América; fuentes para su estudio; catálogo de documentos
conservados en el Archivo General de Indias
de Sevilla, 1. serie. Madrid [Estab. Tip.
de la Sociedad de Publicaciones Históricas]
1912. 6 v.   (721
   Calendar of 8,000 documents numbered consecutively. Vol. 6 consists of indexes.
   Compiler: Pedro Torres Lanzas.---Jones 486.

-----. -----. -----. 2a serie, Sevilla [Tip.
Zarzuela] 1924- . v. 1-2- . (Publ. del Centro Oficial de Estudios Americanistas de
Sevilla. Biblioteca colonial americana,
t. 11, 14-)   (722
   Compiler: Pedro Torres Lanzas.---Jones
487.

-----. -----. Indice de documentos de Nueva
España existentes en el Archivo de Indias de
Sevilla.   (723
   "Contiene un catálogo de documentos relativos a México durante la dominación española según las cédulas que fueron copiadas y
arregladas bajo la dirección del eminente
historiador don Francisco del Paso y Troncoso". v. 1, p. vii.---Jones 2406.

-----. -----. Relación descriptiva de los
mapas, planos, etc. de la audiencia y capitanía general de Guatemala (Guatemala, San
Salvador, Honduras, Nicaragua y Costa Rica)
existentes en el Archivo General de Indias.
Madrid, Tip. de la Revista de Archivos, Bibliotecas y Museos, 1903. 214 p.   (724
   From the Revista de archivos, bibliotecas
y museos. Compiler: Pedro Torres Lanzas.
Jones 1255.

-----. -----. Relación descriptiva de los mapas, planos, etc. de las antiguas audiencias
de Panamá, Santa Fé y Quito existentes en el
Archivo General de Indias. Madrid, Tip. de
la Revista de Archivos, Bibliotecas y museos,
1904. 185 p.   (725

SPAIN. Archivo General de... (Cont.)
From the Revista de archivos, bibliotecas
y museos, año 8-10] Compiler: Pedro Torres
Lanzas.---Jones 488.

-----. -----. Relación descriptiva de los mapas, planos, &c. de Mèxico y Florida, existentes en el Archivo General de Indias.
Sevilla, Impr. de El Mercantil, 1900.
2 v.   (726
Compiler: Pedro Torres Lanzas.---Jones
489.

------. ------. Relación de mapas, planos,
&c. del Virreinato de Buenos Aires existentes en el Archivo General de Indias (Sevilla)
[Madrid] 1900. 46 p.   (727
Published in Revista de archivos, bibliotecas y museos, ép. 3a, año 2, no. 10-12.
Compiler: Pedro Torres Lanzas.---Jones 869.

-----. -----. -----. 2. ed. aum. Buenos Aires,
1921. (Buenos Aires. Universidad. Instituto de Investigaciones Históricas.
Publ. 7)   (728
Compiler: Pedro Torres Lanzas.---Jones
870.

-----. -----. Relación descriptiva de los mapas, planos, etc. del Virreinato del Perú
(Perú y Chile) existentes en el Archivo General de Indias (Sevilla). Barcelona, Impr.
Henrich y Ca., 1906. 135 p.   (729
Compiler: Pedro Torres Lanzas.---Jones
2762.

-----. Archivo General de Marina Don Alvaro
de Bazán. Independencia de América. Indice de los papeles de expediciones de Indias,
por Julio Guillén. Madrid, Instituto Histórico de Marina, 1953. 3 v.   (730
v. 1-2 are a catalog of some 4,500 items,
1807-1839, and v. 3 is an index of names and
subjects.

-----. -----. Indice de los expedientes y papeles de la Sección de Indiferente ... 1,
1730-1794. Madrid, Consejo Superior de Investigaciones Científicas, 1951.
291 p.   (731
Compiler: Julio F. Guillén. Cited in
HLAS 19, item 3191.

-----. -----. Indice de los papeles de la
Sección de Corso y Presas. Madrid, 1953-
1954. 2 v.   (732
Compiler: Julio F. Guillén.

-----. Archivo General de Simancas. Guía del
Archivo General de Simancas. [Madrid] Dirección General de Archivos y Bibliotecas, 1958.
140 p. (Ediciones conmemorativas del Centenario del Cuerpo Facultativo, 1858-1958,
11)   (733

SPAIN. Archivo General de Simancas. Títulos
de Indias ordenado por Ricardo Magdaleno.
Valladolid, 1954. 980 p. (Catálogo,
20)   (734
Cited in HLAS 19, item 3191a.

-----. Archivo Histórico Nacional, Madrid.
Documentos de Indias, siglos XV-XIX; Catá-
logo de la serie existente en la Sección
Diversos. Madrid, 1954. 282 p.   (735
Compiler: María del Carmen Pescador del
Hoyo.

-----. Biblioteca Nacional. Catálogo de manuscritos de América existentes en la Biblioteca Nacional, por Julián Paz. Madrid, Tip.
de Archivos, 1933. viii, 724 p.   (736

-----. -----. Manuscritos sobre Mexico en la
Biblioteca Nacional de Madrid. Madrid, 1932.
277 p. (Cuadernos mexicanos de la Embajada
de México en España)   (737
Compiler: Julián Paz.

------. Consejo de las Indias. Indice general de los papeles del Consejo de Indias.
Madrid, 1923-1926. 6 v. (Colección de documentos inéditos relativos al descubrimiento, conquista y organización de las antiguas
posesiones españolas de ultramar,
v. 14-19)   (738
Jones 213.

SUSTO, Juan Antonio. Catálogo de la Audiencia
de Panamá, sección V del Archivo de Indias
de Sevilla. Madrid, Tip. de la Revista de
Archivos, Bibliotecas y Museos, 1926.
55 p.   (739
Reprinted from the Revista de archivos,
bibliotecas y museos, Madrid, año 30 (1926)
p. 270-95, 441-66.---Jones 1358.

-----. Panamá en el Archivo General de Indias.
Tres años de labor. Panamá, Impr. Nacional,
1927. 48 p.   (740

TORRE REVELLO, José. Adición a la Relación
descriptiva de los mapas, planos, etc. del
Virreinato de Buenos Aires, existentes en
el Archivo General de Indias. Buenos Aires,
Peuser, 1927. 128 p.   (741
Jones 862.

-----. El Archivo de Indias. Paraná, 1939.
22 p.   (742
Jones 862a.

-----. Archivo General Central en Alcalá de
Henares; reseña histórica y clasificación
de sus fondos. Buenos Aires, Impr. de la
Universidad, 1926. 34 p. (Publ. del Instituto de Investigaciones Históricas, no.
30)   (743
Jones 479.

TORRE REVELLO, José. El Archivo General de Indias de Sevilla; historia y clasificación de sus fondos. Buenos Aires, Tall. Casa J. Peuser, 1929. 214 p. (Universidad de Buenos Aires. Instituto de Investigaciones Históricas, Publ. no. 50) (744
Jones 479a.

-----. Los archivos de la República Argentina (Noticias anotadas, extractadas y coordinadas, para un ensayo de guía del investigador) Sevilla, Tip. Zarzuela, 1925. 32 p. (Publ. del Centro Oficial de Estudios Americanistas de Sevilla. Biblioteca colonial americana, Cuaderno, 14) (745

-----. Los archivos españoles. Buenos Aires, Impr. de la Universidad, 1927. 41 p. (Publ. del Instituto de Investigaciones Históricas, no. 34) (746

------. Inventarios del Archivo General de Indias. Buenos Aires, 1926. 24 p. (Universidad de Buenos Aires. Instituto de Investigaciones Históricas, Publ., 28) (747
Jones 481.

-----. Mapas y planos referente al Virreinato del Plata, conservados en el Archivo General de Simancas. Buenos Aires, Jacobo Peuser, 1938. 66 p. (Publ. del Instituto de Investigaciones Históricas, no. 73) (748
48 maps and plans, mostly in manuscript. Jones 867.

------. Relación de mapas y planos relativos al Virreinato de Buenos Aires existentes en el Archivo Histórico Nacional de Madrid. (Boletín del Instituto de Investigaciones Históricas, Buenos Aires, t. 7. p.60-5, 1928. (749
Jones 867g.

TUDELA, José. Los manuscritos de América en las bibliotecas de España. Madrid, Ediciones Cultura Hispánica, 1954. 586 p. (750

VALCARCEL ESPARZA, Carlos Daniel. Biografías hispanoamericanas en el Archivo General de Indias. Lima, 1959. 127 p. (751

WRIGHT, Irene Aloha. Spanish documents concerning English voyages to the Caribbean, 1527-1568, selected from the Archives of the Indies at Seville. London, Printed for the Hakluyt Society, 1929. 167 p. Works issued by the Hakluyt Society ... Second ser. no. 62) (752
Jones 3016.

UNITED STATES

BUTLER, Ruth Lapham. A check list of manuscripts in the Edward E. Ayer collection. Chicago, Newberry Library, 1937. 295 p. (753
Jones 79.

CASTAÑEDA, Carlos Eduardo, and DABBS, Jack Autrey. Guide to the Latin American manuscripts in the University of Texas Library. Cambridge, Harvard Univ. Pr., 1939. 217 p. (754
Jones 87a.

CASTAÑEDA, Carlos Eduardo, and MARTIN, Early. Three manuscript maps of Texas by Stephen F. Austin, with biographical and bibliographical notes. Austin, Texas, 1930. 55 p. (755
List of manuscript maps of Texas, 1822-1835: p. 45-55.---Jones 2118.

FISHER, Mary Ann. Preliminary guide to the microfilm collection in the Bancroft Library. Berkeley, Calif., Univ. of California, 1955. 28 p. mimeogr. (756
Descriptive of two and one-half million frames of microfilm acquired from foreign archives, and some 2,500 reels of newspapers relative to North America, the Pacific Coast, and Latin America.

GARCIA CHUECOS, Héctor. Catálogo de documentos referentes a la historia de Venezuela y de América, existentes en el Archivo Nacional de Washington. Caracas, Impr. Nacional, 1950. 88 p. (757
A total of 331 documents, 1810-1834 are included.

GROPP, Arthur Eric. Manuscripts in the Department of Middle American Research. New Orleans, Tulane University of Louisiana, 1933. p. 221-97. (Middle American pamphlets, no. 5 of Publication 5 in the Middle American research series) (758
Jones 2535a.

-----. -----. Rev. ed. 1934. (759

HARRISON, John Parker. The archives of United States diplomatic and consular posts in Latin America. Washington, D.C., National Archives, 1953. 16 p. (National Archives publ. no. 53-20) (760

-----. Guide to materials on Latin America in the National Archives, v. 1. Washington, D.C., General Services Administration, National Archives, 1961. 246 p. (National Archives publ. no. 62-3) (761

HARRISON, John Parker. Materials in the National Archives relating to the Mexican states of Sonora, Sinaloa, and Baja California. Washington, D.C., 1952. 16 p. (U.S. National Archives publ. no. 53-6; Reference information papers, 42)   (762

HELTON, H. Stephen. Preliminary inventory of the records of the Office of Inter-American Affairs. Washington, D.C., 1952. 138 p. (National Archives, Publ. 52-16; Preliminary inventories, no. 41)   (763

-----. Preliminary inventory of the records of United States in international conferences, commissions, and expositions. (Record group 43) Washington, D.C., National Archives, 1955. 161 p. (National Archives, Publ. 55-8; Preliminary inventories, no. 76)   (764

HINCKLEY, Lyman. Preliminary checklist of the records of the Military Government of Santo Domingo, 1916-1924. [Washington, D.C., 1945] 10 p. (National Archives, Preliminary checklist, no. 27)   (765

HUSSEY, Roland Dennis. Manuscript Hispanic Americana in the Harvard College Library. (Hispanic American historical review, Durham, N.C., v. 17, p. 259-277, 1937)   (766
    Jones 209.

IRVINE, Maria Hunter. Administrative papers: copies relating to New Spain - a collection of manuscripts in the Middle American Research Institute. New Orleans, Middle American Research Institute, Tulane Univ. of Louisiana, 1948. 28 p. (Miscellaneous ser., no. 5)   (767

JORGENSEN, Margareth. Preliminary checklist of the records of the Military Government of Cuba, 1899-1933. [Washington, D.C.] 1946. 52 p.   (768
    Cited in Yang.

------. Preliminary inventory of the records of Military Government of Cuba (Record group 140) Washington, D.C., 1962. 65 p. (National Archives, Publ. 63-11; Preliminary inventories, no. 145)   (769

MUNDEN, Kenneth. List of records of the Bureau of Insular Affairs relating to the Dominican Customs Receivership, 1905-1940. Washington, D.C., 1943. 29 p. (National Archives, Special list, no. 5)   (770

------. Records of the Bureau of Insular Affairs relating to the Unites States Military Government of Cuba, 1898-1902 and the United States Provisional Government of Cuba, 1906-1909; a list of selected files. Washington, D.C., 1943. 43 p. (National Ar-

MUNDEN, Kenneth... (Cont.)
chives, Special list, no. 3)   (771

MUNDEN, Kenneth, and GREENBAUM, Milton. Records of the Bureau of Insular Affairs relating to Puerto Rico, 1898-1934, a list of selected files. Washington, D.C., 1943. 47 p. (National Archives. Special list, no. 4)   (772

THE NATIONAL union catalog of manuscript collections, 1959-1961, based on reports from American repositories of manuscripts. Ann Arbor, J. W. Edwards, 1962. 1061 p. (773
    Compiled by the Library of Congress. Latin American countries and regions listed in the subject index.

NORTH CAROLINA Historical Records Survey. List of the "papeles procedentes de Cuba" (Cuban papers) in the archives in the North Carolina Historical Commission. Raleigh, N.C., 1942. 78 p.   (774
    Cited in Yang.

PARDO, J. Joaquín. Catálogo de los manuscritos existentes en la colección latino americana de la biblioteca de la Universidad de Texas, relativos a la historia de Centro América. [Guatemala, 1958] 45 p. (Publ. de la Sección de Divulgación del Departamento de Historia de la Facultad de Humanidades)   (775

PATTERSON, Jerry E. Bibliographical notes on printed descriptions of Latin American manuscript and transcript collections in the United States (excluding the Library of Congress and the National Archives): a provisional version ... ed. with additional materials by Howard F. Cline. Washington, D.C., 1962. 62 p. (Handbook of Middle American Indians, Working paper, 14)   (776

POMRENZE, Seymour Jacob. Materials in the National Archives relating to Haiti. [Washington, D.C., 1949] 13 p. (National Archives. Publ. 49-27; Reference information circular, no. 40)   (777

QUESADA ZAPIOLA, Carlos A. Catálogo de la documentación referente a las relaciones diplomáticas entre Estados Unidos de América y la República Argentina, 1810-1830, existentes en el Archivo Nacional de los Estados Unidos de América; recopilación cronológica. Buenos Aires, G. Kraft, [1948] 210 p. (778

RHOADS, James Berton. Preliminary inventory of the cartographic records of the Panama Canal. (Record group 185). Washington, D.C., 1956. 72 p. (National Archives, Publ. 56-9; Preliminary inventories, no. 91) (779

SALADO ALVAREZ, Victoriano. Breve noticia de
algunos manuscritos de interés histórico
para México, que se encuentran en los archivos y bibliotecas de Washington. México,
Impr. del Museo Nacional, 1908.
24 p. (780
   From Anales del Museo Nacional, 3a. ép.,
t. 1.---Jones 2481.

SPELL, Lota May. The Mier archives. (The
Hispanic-American historical review, Durham,
N.C., v. 12, p. 359-75, 1932) (781
   The collection, acquired by the University
of Texas, consists of some 1,000 folios of
the papers of José Servando Teresa de Mier
Noriega y Guerra.---Jones 2516.

TEXAS. University. Library. Calendar of the
Manuel E. Gondra manuscript collection, the
University of Texas Library, prepared by
Carlos Eduardo Castañeda and Jack Autrey
Dabbs. México, D.F., Edit. Jus, 1952.
xxii, 467 p. (782

-----. Independent Mexico in documents: independence, empire and republic. A calendar
of the Juan E. Hernández y Dávalos manuscript
collection, prepared by Carlos Eduardo Castañeda and Jack Autrey Dabbs. México, D.F.,
Edit. Jus, 1954 [i.e., 1955] 604 p. (783

TULANE University of Louisiana, New Orleans.
Middle American Research Institute, Calendar of the Yucatecan letters. New Orleans,
1939. 240 p. (Inventory of the collections
of the Middle American Research Institute,
no. 2) (784
   Prepared in cooperation with the Historical Records Survey of the Works Projects Administration. ---Jones 1255a.

-----. Fayssoux collection of William Walker
papers, New Orleans, 1937. 28 p. (Inventory of the collections of the Middle American Research Institute, no. 1) (785
   Prepared in cooperation with the Historical Records Survey of the Works Projects Administration.

TWITCHELL, Ralph Emerson. The Spanish archives
of New Mexico. [Cedar Rapids, Ia.] The
Torch Pr., 1914. 2 v. (786

ULIBARRI, George S. Preliminary inventory of
[the] United States and Mexican claims commissions (Group 76). Washington, D.C.,
1962. 51 p. (U.S. National Archives, Publ.
62-9; Preliminary inventories,
no. 136) (787

U.S. Library of Congress. The Harkness collection in the Library of Congress; Calendar of Spanish manuscripts concerning Peru,

U.S. Library of Congress... (Cont.)
1531-1651. Washington, D.C., Govt. Print.
Off., 1932. 336 p. (788
   Compiler: Stella R. Clemence.

-----. National Archives. List of National
Archives microfilm publications. Washington,
D.C., 1961. 231 p. (Publ. 61-12) (789
   Covers diplomatic relations between the
U.S. and other countries including Latin
America.

-----. -----. Materials in the National Archives relating to Brazil. Washington, D.C.,
1942. 6 p. (Reference information papers,
8) (790

-----. -----. Materials in the National Archives relating to Cuba. Washington, D.C.,
1948. 12 p. (Reference information circular, no. 34) (791

-----. -----. Materials in the National Archives relating to the Dominican Republic.
Washington, D.C., 1948. 12 p. (Reference
information circular, no. 35) (792

-----. -----. Materials in the National Archives relating to Latin America (in Records
of Emergency War Areas, 1917-1919) Washington, D.C., 1942. 14 p. (Reference information circular, no. 11) (793

-----. -----. Materials in the National Archives relating to military government by
the United States in the Caribbean area,
1898-1934. Washington, D.C., 1944. 14 p.
(Reference information circular,
no. 26) (794

-----. -----. Materials in the National Archives relating to the Caribbean region.
Washington, D.C., 1942. 10 p. (Reference
information circular, no. 7) (795

-----. -----. Materials in the National Archives relating to the countries on the
West Coast of South America. Washington,
D.C., 1942. 8 p. (Reference information
papers, 9) (796

-----. -----. Preliminary inventory of the
government of the Virgin Islands of the
United States, compiled by Don Hooker,
Washington, D.C., 1960. 31 p. (Publ.
60-1; Preliminary inventories 126) (797

-----. -----. Preliminary inventory of the
textual records of the Panama Canal, compiled by Richard W. Giroux and revised by
Garry D. Ryan. Washington, D.C., 1963.
36 p. (Publ. 63-20; Preliminary inventories, 153) (798

DOMINICAN REPUBLIC

FLOREN LOZANO, Luis. Bibliografía de las
bellas artes en Santo Domingo. Bogotá, An-
tares, 1956. 53 p. (Materiales para el
estudio de la cultura dominicana,
v. 8)   (836

LATIN AMERICA

JAMES, Concha Romero. A bibliography on the
arts in Latin America. Washington, D.C.,
Pan American Union [1932] 12 p.   (837

LASSALLE, Emilie Dew. Arts, crafts, and customs of our neighbor republics; a bibliography. Washington, D.C., 1943. 52 p.
(U.S. Office of Education, Bull. 1942,
no. 2)   (838
    First issued in mimeograph form in 1942.

SMITH, Robert Chester, and WILDER, Elizabeth.
A guide to the art of Latin America. Washington, D.C., Govt. Print. Off., 1948.
480 p. (Library of Congress, Latin American ser., no. 21)   (839

SOLA, Miguel. Historia del arte hispano-americano: arquitectura, escultura, pintura y
artes menores en la América española durante los siglos XVI, XVII y XVIII. Barcelona
[etc.] Edit. Labor, 1935. 341 p. (Colección Labor, Sección 4: Artes plásticas,
no. 371-72)   (840
    Bibliografía: p. 331-334.---Jones 451.

U.S. Library of Congress. Hispanic Foundation. Bibliography of the fine arts in the
other American republics; prepared by the
Archives of Hispanic Culture for the Office
of the Coordinator of Inter-American
Affairs. [Washington, D.C., 1941]
12 p.   (841

-----. -----. -----. The fine and folk arts
of the other American Republics; a bibliography of publications in English; prepared
by the Archives of Hispanic Culture, Hispanic Foundation, Library of Congress for
the Division of Inter-American Activities
in the United States, Office of the Coordinator of Inter-American Affairs. Washington, D.C., 1942. 18 p. mimeogr.   (842

-----. -----. Prints and Photographs Division. The colonial art of Latin America,
a collection of slides and photographs,
prepared by Robert C. Smith. Washington,
D.C., 1945. 43 p.   (843
    Includes bibliographies

MEXICO

AMERICAN Federation of Arts. Mexican arts;
catalogue of an exhibition, organized for
and circulated by the American Federation
of Arts, 1930-1931. Portland, Me., The
Southworth Pr., 1930. 59 p.   (844
    Books and periodicals: p. 56-8.---Jones
2045a.

ANDERSON, Lawrence Leslie. El arte de la pla-
tería en México, 1519-1936. London, Oxford
Univ. Pr., 1937.   (845
    Jones 2048.

-----. 2a. ed. México, Edit. Porrúa, 1956.
xxiii, 373 p.   (846
    Bibliography: p. ix-xix.

CARPENTER, Edwin H. Copper engraving in Mexico
during the late eighteenth century: an inventory of the engravers found in the New
York Public Library. New York, 1953.
12 p.   (847
    Bibliographical footnotes. Reprinted
from Bulletin of the New York Public Library,
June 1953.

FERNANDEZ, Justino. El arte moderno en México.
México, Porrúa, 1937, 473 p.   (848
    Bibliographies at the ends of chapters.
Jones 2163.

IGUINIZ, Juan Bautista. Las artes gráficas en
Guadalajara. México, Tall. Linotip. Numan-
cia, 1943. 59 p.   (849
    "Contribución del Estado de Jalisco a la
II Feria Nacional del Libro". Cited in
Millares, item 1168.

INSTITUTO Nacional Indigenista, México. Bibliografía de las artes populares plásticas
de México. México, D.F., 1950.   (849a
    p. 83-132. (Memorias, v. 1, no. 2)

JIMENEZ, Guillermo. Fichas para la historia
de la pintura en México. México, Ediciones
de la Universidad Nacional, 1937.
52 p.   (850
    Biographical sketches of 23 Mexican art-
ists.---Jones 2266. Includes bibliographies.

OCAMPO, Maria Luisa, and MEDIZ BOLIO, María.
Apuntes para una bibliografía del arte en
México. México, Secretaría de Educación Pública, 1957. 193 p. (Biblioteca enciclopédica popular, 232)   (851

PEREZ SALAZAR, Francisco. Algunos datos sobre
la pintura en Puebla en la época colonial.
México, Tall. Gráf. de la Nación, 1923.
p. 217-302   (852
    Reprinted from Memorias de la Sociedad
Científica "Antonio Alzate", t. 41. "Documentación y bibliografía": p. 265-302.

PEREZ SALAZAR, Francisco ... (Cont.)
---Jones 2420.

ROMERO DE TERREROS Y VINENT, Manuel. Ensayo
bibliográfico de la pintura en México durante la época colonial. (Boletín de la Biblioteca Nacional, México, t. 12, no. 7, p. 1-8,
abr./sept. 1919)							(853
Jones 2473.

-----. Historia sintética del arte colonial
de México (1521-1821) México, Porrúa Herma-
nos, 1922. 89 p.							(854
Includes biographical and bibliographical
information.---Jones 2474.

SCHMECKEBIER, Laurence Frederick. Modern Mexican art. Minneapolis, Univ. of Minnesota
Pr. 1939. 190 p.							(855
Includes biographical notes on 34 artists
and bibliography (p. 181-83).---Jones 2496.

VELAZQUEZ CHAVEZ, Agustín. Indice de la pintura mexicana contemporánea. Index of contemporary Mexican painting. México, Edicio-
nes Arte Mexicano, 1935. 225 p.				(856
Includes bibliographical references.---Jo-
nes 2569.

VELAZQUEZ CHAVEZ, Agustín. Tres siglos de
pintura colonial mexicana. México, Edit.
Polis, 1939. xxiv, 368 (i.e. 364 p.) (857
Bibliografía: p. 353-69.---Jones 2570.

PERU

MEANS, Philip Ainsworth. A study of Peruvian
textiles. Boston, Museum of Fine Arts, 1932.
83 p.									(858
Bibliographical references: p. 74-82.
---Jones 2689.

-----. A survery of ancient Peruvian art.
New Haven, Conn., Yale Univ. Pr., 1917.
p. 315-422. (Transactions of the Connecticut Academy of Arts and Sciences,
v. 21)								(859
Bibliography: p. 394-401.---Jones 2690.

SOUTH AMERICA

NOEL, Martín S. La historia del arte en Sud
América durante el período colonial. (Handbook of Latin American studies, 1937, Cam-
bridge, Mass., 3, p. 505-27, 1938)		(860
Bibliography of recent publications.---Jo-
nes 336b.

BIBLIOGRAPHY

GENERAL

CARVALHO, Oswaldo de. Documentação, bibliografia, biblioteconomia. São Paulo, 1957.
45 p. mimeogr. (Hemerografia brasileira,
1)									(861

COBLANS, Herbert. Introdução ao estudo de documentação; trad. de Maria Antonieta Requião
Piedade. Rio de Janeiro, Departamento Administrativo do Serviço Público, 1957. 149 p.
(Ensaios de administração, 8)			(862

COLLISON, Robert Lewis. Bibliographical services throughout the world; fifth annual report, 1956. [Paris, 1958] 198 p. (Unesco/
CUA/ 89)								(863
The first and second report were issued in
1955 prepared by Louise Nöelle Malclès. The
third annual report was issed as Unesco/CUA/
80. Includes Latin American countries.

-----. Bibliographical services throughout
the world, 1950-1959. [Paris, 1961] 228 p.
(Unesco bibliographical handbooks, 9) (864
Latin American countries included.

-----. Les services bibliographiques dans le
monde, 1950-1959. [Paris, 1961] 242 p.
(Unesco manuel, 9)						(865
Latin American countries included.

IGUINIZ, Juan Bautista. Disquisiciones bibliográficas; autores, libros, bibliotecas, artes gráficas. [México] El Colegio de Méxi-
co [1943] 310 p.						(867

INTER-AMERICAN Bibliographical and Library
Association. Proceedings. N.Y., H.W. Wilson,
1938-1946. 4 v. (Publ., ser. II,
v. 1-4)								(868
v. 4 has imprint: Washington, 1946.
Contents of Latin American bibliographical
interest: v. 1: Problems in Hispanic American bibliography, by C. K. Jones. - La ri-
queza bibliográfica de América, by Rafael
Heliodoro Valle. - The biography of a Spanish folklore bibliography, by Ralph Steele
Boggs. - Bibliographical and library problems
in geographical research concerning Latin
America, by F. A. Carlson. - Some of Chile's
historians as viewed by their fellow crafts-
men, by Isaac Joslin Cox. - Conversión en
Píritu and some other ecclesiastical writings
of colonial Venezuela, by Mary Watters. -
Some Spanish American poets, by Alice Stone
Blackwell. - A Revista do Instituto Histórico e Geográphico Brasileiro, by Max Fleiuss. -
Bibliography of official publications and
the administrative system in Latin American
countries, by James B. Childs. v. 2 Bibliographical principles and practices in the

INTER-AMERICAN Bibliographical ... (Cont.)
field of Latin American Studies, by Lewis
Hanke. - A few thoughts on inter-American
bibliographic cooperation, by Roduolf Dolge. -
Report on the Inter-American Center of Bibliography of the Pan American Union, by Charles
E. Babcock. - Recents attempts at an economic
bibliography on Latin America, by J. F.
Normano. - La bibliografía en Santo Domingo,
by Emilio Rodríguez Demorizi. - The discovery
of Hispanic American junior books for reading
in the United States of America, by Marie
Kiersted Pidgeon. - Bibliografía sobre la
familia lingüística Tukano, by Fr. Marcelino
de Castellví. - A literatura para crianças
no Brasil, by Adelpha S. R. de Figueiredo. -
Cuban government publications, by James B.
Childs. - Newspaper collections in the Middle
Americas, by Arthur E. Gropp. v. 3: The
three-fold printing centennial, by Iranaeus
Herscher. - Bibliographing Latin American
literatures, by Alfred Coester. - Central
and South American medical literature in the
Army Medical Library, by Harold W. Jones. -
Libros antiguos, by Dr. Jorge Cornejo Bouron-
cle. - Bibliografía sobre los Sibundoyes y
otros de la familia lingüístico Kamsa o Coche, by Marcelino de Castellví. - Bibliografía del idioma Kamsa (o Coche) de Sibundoy
(Putumayo-Colombia), by Marcelino de Castellví. - Bibliografía del Patronato Nacional,
by Enrique Arana (h.). - Colombian government
publications, by James B. Childs.

MALCLES, Louise Nöelle. La bibliografía. Buenos Aires, EUDEBA, Edit. Universitaria de
Buenos Aires, [1960]. 71 p. (Colección cuadernos, 27)   (869

-----. Bibliographical services throughout
the world; first and second reports 1951/
1952-1952/1953. [Paris] UNESCO, 1955.
352 p. (Unesco bibliographical handbooks,
4)   (870
   Reports prepared in accordance with recommendations of the International Advisory
Committee on Bibliography.

MARTINEZ, Angelina, and JAMES, C. Noel. Lista seleccionada de publicaciones sobre investigación. Turrialba, C. R., Instituto
Interamericano de Ciencias Agrícolas, 1955.
15 p. mimeogr.   (871

MEDELLIN. Escuela Interamericana de Bibliotecología. B-14: Bibliografía: bibliografía.
Medellín, 1960. 3 p. mimeogr.   (872

-----. B-45: Documentación: bibliografía.
Medellín, 1960. 3 p. mimeogr.   (873

SCHNEIDER, Georg. Handbuch der bibliographie.
4. gänzlich veränderte und stark vermehrte
aufl. Leipzig, K. W. Hiersemann, 1930.
674 p.   (874

SCHNEIDER, Georg... (Cont.)
Includes list of national bibliographies
and biographies.---Jones 440.

TIGRE, Manoel Bastos. Breve ensaio sôbre bibliografia. Rio de Janeiro, 1915.
35 p.   (875
   Cited in Bibliografia brasileira de doc.,
v. 1, item 223.

ARGENTINA

BECU, Teodoro. La bibliografía en la República Argentina. Buenos Aires, Comité Argentino de Bibliotecarios de Instituciones
Científicas y Técnicas, 1945. 34 p. (Contribuciones al conocimiento de la bibliotecología, 2)   (876
   Cited in Catálogo, Inst. Bibliotecológico,
Buenos Aires, 1964, item 291.

Brazil

BIBLIOGRAFIA brasileira de documentação, v. 1:
1811-1960. Rio de Janeiro, Instituto Brasileiro de Bibliografia e Documentação, 1960.
237 p.   (877

CHILE

MATAS ANGUITA, Blanca. Current bibliography
in Chile. Madison, Wisc., 1963.
12 p.   (878
   Working paper no. 13, submitted the 8th
Seminar on the Acquisition of Latin American Library Materials, Madison, Wis., July
11-13, 1963.

COLOMBIA

PEREZ ORTIZ, Rubén. Enquête sur les services
bibliographiques conduite par l'Unesco et
la Bibliothèque du Congrès des Etats-Unis:
Colombia. Paris, Unesco, 1950. 8 p.
mimeogr.   (879

CUBA

HABANA. Biblioteca Municipal. Publicaciones;
Ser. C: Guías bibliográficas, no. 1- 1936- .
Havana.   (880
   DPU has no. 1-26. Numbers also entered
separately in this bibliography.

DOMINICAN REPUBLIC

RODRIGUEZ DEMORIZI, Emilio. La bibliografía
en Santo Domingo. Proceedings of the Second
Convention of the Inter-American Bibliographical and Library Association, Washington.
New York, The H. W. Wilson Co., 1939.

RODRIGUEZ DEMORIZI, Emilio... (Cont.)
  p. 84-7)   (881
    Jones 3007a.

LATIN AMERICA

GROPP, Arthur Eric. Bibliografía en América.
  Maracaibo, Venezuela, Edit. Universitaria
  L.U.Z., 1963. 22 p.   (882
    Separata of Boletín of the Biblioteca Ge-
  neral, Universidad del Zulia, no. 4.
  Version in Spanish of Bibliography in the
  Americas.

-----. Bibliography in the Americas; an anal-
  ysis of the results of the Inter-American
  Conferences. [Washington, D.C., 1959] 27 p.
  mimeogr.   (883
    Working paper prepared for use at the
  Meeting of Bibliographers Specializing in
  History, Washington, D.C., June 1959.

SEMINAR on the Acquisition of Latin American
  Library Materials, 1956- . Final report,
  1956- . [Gainesville, Fla.], etc.
  1956- .   (884
    The final report includes working papers
  relative to practices, sources, services and
  information concerned with the acquisition
  of Latin American Library materials. Many
  working papers are substantial bibliographies
  Marietta Daniels Shepard is Permanent Secretary of the Seminar.

SEMINARIO bibliográfico de Centro América y
  del Caribe, 1a., La Habana, 1955. Informe
  final. La Habana, 1955. 111 p.   (885
    Organized by the Agrupación Bibliográfica
  Cubana José Toribio Medina with the collaboration of Unesco's Centro Regional en el Hemisferio Occidental and with financial assistance of the Comité Consultivo Internacional de Bibliografía and the Comisión Nacional Cubana de Unesco. This meeting was held
  under the name of Seminario Piloto de Bibliografía. Contains working papers: La nece-
  sidad de docencia bibliotecaria en las escuelas de medicina, por Carlos Cuitiño C. -
  La documentación científica agrícola en América Latina, por Ana María Paz. - Apuntes
  sobre bibliografías salvadoreñas, por Bau-
  dilio Torres. - Actividad y servicios bibliotecarios de la Organización de Estados Americanos, por Arthur E. Gropp. - Centro Cubano de Documentación, por Fermín Peraza. -
  Estado actual de los servicios bibliográficos
  en Cuba; bibliografías especializadas, por
  Elena Vérez de Peraza. - Metodología bibliográfica, por Luis Florén. - El servicio de
  intercambio científico del Centro Interamericano de Vivienda de Bogotá, por Luis Florén. - La bibliografía en Puerto Rico, por
  Gonzalo Velázquez. - Mi "Bibliografía de
  Centro-America", por Rafael Heliodoro Valle.

SEMINARIO bibliográfico ... (Cont.)
  El programa de la Unesco en materia de bibliografía, por Denise Ravage. - Trabajos bibliográficos de la Biblioteca Nacional de Cuba,
  por Lilia Castro de Morales. - Estado actual
  de los servicios bibliográficos en Cuba, por
  María Teresa Freyre de Andrade. - Services
  bibliographiques en Haiti, por Max Bissainthe. - La enseñanza de la bibliografía en
  Cuba, por Ofelia Alvarez Mendoza. - Necesi-
  dad de un centro bibliográfico nacional, por
  John Firth. - Estado actual de los servicios
  bibliográficos en Panamá, por Bonifacio Pereira J. - Anexos.

-----. 2a., Panamá, 1958. Informe final.
  Panamá, 1958. 2 v.   (886
    Contents: v. 1: Bibliografía de Centro
  América y del Caribe, informe de Fermín Peraza. - La compilación de un directorio de
  obras de consulta, por la División de Bibliotecas de la Unesco. - La recopilación de una
  lista de obras de consulta, por Arthur E.
  Gropp. - La bibliografía y su importancia en
  los estudios universitarios, por Inés María
  Herrera. - Estado actual de la bibliografía,
  por Juan Antonio Susto. - Posibilidades de
  organizar en Panamá un centro de documentación, por Otilia de Tejeira. - El servicio
  de intercambio científico y documentación
  del Centro Interamericano de Vivienda y
  Planeamiento y su labor bibliográfica y de
  documentación, informe por Luis Florén Lozano. - Primeras Jornadas Bibliotecológicas
  Rioplatenses. - v. 2: Aspectos bibliográficos de los Seminarios sobre la adquisición
  de los materiales impresos latinoamericanos,
  por Marietta Daniels. - Bibliografía de Coclé con motivo de su centenario, 1855-1955,
  por Rubén Darío Carles, Bonifacio Pereira
  J., Carmen D. de Herrera, Ana María Jaen y
  Diógenes A. Arosemena [publication tipped
  in]. - Bibliografía de la independencia de
  Panamá, por Ernesto de J. Castillero R.
  (Véase Lotería, v.v2, no. 24, nov. 1957). -
  Bibliografía de la producción del profesor
  don Ernesto de J. Castillero R., por Concha
  Peña. - Bibliografía de los trabajos de investigación del Instituto Nacioal de Agricultura, por J. de. C. Contreras. - Bibliografía del historiador don Juan Antonio Susto, por Concha Peña. - Bibliografía retrospectiva de las publicaciones periódicas aparecidas en la República de Panamá, 1957-1954,
  por Carolina M. Rodríguez, con la colaboración de Catalina G. de Freitas y Elena de
  Torrente. - Bibliografía del Servicio Interamericano de Cooperación Agrícola en Panamá
  (SCIAP), por Nuria Ferguson y María Aracely
  Narváez [publication tipped in]. - Bibliografía retrospectiva de libros y folletos,
  1957-1955, por el Grupo Bibliográfico de la
  Universidad, dirigido por Carmen D. de
  Herrera. - Contribución a la bibliografía de
  vivienda y urbanismo en Panamá, 1944-1957,

SEMINARIO bibliográfico ... (Cont.)
por Genarina Arrocha G. - Guía de bibliotecas de Panamá, por Angela Alvarado A. - Guía
de instituciones científicas técnicas y profesionales, por Carmen Cecilia Lasso J. -
Guía de librerías, imprentas y editoras, por
María Teresa Quirós. - Guía de organismos
oficiales y sus publicaciones, por Nery Quirós de Vega. - Lista bibliográfica de las
publicaciones de la Contraloría General de
la República. - Lista de los trabajos de
graduación correspondiente a los años 1957-
1955, por Carmen D. de Herrera, Olivia de
Fierro. - Official publications of the Panama Canal Company/Canal Zone government, 1954-
1957.

SEMINARIO Latinoamericano sobre Documentación
Científica, Lima, 1962. [Miscellaneous pa-
pers] Lima, 1962. 53 pamphlets.
40 cm.   (887

MEXICO

LEON, Nicolás. La bibliografía en México en
el siglo XIX. Memoria leída en el Concurso
Nacional de 1900. México, D.F., Tip. de "El
Tiempo", 1901. 32 p.   (888

LEON, Nicolás. La bibliografía... (Cont.)
Cited in Iguiniz, p. 338. Also printed
in Boletín del Instituto Bibliográfico Mexicano, no. 3, p. 53-66, 1902.---Jones 2287.

URUGUAY

SPERONI VENER, Julio. La bibliografía en el
Uruguay. Montevideo, Florensa & Lafón,
1955. 8 p.   (889
Reissued from the Review of inter-American
bibliography, en./jun. 1954. Also issued as
a reprint from the Review.

VENEZUELA

GRASES, Pedro. Estudios bibliográficos. Caracas, 1961. 387 p.   (890

-----. Nuevos temas de bibliografía y cultura
venezolana. Maracaibo, Universidad de Zulia,
1960. 379 p.   (891

-----. Temas de bibliografía y cultura venezolanas. Buenos Aires, Edit. Nova, 1953.
223 p.   (892

BIBLIOGRAPHY OF BIBLIOGRAPHIES

GENERAL

BESTERMAN, Theodore. A world bibliography of
bibliographies; 3d and final edition, rev.
and greatly enlarged throughout. Genève,
Societas Bibliographica, [1955-1956]
4 v.   (893
V. 4 is an index volume. Editions: 1st,
1939-1940; 2d ed., 1947-1949. Present edition contains about 80,000 references arranged under some 12,000 headings and subheadings. Latin American countries are
found as headings, as well as subheadings
under a specified list of subjects given in
the "Introduction".

The BIBLIOGRAPHIC index, 1938- . N.Y., H. W.
Wilson, 1938- .   (894
A cumulative bibliography of bibliogra-
phies. Includes headings for the various
countries of Latin America.---Jones 57.

BUENOS AIRES. Universidad. Facultad de Agronomía y Veterinaria. Biblioteca. Compilación de las bibliografía existentes en la
Biblioteca. Buenos Aires, 1951. 30 p.
mimeogr.   (895

CARVALHO, Oswaldo de. Catálogos de bibliotecas e arquivos. São Paulo, 1959. vi, 45 p.
mimeogr.   (896

CONOVER, Helen Field. Current national bibliographies. Washington, 1955. 132 p . (897
Includes Latin America: p. 17-27.

COULTER, Edith Margaret, and GERSTENFELD,
Melanie. Historical bibliographies. Berkeley, Univ. of California Pr., 1935.
206 p.   (898
Includes Latin American countries.---Jones
114.

ESCAMILLA GONZALEZ, Gloria. Bibliografía e
investigación bibliográfica. México, 1960.
200 l. (Publ. del Seminario de Investigaciones Bibliotecológicas. Serie B: Bibliografía, no. 1)   (899
Thesis presented for library science de-
gree at the University of Mexico.

FORD, Paul Leicester. Check-list of bibliographies, catalogues, reference lists, and
lists of authorities of American books and
subjects. Brooklyn, N.Y., 1889. 59, [1],
61-4 p.   (900
Based on his "Reference list to bibliographies, catalogues, and reference lists
on America" (Library journal, v. 13, 1888)
1070 titles: classified, with author index.---Jones 153.

JACKSON, James. Liste provisoire des bibliographies géographiques speciales; 2. ed. Paris, Société de Géographie, 1881. 340 p.   (901
  Amérique: no. 314-450.---Jones 220a.

LIMA. Universidad Mayor de San Marcos. Biblioteca Central. Bibliografía de bibliografías y biblioteconomía, 1936-1948. Lima, Compañía de Impresiones y Publicidad, 1949. 28 p.   (902
  Reprinted from Boletín bibliográfico, Lima, año 22, v. 19, no. 1-2, jul. 1949.

MEDELLIN. Escuela Interamericana de Bibliotecología. B-38: Bibliografía especializada (Material de clase) Algunas bibliografías especializadas iberoamericanas desde 1940. [Bogotá, 1962] 20 p. mimeogr.   (903

-----. B-38: Bibliografía especializada: materiales de clase; principales bibliografías especializadas internacionales en curso de publicación en 1961. Medellín, 1962. 4 p. mimeogr.   (904

ARGENTINA

BINAYAN, Narciso. Bibliografía de bibliografías argentinas. Buenos Aires, Tall. Gráf. del Ministerio de Agricultura, 1919. 39 p.   (905
  Reprinted from Revista de la Universidad de Buenos Aires, t. 43, p. 114-49.---Jones 603.

BRAZIL

CARVALHO, Oswaldo de. Hemerografía brasileira. São Paulo, 1957-1959. 2 pts.   (907

-----. Indices de publicações seriadas. São Paulo, 1959. ii, 19 p. (Hemerografías brasileiras, 2) mimeogr.   (908

DORIA, Irene de Menezes. The situations of bibliography in Brazil. 1964. 21, [18] p. (Seminar on the Acquisition of Latin American Library Materials, St. Louis, 9th, 1964, Working paper no. 7)   (909

FIGUEIREDO, Fidelino de. Aristarchos; quatro conferencias sobre methodologia da critica litteraria no Departamento Municipal de Cultura de São Paulo. São Paulo, 1939. 114 p. (Colleção do Departamento de Cultura, v. 23)   (910
  Contains two valuable lectures on general and historical bibliography in Portugal and Brasil, and Appendix; Subsidio para una bibliographia das bibliographias brasileiras. ---Jones 1039.

REIS, Antônio Simões dos. Bibliografia das bibliografias brasileiras. Rio de Janeiro, 1942. 186 p. (Instituto Nacional do Livro. Coleção B 1; Bibliografia 1)   (911
  Contains 712 titles.

CHILE

LAVAL, Ramón A. Bibliografía de bibliografías chilenas. Santiago, Impr. Universitaria, 1915. 71 p.   (912
  From Revista de bibliografía chilena y extranjera, año 3, 1915. Also included in Vaïsse, Emilio, Bibliografía general de Chile, 1915.---Jones 1508.

OCHSENIUS, Herminia Elgueta de. Suplemento y adiciones a la Bibliografía de bibliografías chilenas que publicó en 1915 Ramón A. Laval. Santiago, Impr. Cervantes, 1930. 71 p.   (913
  From Revista de bibliografía chilena, Santiago, 3o sem., p. 115-76, 1929.---Jones 1509.

SILVA, Relávila. Lista de algunas bibliografías publicadas en Chile. (Bibliographical Society of America, Bulletin, Chicago, v. 3. p. 35-7, 1911)   (914
  Jones 1616a.

COLOMBIA

GIRALDO JARAMILLO, Gabriel. Bibliografía de bibliografías colombianas. Bogotá, Edit. Pax, 1954. 192 p. (Publ. de la Biblioteca Nacional)   (915

-----. 2a. ed. corr. y puesta al día por Rubén Pérez Ortiz. Bogotá, 1960. xvi, 204 p. (Instituto Caro y Cuervo, Bogotá. Publ.: Ser. bibliográfica, 1)   (916

PEREZA SARAUSA, Fermín. La documentación en Colombia; 2a. ed. Gainesville, Fla., 1962. 13 p. (Biblioteca del bibliotecario, 66)   (917

CUBA

PERAZA SARAUSA, Fermín. Bibliografías cubanas. Washington, D.C. [Govt. Print. Off.] 1945. xiv, 58 p. (Library of Congress. Latin American ser., no. 7)   (918

VILLAR BUCETA, María. Guías de la bibliografía cubana. (Libros cubanos, La Habana, v. 1, no. 2, p. 1-4, 1940)   (919
  Additions in no. 3, p. 9, of Libros cubanos.---Jones 1938a.

DOMINICAN REPUBLIC

FLOREN LOZANO, Luis. Bibliografía de la bi-
    bliografía dominicana. Ciudad Trujillo,
    Roques Román, 1948. 66 p.   (920

ECUADOR

CHAVES, Alfredo. Fuentes principales de la
    bibliografía ecuatoriana. Quito, Edit.
    Casa de la Cultura Ecuatoriana, 1958. 24 p.
    (Asociación de Bibliotecarios del Ecuador.
    Grupo Bibliográfico Nacional, Publ.,
    no. 1)   (921

GUATEMALA

VELA, David. Bibliografía guatemalteca, com-
    pilaciones hechas hasta el presente y ser-
    vicios que prestan al lector curioso y al
    estudioso. (Boletín de la Biblioteca Na-
    cional, Guatemala, año 8, p. 161-66,
    1940)   (922
        Jones 1312a.

LATIN AMERICA

CANNON, Marie W. Latin American booksellers'
    catalogues and general bibliographies in
    1939. Cambridge, Mass., 1940. 36 p. (923
        Reprinted from Handbook of Latin American
    Studies, 1939.

JONES, Cecil Knight. A bibliography of Latin
    American bibliographies; 2d ed. Washington,
    D.C., Govt. Print. Off., 1942. 307 p.
    (Library of Congress, Latin American
    ser., 2)   (924
        Lists 3,016 bibliographies, compiled with
    the assistance of James A. Granier.

-----. Hispanic American bibliographies in-
    cluding collective biographies, histories
    of literature and selected general works.
    With critical notes on sources, by José To-
    ribio Medina. Baltimore, The Hispanic Amer-
    ican historical review, 1922. 200 p. (925
        Jones 225. Listing of 1281 items in book
    form of the bibliographies included and
    reprinted from the Hispanic American his-
    torical review, v. 3, no. 3/4-v.4, no. 1-4,
    1920-1921.

-----. Supplement, 1-7. [Durham,
    N.C.]   (925a
        Reprinted from the Hispanic American His-
    torical review with variations in title:
    v. 6, no. 1-3; v. 9, no. 3; v. 13, no. 3;
    v. 14, no. 4; v. 17, no. 1; and v. 18, no.
    3, 1927-1938.

JONES, Cecil Knight. Recent contributions to
    Hispanic American bibliography (1926-1938)
    Durham, N.C., Duke Univ. Pr., 1938.
    p. 403-23.   (926
        Reprinted from Hispanic American histori-
    cal review, v. 18.

MATULKA, Barbara. Recent Spanish-American
    bibliographies. (Romanic review, New York,
    v. 24, p. 237-43, 1933)   (927
        Reviews of the Bibliographies of Spanish-
    American literature of the Harvard Council
    on Hispano-American Studies and of Spain
    and Spanish America in the libraries of the
    University of California.---Jones 293.

PAN AMERICAN UNION. Columbus Memorial Library.
    Bibliographies pertaining to Latin America
    in the Library of the Pan American Union.
    Washington, D.C., 1928. 34 p.   (928
        Jones 34. Compiler: Charles E. Babcock.

-----. -----. Fuentes de información sobre
    libros de la América Latina. Washington,
    D.C., 1930. 23 p. (Bibliographic ser.,
    no. 3) mimeogr.   (929
        Jones 354.

-----. -----. -----. 2a ed., rev. y aum.
    Washington, D.C., 1933. 28 p. (Columbus
    Memorial Library. Bibliographic ser.,
    no. 3) mimeogr.   (930

-----. Division of Intellectual Cooperation.
    Bibliographies on Pan American topics sug-
    gested for high schools. Washington, D.C.,
    [1932] 12 p.   (931

-----. -----. 1933. 15 p. (ibliographic
    ser., no. 12)   (932
        Jones 351

PERAZA SARAUSA, Fermín. Bibliografías corrien-
    tes de la América Latina. Medellín, Edicio-
    nes Anuario Bibliográfico Cubano, 1962.
    46 p. (Biblioteca del bibliotecario, 65)
    mimeogr.   (933
        Contains 148 entries. Earlier edition of
    94 entries published in Universidad, Santa
    Fé, no. 52, p. 185-221, 1962.

-----. Bibliografías sobre publicaciones ofi-
    ciales de la América Latina. Gainesville,
    Fla., 1964. 25 p. (Biblioteca del biblio-
    tecario, 70)   (934

U.S. Library of Congress. Division of Bibli-
    ography. Latin America; a list of recent
    bibliographies, compiled by Grace Hadley
    Fuller. [Washington, D.C.] 1942. 16 p.
    mimeogr.   (935

WILGUS, Alva Curtis. Bibliographical activi-
    ties in the United States concerning Latin
    America. n.d. 11 p. mimeogr.   (936

BIBLIOGRAPHY

WILGUS, Alva Curtis. Bibliographical...(Cont.)
Jones 530. Presented at the Second General
Assembly of the Pan American Institute of
Geography and History, Washington, D.C., 1935.
Published in World Affairs, Washington, D.C.,
v. 99, p. 45-51, Mar. 1936.

-----. Some bibliographies in English dealing
with Hispanic America. (Pan-American magazine. Washington, D.C., v. 43, p. 162-64,
1930)   (937
Jones 539.

WISE, Murray M. Development of bibliographical
activity during the past five years; a tentative survey. (Handbook of Latin American
studies, 1939, p. 13-36)   (938
Jones 544a. Continued in subsequent volumes of the Handbook.

MEXICO

IGUINIZ, Juan Bautista. Algunas bibliografías
mexicanas. (El Libro y el pueblo, México,
D.F., t. 11, 1933)   (939
Jones 2250.

LEON, Nicolás. Bibliografía bibliográfica me-
xicana. Primera parte. México, Tall.
Gráf. del Museo Nacional de Arqueología,
Historia y Etnografía, 1923. 66 p.
(A-Stevens)   (940
Issued in signatures with the Boletín del
Museo Nacional de Arqueología, Historia y
Etnografía, ép. 4a. t. 2, 1923-1924.
No more published (cf. p. 4)---Jones 2286.

MILLARES CARLO, Agustín, and MANTECON, José
Ignacio. Ensayo de una bibliografía de bibliografías mexicanas (la imprenta, el libro,
las bibliotecas, etc.) México, D.F., 1943.
xvi, 224 p. (Biblioteca de la II Feria del
Libro y Exposición Nacional del
Periodismo)   (941
Contains some 2,000 references. "Adiciones": p. 195-205.

-----. Adiciones. México, D.F., 1944. 46 p.
(III Feria del Libro y Exposición Nacional
del Periodismo y I de Cine y Radio)   (942

PARAGUAY

BINAYAN, Narciso. Bibliografía de bibliografías paraguayas. Buenos Aires, "Coni",
1922. 13 p.   (943
From Humanidades, v. 3. Lists 17 titles.
---Jones 2599.

DIAZ PEREZ, Viriato. Sobre una "Bibliografía
de bibliografías paraguayas". (Revista paraguaya, Asunción, año 2, p. 26-37,
1926)   (944
Reprint of Binayán's Bibliografía de bib.
paraguayas.---Jones 2600.

PORTUGAL

ANSELMO, Antonio. Bibliografía das bibliografias portuguesas. Lisboa, Oficinas
Gráficas da Biblioteca Nacional, 1923.
158 p.   (945
First published in Annais das bibliotecas e arquivos. Of value also with reference to Brazil.---Jones 958.

SOUTH AMERICA

KAISER, John Boynton. The national bibliographies of the South American republics;
preliminary list. Boston, The Boston
Book Co., 1913. 19 p. (Bulletin of bibliography pamphlets, no. 21)   (946
Reprinted from the Bulletin of bibliography, v. 7, no. 6, July 1913.---Jones 233.

URUGUAY

MUSSO AMBROSI, Luis Alberto. Bibliografía
de Bibliografías uruguayas, con aportes a
la historia del periodismo en el Uruguay.
Prefacio de James B. Childs. Montevideo,
1964. vii, 102 p.   (947
Contains 637 items with index, list of
periodicals analyzed, and institutions
visited.

VENEZUELA

SANCHEZ, Manuel Segundo. Bibliografía de
índices bibliográficos relativos a Venezuela. (Handbook of Latin American studies, 1939, p. 428-42)   (948
Contains 133 items with notes and indexes of authors and subjects.---Jones
2952b.

GRASES, Pedro. General aspects of bibliographical activities in Venezuela. Carbon-
dale, Ill., Southern Illinois University,
1961. 12 p. (Seminar on the Acquisition
of Latin American Library Materials, 6th,
1961; Working paper no. 10)
mimeogr.   (948a

ARGENTINA

ANUARIO bibliográfico de la República Argentina, año [1]-9; 1879-1887. Buenos Aires,
1880-1888.   (949
   Editors: 1879-1884, Alberto Navarro Viola. - 1885-1887, Enrique Navarro Viola.
No more published.---Jones 560.

ARGENTINA. Biblioteca Nacional. Libros argentinos traducidos a diversos idiomas.
Buenos Aires, 1941. 117 p.   (950

-----. -----. Lista de las últimas obras argentinas ingresadas en la Biblioteca Nacional. Buenos Aires, 1932-1934.   (951
   Jones, item 616, reports 42-246 pages.
DPU has issues, jul./dic. 1932 (43-157 p.)
and en./mar. 1933 [48], xvi p.) In La Biblioteca Nacional en 1945-46, p. 89, the
last issue listed is 1935.

-----. Ministerio de Justicia e Instrucción
Publica. Registro nacional de la propiedad
intelectual, catálogo año de 1934- . Buenos
Aires, Tall. Gráf. de la Penitenciaría Na-
cional, 1936- .   (952
   Jones 581.

BIBLIOGRAFIA general argentina, compilada por
Fortunato Mendilaharzu . . . prologada, revista y anotada por Manuel Selva . . . obra
especial para "La Literatura argentina",
dirigida por Lorenzo J. Rosso. Buenos Aires,
Tall. Gráf. Argentinos de L. J. Rosso, 1929.
v.1 (A-B)   (953
   Jones 598.

BIBLIOGRAFIA general argentina, por Manuel
Selva . . . Fortunato Mendilaharzu . . . y
Lorenzo J. Rosso . . . inventario analítico-
crítico de todas las publicaciones argentinas desde el origen de la primera imprenta
en el Río de la Plata, hasta el presente.
Publicación auspiciada por la Comisión Protectora de Bibliotecas Populares. Buenos
Aires, Tall. Gráf. Argentinos de L. J. Rosso,
1931- . t.1- .   (954
   "Principales bibliografías argentinas consultadas": t. 1, p. 3-5.
   A revision of the provisional edition of
1929 having title: Bibliografía general argentina, compilada por Fortunato Mendilaharzu.---Jones 599.

CABOT, Acislo M. Bibliografía de 1866. Buenos Aires, Impr. Española, 1867.
16 p.   (955
   Cited in Binayán.---Jones 639.

LOS CIEN mejores libros argentinos. (Revista
de filosofía, Buenos Aires, t. 4, p. 453-57,
1918)   (956

LOS CIEN mejores libros... (Cont.)
Jones 668.

GARCIA, Perfecto. Bibliografía americana; especialidad en obras de autores argentinos;
repertorio alfabético con un apéndice por
orden cronológica de algunos libros y folletos raros desde 1796 hasta 1853. Buenos Aires, P. García, 1916. 195 p.   (957
Jones 703.

GUIA del libro, 1935-1942. Buenos Aires, PLR,
1943. 373 p., 1 1., lxviii p.   (958

-----. Buenos Aires, Cámara Argentina de Editoriales Técnicas [1959] 133 p.   (959

LA PLATA. Universidad Nacional. Facultad de
Ciencias Jurídicas y Sociales. Registro bibliográfico de obras y artículos publicados
en el país durante el año 1958. La Plata,
1960. 48 p.   (960

-----. -----. Instituto Bibliografico. Anuario bibliográfico; letras, historia, educación y filosofia, t. 1- . 1926- . La Plata,
1927- .   (961
   Jones 559. DPU has t. 2-4, 1927-1929.

REPERTORIO de ediciones, 1960. Buenos Aires,
Cámara Argentina del Libro, 332 p.   (962
   Issued as año 18, no. 104, 1960 of Biblos.

ZEBALLOS, Estanislao Severo. Apuntaciones
para la bibliografía argentina. [Buenos
Aires] 1897-1898.   (962a
   Reprinted from Boletín del Instituto Geográfico Argentino, t. 17, p. 293-307, 483-98,
691-708; t. 18, p. 71-103, 541-47, 632-46;
t. 19, p. 119-33; t. 20, 84-94, 303-16)
Continued in Revista de derecho, historia y
letras, t. 17.---Jones 888.

BOLIVIA

BIBLIOGRAFIA boliviana, 1962- . Cochabamba;
La Paz, Edit. Los Amigos del Libro,
1963- .   (963
   Compiler: Werner Guttentag Tichauer.
Issued annually.

GUTIERREZ, José Rosendo. Bibliografía boliviana en 1878. [La Paz, 1879] 16 p. (964
Jones 915.

-----. Datos para la bibliografía boliviana.
Primera sección. La Paz, Impr. de "La Li-
bertad" de E. Arzadum, 1875. 255 p.   (965
   Nos. 1-2203.---Jones 915a.

-----. Segundo suplemento; últimas adiciones
y correcciones a la primera sección. La Paz,
Impr. de la Unión Americana, 1880.

GUTIERREZ, José Rosendo... (Cont.)
   24, 126 p.   (966
   "Ultimas adiciones a la primera parte de
   la bibliografía boliviana hasta el 31 de diciembre de 1875": p. 67-97. No. 2204-3089.
   Includes (1) books and pamphlets printed
   in Bolivia, 1825-1875, (2) those of Bolivian
   authors printed elsewhere, and (3) books on
   Bolivia by foreign authors printed in other
   countries. No more published.---Jones 916.

RENE MORENO, Gabriel. Biblioteca boliviana.
   Catálogo de la sección de libros i folletos.
   Santiago, Impr. Gutenberg, 1879.
   880 p.   (967
      Preface signed: G. René-Moreno.
      Alphabetical title catalog (3,529 entries)
   with index of authors, translators and
   editors.---Jones 933.

-----. Primer suplemento a la Biblioteca boliviana; epítome de un catálogo de libros y
   folletos, 1879-1899. Santiago, Impr. Barcelona, 1900. 349 p.   (968
      No. 3530-5176 arranged as follows: "Li-
   bros y folletos anteriores a 1879," no.
   3530-3617; "Libros y folletos desde 1879,"
   no. 3618-4641c; "Libros y folletos americanos,"
   nos," no. 4642-5176.---Jones 933.

-----. Segundo suplemento a la Biblioteca boliviana. Libros y folletos, 1900-1908. Santiago, Impr. Universitaria, 1908.
   349 p.   (969
      Publication begun March 26, 1908, contin-
   ued under the direction of E. Barrenechea
   and E. O'Ryan G. after the author's death,
   April 28, 1908.
      No. 5177-6815 arranged as follows: "Li-
   bros y folletos bolivianos," nos. 5177-6031;
   "Libros y folletos americanos," no. 6032-
   6815. Appended: Bolivia. Ensayo de una
   bibliografía general de los periódicos. Suplemento (1905-1907) Santiago de Chile, 1908
   (xvii p.)
      The monumental work of Bolivian bibliogra-
   phy.---Jones 933.

-----. Adiciones a la Biblioteca boliviana
   de Gabriel René-Moreno, por Valentín Abecía
   con un apéndice del editor, 1602-1879. Santiago, Impr. Barcelona, 1899. 440 p. (970
      571 entries; no. 1-350 are the work of
   Abecía; no. 351-571 form part of the appendix by the editor, E. Barrenechea.---Jones
   934.

BRAZIL

BIBLIOGRAFIA brasileira, 1938/1939- . Rio de
   Janeiro, 1941- .   (971
      The following volumes are in the DPU col-
   lection: 1938/1939; 1940; 1941; 1942/1945
   (2 v.); 1946; 1947/1952 (2 v.) Compilation

BIBLIOGRAFIA brasileira ... (Cont.)
   by the Instituto Nacional do Livro.

BLAKE, Augusto Victorino Alves do Sacramento.
   Diccionario bibliographico brazileiro. Rio
   de Janeiro, Typ. Nacional, 1883-1902.
   7 v.   (972
      Jones 978. Now available in microprint.

-----. Indice alphabetico do "Diccionario bibliographico" de Sacramento Blake. Rio de
   Janeiro, 1937. 127 p.   (973
      Jones 979. Now available in microprint.

CARVALHO, Alfredo de. Bibliotheca exotico-
   brasileira. Rio de Janeiro, 1929-1930.
   3 v. (to M)   (974
      Posthumous edition ed. by Eduardo Tavares
   de Mello.
      Contains works of foreign authors on Bra-
   zil, including translations, translations of
   works of Brazilian authors, works of Brazi-
   lians in foreign languages and important
   articles in reviews, with extensive bibliographical notes.---Jones 1014.

CARVALHO, Oswaldo de. Bibliografias paulistas.
   São Paulo, 1957. 46 p.   (975

-----. Suplemento, no. 1. [São Paulo] 1957.
   31 p. mimeogr.   (976
      Cited in Richardson, item 7242.

-----. Suplemento, no. 2. São Paulo, 1959.
   ii, 19 p. mimeogr.   (977
      Cited in Richardson, item 7243.

-----. Suplemento, no. 3. São Paulo, 1960.
   23 p.   (978

FIGUEIREDO, Laura Maia de. Bibliografía
   corrente brasileira. [1961] 6 p.
   mimeogr.   (979
      Paper presented in the Congresso de Biblio-
   grafia e Documentação, 3o, Curitiba, 1961.

HORNBERGER, Theodore. A list of American
   books translated into Portuguese produced
   by Brazilian publishers; compiled by the
   Evaluation Section ... for the American
   Embassy. Rio de Janeiro, 1952.   (980
      Subject sections separately paged. Approx-
   imately 135 pages, listing 1010 items.

LIMA. Universidad Mayor de San Marcos. Facultad de Letras. Donativo bibliográfico brasileño entregado al Seminario de la Facultad
   de Letras por el Prof. Josué Montello, cate-
   drático de estudios brasileños. Lima, [Ed.
   San Marcos] 1955. 21 p.   (981
      Cited in Anuario bibliográfico peruano,
   1955-1957, item 2.

MOREIRA, Júlio Estrella. Diccionário bibliográfico do Paraná. Curitiba, 1953.

MOREIRA, Júlio Estrella. Dicionário...(Cont.)
152 p.   (982
    Published in commemoration of the first
centennial of the state of Paraná.

-----. Ed. comemorativa do centenário da Lei
n. 27 de 7 de março de 1957 [i.e. 1857] que
creou a Bibliotheca Pública do Paraná, com-
preendendo as publicações saidas à luz até
1957, referemtes aos trabalhos publicados
no Paraná, trabalhos de autores paranaenses,
trabalhos relativos ao Paraná. Curitiba,
Impr. Oficial do Estado [1960]
637 p.   (983

PAIVA, Tancredo de Barros. Caxias na bibliographia brasileira. Rio de Janeiro, Impr.
Nacional, 1938. 28 p.   (984
    Reprinted from Revista militar brasileira,
v. 35, no. 3, p. 39-65, 25 ag. 1936.
Cited in Reis, item 551.

REIS, Antônio Simões dos. Bibliografia nacional, 1942-1943. Rio de Janeiro, Z. Valverde, 1942-1943. 14 v.   (985
    Issued in 1942: 8 v.; in 1943: 6 v.

-----. Bibliografia sul-riograndense. Notas,
1o fasc. Rio de Janeiro, Jornal do Comércio, 1939. 16 p.   (986
    Cited in Bibliogr. bras. 1938-1939,
p. 253.

SAMBAQUY, Lydia de Queiroz. Guia das principais instituições culturais brasileiras e
de suas publicações. (Handbook of Latin
American studies, 1937, p. 465-89) (987
    Jones 1149.

CHILE

BRISEÑO, Ramón. Estadística bibliográfica de
la literatura chilena. Santiago, Impr.
Chilena, 1862-1879. 2 v.   (989
    Now available in microprint.
    Contents. - t. 1, 1812-1859. Impresos
chilenos. Obras sobre Chile. Escritores
chilenos. - t. 2, 1860-1876. Prólogo.
Prensa chilena por orden alfabético. Prensa chilena por orden cronológico. Prensa
periodística chilena. Bibliografía chilena en el país, desde 1812 hasta 1859 inclusive. Bibliografía chilena en el extranjero, desde 1860 hasta 1876 inclusive. Cu-
riosidades bibliográficas chilenas.---Jones
1409.

CHILE. Biblioteca Nacional. Anuario de la
prensa chilena, 1886- . Santiago,
1887- .   (990
    Jones 1593.
    Listing of books deposited in the Nation-
al Library under law of 1872. From 1891-
1913 included also deposits of books by

CHILE. Biblioteca Nacional ... (Cont.)
Chilean authors or relating to Chile published in other countries. From 1892-1913,
1895 excepted, the annuals contained an
appendix of "publicaciones omitidas". Musical compositions are entered in volumes
1896-1900. The annuals, 1886-1916 were published from 1887-1927 in 36 v. In 1963 under the direction of Guillermo Feliú Cruz
the National Library renewed publication
with the 1917-1921 coverage. By 1965 the
Anuario was brought up-to-date.

-----. -----. Anuario de la prensa chilena,
1877-1885. I. Libros, folletos y hojas
sueltas. Santiago, Impr. Universitaria,
1952. 621 p.   (991
    Contains 4,170 entries, aimed to supply
fuller national bibliography than that given
by Toro Melo in his Catálogo of 2,453 entries
published in 1893 covering the same period.

LINDSAY, Santiago. Catálogo de las obras publicadas en Chile desde el año 1812 hasta el
de 1858. (Anuario estadístico de la República de Chile. Entrega 2. Santiago, Impr.
Nacional, 1861. p. 144-56)   (992
    Gives 961 books and pamphlets and 278 peri-
odicals, without designation of place or
publisher (cf. Laval, Bibl. de Bibl. chil.
no. 158)---Jones 1515.

MAYORGA URIBE, Luis. Bosquejo de una bibliografía femenina chilena. Santiago, Impr.
"El Esfuerzo", 1933. 14 p.   (993
    Reprinted from Boletín de la Biblioteca
Nacional, Santiago, año 4, no. 2, p. 27-38,
feb. 1933.

MONTT, Luis. Bibliografía chilena [1780-1818]
Santiago, Impr. Universitaria, 1904-1921.
3 v.   (994
    When v. 2 was published in 1904, v. 1, 3
and 4 were announced to appear soon. Of v. 1,
264 pages were printed which the author
intended to revise; these sheets were later
sold as waste paper. Of v. 3, 160 pages
were printed, and destroyed by fire at the
University Press in 1909. The present issue
of v. 1 and 3 is a reprint of the pages as
originally printed (cf. Laval, Bibl. de bibl.
chilenas)---Jones 1552.

OBRAS chilenas para la "Biblioteca Sarmiento".
Santiago, Impr. y Encuad. Fiscal de la Penitenciaría, 1916. 47 p.   (995

SILVA CASTRO, Raúl. Lista de libros selectos
c ilenos; 2. ed. Santiago, Prensa de la
Universidad, 1938? 62 p.   (996
    First published in 1932 in the Boletín de
la Biblioteca Nacional. The present edition
is revised and enlarged (cf. Prólogo)---
Jones 1625.

TORO MELO, David. Catálogo de los impresos
que vieron la luz pública en Chile desde
1877 hasta 1885 inclusives. Santiago, Impr.
"Gutenberg", 1893. 504 p. (997
"Comprende sólo la 1. parte: Libros y
folletos y cataloga 2453 piezas. No existen
de esta publicación más de 5 ejs. formados
con los pliegos que se retiraban de la imprenta a medida que se imprimían. El resto
de la edición desapareció en el incendio que
consumió el establecimiento que lo daba a
luz en 1894". (Laval no. 330).---Jones 1643.
Rafael Heliodoro Valle, in HLAS, 1941,
p. 576, mentions Bibliografía de los años
1876 a 1885 (Santiago) 256 p.

VAISSE, Emilio. Bibliografía general de Chile.
Primera parte. Diccionario de autores y
obras. (biobibliografía y bibliografía)
Precedido de una bibliografía de bibliogra-
fías chilenas por Ramón A, Laval. Santiago,
Impr. Universitaria, 1915. lxix,
331, x p. (998
T. 1: Abalos-Barros Arana.---Jones 1594.

COLOMBIA

ALVAREZ RESTREPO, Mary. Bibliografía de autores antioqueños. [Medellín] Edit. Universidad de Antioquia [1960] 691-838 p. (999
Separata de la revista Universidad de Antioquia, no. 146, jul./sept. 1961.

ANUARIO bibliográfico colombiano, 1951. Ordenado y publicado por la Biblioteca "Jorge
Garcés B." Cali, Impr. J. G. B., 1952.
247 p. (1000
Colophon is dated 1953.

ANUARIO bibliográfico colombiano, 1951/1956- ,
compilado por Rubén Pérez Ortiz. Bogotá,
1958- . (1001
Volumes, 1951/56: 334 p.; 1957/1958:
178 p.; 1959/1960: 242 p.; 1961, 178 p.;
1962, 188 p. All issued by the Departamento de Bibliografía del Instituto Caro y Cuervo.

COLOMBIA. Imprenta Nacional. Informe del director ... (1o de mayo de 1934 a 30 de abril
de 1935) Bogotá, 1935. 26 p. (1002
Lists 121 items and 15 newspapers published during the period. Cited in Giraldo Jaramillo p. 43.

-----. Ministerio de Educación Nacional. Textos para la enseñanza primaria. Bogotá,
1963. (Divulgaciones bibliotecológicas,
no. 7) (1003
Cited in Boletín de adquisiciones, Medellín, no. 11, p. 15, nov. 1965. In the
Anuario bibliográfico colombiano, 1963, p.1,
this item is entered under, Borórquez Ca-
sallas, Luis A., with title, Lista provisio-

COLOMBIA. Ministerio de Educación...(Cont.)
nal (5 p.)

CORPORACION Autónoma Regional del Cauca, Cali,
Col. Folletos existentes. Cali, 1962.
22 p. mimeogr. (1004
Cited in Peraza, Fichas, t. 4-6, item 292.

-----. Publicaciones. Cali, 1962. 8 p.
mimeogr. (1005
Cited in Peraza, Fichas, t. 4-6, item 293.

GIRALDO JARAMILLO, Gabriel. Bibliografía
colombiana, 1953. [Sevilla] 1954. (1006
Reprint of Anuario de estudios americanos, v. 11, p. 629-45.

INTER-AMERICAN Book Exchange, Washington, D.C.
A general bibliography of Colombian publications for 1938. Washington, D.C., 1940.
20 p. (Bibliographical ser., 7) (1007

LAVERDE AMAYA, Isidoro. Bibliografía colombiana. Tomo I. Bogotá, M. Rivas, 1895.
296 p. (1008
No more published.---Jones 1725.

NIETO CABALLERO, Luis Eduardo. Libros colombianos publicados en 1924. [Bogotá] Linotip. de "El Espectador", 1925. 329 p. (1009
Jones 1739.

-----. Segunda serie. Bogotá, Edit. Minerva, 1928. 292 p. (1010
Jones 1739.

-----. Tercera serie. Bogotá, Edit. Minerva, 1928. 272 p. (1011
Jones 1739.

PERAZA SARAUSA, Fermín. Fichas para el anuario bibliográfico colombiano. Gainesville,
Fla., Medellín, Ediciones Anuario Bibliográfico Cubano, 1961- . (Biblioteca del
bibliotecario, 61-62, 67-68, 71-72) (1012
Vol. 8-9 published with title: Bibliografía colombiana.

-----. Libros de Medellín, 1961. Medellín,
Ediciones Anuario Bibliográfico Cubano,
1961. 28 p. (Biblioteca del bibliotecario, 63) (1013

POSADA, Eduardo. Bibliografía bogotana.
Bogotá, Impr. Arboleda y Valencia, 1917-
1925. 2 v. (Biblioteca de historia nacional, v. 16, 36) (1014
Jones 1759

ROA, Jorge. Catálogo de la Biblioteca Popular. Bogotá, Librería Nueva, n.d.
16 p. (1015
Catalog of the series edited by the author on Colombian life and culture. Cited
in Giraldo Jaramillo, p. 55.

COSTA RICA

ANUARIO bibliográfico costarricense, 1956- .
San José, 1958- .   (1016
    Issued by Asociación Costarricense de Bi-
bliotecarios, Comité Nacional de Bibliografía "Adolfo Blen". Last issue received at
DPU: 1963.

BOLETIN bibliográfico de la Biblioteca Nacional, 1938- . San José.   (1017
    Published with title: Publicaciones na-
cionales, 1938-1945, issue in typewritten
form; Boletín bibliográfico, 1946-1955.
For continuation of national bibliography,
see Anuario bibliográfico costarricense.

DOBLES SEGREDA, Luis. Indice bibliográfico
de Costa Rica. San José, Impr. Lehmann,
1927-1936. 9 v.   (1018
    Only 9 of the 12 projected volumes have
been published.---Jones 1267.

LINES, Jorge A. Libros y folletos publicados
en Costa Rica durante los años 1830-1849.
San José, 1944. 151 p.   (1019

CUBA

BIBLIOGRAFIA cubana, 1937- . Habana. 1938-
    Title varies: Anuario bibliogrático cubano,
1937-1952.
    Jones 1882. The 1960 volume was publish-
ed in Medellín, Colombia in the Edit.
Bedout; the 1961 volume in Gainesville,
Florida. Compiler, Fermín Peraza
Sarausa.   (1020

CONFERENCIAS y discursos, 1943-1950. La Habana, Ediciones Anuario Bibliográfico Cubano, 1944-1951. 8 v. (Biblioteca del bibliotecario, 6, 11, 16, 19, 22, 26, 30, 33)
mimeogr.   (1021
    Continues the section "Conferencias" of
the Anuario Bibliográfico Cubano, directed
by Fermín Peraza Sarausa.

PERAZA SARAUSA, Fermín. Bibliografía cubano-
uruguaya. Habana, Ediciones Anuario Bibliográfico Cubano, 1956. 49 p. (Biblioteca
del bibliotecario, 47) mimeogr.   (1022

RODRIGUEZ Y EXPOSITO, César. Apuntes bibliográficos; entre libros. Habana, Edit. Selecta, 1947. 334 p.   (1023
    Contains reviews of over 100 titles ac-
companied by an alphabetical listing of
names.
    Continues review section previously publ-
ished in Avance.

-----. Entre libros (Apuntes bibliográficos)
La Habana, Edit. "Cubanacan", [1944]
297 p.   (1024

RODRIGUEZ Y EXPOSITO, César ... (Cont.)
    Contains reviews of over 100 titles, pre-
viously appearing in Avance.

-----. and CASTRO DE MORALES, Lilia. Los
mejores libros cubanos de 1900 a 1950 según la encuesta iniciada el 19 de julio de
1950 ... en su sección "Entre libros" del
periódico "Avance" adaptado al sistema de
catalogación de la Biblioteca Nacional.
Habana, Biblioteca Nacional, 1952.
18 p.   (1025

SPACE buyers' guide of Cuba. Habana, 1939.
24 p.   (1026
    Directory of Cuban publications. This is
the 8th year of publication. Editor Charles W. Monroe. Cited in HLAS, 5, item 132.

TRELLES Y GOVIN, Carlos Manuel. Bibliografía cubana de los siglos XVII y XVIII; 2a.
ed. Habana, Impr. del Ejército, 1927.
xix, 463 p.   (1027
    This edition contains 2.100 entries.

-----. Bibliografía cubana del siglo XIX.
Matanzas, Impr. de Quirós y Estrada,
1911-1915. 8 v.   (1028
    A continuation of the author's Ensayo de
bibliografía cubana de los siglos XVII y
XVIII with supplement, 1908.---Jones 1913.
Now available in microprint.

-----. Bibliografía cubana del siglo XX.
(1900-1916) Matanzas, Impr. de la Vda. de
Quirós y Estrada, 1916-1917. 2 v.   (1029
    Jones 1914. Now available in microprint.

-----. Bibliografía de autores de la raza
de color en Cuba. (Cuba contemporánea,
Habana, v. 43, p. 33-78, 1927)   (1030
    Jones 1915.

-----. Los ciento cincuenta libros más notables que los cubanos han escrito. Habana, Impr. "El Siglo XX" de A. Miranda,
1914. 61 p.   (1031
    From Cuba y América, v. 17, no. 1. Oct.
1913.---Jones 1924.

-----. Ensayo de bibliografía cubana de los
siglos XVII y XVIII. Seguido de unos apuntes para la bibliografía dominicana y por-
torriqueña. Matanzas, Impr. "El Escritorio", 1907. 228 p.   (1033
    "Notas y adiciones", in El Curioso ame-
ricano, Habana, 1907, p. 27, 30, 43, 46,
62, 94, 96.---Jones 1926.
Now available in microprint.

-----. -----. Suplemento. Matanzas, Impr.
"El Escritorio", 1908. 76 p.   (1034
    A second edition was published in 1927.
---Jones 1926.
Now available in microprint.

VALDES DOMINGUEZ, Eusebio. Bibliografía cubana. (Revista cubana, Habana, t. 5, p. 368-
79, 581-92; t. 6, p. 85-9, 1879)   (1035
    Jones 1934

VEREZ DE PERAZA, Elena Luisa. Publicaciones
de las instituciones culturales cubanas.
Habana, Anuario Bibliográfico Cubano, 1949.
viii, 149 p. (Biblioteca de bibliotecario,
29) mimeogr.   (1036

-----. 2a ed. La Habana, 1954. 246 p. (Biblioteca del bibliotecario, 29)   (1036a

DOMINICAN REPUBLIC

ANUARIO bibliográfico dominicano, 1946-1947.
    Ciudad Trujillo, Oficina de Canje y Difusión
    Cultural, 1947-1948.   (1037
    DPU also has typewritten carbon copy,
    1950-1951.

ECUADOR

ALVARADO, Rafael. Indice de traducciones ecuatorianas. Quito, Casa de la Cultura Ecuatoriana, 1954. 31 p.   (1038

-----. 2a. ed., corr. y aum. con un apéndice
sobre traducciones mundiales. Quito, Edit.
Casa de la Cultura Ecuatoriana, 1957.
54 p.   (1039

ANRIQUE REYES, Nicolás. Noticia de algunas
publicaciones ecuatorianas anteriores a 1792.
Santiago de Chile, 1891. 23 p.   (1040
    Jones 1948. Published also in Revista
ecuatoriana, t. 4, entrega 3, no. 39, mar.
1892.

ECUADOR. Biblioteca Nacional. Producción bibliográfica ecuatoriana, 1938. Quito, 1939.
10 p. mimeogr.   (1041
    Reprinted in Pan American book shelf,
Washington, D.C., v. 2, no. 9, p. 50-60,
Sept. 1939.

ESPINOSA CORDERO, Nicolás. Bibliografía ecuatoriana; noticia de las obras literarias y
científicas que forman el caudal bibliográfico de la Real Audiencia de Quito, hoy República del Ecuador, con breves datos biográficos de sus autores (1534-1809) Cuenca, Impr. del Colegio Nacional "Benigno Malo", 1934. 171 p.   (1042
    Forms part 4 of the author's Estudios li-
terarios y bibliográficos (Cuenca, 1934)
Bibliografía: p. 155-64.---Jones 1978.

HOJAS volantes que se han publicado en las
diversas provincias de la República del
Ecuador 1790-1920. Lista en la que constan
por orden cronológico de fechas, semanarios,

HOJAS volantes que se han...(Cont.)
publicaciones eventuales y ocasionales. Colección del señor Leonardo J. Muñoz. Quito,
Impr. del Ministerio de Gobierno, 1941.
16 p.   (1043
    Cited in HLAS, 7, p. 579, and displayed in
the Primera Exposición del Periodismo Ecuatoriano, Quito, 1941.

INTER-AMERICAN Book Exchange, Washington, D.C.
A general bibliography of Ecuadorian publications for 1936 and 1937. Washington, D.C.,
1938. 15 p. (Bibliographical ser.,
no. 1)   (1044

-----. 1938. Washington, D.C., 1939. 7 p.
(Bibliographical ser., no. 4)   (1044a

ROLANDO, Carlos A. Catálogo de la bibliografía
nacional del dr. Carlos A. Rolando. Guayaquil, Impr. Mercantil, 1913. 135 p.   (1045
    "El catálogo está arreglado hasta el 31 de
diciembre de 1912".---Jones 2006.

TERAN, Enrique. National bibliography of Ecuador ... books published in Ecuador in 1938.
(Pan American book shelf, Washington, D.C.,
v. 2, no. 9, p. 50-60, 1939)   (1046
    Jones 2017.

EL SALVADOR

ANUARIO bibliográfico salvadoreño, 1952. San
Salvador, Edit. Casa de la Cultura, 1954.
39 p. (Anexo de "Anaqueles", ép. 5, no. 4,
1954)   (1047
    Previous years published in Revista and in
Anaqueles of the Biblioteca Nacional.

EL SALVADOR. Biblioteca Nacional. Bibliografía salvadoreña; lista preliminar por autores.
[San Salvador, 1953] 430 p. mimeogr. (1048

-----. ------. Bibliografía salvadoreña; publicaciones impresas en El Salvador durante
los años de 1945 y 1946. San Salvador, 1948.
16 p.   (1049
    Cited in HLAS, 14, item 7.
    List covering same period published in Re-
vista de la Biblioteca Nacional, ép. 4, v. 1,
p. 183-95, en./abr. 1947; and continued other
years in subsequent issues: v. 2, p. 173-207,
mayo/ag. 1947; v. 5, p. 157-84, mayo/ag.
1949. Later years in Anaqueles.

-----. Imprenta Nacional. Nómina de las obras
editadas. San Salvador, 1944. 54 p. (1050
    Cited in HLAS, 11, item 56.

GUATEMALA

ANUARIO bibliográfico guatelamteco; por autores.
1960. Guatemala, 1961- .   (1051

ANUARIO bibliográfico...(Cont.)
  Issued 1960- by Biblioteca Nacional de
Guatemala.

DARDON CORDOVA, Gonzalo. Bibliografías de
autores guatemaltecos. v. 1. Guatemala,
Universidad de San Carlos, Facultad de Humanidades, 1962. 28 p. (Publicaciones de
la Escuela de Biblioteconomía de la Facultad de Humanidades, 3)   (1052

-----. Series guatemaltecas en el campo de
las humanidades (1886-1962) Guatemala,
Instituto Guatemalteco-Americano, 1962.
137 p. (Cooperación interbibliotecaria,
3)   (1053

INDICE bibliográfico guatemalteco, 1951- .
Guatemala, 1952- .   (1055
  1951-1952 published by the Servicio Extensivo of the Biblioteca Nacional, and
1958 by the Instituto Guatemalteco-Americano. Publication suspended 1953-1957.
Last issue received at DPU: 1959-1960.

INTER-AMERICAN Book Exchange, Washington, D.C.
A general bibliography of Guatemalan publications for 1938. Washington, D.C., 1939.
8 p. (Bibliographical ser., no. 3) (1056

O'RYAN, Juan Enrique. Bibliografía de la
imprenta en Guatemala en los siglos xvii y
xviii. Santiago de Chile, Impr. Elzeviriana, 1897. 120 p.   (1057
  Bibliografía: p. 17-20.---Jones 1305.

-----. Bibliografía guatemalteca de los siglos XVII y XVIII; 2. ed. Guatemala, Edit.
del Ministerio de Educación Pública "José
de Pineda Ibarra", 1960. 19 p. facsims.:
120 p. (Colección bibliográfica del 3o
Centenario de la Fundación de la Primera
Imprenta en Centro América, t. 1)   (1058

VALENZUELA, Gilberto. Bibliografía guatemalteca; catálogo de obras, folletos, etc.,
publicados en Guatemala desde la independencia hasta el año de 1850. T. 1. [1821-
1830]. Guatemala, 1933. 459 p. (Folletín
del "Diario de Centro América")   (1059
  Jones 1311.

-----. Bibliografía guatemalteca, y catálogo
general de libros, folletos, periódicos, revistas, etc., 1821-1830. Guatemala, [Tip.
Nacional] 1961. 319 p. (Colección bibliográfica del 3o Centenario de la Fundación
de la Primera Imprenta en Centro América,
t. 3)   (1060

-----. -----. 1831-1840. Guatemala [Edit.
del Ministerio de Educación Pública "José
de Pineda Ibarra"] 1961. 206 p. (Colección bibliográfica del 3o Centenario de la
Fundación de la Primera Imprenta en Centro

VALENZUELA, Gilberto ... (Cont.)
  América, t. 4)   (1061

-----. -----. 1841-1860. Guatemala [Tip. Na-
cional] 1961. 185 p. (Colección bibliográfica del 3o Centenario de la Fundación de la
Primera Imprenta en Centro América,
t. 5)   (1062

VALENAUELA REYNA, Gilberto. Bibliografía guatemalteca, y catálogo general de libros,
folletos, periódicos, revistas, etc., 1861-
1900. Guatemala [Tip. Nacional] 1962.
485 p. (Colección bibliográfica del 3o Centenario de la Fundación de la Primera Imprenta en Centro América, t. 6)   (1063

-----. 1901-1930. Guatemala [Tip. Nacional]
1962 [i.e. 1963] 537 p. (Colección bibliográfica del 3o Centenario de la Fundación de
la Primera Imprenta en Centro América,
t. 7)   (1064

-----. 1931-1940. Guatemala [Tip. Nacional]
1963. 288 p. (Colección bibliográfica del
3o Centenario de la Fundación de la Primera
Imprenta en Centro América, t. 8)   (1065

VILLACORTA CALDERON, José Antonio. Bibliografía guatemalteca, Tip. Nacional, 1944.
638 p.   (1066
  Contents: --Dos siglos de imprenta en
Guatemala, 1660-1860. -- Dos siglos de grabado en Guatemala, 1660-1860. -- Dos siglos
de periodismo en Guatemala, 1729-1929. -- El
libro y el folleto modernos en Guatemala.

HAITI

BISSAINTHE, Max. Dictionnaire de bibliographie haitienne. Washington, D.C., Scarecrow
Pr., 1951. 1052 p.   (1067
  Contains pt. 1: 4,318 works by Haitians,
1804-1950. - pt. 2: 4,151 titles by non-
Haitian authors about Saint Domingue and
Haiti. - pt. 3: periodical publications,
1764-1949. - pt. 4: names of journalists
related to publications mentioned in pt. 3.

DUVIVIER, Ulrick. Bibliographie générale et
méthodique d'Haiti. Port-au-Prince, Impr.
de l'Etat. 1941. 2 v.   (1068
  Jones 2990a.

HONDURAS

ANUARIO bibliográfico, 1961. Tegucigalpa,
Edit. del Ministerio de Educación Pública,
1963. 49 p.   (1069
  Prepared in the Biblioteca Nacional by
Miguel Angel García.

DURON, Jorge Fidel. Indice de la bibliografía
hondureña. [Tegucigalpa] Impr. Calderón,
1946. 211 p.   (1070

-----. Repertorio bibliográfico hondureño.
Tegucigalpa, 1943. 68 p.   (1071

INTER-AMERICAN Book Exchange, Washington, D.C.
A general bibliography of Honduran and Costa
Rican publications for 1938. Washington,
D.C., 1940. 8 p. (Bibliographical ser.,
no. 5)   (1072

VALLE, Rafael Heliodoro. Indice bibliográfico
hondureño. (Centro-América, Guatemala, v.5,
p. 583-87, 1913)   (1073
Jones 1329.

MEXICO

ANUARIO bibliográfico de Yucatán, 1938-1942.
Mérida, Yucatán, Museo Arqueológico e Histórico de Yucatán, 1939-1943. 5 v. (Boletín de bibliografía yucateca, no. 4/5, en./
feb. 1939; no. 11, 15 mayo 1940; no. 13,
1 abr. 1941; no. 15, 1 abr. 1942; no. 17,
abr./mayo 1943)   (1074

ANUARIO bibliográfico mexicano, 1931-1942.
México, 1933-1944. 9 v.   (1075
Issues for 1931-1933 compiled by Felipe
Teixidor; for July 1938-1940 (incomplete)
compiled under the title Bibliografía mexicana, by Francisco J. Gamoneda under the
auspices of the Asociación de Libreros de
México; for 1940-1941/1942 compiled by Julián Amo and published as Serie Bibliografías mexicanas, no. [1], 3; and for 1942 by
the Comisión Mexicana de Cooperación Intelectual. Issue for 1940 contains Catálogo
de catálogos of dealers and Indice de periódicos y revistas que se editan actualmente
en la República.---Jones 2059, 2079.

ANUARIO bibliográfico nacional (1888) por
Luis González Obregón; año I. México, Oficina Tip. de la Secretaría de Fomento, 1889.
155 p.   (1076
No more published.
Pt. 1, Catálogo de libros impresos en 1888
(167 titles); pt. 2, Periódicos (266 titles,
without bibliographical details); pt. 3,
Propiedades concedidas.---Jones 2060.

BERROA, Josefina. México bibliográfico, 1957-
1960; catálogo general de libros impresos en
México. México, 1961. 189 p.   (1077

CAMPECHE, México (State). Bibliografía del
estado de Campeche. Campeche, [Tall. Linotip. del Gobierno 1943. xxiv, 377 p. (1078
Compilation by Héctor Pérez Martínez y
Juan de Dios Pérez Galaz.

CHAVEZ OROZCO, Luis. Bibliografía de Zacatecas. México, Impr. de la Secretaría de Relaciones Exteriores, 1932. 231 p. (Monografías bibliográficas mexicanas,
no. 26)   (1079
Jones 2129.

COLIN, Mario. Bibliografía general del Estado
de México. México, [Edit. Jus, 1963] t. 1.
(xvi, 425 p.) (Biblioteca enciclopédica del
Estado de México, 1)   (1080

CUELLAR ABAROA, Crisanto. Bibliografía de
Tlaxcala. [Tlaxcala, México] 1960.
98 p.   (1081
Compilation of the work by Ramos Cuéllar.

DIAZ MERCADO, Joaquín. Bibliografía general
del estado de Veracruz. México, D.A.P.P.,
1937. v. 1 (715 p.) (Bibliografías mexicanas, no. 1)   (1082
Covers the years 1794-1910.---Jones 2148.

-----. Bibliografía sumaria de la Baja California. México, 1937. 179 p. (Bibliografías mexicanas, no. 2)   (1083
Jones 2149.

DIEZ, Domingo. Bibliografía del estado de
Morelos. México, Impr. de la Secretaría de
Relaciones Exteriores, 1933. 427 p. (Mono-
grafías bibliográficas mexicanas,
no. 27)   (1084
Jones 2151.

DOSSICK, Jesse J. Bibliography of Mexicana
written in English during the year 1939
(750 items). (Mexicana review, New York,
v. 1, p. 7-34, 1940)   (1085
Jones 2153a.

EGUIARA Y EGUREN, Juan José de. Bibliotheca
mexicana ... Tomus primus, exhibens litter-
as A B C. Mexici, ex nova typographia in
awdibus authoris editioni ejusdem Bibliothecae destinata, 1755. 543 p.   (1086
No more published.
"Das werk ist die bedeutendste bibliogra-
phische leistung des XVIII jahrhundert in
Mexico; auch heute noch für die mexicanische
missionsgeschichte von bedeutung" (Streit)
---Jones 2155.

-----. Prólogos a la Biblioteca mexicana;
nota preliminar por Federico Gómez de Orozco,
versión española anotada, con un estudio
biográfico y la bibliografía del autor por
Agustín Millares Carlo. México, Fondo de
Cultura Económico, [1944] 303 p. (Biblioteca americana de obras latinas)   (1087
First Latin edition: 1755; Second Latin
edition: 1944; First Spanish edition: 1944.

ESTRADA, Genaro. 200 notas de bibliografía
mexicana. México, Impr. de la Secretaría
de Relaciones Exteriores, 1935. 123 p.
(Monografías bibliográficas mexicanas,
no. 31)   (1088
    Jones 2161.

-----. Nuevas notas de bibliografía mexicana.
México, D.F., Secretaría de Relaciones Exteriores, 1954. xviii, 89 p. Monografías
bibliográficas mexicanas, 2a ser.,
no. 6)   (1089

FERNANDEZ DE CORDOBA, Joaquín. Rextificacio-
nes bibliográficas a un erudito. México,
Edit. Arana, 1961. 27 p. (Biblioteca de
bibliografía mexicana)   (1090

-----. Tesoros bibliográficos de México en
los Estados Unidos. México, D.F., Edit.
Cultura, 1959. 151 p.   (1091
    First published in Historia mexicana,
    v. 5-6, no. 17, 21, 1955-1957.

FRIAS, Valentín F. Ensayos bibliográficos de
Querétaro. Opúsculo presentado a la Sociedad "Antonio Alzate". Publicados por primera vez en el Boletín de la misma, t. 19,
no. 7, p. 85. Santiago de Querétaro, Deme-
trio Contreras, 1904. 18 p.   (1092
    Cited in Ayala, item 459.

GARCIA ICAZBALCETA, Joaquín. Bibliografía
mexicana del siglo XVI. Primera parte.
Catálogo razonado de libros impresos en México de 1539 a 1600. Con biografías de autores y otras ilustraciones. Precedida de
una noticia acerca de la introducción de la
imprenta en México. México, Andrade y Morales, 1886. 419 p.   (1093
    The second part (intended to cover 16th.
    century writers whose works were either
    published after 1600, or remained in ms.)
    was never published.
    116 titles, trancribed line for line.---
    Jones 2191. Now available in microprint.

-----. Nueva ed, por Agustin Millares Carlo.
México, Fondo de Cultura Económica, 1954.
484 p., 66 plates. (Biblioteca americana.
Ser. de literatura moderna: historia y biografía)   (1094

-----. Obras. México, Impr. de V. Agüeros,
editor, 1896-1899. 10 v. (Biblioteca de
autores mexicanos. Historiadores, 1-3, 6,
9, 12, 14, 18, 20, 23)   (1095
    Includes some 99 biographies of prominent
    men of the colonial period.---Jones 2199.

GOMEZ UGARTE, Elena, and PAGAZA, Aurora. Bibliografía sumaria del territorio de Quintana Roo. México, D.A.P.P., 1937. 142 p.
(Bibliografías mexicanas, no. 3)   (1097
    390 items listed.---Jones 2210.

GONZALEZ, Héctor, and ORDOÑEZ, Plinio D. Bibliografía del estado de Nuevo León de 1820
a 1946. Reseña de libros por Héctor González. Reseña de periódicos por Plinio D. Ordoñez. [Monterrey, Sociedad Nuevoleonesa de
Historia y Geografía y Estadística, 1946]
63 p.   (1098

HERRERA, Moisés. Contribución para una bibliografía de obras referentes al estado de Puebla. [Puebla] 1943. 112 p. (Biblioteca de
la Segunda Feria del Libro y Exposición Nacional del Periodismo)   (1099

INSTITUTO Mexicano del Libro. Catálogo de libros impresos en México. VI Feria Mexicana
del Libro [20 noviembre-15 diciembre 1954.
México] 121 p.   (1100

-----. VII Feria Mexicana del Libro. [Méxi-
co] 1956. xiv, 144 p.   (1101

LEON, Nicolás. Adiciones a la Bibliografía
mexicana del siglo XVI del señor don Joaquín
García Icazbalceta. (Boletín del Instituto
Bibliográfico Mexicano, México, núm. 2, p.
41-64, 1903)   (1102
    Jones 2193.

-----. Bibliografía mexicana del siglo XVIII.
México, 1902-08. 5 v. in 6. (Boletín del
Instituto Bibliográfico Mexicano)   (1103
    Publication first begun in Anales del Mu-
    seo Michoacano, 1890.
    Sección 1: 1. pte., A-Z (1000 titles)
    1902; 2. pte. A-Z (999 titles including
    reprint of the Gaceta de México and Mercu-
    rio de México) 1903-05; 3. pte., A-Z (400
    titles) 1906; 4. pte., A-Z (400 titles)
    1907; 5. pte., A-Z (500 titles)
    Parts 6-7, and "Sección segunda (biográ-
    fica, histórica y crítica) remain unpublish-
    ed.---Jones 2288.
    Now available in microprint.

LOPEZ, E. Y. Bibliografía de Sonora, Hermosillo. México, D.F., Ediciones Fátima,
1960. 200 p.   (1104
    Contains 1,631 entries.

MANTECON, José Ignacio. Indice de las traducciones impresas en México, 1959. México,
Universidad Nacional, 1964. 247 p. (Anexos
del Boletín de la Biblioteca Nacional,
1)   (1105

MEXICO, Comisión Mexicana de Cooperación Intelectual. Bibliografía mexicana, 1942.
México, D.F., [Depto. de Publicidad y Propaganda, Tall. Gráf. no. 1 de la S. E. P.]
1944. 89 p.   (1106
    Contains works published in México; Mexi-
    can authors published abroad; works publish-
    ed abroad about México; and Exchange.

PRIEGO DE ARJONA, Mireya. Notas acerca de
bibliografía yucateca. Mérida, Tall. Graf.
del Sudeste, 1937. 14 p. (Ediciones del
Museo Arqueológico e Histórico de Yucatán.
Publ. no. 4)   (1107
   "Las obras cotejadas a que se refiere este trabajo fueron: Disertación sobre la
historia de la lengua maya o yucateca, por
d. Crescencio Carillo y Ancona. 4a. ed.
... Bibliografía yucateca, por Felipe Teixidor ... i A Maya grammar, por Alfred M.
Tozzer."---Jones 2433.

RAMOS, Roberto, and CUELLAS ABAROA, Crisanto.
Bibliografía del estado de Tlaxcala.
Tlaxcala, México, 1949. 59 p. (Publ. de la
Dirección de Bibliotecas, Museos, e Inves-
tigaciones Históricas)   (1108

REIMERS FENOCHIO, G. Breves apuntes sobre
bibliografías oaxaqueñas del siglo XVI.
(Investigaciones lingüísticas, México, v. 2,
p. 74-5, 1934)   (1109
   Jones 2454.

ROMERO FLORES, Jesús. Apuntes para una bibliografía geográfica e histórica de Michoacán. México, Impr. de la Secretaría de Relaciones Exteriores, 1932. 325 p. (Monografías bibliográficas mexicanas,
no. 25)   (1110
   Jones 2477.

SAN LUIS POTOSI. Universidad. Fichas de bibliografía potosina. San Luis Potosí,
1955. 29 p.   (1111
   Cited in Bol., Biblioteca Nacional, México, oct./dic. 1955, p. 73.

SANTAMARIA, Francisco Javier. Bibliografía
general de Tabasco. México. [Impr. de la
Secretaría de Relaciones Exteriores] 1930-
1946. 3 v.   (1112
   Vol. 1 (608 p.) cited in Jones 2484;
vol. 2 (1945, 414 p.) cited in González,
item 111; and vol. 3 (1946) cited in HLAS
15, item 36.

-----. 2a. ed. Villahermosa, México, Gobierno del Estado, 1949. xxxi, 512 p. (Escritores tabasqueños, 37)   (1113

SUAREZ, Víctor M. Libros yucatecos de 1947.
Mérida, Yucatán, 1948. 38 p.   (1114
   Lists 67 titles.

TEIXIDOR, Felipe. Bibliografía yucateca.
Mérida, 1937. 263 p. (Publ. del Museo Arqueológico e Histórico de Yucatán,
no. 1)   (1115
   Lists 239 items on the Maya language, 38
manuscripts and 1460 titles including
history, literature and science.---Jones
2522.

VALLE, Rafael Heliodoro. Bibliografía mexicana de 1933. (El Libro y el pueblo, México, D.F., t. 12, p. 36-43, en. 1934) (1116
   Jones 2550.

-----. Bibliografía mexicana. (1937-1938)
(The Hispanic American historical review.
Durham, N.C., v. 20, p. 294-334, 686-746,
May, Nov. 1940; v. 21, p. 143-81,
Feb. 1951)   (1117
   Jones 2550a.

-----. Mexican bibliography in 1934. (The
Hispanic American historical review, Durham,
N.C., v. 15, p. 523-47, 1935)   (1118
   Jones 2555.

-----. -----, in 1935. (Ib., v. 17, p. 370-
416, Aug. 1937)   (1119

-----. Mexican bibliography in 1936. (The
Hispanic American historical review, Durham,
N.C., v. 18. p. 580-99, 1938)   (1120
   Jones 2556.

VELDE, Paul van de. Breves apuntes sobre la
bibliografía mexicana. (Memorias y Revista
de la Sociedad Científica "Antonio Alzate",
México, D.F., v. 51, p. 89-97, 1931) (1121
   Jones 2571.

VILLASEÑOR Y VILLASEÑOR, Ramiro. Bibliogra-
fía general de Jalisco. Guadalajara, Méxi-
co, 1958. 401 p. (Publ. del Gobierno del
Estado)   (1122
   Vol. 1 of the bibliography aimed to cover
Jalisco from the conquest through 1956.
Contains entries A-F.

-----. La Constitución en la bibliografía
jalisciense. Guadalajara, 1957. 40 p.
(Publ. del Gobierno del Estado)   (1122a

WAGNER, Henry Raup. Nueva bibliografía mexicana del siglo XVI. Suplemento a las bibliografías de Don Joaquín García Icazbel-
ceta, José T. Medina y Nicolás León. Escrito en inglés, la tradujeron don Joaquín
García Pimentel y Federico Gómez de Orozco,
México, D.F., Antigua Libr. Robredo, 1946.
548 p.   (1123

NICARAGUA

BIBLIOTECA Americana, Managua, Nicaragua.
Bibliografía de trabajos publicados en Ni-
caragua. A bibliography of works publish-
ed in Nicaragua, 1943-1945/1947. [Managua]
Edit. Nuevos Horizontes, 1944-1948. 3 v.
(Bibliographical series of the American
Library of Nicaragua, no. 1, 6-7/9)   (1124

PANAMA

HERRERA, Carmen D. Bibliografía panameña de
libros y de folletos, 1958-1960. Panamá,
1960. 44 p.   (1125
  Prepared for the Third Bibliographical Seminar of Central America, the Caribbean and
Panama, México, 1960.

PANAMA. Biblioteca Nacional. Bibliografía
panameña. Panamá, Ministerio de Educación,
Comité Nacional Pro-Bibliotecas, Biblioteca
Nacional, 1954. 66 p.   (1126

-----. Universidad. Biblioteca. Bibliografía panameña existente en la Biblioteca de
la Universidad. [Panamá, 1953] 109 p.
(loose leaf) mimeogr.   (1127

-----. -----. Bibliografía retrospectiva de
libros y folletos, 1955/1957. Panamá, Oficina de Información y Publicaciones, 1958.
63 p.   (1128
  Working paper prepared by the "Grupo Bibliográfico" under the supervision of Carmen
D. Herrera for the Seminario Bibliográfico
de Centro América y el Caribe.

SUSTO, Juan Antonio. Bibliografía de Panamá,
1938. Panamá, 1939. 15 p. mimeogr. (1129
  Jones 1349a, 1359. Reprinted with title
"National bibliography of Panama ... books
published in Panama in 1938" in Pan American
book shelf (2(9): 61-70, Sept. 1939)

-----. Introducción a la bibliografía panameña (1619-1945) Panamá, 1946. 35 p.
(Publ. de la Biblioteca Nacional,
no. 4)   (1130

PARAGUAY

BIBLIOGRAFIA paraguaya. Asunción, Librerías
Nizza [1959?] 3 p.   (1130a
  HLAS no. 22, item 6282.

PERU

ANUARIO bibliográfico peruano, 1943- . Lima
[Tall. Gráf. de la Edit. Lumen]
1945- .   (1131
  Issued in series, Ediciones de la Biblioteca Nacional, v. 1-2, 4-7, 9- . Editor:
Alberto Tauro, 1943- . Last vol. received
at DPU: 1958/1960 published in 1964.

BASADRE, Jorge. La producción bibliográfica
del Perú, 1937-1938. (Boletín bibliográfico, Biblioteca Central de la Universidad,
Lima, v. 11, p. 237-55, 1938)   (1132
  Jones 2631.

BIBLIOTHECA peruviana; a catalogue of books,
tracts and manuscripts chiefly relating to
North and South America, comprising works
printed at Lima. London, 1873.   (1133
Jones 2636.

DEUSTUA PIMENTEL, Carlos, and PACHECO VELEZ,
César. Bibliografía peruana. Sevilla,
1954. p. 97-120.   (1134
  Reprinted from Anuario de estudios americanos, t. 11, p. 659-82.

ORTIZ, Pedro. Bibliografía básica de Puno.
Lima, Perú, Ministerio de Trabajo y Asuntos
Indígenas, 1964. 39 p. (Serie bibliográ-
fica, no. 1)   (1134a

PAZ SOLDAN, Mariano Felipe. Biblioteca peruana. Lima, Impr. Liberal, 1879.
544 p.   (1135
  "Menos que un epítome bibliográfico es
apenas una lista o índice de las piezas hecho a estilo comercial, sin los reclamos de
estilo." (Bib. peruana, v. 1, no. 176)
---Jones 2712.

PERU. Dirección de Propaganda e Informaciones. Producción bibliográfica peruana,
1940-1941. Lima [1942] 109 p.   (1136
  Reprinting of Bibliografía de libros y
folletos peruanos, 1940-1941 por Federico
Schwab; and Esquema de la producción bibliográfica peruana en el bienio 1940-1941 por
Antonio Olivas, from Boletín bibliográfico,
Biblioteca Central, Universidad Mayor de
San Marcos, año 14, no. 1-4, p. 51-155,
dic. 1941.

PRINCE, Carlos. Bibliografía nacional. Los
peruanófilos anticuarios del siglo XIX.
Lima, Impr. de la Escuela de Ingenieros,
1908. 283 p.   (1137
  First published in Revista de ciencias.
The lack of an index impairs the usefulness
of the work.---Jones 2729.

SCHWAB, Federico. Bibliografía de libros y
folletos peruanos publicados en 1937. (Boletín bibliográfico, Universidad Mayor de
San Marcos, Lima, v. 11, p. 256-323,
1938)   (1138
  Continued for 1938- , in suceeding volumes
of the Boletín.---Jones 2750.

-----. Bibliografía de libros y folletos peruanos publicados en 1940-1941. Lima, Compañía de Impresiones y Publicidad, 1942.
102 p.   (1139

-----. Bibliografía de libros y folletos peruanos publicados en 1942. Lima, Compañía
de Impresiones y Publicidad, 1943.
48 p.   (1140
  Cited in Anuario bibliográfico peruano,
1941, item 496.

SCHWAB, Federico. Bibliografía de libros y
folletos peruanos publicados en 1943 y 1944.
Lima, Compañía de Impresiones y Publicidad,
1944. 48 p.   (1141
    Cited in Anuario bibliográfico peruano,
1944, item 703.

VALCARCEL, Luis Eduardo. Los estudios peruanistas en 1937. (Revista del Museo Nacional, Lima, t. 7, no. 1, p. 6-20, 1o. sem.
1938)   (1142
    Contains bibliography.---Jones 2766.

VARGAS UGARTE, Rubén. Impresos peruanos. Lima, 1953-1957. 7 v. (Biblioteca peruana,
6-12)   (1143
    The author brings this work through 1825,
adding numerous items not in La Imprenta en
Lima, 1584-1824, by José Toribio Medina.
Title of no. 6 of series: Impresos peruanos
publicados en el extranjero. Supplement to
the series published in 1961 (See item 440)

PUERTO RICO

ANUARIO bibliográfico puertorriqueño, 1948- .
Río Piedras, Biblioteca de la Universidad.   (1144
    Imprint varies: Editorial Universitaria:
1951-1952; San Juan, Depto. de Instrucción
Pública: 1953- .
    Issue 1957-1958 appeared in 1964.

GEIGEL Y ZENON, José, and MORALES FERRER, Abelardo. Bibliografía puertorriqueña escrita
en 1892-1894. Barcelona, Edit. Araluce,
1934. 453 p.   (1145
    Jones 2792.

PEDREIRA, Antonio S. Bibliografía puertorriqueña (1493-1930) Madrid, Impr. de la Librería y Casa Editorial Hernando, 1932.
707 p. (Monografías de la Universidad de
Puerto Rico. Serie A: Estudios hispánicos, no. 1)   (1146
    Jones 2801.

SAMA, Manuel María. Bibliografía puerto-
riqueña. Trabajo premiado en el certamen
del Ateneo Puertorriqueño, celebrado el 29
de enero de 1887, de conformidad con el
laudo del jurado calificador de la Asociación de Escritores y Artistas de Madrid.
Mayagüez, Tip. Comercial-Marina, 1887.
159 p.   (1147
    Largely supplanted by the later works of
Pedreira and Géigel y Zenón.---Jones 2807.

URUGUAY

ANUARIO bibliográfico uruguayo, 1946- .
Montevideo, Biblioteca Nacional,
1947- .   (1148

ANUARIO bibliográfico... (Cont.)
The last issue received at DPU: 1949.

INTER-AMERICAN Book Exchange, Washington, D.C.
A general bibliography of Uruguayan publications for 1938. Washington, D.C., 1939.
15 p. (Bibliographical ser., no. 2) (1149

URIOSTE, Antero. Algunas papeletas bibliográficas de Rocha. Montevideo, Ediciones Ceibo,
Impr. L.I.G.U., 1943. 35 p.   (1150
    Published in Revista nacional, Montevideo,
no. 59, nov. 1942.

URUGUAY. Biblioteca Nacional. Anales de la
bibliografía uruguaya; t. 1. (año 1895)
Montevideo, Impr. de la Nación, 1896.
127 p.   (1151
    Jones 2851. Compiled by Pedro Mascaró.
No more published.

-----. Oficina de Depósito, Reparto y Canje
Internacional de Publicaciones. Lista de
las publicaciones existentes. Montevideo,
1890.   (1152
    Jones 2876.

VENEZUELA

ANUARIO bibliográfico de Venezuela, 1916 (Año
primero de su publicación) Caracas, Lit.
del Comercio, 1917. 71 p.   (1153
    Compiled by Manuel Segundo Sánchez.
    Books, pamphlets and periodicals received
by the Biblioteca Nacional, with addition
of some titles from other sources.
    1917 issued in Boletín de la Biblioteca
Nacional, no. 41-2, 1936.---Jones 2883.

ANUARIO bibliográfico venezolano, 1942- ,
Caracas, 1944- .   (1154
    Last issue received at DPU: 1949/1954,
in 2 v., published in 1960. Separate Alcance to Anuario published in 1948 with title
Escritores venezolanos fallecidos durante
1942 y 1947.

GODOY, Pedro Luis. Estadística bibliográfica
de la ciudad de Mérida. (Gaceta médica,
Mérida, no. 57-8, p. 434-38, 1906)   (1154a
    Jones 2914.

LOLLETT C., Carlos Miguel. Introducción a la
bibliografía venezolana. Caracas, Impr. de
la Dirección de Cultura, n.d. 18 p.   (1155
    Reprinted from Revista nacional de cultu-
ra, no. 77, p. 49-64, nov./dic. 1949. Cited
in An. bibliog. venezolano, 1949/1954, item
2125.

SANCHEZ, Manuel Segundo. Bibliografía de
las ediciones nacionales y de las extranjeras relativas a Venezuela, incompletas o
truncas. Caracas, Tip. Vargas, 1925.

SANCHEZ, Manuel Segundo ... (Cont.)
  xxxiv p.   (1156
    List 53 works, 1723-1917.---Jones 2952c.

-----. Bibliografía de obras didácticas publicadas en Venezuela o por autores venezolanos en el extranjero. Caracas, Tip. Americana, 1946. xxvii, 111 p.   (1157
  Published under auspices of the Biblioteca
Nacional.

-----. Bibliografía venezolanista; contribución al conocimiento de los libros extranjeros relativos a Venezuela y sus grandes hombres, pub. o reimpresos desde el siglo XIX.
Caracas, Empresa El Cojo, 1914.
494 p.   (1158
  1439 titles cited. Includes a reprint of
Hermann Ahrensburg's Bibliographia prof. dr.
phil. A. Ernst (Caracas, Jena Universi-
tätsbuchdr. G. Neuenhahn, 1899) giving 381
titles of Ernst's publications.---Jones 2954.
Now available in microprint.

-----. Bibliografía venezolana; nómina de los
principales libros y folletos venezolanos
publicados en los primeros meses de 1918.
Santiago de Chile, Impr. Universitaria,
1919. 8 p.   (1159
  Reprinted from Revista de bibliografía
chilena y extranjera, año 6, p. 339-44.---
Jones 2953.

SANCHEZ, Manuel Segundo. Obras; prólogo de
Pedro Grases. Caracas, Banco Central de Venezuela, 1964. 2 v. (Col. Cuatricentenario
de Caracas)   (1160
  Contents: v. 1, Bibliografía venezolanista. - v. 2, Estudios bibliográficos e históricos. Cited in HLAS 26, item 74c.

VENEZUELA. Biblioteca Nacional. Fichas bibliográficas. [Caracas] Impr. Nacional,
1946. 67 p.   (1161
  Compilers: Yolanda Alemán and Olga Mazzei.
264 titles included.

-----. -----. Publicaciones venezolanas y relativas a Venezuela recibidas en la Biblioteca Nacional desde el 1o. de junio hasta el
30 de septiembre de 1940. Caracas, 1940.
32 p.   (1162
  209 titles listed with index.---Jones
2967a.

-----. Ministerio de Fomento. Memoria, 1911.
Caracas, Empresa Guttenberg, 1911.
119 p.   (1163
  Includes (p. 1057-1091): (1) Bibliografía
nacional; (2) Biblioteca estadística; (3)
Obras compradas.---Jones 2968a.

BIBLIOGRAPHY - PROCEDURE

ASSOCIAÇÃO Brasileira de Normas Técnicas, Rio
de Janeiro. Normalização de documentação no
Brasil. Rio de Janeiro, Conselho Nacional
de Pesquisas, Instituto Brasileiro de Bibliografia e Documentação, 1960. 104 p. (1164

BONFANTI, Celestino. Curso de instrucción en
el uso de la biblioteca y preparación de bibliografías. [Maracay] Universidad Central
de Venezuela, [1956] 86 p. (Revista de la
Facultad de Agronomía; Alcance no. 1, mar.
1956)   (1165

BONILLA NAAR, Alfonso. Bases para escribir
un trabajo científico. Bogotá, 1952.
27 p.   (1166
  Cited in Giraldo Jaramillo, p. 134.

BOSCH GARCIA, Carlos. La técnica de investigación documental. México, D.F., Universidad Nacional Autónoma, 1959. 62 p. (1167

CARVALHO, Oswaldo de. Bibliografia de normalização bibliográfica. São Paulo, 1960.
9 p. mimeogr.   (1168
  Cited in Richardson 7240.

DORIA, Irene de Menezes. Processos técnicos
da compilação bibliográfica. [Rio de Janei-
ro] Ministério das Relações Exteriores,
Seção de Publicações [1955] 30 p.   (1169

DUARTE BLASCHKA DE MORALES, Cristina. Introducción bibliográfica para estudiantes de
medicina. [Lima, Tall. Gráf. Cecil] 1958.
65 p.   (1170

GARCES G., Jorge A. Cómo han de traducirse
los documentos paleográficos de Hispanoamérica; acotaciones al libro Normas para la
transcripción y edición de documentos históricos, publicado por la Universidad de
Córdoba, 1957, Argentina. Quito [1961]
82 p. (Publicaciones del Museo Municipal
de Arte e Historia, v. 31)   (1171

IGUINIZ, Juan Bautista. Instrucciones para
la redacción y formación de los catálogos
bibliográficos según el sistema Melvil
Dewey adaptadas a las Bibliotecas Hispano-
Americanas. México, Biblioteca Nacional,
1919. 185 p.   (1172

INTER-AMERICAN Institute of Agricultural Sciences. Lista seleccionada de publicaciones sobre investigación. Selected list of publications on research. Turrialba, 1955. 15 p. (1173

-----. Redacción de referencias bibliográficas; normas de estilo oficiales del IICA. San José, C.R., 1964. 24 p. (Bibliotecología y documentación, no. 4) (1174

LINARES, Emma. Normas elementales a seguir en la preparción de bibliografías o listas de libros u otras publicaciones. Washington, D.C., Unión Panamericana, 1960. 9 p. (Cuadernos bibliotecológicos, no. 2) (1175
"Un reimpreso de las normas compiladas por Emma Linares publicadas en la List of Books Accessioned...Sept. 1959, p. 33-9"

LÜTHOLD, Rosmarie. Normas para a compilação de bibliografias (referências bibliográficas) São Paulo, Reitoria da Universidade de São Paulo, 1958. 9 p. (1176

-----. Normas para a compilação de um catálogo coletivo de periódicos...baseadas nas anteriormente estabelecidas pela Comissão constituída pelas bibliotecarias DD. Guiomar Carvalho Franco [et.al.] São Paulo, Reitoria da Universidade de São Paulo, Biblioteca Central, 1953. 10 p. (1177

MARTINEZ, Angelina. Curso de instrucción en el uso de la biblioteca y preparación de bibliografías. Turrialba, C.R., Instituto

MARTINEZ, Angelina. Curso de (Cont.) Interamericano de Ciencias Agrícolas, 1952. 45 p. (1178

PLACER, Xavier. A bibliografia e sua técnica. [Rio de Janeiro] Ministério da Educação e Cultura, Serviço de Documentação [1955] 46 p. (Coleção Aspectos, 21) (1179

RIO DE JANEIRO. Instituto Oswaldo Cruz. Biblioteca. Bibliografia sôbre composição de trabalhos científicos. Rio de Janeiro, 1957. 5 p. (1180

RIVERA, Rodolfo Osvaldo. Methods and technique in compiling Latin American bibliography. [Durham, N.C.] 1938. 1 p. (1181

SÃO PAULO. Universidade. Biblioteca Central. Normas para a compilação de um catálogo coletivo de periódicos; primeira contribução para os suplementos do catálogo coletivo de periódicos nacional (A-Annals) São Paulo, Biblioteca Central, 1957. 15, 95 p. (1182

VATICAN. Biblioteca Vaticana. Normas para catalogação de impresos; 2. ed. brasileira. Rio de Janeiro, Instituto Brasileiro de Bibliografia e Documentação, 1962. 502 p. (1183

ZAHER, Célia Ribeiro. Guia para pesquisas bibliográficas em ciências e tecnologia; para uso da cadeira de técnica da organização e da pesquisa bibliográfica do curso de pesquisas bibliográficas em tecnologia. Rio de Janeiro, 1961. 104 p. (1184

BIOGRAPHY (COLLECTIVE)

GENERAL

AZPURUA, Ramón. Biografías de hombres notables de Hispano-América. Caracas, Impr. Nacional, 1877. 4 v. (1185
Jones 33.
Authorship shown in biographies.

BARROS ARANA, Diego. Los cronistas de Indias, estudio bibliográfico. (Revista del Pacífico, Valparaíso, t. 4, 1861) (1186
Jones 1401a.
Also in the author's Obras, v. 8.

BERMUDEZ, J. A. Los cronistas de la conquista. (Ensayo de una bibliografía). (Senderos, Bogotá, v. 1, p. 302-10, 1934) (1187
Jones 55.

CABRAL, Jorge. Los cronistas jurídicos y religiosos de la conquista. (Anales de la Facultad de Derecho y Ciencias Sociales,

CABRAL, Jorge. Los cronistas... (Cont.) Buenos Aires, t. 3, 2a. pte. (2a. ser.), p. 461-541, 1913) (1188
A discussion of the works of Agustín de Zárate, Diego Fernández, Polo de Ondegardo, Juan de Matienzo, Fernando de Santillán, Fernando Montesinos, Vicente de Valverde, José de Acosta, Cristóbal de Molina, Miguel Cabello de Balboa, Martín de Murúa, Reginaldo de Lizárraga and Bernabé Cobo.---Jones 80.

CORTES, José Domingo. Diccionario biográfico americano. Este volumen contiene los nombres, con los datos biográficos i enumeración de las obras de todas las personas que se han ilustrado en las letras, las armas, las ciencias, las artes, en el continente americano. Paris, Tip. Lahure, 1875. 552 p. (1189
Jones 112.

DIRECTORY of Caribbean scholars. Río Piedras,
P.R., University of Puerto Rico, Institute
of Caribbean Studies, 1962. unpaged. Loose-
leaf binder. Editor: William A. Trem-
bley.   (1189a

-----. 2d ed. 1964.   (1189b

FELIU CRUZ, Guillermo. Advertencias saluda-
bles a un criticastro de mala ley. Buenos
Aires, 1929. 56 p.   (1190
     From the Boletín del Instituto de Investi-
gaciones Históricas, v. 8-9.---Jones 302.

FIGUEROA, Pedro Pablo. Pensadores americanos.
Santiago de Chile, Impr. de "El Correo,"
1890. 137 p.   (1191
     Contents. - Bartolomé Mitre - Alberto Palo-
meque - Lázaro María Pérez - Ignacio Ramírez
- Juan Carlos Gómez - Familias de escritores
americanos - José Antonio Soffia - Novelistas contemporáneos de América - Francisco
Sosa - Dardo Rocha - Héctor F. Varela - Francisco Octaviano - Poetas de Venezuela - Periodistas del Brasil - Ramón J. Cárcano -
Sarmiento artista.---Jones 145, 1485.

GARCIA CALDERON, Ventura. Semblanzas de América. Rodó, Silva, Herrera y Reissig, Palma,
Chocano, Gómez Carrillo, Almafuerte, Zorrilla
de San Martín, Reyles, Prada y Montalvo.
Madrid, Impr. de G. Hernández y G. Sáez
[1920] 206 p.   (1192
     Interesting studies of Spanish American
men of letters.---Jones 157.

GODOY, José Francisco. Enciclopedia biográfica de contemporáneos. Washington, Estab.
Tip. de T. W. Cadick, 1898. 322 p.   (1193
     A useful reference work for the period
covered.---Jones 167.
     Publications mentioned in biographies.

JUNTA de Historia y Numismática Americana; bibliografía de los miembros. (Boletín de la
Junta, Buenos Aires, v. 2, 1924)   (1194
     Jones 731.

MARTINEZ, Benigno T. Diccionario biográfico-
bibliográfico de escritores antiguos y modernos nacidos en los países del habla castellana, escrito en vista de las fuentes más autorizadas, extractado y traducido de los diccionarios, revistas, periódicos, catálogos y
otras obras biográficas y bibliográficas publicadas en Europa y en América. Introducción. Buenos Aires, Impr. de Stiller y Laass,
1886. 100 p.   (1195
     Contents - 1a. pte. Plan de la obra y su
alcance. - 2a. pte. Fuentes biográficas
(p. 6-7) Fuentes bibliográficas (p. 7-20)
- 3a. pte. Indicadores bibliográficos del tomo I (Title index of works by authors whose
names begin with A) - 4a. pte. Biografías
comprendidas en el tomo I, letra A.

MARTINEZ, Benigno T. Diccionario...(Cont.)
     No more published.---Jones 288.

-----. Gallegos ilustres en América, desde
la conquista hasta nuestros días. Notas
biográficas. Buenos Aires, 1901.
94 p.   (1196
     Viuda do Rico, Bol., May 1906.---Jones 289.

MEDINA, José Toribio. Diccionario de anónimos
y seudónimos hispanoamericanos. Buenos Aires, Impr. de la Universidad, 1925. 2 v.
(Publ. del Instituto de Investigaciones Históricas, no. 26-7)   (1197
     Jones 301.

-----. Escritores hispanoamericanos celebra-
dos por Lope de Vega en el Laurel de Apolo.
Santiago de Chile, Impr. Universitaria,
1924. 134 p.   (1198
     Jones 304.

MENDEZ BEJARANO, Mario. Bio-bibliografía
hispálica de ultramar, o papeletas bio-
bibliográficas de escritores nacidos en la
provincia de Sevilla que han tratado de las
tierras y misiones de ultramar. Madrid,
Impr. de Patronato de Huérfanos de Intendencia e Intervención Militares, 1915.
218 p. (Biblioteca sevillana,
1. serie)   (1199
     Published also in the Boletín de la R.
Sociedad Geográfica, Madrid, v. 57-8, 1915-
1916.---Jones 312.

MILLARES CARLO, Agustín. Investigaciones
biobibliográficas iberoamericanas; época
colonial. México, 1950. 153 p. (Publicaciones del Instituto de Historia, 1a.
ser., no. 17)   (1200

MILLARES CARLO, Agustín, and CALVO, Julián.
Los protomártires del Japón (Nagasaki,
1557) Ensayo biobibliográfico. México,
1954. unpaged.   (1201
     Cited in HLAS, 19, item 3326. Listing
of 416 items, 1592-1953 Reprinted from
Testimonios auténticos acerca de los protomártires del Japón, edited by Eduardo
Enrique Ríos.

MILLARES CARLO, Agustín. Tres estudios bio-
bibliográficos. Maracaibo, Vene., 1961.
215 p.   (1202
     Publication of the Facultad de Humanida-
des y Educación of the Universidad del
Zulia. Contains 44 entries of Juan López
de Palacios Rubios; 34 of Antonio de León
Pinelo and a study of his Epítome; and 24
of Gil González Dávila supplemented by
description of 13 documents and the Teatro
Eclesiástico de la Santa Iglesia de Venezuela y Vida de Sus Obispos.

OSSA VARELA, Peregrino, 1882. Catálogo alfabético de algunos geógrafos y exploradores
que por medio de sus informaciones han hecho
conocer la corteza terrestre. Bogotá, 1951.
79 p.   (1203

OSSORIO Y BERNARD, Manuel. Apuntes para un
diccionario de escritoras americanas del siglo XIX. (España moderna, Madrid, año 3,
no. 36, p. 198-202; año 4, no. 37, p. 196-
206; no. 38, p. 166-73, 1891-1892)   (1204
Jones 345.

PAN AMERICAN Institute of Geography and History, México, D.F. Guía de personas que cul-
tivan la historia de América. México, D.F.,
1951. 507 p. (Publ. del Instituto Panamericano de Geografía e Historia, no.
121)   (1205
Issued also as publication of the Comisión de Historia, 34, and as Vol. 2 of the
series, Guías. Contains 1,399 names, giving
under each a listing of publications.

PEDRELL, Felipe. Diccionario biográfico y bibliográfico de músicos y escritores de música españoles, portugueses e hispano-americanos antiguos y modernos, acopio de datos
y documentos para servir a la historia del
arte musical en nuestra nación. Barcelona,
Tip. de V. Berdós y Feliú, 1894-1897.
715 p.   (1206
"Tomo 1, único publicado, comprendiendo
las letras A-F... Del tomo 2 hemos visto
G-Gaz, 88 págs." (Palau y Dulcet, Manuel
del libreo)---Jones 366a.

PETERSON, Viola E. Discoverers, conquerors,
colonial settlers, liberators, national
leaders of Latin America; a bibliography.
Washington, D.C., Pan American Union, Division of Intellectual Cooperation, 1946.
22 p. mimeogr.   (1207

SABIN, Joseph. A list of the editions of the
works of Louis Hennepin and Alonso [i.e. An-
tonio] de Herrera. New York, J. Sabin &
Sons, 1876. 16 p.   (1207a
Extracted from a Dictionary of books relating to America.

SANCHEZ, José Rogerio. Autores españoles e
hispano-americanos (estudio crítico de sus
obras principales) Madrid, Perlado, Páez y
Cía., 1911. 913 p.   (1208
Jones 429.

SOSA, Francisco. Escritores y poetas sud-ame-
ricanos. México, Of. Tip. de la Secretaría
de Fomento, 1890. 290 p.   (1209
Jones 452.

TORO, Josefina del. A bibliography of the
collective biography of Spanish America.
Río Piedras, P.R., The University, 1938.

TORO, Josefina del ... (Cont.)
140 p. (The University of Puerto Rico Bulletin, series 9, no. 1, Sept. 1938)   (1211
Jones 477.

TORRE REVELLO, José. Los maestros de la bibliografía en América. Buenos Aires, Instituto Argentino de Artes Gráficas, 1941.
24 p.   (1212

TORRES CAICEDO, José María. Ensayos biográficos y de crítica literaria sobre los principales poetas y literatos hispano-americanos; 1. serie. París, Guillaumin y Cía.,
1863. 2 v.   (1213
Jones 483.

-----. -----. 2. ser. París, Dramard Baudry
y Cía., 1868. 480 p.   (1214
Jones 483.

TORRES RIOSECO, Arturo. Novelistas contempo-
ráneos de América. Santiago de Chile, Edit.
Nascimento, 1939. 422 p.   (1215
Jones 491a.
Contents. - Mariano Azuela. - José Eusta-
sio Rivera. - Rómulo Gallegos. - Ricardo
Güiraldes. - Benito Lynch. - Eduardo Barrios.
- Manuel Gálvez. - Joaquín Edwards Bello. -
Carlos Reyles. - Manuel Díaz Rodríguez. -
Pedro Prado. - Rafael Arévalo Martínez.

URIBE MUÑOZ, Bernardo. Mujeres de América.
Medellín, Impr. Oficial, 1934. 460 . (1216
Jones 505. Occupations listed in index.
Publications noted in biographical sketches.

VELAZQUEZ BRINGAS, Esperanza, and VALLE, Rafael Heliodoro. Indice de escritores. México, Herrero Hermanos Sucs., 1928.
320 p.   (1217
Jones 511, 2567.

VICTORICA, Ricardo. Errores y omisiones del
Diccionario de anónimos y seudónimos de
José Toribio Medina. Buenos Aires, 1928.
338 p.   (1218
Jones 302.

-----. Nueva epanortosis al Diccionario de
anónimos...de Medina. Buenos Aires, L. J.
Rosso, 1929. 207 p.   (1219
Jones 302.

WHO'S who in Latin America. Stanford University, Univ. Pr., 1935. 438 p.   (1220
Jones 286. Editor: Percy A. Martin assisted by Manoel da Silveira Soares Cardozo.

-----. 2d ed. 1940. 558 p.   (1221
Editors: Percy A. Martin and Manoel da
Silveira Soares Cardozo.

-----. 3d ed. and enl. 1951. ts. 1-7. (1222
Editor: Ronald Hilton.

WHO'S who in Latin America... (Cont.)
First printing of this edition was released in 1946.

ARGENTINA

ARGENTINA. Comisión Nacional de Cultura.
Obras y autores presentados en los distin-
tos concursos, 1933-1937. Buenos Aires,
1938. 146 p. (1223
Jones 570.

CARBIA, Rómulo D. Los historiógrafos argentinos menorès; su clasificación crítica. Buenos Aires, J. Peuser, 1923. 22 p. (Facultad de Filosofía y Letras; Publ.
no. 17) (1224
Jones 653.

CUTOLO, Vicente Osvaldo. Diccionario de al-
fónimos y seudónimos de la Argentina, 1800-
1930. Buenos Aires, Edit. Elche, 1962.
160 p. (1224a

DURAN, Leopoldo. Contribución a un diccionario de seudónimos en la Argentina. Noticia
preliminar de León Benarós. Buenos Aires,
Librería Huemul [1961] 60 p. (1224b

GALERIA de celebridades argentinas; biografías de los personajes más notables del Río
de la Plata, por los señores Bartolomé Mitre, Domingo F. Sarmiento, Juan M. Gutiérrez, Félix Frías, Luis Domínguez, general Ignacio Alvarez y Thomas, y otros más.
Con retratos litografiados por Narciso Desmadryl. Buenos Aires, Ledoux y Vignal,
1857. 276 p. (1225
Jones 700.

GUIA de autores mendocinos nacionales y extranjeros que se ocupan de Mendoza. Mendoza, Arg., Dirección General de Turismo,
1940. 131 p. (1226
Jones 715a.

GUTIERREZ, Juan María. Apuntes biográficos
de escritores, oradores y hombres de estado
de la República Argentina. Buenos Aires,
Impr. de Mayo, 1860. 294 p. (1227
Jones 718.

LA PLATA. Facultad de Humanidades y Ciencias
de la Educación. El valor testimonial de
cuatro cronistas americanos, Funes, Rui
Díaz, Las Casas y Acosta; con advertencia
del profesor Rómulo D. Carbia. Buenos Aires, "Coni", 1929. 101 p. (Trabajos de
los alumnos en los cursos de seminario y
de lectura y comentario de textos, III:
Historia) (1228
Jones 243.

LEVILLIER, Roberto. Biografías de conquistadores de la Argentina en el siglo XVI; Tucumán. Madrid, Impr. de J. Pueyo, 1933.
250 p. (1229
"Fuentes" at the end of each chapter.---
Jones 754.

MARTINEZ, Teófilo. Contemporáneos ilustres
(argentinos) 1. ser. Paris, Garnier, 1910.
331 p. (1230
Jones 772.

MOLINA ARROTEA, Carlos, GARCIA, Servando, and
CASABOL, Apolinario C. Diccionario biográfico nacional que contiene la vida de todos
los hombres de estado, escritores, poetas,
militares, etc. (fallecidos) que han figu-
rado en el país desde el descubrimiento
hasta nuestros días. v. 1. A-Ch. Buenos
Aires, Impr. Rivadavia de M. Sánchez y Cía.,
1877-1881. 279 p. (1231
No more published. Cited in Salas, Bibl.
de San Martín, t.3, p. 143.---Jones 785.

PARKER, William Belmont. Argentines of today.
New York, The Hispanic Society of America,
1920. 2 v. (Hispanic notes and monographs,
v. 5) (1232
Jones 809.

QUIEN ES QUIEN en la Argentina, biografías
contemporáneas, año 1939. Buenos Aires,
G. Kraft, 1939. 456 p. (1233
Jones 824. Latest ed. at DPU: 1963.

SCOTTO, José Arturo. Los pseudónimos en el
periodismo argentino. (Revista nacional,
Buenos Aires, v. 25, p. 259-62, v. 28,
p. 206-07, v. 29, p. 172-73, 1898-
1900) (1234
Jones 840.

VICTORICA, Ricardo. Crítica estéril. Buenos
Aires, Viau y Zona, 1927. 283 p. (1235
"Diccionario de anónimos y seudónimos
hispanoamericanos, apuntaciones reunidas
por José Toribio Medina": p. 31-58.
"Los incunables bonaerenses por J. Lázaro": p. 79-94.---Jones 513.

BOLIVIA

ARANZAES, Nicanor. Diccionario histórico del
departamento de la Paz; expedientes matri-
moniales, libros de bautizos, archivos oficiales e historiadores contemporáneos consultados. La Paz, J. L. Calderón, 1915.
813 p. (1236
Jones 898.

BLANCO, Federico. Reseña histórica de los
escritores que se han ocupado de la historia natural de Bolivia y de los exploradores de la hoya del Amazonas. Cochabamba,

BLANCO, Federico. Reseña... (Cont.)
Heraldo, 1884. 24 p.   (1237
    Primer sup. a la Biblioteca boliviana de
G. René-Moreno, no. 3790.---Jones 901.

BOLIVIA en el primer centenario de su independencia. New York, The University Society
[1925?] 1142 p.   (1238
    "Apuntes para un diccionario biográfico
boliviano (1825-1925)." p. 362-420.---Jones
907.
    El arte y la literatura en Bolivia, p.
261-361, with bibliographies. Works also
noted in biographies.

CORTES, José Domingo. Galería de hombres cé-
lebres de Bolivia. Santiago, Impr. de la
República, 1869. 187 p.   (1239
    Contents. - Casimiro Olañeta, por F. Re-
yes Ortíz. - Clemente Díez de Medina, por
Agustín Aspiazu. - Antonio José Sucre, por
Manuel Ancízar. - Manuel Sagárnaga, por J.
V. Saravia. - Ildefonso de las Muñecas, por
Santos Machicado. - Simón Bolívar, por J.
M. Loza. - José Manuel Indaburo, por J. J.
Solís. - José Manuel Loza, por F. Reyes Or-
tíz. - Andrés Santa-Cruz, por M. J. Cortés.
- José Ballivián, por Tomás Frías. - Pedro
Domingo Murillo, por J.R. Muñoz Cabrera. -
Al primer campeón paceño, por R. J. Busta-
mante.---Jones 911.

DIAZ A., Julio. Los generales de Bolivia
(Rasgos biográficos) 1824-1925. La Paz,
Impr. Intendencia General de Guerra, 1929.
718 p.   (1240
    Jones 912. Bibliography: p. 717-18.

PARKER, William Belmont. Bolivians of today.
Santiago de Chile, New York [etc.] G. P.
Putnam's Sons, 1920. 319 p.   (1241
    Jones 928.

-----. -----. 2d ed. rev. and enl. London,
New York, The Hispanic Society of America,
1922. 332 p.   (1242
    Jones 929.

URQUIDI, José Macedonio. Bolivianas ilustres.
Prólogo de Ismael Vásquez. La Paz, 1918.
2 v.   (1243
    Jones 943.

BRAZIL

BATISTA, Nair. Pintores do Rio de Janeiro
colonial (notas bibliográficas) (Revista
do Serviço do Patrimonio Histórico e Artístico Nacional, Rio de Janeiro, no. 3,
p. 103-21, 1939)   (1244
    Bibliographical references to 14 colonial
artists.---Jones 972a.

FERNANDES, João Ribeiro. Autores contemporaneos; excerptos de escritores brazileiros e
portuguezes do seculo XIX; 11. ed. refun-
dida. Rio de Janeiro, F. Alves, 1917.
359 p.   (1245
    Bibliographical notes.---Jones 1157.

GALVÃO, Francisco. A Academia de Letras na
intimidade. Rio de Janeiro, A Noite, 1937.
234 p.   (1246
    Brief biographical sketches of 40 members
of the Academy, each sketch preceded by a
bibliography.---Jones 1046a.

GUARANA, Armindo. Diccionario biobibliogra-
phico sergipano. Rio de Janeiro, 1925.
282 p.   (1247
    Jones 1053.

GUIMARÃES, Argeu. Diccionario biobibliogra-
phico brasileiro de diplomacia, política
exterior e direito internacional. Rio de
Janeiro, 1938. 478 p.   (1248
    Jones 1053a.

LIMA, Mario de. Collectanea de auctores mineiros. Bello Horizonte, Imprensa Official,
1922- .   (1249
    Contents: v. 1- Poetas, Prosadores.
    Contains biobibliographical notices.---
Jones 1078.

MACEDO, Joaquim Manuel de, Anno biographico
brazileiro. Rio de Janeiro, Typ. e Lith.
do Imperial Instituto Artistico, 1876.
4 v.   (1250
    "Escripta á convite da illustrada Commi-
ssão Superior da Exposição Nacional de 1875
com o fim de apparecer na Exposição de Philadelphia".
    Brief biographies of 365 persons, one for
each day of the year. Each individual
appears under the date corresponding to
that of his birth or death, or to the date
of some prominent event in the history of
Brazil, with which he was connected.---Jones
1083.
    Publications noted in biographies.

-----. Brazilian biographical annual. Rio
de Janeiro, Typ. e Lith. do Imperial Instituto Artistico, 1876. 3 v.   (1251
    Jones 1084. Publications noted in bio-
graphies.

MARIZ, Vasco. Diccionario bio-bibliográfico
musical; brasileiro e internacional. Rio
de Janeiro, Livraria Kosmos, 1948.
246 p.   (1251a

MELLO, Joaquim Antonio. Biographias de alguns
poetas e homens illustres da provincia de
Pernambuco. Recife, Typ. Universal, 1858-
1860. 3 v.   (1252
    Jones 1097.

MORAES, Alexandre José de Mello, filho. Poetas brasileiros contemporaneos. Rio de Janeiro, Paris, H. Garnier, 1903.
344 p.   (1253
   25 biographical notes.---Jones 1100.

PAIVA, Tancredo de Barros. Achêgas a um diccionario de pseudonymos, iniciaes, abreviaturas e obras anonymas de auctores brasileiros e de estrangeiros, sobre o Brasil ou no mesmo impressas. Rio de Janeiro, J. Leite & Ca., 1929. 248 p.   (1254
   1. pte., Pseudonymos, iniciaes e abreviaturas. - 2. pte., Obras anonymas. - Indice e indicações bio-bibliographicas.---Jones 1123.

REIS, Antonio Simões dos. Pseudonimos brasileiros; pequenos verbetes para um diccionário; 1-5 ser. Rio de Janeiro, Z. Valverde, 1941-1943. 5 v.   (1254a
   Ser. 1, v. 2 published in 1943. Ser. 5, v. 1, published in 1942.

-----. Poetas do Brasil; bibliografia. Rio de Janeiro, Organização Simões, 1949. 2 v. (Bibliografia brasileira, 3)   (1255
   v. 1 (p. 1-176): Arthur de Sousa Abalo; Maria Nunes de Andrade. - v. 2 (p. 177-303): Mário Raul de Morais de Andrade; I. Serro Azul.
   Cited in HLAS, 17, item 2575.

SILVA, João Manuel Pereira da. Os varões illustres do Brazil durante os tempos coloniaes. Pariz, A. Franck, 1858.
2 v.   (1256
   First edition, Rio de Janeiro, 1847, issued under title: Plutarco brasileiro.
   "Notas para uma bibliographia brazileira": t. 2, p. 345-369.---Jones 1137.

SILVA, Manuel Francisco Dias da. Diccionario biographico de brasileiros celebres nas letras, artes, política, philantropia, guerra, diplomacia, industria, sciencias e caridade, desde o anno 1500 até nossos dias. (Contendo cento e tres biographias) Rio de Janeiro, E. & H. Laemmert, 1871.
192 p.   (1257
   Jones 1028.

SISSON, Sebastião Augusto. Galeria dos brasileiros illustres (os contemporaneos); retratos dos homens mais illustres do Brasil, na política, sciencias e letras desde a guerra da independencia até os nossos dias. Rio de Janeiro, Lith. de S. A. Sisson, 1861.
2 v.   (1258
   Jones 1199.

STUDART, Guilherme, barão de. Diccionario bio-bibliographico cearense. Fortaleza, 1910-1915. 3 v.   (1259
   Cited in Apontamentos bio-bibliographicos,

STUDART, Guilherme, barão de ... (Cont.)
   p. 9. "1o. vol. com 480 biographias em 1910, 2o. vol. com 375 biographias em 1913 e 3o. vol. com 252 biographias em 1915".---Jones 1209.

TAUNAY, Affonso de Escragnolle. Escriptores coloniaes; subsidios para a historia da litteratura brasileira. São Paulo, Of. do "Diario official", 1925. 292 p.   (1260
   "Separata do tomo 2 dos Annaes do Museo Paulista."
   Includes "Bibliographia" for each author.
   Contents. - Manuel de Moraes. - Pero de Moraes Madureira. - Diego Garção Tinoco. - André João Antonil. - Frei Gaspar da Madre de Deus. - Manuel Cardoso de Abreu. - Frei Miguel Archanjo da Annunciação. - Theotonio José Juzarte. - Diego de Toledo Lara e Ordonhes. - Addenda á biographia de Manuel de Moraes.---Jones 1034.

VELHO, João Francisco (sobrinho) Diccionario bio-bibliographico brasileiro. Rio de Janeiro, Irmãos Pongetti, 1937-1940.
2 v.   (1261
   Published under the direccion of the Ministerio de Educação e Saude.---Jones 1222.
   The two volumes include the letters A-B.

WELLER, Emile. Les pseudonymes portugais et brésiliens; supplément à l'Index pseudonymorum. (Le Bibliophile belge, Bruxelles, 6. année, p. 183-92, 1871)   (1262
   299 pseudonyms.---Jones 1226.

CHILE

AMUNATEGUI Y SOLAR, Domingo. Hijos ilustres de Chillán. Santiago, Prensas de la Universidad de Chile, 1935. 87 p.   (1263
   Jones 1385. Contains bibliographical footnotes.

CHILEAN Who's who (Quién es quién en Chile) Santiago, Edit. Nascimento, 1937.
530 p.   (1264
   Includes more than 5000 biographies.---Jones 1438.

DESMADRYL, Narciso. Galería nacional, o Colección de biografías y retratos de hombres célebres de Chile, escrita por los principales literatos del país. Santiago, Impr. Chilena, 1854-1861. 2 v.   (1265
   Jones 1446.

DICCIONARIO biográfico de Chile. Santiago, Soc. Impr. y Lit. Universo, 1936.
737 p.   (1266
   Jones 1447.

-----. 2. ed. Santiago, Soc. Impr. y Lit. Universo, 1938. 842 p.   (1267

DICCIONARIO biográfico... (Cont.)
Jones 1448. Newer editions have appeared.
Publications noted in biographies.

ESPEJO, Juan Luis. Relaciones de méritos y
servicios de funcionarios del reino de Chile
(siglos XVIII y XIX) Santiago, Zamorano y
Caperán, 1926. 160 p.   (1268
335 numbers, 215 of which are reprinted
from Medina's Biblioteca hispanochilena
(Santiago de Chile, 1897-1899).---Jones 1470.

FELIU CRUZ, Guillermo. Bio-bibliografía. (Revista chilena de historia y geografía, Santiago, v.47, p. 403-52, 1923)   (1269
Jones 1474.

FIGUEROA, Pedro Pablo. Diccionario biográfico
de Chile; 4a. ed. ilus. con retratos. Santiago, Impr. Barcelona, 1897-1902.
3 v.   (1270
Jones 1482.

-----. Diccionario biográfico de extranjeros
en Chile, Santiago de Chile, Impr. Moderna,
1900. 258 p.   (1270a
Jones 1483. Publications noted in biographies.

GLIGO, María Eugenia, y QUIROGA MORALES, Carmen. Escritores eclesiásticos en Chile,
1842-1956. Santiago, 1957.   (1270b
Thesis presented in the Facultad de Filosofía y Ciencias de la Educación of the Universidad Católica. Cited in Bibliografía
eclesiástica de Chile, p. 323.

LOPEZ L., Guillermo. Indice de seudónimos.
Santiago, Prensas de la Universidad, 1939.
108 p.   (1271
From Anales de la Universidad de Chile,
XCVII, 33-4 (1o. y 2o. trimestres de 1939)
p. 56-159.
Includes "un registro de seudónimos... por
orden alfabético y numerados (1224); una
lista de "firmas y seudónimos de dibujantes
y caricaturistas (38); un índice de autores
...; en seguida van los'impresos seudónimos
chilenos (113), anteriores a 1926, no in-
cluidos en el Diccionario ... de Medina'"
(E. R. Moore).---Jones 1519b.

MEDINA, José Toribio. Diccionario biográfico
colonial de Chile. Santiago, Impr. Elzeviriana, 1906. 1004 p.   (1272
Jones 1539. Publications noted in biographies.

PARKER, William Belmont. Chileans of to-day.
Santiago, New York, 1920. 633 p.   (1273
Jones 1562.

SOLAR CORREA, Eduardo. Escritores de Chile.
Santiago, Impr. Universitaria, 1932- .
v. 1- .   (1274

SOLAR CORREA, Eduardo. Escritores...(Cont.)
v.1, Epoca colonial; v.2, Siglo XIX.---
Jones 1631.

-----. Semblanzas literarias de la colonia.
Santiago, Nascimento, 1933. 320 p.   (1275
Biographical information of Alonso de Er-
cilla, Pedro de Oña, Alonso de Ovalle, Die-
go de Rosales, Miguel de Olivares, Felipe
Gómez de Vidaurre.---Jones 1632.

THAYER OJEDA, Tomás. Los conquistadores de
Chile. Santiago, Impr. Cervantes, 1908-
1913. 3 v.   (1276
Jones 1638. References to publications
in biographies and to sources in footnotes.

-----. Reseña histórico-biográfica de los
eclesiásticos en el descubrimiento y conquista de Chile. Santiago, Impr. Universitaria, 1921. 218 p.   (1277
Reprinted from Revista chilena de historia y geografía, Santiago de Chile, año 11,
t. 35-9, 1919-1923.
Jones 1640.

COLOMBIA

ACHURY VALENZUELA, Darío. El libro de los
poetas. Bogotá, Tip. "Colón", 1937.
128 p.   (1278
Contains biobibliographical notes on contemporary Colombian poets.---Jones 1666.

ACOSTA DE SAMPER, Soledad. Biografías de hombres ilustres o notables de la época del descubrimiento o colonización de Colombia.
Bogotá, Impr. de "La Luz", 1883.
447 p.   (1279
"Lista de las obras": p. 445-47. Includes 287 biographies.---Jones 1668.

LAVERDE AMAYA, Isidoro. Fisonomías literarias de colombianos. Curazao, A. Bethencourt e Hijos, 1890. 341 p.   (1280
Jones 1726.

LIMA, Silvio Julio de Albuquerque. Escritores
de Colombia e Venezuela. Rio de Janeiro,
Federação das Academias de Letras do Brasil,
1942. 210 p.   (1281
Cited in Giraldo Jaramillo, p. 185.

OSPINA, Joaquín. Diccionario biográfico y
bibliográfico de Colombia. Bogotá, "Cromos",
1927- . v. 1 (A-F)- .   (1282
Jones 1742.

OTERO MUÑOZ, Gustavo. Antología de poetas
colombianos, 1800-1930. Bogotá, Edit. de
Cromos, 1930. 342 p.   (1283
Includes information about 85 authors.
---Jones 1743.

OTERO MUÑOZ, Gustavo. Ensayo sobre una bio-
  bibliografía colombiana. (Boletín de historia y antigüedades, Bogotá, v. 23- .
  1936-).   (1284
    Jones 1744.

-----. Semblanzas colombianas. Bogotá, Edit.
  A B C, 1938. 2 v. (Biblioteca de la historia nacional, v. 55-6)   (1285
    Jones 1751. Publications noted in biogra-
  phies.

PARIS, Gonzalo. The young writers of Colombia. (Inter-America, New York, v. 2,
  p. 241-48. 1919)   (1286
    Translated from Cuba contemporánea, v. 19,
  p. 395-402, 1919.---Jones 1753.

PEREZ ARBELAEZ, Enrique. Tentamen de un directorio colombiano de ciencias naturales,
  o quién es quién en ciencias naturales en
  Colombia. Bogotá, Prensas del Ministerio
  de Educación, 1948. 36 p.   (1287

PEREZ ORTIZ, Rubén. Seudónimos colombianos.
  Bogotá, Instituto Caro y Cuervo, 1961.
  276 p.   (1287a
    Titles of books given in many instances
  in which pseudonym was used.

RESTREPO SAENZ, José María. Gobernadores de
  Antioquia, 1571-1819. Bogotá, Impr. Nacional, 1931. 387 p.   (1288
    Jones 1764. Documented with footnotes.

RIVAS, Raimundo. Los fundadores de Bogotá
  (Diccionario biográfico). Bogota, Impr.
  Nacional, 1923. 442 p. (Biblioteca de historia nacional, t. 31)   (1289
    Jones 1768. Contains bibliographical
  footnotes.

COSTA RICA

MacDONALD, Mary B., and McLOUGHLIN, Dwight H.
  Vida y obra de autores de Costa Rica. La
  Habana, Edit. "Alfa", 1941. 79 p.   (1290
    Biobibliographies of 22 authors.---Jones
  1272b.

SOTELA, Rogelio. Escritores y poetas de Costa Rica. San José, Sauter y Cía., 1923.
  703 p.   (1291
    The author is a recognized authority on
  Costa Rican literature.---Jones 1278.

CUBA

CALCAGNO, Francisco. Diccionario biográfico
  cubano. (Comprende hasta 1878) New York,
  N. Ponce de León, 1878-[86] 727 p. (1292
    Jones 1793. Note on back cover gives in-
  formation that the first 120 pages were

CALCAGNO, Francisco. Diccionario... (Cont.)
  printed in New York in 1878, the others in
  Havana in 1886.

FIGAROLA CANEDA, Domingo. Diccionario cubano
  de seudónimos. Habana, Impr. "El Siglo XX,"
  1922. xvi, 182 p.   (1293
    Jones 1824.

GARCIA GAROFALO Y MESA, Manuel. Diccionario
  de pseudónimos de escritores, poetas y periodistas villaclareños. La Habana, J.
  Arroyo, 1926. 61 p.   (1294
    125 pseudonyms noted.---Jones 1832.

GRISMER, Raymond L., and RODRIGUEZ SAAVEDRA,
  Manuel. Vida y obras de autores cubanos.
  La Habana, Edit. "Alfa", 1940. 162 p. (1295
    Biobibliographical studies of 37 authors.
  ---Jones 1836b.

LIZASO, Félix. Ensayistas contemporáneos,
  1900-1920. La Habana, Edit. Trópico, 1938.
  281 p. (Antologías cubanas, 2)   (1296
    Includes useful biobibliographical appen-
  dix on 24 authors.---Jones 1864.

MUÑOZ SAÑUDO, Lisardo. Periodistas y periódicos masónicos de Cuba; 2a. ed. Habana,
  Impr. "El Siglo XX", 1916. 17 p.   (1297
    Jones 1878a.

PARKER, William Belmont. Cubans of to-day.
  New York and London, G. P. Putnam's Sons,
  1919. 684 p. (Hispanic notes and monographs ... issued by the Hispanic Society
  of America)   (1298
    Jones 1880.

VALLE, Rafael Heliodoro. Cuban authors and
  thinkers. (The Hispanic American historical
  review, Baltimore, v. 3, p. 634-38, Nov.
  1920)   (1299
    Jones 1936.

DOMINICAN REPUBLIC

FLOREN LOZANO, Luis. Bibliografía de los profesores universitarios, 1947-1948. [Santo
  Domingo, 1949] 10 p. (Anales, Universidad
  de Santo Domingo, 49/52)   (1300
    Extract.

-----. Bibliografía de los profesores universitarios en 1949. [Santo Domingo, 1950]
  9 p. (Anales, Universidad de Santo Domingo,
  53/56)   (1301
    Extract.

-----. Bibliografía de los profesores universitarios, 1945-51. [Santo Domingo, 1952]
  78 p. (Anales, Universidad de Santo Domingo, 63/64)   (1302
    Cumulated bibliography; includes the pre-

FLOREN LOZANO, Luis. Bibliografía... (Cont.)
viously published separates.

RODRIGUEZ DEMORIZI, Emilio. Seudónimos dominicanos. Ciudad Trujillo, Edit. Montalvo,
1956. 280 p.   (1302a

ECUADOR

CALLE, Manuel J. Biografías y semblanzas.
Quito, Tall. Tip. Nacionales, 1920.
294 p.   (1303
     Jones 1963.

CASTILLO, Abel Romeo. Los gobernadores de
Guayaquil del siglo XVIII (notas para la
historia de la ciudad durante los años de
1763 a 1803); prólogo de Rafael Altamira.
Madrid, Impr. de G. Sáez, 1931.
397 p.   (1304
     Bibliografía: p. 351-61.---Jones 1965.

DESTRUGE, Camilo. Album biográfico ecuatoriano. Guayaquil, Tip. "El Vigilante", 1903-
1905. v. 1-5.   (1305
     310 biographies of prominent men.---Jones
1970.
     Publications mentioned in biographies.

ESPINOSA CORDERO, Nicolás. Estudios literarios y bibliográficos. Cuenca, Impr. del
Colegio Nacional "Benigno Malo", 1934.
265 p.   (1306
     Contents: Don Luis Cordero. - Don Juan
Montalvo. - Inventario bibliográfico de la
ciencia azuaya. - Bibliografía ecuatoriana.
---Jones 1980.

GALLO ALMEIDA, Luis. Literatos ecuatorianos.
Quito, Tip. de la "Prensa Católica", 1921.
249 p.   (1307
     Jones 1982.

-----. 2. ed., corr., aum. y arreglada según
el programa oficial. Riobamba, Tip. "La
Buena Prensa del Chimborazo", 1927.
326 p.   (1308
     Includes bibliographies.---Jones 1983.

RENDON, Víctor Manuel. Escritoras ecuatorianas. (Boletín del Centro de Investigaciones Históricas, Guayaquil, t. 4, p. 112-14,
1936)   (1309
     Jones 2003.

ROLANDO, Carlos A. Los centenarios de 1933.
Doctor Luis Cordero, don Julio Zaldumbide,
doctor Antonio Flores Jijón, doctor José
Modesto Espinoza. Guayaquil, 1933.
79 p.   (1310
     Jones 2007.

-----. Los centenarios de 1950: Dr. Pedro
José Boloña y Roca, Dr. Francisco Javier

ROLANDO, Carlos A. Los centenarios... (Cont.)
Martínez Aguirre, Rvmo. Dr. Juan Félix Proaño, Excmo. Sr. Dr. Andrés Machado, Sr. Dn.
Daniel Enrique Proaño. Guayaquil, Impr. de
la Universidad, 1950. 34 p.   (1311
     Reprinted from Boletín del Centro de In-
vestigaciones Históricas, t. 8, no. 18-20,
p. 167-88, 1950.

-----. Pseudónimos de escritores nacionales
y extranjeros en la prensa guayaquileña.
(Boletín de la Sociedad Ecuatoriana de Estudios Históricos Americanos, Quito, t. 3,
p. 273-75, 1919)   (1312
     Jones 2012.

TORO RUIZ, T. Más próceres de la independen-
cia, otros complementos y rectificaciones.
[Latacunga, Ecuador, 1934] iii, 359 p.   (1313
     Bibliografía: p. ii-iii.
     Additions to and corrections of "Ecuador.
Próceres de la independencia", by Manuel de
Jesús Andrade.---Jones 2020.

EL SALVADOR

ACADEMIA Salvadoreña de la Historia. Biografías de vicentinos ilustres; homenaje al
tercer centenario de la fundación de la ciudad de San Vicente. San Salvador, Impr.
Nacional, 1935. 214 p.   (1314
     Jones 1364.

GUATEMALA

ACADEMIA Guatemalteca. Biografías de litera-
tos nacionales. t. 1. Guatemala, Estab.
Tip. "La Unión," 1889. v. 1.   (1315
     Contents. - R. García Goyena, I. Gómez,
M. Diéguez Olaverri, J. Batres Montúfar, J.
Dieguez Olaverri, A. Marure.---Jones 1283.

ESCRITORES del antiguo reino de Guatemala,
extracto de la Biblioteca hispano-americana
de Beristain. (Anales de la Sociedad de
Geografía e Historia de Guatemala, Guatemala, v. 4, p. 290-320; v. 5 p. 211-41, 336-
50, 454-68, 1927-1928)   (1316
     Jones 1290.

DARDON CORDOVA, Gonzalo. Monografía bibliográfica de libros escritos por los catedráticos de la Facultad de Humanidades. Guatemala, 1953. 7 p.   (1317

LITERATOS que han publicado obras nacionales
desde el año 1871 hasta nuestros días.
Guatemala, Secretaría de Instrucción Pública, 1907. p. 27-30.   (1318
     From the Memoria de la Secretaría de Ins-
trucción Pública.---Jones 1300.

HONDURAS

ALBIR, Francisco José. Writers of Honduras.
(Bulletin of the Pan American Union, Washington, D.C., v. 49, p. 187-90,
1919)   (1319
　　Published also in the Spanish edition of
the Bulletin, June, 1919.---Jones 1318.

ABREU GOMEZ, Ermilo. Clásicos, románticos,
modernos. México, Ediciones Botas, 1934.
217 p.   (1320
　　Critical essays on Sigüenza y Góngora,
Juana Inés de la Cruz, Ruiz de Alarcón, Justo Sierra, Alfonso Reyes, Genaro Estrada,
Peón y Contreras, Torres Bodet, Marinello,
and Silva y Aceves, with bibliographical
notes.---Jones 2025.

MEXICO

AGÜEROS, Victoriano. Escritores mexicanos
contemporáneos. México, I. Escalante, 1880.
224 p.   (1321
　　Jones 2033.

BERMUDEZ DE CASTRO, Diego Antonio. Theatro
angelopolitano, o Historia de la ciudad de
Puebla. Lo publica por vez primera el dr.
N. León. (León, Nicolás. Bibliografía mexicana del siglo XVIII. México, 1908. Sec,
l., 5a. pte., p. 121-354)   (1322
　　Jones 2076.

BERRUETE RAMON, Fernando, and FLORES AGUIRRE,
Jesús. Once poetas de Nueva Extremadura;
con datos bibliográficos y juicios críticos.
México, Herrero Hnos. Sucrs., 1927.
157 p.   (1323
　　Cited in Millares 1026.

CARREÑO, Alberto María. La obra personal de
los miembros de la Academia Mexicana, correspondiente de la Española. México, D.F.,
Tall. Gráf. de la Secretaría de Educación
Pública, 1946 [colophon: 1947]
347 p.   (1324
　　Contains bibliographies of 125 members.

CASTILLO LEDON, Luis. Los mexicanos autores
de óperas. (Anales del Museo Nacional de
Arqueología, Historia y Etnología, México,
t. 2, p. 313-54, 1911)   (1325
　　Jones 2120.

LOS CONTEMPORANEOS; datos para la biografía
de algunos mexicanos distinguidos en las
ciencias, en las letras y en las artes. t.1.
México, Impr. de G. A. Esteva, 1884.
386 p.   (1326
　　No more published; 26 biographies.---Jones
2134a.

DAVILA GARIBI, José Ignacio Paulino. La sociedad de Zacatecas en los albores del régimen
colonial, actuación de los principales fundadores y primeros funcionarios públicos de
la ciudad. México, Antigua Librería Robredo,
1939. 132 p. (Biblioteca histórica mexicana de obras inéditas, 13)   (1327
　　Bibliografía: p. 111-18.---Jones 2144.

DOMINGUEZ, Ricardo. Galería de escritores y
periodistas de la "Prensa asociada". México, Impr. de "El Partido Liberal", 1890.
123 p.   (1328
　　Jones 2153.

EDELMAN, Lily. Mexican mural painters and
their influence in the United States. New
York, Service Bureau for Intercultural Education [1938] 14 p. mimeogr.   (1329
　　Includes a short bibliography.---Jones
2154a.

ESCANDON, Luis A. Poetas y escritores mexicanos. México, Impr. de I. Paz, 1889.
126 p.   (1330
　　Jones 2156.

ESTRADA, Genaro. Poetas nuevos de México;
antología con noticias biográficas, críticas y bibliográficas. México, Ediciones
Porrúa, 1916. 338 p.   (1331
　　Includes biobibliographical notes.---Jones
2162.

FERNANDEZ MacGREGOR, G. Carátulas. México,
Botas, 1935. 284 p.   (1332
　　On contemporary Mexican authors.---Jones
2166.

FRIAS, Valentín F. Noticia bibliográfica de
sus escritos. Santiago de Querétaro, Deme-
trio Contreras, 1906. 16 p.   (1333
　　Cited in Ayala 462.

GONZALEZ OBREGON, Luis. Breve noticia de los
novelistas mexicanos en el siglo XIX. México, Tip. O. R. Spíndola y Cía., 1899.
63 p.   (1334
　　Cited in Millares 1030.

-----. Cronistas e historiadores. México,
Botas, 1936. 223 p.   (1335
　　Contents. - El capitán Bernal Díaz del
Castillo, conquistador y cronista de Nueva
España. - El abate Francisco Javier Clavijero; noticias biobibliográficas. - Vida y
obras de don José Fernando Ramírez. - Don
Francisco del Paso y Troncoso, sabio ar-
queólogo y lingüista mexicano. - Dr. d. José María Marroquí, cronista de la ciudad
de México. - Genaro García, su vida y su
obra.---Jones 2215.

IGUINIZ, Juan Bautista. Bibliografía biográfica mexicana. México, 1930. t. 1 (546 p.)

IGUINIZ, Juan Bautista. Bibliografía...(Cont.)
(Monografías bibliográficas mexicanas,
no. 18) (1336
   Jones 2251.
   Contents: v. 1: Repertorios biográficos.

-----. Bibliografía de novelistas mexicanos;
ensayo biográfico, bibliográfico y crítico;
precedido de un estudio histórico de la novela mexicana por Francisco Monterde García
Icazbalceta. México, 1926. 432 p. (Monografías bibliográficas mexicanas,
no. 3) (1337
   Jones 2252.

-----. Catálogo de seudónimos, anagramas e
iniciales de escritores mexicanos. París,
México, Librería de la Vda. de Ch. Bouret,
1913. 62 p. (1338
   Includes a list of 18 members of the Academia de los Arcades de Roma.
   Additions to the Catálogo (89 pseudonyms)
are given in Biblos, v. 1, no. 46 (Nov. 29,
1919).---Jones 2254.

-----. Los historiadores de Jalisco; epítome
bibliográfico. México, Of. Impr. de la
Secretaría de Hacienda, 1918.
114 p. (1339
   Jones 2259, 2349.

LEON, Nicolás. Hombres ilustres y escritores
michoacanos; galería fotográfica y apuntamientos biográficos. Morelia, Impr. del
Gobierno, a cargo de J. R. Bravo, 1874.
104 p. (1340
   Jones 2293.

-----. Los precursores de la literatura mé-
dica mexicana en los siglos XVI, XVII,
XVIII y primer tercio del siglo XIX (hasta
1833). (Gaceta médica de México, México,
D.F., t. 10, p. 3-94, 1916) (1341
   Jones 2298.

MANEIRO, Juan Luis. De vitis aliquot Mexi-
canorum aliorumque qui sive virtute, sive
litteris Mexici imprimis floruerunt.
Bononiae, ex. Type. Laelii a Vulpe, 1791-
1792. 3 v. (1342
   Jones 2314.

MARTINEZ ALOMIA, Gustavo. Historiadores de
Yucatán. Apuntes biográficos y bibliográficos de los historiadores de esta península desde su descubrimiento hasta fines
del siglo XIX. Campeche, Tip. "El Fénix",
1906. 360 p. (1343
   Jones 2320.

MEXICO. Universidad Nacional. Instituto de
Investigaciones Estéticas. Bibliografías
de investigadores. México, D.F., 1961.
233 p. (1344
   Suplemento no. 2 del no. 30 de los Anales

MEXICO. Universidad Nacional ... (Cont.)
del Instituto de Investigaciones Estéticas.
Compiler: Justino Fernandez.

MOORE, Ernest Richard. Bibliografía de novelistas de la revolución mexicana. México, Fondo de Cultura Económica, 1941.
190 p. (1345
   Jones 2371a.

NARANJO, Francisco. Diccionario biográfico
revolucionario. México, D.F., Impr. Edit.
"Cosmos," 1935. 317 p. (1346
   Bibliografía: p. 12.---Jones 2375.

OSORES Y SOTOMAYOR, Félix. Noticias bio-
bibliográficas de alumnos distinguidos del
Colegio de San Pedro, San Pablo y San Ildefonso de México (hoy Escuela n. preparatoria) México, Vda. de C. Bouret, 1908.
2 v. (Documentos inéditos o muy raros para
la historia de México, publ. por Genaro
García, t. 19-21) (1347
   Jones 2399.

PEZA, Juan de Dios. La vida intelectual mexicana; poetas y escritores modernos en
México, revista crítico-biográfica del estado intelectual de la República Mexicana.
(Nueva revista de Buenos Aires, v. 8,
p. 550-79; t. 9, 124-44, 448-71, 598-618,
1883) (1348
   Jones 2424.

PIMENTEL, Francisco. Novelistas y oradores
mexicanos. (His Obras. México, 1904.
t. 5, p. 259-508) (1349
   Jones 2430.

ROMERO DE TERREROS Y VINENT, Manuel. Los
grabadores en México. México, Of. Impr.
de la Secretaría de Hacienda, 1918.
28 p. (1350
   Jones 2349. In prize winning compilation
of bibliographies chosen by the National
Library in 1915. Includes 89 entries of
engravers with references to the works in
which engravings appeared.

SOSA, Francisco. Biografías de mexicanos distinguidos. México, Of. Tip. de la Secretaría de Fomento, 1884. 1115 p. (1351
   Jones 2506. Occupations identified in
index of names. Publications noted in biographies.

-----. Manual de biografía yucateca. Mérida,
Impr. de J. B. Espinosa e Hijos, 1866.
228 p. (1352
   Jones 2509.

VELAZQUEZ CHAVEZ, Agustín. Contemporary Mexican artists. New York, Covici-Friede,
1937. 304 p. (1353
   Selected bibliography: p. 285-304.---

VELAZQUEZ CHAVEZ, Agustín ... (Cont.)
   Jones 2568.

VERA, Fortino Hipólito. Escritores eclesiásticos de México, o Bibliografía histórica
   eclesiástica mexicana. Amecameca, 1880.
   49 p.   (1354
   Jones 2572.

WRIGHT DE KLEINHAUS, Laureana. Mujeres notables mexicanas. México, Tip. Económica,
   1910. 246 p.   (1355
   Jones 2589.

PANAMA

LAURENZA, Roque Javier. Los poetas de la ge-
   neración republicana (conferencia leída en
   el Instituto Nacional de Panama la tarde
   del 17 de enero de 1933) Panamá, Edit. La
   Moderna, 1933, 121 p.   (1356
   Jones 1352.

PARAGUAY

PARKER, William Belmont. Paraguayans of to-
   day. Buenos Aires, New York, The Hispanic
   Society of America, 1921. 317 p.   (1357
   A second edition was published in London,
   1921.---Jones 2616.

PERU

BERMEJO, Vladimiro. Arequipa (bio-bibliografía de Arequipeños contemporáneos) v. 1.
   Arequipa, Establecimientos Gráf. "La Colmena", 1954. 478 p.   (1358
   Contains summaries of 58 authors of the
   region with a listing of their works.
   Cited in An. Bibliog. Peruano, 1953/1954,
   item 139.

MENDIBURU, Manuel de. Diccionario histórico-
   biográfico del Perú. Parte primera que
   corresponde a la época de la dominación española. Lima, Impr. de J. F. Solís, 1874-
   1890. 8 v.   (1359
   "Catálogo de las obras y manuscritos que
   deben consultarse": v. 1, 25 p.---Jones
   2697.

-----. Segunda edicion con adiciones y notas
   bibliográficas publicadas por Evaristo San
   Cristóval; estudio biográfico del general
   Mendiburu por el dr. d. José de la Riva-
   Agüero y Osma. Lima, Impr. "Enrique Pala-
   cios" 1931-1935. 11 v.   (1360
   "Catálogo de las obras y manuscritos que
   deben consultarse para la historia de la
   América Latina y particularmente del Perú":
   v. 1, p. 15-52.---Jones 2698.

MOSTAJO, Francisco. Contribución al catálogo
   de pseudónimos. (Boletín bibliográfico, Biblioteca Central de la Universidad, Lima,
   año 12, p. 13-25, 1909)   (1361
   Includes "Pseudónimos de escritores arequipeños" (104); "Pseudónimos de escritores
   de otros departamentos" (71); "Pseudónimos
   de extranjeros que escribieron en el Perú"
   (10).---Jones 2704.

LA OBRA de los médicos en el progreso del Perú,
   prólogo del prof. Leónidas Avendaño, palabras del prof. dr. Hermilio Valdizán.
   Lima, Edit. Perú Moderno, 1934.
   213 p.   (1362
   Jones 2706.

PARKER, William Belmont. Peruvians of to-day.
   Lima, Southwell Pr., 1919. 616 p.   (1363
   Jones 2709.

POLO, José Toribio. Historia nacional. Crítica del Diccionario histórico-biográfico
   del Perú del señor general Mendiburu. Lima,
   Impr. de "El Comercio", por J. R. Sánchez,
   1891. 83 p.   (1364
   Jones 2700.

SAN CRISTOVAL, Evaristo. Apéndice al Diccio-
   nario histórico biográfico del Perú. Lima,
   Gil, 1935-1938. 4 v.   (1365
   Useful as supplementing Mendiburu.---
   Jones 2699.

PORTUGAL

FONSECA, Martinho Augusto Ferreira da. Subsidios para um diccionario de pseudonymos,
   iniciaes e obras anonymas de escriptores
   portuguezes, contribução para o estudo da
   litteratura portugueza ... com poucas pa-
   lavras servindo de prologo pelo academico
   dr. Theophilo Braga. Lisboa, Por ordem e
   na Typ. da Academia Real das Sciencias,
   1896. 298 p.   (1366
   Jones 1040.

MACHADO, Diogo Barbosa. Bibliotheca lusitana
   histórica, crítica e cronológica. Na qual
   se comprehende a noticia dos authores portuguezes, e das obras que compuserão desde
   o tempo da promulgação da ley da graça até
   o tempo prezente. Lisboa, 1741-1759.
   4 v.   (1367
   A new edition in 4 volumes was published
   in Lisbon, 1930-1935.---Jones 969.

PUERTO RICO

ASENJO, Conrado. Quién es quién en Puerto
   Rico, diccionario biográfico de record personal, 1933-1934- . San Juan, Real Hnos.,
   n.d. v. 1- .   (1368

ASENJO, Conrado. Quién es quién... (Cont.)
Jones 2781.
Authorship shown in biographies.

CUCHI COLL, Isabel. Oro nativo: colección
semblanzas puertorriqueñas contemporáneas.
San Juan, 1936. 125 p.   (1369
Jones 2788.

GRISMER, Raymond L., and ARROYO, César I. Vi-
da y obras de autores puertorriqueños. La
Habana, Edit. "Alfa", 1941. 71 p.   (1370
Jones 2793a.

LIMON DE ARCE, José Ramón. Poetas arecibeños,
1832-1904. Arecibo, H. C. del Pozo, 1926.
292 p.   (1371
Jones 2794.

SPAIN

RAMIREZ DE ARELLANO, Carlos. Ensayo de un catálogo biográfico-bibliográfico de los escritores que han sido individuos de las cuatro órdenes militares de España. (Colección
de documentos inéditos para la historia de
España. Madrid, 1894. t. 109,
p. 1-243)   (1372
Jones 389.

REZABAL Y UGARTE, José de. Biblioteca de los
escritores que han sido individuos de los
seis colegios mayores: de San Ildefonso de
la Universidad de Alcalá, de Santa Cruz de
la Valladolid, de San Bartolomé, de Cuenca,
San Salvador de Oviedo, y del Arzobispo de
la de Salamanca. Madrid, Impr. de Sancha,
1805. 472 p.   (1373
Jones 398.

URUGUAY

ARAUJO, Orestes. Gobernantes del Uruguay.
Montevideo, Dornaleche y Reyes, 1903.
2 v.   (1374
Jones 2812.
Contains bibliographical footnotes.

ARECHAVALETA, José. Naturalistas en el Uruguay. (Revista histórica de la Universidad,
Montevideo, v. 1, p. 478-506, 828-42,
1907)   (1375
Biobibliographical data concerning natu-
ralists who have studied the flora and fauna
of Uruguay.---Jones 2814.

CARVE, Luis. Apuntaciones biográficas (Revista histórica de la Universidad, Montevideo,
v. 1, p. 30-57, 355-371, 651-70; v. 2, p.
99-108, 430-34, 459-65, 724-34,
1907-1909)   (1376
Contents. - S. Vázquez, J. B. Blanco, M.
Herrera y Obes, L. J. de la Peña, J. B.

CARVE, Luis. Apuntaciones... (Cont.)
Lamas, C. Juanicó, E. Echeverría, F. Cas-
tellanos, L. A. Fernández, F. Ferreira, A.
Lamas, J. G. Palomeque, F. A. Antuña, F. Acu-
ña de Figueroa, F. Ferreira y Artigas, J. A.
Varela, G. Pérez Gomar, F. Araucho, J. M.
Besnes Irigoyen, C. M. Ramírez, T. Narvaja,
A. de Villegas, J. L. Terra, J. J. de Herre-
ra, M. Herrero y Espinosa, J. C. Blanco.---
Jones 2825.

DE-MARIA, Isidoro. Rasgos biográficos de hom-
bres notables de la República Oriental del
Uruguay. Montevideo, 1879-1880. 3 v.   (1377
Jones 2827.

-----. Another ed. Montevideo, C. García y
Cía., 1939. 4 v.   (1378
Bibliografía; v. 4, p. 8-10.

FERNANDEZ SALDAÑA, José María. Diccionario
uruguayo de biografías, 1810-1940. Montevideo, Amerinda, 1945. 1366 p.   (1379
First edition entitled: Fichas para un
diccionario uruguayo de biografías. Writings
are noted in biographies.

-----. Fichas para un diccionario uruguayo
de biografías. Montevideo, Tall. Gráf. 33,
1945. 2 v.   (1380
Second edition entitled: Diccionario uruguayo de biografías. Writings are mentioned
in biographies.

SCARONE, Arturo. Apuntes para un diccionario
de seudónimos y de publicaciones anónimas.
(Contribución al estudio de la bibliografía
del Uruguay) Montevideo, Impr. "El Siglo
Ilustrado", 1926. 75 p.   (1381
Jones 2862.

-----. -----. 2. ed., notablemente aum. y corr.
Prólogo de Ariosto D. González. Montevideo,
Impr. Nacional, 1934. 351 p. (Publ. de la
Biblioteca Nacional de Montevideo)   (1382
Jones 2863.

-----. Diccionario de seudónimos y de algunos anónimos [uruguayos] (Boletín de la
Biblioteca Nacional, Caracas, año 2, no. 8,
p. 225-40, 1925)   (1383
Jones 2866.

-----. Diccionario de seudónimos del Uruguay;
prólogo de Ariosto. D. González. Montevideo,
García, 1941. 532 p.   (1384
Cited in Musso 599.

-----. -----. 2a ed. Montevideo, Claudio
García, 1942. 632 p.   (1385
Cited in Musso 600.

-----. Uruguayos contemporáneos; obra de consulta biográfica. Diccionario de datos referentes a compatriotas ... y de algunos ex-

SCARONE, Arturo. Uruguayos... (Cont.)
tranjeros desde largo tiempo incorporados y
descollantes en nuestra vida pública. 1. ed.,
con un apéndice. Montevideo, "Renacimiento",
1918. 676 p.   (1386
  Jones 2868.

-----. -----. nuevo diccionario de datos biográficos y bibliográficos. Montevideo, "Casa A. Barreiro y Ramos", s.a., 1937.
610 p.   (1387
  "Apéndice: Destacados compatriotas que
han fallecido desde 1918 - año de la primera publicación de esta obra - hasta la fecha de aparecer esta edición": p. 545-610.
---Jones 2869.

SEIJO, Carlos. Carolinos ilustres, patriotas
y beneméritos. Montevideo, Impr. "El Siglo
Ilustrado", 1936. 244 p.   (1388
  Jones 2871. In addition to publications
noted in biographies, the author has given
considerable bibliographic information in
the 299 footnotes.

URUEÑA GONZALEZ, Camilo. Crónicas de Treinta
y Tres; siete lustros de periodismo bravío.
V. I, Los periodistas. [Montevideo, Prome-
teo, 1948] 83 p.   (1389
  Musso, 409, notes that this is only volume published.

ʼCHARDON, Carlos Eugenio. Resumen de los trabajos bio-bibliográficos llevados a cabo en
Caracas y Puerto España (Trinidad) de diciembre 26 de 1944 a febrero 9 de 1945, para el libro "Los Naturalistas en la América
Latina". [Caracas, 1945] 8 h.
mimeogr.   (1390
  Cited in An. venez. 1945, item 218.

MACHADO, José Eustaqui. Seudónimos y anónimos en la literatura y en la política venezolanas. (Boletín de la Biblioteca Nacional, Caracas, no. 5, p. 131-34, 1924) (1391
  Jones 2929.

MONTENEGRO, M. V. Esbozos de venezolanos notables. Cartagena, Tip. de García e Hijos,
1902. 154 p.   (1392
  Jones 2935.

TEJERA, Felipe. Perfiles venezolanos; o, Galería de hombres célebres de Venezuela en
las letras, ciencias y artes. Caracas, Impr.
Sanz, 1881. 478 p.   (1393
  Jones 2962.

VENEZUELA. Biblioteca Nacional. Escritores
venezolanos fallecidos entre 1942 y 1947.
Caracas, 1948. 72 p. (Alcance al Anuario
bibliográfico venezolano)   (1394

BIOGRAPHY (INDIVIDUAL)

ABREU, JOÃO CAPISTRANO DE

CARMO, José Arimateia Pinto do. Bibliografía
de Capistrano de Abreu. Rio de Janeiro, Imprensa Nacional, 1943. 133 p. (Instituto
Nacional do Livro, Coleção B 1; Bibliografía 3)   (1395

PAIVA, Tancredo de Barros. Bibliografía ca-
pistraneana. São Paulo, Diario Official,
1931. 31 p.   (1396
  Bibliography of the works of João Capistrano de Abreu, 1853-1927, Brazilian histo-
rian.---Jones 1124a.
  Reprinted from Annaes, Museu Paulista,
São Paulo, t. 4, p. 481-512.

VIANNA, Helio. Capistrano de Abreu; ensaio
bio-bibliográfico. Rio de Janeiro, Serviço
de Documentação. Ministério da Educação e
Cultura, 1955. 126 p. (Coleção "Vida brasileira," no. 3)   (1397

ABREU GOMEZ, ERMILO

VALLE, Rafael Heliodoro, and VARGAS SALAS, José E. Ermilo Abreu Gómez; notas bibliográ-

VALLE, Rafael Heliodoro, and VARGAS... (Cont.)
ficas. Washington, Ateneo Americano de Washington, 1953. 14 p.   (1398
  Also published in Hispania, v. 33, Aug.
1950.

ACEVEDO DIAZ, EDUARDO

URUGUAY. Biblioteca Nacional. Bibliografía
crítica de Eduardo Acevedo Diaz. [Montevi-
deo] n.d. 4 p. mimeogr.   (1399
  Cited in Musso 261.

ACOSTA SAIGNES, MIGUEL

VENEZUELA. Universidad Central. Escuela de
Biblioteconomía y Archivos. Miguel Acosta
Saignes. Caracas, 1963. 36 p. (Serie bi-
bliográfica, 1)   (1400

ACOSTA SOLIS, MISAEL

ACOSTA SOLIS, Misael. Bio-bibliografía ...
Actuación científica, distinciones y carre-

ACOSTA SOLIS, Misael ... (Cont.)
ra docente, ordenadas cronológicamente hasta 1940. [Quito, Impr. "Ecuador", 1940?]
27 p.   (1401

ACUÑA, MAMERTO

ACUÑA, Mamerto. Reseña de trabajos científicos y labor docente. Buenos Aires, Librería "Las Ciencias", 1918. 51 p.   (1402
Cited in Binayan, item 36.

AGOTE, LUIS

AGOTE, Luis. La cátedra de clinica medica
(su concurso) Buenos Aires, Impr. de Martino y Gutiérrez, 1915. 147 p.   (1403
Banayan, item 37: Bibliography of the
author, p. 29-47.

AGRAMONTE Y LOYNAZ, IGNACIO

PERAZA SARAUSA, Fermin. Ignacio Agramonte y
Loynaz. Habana, 1943. 7 p. (Publicaciones de la Biblioteca Municipal de La Habana, Ser. C: Guías bibliográficas, 6) (1404

AGUAYO, ALFREDO MIGUEL

AGUAYO, Jorge. Bibliografía de Alfredo M.
Aguayo. Habana, Cultural, 1950.
119 p.   (1404a

ALBERDI, JUAN BAUTISTA

KREIBOHM, Enrique. Aquel "muchacho" Alberdi
y ensayo de bibliografía "alberdiana". Tucumán, Facultad de Derecho y Ciencias Sociales, Universidad Nacional de Tucumán,
1960. 121-64 p.   (1405
"Separata del Cuaderno no. 5 del Instituto de Derecho del Trabajo 'Juan B. Alberdi'"

ALAMAN, LUCAS

VALADES, José C. Alamán, estadista e historiador. Mexico, Antigua Librería Robredo,
1938. 576 p.   (1406
Bibliografía: p. 541-57.---Jones 2542.

ALENCAR, JOSE MARTINIANO

LEÃO, Mucio. José de Alencar; ensaio bio-
bibliográfico. Rio de Janeiro, 1955.
71 p. (Publ. da Academia Brasileira) (1407

ALMEIDA, MANUEL ANTÔNIO DE

CRUZ, Eddy Dias da (Marques Rebêlo, pseud.)
Bibliografia de Manuel Antônio de Almeida.
Rio de Janeiro, Departamento de Imprensa
Nacional, 1951. 188 p. (Instituto Nacio-
nal do Livro, Coleção B 1; Bibliografia
7)   (1408
Contains 258 entries.

ALTAMIRA Y CREVEA, RAFAEL

BIBLIOGRAFIA y biografía de Rafael Altamira
y Crevea. [México, D.F.] Edit. Mediterrani, [1946] 67 p.   (1409

-----. Apendice. [México, D.F.,] Ediciones
Mediterrani, [1948] 41 p.   (1410

ALTAMIRANO, IGNACIO MANUEL

VALLE, Rafael Heliodoro. Bibliografía de Ignacio Manuel Altamirano. México, D. A. P.
P., 1939. 155 p. (Bibliografías mexicanas,
no. 8)   (1411
Jones 2548.

WARNER, Ralph Emerson. Bibliografía de Ignacio Manuel Altamirano. México, Impr. Universitaria, 1955. 219 p. (Serie Letras,
no. 19)   (1412

ALURRALDE, MARIANO

ALURRALDE, Mariano. Títulos, cargos, y trabajos experimentales y clínicos. Buenos
Aires, Agustín Etchepareborda 1909.
12 p.   (1413
Cited in Binayán, item 38.

ALVAREZ, ALEJANDRO

INSTITUT de France. Académie des Sciences
Morales et Politiques. Notice biographique
sur Alejandro Alvarez ... [Paris, Imprimerie
et Librairie Centrales des Chemins de Fer,
Imprimerie Chaix, 1930] p. 237-47.   (1414
"Extrait des notices de l'Académie des
Sciences Morales et Politiques de l'Insti-
tute de France.

ALVAREZ DE TOLEDO, JOSE

TRELLES Y GOVIN, Carlos Manuel. Discursos
leídos en la recepción pública del Sr. Carlos M. Trelles y Govin. Contesta en nombre
de la corporación el Capitán Sr. Joaquín
Llaverías. Habana, Impr. "El Siglo XX",
1926. 207 p.   (1415
At head of title: Academia de la Historia.

TRELLES Y GOVIN, Carlos Manuel ... (Cont.)
"Bibliografía de Alvarez de Toledo".
p. 131-39.
"Bibliografía revolucionaria cubana, 1803-
1830": p. 139-50.
"Bibliografía del sr. Carlos M. Trelles y
Govín, 1920 a 1926": p. 188-90.---Jones 1925.

ALVES, ANTÔNIO DE CASTRO

HORCH, Hans Jürgen Wilhelm. Bibliografia de
Castro Alves. Rio de Janeiro, Instituto
Nacional do Livro, 1960. 259 p. (Coleção
B-1, Bibliografia, 12)   (1416

PEIXOTO, Afrânio. ... Castro Alves, ensaio
bio-bibliográfico. Rio de Janeiro, Off.
Industrial Graphica, 1931. 111 p. (Publ.
da Academia Brazileira. [Bibliotheca de
cultura nacional; classicos brasileiros]
III: Bibliografia [1])   (1417

AMADO, JORGE

BRAZIL. Biblioteca Nacional. Jorge Amado:
30 años de literatura. [Rio de Janeiro,
1961] 36 p.   (1418
Exhibition. Cited in Rev. do livro, 6
(23-4): 236, set./dez. 1961.

AMBROSETTI, JUAN BAUTISTA

AMBROSETTI, Juan Bautista. Trabajos publicados. Buenos Aires, Impr. de Juan A. Alsina,
1904.   (1419
Cited in PAU Bibliographies 1928.

AMEGHINO, FLORENTINO

AMBROSETTI, Juan Bautista. Doctor Florentino
Ameghino, 1814-1911. (Anales del Museo Nacional de Historia Natural, Buenos Aires,
t. 15, p. xi-lxxxi, 1912)   (1420
Bibliografía, p. xlix-lxi. A list of
Ameghinos' works will also be found in José
Ingenieros' Las Doctrinas de Ameghino (Buenos Aires, 1919, p. 203-216) See also Debenedetti's "Nómina de los trabajos de Ambrosetti" in Ambrosetti's Superticiones y
leyendas (Buenos Aires, 1917. p. 227-35)
and his article in Revista de filosofía,
Buenos Aires, v. 1, p. 241-59, 1917.---
Jones 555.

CASTELLANOS, Alfredo. Florentino Ameghino,
su obra arqueológica, antropológica, psí-
quica. (Revista de la Universidad de Córdoba, Córdoba, t. 4, p. 228-75,
1916)   (1421
Bibliografía: p. 245-75.---Jones 659.

SOCIEDAD "Luz" (Universidad Popular) Buenos
Aires. Ameghino. Homenaje de la Sociedad
Luz en el XXV aniversario de su muerte,
1911-agosto 6-1936. Buenos Aires, Impr. Fe-
deración Gráfica Bonaerense, 1936. 239 p.
(Sociedad Luz (Universidad Popular) [Publ.]
Ser. 1, t. 7)   (1422
Includes bibliographies.---Jones 847.

AMUNATEGUI, MIGUEL LUIS

BRISEÑO, Ramón. Catálogo bibliográfico y un
tanto razonado, de las obras de don Miguel
Luis Amunátegui. Santiago de Chile, Impr.
Gutenberg, 1890. 30 p.   (1423
Cited in Laval, item 69.

ROSALES, Justo Abel. Bibliografía del literato don Miguel Luis Amunátegui. Santiago
de Chile, Impr. de la Libertad Electoral,
1888. 30 p.   (1424
Jones 1378.

AMUNATEGUI SOLAR, DOMINGO

FELIU CRUZ, Guillermo. Ensayo de una bibliografía de Domingo Amunátegui Solar, 1876-
1946; setenta años de labor pública consa-
grada a las disciplinas históricas y literarias, a la enseñanza y a la administración. Precedida de una "Historia de mis
libros" del mismo Amunátegui Solar. Santiago de Chile, Edit. Nascimento, 1961.
430 p.   (1425
Reprinted from Anales de la Universidad
de Chile, no. 121-22.

GIMENEZ PASTOR, Arturo. Una época bonaerense: el ochenta. (Homenaje de la Universidad de Chile a ... don Domingo Amunátegui.
Santiago de Chile, 1935. v. 2,
p. 217-40)   (1426
Jones 1491.

ANCHIETA, JOSE DE

ANCHIETA, José de. Cartas, informações,
fragmentos históricos e sermões. Rio de
Janeiro, Civilização Brasileira, 1933.
567 p. (Cartas jesuíticas, 3)   (1427
Publicações da Academia Brasileira. "Bibliografía do padre Joseph de Anchieta,
S. J.": p. 27-31.---Jones 953.

ANDRADE, MARIO DE

REIS, Antônio Simões dos. Mario de Andrade;
bibliografia sôbre a sua obra. [Rio de Ja-
neiro] Ministério da Educação e Cultura,
Instituto Nacional do Livro [1960?] 47 p.
(Suplemento da Revista do livro, 3)   (1428

ANDRADE, MARTIM FRANCISCO RIBEIRO DE

BELLIDO, Remigio de. Bibliografia andradina.
São Paulo, 1915. 87 p.   (1429
A bibliography of the works of José Boni-
facio de Andrade e Silva, Martim Francisco
Ribeiro de Andrade, and Antonio Carlos de
Andrade e Silva.---Jones 973.

ANDRADE, OLEGARIO VICTOR

BURZIO, Blas F. A. La obra poética de Olega-
rio V. Andrade. (Ensayo crítico) Buenos
Aires, 1930. 236 p.   (1430
Bibliografía: p. 1-11.---Jones 638c

ANDRADE, VICENTE DE P.

SOCIEDAD Mexicana de Geografía y Estadística.
Sesión celebrada la noche del día 9 de septiembre de 1915 en memoria del socio Sr. Lic.
Canónigo Don Vicente de P. Andrade (1844-
1915) México, D.F., Impr. Stephan y Torres,
1915. 102 p.   (1431
Catálogo de obras por Juan B. Iguíniz:
p. 50-99.

ANGELIS, PEDRO DE

ARANA, Enrique. Bibliografía de Pedro de Angelis, 1784-1859, su labor histórica, periodística, y literaria. Buenos Aires, 1933.
75 p.   (1432
First published in Boletin de la Biblioteca de la Facultad de Derecho y Ciencias Sociales, año 1, no. 5.---Jones 565.

ANGHIERA, PIETRO MARTIRE D'

SALAS, Carlos I. Estudio biográfico-biblio-
gráfico de la vida y obras del doctor Pedro
Mártir de Anglería. Córdoba, Est. Gráfico
"Los Principios", 1917. 96 p.   (1433
Only 50 copies printed. Reviewed in La
Prensa, New York, May 25, 1921.---Jones 426.

APARICIO, FRANCISCO DE

BUENOS AIRES. Universidad. Facultad de Filosofía y Letras. Publicaciones de Francisco
de Aparicio. Buenos Aires, Tall. Gráf. A.
Plantié, 1939. 14 p.   (1434
Listing of 94 entries. Cited in HLAS 5,
item 212.

ARAI, ALBERTO T.

BIBLIOGRAFIA del Arquitecto Alberto T. Arai.
México, D.F., 1956. 15 p. mimeogr. (VIIa

BIBLIOGRAFIA del Arquitecto... (Cont.)
Feria Mexicana del Libro)   (1435
Cited in Bol., Bibl. Nac., Mexico, jul./
sept. 1956, p. 52.

ARANGO, IGNACIO

ANTUNEZ, Francisco. Un gran impresor del siglo XIX. Morelia, Impr. de la Escuela Federal Tipo, 1933.   (1436
Cited in Millares, item 1104.

ARAOZ ALFARO, GREGORIO

ARAOZ ALFARO, Gregorio. Exposición de titulos
y trabajos. Buenos Aires, A. Etchepareborda, 1910. 12 p.   (1437
Cited in Binayán, item 40.

ARCE, JOSE

ARCE, José. Concurso de clínica quirúrgica.
1918. 24 p.   (1438
Cited in Binayán, item 41.

ARGÜELLO, SANTIAGO

MOORE, Ernest Richard. Bibliografía de Santiago de Argüello (1872-1940) [México, D.
F.]   (1439
Reprinted from Revista Iberoamericana,
5(10): 427-37, oct. 1942.

ARMAS Y CARDENAS, JOSE DE

VALVERDE Y MARURI, Antonio L. Elogio del Lic.
José de Armas y Cárdenas (Justo de Lara)
Habana, Impr. "El Siglo XX", 1923.
225 p.   (1440
Bibliografía: p. 148-76.---Jones 1937.

ARLT, ROBERTO

BECCO, Horacio Jorge, and MASOTTA, Oscar.
Roberto Arlt. Buenos Aires, Instituto de
Literatura Argentina "Ricardo Rojas", Uni-
versidad de Buenos Aires, 1959. 10 p.
(Guías bibliográficas, 2)   (1440a

ARTIGAS, JOSE GERVASIO

ARDAO, María Julia, and CAPILLAS DE CASTELLA-
NOS, Auróra. Bibliografía de Artigas. Montevideo, Comisión Nacional Archivo Artigas
[1953-1958] 2 v.   (1441

BEALER, Lewis W. Contribution to a bibliography on Artigas and the beginnings of Uruguay,

BEALER, Lewis W. Contribution... (Cont.)
1810-1820. [Durham, N.C.] p. 108-34. (1442
Reprinted from the Hispanic American historical review, v. 11, 1931.
Jones 2821.

URUGUAY. Biblioteca Nacional. Bibliografía;
José Artigas. Montevideo, n.d. 4 p.
mimeogr.   (1443
Cited in Musso 260.

ASCASUBI, HILARIO

RODRIGUEZ MOLAS, Ricardo. Contribución a la
bibliografía de Hilario Ascasubi (1807-1875)
Buenos Aires, Fondo Nacional de las Artes
[1962]   (1444
Section 2 of Bibliografía argentina de artes y letras, no. 12, p. 51-85, oct./dic.
1961.

SPERONI VENER, Julio. Un folleto raro de
Ascasubi: la edición original del Paulino
Lucero. Montevideo, 1960. 36 p.   (1445
Reprinted from Revista histórica, Monte-
video, t. 30, no. 88-90, p. 510-43, ag. 1960
Cited in Musso 583.

AYERZA, ABEL

AYERZA, Abel. Títulos y trabajos (1886-1914)
Buenos Aires, Tall. Gráf. Duilio Sorrentino,
1914. 47 p.   (1446
Cited in Binayán, item 42

AZARA, FELIX DE

GONZALEZ, Julio César. Don Félix de Azara,
apuntes bio-bibliográficos. Buenos Aires,
Edit. Bajel, 1943. 125 p.   (1447
Bibliografía: p. 91-106 with 19 entries.

TORRES, Luis María. Los estudios geográficos
y etnográficos de Azara. Buenos Aires,
1923. 11 p.   (1448
Jones 868d.

-----. Les études géographiques et historiques de Félix d'Azara. Buenos Aires, 1905.
20 p.   (1449
Jones 868e.

AZEVEDO, ARTUR

SEIDL, Roberto. Artur Azevedo; ensaio bio-
bibliografico. Rio de Janeiro, Empresa
Editora ABC, 1937. 175 p. (Publ. da Academia Brasileira) [Classicos brasileiros]
3: Bibliografia [8])   (1450
Jones 1193.

AZEVEDO, MANUEL ANTONIO ALVARES DE

PIRES, Homero. Alvares de Azevedo; ensaio
bio-bibliográfico. Rio de Janeiro, Off.
Industrial Graphica, 1931. 96 p. (Publ.
da Academia Brasileira. Classicos brasileiros, 3: Bibliografia, 3)   (1451
Jones 1147.

AZUELA, MARIANO

GONZALEZ, Manuel Pedro. Bibliografía del novelista Mariano Azuela. La Habana,
1941.   (1452
Cited in Millares 499, and appearing in
Revista bimestre cubano, Habana, 48 (1):
50-72, jul./ag. 1941.

MOORE, Ernest Richard. Biografía y bibliografía de don Mariano Azuela. Libros, artículos, crítica. (Abside, México D.F., v. 4,
no. 2, p. 53-62; no. 3, 50-64, 1940) (1453
Jones 2371b.

VILLASEÑOR Y VILLASEÑOR, Ramiro. Bibliografía de Mariano Azuela. (Letras de México,
México D.F., 6, p. 8, 16 de abril,
1937)   (1454
Jones 2577.

BACHILLER Y MORALES, ANTONIO

NUÑEZ GONZALEZ, Ana Rosa. La vida bibliográfica de Don Antonio Bachiller y Morales.
Habana, Librería Martí, 1955. 20 p. (1455

PERAZA SARAUSA, Fermín. Antonio Bachiller y
Morales. Habana, 1942. 7 p. (Publ. de
la Biblioteca Municipal de la Habana; ser.
C: Guías bibliográficas 5)   (1456

-----. Bachiller, el primer bibliógrafo cubano. Habana, Biblioteca Municipal de la
Habana, 1951. 4 p. (Publ., ser. C: Guías
bibliográficas, 18)   (1457

BALLIVIAN, ADOLFO

SANTIBAÑEZ, José María. Rasgos biográficos
de Adolfo Ballivián. Santiago de Chile,
Impr. de "La República" de J. Núñez, 1878.
145 p.   (1458
"Escritos de don Adolfo Ballivián":
Apéndice, p. 3-19.---Jones 1612.

BAÑADOS, FEDERICO MATIAS

BIBLIOGRAFIA de los señores d. Federico Matías Bañados, d. Guillermo M. Bañados Honorato y d. Amable Bañados Honorato. Santiago de Chile, Impr. Universitaria, 1915.

BIBLIOGRAFIA de los señores... (Cont.)
27 p.   (1459
    In part from Revista de bibliografía chi-
lena y extranjera, t. 3, p. 213-16.---Jones
1404.

BANCHS, ENRIQUE

FERNANDEZ, Belisario. Bibliografía de Enrique
Banchs. Buenos Aires, Fondo Nacional de las
Artes, [1960]   (1460
    Section 2 of Bibliografía argentina de ar-
tes y letras, no. 7, p. 51-99, jul./set.
1960.

BANDELIER, ADOLPH FRANCIS ALPHONSE

HODGE, Frederick Webb. Bibliografía de Adolph
Francis Alphonse Bandelier. (Boletin bibliográfico de la Biblioteca Central de la Universidad de San Marcos, Lima, v. 1, no. 8-9,
1923)   (1461
    Jones 2246.

BARAHONA VEGA, CLEMENTE

BARAHONA VEGA, Clemente. Bibliografía de Don
Clemente Barahona Vega, 1879-1915. Santiago
de Chile, Impr. Universitaria, 1915.
59 p.   (1462
    Reprinted from Revista de bibliografía
chilena y extranjera, t. 3, p. 219-71.---
Jones 1400.

BARALT, RAFAEL MARIA

GRASES, Pedro. Ficha bio-bibliográfica de
Rafael María Baralt. Caracas, 1959.
10 p.   (1463
    Reprinted from Revista nacional de cultu-
ra, Caracas, no. 136, set./oct. 1959.

-----. Rafael María Baralt, notas y bibliografía. Caracas, 1960. p. 49-90.   (1464
    Reprinted from Boletin de la Academia Na-
cional de la Historia, no. 169.

BARBOSA, RUY

NERY, Fernando. Ruy Barbosa (Ensaio bio-bibliográfico) Rio de Janeiro, Edit. Guanabara,
Waissmann-Koogan, [1932] 282 p.   (1465

PEREIRA, Antonio Baptista. Ruy Barbosa, catálogo das suas obras. Rio de Janeiro, 1929.
226 p.   (1466
    Jones 968.

PIRES, Homero. Rui Barbosa e os livros, [con-
ferencia na Casa de Rui Barbosa, a 5 de no-

PIRES, Homero ... (Cont.)
vembro de 1938] 5. ed. Rio de Janeiro, Casa de Rui Barbosa, 1949. 106 p.   (1467

BARNET, ENRIQUE BUENAVENTURA

LE ROY Y CASSA, Jorge Eduardo. Elogio del dr.
Enrique B. Barnet. Habana, Impr. El Debate,
1918. 36 p.   (1468
    81 publications of Dr. Barnet are listed.
---Jones 1859.

BARRIGA, VICTOR M.

VALLE GOICOCHEA, Luis. Bibliografia de obras
y artículos publicados por Fr. Victor M.
Barriga. Arequipa, 1947. 50 p.   (1468a

BARRIOS, JUSTO RUFINO

BIBLIOGRAFIA sobre el general Justo Rufino
Barrios. (Boletin de la Biblioteca Nacional, Guatemala, año 4, no. 14, p. 580-83,
1935)   (1469
    Jones 1285.

BARROS ARANA, DIEGO

CHIAPPA, Víctor M. Bibliografía de don Diego
Barros Arana (ensayo) Temuco, Impr. Alemana, 1907. 112 p.   (1470
    Jones 1421.

DONOSO, Ricardo. Barros Arana, educador, historiador y hombre público. Santiago, Universidad de Chile, 1931. 337 p.   (1471
    Bibliografía: p. 279-329.---Jones 1451.

BAUZA, FRANCISCO

XALAMBRI, Arturo E. Rememoración de Francisco
Bauzá. Montevideo, Mosca, 1950.
40 p.   (1472
    Cited in Musso 299.

BECQUER, GUSTAVO ADOLFO

BENITEZ, Rubén. Ensayo de bibliografía razonada de Gustavo Adolfo Bécquer. Buenos Aires, Univ. de Buenos Aires, Facultad de Filosofía y Letras, 1961. 158 p. (Instituto
de Literatura Española. Bibliografías críticas, 1)   (1473

BELLO, ANDRES

BELLO, Andrés. The Odes of Bello, Olmedo and
Heredia, with an introduction by Elijah

BELLO, Andrés. The Odes of Bello... (Cont.)
Clarence Hills. New York and London, G.P.
Putnam's Sons, 1920. 153 p. (Hispanic notes
& monographs, issued by the Hispanic Society
of America. Peninsular series, 3)   (1474
Bibliography: p. 137-53.---Jones 203b.

CARO, Miguel Antonio. Homenaje del "Repertorio
colombiano" a la memoria de Andrés Bello en
su centenario. Bogotá, 1881.   (1475
Jones 1696.

GRASES, Pedro. Contribución al estudio de la
bibliografía caraqueña de don Andrés Bello.
Caracas, Tip. Americana, 1944 53 p.   (1476
Includes some 50 titles of works of Bello
printed in Caracas.

ORREGO VICUÑA, Eugenio. Don Andrés Bello.
Santiago de Chile, Prensas de la Universidad,
1935. 285 p.   (1477
Contains bibliography.---Jones 1559.

VAÏSSE, Emilio. Bibliografía de Don Andrés
Bello, y de sus descendientes, 1781-1916.
Santiago de Chile, Impr. Universitaria, 1917.
125 p.   (1478
Jones 2963.

VENEZUELA. Biblioteca Nacional. Don Andrés
Bello; bibliografía de trabajos sobre su
vida y su obra. [Caracas, 1956.] 119 p.
(Catálogo analítico, entrega no. 1)   (1479
Compiled by Martín Perea Romero.

BENAVIDES, ALONSO DE

HODGE, Frederick Webb. Bibliography of fray
Alonso de Benavides. New York, Museum of
the American Indian, Heye Foundation, 1919.
39 p. (Indian notes and monographs, v. 3,
no. 1)   (1480
Jones 2247.

BERG, CARLOS

GALLARDO, Angel. Carlos Berg; reseña biográfica. Buenos Aires, 1902.
p. xxiii-xl.   (1481
Reprinted from Anales del Museo Nacional,
Buenos Aires, 2a., IV, 1902. The article
in the Anales is paged: ix-xl.
Cited in Binayán, item 54.

BERISTAIN, DE SOUZA, JOSE

MEDINA, José Toribio. D. José Mariano Beristain de Souza; estudio bio-bibliográfico.
Santiago de Chile, Impr. Elzeviriana, 1897.
52 p.   (1482
Jones 2075.

BERNARDEZ, FRANCISCO LUIS

LACUNZA, Angélica Beatriz. Bibliografía de
Francisco Luis Bernárdez. Buenos Aires,
1962. 26 p. (Universidad de Buenos Aires,
Facultad de Filosofía y Letras, Instituto
de Literatura Argentina "Ricardo Rojas"
Guías bibliográficas, 7)   (1482a

BIEDMA, JOSE JUAN

CANTER, Juan. Bio-bibliografía de José Juan
Biedma. Buenos Aires, Tall. Casa Jacobo
Peuser, 1934. p. 603-792.   (1483
"Del Boletín del Instituto de Investiga-
ciones Históricas...año 12, t. 17, p. 603-
792, Buenos Aires, oct. 1933-jun. 1934".---
Jones 646.

BOERGER, ALBERTO

BOERGER, Alberto. Publicaciones técnicas del
Dr. Alberto Boerger desde su llegada al Uruguay, 1912-1936. Montevideo, Urta & Curbelo, 1937. 8 p.   (1484
Cited in Musso 274.

BOLIVAR, SIMON

ACADEMIA Nacional de la Historia, Caracas.
Biblioteca General. Catálogos de las bibliotecas bolivariana i mirandina de la
misma institución. Trabajos efectuados por
Erasmo Colina y Dolores Bonet de Sotillo,
bajo la dirección [de] J. A. Cova. Edición
acordada por el Ministerio de Relaciones
Exteriores. Caracas, Impr. Nacional, 1957.
146 p.   (1485

BELAUNDE, Víctor Andrés. Bolívar and the
political thought of the Spanish American
revolution. Baltimore, The Johns Hopkins
Pr., 1938. 451 p.   (1486
Selective bibliography: p. 407-27.---
Jones 2888.

KEY-AYALA, Santiago. Series hemerobibliográ-
ficas; la. serie bolivariana. Caracas,
Tip. Americana, 1933. 202 p.   (1487
1,000 references to articles on Bolívar
in periodicals, mostly Venezuelan.---Jones
2923.

LaFOND, Georges. Bolivar et la libération de
l'Amérique du Sud. Paris, Payot, 1931.
355 p.   (1488
Bibliographie: p. 338-46.---Jones 2924.

OSORIO JIMENEZ, Marcos A. Bibliografía crítica de la detracción bolivariana. Poema
de Angel Francisco Brice. Caracas, Ediciones de la Sociedad Bolivariana de Venezuela,

BIOGRAPHY

OSORIO JIMENEZ, Marcos A. ... (Cont.)
1959. 331 p.   (1489

PAN AMERICAN UNION. Columbus Memorial Library.
Bibliography of the Liberator, Simón Bolívar.
Washington, D.C., 1930. 22 p. (Bibliogra-
phic ser., no. 1) mimeogr.   (1490
Jones 2938.

-----. -----. Washington, D.C., 1933.
107 p. (Bibliographic ser., no. 1. rev.
and enlarged)   (1491
Commemorative of the 150th anniversary of
the birth of Simón Bolívar. Title also in
Spanish. Includes all publications on Bolívar in the public catalogue of the Library
of Congress, in the National Library at Caracas, and in the Columbus Memorial Library
of the Pan American Union.---Jones 2939.

-----. Simón Bolívar; bibliography of the li-
berator Simón Bolívar. Washington, D.C.,
Govt. Print. Off., 1931. 21 p. (U.S. 71st.
Cong., 3rd. sess. Senate. doc. 231)   (1492

PEREYRA, Carlos. La juventud legendaria de
Bolívar. Madrid, M. Aguilar, 1932.
523 p.   (1493
Bibliography: p. 7-21.---Jones 2942.

VALLE, Rafael Heliodoro. Bibliografía Bolivariana. (Revista de revistas, México, D.F.
14 dic., 1930)   (1494
See also his Bibliografía mínima de Bolívar, in Eurindia, Mexico, D.F., p. 563-75,
1930.---Jones 2963a.

VIVANCO, Carlos A. Contribution to the Boli-
varian bibliography of Ecuador (1825 to
1930) (Pan American book shelf, Washington,
v. 3, no. 2, p. 74-92, 1940)   (1495
Jones 2974.

BONILLA, POLICARPO

SANSO, Aro, ALDUVIN, Ricardo D., etc. Policarpo Bonilla; algunos apuntes biográficos
por Aro Sanso; un estudio del dr. Ricardo
D. Alduvín; y esquema para una biografía
por Rafael Heliodoro Valle. México, Impr.
Mundial, 1936. 558 p.   (1496
Bibliografía sumaria: p. 553-56.---Jones
1327a.

BONILLA NAAR, ALFONSO

CURRICULUM vitae, 1936-1944. 100 trabajos
científicos. Bogotá, Edit. Cromos, 1945.
16 p.   (1497
Medical studies of Alfonso Bonilla Naar.
Cited in Giraldo Jaramillo, p. 160.

BORGES, JORGE LUIS

LUCIO, Nodier, and REVELLO, Lydia. Contribución a la bibliografía de Jorge Luis Borges.
Buenos Aires, Fondo Nacional de las Artes
[1962]   (1498
Section 2 of Bibliografía Argentina de artes y letras, no. 10-11, 43-112, abr./sept.
1961.

BOSE, MARGARITA ELISABETH

BOSE, Margarita Elisabeth Heiberg de. Antecedentes, trabajos y títulos. [La Plata, Olivieri y Domínguez, 1939] 25 p.   (1499

BOSE, WALTER BJÖRN LUDOVICO

BOSE, Walter Björn Ludovico. Antecedentes,
trabajos y publicaciones. [La Plata, Tall.
de Olivieri y Domínguez, 1938] 47 p. (1500

-----. Trabajos y publicaciones, 1924-1940.
[La Plata, Olivieri y Domínguez, 1944]
45 p.   (1501

-----. Veinte años de labor historiográfica
(1924-1944) Buenos Aires [La Plata, Tall.
Graf. Olivieri & Domínguez] 1945.
62 p.   (1502

BRANCO, CAMILLO CASTELLO

MOTA, João Xavier da. Camilleana; collecção
das obras de Camillo Castello Branco. Rio
de Janeiro, Companhia Impr., 1891.
24 p.   (1503
Cited in Reis, item 140.

BRANDSEN, FEDERICO

SALAS, Carlos I. Bibliografía del coronel
don Federico Brandsen. Buenos Aires, Compañía Sud-Americana de Billetes de Banco,
1909. 311 p.   (1504
Jones 2738.

-----. 2a ed., considerablemente aum. Buenos
Aires, Compañía Sudamericana de Billetes de
Banco, 1910. 418 p.   (1505
Valuable for the period of the war of in-
dependence.---Jones 2739.

BRICEÑO, SANCHO

DAVILA, Vicente. Don Sancho Briceño; su monumento en Trujillo. El arbol de los Bri-
ceños. Caracas, Tip. Americana, 1927.
72 p.   (1506
Jones 2903.

BRISEÑO, RAMON

BRISEÑO, Ramón. Breve reseña biográfica y bibliográfica del señor Don Ramón Briseño.
Santiago de Chile, Impr. y Encuad. Barcelona, 1897. 35 p.   (1507
Ochsenius, item 32, states that the pamphlet is signed by Baltasar Alemany, Luis
Montt and Ramón C. Briseño, but that it is
said that the work was done by Ramón Briseño.

BRUNER, J. JUAN

BRUNER PRIETO, Fernando. Bibliografía del Dr.
J. Juan Bruner, 1825-1899. Santiago, Impr.
Universitaria, 1916. 98 p.   (1508
Reprinted from Revista de bibliografía chi-
lena y extranjera, año 4, p. 158-80. Cited
in Ochsenius, item 38.

BUNGE, CARLOS OCTAVIO

LLAMBI, Carlos E. Noticia bibliográfica sobre
los escritos publicados e inéditos de Carlos
Octavio Bunge. (Revista de filosofía, Buenos Aires t. 4, no. 4, 1918)   (1509
Jones 759.

BURMEISTER, CARLOS GERMAN

BERG, Carlos. Carlos Germán Conrado Burmeister. (Anales del Museo Nacional de Historia
Natural, Buenos Aires, 2a. ser., t. 1,
p. 313-57, 1895)   (1510
Bibliografía: p. 325-57.---Jones 596.

BYRNE, BONIFACIO

MOLINER, Israel M. Indice bio-bibliográfico
de Bonifacio Byrne, [Matanzas] Atenas de
Cuba, 1943. 11 p.   (1511

CABALLERO Y RODRIGUEZ, AGUSTIN

HOMENAJE al ilustre habanero pbro. dr. José
Agustín Caballero y Rodríguez en el cente-
nario de su muerte, 1835-1935. Habana, Mu-
nicipio de la Habana, 1935. 75 p. (Cuader-
nos de historia habanera)   (1512
Bibliografía de José Agustín Caballero y
Rodríguez por F. González del Valle y E.
Roig de Leuchsenring.---Jones 1848.

CABRAL, ALFREDO DO VALLE

RODRIGUEZ, José Honório. Alfredo do Valle
Cabral. [Rio de Janeiro] Biblioteca Na-
cional, 1954. 38 p.   (1513
Reprinted from Anais da Biblioteca Nacio-

RODRIGUES, José Honório ... (Cont.)
nal, v. 73.

CABRERA, LUIS

LUIS CABRERA: bibliografía; aspectos de su vida; páginas escogidas. México, Edit. Cultura, 1951. 129 p.   (1514

CALLEGARI, GUIDO VALERIANO

CALLEGARI, Guido Valeriano. Bibliografía americana, 1906-1936. Trento, Tip. Editrice
Mutilati e Invalidi, 1936. 20 p.   (1515

CAMOES, LUIZ DE

BIBLIOGRAFIA camoneana; resenha chronologica
das edições das obras de Luiz de Camões e
das suas traduções impressas. Rio de Janeiro, Typ. da Gazeta de Noticias, 1880.
53 p.   (1516
Cited in Reis, item 86.

LUIZ de Camões; homenagem da "Gazeta de Noticias" de 10 de junho de 1880. Rio de Janeiro, Typ. da Gazeta de Noticias, 1880.
223 p.   (1517
Cited in Reis 84.

SILVA, João Alves Mendes da. Catalogo de Camoneana. Rio de Janeiro, Typ. do Jornal do
Commercio de Rodrigues & C., 1900.
20 p.   (1518
Cited in Reis, item 187.

CAMPO, ESTANISLAO DEL

AYESTARAN, Lauro. La primera edición del
Fausto de Estanislao del Campo. Montevideo,
Universidad, 1959. 12 p.   (1519
Reprinted from Revista iberoamericana de
literatura, Montevideo, año 1, no. 1, p. 9-
20, ag. 1959. Cited in Musso 542.

CARO, MIGUEL ANTONIO

CARO, Víctor E., and TOLEDO, Augusto. Bibliografías de don Miguel Antonio Caro por Víctor E. Caro y de don Rufino José Cuervo por
Augusto Toledo. Bogotá, Edit. ABC, 1945.
xiv, 183 p.   (1520
Cited in Torres Quinteros.

CARRASCO, GABRIEL

CARRASCO, Gabriel. Bibliografía y trabajos
públicos. Buenos Aires, Impr. Lit. y
Encuad. de Jacobo Peuser, 1894. 59 p. (1521

CARRASCO, Gabriel. Bibliografía... (Cont.)
Cited in Binayán, item 69. Jones, 657,
cites 60 p.

CARRERA, JOSE MIGUEL

MEDINA, José Toribio. Bibliografía de don José Miguel Carrera. (Revista chilena de historia y geografía, Santiago, v. 40, p. 326-
71, 1921)   (1522
Adiciones, por Ramón A. Laval: v. 40.
p. 458-99.---Jones 1530.

-----. Ensayo de una bibliografía de las obras
de don José Miguel Carrera. La Plata, Tall.
del Museo de la Plata, 1892. 36 p.   (1523
"Del tomo 4 de la Revista del Museo de la
Plata, p. 53 y siguientes".---Jones 1542.

CARRILLO Y ANCONA, CRESCENCIO

CANTON ROSADO, Francisco, and RIVERO FIGUEROA,
José. Dos vidas ejemplares; ensayos biográ-
ficos del Ilmo. Sr. Obispo de Yucatán D.
Crescencio Carrillo y Ancona, y de Monseñor
Norberto Domínguez. Habana, Impr. "Avisador
Comercial", 1918. 86 p.   (1524
Bibliografía de Monseñor Carrillo, p. 65-
78.

CASAS, BARTOLOME DE LAS

BECERRA DE LEON, Berta. Bibliografía del Pa-
dre Bartolomé de las Casas. La Habana [Ucar
García] 1949. 67 p. (Sociedad Económica de
Amigos del País. Biblioteca. Ediciones
4)   (1525
Contains 256 items.

HANKE, Lewis, and GIMENEZ FERNANDEZ, Manuel.
Bartolomé de las Casas 1474-1566; bibliografía crítica y cuerpo de materiales para el
estudio de su vida, escritos, actuación y
polémicas que suscitaron durante cuatro siglos. Santiago de Chile, Fondo Histórico y
Bibliográfico José Toribio Medina, 1954.
xxxi, 394 p.   (1526

SABIN, Joseph. A list of the printed editions
of the works of Fray Bartolomé de las Casas,
Bishop of Chiapa. New York, J. Sabin &
Sons, 1870. 27 p.   (1526a
Extracted from A Dictionary of books re-
lating to America.

CASAVALLE, CARLOS

PICCIRILLI, Ricardo. Carlos Casavalle, impresor bibliófilo; una época de la bibliografía
americana. Buenos Aires, Edit. J. Suárez,
1942. 328 p.   (1527

PICCIRILLI, Ricardo. ... (Cont.)
Contains "Colección periódicos que poseyó
y clasificó d. Carlos Casavalle" and "Algunas de las obras impresas por Carlos Casavalle".

CASTAÑO, CARLOS ALBERTO

CASTAÑO, Carlos Alberto. Antecedentes, títu-
los y trabajos. Buenos Aires, "La Semana
Médica", 1918. 42 p.   (1528
Cited in Binayán, item 45.

CASTEX, MARIANO RAFAEL

CASTEX, Mariano Rafael. Títulos y trabajos.
Buenos Aires, Impr. de Coni Hnos. 1910.
96 p.   (1529
Cited in Binayán, item 47.

-----. Another edition. Buenos Aires, A. G.
Buffarini. [1927?] 42 p.   (1530

CASTRO BARROS, PEDRO IGNACIO

ARANA, Enrique. El doctor Pedro Ignacio de
Castro Barros; rasgos de su actuación política; bio-bibliografía. (Estudios, revista
mensual, Buenos Aires, t. 57. p. 171-244,
1937)   (1531
Jones 566.

CATARINA DE SAN JUAN

CARRASCO PUENTE, Rafael. Bibliografía de Catarina de San Juan y de la china poblana.
Prólogo de Carlos González Peña. México,
Secretaría de Relaciones Exteriores, Departamento de Información para el Extranjero,
1950. xvii, 149 p. (Monografías bibliográficas mexicanas, 2a. ser., no. 3)   (1532

CERVANTES SAAVEDRA, MIGUEL DE

ELIZ, Leonardo. En el tricentenario del Principe de los ingenios. Apuntes para una bibliografía chilena sobre Cervantes. Valparaíso, Impr. Royal, 1916. 10 p.   (1533
From España en Chile (periodical) Cited
in Ochsenius, item 60.

COSTAGLIOLA C., Sergio. Cervantes en la Biblioteca Nacional; ensayo bibliográfico.
Santiago de Chile, Edit. Universitaria, 1950.
151 p.   (1534
Reprinted from Anales de la Universidad
de Chile, 3/4 trim. 1949.

MEDINA, José Toribio. Cervantes en las letras
chilenas (Notas bibliográficas) Santiago de

MEDINA, José Toribio ... (Cont.)
Chile, Impr. Universitaria, 1923.
80 p.   (1535
Jones 1538.

ORTEGA TORRES, José J. Cervantes en la litera-
tura colombiana. Bogotá, Instituto Caro y
Cuervo, 1949. 31 p.   (1535a
Cited in Bryant 240.

TORRES QUINTERO, Rafael. Cervantes en Colombia; ensayo de bibliografía crítica de los
trabajos cervantinos producidos en Colombia.
Bogotá, Instituto Caro y Cuervo, 1948.
63 p.   (1536
From the Boletin del Instituto Caro y Cuervo. t. 4, no. 1, 1948.

VALLE, Rafael Heliodoro, and ROMERO, Emilia.
Bibliografía cervantina en la America Española. México, Impr. Universitaria, 1950.
xiv, 313 p.   (1537

CHAGAS, CARLOS

RIO de Janeiro. Instituto Oswaldo Cruz. Biblioteca Carlos Chagas; bio-bibliografia.
Rio de Janeiro, 1959. 44 p.   (1538

CIEZA DE LEON, PEDRO DE

OTERO D'ACOSTA, Enrique. Pedro de Cieza de
Leon; estudio cronológico-bibliográfico.
(2o. Congreso Internacional de Historia de
América, Buenos Aires, 1938. v. 5,
p. 250-75)   (1539

CIPRIANO DE UTRERA (Fray)

ALFAU Durán, Vetilio. Fray Cipriano de Utrera (notas bibliográficas) Ciudad Trujillo,
Impr. Dominicana, 1951. 33 p.   (1540

CLAVIJERO, FRANCISCO JAVIER

GARCIA, Rubén. Bio-bibliografía del historiador Francisco Javier Clavijero. México,
D.F., 1931. 22 p. (México. Departamento
del Distrito Federal. Dirección General de
Acción Cívica, publ. no. 153)   (1541

GARCIA GRANADOS, Rafael. Clavijero; dato bibliográfico. México, D.F., Impr. Mundial,
1932. 15 p.   (1542
Publication of the Universidad Nacional
Autónoma de México --- Millares, item 522.

GONZALEZ OBREGON, Luis. El abate Francisco
Javier Clavijero; noticias bio-bibliográficas. México, Departamento Edit. de la Dirección General de Bellas Artes, 1917.

GONZALEZ OBREGON, Luis. El abate... (Cont.)
30 p.   (1543
Cited in Millares, item 523. Also appeared in Gonzalez Obregón, Cronistas e historiadores (México, Botas, 1936. p. 81-123)
---Jones 2215.

COELHO NETTO, HENRIQUE

COELHO NETTO, Paulo. Bibliografia de Coelho
Netto. Rio de Janeiro, Borosoi, 1956.
34 p.   (1544

COMAS, JUAN

COMAS, Juan. Curriculum vitae. México, D.F.,
1960. 43 p.   (1545

CONI, EMILIO R

CONI, Emilio R. El dr. Emilio R. Coni; su la-
bor científica (1867-1910) Buenos Aires,
Impr. de Coni Hnos., 1910. 96 p.   (1546
Cited by Binayán.---Jones 672.

COLUMBUS, CHRISTOPHER

R. ACADEMIA de la Historia, Madrid. Bibliografía colombina, enumeración de libros y
documentos concernientes a Cristóbal Colón
y sus viajes; obra que publica la Real Academia de la Historia por encargo de la Junta Directiva del Cuarto Centenario del Descubrimiento de América. Madrid, Est. Tip.
de Fortanet, 1892. 680 p.   (1547
Compilers: E. Saavedra, Juan de la Rada
y Delgado, M. Menéndez y Pelayo, A. M. Fa-
bié and C. Fernández Duro. For criticism
and additions, see H. Harrisse, Christophe
Colomb et les académiciens espagnols.
(Zentralblatt für bibliothekswesen, v. 11.
p. 1-70, 1894).---Jones 1.

FUMAGALLI, Giuseppe and AMAT DI S. FILIPPO,
Pietro. Bibliografia degli scritti italiani o stampati in Italia sopra Cristoforo
Colombo, la scoperta del Nuovo Mondo, e i
viaggi degli italiani in America. Roma,
Auspice il Ministero della Pubblica Istru-
zione, 1893. 217 p. (Raccolta di documen-
ti e studi, pub. della R. Commissione Colombiana, pte. 6)   (1548
Jones 155.

MAJOR, Richard Henry. The bibliography of
the first letter of Christopher Columbus,
describing his discovery of the New World.
London, Ellis & White, 1872. 61 p.   (1549
Jones 277.

BIOGRAPHY

MUGRIDGE, Donald Henry. Christopher Columbus; a selected list of books and articles by American authors or published in America, 1892-1950. Washington, Library of Congress, 1950. 37 p. (1550

SANZ, Carlos. Bibliografía general de la Carta de Colón. Madrid, Libr. General V. Suarez, 1958. 305 p. (1551

SILVA ARRIAGADA, Luis Ignacio. Apuntes bibliográficos. Cristobal Colón en Chile. Santiago de Chile, Impr. Lit. y Encuad. Barcelona, 1902. 25 p. (1552
Reprinted from Ensayo de una bibliografía histórica y geográfica de Chile, by Nicolás Anrique Reyes and L. Ignacio Silva A., p. 218-32. Laval, item 313, ascribes authorship to Luis Ignacio Silva Arriagada.

VEREZ DE PERAZA, Elena Luisa. Bibliografía colombina. Habana, Sociedad Colombista Panamericana, 1951. 14 p. (Biblioteca Pública Panamericana "Habana", Bibliografías panamericanas, 1) mimeogr. (1553

CORDERO, LUIS

ESPINOSA CORDERO, Nicolás. Don Luis Cordero, ensayo bibliográfico. Cuenca, Impr. del Colegio Nacional, 1933. 91 p. (1554
Jones 1979.

CORTES, HERNAN

HARRISSE, Henry. Bibliography of Cortés and the conquest of México. New York, 1886. (1555
Reprinted from the author's Bibliotheca Americana Vetustissima, p. 20-224, 233-41. Cited in Millares, item 528.

MEDINA, José Toribio. Ensayo bio-bibliográfico sobre Hernán Cortés; obra póstuma. Introducción de Guillermo Feliú Cruz. Santiago, Fondo Histórico y Bibliográfico José Toribio Medina, 1952, cviii, 243 p. (1556

VALLE, Rafael Heliodoro. Bibliografía de Hernán Cortés. México, Edit. Jus, 1953. 269 p. (Publ. de la Sociedad de Estudios Cortesianos, no. 7) (1557

WINSOR, Justin. Cortés and his companions, [with a critical essay on the documentary sources of Mexican history and notes] (Narrative and critical history of America. Boston and New York, 1884-1889. v. 2, p. 349-430) (1558
Jones 2586.

COSTA, FRANCISCO AUGUSTO PEREIRA DA

ABRANTES, Jorge, and CAETE, Francisco Barreto. Bibliografía de Pereira da Costa. Recife, 1951. p. [87]-135. (1559
Reprinted from Homenagem do Arquivo Público a Pereira da Costa.

COUTURE, EDUARDO J.

ROCCA COUTURE, Eduardo. Eduardo J. Couture; bibliografía. n.d. 20 p. (1560
Cited in Musso 276.

CRESPO TORAL, REMIGIO

ROMERO ARTETA, Oswaldo. Bibliografía [de Remigio Crespo Toral] e introduccion. Advertencia preliminar de Aurelio Espinosa Polit. Quito, 1957. xvii, 179 p. (Obras completas de Remigio Crespo Toral, 1) (1561
Publication of the Academia Ecuatoriana de la Lengua. Lists 1,310 items.

CUERVO, RUFINO JOSE

MARTINEZ, Fernando Antonio, and TORRES QUINTERO, Rafael. Rufino José Cuervo; estudio y bibliografía. Bogotá, 1954. 221 p. (Filólogos colombianos, 1) (1562

TORRES QUINTEROS, Rafael. Bibliografía de Rufino José Cuervo. Bogotá, 1951. 104 p. (Publ. del Instituto Caro y Cuervo, Ser. minor, 2) (1563

CUNHA, EUCLYDES DA

SOUSA, José Galante de. Algumas fontes para o estudo de Euclydés da Cunha. Rio de Janeiro, Instituto Nacional do Livro, 1959. (1564
Reprinted from Revista do Livro (15): 183-219, set. 1959. Cited in Doria Menezes 124.

VENÂNCIO, FRANCISCO. Euclydés da Cunha; ensaio bio-bibliographico. Rio de Janeiro, Off. Industrial Graphica, 1931. 165 p. (Publ. da Academia Brasileira. [Classicos brasileiros] 3: Bibliografia, 2) (1565
Jones 1223.

-----. Euclydes da Cunha. Edição do Conselho Nacional de Geografia especialmente dedicada às "Comemorações Euclidianas". São José do Rio Pardo, São Paulo, agôsto de 1949. Rio de Janeiro, Serviço Gráfico do Instituto Brasileiro de Geografia e Estatística. 1949. 37 p. (1566

DARIO, RUBEN

CONTRERAS, Francisco. Rubén Darío. Barcelona, 1930. 319 p.   (1567
   Bibliografía: p. 315-19.---Jones 1334.

DARIO, Rubén. Obras desconocidas... escritas en Chile y no recopiladas en ninguno de sus libros. Edición recogida por Raúl Silva Castro. Santiago de Chile, Prensas de la Universidad, 1934. CXXXII, 316 p.   (1568
   Bibliografía: p. LXXXII-CXXXII.---Jones 1335.

DOYLE, Henry Grattan. A bibliography of Rubén Darío (1867-1916) Cambridge, Mass., Harvard University, 1935. 27 p. (Bibliographies of Spanish-American literature)   (1569
   Jones 1336.

MAPES, Erwin Kempton. Escritos inéditos de Rubén Darío, recogidos de periódicos de Buenos Aires y anotados. New York, Instituto de las Españas, 1938. 224 p.   (1570
   Jones 1340.

-----. L'influence français dans l'oeuvre de Rubén Darío. Paris, H. Champion, 1925. 183 p. (Bibliotèque de la Revue de littérature comparée, t. 23)   (1571
   Bibliographie: p. 154-70.---Jones 1341.

SAAVEDRA MOLINA, Julio. Bibliografía de Rubén Darío. Santiago, Edición de la "Revista Chilena de Historia y Geografía", 1946. 114 p.   (1572
   Reprinted from Revista chilena de historia y geografía, no. 105, p. 3-23, jul./dic. 1944; no. 106 p. 24-66, en./dic. 1945; no. 107, p. 67-144, en./jun. 1946.

SILVA CASTRO, Raúl. Rubén Darío y Chile; anotaciones bibliográficas precedidas de una introducción sobre Rubén Darío en Chile. Santiago de Chile, Impr. "La Tracción", 1930. 127 p.   (1573
   Reprinted from Boletin de la Biblioteca Nacional.---Jones 1346, 1626.

TORRES RIOSECO, Arturo. Rubén Darío, casticismo y americanismo. Cambridge Mass. Harvard Univ. Pr., 1931. 253 p. (Bibliographies of Spanish-American literature)   (1574
   Published also with thesis note: PH.D. University of Minnesota, 1931.
   Bibliografía: p. 243-53.---Jones 1347.

DAVILA GARIBI, IGNACIO PAULINO

DAVILA GARIBI, José Ignacio Paulino. Recuerdo de mis bodas de plata de escribir para el público. (Enero 3 de 1904 a enero 3 de 1929) T. 1: Efemérides bibliográficas.

DAVILA GARIBI, José Ignacio Paulino... (Cont.) Guadalajara, Tip. J.M. Iguíniz Sucs., 1929. xv, 264 p.   (1575

DEBENEDETTI, SALVADOR

APARICIO, Francisco de. Salvador Debenedetti (nota biográfica y bibliográfica) (Solar, Buenos Aires, t. 1, p. 375-84, 1931) (1576
   See also Ricardo R. Caillet-Bois' Salvador Debenedetti, contribución a su bibliografía in Bol. del Inst. de Investig. Hist., Buenos Aires, t. 12, p. 392-411, 1931.
   A list of the "Publicaciones" of Aparicio (14 p.) was published in Buenos Aires, 1939. ---Jones 563a.

DELETANG, LUIS F.

LIZER, Carlos. Contribución a la bibliografía de Luis F. Deletang. (Boletin del Instituto de Investigaciones Históricas, Buenos Aires, t. 15, p. 304-08, 1932)   (1577
   Jones 757a.

DELGADO, RAFAEL

MOORE, Ernest Richard, and BICKLEY, James G. Rafael Delgado; notas bibliográficas y críticas. [México, D.F.,] 1943. 50 p. (1578
   Reprinted from Revista iberoamericana, 6 (11): 155-200, feb. 1943.

DELIGNE, GASTON FERNANDO

AMIAMA TIO, Fernando A. Contribución a la bibliografía de Gastón Fernando Deligne. Ciudad Trujillo, Edit. L. Sánchez Andújar, 1944. 28 p.   (1579

DEMARIA, ENRIQUE B.

DEMARIA, Enrique B. Títulos y trabajos. Buenos Aires, "La Semana Médica", 1916. 36 p.   (1580
   Cited in Binayán, item 50.

DENIS, FERDINAND

McNEIL, Paul Alexander. Notes on the works of Ferdinand Denis, 1789-1890, Americanist, in the Oliveira Lima Collection, Catholic University of America. Washington, D.C., 1941. 8 p.   (1581

DERBY, ORVILLE ADELBERT

BIBLIOGRAPHICAL list of scientific publications

BIBLIOGRAPHICAL list... (Cont.)
of Orville A. Derby. Rio de Janeiro, Typ.
Leuzinger, 1908. 17 p.   (1582
Cited in Reis, item 230.

DESSY, SILVIO

DESSY, Silvio. Curriculum Vitae. Buenos Aires, [Tall. Gráf. de la Compañía de Fósfo-
ros] 1919. 19 p.   (1583
Cited in Binayán, item 51.

DEUSTUA, ALEJANDRO OCTAVIO

ARIZOLA TIRADO, Gonzalo, and BUSE DE LA GUERRA,
Hermann. Bibliografía de las obras del dr.
Dn. Alejandro O. Deustua. Lima, Gil, 1939.
29 p.   (1584

DIAS, ANTONIO GONÇALVES

SILVA, Manoel Nogueira da. As edições allemãs
dos "Cantos" de Gonçalves Dias. Niteroi,
1929. 34 p.   (1585
Jones 1109.

-----. Bibliografia de Gonçalves Dias. Rio
de Janeiro, Impr. Nacional, 1942. 203 p.,
37 plates. (Instituto Nacional do Livro,
Coleção B 1; Bibliografia 2)   (1586

DIAZ, PORFIRIO

GARCIA, Genaro. Porfirio Díaz; sus padres,
niñez y juventud. México, Impr. del Museo
Nacional, 1906. 64 p.   (1587
Second edition. Bibliography: p. 12-59.

DIAZ DE GAMARRA, JUAN BENITO

RAMIREZ, Esteban. Díaz de Gamarra; biobibliografía. México, 1955. 146 p.   (1588

DIAZ DE SOLIS, JUAN

MEDINA, José Toribio. Juan Díaz de Solis; estudio histórico. Santiago de Chile, Impr.
en casa del autor, 1897. 2 v.   (1589
"Documentos y bibliografía": v. 2.---Jones
306.

DIAZ DEL CASTILLO, BERNAL

GARCIA, Genaro. Bernal Díaz del Castillo;
noticias bio-bibliográficas. México, Impr.
del Museo Nacional, 1904. 75 p.   (1590
From Anales del Museo Nacional de México,
2a. ep., v. 1, p. 306-75.---Jones 2179.

GONZALEZ OBREGON, Luis. El Capitán Bernal
Díaz del Castillo, conquistador y cronista
de Nueva España. Noticias biográficas y bibliográficas. México. Tip. de la Secretaría
de Fomento, 1894. 88 p.   (1591
Jones 2214.

PEREYRA, Carlos. Bernal Díaz del Castillo y
su obra. (El Consultor bibliográfico, Barcelona, t. 4, p. 393-422, 1927)   (1592
Jones 2417.

VILLACORTA CALDERON, José Antonio. Noticias
bibliográficas de la obra de Bernal Díaz del
Castillo. (Anales de la Sociedad de Geografía e Historia, Guatemala, v. 10, p. 478-89,
1934)   (1593
Jones 1261.

DIAZ GARCES, JOAQUIN

MUNDY, E. Evangelina. Joaquín Díaz Garcés
(Angel Pino) su vida y su obra (1878-1921)
Primera parte, bibliografía general. Santiago, Prensas de la Univ. de Chile, 1944.
186 p.   (1594

DOBLES SEGREDA, LUIS

DOBLES SEGREDA, Luis. Obras del profesor Luis
Dobles Segreda. San José, Costa Rica, 1935.
56 p.   (1595
Bibliographical notes.---Jones 1269.

ECHEVARRIA, ESTEBAN

KISNERMAN, Natalio. Contribución a la bibliografía de Esteban Echevarría, 1805-1959.
[Buenos Aires] 1960. 75 p. (Universidad
de Buenos Aires, Facultad de Filosofía y
Letras, Instituto de Literatura Argentina
"Ricardo Rojas", Guías bibliográficas,
4)   (1596

EDWARDS, ALBERTO

SILVA CASTRO, Raúl. Don Alberto Edwards;
biografía y bibliografía. Santiago de Chile, Impr. Universitaria, 1933. 64 p. (1597
Jones 1622.

EGAÑA, JUAN

EGAÑA, Juan. Escritos y servicios del ciudadano Dr. D. Juan Egaña. [Santiago], Impr.
de R. Rengifo, [1828] 23 p.   (1598
Cited in Ochsenius, item 58.

-----. Escrits publiés et services par le
citoyen Dr. Don Juan Egaña; trad. de l'es-

EGAÑA, Juan. Escrits publiês... (Cont.)
pagnol par M. W. Paris, Impr. de David,
1830. 23 p.   (1599
    Cited in Ochsenius, item 59.

SILVA CASTRO, Raul. Bibliografía de don Juan
Egaña, 1768-1836. Santiago de Chile, Impr.
Universitaria, 1949. x, 281 p.   (1600

EGUIARA Y EGUREN, JUAN JOSE DE

MILLARES CARLO, Agustín. Don Juan José de
Eguiara y Eguren y su Biblioteca mexicana,
México, Universidad de México, 1957.
187 p.   (1601

-----. Don Juan José de Eguiara y Eguren y
su Biblioteca mexicana. Maracaibo, Universidad del Zulia, Dirección de Cultura,
1963. 165 p.   (1602

ERNST, ADOLF

AHRENSBURG, Hermann. Bibliographia prof. dr.
phil. A. Ernst, Caracas. [Jena Univer-
sitätsbuchdruckerei G. Neuenhahn, 1901]
32 p.   (1603
    Reprinted in Sánchez, Manuel Segundo.
Bibliografía venezolanista. 381 titles are
registered.

ERRAZURIZ, CRESCENTE

ERRAZURIZ, Crescente. Obras. Santiago de
Chile, Impr. Zig-Zag, 1936. 3 v.   (1604
    Tomo 1, Páginas escogidas, selección y
bibliografía de Raúl Silva Castro.
    Bibliografía (p. xvii-xciii): 1a. pte.,
Libros y folletos; 2a. pte., Publicaciones
hechas en diarios y revistas; 3a. pte., Bio-
bibliografía hasta 1934. Includes 290 items
---Jones 1463a.

ESCOMEL, EDMUNDO

ESCOMEL, Edmundo. Títulos comisiones y trabajos hechos por el Dr. Edmundo Escomel,
Arequipa, Perú, 1926. 20 p.   (1605
    Lists 357 items.

ESCUDERO, PEDRO

ESCUDERO, Pedro. Títulos y trabajos. Buenos
Aires, "Las Ciencias", 1919. 24 p.   (1606
    Cited by Binayán, item 52.

ESPINOSA, ANTONIO DE

STOLS, Alexander Alphonse Marius. Antonio

STOLS, Alexander Alphonse... (Cont.)
de Espinosa; el segundo impresor mexicano.
México [1962] 120 p. (Biblioteca Nacional,
México. Instituto Bibliográfico Mexicano.
[Publicación] 7)   (1607
    25 items are described.

ESPINOSA PÓLIT, AURELIO

ROMERO ARTETA, Oswaldo. Bibliografía del P.
Aurelio Espinosa Pólit, S.I., y reseña de
los críticos de sus obras. Quito, Edit.
"Don Bosco", 1961. 194 p. (Publ. de la Academia Ecuatoriana de la Lengua)   (1608

ESTABLE, CLEMENTE

TRINKLE, Elsa. Clemente Estable; su bibliografía científica. [Montevideo, 1959]
p. 169-76.   (1609
    Reprinted from Anales de la Facultad de
Medicina, Montevideo, t. 44, no. 3-4, 1959.

ESTRADA, GENARO

VALLE, Rafael Heliodoro. Bibliografía de Genaro Estrada. (Letras de México, México,
D.F., no. 18, p. 14, nov. 1, 1937)   (1610
    Jones 2547.

-----. A contribution toward the bibliography
of Genaro Estrada. Durham, N.C., 1938.
p. 243-48, 423-25.   (1611
    Reprinted from the Hispanic American his-
torical review, v. 18.---Jones 2552.

FALKNER, TOMAS

FURLONG CARDIFF, Guillermo. La personalidad
y la obra de Tomás Falkner. Buenos Aires,
Tall. S.A., Casa Jacobo Peuser, 1929. 109 p.
(Buenos Aires. Universidad Nacional. Instituto de Investigaciones Históricas. Publ.
no. 48)   (1612
    Jones 699b.

FERNANDEZ, UBALDO

FERNANDEZ, Ubaldo. Cátedra de puericultura.
Concurso para la designación de su profesor
titular. Reseña de los antecedentes, títulos y trabajos presentados. Buenos Aires,
Impr. Flaiban y Camilloni, 1915. 29 p. (1613
    Cited by Binayán, item 53.

FERNANDEZ DE CASTRO, JOSE ANTONIO

CASTRO DE MORALES, Lilia, and FERNANDEZ DE
CASTRO, José Antonio, etc. Bibliografía de

BIOGRAPHY

CASTRO DE MORALES, Lilia, and... (Cont.)
José Antonio Fernández de Castro. La Habana, Biblioteca Nacional, 1955. 48 p. (Biblioteca Nacional, Habana, Publicaciones)   (1614

FERNANDEZ DE LIZARDI, JOSE J.

CALIFORNIA. State Library. Sutro Branch.
An annoted bibliography of the poems and
pamphlets of J. J. Fernández de Lizardi.
First period, 1808-1819. San Francisco,
1939. (Occasional papers; Mexican history
ser., no. 2, pt. 1)   (1615
Jones 2105b. Prepared by the personnel
of the Works Progress Administration.

-----. The Opponents and friends of Lizardi.
[San Francisco], 1939. 134 p. (Occasional
papers; Mexican history ser., no. 2,
pt. 2)   (1616
Jones 2105b. Prepared by the personnel
of the Works Progress Administration. Bibliography, p. 69-134.

-----. Some newly discovered poems and pamphlets of J. J. Fernández de Lizardi (El
Pensador Mejicano) San Francisco, 1939.
78 p. (Occasional papers, Mexican history
ser., no. 1)   (1617
Jones, item 2105b. Prepared by the personnel of the Works Progress Administration.

GONZALEZ OBREGON, Luis. Bibliografía del Pensador mexicano (José Joaquín Fernández de
Lizardi) (El Libro y el pueblo, México,
t. 4, no. 1/3, p. 21-39, 1925)   (1618
Jones 2212.

-----. Don José Joaquín Fernández de Lizardi
(El Pensador mexicano) apuntes biográficos
y bibliográficos. México, Of. Tip. de la
Secretaría de Fomento, 1888. 91 p.   (1619
Jones 2216.

-----. Don José Joaquín Fernández de Lizardi
(el Pensador mexicano) México, Ediciones
Botas, 1938. 223 p.   (1620
First published 1888. Includes bibliography.---Jones 2217.

SPELL, Jefferson Rea. Fernández de Lizardi;
a bibliography. (Hispanic American historical review, Durham, N.C., v. 7, p. 490-
507, 1927)   (1621
See also Ernest R. Moore's article, "El
compendio del tomo cuarto de El Periquillo
Sarniento, ensayo crítico", (with bibliography) in Abside, v. 3, no. 11, p. 1-13,
nov. 1939).---Jones 2513.

-----. The life and works of José Joaquín
Fernández de Lizardi. Philadelphia, 1931.
141 p. (University of Pennsylvania; Publ.

SPELL, Jefferson Rea. The life... (Cont.)
of the series in romantic languages and literatures, no. 23)   (1622
Bibliography: p. 118-38.---Jones 2514.

FERNANDEZ MORENO, BALDOMERO

FERNANDEZ MORENO, César, y FERNANDEZ MORENO,
Manrique. Bibliografía de Fernández Moreno;
con un apéndice por Horacio Jorge Becco.
Buenos Aires, Instituto de Literatura Argentina "Ricardo Rojas", 1960. 105 p. (Universidad de Buenos Aires, Facultad de Filosofía y Letras, Instituto de Literatura Argentina "Ricardo Rojas"; Guías bibliográficas, 5)   (1623

FERREIRA, ALEXANDRE RODRIGUES

BRAZIL. Biblioteca Nacional. Alexandre Rodrigues Ferreira; catálogo de manuscritos e bibliografias. Rio de Janeiro, 1952.
162 p.   (1624
Reprinted from Anais, v. 72.

FIGUEROA, ANDRES A.

LEDESMA MEDINA, Luis A. Adición a la bibliografía de Andrés A. Figueroa. Buenos Aires,
1943. 61 p.   (1625
Reprinted from Boletín del Instituto de
Investigaciones Históricas, Buenos Aires.
t. 26, no. 89-92. jul. 1941-jun. 1942.
Cited in HLAS, 9, item 45a.

FINLAY, CARLOS JUAN

FINLAY, Carlos Juan. Trabajos selectos. Selected papers. Habana, [Secretaría de Sanidad y Beneficencia] 1912. 657 p.   (1626
"Bibliografía del dr. Carlos J. Finlay,
por el dr. Jorge Le-Roy y Cassá": p. 623-54.
---Jones 1829a.

FINO, JOSE FEDERICO

FINO, José Federico. Publicaciones de J. F.
Finó. I, 1931-1957. Buenos Aires, 1957.
10 p.   (1627
Cited in Catálogo, Instituto Bibliotecológico, item 190.

FLORIT, EUGENIO

EUGENIO Florit: vida y obra - bibliografía-
antología. New York, Hispanic Institute
in the United States, 1943. 50 p. (Autores modernos 10)   (1627a

FREIRE, LUIZ JOSE JUNQUEIRA

BRAZIL. Biblioteca Nacional. Luiz José Junqueira Freire, 1832-1855; bibliografia organizada pela Seção de Referência. Rio de
Janeiro, 1955. 15 p. mimeogr.   (1628
    Cited in Bol. bibliog., Rio de Janeiro,
    v. 5, t. 1, p. 17, 1955.

PIRES, Homero. Junqueira Freire; ensaio bio-
bibliográfico. Rio de Janeiro, Off. Industrial Graphica, 1932. 91 p. (Publ. da Academia Brasileira. [Classicos brasileiros]
3: Bibliografia 1)   (1629
    Jones 1148.

FRERS, EMILIO

FRANCO, Pedro B. Bibliografia analítica de
las obras completas de Emilio Frers. Buenos
Aires, 1925.   (1630
    Jones 696.

FREYRE, GILBERTO

HANKE, Lewis. Gilberto Freyre. Vida y obra-
bibliografías- antología. New York, Instituto de las Españas en los Estados Unidos,
1939. 30 p. (Autores modernos 7)   (1631

FRIAS, VALENTIN F. (ALTER)

VALENTIN F. Frías; noticia bibliográfica de
sus escritos. Santiago de Querétaro, Deme-
trio Contreras, 1904. 16 p.   (1632
    Cited in Millares, item 578; also Ayala,
    item 462.

FUNES, GREGORIO

FURLONG CARDIFF, Guillermo. Bio-bibliografía
del deán Funes; con una introducción de Enrique Martínez Paz. Córdoba, Arg., Impr.
de la Universidad, 1939. xxxi, 413 p. (Universidad Nacional de Córdoba, Instituto de
Estudios Americanistas. [Publ.]
no. 4)   (1633

ZINNY, Antonio. Monobibliografía del Dr. D.
Gregorio Funes deán de la Santa Iglesia Ca-
tedral de Córdoba, seguida de su bosquejo
histórico hasta la batalla de Maipú; trad.
del inglés y anotado. Buenos Aires, Impr.
de Mayo, 1868. 136 p.   (1634
    Binayán notes, item 75, that this work was
    also published in the Revista de Buenos Ai-
    res, XV, p. 135-60, 291-320, 452-78, 607-34,
    1868. See also the author's Efemeridografía
    argirometropolitana (1869)

FURLONG CARDIFF, GUILLERMO

GEOGHEGAN, Abel Rodolfo. Bibliografía de Guillermo Furlong, S.J. Buenos Aires [Tall.
Gráf. San Pablo], 1957. 221 p.   (1635

GABALDON MARQUEZ, JOAQUIN

VENEZUELA. Universidad Central. Escuela de
Biblioteconomía y Archivos. Bibliografía de
Joaquín Gabaldón Márquez. Caracas, 1964.
75 p. (Ser. bibliográfica, 3)   (1635a

GALINDO Y VILLA, JESUS

GALINDO Y VILLA, Jesús. Noticias bibliográficas de la labor literaria de Jesús Galindo y
Villa, de 1887 a 1937. México, 1937. 140 p.
(Boletín de la Sociedad Mexicana de Geografía y Estadística, t. 45)   (1636
    Cited by Valle, Bibliog. mex. (1937-1938)

-----. Noticias de algunos escritos de Jesús
Galindo y Villa. publicados 1887-1908. n.d.
10 p.   (1637
    Cited in Millares 583.

-----. Noticias de algunos escritos de Jesús
Galindo y Villa. México, Tall. Tip. de "El
Tiempo", 1906. 16 p.   (1638
    Cited in Millares, item 582.

-----. Noticia de diversos escritos de Jesús
Galindo y Villa. publicados de 1887 a 1912.
México, D.F., Impr. del Museo Nacional de
Arqueología, Historia y Etnografía, 1913.
iv., 43 p.   (1639
    Cited in Millares 584.

GALVEZ, BERNARDO DE

CAUGHEY, John Walton. Bernardo de Gálvez en
Louisiana, 1776-1783. Berkeley, Univ. of
California Pr., 1934. 290 p. (Publ. of
the University of California at Los Angeles
in social sciences, 4)   (1640
    Bibliography: p. 259-72.---Jones 91.

GALVEZ, JOSE DE

PRIESTLEY, Herbert Ingram. José de Gálvez,
Visitor-General of New Spain (1765-1771)
Berkeley, Univ. of California Pr., 1916.
449 p. (University of California, Publ. in
history, v. 5)   (1641
    Bibliography: p. 301-403.---Jones 2434

GALVEZ, MANUEL

KISNERMAN, Natalio. Bibliografía de Manuel

KISNERMAN, Natalio ... (Cont.)
Gálvez. Buenos Aires, Fondo Nacional de las
Artes, 1964. 75 p. (Bibliografía argentina
de artes y letras; compilaciones especiales,
17)   (1642

OLIVARI, Nicolás, and STANCHINA, Lorenzo.
Manuel Gálvez; ensayo sobre su obra. Buenos
Aires, Agencia General de Librería y Publi-
caciones, 1924. 130 p.   (1643
Bibliografía: p. 125-30.---Jones 798.

GAMBOA, FEDERICO

MOORE, Ernest Richard. Bibliografía de Federico Gamboa (1864-1939) (Letras de México,
México, v. 2, no. 12-3, 1939-1940)   (1644
See also his article: "Bibliografía de
obras y crítica de Federico Gamboa" in Revista iberoamericana, p. 271-79, abr. 1940.
---Jones 2370a.

GARCIA, JUAN AGUSTIN

RAVIGNANI, Emilio. Juan Agustín García biobibliografía) (Boletín del Instituto de Investigaciones Históricas, Buenos Aires, t. 1,
397-410, 1923)   (1645
Jones 824c.

TORRES, Luis María. Juan Agustín García, examen general de su obra histórica. (Verbum,
Buenos Aires, año 17, no. 61, p. 21-34,
1923)   (1646
Jones 868f.

GARCIA CUBAS, ANTONIO

AGUILAR Y SANTILLAN, Rafael. Bibliografía y
cartografía de Antonio García Cubas. México, D.F., 1935.   (1647
Reprinted from Boletín de la Sociedad Mexicana de Geografía e Historia, v. 44, p.
371-81.

GARCIA ICAZBALCETA, JOAQUIN

GALINDO Y VILLA, Jesús. Don Joaquín García
Icazbalceta (1867-1937); notas biográficas
y bibliográficas. México, Impr. del Sagrado Corazón de Jesús, 1889. 40 p.   (1648

-----. D. Joaquín García Icazbalceta; biografía y bibliografía. (Boletín del Instituto
Bibliográfico Mexicano, México, no. 2,
p. 1-39, 1903)   (1649
Jones 2200.

-----. -----. 3. ed., muy aumentada. México,
Impr. del Museo Nacional, 1904.

GALINDO Y VILLA, Jesús. Don Joaquín... (Cont.)
87 p.   (1650
Reprinted from Anales del Museo Nacional
de México, v. 7, p. 520-62.---Jones 2201.

-----. Don Joaquín García Icazbalceta, su
vida y sus obras. (El Libro y el pueblo,
México, v. 4, no. 7-9, p. 45-75,
1925)   (1651
A translation of this article will be
found in Inter-America (English) v. 9, no.
4, p. 331-44, Apr. 1926.---Jones 2202.

-----. Don Joaquín Icazbalceta; su vida y
sus obras. (Boletín del Instituto de Investigaciones Históricas, Buenos Aires,
t. 4, p. 506-69, 1926)   (1652
Jones 2203.

GARCIA ICAZBALCETA, Joaquín. Cartas de Joaquín García Icazbalceta a José Fernando Ramírez, José María de Agreda, Manuel Orozco
y Berra, Nicolás León, Agustín Fischer,
Aquiles Gerste, Francisco del Paso y Troncoso; compiladas y anotadas por Felipe Teixidor. México, Ediciones Porrúa, 1937.
433 p.   (1653
"Autores, ediciones y manuscritos que se
citan en el texto de las cartas y en las
notas": p. 359-93.---Jones 2195.

WAGNER, Henry Raup. Joaquín García Icazbalceta. (American Antiquarian Society.
Proceedings. Worcester, Mass., 1935. n.s.,
v. 44, p. 103-53)   (1654
List of Icazbalceta's works: p. 120-53.
---2579a

GARRETT, JOÃO BAPTISTA ALMEIDA

BRAZIL. Biblioteca Nacional. Garrettiana da
Biblioteca Nacional. Rio de Janeiro, Typ.
Leuzinger, 1900. 18 p.   (1655
Reprinted from Annaes, v. 21, p. 165-92.
Published in commemoration of the hun-
dredth anniversary of the birth of João
Baptista de Almeida-Garrett. Compiled by
José Alexandre Teixeira de Mello. Cited in
Reis 183.

LIMA, Henrique de Campos Ferreira. Garrett e
o Brasil; notas bibliographicas. Rio de
Janeiro, 1923.   (1656
Cited in Reis 351.

GAY, CLAUDIO

CHILE. Archivo Nacional. Catálogo del archivo de Claudio Gay. [Santiago] Dirección
de Bibliotecas, Archivos y Museos, 1963.
153 p.   (1657

GENIN, AUGUSTO

GOMEZ DE OROZCO, Federico. Don Augusto Genin;
nota bibliográfica. México, Tall. Graf. del
Museo Nacional de Arqueología, Historia y
Etnografía, 1933. 8 p. (1658
  Assumed to be a reprint from Boletín del
Museo Nacional de Historia y Antropología,
5a. ep., t. 1, p. 238-43, 1932. Cited in
González, item 126.

GERCHUNOFF, ALBERTO

ALBERTO GERCHUNOFF: vida y obra - bibliografía
- antología. New York, Hispanic Institute
in the United States, [1957] (Autores modernos 26) (1658a
  Bibliography by Olga Blondet Tudisco.
Reprinted from Revista hispánica moderna,
año 23, no. 3/4, p. 344-56, jul./oct. 1957.

GOMEZ DE AVELLANEDA, GERTRUDIS

COTARELO Y MORI, Emilio. Doña Gertrudis Gómez de Avellaneda; indicaciones bibliográficas con motivo de un libro reciente. Madrid, Tip. de la Revista de Archivos, Bibliotecas y Museos, 1915. 24 p. (1659
  "Del Boletín de la Real Academia Española"; also in Cuba intelectual, no. 40-2.---
Jones 1803.

KELLY, Edith L. Bibliografía de la Avellaneda. (Revista bimestre cubana, Habana, v.
35, p. 107-39, 261-95, 1935) (1660
  Jones 1851.

-----. Observaciones sobre algunas obras de
la Avellaneda publicadas en México. [Méxi-
co, D.F.] Revista iberoamericana, 1941.
p. 123-32. (1661
  Reprinted from Revista iberoamericana,
feb. 1941.

WILLIAMS, Edwin Bucher. The life and dramatic works of Gertrudis Gómez de Avellaneda.
Philadelphia, 1924. 116 p. (Publ. of the
University of Pennsylvania; ser. in romance languages and literatures,
no. 11) (1662
  Bibliography: p. 114-16.---Jones 1939.

GOMEZ RESTREPO, ANTONIO

RAMIREZ, Virginio. Bibliografía crítico-li-
teraria y poética del dr. Antonio Gómez
Restrepo. (Arte, Ibagué, Colombia, año 1,
p. 384-89; año 2, p. 548-53, 1935) (1663
  Jones 1763.

GOMEZ Y BAEZ, MAXIMO

HAVANA. Biblioteca Municipal. Guia bibliográfica sobre Máximo Gómez y Baez. Habana,
1936. [4] p. (Publ., Ser. C: Guías bibliográficas 1) (1664

GONZAGA, THOMAZ ANTONIO

BRAZIL. Biblioteca Nacional. Gonzagueana da
Bibliotheca Nacional, catalogo organizado
pelo bibliothecario Emmanuel Eduardo Gaudie
Ley. Rio de Janeiro, Bibliotheca Nacional,
1936. 76 p. (1665

OLIVEIRA, Oswaldo Mello Braga de. As edições
de Marilia de dirceo; bibliographia. Rio
de Janeiro [Edição Benedicto Souza] 1930.
58 p. (1666
  Jones 1098.

GONZALEZ, JOAQUIN VICTOR

CONDE MONTERO, Manuel. Bibliografía de Joaquín V. González. Buenos Aires, Tall. Gráf.
Rodriguez Giles, 1928. 30 p. (1667
  Jones 670. Probably a reprinting of the
bibliography appearing in Boletín de la Junta de Historia y Numismática Americana,
v. 4, p. 295-320.

GONZALEZ, Joaquín Victor. Homenajes tributa-
dos a su memoria con motivo de la traslación de sus restos a la tierra natal, a pe-
dido del pueblo y gobierno de La Rioja.
Buenos Aires, 1927. 527 p. (1668
  Bibliografía: p. 44-54.---Jones 712.

GONZALEZ ALCORTA, LEANDRO

SANTOVENIA Y ECHAIDE, Emeterio Santiago. Leandro González Alcorta; estudio bibliográfico.
Habana, Impr. Pérez, Sierra, y Cía., 1926.
196 p. (1669

GONZALEZ DE SANTA CRUZ, ROQUE

TESCHAUER, Carlos. Vida e obras do padre Roque Gonzalez de Santa Cruz, S.J., primeiro
apostolo do Rio Grande do Sul (contribuição
para a historia da civilização no Brasil)
3. ed. cuidadosamente revista e publicada
pelo Instituto Histórico e Geographico do
Rio Grande do Sul. Porto Alegre, Typ. do
Centro, 1928. 136 p. (1670
  "Notas bio-bibliographicas sobre os autores que foram com preferencia consultados:"
p. 127-34.---Jones 1214.

GONZALEZ DEL VALLE, FRANCISCO

PERAZA SARAUSA, Fermín, 1907-   Bibliografía de Francisco González del Valle. Trabajo presentado al II Congreso Nacional de
Historia. [Havana] Anuario Bibliográfico
Cubano, 1943. 19 p. (Biblioteca del bibliotecario, 4) mimeogr.   (1671

-----. 2a. ed. Gainesville, Fla. 1964. 15 p.
(Biblioteca del bibliotecario, 4)   (1671a

GONZALEZ OBREGON, LUIS

WARNER, Ralph Emerson. A bibliography of the
works of Luis González Obregón. (The Hispanic American historical review, Durham,
N.C., v. 19, p. 577-94, 1939)   (1672
Jones 2580.

GONZALEZ PRADA, MANUEL

GONZALEZ PRADA: vida y obra - bibliografía -
antología. New York, Hispanic Institute in
the United States, 1938. 51 p. (Autores
modernos 6)   (1672a

GONZALEZ PRADA, Alfredo. Manuel González Prada: bibliografía. (Revista hispánica moderna, New York, año 4, p. 27-39,
1937)   (1673
Jones 2657.

GONZALEZ SUAREZ, FEDERICO

BUENO C., Ricardo. Ensayo bibliográfico de
los escritos del Illmo. y Rvmo. Señor Doctor Don Federico González Suárez. (Dios y
patria, Riobamba, t. 1, p. 277-301; t. 2,
p. 7-17, 164-77, 370-424, 1924-
1925)   (1674
Jones 1962.

-----. Homenaje a la memoria del Ilmo. y
Rvmo. Sr. Dn. Federico González Suárez en
el centenario de su nacimiento; ensayo bi-
bliográfico de sus obras y escritos; 2a. ed.
Quito, 1943. 149 p.   (1675
Cited in Chaves p. 20.

GONZALEZ VIGIL, FRANCISCO DE

LEGUIA, Jorge Guillermo. Francisco de Paulo
González Vigil)1792-1875) (Boletín bibliográfico, Biblioteca Central de la Universidad de San Marcos, Lima, v. 1, no. 2-3,
1923)   (1676
Jones 2671.

GONZALEZ ZELEDON, MANUEL

ARCE, José M. Manuel González Zeledón: vida
y obra - bibliografía - antología. New York,
Hispanic Institute in the United States,
1948. 37 p. (Autores modernos 14)   (1676a

GOROSTIZA, MANUEL EDUARDO DE

AGUILAR M., María Esperanza. Estudio bibliográfico de don Manuel Eduardo de Gorostiza.
México, [Impr. "Renacimiento"] 1932.
114 p.   (1677

GOYA Y LUCIENTES, FRANCISCO JOSE DE

ESTRADA, Genaro. Bibliografía de Goya. La
Casa de España en México. [México, D.F.,
Impr. Industrial Gráfica] 1940.
117 p.   (1678

GRAHAM, ROBERT CUNNINGHAM

ROBERT Cunningham Graham, 1852-1936: vida y
obra - bibliografía - antología. New York,
Hispanic Institute in the United States,
1947. 47 p. (Autores modernos 15)   (1678a

GRASES, PEDRO

GRASES, Pedro. Publicaciones, Caracas, 1961.
31 p.   (1679

-----. Publicaciones. Caracas, 1964.
73 p.   (1680

GROUSSAC, PAUL

CANTER, Juan. Contribución a la bibliografía
de Paul Groussac. Buenos Aires, El Ateneo,
1930. 329 p.   (1681
Reprinted from Boletín del Instituto de
Investigaciones Históricas, t. 9, p. 484-
710, 1929.---Jones 647.

GUANES, ALEJANDRO

RODRIGUEZ-ALCALA, Hugo. Alejandro Guanes,
1872-1920: vida y obra - bibliografía - antología. New York, Hispanic Institute in
the United States, 1948. 68 p. (Autores
modernos 17)   (1682

GUIMARAES, LUIZ

VILELA, Iracema Guimarães. Luís Guimarães
Junior; ensaio bio-bibliográfico. Rio de
Janeiro, Of. Industrial Gráfica, 1934.

VILELA, Iracema Guimarães ... (Cont.)
119 p. (Publ. da Academia Brasileira.
[Classicos brasileiros] 3: Bibliografia,
5)   (1683
   Jones 1054.

GUIRALDES, RICARDO

BECCO, Horacio Jorge. Contribucion a la bibliografía argentina contemporánea: Ricardo
Güiraldes (1886-1927) Buenos Aires,
1954.   (1684
   Reprinted from Alada, no. 8, oct. 1954.

-----. Ricardo Güiraldes. Buenos Aires, Instituto de Literatura Argentina "Ricardo Rojas", Universidad de Buenos Aires. 1959.
35 p. (Guías bibliograficas, 1)   (1685

PREVITALE, Giovanni. Ricardo Güiraldes and
Don Segundo Sombra; life and works. New
York, Hispanic Institute in the United
States, 1963. 225 p.   (1686

-----. Vida y obra de Ricardo Güiraldes; ed.
rev. por Adelina del Carril de Güiraldes;
trad. del inglés por Pablo Max Ynsfran.
St. Petersburg, Fla., 1963.
277 p.   (1687

GUTIERREZ, JOSE ROSENDO

PAREDES, Manuel Rigoberto. José Rosendo Gutiérrez; apuntes bio-bibliográficos (Kolla-
suyo, La Paz, año 1, no. 8, p. 19-38,
1939)   (1688
   Jones 927a.

GUTIERREZ, JUAN MARIA

URIEN, Carlos María. Apuntes sobre la vida
y obras del doctor Juan María Gutiérrez.
Buenos Aires, Maucci Hnos. [1909?]
400 p.   (1689
   Jones 880a.

GUTIERREZ NAJERA, MANUEL

GOMEZ BAÑOS, Virginia. Bibliografía de Manuel Gutiérrez Nájera y cuatro cuentos inéditos. México, 1958. 88 p.   (1690

PEREZ TREJO, C. Bibliografía de Manuel Gutiérrez Nájera. (El Libro y el pueblo, México, v. 12, p. 129-36, 1934)   (1691
   Jones 2422.

HARRISSE, HENRY

BINAYAN, Narciso. Henry Harrisse; ensayo
biobibliográfico. Buenos Aires, J. Peuser,

BINAYAN, Narciso ... (Cont.)
1923. 36 p.   (1692
   Jones 191.

CORDIER, Henri. Henry Harrisse, 1830-1910.
[Chartres, Impr. Durand, 1910?]
39 p.   (1693
   "Extrait du Bulletin du bibliophile".
Bibliographie: p. 9-39.---Jones 192.

GROWELL, Adolf. Henry Harrisse; biographical
and bibliographical sketch. New York, 1899.
13 p. (Dibdin Club, New York. Leaflets,
no. 3)   (1694
   Jones 193.

SANZ, Carlos. Henry Harrisse (1829-1910)
príncipe de los americanistas: su vida, su
obra. Con nuevas adiciones a la Bibliotheca Americana Vetustissima. Madrid, Libr. General Victoriano Suárez, 1958.
282 p.   (1695

VIGNAUD, Jean Henry. Henry Harrisse; étude
biographique et morale, avec la bibliographie critique de ses écrits. Paris, C.
Chadenat, 1912. 83 p.   (1696
   Jones 194.

HARTH-TERRE, EMILIO

TAURO, Alberto. Bio-bibliografía de Emilio
Harth-Terre. Conmemorativa de sus bodas
de plata profesionales (1920-1945) Lima
[Impr. Torres Aguirre] 1945. 78 p.   (1697

HENRIQUE, INFANTE OF PORTUGAL

RIO DE JANEIRO. Gabinete Português de Leitura. Catálogo henriquino do Real Gabinete
Português de Leitura do Rio de Janeiro.
Lisboa, Comissão Executiva do V Centenário
da Morte do Infante D. Henrique, 1960.
60 p.   (1698

HEREDIA, CARLOS M.

IGUINIZ, Juan Bautista. La producción del
Padre Heredia, en celebración del R. P.
Carlos M. Heredia al cumplir 50 años en la
Compañía de Jesús. México, [n.d.]
53 p.   (1699
   Cited in Millares 615a. Adiciones.

HEREDIA, JOSE M.

ESCOTO, José Augusto. Ensayo de una biblioteca herediana. (Cuba y América, Habana,
v. 14, p. 148-49, 261-69, 1904)   (1700
   Jones 1820.

GONZALEZ DEL VALLE Y RAMIREZ, Francisco.
Cronología herediana (1803-1839) La Habana, [Secretaría de Educación] 1938.
331 p.   (1701
    Jones 1836a.

HEREDIA, José María. Poesías, discursos y
cartas, con una biografía del poeta por
María Lacoste de Arufe y juicios de José
Martí, Manuel Sanguily, Enrique Piñeyro y
Rafael Esténger. Habana, Cultural, 1939.
2 v. (Colección de libros cubanos, v. 41-
2)   (1702
    Bibliografía: v. 1, p. clxxv-cxcvi.---
Jones 1847.

TOUSSAINT, Manuel. Bibliografía mexicana de
Heredia. México, Secretaría de Relaciones
Exteriores, Departamento de Información pa-
ra el Extranjero, 1953. xviii, 146 p.
(Monografías bibliograficas mexicanas, 2a.
ser., no. 5)   (1703

HERNANDEZ, FRANCISCO

SOMOLINOS, Germán. Bibliografía del Dr. Francisco Hernández, humanista del siglo XVI.
Washington, D.C., Unión Panamericana, 1958.
82 p.   (1704
    Reprinted from Revista interamericana de
bibliografía, v. 7, no. 1, p. 1-76, 1957.

HERNANDEZ, JOSE

CORTAZAR, Augusto Raúl. José Hernández,
"Martín Fierro" y su crítica; aportes para
una bibliografía. Buenos Aires, Fondo Nacional de las Artes [1960]   (1705
    Section 2 of Bibliografía argentina de
artes y letras, no. 5-6, p. 51-129, en./jun.
1960.

MAUBE, José Carlos. Itinerario bibliográfico
y henerografico del "Martín Fierro". Buenos Aires, Edit. El Ombú, 1943.
187 p.   (1706

HERNADEZ DE ALBA, GUILLERMO

OSORIO DE HERNANDEZ DE ALBA, Paulina. Guillermo Hernández de Alba: Publicaciones. Madrid, 1951. 36 p.   (1707
    Hernández de Alba is Colombian.

HERRERA Y REISSIG, JULIO

BULA PIRIZ, Roberto. Herrera y Reissig (1875-
1910): vida y obra - bibliografía - antología. New York, Hispanic Institute in the
United States, 1952. 113 p. (Autores modernos, 20)   (1708

PINO SAAVEDRA, Yolando. La poesía de Julio
Herrera y Reissig. Sus temas y su estilo.
Santiago, Prensas de la Universidad de Chi-
le, 1932. 148 p.   (1709
    Bibliografía: p. 7-11.---Jones 2858.

HORATIUS FLACCUS, QUINTUS

MENDEZ PLANCARTE, Gabriel. Horacio en México.
México, La Universidad Nacional, 1937.
333 p.   (1710
    Bibliografía at end of each chapter.---
Jones 2338.

HOSTOS Y BONILLA, EUGENIO M. DE

BIBLIOGRAFIA hostosiana; trabajos referentes
a Hostos y trabajos en que se menciona a
Hostos. (Boletín de la Comisión del Centenario de Hostos, San Juan, P.R., no. 7,
p. 11-60, 1938)   (1711
    Jones 2786.

COMISION pro Celebración del Centenario del
Natalicio de Eugenio María de Hostos. América y Hostos, coleccion de ensayos acerca
de Eugenio María de Hostos, recogidos y publicados por la Comisión pro Celebración
del Centenario del Natalicio de Eugenio María de Hostos. Habana, Cultural, 1939.
391 p.   (1712
    Complemento biográfico y bibliográfico,
p.341-54. Bibliografía hostosiana, trabajos referentes a Hostos: p. 355-91.---Jones
2780.

EUGENIO M. de HOSTOS (1839-1903): vida y obra
- bibliografía - antología. New York, Hispanic Institute in the United States, 1940.
44 p. (Autores modernos, 8)   (1713
    Bibliography by Sidonia C. Rosenbaum.

HOSTOS, Adolfo de. Indice hemero-bibliográ-
fico de Eugenio María de Hostos (incluye
material inédito, iconografía y hostosiana)
1863-1940. San Juan, P.R., [Havana, Printed
by Cultural] 1940. 756 p.   (1714
    Published under the auspices of the
Comisión pro Celebración del Centenario del
Natalicio de Hostos. "Gran parte del material utilizado en este libro ha sido colec-
cionado por el señor Eugenio Carlos de Hostos".

HOSTOS, Eugenio María de. Biografía y bibliografía. Santo Domingo, Impr. "Oiga", 1905.
384 p.   (1715
    Cited in Ochsenius 86.

PEDREIRA, Antonio S. Hostos, ciudadano de
América. Madrid, Tall. Tip. de Espasa-
Calpe, 1932. 264 p.   (1716
    Bibliografía: 249-64.---Jones 2802.

HOUSSAY, BERNARDO ALBERTO

HOUSSAY, Bernardo Alberto. Antecedentes, títulos y trabajos. Buenos Aires, Tall. Gráf.
de A. Plaiban, 1919. 38 p.   (1717
Cited in Binayán, item 56.

HRDLĬCKA, ALES

RUBIN DE LA BORBOLLA, Daniel. Bibliografía
del Dr. Ales Hrdlĭcka. México, 1939.
p. 53-76.   (1718
Reprinted from Boletín bibliográfico de
antropología americana, v. 2, no. 1/3,
en./sept. 1938.

HUDSON, WILLIAM HENRY

BECCO, Horacio Jorge. Contribución a la bibliografía argentina: W. H. Hudson (1841-
1922) Buenos Aires, 1955.   (1719
Reprinted from Alada no. 10, oct. 1955.

GUILLERMO HENRIQUE HUDSON: vida y obra - bi-
bliografía - antología. New York, Hispanic
Institute in the United States, [1944]
(Autores modernos, 12)   (1720
Bibliography by Sidonia C. Rosenbaum.
Reprinted from Revista hispánica moderna,
año 10, no. 3/4.

WILSON, George Francis. A bibliography of the
writings of W. H. Hudson. London, The Book-
man's Journal, 1922. 79 p.   (1720a

HUMBOLDT, ALEXANDER VON

LEIPZIG. Deutsche Bücherei. Alexander von
Humboldt; bibliographie seiner ab 1860 in
deutscher Sprache herausgegebenen Werke und
der seit 1900 erschienenen Veröffentlichungen über ihn. Im Auftrage des Alexander von
Humboldt-Komitees der Deutschen Demokrati-
schen Republik herausgegeben von der Deutschen Bücherei. Leipzig, Deutsche Bücherei,
1959. 44 p. (Sonderbibliographien der Deutschen Bücherei, 16)   (1721

HUSSEY, RONALD D.

GRASES, Pedro. La obra de Hussey y la biblio-
grafía relativa al siglo XVIII de Venezuela.
Caracas, 1962. 23 p.   (1722
Reprinted from the study published in
La Compañía de Caracas, 1728-1784, by Roland
D Hussey. Lists 68 references.

ICAZA, JORGE

JORGE ICAZA: vida y obra - bibliografía - an-

JORGE ICAZA: vida y obra... (Cont.)
tología. New York, Hispanic Institute in
the United States, 1947. 70 p. (Autores
modernos, 16)   (1723

IMBELLONI, JOSE

MARTINEZ SOLER, Benigno J. Bibliografía de
José Imbelloni. [México] 1945. p. 100-
17.   (1724
Reprinted from the Boletín bibliográfico
de antropología americana, v. 8, 1945.

INGENIEROS, JOSE

INGENIEROS, José. Estudios y trabajos médicos.
Buenos Aires, A. Etchepareborda, 1907.
27 p.   (1725
Cited in Binayán, item 58.

BAGU, Sergio. Vida ejemplar de José Ingenie-
ros, juventud y plenitud. Buenos Aires,
Edit. Claridad, 1936. 244, [25] p.   (1726
Bibliografía de Ingenieros: 24 p. at end.
---Jones 591.

IRISARRI, ANTONIO JOSE DE

FELIU CRUZ, Guillermo. Un libro raro americano. El Cristiano errante. Santiago de Chile, Dirección General de Tall. Fiscales de
Prisiones, 1928. 12 p.   (1727
Reprinted from Revista chilena, no. 97.

DONOSO, Ricardo. Antonio José de Irisarri,
escritor y diplomático. Santiago, Prensas
de la Universidad de Chile, 1934.
319 p.   (1728
Bibliografía: p. 315-17.---Jones 131.

FELIU CRUZ, Guillermo. Antonio José Irisarri
y sus libros. (Anales de la Sociedad de
Geografía e Historia de Guatemala, Guatemala,
v. 5, p. 297-305, 1929)   (1729
Cf. H. M. Lyndenberg's article "Where are
the Irisarri books", in Bulletin of the New
York Public Library, Feb., 1929.---Jones
143.

-----. Apostillas bibliográficas. Las obras
de Irisarri y su biblioteca. Santiago de
Chile, 1928. 18 p.   (1730
Jones 1472.

IRISARRI, Antonio José de. Defensa de la historia critica del asesinato cometido en la
persona del gran mariscal de Ayacucho. Con
prólogo y notas de Alfredo Flores y Caamaño.
Santiago de Chile, Impr. Universitaria,
1922. 192 p.   (1731
Includes a bibliography of Irisarri.---
Jones 218.

ISAACS, JORGE

JORGE ISAACS, 1837-1937; the tribute of a
continent. (Panorama, Washington, D.C.,
Pan American Union, no. 9, p. 1-6,
1937)   (1732
   Includes bibliography.---Jones 1722.

ITURBIDE, AGUSTIN DE

VALLE, Rafael Heliodoro. Como era Iturbide.
México, Impr. del Museo Nacional de Arqueología, Historia y Etnografía, 1922.
115 p.   (1733
   Bibliografía: p. 35-114.---Jones 2551.

JUANA INES DE LA CRUZ (Sor)

ABREU GOMEZ, Ermilo. Sor Juana Inés de la
Cruz; bibliografía y biblioteca. México
[Impr. de la Secretaría de Relaciones Exte-
riores, 1934] xviii, 455 p. (Monografías
bibliográficas mexicanas, no. 20)   (1734
   Jones 2027.

HENRIQUEZ UREÑA, Pedro. Bibliografía de Sor
Juana Inés de la Cruz. (El Libro y el pueblo, México, D.F., v. 12, p. 72-8, 137-43,
175-79, 1934)   (1735
   Reprinted with notes by Ermilo Abreu Gómez,
from Revue hispanique, v. 40.---Jones 2237.

-----. -----. (Revue hispanique, New York,
v. 40, no. 97, p. 161-214, 1917)   (1736
   Jones 2236.

SCHONS, Dorothy. Bibliografía de Sor Juana
Inés de la Cruz. México, 1927. 67 p. (Monografías bibliográficas mexicanas,
no. 7)   (1737
   Jones 2498.

-----. Some bibliographical notes on Sor Juana Inés de la Cruz. Austin, Tex., The University, 1925. 30 p. (University of Texas
bulletin, no. 2526)   (1738
   Jones 2499.

JUAREZ, BENITO

GARCIA, Genaro. Juárez; refutación a don Francisco Bulnes. México, Vda. de C. Bouret,
1904. 276 p.   (1739
   Bibliografía: p. 195-276.---Jones 2184.

KELSEN, HANS

HERMIDA, Ernesto C., and CAMINOS, Hugo. Bibliografía de Hans Kelsen. Buenos Aires,
Tip. Edit. Argentina, 1949. 51 p.   (1740

LACERDA, JOÃO BAPTISTA DE

SYNOPSE das publicações scientificas do Dr.
João Baptista de Lacerda. Rio de Janeiro,
Papelaria Luiz Macedo, 1913. 12 p.   (1741
   Cited in Reis 281.

LACUNZA, MANUEL

SCHAIBLE, Carl H. Las primeras ediciones de
la obra del padre Lacunza: Venida del Me-
sías en gloria y magestad. Ensayo filoló-
gico-bibliográfico. Santiago de Chile, Impr.
Universitaria, 1918. 60 p.   (1742

LAFONE QUEVEDO, SAMUEL A.

TORRES, Luis María. Dr. Samuel A. Lafone Quevedo, director del Museo (1906-1920), noticia bibliográfica. (Revista del Museo de
La Plata, Buenos Aires, t. 25, p. ix-xxvi,
1921)   (1743
   Jones 868a.

LAMAS, ANDRES

ARREDONDO, Horacio. Los "Apuntes estadísticos" del Dr. Andrés Lamas. Montevideo, El
Siglo Ilustrado, 1928. 175 p.   (1744
   Reprinted from Revista del Instituto Histórico y Geográfico del Uruguay, Montevideo,
t. 6, no. 1, p. 25-195, 1928. Cited in
Musso 538.

FURLONG CARDIFF, Guillermo. Bibliografía de
Andrés Lamas. Buenos Aires, 1944. 366 p.
(Publicaciones del cincuentenario de la Aca-
demia Nacional de Historia, 2)   (1745
   Includes 888 items.

LANDAETA ROSALES, Manuel

LANDAETA ROSALES, Manuel. Hoja de servicios
e índice de publicaciones históricas y estadísticas. Caracas, Empresa El Cojo,
1920. 30 p.   (1746
   First edition published with title: Indice de los trabajos históricos y estadísticos (Caracas, Tip. Americana, 1909)

-----. Indice de los trabajos históricos y
estadísticos de Manuel Landaeta Rosales.
Caracas, Tip. Americana, 1909. 30 p. (1747
   A second edition was published in Caracas
in 1920, under title Hoja de servicios e
índice de publicaciones históricas y estadísticas.---Jones 2926.

LANDIVAR, RAFAEL

BENDFELDT ROJAS, Lourdes. Tópicos en la bibliografía landivariana. Guatemala, Universidad de San Carlos, Facultad de Humanidades, 1962. 170 p. mimeogr.   (1748

VALLE, Rafael Heliodoro. Bibliografía de Rafael de Landívar. Bogotá, Instituto Caro y
Cuervo, 1953. 48 p.   (1749
   Reprinted from Thesaurus, v. 8, p. 35-80,
1952.

VILLACORTA CALDERON, José Antonio. Estudios
bio-bibliográficos sobre Rafael Landívar.
Guatemala, Tip. Nacional, 1931.
157 p.   (1750
   Bibliografía: p. 153-57.
   Published also in Anales de la Sociedad
de Geografía e Historia, Guatemala, v. 8,
1931-1932.---Jones 1315.

LARRABURE Y UNANUE, EUGENIO

LARRABURE Y UNANUE, Eugenio. Manuscritos y
publicaciones. Lima, 1934-1936.
2 v.   (1751
   Vol. 1, Literatura y crítica literaria;
v. 2, Historia y arqueología.---Jones 2661.

LARRETA, ENRIQUE

MONTERO, María Luisa, and TORTOLA, Angélica L.
Contribución a la bibliografía de Enrique
Larreta. Buenos Aires, Fondo Nacional de
las Artes [1964] 59 p. (Bibliografía argentina de artes y letras; compilaciones
especiales, no. 19)   (1752

LASTARRIA, JOSE VICTORINO

FUENZALIDA GRANDON, Alejandro. Lastarria i
su tiempo (1817-1888); su vida, obras e influencia en el desarrollo político e intelectual de Chile. Santiago de Chile, Impr.
Barcelona, 1911. 2 v.   (1753
   1st edition published in 1893.
   Bibliografía i notas bibliográficas: v. 2,
p. 273-315.---Jones 1488.

ZAÑARTU, Sady. Lastarria, el hombre solo.
Prólogo de Ricardo A. Latcham. Santiago
de Chile, Ediciones Ercilla, 1938. 266 p.
(Colección Contemporáneos)   (1754
   "Obras principales de don José Victorino
Lastarria": p. 263-64. "Fuentes bibliográ-
ficas": p. 265-66.---Jones 1664.

LATORRE, MARIANO

MARIANO LATORRE: vida y obra - bibliografía -

MARIANO LATORRE: vida y obra... (Cont.)
antología. N.Y., Hispanic Institute in the
U.S., 1944. 88 p.   (1755
   Bibliography by Magda Arce and Sidonia C.
Rosenbaum.

LAVAL, RAMON A.

LAVAL, Ramón A. Bibliografía de Ramón A. Laval. (Revista chilena de historia y geografía, Santiago, t. 63, p. 48-62, 1930) (1756
   Jones 1507.

LAVALLE, JUAN BAUTISTA DE

NOMBRAMIENTOS, servicios y publicaciones del
Dr. Juan Bautista de Lavalle. Lima, [Tip.
R. Varese] 1945. 8 p.   (1757
   Cited in Anuario bibliográfico peruano,
1945, item 740.

LAVALLEJA, JUAN ANTONIO

URUGUAY. Biblioteca Nacional. Bibliografía:
Juan Antonio Lavalleja. [Montevideo, 1953]
9 p. mimeogr.   (1758
   Cited in Musso 262.

LAZO, BENITO

LEGUIA, Jorge Guillermo. Bibliografía de Benito Lazo. (Boletín bibliográfico, Biblioteca Central, Universidad de San Marcos,
Lima, v. 3, no. 6, 1928)   (1759
   Jones 2669.

LEGUIA, JORGE GUILLERMO

ROMERO, Emilia. Bibliografía de Jorge Guillermo Leguía. Lima, Cía. de Impresiones
y Publicidad, 1940. 68 p.   (1760
   Jones 2736b. Reprinted from Boletín bibliográfico, Biblioteca Central, Universidad Mayor de San Marcos, año 13, no. 3,
p. 159-224, oct. 1940.

LEGUIZAMON, MARTINIANO

TORRE REVELLO, José. Martiniano Leguizamón,
el hombre y su obra. Paraná, Arg., 1939.
40 p.   (1761
   Jones 867a.

LENZ, RODOLFO

CHILE. Universidad. Homenaje a la memoria
del dr. Rodolfo Lenz. Santiago, 1938.
169 p. (Anales de la Facultad de Filosofía

CHILE. Universidad. Homenaje... (Cont.)
y Educación. Sección de Filología,
t. 2)   (1762
   "Bibliografía de las publicaciones ... del
dr. Lenz": p. 160-69.---Jones 1435a.

LENZ, Rodolfo. Bibliografía de las publicaciones científicas y pedagógicas del Dr. Rodolfo Lenz. Santiago de Chile, Impr. Universitaria, 1914. 41 p.   (1763
   Published in Revista de bibliografía chilena y extranjera, mayo 1914. Cited in Laval 154. Includes 81 citations.

LEON, NICOLAS

LEON, Nicolás. Noticia de las publicaciones
originales y de varios autores hechas hasta
el presente por el Dr. Nicolás León; 3a. ed.
México, El Tiempo, 1901. 12 p.   (1764
   Millares 640 notes that this work was privately printed in an edition of 100 copies.

-----. Noticia de sus obras originales impresas e inéditas, las de varios autores por él
editadas, sociedades científicas a que pertenece, comisiones y empleos públicos por él
desempeñados hasta el año 1908, 25 de su
graduación médica. México, Tip. Vda. de F.
Díaz de Leon, Sucs., 1908. 34 p.   (1765
   Jones 2300.

-----. -----. Suplemento no. 1. México,
1919. 17 p. Covers the period 1909-
1919.   (1766
   Cited in Millares 641.

-----. Noticia de sus obras originales impresas e inéditas ... desde el año de 1874
hasta el de 1920. [México, 1920]
20 p.   (1767
   Reprinted from the author's Biblioteconomía. [México, 1920] p. 148-67. Cited in
Millares 643.

-----. Noticia de sus escritos originales
impresos e inéditos. Los de varios autores
por él editados. Traducciones de obras, impresas e inéditas. Sociedades científicas a
las cuales pertenece, comisiones y empleos
públicos que ha servido, 1874 a 1925. [Mé-
xico, Impr. de M. León Sánchez, 1925]
60 p.   (1768
   Jones 2301.

QUINTANA, José Miguel. El doctor Nicolás
León, historiador y bibliógrafo mexicano.
(2o. Congreso Internacional de Historia de
América. Buenos Aires, 1938. v. 5, p. 287-
95)   (1769
   Jones 2302.

VALLES, Roberto. Indice de anónimos de la
Bibliografía mexicana del siglo XVIII del

VALLES, Roberto. Indice de... (Cont.)
Dr. Don Nicolás León. México, D.F., Vargas
Rea, 1946. 43 p. (Biblioteca aportación
histórica, no. 92)   (1770

-----. Indice de impresos de la Bibliografía
mexicana del siglo XVIII del Dr. Don Nicolás
León. México, D.F., Vargas Rea, 1946. 28 p.
(Biblioteca aportación histórica,
no. 108)   (1771

-----. Indice de nombres de la Bibliografía
mexicana del siglo XVIII del Dr. Don Nicolás
León. México, Edit. Vargas Rea, 1945. 60 p.
(Biblioteca aportación histórica, no.
111)   (1772

LEON PINELO, ANTONIO RODRIGUEZ DE

LEON PINELO, Antonio Rodríguez de. Discurso
sobre la importancia, forma y disposición
de la recopilación de leyes de las Indias
Occidentales, que en su Real Consejo presenta el licenciado Antonio de León, 1623. Estudios biobibliográficos por José Toribio
Medina; prólogo de Aniceto Almeyda. Santiago de Chile, Fondo Histórico y Bibliográfico José Toribio Medina, 1956. xix,
176 p.   (1773

O'RYAN, Juan Enrique. Biblioteca de "Chile
moderno". Don Antonio de León Pinelo. Notas y rectificaciones. Valparaíso, Lit. e
Impr. Sud-Americana de Babra y Cía., 1903.
23 p.   (1774
   Cited in Laval 245.

LISBOA, ANTONIO FRANCISCO

MARTINS, Judite. Apontamentos para a bibliografia referente a Antonio Francisco Lisboa.
(Revista do Serviço do patrimonio historico
e artistico nacional, Rio de Janeiro, no.
3, p. 179-205, 1939)   (1775
   100 items; annotated.---Jones 1095c.

LLAMES MASSINI, JUAN CARLOS

LLAMES MASSINI, Juan Carlos. Antecedentes,
títulos y trabajos. Buenos Aires, Impr. y
Casa Edit. Coni, 1918. 45 p.   (1776
   Cited in Binayán 59.

LLORENS TORRES, LUIS

LUIS LLORENS TORRES: vida y obra - bibliografía - antología. New York, Hispanic
Institute in the United States [1953] (Autores modernos, 22)   (1777
   Bibliography by Félix L. Alegría. Reprinted from Revista hispánica moderna,

LUIS LLORENS TORRES: vida y obra ... (Cont.)
año 19, no. 1.

LOPEZ PORTILLO Y ROJAS, JOSE

VILLASEÑOR Y VILLASEÑOR, Ramiro. Bibliografía
de José López Portillo y Rojas, 1850-1923.
Guadalajara, 1950. 20 p. (Suplemento a Et
Caetera, Guadalajara, año 1, no. 4, en./dic.
1950)   (1778
    Cited in González 131.

LOPEZ Y GARCIA, GUSTAVO

LE ROY Y CASSA, Jorge Eduardo. Elogio del dr.
Gustavo López y García. Habana, Impr. de
Lloredo y Cía., 1915. 49 p.   (1779
    "Bibliografía del dr. López y García"(157
items): p. 31-49.---Jones 1860.

LORENTE, SEBASTIAN

ZULEN, Pedro Salvino. Bibliografía de Sebastián Lorente (1813-1884) (Boletín bibliográfico, Biblioteca Central, Universidad Mayor de San Marcos, Lima, v. 1, no. 6,
1923)   (1780
    Jones 2779.

LOSADA Y PUGA, CRISTOBAL DE

BIO-BIBLIOGRAFIA de Cristóbal de Losada y Puga. Lima, Tall. Gráf. de la Edit. Lumen,
1945. p. 180-88.   (1781
    Reprinted from Boletín de la Biblioteca
Nacional, Lima, año 2, no. 6, en. 1945.
Cited in Anuario bibliográfico peruano,
1945.

LOZANO, PEDRO

FURLONG CARDIFF, Guillermo. El p. Pedro Lozano, S.J.; su personalidad y su obra; bio-
bibliografía. Montevideo, Impr. "El Siglo
Ilustrado", 1930. 104 p.   (1782
    Reprinted from Revista de la Sociedad
Amigos de la Arqueología, t. 4, 1930.
"Obras consultadas": p. 103-04.---Jones
2837.

GARCIA ACEVEDO, Daniel. Documentos inéditos
de Lozano. (Revista histórica de la Universidad, Montevideo, año 1, p. 862-94;
año 2, p. 147-70, 1907-1909)   (1783
    Jones 2838.

LEONHARDT, Carlos. El p. Pedro Lozano (S.J.);
historiador rioplatense, nuevas noticias
para su biografía. (Boletín del Instituto
de Investigaciones Históricas, Buenos Aires,

LEONHARDT, Carlos ... (Cont.)
    t. 3, p. 201-32, 1925)   (1784
    Jones 751a.

LUZ Y CABALLERO, JOSE CIPRIANO DE

FIGAROLA CANEDA, Domingo. Bibliografía de Luz
y Caballero; 2a. ed. corr. y aum. Habana,
Impr. "El Siglo XX", de A. Miranda, 1915.
272 p.   (1785
    "Las cinco primeras partes de esta obra se
dieron a la estampa en la Revista de la Facultad de Letras y Ciencias de nuestra Universidad (1914-1915) Ahora se reproducen
corregidas, aumentadas, completas con las
abreviaturas y una tabla metódica."---Jones
1822.

LYNCH, BENITO

BECCO, Horacio Jorge, and NASON, Marshall R.
Bibliografía de Benito Lynch. Buenos Aires,
Fondo Nacional de las Artes [1961]   (1786
    Section 2 of Bibliografía argentina de ar-
tes y letras, no. 8, p. 51-88, oct./dic.
1960.

MACEO Y GRAJALES, ANTONIO

PERAZA SARAUSA, Fermín. Bibliografía de Antonio Maceo y Grajales. La Habana, Anuario
Bibliográfico Cubano, 1945. 63 p. (Biblioteca del bibliotecario, 12)   (1787

-----. -----. Habana, Depto. de Cultura,
1946. 72 p. (Publ. de la Biblioteca Municipal de Habana, Ser. C: Guías bibliográficas, 12)   (1788

-----. Maceo en El Fígaro. Habana, Depto.
de Cultura, 1946. 21 p. (Publ. de la Biblioteca Municipal de la Habana, Ser. C:
Guías bibliográficas, 11)   (1789

MACHADO, J. GABRIEL

MACHADO, J. Gabriel. Indice bibliográfico.
Caracas, C. A. Artes Gráficas Scra., 1945.
47 p.   (1790

MACHADO DE ASSIS, JOAQUIM MARIA

SOUSA, José Galante de. Bibliografía de Machado de Assis. Rio de Janeiro, 1955.
772 p. (Instituto Nacional do Livro, Coleção B 1; Bibliografia, 10)   (1791
    17 leaves at end: facsimiles of title
pages of works by Machado de Assis and sam-
pling of text in his own handwriting.

SOUSA, José Galante de. Fontes para o estudo de Machado de Assis. Rio de Janeiro, Instituto Nacional do Livro, 1958. 310 p. (Coleção B 1, bibliografia, 11) (1792

MAGALHÃES, ADELINO

PLACER, Xavier. Bio-bibliografía de Adelino Magalhães. 2a. ed. revista e atualizada. Rio de Janeiro, Edições "Margem", 1953. 29 p. (1793
First edition mimeographed in 1951.

MAGALHÃES, BASILIO DE

PAIVA, Tancredo de Barros. Basilio de Magalhães, ligeiras notas bio-bibliographicas. Rio de Janeiro, Livraria Martins, 1930. 64 p. (1794
"Principaes referencias": p. 60-4.---Jones 1124.

MALLEA, EDUARDO

BECCO, Horacio Jorge. Eduardo Mallea. Buenos Aires, Instituto de Literatura Argentina "Ricardo Rojas", Universidad de Buenos Aires, 1959. (Guías bibliográficas, 3) (1795

MARCO DEL PONT, JOSE

CONDE MONTERO, Manuel. Bibliografía de Alejandro Rosa, José Marcó del Pont, Enrique Peña. Buenos Aires, Tall. Graf. Rodríguez Giles, 1927. 16 p. (1795a

MARIATEGUI, JOSE CARLOS

ROUILLON, Guillermo. Bio-bibliografía de José Carlos Mariátegui. Lima, Universidad Nacional Mayor de San Marcos, 1963. 345 p. (Biblioteca de estudios superiores) (1796

MARKHAM, CLEMENTS ROBERT

OLIVAS, Antonio. Contribución a la bibliografía de Sir Clements Robert Markham (julio 20 de 1830-enero 30 de 1916) Lima, Compañía de Impresiones y Publicidad, 1924 [i.e. 1942] (1797
Reprinted from Boletín bibliográfico, Lima, año 15, no. 1-2, p. 69-91, jul. 1942.

MARTI, JOSE

CUBA. Biblioteca Nacional. Relación de las obras de y sobre José Martí que posee la

CUBA. Biblioteca Nacional ... (Cont.) Biblioteca Nacional. La Habana, 1953. 47 p. (Publicaciones) (1798

DOMINICAN REPUBLIC. Universidad de Santo Domingo. Biblioteca. Contribución a la bibliografía Martiana; centenario del nacimiento de José Martí, 1853-1953. [Ciudad Trujillo] 1953. 10 p. mimeogr. (1799

FIGAROLA CANEDA, Domingo. Para la biografía de José Martí. (Revista de la Biblioteca Nacional, Habana, t. 1, p. 138-60, 1909) (1800
Jones 1828.

GONZALEZ, Manuel Pedro. Fuentes para el estudio de José Martí, ensayo de bibliografía clasificada. La Habana, Ministerio de Educación, Dirección de Cultura, 1950. 517 p. (Bibliografía cubana, 1) (1801

HAVANA. Biblioteca Municipal. Guía bibliográfica sobre José Martí. Habana, 1937. [4] p. (Publicaciones, Ser. C: Guías bibliográficas, 2) (1802

JOSE MARTI (1853-1895): vida y obra - bibliografía - antología. New York, Hispanic Institute in the United States, 1953. 243 p. (Autores modernos, 21) (1803

LLAVERIAS Y MARTINEZ, Joaquín. Los periódicos de Martí. La Habana, Impr. Pérez, Sierra y Cía., 1929. 131 p. (1804
Jones 1867.

MARTI, José Julián. Ideario; ordenado por M. Isidro Méndez. Habana, Cultural, 1930. 410 p. (Colección de libros cubanos, v. 15) (1805
Bibliografía: p. 385-410.---Jones 1871.

PERAZA SARAUSA, Fermín. Bibliografía de José Martí. 1949-1950. Habana, Anuario Bibliográfico Cubano, 1950-1951. 2 v. (Biblioteca del bibliotecario, 32, 35) 1949: 56 p.; 1950: 46 p. (1806

-----. Bibliografía martiana, 1853-1953. Ed. del centenario. Habana, Comisión Nacional Organizadora de los Actos y Ediciones del Centenario y del Monumento de Martí, 1954. xvi, 692 p. (1807

-----. -----. Another edition, Havana, 1956. 720 p. (1807a

-----. Bibliografía martiana, 1940-1958/1959. Habana, 1941-1960. 18 v. (Habana. Biblioteca Municipal. Publicaciones, Ser. C: Guías bibliográficas, 4, 7-10, 13-17, 19-26) (1808
Each issue of the series from 12 to 64 pages.

PERAZA SARAUSA, Fermín. Cronología de la obra
martiana. [Habana, Anuario Bibliográfico
Cubano, 1955] 41 p. (Biblioteca del bibliotecario, 45)   (1809
"Publicada por primera vez como un índice
de la Bibliografía martiana, 1853-1953, edición del centenario."

URUGUAY. Universidad. Facultad de Humanidades y Ciencias. Biblioteca. Aportes para
una bibliografía de José Martí. Montevideo,
1954. 40 p.   (1810

VEREZ DE PERAZA, Elena Luisa. José Martí, compilación bibliográfica de los fondos que posee la Biblioteca Pública Panamericana "Habana". Habana, Sociedad Colombista Panamericana, 1953. 21 p. (Biblioteca Pública
Panamericana "Habana". Bibliografías panamericanas, 2) mimeogr.   (1811

MARTINO, PEDRO J.

ESCARDO Y ANAYA, Víctor. Bibliografía del Dr.
Pedro J. Martino. Montevideo, Garcia Morales, 1939. 3 p.   (1812
Reprinted from Archivos del Hospital Pereira Rossell, Montevideo, año 1, no. 3, p. 199-
203, dic. 1938. Cited in Musso 242.

MEDINA, JOSE TORIBIO

AMUNATEGUI Y SOLAR, Domingo. José Toribio Me-
dina, Santiago, Prensa de la Universidad de
Chile, 1932. 48 p.   (1813
Jones 1387.

CHIAPPA, Víctor M. Biblioteca Medina. Noticias acerca de la vida y obras de don José
Toribio Medina. Santiago de Chile, Impr.
Barcelona, 1907. 276 p.   (1814
One of the best sources for Medina bibliography; see also Guillermo Feliú Cruz "Continuación de la bibliografía de ... Chiappa",
in Revista chilena de historia y geografía,
v. 47, p. 382-542 and in Boletín del Instituto de Investigaciones Históricas Buenos
Aires v. 13, p. 220-492.---Jones 1422.

-----. Epítome de las publicaciones de D.
José Toribio Medina. Santiago de Chile,
Impr. Universitaria, 1914. 88 p.   (1815
226 items listed.

CHILE. Biblioteca Nacional. Homenaje a don
José Toribio Medina con ocación de su falle-
cimiento, 21 de octubre 1852, 11 de diciem-
bre de 1930. Santiago de Chile, Impr. "La
Tracción", 1931. 115 p.   (1816
Jones 1606.

FELIU CRUZ, Guillermo. Bibliografía de don
José Toribio Medina (1923-1930) [Santiago]
Impr. "La Tracción," 1931. 108 p.   (1817

FELIU CRUZ, Guillermo. Bibliografía...(Cont.)
Also printed with additional "Notas críticas" for each entry by the Imprenta de la
Universidad, Buenos Aires, 1931. See item
1818.

-----. Bibliografía de don José Toribio Medina; notas críticas con retrato. Buenos Aires, Impr. de la Universidad, 1931.
177 p.   (1818
Reprinted from Boletín del Instituto de
Investigaciones Históricas de la Facultad
de Filosofía y Letras, año 10, t. 13, no.
49-50, p. 316-492, jul.-dic. 1931.
Jones, item 1472a, notes contents as
follows: pt. 1, Catálogo formado por Víctor
M. Chiappa, 1873-1914 (no. 1-226); pt. 2,
Contiuación...por G. Feliú Cruz, 1910-1923
(no. 227-307); pt. 3, Bibliografía de...Medi-
na hasta su muerte, por G. Feliú Cruz, con
una lista de obras póstumas, 1923-1930
(no. 308-408)

-----. La biblioteca americana de don José
Toribio Medina. (Revista chilena de historia y geografía, Santiago, t. 51, p. 276-87,
1925-1926)   (1819
Jones 1473.

-----. Continuación de la Bibliografía de
Víctor M. Chiappa. (Revista chilena de historia y geografía, Santiago, t. 47, p. 382-
452, 1924)   (1820
Continues Chiappa's list of Medina's
works from no. 227-307.---Jones 1475.

-----. José Toribio Medina, la formación del
bibliógrafo; estudio crítico. Santiago de
Chile, 1958. 85 p.   (1821

-----. La labor literaria y científica de
José Toribio Medina en 1910. Santiago de
Chile, 1961. 64 p.   (1822

GALVEZ GARCIA, María Albertina. Síntesis bio-
bibliográfico de don José Toribio Medina y
su Historia de la Imprenta en Guatemala.
Guatemala, Edit. del Ministerio de Educación Pública "José de Pineda Ibarra", 1960.
46 p. (Colección "José de Pineda Ibarra",
3)   (1823

LOOSER, Gualtero. Don José Toribio Medina y
las ciencias naturales y antropológicas.
Santiago de Chile, 1931. 27 p.   (1824
"Bibliografía antropológica de...Medina":
p. 21-7. From the Boletín de la Biblioteca Nacional.---Jones 1519a

MEDINA, José Toribio. Escritos inéditos;
introducción y notas de Alberto Tauro.
Lima, 1954. 52 p. (Ediciones de la Biblioteca Nacional, 10)   (1825

PRIETO DEL RIO, Luis Francisco. Muestras de
errores y defectos del "Diccioario biográfico colonial de Chile por José Toribio Medina". Santiago, Impr. Chile, 1907.
124 p.   (1826

RAMOS, Roberto. Bibliografía de Don José Toribio Medina. México, Graficos Herber, 1953.
44 p.   (1827
    Reprinted from Boletín de la Biblioteca
Nacional, México D. F., t. 3, no. 4.

ROBERTS, Sarah Elizabeth. José Toribio Medi-
na, his life and works. Washington, D.C.,
Inter-American Bibliographical and Library
Association, 1941. 192 p.   (1828
    Jones 1588a

SCHAIBLE, Carl H. Bibliografía de José Toribio Medina; introducción de Alamiro de Avi-
la Martel. Santiago, Sociedad de Bibliófilos Chilenos, 1952. xviii, 251 p.   (1829

SOCIEDAD CHILENA de Historia y Geografía, Santiago. Homenaje que la Sociedad de Historia
y Geografía tributa a su socio honorario don
José Toribio Medina con ocasión de enterar
cincuenta años de labor histórica y literaria. Santiago, Impr. Cervantes, 1924.
452 p.   (1830
    Issued also as Revista de historia y geo-
grafía, Santiago, t. 47, 1924.
    Contains 17 contributions, including Ca-
tálogo de las publicaciones de don José Toribio Medina (1873-1914) por Víctor M. Chiappa (226 titles, p. 333-82) and Continuación
del Catálogo...seguido de una biobibliografía de don José Toribio Medina, por Guillermo Feliú Cruz (no. 227-307, p. 383-452)
    An earlier edition of the Catálogo by V.
M. Chiappa was published separately in 1914
under the title: Epítome de las publicaciones de d. José Toribio Medina (226 titles,
1873-1914) A further continuation of the
Catálogo with title Bibliografía de don José Toribio Medina was published by G. Feliú
Cruz in v. 13 of the Boletín del Instituto
de Investigaciones Históricas, Buenos Aires,
1931, and also separately.---Jones 1545.

TOWNSEND EZCURRA, Andrés. José Toribio Medina; síntesis bio-bibliográfica. [Guatema-
la, 1952] 18 p. (Colección mínima,
4)   (1831

VILLALOBOS R., Sergio. Medina: su vida y sus
obras (1852-1930) Santiago, Comisión Nacional de Conmemoración del Centenario del
Nacimiento de José Toribio Medina, 1952.
52 p. (Publicación 2)   (1832
    Medina's works are listed under broad
subjects.

ZAMUDIO Z., José. Medina y la bibliografía.
Santiago, Nascimento, 1952. 100 p.   (1832a

MENDEZ, JULIO

MENDEZ, Julio. Indice de los estudios y trabajos médicos. Buenos Aires, A. Etchepareborda, 1905. 16 p.   (1833
    Cited in Binayán, item 60.

MENDEZ PEREIRA, OCTAVIO

PANAMA. Universidad. Biblioteca. Bibliografía de y sobre Méndez Pereira y la Universidad. Panamá, 1961. 18 p.
mimeogr.   (1834

SUSTO, Juan Antonio. "Dr. Octavio Méndez Pereira" (bio-bibliografía) Panamá, Impr.
en la U. P., 1954. 16 p.   (1835

MENDIETA, JERONIMO R.

LARRIÑAGA, Juan R. Fray Jerónimo de Mendieta,
historiador de Nueva España (1525-1604)
Apuntes bibliográficos. (Archivo ibero-
americano, Madrid, v.1, p. 290-300, 488-99;
v.2, p. 188-201, 387-404; v.4, p. 341-73,
1914-1915)   (1836
    Jones 2277.

MENDONÇA, LUCIO

MENDONÇA, Edgar Süssekind de, and MENDONÇA,
Carlos Süssekind de. Ensaio bio-biblio-
gráfico. Rio de Janeiro, Civilização Bra-
sileira, 1934. 184 p. (Publ. da Academia
Brasileira, 3: Bibliografia, 6)   (1837
    Ensaio de bibliografia: p. 81-111.---
Jones 1212a.

MENDONÇA, SALVADOR DE

LEÃO, Múcio. Salvador de Mendonça; ensaio
biobibliográfico. Rio de Janeiro, Academia Brasileira, 1952. 133 p. (Coleção
Afrânio Peixoto, 3; Biobibliografia) (1838

MENENDEZ Y PELAYO, MARCELINO

SANCHEZ AREVALO, Francisco. Marcelino Menéndez y Pelayo y Colombia. Bogotá, Edit.
Kelly, 1957. 65 p. (Ediciones de la Re-
vista "Ximénez de Quesada")   (1839

MERA, JUAN LEON

ROLANDO, Carlos A. Don Juan Leon Mera, 1832-
1932. Gauyaquil, Impr. i Tall. Municipa-
les, 1932. 28 p.   (1840
    Jones 2010.

MERCHAN, RAFAEL MARIA

FIGAROLA CANEDA, Domingo. Bibliografía de
Rafael M. Merchán; 2a. ed., corr. y aum.
Habana Impr. La Universal, 1905
48 p.   (1841
Jones 1823.

MEZA Y SUAREZ INCLAN, RAMON

FIGAROLA CANEDA, Domingo. El doctor Ramón
Meza y Suárez Inclán; noticia biobiblio-
gráfica, 2a. ed. corr. Habana, Impr. de la
Biblioteca Nacional, 1909. 21 p.   (1842
From "Revista de la Biblioteca Nacional",
v. 1, p. 31-51.---Jones 1825.

GONZALEZ DEL VALLE Y RAMIREZ, Francisco. Bibliografía del dr. Ramón Meza y Suárez Inclán. (Anales de la Academia de la Historia
de Cuba, Habana, t. 1, 1919)   (1843
Jones 1836

RODRIGUEZ LENDIAN, Evelio. Elogio del doctor
Ramón Meza y Suárez Inclán. Habana, Impr.
"El Siglo XX" de A. Miranda, 1915.
68 p.   (1844
Published also in Anales de la Academia
de la Historia, Habana, t. 1, p. 24-63, 210-
35; t. 2, p. 14-40, 1919-1920, including
bibliography (539 items).---Jones 1904.

MIRANDA, FRANCISCO DE

DAVILA, Vicente. Biografía de Miranda. Caracas, Tip. Americana, 1933. 50 p.   (1846
Bibliografía: p. 41-50.---Jones 2901

MIRANDA, Francisco de. The diary of Francisco de Miranda, tour of the United States,
1783-1784. The Spanish text, ed. with introduction and notes by William Spence
Robertson. New York, 1928. 206 p.   (1847
Bibliography: p. 173-78.---Jones 2934.

ROBERTSON, William Spence. Francisco de Miranda and the revolutionizing of Spanish America. (American Historical Association.
Annual report, 1906. Washington, D.C., 1908,
p. 189-539)   (1848
"Critical bibliography": p. 481-511.---
Jones 413.

-----. Francisco de Miranda y la revolución
de la América española. Traducción por Diego Mendoza. Bogotá, Impr. Nacional, 1918.
436 p. (Biblioteca de historia nacional,
v. 21)   (1849
Bibliografía crítica: p. 375-404.---Jones
2947.

-----. The life of Miranda. Chapel Hill,
Univ. of North Carolina Pr., 1929.

ROBERTSON, William Spence. The life...(Cont.)
2 v.   (1850
Bibliography: v. 2, p. 257-76.---Jones
2948.

MISTRAL, GABRIELA

ESCUDERO, Alfonso María. La prosa de Gabriela
Mistral; fichas de contribución a su inven-
tario. Santiago, [Escuela Tip. Salesiana
"La Gratitud Nacional"] 1950. 64 p.   (1851
Reprinted from Revista Universitaria.

-----. -----. 2a. ed. [Santiago de Chile]
1957. 60 p. (Ediciones de los Anales de
la Universidad de Chile. Serie roja: Letras, no. 14)   (1852

GABRIELA MISTRAL: vida y obra - bibliografía
- antología. New York, Hispanic Institute
in the United States, 1936. 53 p. (Autores modernos, 5)   (1853
Reprinted from Revista hispánica moderna,
año 3, no. 2. Bibliography by Sidonia C.
Rosenbaum.

PAN AMERICAN UNION. Inter-American Committee
on Bibliography. Gabriela Mistral, 1889-
1957. Washington, D.C., Pan American, 1958.
90 p.   (1854
A collection of the papers read as a tribute to the memory of Gabriela Mistral at a
literary gathering held in Washington on
Feb. 8, 1957.
Contents: - Recuerdo de Gabriela Mistral,
por Juan Marín. - Gabriela Mistral; aspectos
de su vida y de su obra, por Juan Uribe
Echevarría. - Alabanza de Gabriela Mistral,
por Rafael Heliodoro Valle. - Las ideas americanistas de Gabriela Mistral, por José A.
Mora. - Los escritos de Gabriela Mistral y
estudios sobre su obra, por Norah Albanell
y Nancy Mango.

PINILLA, Norberto. Bibliografía crítica sobre
Gabriela Mistral. Santiago, Edición de la
Universidad de Chile, 1940. 69 p.   (1855
Jones 1566a.

ROSENBAUM, Sidonia C. Gabriela Mistral, bi-
bliografía. (Revista hispánica moderna,
New York, año 3, p. 135-40, 1937)   (1856
Jones 1589.

SILVA CASTRO, Raúl. Estudios sobre Gabriela
Mistral. Santiago de Chile, Zig-Zag, 1935.
253 p.   (1857
Bibliography: p. 229-49.---Jones 1623.

MITRE, BARTOLOME

CONDE MONTERO, Manuel. Bibliografía de Bartolomé Mitre. (Boletín de la Juta de His-

CONDE MONTERO, Manuel. Bibliografía... (Cont.)
toria y Numismática Americana, Buenos Aires,
1925. v. 2, p. 207-47, 1925) (1858
The author has published various personal
bibliographies in the Boletín de la Junta:
Enrique Peña. (v. 3, p. 155-60), José Marcó
del Pont (v. 3, p. 152-54), Alejandro Rosa
(v. 3, p. 149-51), Manuel F. Mantilla (v. 5,
p. 171-76), Joaquín V. González (v. 4, p.
295-320), Carlos I. Salas (v. 7, p. 391-94),
Carlos M. Urién (v. 6, p. 197-207), Gregorio
F. Rodríguez (v. 5, p. 179-91).---Jones 670.
Of the bibliographies those of Mitre, Peña,
Marcó del Pont, Rosa and González appeared
as separates.

-----. Bibliografía de Bartolomé Mitre.
I: libros y folletos. Buenos Aires, Tall.
Gráf. Rodríguez Giles, 1927. 43 p. (1859
Jones, 670, cites this bibliography as
published in Boletín de la Junta de Historia
y Numismática Americana, Buenos Aires, v. 2,
p. 207-47, 1925.

MITRE, Adolfo, CONDE MONTERO, Manuel, etc.
Apuntes de la juventud de Mitre y bibliogra-
fía de Mitre. Buenos Aires, Tall. Gráf.
Didot, 1947. 294 p. (Cincuentenario de la
Academia Nacional de Historia, Publ.
3) (1860
The bibliography lists 150 items.

MOLINA, JUAN RAMON

MOLINA, Juan Ramón. Tierras, mares y cielos.
Prefacio de Enrique González Martínez, bibliografía de Rafael Heliodoro Valle. Tegucigalpa, Impr. Calderón, 1937.
253 p. (1861
Bibliografía: p. 235-53.---Jones 1326a.

MOLINA, PEDRO

GUATEMALA. Comité del Centenario de los Pro-
ceres Pedro Molina y José Francisco Barrun-
día. Bibliografía del doctor Pedro Molina.
Guatemala, Edit. del Ministerio de Educación
Pública, 1954. 55 p. (Colección Documentos,
16) (1862

MOLL, BRUNO

MOLL, Bruno. Publicaciones del Dr. Bruno Moll
en castellano de 1937 a jun. de 1944. [Li-
ma, 1948] 4 p. (1863

-----. -----. julio de 1944 a junio de 1947.
[Lima, 1948] [2] p. (1864

PUBLICACIONES del Dr. Bruno Moll en castellano
de 1937 a 1954, y 1954-1960. [Lima, 1960]
2 v. (1865

PUBLICACIONES del Dr. Bruno Moll ... (Cont.)
Cited in Anuario bibliográfico peruano,
1948-1960, item 11b.

MONCORVO, ARTHUR (filho)

MONCORVO, Arthur, (filho) Trabalhos originaes
publicados pelo Dr. Arthur Moncorvo filho.
[E principaes investigações scientificas do
Dr. Moncorvo filho.] n. p. [1928?] [5]-21,
7 p. (1866

MONTALVO, JUAN

REYES, Oscar Efrén. Vida de Juan Montalvo.
Quito, Tall. Gráf. Nacionales, 1935.
418 p. (1867
Bibliography: p. 411-18.---Jones 2004.

ROLANDO, Carlos A. Don Juan Montalvo, 1832-
1932. Guayaquil, Impr. i Tall. Municipales,
1932. 22 p. (1868
Datos biográficos - Bibliografía de don
Juan Montalvo - Bibliografía que trata de
Montalvo - En honor de Juan Montalvo.---
Jones 2011.

MONTEAGUDO, BERNARDO

SALAS, Carlos I. Bibliografía de Bernardo
Monteagudo. Buenos Aires, 1924. 104 p.
(Buenos Aires, Universidad Nacional. Ins-
tituto de Investigaciones Históricas. Publ.,
no. 23) (1869
Jones 832.

MONTORO Y VALDES, RAFAEL

BARRIAL DOMINGUEZ, José. Bibliografía de Rafael Montoro y Valdés. La Habana, Biblioteca Nacional, 1952. 134 p. (1870

MORENO, FRANCISCO PASCASIO

TORRES, Luis María. Dr. Francisco P. Moreno,
fundador y primer director del Museo; noticia biobibliográfica. Buenos Aires, 1921.
18 p. (1871
From Revista del Museo de La Plata, t. 26.
---Jones 868.

MORENO, MARIANO

PIÑERO, Norberto. Los escritos de Mariano
Moreno. Buenos Aires, 1938. 234 p. (1872
Jones 815b.

MORQUIO, LUIS

ESCARDO Y ANAYA, Víctor. Bibliografía del
Profesor Morquio. Montevideo [Garcia Mo-
rales] 1938. 24 p.   (1873
Reprinted from Archivos del Hospital Pereira Rossell, Montevideo, año 1, no. 1,
p. 11-34, jun. 1938. Cited in Musso 245.

MOTOLINIA, TORIBIO

GIL SALCEDO, J. J. Estudio bibliográfico de
Motolinia. México, 1953. 263 p.   (1874
Cited in Revista interamericana de biblio-
grafía, v. 4, p. 334.

MÜLLER, LAURO SEVERIANO

REIS, Marcos Konder. Lauro Müller; ensaio
biobibliográfico. Rio de Janeiro, Academia Brasileira de Letras, 1953.
98 p.   (1874a

MUÑOZ, JUAN BAUTISTA

MURO OREJON, Antonio. Juan Bautista Muñoz.
Las fuentes bibliográficas de la Historia
del Nuevo Mundo. Sevilla, Escuela de Estudios Hispano-Americanos, 1953.
73 p.   (1875
Reprinted from Anuario de estudios americanos, t. 10, p. 265-337, 1953.

MURATORI, LUDOVICO ANTONIO

GEOGHEGAN, Abel Rodolfo. Bibliografía sobre
Ludovico A. Muratori y su obra sobre las
misiones jesuíticas del Paraguay, 1743-
1749. Buenos Aires, 1960. 23 p.   (1875a

NABUCO, JOAQUIM

BRAZIL. Ministério das Relações Exteriores.
Serviço de Documentação. Bibliografia de
Joaquim Nabuco. [Rio de Janeiro] 1949.
93 p.   (1876

OLIVEIRA, Oswaldo Mello Braga de. Bibliografia de Joaquim Nabuco. Rio de Janeiro, Departamento de Imprensa Nacional, 1952.
265 p. (Instituto Nacional do Livro, Coleção B 1; Bibliografia, 8)   (1877
In Bibliografia brasileira author is entered under Braga, Oswaldo Mello.

NANDINO, ELIAS

ARCE, David N. Poesía y mensaje de Elías
Nandino. México, Biblioteca Nacional, 1959.

ARCE, David N. Poesía y mensaje... (Cont.)
24 p. (Bibliografías mexicanas contemporáneas, 9)   (1878

NARIÑO, ANTONIO

GIRALDO JARAMILLO, Gabriel. Bibliografía selecta de [Antonio] Nariño. Bogotá, Edit.
Sucre, 1953. 24 p.   (1879

POSADA, Eduardo, and IBAÑEZ, Pedro M. El precursor. Documentos sobre la vida pública
y privada del General Antonio Nariño. Bogotá, Impr. Nacional, 1903. xxxii, 653 p.
(Biblioteca de historia nacional, 2) (1880
p. 164-91: Contains catalog of the Library of General Nariño.

NAVARRO, N. E.

RASGOS biográficos de Monseñor N. E. Navarro.
Resumen de sus labores. Caracas, Edit. Ve-
nezuela, 1943. 23 p.   (1881
Biographical sketch precedes bibliography
of over 80 entries.
Cited in HLAS, 9, item 80.

NERUDA, PABLO

PABLO NERUDA: vida y obra - bibliografía - antología. New York, Hispanic Institute in
the United States [1936] (Autores modernos,
4)   (1882
Bibliography by Sidonia C. Rosenbaum.

ROSENBAUM, Sidonia C. Pablo Neruda: biblio-
grafía. (Revista hispánica moderna, New
York, año 3, p. 32-4, 1936)   (1883
Jones 1590.

NERVO, AMADO

ESTRADA, Genaro. Bibliografía de Amado Nervo.
México, Impr. de la Secretaría de Relaciones Exteriores, 1925. 36 p. (Monografías
bibliográficas mexicanas, no. 1)   (1884
Jones 2160.

WELLMAN, Esther Turner. Amado Nervo, México's
religious poet. New York, Instituto de las
Españas en los Estados Unidos, 1936.
293 p.   (1885
Bibliography: p. 291-92.---Jones 2582.

NOGUES, M. A. F.

LISTE bibliographique des travaux scientifiques
de M. A. F. Noguès. Santiago de Chile, Impr.
Cervantès, 1892. 14 p.   (1886
Cited in Laval, item 159.

NOVO, SALVADOR

ARCE, David N. Nómina bibliográfica de Salvador Novo. México, 1963. 37 p. (Publ. de
la Biblioteca Nacional, 9; Bibliografías mexicanas contemporáneas, 13)   (1887
    Reprinted from Boletín de la Biblioteca
Nacional, México, v. 13, no. 4, p. 61-89,
oct./dic. 1962.

NUÑEZ, ENRIQUE BERNARDO

NUÑEZ, Enrique Bernardo. Indice de sus trabajos publicados. Caracas, 1963.
19 p.   (1888

NUTTAL, ZELIA

GOMEZ DE OROZCO, Federico. Doña Zelia Nuttall.
Nota bibliográfica. México, Tall. Gráf. del
Museo de Arqueología, Historia y Etnografía,
1933. 11 p.   (1889
    Cited in González, item 127.

OBEJERO, EDUARDO

OBEJERO, Eduardo. Títulos y trabajos (1880-
1914) Buenos Aires, Impr. Somoza Hnos.
[1914] 7 p.   (1890
    Cited in Binayán, item 63.

OCAMPO, VICTORIA

TUNINETTI, Beatriz T. Contribución a la bibliografía de Victoria Ocampo. Buenos Aires,
Instituto de Literatura Argentina "Ricardo
Rojas", Universidad de Buenos Aires, 1962.
32 p. (Guías bibliográficas, 6)   (1891

OCANTOS, CARLOS MARIA

ANDERSSON, Theodore. Carlos María Ocantos,
Argentine novelist; a study of indigenous,
French and Spanish elements in his work.
New Haven, Yale Univ. Pr., 1934. 136 p.
(Yale romanic studies, v. 8)   (1892
    Bibliography: p. 130-36.---Jones 556.

OCHARTE, PEDRO

STOLS, Alexander Alphonse Marius. Pedro
Ocharte; tercer impresor mexicano. México,
D.F., Impr. Nuevo Mundo, 1962.
138 p.   (1893

OCHOTERENA, ISAAC

VEGA, Crisoforo. Folleto bio-bibliográfico

VEGA, Crisoforo. Folleto... (Cont.)
del señor profesor y doctor don Isaac Ochoterena. [México, D.F.] Instituto de Biología, 1945. 30 p.   (1894
    Cited in Boletín de la Biblioteca Nacio-
nal, México, 2a. ép., año 14, no. 1/2,
p. 108, en./jun. 1963.

O'HIGGINS, BERNARDO

VICUÑA MacKENNA, Benjamín. Bibliografía del
general O'Higgins. (La corona del héroe.
Recopilación de datos i documentos para per-
petuar la memoria del general don Bernardo
O'Higgins. Santiago, 1872. p. 561-
72)   (1895
    Laval, 341.---Jones 1655.

ZAMUDIO Z., José. Fuentes bibliográficas para el estudio de la vida y de la época de
Bernardo O'Higgins. Santiago, Impr. "El
Esfuerzo", 1946. 286 p.   (1896
    The first and second part of this work
appeared in Boletín de la Academia Chilena
de la Historia, no. 25, 32.

OLIVAS ESCUDERO, FIDEL

ANGELES CABALLERO, César Augusto. Contribución a la bibliografía de Mons. Fidel Olivas
Escudero. [Lima, Impr. la "Crónica", 1950]
8 p.   (1897
    Reprinted from La Crónica, Lima, sept.
1950.

OLMOS, ANDRES DE

PILLING, James Constantine. The writings of
Padre Andrés de Olmos in the languages of
Mexico. Washington, Judd & Detweiler, 1895.
18 p.   (1898
    From American anthropologist, v. 8, no. 1
---Jones 2427.

OÑATE, JUAN DE

HAMMOND, George Peter. Don Juan de Oñate and
the founding of New Mexico; a new investi-
gation into the early history of New Mexico
in the light of a mass of new materials recently obtained from the Archivo General de
Indias, Seville, Spain. Santa Fe, N. M.,
El Palacio Pr. [1927] 228 p. (Historical
Society of New Mexico, Publ. in history,
v. 2)   (1899
    Bibliography: p. 211-20.---Jones 2233.

OROZCO Y BERRA, MANUEL

GARCIA, Rubén. Biografía, bibliografía e ico-

GARCIA, Rubén. Biografía... (Cont.)
nografía de don Manuel Orozco y Berra. México, D.F., 1934? 185 p.   (1900
    Bibliografía: p. 131-44. - Bibliografía
sobre Orozco y Berra: p. 145-46.
    Reprinted from Boletín de la Sociedad Me-
xicana de Geografía y Estadística, t. 44,
oct. 1934.---Jones 2186.

SOTO, Jesús S. Divagación sobre la biografía
y algo en explicación de la de Orozco y
Berra. (Boletín de la Sociedad Mexicana de
Geografía y Estadística, México, D.F., v. 44,
p. 423-93, 1935)   (1901
    Jones 2511. Bibliografía: p. 485-92.
Iconografía: p. 493.

OROZCO Y JIMENEZ, FRANCISCO

DAVILA GARIBI, José Ignacio Paulino. Labor
científica y literaria del Excmo. y Revmo.
Sr. Dr. Mtro. don Francisco y Jiménez. Intento bio-bibliográfico. Guadalajara, Tip.
Jaime, 1936. 44 p.   (1902
    Reprinted from Boletín de la Junta Auxi-
liar Jaliciense de la Sociedad Mexicana de
Geografía y Estadística, México, D.F., t.5,
no. 1. Cited in Millares, item 679.

ORTIZ, JOSE JOAQUIN

ARRIETA, Diógenes A. Colombianos contemporáneos, t. 1. Caracas, 1883. 175 p. (Primera serie)   (1903
    Jones 1677. Vol. 1: José Joaquín Ortiz.

OSORIO, MIGUEL ANGEL

VALLE, Rafael Heliodoro. Bibliografía de Porfirio Barba-Jacob. Ordenada por Emilia Romero de Valle. Bogotá, Instituto Caro y
Cuervo, 1961. 107 p.   (1904
    Reprinted from Thesaurus, boletín del
Instituto Caro y Cuervo, Bogotá, t. 15,
1960.

OTHON, MANUEL JOSE

MONTEJANO Y AGUIÑAGA, Rafael. Lo que escribió
Manuel José Othón; bibliografía esencial.
San Luis Potosí, Universidad Autónoma, 1959.
46 p.   (1905

OUTES, FELIX FAUSTINO

OUTES, Félix Faustino. Félix F. Outes; nómina de sus publicaciones, 1897-1922; ed.
privada, con motivo del XXV aniversario de
su labor de publicista. Buenos Aires, Impr.

OUTES, Félix Faustino. Félix F... (Cont.)
y Casa Editora "Coni", 1922. 57 p.   (1906
    Jones 807.

PACHECO, CARLOS MAURICIO

PAZ, Marta Lena. Bibliografía crítica de Carlos Mauricio Pacheco. Buenos Aires, Fondo
Nacional de las Artes [1963] 90 p. (Bibliografía argentina de artes y letras; compilaciones especiales, no. 14)   (1907

PABLOS, JUAN

MILLARES CARLO, Agustín, and CALVO, Julián.
Juan Pablos, primer impresor que a esta
tierra vino. México, D.F., Librería de Manuel Porrúa [1953] 220 p.   (1908
    62 items are described.

PAGES LARRAYA, ANTONIO

KISNERMAN, Natalio. Bibliografía de Antonio
Pagés Larraya. Buenos Aires, Grupo Editor
Argentino, 1963. 25 p. (Seria Bibliografías)   (1909
    Cited in Bibliografía argentina de artes y
letras no. 19, item 9328.

PALACIOS, ALFREDO

URUGUAY. Poder Legislativo. Biblioteca. Alfredo Palacios. Montevideo, 1955. 102,
66 p. (Referencia, no. 27) mimeogr. (1910
    Cited in Musso 286.

PALAFOX Y MENDOZA, JUAN DE

GARCIA, Genaro. Don Juan de Palafox y Mendoza,
obispo de Puebla y Osma, visitador y virrey
de la Nueva España. México, D.F., Bouret,
1918. 426 p.   (1911
    Bibliografía: p. 319-423.---Jones 2181.

PALMA, RICARDO

FELIU CRUZ, Guillermo. En torno de Ricardo
Palma. Santiago, Universidad de Chile, 1933.
2 v.   (1912
    Contents: v. 1, La estancia en Chile; -
v. 2, Ensayo crítico-bibliográfico.---Jones
2654.

SOCIEDAD "Amigos de Palma", Lima. Ricardo Palma, 1833-1933. Lima, Sociedad Amigos de Palma, 1934. 341 p.   (1913
    Jones 2753.

BIOGRAPHY

PASO Y TRONCOSO, FRANCISCO DEL

GALINDO Y VILLA, Jesús. Don Francisco del
Paso y Troncoso; su vida y sus obras. (Me-
morias y revista de la Sociedad Científica
"Antonio Alzate", México, D.F., t. 42,
p. 135-304, 491-670, 1923) (1914
Includes bibliography.---Jones 2174.

PASTEUR, LUIS

ROLANDO, Carlos A. Bibliografía de Luis
Pasteur. Guayaquil, Monteverde & Velarde,
1922. 15 p. (1915

PAYRO, ROBERTO JORGE

FERNANDEZ DE VIDAL, Stella Maris. Bibliografía de Roberto J. Payró (1867-1928) Buenos
Aires, Fondo Nacional de las Artes, 1962.
73 p. (Bibliografía argentina de artes y
letras; compilaciones especiales,
13) (1916

PAZ SOLDAN, CARLOS ENRIQUE

PAZ SOLDAN, Carlos Enrique. Mi foja de servicios a la causa de la cultura médico-social peruana. Lima, [Impresa en los Tall.
Gráf. del Asilo "Víctor Larco Herrera",
1922] 29 p. (1917
620 books, pamphlets and articles by the
author are cited.

PENA, PRUDENCIO DE

ESCARDO Y ANAYA, Víctor. Bibliografía del
profesor de Pena. Montevideo [García Mora-
les] 1938. 8 p. (1918
Reprinted from Archivos del Hospital Pereira Rossell, Montevideo, año 1, no. 2,
p. 95-101, set. 1938. Cited in Musso 247.

PEÑAFIEL, ANTONIO

OBRAS del Doctor Antonio Peñafiel y su biografía. México, D.F., Tip. de la "Sociedad Impresora", 1904. 44 p. (1919
Cited in Millares 700.

PEREZ DE SOTO, MELCHOR

ROMERO DE TERREROS Y VINENT, Manuel. Un bibliófilo en el Santo Oficio. México, D.F.,
Librería de Pedro Robredo, 1920.
47 p. (1920

PESSOA, FERNANDO

NEMESIO, Jorge. A obra poética de Fernando
Pessoa; estrutura das futuras edições.
[Salvador] 1958. 189 p. (Salvador, Brazil,
Universidade. Publicações II: Introduções
e ensaios, 13) (1921

PEZOA VELIZ, CARLOS

PINILLA, Norberto. Bibliografía crítica sobre
Carlos Pezoa Véliz. Santiago de Chile, Prensas de la Escuela Nacional de Artes Gráficas,
1945. 28 p. (1922

PHILIPPI, FEDERICO

GOTSCHLICH, Bernardo. Catálogo de las publicaciones científicas de don Federico Philippi (1859-1898) (Boletín del Museo Nacional
de Chile, Santiago, t. 2, p. 288-97,
1910) (1923
Jones 1492.

PHILIPPI, RUDOLPH AMANDUS

BARROS ARANA, Diego. El doctor don Rodolfo
Amando Philippi; su vida i sus obras. Seguida de una bibliografía de las obras del
Doctor Philippi por don Carlos Reiche. Santiago de Chile, Impr. Cervantes, 1904.
248 p. (1924
Jones 1402.

PIÑEYRO, ENRIQUE

PIÑEYRO, Enrique. Bibliografía de Enrique Piñeyro, con una introducción, notas y un complemento por Domingo Figarola-Caneda. Habana, Impr. "El Siglo XX", 1924.
98 p. (1925
Edited from the author's manuscript presented to la Biblioteca Nacional de Cuba
in 1907.
"La primera edición apareció en los Anales de la Academia de la Historia, Habana,
t. 1-2, 1919-1920. La presente es la segunda edición, corregida y aumentada."---
Jones 1895.

PITTIER, HENRI FRANÇOIS

JAHN, Alfredo. Bibliografía del dr. H. Pit-
tier, 1878-1937. (Boletín de la Sociedad
Venezolana de Ciencias Naturales, Caracas,
v. 4, p. 25-43, 1937) (1926
Jones 2920.

PLANCHER DE LA NOE, PIERRE

PACHECO, Félix. Un français-brésilien; préf-
ace de Constancio Alves, trad. de Clément
Gazet. Rio de Janeiro, Typ. do Jornal do
Commércio, 1924. 236 p.   (1927
    On the life and activities of Pierre Plan-
cher, founder of the Jornal do Commércio,
with "Relação das obras de 1824 a 1835".---
Jones 1122.

PLASENCIA Y LIZASO, IGNACIO JERONIMO

LEROY Y CASSA, Jorge Eduardo. Elogio del dr.
Ignacio Plasencia y Lizaso. Habana, Impr.
de Rambla, Bouza, 1915. 38 p.   (1928
    Bibliografía del dr. Plasencia y Lizaso
(68 items): p. 25-38.---Jones 1861.

POE, EDGAR ALLAN

ENGLEKIRK, John Eugene. Edgar Allan Poe in
Hispanic literature. New York, Instituto
de las Españas, 1934. 504 p.   (1929
    Bibliography: p. 478-504.---Jones 141.

POLIT LASO, MANUEL MARIA

ESPINOSA POLIT, Aurelio. Datos bibliográficos
de Monseñor Manuel María Polit Laso. Quito,
Edit. "La Sociedad", 1943. 50 p.   (1930
    Cited in Chaves, p. 20.

PORTER, CARLOS EMILIO

PORTER, Carlos Emilio. Bibliografía del Prof.
Carlos E. Porter. Santiago, Impr. Universitaria, 1914. 7 p.   (1931
    Extract from Boletín de bibliografía nacio-
nal y extranjera, año 2, p. 233-39, 1914.
Laval, item 263, notes that the compilation
contains 150 references to published and 12
to unpublished works.

-----. Bosquejo de la hoja de servicios, ac-
tuación científica y premios del prof. dr.
Carlos E. Porter. Santiago, Impr. y Lit. La
Ilustración, 1935. [14] p.   (1932
    Contains bibliography of the author.

-----. Catálogo razonado de los trabajos histórico-naturales hechos desde 1894 hasta 1903.
Valparaíso, Impr. L. de la Cruz, 1904.
34 p.   (1933
    Cited in Laval, item 265.

-----. -----, hechos desde enero de 1894 hasta
junio de 1905. Valparaíso, Impr. Gillet,
1905. 32 p.   (1934
    Jones 1574.

PORTER, Carlos Emilio. Catálogo razonado de
los trabajos histórico-naturales. 1908.
40 p.   (1935
    Jones 1575. Includes "Publicaciones desde
enero de 1894 hasta dic. de 1908.

PORTO ALEGRE, MANOEL DE ARAUJO

LOBO, Hélio. Manoel de Araujo Porto-Alegre.
Ensaio biobibliográfico. Rio de Janeiro, Empresa Edit. A.B.C., 1938. 180 p. (Publ. da
Academia Brasileira [Clásicos brasileiros]
3; Bibliografia [9])   (1936

POSADA, EDUARDO

ELIAS ORTIZ, Sergio. Bibliografía de Eduardo
Posada. (Boletín de estudios históricos,
Pasto, v. 5, p. 217-34, 1934)   (1937
    Jones 1708.

POU ORFILA, JUAN

POU ORFILA, Juan. Títulos, méritos y trabajos.
Montevideo, "El Siglo Ilustrado", 1920.
12 p.   (1938
    Contains a listing of "publicaciones cien-
tíficas" of the author.

PRADO, PEDRO

PEDRO PRADO (1886-1952): vida y obra - bibliografía - antología. New York, Hispanic Institute in the United States, 1960. 107 p.
(Autores modernos [29])   (1939
    Bibliography by Olga Blondet Tudisco.

PRESCOTT, WILLIAM HICKLING

GARDINER, C Harvey. William Hickling Prescott;
an annotated bibliography of published works,
prepared for the Library of Congress. Washington, D.C., Hispanic Foundation, Reference
Dept., Library of Congress, 1958 [i.e.1959]
xvi, 275 p. (Hispanic Foundation Bibliographical ser., no. 4)   (1940

PROAÑO, MANUEL JOSE

HEREDIA, José Félix. Notas bio-bibliográficas
acerca del r. p. Manuel José Proaño. Quito,
1935. 211, cxxxiv p.   (1941
    Jones 1989.

PUTNAM, SAMUEL

SILVEIRA, Brenno. Samuel Putnam, 1892-1950;
notas bio-bibliográficas. São Paulo, União

SILVEIRA, Brenno. Samuel... (Cont.)
Cultural Brasil-Estados Unidos, 1950.
32 p.   (1942

QUIROGA, HORACIO

ABREU GOMEZ, Ermilo. Horacio Quiroga; bibliografía por Bernice D. Matlowsky. Washington,
D.C., División de Filosofía, Letras y Ciencias, Departamento de Asuntos Culturales,
Unión Panamericana, 1951. 26 p. (Semblanzas literarias, 2)   (1943

QUIROGA, JOSE

FURLONG CARDIFF, Guillermo. El padre José Qui-
roga. Buenos Aires, Tall. S.A., Casa Jacobo
Peuser, 1930. 96 p. (Buenos Aires, Univer-
sidad Nacional. Instituto de Investigaciones
Históricas. Publ., no. 54)   (1944
Bibliografía: p. 89-92.---Jones 699a.

QUIROGA, JUAN FACUNDO

PEÑA, David. Guía bibliográfica: Juan Facundo
Quiroga. (Estudios, Buenos Aires, t. 5,
p. 315-28, 1903)   (1945
Jones 811a.

RADAELLI, SIGFRIDO A.

RADAELLI, Sigfrido A. Antecedentes y trabajos,
1930-1939. Buenos Aires, 1939. 15 p. (1946
Cited in HLAS, 5, item 144.

RAMIREZ, FRANCISCO

CASTRO, Antonio P. Ramírez a través de las
publicaciones de Zinny; la Gaceta de Buenos
Aires y Bibliografía histórica, contribución
a su historia. Concordia, E. R., 1935.
128 p.   (1947
"Obras consultadas": p. 121.---Jones 660.

RAMIREZ, JESUS EMILIO

RAMIREZ, Jesús Emilio. Conferencia. Medellín,
Escuela Interamericana de Bibliotecología,
1961. Unpaged. mimeogr.   (1948
Contains "Curriculum vitae" with a listing
of 85 works by Jesús Emilio Ramírez.

RAMIREZ, JOSE FERNANDO

GONZALEZ OBREGON, Luis. Don José Fernando Ramírez; datos bio-bibliográficos. México,
D.F., Tip de "El Tiempo", 1898.
xlvii p.   (1949

GONZALEZ OBREGON, Luis. Don José... (Cont.)
Cited in Iguínez, p. 461. Forms introduction to Obras del Lic. Don José Fernando Ramírez in Biblioteca de autores mexicanos,
t. 15.

-----. Vida y obra de don José Fernando Ramírez. México, D.F., Impr. del Gobierno Federal, 1901. 44 p.   (1950
Reprinted from Memoria de la Sociedad Científica "Antonio Alzate", t. 16, 1901. Also
appeared in the author's Cronistas e historiadores (México, Botas, 1936. p. 125-71)

RAMON Y CAJAL, SANTIAGO

CUBA. Biblioteca Nacional. Catálogo de la
exhibición de impresos referentes a Don Santiago Ramón y Cajal, con motivo del centenario de su nacimiento. Habana, 1952.
31 p.   (1951
Cited in Anuario bibliográfico cubano,
1952, item 218.

RAMOS, JOSE ANTONIO

PERAZA SARAUSA, Fermín. Bibliografía de José
Antonio Ramos. Habana, Anuario Bibliográfico Cubano, 1947. 65 p. (Biblioteca del bibliotecario, 18)   (1952

-----. 2a. ed. 1956. 68 p. (Biblioteca del
bibliotecario, 18)   (1952a

RATTO, HECTOR RAUL

TORRE REVELLO, José. Bibliografía del Capitán
de Fragata Don Héctor Raúl Ratto. Buenos
Aires, 1956. 62 p.   (1953
Cited in Revista interamericana de bibliografía, v. 7, p. 444.

RAZETTI, LUIS

HOMENAJE del panamericanismo médico a la memoria del dr. Luis Razetti, gloria de la medicina social contemporánea. Caracas, Tip.
Casa de Especialidades, 1934.
138 p.   (1954
"Bibliografía y carrera profesional del
doctor Razetti": p. 105-34.---Jones 207,
2916.

REED, CARLOS SAMUEL

REED, Carlos Samuel. 1904-1915; bibliografía
de Carlos S. Reed. Mendoza, Impr. y Lit. G.
Kraft [1915] 10 p.   (1955

REED, Carlos Samuel. Enumeración de los tra-
bajos publicados...1904-1919. Mendoza,
Establ. Tip. de la Escuela "Alberdi", 1916.
18 p.   (1956
   Binayán, item 62, notes the following:
Bibl. de Carlos S. Reed, F.Z.S. (Mendoza,
Impr. y Lit. de G. Kraft, 1915. 10 p.) and
Cargos desempeñados en la República Argenti-
na y bibliografía de Carlos S. Reed (Mendoza,
Impr. del Colegio, 1917. 10 p.

RESTREPO, FELIX

KIMSA, Antanas. Bibliografía del R. P. Félix
Restrepo, S. I. Bogotá, Instituto Caro y
Cuervo, 1950. 79 p.   (1957
   From Boletín del Instituto Caro y Cuervo,
Bogotá, t. 5, no. 1-3, 1949.

REYES, ALFONSO

ALFONSO REYES: vida y obra - bibliografía -
antología. New York, Hispanic Institute in
the United States, 1956. 112 p. (Autores
modernos 25)   (1958

ARCE, David N. Estos y "Aquellos días" de Alfonso Reyes. México, D.F., Biblioteca Nacional, 1956. 51 p. (Bibliografías mexicanas
contemporáneas, 3)   (1959
   Reprinted from Boletín de la Biblioteca
Nacional, México, D.F., v. 7, no. 4)

NUEVO LEON, México. Universidad. Biblioteca.
Catálogo de índices de los libros de Alfonso
Reyes. Monterrey, Universidad de Nuevo León,
1955. 89 p. (Biblioteca universi-
taria)   (1960
   Compiler: Alfonso Rangel Guerra.

REYES, Alfonso. Algunos datos biográficos y
bibliográficos. Rio de Janeiro, 1934.
21 p.   (1961
   Jones 2456.

REYNAUD, PAUL

URUGUAY. Poder Legislativo. Biblioteca. Paul
Reynaud; biografía. Montevideo, 1952. 129,
6, 4 p. (Referencia, no. 17)   (1962
   Cited in Musso 287.

RIBEIRO, MUCIO

LEÃO, Múcio. João Ribeiro; ensaio biobibliográfico. Rio de Janeiro, Academia Brasileira de Letras, 1964. 89 p.   (1963
   Cited in Revista interamericana de bibliografía, v. 5, no. 1.

REIS, Antônio Simões dos. João Ribeiro; bibliografia sôbre a sua obra. [Rio de Janei-
ro] Ministério da Educação e Cultura [1960]
45 p. Suplemento da Revista do livro,
4)   (1964

RIPALDA, JERONIMO DE

SANCHEZ, Juan Manuel. Doctrina cristiana del
p. Jerónimo de Ripalda e intento bibliográfico de la misma, años 1591-1900. Madrid,
Impr. Alemana, 1909. 46, 110 p.   (1965
   Jones 430

RIVERA, DIEGO

WOLFE, Bertram David. Diego Rivera, his life
and times. New York, A. A. Knopf, 1939.
420 p.   (1966
   Partial bibliography: p. 411-20.---Jones
2588a.

RIVERA CAMBAS, MANUEL

DENEGRE VAUGHT, Jorge. Apuntes para una bibliografía de Manuel Rivera Cambas. México, D.F., Edit. Academia Literaria, 1962.
33-210 p.   (1967
   Reprinted from Historia de la intervención europea y norteamericana en México y
del imperio de Maximiliano de Hapsburgo, by
Manuel Rivera Cambas.

RIVERA Y SANROMAN, AGUSTIN

RIVERA Y SANROMAN, Agustín. Bodas de oro de
Agustín Rivera como escritor público, cele-
bradas el día 11 de mayo de 1897. Folleto
escrito por él mismo quien lo dedica a su
tipógrafo...el Sr. Ausencio López Arce.
Lagos de Moreno, Ausencio López Arce e Hijo,
1897. 2, 27 p.   (1969
   Chronological order with descriptions of
writings 1849-1897. Cited in Millares 728

-----. 2a ed. Guadalajara, Escuela de Artes
y Oficios, Tall. de Tip. dirigido por José
Gómez Ugarte, 1897. 30 p.   (1970
   Cited in Millares 728.

TORO, Alfonso. El dr. dn. Agustín Rivera y
San Román. Biografía por...Alfonso Toro;
bibliografía por...Juan B. Iguíniz. México,
D.F., "Revista de revistas", 1917. 86 p.
(Publ. de la Academia Mexicana de la His-
toria)   (1971
   Jones 2528.

RIVERA Y USTARIZ, MARIANO EDUARDO DE

ALCALDE MONGRUT, Arturo. El "Memorial de
Ciencias Naturales", Lima, 1827-1828; contribución a la bibliografía de Mariano E.
de Rivero y Ustariz. Lima, [1954] p. 82-
150.   (1972
Reprinted from Boletín bibliográfico, Universidad Mayor de San Marcos, Lima, v. 27.
Lists 84 titles.

ROCA, JULIO ARGENTINO

MARCO DEL PONT, Augusto. Roca y su tiempo
(cincuenta años de historia argentina) Bue-
nos Aires, Tall. Gráf. Argentinos L. J.
Rosso, 1931. 481 p.   (1973
Las fuentes de este libro: p. 465-68.---
Jones 764.

RODO, JOSE ENRIQUE

HENRIQUEZ UREÑA, Max. Rodó y Rubén Darío.
La Habana, Sociedad Edit. Cuba Contemporánea, 1918. 152 p.   (1974
Bibliografía: p. 63-9, 141-49.---Jones
2842.

RODO, José Enrique. The motives of Proteus;
tr. by Angel Flores. New York, Brentano's,
1928. 378 p.   (1975
Bibliography: p. 363-69.---Jones 2860.

SCARONE, Arturo. Bibliografía de Rodó. Montevideo, Impr. Nacional, 1930. 2 v. (Publ.
de la Biblioteca Nacional)   (1976
Jones 2864. "Rodó, su bibliografía y sus
críticos, por Ariosto D. González": v.1,
p. v-xxvi.

RODRIGUES, JOSE HONORIO

RODRIGUES, Leda Boechat. Bibliografía de
José Honorio Rodrigues. Rio de Janeiro,
1956. 50 p.   (1976a

RODRIGUEZ, SIMON

GRASES, Pedro. Los escritos de Simón Rodríguez. Caracas, Ediciones de la Sociedad
Bolivariana de Venezuela, 1953.
16 p.   (1977

RODRIGUEZ GUERRERO, IGNACIO

ACOSTA HOYOS, Luis Eduardo. Reseña biográfica y bibliográfica del Doctor Ignacio Rodríguez Guerrero. Pasto, Col., Impr. del Departamento, 1962. 67 p. (Pasto, Col. Universidad de Nariño. Biblioteca. Numen uni-

ACOSTA HOYOS, Luis Eduardo ... (Cont.)
versitario, "A"; Bibliografías 1)   (1978

ROFFO, ANGEL HONORIO

LIBRO de oro dedicado al prof. dr. Angel H.
Roffo en ocasión de sus bodas de plata con
la cancerología, 1910-1935. Buenos Aires,
A. Guidi Buffarini, 1935? clxxiii,
2133 p.   (1980
Includes bibliographies. Dr. Roffo began
publishing in 1925/1926 a "Bibliografía de
cancerología".---Jones 755.

ROJAS, ARISTIDES

VENEZUELA. Biblioteca Nacional. Bibliografía de don Arístides Rojas, 1826-1894. Caracas, Tip. Americana, 1944. xv,
142 p.   (1981

ROJAS, RICARDO

SALVADOR, Nélida. Ensayo de bibliografía de
Ricardo Rojas. [Buenos Aires] Universidad
de Buenos Aires, Departamento Editorial
[19] p. 479-90.   (1982
"De la Revista de la Universidad de Buenos
Aires, ép. 5, año 3, no. 3".

ROMERO, CARLOS A.

LEGUIA, Jorge Guillermo. Bio-bibliografía de
D. Carlos A. Romero. Lima, Librería e Impr.
Gil, 1942. 18 p.   (1983

ROMERO, FRANCISCO

BECCO, Horacio Jorge. Bibliografía de Francisco Romero. Buenos Aires, 1956.   (1984
Reprinted from Ciudad, p. 5-6.---Bryant
35.

FRANCISCO ROMERO: vida y obra - bibliografía
- antología. New York, Hispanic Institute
in the United States [1954] (Autores modernos, 23)   (1985
Reprinted from Revista hispánica moderna,
año 20, no. 1.

ROMERO, JOSE RUBEN

CORD, William O. José Rubén Romero; estudio y bibliografía selecta con cuentos y
poemas inéditos. México, D.F., Privately
published by the Author, 1963.
111 p.   (1986
Cited in Bryant 86.

JOSE RUBEN ROMERO: vida y obra - bibliografía
- antología. New York, Hispanic Institute
in the United States, 1946. 74 p. (Autores
modernos, 13)   (1987
  Bibliography by Ernest Richard Moore,
  p. 41-6.

MOORE, Ernest Richard. Bibliografía de José
Ruben Romero. (Letras de México, México, D.
F., no. 33, p. 8, nov. 1, 1938)   (1988
  Jones 2371.

ROSA, ALEJANDRO

CONDE MONTERO, Manuel. Bibliografía de Ale-
jandro Rosa, José Marcó del Pont, Enrique
Peña. Buenos Aires, Tall. Gráf. Rodríguez
Giles, 1927. 16 p.   (1989
  Jones 670. Probably a reprinting of the
same bibliographies which appeared in Bole-
tín de la Junta de Historia y Numismática
Americana: v. 3, p. 149-51 (Rosa); v. 3
p. 152-54 (Marcó del Pont); v. 3, p. 155-60
(Peña).

ROSAS, JUAN MANUEL JOSE DOMINGO ORTIZ DE

PRADERE, Juan A. Juan Manuel de Rosas, su
iconografía. Buenos Aires, J. Mendesky e
Hijo, 1914. 271 p.   (1990
  Jones 815 c

ROTH, SANTIAGO

TORRES, Luis María. Doctor Santiago Roth
(1850-1924) (Revista del Museo de La Plata,
Buenos Aires, t. 30, p. 165-69,
1927)   (1991
  Jones 868b

ROUSSEAU, JEAN JACQUES

SPELL, Jefferson Rea. Rousseau in the Spanish
world before 1833. Austin, Univ. of Texas
Pr., 1938. 325 p.   (1992
  Contains a chapter on "Rousseau in Spanish
America" and a bibliography.---Jones 459.

RUIZ DE ALARCON Y MENDOZA, JUAN

ABREU GOMEZ, Ermilo. Ruiz de Alarcón; bibliografía crítica. México, D.F., Ediciones Botas, 1939. 172 p.   (1993
  Contents. - Prólogo. - Advertencia. - Bibliografía de Ruiz de Alarcón, por Nicolás
Rangel, 1927. - Bibliografía de Juan Ruiz
de Alarcón, por Dorothy Schons, 1929. - Bibliografía de Juan Ruiz de Alarcón, por Alfonso Reyes, 1931. - Bibliografía de Juan
Ruiz de Alarcón, por Pedro Henríquez Ureña,

ABREU GOMEZ, Ermilo ... (Cont.)
1938. - Adiciones. - Catálogo del teatro de
Ruiz de Alarcón.---Jones 2026.

RANGEL, Nicolás. Bibliografía de Juan Ruiz de
Alarcón. México, D.F., 1927. 44 p. (Mo-
nografías bibliográficas, no. 11)   (1994
  Jones 2449.

SCHONS, Dorothy. Apuntes y documentos nuevos
para la biografía de Juan Ruiz de Alarcón y
Mendoza. [Chicago, 1929] 95 p.   (1995
  Reprinted from Boletín de la Real Academia Española de la Historia, v. 95, no. 3,
1929. Bibliografía: p. 52-6.---Jones 2497.

RUSCONI, CARLOS

FONTANA COMPANY, Mario A. La destacada obra
geopaleontológica de don Carlos Rusconi.
Montevideo, Impr. "El Siglo Ilustrado",
1933. 28 p.   (1996
  Bibliografía: p. 14-25. Reprinted from
Revista de la Sociedad "Amigos de la Arqueología", t. 6, 1932.

SA, MANOEL FERREIRA DA CAMARA BETHENCOURT E

CARNEIRO DE MENDONÇA, Marcos. O intendente
Camara, Manoel Ferreira da Camara Bethencourt
e Sá, intendente geral das minas e dos dia-
mantes, 1764-1835. Rio de Janeiro, Imprensa
Nacional, 1933. 498 p.   (1997
  Bibliografía: p. 469-85.---Jones 1012.

SAHAGUN, BERNARDINO DE

CHAVERO, Alfredo. Sahagún; estudio. México,
D.F., Impr. de J. M. Sandoval, 1877.
109 p.   (1998
  Jones 2128.

-----. Sahagún. México, D.F., Vargas Rea,
1948. 106 p. (Biblioteca Aportación histórica, 2a. ser.)   (1999

JIMENEZ MORENO, Wigberto. Fray Bernardino de
Sahagún y su obra. (Este trabajo se publicó
en el tomo I de la Historia general de las
cosas de Nueva España, de Sahagún, en su 4a.
ed. castellana que acaba de imprimirse)
México, D.F., P. Robredo, 1938. 76 p.   (2000
  Jones 2267a

SALLABERRY, JUAN F.

XALAMBRI, Arturo E. La figura del Padre Juan
F. Sallaberry sobre el pedestal de sus libros.
La tradición de cultura de la Compañía de Je-
sús en un jesuita uruguaya. [Montevideo,
Florensa y Lafón] 1947. 64 p.   (2001

XALAMBRI, Arturo E. La figura... (Cont.)
    Cited in Musso 296.

SALVADOR, JAIME

SALVADOR, Jaime. Exposición de títulos, tra-
    bajos y actuación docente. Buenos Aires,
    "La Semana Médica", 1918. 59 p.   (2002
    Cited in Binayán, no. 65.

SAN MARTIN, JOSE DE

ARGENTINA. Caja Nacional de Ahorro Postal.
    Biblioteca. Gral. José de San Martín; mate-
    rial para uso de educadores y estudiantes
    existentes en la Biblioteca "Domingo F. Sar-
    miento" de la Caja Nacional de Ahorro Pos-
    tal. Buenos Aires, 1961. 15 p.   (2003

-----. Congreso. Biblioteca. Bibliografía
    de San Martín. Buenos Aires, 1950. 83 p.
    (Información bibliográfica, publ. no.
    7)   (2004

GARCIA DEL RIO, Juan. Bibliografía del Gene-
    ral San Martín. Buenos Aires, Biblioteca
    Nacional. 1950. xxiv, 47 p.   (2005
    Reprint of original ed., London, 1823,
    entitled Biografía; el general San Martín.

INSTITUTO Sanmartiniano, Buenos Aires. Expo-
    sición iconográfica del Libertador, San Mar-
    tín; conferencias y cuadros expuestos. Bue-
    nos Aires, 1934. 81 p.   (2006
    Jones 729a.

OTERO, José Pacífico. Historia del Libertador
    don José de San Martín. Buenos Aires, Ca-
    baut y Cía., 1932. 4 v.   (2007
    Bibliografía: v. 4, 831-37.---Jones 801.

SALAS, Carlos T. Bibliografía del general don
    José de San Martín y de la emancipación sud-
    americana. Pub. bajo los auspicios de la
    honorable Comisión del Centenario de la In-
    dependencia Argentina, 1778-1910. Buenos
    Aires, Compañía Sud-americana de Billetes de
    Banco, 1910. 5 v.   (2008
    Jones 833.

SAN MARTIN y la emancipación sud-americana,
    bibliografía. Adhesión al año sanmartinia-
    no. Buenos Aires, Librería del Plata
    [1950] 80 p.   (2009

VICTORICA, Ricardo. Errores y omisiones de
    la obra "Bibliografía del general José de
    San Martín y de la emancipación sudameri-
    cana" Buenos Aires, "El Comercio", 1912.
    600 p.   (2010
    Jones 834.

FLORENCIO, SANCHEZ

RICHARDSON, Ruth. Florencio Sánchez and the
    Argentina theatre. New York, Instituto de
    las Españas, 1933. 243 p.   (2011
    Bibliography: p. 229-43.---Jones 827.

SANCHEZ, MANUEL SEGUNDO

GRASES, Pedro. Manuel Segundo Sánchez, 1868-
    1945. Caracas, 1964. 38 p.   (2012

SANCHEZ ALBORNOZ, CLAUDIO

BIBLIOGRAFIA de Claudio Sánchez Albornoz; ho-
    menaje en ocasión de sus cuarenta años de
    docencia universitaria. Buenos Aires, Impr.
    y Casa Edit. Coni, 1957. 45 p.   (2013

SANCHEZ DE BUSTAMANTE Y SIRVEN, ANTONIO

SANCHEZ DE BUSTAMANTE Y SIRVEN, Antonio. In-
    dice alfabético de mil obras y trabajos,
    cuyos autores pertenecen a cuarenta y ocho
    países, que se refieren a libros u opinio-
    nes científicas del dr. Antonio S. de Busta-
    mante y Sirvén. Habana, Carasa y Cía.,
    1938. 100 p.   (2014
    Jones 1906.

SANCHEZ LABRADOR, JOSE

FURLONG CARDIFF, Guillermo. La enciclopedia
    rioplatense de Jose Sánchez Labrador, S.J.
    Montevideo, El Siglo Ilustrado, 1932.
    47 p.   (2015
    Reprinted from Revista de la Sociedad
    "Amigos de la Arqueología", Montevideo,
    t. 5, p. 263-307, 1931.
    Cited in Musso 555.

SANGUILY Y GARRITTE, JOSE MANUEL

RODRIGUEZ GARCIA, José Antonio. Manuel San-
    guily. Habana, Impr. "Cuba Intelectual",
    1926. 266 p.   (2016
    Jones 1903.

SANTA ANNA, ANTONIO LOPEZ DE

CALLCOTT, Wilfred Hardy. Santa Anna; the sto-
    ry of an enigma who once was Mexico. Norman,
    Univ. of Oklahoma, Pr., 1936. 391 p. (2017
    Bibliography: p. 370-81.---Jones 2109.

VALADES, José C. Santa Anna y la guerra de
    Texas. México, Impr. Mundial, 1936.
    315 p.   (2018
    Bibliografía: p. 291-301.---Jones 2543.

128

SANTOS CHOCANO, JOSE

MORTHEIRU SALGADO, Pedro. Sobre José Santos
Chocano [bibliografía] (Atenea, Concepción,
Chile, año 14, t. 40, p. 438-47,
1937)   (2019
    Jones 2702.

ROSENBAUM, Sidonia C. José Santos Chocano:
bibliografía. (Revista hispánica moderna,
New York, v. 1, p. 191-93, 1935)   (2020
    Jones 2737.

SANTOS FERNANDEZ, JUAN

LE ROY Y CASSA, Jorge Eduardo. Bibliografía
del dr. Juan Santos Fernández. Habana, Impr.
de Lloredo y Cía., 1916. 98 p.   (2021
    Contains 928 items.---Jones 1857.

SARMIENTO, DOMINGO FAUSTINO

LA PLATA. Universidad Nacional. Biblioteca.
Bibliografía sobre Sarmiento (piezas bibliográficas existentes en la Biblioteca Pública
de la Universidad. Con una nómina de las
obras de Sarmiento pertenecientes a la institución) La Plata, 1938. 62 p.   (2022
    "La confección de la bibliografía ... ha
sido confiada al señor Alfredo Amaral Insiarte" (Pref.)---Jones 554b, 741b.

-----. -----. Facultad de Ciencias Jurídicas
y Sociales. Bibliografía de Sarmiento, con
prólogo de Ricardo Rojas. Trabajo realizado
por los alumnos de letras. Buenos Aires,
Impr. de Coni Hermanos, 1911.
582 p.   (2023
    Analysis of the contents of the 52 volumes
of Sarmiento's works.---Jones 743.

MONTT, Luis. Noticias de las publicaciones
hechas en Chile por don Domingo F. Sarmiento
(1841-1871) Santiago, Impr. Gutenberg, 1884.
83 p.   (2024
    Also in Obras de Sarmiento, t. 1, Santiago
de Chile, 1887 (Cf. Laval, 233-34)---Jones
786a.

SASTRE, MARCOS

SASTRE, Marcos. Catálogo analítico de las
obras de Marcos Sastre. Buenos Aires, Impr.
de Ostwald y Martínez, 1881. 19 p.   (2025
    Binayán, 73, mentions that another catalog
was published in 1871 on the occasion of the
Exposición Nacional de Córdoba.

SCHMIDEL, ULRICH

ARANA, Enrique. Ulrich Schmidel, primer his-

ARANA, Enrique. Ulrich... (Cont.)
toriador del Río de La Plata, notas históricas y bibliográficas. (Boletín del Instituto de Investigaciones Históricas, Buenos Aires, t. 12, p. 193-228, 1913) (2026
    Jones 566a.

MITRE, Bartolomé. Ulrich Schmidel, primer
historiador del Río de la Plata, con notas
bibliográficas y biográficas. La Plata,
1890. 17 p. (Anales del Museo de La Plata.
Sección de Historia Americana)   (2027
    Jones 784.

SHAKESPEARE, WILLIAM

GOMES, Celuta Moreira. William Shakespeare
no Brasil; bibliografia; colaboração de The-
reza da Silva Aguiar. Rio de Janeiro, Biblioteca Nacional, 1961. 352 p.   (2028
    Reprinted from Anais da Biblioteca Nacio-
nal, v. 79, 1959.

SCHULLER, RUDOLPH R.

SCHULLER, Rudolph R. Bibliografía. (El Libro
y el pueblo, México, D.F., t. 1, no. 8-10,
p. 244-45, 1923)   (2029
    Jones 441.

SENNA, NELSON COELHO DE

SENNA, Nelson Coelho de. Notas bibliográficas,
com indicação não só dos estudos e trabalhos
escriptos, como ainda das obras e livros publicados. [Bello Horizonte?, 1944]
23 p.   (2030
    Works published 1895-1944.

SIERRA, CARLOS J.

HEMERO-BIBLIOGRAFIA de Carlos J. Sierra, 1954-
1964. México, D.F., Ediciones San Ildefonso, 1964. 64 p.   (2030a
    Cited in Revista interamericana de biblio-
grafía, no. 34.

SIERRA, JUSTO

MEXICO. Universidad Nacional. Biblioteca.
Notas para la bibliografía del maestro Justo
Sierra. Contribución de la Biblioteca de la
Universidad, en la conmemoración del XXVIII
aniversario de la fundación de la Universidad Nacional. México, D.F., 1938.
8 p.   (2031

SIGÜENZA Y GONGORA, CARLOS

FRIAS, Valentín. Noticia bibliográfica de los
escritores Sigüenza y Góngora y Presbítero
José M. Zelaá sobre la obra "Glorias de Querétaro", de ambos, y principalmente sobre el
Poema "Primavera Indiana", del primero. México, D.F., Impr. del Gobierno Federal,
1906.   (2032
   Reprinted from Boletín de la Sociedad "Antonio Alzate", p. 131-57. Cited in Ayala
460.

LEON, Nicolás. Tres obras de Sigüenza y Góngora, nota bibliográfica. Morelia, Impr.
del Gobierno, 1886. 22 p.   (2033
   From Gaceta Oficial del gobierno del estado de Michoacán, 1886.---Jones 2299.

LEONARD, Irving Albert. Ensayo bibliográfico
de don Carlos de Sigüenza y Góngora. México, 1929. 65 p. (Monografías bibliográficas mexicanas, no. 15)   (2034
   Jones 2303.

TOUSSAINT, Manuel. Compendio bibliográfico
del Triunfo Parténico de don Carlos de Sigüenza y Góngora. México, D.F., Impr. Universitaria, 1941. 45 p.   (2035

SOLER, MARIANO

VIDAL, José María. El primer arzobispo de
Montevideo, doctor don Mariano Soler. Montevideo, Escuela Tip., 1935. 2 v. (Biblioteca uruguaya de autores católicos)   (2036
   "Bibliografía de monseñor Soler, compuesta
por A. E. Xalambrí:" v. 2, p. 119-27.---
Jones 2877.

XALAMBRI, Arturo E. La bibliografía de Monseñor Soler. [Montevideo, El Demócrata,
1928] 4 p.   (2037
   Cited in Musso 290.

SOSA, FRANCISCO

FERRER DE MENDIOLEA, Gabriel. Don Pancho Sosa.
México, Tall. Tip. "Don Bosco", 1943.
62 p.   (2038
   Cited in Millares, Adiciones 768a.

SOTELO, J. ROBERTO

TRINKLE, Elsa. J. Roberto Sotelo; lista de
sus trabajos científicos; List of his scientific papers, 1940-1962. Montevideo, 1963.
8 p. mimeogr.   (2039

SQUIER, EPHRAIM GEORGE

SQUIER, Frank. A collection of books by
Ephraim George Squier. His own copies, with
some recently acquired additions, and a few
books by others. N.Y., 1939. 44 p.
mimeogr.   (2040

VALLE, Rafael Heliodoro. Ephraim George
Squier (notas biobibliográficas) México,
Secretario de Gobernación, 1922.   (2041
   Reprinted from Memorias y revista de la
Sociedad Científica "Antonio Alzate", t. 40,
p. 509-25.

-----. -----. (The Hispanic American historical review. Baltimore, v. 5, p. 777-89,
1922)   (2042
   In Spanish and English.
   Cf. also Revista de Costa Rica, v. 3,
p. 273-77, 1922.---Jones 2554.

STORNI, ALFONSINA

BARALIS, Marta. Contribución a la bibliografía de Alfonsina Storni. Buenos Aires, Fondo Nacional de las Artes [1964] 64 p. (Bibliografía argentina de artes y letras; Compilaciones especiales, no. 18)   (2042a

STUDART, GUILHERME, BARÃO DE

APONTAMENTOS bio-bibliographicos. Fortaleza,
1900. 23 p.   (2043
   Cited in Reis, item 185.

-----. Fortaleza, 1910. 12 p.   (2044
   Jones 1206.

-----. Dr. Guilherme Studart, Barão de Studart.
Fortaleza, Typ. Commercial a Vapor, 1915.
12 p.   (2045
   Jones 1207.

-----. Dr. Guilherme Studart (barão de Studart) Ceará-Fortaleza, Est. Graphico A. C.
Mendes, 1921. 14 p.   (2046

SUAREZ, BUENAVENTURA

FURLONG CARDIFF, Guillermo. Glorias santafe-
sinas: Buenaventura Suárez, Francisco Javier
Iturri, Cristóbal Altamirano; estudios bibliográficos. Buenos Aires, Edit. "Surgo",
1929. xv, 302 p.   (2047
   "Libros citados en esta obra": p, vii-xi;
"Manuscritos y archivos citados": p. xiii-
xv.---Jones 698b.

SUAREZ, MARCO FIDEL

ORTEGA TORRES, Jorge. Marco Fidel Suárez: bibliografía. Bogotá, Instituto Caro y Cuervo,
1956. 547 p. (Filólogos colombianos,
2)   (2048

TAUNAY, ALFREDO D'ESCRAGNOLLE

SERPA, Phocion. Visconde de Taunay; ensaio
bibliográfico. Rio de Janeiro, Academia Brasileira, 1952. 135 p. (Coleção Afrânio Peixoto; Biblioteca de cultura nacional, 3: Bio-
bibliografía)   (2049

TEIXEIRA, ANISIO

CENTRO Brasileiro de Pesquisas Educacionais.
Bio-bibliografia do professor Anísio Teixeira, 1924-1960. Rio de Janeiro, 1960. 36 p.
mimeogr.   (2050
    Cited in Doria Menezes, 36.

TEJERA Y GARCIA, DIEGO VICENTE

PERAZA SARAUSA, Fermín. Bibliografía de Diego Vicente Tejera y García. Habana, Anuario
Bibliográfico Cubano, 1945. 21 p. (Biblioteca del bibliotecario, 14)   (2051

TERAN, JUAN BAUTISTA

SOCIEDAD de Historia Argentina. Estudios sobre la vida y la obra de Juan B. Terán.
Buenos Aires, Edit. "La Facultad", 1939.
345 p.   (2052
    "Contiene colaboraciones de miembros de
la Sociedad, en las que se estudia la vida
y obra del Doctor Terán". (Torre Revello)
---Jones 846.

TERAN, Juan B, hijo, and TERAN ETCHECOPAR,
Gastón. Bibliografía de don Juan B. Terán.
(Boletín de la Academia Argentina de Letras,
Buenos Aires, t. 6, p. 377-81,
1938)   (2053
    Jones 858a.

THAYER OJEDA, LUIS

BLANCHARD-CHESSI, Enrique. Publicaciones ge-
nealógicas y literarias de don Luis Thayer
Ojeda. Indicaciones bibliográficas por Miguel de Lanuza. Santiago de Chile, Tall.
particular de E. Blanchard-Chessi, 1909.
35 p.   (2054
    Cited in Laval, item 64.

TOLEDO, FRANCISCO DE

ZIMMERMAN, Arthur Franklin. Francisco de Toledo, fifth viceroy of Peru, 1569-1581.
Caldwell, Id., The Caxton Printers, 1938.
307 p.   (2055
    Bibliography: p. 289-300.---Jones 2778.

TORIBIO, SAINT, ABP. of LIMA

MEDINA, José Toribio. Bibliografía de Santo
Toribio Mogrovejo, Arzobispo de Lima. Lima,
Impr. S. Pedro, 1907. lxxxii p.   (2056
    "Publicado en Estudios históricos sobre
Santo Toribio, por Monseñor Manuel Tovar,
Arzobispo de Lima, t. 3, impreso en 1907"
(Laval. Bibl. chilenas, no. 171)---Jones
1533, 2691.

TORQUEMADA, JUAN DE

MORENO TOSCANO, Alejandra. Fray Juan de Tor-
quemada y su Monarquía Indiana. Xalapa, Veracruz, Univ. Veracruzana, 1963. 100 p.
(Cuadernos de la Facultad de Filosofía, Letras y Ciencias, 19)   (2057

TORRALBAS, FEDERICO

TORRALBAS, Federico. Bibliografía del dr. José I. Torralbas. Habana, Impr. Avisador Comercial, 1910. 53 p.   (2058
    Jones 1911.

TORRE REVELLO, JOSE

LEONARD, Irving Albert. Bibliografía de José
Revello. Sevilla, Impr. de M. Carmona, 1934.
15 p.   (2059
    Jones, 751, notes that the "Advertencia"
of this edition is by José Rumazo González.

-----. Bibliography of José Torre Revello.
(Hispanic American historical review, Durham,
N.C., v. 14, p. 262-68, 1934)   (2060
    Jones 751.

TORRE REVELLO, José. Publicaciones de José
Torre Revello. Buenos Aires, Impr. de la
Edit. Araujo, 1942. 39 p.   (2061

TORRES, LUIS MARIA

TORRES, Luis María. Doce años de labor en la
dirección del Museo de La Plata. Buenos Aires, 1935. 25 p.   (2062
    Jones 867i

TORRES BODET, JAIME

ARCE, David N. Sin tregua y con fervor, la
obra de Jaime Torres Bodet. México, D.F.,
Biblioteca Nacional, 1958. 21 p. (Bibliografías mexicanas contemporáneos, 7)   (2063

TOSCANELLI, PAOLO DEL POZZO

VIGNAUD, Jean Henry. Bibliografía della pole-
mica concernente Paolo Toscanelli e Cristoforo Colombo originate dalle communicazioni
di González de la Rosa e di Enrico Vignaud
al Congresso degli americanisti tenuto a Pa-
rigi nel settembre del 1900. Saggio compi-
lato da Enrico Vignaud...tradotto con introduzione e aggiunte da Gustavo Uzielli. Napoli, Tip. Ed. Cav. A. Tocco-Salvietti,
1905. 36 p.   (2064
"Estrato dagli Atti del V Congresso Geografico Italiano, tenuto in Napoli dal 6 a
11 aprile 1904. V. 2, Sezione 4 (Storica)
p. 479-514."---Jones 515.

TOUSSAINT, MANUEL

MANTECON, José Ignacio. Bibliografía de Manuel Toussaint. [México, 1957] 36 p.
(Suplemento no. 1, del núm. 25 de los Anales del Instituto de Investigaciones Estéticas, México)   (2065

TRELLES Y GOVIN, CARLOS MANUEL

ASOCIACION de la Prensa Médica de Cuba. Homenaje al señor Carlos M. Trelles y Govín, socio de honor. Matanzas, Impr. de J. F. Oliver, 1919. 90 p.   (2066
"Bibliografía del señor Carlos Manuel
Trelles y Govín por el dr. Jorge Le-Roy y
Cassá" p. 24-35.---Jones 1785.

TRUJILLO MOLINA, RAFAEL LEONIDAS

FLOREN LOZANO, Luis. Bibliografía Trujillis-
ta. Ciudad Trujillo, 1954. 2 v.   (2067
Typewritten, carbon copy.

UHLE, MAX

SCHWAB, Federico. Max Uhle y la arqueología
peruana. (Revista chilena de historia y
geografía, Santiago, t. 80, p. 198-212,
1936)   (2068
Bibliografía del dr. Max Uhle: p. 204-12.
---Jones 2752.

VALCARCEL, DANIEL

BIBLIOGRAFIA de Daniel Valcárcel. Lima,
[Impr. de la Universidad Nacional Mayor de
San Marcos] 1961. p. 278-86.   (2069
Reprinted from Boletín bibliográfico, Li-
ma, 1960.

VALDES, GABRIEL DE LA CONCEPCION

CERVANTES, C. A. Bibliografía placidiana.
(Revista cubana, Habana, v. 8, p. 155-86,
1937)   (2070
On Gabriel de la Concepción Valdés (Plá-
cido).---Jones 1800.

VALDIVIA, PEDRO DE

CHIAPPA, Víctor M. Anotaciones bibliográficas
sobre Pedro de Valdivia. Santiago de Chile,
Impr. Cervantes, 1930. 99 p.   (2071
Jones 1420.

VALLE, JOSE CECILIO DEL

VALLE, Rafael Heliodoro. Bibliografía de don
José Cecilio del Valle. México, Ediciones
de "Número", 1934. 38 p.   (2072
Jones 1260, 2546.

VALLEJO, CESAR

MONGUIO, Luis. César Vallejo, 1892-1938: vida y obra - bibliografía - antología. New
York, Hispanic Institute in the United
States, 1952. 141 p. (Autores modernos
19)   (2073

VARGAS UGARTE, RUBEN

BIO-BIBLIOGRAFIA de. R. P. Rubén Vargas Ugarte. Lima, Edit. San Marcos, 1955.
27 p.   (2074
Reprinted from Boletín bibliográfico, Universidad Mayor de San Marcos, v. 24, no. 1-
4.

VARNHAGEN, FRANCISCO A.

BELLIDO, Remigio de. Varnhagen e a sua obra...
commemoração do centenario; com um estudo-
prefacio de Antonio de Oliveira. S. Paulo,
Rothschild & Cía., 1916. 41 p.   (2075
Jones 974a.

FONTES, Armando Ortega. Bibliografia de Varnhagen. Rio de Janeiro, Ministério das Relações Exteriores, 1945. 42 p.   (2076
Published by the Comissão de Estudo dos

FONTES, Armando Ortega ... (Cont.)
Textos da História do Brasil.

MAGALHÃES, Basilio de. Bibliographia varnha-
geniana. (Revista da Academia Brasileira de
Letras, Rio de Janeiro, anno 19, p. 332-74,
1928)   (2077
Jones 1085.

-----. Francisco Adolpho de Varnhagen (visconde de Porto-Seguro) Rio de Janeiro, Imprensa Nacional, 1928. 100 p. (Revista do
Instituto Histórico e Geographico Brasileiro ... Boletim)   (2078
Pt. 2: Bibliographia methodizada e razoa-
da.---Jones 1088.

VARONA, ENRIQUE JOSE

PERAZA SARAUSA, Fermín. Bibliografía de Enrique José Varona. (Revista bimestre cubana,
Habana, v. 26, p. 161-77; v. 27, p. 100-16,
1930-1931)   (2079
Jones 1883.

-----. Bibliografía de Enrique José Varona.
Habana, Impr. Molina y Cía., 1932. 299 p.
(Colección cubana de libros y documentos
inéditos o raros, v. 11)   (2080
Jones 1884.

-----. -----. Complemento. (Revista bimestre cubana, Habana, v. 39, p. 240-72,
1937)   (2081
Jones 1885.

-----. -----. Bibliografía del primer centenario del nacimiento de Enrique Varona.
Habana, Anuario Bibliográfico Cubano, 1949.
44 p. (Biblioteca del bibliotecario,
28)   (2082

-----. Iconografía de Enrique José Varona.
[Habana] Municipio de la Habana (Departa-
mento de Cultura) 1942. xii, 132 p.
(Publ. de la Biblioteca Municipal de la
Habana. Serie E: Iconografías cubanas,
1.)   (2083
Reprinted from Revista bimestre cubana,
Habana, 1939 a 1942.

TRELLES Y GOVIN, Carlos Manuel. Bibliografía
de Varona. (Homenaje a Enrique José Varona)
La Habana, Secretaría de Educación, 1935.
p. 495-518)   (2084
Jones 1919.

VASCONCELOS, JOSE

ARCE, David N. Bibliografía de José Vasconcelos. México, Biblioteca Nacional, 1958.
22 p. (Bibliografías mexicanas contemporáneas de la Biblioteca Nacional, 6)   (2085

ARCE, David N. Bibliografía... (Cont.)
Reprinted from the Boletín of the Biblioteca Nacional de México, v. 8, no. 4)

VAZQUEZ, HONORATO

DIAZ CUEVA, Miguel. Bibliografía de Honorato
Vazquez. Cuenca [Edit. del Núcleo del Azuay
de la Casa de la Cultura Ecuatoriana] 1955.
xvii, 187 p. (Biblioteca ecuatoriana,
v. 1)   (2086

VAZ FERREIRA, CARLOS

URUGUAY. Biblioteca Nacional. Aportes a una
bibliografía de Carlos Vaz Ferreira; obra y
crítica. Montevideo, 1953. 2 v.   (2087
v. 1, contains lists of works by and about
Carlos Vaz Ferreira, and v. 2, contains a
listing of the same by subject. Musso 259
attributes authorship to the Biblioteca Nacional.

-----. Universidad. Facultad de Humanidades y
Ciencias. Bibliografía de Carlos Vaz Ferreira; libro, folleto, hoja suelta ... en orden
cronológico de primeras ediciones, seguida
cada una de sus reediciones respectivas. Montevideo, 1962 [cover 1963] 14 p.   (2088

VEGA CARPIO, FELIX DE LOPE

BROWN, Robert B. Bibliografía de las comedias
históricas, tradicionales y legendarias de
Lope de Vega. México, D.F., Edit. Academia,
1958. 151 p. (Iowa. State University. Studies in Spanish language and literature, no.
10)   (2089

VELASCO, JUAN DE

BATALLAS, Leónidas. Vida y escritos del r. p.
Juan de Velasco, con un estudio crítico del
sr. dr. Alfredo Flores y Caamaño. Quito,
Impr. Nacional, 1927. 202 p.   (2090
Notas bibliográficas: p. 187-97.---Jones
1961.

VELAZQUEZ, PRIMO FELICIANO

VELAZQUEZ, Primo Feliciano. Obras. México, D.
F., Impr. de V. Agüeros, 1901. 454 p. (Biblioteca de autores mexicanos, 34)   (2091
Bibliografía científica potosina: p. 273-
449.---Jones 2566.

VELEZ SARSFIELD, DALMACIO

CHANETON, Abel. Historia de Vélez Sársfield.

BIOGRAPHY

CHANETON, Abel ... (Cont.)
Buenos Aires, 1937. 2 v.   (2092
Jones 665b.

VERACRUZ, ALONSO DE LA

BOLANO E ISLA, Amancio. Contribución al estudio biobibliográfico de Fray Alonso de la
Vera Cruz. Prólogo de Agustín Millares Carlo. México, D.F., Robredo, 1947. xi, 156 p.
(Biblioteca histórica mexicana de obras inéditas, 21)   (2093

VESPUCCI, AMERICO

ABOAL AMARO, José Alberto. Amerigho Vespucci;
ensayo de bibliografía crítica. Madrid, Librería para Bibliófilos, 1962. 149 p.
(Publ. de la Biblioteca Colombina,
no. 3)   (2094

COMITATE Onoranze ad Amerigo Vespucci nel
Quinto Centenario della Nascita. Mostra
Vespucciana; catalogo. Prefacio de Alberto
Giraldo. [Firenze, 1955] 188 p.   (2095
Listing of some 300 items, exhibited from
June 1954 to Sept. 1955.

VEYGA, FRANCISCO DE

VEYGA, Francisco de. Trabajos publicados y
concursos en que ha tomado parte, 1890-1899.
Buenos Aires, "La Semana Médica", 1899.
14 p.   (2096
Cited in Binayán, item 67.

VICUÑA CIFUENTES, JULIO

DINAMARCA, Salvador. Julio Vicuña Cifuentes;
bibliografía. (Revista hispánica moderna,
New York, año 4, p. 117-20, 1938)   (2097
Jones 1450.

VICUÑA MACKENNA, BENJAMIN

BENELLI BOLIVAR, Alejandro. Bibliografía general de Vicuña Mackenna, integrada con trabajos de Ramón Briseño, Carlos Vicuña M.,
Guillermo Feliú Cruz y Eugenio Orrego Vicuña. [Santiago] Universidad de Chile (1940]
279 p. (Obras completas de Vicuña Mackenna,
v. 1)   (2098
Jones, 1402a.

BRISEÑO, Ramón. Catálogo por el orden alfabético de sus títulos de las publicaciones
que por la prensa hizo don Benjamín Vicuña
Mackenna. Santiago, Impr. Nacional, 1886.
29 p.   (2099
Also in Anales de la Universidad de Chile,

BRISEÑO, Ramón. Catálogo... (Cont.)
2a. sección, v. 70, 1886.---Jones 1407.

CHILE. Biblioteca Nacional. Homenaje a d. Benjamín Vicuña Mackenna en el centenario de su
nacimiento, 1831 - 25 de agosto - 1931. Santiago, Impr. "La Tracción", 1932.
237 p.   (2100
Reprinted from Boletín de la Biblioteca
Nacional, no. 3, sept. 1931. Includes Ensayo de una bibliografía de las obras de don
Benjamín Vicuña Mackenna, por Guillermo Feliú Cruz.---Jones 1605.

-----. Universidad. Homenaje a Vicuña Mackenna. Santiago, 1931-1932. 2 v.   (2101
Includes bibliography.---Jones 1436.

DONOSO, Ricardo. Don Benjamín Vicuña Mackenna;
su vida, sus escritos y su tiempo, 1831-1886.
Santiago, Impr. Universitaria, 1925.
671 p.   (2102
Bibliografía: p. 525-656.---Jones 1452.

FELIU CRUZ, Guillermo. Ensayo de una biblio-
grafía de las obras de d. Benjamín Vicuña
Mackenna, 1850-1931. Santiago, Impr. "La
Tracción", 1932. 102 p.   (2103
Reprinted from Boletín de la Biblioteca
Nacional, no. 3, sept. 1931.---Jones 1476.

-----. Las obras de Vicuña Mackenna; estudio
bibliográfico precedido de un panorama de
la labor literaria del escritor. [Santiago]
Prensas de la Universidad de Chile, 1932.
226 p.   (2104
"Bibliografía parlamentaria de Vicuña
Mackenna, por Carlos Vicuña Mackenna"
(p. 121-47) is reprinted from the Revista
de bibliografía chilena y extranjera, año 3,
1915.---Jones 1477.

ORREGO VICUÑA, Eugenio. Vicuña Mackenna en
la Universidad de Chile. Santiago, Prensas
de la Universidad, 1934. 45 p.   (2105
Bibliografía: p. 37-45. Reprinted from
Anales de la Universidad de Chile.---Jones
1560.

VICUÑA MACKENNA, Benjamín. Bibliografía completa de las obras de don B. Vicuña Mackenna.
Santiago, Impr. del Centro Editorial, 1879.
15 p.   (2106
Jones 1654.

VIDAURRE ENCALADA, MANUEL LORENZO DE

LEGUIA, Jorge Guillermo. Contribución a la
bibliografía de d. Manuel Lorenzo de Vidaurre Encalada. (Boletín bibliográfico, Biblioteca Central, Universidad Mayor de San
Marcos, Lima, v. 3, no. 5, 1928)   (2107
Jones 2670.

LEGUIA, Jorge Guillermo. Manuel Lorenzo de
Vidaurre; contribución a un ensayo de interpretación sicológica. Lima, Impr. "La
Voce d'Italia", 1935. 231 p.   (2108
"Contribución a la bibliografía de Manuel Lorenzo de Vidaurre y Encalada":
p. 211-30.---Jones 2672.

VILLARROEL, GASPAR DE

VARGAS UGARTE, Rubén. El Ilmo. d. fray Gaspar de Villarroel, obispo de Santiago de
Chile, de Arequipa y arzobispo de Charcas.
(Instituto de Investigaciones Históricas
de la Universidad Católica del Perú. Cuadernos de estudio, Lima, t. 1, p. 1-44,
1939)   (2109
Obras de Villarroel: p. 39-44.---Jones
2768.

VITERBO, FRANCESCO MARQUES DE SOUSA

RIBEIRO, Victor. Sousa Viterbo e sua obra;
notas biobibliographicas. Lisboa, Typ.
Castro Irmão, 1913. 253 p.   (2110
"Terminou-se a impressão da presente
obra, anno MCMXV".---Jones 1158.

VITON, JUAN JOSE

VITON, Juan José. Exposición de títulos,
trabajos y actuación docente. Buenos
Aires, "La Semana Médica", 1899.
20 p.   (2111
Cited in Binayán, item 68.

XEREZ, FRANCISCO DE

POGO, Alexander. Early editions and translations of Xerez, Verdadera relación de
la conquista del Perú [Chicago, 1936]
p. 57-84.   (2112

POGO, Alexander. Early editions... (Cont.)
Reprinted from the Papers of the Bibliographical Society of America, v. 30, pt. 1,
1936.---Jones 2777.

ZINNY, ANTONIO

BINAYAN, Narciso. Antonio Zinny; ensayo bio-
bibliográfico. Buenos Aires, J. Menéndez,
1922. 73 p.   (2113
Jones 602.

ZORRILLA DE SAN MARTIN, JUAN

SPERONI VENER, Julio. Sobre la edición original de "Tabaré" de Zorrilla. Montevideo,
Universidad [1961] 4 p.   (2114
Reprinted from Revista iberoamericana de
literatura, Montevideo, año 2-3, no. 2-3,
p. 131-34, 1960/1961. Cited in Musso 585.

XALAMBRI, Arturo E. Bibliografía fragmenta-
ria y sintética del doctor Juan Zorrilla de
San Martín. Montevideo, 1956. 39 p. (2115
Reprinted from Tribuna católica, Montevideo, año 21, no. 3, 1955 with additional
entries. Cited in Musso 294.

ZUMARRAGA, JUAN DE

GARCIA ICAZBALCETA, Joaquín. Biografía de d.
fr. Juan de Zumárraga. Madrid, M. Aguilar,
1929. 471 p. (Biblioteca histórica ibero-
americana)   (2116
Noticia de los escritos de Zumárraga:
p. 296-372.---Jones 2194.

-----. Don fray Juan de Zumárraga, primer
obispo y arzobispo de México; estudio biográfico y bibliográfico; con un apéndice de
documentos inéditos o raros. México, D.F.,
Andrade y Morales, 1881. 371, 270 p. (2117
Also published in Madrid, 1929.---Jones
2198.

BIOLOGY

SECKT, Hans. Bibliografía hidrobiológica
(relativa a la Argentina y otras repúblicas sudamericanas) (Revista de la Universidad Nacional, Córdoba, v. 11, no. 104-10,
1924)   (2118
Jones 841.

SPARN, Enrique. Nómina y bibliografía de
las algas recolectadas en el Atlántico argentino por las expediciones del "Hassler",
"Albatros" y Dr. Schmitt, según W. R. Taylor. Córdoba, Impr. de la Universidad,

SPARN, Enrique. Nómina y... (Cont.)
1940. 12 p.   (2119
Cited in Catálogo, Inst. Bibliotecológico, Buenos Aires, 1964, item 662.

UNITED NATIONS Educational, Scientific and
Cultural Organization. Science Cooperation
Office for Latin America, Montevideo. Catálogo general de colecciones micológicas
latinoamericanas. Montevideo, 1952-1955.
2 v.   (2120

UNITED NATIONS Educational, Scientific and
Cultural Organization. Science Cooperation
Office for Latin America, Montevideo. Contribución a la bibliografía latinoamericana
sobre biología marina, 1955-1960; lista provisional. Montevideo, [1961] 106 p. (2121
Working paper presented to the Seminario
Latinoamericano sobre Estudios Oceanográfi-
cos in cooperation with the Universidad de
Concepción, Chile, 20-25 Nov. 1961. Cited
in Musso 49.

-----. Oceanografía: física del mar; bentos;
equinodermos; biología de peces. Montevideo, 1963. Various paging. (Bibliografías
latinoamericanas) mimeogr. (2122
Contents: - Contribuição a bibliografia
latinoamericana sobre física do mar, 1950-
1962, por I. Emilsson. - Contribución a la

UNITED NATIONS Educational... (Cont.)
bibliografía latinoamericana sobre Bentos,
1956-1961, por L. Forneris. - Contribución
a la bibliografía latinoamericana sobre equinodermos, 1648-1962, por I. Bernasconi. -
Contribución a la bibliografía sobre investigaciones en biología de peces marinos en
América Latina, 1956-1961 (Primera parte),
por V. Angelescu.

VIQUEZ SEGREDA, Carlos. Animales venenosos de
Costa Rica; parásitos intestinales de nuestros animales encontrados en sus investigaciones. San José, Impr. Nacional, 1935.
313 p. (2123
"Algunos trabajos de química biológica,
hematología, etc."; p. 221-78. Bibliografía: p. 301-02.---Jones 1282. Another edition, 1940, with title Nuestros animales venenosos.

BOOKS

ALCOVER Y BELTRAN, Antonio Miguel. Los libros
de producción latino-americana; ensayo acerca del problema de su expansión comercial
dentro del continente. Habana, "El Siglo
XX", 1912. 76 p. (2124

BUONOCORE, Domingo. Bibliografía literaria y
otros temas sobre el editor y el libro.
Santa Fe, 1956. 47 p. (Temas bibliotecológicos, no. 7) (2125
Originally published in Universidad, Santa Fe, no. 33, p. 187-206.

CASTAGNINO, Raúl Héctor. Biografía del libro.
Buenos Aires, Edit. Nova, [1961]
150 p. (2126

FRIEIRO, Eduardo. Os livros nossos amigos;
nova ed. acrescida de nove capítulos novos.
Belo Horizonte, Liv. Inconfidência, 1945.
221 p. (2127
Cited in Bibliografia brasileira, 1942-
1945, p. 364.

HENRIQUEZ UREÑA, Pedro. El primer libro de
escritor americano. (Revista de filosofía,
Buenos Aires, año 4, p. 317-20, 19180 92128
Jones 198.

LEON, Nicolás. Ex libris de bibliófilos mexicanos. (Anales del Museo Nacional de Arqueología, Historia y Etnología, México, D.
F., t. 5, p. 65-124, 1913) (2129
Jones 2291.

-----. Los ex libris simbólicos de los bibliófilos mexicanos. (Boletín del Instituto Bibliográfico Mexicano, México, D.F.,
no.2, p.65-8; no. 6, p.3-6, 1903-

LEON, Nicolás. Los ex libris... (Cont.)
1905) (2130
Jones 2292.

MAYOL, Josefina. Ex-libris cubanos. Habana
[Tall. de Ucar García] 1950.
193 p. (2131
Reprinted with additions from Boletín de
la Asociación Cubana de Bibliotecarios, v.1,
no. 3-4, p. 103-55, 1950.

MENA, Ramón. Filigranas o marcas transparen-
tes en papeles de Nueva España del siglo
XVI. México, D.F., 1926. 29 p. (Monografías bibliográficas mexicanas, 5) (2132
Jones 2337.

PAN AMERICAN Union. Columbus Memorial Library. Books and libraries in Mexico. Washington, D.C., [1930] 16 p. (Library and
bibliography ser., no. 3) (2133

-----. Cuban books and libraries. Washington, D.C., [1930] 10 p. (Library and
bibliography ser., no. 4) (2134

-----. Libros y bibliotecas en México.
Washington, D.C., [1930] 17 p. (Serie
sobre bibliotecas y bibliografía, no.
5) (2135
Reprinted from Boletín de la Unión Panamericana, nov. 1930.

RAMOS, Roberto. Libros que leyó Don Miguel
Hidalgo. Washington, D.C., Pan American
Union, 1954. 8 p. (2136
Reprinted from Inter-American review of
bibliography, v. 4, no. 1-2, Jan./June 1954.

ROMERO DE TERREROS Y VINENT, Manuel. Encua-
dernaciones artísticas mexicanas, siglos
XVI al XIX. México, D.F. Impr. de la Secretaría de Relaciones Exteriores, 1932.
xxviii, 25 p. (Monografías bibliográficas
mexicanas, no. 24)   (2137
   Jones 2472.

-----. 2a. ed. México, D.F., 1943. 10 p.,
20 plates on 11 p. (Biblioteca de la 2a.
Feria del Libro y Exposición Nacional del
Periodismo)   (2137a

STARR, Frederick. Mexican bookplates. [Mex-
ico, D.F., 1923. 6 p.]   (2138
   Reprinted from the Bookplate annual, 1923.

-----. Mexican Indian motifs in bookplates.
Washington, D.C., [1928?] 12 p.   (2139
   Reprinted from the Year book, 1928 of the
American Society of Bookplate Collectors and
Designers, Washington, D.C.

TEIXIDOR, Felipe. Ex libris y bibliotecas de
México. México, D.F., 1931. 550 p. (Monografías bibliográficas mexicanas, no.
20)   (2140
   Bibliografía: p. 485-508. Obras citadas
en el texto: p. 537-42.---Jones 2523.

TORRE REVELLO, José. La expansión del libro
en la colonia. (Boletín de la Comisión de
Bibliotecas Populares, Buenos Aires, año 5,
no. 21, p. 5; no. 22, p. 6, 1937-
1938)   (2141
   Jones 866c.

-----. Lista de libros embarcados para Buenos
Aires en los siglos XVII y XVIII. (Boletín
del Instituto de Investigaciones Históricas,
Buenos Aires, t. 11, p. 45-66, 1930) (2142
   Jones 866f.

-----. El libro, la imprenta y el periodismo
en América durante la dominación española.
Buenos Aires, Tall. Jacobo Peuser, 1940.
269, ccxxxviii, 20 p. (Buenos Aires. Universidad. Instituto de Investigaciones Históricas, Publ. no. 74)   (2143
   Jones 866e

VILAFRANCA Y FERRES, José. Catálogo general
de la ilustración colombiana. Bogotá, 1878.
32 p.   (2144
   Cited in Giraldo Jaramillo, p. 79.

VINDEL, Pedro. Catálogo descriptivo de ex
libris hispano-americanos (1588-1900) Publica su descripción con notas y 403 facsí-
miles Francisco Vindel. Madrid, [Tip. Gón-
gora] 1929. 144 p., 120 plates.   (2145

YAÑEZ, Agustín. Los libros fundamentales de
nuestra época; encuesta realizada. Guadalajara, Méx., Ediciones Et Caetera, 1957.

YAÑEZ, Agustín. Los libros... (Cont.)
43 p.   (2146

BOOKS - Children's

ASSOCIAÇÃO Brasileira de Educação. Bibliotheca para creanças e adolescentes, organizada
pela secção de cooperação da familia. Rio
de Janeiro, Escola Profissional de Artes
Graphicas, 1930. 31 p.   (2147

BARRY, Mary Elizabeth, and GOETZ, Delia.
Children of the other Americas. A guide to
materials in English on the other Americas
suitable for the elementary and junior high
school grades. Prepared with the assistance
of Dorothy Conzelman under the supervision
of the Division of Intellectual Cooperation
of the Pa American Union. Washington, D.C.,
Govt. Print. Off., 1942. 172 p.   (2148

BEUST, Nora Ernestine. Our neighbor republics;
a selected list of readable books for young
people. [Washington, D.C., Govt. Print.
Off., 1942] 50 p. (Office of Education:
Bulletin 1942, no. 5)   (2149
   Collaborators: Emilie Sandsten Lasalle
and Jean Gardiner Smith.

BUENAVENTURA, Emma. Bibliografía de literatura infantil. Washington, D.C., Unión Panamericana, 1959. 40 p. (Columbus Memorial
Library. Bibliographic ser., no.
47)   (2150
   The second portion of this number is: La
Biblioteca como auxiliar de la educación,
by Emma Linares and Marietta Daniels,
p. 41-70.

CAMARÃO, Maria Leonor. Bibliografia para o
jardim da infância. Belo Horizonte, Departamento de Educação, n.d. mimeogr.   (2151
   Cited in Doria Meneses 62.

CASTILLA BARRIOS, Olga. Breve bosquejo de la
literatura infantil colombiana. Bogotá,
Aedita, 1954. 371 p.   (2152
   Thesis presented to the Pontificia Universidad Católica Javeriana.

CHAVEZ ZELAYA, Enrique. Indice de libros escolares; autores guatemaltecos. [Guatema-
la] Instituto de Investigaciones y Mejora-
miento Educativo (IIME), 1963.
34 p.   (2153
   "Colaboración del Archivo Nacional y la
Facultad de Humanidades".

CHILD STUDY Association of America. Children's
Book Committee. Latin America in books for
boys and girls. Washington, D.C., Pan American Union, Department of Cultural Affairs,
1956. v., 23 p.   (2154
   Published as a supplement to the List of

CHILD STUDY Association of America ... (Cont.)
books accessioned and periodical articles
indexed, Nov. 1956.

ESPINOSA CALISTO, Emma. Bibliografía infantil para los grados superiores de la escuela primaria (4o., 5o. y 6o.) [Quito] Servicio Cooperativo Interamericano de Educación, 1957. [14] p.   (2155
  Issued as "Trabajo no. 1".

-----. Bibliografía infantil para los primeros grados de la escuela primaria (1o., 2o.
y 3o.) [Quito] Servicio Cooperativo Interamericano de Educación, 1957.
6 [i.e., 9] p.   (2156

FRACCAROLI, Lenyra C. Bibliografia de litera-
tura infantil em língua portuguêsa. São
Paulo, Secretaria de Educação e Cultura,
Departamento de Cultura, Divisão de Biblio-
tecas Infanto-juvenis, 1953. 216 p. (2157
  Contains 1,843 entries.

-----. 2a. ed. aumen. São Paulo, Edit. Jornal dos Livros, 1955. 280 p.   (2158
  Contains 2,388 entries of books, and 26
  of periodicals.

-----. Suplemento à bibliografia de literatura infantil em língua portuguêsa, anos 1956-
1957. São Paulo, Departamento de Cultura,
1960. 47 p.   (2159
  Cited in Doria Menezes 94.

GOETZ, Delia. Bibliography of Spanish books
for children. Washington, D.C., Dept. of
Health, Education and Welfare, Office of
Education, [1953] 11 p. mimeogr.   (2160

HAVANA. Biblioteca Municipal. Cuales son los
veinticinco libros cuya lectura usted reco-
mienda en primer lugar a la juventud cubana? Habana, 1939. 3 p. (Ser. C: Guías
bibliográficas, 3)   (2161
  Compilation by Enrique José Varona.

INTER-AMERICAN Children's Institute, Montevideo. Bibliografía; literatura infantil y
juvenil. Montevideo, 1957. 36 p.   (2162
  Reprinted from Boletín del Instituto Interamericano del Niño, t. 31, no. 3,
p. 344-79, 1957. Cited in Musso 165.

MAZZEI DE GIORGI, Olga. Bibliografía infantil venezolana. Caracas, División de Divulgación y Publicaciones del Consejo Venezolano del Niño, 1956. 39 p.   (2163

OLIVAS, Antonio. Hacia la formación de una
bibliografía sobre la literatura infantil
peruana. (Boletín bibliográfico, Biblioteca Central, Universidad Mayor de San Marcos,
Lima, año 13, p. 255-74, 389-96,
1940)   (2164

OLIVAS, Antonio. Hacia la formación... (Cont.)
Jones 2708a.

PAN AMERICAN Union. Columbus Memorial Library.
Children's books in English on Latin America.
Washington, D.C., 1941. viii, 41, vii p.
(Bibliographic ser., no. 25) mimeogr. (2165
  Prepared by Leila Fern.---Jones 352a.

-----. Division of Intellectual Cooperation.
Books on Latin America for young readers.
Washington, D.C. [1940] 7 p.   (2166

PANAMA. Biblioteca Nacional. Bibliotecas ju-
veniles (una bibliografia selecta) con motivo de la inaguración de la Sección Juvenil
de la Biblioteca Nacional. Panamá, Impr.
Nacional, 1952. 34 p. (Publ., v. 2, no.
10)   (2167
  Compiler: Galileo Patiño.

PERDIGÃO, Domingos de Castro. O que se deve
ler; vade-mecum bibliographico. S. Luiz do
Maranhão, Impr. Off., 1922. 348, vi p. (2168
  A reading list for young people.

PORTO ALEGRE, Brazil. Biblioteca Publica Infantil. Nossa bibliotequinha; boletim bibliográfico, 1955 e 1956. Porto Alegre,
Secretaria de Educação e Cultura, n.d. 2 v.
in 1v. (168 p.)   (2169

PRESSON, Mary Louise. A bibliography of juve-
nile holdings in the Library of Congress in
classification F 1401-2239, Latin America.
Washington, D.C., 1961. 128 p.   (2170
  Thesis: Catholic University of America.

PRIETO FIGUEROA, Luis Beltrán. La magia de
los libros; libros estimulantes para la juventud. Tegucigalpa, Publicaciones del Ministerio de Educación Pública, 1955. 75 p.
(Colección Ramón Rosa, 2)   (2171
  Apendice, p. 49-75: Lista de obras estimulantes para la juventud.

-----. Another edition. Caracas, Ministerio
de Educación, Dirección Técnica, Departamento de Publicaciones [1961] 73 p. (Colección Vigilia, 1)   (2172

RITTER, Helen L. Stories of Latin America
for seventh grade; introduction and annotated bibliography. Workshop in Inter-
American Education, Summer Session, 1944,
University of Louisville, Louisville,
Kentucky, in cooperation with Office of
Inter-American Affairs. New York, Curriculum Service Bureau for International Studies
[1944?] 30 p.   (2173

SCALA DE INTERGUGLIELMO, Marta N. S. de. Libros para niños en la República Argentina.
Contribución a las segundas jornadas bibliotecarias argentinas. Buenos Aires, 1951.

SCALA DE INTERGUGLIELMO, Marta... (Cont.)
31 p.   (2174
   Contains listing of works referred to:
p. 27-31.

SECRETARIADO CATOLICO del Libro, Montevideo.
Guía de orientación de lecturas para niños
y jóvenes. [Montevideo, Barreiro y Ramos]
1962. 55 p.   (2175
   Cited in Musso 158.

SMITH, Jean Gardiner. Latin America; books
for young readers. Chicago, American Library Association, 1941. p. 369-80. (2176
   Reprinted from Booklist, v. 37, no. 14,
Apr. 1941.

SOUZA, Ruth Villela Alves de. Seleção de livros para biblioteca escolar de nivel se-
cundário. Rio de Janeiro, MEC, CADES, 1961.
59 p.   (2177
   Cited in Doria Menezes 78.

UNITED NATIONS Educational, Scientific and
Cultural Organization. Centro Regional en
el Hemisferio Occidental, Habana. Bibliografía infantil selectiva. Bogotá, Ministerio de Educación Nacional, Sección de Servicios Bibliotecarios, 1963. (Divulgaciones bibliotecológicas, no. 6)   (2178
   Cited in Boletín de adquisiciones, Medellín, Col., no. 11, p. 16, nov. 1963.

U.S. Office of Education. Concerning the
other Americas; annotated list of non-fiction material available in inexpensive form.
Washington, D.C., 1943. 18 p.
mimeogr.   (2180
   Compiler: Jessie A. Lane.

URIOSTE, Antero. Algunos libros que pueden
servir para establecer una biblioteca infantil. Montevideo, Barreiro y Cía., 1923.
74 p.   (2181

-----. Another edition. San José, C.R.,
Impr. María v. de Lines, 1924. 45 p. (2182

URUGUAY. Consejo Nacional de Enseñanza Primaria y Normal. Boletín bibliográfico; libros indicados para la formación de bibliotecas escolares. Montevideo, Dept. Editorial, 1946. 181 p. (Colección Ceibo,
v. 5)   (2183
   Compiler: Carlos Alberto Garibaldi.

BOOKS - Rare

ABOAL AMARO, José Alberto. Diez raros "ame-
ricanos" del Siglo XVI. Montevideo, [L. I.
G.U.] 1959. 16 p.   (2184
   Cited in Musso 535.

ALBUQUERQUE, Alexandre de. As duas edições
dos Lusiados de 1572. Rio de Janeiro,
1921.   (2185
   Cited in Reis, 332.

AMIGOS DEL ARTE, Montevideo. Exposición del
libro antiguo. Montevideo, Impresora Uruguaya, 1946. 237 p.   (2186

ARAUJO ESPINOZA, Graciela. Adiciones a "La
Imprenta en Lima, 1584-1824". Lima, P. L.
Villanueva, 1954. 238 p.   (2187
   Reprinted from Fénix, no. 8, p. 467-704,
[1954] Thesis presented in the Facultad de
Letras of the Pontificia Universidad Cató-
lica, 1954.

BANCO de la República, Bogotá. Biblioteca
"Luis Angel Arango". Incunables bogotanos
- Siglo XVIII. [Bogotá] 1959. 240 p. (2188

BARTLETT, John Russell. A list of books printed in Mexico, 1540-1600. Providence,
1875.   (2189
   Cited in Millares, item 1108. See also
item 6659.

BIBLIOTHECA americana; or, A chronological
catalogue of the most curious and interesting books, pamphlets, state papers, &c. upon
the subject of North and South America, from
the earliest period to the present, in print
and manuscript; for which research has been
made in the British Museum, and the most
celebrated public and private libraries,
reviews, catalogues, &c. London, Printed
for J. Debrett, J. Sewell, R. Baldwin and
J. Bew; and E. Harlowe, 1789. 270 p. (2190
   Attributed to Arthur Homer, to a "Mr. Reid,
American resident in London," to J. Debrett,
the publisher of the work, and to Alexander
Dalrymple. "A worthless compilation" (B.A.
V. Harrisse)---Jones 59a.

BRAZIL. Biblioteca Nacional. Catálogo de incunábulos. Rio de Janeiro, Ministério de
Educação e Cultura, 1956. 377 p.   (2193

BRUNER PRIETO, Fernando. Notas bibliográficas
sobre algunos incunables hallados en Chile.
Palma Mallorca, F. Soler, 1923. 9 p. (2194
   Ochsenius, item 43, notes that only the
prologue was published.

CINCINNATI. Public Library. Rare Book Dept.
A checklist of books relating to the discovery, exploration and description of America,
from Columbus to Mackenzie 1492-1801. Compiled by Yeatman Anderson, III, curator.
[Cincinnati] Public Library of Cincinnati
and Hamilton County, 1961. Unpaged. (2195
   Contains 196 items.

COLOMBIA. Biblioteca Nacional. Exposición
de libros incunables, raros y curiosos, ju-

COLOMBIA. Biblioteca Nacional ... (Cont.)
lio 7-14, 1962. [Bogota, 1962] Unpaged.
mimeogr.   (2196
    Florén, 1961-1962, item 2, notes that 256
titles are described.

DIAS, Antonio Caetano. Catálogo das obras raras ou valiosas da Biblioteca da Escola Nacional de Belas Artes. Rio de Janeiro, Imprensa Nacional, 1945. 67 p. (Instituto
Nacional do Livro, Coleção B 1; Bibliografia 5)   (2197

DRAUD, Georg. Bibliotheca classica, sive Catalogus officinalis...Usque ad annum MDCXXIV.
Francofurti ad Moenum, 1625. 1761 p. (2198
    Contains a chapter, De scriptoribus rerum
americanarum. "The only special list of
books relating to America which seems to
have been published from the time when the
Roman presses first published the Epistle of
Columbus in 1493 to the year 1625" (B.A.V.
Harrisse, p. xiii).---Jones 132.

ECUADOR. Biblioteca Nacional. Incunables y
libros raros y curiosos de los siglos XV,
XVI, XVII, XVIII, de la sección llamada "Hispanoamericana". Quito, Edit. Casa de la Cultura Ecuatoriana, 1959. 108 p.   (2199

FINA, José Augusto. Los tesoros de nuestra
Biblioteca Nacional. Habana, Impr. de F. V.
O'Reilly, 1931. 35 p.   (2200
    Jones 1829.

FORERO, Manuel José. Incunables bogotanos.
Bogotá, Edit. Minerva, 1946. 47 p.   (2201

GALLARDO, Bartolomé José. Ensayo de una biblioteca española de libros raros y curiosos,
formado con los apuntamientos de don Bartolomé José Gallardo, coordinados y aumentados
por d. M. R. Zarco del Valle y d. J. Sancho
Rayón. Madrid, M. Rivadeneyra, 1863-1866;
M. Tello, 1888-1889. 4 v.   (2202
    Vol. 3-4 ed. by Marcelino Menéndez y Pela-
yo.---Jones 156.

GARDEL, Luis Delgado. A brief description of
some rare & interesting books from the XVIth
& XVIIth centuries which can be found in the
Columbus Memorial Library. Washington, D.C.,
Pan American Union, 1958. 70 p.   (2203
    Bibliographical notes: p. 67-70.

GRASES, Pedro. Más incunables venezolanos.
Caracas, 1960. 30 p.   (2204

GROPP, Arthur Eric. Rare americana. New Orleans, La., Tulane University of Louisiana,
1932. 26 p. (Pamphlet of the Department of
Middle American Research, 2)   (2205
    Description of rarities in the Library of
the Department prepared on the occasion of
the 54th Annual Conference of the American

GROPP, Arthur Eric. Rare americana ... (Cont.)
Library Association.

GUADALAJARA, Mexico. Biblioteca Pública del
Estado. Catálogo de incunables. Prologo
de José Cornejo Franco. México, D.F., Impr.
Nuevo Mundo, 1948. xxii, 66 p.   (2206
    Description of 15 volumes of incunabula,
1484-1500. Compiler: Lorna Lavery Stafford.

HISPANIC SOCIETY of America, New York. Library.
List of books printed before 1601 in the Library of the Hispanic Society of America,
compiled by Clara Louise Penny. New York,
1929. 247 p.   (2207
    Includes imprints from Mexico and Lima.

-----. Reissued with additions. New York,
1955. xiv, 305 p. (Hispanic notes and monographs; Catalogue ser.)   (2208

HOLMES, Ruth E. V. Bibliographical and historical description of the rarest books in
the Oliveira Lima collection at the Catholic
University of America. Washington, D.C.,
1926. vi, 367 p.   (2209
    209 items described.

LAVAL, Ramón A. Un incunable chileno, Modo de
ganar el jubileo santo, año de 1776; noticia
bibliográfica. Santiago, Impr. Universitaria, 1910. 16 p., 8 facsims.   (2210
    Jones 1510.

LAZARO, José de. Los incunables bonarenses.
Madrid, Tip. Blass, 1925. 102 p.   (2211
    Jones 747.

MATTOS, Ricardo Pinto de. Manual bibliographico portuguez de livros raros, classicos
e curiosos. Porto, Livraria Portuguesa,
1878. 582 p.   (2212
    Jones 1145.

MEDINA, José Toribio. Un incunable limeño
hasta ahora no descrito, reimpreso a plana
y renglón, con un prólogo. Santiago, Impr.
Elzeviriana, 1916. 15 p.   (2213
    Jones 2695.

MEXICO. Biblioteca Nacional. Catálogo de incunables de la Biblioteca Nacional de México.
(Boletín, México, D.F., año 10, p. 49-61,
1913)   (2214
    Compiled by José María de Agreda y Sán-
chez.---Jones 2345.

MILLARES CARLOS, Agustín. Los incunables de
la Biblioteca Universitaria de La Plata.
(Humanidades, La Plata, v.9, p. 9-24,
1924)   (2215
    Jones 781.

MORAES, Rubens Borba de. Bibliographia brasiliana; a bibliographical essay on rare

MORAES, Rubens Borba de ... (Cont.)
books about Brazil published from 1504 to
1900 and works of Brazilian authors published abroad before independence of Brazil in
1822. Amsterdam, Rio de Janeiro, Colibris
Editora [1958] 2 v. (v. 1: 427 p.; v. 2:
448 p.)   (2216

OLAGUIBEL, Manuel de. Impresiones célebres y
libros raros. México, Impr. del "Socialis-
ta" de M. López y Comp., 1878.
142 p.   (2217
    Jones 2386.

-----. Another edition. México, D.F., Impr.
de F. Díaz de León, 1884. 153 p.   (2218
    Jones 2387.

PACHECO, Felix. Duas charadas bibliographicas.
Carta ao director do Museu Paulista a pro-
posito do primeiro livro editado no Brasil,
e sobre o "Exame de Artilheiros", e o "Exame de Bombeiros" de Alpoym. Com uma segunda parte concernente ao "Luzeiro Evangeli-
co" e a outros trabalhos mais antigos impressos em portuguez na America, e um volume de appendice reproduzido em photozinco a
"Relação da Entrada", do Dr. Rosario da
Cunha, as "Conclusões Metaphysicas", de
Francisco Fraga, e as Composições poeticas
impressas no Rio de Janeiro por Antonio Isidoro da Fonseca. Rio de Janeiro, Typ. do
Jornal do Commercio, Rodrigues & C., 1931.
434, 64 p.   (2219
    Cited in Reis, item 430.

RAMIREZ DE ARELLANO, Angel. Apuntes para un
catálogo de libros notables impresos en México de 1539 a 1599. México, D.F., 1895.
45 p.   (2220

RAMIREZ DE ARELLANO, Angel. Apuntes...(Cont.)
    Jones 2446.

SANCHEZ, Manuel Segundo. El Publicista de Venezuela; capítulo del libro en preparación
"Los incunables venezolanos". Caracas, Tall.
de "El Universal", 1920. 25 p.   (2221
    Jones 2958.

STILLWELL, Margaret Bingham. Incunabula and
Americana, 1450-1800. New York, Columbia
Univ. Pr., 1931. xviii, 438 p.   (2222

URUGUAY. Universidad. Facultad de Humanidades
y Ciencias. Instituto de Investigaciones
Históricas. Biblioteca de impresos raros
americanos. Montevideo, 1948-1951.
2 v.   (2223
    Contents: - v.1, Gazeta de Montevideo. -
v. 2, Descripción de las fiestas cívicas ce-
lebradas en Montevideo, mayo de 1816; Ora-
ción inaugural pronunciada por Larrañaga en
la apertura de la Biblioteca Pública de Montevideo, 1816. Includes also "Reconstrucción bibliográfica" por Arbelio Ramírez, and
"Apéndice documental".

VINDEL, Francisco. Catálogo de la Librería F.
Vindel... 100 obras: América, varios, en-
cuadernaciones. Madrid, 1930. 115 p. (2224
    Jones 518.

-----. Manual gráfico-descriptivo del bibliófilo hispano-americano, 1475-1850. Madrid,
1930-1931. 11v.   (2225
    Jones 518.

-----. -----. Suplemento, t. 12- . Madrid,
1934- .   (2226
    Jones 519.

BOOKSELLERS AND PUBLISHERS

GENERAL

AHRENSBURG, Hermann, Bookseller, Berlin. Catálogo. Colección de libros, folletos, periódicos, hojas volantes, proclamas, extra-
ordinarios, y documentos manuscritos, en su
mayor parte muy raros, del tiempo de la
guerra de la independencia surmamericana
[sic] y del gobiero [sic] colonial español.
Berlin, Lichterfelde, 1930. 39 p.   (2227

ANDRADE, José María. Catalogue de la riche
bibliothèque de d. José María Andrade. Livres manuscrits et imprimés. Littérature
française et espagnole. Histoire de l'Afrique, de l'Asie et de l'Amérique. 7000 piè-
ces et volumes ayant rapport au Mexique ou
imprimés dans ce pays. Leipzig, List &
Francke, 1869. 368 p.   (2228
    Jones 2049.

---

* The compilation of an extensive listing of booksellers' and publishers' catalogs was not attempted. Reference is made
to several substantial listings in the early volumes of the Handbook of Latin American studies, the Ensayo de una bibliografía de bibliografías mexicanas by Agustín

Millares Carlo (item 343-403, 1442-78),
Fuentes de la historia contemporánea de México by Luis González y González (items
204-253), and Bibliografía bibliotecológica
colombiana 1961/1962 by Luis Florén y Lozano (items 244-59)

ANDRADE, José María. Prix d'adjudication des
articles de la bibliothèque de d. J. M. Andrade; vente faite à Leipzig le 18 janvier
1869 et jours suivants. Leipzig, List &
Francke, 1869. 11 p.   (2229
Jones 2050.

ANUARIO de la librería española, portuguesa e
hispano-americana. Madrid, A. Romo [1913]
566 p.   (2230
Jones 23.

ARCHIVO bibliográfico hispano-americano; lo
publica la Librería General de Victoriano
Suárez, 1909-1926. 16 v.   (2231
Includes "Notas bibliográficas".---Jones
27. Not published in 1919 and 1922. Now
available in microprint.

BIBLIOTHECA mejicana, a catalogue of an extraordinary collection of books relating to
Mexico and North and South America, from
the first introduction of printing in the
New World, A.D. 1544 to A. D. 1868. Collected during 20 years' official residence
in Mexico. [n.p., n.d.] 312 p.   (2232
Jones 2080, 2440. The collection of about
2,962 items was brought together by Father
A. Fischer and Dr. C. Hermann Berendt. (See
also item 2234) and sold at auction by Puttick and Simpson in London.

-----. Sold by auction, June 1st to June 10th
1869. Prices and purchasers' names. [Lon-
don, G. Norman and son, Printers, 1869]
41 p.   (2233
Jones 2440. Auctioned by Puttick and
Simpson in London.

BIBLIOTHECA mexicana; catalogue d'une collection de livres rares (principalement sur
l'histoire et la linguistique) réunie au
Mexique par M ... attaché à la cour de l'em-
pereur Maximilien. Paris, Librairie Tross,
1868. 47 p.   (2234
Jones 2081. Collection of about 233 items
coming from the Fischer-Berendt collection,
sold separately in Paris. The main collection was auctioned in London by Puttick and
Simpson (see item 2232)

CHADENAT, C. Bibliophile américain: cata-
logue de livres, cartes & documents rela-
tifs à l'Europe, Asie, Afrique, Amérique,
Océanie. Bulletin trimestriel. Paris, C.
Chadenat, 1889- .   (2235
Jones 94.

THE DOLPHIN Co., Oxford. One hundred manuscripts relating to Latin America. Oxford
[1957] 36 p. (Catalogue no. 35)   (2236

HESPERIA; Librería Anticuaria Luis Marquina
y Marín, Zaragoza, Spain. Americana, II;
una selección de libros y folletos antiguos

HESPERIA; Librería Anticuaria... (Cont.)
y modernos referentes a temas americanos.
Zaragoza [1964] Unpaged. (Lista especial,
6)   (2237
Contains 2,840 entries arranged alphabetically by author.

HIERSEMANN, Bookseller, Leipzig. Katalog. 51:
Americana. Karten und Bücher über oder
gedruckt in Nord-und Sur-America. Leipzig,
58 p.   (2238

-----. 70: Americana. Maps and works on or
printed in North and South-America. Leipzig,
1891. 90 p.   (2239

-----. 82: Amerikanische Sprachen. Leipzig,
1891. 18 p.   (2240

-----. 119: American books, maps, views,
costumes, and portraits. American aboriginal languages. Leipzig, 1893. 96 p. (2241

-----. 143: America. Geographie, topogra-
phie, etnographie, ursprachen, geschichte,
bücherkarten und pläne kunstblätter.
Leipzig, 1895. 161 p.   (2242

-----. 179: Bibliotheca Americana. I. Theil:
America im Allegemeinen. Leipzig, 1897.
64 p.   (2243

-----. -----. 181: III. Theil: Central-
Amerika und Sud-Amerika. Westindischer
Archipiel. Mexico. Die Republiken von
Central-Amerika. Leipzig, 1897.
48 p.   (2244

-----. 279: America Vetustissima, früe
gestichte und geographie bis zur mitte des
17. Jahrhunderts. Leipzig, 1902.
73 p.   (2245

-----. 280: Las Indias Occidentales, la
América Central y Meridional, desde 1650
hasta nuestros días. Periódicos, libros,
vistas, pinturas originales, Leipzig, 1902.
80 p.   (2246

-----. 301: Amerikanische linguistik und
americana im allgemeinen. Enthaltend u.a.
einen theil der Bibliothek des Amerikanisten Prof. Dr. J. Platzmann. Leipzig,
1904. 46 p.   (2247
Supplement to Katalog, 279, 281.

-----. 311: Bd. II. Westindien, Mittel-und
Süd-Amerika. Leipzig, 1905.   (2248

-----. 321: Biblioteca latino-americana.
Colección de libros y manuscritos antiguos
y raros sobre la América Central y Meridional, Indias Occidentales y Filipinas.
Leipzig, 1906. 156 p.   (2249

HIERSEMANN, Bookseller, Leipzig. 327: Colección de libros y manuscritos antiguos y raros sobre América del Norte, Central.
Tournon Collection. Leipzig, 1907.
31 p.   (2250

-----. 335: Amerikanische linguistik.
Allgemeines. Die einzelnen ursprachen,
enthalten u.a. einen Theil der Bibliotheken
des Amerikanisten Lucien Adam im Rennes.
Sowie zwei der Pariser Diplomaten. Leipzig,
1907. 31 p.   (2251

-----. 336: America Central y Meridional,
Indias Occidentales y Filipinas, España y
Portugal. Leipzig, 1907. 274 p.   (2252

-----. 346: América Central y Meridional.
Manuscritos, libros, mapas. Leipzig, 1907.
148 p.   (2253

-----. 362: Eine seltene Kollektion von
werken über Amerikanische linguistik, enthaltend einen Theil der Bibliothek des
verstor benen Amerikanisten León Léjeal,
Professor am Collège de France. Leipzig,
1908. 30 p.   (2254

-----. 363: A choice collection of scarce
and valuable books, pamphlets, manuscripts
and maps relating to Central and South-
America, the West-India and the Philippine
Islands, containing the geographical and
ethnographical part of the library of the
late Geh. Regierungs-Rat Dr. W. Reiss
(author of Reiss and Stübel, the Necropolis
of Ancon) the library of a South-American
bibliophile. Leipzig, 1909. 222 p.   (2255

-----. 376: Biblioteca latino-americana histórica. Colección de libros y manuscritos
sobre la historia, política y legislación
de la América Central y Meridional, Indias
Occidentales y Filipinas. Leipzig, 1909.
56 p.   (2256

-----. 395: America. II. Middle and South
America, including the West Indies, America
Central y-Meridional, Mittel und Sud-Ameri-
ka. Leipzig, 1911. 150 p.   (2257

-----. 420: Spanien u. Portugal, das Lateini-
sche Amerika und die Philippinen. (Retrato
de Brasseur de Bourbourg) Leipzig, 1913.
141 p.   (2258

HIERSEMANN, Karl W., Leipzig. Brasilien;
eine sammlung älterer und neurer werke zur
geschichte, geographie und literatur des
landes. Leipzig, n.d., 21 p. (Neuerwerbun-
gen, Feb. 1927)   (2259

LECLERC, Charles. Bibliotheca americana.
Catalogue raisonné d'une très précieuse
collection de livres anciens et modernes

LECLERC, Charles. Bibliotheca... (Cont.)
sur l'Amérique et les Philippines, classés
par ordre alphabétique de noms d'auteurs.
Paris, Maisonneuve, 1867. 407 p.   (2260
1,647 titles; bibliographical and critical
notes.---Jones 253.

-----. -----. Histoire, géographie, voyages,
archéologie et linguistique des deux Améri-
ques et des îles Philippines. Paris,
Maisonneuve, 1878. 737 p.   (2261
A second catalog of Americana for sale by
Maisonneuve, the first having appeared in
1867.
2,638 titles, classified; with author and
title index.---Jones 254.

-----. Supplément, no. 1. Novembre 1881.
Paris, Maisonneuve, 1881. 102 p.   (2262
Titles numbered, 2,639-3,029.---Jones 254.

-----. Supplément, no. 2. Paris, Maisonneuve
frères & C. Leclerc, 1887. 127 p.   (2263
Titles numbered 3,030-3,620.
"Publications relatives à l'histoire et à
la linguistique de l'Amérique, en vente chez
Maisonneuve et Ch. Leclerc": p. 111-27.---
Jones 254.

LIBRERIA de Victoria Vindel, Madrid. Catálogos. Madrid, 1920-1933.   (2264

MAGGS Bros., London. Bibliotheca americana,
pt. 1-9. London [1922-   ]   (2265
Items in pt. 1-5 numbered continuously.
Catalogues, no. 429, 432, 442, 479, 496, 503.
Pt. 2: Father Kino, "Apostle of California".

-----. Bibliotheca brasiliensis; catalogo
annotado de livros raros, de alguns autographos e manuscriptos importantissimos e
de gravuras sôbre o Brasil e o descobrimento da America, 1493-1930 A.D. London,
[1930] 369 p.   (2266
Jones 1091. Catalog no. 546, describing
411 works.

-----. Catalogue of fifty-three rare Americana selected from the stock of Maggs Bros.
London, 1928. 97 p.   (2267

-----. From Panama to Peru; the conquest of
Peru by the Pizarros, the rebellion of Gon-
zalo Pizarro and the pacification by La
Gasca. London, 1925. 620 p.   (2268
Collection of 3,000 manuscript pages now
in Henry E. Huntington Library and Art
Gallery.---Yang.

-----. An illustrated catalogue raisonné of
one hundred and six original manuscripts,
autographs, maps, and printed books illus-
trating the discovery & history of America
from 1492 to 1814. [Leamington Spa, Courier
Pr., 1929] 232 p.   (2269

BOOKSELLERS

MAGGS Bros., London. An illustrated...(Cont.)
Items exhibited at the Library of Congress,
Spring 1929.

-----. Spanish America and the Guianas. London, 1935. 118 p. (Cat., no. 612) (2270
Jones 275.

MULLER, Frederik. Americana; livres et cartes
provenant en partie de la collection d'un
ancien ministre aux Etats-Unis. Amsterdam,
F. Muller & Co., 1896. 191 p. (2271
Jones 325.

-----. Catalogue of books, maps, plates on
America, and of a remarkable collection of
early voyages, offered for sale by Frederick
Muller...including a large number of books
in all languages with bibliographical and
historical notes and presenting an essay
towards a Dutch-American bibliography. Amsterdam, F. Muller, 1872-1875. 3 v. (2272
Jones 324.

-----. Catalogue of books and pamphlets, atlases, maps, plates and autographs relating
to North and South America. Amsterdam,
1877. (2273
Cited in Giraldo Jaramillo, p. 48.

-----. Catalogue of books relating to America,
including a large number of rare works printed before 1700 amongst which a nearly complete collection of the Dutch publications
on New Netherland from 1612 to 1820. Amsterdam [1850] 104 p. (2274
Cited in Giraldo Jaramillo, p. 68.

NEBENZAHL, Kenneth, Inc., firm, Chicago. Mexico, Texas and the Southwest in the Nineteenth Century. Chicago, n.d. 85 p. (Catalogue 15) (2275
Lists 439 items.

PAN AMERICAN Union. Latin American publications and their representatives in the United
States. Washington, D.C., 1941.
7 p. (2276
Includes directory of publications.

QUARITCH, Bernard. A catalogue of geography,
voyages, travels, Americana. London, 1895.
200 p. (2277
Jones 383.

-----. A general catalogue of books offered
to the public at the affixed prices. London,
1887-1892. 7 v. (2278
v. 4, Spanish and Portuguese books; v. 5,
Geography and travels, with American languages; v. 7, General index; supp. 7, Bibliotheca hispana.---Jones 384.

SAVILE Book Shop, Washington, D.C. A catalogue of books recent and forthcoming in

SAVILE Book Shop, Washington, D.C. ... (Cont.)
English and Spanish on Latin America. Washington, 1964. 11 p. (2279

STECHERT-HAFNER, Inc., New York. Latin Amer-
ica; publications acquired under the Latin
American Cooperative Acquisitions Project.
New York, 1960- . (Catalog, 283-) (2280
In 1964 DPU had received Catalogs, 1-11,
each with 1500 to 2100 entries.

STEVENS, Henry, Son and Stiles, London. Rare
americana; a catalogue of historical and
geographical books and pamphlets & manuscripts relating to America. London.
578 p. (2281
Millares, item 387, does not give date of
publication.

-----. [London, Dryden Pr., 1911] x,
210 p. (2282
"Manuscripts" is omitted in the title of
this publication.

TORRE REVELLO, José. Un catálogo impreso de
libros para vender en las Indias Occidentales en el siglo XVII. Madrid, F. Beltrán
[1930] 30 p. (2283
Jones 480. "Este trabajo apareció por primera vez en el Boletín del Instituto de Investigaciones Históricas de Buenos Aires,
en el no. 40, de abr.-jun. de 1929, y pos-
teriormente en los no. 1-2 de en.-feb. de
1930, del Boletín de las Cámaras Oficiales
del Libro de Madrid y Barcelona".

TRÖMEL, Paul Friedrich. Bibliothèque américaine. Catalogue raisonné d'une collection
de livres précieux sur l'Amérique, parus
depuis sa découverte jusqu'à l'an 1700, en
vente chez F. A. Brockhaus à Leipzig, F. A.
Brockhaus, 1861. 133 p. (2284
435 items described.---Jones 492.

TRÜBNER, Publishers, London. Bibliotheca hispano-americana. A catalogue of Spanish books
printed in Mexico, Guatemala, Honduras, the
Antilles, Venezuela, Colombia, Ecuador, Peru,
Chile, Uruguay, and the Argentine Republic;
and of Portuguese books printed in Brazil.
Followed by a collection of works on the
aboriginal languages of America. London,
1870. 184 p. (2285
Jones 493.

VINDEL, Pedro (Librería), Madrid. Catálogo de
la Librería de P. Vindel. Madrid, 1896-1903.
3 v. (2286
Jones 520.

-----. Madrid, 1929. (2286a

-----. Biblioteca ultramarina. Manuscritos
muchos de ellos originales e inéditos, referentes a América, China, Filipinas, Japón,

VINDEL, Pedro (Librería), Madrid ... (Cont.)
y otros países. Madrid, 1917. (Catálogo,
n.s., t. 6, no. 18)   (2287

WEISS & Cía, Antiquariat, München. Opera
meddi aevi manu conscripta, incunabula typo-
graphica, libri cum figuris xylographicis,
americana vetustissima, opera geographica y
historica, opera medicinalia, varia. Catalogus quintus. München, 1929.
206 p.   (2288
    Items 108-130 relate to the New World.

ARGENTINA

ARRIETA, Rafael Alberto. La ciudad y los libros; excursión bibliográfica al pasado por-
teño. Buenos Aires, Libr. del Colegio
[1955] 207 p.   (2289

EL ATENEO, Librería Científica y Literaria,
Buenos Aires. Catálogo general de la sección derecho y ciencias sociales. Buenos
Aires, Casa Editora, Pedro García, 1926.
480 p.   (2290

CARLOS CASAVALLE, hijo, Librería, Buenos Ai-
res. Catálogo. n.d. 90 p.   (2292

EDITORIAL Atlántida, Buenos Aires. Libros
publicados. Buenos Aires, 1944.
112 p.   (2293
    Cited in HLAS, no. 10, item 22.

LIBRERIA del Plata, S.R.L., Buenos Aires.
San Martín y la emancipación Sud-Americana;
bibliografía. Adhesión al Año Sanmartiniano. Buenos Aires [1950] 80 p.
(no. 27)   (2294

LIBRERIA del Saber, Buenos Aires. Bibliografía referente a Rosas y su época. Buenos
Aires, Matera y Cía., 1951. 68 p. (Bole-
tín, no. 12)   (2295
    Cited in Catálogo, Instituto Biblioteco-
lógico, Buenos Aires, 1964, item 802.

LIBRERIA Panamericana, Buenos Aires. Bibliografía hispanoamericana; libros antiguos y
modernos referentes a América y España.
Buenos Aires, 1947. xxiii, 371,
28 p.   (2296
    Compilers: David Behar and Raúl Behar.

-----. Catalogo de literatura hispanoameri-
cana. Buenos Aires, 1948.   (2297
    Cited in Bryant 194.

SUAREZ, Julio, Librería, Buenos Aires. Catálogo de libros americanos. Buenos Aires,
Tall. Gráf. Contreras, 1933-1935.
2 v.   (2298
    Jones 468.

SUAREZ, Julio, Librería, Buenos Aires. Catá-
logo de libros americanos y referentes a la
América del Sud de la "Librería Cervantes".
Buenos Aires, 1939. 291 p.   (2299
    Cited in Catálogo, Inst. Bibliotecológico,
Buenos Aires, 1964, item 828.

BOLIVIA

CARVAJAL R., Walter. Cultura patria [Comenta-
rios a las obras nacionales publicadas por
la casa González y Medina] La Paz, Gonzá-
lez y Medina, 1920. 264 p.   (2300
    Jones 909.

GISBERT y Cía., S. A. Obras nacionales, catálogo no. 1. La Paz, 1956. 23 p.
mimeogr.   (2301
    Cited in HLAS, 23, item 6402.

BRAZIL

ALVES, Francisco & Cia. Edições. Rio de Ja-
neiro, 1917. 216 p.   (2301a

LAEMMERT & Cia. Catalogo geral das obras de
fundo e outros livros. Rio de Janeiro, 1906.
352 p.   (2302
    Jones 1073.

LIVRARIA Casa Cruz. Catálogo geral de livra-
ria. Rio de Janeiro, n.d.   (2303
    Cited in PAU Bibliographies, 1928, p. 7.

LIVRARIA da Federação Espirita Brasileira.
Catálogo geral, no. 2. Rio de Janeiro, Typ.
Martins de Araujo, 1919. 130 p.   (2304
    Cited in PAU Bibliographies, 1928, p. 7.

LIVRARIA Econômica João Gazeau & Cia., São
Paulo. Bibliografia abreviada americana
brasileira classificada por assuntos. São
Paulo [1939] 32 p. mimeogr.   (2305
    Cited in Reis, item 590.

LIVRARIA Freitas Bastos, Rio de Janeiro. Bibliografia das obras editadas. [Rio de Ja-
neiro] 1956. 102 p.   (2306
    Cited in Richardson, item 7261.

-----. Bibliografia das obras jurídicas publicadas no Brasil. Rio de Janeiro, 1951.
107 p.   (2307
    Cited in Richardson, item 7262.

LIVRARIA H. Garnier, Rio de Janeiro. Catálogo completo. Rio de Janeiro, n.d.
80 p.   (2308

LIVRARIA Magalhães. Catálogo, 1918-1919.
São Paulo, 1919. 167 p.   (2309
    Cited in PAU Bibliographies, 1928, p. 7.

LIVRARIA Universal de Echenique y Irmão, Porto
Alegre. Catálogo geral das obras existentes
e a venta. Porto Alegre, n.d.   (2310
    Contents: Catálogo 2: Litteratura. - 3:
Educação e ensino. - 4: Agricultura, commercio, artes, industria, economia rural e do-
méstica e conhecimentos uteis. - 5: Medicina,
cirugia, hygiene, pharmacia, homoeopathia. -
6: Direito, política, philosophia.

MARTINS, José de Barros. Dez anos de ativida-
des editoriais de José de Barros Martins.
[São Paulo, Empresa Graf. da "Revista dos
Tribunais", 1950] 96 p.   (2311
    Contains 401 items published during 1940-
1950.

CHILE

FIGUEROA, Pedro Pablo. La librería en Chile;
estudio histórico y bibliográfico del canje
de obras nacionales establecido y propagado
en Europa y America, por el editor y librero don Roberto Miranda, 1884-1894; 2a. ed.
Paris, Garnier Hermanos, 1896. 136 p. (2312
    First issued in 1894.---Jones 1484.

LIBRERIA Inglesa, Santiago. Catálogo de obras
americanas y de algunas relativas al Oriente, en su mayor parte antiguas. A catalogue
of old and rare books relating to Latin America and to the Orient, for sale by Hume and
Co. Santiago, [Impr. de Enrique Blanchard-
Chessi, n.d. 158 p.   (2313
    Cited in Laval, item 351.

LIBRERIA M. C. Jorge Nascimento, Santiago. Catálogo de las obras nacionales o impresas en
el país de derecho, historia, literatura,
etc. Santiago, n.d.   (2314
    Cited in Ochsenius, item 46.

MEDINA, José Toribio. Catálogo de una pequeña colección de libros antiguos sobre la
América Española. [Santiago, Impr. del autor, 1888] 114 p.   (2315
    Cited in Millares item 384. Schaible,
item 36, notes that the catalog is a short
list of duplicates which Medina offered for
sale in 1888.

-----. Catálogo de obras americanas y de algunas relativas al Oriente, en su mayor parte antiguas. A catalogue of old and rare
books relating to Latin America and the
Orient. For sale by Hume and Co., Librería
Inglesa. Santiago, Impr. de Enrique Blanchard-Chessi [1902] 167 p.   (2316
    Millares, 385, notes that 1,552 titles
with facsimiles are included. Schaible,
item 116, states "El catálogo es obra de Medina, según Feliú, no. 228".

CATALOGO de la Librería Americana. Bogotá,
Impr. de "La Luz", 1889. 28 p.   (2317

CATALOGO de la Librería Barcelonesa de Solde-
villa y Curriols. Bogotá, 1878.
136 p.   (2318
    Cited in Giraldo Jaramillo, p. 66.

CATALOGO de la Librería y Papelería de Manuel
Gómez Calderón. Bogotá, Impr. de Gaitán
[1880?] 24 p.   (2319
    Cited in Ib. p. 66.

CATALOGO de libros antiguos de la Librería
Americana. Bogotá, 1891. 14 p.   (2320
    Cited in Ib., p. 66.

CATALOGO de una librería particular que está
de venta total o parcialmente. Bogotá, Impr.
de Cualla, 1844. 16 p.   (2321
    Perhaps the first catalog published in Bo-
gotá, grouped by languages in which the books
were written. Cited in Ib., p. 67.

CATALOGO general de "La Ilustración Colombiana" Librería Torres Amaya. Bogotá, 1881.
32 p.   (2322
    Cited in Ib., p. 67.

CATALOGO general de la Librería "El Mensajero". Bogotá, Tip. de Eugenio Pardo, 1897.
62 p.   (2323
    Cited in Ib., p. 67.

CATALOGO general ilustrado de la Librería y
Papelería de "El Mensajero". Bogotá, Impr.
de Luis M. Holguín, 1898. 129 p.   (2324
    Cited in Ib., p. 67.

COLOMBIA. Universidad, Bogotá. Catálogo de
la Librería Universitaria. Obras de autores
colombianos y extranjeros. Bogotá, Ediciones Nacionales, 1951. 30 p.   (2325
    Cited in Ib., p. 78.

EDICIONES Paulinas, Bogotá. Catálogo general.
[Bogotá, 1963] 46 p.   (2326
    Cited in Peraza, Fichas, t. 4-6, item 362.

LIBRERIA Colombiana, Bogotá. Catálogo. [Bo-
gotá, Impr. Patriótica del Instituto Caro
y Cuervo, 1961. 19 p.   (2327
    Cited in Peraza, Fichas, t. 2, item 178.

-----. Catálogo de textos escolares. Bogotá
[1962] 41 p. mimeogr.   (2328
    Cited in Ib., t. 3, item 195.

LIBRERIA Colombiana, Bogotá. Catálogo de algunas publicaciones colombianas aparecidas
en 1958 y 1959. Bogotá, 1959. 20 p. (Catálogo no. 46) mimeogr.   (2329
    Cited in Giraldo Jaramillo, p. 72.

LIBRERIA Colombiana, Bogotá. Catálogo de libros colombianos publicados de 1934 a julio
de 1942. Bogotá, Edit. Antena, 1942.
217 p.   (2330
     Cited in Giraldo Jaramillo., p. 72.

-----. -----. Sección de historia. Bogotá,
1945. 64 p.   (2331
     Cited in Ib., p. 64.

-----. -----. no. 1: Historia. Bogotá
[1955?] 23 p.   (2332
     Cited in Ib., p. 72.

-----. -----. no. 2: Libros raros, ediciones
agotadas. Bogotá, 1955. 27 p.   (2333
     Cited in Ib., p. 72.

-----. -----. no. 3: Literatura. Bogotá,
[1956] 48 p.   (2334
     Cited in Ib., p. 72.

-----. Catalogue of books published in the
Republic of Colombia. Bogotá, 1934.
160 p.   (2335
     Cited in Ib., p. 73.

-----. Libros colombianos (autores, temas y
ediciones nacionales) Bibliografía completa, 1934-1939. Bogotá, 1939. 74 p. (2336
     Cited in Ib., p. 73.

-----. -----. (Complemento de los publicados
en 1934 y 1939) Bogotá, Edit. Andes. 1940.
61 p.   (2337
     Cited in Ib., p. 73.

-----. Obras colombianas (publicados de 1940
a 1951) Bogotá, Edit Minerva [1951]
16 p.   (2338
     Cited in Ib., p. 73.

LIBRERIA Siglo XX, Bogotá. Catálogo especial,
editado para información de los socios del
Club de Libros. Bogotá, Edit. Centro, 1943.
128 p.   (2339
     Cited in Ib., p. 73.

-----. Catálogo general de literatura, ensayos, arte, filosofía, historia, biografías
y obras de orientación religiosa. Bogotá,
Edit. El liberal, 1946. 448 p.   (2340
     Cited in Ib., p. 73.

LIBRERIA VOLUNTAD, Ramón de Bedout e Hijos,
Bogotá. Catálogo de textos escolares, libros varios, libros para niños, libros religiosos, diccionarios, material pedagógico,
mapas y atlas. Bogotá [1961] 55 p. (2341
     Cited in Peraza, Fichas, t. 2, item 319.

CUBA

CULTURAL, S.A., Habana. Curso escolar de

CULTURAL, S.A., Habana. Curso... (Cont.)
1943-1944; extracto del catalogo de libros de
educación; libros de texto para la enseñanza
elemental y superior. Institutos de segunda
enseñanza. Escuelas normales y escuelas de
comercio. Catálogo de diccionarios. Habana,
1943. 104 p.   (2342

-----. Latin-American bibliography for this
Session. Habana, [1941] 55 p.   (2343
     Prepared for the Summer Session students
enrolled at the University of Havana.

EDITORIAL LEX, La Habana. Catálogo de las
obras de Editorial Lex. Comentarios, anéc-
dotas, índice de términos judiciales, leyes
y decretos inconstitucionales, almanaque judicial, 1945. Habana, 1944. 192 p.   (2344
     Cited in HLAS, no. 11, item 12.

ECUADOR

JANER e Hijo. Catálogo general de la Librería
Española de Janer e Hijo. Guayaquil, 1915.
388 p.   (2345
     Cited in PAU, Bibliographies 1928. p. 16.

MUÑOZ, Bonifacio. Obras de autores ecuatorianos; catálogo especial de las librerías "Sucre". Quito, Tip. y Encuad. Salesianas,
1920. 144 p.   (2346
     Jones 1996.

GUATEMALA

LIBRERIA de Autores Nacionales, Guatemala.
Obras de autores nacionales; catálogo, no. 1,
Guatemala, 1964. 24 p.   (2347
     Cited in HLAS 26, item 65.

HAITI

LAURENT, Mentor. A la bonne ménagère; Oficine
Général des Livres d'Haiti et des Autres Antilles. Port-au-Prince, Impr. Telehomme,
1937. 98 p.   (2348
     Cited in Bissainthe 2695, listing of books
for sale in bookstore of the compiler.

MEXICO

ANDRADE Y MORALES, Sucesores, Librería. Catálogo general de las obras de surtido. Antigua librería establecida en 1814 en el Por-
tal de Agustinos, núm. 3. México, Impr. de
Ignacio Escalante, 1887. 126 p.   (2349
     Cited in Millares 1437.

ANTIGUA Librería Robredo de José Porrúa e Hijos, México, D.F. Catálogo 16. México, D.F.,
1954.   (2350

ANTIGUA Librería Robredo de José Porrúa e Hijos, México, D.F. Catálogo de libros de ocasión, no. 2. México, D.F., A. del Bosque, 1940. 225 p.   (2351
Cited in Millares, Registro. p. 1.

-----. Catálogo de libros de textos: primaria, secundaria, preparatoria, escuelas superiores, obras de consulta. México, 1941. 80 p.   (2352
Cited in Millares, Registro, p. 1.

BLAKE, A. M. Collection of rare books, mostly Mexicana, n.d. 237 p. mimeogr.   (2353
Contains 3112 items which were to be sold at auction.

BLAKE, Willson Wilberforce. Catalogue of second hand books. México, D.F., 1892-1902.   (2354
Jones 2084.

BOURET, Viuda de Ch. Catálogo de novelas en español y francés. México, D.F., Bouret, 1913. 294 p.   (2355

-----. Catálogo general de las obras de derecho. México, D.F., Bouret, 1913. 175 p.   (2356

-----. Catálogo general de obras de agricultura y construcciones. México, D.F., Impr. Francesa, 1918. 36 p.   (2357

-----. Catálogo general de obras de artes y oficios. México, D.F., Impr. Francesa, 1918. 70 p.   (2358

FERNANDEZ DEL CASTILLO, Francisco. Libros y libreros en el siglo XVI. México, D.F., Tip. Guerrero Hnos., 1914. 608 p. (Publ. del Archivo General de la Nación, 6) (2359
Jones 2164.

FONDO de Cultura Económica, México. Catálogo general. México, D.F., 1943. 115 p. (2360

-----. Catálogo general, México, D.F., [1955] xxvi, 487 p.   (2361

-----. Catálogo general. México, D.F., 1964. 627 p.   (2362

PORRUA, José e Hijos. Catálogo de libros de ocasión. México, D.F., 1938- . no. 1- .   (2363
Jones 2431b.

PORRUA, Manuel, Librería, México. Bibliografía de la imprenta en Puebla, 1643-1941. México, D.F., 1949. unpaged. (Oferta especial, 1950, no. 2) mimeogr.   (2364

-----. Catálogo bibliográfico; advertencia preliminar por Agustín Millares Carlo. Mé-

PORRUA, Manuel, Librería, México, D.F...(Cont.) xico, D.F., 1948. 124 p. ("Libros"; suplemento, no. 2)   (2365
Contents:- 1, Impresos mexicanos del siglo XVI. - 2, Impresos raros. - 3, Otros libros importantes.

-----. Catálogo de libros de ocasión; México jurídico y político, relaciones y antecedentes. México, D.F., 1951. 168 p. ("Libros", suplemento, no. 3)   (2366

-----. Catálogo de una biblioteca de literatura mexicana. Prólogo de Andrés Henestrosa. México, D.F., 1952. unpaged. (Oferta especial, no. 1)   (2367

PORRUA Hermanos, Librería, México. Bibliografía americana. Catálogo. México, D.F., 1923. 135 p.   (2368

-----. Catálogo de libros mexicanos o que tratan de América y de algunos otros impresos en España. México, D.F., 1949. xxii, 889 p. (Bibliografía americana, no. 5)   (2369
Lists 9,088 items.

SOCIEDAD de Edición y Librería Franco-Americana. Catálogo de ciencias aplicadas, artes y oficios. México, 1924. xvi, 207 p.   (2370
Cited in PAU, Bibliographies, 1928. p. 21.

UNION Tipográfica Editorial Hispano Americana, México. Catálogo general. México, 1963. 138 p.   (2371

PERU

LIBRERIA Internacional del Perú, Lima. Catálogo, no. 1. Lima, 1944. 68 [1] p. (2372
Listed are 574 items many of which are imprints from Peru and other Latin American countries.

-----. Catálogo, no. 2. Lima, 1945. 102 p.   (2373

-----. Catálogo, V. [Lima, 1949] 179 [3] p.   (2374

-----. Catálogo, VI. Lima, 1954. 159 p.   (2375

-----. Ciencias jurídicas: I: Derecho peruano; II: Folletos; III: Derecho americano; IV: Derecho. Lima, n.d. 120 p.   (2376

-----. Derecho. [Lima] 1950. 28 p. (Número 1)   (2377

-----. Derecho peruano. [Lima] 1950. 11 p.

LIBRERIA Internacional del Perú, Lima...(Cont.)
(Número 1)   (2378

-----. Filosofía [Lima] 1950. 23 p. (Número 2)   (2379

URUGUAY

BARREIRO Y RAMOS, Antonio. Obras de fondo y
algunas de surtido. Montevideo, 1918.
40 p.   (2380

BERTRAN, Luis. Notas para una historia de la
producción editorial del país en el primer
centenario de su independencia. Montevideo,
"La Impresora Uruguaya", 1931.
xlvi p.   (2381
Jones 2822.

BOLETIN bibliográfico Barreiro. Montevideo,
Barreiro y Ramos, 1955- . Annual   (2382
Cited in Musso 611.

BOTANY

GENERAL

RIZZINI, Carlos Toledo. Esboço de um guia da
literatura botânica. Rio de Janeiro, Conselho Nacional de Pesquisas, Instituto Brasileiro de Bibliografia e Documentação,
1957. 81 p.   (2383

ARGENTINA

CASTELLANOS, Alberto, and PEREZ-MOREAU, Román
A. Contribución a la bibliografía botánica
argentina. Buenos Aires, Impr. Coni, 1941.
2 v.   (2383a
Cited in Besterman, 4th ed., 952.

-----. Los tipos de vegetación de la República Argentina. [Tucumán, 1945] 154 p. (Tucumán, Universidad Nacional. Facultad de
Filosofía y Letras, Instituto de Estudios
Geográficos, Monografías, 4)   (2384

DOMINGUEZ, Juan Aníbal. Contribuciones a la
materia médica argentina. Buenos Aires,
Casa J. Peuser, 1928. 433 p.   (2385
Includes bibliographies and a section on
"Los investigadores de la flora médica americana desde el descubrimiento hasta mediados del siglo XIX".---Jones 684.

KURTZ, Federico. Essai d'une bibliographie
botanique de l'Argentine; 2. éd. Córdoba,
Est. Tip. F. Domenici, 1913-1915. p. 221-
376, 369-467.   (2386
Academia Nacional de Ciencias, Córdoba,
Boletín, t. 19-20. The first edition was
published in the Boletín, v. 16, p. 117-205,
1899.
The literature from 1914 to 1921 is cov-
ered by L. Haumann and A. Castellanos in
Physis, Buenos Aires, v. 5, p. 263-91 (cf.
Quelle, no. 385a.)---Jones 737.

SPARN, Enrique. Bibliografía de la yerba ma-
te. Córdoba, 1937. 21 p. (Academia Nacional de Ciencias. Miscelánea, 22)   (2387

SPARN, Enrique. Bibliografía... (Cont.)
Jones 853.

BRAZIL

ANGELY, João. Bibliografia sôbre plantas tó-
xicas. Curitiba, Instituto Paranaense de
Botânica, 1960. 15 p. (Boletim, no.
4)   (2388
Cited in Revista interamericana de bibliografía, v. 12, p. 180.

BIBLIOGRAFIA brasileira de botânica, v. 1- .
1950/55- . Rio de Janeiro, Instituto Brasileiro de Bibliografía e Documentação
[1957-]   (2389
Latest at DPU: v. 3, 1959/1960.

NEIVA, Arthur. Esboço historico sôbre a botâ-
nica e zoologia no Brasil (1587-1922) São
Paulo, 1929. 143 p.   (2390
Jones 1108.

SAMPAIO, Alberto José de. Apontamentos para
a bibliographia botânica referente a flora
brasileira e as plantas cultivadas no Brasil.
Rio de Janeiro, Impr. Nacional, 1914.
50 p.   (2391
Cited in Reis 284.

-----. Bibliographia botânica (relativa á flora brasileira) (Boletim do Museu Nacional,
Rio de Janeiro, v. 1, no. 2, p. 111-25,
1924)   (2392
Jones 1182.

CHILE

LOOSER, Gualterio. Bibliografía botánica chilena. (Revista de bibliografía chilena, Santiago, 3r. trim. p. 212-30, 364-90,
1927)   (2393
An amplification of the bibliography of
Karl Reiche, Grundzüge der pflanzenverbrei-
tung in Chile, Leipzig, 1907, p. 27-45.---

LOOSER, Gualterio. Bibliografía... (Cont.)
Jones 1519.

PORTER, Carlos Emilio. Bibliografía chilena
razonada de botánica agrícola e industrial.
(Anales de la Universidad de Chile, Santiago,
año 7, 2a. ser., p. 861-917, 3r. trim.
1929)   (2394
"Forma parte de...Reseña histórica y bibliografía chilena razonada de ciencias naturales
que viene publicando el autor, desde 1898,
en la Revista chilena de ciencias naturales".
Cited in Ochsenius, no. 167.---Jones 1572.

REICHE, Karl Friedrich. Grundzüge der pflanzen
verbreitung in Chile. Leipzig, W. Engelmann,
1907. 374 p. (Die vegetation der erde, hrsg.
von A. Engler und O. Drude, 8)   (2395
"Literarische Hilisquellen" (p. 1-47) lists
627 publications.---Jones 1581.

-----. Geografía botánica de Chile. Traducción del alemán de Gualterio Looser. Santiago, Impr. Universitaria, 1934- .
v. 1- .   (2396
"Bibliografía de la flora chilena, literatura, mapas, colecciones": v. 1, p. 44-85.
---Jones 1582.

MEXICO

BIBLIOGRAFIA botánica mexicana. (El Libro y
el pueblo, México, D.F., año 2, t. 2, no.
6-7, 1923)   (2397
Jones 2077.

LANGMAN, Ida Kaplan. A selected guide to the
literature on the flowering plants of Mexico.
Philadelphia, Univ. of Pennsylvania Pr.,
[1964] 1015 p.   (2398
DPU has copy of typewritten manuscript
prepared in 1950. 726 p.

-----. Títulos de los 73 trabajos de la obra
"Biblioteca Botánica Mexicana" de Nicolás
León, en cuya localización esta interesada
la Sra. Ida Langman. Philadelphia, Univ.
of Pennsylvania, Dept. of Botany [1960] 5 p.
mimeogr.   (2399

LEON, Nicolás. Biblioteca botánico-mexicana.
Catálogo bibliográfico, biográfico y crítico de autores y escritos referentes a vege-
tales de México y sus aplicaciones, desde
la conquista hasta el presente. Suplemento
a la materia médica mexicana publicada por

LEON, Nicolás. Biblioteca... (Cont.)
el Instituto Médico Nacional. México, D.F.,
Of. Tip. de la Secretaría de Fomento, 1895.
372 p.   (2400
Jones 2289.

MARTINEZ, Maximino, and ROVIROSA, Gustavo.
Bibliografía botánica mexicana. (El Libro y
el pueblo, México, D.F., t. 2-3, 1923-
1924)   (2401
Jones 2317.

MARTINEZ, Maximino. Catálogo de nombres vul-
gares y científicos de plantas mexicanas.
México, D.F., Impr. Mexicana, 1937.
551 p.   (2402
Bibliografía: p. 547-51.---Jones 2318.

-----. Las plantas más útiles que existen en
la República Mexicana. México, 1928.
381 p.   (2403
Includes bibliography.---Jones 2319.

-----. Las plantas medicinales de México; 2a.
ed. México, Ediciones Botas, 1939.
628 p.   (2404
Includes bibliography.---Jones 2319a.

OLAGUIBEL, Manuel de. Memoria para una biblio-
grafía científica de México en el siglo XIX.
México, D.F., Of. Tip. de la Secretaría de
Fomento, 1889. 99 p.   (2405
"Sección primera: Botánica". No more
published.---Jones 2388.

ROYS, Ralph Loveland. The ethno-botany of the
Maya. New Orleans, Tulane University, 1931.
539 p. (The Tulane University of Louisiana,
Middle American series, publ. no. 2)   (2406
Bibliography: p. 352-59.---Jones 2478.

PERU

WILLIAMS, Llewelyn. Woods of northeastern Peru. Chicago, 1936. 587 p. (Field Museum
of Natural History. Botanical ser.,
v. 15)   (2407
Bibliography: p. 568-74.---Jones 2774.

PUERTO RICO

STAHL, Agustín. Estudios sobre la flora de
Puerto Rico; 2a. ed. San Juan, Impr. Vene-
zuela, 1936. 2 v.   (2408
Literatura: v. 33-52.---Jones 2808.

CATALOGS - LIBRARY

GENERAL

BOSTON College. Library. Catalogue of books, manuscripts, etc. in the Caribbeana section (specializing in Jamaicana) of the Nicholas M. Williams memorial ethnological collection. Chestnut Hill, Mass., 1932. 133 p. (2409

BRITISH Museum. Dept. of Printed Books. Short-title catalogue of Spanish-American books printed before 1601, now in the British Museum. London, Printed by order of the Trustees, 1944. 19 p. (2409a
Compiler: Hernry Thomas.

CALIFORNIA. State Library. Sutro Branch. Catalogue of Mexican pamphlets in the Sutro collection, 1623-1888. San Francisco, 1939-1940. 10 v. (2410
A list mimeographed, without annotations, alphabetical by year. Prepared by the personnel of the Works Progress Administration, P. Radin, Editor.---Jones 2105a.

-----. -----. Supplements 1-2, 1605-1828. San Francisco, 1941. 198 p. (2411
Compiled by A. L. Gans.

-----. -----. Supplement, 1605-1888. 290 p. (2412

-----. -----. Author index. 1623-1888. San Francisco, 1941. 65 p. (2413
Compiled by A. L. Gans.

-----. University. Bancroft Library. Catalog of printed books of the Bancroft Library. Boston, G. K. Hall, 1964. 22 v. (2414

-----. -----. -----. Index to printed maps. Boston, G. K. Hall, 1964. 521 p. (2415

-----. -----. Library. Spain and Spanish America in the libraries of the University of California; a catalogue of books. Berkeley, 1928-1930. 2 v. (2416
Contents: v. 1, The General and Departmental libraries, prepared by Alice I. Lyser. - v. 2, The Bancroft Library.---Jones 81.

CENTRO di Studi Americani, Rome. Biblioteca. Catalogo, Roma, 1935- . v. 1- . (2417
The first volume contains Ada Marchino's Bibliografía americana.---Jones 420.

EZELL, Paul Howard, and EZELL, Greta. The Aguiar collection in the Arizona Pioneers' Historical Society. San Diego, Calif., San Diego State College Pr., 1964. 100 p. (Social science monograph ser., 1: 1) (2417a
Contains material related to states of northern Mexico.

GENOA. Biblioteca Civica Berio. Catalogo

GENOA. Biblioteca... (Cont.)
delle opere componenti la raccolta colombiana esistente nella civica Biblioteca Berio di Genova. Genova, Fratelli Pagano, 1906. 126 p. (2418
Jones 162.

-----. Catalogo della raccolta colombiana (Catalog of the Columbus Collection) Boston, G. K. Hall, 1963. 151 p. (2418a

GROSVENOR Library, Buffalo, N. Y. Catalogue of books on Latin-America. Buffalo, The Library, 1901. 30 p. (Bulletin, no. 1) (2419
Jones 180.

HISPANIC Society of America, N.Y. Library. Catalogue. Boston, G. K. Hall, 1962. 10 v. (10048 p.) (2420

-----. List of books printed 1601-1700, in the Library of the Hispanic Society of America, by Clara Louisa Penney. N. Y., 1938. xxvi, 972 p. (Hispanic notes and monographs; essays, studies, and brief biographies. [Catalogue ser.]) (2421
Contains appendices: Fifteenth-Sixteenth century books not included in List of books printed before 1601; Check list of printing sites and printers of Hispanic books 1468?-1700. Includes Hispanic American imprints.

JONES, Cecil Knight. Hispano-Americana in the Library of Congress. [Baltimore, 1919] p. 96-104. (2422
Reprinted from the Hispanic American historical review, v. 2, no. 1, Feb. 1919. Published in Spanish in Inter-America, Jul. 1919.---Jones 226.

LUTRELL, Estelle. Mexican writers, a catalogue of books in the University of Arizona Library, with synopsis and biographical notes. Tucson, 1920. 83 p. (University of Arizona record, v. 13, no. 5, Library bibliography, no. 5) (2423
Authors' names are given in full with dates, followed by biobibliographical notes. Contents: 1, Mexican writers; 2, Literature in Spanish upon Mexican themes by authors native to other countries; 3, Collections, Literary criticism, Biography; 4, Bibliographies; 5, Mexican language.---Jones 2310.

MADRID. Museo-Biblioteca de Ultramar. Catálogo. Madrid, Sucesora de M. Minuesa de los Ríos, 1900. ix, [2] 350 p. (2424
Jones 272. Compiler Francisco de P. Vigil.

MANCHESTER, Alan Krebs. Descriptive bibliography of the Brazilian section of the Duke University Library. 1933. 69 p. (2425
Reprinted from Hispanic American historical

MANCHESTER, Alan Krebs. Descriptive... (Cont.)
review, v. 13, no. 2, p. 238-66, May 1933;
no. 4, p. 495-523, Nov. 1933.---Jones 1095.

MATHEWS, Thomas G. General survey of the material related to Puerto Rico held by the
Library of Congress; report submitted August
8, 1956. [n.p., 1956?] 56 p.   (2426

MONTIGNANI, John Brommer. Books on Latin America and its art in the Metropolitan Museum
of Art Library. New York, 1943.
63 p.   (2427

NEWBERRY Library, Chicago. Dictionary catalog
of the Edward E. Ayer collection of Americana
and American Indians. Boston, G. K. Hall,
1961. 16 v.   (2428
Includes North and South America.

NEW YORK. Public Library. Dictionary catalog
of the history of the Americas collection of
the New York Public Library. Boston, G. K.
Hall, 1964. 28 v.   (2429

SANTIAGO DE COMPOSTELA. Universidad. Catálogos de la biblioteca "América" ... Redactado por d. José Ma. de Bustamante y Urrutia.
[Santiago] Tip. de "El Eco de Santiago",
1927-1929. 2 v. (Anales de la Universidad
de Santiago)   (2429a
"Catálogo alfabético de autores, de obras
de más de 200 páginas con un apendice de las
obras que llegaron con posterioridad a la
impresión de su letra respectiva".---Jones
434.

SCHNITZLER, Mario C. An annotated bibliography of the Henry Raup Wagner collection
of early Hispanic-American history and geography, Honnold Library, Claremont College.
Claremont, Calif., 1955. 73 p. typewritten?   (2430
Presented as thesis for the M. A. degree.
Winston L. Yang notes that 479 titles are
described.

SEVILLA. Biblioteca Colombina. Catálogo de
sus libros impresos; publicado por primera
vez en virtud de acuerdo del excmo. e ilmo.
sr. deán y cabildo de la Santa Metropolitana y Patriarcal Iglesia de Sevilla, bajo la
inmediata dirección de su bibliotecario el
ilmo. sr. dr. d. Servando Arbolí y Faraudo
... con notas bibliográficas del dr. d. Simón de la Rosa y López --- Sevilla, Impr.
de E. Rasco [etc] 1888-1948. 7 v.   (2431
Caption title, v. 1: Indice alfabético
de los libros impresos procedentes de la librería de don Fernando Colón, que se conservan en la Biblioteca del excmo. e ilmo. cabildo eclesiástico de Sevilla.---Jones 447.

SPAIN. Biblioteca Nacional. Catálogo de
obras iberoamericanas y filipinas en la Bi-

SPAIN. Biblioteca Nacional. Catálogo...(Cont.)
blioteca Nacional, redactado y ordenado por
Luisa Cuesta con la colaboración de Modesta
Cuesta. Prólogo de Francisco Sintes Obrador.
Madrid, Dirección General de Archivos y Bi-
bliotecas, 1953. 322 p. (Catálogos de ar-
chivos y bibliotecas, 1)   (2432
Lists 3,364 items.

-----. Junta de Relaciones Culturales. Catálogo de las bibliotecas españolas en las repúblicas hispanoamericanas. Madrid, 1934.
143 p.   (2433
Jones 457.

-----. -----. Catálogo de las bibliotecas populares españolas en las repúblicas hispano-
americanas. Madrid, 1934. 61 p.   (2434
Jones 458.

STEIN, Barbara H. Latin America: social
sciences and humanities. Serials (periodicals, monographs in series, documents) currently received in the Princeton University
Library. Princeton, N.J., 1964. 41 p.
mimeogr.   (2435
Cited in HLAS 27, item 68.

TEXAS. University. Library. Recent Venezuelan acquisitions of the Latin American Collection, no. 1. 1962/1964. Austin, 1964.
62 p.   (2436
Photo-offset reproduction of Library cards.
Contains approximately 1,100 entries. Cited
in HLAS 26, item 85f.

THOMAS Gilcrease Institute of American History
and Art, Tulsa, Okla. A catalog of Hispanic
documents in the Thomas Gilcrease Institute.
Tulsa, Okla., 1962. 155 p. mimeogr. (2437
Compiler: Clevy Lloyd Strout.

UNION Ibero-Americana. Memoria correspondiente al año 1930. Madrid, 1931.
124 p.   (2438
Libros ingresados en la Biblioteca:
p. 33-102.---Jones 498.

YALE University. Library. Spanish American
literature in the Yale University Library;
a bibliography [by] Frederick Bliss Luquiens.
New Haven, Yale Univ. Pr.; London, H. Milford,
Oxford Univ. Pr., 1939. 335 p.   (2439
Jones 546.

ARGENTINA

ARGENTINA. Arsenal Principal de Guerra. Catálogo de la Biblioteca. Buenos Aires, 1909-
1910. 2 v.   (2440
Binayán, item 103, notes that he did not
examine this item but that it was cited in
the Catalogo de la Biblioteca of the Estado
Mayor del Ejército.

ARGENTINA. Biblioteca Nacional. Catálogo de
la donación Leguina. Buenos Aires, 1946.
193 p.   (2441

-----. -----. Catálogo de la donación Félix
Buxareo Oribe. Buenos Aires, Impr. de la
Biblioteca Nacional, 1935. 195 p.   (2442
Contains "obras sobre hipología".---Jones
610.

-----. -----. Catálogo de las obras que los
lectores pueden consultar en los pupitres
laterales del salón de lectura. Buenos Aires, 1922. 24 p.   (2443
Jones 610a.

-----. -----. Catálogo metódico de la Biblioteca Nacional, seguido de una tabla alfabética de autores. Buenos Aires, Impr. de P.
E. Coni e Hijos, 1893-1931. 7 v.   (2444
Contents. - t. 1, Ciencias y artes, 1893,
- t. 2, Historia y geografía, 1900. - t. 3,
Literatura, 1911. - t. 4, Derecho, 1915. -
t. 5, Ciencias y artes, 1919. - t. 6, Historia y geografía (t. 2), 1925. - t. 7, Literatura (t. 2), 1931.---Jones 613.

-----. -----. Los 5,300 libros más pedidos
en la Biblioteca Nacional y algunas indicaciones útiles; 4a. ed. Buenos Aires, 1950.
319 p.   (2445

-----. -----. Los 2,600 libros más pedidos
en la Biblioteca Nacional. Buenos Aires,
Impr. de la Biblioteca Nacional, 1936.
106 p.   (2446
Jones 615.

-----. -----. Ediciones del Quijote en la
Biblioteca Nacional. Buenos Aires, 1947.
62 p.   (2447
Lists 123 items.

-----. -----. Los 3,000 libros más pedidos
en la Biblioteca Nacional y algunas indicaciones útiles; 3a. ed. Buenos Aires, Impr.
de la Biblioteca Nacional, 1941.
212 p.   (2448

-----. Círculo de Aeronáutica. Biblioteca
Nacional de Aeronáutica. Catálogo de la
Biblioteca escolar. Buenos Aires, 1949.
128 p.   (2449

-----. Congreso. Biblioteca. Catálogo de
los libros que contiene la Biblioteca. Buenos Aires, Impr. Lit. y Encuad. de Stiller
y Laass, 1886. 110 p.   (2450
Cited in Catálogo, Inst. Bibliotecológico,
Buenos Aires, 1964, item 890.

-----. -----. Catálogo de los libros que con-
tiene la Biblioteca del Congreso. Buenos
Aires, 1887. 68 p.   (2451
Jones 571.

ARGENTINA. Congreso. Biblioteca. Catálogo
general. Buenos Aires, "El Comercio", 1913.
t. 1.   (2452
Jones 572.

-----. -----. Catálogo general (por orden de
materias), Buenos Aires [1918] 704 p. (2453
On verso of title page: Este pliego subs-
tituye al aparecido en el no. 1 de este Boletín, correspondiente a septiembre de 1918.

-----. -----. Catálogo metódico de la biblioteca: t. 2, Historia y geografía. Ciencias.
Artes e industrias. Literatura. Administración (publicaciones oficiales). Instituciones particulares. Buenos Aires, 1934.
388 p.   (2454

-----. Dirección de Meteorología, Geofísica e
Hidrología. Catálogo de publicaciones perió-
dicas existentes en la Biblioteca. Buenos
Aires, 1938-1939. 124 p.   (2455
Classified by country.---Jones 577a.

-----. Dirección General de Correos y Telégrafos. Catálogo de la Biblioteca de Correos
y Telégrafos. Anexo A del folleto no. 46
"Secretaría General y Dependencias". Buenos
Aires, Tall. Gráf. de Correos y Telégrafos,
1937. 319 p.   (2456
Jones 578.

-----. -----. Biblioteca. Primer suplemento
al Catálogo. Buenos Aires, Tall. Gráf. de
Correos y Telégrafos, 1939. 94 p.   (2457
Cited in Catálogo, Instituto Bibliotecológico, Buenos Aires, 1964., item 892.

-----. Dirección General de Navegación, Biblioteca y Archivo. Catálogo de la Biblioteca.
[Buenos Aires] 1944. 71 p. mimeogr. (2458
Cited in Catálogo, Instituto Bibliotecológico, Buenos Aires, 1964, item 893.

-----. Ejército. Estado Mayor. Catálogo de
la Biblioteca. Buenos Aires, Tall. Gráf. del
Estado Mayor del Ejército, 1914. xii,
409 p.   (2459
Jones 580.

-----. -----. Biblioteca. Catálogo de la Biblioteca. Buenos Aires, Tall. Gráf. del Instituto Geográfico Militar, 1933.
791 p.   (2460
Cited in Catálogo, Instituto Bibliotecológico, Buenos Aires, 1964, item 894.

-----. Escuela Naval Militar. Catálogo de la
Biblioteca; 4a. ed. Buenos Aires, Tall. Tip.
de la Escuela Naval Militar, 1906.
60 p.   (2461
Cited in Binayán 105.

-----. Instituto de Sanidad Vegetal. Laboratorio Central de Fitopatología. Biblioteca.

ARGENTINA. Instituto de Sanidad... (Cont.)
Catálogo de la Biblioteca ... e instrucciones para su uso, por Ricardo J. Lois. Buenos Aires, Ministerio de Agricultura, 1948.
95 p.   (2462

-----. Ministerio de Marina. Biblioteca.
Catálogo de la Biblioteca Nacional de Marina. Buenos Aires, Tall. Gráf. del Ministerio de Agricultura, 1917. 344 p.   (2463
Later editions, 1927 and 1934.---Jones 582.

-----. -----. Buenos Aires, Ferrari Hnos.,
1922. 122 p.   (2464

-----. -----. Buenos Aires, Ferrari Hnos.,
n.d. 183 p.   (2465
Cited in Pan American Union, Bibliographies. 1928.

-----. -----. Buenos Aires, G. Kraft, 1927.
188 p.   (2466

-----. -----. Buenos Aires, T. Palumbo, 1934.
217 p.   (2467

ASOCIACION Bernardino Rivadavia, Bahía Blanca.
Biblioteca. Catálogo de la Biblioteca Popular del Municipio. Buenos Aires, Tall. Gráf.
de la Penitenciaría Nacional, 1904.
2 v.   (2468
Jones 588.

-----. 1o.-2o. suplementos. Buenos Aires,
Tall. Gráf. de la Penitenciaría Nacional,
1915. 2 v.   (2469
Jones 588.

-----. Catálogo metódico. Buenos Aires, M.
Zaragoza, 1916. 210 p.   (2470
Jones 589.

-----. Catálogo general. [Bahía Blanca, Biblioteca Popular de la Asociación Bernardino Rivadavia, 1932] 459 p.   (2471
Cited in Catálogo, Instituto Bibliotecológico, Buenos Aires, 1964, 896.

ASOCIACION "Biblioteca Sarmiento", Tucumán.
Catálogo de la Biblioteca Pública. Tucumán,
"La Velocidad", 1910. 181 p.   (2472
Cited in Binayán 125.

BANCO Industrial de la República Argentina.
Departamento de Biblioteca y Difusión. Bi-
blioteca. Catálogo bibliográfico. Buenos
Aires, 1959.   (2473
Various pagings by some 64 subjects.

BIBLIOTECA Obrera "Juan B. Justo", Buenos Aires. Catálogo de la Biblioteca Obrera fundada el 25 de septiembre de 1897. Buenos
Aires, Impr. y Encuad. de Lotito & Barberis,
1914. 117 p.   (2474

BUENOS AIRES. Colegio Nacional. Biblioteca.
Catálogo. Buenos Aires, Universidad de Buenos Aires, 1928. 527 p.   (2475

-----. -----. Suplemento, 1o. al 3o. Buenos
Aires, Impr. de la Universidad, 1930-1932.
3 v.   (2476

-----. -----. Catálogo de obras de la sección
Sanmartiniana. Buenos Aires, 1950. 30 p.
mimeogr.   (2477
Cited in Catálogo, Instituto Bibliotecológico, Buenos Aires, 1964, item 909.

-----. Departamento de Policía. Catálogo ge-
neral de la Biblioteca. Buenos Aires, Tall.
Gráf. de la Policía, 1939. 278 p.   (2478
Jones 619.

-----. Escuela Industrial de la Nación. Catálogo de la Biblioteca. Buenos Aires, Tall.
Gráf. de la Penitenciaría Nacional, 1914.
132 p.   (2479
Jones 620.

-----. -----. Catálogo de la Biblioteca tecnológica. Comprende las obras ingresadas
hasta el 15 de marzo de 1926. Buenos Aires,
1926. 305 p.   (2480
Jones 661. Classified with author index.

-----. -----. Suplemento al Catálogo de la
Biblioteca tecnológica ... 1-4, 1926/1927-
1929/1930. Buenos Aires, 1927-1930.   (2481
Classified with author index.

-----. Museo Mitre. Catálogo de la Biblioteca. Buenos Aires, Impr. de M. Biedma e Hijo,
1907. 704 p.   (2482
"La sección 10a., Lenguas americanas ...
no está agregada a este catálogo".---Jones
622.

-----. -----. Catálogo general, sección 1,
Museo. Buenos Aires, 1937. 92 p.   (2483
Jones 623.

-----. -----. Obras del general Mitre, catálogo de la sección XXIV. Buenos Aires, 1913.
22 p.   (2484
Jones 625a.

-----. Universidad. Catálogo-guía de la sección Arquitectura. Buenos Aires, 1934.
75 p. mimeogr.   (2485
Classified with author and subject index.
---Jones 629a.

-----. -----. Repertorio de las obras existentes en la Biblioteca, enero 1915. Buenos Aires, Tall. de R. Radaelli, 1915.
144 p.   (2486
Jones 630.

BUENOS AIRES. Universidad. Facultad de Arquitectura y Urbanismo. Biblioteca. Catálogo alfabético. Buenos Aires, 1941.
188 p.   (2486a
    Cited in Geoghegan 2170.

-----. -----. Facultad de Ciencias Exactas, Físicas y Naturales. Catálogo de la Biblioteca. Buenos Aires, 1930-1931. 1359 p.
(Ser. A, Publ. 6)   (2487
    Jones 628.

-----. -----. Facultad de Ciencias Médicas. Catálogo metódico de la Biblioteca; antecedentes de su fundación y desarrollo desde 1863 hasta 1904. Buenos Aires, Impr. Europea de M. A. Rosas, 1904. xxviii, 202 p.   (2488
    Cited in Binayán 83.

-----. ------. -----. Catálogo metódico de la Biblioteca. Primer suplemento. Buenos Aires, Impr. Europea de M. A. Rosas, 1904. 97 p.   (2489
    Cited in Ib. 84.

-----. -----. -----. Segundo suplemento. Buenos Aires, Impr. Europea de M. A. Rosas, 1905. xxiv, 86 p.   (2490
    Cited in Ib. 85.

-----. -----. -----. Tercer suplemento. Buenos Aires, Impr. Europea de M. A. Rosas, 1907. xiii, 76 p.   (2491
    Cited in Ib. 86.

-----. -----. -----. Cuarto suplemento. Buenos Aires, Impr. Europea de M. A. Rosas, 1908. xv, 78 p.   (2492
    Cited in Ib. 87.

-----. -----. Facultad de Derecho y Ciencias Sociales. Catálogo metódico de la Biblioteca ... seguido de una tabla alfabética de autores. Buenos Aires, Impr. de M. Biedma e Hijo, 1898. 426 p.   (2493
    Jones 634.

-----. -----. -----. -----. 1o.-3o. Suplemento. Buenos Aires, Impr. de M. Biedma e Hijo, 1899-1902. 3 v.   (2494
    Jones 634.

-----. -----. -----. Catálogo metódico de la Biblioteca. Antecedentes de su fundación y desarrollo desde 1863 hasta 1904. Buenos Aires, Impr. Europea de M. A. Rosas, 1904. 202 p.   (2495
    Jones 633.

-----. -----. -----. -----. 1o.-4o. Suplemento. Buenos Aires, Impr. Europea de M. A. Rosas, 1904-1908. 4 v.   (2496
    Jones 633.

BUENOS AIRES. Universidad. Facultad de Derecho y Ciencias Sociales. Obras ingresadas a la Biblioteca. Buenos Aires, 1909-1916. 8 v.   (2497
    Jones 631c.

-----. -----. Facultad de Filosofía y Letras, Catálogo de la Biblioteca. Buenos Aires, Compañía Sud-Americana de Billetes de Banco, 1912. 167 p.   (2498
    Jones 635.

-----. -----. -----. Buenos Aires, 1928-1930. 2 v.   (2499
    Jones 635.

-----. -----. Instituto Bibliotecológico. Catálogo de la Biblioteca; obras. Buenos Aires [1964] 146 p.   (2500
    Compiled under the supervision of Hans Gravenhorst.

BUENOS AIRES (Province). Dirección de Vialidad. Biblioteca Técnica. Catálogo de la Biblioteca Técnica. La Plata, División Publicaciones y Biblioteca, 1963. 350 p. (Publ., no. 37)   (2501

-----. Legislatura. Biblioteca. Catálogo. La Plata Tall. de Impresiones Oficiales, 1936. 205 p.   (2502
    Jones 638a.

------. ------. Catálogo metódico. La Plata, Tall. Gráf. Olivieri & Domínguez, 1938. xix, 196 p.   (2503
    Advertencia signed: Juan Carlos Bordoni, encargado.

-----. -----. -----. Suplemento no. 1. La Plata, 1943. 196 p.   (2504

-----. -----. -----. Suplemento no. 2. La Plata, Peuser. 1949. 448, [8] p.   (2505

-----. -----. El folklore argentino en la Biblioteca. Catálogo complementario de las obras adquiridas. La Plata, 1950. 166 p.   (2505a
    Compiler: Francisco M. Timpone.

-----. Ministerio de Gobierno. Catálogo metódico de la Biblioteca. La Plata. Tall. de Impresiones Oficiales, 1939. 346 p.   (2506
    Jones 638b.

-----. -----. Biblioteca. Catálogo metódico. La Plata, Tall. de Impresiones Oficiales, 1945, xxvi, 868 p.   (2507
    2a. ed. ampliada.

CENTRO Argentino de Ingenieros Agrónomos, Buenos Aires. Biblioteca. Catálogo metódico de la biblioteca. Buenos Aires, Impr. de la Universidad, 1942. 167 p.   (2508

CENTRO Argentino de Ingenieros... (Cont.)
   Cited in Catálogo, Instituto Bibliotecológico, item 925.

COLEGIO de Doctores en Ciencias Económicas y
   Contadores Públicos Nacionales, Buenos Aires.
   Biblioteca. Catálogo. Buenos Aires, Impr.
   Tomatis y Sella, 1933. 96, [2] p.   (2509

-----. -----. Supl. 5. Buenos Aires, 1936.
   8 p. mimeogr.   (2510

-----. Catálogo metódico. Buenos Aires, 1950.
   235 p.   (2511

-----. -----. Primer suplemento. Buenos Aires, 1950. 35 p.   (2512

COLEGIO de Escribanos de la Provincia de Buenos Aires, La Plata. Biblioteca "Dalmacio
   Vélez Sarsfield". Catálogo. La Plata, 1956.
   255 p.   (2513
      Cited in Catálogo, Instituto Bibliotecoló-
   gico, item 927.

CORDOBA. Universidad Nacional. Biblioteca.
   Córdoba, Establ. Gráf. La Moderna, 1906-1911.
   3 v.   (2514
      Jones 673a.

-----. Catálogo de la Biblioteca Dalmacio
   Vélez Sarsfield; prólogo del dr. Enrique
   Martínez Paz. Córdoba [Impr. de la Univer-
   sidad Nacional] 1940. 4, xxix, [2], 229 p.
   (Publ. de la nueva serie II)   (2515
      Jones 673b.

INSTITUTO del Cemento Portland Argentino, Buenos Aires. Biblioteca. Catálogo. [Buenos
   Aires, Tall. Gráf. Gotelli, 1943]
   48 p.   (2516
      Cited in Catálogo, Instituto Bibliotecoló-
   gico, item 928.

-----. -----. Suplemento, no. 1. [Buenos
   Aires, Tall. de Plat, 1946] 30 p.   (2517
      Cited in Ib.

-----. Catálogo de la Biblioteca. Buenos
   Aires [1958] 207 p.   (2518

JOCKEY CLUB, Buenos Aires. Catálogo de la Biblioteca. Buenos Aires, Tall. Gráf. Argentinos de L. J. Rosso, 1919.   (2519
      Binayán, item 114, notes that this edition
   was in press at the time of his compilation,
   and that editions appeared in 1906 and in
   1913, the latter with 115 p.

-----. Catálogo de la biblioteca, seguido de
   una tabla de autores y otra de colaborado-
   res. Buenos Aires, Tall. Gráf. del Jockey
   Club, 1928. 1218 p.   (2520
      "La Biblioteca del Jockey Club se especia-
   lizó desde sus comienzos, en historia y li-

JOCKEY CLUB, Buenos Aires. Catálogo...(Cont.)
   teratura argentinas...Siguen después, en orden de importancia, las secciones de historia y literatura americana". (Preface).---
   Jones 730.

-----. Biblioteca. Catálogo de la sección argentina. Buenos Aires, Tall. Gráf. del Jockey Club, 1937. 293 p.   (2521
      Cited in Catálogo, Instituto Bibliotecoló-
   gico, item 931.

-----. Catálogo temático de bellas artes.
   [Buenos Aires, Tall. Gráf. del Jockey Club,
   1939] 237 p.   (2522
      Cited in Ib., item 932.

LA PLATA. Universidad Nacional. Biblioteca
   Pública. Anuario bibliográfico, 1937- . La
   Plata, 1937- .   (2523
      DPU has 1937-1938, 1945. Replaces Indice,
   órgano informativo bimestral de la Biblioteca Pública. Contains listing of acquisitions
   to the Library.

-----. -----. Catálogo general razonado de las
   obras adquiridas en las provincias argentinas
   a las que se agregan muchas otras más o menos
   raras, por Antonio Zinny. San Martín, Escuela de Artes y Oficios de la Provincia, 1887.
   344 p.   (2524
      Jones 740.

-----. -----. Lista de algunos de los libros
   entrados en el año 1942. La Plata, Escuela
   de Artes y Oficios de San Vicente de Paul,
   1943. 147 p.   (2525
      Cited in Catálogo, Instituto Bibliotecoló-
   gico, item 933.

-----. Facultad de Ciencias Jurídicas y Sociales. Biblioteca. Boletín bibliográfico, año
   1945-1947. [La Plata, Tall. Gráf. "Das Neves
   Hnos"] 1947. 83 p.   (2526

-----. -----. Catálogo de la Biblioteca. Buenos Aires, Compañía Sudamericana de Billetes
   de Banco, 1917-1918. 2 v. (v. 1: 331 p.;
   v. 2: 181 p.)   (2527
      Jones 743a.

-----. -----. -----. Suplemento al tomo 1 (Autores) La Plata, Olivieri y Domínguez, 1919.
   31 p.   (2528
      Jones 744.

-----. -----. Catálogo general de obras y autores. La Plata, Tall. Gráf. Das Neves Hnos.,
   1939. 1105 p.   (2529
      The name of the library in this edition:
   Biblioteca Pública "Joaquín V. González".

LOIS, Ricardo J. Catálogo de la Biblioteca del
   Laboratorio Central de Fitopatología e instrucciones para su uso. Buenos Aires, 1948.

LOIS, Ricardo J. Catálogo de la... (Cont.)
95 p. (Argentina. Instituto de Sanidad
Vegetal. Publicaciones, ser. B. No.
12)   (2530

MENDOZA, Arg. Universidad Nacional de Cuyo.
Instituto de Investigaciones Económicas y
Tecnológicas. Biblioteca. Catálogo. Men-
doza, 1958. 122 p.   (2531

MENDOZA (Province) Legislatura. Biblioteca.
Catálogo. Mendoza, Best Hnos., 1938.
413 p.   (2532
    Jones 779a.

MERCEDES, Arg. Biblioteca Popular "Domingo
Faustino Sarmiento". Catálogo general. Mercedes, 1929. 312 p.   (2533

PERGAMINO, Arg. Biblioteca Pública Municipal
"Doctor Menéndez". Catálogo de libros antiguos. Pergamino, 1938. 14 p.   (2534

LA PRENSA, Buenos Aires. Biblioteca. Catálogo de la Biblioteca de "La Prensa". Buenos
Aires, Impr. y Encuad. de G. Kraft, 1916.
116 p.   (2535

-----. Catálogo de la Biblioteca Pública gra-
tuita de "La Prensa", orden de obras y de
autores. Buenos Aires, 1906. 81 p. (2536

ROSARIO, Arg. Universidad Nacional del Litoral. Biblioteca "Estanislao S. Zeballos".
Catálogo metódico. Rosario, 1945. v.1
(603 p.)   (2537
    Contents: Economics, finance, banks and
stock exchanges.

-----. Facultad de Ciencias Jurídicas y Sociales. Biblioteca. Catálogo metódico.
Santa Fe, 1937. 616 p.   (2538
    Jones 836b.

-----. -----. -----. Suplemento, no. 1-2,
1938/1939-1940/1943. Santa Fe, Arg., 1940-
1943. 2 v.   (2539

-----. -----. Catálogo metódico; sección de
educación e instrucción pública. Santa Fe,
1957. 120 p.   (2540

-----. -----. Indice alfabético de autores
del Catálogo metódico de la biblioteca. Santa Fé, [Impr. de la Universidad Nacional del
Litoral] 1938. 110 p.   (2541

SANTA FE, Arg. (Province) Ministerio de Salud
Pública y Bienestar Social. Biblioteca Cen-
tral. Catálogo general de libros y revistas
Santa Fé, 1952. 296 p.   (2542

TUCUMAN. Universidad Nacional. Instituto de
Física y Matemática. Biblioteca. Catálogo
de libros y publicaciones periódicas; sec-

TUCUMAN. Universidad Nacional ... (Cont.)
ción física. San Miguel de Tucumán, 1955.
103 p. (Publ., no. 689)   (2543
    Cited in Catálogo, Instituto Bibliotecoló-
gico, item 668.

BOLIVIA

BIBLIOTECA y Museo Pedagógicos, La Paz. Catálogo. La Paz, Impr. Velarde, 1912.
228 p.   (2545

BOLIVIA. Congreso. Biblioteca. Catálogo.
La Paz, Impr. y Lit. Boliviana, H. Heitmann
& Cía., 1915. 72 p.   (2546
    Jones 903.

-----. Dirección de Estadística Occidental.
Biblioteca Pública. Catálogo general por
P. Kramer B. [La Paz] n.d. 97 p.   (2547

-----. Ministerio de Colonización y Agricultura. Sección de Estadística y Biblioteca.
Catálogo general de las publicaciones ingresadas durante el año de 1906- . La Paz,
1907- . Año 1- , v. 1- .   (2548
    Jones 905.

COCHABAMBA, Bolivia. Universidad Autónoma Simón Bolívar. Biblioteca. Catálogo...cien-
cias sociales y derecho; faccionado bajo la
dirección de José Francisco Lora J. Cochabamba, Impr. Universitaria, 1945.
259 p.   (2549

LA PAZ. Biblioteca Municipal "Mariscal Andrés
de Santa Cruz". La sala colombiana. La Paz,
Edit. Artística, 1951. 79 p. (Publicaciones pro-cultura cívica)   (2550

SUCRE, Bolivia. Universidad Mayor de San Francisco Xavier. Facultad de Derecho, Ciencias
Políticas y Sociales. Biblioteca. Catálogo.
Sucre, 1946-1952. 2 v. (Publicacio-
nes)   (2550a
    Compiler: Manuel Giménez Carranza.

BRAZIL

ALBUQUERQUE FILHO, Mata. Catálogo de Biblioteca do Ginásio Pernambucano. Recife, Impr.
Oficial, 1939. 195 p.   (2551
    Cited in Reis, item 556.

ALMEIDA JUNIOR, A. Catalogo da Bibliotheca
Infantil Modelo. São Paulo, Impr. Official
do Estado, 1936. 78 p.   (2552
    Cited in Reis, item 489.

AMAZONAS. Bibliotheca Publica do Estado. Catalogo. Manáos, Diario Official, 1916-
1917.   (2553
    Cited in Reis, item 298.

ASSOCIAÇÃO Commercial da Bahia. Catalogo da
Bibliotheca. Bahia, 1909.   (2554
     Compiler: Gabriel Godinho. Cited in Reis,
item 264.

ASSOCIAÇÃO dos Empregados no Commercio, Porto
Alegre. Catalogo da Bibliotheca. Porto Alegre, Off. Graph. da Livraria Americana, 1909,
104 p.   (2555
     Cited in Reis, item 260.

ASSOCIAÇÃO dos Guardas Livros, Rio de Janeiro.
Primeiro catalogo da Bibliotheca. Rio de
Janeiro, Typ. Cosmopolita, 1870.   (2556
     Cited in Reis, item 55. Ascribes compila-
tion to I. I. de Souza Machado.

ASSOCIAÇÃO Gremio Litterario, Salvador. Catalogo das obras existentes na Bibliotheca..
organizado no anno social de 1868 a 1869.
Bahia, 1869. 94 p.   (2557
     Cited in Reis, item 52. Compiler: Luiz
Tarquinio dos Santos.

-----. -----. Appendice ao Catalogo das obras
existentes na Bibliotheca. Bahia, Typ.
Masson, 1872. 61 p.   (2558
     Cited in Reis, item 59. Compiler: Cons-
tancio José dos Santos.

-----. Catalogo da Bibliotheca. Bahia, Lit.-
Typ. de João Gonçalves Tourinho, 1883.
87 p.   (2559
     Cited in Reis, item 102. Compiler: Hen-
rique de Almeida Costa.

BAHIA. Bibliotheca Publica. Catalogo dos livros que se achão no Bibliotheca Publica da
cidade da Bahia. [Bahia, Typ. de M. A. da
Silva Serva, 1818] 54 p.   (2560
     "Foi o primeiro catalogo de livros de bi-
bliotheca que se imprimiu no Brazil" (Reis,
item 5)---Jones 967.

-----. -----. Catalogo geral. Bahia, Typ. de
Antonio Olavo da França Guerra, 1858.
935 p.   (2561
     Cited in Reis, item 27.

-----. -----. Catalogo geral das obras de
sciencias e litteratura que contem a Bibliotheca Pública da Provincia da Bahia. Bahia,
Typ. Constitucional, 1878. 540 p.   (2562
     Cited in Reis, item 80. Attributes au-
thorship to Antônio Ferrão Muniz.

-----. Faculdade de Medicina. Catalogo das
obras da Bibliotheca. Bahia, Typ. do Diario, 1876.   (2563
     Cited in Reis, item 64.

-----. -----. Catalogo dos livros. Bahia,
1877.   (2564
     Cited in Reis, item 72.

BAHIA. Faculdade de Medicina. Catalogo dos
livros. Bahia, 1885.   (2565
     Cited Reis, item 112.

-----. -----. Catalogo da Bibliotheca. Bahia,
Litho-Typ. de João Gonçalves Tourinho, 1886.
132 p.   (2566
     Cited in Reis, item 120.

-----. -----. Catalogo dos livros da Bibliotheca. Bahia, Livraria Catilina de Romualdo
dos Santos, 1910. 455 p.   (2567
     Compiler: Pedro Rodrigues Guimarães.
Cited in Reis, item 267.

-----. Faculdade de Medicina e Pharmacia. Catalogo dos livros da Bibliotheca. Bahia, Typ.
Catilina, 1900.   (2568
     Cited in Reis, item 180.

-----. Gabinete Portuguez de Leitura. Catalogo dos livros com que foi aberto. Bahia,
Tourinho Dias & Cia., 1867. 12 p.   (2569
     Cited in Reis, item 45.

-----. -----. Catalogo das obras existentes.
Bahia, Tourinho & Cia., 1868. 66 p.   (2570
     Cited in Reis, item 49.

-----. -----. Bahia, Camillo de Lellis Masson
& Cia., 1871. 125 p.   (2571
     Cited in Reis, item 57.

-----. -----. Bahia, Typ. do Diario de Noticias, 1877. 183 p.   (2572
     Cited in Reis, item 71.

-----. -----. Bahia, Litho-Typ. de João G.
Tourinho, 1882. 126 p.   (2573
     Cited in Reis, item 95.

-----. -----. Catalogo das obras da Bibliotheca. Bahia, 1902.   (2574
     Cited in Reis, item 193.

BANCO do Brasil. Biblioteca. Catalogo das
obras incorporadas até 31 de dezembro de
1947, classificados por asuntos. [Rio de
Janeiro] 1948. 196 p. mimeogr.   (2574a

BANCO do Estado de São Paulo. Biblioteca. Catalogo das obras da Biblioteca. [São Paulo,
Saraiva] 1956. 310 p.   (2575
     Cited in Richardson 7199.

BELLO HORIZONTE. Faculdade Livre de Direito.
Catalogo da Bibliotheca. Bello Horizonte,
Impr. Official, 1909.   (2576
     Reis, item 266, attributes authorship to
Angenor de Sena.

BIBLIOTHECA Fluminense, Rio de Janeiro. Catha-
logo [sic] dos livros. Rio de Janeiro, Typ.
de M. A. da Silva Lima, 1848. 122 p.   (2577
     Cited in Reis, item 15.

BIBLIOTHECA Fluminense, Rio de Janeiro. Primer suplemento. Rio de Janeiro, Typ. do Archivo Medico Brasileiro, 1849.   (2578
    Cited in Reis, item 16.

-----. Catalogo dos livros. Rio de Janeiro, Typ. Commercial de Soares & Cia., 1852. 290 p.   (2579

-----. Catalogo dos livros. Rio de Janeiro, Typ. Thevenet & Cia., 1866. 312 p. (2580
    Cited in Reis, item 43.

-----. -----. [Additions] no. 1. [Rio de Janeiro, Typ. do Commercio de Pereira Braga, 1866?]   (2581
    Cited in Reis, item 44.

BONSUCESSO, Anastacio Luiz de. Bibliotheca do Instituto dos Bachareis em Lettras. Rio de Janeiro, Typ. do Correio Mercantil, 1867.   (2582
    Cited in Reis, item 47.

BRAZIL. Arquivo Nacional. Catalogo da Bibliotheca do Archivo Público Nacional. Rio de Janeiro, 1911. 119 p.   (2583

-----. -----. Catalogo da Bibliotheca. Rio de Janeiro, Impr. Nacional, 1901. 90 p.   (2584
    Jones 985.

-----. Biblioteca Nacional. Catalogo dos documentos sôbre Bahia existentes na Biblioteca Nacional. Rio de Janeiro [1949] 431 p. (Anais, v. 68)   (2585
    Lists 2,178 documents beginning with 1534.

-----. -----. Catalogo de manuscritos sôbre o Paraná existentes na Biblioteca Nacional. [Rio de Janeiro] 1953. 48 p.   (2586
    Reprinted from Anais, v. 74, p. 15-48.

-----. Congresso. Câmara dos Deputados. Biblioteca. Biblioteca da Câmara dos Deputados; relação das publicações encadernadas da Organização das Nações Unidas, e outras em inglês, francês e espanhol, com o respectivo índice. Rio de Janeiro, Impr. Nacional, 1951. 44 p.   (2587
    Cited in Richardson 7218.

-----. -----. Senado. Catalogo da livraria. [Rio de Janeiro, Typ. Nacional, 1876] 24 p.   (2588
    Cited in Reis, item 63.

-----. -----. -----. Catalogo alphabetico. Bibliotheca do Senado Federal. Rio de Janeiro, Impr. Nacional, 1898. 344 p. (2589
    Jones 988.

BRAZIL. Congresso. Senado. Indice das obras por autores, Bibliotheca do Senado Federal. Rio de Janeiro, Impr. Nacional, 1919. 429 p.   (2590
    Jones 989.

-----. Directoria Geral de Estatistica. Catalogo da Bibliotheca. Primeira parte. Rio de Janeiro, Typ. da Directoria Geral de Estatistica, 1921-1922. fasc. 1-2 (256 p., 257-544 p.)   (2591
    Cited in Reis 331, 344.

-----. Exercito. Catalogo da Bibliotheca. Rio de Janeiro, Impr. Nacional, 1885. 358 p.   (2592
    Compiler: Joaquim Alves da Costa Matos.

-----. -----. Catálogo da Bibliotheca. Rio de Janeiro, Impr. Nacional, 1895. 30 p.   (2593
    Compiler Juvenal Rodopiano Gonçalves dos Santos.
    Cited in Reis, item 155.

-----. -----. Catalogo da Bibliotheca (Ordem alphabetica de autores) Rio de Janeiro, Impr. Militar, 1922. 199 p.   (2594
    Cited in Reis, item 330.

-----. -----. Catalogo da Bibliotheca. (Assumptos - Séries) Rio de Janeiro, Impr. Militar, 1924. 117 p.   (2595
    Cited in Reis, item 353.

-----. Ministério da Agricultura. Serviço de Estatistica da Produção. Catalogo geral da Biblioteca (classificação decimal universal) Rio de Janeiro, 1938- .   (2596
    DPU has v. 6: Catalogo geográfico colectivo: Fascículo 5 (8) America do Sul: Parte I (81) Brasil, 110 p. mimeogr.

-----. Ministério da Justiça e Negócios Interiores. Catalogo da Biblioteca; direito, 1941-1945. [Rio de Janeiro] Serviço de Documentação, 1961. 572 p.   (2597

-----. -----. Suplemento, 1-5, 1956-1960. [Rio de Janeiro] 1958-1961. 5 v.   (2598

-----. Ministério da Marinha. Catalogo methodico dos livros existentes na Bibliotheca da Marinha organisado segundo o systema de Mr. Brunet. Rio de Janeiro, 1850.   (2599
    Cited in Reis, item 18.

-----. -----. -----. Supplemento. Rio de Janeiro, Typ. do Diario de N. L. Vianna, 1851. 16 p.   (2600
    Cited in Reis, item 20.

-----. -----. Catalogo methodico dos livros. Rio de Janeiro, Typ. de Francisco de Paula Brito, 1858. 152 p.   (2601

BRAZIL. Ministerio da Marinha ... (Cont.)
    Compiler: Primeiro Tenente Sabino Eloi
    Pessoa.---Jones 1000.

-----. -----. Rio de Janeiro, 1878.   (2602
    Compiler Luiz Filipe Saldanha da Dama.

-----. -----. Rio de Janeiro, Typ. Esperança,
    1879. 366 p.   (2603
    Jones 1001.

-----. -----. Rio de Janeiro, Impr. Nacional,
    1904. pt. 1 (928 p.); pt. 2 (180 p.) (2604
    Jones 999.

-----. -----. -----. Supplemento, 1-4. Rio
    de Janeiro, 1905-1909.   (2605
    Reis, item 285, cites the 8th (Octavo)
    supplement, Rio de Janeiro, 1914.

-----. -----. Segundo catalogo da Bibliothe-
    ca pelo systema decimal de Mervil [sic]
    Dewey (de 1905-1921) organizado durante a
    administração do capitão de mar e guerra A.
    Thompson. Rio de Janeiro, Impr. Naval, 1925.
    664 p.   (2606
    Cited in Catálogo, Instituto Biblioteco-
    lógico, item 898.

-----. Ministério da Viação e Obras Públicas.
    Catalogo de Biblioteca; 2. ed. atual. Rio
    de Janeiro, 1954. 396 p.   (2607
    Cited in Richardson, item 7230.

-----. Ministério das Relações Exteriores.
    Biblioteca. Bibliografía anual, 1958- .
    Rio de Janeiro, Seção de Publicações,
    1958- .   (2608
    Last issue received at DPU: 1962.

-----. -----. Catalogo alphabetico da Biblio-
    theca. Rio de Janeiro, Impr. Nacional,
    1917-1919. v. 1 (537 p.), v. 2
    (394 p.)   (2609
    Compiler: Juvenal Meireles Mesquita.

-----. Ministério do Trabalho, Indústria e
    Comércio. Biblioteca. Boletim bibliográ-
    fico. Rio de Janeiro, 1954. 214 p. (2610

-----. -----. Catalogo, 1945/1949. [Rio de
    Janeiro] Serviço de Documentação, 1951.
    312 p.   (2611

-----. -----. Registro bibliográfico, 1945-
    1948. Rio de Janeiro, 1946-1949.
    4 v.   (2612

-----. Supremo Tribunal Federal. Catalogo
    da Biblioteca, organisado pelo Bibliothe-
    cario Bacharel Francisco de Paulo de Olivei-
    ra em collaboração com o Bacharel Francis-
    co Couto de Oliveira. Rio de Janeiro, Impr.
    Nacional, 1931. v. 1 (306 p.)   (2613

BRAZIL. Supremo Tribunal Federal. Catalogo
    da Biblioteca. Rio de Janeiro, Impr. Nacio-
    nal, 1940. 409 p.   (2614
    Compiler: Francisco Couto de Oliveira.
    Cited in Reis, item 609.

-----. Tribunal de Contas. Catalogo da Bi-
    bliotheca. Autores. Rio de Janeiro, Impr.
    Nacional, 1920. 215 p.   (2615
    Cited in Reis, item 320.

-----. -----. Assumptos. Rio de Janeiro, Impr.
    Nacional, 1927. 226 p.   (2616
    Cited in Reis, item 364.

CAIXA Económica Federal, São Paulo. Bibliote-
    ca. Regulamento e catalogo. São Paulo
    [1940] 162 p.   (2617
    Cited in Reis, item 599.

CAMETA, Brazil. Gabinete Litterario Cametaen-
    se. Catalogo. Cametá, O Commercial, 1889.
    39 p.   (2618
    Cited in Reis, item 134.

CATALOGO da Bibliotheca da Secretaria de Esta-
    do dos Negocios da Justiça. Rio de Janeiro,
    Typ. de Barboza Janner & Polary, 1889. 293,
    3, 31 p.   (2619
    Cited in Reis, item 133.

CATALOGO da Bibliotheca do Palacio do Cattete.
    Rio de Janeiro, Impr. Nacional, 1902. (2620
    Cited in Reis, item 192. Also item 199
    with title: Catalogo de uso privativo da
    Bibliotheca do Palacio do Catete.

CERCLE SUISSE, São Paulo. Catalogo da Biblio-
    theca. São Paulo, Typ. Hennies Irmãos, 1914.
    15 p.   (2621
    Cited in Reis, item 286.

CLUB GERMANIA, Rio de Janeiro. Catalog der
    bibliothek. Rio de Janeiro, Universal-
    Buchdruckerei von E. & H. Laemmert, 1852.
    71 p.   (2622

-----. -----. Nachtrag, no. 1. Rio de Ja-
    neiro, Universal-Buchdruckerei von E. & H.
    Laemmert, 1856. 62 p.   (2623

-----. Catalog der Bibliothek. Rio de Janei-
    ro, Gedruckt bei Lorenz Winter, 1870.
    216 p.   (2624
    Cited in Reis, item 53.

-----. -----. Nachtrag der Catalog der Bi-
    bliothek, Rio de Janeiro, Gedruckt bei Lo-
    renz Winter, 1878. 39 p.   (2625
    Cited in Reis, item 75.

CLUBE 12 de Agosto, Florianópolis. Catalogo
    da Bibliotheca. Desterro, Graf. Brazil,
    1901. 72 p.   (2626
    Today Desterro is Florianópolis. Cited

CLUBE 12 de Agosto, Florianópolis. ... (Cont.)
in Reis, item 188.

-----. Catalogo de Bibliotheca. Florianópo-
lis, [1938] 224.   (2627
Cited in Reis, item 538.

GOIÂNIA, Brazil. Gabinete Literario Goyano .
Catalogo geral da Bibliotheca. Goyaz,
1894.   (2628
Cited in Reis, item 147.

INSTITUTO Brasileiro de Bibliografia e Docu-
mentação. Biblioteca. Catalogo da biblio-
teca de energia atômica. Rio de Janeiro,
1956-1959. 4 v.   (2629
Contents: Coleção de relatórios científi-
cos ofrecida á Comissão Nacional de Energia
Atômica: v. 1-2 (1956-1957): Estados Unidos.
- v. 3 (1958): Estados Unidos, França, Gran
Bretanha. - v. 4 (1959): Argentina, Belgica,
Canadá, Dinamarca, Estados Unidos, França,
Holanda-Noruega, Italia, México, Polonia,
Portugal.

INSTITUTO Brasileiro de Cultura Japonesa. Catalogo dos livros da Biblioteca. Rio de Janeiro, [Jornal do Brasil], 1940.
73 p.   (2630
Cited in Reis, item 597.

INSTITUTO de Belas Artes do Rio Grande do Sul,
Pôrto Alegre. Biblioteca. Boletim informa-
tivo, no. 2. Pôrto Alegre, 1960. 10 p.
mimeogr.   (2631
Compiler: Jahyra Corrêa Santos. Cited in
Revista do livro, 5 (20): 237, dez. 1960.

INSTITUTO Historico e Geographico Brasileiro,
Rio de Janeiro. Biblioteca. Catalogo dos
livros. Rio de Janeiro, Typ. de D. L. dos
Santos, 1860. 203, xxii p.   (2632
Jones 1063.

-----. -----. Rio de Janeiro, 1893.   (2633
Cited in Reis, item 144.

MACHADO, Cezário Pereira. Catalogo da Bibliotheca Municipal de Itaguahi. Rio de Janeiro, Typ. Universal de E. & H. Laemmert, 1881.
27 p.   (2634
Cited in Reis, item 93.

MINAS GERAIS. Secretaria de Estados dos Negócios do Interior. Catalogo da Biblioteca.
Belo Horizonte, Impr. Oficial, 1939. 2 v.
(v. 1: 452 p.; v. 2: 272 p.)   (2635
Contents: v. 1: classes 0-3; v. 2: clas-
ses 4-9. Compiler: Marina A. G. Brandão.
Cited in Bibliografia brasileira, 1938-
1939, p. 199.

-----. Catalogo provisório da Biblioteca.
(Indice alfabético de autores) Belo Horizonte, 1934. 208 p.   (2636

MINAS GERAES. Secretaria de Estado... (Cont.)
Cited in Reis, item 466.

PARA (State). Bibliotheca Pública. Catalogo.
Belem, Impresso na Typ. do Diario Official,
1893. 132 p.   (2637
Jones 1130.

PARANAGUA. Clube Litterario. Catalogo da Biblioteca. Paraná, 1905.   (2638
Cited in Reis, item 211.

PELOTAS. Bibliotheca Pública. Annaes. Pelotas, 1904(?)- .   (2639
Library founded in 1875; the Annaes contain
articles, lists of accessions, etc.---Jones
1134.

-----. Catalogo das obras do Gabinete de Leitura. [Pelotas] Impr. a Vapor "Correio Mercantil", 1898. 76 p.   (2640
Cited in Reis, item 165.

-----. Catalogo dos livros. Pelotas, 1917.
71 p.   (2641
Cited in Reis, item 299.

PERNAMBUCO. Bibliotheca Pública do Estado.
Catalogo dos livros pertencentes a Bibliote-
ca Provincial de Pernambuco. Recife, Typ.
Universal, 1854. 112 p.   (2642
Cited in Reis, item 25.

-----. Catalogo geral. Recife, Livraria e
Typ. de F. P. Baulitreay, 1896.
564 p.   (2643
Compilers: Clovis Bevilaqua and Lourenço
Cavalcanti. Cited in Reis, item 159.

-----. Catalogo da collecção França Pereira.
Recife, Impr. Off., 1927. 100 p.   (2644

-----. Bibliotheca Pública. Catalogo da
collecção Martins junior. Recife, Impr. Off.,
1927. 126 p.   (2645

PETROPOLIS. Prefeitura Municipal. Biblioteca.
Catalogo suplementar; romances e livros de
literatura ligeira, em português, recebidos
durante o ano de 1942. Petrópolis, Tip.
Ipiranga, 1943. 14 p.   (2646
Cited in Catálogo, Instituto Bibliotecológico, item 753.

PORTO ALEGRE, Brazil. Bibliotheca Rio-Gran-
dense. Catalogo. [Pelotas e Rio Grande,
Livraria Central] 1907. 698 p.   (2647
Compiler: Vigário Josué Silveira de Ma-
tos. Cited in Reis, item 228.

-----. -----. Supplemento. Rio Grande, Livraria Americana, 1912. 145 p.   (2648
Compiler: Alfredo Assunção. Cited in Reis,
item 280.

PORTO ALEGRE, Brazil. Bibliotheca Rio-Gran-
dense. Novo supplemento ao catalogo de livros. Rio Grande, Typ. "Artista", 1887.
126 p.   (2649
   Cited in Reis, item 124.

-----. Facultad Livre de Direito. Catalogo
da Biblioteca, no. 1. Porto Alegre, Off.
Graph. da Livraria Americana, 1911.
34 p.   (2650

-----. Universidade. Instituto de Fisiologia
Experimental. Catalogo da Biblioteca "Noely
Carvalho". Pôrto Alegre, 1959.
77 p.   (2651
   Cited in Revista do livro, 5 (19): 243,
set. 1960.

RECIFE. Faculdade de Direito. Catalogo da
Bibliotheca, no. 1. Pernambuco, Typ. Commercial de Feraldo Henrique de Meira & C.,
1860. 32 p.   (2652
   Cited in Reis, item 34.

-----. -----. Catalogo geral da Bibliotheca.
Recife, Empreza d'a Provincia, 1896.
420 p.   (2653
   Jones 1139.

-----. -----. -----. Primeiro supplemento.
Recife, Impr. Industrial, 1913.
439 p.   (2654
   Jones 1139.

-----. -----. Novo catalogo geral sistemati-
co. Recife, Impr. Industrial, J. Nery da
Fonseca, 1930-1932. 2 v. (635,
426 p.)   (2655
   Compiler of v. 1: José Rodrigues dos
Anjos; of v. 2: João Barreto de Menezes.
Cited in Reis, item 400, 450.

-----. -----. Tombamento geral dos livros da
Bibliotheca em lo. de setembro de 1929.
Recife, Impr. Imperial, J. Nery da Fonseca,
1929. v. 1 (155 p.)   (2656
   Cited in Reis, item 393.

-----. Gabinete Litterario. Catalogo dos
livros. Pernambuco, 1841.   (2657
   Cited in Reis, item 11.

-----. Gabinete Portuguêz de Leitura. Catalogo da Livraria. Havre, Typ. Alf. Lemale,
1863.   (2658
   Cited in Reis, item 41.

-----. -----. Catalogo geral da Bibliotheca.
Porto, Impr. Portugueza, 1882.
492 p.   (2659
   Compiled by A. de Sousa Pinto and Feliciano de Azevedo Gomes.
   Supplemento...no. 1, 1880-1881: p. 473-
92.---Jones 1140.

RIO GRANDE DO SUL. Bolsa de Valores. Catalogo
da Biblioteca. Pôrto Alegre, 1959.
104 p.   (2660
   Compiler: Therezinha de Jesus Barcellos.
Cited in Revista do livro, 5 (18): 233, jun.
1960.

RIO DE JANEIRO. Bibliotheca Circulante (Fran-
co-Brasileira) Catalogo. [Rio de Janeiro,
Typ. do Jornal do Commercio, 1936]
135 p.   (2661
   Cited in Reis, item 509.

-----. Biblioteca Circulante dos Empregados
nos Serviços de Carris, Luz, Força, Gás e
Telefones. [Rio de Janeiro] 1941.
91 p.   (2662
   Cited in Reis, item 635.

-----. -----. Catalogo geral. [Rio de Janei-
ro], 1948. 81 p.   (2663

-----. Bibliotheca Municipal. Catalogo. Rio
de Janeiro, Typ. Central de Brown & Evaristo,
1878. 815 p.   (2664
   Jones 1160. Alonso Herculano de Lima, director of Library. Reis cites the "Catalogo" with 185 p.

-----. Casa de Rui Barbosa. Biblioteca. Catalogo. Rio de Janeiro, Impr. Nacional,
1944-1951. 2 v. (A-B; C-E).   (2665

-----. -----. Catalogo da Biblioteca de Rui
Barbosa. Rio de Janeiro, 1957-1959.
3 v.   (2666
   Cited in Doria Menezes 149.

-----. Escola Militar. Catalogo da Bibliotheca da Escola Militar da Corte. Rio de Janeiro, Impr. Nacional, 1889. 226 p.   (2667
   Compiler: Cláudio do Amaral Savaget.
Cited in Reis, item 136.

-----. -----. Catalogo da Bibliotheca. Rio
de Janeiro, Impr. Nacional, 1902.
288 p.   (2668
   Jones 993. Compiler: Adolpho José de
Carvalho.

-----. Escola Normal do Districto Federal.
Catalogo da Bibliotheca. 1. Secção de geo-
graphia e historia. Rio de Janeiro, Typ.
Leuzinger, 1896. 98 p.   (2669
   Prepared by F. Cabrita. 187 titles
given.---Jones 1170.

-----. Escola Polytecnica. Catalogo da Bibliotheca. Rio de Janeiro, Typ. Nacional,
1878.   (2670
   Cited in Reis, item 74.

-----. -----. Rio de Janeiro, Impr. Nacional,
1882. 211 p.   (2671

RIO DE JANEIRO. Escola Polytecnica. Catalogo da Bibliotheca. Rio de Janeiro, Typ. do
Jornal do Commercio, 1923-1925. 2 v. (2672

-----. Faculdade de Medicina. Catalogo das
obras existentes na Bibliotheca. Rio de Janeiro, Typ. Nacional, 1877. 64 p.   (2673
Cited in Reis, item 73. Compiler: José
Pinto de Sá.

-----. -----. Catalogo systematico da Bibliotheca. Rio de Janeiro, 1884.   (2674
Cited in Reis, item 107.

-----. -----. Rio de Janeiro, Impr. Nacional,
1892. 556 p.   (2675
Compiler: Carlos Antônio de Paula Costa.
Jones 1171.

-----. -----. -----. 1. supplemento. 1894.
124 p.   (2676
Jones 1171.

-----. -----. -----. 2. supplemento. 1895.
18 p.   (2677
Jones 1171. Reis, item 153, cites an
edition of the Catalogo systematico for the
same year, 1895.

-----. -----. -----. 3. supplemento. 1895.
20 p.   (2678
Jones 1171.

-----. -----. -----. 4. supplemento. 1896.
34 p.   (2679
Jones 1171.

-----. -----. Catalogo systematico da Bibliotheca. Rio de Janeiro, 1900.   (2680
Cited in Reis, item 182.

-----. -----. [Rio de Janeiro, 1915]   (2681
Cited in Reis, item 289.

-----. -----. Rio de Janeiro, Impr. Nacional,
1916. 163 p.   (2682
Publications entered from 1900 to 1915.
Compiler: Alvaro Paulino Soares de Souza.
Cited in Reis, item 296.

-----. -----. Rio de Janeiro, 1930.   (2683
Publications entered from 1916-1929.
Cited in Reis, item 399.

-----. -----. Rio de Janeiro, Impr. Nacional,
1936. 34 p.   (2684
Publications entered from 1930 to 1934.
Compilation attributed to Alvaro Paulino
Soares de Souza. Cited in Reis, item 505.

-----. Gabinete Portuguez de Leitura. Catalogo dos livros. Rio de Janeiro, Impr. Nacional Americana de I. P. da Costa, 1840.
194 p.   (2685
Cited in Reis, item 10.

RIO DE JANEIRO. Gabinete Portuguez de Leitura.
Catalogo dos livros, seguido de um supplemento das obras entradas no Gabinete depois de
começada a impressão. Rio de Janeiro, Impr.
Americana de I. P. da Costa, 1844.
168 p.   (2686

-----. -----. -----. 2. supplemento do catalo-
go dos livros. [Rio de Janeiro, Typ. de
Carlos Haring, 1846] 41 p.   (2687
Cited in Reis, item 13.

-----. -----. -----. 4. supplemento do catalogo dos livros. Rio de Janeiro, Typ. Commercial de Soares & Cia., 1852. 50 p. (2688
Cited in Reis, item 22.

-----. -----. Catalogo dos livros. Rio de
Janeiro, Typ. Commercial de F. de O. Q. Re-
gadas, 1858. 425 p.   (2689
Jones 1172.

-----. -----. Catalogo supplementar dos livros. Rio de Janeiro, Typ. Perseverança,
1868. 430 p.   (2690
Compiled by Manuel da Silva Melo Guimarães.

-----. -----. Catalogo. Rio de Janeiro, Typ.
do "Jornal do Commercio", de Rodrigues & C.,
1906. 2 v.   (2691
Jones 1173. Compiler: Benjamin Franklin
Ramiz Galvão.

-----. Museu Escolar Nacional. Catalogo da
Bibliotheca do Museu Escolar Nacional. Rio
de Janeiro, Typ. de G. Leuzinger & Filhos,
1885. 394 p.   (2692
Compiler: Julio de Lima Franco.

-----. -----. Rio de Janeiro, Impr. Nacional,
1887. 158 p.   (2693
Cited in Reis, item 126. Compiler: Julio
de Lima Franco.

-----. Universidade. Faculdade de Direito.
Catalogo da Biblioteca. Rio de Janeiro,
Impr. Nacional, 1933. 77 p.   (2694
Cited in Reis, item 462.

-----. -----. Rio de Janeiro, Est. Graf. Canton & Reile, 1936. 101 p.   (2695
Cited in Reis, item 488.

SÃO LUIZ, Maranhão. Gabinete Portuguez de Leitura. Catalogo de Bibliotheca Publica. Maranhão, 1876. 176 p.   (2696
Cited in Reis, item 62.

-----. -----. Maranhão, 1900.   (2697
Cited in Reis, item 181.

SÃO PAULO (City). Biblioteca Municipal. Catálogo da Biblioteca "Paulo Prado" doada em
1944 a Biblioteca Municipal de São Paulo.
São Paulo, Departamento de Cultura, 1945.

SÃO PAULO (City) Biblioteca... (Cont.)
148 p. (Boletín bibliográfico, Suplemento 5)   (2698

-----. Departamento Jurídico. Repertório ge-
ral da Biblioteca. I. Catálogo onomástico.
São Paulo, 1938. 304 p.   (2699
Jones 1188.

-----. Escola Polythechnica. Catalogo da Bibliotheca. [São Paulo] 1897.   (2700
Cited in Reis, item 164.

-----. Faculdade de Direito. Catalogo da Bi-
bliotheca. São Paulo, Typ. a Vapor de Jorge
Seckles & C., 1887. 376 p.   (2701
Cited in Reis, item 125.

-----. -----. São Paulo, Augusto Siqueira &
Cia., 1920. 843 p.   (2702
Cited in Reis, item 319.

-----. -----. Catalogo dos diccionarios.
São Paulo, Typ. Sigueira, Nogel & Comp.,
1915. 35 p.   (2703
Cited in Reis, item 288.

-----. -----. Relatorio, 1936. São Paulo,
1937. 288 p.   (2704
Includes Relação das obras entradas no Bibliotheca, por compra, doação e permuta.---
Jones 1190. Includes also a listing of periodical publications received.

SÃO PAULO (State). Bibliotheca Publica. Catalogo systematico, organizado segundo a
classificação decimal de Melvil Dewey...
Classes 0-5. São Paulo, Off. do Diario
Official, 1924. v. 1 (498 p.)   (2705
Compiler: Alfredo Freire. Cited in Reis,
item 356.

-----. Departamento de Assistencia ao Cooperativismo. Catálogo da Biblioteca. São
Paulo, 1940. 32 p. (Bibliografia cooperativista, Publ. no. 81)   (2706

-----. Secretaria da Viação e Obras Publicas.
Departamento de Aguas e Energia Eléctrica.
Catálogo da Biblioteca. São Paulo,
1956.   (2707
Cited in Boletín de adquisiciones, Mede-
llín, jul. 1964, p. 11.

-----. Tribunal de Apelação. Biblioteca.
Catalogo das obras. São Paulo, Empresa
Gráf. da "Revista dos Tribunais" [1940]
669 p.   (2708

-----. Tribunal de Justiça. Biblioteca.
Catálogo onomástico. São Paulo, 1952.
371 p.   (2708a

-----. -----. Suplemento. 1952.
78 p.   (2708b

SOCIEDADE Brasileira de Cultura Inglesa, Rio
de Janeiro. Library catalogue. Rio de Janeiro [1941]. 75 p.   (2709
Cited in Reis, item 638.

SOCIEDADE de Geographia, Rio de Janeiro. Cata-
logo da Bibliotheca. Rio de Janeiro, Typ
Perseverança [1888]   (2710
Compiler Antônio Alvares Pereira Coruja
Júnior. Cited in Reis, item 129.

SOCIEDADE Propagadora das Bellas Artes, Rio de
Janeiro. Catalogo da Bibliotheca Popular.
Rio de Janeiro, Typ. Leuzinger, 1911.
239 p.   (2711
Cited in Reis, item 273.

SOCIEDADE Recreio Litterario, Bahia. Catalogo
da Bibliotheca. Bahia [Typ. de Pagessi]
1860.   (2712
Cited in Reis, item 35.

SOROCABA, Brazil. Gabinete de Leitura Soroca-
bana. Catalogo dos livros. Sorocaba, Typ.
Americana, 1874. 14 p.   (2713
Cited in Reis, item 61.

-----. Sorocabana, Typ. Americana,
1876.   (2713a
Cited in Reis, item 65.

YPIRANGA Sport-Club, Mossoró, Brazil. Bibliotheca Dr. Hemeterio Fernandes de Queiroz.
Catalogo, no. 1. Mossoró, Ateliér Escossia,
1930. [10] p.   (2714

CHILE

BROWN University. Library. List of Latin American imprints before 1800, selected from bibliographies of José Toribio Medina, micro-
filmed by Brown University. Providence, 1952.
140 p.   (2715
Supersedes preliminary lists no. 1, and 2,
which were distributed in 1942 and 1943.
Entries: 2,339 titles.

-----. Photographic Laboratory. Latin Americana. Providence, R. I.,1942-1943.
no. 1-2.   (2716
Titles filmed by the University for its
collection of the Biblioteca Nacional in Santiago, Chile.

CHILE. Biblioteca Nacional. Catálogo de autores griegos y latinos. Santiago, 1898.
391 p.   (2718

-----. -----. Catálogo de la sección america-
na. América en general. Santiago de Chile,
Impr. Universitaria, 1902. 152 p.   (2719
Jones 1602.

CHILE. Biblioteca Nacional. Catálogo por orden alfabético de los libros que contiene la Biblioteca Nacional de Santiago de Chile. Santiago, Impr. de la Sociedad, 1854. 216 p.   (2720
   Jones 1604.

-----. Congreso. Biblioteca. Catálogo, 1921-1922. Santiago, Impr. Cervantes, 1922. 526 p.   (2721
   "Prefacio" signed: Adolfo Labatut.---
   Jones 1425.

-----. Instituto Nacional. Biblioteca peruana. Apuntes para un catálogo de impresos. Santiago de Chile, Biblioteca del Instituto Nacional, 1896. 2 v.   (2722
   Contents: v. 1, Libros y folletos peruanos de la Biblioteca del Instituto Nacional (558 p.). - v. 2, Libros y folletos peruanos de la Biblioteca Nacional y Notas bibliográficas (618 p.). Compiler: Gabriel René-Moreno.---Jones 2635.

-----. Universidad. Escuela de Medicina. Nuevos títulos; lista de libros de tesis, etc. incorporados a la biblioteca entre julio y septiembre de 1962. Santiago, 1962.   (2723
   Cited in Boletín de adquisiciones, Medellín, no. 9, p. 18, sept. 1963.

-----. -----. Facultad de Ciencias Jurídicas y Sociales. Biblioteca. Catálogo. [Santiago de Chile, 1940] 226 p.   (2724

INSTITUTO Pedagógico, Santiago. Catálogo de la biblioteca del Instituto Pedagógico. (Memoria del Ministerio de Justicia e Instrucción Pública. Santiago, 1896. p. 72-196)   (2725
   Jones 1609.

NUÑOA, Chile. Biblioteca Pública Municipal. Catálogo de las obras existentes en la Biblioteca Pública Municipal de Ñuñoa. Ñuñoa, El Globo, 1938. 36 p.   (2726

SANTIAGO DE CHILE. Biblioteca de la Recolección Dominicana. Catálogo general por orden alfabético de autores. Santiago, Impr. La Ilustración, 1910. 563 p.   (2727
   Cited in Bibliografía eclesiástica de Chile, p. 323.

-----. Universidad Católica. Biblioteca de la Universidad Católica de Santiago. Santiago, Impr. de E. Pérez L., 1902. 227 p.   (2728
   Jones 1610.

VALPARAISO, Chile. Escuela de Derecho. Biblioteca. Catálogo. [Santiago de Chile] Universidad de Chile, 1947. 125 p.   (2729

COLOMBIA

ACADEMIA de Historia de Cartagena. Biblioteca. Primer catálogo levantado por ... don Gabriel Jiménez M. Cartagena, 1935. 57 p.   (2730

ANTIOQUIA, Col. Archivo del Departamento. Catálogo de los libros y folletos impresos pertenecientes al Archivo del Departamento de Antioquia. Medellín, Impr. del Departamento, 1896. 63 p.   (2731
   Cited in Giraldo Jaramillo, p. 67.

-----. Biblioteca Departamental. Catálogo. Medellín, Impr. Oficial, 1903. x, 123 p.   (2732
   This library is now incorporated in the Library of the University of Antioquia. Cited in Giraldo Jaramillo, p. 62.

BANCO de la República, Bogotá. Biblioteca Luis Angel Arango. Catálogo. Libros de texto. Bogotá, 1956. 38 p. mimeogr.   (2733
   Cited in Giraldo Jaramillo, p. 91.

-----. Catálogo general. Bogotá, Impr. del Banco de la República, 1961. v. 1: 236 p.   (2734
   Contains sections 000 to 299.

-----. Catálogo general de libros. Bogotá, Impr. del Banco de la República, 1948-1950. 3 v.   (2735

BOGOTA. Biblioteca Central Municipal. Catálogo de las obras: Literatura. Bogotá, Impr. Municipal, 1954. 10, 41 p. (Ediciones de la Sección de Publicaciones y Bibliotecas Municipales, no. 1)   (2736
   Cited in Giraldo Jaramillo, p. 62 and p. 126. Contains two sections: General literature and Colombian literature.

-----. -----. Literatura inglesa y de Estados Unidos de Norte América. Bogotá, Impr. Municipal, 1954. 12 p.   (2737
   Cited in Anuario bibliográfico colombiano, 1951-1956, p. 1.

CARTAGENA. Universidad. Facultad de Derecho y Ciencias Políticas. Biblioteca. Catálogo general de obras. Cartagena, Edit. Bolívar, 1942. 155 p.   (2738

CENTRO Interamericano de Vivienda, Bogotá. Lista de nuevas adquisiciones de la Biblioteca: 1a. acumulación anual-6a. acumulación anual, 1954-1962. Bogotá, 1955-1964. 6 v. mimeogr.   (2739

CENTRO Nacional de Investigaciones Agrícolas "Tibaitatá". Biblioteca. Lista de publicaciones que se reciben actualmente. Bogotá, 1959. (Boletín bibliográfico, v. 6, no. 5-6, nov./dic. 1959) mimeogr.   (2740

COLEGIO Mayor de Nuestra Señora del Rosario,
Bogotá. Biblioteca. Catálogo. Bogotá,
Impr. de "La Luz", 1925. 287 p.   (2741
    Compiled by Jenaro Jiménez. Cited in Gi-
raldo Jaramillo, p. 70.

-----. Suplemento. Bogotá, Edit. Centro
1938.   (2742
    Tomás Lombo, Librarian. Cited in Giraldo
Jaramillo, p. 73.

-----. Suplemento. Bogotá, Impr. de "La Luz",
1928. 50 p.   (2743
    Primitivo Vergara Crespo, Librarian.
Cited in Giraldo Jaramillo, p. 79.

COLEGIO Salesiano de León XIII, Bogotá. Biblioteca. Catálogo. Bogotá, Escuelas Gráficas Salesianas, 1945. 83 p.   (2744
    Cited in Giraldo Jaramillo, p. 62.

COLOMBIA. Biblioteca Nacional. Catálogo de
las obras...existentes en la Biblioteca Nacional. Bogotá, Impr. del Estado, 1855-1857.
6 v.   (2745
    Jones 1681. Primera ser.: Obras en fran-
cés. - Segunda ser.: Obras en inglés. - Tercera ser.: Obras en español. - Cuarta ser.:
Obras en latín. - Quinta ser.: Obras en italiano, portugués, alemán, etc. - Unnumbered
ser.: Obras nacionales: Biblioteca Pineda.

-----. -----. Catálogo de las obras hispano-
americanas existentes en la Biblioteca Nacional. Bogotá, Impr. de Zalamea Hermanos,
1897. 360 p.   (2746
    Jones 1682.

-----. -----. Catálogo de los mapas, planos,
cartas hidrográficas &c, existentes en la
Biblioteca Nacional, formado por Saturnino
Vergara, 1881. (Anales de la instrucción
pública en los Estados Unidos de Colombia.
Bogotá, no. 16, p. 456-66, en. 1882) (2747
    Jones 1683.

-----. -----. Catálogo del fondo "Anselmo
Pineda". Bogotá, Edit. "El Gráfico", 1935.
2 v.   (2748
    Jones 1686.

-----. -----. Catálogo del fondo "José María
Quijano Otero" dispuesto por orden alfabético de autores y de personas a quienes se
refieren las piezas contenidas en los volúmenes de la sección respectiva. Bogotá,
Edit. "El Gráfico, 1935. 318 p.   (2749
    On cover: Catálogo ... dispuesto por
orden alfabético de autores y por orden
cronológico de obras colombianas. Seguido
de una descripción bibliográfica de los periódicos de la época de la Gran Colombia.
---Jones 1687.

COLOMBIA. Biblioteca Nacional. Catálogo topográfico de los mapas, planos [etc.] de la Biblioteca Nacional. (Revista de la Biblioteca Nacional, Bogotá, t. 1, p. 170-75, 190-
205, 1923)   (2750
    Jones 1688.

-----. -----. Libros adquiridos recientemente
por la Biblioteca Nacional. [Bogotá], 1953.
7 p.   (2750a

-----. Congreso. Biblioteca. Indice general.
Bogotá, Impr. Nacional, 1936. 203 p. (2751
    Jones 1701.

-----. Contraloría General de la República.
Biblioteca. Catálogo de la Sección "Autores".
Bogotá, 1955. 47 p.   (2752

-----. -----. -----. Bogotá, 1956. 227 p.
mimeogr.   (2753
    Cited in Giraldo Jaramillo, p. 37.

-----. -----. Catálogo de la Sección Colombia.
Bogotá, Contraloría-Multilith, 1955.
25 p.   (2754

-----. -----. -----. Bogotá, 1956.
81 p.   (2755
    Cited in Giraldo Jaramillo, p. 62.

-----. -----. Catálogo de la Sección "Departamentos". Bogotá, 1955. 14 p.   (2756

-----. Departamento Administrativo de Planea-
ción y Servicios Técnicos. Biblioteca. Catálogo de las publicaciones donadas por el
Banco Internacional de Reconstrucción y Fomento sobre Desarrollo Económico. Bogotá,
1963.   (2757
    Cited in Boletín de adquisiciones, Medellín,
no. 10, p. 20, oct. 1963.

-----. Dirección Nacional de Estadística. Biblioteca. Lista de publicaciones catalogadas
en la Biblioteca del Punto Focal de la Dirección Nacional de Estadística. Bogotá, 1951.
various pagings.   (2758

-----. Laboratorio Químico Nacional. Catálogo general de libros y revistas. Bogotà,
1961. 69 p. mimeogr.   (2759
    Cited in Peraza, Fichas, t. 4-6, item 193.

-----. Ministerio de Relaciones Exteriores.
Catálogo de la Biblioteca de Información;
2a. ed. arreglado por Alberto Sánchez. Bogotá, Impr. Nacional, 1914. 86 p.   (2760
    Jones 1704.

-----. Servicio Geológico Nacional. Catálogo
de libros del Servicio Geológico Nacional;
índice alfabético por autores, por Alicia
Venegas Leyva. Bogotà, 1963. 113 p.
mimeogr.   (2761

COLOMBIA. Universidad Nacional. Facultad de
Derecho y Ciencias Políticas. Biblioteca.
Catálogo. Bogotá, Casa Edit. de Arboleda &
Valencia, 1919. 80 p.   (2762
   Cited in Giraldo Jaramillo, p. 78.

-----. -----. Facultad de Ingeniería e Ingeniería Química. Biblioteca. Catálogo general de la Biblioteca A. García Bonus, 1939-
1959. Bogotá, 1959. 123 p. (Boletín bibliográfico, año 1, no. 1.)   (2763
   Cited in Revista interamericana de bibliografía, v. 10, p. 432.

ESCUELA Superior de Administración Pública,
Bogotá. Biblioteca. Catálogo de la colección "Alfredo Michelsen" adquirida por la
Biblioteca de la ESAP, en abril 1962. [Bo-
gotá, 1962] 61 p. mimeogr.   (2764

-----. Lista provisional por arden alfabético
de autores de las publicaciones existentes
en la Biblioteca, marzo 1o. de 1962. [Bogo-
tá, 1962] 66 p. mimeogr.   (2765
   Cited in Florén, Bibliografía bibliotecológica, 1961/1962, item 226.

INSTITUTO Cultural Colombo Británico, Medellín.
Library catalogue, 1945. Medellín, n.d.
62 p.   (2766
   Cited in Giraldo Jaramillo, p. 70.

PASTO, Col. Universidad de Nariño. Biblioteca. Catálogo, preparado por Angela Hernández de Caldas con la colaboración de Ruth
Baena Velasco. Pasto, Intergráficas, 1960.
347 p.   (2767

SONSON, Col. Biblioteca Municipal. Catálogo;
2a. ed. [Sonsón, Impr. Municipal] 1939.
38 [2] p.   (2768

URIBE, María. Boletín bibliográfico de la Biblioteca de Malterías Unidas, S.A. Bogotá,
1961. 14 p. mimeogr.   (2769
   Cited in Floren, Bibliografía bibliotecológica, 1961/1962, item 243.

VENEZUELA. Biblioteca Nacional. Libros venezolanos, catálogo de la colección donada por
el gobierno de los E.E.U.U. de Venezuela a
la Biblioteca Nacional de Bogotá. Caracas,
Tip. Americana, 1945. 147 p.   (2770

COSTA RICA

COSTA RICA. Biblioteca Nacional. Catálogo
de la Biblioteca Nacional seguido de un ín-
dice alfabético de autores. Autor Adolfo
Blen. t. 1: Bellas Artes. San José, 1920-
1929. 584 p.   (2771
   Cited in Gropp, Guide p. 16, footnote.
In 1937 seven additional signatures and the
"Indice alfabético were ready for publication

ESCUELA Superior de Administración Pública América Central, San José. Catálogo de la Biblioteca, 1954-1957. San José, 1958. 212 p.
(Ser. bibliográfica, no. 5)   (2772

-----. Catálogo de la Biblioteca, 1958-1959.
[San José, 1960] 124 p. (Ser. bibliográfica no. 7)   (2773

CUBA

BIBLIOTECA Menéndez y Pelayo, Havana. Católo-
go. Habana, Cultural, 1930. 688 p.   (2774
   Jones 1840. At head of t.-p.: Asociación
de Dependientes de Comercio de la Habana.

CENTRO Asturiano, Havana. Biblioteca "Labra-
Parajón". Catalogo. Habana, 1936. xvi,
458 p.   (2775
   Cited in Caribbean acquisitions, 1957/1958,
p. 4.

COLEGIO de Abogados, Havana. Biblioteca. Habana, Edit. Forum, 1947. x, 259 p.   (2776

CUBA. Congreso. Cámara de Representantes.
Biblioteca. Catálogo de las obras existen-
tes en la Biblioteca. Habana, Impr. de
Rambla y Bouza, 1905. 30 p.   (2777
   Jones 1809.

-----. -----. Catálogo de las obras que forman su biblioteca; ciencia política. Habana, Impr. y Almacén de Papel de Suárez, Carasa y Cía., 1916- . t. 1 (349p.)- .   (2778

-----. -----. -----. Derecho internacional.
Habana, 1917. 72 p.   (2779
   Jones 1810.

-----. -----. -----. Secciones de hacienda
pública y de comercio y transporte. Habana, Impr. de Suárez, Carasa y Cía., 1913.
272 p.   (2780
   Prepared by Luis Marino Pérez.---Jones
1811.

-----. Senado. Biblioteca. Catálogo de las
obras existentes en la Biblioteca, año de
1916. Habana, Impr. de Rambla, Bouza y Cía.,
1917. 350 p.   (2781
   Jones 1812.

HAVANA. Museo Nacional. Catálogo de la Biblioteca de arte. La Habana, [1958]
39 p.   (2782

PINAR DEL RIO (City). Instituto de Segunda
Enseñanza. Catálogo de la Biblioteca "Hermanos Saiz". Pinar del Río, Edicion INS,
1960. 38 p.   (2783
   Cited in Caribbean acquisitions, 1961,
p. 5.

SOCIEDAD Cubana de Ingenieros. Catálogo abre-
viado de la Biblioteca. Habana, Impr. de P.
Fernández y Cía., 1915. 42 p.   (2784
    Jones 1907.

SOCIEDAD Económica de Amigos del País, Havana.
Catálogo de la Biblioteca. (Revista bimestre cubana, Habana, t. 14-17, 1920-
1922)   (2785
    Includes only sections A-Artiga.---Jones
1908.

DOMINICAN REPUBLIC

SOCIEDAD Literaria "Amantes de la Luz". Catálogo de las obras, novelas, folletos y periódicos que contiene la Biblioteca. Santiago de los Caballeros, Impr. de José Ma.
Vila Morel, 1905. 15 p.   (2786
    Cited in Floren Lozano, Bibl. de la bibl.
dominicana, item 1.

-----. Catálogo de las obras, novelas, folle-
tos y periódicos que contiene la Biblioteca.
Santiago de los Caballeros, Tip. de Ulises
Franco Bido, 1911. 20 p.   (2787

ECUADOR

BIBLIOTECA de Autores Nacionales Carlos A. Rolando, Guayaquil. Catalogo decimal de la
Biblioteca. [Guayaquil] Impr. y Tall. Municipales, 1947. 268 p.   (2788

BIBLIOTECA del Maestro, Cuenca, Ecuador. Catálogo general y reglamento de la "Biblioteca del Maestro". Cuenca, Tip. de la Universidad, 1933. 16 p.   (2789

CUENCA. Biblioteca Pública Azuay. Catálogo.
Cuenca, Impr. de la Universidad, 1890-1891.
8 v.   (2790
    Cited in Chaves, p. 12, with following
contents: - v.1, Ciencias eclesiásticas. -
v. 2, Jurisprudencia. - v. 3, [Lacking]. -
v. 4, Historia. - v. 5, Literatura, through
letter R. - v. 6, Ciencias. - v. 7, Medicina. - v. 8, Artes y oficios.

ECUADOR. Biblioteca Nacional. Catálogo de
las obras que componen la Sección Argentina
de la Biblioteca Nacional de Quito, inaugurada en 1926. Quito, Impr. Nacional, 1926.
63 p.   (2791
    Jones 1974.

JARAMILLO, Miguel Angel. Indice bibliográfico
de la Biblioteca "Jaramillo" de escritos nacionales. Cuenca, Impr. de la Universidad,
1932. v. 1 (356 p.)   (2792
    Contents: - Sección I: Obras generales.---
Jones 1990a.

MUÑOZ, Bonifacio. Biblioteca de alquiler; catalogo especial de 30,000 obras dedicado al
pueblo ecuatoriano; Librería "Sucre" de Bonifacio Muñoz. Quito, Impreso por N. Romero
D., 1918. 424 p.   (2793
    "Sección nacional": p. 335-65.---Jones 1995.

QUITO. Universidad Central. Biblioteca General. Libros coloniales de la Universidad
Central; catálogo general. Quito, Edit. Universitaria [1963] 105 p.   (2793a

-----. -----. Facultad de Derecho. Biblioteca. Catálogo de obras. Quito, Edit. Universitaria, 1957. 100 p.   (2794
    Cited in Chaves, p. 23.

EL SALVADOR

EL SALVADOR. Biblioteca Nacional. Catálogo
alfabético y por materias de todos los libros que contiene la Biblioteca Nacional de
El Salvador, formado por Rafael U. Palacios.
San Salvador, Tip. el Cometa, 1887.
152 p.   (2795
    Jones 1374.

-----. -----. -----. 1o. Apéndice, por Eduardo Martínez López. San Salvador,
1890.   (2796
    Jones 1374a

-----. -----. Catálogo general alfabético.
San Salvador, 1896-1897. 3 v.   (2797
    Jones 1375.

-----. -----. -----. San Salvador,
1905.   (2798
    Jones 1376.

-----. -----. Catálogo de la Biblioteca Nacional arreglado por materias según el sistema "Dewey decimal" por Rafael García Escobar. San Salvador, Impr. "La Salvadoreña",
1930 [i.e., 1930-1932] 2 v.   (2799
    "Sección Argentina": t. 2, p. 3-101.---
Jones 1377.

-----. -----. Obras enviadas por la Bibliote-
ca Nacional de Montevideo a la Biblioteca
Nacional de San Salvador. San Salvador,
Impr. Nacional, 1928. 15 p.   (2800

-----. Dirección General de Estadística y
Censos. Publicaciones catalogadas, 1952-
1954. San Salvador, 1954. 57 p.   (2801

-----. Universidad. Biblioteca Universitaria.
Catálogo de las obras de la Biblioteca Universitaria arreglado por orden alfabético
de autores. San Salvador, Impr. Nacional,
1909. 27 p.   (2802

GUATEMALA

GUATEMALA. Biblioteca Nacional. Catálogo.
Guatemala, 1932. 257 p.   (2803
"Lista de la prensa del país existente en
la Biblioteca Nacional": p. 182-87. Prepared by Rafael Arévalo Martínez.---Jones
1293.

-----. Instituto Nacional. Biblioteca. Guatemala, 1887.   (2804
Cited in Catálogos de periódicos y libros
de la Biblioteca Nacional de Bogotá, 1914,
p. 189.---Jones 1298.

GUATEMALA. Universidad de San Carlos. Facultad de Derecho. Catálogo de la Biblioteca
de la Facultad de Derecho y Notariado del
Centro. Sección latino-americana. Guatemala, Siguere y Cía., 1898. p. 217-300. (Publicación mensual, t. 8, no. 7)   (2805
Jones 1297.

HONDURAS

HONDURAS. Biblioteca Nacional. Catálogo metódico, seguido de un índice alfabético de
autores y otro de materias. Tegucigalpa,
Tip. Nacional [1915] 293 p.   (2806
Jones 1326.

JAMAICA

INSTITUTE of Jamaica, Kingston. Library.
Catalogue of books in the Library. Kingston,
1895. 351 p.   (2806a

-----. First supplement. Kingston, 1915.
78 p.   (2806b
Cited in Gropp Guide, p. 250.

-----. Second supplement. Kingston, 1919.
66 p.   (2806c
Cited in Gropp, Guide, p. 250.

MEXICO

ALIANZA Francesa, México. Bibliothèque Circulante. Catalogue, no. 5. México, D.F.,
1954. 445 p.   (2807
Cited in Boletín, Biblioteca Nacional, México, D.F., jul./sept. 1954, p. 47.

CARRILLO F., Arsenio. Catálogo general de la
Biblioteca. Mérida, Yucatán, Tall. de la
Revista de Yucatán, 1920. 163 p.   (2808
Cited in González, item 175.

DUCLAS, Robert. Catálogo descriptivo de los
libros impresos en la ciudad de Salamanca
en el siglo XVI existentes en la Biblioteca
Pública de Guadalajara. México, D.F., 1961.

DUCLAS, Robert. Catálogo... (Cont.)
247 p. (Biblioteca Nacional de México. Instituto Bibliografico Mexicano. Publ.
6)   (2809

GUADALAJARA. Biblioteca Pública del Estado.
Catálogo de los libros que existen en la Bi-
blioteca Pública del Estado. Guadalajara,
Tip. de S. Banda, 1874. 2 v.   (2810
Jones 2224.

INSTITUTO Científico y Literario del Estado,
San Luis Potosí. Catálogo de las obras de
la Biblioteca Pública. San Luis Potosí,
Impr. de Silverio M. Vélez, 1879.
186 p.   (2811
Cited in Millares, item 1410.

INVENTARIO formado por el inspector general de
las obras de la Biblioteca "Cepeda" por orden superior del Gobierno del Estado. Mérida, Yucatan, Tall. del Gobierno del Estado,
1923. 115 p.   (2812
Cited in González, item 183.

MEXICO. Biblioteca Nacional. Catálogo espe-
cial de las obras mexicanas o sobre México.
México, D.F., 1911. 486 p.   (2813
Jones 2346.

-----. -----. Catálogo de la Biblioteca Nacional de México, formados por el director
José M. Vigil. México, D.F., Of. Tip. de
la Secretaría de Fomento, 1889-1908.
v. 1-9   (2814
Jones 2347. DPU collection contains 1,
3-9.

-----. -----. -----. Primeros suplementos de
las divisiones 3a., 5a. a 8a. México, D.F.,
Of. Tip. de la Secretaría de Fomento, 1895.
Various pagings.   (2815
Jones 2347.

-----. -----. -----. Segundos suplementos;
divisiones 1a. a 3a., 5a. a 9a. México,
1903. 396 p.   (2816

-----. -----. Catálogos de la Biblioteca Na-
cional de México, formados por el director
José M. Vigil. Biblioteca Nocturna. Mé-
xico, D.F., Of. Tip. de la Secretaría de
Fomento, 1897. 251 p.   (2817
Jones 2348.

-----. Congreso. Cámara de Senadores. Biblioteca: catálogo clasificado. México, D.F.,
Tip de la Of. Impresora de Estampillas,
1913. 145 p.   (2818
Cited in González, item 177.

-----. Dirección General de Correos. Oficina
de Museo y Biblioteca Postal. Catálogo de
documentos históricos de la Biblioteca Postal. México, D.F., 1954. 110 p.   (2819

CATALOGS, LIBRARY

MEXICO. Escuela Nacional de Jurisprudencia.
Biblioteca. Catálogo alfabético de una par-
te de las obras impresas. México, D.F., Tip.
Económica, 1904. 337 p. (2820
Cited in Millares, item 1397.

-----. Escuela Nacional de Medicina. Biblio-
teca. Catálogo de las obras existentes.
México, D.F., Impr. del Gobierno en el ex-
Arzobispado, 1894. 171 p (2821
Cited in Millares, item 1398.

-----. Escuela Nacional Preparatoria. Catálogo de las obras de la Biblioteca. México,
D.F., Tip de "La Voz de Oriente", 1889.
276 p. (2822
Jones 2358.

-----. Museo Nacional de Arqueología, Historia y Etnografía. Catálogo general de las
obras que contiene la Biblioteca. México,
1911-1913. 152 p. (2823
Issued in signatures with the Boletín
del Museo Nacional, v. 1-2, 1911-1913, when
the Boletín suspended publication. No more
published?---Jones 2364.

-----. Secretaría de Comunicaciones y Obras
Públicas. Biblioteca. Catálogo general de
las obras. México, D.F., Tall. Graf. de la
S.C.O.P., 1914. 202 p. (2824
Cited in González, item 182.

OAXACA. Biblioteca del Estado. Catálogo alfabético. Oaxaca, Impr. del Estado, 1887.
270 p. (2825
Jones 2381.

PAN AMERICAN Institute of Geography and His-
tory. Catálogo de la Biblioteca (1930-1939)
Tacubaya, D.F., 1940. 412 p. (Publ. del
Instituto Panamericano de Geografía e His-
toria, no. 47) (2826
Jones 349a. Compiler: Jorge A. Vivó.

-----. Catálogo de la Biblioteca. México,
D.F., 1945. 2 v. (Publ. del Instituto Panamericano de Geografía e Historia, no.
79) (2827
Contents: v.1 (264 p.), Hemeroteca y mapoteca. - v. 2 (359 p.), Biblioteca. Compilers: Jorge a Vivó and Fernando Jordan.

SOCIEDAD Mexicana de Geografía y Estadística.
Memoria presentada...por el primer secretario lic. Ignacio M. Altamirano, en enero
de 1880. México, D.F., Impr. de F. Díaz
de León, 1887. 348 p. (2828
"Catálogo de libros de la Sociedad: Anexo 3, p. 71-207. Catálogo de cartas. -
Cuadros sinópticos, geográficos, estadísticos e históricos. - Vistas. - Retratos:
p. 208-334".---Jones 2504.

SONORA (State) Biblioteca del Gobierno. Catálogo. Hermosillo, 1903.
378, x p. (2829
Cited in Millares, item 1411.

TOLUCA, México. Biblioteca Pública Central.
Catálogo; ciencias eclesiásticas. Toluca,
Of. Tip. del Gobierno en la Escuela de Artes
y Oficios para Varones, 1908. 199 p. (2830
Millares, item 1412, gives compilers: Ame-
lio J. Venegas and José María Crespo.

NICARAGUA

BIBLIOTECA Americana, Managua. Lista de los
libros adquiridos...durante el segundo semestre de 1944. List of books added...
during the last six months of 1944. [Mana-
gua] 1945. 31 p. (Bibliographical ser.,
no. 5) (2832

NICARAGUA. Biblioteca Nacional. Catálogo general de los libros de que consta la Biblioteca Nacional. Managua, Tip. de Managua,
1882. 90 p. (2833
Jones 1342.

-----. -----. Managua, 1906. (2834
Jones 1343.

PANAMA

COLON, Panamá. Biblioteca Colón. Catálogo de
libros. Colón, Impr. The Independent, 1910.
42 p. (2835

PARAGUAY

PARAGUAY. Biblioteca Nacional. Bibliografía
paraguaya; catálogo de la Biblioteca Paraguaya "Solano López". Asunción, Tall. Nacionales de H. Kraus, 1906. 984 p. (2836
The collection was acquired in part by the
government from the former owner, Enrique
Solano López. It is now in the public library in Asunción.---Jones 2614.

-----. Catálogo. Asunción, Impr. de El País,
1904. 97 p. (2837
Jones 2615.

PERU

BIBLIOTECA Entre Nous, Lima. Catálogo general,
1912-1926. Lima [La Opinión Nacional, 1926?]
167 p. (2838

CLUB NACIONAL, Lima. Biblioteca. Catálogo de
la Biblioteca. Suplemento II. Lima, 1952.
45, 4, 8 p. mimeogr. (2839
Cited in Anuario bibliográfico peruano,

CLUB NACIONAL, Lima. Biblioteca ... (Cont.)
1957/1959, item 2132.

COLEGIO de Abogados, Lima. Biblioteca. Historia, reglamento, relación de libros. Lima,
Empresa Edit. "La Crónica y Variedades",
1950. 80 [2] p., 3 l.   (2840

CUZCO. Universidad. Catálogo general de la
Biblioteca moderna de la Universidad, arreglado por materias según el sistema "Dewey
decimal". Cuzco, H. G. Rozas Sucs., 1940.
415 p.   (2841
    Compiler: Rafael Yépez La Rosa.---Jones
2648a.

-----. Inventario de la "Biblioteca de los
Jesuítas". Cuzco, H. G. Rozas Sucs., 1938.
200 p.   (2842
    Apéndice no. 1 al Catálogo general de la
biblioteca.---Jones 2649.

LIMA. Gran Unidad Escolar Melitón Carvajal.
Biblioteca. Catálogo de la Biblioteca.
Lima [Tall. Gráf. de la G.U.E. "Melitón Carvajal"] 1954. 84 p.   (2843
    Cited in Anuario bibliográfico peruano,
1953/1954, item 1494; also 1957/1959, item
2134.

-----. Universidad Mayor de San Marcos. Biblioteca. Catálogo de la Biblioteca. Lima,
Impr. San Pedro, 1907. 113 p.   (2844
    Jones 2680.

-----. -----. -----. Suplemento, 1-3. Lima,
Impr. San Pedro, 1908-1911. 3 v.   (2845
    Jones 2680.

LIMA. Universidad Mayor de San Marcos. Biblioteca. Sección peruana de la Biblioteca.
Lima, n.d. 166 p. Typewritten.   (2846

-----. -----. Facultad de Farmacia y Bioquí-
mica. Relación de obras existentes en la
Biblioteca. Indices de materias y autores.
Lima [Empresa Edit. "La Crónica y Varieda-
des", 1946] 27 p.   (2847
    Reprinted from Revista de la Facultad de
Farmacia y Bioquímica, t. 12, no. 31/32.
Cited in Anuario bibliográfico peruano,
1946, item 701b.

PERU. Biblioteca Nacional. Catálogo de los
libros que existen en el salón América, por
Ricardo Palma. Lima, Impr. de T. Aguirre,
1891. 217 p.   (2848
    Jones 2678.

-----. Congreso. Cámara de Senadores. Catálogo de las obras de la Biblioteca. Lima, Impr. La Industria, 1906.
67 p.   (2849
    Jones 2718.

PERU. Congreso. Cámara de Senadores. Catálogo de la Biblioteca, formado por el oficial
primero don Rafael Belaúnde. Lima, Empr.
Tip. "Unión", 1913. 75 p.   (2850
    Jones 2719.

SOCIEDAD Geográfica de Lima. Catálogo de la
Biblioteca primera sección. Lima, L. H. Jiménez, 1898. v.1   (2851
    Jones 2754. v.1, Obras de la Sociedad Geo-
gráfica.

VENEZUELA. Biblioteca Nacional. Libros vene-
zolanos; catálogo de la colección donada por
el gobierno de los EE.UU. de Venezuela a la
Biblioteca Nacional de Lima. Caracas, Tip.
Americana, 1946. xiii, 187 p. (Publ. de la
Biblioteca Nacional)   (2852

PUERTO RICO

ATENEO Puertorriqueño. Catálogo por orden alfabético de autores y de materias, de las obras
existentes en la Biblioteca del Ateneo Puertorriqueño. Puerto-Rico, Tip. de "El País",
1897. 63 p.   (2853
    Jones 2782.

URUGUAY

ARGENTINA. Comisión Protectora de Bibliotecas
Populares. Sección Argentina en la Biblioteca de Montevideo. Buenos Aires, Coni, 1926.
134 p.   (2854
    "Nómina de las obras": p. 89-119.

ATENEO del Uruguay. Reglamento y catálogo general de la Biblioteca Pública del Ateneo
del Uruguay. Montevideo, Impr. de la Idea,
de Flores Hermanos, 1880. 38 p.   (2855
    Jones 2815.

CENTRO Protección Choferes, Montevideo. Biblioteca Social. Catálogo alfabético de autores. Montevideo, Impr. Central, n.d.
458 p.   (2856
    Cited in HLAS, 10, item 4312.

CENTRO Social y Biblioteca Popular "Villa Colón", Montevideo. Catálogo, no. 1-4. Montevideo, Edit. Monteverde y Cía., 1941-
1944.   (2857
    Each catalog contains from 16-32 pages.
Cited in HLAS, 7, item 5374; 10, item 4314.

FLORIDA, Uruguay. Biblioteca Pública Municipal y Liceal. Catálogo general de obras;
2a. ed. Florida, Impr. Fénix, 1944.
225 p.   (2858
    Cited in HLAS, 10, item 4311.

URUGUAY. Biblioteca Nacional. Memoria. Montevideo, 1881-1885. 3 v.   (2859

URUGUAY. Biblioteca Nacional ... (Cont.)
Includes catalogs of accessions to the
library. "Relación de todos los periódicos
que aparecen en la República: 1880, fold.
tabl. following p. 197. "Relación de los
grabados, mapas, planos y fotografías que
posee la Biblioteca Nacional": p. 211-37.---
Jones 2852.

-----. -----. Relación de las obras que forman la "Sección Argentina" donada por la Comisión Protectora de Bibliotecas Populares
de aquel país, e inaugurada oficialmente el
16 de enero de 1926. Montevideo, 1926.
36 p.   (2860

-----. Biblioteca Pedagógica Central. Catálogo metódico de la Biblioteca Pedagógica
Central, preparado de acuerdo con el sistema de nomenclatura binaria por Sebastián Morey Otero. Vol. 1. Montevideo, Peña Hnos.,
1930. 902 p.   (2861
"Nota bibliográfica": t. 1, p. xii-xiv.---
Jones 2853.

-----. Consejo Nacional de Enseñanza Secundaria y Preparatoria. Biblioteca Central y
Publicaciones. Obras leídas en la Biblioteca Central durante los años 1948, 1949 y
1950. Montevideo, 1951. 9 p.   (2862
Part II: Los libros más pedidos.
Working paper presented in the Conference
for Development of Public Library Services
in Latin America, São Paulo, 1951, by Miguel
Angel Piñeiro.

-----. Poder Legislativo. Biblioteca. Catálogo de derecho constitucional y político,
por autores. Montevideo, Peña Hnos., 1931.
221, xiv p.   (2863
Jones 2850ab.

-----. -----. Catálogo por autores. I, Ciencias. 1. Ciencias jurídicas. Montevideo,
Impr. Rosgal, 1940. 1250 p.   (2864

-----. -----. -----. Por materias. Montevideo, 1938-1939. 20 parts separately
paged.   (2865
Jones 2850b. Subject catalog of Class I,
Ciencias; 1, Ciencias jurídicas.

-----. -----. Lista de obras incorporadas.
Montevideo, 1939-1964. 14, 3 numbers (2866

-----. -----. Cámara de Representantes. Bi-
blioteca. Catálogo. Montevideo, Tip.
Oriental, 1885. 20 p.   (2866a
Cited in Musso, item 814.

-----. -----. -----. Catálogo. Montevideo,
El Siglo Ilustrado, 1910. 264 p.   (2866b
Cited in Musso, item 815.

URUGUAY. Poder Legislativo. Cámara de Representantes. Biblioteca. Catálogo. Montevideo, Impr. Nacional, 1917. 402 p.   (2866c
Cited in Musso, item 816.

-----. Universidad. Facultad de Derecho y
Ciencias Sociales. Biblioteca. Catálogo de
derecho administrativo. Montevideo, Impr.
"Moderna", 1942. 116 p.   (2867

-----. -----. -----. Catálogo de derecho civil.
Montevideo, Impr. "Moderna", A. Amit, 1939.
187 p.   (2868

-----. -----. -----. Catálogo de derecho comercial. Montevideo, Impr. "Moderna", A.
Amit, 1940. 89 p.   (2869
Cited in Catálogo, Instituto Bibliotecológico, item 589.

-----. -----. -----. Catálogo de derecho internacional privado. Montevideo, Impr. Moderna, 1944. 41 p.   (2870

-----. -----. -----. Catálogo de derecho penal.
Montevideo, Impr. "Moderna", 1942.
89 p.   (2871

-----. -----. -----. Catálogo de derecho procesal. Montevideo, Impr. "Moderna", A. Amit,
1940. 73 p.   (2872
Cited in Catálogo, Instituto Bibliotecológico, item 592.

-----. -----. -----. Catálogo de derecho rural y minería. Montevideo, Milton Reyes,
1945. 19 p.   (2873

-----. -----. Facultad de Humanidades y Ciencias. Biblioteca. Las obras de arte, cine-
matografía y fotografía (incorporados en
1952) Montevideo, 1953. 114 p.
mimeogr.   (2874

-----. -----. Facultad de Ingeniería y Ramas
Anexas. Biblioteca. Catálogo. Montevideo,
Impr. Nacional, 1923. 737 p.   (2875

-----. -----. -----. Instituto de Electrotécnica. Catálogo de la Biblioteca del Instituto de Electrotécnica. Montevideo [Lit. e
Impr. del Comercio] 1945. 41 p.   (2876
Cited in HLAS, 11, item 3751.

-----. -----. Facultad de Odontología. Biblioteca. Catálogo. [Montevideo, 1951]
86 p.   (2877

VENEZUELA

CARACAS. Colegio América. Catálogo de la Biblioteca. Caracas, 1948. 12 p.   (2878
Cited in Anuario bibliográfico venezolano,
1947/1948, item 218.

CARACAS. Escuela de Artes Plásticas y Artes Aplicadas Cristóbal Rojas. Biblioteca. Catálogo de los libros existentes. Caracas, 1959.   (2879
    Cited in Revista interamericana de bibliografía v. 10, p. 432.

FUNDACION Shell, Caracas. Biblioteca López Méndez. [Catálogo] Caracas, Academia Nacional de la Historia, 1963. 58 p. (2882
    Cited in HLAS 26, item 44.

INTER-AMERICAN Conference on Agriculture, 3d., Caracas, 1945. Catálogo de la Biblioteca. Caracas, 1945. Various pagings. mimeogr.   (2883
    Cited in Anuario bibliográfico venezolano, 1945, item 163.

MERIDA, Venezuela. Universidad de los Andes. Facultad de Derecho. Biblioteca. Catálogo de la Biblioteca. Mérida, 1959. 286 p.   (2884
    Cited in Revista interamericana de bibliografía, v. 10, p. 432.

VENEZUELA. Biblioteca Nacional. Catálogo de la sección de bibliografía nacional. Caracas, Impr. Nacional, 1921. 66 p.   (2885
    Jones 2965.

-----. -----. -----. 2. ed., aum. y corr. por el br. Ciro Nava. Caracas, Edit. "Elite", 1930. 74 p.   (2886
    Jones 2966.

-----. -----. Cuarto catálogo de la Biblioteca Circulante. Caracas, 1930. 148 p.   (2887
    Jones 2967.

-----. -----. Libros recientemente recibidos de la Biblioteca Nacional de Montevideo. Caracas, Lit. y Tip. Vargas, 1927. 10 p. (Publicaciones)   (2888

-----. -----. Segundo catálogo de la Biblioteca Circulante. Caracas, 1914. 94 p.   (2889
    Cited in Cuarto catálogo (sección nacional) p. 16.

VENEZUELA. Biblioteca Nacional. Segundo catálogo de la Biblioteca Circulante. Suplemento. Caracas, 1918. 36 p.   (2890

-----. -----. Tercer catálogo de la Biblioteca Circulante. Caracas, 1922.   (2891
    Cited in Cuarto catálogo (sección nacional) p. 16.

-----. Dirección de Agricultura. Servicio de Biblioteca. Lista de publicaciones nacionales y extranjeras llegadas en abril, septiembre de 1947. El Valle, [1947] 2 v. mimeogr.   (2892
    Cited in Anuario bibliográfico venezolano, 1947/1948, item 320, 845.

-----. -----, feb., abr., jun., sept., nov., 1948.   (2893
    Compiler: Marcos Moreno Terán.

-----. Estado Mayor General. Biblioteca. Catálogo general de las obras existentes en la Biblioteca. Caracas, Edit. Grafolit, 1949. 236 p. (Suplemento no. 21 de la Revista de las Fuerzas Armadas, jul. 1949)   (2894
    Cited in Anuario bibliográfico venezolano, 1949/1954, item 3776.

-----. Ministerio de Hacienda. Biblioteca. Catálogo de los libros existentes. [Caracas, 1954] 174 p. mimeogr.   (2895
    Cited in Ib., item 46.

-----. Ministerio de Sanidad y Asistencia Social. Biblioteca. Catálogo de los libros de la Biblioteca, organizado por Cecilia Ospina. Caracas, 1943. 245 p.   (2896
    Cited in Archila, p. xv.

-----. Universidad Central. Biblioteca. Catálogo. Caracas, F. T. de Aldrey, 1875. 279 p.   (2897
    Prepared by Adolfo Ernst.---Jones 2973.

-----. -----. -----. Obras que posee la Biblioteca Central de la Universidad Central de Venezuela. Caracas, 1953. 76 p. (2898

CHEMISTRY

BIBLIOGRAFIA brasileira de química, v. 1, 1950/1955- . Rio de Janeiro, Instituto Brasileiro de Bibliografia e Documentação, 1957- .   (2899
    Vol. 1 covers the period 1950/1955 (185 p.); v. 2, 1956/1958 (159 p.); v. 3, 1959/1960 (84 p.)

HERRERO DUCLOUX, Enrique. Las ciencias químicas. Buenos Aires, "Coni", 1923. 75 p. (Evolución de las ciencias en la República Argentina, v. 4)   (2900
    "Bibliografía selecta": p. 48-75.---Jones 723.

HERRERO DUCLOUX, Enrique. Los estudios químicos en la República Argentina (1810-1910).
Buenos Aires, Coni Hermanos, 1912.
431 p.   (2901
    Reprinted from Revista de la Universidad
de Buenos Aires, t. 17, p. 5 and following
issues.
    "He reunido ... todo lo publicado en la
República Argentina por argentinos y extranjeros y fuera del país por argentinos": p. 7.

HERRERO DUCLOUX, Enrique ... (Cont.)
    "Bibliografía química argentina": p. 38-431.
    "Indice alfabético de materias redactado
por María Luisa Cobanera": p. 355-431.---
Jones 722.

SERVIÇO especial de abstractos para a indústria
química brasileira. Rio de Janeiro, Confederação Nacional da Indústria, 1950.   (2902
    Cited in Doria Menezes 180.

COMMERCE AND TRADE

ANUARIO de la América latina (Bailly-Baillière-
Riera) Información general del comercio de
importación y exportación, industria, agricultura, ganadería, minería y elemento oficial de las Américas, año 2. Barcelona (España) Sociedad Anónima "Anuarios Bailly-
Baillière y Riera reunidos", 1914.   (2903
    Jones 22. Lists "periódicos" under names
of cities in each country. Later editions
issued.

BANCO Nacional de Comercio Exterior, México.
México exportador. México D.F., Edit. Cultura, 1939. 856 p.   (2904
    Notas y bibliografía: p. 837-53.---Jones
2065.

BOSTON. Public Library. A selected list of
books on the commercial relations of South
America, principally with the United States.
Boston, The Trustees, 1918. 19 p. (Brief
reading lists, no. 4)   (2905
    Jones 69.

CARIBBEAN Commission, San Juan, P.R. Select
bibliography of trade publications with special reference to Caribbean trade statistics;
a manual for the guidance of research work-
ers in identifying useful sources of trade
statistics and of published ground rules in
the preparation of trade accounts. [Port of
Spain, Trinidad, 1954] 54 p.   (2906

FILSINGER, Ernst B. Commercial travelers'
guide to Latin-America. Washington, Govt.
Print. Off., 1920. 592 p. (U.S. Bureau of
Foreign and Domestic Commerce. Misc. ser.,
no. 89)   (2907
    Bibliography: p. 580-92.---Jones 147.

-----. -----. 2d rev. ed. Washington, Govt.
Print. Off., 1926. 617 p. (U.S. Bureau of
Foreign and Domestic Commerce. Misc. ser.,
no. 89)   (2908
    Bibliography: p. 594-608.---Jones 148.

-----. Exporting to Latin America; a handbook
for merchants, manufacturers and exporters.
New York, D. Appleton and Co., 1916.

FILSINGER, Ernst B. Exporting... (Cont.)
565 p.   (2909
    Bibliography: p. 465-505.
    A later edition was published in 1919.---
Jones 149.

HARING, Clarence Henry. Comercio y navegación
entre España y las Indias, versión española
revisada por Emma Salinas. México, 1939.
xxvi, 460 p.   (2910
    Bibliography: p. ix-xxiii.---Jones 187b.

-----. Trade and navigation between Spain and
the Indies in the time of the Hapsburgs.
Cambridge, Harvard Univ. Pr., 1918. xxviii,
371 p. (Harvard economic studies,
v. 19)   (2911
    Annotated bibliography: p. xv-xxvi.---
Jones 187a.

HUSSEY, Roland Dennis. The Caracas Company,
1728-1784, a study in the history of Spanish
monopolistic trade. Cambridge, Harvard
Univ. Pr., 1934. 358 p. (Harvard historical
studies, v. 37)   (2912
    Bibliography: p. 323-46. The most com-
plete bibliography on the Real compañía
guipuzcoana.---Jones 2918.

JONES, Clarence Fielden. Commerce of South
America. Boston, New York [etc.] Ginn and
Co., 1928. 584 p.   (2913
    References: p. 555-71.---Jones 230.

PAN AMERICAN UNION. Columbus Memorial Library.
A reference list on commerce, exporting and
importing, compiled by Chas. E. Babcock.
Washington, D.C., 1919. 19 p.   (2914

PEREZ, Luis Marino. Fuentes de información
sobre los mercados azucareros. Habana, Cárdenas y Cía., 1960. 16 p.   (2915
    Cited in Caribbean acquisitions, 1963,
item 72.

U.S. Bureau of Foreign Commerce. A guide to
foreign business directories. Washington,
D.C., Govt. Print. Off., 1955.
132 p.   (2916

U.S. Bureau of Foreign Commerce ... (Cont.)
"First issued by the U.S. Department of
Commerce in 1931 ... under the title "Foreign
directories". Contains, among other coun-
tries, a listing of directories in Argentina,
Brazil, Colombia, Costa Rica, Cuba, Dominican
Republic, Ecuador, Guatemala, Honduras, Me-
xico, Nicaragua, Panama, Peru, El Salvador,
Uruguay, and of British and French posses-
sions in the West Indies.

-----. Bureau of Foreign and Domestic Commerce. Publications on Latin America and
the West Indies. Brief review of information available to manufacturers and exporters in bulletins issued by the Bureau of
Foreign and Domestic Commerce. Washington,
D.C., Govt. Print. Off., 1914. 15 p. (Misc.
ser., no. 17)   (2917
    Jones 499.

U.S. Bureau of Foreign and Domestic Commerce.
Publications on South America. Brief review
of information available to manufacturers and
exporters in bulletins issued by the Bureau
of Foreign and Domestic Commerce. Washington,
D.C., Govt., Print. Off., 1913. 11 p. (Misc.
ser., no. 12)   (2918
    Jones 500.

-----. -----. Washington, D.C., Govt. Print.
Off., 1914. 11 p. (Misc. ser., no.
12)   (2919
    Jones 501.

-----. Library of Congress. Brief list of
books relating to South America, with special
view to trade development. Washington, D.C.,
1919. 4 p.   (2920
    Cited in Yang.

DEFENSE

ANRIQUE REYES, Nicolás. Bibliografía marítima chilena (1840-1894) Santiago de Chile,
Impr. Cervantes, 1894. 205 p.   (2921
    639 titles listed with bibliographical
data, notes and historical introduction.
Classified in sections: Artillería, Balís-
tica i torpedos, estratejia i táctica, Astronomía i navegación, Construcción naval,
Faros i valizas, Legislación, etc., Ciencias, Instrucción, Historia i biografía, Hidrografía, etc., Periódicos, Miscelánea, Medicina, Cartografía, Indices.---Jones 1394.

BARRA, Felipe de la. La historia militar y
sus fuentes. Lima [Impr. del Ministerio de
Guerra] 1959. 40 [1] p.   (2922

CIRCULO Militar, Buenos Aires. Biblioteca
Nacional Militar. Catálogo de la sección
materias militares. Buenos Aires [Tall.
Gráf. Edit. Molino] 1940. 207 p.   (2022a

-----. Catálogo de materias militares. Buenos Aires, Tall. de la Cooperativa Poligrá-
fica Mariano Moreno, 1957. 484 p.   (2923

HERRERA GOMEZ, Néstor, and GONZALEZ, Silvino
M. Apuntes para una bibliografía militar
de México, 1536-1936. México, D.F., Sección de Estudios Militares del Ateneo, 1937.
469 p.   (2924
    Bibliographical details with locations of
copies and references to bibliographical
sources. 1,888 titles with index of authors

HERRERA GOMEZ, Néstor, and GONZALEZ... (Cont.)
and translators.
    "Bibliografía sobre el servicio militar
obligatorio": p. 435-43.---Jones 2244.

MEXICO. Comisión de Estudios Militares. Apuntes para una bibliografía militar de México,
1536-1936. Recopilación de fichas bibliográficas hecha por los delegados de la Secretaría de Guerra y Marina, con ocasión del primer Congreso Bibliográfico convocado por el
Ateneo Nacional de Ciencias y Artes de México, ... Néstor Herrera Gómez ... Silvino M.
González. México, 1937. 469 p.   (2925

SANTOS, Francisco Ruas. Fontes para a história
da F. E. B.; ensaio. Rio de Janeiro, Biblioteca do Exército, 1958. 154 p.   (2926
    465 entries with descriptive summaries to
printed material, documents, films, photographs and paintings about the Força Expedi-
cionária Brasileira, 1944-1945 in World War
II.

U.S. Bureau of Foreign and Domestic Commerce.
Some references to material on Western Hemisphere defense. [Washington, D.C., 1940]
8 p. mimeogr.   (2927

-----. Library of Congress. Division of Bibliography. A list of references on Western
Hemisphere defense compiled by Helen F.
Conover. Rev. ed. [Washington] 1942.
39 p.   (2927a

ECONOMICS

GENERAL

ANTWERP. Institut Universitaire des Territoires d'Outremer. Bibliografie overhet derde wereldblok. Developing countries bibliographic compendium. Recopilación bibliográfica relativa a los problemas del tercer mundo. Antwerpen, 1964. 157 p. (2928
"Organizations and revues interested in developing countries": p. [133]-57.

ARGENTINA. Congreso. Biblioteca. Integración económica latinoamericana. Buenos Aires, 1963. 180 p. (Serie: Asuntos económicos, 1) (2929
Summary of documentation leading to a Latin American common market, and bibliography (p. 85-180)

BRIEN, Richard H., SANDERS, Richard D., etc. A selected, annotated bibliography on Latin American business; preliminary version. [Austin] 1964. 50 p. (2930

BUENOS AIRES. Universidad. Instituto de Economía. Bibliografía sobre economía internacional, año 1950. Buenos Aires, 1951. 112 p. (2931
Reprinted from Revista de la Facultad de Ciencias Económicas, jul. 1951.

CARTAGENA. Universidad. Facultad de Economía. Departamento de Investigaciones Económicas. Bibliografía económica existente en las diferentes bibliotecas de la Universidad para uso de profesores y estudiantes. Cartagena, 1962. various pagings. (2932
Cited in Florén, Bibliografía bibliotecológica, 1961/62, item 272.

COLMEIRO, Manuel. Biblioteca de los economistas españoles de los siglos XVI, XVII y XVIII. México, D.F., Univ. Nacional Autónoma de México, Escuela de Economía, 1942. vii, 35-212 p. (2933
Reprinting of bibliography from the Memorias of the Real Academia de Ciencias Morales y Políticas, Madrid, v. 1, p. 33-212.

CRUZ, Salviano. Bibliografia da ciência econômica. Rio de Janeiro, 1949. vii, 112 p. (2934
Reprinted from Teoria da metodologia e bibliografia de pesquisas econômicas. Cited in Richardson, item 7250.

DOCUMENTATION Incorporated, Washington, D.C. Technical assistance in Latin America; a bibliographical study prepared for the Ford Foundation. Washington, D.C., 1952. 83 p. (2935

HAMILTON, Earl Jefferson. American treasure and the price revolution in Spain, 1501-1650. Cambridge, Mass., Harvard Univ. Pr., 1934. xxxv, 428 p. (2936
Bibliography: p. xvii-xxxv.---Jones 184.

HARVARD University. Bureau for Economic Research in Latin America. The economic literature of Latin America, a tentative bibliography, compiled by the staff of the Bureau for Economic Research in Latin America, Harvard University. Cambridge, Harvard Univ. Pr., 1935-1936. 2 v. (2937
Jones 195.

-----. International Program in Taxation. Bibliography on taxation in underdeveloped countries. Cambridge, Law School of Harvard University, 1962. 75 p. (2938
Includes Latin American countries.

INTERNATIONAL bibliography of economics. Bibliographie internationale de science économique, v. 1- . 1952- . (2939
[Paris] UNESCO, [1955]- . Annual. (Documentation in the social sciences)
Arrangement is by subject. Accompanying subject and geographic indexes have references to items under the names of Latin American countries in the bibliography.

JONES, Tom Bard, and WARBURTON, Elizabeth Anne, etc. A bibliography of South American economic affairs; articles in nineteenth century periodicals. Minneapolis, Univ. of Minnesota Pr., [1955] xv, 146 p. (2939a

KEPNER, Charles David, and SOOTHILL, Jay Henry. The banana empire, a case of economic imperialism. New York, The Vanguard Pr., 1935. 392 p. (2940
Abridged bibliography: p. 361-63.---Jones 1236.

NORMANO, João Federico. Recent attempts at an economic bibliography on Latin America. [Washington, D.C.? 1939] p. 75-83. (2941
Reprinted from the Proceedings of the Second Convention of the Inter-American Bibliographical and Library Association, Washington, D.C., 1939.

PAN AMERICAN UNION. Department of Economic Affairs. Unit of Planning and Programming. Latin America; index of final reports issued as United Nations documents or prepared as papers for governments through 1 April 1961. [Washington, D.C.] 1962. [26] p. (2942

-----. Division of Economic Research. List of references and sources of information, economic development of Latin America. [Washington, D.C., 1948] 2 p. (2943

PAN AMERICAN UNION. Unit of International
Economics. List of publications on economic
integration in Latin America. Washington,
D.C., 1962. 10 p.   (2944

ReQUA, Eloise G., and STATHAM, Jane. The developing nations; a guide to information
sources concerning their economic, political,
technical, and social problems. Foreword by
George I. Blanksten. Detroit, Gale Research
Co. [1965] 339 p. (Management information
guide, 5)   (2945
    Latin America, p. 191-206.

SMITH, Robert Sidney. Bibliografía económica
y bibliotecas económicas. Buenos Aires, Instituto de Política Económica, Universidad de
Buenos Aires, 1957. 19 p.   (2946

STANFORD Research Institute. International
Development Center. Human resources and
economic growth; an international annotated
bibliography on the role of education and
training in economic and social development.
Edited by Marian Crites Alexander-Frutschi.
Menlo Park, Calif., 1963. xv,
398 p.   (2947
    Latin America: p. 338-51.

TRIGUEIROS, Florisvaldo dos Santos. Economia,
pequena bibliografia. Rio de Janeiro, 1957.
51 p. (Associação Atlética Banco do Brasil,
Cadernos, no. 24)   (2948

UNITED NATIONS. Committee on Economic Cooperation in Central America. Lista de documentos del Comité de Cooperación del Istmo Centroamericano. New York [1961] 16 p. (UN/
Misc. Doc. 10) mimeogr.   (2949

-----. Dag Hammarskjold Library. Economic
and social development plans: Africa, Asia,
and Latin America. New York, 1964. 25 p.
(ST/LIB/SER.B/9)   (2950

U.S. Bureau of Foreign and Domestic Commerce.
Index of Latin American publications. [Wash-
ington, D.C., 1943] Various pagings.
mimeogr.   (2951

-----. Department of State. Division of Library and Reference Services. Economic
studies of under-developed countries, Latin
America and Caribbean area. Washington, D.C.
1950. 90 p. (Bibliography, no. 52) (2952

-----. -----. Point Four; a selected bibliography of materials on technical cooperation
with foreign governments. Washington, D.C.,
1950. 10 p. (Bibliography, no. 54) (2953

-----. -----. Point Four. Latin America and
European dependencies in the Western Hemisphere; a selected bibliography of studies
on economically under-developed countries.

U.S. Department of State. Division...(Cont.)
Washington, D.C., 1950. 110 p. (Bibliography, no. 55)   (2954
    Revision of Bibliography no. 52 and supple-
ment of Bibliography, no. 54.

-----. Embassy. Brazil. Economics in the
United States; a bibliography. Rio de Janeiro, 1958. 54 p. (Biblioteca Thomas Jefferson; Bibliography, no. 3)   (2955
    Cited in Revista interamericana de biblio-
grafía, v. 9. p. 288.

URUGUAY. Poder Legislativo. Biblioteca. Turismo [obras existentes en la Biblioteca]
Con motivo de la celebración en el Palacio
Legislativo, del VII Congreso Interamericano
de Turismo, bajo los auspicios de la Organización de los Estados Americanos. Montevideo [1958] 143 p. (Referencia, no.
32)   (2956

-----. Universidad. Facultad de Ciencias Económicas y de Administración. Biblioteca.
Bibliografía: curso intensivo de capacitación en problemas de desarrollo económico.
Montevideo, 1963. 17 p. mimeogr.   (2957
    Cited in Musso 88.

WHITBECK, Ray Hughes. Economic geography of
South America. New York, McGraw-Hill, 1926.
430 p.   (2958
    Includes bibliographies.---Jones 528.

-----. 2d ed. New York and London, McGraw-
Hill, 1931. 430 p.   (2959
    "The bibliographies...include the more
readily accessible primary and secondary
sources in English".---Jones 529.

-----. 3d ed. New York and London, McGraw-
Hill, 1940. 469 p.   (2960
    Bibliography: p. 437-69.---Jones 529a.

LAND TENURE AND REFORM

BRAZIL. Serviço de Informação Agricola. Bibliografia sôbre reforma agrária. Rio de
Janeiro, 1953. 6 p.   (2961
    Cited in Revista interamericana de biblio-
grafía, v. 4. no. 1, p. 124.

CARDOSO GONZALES, Armando. Contribución al
conocimiento de la bibliografía de la reforma agraria en Bolivia. [La Paz? 1962] 5 p.
(Sociedad de Ingenieros Agrónomos de Bolivia.
Boletín bibliográfico, no. 1)   (2962

CARROLL, Thomas F. Land tenure and land
reform in Latin America; a selective annotated bibliography. Régimen de tierras y
reforma agraria en América Latina; una bibliografía anotada de carácter selectivo.
Washington, D.C., Inter-American Development

CARROLL, Thomas F. Land tenure... (Cont.)
Bank, Economic Development Division, 1962.
256 p. mimeogr.   (2963
  Preliminary version, subject to revision.

CENTRO Latino Americano de Pesquisas em Ciências Sociais, Rio de Janeiro. Estrutura y
reforma agrária en America Latina; bibliografia. Rio de Janeiro, Serviço de Documentação, 1962. 51 p. mimeogr.   (2964
  Cited in Doria Menezes 46.

CHILE. Congreso. Biblioteca. Reforma agraria; bibliografía preparada por la Sección
Catalogación y Referencias Bibliográficas.
Santiago, 1961-1962. 2 pts. (Ser. Bibliografías 11, suppl. 1)   (2965

DELGADO, Oscar. Bibliografía latinoamericana
sobre reforma agraria y tenencia de la tierra. Con un apéndice bibliográfico sobre
economía agrícola, política agraria, sociología rural, historia social agraria y derecho agrario, 1950-1961. México, D.F.,
1962. 37 p. mimeogr.   (2966

FOOD and Agriculture Organization of the United
Nations, Rome. Bibliography on land tenure;
bibliographie des régimes fonciers; bibliografía sobre tenencia de la tierra. Rome
[1955] 386 p.   (2967
  Includes Latin America as a section as
well as individual countries of Latin America.

-----. Supplement. 1959. 282 p.   (2968

GUERRA, D'Almeida, filho, and PLACER, Xavier.
Indicações bibliográficas sôbre reforma agraria. Rio de Janeiro, Serviço de Informação
Agrícola, 1961. 32 p. (Sér. documentária,
no. 14)   (2969

McBRIDE, George McCutchen. Chile: land and
society. New York, American Geographical
Society, 1936. 408 p. (Research ser., no.
19)   (2970
  Bibliography: p. 387-400. A Spanish
translation was published in Santiago de
Chile, 1938.---Jones 1522.

-----. The land systems of Mexico. New York,
American Geographical Society, 1923.
204 p.   (2971
  Bibliography: p. 182-95.---Jones 2311.

MAGARIÑOS TORRES, Santiago. El problema de
la tierra en Méjico y la constitución socia-
lista de 1917. Madrid, C. Bermejo, 1932.
386 p. (Publ. del Instituto de Derecho Comparado Hispano-Português-Americano) (2972
  Bibliografía: p. 360-84.---Jones 2313.

RIO DE JANEIRO. Universidade. Instituto de
Ciências Sociais. Bibliografia sôbre refor-

RIO DE JANEIRO. Universidade ... (Cont.)
ma agrária. Rio de Janeiro [1962]
89 p.   (2974
  Cited in Doria Menezes 61.

SIMPSON, Eyler Newton. The ejido; Mexico's
way out. Chapel Hill, Univ. of North Carolina Pr., 1937. 849 p.   (2975
  Bibliography: p. 809-23.---Jones 2502.

WISCONSIN. University. Land Tenure Center.
Library. Bibliography: agrarian reform &
tenure, with special sections on agricultural
finance, taxation and agriculture, agricultural statistics, and bibliographical sources.
Madison, 1964. 78, 10 p.   (2975a

COMMON MARKET

BANCO de México. Departamento de Investigaciones Industriales. Servicio Bibliográfico y
Archivo Técnico. Información del mercado común y bibliografía preliminar sobre actividades económicas de los países latino-ameri-
canos. [México] 1960. 86 p.   (2976

BARNES, Roberto. Bibliografía preliminar sobre el mercado común latinoamericano.
[n.p.] 1961. 9 p. mimeogr.   (2977

-----. Bibliografía preliminar sobre la integración económica centroamericana. [n.p.]
1961. 5 p. mimeogr.   (2978

ROSARIO. Universidad Nacional del Litoral.
Biblioteca "Estanislao S. Zeballos". Desarrollo económico, mercado común y Alianza
para el Progreso. Bibliografía actualizada;
2a. ed. Rosario, Facultad de Ciencias Eco-
nomicas, Comerciales y Políticas, 1963.
265, xxxviii p.   (2979

UNITED NATIONS. Library, Mexico. Mercado común latinoamericano; integración económica
centroamericana. Bibliografía inicial.
[México, D.F.] 1961. 24, 3 p.
mimeogr.   (2980

ARGENTINA

ARGENTINA. Congreso. Biblioteca. Servicios
públicos. [Buenos Aires, 1951] 66 p. (Información bibliográfica, Publ. no. 8) (2981

BANCO de la Nación Argentina, Buenos Aires.
Biblioteca. Planificación; selección bibliográfica (libros, folletos, artículos aparecidos en los diarios y revistas) Buenos Aires,
1947. 47 p. (Ser. bibliográfica,
no. 1)   (2982
  Cited in Catálogo, Instituto Bibliotecológico, item 552.

BUENOS AIRES. Universidad, Instituto Bibliotecológico. Bibliografía sobre planificación, producción y racionalización. Preparada...con motivo del Congreso Nacional de
Productividad y Bienestar Social. Buenos
Aires, 1955. 4 v.   (2983
   Cited in Catálogo, Instituto Bibliotecológico, item 554.

-----. -----. Instituto de Economía. Bibliografía sobre ciclos económicos, 1948- .
Buenos Aires, 1949- .   (2984
   DPU collection through 1952. Reprinted
from Revista de la Facultad de Ciencias Económicas, 2 (14): 611-18, jun. 1949; 2 (15):
740-70, jul. 1949; 3 (24): 467-506, jun.
1950; 4 (33): 283-328, mayo 1951; 5 (47-48):
915-71, sept./oct. 1952; 6 (53-54): 377-432,
mayo/jun. 1953.

-----. -----. Instituto de la Producción.
Serie bibliográfica, Buenos Aires, 1941- .
v. 1- .   (2985
   Contents: v. 1 (1941), Producción de gra-
nos. - v. 2 (1942), Perspectivas agropecuarias de postguerra. - v. 3 (1943), La industria azucarera en la República Argentina. -
v. 4 (1943), Las industrias originadas por
la actual guerra en la República Argentina;
su estabilidad y consolidación. - v. 5 (1943)
Los combustibles sólidos en la Republica Argentina; posibilidades de su explotación económica. - v. 6 (1944), Función de la navegación en la economía mundial. - v. 7 (1945),
Consumo de energía en la República Argentina. Fomento de la explotación de las fuentes nacionales de energía. - v. 8 (1946),
La industria aceitera en la República Argentina. - v. 9 (1947), La energía hidroeléc-
trica en la República Argentina. - v. 10
(1948), Geografía económica en las provincias y territorios nacionales. - v. 11
(1951), La evolución industrial argentina.
- v. 12 (1952), Las industrias forestales
argentinas. - v. 13 (1953), Estudio integral
de la provincia Presidente Perón. - v. 14
(1953), Estudio integral de la provincia Eva
Perón.

PAN AMERICAN UNION. Department of Economic
Affairs. Unit of Planning and Programmimg.
List of publications on Argentina. Wash-
ington, D.C., 1962. 32 p.   (2986

SMITH, L. Brewster, COLLINGS, Harry T., and
MURPHEY, Elizabeth. The economic position
of Argentina during the war. Washington,
D.C., Govt. Print. Off., 1920. 140 p.
(U.S. Bureau of Foreign and Domestic Com-
merce. Misc. ser., no. 88)   (2987
   Bibliography: p. 132-40.---Jones 844.

BRAZIL

ANDREONI, João Antonio. Cultura e opulencia
do Brazil por suas drogas e minas, com um
estudo bio-bibliographico, por Affonso de
E. Taunay. São Paulo, Companhia Melhoramen-
tos de São Paulo (Weizflog Irmãos) [1923]
280 p.   (2988
   The original edition was published at
Lisbon in 1711.---Jones 955.

CENTRO Brasileiro de Pesquisas Educacionais.
Bibliografia sôbre diversos aspectos do desenvolvimento cultural, social e econômico
do Brasil por solicitação da Delegação do
Brasil junto a Unesco. Rio de Janeiro, n.d.
9 p. mimeogr.   (2989
   Cited in Doria Menezes 31.

NORMANO, João Frederico. Brazil, a study of
economic types. Chapel Hill, Univ. of North
Carolina, 1935. 254 p.   (2990
   Bibliography: p. 231-44.---Jones 1110.

-----. Evolução economica do Brasil; tr. de
Theodoro Quartim Barbosa, Roberto Peake Rodrigues e Laercio Brandão Teixeira. São
Paulo, Companhia Edit. Nacional, 1939.
313 p. (Biblioteca pedagógica brasileira,
ser. 5: Brasiliana, v. 52)
   Bibliographia: p. 301-13.---Jones 1111.

PERNAMBUCO. Comissão de Desenvolvimento Econômico de Pernambuco. Bibliografia de assuntos de Noreste. Recife, 1957. 166 p. (Ser.
Problemas de região, 3)   (2992

CHILE

MACCHIAVELLO VARAS, Santiago. Política económica nacional. Santiago, Balcells & Co.,
1931. 2 v.   (2993
   Bibliografía: v. 1, p. XVII-XXII.---Jones
1523.

PAN AMERICAN UNION. Department of Economic
Affairs. Unit of Planning and Programming.
List of publications on Chile. Washington,
D.C., 1962. 29 p.   (2994

COLOMBIA

BANCO de la República, Bogotá. Seleccion de
artículos de varias publicaciones relacionadas en el Boletín bibliográfico, I-V. Bogotá, 1958-1959. 5 v. mimeogr.   (2995
   Lists are formed from nos. 34-37, 40-42,
44 of the Boletín bibliográfico, each from
6 to 10 pages in length. Cited in Giraldo
Jaramillo, p. 91-2.

BOGOTA. Universidad de los Andes. Centro de Estudios sobre Desarrollo Económico. Bibliografía comentada sobre el desarrollo económico y la economía colombiana. Bogotá, 1959-1961. 2 v. (2996
Vol. 1 edited by Humberto Vegalara; vol. 2, by Eduardo Wiesner Durán.

LOPEZ, J. Emilio. Bibliografía de economía general y colombiana. Medellín [Impr. de la Universidad de Antioquia, 1954]
16 p. (2997
Cited Giraldo Jaramillo, p. 93.

PAN AMERICAN UNION. Department of Economic Affairs. Unit of Planning and Programming. List of publications on Colombia. Washington D.C., 1962. 21 p. (2998

COSTA RICA

COSTA RICA. Oficina de Planificación. Departamento de Financiación. Lista de estudios e informes realizados para uso de ministerios, instituciones autónomas y otros organismos nacionales. San José, 1963. 22 p. mimeogr. (2999
Cited in Anuario bibliográfico costarricense, 1963, p. 14.

ECUADOR

PAN AMERICAN UNION. Department of Economic Affairs. Unit of Planning and Programming. List of publications on Ecuador. Washington, D.C., 1962. 20 p. (3000

HONDURAS

PAN AMERICAN UNION. Department of Economic Affairs. Unit of Planning and Programming. List of publications on Honduras. Washington D.C., 1962. 7 p. (3001

MEXICO

BANCO de México. Biblioteca. La bibliografía económica de México en 1956 y 1957. México, D.F., Departamento de Estudios Económicos. Biblioteca del Banco de México, 1960.
141 p. (3002
This compilation continues Bibliografía económica de México en 1954 y 1955, by Bullejos (item 3005)

-----. Departamento de Investigaciones Industriales. Indice de monografías e informes técnicos del Departamento de Investigaciones Industriales, 1943-1962. [México, D.F., 1963] 95 p. (3003

BARNES, Winthrop M., and ETIENNE B., Guillermo. Sources of industrial marketing and economics information for Mexico. Presented before Instituto Mexicano de Ingenieros Químicos, México, D.F. [San Antonio, Texas, Southwest Research Institute] 1962. 55 p. (Elements of industrial development in Mexico, pt. 1) (3004

BULLEJOS, José. La bibliografía económica de México en 1954 y 1955. [México, D.F.] Banco de México, Departamento de Estudios Económicos, 1956. 119 p. (3005
Supplements the author's compilation, Diez años de literatura económica.

-----. Diez años de literatura económica; bibliografía básica sobre la economía de México, 1943-1953. México, D.F., Instituto de Investigaciones Económicas, 1954.
162 p. (3006

MEXICO. Departamento de Prensa y Publicidad. Bibliografía sobre salarios y costos de la vida. México, D.F., [Tall. Gràf. de la Nación] 1937. 57 p. (Manuales D.A.P.P. Serie Trabajo) (3007

-----. Secretaría de Relaciones Exteriores. Departamento Consular. Indice de los informes económicos rendidos por el Servicio Consular Mexicano durante 1930 y 1931. México, D.F., Impr. de la Secretaría de Relaciones Exteriores, 1932. 225 p. (3008

REICHWEIN, Adolf. El despertar de Méjico. Madrid, Edit. Cenit, 1931. 294 p. (3009
Translated from the German by E. Sadia. "Bibliografía y notas": p. 273-85.---Jones 2453.

-----. Mexiko erwacht. Leipzig, Bibliographisches Institut, 1930. 274 p. (3010
Literatur und anmerkungen: p. 253-65.---Jones 2452.

VELASQUEZ G., Pablo, and NADURILLE T., Ramón. A selected bibliography of economic, social and agricultural development in Mexico. México, Instituto Nacional de Investigaciones Agrícolas, 1964. 22 p. (3011

PANAMA

PAN AMERICAN UNION. Department of Economic Affairs. Unit of Planning and Programming. List of publications on Panama. Washington, D.C., 1962. 9 p. (3012

PANAMA. Instituto de Fomento Económico. Biblioteca. Bibliografía de economía de la República de Panamá. Panamá, 1958.
63 p. (3013
Compiled by Genarina Arrucha.

PERU

UGARTE, César Antonio. Bosquejo de la historia económica del Perú. Lima, Impr. Cabie-
ses, 1926. 214 p.   (3014
    Indice bibliográfico: p. 205-10.---Jones
2764.

URUGUAY

MORI, Mario. Uruguay, condizioni naturali ed
economiche. Roma, Treves, 1928. 215 p.
(Publ. dell' Instituto Cristoforo Colombo,
no. 36)   (3015
    Bibliografía: p. 209-15.---Jones 2855.

URUGUAY. Poder Legislativo. Biblioteca.
Consejo de la Economía Nacional. Montevideo [1950?] 3 pts. in 6 v. (Referencia, 14)
mimeogr.   (3016
    "El presente trabajo sobre el Consejo de
la Economía Nacional, ha tenido por objeto
reunir todo el material bibliográfico y legislativo pertinente." Compiler: Luis Felipe Rodriguez Vildósola.

-----. -----. Impuesto a la renta. [Monte-
video] n.d. 14 p. mimeogr.   (3017
    Cited in Musso 92.

-----. -----. -----. Montevideo, 1960. 68 p.
(Referencia no. [38])   (3017a
    Cited in Musso, Poder Legislativo, no. 761.

URUGUAY. Poder Legislativo. Biblioteca. Impuesto a la renta. Montevideo, 1960. 55 p.
(Referencia 47)   (3018
    Cited in Musso 93.

-----. Universidad. Instituto de Teoría y Política Económicas. Bibliografía básica para
una evaluación de las tendencias del desarrollo económico del Uruguay en el último decenio. Montevideo, Comisión de Inversiones y
de Desarrollo Económico, 1960. 52 p.   (3019

VENEZUELA

PALENZONA, Armando. La Republica del Venezuela sotto l'aspetto economico e le sue rela-
zioni con l'Italia. Milano, Tip. M. Borroni,
1931. 237, ix p.   (3020
    Bibliografía: p. i-iii.---Jones 2937.

PAN AMERICAN UNION. Department of Economic
Affairs. Unit of Planning and Programming.
List of publications on Venezuela. Wash-
ington, D.C., 1962. 25 p.   (3021

WEST INDIES

CARIBBEAN Organization, Hato Rey, P.R. Library.
Bibliography of development plans. Biblio-
graphie des plans de développement. Hato Rey,
P.R., 1963. 9 p.   (3022

EDUCATION

GENERAL

BAYLE, Constantino. España y la educación
popular en América. Madrid, F.... A. E.
[1934] 388 p. (Institutto Pedagógico F. A.
E. Estudios e investigaciones, 1) (3023
    Bibliografía: p. 7-22.---Jones 48.

BERROA, Josefina. Spanish-language books in
the field of education. A bibliography of
books translated from the English and com-
mercially available in Spanish-language editions. México, Regional Technical Aids Center [Institute of Inter-American Affairs,
American Embassy] 1959. 44 p.   (3024

BLANCO Y SANCHEZ, Rufino. El año pedagógico
hispanoamericano. Monografías pedagógicas,
crónica mundial de la enseñanza, 2,000 notas
bibliográficas. Madrid, Perlado, Páez y
Cía., 1920. 320 p.   (3025
    Jones 63.

BUENOS AIRES. Biblioteca Nacional del Docente
y del Estudiante Argentinos. Obras de edu-

BUENOS AIRES. Biblioteca Nacional... (Cont.)
cación; catálogo. [Buenos Aires, Tall.
Gráf. del Consejo Nacional de Educación]
1941. 302 p.   (3026
    Cited in Catálogo, Instituto Biblioteco-
lógico, item 907.

-----. Universidad. Instituto Bibliotecológico. Bibliografía sobre reforma y autonomía universitaria. Buenos Aires, 1956.
87 p.   (3027

-----. -----. -----. Suplemento a la bibliografía. Buenos Aires, 1956. 17 p.   (3028

-----. -----. Medios audiovisuales; bibliografía selectiva. Buenos Aires, 1963.
10 p. (Publ. no. 18) mimeogr.   (3029
    Compiler: Susana Luisa Urreaga.

CASANOVA, Teobaldo. Educational psychology
and some aspects of education in Latin
America. San Juan, P.R., Impr. Venezuela,
1934. 169 p.   (3030
    Bibliography: p. 145-53.---Jones 86.

CENTRO Brasileiro de Pesquisas Educacionais.
Bibliografia analítica dos documentos de
trabalho apresentados a Conferência sôbre
Educação e desenvolvimento Econômico e Social na América Latina, Santiago de Chile,
5-19 de março de 1962. Rio de Janeiro,
1962. 24 p.   (3031
    Preliminary edition. Cited in Doria Me-
nezes 27.

-----. Bibliografia de educação. Rio de Janeiro, 1961. 30 p.   (3032
    Cited in Doria Menezes 28.

-----. Bibliografia de pesquisa educacional.
Rio de Janeiro, 1963. 29 p.
mimeogr.   (3033
    Cited in Doria Menezes 30.

CENTRO Latino-Americano de Pesquisas em
Ciencias Sociais. Pesquisa educacional na
América Latina; fontes bibliográficas. Rio
de Janeiro, 1964. 56 p.   (3034

CONNOR, John M. Bibliografía de la literatura sobre educación de adultos en la América
Latina ... con Addenda recopilada por Germania Moncayo de Monge. Washington, D.C.,
Unión Panamericana, 1952. 88 p. (Bibliographic ser., no. 37)   (3035
    Based on thesis, Latin America: Litera-
ture of adult education, presented by the
author at Teachers College, Columbia University.

COSTA RICA. Inspección General de Enseñanza.
Bibliografía pedagógica y medios materiales
de enseñanza, por B. Corrales. San José,
Tip. Nacional, 1896. 45 p.   (3036
    Jones 1263.

EELLS, Walter Crosby. American dissertations
on foreign education ... 1884-1958. Washington, D.C., National Education Association, 1959. 300 p.   (3037
    Central and South America and the West
Indies: p. 30-66.

ESPINOSA CALISTO, Emma. Biblioteca de cultura pedagógica; libros de consulta para el
maestro sugeridos por Servicio Cooperativo
Interamericano de Educación. [Quito] 1957.
8 p.   (3038
    Issued as "Trabajo 3".

-----. Libros para el alumno; bibliografía
básica para la escuela primaria. Quito,
1959. 15 p.   (3039
    Issued by the Servicio Cooperativo Inter-
americano de Educación, as "Trabajo 15".

-----. Libros para el maestro; bibliografía
de educación primaria. Quito, 1959.
16 p.   (3040
    Issued by the Servicio Cooperativo Inter-

ESPINOSA CALISTO, Emma. Libros ... (Cont.)
americano de Educación as "Trabajo 14".

GRECO ABAL, Rogelio. Bibliografía para maestros. [Montevideo, 1940] 12 p.
mimeogr.   (3041
    Cited in Musso 196.

INTER-AMERICAN Children's Institute, Montevideo. Bibliografía: educación de adultos;
libros, folletos y artículos de revistas
existentes en la Biblioteca. Montevideo,
1951. 5 p. mimeogr.   (3042
    Cited in Musso 198.

-----. Bibliografía: psicología y psicopeda-
gogía. Montevideo, L.I.G.U., 1944.
51 p.   (3043
    Reprinted from Boletín, Instituto Inter-
nacional Americano de Protección a la Infancia, set. 1944. Cited in Musso 204.

-----. Publicaciones sobre tests y asuntos
relacionados con ellos. Montevideo, L.I.G.
U., 1945. 22 p.   (3044
    Reprinted from Boletín, Instituto Inter-
nacional Americano de Protección a la Infancia, t. 19, p. 320-39, 1945. Cited in Musso
206.

INTER-AMERICAN Seminar on Vocational Education,
College Park, Maryland, 1952. Lista de documentos técnicos en castellano y portugués.
Washington, D.C., Unión Panamericana, 1953.
34 p. (Serie A de educación vocacional,
no. 2)   (3045
    202 technical documents and 7 bibliogra-
phies are listed.

-----. Vocational education texbooks; exhibit
catalog. Washington, D.C., 1953. 57 p.
(VOC.EDU./Tecd. 196)   (3046
    Includes Latin American countries. Com-
pilation by Estellita Hart.

MOYA DE PERERA, Ana M. Bibliografía. [Mon-
tevideo, 1950] 61, [4] p.   (3047
    Working paper presented in the Seminario
Interamericano de Educación Primaria, document 16. 630 items listed.

NICHOLS, Madeline Wallis, and KINNAIRD, Lucia
Burk. A bibliography of articles on education in Nosotros. Boston, Faxon, 1935.
24 p. (Bulletin of bibliography pamphlets,
no. 31)   (3048
    Reprinted from Bulletin of bibliography,
Boston, v. 15, no. 7, May/Aug. 1935.

PAN AMERICAN UNION. General references on
education in Latin America. [Washington,
D.C., 1941] 1 p.   (3049

-----. Latin American secondary schools;
courses of study. Washington, D.C., 1920.

PAN AMERICAN UNION. Latin American... (Cont.)
32 p. (Monograph, no. 1)   (3050
  Prepared by Arturo Torres. Contains references to sources.---Jones 355.

-----. Division of Education. Bibliografía
de la educación primaria en América. Washington, D.C., [1958] 85 p.   (3051

-----. -----. Bibliografía sobre educación
y desarrollo económico y social (fuentes
americanas) Washington, D.C., [1961] 66 p.
(La educación en América, Ser. de información, boletín 1962, no. 2)   (3052
  Prepared for the Conferencia sobre Educación y Desarrollo Económico y Social en América Latina, Santiago, 1962. Issued also
in English.

-----. -----. Bibliography on education and
economic and social development (American
sources) Washington, D.C., [1961] 62 p.
(Education in the Americas, Information ser.,
bulletin 1962, no. 2)   (3053
  Prepared as a document for the OAS-UNESCO-
ECLA Conference on Education and Economic
and Social Development in Latin America, Santiago, 1962. Issued also in Spanish.

-----. -----. Education in Latin America; a
partial bibliography. Washington, D.C.,
1957. 20 pts. in 1v. (Information ser.
bulletin, 1957, no. 1-21)   (3054
  pt. 1, Latin America; pt. 2-21 include individual countries of Latin America.

-----. -----. Education in Latin America: a
partial bibliography. Washington, D.C.,
1958. v, 50 p.   (3055
  The first edition was published as Bulletin 1957, no. 1-21 of the Information Series.

-----. -----. Higher education and economic
and social development in Latin America.
Washington, D.C. [1961] 39 p. (Education
in the Americas, Information ser., bulletin
1962, no. 1)   (3056

-----. -----. Secondary education in the Amer-
icas: a bibliography. La educación secun-
daria en las Américas: una bibliografía.
Washington, D.C., 1955. 41 p.   (3057
  Most references are to education in the
United States.

-----. -----. Texbooks and principal reference works. [Washington, D.C., 1948]
xlvi p.   (3058

-----. Division of Intellectual Cooperation.
Latin American studies in American institu-
tions of higher learning, academic year
1938-1939. Washington, D.C., Pan American
Union, 1940. 96 p. mimeogr.   (3059
  Compiled by Raul d'Eça. "Books used in

PAN AMERICAN UNION. Division of... (Cont.)
classes": p. 79-96.---Jones 355a.

SMITH, Henry Lester and Littell, Harold. Edu-
cation in Latin America. New York, [etc.]
American Book Co., 1934. 431 p.   (3061
  Bibliography: p. 413-21.---Jones 449.

TUCUMAN, Argentina. Universidad Nacional. Biblioteca. Bibliografía de educación, pedagogía general y especial, historia y legislación universitaria. Tucumán, Impr. La Velocidad, 1935. 76 p. (Universidad Nacional
de Tucumán. Publ. no. 207. Boletín de la
Biblioteca no. 1)   (3062
  Jones 597, 871.

UNITED NATIONS Educational, Scientific and Cultural Organization. An international bibliography of technical and vocational education.
[Paris, 1959] 72 p. (Educational studies
and documents, no. 31)   (3063
  Geographical arrangement. Latin American
countries included.

-----. International guide to educational documentation, 1955-1960. [Paris, 1963]
700 p.   (3064
  Produced in collaboration with the International Bureau of Education, Geneva. Includes Latin American countries and Caribbean territories.

-----. Education Clearing House. Alfabetización; bibliografía selecta. Paris [1950]
43 p. (Unesco. Dept. de Educación; Centro
de Información. Documentos especiales de
educación, 5)   (3065
  Contains 97 references: América Latina:
no. 76-97.

-----. -----. L'éducation des analphabètes;
bibliographie choisie. Paris [1950] 47 p.
(Unesco. Dépt. de l'Education, Centre d'Information. Documents spéciaux d'éducation,
5)   (3066
  Contains 97 references; Amérique Latine:
no. 76-97.

-----. -----. La enseñanza profesional y técnica; bibliografía internacional. Paris,
1960. 68 p. (Estudios y documentos de educación, no. 31)   (3067

-----. -----. Literacy education; selected
bibliography. Paris, [1950] 43 p. (Unesco.
Education Clearing House, Occasional papers
in education, 5)   (3068
  Contains 97 references; Latin MERICA: no.
76-97.

URIOSTE, Antero. Algunos libros de texto, de
consulta y de cultura general y profesional.
[Montevideo] 1921. 147 p. (Consejo Nacional de Enseñanza Primaria y Normal. Biblio-

URIOSTE, Anero. Algunos libros.. (Cont.)
teca de maestros no. 1)   (3069

ZEPEDA RINCON, Tomás. La instrución pública
en la Nueva España en el siglo I. Mxco,
1933. 138 p.   (3070
Bibliografía: p. 135-38.---Jones 2593.
Published under auspices of the Facultad
de Filosofía y Letras of the Universidad Nacional de Mexico.

ARGENTINA

BUENOS AIRES (Province) Instituto Bibliográfico. Bibliografía argentina de ciencias de
la educación, obras y artículos publicados
durante 1960, no. 2, nov. de 1961. La Plata,
Ministerio de Educación [1962]
115 p.   (3071
No. 1 of this series forms a part of Bibliografía argentina de filosofía y ciencias
de la educación, 1958/1959, no. 1, jun. 1960.
Latest received at DPU: no. 3, nov. 1962.

-----. Bibliografía argentina de psicología;
obras y artículos publicados, 1960/1961- .
no. 1/2- . La Plata, Ministerio de Educación [1963]- .   (3072
Publications issued during 1958-1959 included in no. 1 of Bibliografía argentina de
filosofía y ciencias de la educación.

CHANETON, Abel. Libros didácticos impresos en
Buenos Aires hasta 1810; noticia preliminar
y catálogo. (In La Instrucción primaria en
la época colonial, Buenos Aires, p. 137-48,
1936)   (3073
Jones 665c

GUTIERREZ, Juan María. Noticias históricas sobre el orijen y desarrollo de la enseñanza
pública superior en Buenos Aires, desde la
época de la estinción de la Compañía de Jesús
en el año 1767, hasta poco después de fundada la Universidad en 1821; con notas, biografías, datos estadísticos y documentos curiosos inéditos o poco conocidos. Buenos Aires,
Impr. del Siglo - de J. M. Cantilo, 1868.
941 p.   (3074
"Catálogo de los libros didácticos que se
han publicado o escrito en Buenos Aires, desde el año 1790 hasta el año 1867 inclusive,
con esclusión de los elementales destinados
a las escuelas de primeras letras": p. 573-
618.
Issued also in the series La Cultura argentina, Buenos Aires, 1915. Includes "Escritos
del dr. Maziel, inéditos todos, que han lle-
gado a nuestro conocimiento, 1775-1786".---
Jones 720.

LA PLATA. Universidad Nacional. Programas,
curso de 1922. La Plata, Olivieri y Domínguez, 1922. 144 p.   (3075

LA PLATA. Universidad Nacional ... (Cont.)
Each course contains "programa, bibliografía y plan de trabajos prácticos".---Jones
745.

BRAZIL

BIBLIOGRAFIA brasileira de educação, v. 1,
1953- . Rio de Janeiro, Centro Brasileiro
de Pesquisas Educacionais, [1954]- .   (3076
Last volume received at DPU: v. 11, no. 3,
jul./set. 1963.

Centro Brasileiro de Pesquisas Educacionais.
Bibliografia de ensino superior no Brasil.
Rio de Janeiro, 1961. 64 p. mimeogr. (3077
Cited in Doria Menezes 29.

-----. Bibliografia sôbre planejamento da educação no Brasil. Rio de Janeiro, n.d. 12 p.
mimeogr.   (3078
Cited in Doria Menezes 34.

-----. -----. Suppl. 1963. 4 p.   (3079
Cited in Doria Menezes 34.

-----. Bibliography of education in Brazil.
Rio de Janeiro, n.d. 7 p.   (3080
Cited in Doria Menezes 35.

-----. A educação no Distrito Federal; bibliografia abrangondo o período 1930-1957. Rio
de Janeiro, n.d. 13 p.   (3081
Cited in Doria Menezes 37.

-----. Fontes para o estudo da educação no
Brasil. [Rio de Janeiro] INEP, Ministério
da Educação e Cultura [1959] v. 1: 436 p.
(Publ., ser. 9: Levantamentos bibliográficos,
v. 1, t. 1)   (3082
Vol 1: Bahia, fontes oficiais.

-----. Lista de livros e folhetos sobre educação no Brasil, organizada para o "Clearing
House" -Divisão de Informação do Departamento de Educação da Unesco. Rio de Janeiro,
n.d. 5 p.   (3083
Cited in Doria Menezes 39.

-----. Lista de publicações sôbre oportuni-
dades educacionais no Brasil. Rio de Janeiro, 1959. 3 p.   (3084
Cited in Doria Menezes 40.

-----. Selective bibliography of works in
English and French on Brazilian education.
Rio de Janeiro [1962?] 2 p.   (3085
Cited in Doria Menezes 41.

SÃO PAULO. Centro Regional de Pesquisas Educacionais. Uma bibliografia sôbre instru-
ção programada e máquinas de aprender.
São Paulo, 1963. 30 p.   (3086
Cited in Doria Menezes 76.

CHILE

DOCUMENTOS relativos a la Real Universidad de
San Felipe; libro índole de los libros de
matrícula, de acuerdos, de exámenes y de co-
lación de grados. Santiago, Impr. Cervantes,
1900. 568 p.   (3087
    Published in Anales of the Universidad de
Chile. Cited in Laval, item 98.

LABARCA HUBERTSON, Amanda Pinto de. Historia
de la enseñanza en Chile. Santiago, Impr.
Universitaria, 1939. 399 p.   (3088
    Bibliografía: p. 385-99.---Jones 1499.

PONCE, Manuel Antonio. Bibliografía pedagóji-
ca chilena (anotaciones) Santiago, Impr.
Elzeviriana, 1902. 307 p.   (3089
    665 titles classified "en seis secciones
cronolójicas...pedagojía jeneral, sistemática (organización escolar jeneral e interna),
metodolojía, lejislación, historia de la enseñanza i periódicos profesionales".---Jones
1568.

-----. Reseña histórica de la enseñanza de
lectura en Chile (siglos XVI-XIX) Santiago,
Impr. Barcelona, 1905. 135 p.   (3090
    Inventory of readers and spellers (Cf. La-
val, no. 257).---Jones 1569.

COLOMBIA

BOGOTA. Colegio Mayor de Nuestra Señora del
Rosario. Constituciones...publ. por d. Rafael María Carrasquilla. Bogotá, Medardo
Rivas & C., 1893. 86 p.   (3091
    "Catálogo de los señores rectores del Co-
legio", p. 67-80, gives names and, in most
cases, dates.---Jones 1691.
    Publications cited in biographical
sketches.

COSTA RICA

COSTA RICA. Ministerio de Instrucción Pública. Memoria. San José, 1897. 156 p. (3092
    List of Costa Rican newspapers: p. 145-56.
---Jones 1265.

GONZALEZ, Luis Felipe. Historia de la influencia extranjera en el desenvolvimiento educacional y científico de Costa Rica. San José,
Impr. Nacional, 1921. 317 p.   (3093
    Bibliographical references.---Jones 1271.

CUBA

AGUAYO, Alfredo Miguel. La Universidad y sus
problemas; discurso inaugural del curso académico de 1921 a 1922. Habana, Impr. "El
Siglo XX", 1921. 110 p.   (3094

AGUAYO, Alfredo Miguel. La Universidad...(Cont.)
    Bibliografía cubana de enseñanza superior"
p. 87-96 (112 titles). "Bibliografía extranjera y adiciones": p. 97-110 (113-273 titles).
---Jones 1782.

DIHIGO Y MESTRE, Juan Miguel. Bibliografía de
la Universidad de La Habana. Habana, "La
Propagandista", 1936. 315 p.   (3095
Jones 1814.

TRELLES Y GOVIN, Carlos Manuel. Bibliografía
de la Universidad de la Habana. Habana, Impr.
de Rambla, Bouza y Cía., 1938. 337 p. (Publ.
de la revista "Universidad de la Habana",
t. 5)   (3096
    Cf Revista bibliográfica cubana, 1936, año
1, p. 125-44, supplementing Juan M. Dihigo y
Mestre's Bibliografía de la Universidad de
La Habana.---Jones 1918.

GUATEMALA

GUATEMALA. Departamento de Orientación Escolar y Vocacional. Centro de Documentación.
Documentación psicopedagógica y materias afines (fichas clasificadas), no. 1-2. Guatemala [Edit. del Ministerio de Educación Pública "José de Pineda Ibarra"] 1960.
2 v.   (3097
    Semi-annual publication. No. 2 includes:
"bibliografía sobre orientación escolar y
profesional", by María J. Alcaraz Lledo, p.
3-96.

-----. Secretaría de Educación Pública. Biblioteca mínima: obras de ilustración y de
auxilio para los maestros de las escuelas
urbanas de la República; 66 volúmenes cada
biblioteca. Guatemala [Tip. Nacional] 1947.
87 p.   (3098

HAITI

DARTIGUE, Maurice. L'enseignement en Haiti
(1894-1938). Port-au-Prince, Impr. de
l'Etat, 1939. 50 p. (Service National de
la Production Agricole et de l'Enseignement
Rural, Bull. 14)   (3099
    Includes bibliography.---Jones 2988a.

MEXICO

COOK, Katherine Margaret, and REYNOLDS, Florence
E. Good references on the education of the
indigenous peoples of Mexico. Washington,
D.C., 1933. 11 p. (U.S. Office of Educa-
tion, Bibliography, no. 8)   (3100
Jones 2135.

EBAUGH, Cameron Duncan. The national system
of education in Mexico. Baltimore, 1931.

EDUCATION

EBAUGH, Cameron Duncan ... (Cont.)
149 p. (Johns Hopkins studies in education,
no. 16)   (3101
    Bibliography: p. 146-49.---Jones 2154.

PERU

BARREDA Y LAOS, Felipe. Vida intelectual de
la colonia (educación, filosofía y ciencias)
ensayo histórico crítico. Lima, Impr. "La
Industria", 1909. 422 p.   (3102
    Jones 2627.

-----. Another edition. Buenos Aires, Tall.
Graf. Argentinos L. J. Rosso, 1937.
391 p.   (3102a
    Bibliografía: p. 385-87.

PUERTO RICO

MENDOZA, Antonio Cuesta. Historia de la educación en Puerto Rico (1512-1826) Washington, D.C., Catholic University of America,
1937. xxvi, 191 p.   (3103
    Bibliografía: p. xi-xxvi.---Jones 2796.

URUGUAY

URUGUAY. Consejo Nacional de Enseñanza Primaria y Normal. Lista de los libros de texto adoptados para uso de los alumnos de las
escuelas primarias durante el año 1902. Montevideo, El Siglo Ilustrado, 1902.
10 p.   (3104
    Cited in Musso 223.

-----. -----, durante el año 1904. Barreiro
y Ramos, 1904. 16 p.   (3105
    Cited in Musso 224.

URUGUAY. Consejo Nacional de Enseñanza Primaria
y Normal. Lista de los libros de texto adoptados para uso de los alumnos de las escuelas
primarias durante el año 1906. Montevideo,
Barreiro y Ramos, 1906. 16 p.   (3106
    Cited in Musso 225.

-----. -----, durante 1907. Montevideo, Barreiro y Ramos 1907. 16 p.   (3107
    Cited in Musso 226.

-----. -----, durante 1908. Montevideo, Barreiro y Ramos, 1908. 18 p.   (3107a
    Cited in Musso 227.

-----. -----, durante el año 1910. Montevideo,
El Siglo Ilustrado, 1910. 22 p.   (3108
    Reprinted from Anales de instrucción prima-
ria, Montevideo, t. 8, no. 1-6, p. 852-65,
en./jun. 1910. Cited in Musso 229.

-----. -----, durante el año 1913. Montevideo,
Barreiro y Ramos, 1913. 15 p.   (3109
    Cited in Musso 230.

VENEZUELA

PARRA, Caracciolo. La instrucción en Caracas,
1567-1725. Caracas, Parra León Hermanos, 1932.
310, 99 p.   (3110
    Contains biographical information, referen-
ces to source material, etc.---Jones 2941.

WEST INDIES

CARIBBEAN Commission. A bibliography of education in the Caribbean. [Port-of-Spain] 1959.
144 p.   (3111
    Compiled by V. O. Alcalá.

EDUCATION (THESES)

BOGOTA. Universidad Javeriana. Facultad de
Bacteriología. Tesis de grado. Bogotá,
1958. Various pagings.   (3112

BOLLINI FOLCHI, Hebe. Tesis de doctorado y
para optar a las cátedras presentadas a la
Facultad de Medicina, 1878-1902. Montevideo,
1962. 37 p.   (3113

BUENOS AIRES. Universidad. Facultad de Ciencias Económicas. Biblioteca. Tesis docto-
rales de la Facultad de Ciencias Económicas:
1916-1951. Buenos Aires, Impr. de la Universidad, 1952. 83 p.   (3114

-----. -----. Facultad de Ciencias Médicas.
Catálogo de la colección de tesis, 1827-1917.

BUENOS AIRES. Universidad. Facultad...(Cont.)
Buenos Aires, Tall. Gráf. de A. Flaiban, 1918.
495 p.   (3115
    Jones 631.

CANDIOTI, Marcial R. Bibliografía doctoral de
la Universidad de Buenos Aires y catálogo
cronológico de las tesis en su primer centenario 1821-1920. Buenos Aires, 1920.
804 p.   (3116
    "Las tesis de jurisprudencia, incluyendo
las de derecho canónico, son 3,450, las de
teología 22, las de medicina son 3,860, los
proyectos de la Facultad de Ciencias Exactas
1,014, las tesis de la Facultad de Filosofía
y Letras 46, Agronomía y Veterinaria 215 y
Ciencias Económicas 79; lo que hace el total

CANDIOTI, Marcial R. Bibliografía...(Cont.)
de 8,636 de la colección. Los diez y nueve
capítulos que sirven de introduccion a la
obra, son un verdadero tratado de crítica
literaria sobre las tesis" (Cf. E. S. Zeballos' review in Revista de derecho, historia
y letras, abr. 1921).---Jones 645.

COLOMBIA. Universidad Nacional. Facultad de
Agronomía. Tesis presentadas a la Facultad
Nacional de Agronomía. Medellín, 1963. (3117
Cited in Boletín de adquisiciones, Mede-
llín, no. 8, p. 9, ag. 1963.

COSTA RICA. Universidad Nacional. Biblioteca.
Lista de tesis de grado de la Universidad de
Costa Rica hasta 1957. [San José] 1961.
380 p. (Ser. bibliotecología, no. 10) (3118
Covers period 1941 to 1957, listing 2,649
theses.

-----. -----. -----. Tesis de grado, 1958- .
San José, 1959- . (Ser. bibliotecología,
11-)   (3119
Last issue, no. 20, 1963, of the series
received at DPU.

-----. -----. Facultad de Agronomía. Bibliografía de tesis de grado, 1931-1954. [San
José, 1955?] 20 p. (Departamento de Publicaciones, Publ., no. 428) mimeogr.   (3120

DOCKSTADER, Frederick J. The American Indian
in graduate studies; a bibliography of theses
and dissertations. New York, Museum of the
American Indian, 1957. 399 p.   (3121
Contains 3,684 entries relating to Indians
of North, Central and South America, and to
the Eskimos.

FLOREN LOZANO, Luis. Catálogo de tesis de la
Universidad de Santo Domingo de 1938/1939 a
1948/1949. Santo Domingo [1956]. p. 177-
359. (Anales, Universidad de Santo Domingo,
XXI (77-78) en./jun. 1956)   (3122
Extract. Authorship in caption: Luis y Caridad Florén. In the Anales, this Catálogo
de tesis is preceded, p. 115-73, with "Catálogo de tesis de farmacéuticos dominicanos,
1909/1910 - 1950/1951".

FLORES, Raul Humberto. Catálogo de tésis doc-
torales de las facultades de la Universidad
de El Salvador. San Salvador, Edit. Universitaria, 1960. 582 p.   (3123

GUATEMALA. Universidad de San Carlos. Escuela de Biblioteconomía. Tesario universitario, 1945-1960. v. 1. Guatemala, 1961.
44 p. (Publicaciones, no. 1)   (3124
Vol. 1 contains: Facultades de Humanidades,
Ciencias Jurídicas y Sociales y Ciencias Económicas, por Alba Rosa Calderón y Lourdes
Bendfeldt R.

HERNANDEZ DE CALDAS, Angela, and VALENCIA M.,
Lucía. Tesis de grado presentadas a la Fa-
cultad Nacional de Agronomía de Medellín.
Medellín, 1954. 27 p. mimeogr.   (3125
Lists 246 theses.

-----. Edición de 1953. 10 p.   (3125a

HERRERA, Carmen D. de. Lista bibliográfica de
los trabajos de graduación y tesis presentados en la Universidad, 1939-1960. Panamá,
Universidad de Panamá, Biblioteca, 1960.
186 p.   (3126
"Contribución al Tercer Seminario Bibliográfico de Centro América y el Caribe".

-----, and FIERRO, Olivia de. Lista de los
trabajos de graduación correspondiente a los
años 1957-1955 [sic]. Panamá, Of. de Información y Publicaciones, 1958. 73 p.   (3126a
Prepared at the Library of the Universidad
de Panamá as a contribution to the Seminario
Bibliográfico de Centro América y el Caribe,
2o., 1958.

INTER-AMERICAN Institute of Agricultural Sciences, Turrialba. Tesis de Magister Agriculturae de la Escuela para Graduados, 1947-1963;
resúmenes analíticos. Turrialba, 1964. 81 p.
(Bibliotecología y documentación, no.
3)   (3127
Contains 178 entries.

-----. Tesis para optar al grado de Magister
Agriculturae presentadas a la Escuela para
graduados del Centro Tropical de Investigación
y Enseñanza para graduados, 1947-1963. Turrialba, Biblioteca y Servicio de Documentación, 1963. [17] p.   (3128
Contains 158 entries. "Indice de materias"
continues running item indications at top of
previous pages: 159-163.

KANTOR, Harry. A bibliography of unpublished
doctoral dissertations and masters theses
dealing with the governments, politics, and
international relations of Latin America.
Prepared for the Committee on Latin American
Affairs of the Committee on Latin American
Affairs of the American Political Science
Association. Gainesville, Fla., 1953. 85 p.
(Inter-American Bibliographical and Library
Association, Ser. I, v. 13)   (3129

KIDDER, Frederick Elwyn. Doctoral dissertations
in Latin American area studies, 1960/1961- .
Washington, D.C. Academy of American Franciscan History, 1962- .   (3130
Reprinted from The Americas, v. 19, no. 2,
Oct. 1962- . These issues are supplements to
the Bibliographic Series no. 5, 4th ed. published by the Columbus Memorial Library of
the Pan American Union. See item 3139.

LA PLATA. Universidad Nacional. Biblioteca.
Catálogo de la colección de tesis jurídi-
cas arreglada según clasificación decimal.
Buenos Aires, Impr. de Coni Hermanos, 1914.
101 p.   (3131
     Alphabetical subject and author indexes.
---Jones 742.

LEAVITT, Sturgis Elleno. A bibliography of
theses dealing with Hispano-American literature. Stanford University, 1935. p. 169-
82.   (3132
     From Hispania, v. 18, no. 2, May 1935.
Continued in v. 21.---Jones 251.

LIMA. Escuela Nacional de Agricultura. Biblioteca. Relación de la existencia de tesis a
diciembre de 1953. [Lima, 1954]
47 p.   (3133
     Compiler: Susana Riedner.

MEXICO (City). Mexico City College. A descriptive list of research papers and theses,
accepted by the Graduate School, 1947-1954;
compiled by the staff of the College Library.
[México D.F.] 1954. 48 p.   (3134
     Contribution to the VI Feria Mexicana del
Libro.

-----. -----. 1954/1960. México, D.F. [1960]
38 p.   (3135

PAN AMERICAN UNION. Columbus Memorial Library.
Theses on Pan American topics, prepared by
candidates for degrees in colleges and universities in the United States. Washington, D.
C., 1931. 52 p. (Bibliographic ser., no. 5)
mimeogr.   (3136

-----. 2d ed., rev. and enl. Washington, D.
C., 1933. 113 p. (Bibliographic ser, no. 5)

PAN AMERICAN UNION. Columbus Memorial (Cont.)
mimeogr.   (3137
     Jones 363.

-----. 3d., rev. and enl. Washington, D.C.,
1941. 170 p. (Bibliographic ser., no. 5)
mimeogr.   (3138

-----. 4th ed. compiled by Frederck Elwyn
Kidder and Allen Bushong. Washington, D.C.,
1962. 124 p. (Bibliographic ser.,
no. 5)   (3139
     The compiler began annual supplements to
this issuance in The Americas, v. 19, no. 2,
Oct. 1962. See item 3130.

PARKER, Franklin. Latin American education
research; an annotated bibliography of 269
United States doctoral dissertations. Austin,
Institute of Latin American Studies, University of Texas [1963?] 63 p.   (3140

SALVADOR, Brazil. Faculdade de Medicina. Catalogo de thesis. [Bahia, 1910?]
304 p.   (3141
     Compiler Pedro Rodrigues Guimarães. Cited
in Reis, 267a.

SCHOENBERG DE SCHEINER, Marta. Tesis de doctorado presentadas en la Facultad de Química
y Farmacia; ordenadas y clasificadas. Montevideo, 1954. 7 p. mimeogr.   (3142
     Lists 32 theses.

TEXAS. University. Institute of Latin American Studies. Seventy-five years of Latin
American research at the University of Texas.
Masters theses and doctoral dissertations
1893-1958 and publications of Latin American
interest 1941-1958. Austin, [1959] 67 p.
(Latin American studies, 18)   (3143

ENGINEERING

BUENOS AIRES. Universidad. Facultad de Ingeniería. Biblioteca. Bibliografía sobre enseñanza de la ingeniería. Buenos Aires,
1960. 59 p. mimeogr.   (3144

URUGUAY. Universidad. Facultad de Ingeniería
y Agrimensura. Bibliografía correspondiente
a los cursos dictados...en el año 1934. Montevideo, Peña, 1935. 84 p.   (3145
     Cited in Musso item 47.

ETHNOLOGY

GENERAL

BALDUS, Herbert, and WILLEMS, Emilio. Dicionário de etnologia e sociologia. S. Paulo,
Editôra Nacional, 1939. 245 p. (Biblioteca
pedagogica brasileira, ser. 4: Iniciação
cientifica, v. 17)   (3146
     Includes bibliography.---Jones 967a.

BANDELIER, Adolph Francis Alphonse. On the
sources for aboriginal history of Spanish
America. (Proceedings of the American Association for the Advancement of Science. 27th
meeting, 1878. Salem, 1879. p. 315-
37.   (3147
     Jones 39.

BRINTON, Daniel Garrison. The American race;
a linguistic classification and ethnographic
description of the native tribes of North
and South America. Philadelphia, D. McKay,
1901. 392 p.   (3148
  Previously published in 1891. Bibliographic footnotes.---Jones 73.

COMAS, Juan. Bibliografía selectiva de las
culturas indígenas de América. México, D.F.,
1953. xxviii, 284 p. (Publ. del Instituto
Panamericano de Geografía e Historia,
no. 166)   (3149
  Issued also as publication of the Comisión
de Historia, no. 64.

JIMENEZ MORENO, Wigberto. Materiales para una
bibliografía etnográfica de la América Latina. 1a. pte. Bibliografía etnográfica de
México. (Boletín bibliográfico de antropología americana, México, D.F., v. 1, p. 47-
77, 167-97, 289-421, 1937)   (3150
  Jones 2268.

PARDAL, Ramón. Medicina aborigen americana.
Buenos Aires, J. Anesi, 1937. 377 p. (3151
  Bibliography at end of each chapter.---
Jones 363a.

ARGENTINA

TARNOPOLSKY, Samuel. Libros con indios pam-
pas y conquistadores del desierto. Buenos
Aires, Edit. Expansión Bibliográfica Argentina, 1958. 54 p.   (3152
  Cited in Catálogo, Instituto Bibliotecológico, item 307.

BRAZIL

BALDUS, Herbert. Bibliografia comentada de
etnologia brasileira (1943-1950). Rio de
Janeiro, Editôra Souza, 1954. 142 p. (Ser.
bibliográfica de estudos brasileiros,
1)   (3153
  "Suplemento ao Manual bibliográfico de estudos brasileiros".

-----. Bibliografia crítica de etnologia brasileira. São Paulo, Comissão do IV Centenário da Cidade de São Paulo, 1954.
859 p.   (3154

-----. Ensaios de etnologia brasileira; com
um prefácio de E. Taunay ... Edição ilustrada. São Paulo, Editôra Nacional, 1937.
346 p. (Biblioteca pedagogica brasileira,
ser. 5: Brasiliana, v. 101)   (3155
  Includes a bibliography on the subject.---
Jones 967b.

CENTRAL AMERICA

ARPEE, Levon Harris. Bibliographical notes on
the Mayas of Central America. Chicago, 1937.
19 numb. 1. mimeogr.   (3156
  Jones 1227a.

CONZEMIUS, Eduard. Ethnographical survey of
the Miskito and Samu Indians of Honduras and
Nicaragua. Washington, D.C., Govt. Print.
Off., 1932. 191 p. (Bureau of American
Ethnology. Bulletin 106)   (3157
  Bibliography: p. 173-78.---Jones 1322.

KRICKEBERG, Walter. Los totonacas; contribución a la etnografía histórica de la América
Central. Traducción del alemán por Porfirio
Aguirre. México, D.F., Tall. Graf. del Museo Nacional de Arqueología, Historia y Etnografía, 1933. 241 p.   (3158
  "Indice de las fuentes de información:"
p. 207-16. The Totonac Indians were located
in Mexico.---Jones 1238.

THOMPSON, John Eric. Ethnology of the Mayas
of southern and central British Honduras.
Chicago, 1930. p. 27-213. (Field Museum of
Natural History. Publ. 274. Anthropological
ser., v. 17, no. 2)   (3159
  Bibliography: p. 196-203.---Jones 1328.

CHILE

GERDTS-RUPP, Elisabeth. Magische vorstellungen
und bräuche der Araukaner in spiegel spani-
scher quellen seit der conquista. Hamburg,
C. Behre, 1937. 166 p. (Ibero-amerikanische
studien des Ibero-Amerikanischen Instituts,
9)   (3160
  Literaturverzeichnis: p. 157-61.---Jones
1490.

GUSINDE, Martin. Bibliografía de la isla de
Pascua. (Publ. del Museo de Etnología y Antropología de Chile. Santiago de Chile,
t. 2, p. 201-383, 1922)   (3161
  Jones 1493.

SUNDT, Roberto. Bibliografía araucana. (Revista de bibliografía chilena y extranjera,
Santiago de Chile, t. 5, p. 300-15, 1917;
t. 6, p. 3-21, 87-101, 182-213, 269-86,
1918)   (3162
  Jones 1634.

COLOMBIA

CASTELLVI, Marcelino de. Bibliografía sobre
los sibundoyes y otros de la familia lingüística kamsá o coche. (Proceedings of the
Third Convention of the Inter-American Bibliographical and Library Association. New
York, H. W. Wilson, 1941. p. 86-97) (3163

CASTELLVI, Marcelino de. Bibliografía...(Cont.)
Jones 1696b.

ORTIZ, Sergio Elías. Contribución a la bibliografía sobre ciencias etnológicas de Colombia. Pasto, Impr. del Departamento, 1937.
66 p. (Idearium; órgano de la Escuela Normal de Occidente; Suppl. no. 1)   (3164
A classified list. A supplement by C.
Loukotka was published in Idearium, Pasto,
1938, v. 1, p. 353-56.---Jones 1709.

REICHEL DOLMATOFF, Gerardo. Bibliografía etnológica del Departamento del Magdalena. Santa Marta, 1949. 27 p. (Divulgación cultural
del Instituto Etnológico del Magdalena,
no. 3)   (3165
Cited in Giraldo Jaramillo, p. 100.

CUBA

FEBRES CORDERO G., Julio. Bibliografía sobre
indigenismo en Cuba. La Habana, 1950. (Revista de la Biblioteca Nacional, 2a. ser.,
t. 1, no. 4, p. 113-204, ag. 1950)   (3165a

ECUADOR

RIVET, Paul. Costumbres funerarias de los indios del Ecuador (Boletín de la Biblioteca
Nacional, Quito, t. 2, p. 1-36, 1927) (3166
Indice bibliográfico: p. 32-6.---Jones
2005.

UHLE, Max. Bibliografía ampliada sobre etnología y arqueología en el Ecuador. (Anales
de la Universidad Central, Quito,
1929)   (3167
Jones 2022.

-----. Bibliografía sobre etnología y arqueología del Ecuador. (Boletín de la Biblioteca
ca Nacional, Quito, nueva ser. no. 7, p. 435-
46, 1926)   (3167a
Jones 2021.

MEXICO

LEON, Nicolás. Las castas de México colonial
o Nueva España. México, D.F., 1924. (Museo
Nacional de Arqueología, Historia y Etnografía. Publ. del Departamento de Antropología Anatómica, no. 1)   (3168
Bibliografía: p. 72-6.---Jones 2290.

MARTINEZ RIOS, Jorge. Bibliografía antropológica y sociológica del Estado de Oaxaca.
México, D.F., Instituto de Investigaciones
Sociales, Universidad Nacional, 1961.
154 p.   (3168a

THE MAYA and their neighbors. New York, D.
Appleton-Century Co., 1940. 606 p.   (3169
Bibliography: p. 491-594.---Jones 2323a.

MENDIZABAL, Miguel O. de. Influencia de la
sal en la distribución geográfica de los gru-
pos indígenas de México. México, D.F., Impr.
del Museo Nacional de Arqueología, Historia
y Etnografía, 1928. 226 p.   (3170
Bibliografía: p. 213-224.---Jones 2339.

PARSONS, Elsie Clews. Mitla, town of the souls,
and other Zapoteco-speaking pueblos of Oaxaca, Mexico. Chicago, Ill., The Univ. of Chicago Pr., 1936. 590 p. (The University of
Chicago publications in anthropology. Ethnological series)   (3171
Bibliography: p. 570-73.---Jones 2405.

SAUER, Carl Ortwin. The distribution of aboriginal tribes and languages in Northwestern
Mexico. Berkeley, Univ. of California, Pr.,
1934. 94 p.   (3172
Bibliography: p. 85-90.---Jones 2488.

TRISTAN, José M. Bibliografía maya yucateca.
Rochester, N.Y., 1949. 125 p.   (3173

VALLE, Rafael Heliodoro. Bibliografía maya.
México, D.F. [1937-1941] 404 p.   (3175
Jones 2549. "Issued as an appendix to the
Boletín bibliográfico de antropología ameri-
cana (v. 1-5, 1937-1941) of the Instituto
Panamericano de Geografía e Historia."

PERU

LOCKE, Leslie Leland. The ancient quipu or
Peruvian knot record. New York, The American
Museum of Natural History, 1923. 84 p. (3177
Bibliography: p. 72-80.---Jones 2681.

SCHWAB, Federico. Bibliografía de etnología
peruana. (Boletín bibliográfico, Biblioteca
Central, Universidad Mayor de San Marcos,
Lima, v. 9, no. 1, p. 1-26. (Etnología);
no. 2, p. 4-27 (Arqueología); no. 3-4, p.
101-15 (Antropología, física y lingüística;
1936)   (3178
Jones 2749.

-----. Bibliografía etnológica de la Amazonia
peruana, 1542-1942, Lima, Compañía de Impresiones y Publicidad, 1942. 76 p.   (3179
Publication sponsored by the Comité del
IV Centenario del Descubrimiento del Río Amazonas.

SOUTH AMERICA

BALDUS, Herbert. Indianerstudien im nordöstli-
chen Chaco. Leipzig, C. L. Hirschfeld, 1931.
230 p. (Forschungen zur völkerpsychologie

BALDUS, Herbert. Indianerstudien...(Cont.)
und soziologie, bd. 11)   (3180
    Literatur: p. 218-25.---Jones 592.

COOPER, John Montgomery. Analytical and cri-
tical bibliography of the tribes of Tierra
del Fuego and adjacent territory. Washington
D.C., Govt. Print. Off., 1917. 233 p.
(Smithsonian Institution. Bureau of American
Ethnology, Bulletin 63)   (3181
    Jones 1439.

DABBENE, Roberto. Los indígenas de la Tierra
del Fuego. (Boletín del Instituto Geográfico Argentino, Buenos Aires, t. 25, p. 163-
226, 247-300, 1911)   (3182
    Bibliografía: p. 288-300.
    A bibliography of Doctor Dabbene by Emilia-
no J. MacDonagh will be found in Revista del
Museo de La Plata (nueva serie) Sección oficial, Buenos Aires, p. 135-42, 1939.---Jones
677.

IZIKOWITZ, Karl Gustav. Musical and other
sound instruments of the South American
Indians. Göteborg, Elanders Boktryckeri
Aktiebolag, 1935. 433 p. (Göteborgs kungl.
vetenskapsoch vitterhets samhälles handlingar.
5. foljden, ser. A, bd. 5, no. 1)   (3183
    Bibliography: p. 417-33.---Jones 220.

KOCK-GRUNBERG, Theodor. Vom Roroima zum Orinoco. Berlin, D. Reimer, 1917-1928.
5 v.   (3184
    Includes bibliographies.---Jones 239.

METRAUX, Alfred. La civilisation matérielle
des tribus Tupi-Guarani. Paris, P. Geuthner,
1928. 331 p.   (3185
    Index bibliographique: p. 314-31.---Jones
314.

NORDENSKIÖLD, Erland. The changes in the material of two Indian tribes under the influence
of new sourroundings. Göteborg, Elanders
Bocktryckeri Aktiebolag, 1920. 245 p. (Comparative etnographical studies, 3)   (3186
    Includes bibliography.---Jones 337.

NORDENSKIÖLD, Erland. An ethno-geographical
analysis of the material culture of two Indian tribes in the Gran Chaco. Göteborg,
Elanders Boktryckeri Aktiebolag, 1919.
295 p.   (3187
    Bibliography: p. 270-93.---Jones 795.

-----. Origin of the Indian civilizations in
South America. Göteborg, Elanders Boktryckeri Aktiebolag, 1931. 205 p. (Comparative
ethnographical studies, 9)   (3188
    Bibliography: p. 134-53.---Jones 339.

O'LEARY, Timothy J. Ethnographic bibliography
of South America. New Haven, Human Relations
Area Files, 1963. 387 p. (Behavior science
bibliographies)   (3189

URUGUAY

SCHULLER, Rudolph R. Sobre el orijen de los
charrua; réplica al doctor Jorje Friederici.
Santiago de Chile, Impr. Cervantes, 1906.
158 p.   (3190
    Contains bibliographies. Published in Ana-
les de la Universidad de Chile, v. 118.---
Jones 2870.

SERRANO, Antonio. Etnografía de la antigua
provincia del Uruguay. Paraná, Tall. Graf.
"Melchior", 1936. 207 p.   (3191
    Bibliografía: p. 191-207.---Jones 2872.

VENEZUELA

ERNST, Adolf. Ensayo de una bibliografía de
la Guajira y de los guajiros. (Revista científica de la Universidad Central de Venezuela,
Caracas, no. 20, p. 341-57, 1890)   (3192
    Jones 2910.

FUCHS, Helmuth. Bibliografía básica de etnología de Venezuela. Sevilla, 1964. 251 p.
(Publ. del Seminario de Antropología Americana, v. 5)   (3193

EXHIBITIONS

ARGENTINA

AGRUPACION Argentina de Amigos del Libro, Buenos Aires. 1a. Exposición de incunables,
manuscritos, mapas y grabados antiguos en
el Salón Kraft. [Buenos Aires, 1947]
44 p.   (3193a

ARGENTINA. Comisión Nacional Ejecutiva del
150. Aniversario de la Revolución de Mayo.
Catálogo del periodismo e imprenta argentina;

ARGENTINA. Comision Nacional... (Cont.)
inauguracion del salón exposición en el Museo
Histórico Nacional, 7 de junio de 1960. Buenos Aires, Ministerio de Educación y Justicia,
Dirección General de Cultura, 1960.
233 p.   (3193b

-----. Ministerio de Agricultura y Ganadería.
Departamento de Bibliotecas. Exposición Internacional del libro cooperativo, Buenos Aires, 15-30 de septiembre de 1959; catálogo.

ARGENTINA. Ministerio de Agricultura...(Cont.)
63 p. (Circular bibliográfica, no.
9)   (3194

ASOCIACION de Escritores Riojanos. El libro
riojano. La Rioja [Impr. del Estado] 1960.
85 p.   (3194a
     Exhibition on the occasion of the 150th.
Anniversary of the "Revolución de Mayo".

BECU, Teodoro. Catálogo de la exposición del
libro...para conmemorar el quinto centenario
de la invención de la imprenta. Buenos Aires [Tall. Gráf. de G. Kraft] 1940. xlvii,
275 p.   (3195

BUENOS AIRES. Exposición Alemana de Libros y
Artes Gráficas. Exposición alemana de libros y artes gráficas en Buenos Aires. [Ca-
tálogo. Leipzig, Durck A. Pries, 1932?]
349 p.   (3196
     Cited in Catálogo, Instituto Bibliotecoló-
gico, item 256.

-----. Instituto Bibliotecológico. Bibliografía filosófica del siglo XX; catálogo de la
Exposición Bibliográfica Internacional de
la Filosofía del Siglo XX. Buenos Aires,
Ediciones Peuser [1952] 465 p.   (3197

-----. (Province). Instituto Bibliográfico.
Exposición del libro latinoamericano; catálogo, 1- . 1950- .   (3197a

BUSANICHE, José Luis. Exposición de libros,
manuscritos, autógrafos y documentos de la
biblioteca del Dr. José Luis Busaniche.
Santa Fé [Impr. de la Provincia] 1951.
146 p.   (3198

CAMARA Española de Comercio de la República
Argentina, Buenos Aires. Relación de algunas de las obras publicadas en España durante los últimos siete años, que exhibe la Cámara Española de Comercio en las salas de
la Exposición de la Dirección General de Cultura. [Buenos Aires, 1946] 215 p.   (3199
     Cited in Catálogo, Instituto Bibliotecoló-
gico, item 257.

CIRCULO Cultural Tolosano, Tolosa, Arg. Biblioteca Popular. Primera Exposición de libros de las tres Américas; catálogo. La
Plata, 1941. 24 p.   (3200

EXPOSICION del Libro Español, Buenos Aires,
1933. Catálogo bibliofílico; suplemento.
Buenos Aires, 1933. 18 p.   (3201

INSTITUTO Bonaerense de Numismática y Antigüedades, Buenos Aires. Descubrimientos y exploraciones en mares australes americanos
en los siglos XVI, XVII y XVIII; exposición
bibliográfica. Buenos Aires, 1957.
57 p.   (3202

INSTITUTO Cultural Argentino-Uruguayo, Buenos
Aires. Exposición de libros de autores uruguayos editados en la Argentina; catálogo documental. Buenos Aires, 1959. 63 p. (3203
     Lists 351 items. Cited in Musso item 110.

INTER-AMERICAN Congress of Philosophy, 6th.
Buenos Aires, 1959. Exposición del libro
americano de filosofía. Buenos Aires, 1959.
131 p.   (3204

LA PLATA. Universidad Nacional. Facultad de
Ciencias Económicas. Catálogo de la primera
exposición internacional de ciencias administrativas, organizada por el Instituto Superior de Ciencias Administrativas, 16 al 23
de mayo de 1960. La Plata, 1960.
120 p.   (3205

-----. -----. Instituto de Economía y Finanzas. Catálogo de la 1a. Exposición Interlatina de Ciencias Económicas, noviembre de
1956. La Plata, 1956. 126 p.   (3206

SANTA FE (City) Arg. Museo Municipal de Bellas
Artes. Primera exposición del libro santafe-
sino. San Fé [Tall. Gráf. "Colmegna"] 1941.
53 p., 3 p.   (3207
     Issued in conmemoration of the 368th anni-
versary of the founding of Santa Fé.

UNION de Universidades de América Latina.
Asamblea General, 3a., Buenos Aires, 1959.
Catálogo; exposición interlatina de publica-
ciones de universidades, patrocinada por la
Universidad de Buenos Aires. [Buenos Aires,
1959, 170 p.]   (3207a
     Cited in Geoghegan, 1318.

BRAZIL

ACADEMIA das Bellas Artes, Rio de Janeiro. Catalogo das obras expostas, em 15 de março de
1879. Rio de Janeiro, Pereira Braga & Cia.
[1879]   (3208
     Cited in Reis, item 81.

-----. Catalogo das obras expostas em 23 de
agosto de 1884. Rio de Janeiro, Typ. a Vapor de P. Braga & Comp., 1884.   (3209
     Cited in Reis, item 106.

AUTORES alagôanos; catalogo alphabético dos
livros de autores alagôanos que figuraram
na exposição organizada pela secção de publicidade do D.M.E. Maceió, Depto. Municipal
de Estatística, 1940. 51 p.   (3210
     Cited in HLAS, 6, item 104.

BANCO de la República, Bogotá. Contribución
al "Segundo Festival del Libro de América"
que se celebrará en Rio de Janeiro del 21
de junio al 5 de julio de 1958. Bogotá,
Impr. del Banco de la República, 1958.

BANCO de la República, Bogotá ... (Cont.)
31 p.   (3211
   Catalog of the gift made by the Bank of
the Republic on occasion of the Second Festival of the Book in the Americas, to the
University of Brazil in Rio de Janeiro. Cited in Giraldo Jaramillo, p. 38.

BRAZIL. Biblioteca Nacional. Catalogo da
colleção Cervantina com que a Biblioteca Nacional do Rio de Janeiro concorreu a Exposição Commemorativa do 3. Centenário de D.
Quixote, realisada pelo Gabinete Portuguez
de Leitura a 15. de junho de 1905. Rio de
Janeiro, Off. de Artes Graphicas da Bibliotheca Nacional, 1909. 96 p.   (3212
   Reprinted from Annaes, v. 29. Compiler:
Antônio Jansen do Paço.

-----. -----. Catalogo da Exposição Bibliográfica Commemorativa do Primeiro Centenário do
Nascimento de Marcelino Menéndez y Pelayo.
Rio de Janeiro, Ministério da Educação e Cultura, 1956. 119 p.   (3213

-----. -----. Catalogo da exposição Biblio-
iconographica organisada pela Bibliotheca Nacional do Rio de Janeiro commemorativa do
sexto centenário de Dante. Rio de Janeiro,
Off. Graph. da Bibliotheca Nacional, 1925.
45 p.   (3214
   Published as a separate from Annaes v. 41-
42, p. 223-69, 1919/1920-1925.

-----. -----. Catalogo da Exposição Camoneana,
10 de junho de 1880. por ocasião do centenário de Camões. Rio de Janeiro, Typ. Nacional, 1880. 71 p.   (3215
   Cited in Reis, item 85.

-----. -----. Catalogo da exposição commemora-
tiva do primeiro centenário de Artur Azevedo.
Rio de Janeiro, 1955. 23 p.   (3216
   Cited in Boletín bibliografico, Biblioteca
Nacional, v. 5, t. 2, 1955, p. 296.

-----. -----. Catalogo da exposição de historia do Brasil. Rio de Janeiro, Typ. G. Leuzinger & Filho, 1881. 2 v. (991, 993-
1612 p.)   (3217
   Published also in Annaes, v. 9, 1881-1882.
Jones 1164.

-----. -----. -----. Suplemento. Rio de Janeiro, Typ. de G. Leuzinger, 1883. p. 1613-1758,
98 p.   (3218
   Also included in Annaes, v. 9, paged continuously with main catalog.

-----. -----. Catalogo da exposição Nassoviana,
comemorativa do 3. centenário da chegada de
Mauricio de Nassau. (Anais da Biblioteca Nacional, Rio de Janeiro, v. 51, p. 1-133,
1938)   (3219
   Jones 1165. Issued also as a reprint of

BRAZIL. Biblioteca Nacional. Catalogo...(Cont.)
Anais.

-----. -----. Catalogo da exposição permanente
dos cimelios da Bibliotheca Nacional. Rio de
Janeiro, Typ. de G. Leuzinger & Filhos, 1885.
1059, 12 p.   (3220
   Also issued as Annaes, v. 11. Compiler:
João Saldanha da Gama.
   Contents. - Prefácio por João de Saldanha
da Gama. - Secção de impressos e cartas geographicas: Esboço historico, por J. A. Teixeira de Mello. Catalogo, por Saldanha da
Gama, Teixeira de Mello, A. Jansen do Paço e
J. Ribeiro Fernandes. Indices, por Saldanha
da Gama. - Secção de manuscriptos: Esboço
historico, catalogo, indice, por A. do Valle
Cabral. - Secção de estampas: Introdução,
esboço historico, catalogo taboa dos mono-
grammas, indices, por J. Z. de Menezes Brum.
- Numismatica: Esboço historico, por A. J.
Fernandes de Oliveira; Catalogo, por L. Fe-
reira Lagos e A. Jansen do Paço. Indice,
por J. de Saldanha da Gama e A. Jansen do
Paço.---Jones 1166.

-----. -----. Exposição: O Brasil visto por
viajantes estrangeiros. Rio de Janeiro,
1952. 11 p.   (3221
   Cited in Bibliografia brasileira, 1947-
1952, p. 1083.

-----. -----. Exposição Alvares de Azevedo e
o Romantismo (1831-1852) Rio de Janeiro,
1952. 15 p.   (3222
   Cited in Bibliografia brasileira, 1947-
1952, p. 1083.

-----. -----. Exposição camoniana. [Rio de
Janeiro] Ministério da Educação e Cultura
[1957?] 79 p.   (3223

-----. -----. Exposição cem anos de ativida-
des (1853-1953). Rio de Janeiro, 1953.
14 p.   (3224
   "Catalogo". Cited in Boletín bibliografico, Biblioteca Nacional, v. 4, t. 2, 1954,
p. 20.

-----. -----. Exposição comemorativa, 1810-
1960. [Rio de Janeiro] Biblioteca Nacional
[1960] 49 p.   (3225
   Exposição realizada em 29 de out. de 1960.

-----. -----. Exposição comemorativa do nascimento de Ernesto Nazareth, 1863-1934. Rio
de Janeiro, 1963. 66 p.   (3226
   Cited in Revista interamericana de bibliografía, no. 30, p. 190.

-----. -----. Exposição de incunábulos da Biblioteca Nacional. [Rio de Janeiro] Biblioteca Nacional, [1960?] 25 p.   (3227

BRAZIL. Biblioteca Nacional. Exposição "Independência do Brasil", catálogo. Rio de Janeiro, 1952. 16 p. mimeogr. (3228
Cited in Bibliografia brasileira, 1947-1952, p. 1083.

-----. -----. Guia da exposição permanente da Bibliotheca Nacional. Rio de Janeiro, Typ. de G. Leuzinger & Filhos, 1885.
45 p. (3229
The collections are fully described in the elaborate "Catalogo da exposição permanente dos cimelios da Bibliotheca Nacional".---
Jones 1169. See item 3220.

-----. -----. 1o. [i.e. Primeiro] Congresso Brasileiro de Critica e História Literária, Recife, 7 a 14 de agôsto de 1960. [Exposição; catalogo dos livros. Rio de Janeiro, 1960] 53 p. (3230

-----. -----. Relação das peças constantes da exposição sôbre o livro através dos tempos, inaugurada em 16 de novembro de 1951. Rio de Janeiro, 1951. 13 p. mimeogr. (3231
Cited in Bibliografia brasileira, 1947-1952, p. 1084.

-----. Ministério da Educação e Saude. Exposição José Bonifacio: centenário da morte do Patriarcha da independência: 1838-1938. Rio de Janeiro, Ministério da Educação e Saude, 1938. 131 p. (Exposições, 1) (3232
Bibliography of José Bonifacio de Andrade e Silva, 1763-1838, called the "Patriarch of the Independence".---Jones 996a.

-----. -----. Exposição Machado de Assis: centenário do nascimento de Machado de Assis: 1839-1939. Rio de Janeiro, Ministerio da Educação e Saude, 1939. 238 p. (Exposições, 2) (3233
Complete bibliography of the works of Joaquim Maria Machado de Assis, 1839-1908.---Jones 996b.

CASCUDO, Luis da Câmara. Exposição bibliográfico-documentária. Natal, Brasil, Prefeitura Municipal, 1961. 12 p. (3234
Cited in Revista interamericana de bibliografía, v. 12, p. 326.

COSTA, Carlos Antônio de Paula. Catalogo da exposição medica brasileira, realizada pela Bibliotheca da Faculdade de Medicina do Rio de Janeiro a 2 de dezembro de 1884. Rio de Janeiro, Typ. Nacional, 1884. 638 p. (3235
Cited in Reis, item 109.

EXPOSIÇAO de livros da Biblioteca do Caraça; promovida sob os auspícios da Sucursal de "O Globo" de Belo Horizonte, setembro de 1960. [Belo Horizonte, Impr. Oficial, 1960] 45 p. (3236
Cited in Revista do livro, 6(23-24); 236,

EXPOSIÇAO de livros da Biblioteca... (Cont.) set./dez. 1961. Exhibit organized by Etelvina Lima.

EXPOSIÇAO do Centenário Farroupilha. A imprensa e o livro no Pavilhão Cultural, 1835-1935. Porto Alegre, Typ. do Centro, 1935. (3237
Cited in Reis, item 477.

FERREIRA, Felix. A exposição da história do Brasil. Notas bibliographicas ... reproduzidas das editoriais "Cruzeiro". Rio de Janeiro, 1882. 102 p. (3238
Exposition was displayed in the National Library. Cited in Reis, item 96.

INSTITUTO da Ordem dos Advogados Brasileiros, Rio de Janeiro. Catalogo da exposição de trabalhos juridicos realizada pelo Instituto ... a 7 de setembro de 1894, 51. anniversario da sua fundação; organisado por Deodato C. Vilella dos Santos. Rio de Janeiro, Impr. Nacional, 1894. 221 p. (3239
Jones 1174.

PAÇO, Antônio Jansen do. Catalogo da Exposição Cervantina, realizada a 12 de junho de 1905. Rio de Janeiro, Typ. do "Jornal do Comercio" de Rodrigues & Cia., 1905. 156 p. (3240
Cited in Reis, item 214.

REMINGTON RAND, Inc., Brasil. Mostra de livros raros de taquigrafia na Biblioteca Nacional de 16 a 30 de setembro de 1960. Rio de Janeiro, 1960. 44 p. (3241

RIBEIRO, Duarte da Ponte, barão. Exposição dos trabalhos históricos geographicos e hydrographicos que serviram de base a carta geral do imperio exhibida na Exposição Nacional de 1875. Rio de Janeiro, Typ. Nacional, 1876. 90 p. (3242

RIO DE JANEIRO. Exposição Internacional do Livro Infantil, 1957. Catalogo. [Rio de Janeiro] 1957. 2 v. (3243
The catalog was prepared by the Biblioteca Infantil "Carlos Alberto" with the collaboration of the Instituto Brasileiro de Bibliografia e Documentação. Contains 2,543 items.

SALVADOR, Brazil. Exposição de livros e periódicos brasileiros; Université de Dakar - Exposition des Livres et périodiques brésiliens, janvier 1961. (Salvador, 1960] 80 p. (3244
Cited in Revista do livro, 6(23-24): 235, set./dez. 1961.

SÃO PAULO (City). Exposição Nacional do Livro e das Artes Gráficas, 1o., 1940. Catalogo. São Paulo, 1940. 55 p. (3246

-----. Universidade. Biblioteca Central. Catalogo das publicações periódicas da Univer-

SÃO PAULO (City) Universidade ... (Cont.)
sidade de São Paulo, apresentado na exposição realizada na Biblioteca Municipal, por
ocasião da Conferência Internacional de Bibliotecas Públicas de 3 a 12 de out. de 1951.
São Paulo, 1951. 52 p.   (3247

SOCIEDADE de Geographia, Rio de Janeiro. Catalogo da exposição de geographia Sul-Ameri-
cana...inaugurada em 23 de fevereiro de 1889.
[Rio de Janeiro] Impr. Nacional, 1891. xx,
473 p.   (3248
     Jones 1201.

SOCIEDADE Nacional de Agricultura, Rio de Ja-
neiro. Catalogo de Publicações agricolas.
Rio de Janeiro, 1908. 51 p.   (3249
     Displayed in the Exposição Nacional, 1908.
Cited in Reis, item 231.

CHILE

CHILE. Biblioteca Nacional. Catálogo de la
exposición bibliográfica de las obras de José Toribio Medina. [Santiago] Impr. Universitaria, 1952. 94 p. (Chile. Comisión Nacional de Conmemoración del Centenario del
Nacimiento de José Toribio Medina (1852-1952)
Publ. no. 3)   (3250

-----. -----. Catálogo de la exposición bibliográfica e iconográfica de Alejandro Humboldt, con motivo del centenario de su muerte, 1859-6-V-1959. [Santiago, Edit. Universitaria, 1959?] 69 p.   (3251

-----. -----. Catálogo de la exposición bibliográfica e iconográfica de Diego Barros
Arana, con motivo del cincuentenario de su
muerte, 1907-4-XI-1957. [Santiago de Chile,
1957] 58 p.   (3252
     The exposition was under the joint auspi-
ces of the Biblioteca Nacional and the Facultad de Filosofía y Educacion of the University of Chile.

-----. -----. Catálogo de la exposición celebrada... en conmemoracion del Centenario de
la Aurora de Chile, 13 de febrero de 1913
[i.e. 1912] Santiago de Chile, Impr. Universitaria, 1912. 37 p.   (3253
     Cited in Laval, item 81.

-----. -----. Catálogo de la exposición retrospectiva de la prensa chilena, abierta el
13 de febrero de 1912 en conmemoración del
centenario de la "Aurora de Chile"; 2. ed.,
corr. y aum. [Santiago de Chile] Impr.
Universitaria, 1912. 75 p.   (3254
     Contents. - Incunables chilenos, o sea
primeros trabajos tipográficos hechos en el
país. - La "Aurora de Chile". - Periódicos
publicados en Santiago hasta el año 1826. -
Primeros periódicos fundados en cada una de

CHILE. Biblioteca Nacional ... (Cont.)
las demás ciudades, pueblos y comunas. - Revistas y anuarios principales (1821-1912). -
Publicaciones periódicas en idioma extranjero. - Periódicos de caricatura. - Diarios y
periódicos con más de 25 años de duración. -
Epocas de las guerras de 1879 y 1891. - Periódicos chilenos impresos en el extranjero.
- Bibliografía concerniente a la introducción de la imprenta en Chile, etc.
     Prepared by Enrique Blanchard-Chessi.---
Jones 1601.

-----. Ministerio de Instrucción Pública. Exposición retrospectiva de la enseñanza. Obras
de los profesores, catálogo. Santiago de Chile, Impr. Universitaria, 1941. 325 p. (3255
     Compiled for the "IV Centenario de la fun-
dación de Santiago".

EXPOSICION Internacional de las Artes Graficas,
1a., Santiago de Chile, 1951. Catálogo.
Santiago, 1951. 188 p.   (3256

COLOMBIA

ACADEMIA Colombiana de Historia, Bogotá. Catálogo de la exposición, 12 de octubre de 1942.
Bogotá, Prensas de la Biblioteca Nacional,
1942. 30 p.   (3257

-----. Feria del Libro Colombiano de Cali, jul.
de 1961. [Bogotá, Impr. Patriótica del Instituto Caro y Cuervo, 1961] 7 p.   (3258
     Cited in Peraza, Fichas, t. 2, item 79.

-----. Guía de la Exposición "20 de julio".
Bogotá, Impr. Nacional, 1933. 8 p.   (3259
     Compiled by Guillermo Hernández de Alba.

BANCO de la República, Bogotá. Biblioteca Luis
Angel Arango. Exposición bibliográfica; relaciones literarias y editoriales entre Francia y Colombia; catálogo. Bogotá,
1964.   (3260
     Cited in Boletín de Adquisiciones, Mede-
llín, no. 9, p. 11, sept. 1964.

COLOMBIA. Biblioteca Nacional. La Biblioteca
Nacional y su exposición del libro. Bogotá,
1940. 141 p.   (3261

-----. -----. Catálogo de la exposición del
libro. Bogotá, 1942. 82 p.   (3262
     Contains 494 items.

-----. -----. Exposición bio-bibliográfica
en honor del Ilustrísimo Señor Don Manuel
José Mosquera ... y del Doctor Rufino Cuervo
... con ocasión del primer centenario de su
muerte. Bogotá, 1953. 58 p.   (3263

-----. -----. Exposición del libro, 26 de julio a 26 de agosto 1942, auspiciada por la

COLOMBIA. Biblioteca Nacional ... (Cont.)
Dirección de Extensión y Bellas Artes del
Ministerio de la Educación Nacional y la Bi-
blioteca Nacional. Bogotá, Prensas de la Bi-
blioteca Nacional, 1942. 82 p.   (3264
Cited in HLAS, 9, item 4651.

-----. -----. Primera exposición bibliográfica bolivariana, con ocasión de cumplir el
143. aniversario de la independencia de Venezuela. Bogotá, Edit. Minerva, 1954.
240 p.   (3265

COSTA RICA

ARGENTINA. Embajada. Costa Rica. [Catálogo
de la] Feria del libro argentino. San José,
C.R., 1958. 63 p.   (3266
Cited in Catálogo, Instituto Bibliotecológico, item, 290.

CUBA

CONGRESO Nacional y Panamericano de Prensa,
2a., La Habana. Exhibición de la prensa cu-
bana contemporánea. Catálogo. Habana, Impr.
Alfa, 1943. 45 p.   (3267
Listing of Cuban periodical publications.
Cited in HLAS, 9, item 76.

CUBA. Biblioteca Nacional. Los 120 primeros
años de la imprenta en Cuba (1723-1843); catálogo de la exhibición de impresos de la
Biblioteca Nacional. Habana, 1951.
29 p.   (3268
Introduction and compilation by Rodolfo
Tro.

-----. -----. Contribución de la Biblioteca
Nacional al Día del Libro Cubano. [Habana,
1955] 48 p.   (3269
Cited in Anuario bibliográfico cubano,
1955, item 236.

-----. -----. El libro en Cienfuegos; catálogo de las obras relacionadas con Cienfuegos
que se exhiben en la Biblioteca Nacional como homenaje al libro cubano, por Lilia Castro de Morales, con la colaboración del Ateneo de Cienfuegos. Habana, 1954.
80 p.   (3270
Contents: - Luis J. Bustamante. - La Bibliografía de Cienfuegos, por Florentino Morales Hernández. - Extracto de la conferencia pronunciada el 21 de abril de 1940, en
el Ateneo de Cienfuegos bajo el título Periódicos y revistas de Cienfuegos, por Luis
J. Bustamante y Hernández. - Catálogo de los
periódicos y revistas publicadas en Cienfuegos de 1846 a 1899. - Significado de las
abreviaturas, algunas erratas más importantes.

LYCEUM y Lawn Tennis Club, Habana. Exposición
de libros navales y sobre descubrimientos en
América, Siglos XVI a XIX, que con la cooperación de la Sociedad Colombista Panamericana celebra el Lyceum Lawn Tennis para conmemorar el IX cincuentenario del descubrimiento de América. [La Habana, 1943]
26 p.   (3271

PANAMA. Biblioteca Nacional. Catálogo de los
libros panameños enviados a la Exposición de
Artemisa, Cuba, con motivo de cumplirse el
95 aniversario del nacimiento del Apóstol
José Martí. Panamá, 1948. mimeogr.   (3272
Cited in Gropp, Bibliografía de bibliotecas nacionales, item 1075.

PERAZA SARAUSA, Fermín. Catálogo. La Habana,
1943. 45 p.   (3273
"La Exhibición de la Prensa Cubana Contemporánea a que se refiere este catálogo, cons-
tituye un aporte de la Hemeroteca Pública
Americana "Colón" al Segundo Congreso Nacional y Panamericano de Prensa, 7 al 11 de junio 1943".

ECUADOR

BIBLIOTECA de Autores Nacionales "Carlos A. Rolando". Catálogo de la exposición de libros
"en el XXV aniversario de su fundación, 1913-
1938" Guayaquil, Tip. y Lit. de la Sociedad
Filantrópica del Guayas, 1938. 12 p.   (3274

ECUADOR. Biblioteca Nacional. Exposición del
libro; biblioteca ecuatoriana que comprende
los diez últimos años de publicaciones [1930-
1940] Quito, Tall. Gráf. de la Nación, 1940.
77 p.   (3275
Jones 1974a.

-----. -----. Exposición del periodismo ecuatoriano. Contribución de la Biblioteca Nacional del Ecuador. Quito, Tall. Gráf. de
Educación, [1941] 119 p. (Publicaciones)   (3276
Jones 1974b.

GRUPO América, Quito. Exposición del libro venezolano; homenaje al General Isaías Medina
Angarita, Presidente de los Estados Unidos
de Venezuela, con ocasión de su visita a la
República del Ecuador. [Quito] Impr. del
Ministerio de Gobierno, 1943.
32 [3] p.   (3277

-----. Exposición del libro venezolano, 1943.
Catálogo adicional de la exposición del libro
venezolano. [Quito] Ecuador, Impr. del Ministerio de Gobierno, 1943. viii p.   (3278

GUAYAQUIL. Biblioteca Municipal. Exposición
y feria anual del libro ecuatoriano. Guayaquil. 1933. 56 p.   (3279

GUAYAQUIL. Biblioteca Municipal ... (Cont.)
Jones 1988.

JARAMILLO, Miguel Angel. Exposición del libro
azuayo; índice bibliográfico. Cuenca, Impr.
de la Universidad, 1939. xiv,
142 p.   (3280

QUITO. Biblioteca Municipal. Primera exposición del periodismo ecuatoriano. Contribución de la Biblioteca Municipal de Quito.
Quito, Impr. Nacional, 1941. 17 p. (3281
Cited in HLAS, 7, item 5381.

-----. Casa de la Cultura Ecuatoriana. Catalogo de la primera exposición cartográfica
nacional. [Quito, 1954?] 19 p.   (3282

EL SALVADOR

EL SALVADOR. Biblioteca Nacional. Exposición
de libros de historia y geografía americana
abierta ... a iniciativa del Ateneo de El
Salvador. Lista de las obras expuestas.
[San Salvador] Impr. Nacional [1933]
25 p.   (3283

-----. Exposición Continental del Periódico
Americano, 1960. Exposición Continental del
Periódico Americano, celebrada en San Salva-
dor, del 1o. al 31 de julio de 1960. San
Salvador, Ministerio de Cultura [1960]
409 p.   (3284
Gives listing, facsimiles and historical
information of newspapers exhibited.

FRANCE

MASA, Nicolás, and QUESADA, Ernesto. La Biblioteca Pública de Buenos Aires en la Exposición
Universal de París, 1878. Catálogo sistemático y alfabético de la colección de obras
argentinas que se envía, con su correspondiente informe. Buenos Aires, Impr. de la
Penitenciaría, 1878. 77 p.   (3285
Jones 773.

GUATEMALA

GUATEMALA. Secretaría de Educación Pública.
Catálogo general de la primera Exposición del
libro pedagógico del 3 al 31 de marzo de
1950, pasaje del Palacio Nacional. Guatemala, [1950] 23 p.   (3286

PANAMA. Biblioteca Nacional. Catálogo de los
libros panameños enviados en esta fecha a
las exposiciones de Guatemala y Rio de Janeiro. Panamá, 1946. 14, [1] p.
mimeogr.   (3287
Cited in Gropp Bibliografía de bibliotecas
nacionales, item 1016.

SPAIN. Embajada. Guatemala. Exposición del
libro español contemporáneo. Guatemala,
1956. 44 p.   (3288
Cited in Revista interamericana de biblio-
grafía, v. 7, p. 201.

MEXICO

BIBLIOTECA Benjamín Franklin, México. Catálogo de la exposición de libros norteamerica-
nos. n.d. 44 p.   (3289
Cited in Boletín, Biblioteca Nacional, Mé-
xico, D.F., jul./sept. 1954, p. 47.

CATALOGO de la exposición de libros mexicanos
de historia. México, D.F., 1949.
47 p.   (3290
"Presentada en relacion con el Primer Con-
greso de Historiadores de México y de los
Estados Unidos en Monterrey, N.L., del 4 al
9 de septiembre de 1949".   (3290
Cited in Boletín, Biblioteca Nacional, Mé-
xico, D.F., jul./sept. 1953, p. 54.

EXPOSICION de la prensa regional mexicana, organizada por el Centro Periodístico "Graphos",
1922. México, D.F., Edición de la National
Paper and Type Co., 1922. 44 p.   (3291
Cited in González, item 145.

EXPOSICION de libros científicos de Holanda
del 30 de octubre al 13 de noviembre 1952.
En el vestíbulo de la Biblioteca Nacional.
México, D.F., Amsterdam, n.d. 76 p. (3292
Cited in Boletín, Biblioteca Nacional,
México, en./mar. 1955, p. 53.

EXPOSICION Editorial del Continente Americano,
1a., México. Memoria. México, 1964.
270 p.   (3292a
Cited in Revista interamericana de biblio-
grafía, no. 35, p. 340.

FERIA Internacional del libro, 4a., México,
1946. Obras expuestas en la IV Feria Internacional del Libro. México, D.F., 1946.
39 p.   (3293
Cited in Anuario bibliográfico venezolano,
1946, item 326.

MEXICO. Servicio de Bibliotecas. Exposición
retrospectiva del libro mexicano. México,
D.F., 1943. [15 p.] (Biblioteca de la Segunda Feria del Libro y Exposición Nacional
del Periodismo)   (3294
Cited in HLAS, 9, item 62. Contains
chronological list of books exhibited.

MEXICO (Distrito Federal) Dirección de Acción
Social. Oficina de Bibliotecas. Exposi-ción
retrospectiva del libro mexicano. México,
D.F., Biblioteca de la II Feria del Libro y
Exposición Nacional del Periodismo, 1943.
[15 p.] incl. t.-p. and plates.   (3295

EXHIBITIONS

MEXICO (Distrito Federal) ... (Cont.)
Locations are shown for the editions of
the XVI Century. Prepared by Francisco
Gamoneda, Agustín Millares Carlo, and José
Ignacio Mantecón.

SAN LUIS POTOSI. Universidad. Biblioteca.
Exposición bibliográfica medica potosina.
San Luis Potosí [1950] 56, [8] p. (3296
Cited in Boletín, Biblioteca Nacional, Mé-
xico, D.F., jul./sept. 1953, p. 54.

-----. Primera exposición de bibliografía jurídica potosina presentada en la Facultad
de Derecho, 9 de octubre de 1953. [San Luis
Potosí, 1953] 183 p. (3297

-----. Primera exposición bibliográfica
potosina, 2-18-iv 1949. San Luis Potosí,
Tall. Gráf. Edit. Universitaria, 1949.
48 p. (3298

-----. V Exposición bibliográfica potosiana:
manuscritos y obras de Manuel José Othón.
San Luis Potosí, 1956. 15 p. (3299

SOCIEDAD Mexicana de Geografía y Estadística.
Catálogo de la exposición de cartografía mexicana (organizada por la Sociedad Mexicana
de Geografía y Estadística) Preparado por
Jorge L. Tamayo y Ramón Alcorta G. México,
D.F., Edit. Cultura, 1941. 160 p. (Instituto Panamericano de Geografía e Historia.
Publ. no. 59) (3300
Prepared for the Primer Congreso Mexicano
de Ciencias Sociales, 20 al 26 de julio
1941.

PANAMA

EXPOSICION Internacional del Libro, 5a., Panamá, 1961. Catálogo. Panamá, 1961. various
pagings. (3301

-----, 6a., Panamá, 1962. Catalogo. Panamá,
1962. various pagings. (3301a

-----, 7a,, Panamá, 1963. Catálogo. Panamá,
Universidad, 1963. 100 p. (3301b

-----, 8a., Panamá, 1964. Catálogo. Panamá,
1964. various pagings. (3302

PARAGUAY

BRAZIL. Biblioteca Nacional. Exposição do
livro brasileiro contemporâneo, Assunção,
1960. Rio de Janeiro [1961] 167 p. (3303

PERU

AREQUIPA, Perú. Universidad Nacional de San

AREQUIPA, Perú. Universidad... (Cont.)
Agustín. Catálogo de la primera Exposición
del Libro Peruano. [Arequipa], Tip. S. Quiroz [1940] 242 p. (3304
In commemoration of the 400th anniversary
of the founding of Arequipa, 1540-1940.

INSTITUTO de Cultura Italo-Peruano, Lima. Catalogo della mostra del libro italiano, 18-
25 giugno 1955. [Lima, Tall. Gráf. P. L.
Villanueva, 1955] 203 p. (3305
Cited in Anuario bibliográfico peruano,
1955/1957, item 1.

LIMA. Exposición de la Prensa Peruana, 1st,
1941. Primera exposición de la prensa peruana organizada por la Dirección de Propaganda
e Informaciones en el Palacio Municipal de
Lima del 25 de julio al 4 de agosto de 1941.
[Lima, Edit. "El Universal", 1941]
124 p. (3306
Contains list of publications preceding
the first newspaper, followed by a list of
periodical publications 1790-1821, and those
still current 1790-1940. Arrangement by
provinces.

-----. Exposición del Libro Mexicano, 1946.
Catálogo de la Exposicion del Libro Mexicano
organizada por la Cámara Mexicana del Libro
bajo el patrocinio de los gobiernos de México y Perú en la Ciudad de Lima. México,
[Tall. de la Edit. Stylo], 1946. xvi,
416 p. (3307
Collection from Mexico for the restoration
of the National Library of Peru, compiled by
Rafael Aguayo Spencer. HLAS, 12, item 2 cites
424 p.

PERU. Biblioteca Nacional. Exposición del libro austríaco. [Lima, 1954] 26 p. (3308
Catalog. Cited in Anuario bibliográfico
peruano, 1953/1954, item 1493.

PORTUGAL

BRAZIL. Biblioteca Nacional. Exposição do livro brasileiro contemporânio. Lisboa, 1957.
245 p. (3309

PORTUGAL. Secretariado Nacional da Informação,
Cultura Popular. Exposição histórica comme-
morativa do tricentenário da restauração per-
nambucana, 1654-1954, Palacio Foz, Lisboa,
Gabinete Português de Leitura, Recife, 1954.
[Lisboa, 1954] 160 p. (3310
Listings from Portuguese depositories
pertaining to the expilsion of the Dutch from
Brazil: documents, maps, paintings and en-
gravings.

SPAIN

BARCELONA. Biblioteca Central. Catálogo de
la exposición del libro en España e Hispano-
américa. Barcelona, Instituto Nacional del
Libro Español, 1962. 233 p.   (3311

BRAZIL. Biblioteca Nacional. Exposición del
libro brasileño contemporáneo, Madrid, abril
1959. [Catálogo redactado por María Amelia
Martins de Araujo; 3er. ed.] Rio de Janeiro,
1959. 229 p.   (3312

EXPOSICION Bibliográfica Simón Bolívar, Bilbao,
Spain, 1960. Catálogo. Bilbao, Archivo y
Biblioteca de la Excma. Diputación de Vizca-
ya, 1960. 51 p.   (3313
   Cited in Revista interamericana de biblio-
grafía, v. 11, p. 261.

MADRID. Exposición Historica-Americana.
Commemoração no descobrimento da America.
Elencho dos livros, mapas, etc. enviados a
secção portuguesa da Exposição de Madrid.
Lisboa, 1892. 20 p.   (3314
   Cited in Reis, item 142, with Joaquim de
Araujo as author. Another edition cited by
the Library of Congress with subtitle Cata-
logo da Secção maritima portugueza na Expo-
sição de Madrid en 1892. (1892, 34 p.)

UNITES STATES

AMERICAN Library Association, Chicago. Latin
American books; a check list of an exhibit
sponsored by the American Library Association, 1939 and 1940. Chicago, 1940.
23 p.   (3315

BROWN University. John Carter Brown Library.
The British West Indies; an exhibition of
books, maps, and prints opened at the annual
meeting of the Associates of the John Carter Brown Library, May 12, 1961.
[16] p.   (3316
   Cited in Current Caribbean bibliography,
1959/1961.

-----. In retrospect, 1923-1949. An exhibition commemorating twenty-six years of service. Providence, 1949. 40 p.   (3317
   Catalog with annotations of 113 items,
many relative to Latin America. Compilation
by Lawrence C. Wroth.

CALIFORNIA. University. Bancroft Library.
México: ancient and modern, as represented
by a selection of works in the Bancroft Library. An exhibition celebrating the acquisition of the Silvestre Terrazas Collection. Berkeley, 1962. 95 p. (The Friends
of the Bancroft Library)   (3318

DECOUD, Diogène. Expos9io Internationale de
Chicago, 1893. Les sciences médicales dans
la République Argentine. Buenos Aires, Impr.
Européenne, 1893. 80, CLXV p.   (3319
   "Bibliographie argentina médicale": p. 78-
80 and Appendix: "Index bibliográfico,"
CLXV p.---Jones 680.

HENRY E. HUNTINGTON Library and Art Gallery,
San Marino, Calif. Mexican imprints, 1544-
1600, in the Huntington Library; an exhibition prepared and described by Henry R. Wagner. San Marino, 1939. 35 p.   (3320
   Jones 2240.

-----. Mexico in the sixteenth century; an
exhibition at the Huntington Library. San
Marino, 1938. 18 p.   (3321

INDIANA. University. Lilly Library. The Bernardo Mendel collection; an exhibit. Dedication of the Mendel Room, Lilly Library. April
15, 1964. Bloomington, Ind., 1964.
83 p.   (3322
   Volume describes 104 items related primarily to the discovery of the New World, the
Spanish conquest, and the independence movements in Latin America. Descriptive notes
written by Cecil K. Byrd, Douglas G. Parson-
age, Otto H. Ranschburg, and Richard B.
Reed. The Mendel Collection contains over
30,000 items.

INTER-AMERICAN Seminar on Vocational Education,
College Park, Maryland, 1952. Catálogo de
la exposición de textos de educación vocacional. Washington, D.C., Unión Panamericana, 1953. 41 p. (VOC.EDU./Tecd.196) (3323
   Latin American countries are represented.
Compilation by Estellita Hart.

PAN AMERICAN UNION. Catalog of the Second Pan
American Book Exposition [Hall of the Amer-
icas, May 11-June 6, 1947] Washington, D.
C., 1947. 102, [20] p.   (3324

TEXAS. University. Library. An exhibit
commemorating the one hundredth anniversary
of the Constitution of 1857 of the Republic
of Mexico, by Nettie Lee Benson. Austin,
1957. 4 p.   (3325
   Cited in Yang.

URUGUAY

BRAZIL. Ministério da Educação e Saude. Exposição do livro brasileiro em Montevideo.
Catalogo. Rio de Janeiro, 1939.
117 p.   (3326
   Cited in Reis, item 576.

IBAÑEZ, Roberto. Originales y documentos de
Zorrilla de San Martín. [Exposición. 28
de dic. 1955-5 de en. 1956, Salón de Actos

IBAÑEZ, Roberto. Originales... (Cont.)
del Teatro Solís. Indice crítico] Montevideo, Ministerio de Instrucción Pública y
Previsión Social, Instituto Nacional de Investigaciones y Archivos Literarios, 1955.
102 p.   (3327

URUGUAY. Biblioteca Nacional. Exposición Francisco Acuña de Figueroa; manuscritos, impresos, piezas iconográficas y bibliografía.
[Montevideo] Comisión Nacional de Homenaje,
1941. 29 p. mimeogr.   (3328
    Cited in Musso 264.

-----. -----. Exposición Goethe; organizada
por la Biblioteca Nacional, Montevideo 14-25
de noviembre de 1949. Amigos del Arte...
Montevideo [Antuña Yarzal] 1949.
24 p.   (3329
    Cited in Musso 267, with note that 122
titles were included.

-----. -----. Exposición Isidoro de María;
centenario del primer ensayo biográfico sobre Artigas. Montevideo, 1960.
24 p.   (3330
    Cited in HLAS, 26, item 1185.

-----. -----. Exposición Pedro Figari; centenario de su nacimiento, 1861-1961. Montevideo, Biblioteca Nacional, 1961.
51 p.   (3331
    Cited in Musso 266.

-----. Ministerio de Instrucción Pública y
Previsión Social. Comisión de Investigaciones Literarias. Originales y documentos de
José Enrique Rodó; exposición inaugurada el
19 de diciembre de 1947. Montevideo, 1947.
pages unnumbered.   (3332
    Cited in Musso 285.

-----. Universidad. Facultad de Humanidades
y Ciencias. Biblioteca. Catálogo de la exposición del libro del S. XVIII. Montevideo,
1955. 72 p. mimeogr.   (3333

-----. -----. Facultad de Medicina. Exposición de actividades científicas y extra-cien-
tíficas de los médicos del país. [Montevi-
deo, Impr. Rosgal] 1939. 32 p.   (3334
    Pamphlet largely devoted to a listing of
medical journals, and theses by years, 1832-
1937, displayed on the occasion of the 64th
anniversary of the founding of the School
of Medicine.

VENEZUELA

BANCO de la República, Bogotá. Contribución
al Primer Festival del Libro de América que
se celebrará en Caracas - Ciudad Universitaria - del 15 al 30 de noviembre de 1956.
Bogotá, Impr. del Banco de la República,

BANCO de la República, Bogotá... (Cont.)
1956. 95 p.   (3334a
    Contains a listing of Colombian publications
printed during the first half of the XX Century. Cited in Giraldo Jaramillo, p. 36.

CARACAS. Exposición Bibliográfica sobre Caracas, 1956. Catálogo de la primera Exposición Bibliográfica sobre Caracas, organizada
como uno de los actos conmemorativos del 389.
aniversario de la fundación de la ciudad de
Santiago de León de Caracas, 25 de julio de
1956. Caracas, Consejo Municipal del Distrito Federal, 1956. 117 p.   (3335

-----. Exposición Bibliográfica sobre Caracas,
2a., 1957. Guía de la II Exposición Bibliográfica sobre Caracas. [Caracas] Consejo
Municipal del Distrito Federal [1957]
31 p.   (3336

-----. Exposición del Libro Ecuatoriano. Catálogo ... presentado en Caracas por el escritor Jorge Guerrero con los auspicios del Ministerio de Educacion Nacional. Caracas, Escuela Técnica Industrial, 1942. 21 p. (3337
    Cited in Anuario bibliográfico venezolano,
1942, item 124.

-----. Exposición del Libro Venezolano, 2a,
1940. Catálogo. Prólogo de Pedro Grases.
Caracas, Tip. Americana, 1942. xxxii, 85
[2] p.   (3338

-----. -----. Segunda exposición del Libro
Venezolano, 29 de noviembre-17 de diciembre,
1940. Caracas, Tip. Americana, 1940.
23 p.   (3339
    Lists 298 titles covering period, 1806-
1830.

-----. Feria del Libro Venezolano, 4a., 1943.
Catálogo de Venta. [1943] 12 p.   (3340
    Cited in Anuario bibliográfico venezolano,
1943, item 256.

CENTRO Venezolano-Americano, Caracas. Lista
de obras de escritoras venezolanas exhibi-
das en el Centro Venezolano-Americano.
[Caracas] 1950 [8] p.   (3342
    Cited in Anuario bibliográfico venezolano,
1949/1954, item 880.

COLOMBIA. Embajada. Venezuela. Libros y
autores colombianos; Biblioteca de la Embajada de Colombia. [Caracas, Edit. "Elite",
1943] 217 p.   (3343
    Catalog of the exhibition of Colombian
books, opened in Caracas on Feb. 13, 1943.
Cited in Anuario bibliográfico venezolano,
1943, item 197.

CONGRESO Internacional de Sociedades Bolivia-
rianas, 1o., Caracas, 1960. Catálogo de la
exposición bibliográfica bolivariana, orga-

CONGRESO Internacional .... (Cont.)
nizada en ocasión del Primer Congreso Internacional de Sociedades Bolivarianas, por Pedro Grases. Caracas, Impr. Nacional, 1962.
80 p. (Ediciones de la Sociedad Bolivariana
de Venezuela)   (3344

INSTITUTO Cultural Venezolano-Británico, Caracas. Exposición del libro inglés, enero-fe-
brero de 1945. [Caracas, 1945] 21 p.
mimeogr.   (3345
   Cited in Anuario bibliográfico venezolano,
1945, item 339.

-----. Exposición ilustrativa de la contribucion de la comunidad británica a la agrono-
mia tropical y de otras zonas. [Caracas,
Edit. "Elite"] 1946. 158 p.   (3346
   Contains "Lista de revistas y libros ex-
puestos" and "Bibliografía veterinaria".
Cited in Anuario bibliográfico venezolano,
1946, item 262.

LOPEZ DE SAGREDO Y BRU, José. Reseña de las
obras presentadas en la Primera Exposición
del Libro Zuliano, 1944. [Maracaibo, 1954]
44 p. mimeogr.   (3347
   Cited in Anuario bibliográfico venezolano,
1949-1954, item 2150.

PAN AMERICAN Institute of Geography and History. Fourth General Assembly, Caracas, 1946.
Catálogo de la exposición de libros de geografía e historia de Venezuela. Caracas,
1946. 246 p. mimeogr.   (3348
   Lists 1691 titles. Prepared by the National Library.

VENEZUELA. Biblioteca Nacional. Catálogo de
la Exposición de libros bolivarianos, organizada con motivo del centenario del tras-
lado de los restos del Libertador a Caracas.
16 de diciembre de 1942-20 de enero de 1943.
Caracas, Artes Graficas, 1943.
237 p.   (3349

FINANCE

GENERAL

BUENOS AIRES. Universidad. Instituto de Economia Bancaria. Bibliografía bancaria por
autores. Buenos Aires, 1936- . v.1- . (3350
   Jones 636. Vol. 7 (270 p.) appeared in
1959. DPU collection v. 1-7.

BULLEJOS, José. Bibliografía monetaria y bancaria de los países subdesarrollados, America Latina y México, 1943-1958. México,
D.F., 1959. 62 p. (Banco de México.
Depto. de Estudios Económicos. Serie de
bibliografías especiales, 3)   (3351

MEXICO. Universidad Nacional. Escuela Nacional de Economía. Bibliography of foreign investments in Latin America. [Mexico,
1955] 13 p. mimeogr.   (3352
   "The major part of this bibliography was
taken from Investigación Económica, quarterly publication of the Escuela Nacional
de Economía, Universidad Nacional Autónoma
de México, first quarter 1955. Other references were compiled in the Division of
Economic Research, Pan American Union,
Washington, D.C., 1955".

PAN AMERICAN UNION. Division of Economic
Research. References and sources of information pertaining to investments in
Latin America. [Washington, D.C., 1948]
4 p.   (3353

STEWART, Charles F., and SIMMONS, George B.
A bibliography of international business.
N.Y., Columbia Univ. Pr., 1964.

STEWART, Charles F., and SIMMONS... (Cont.)
603 p.   (3354
   Latin America, general and by regions,
p. 370-93.

WINIZKY, Ignacio. Cheque, guía bibliográfica
e índice legislativo. [Buenos Aires] Universidad de Buenos Aires, Facultad de Derecho y Ciencias Sociales, 1936. 202 [24] p.
(Guias bibliográficas del Seminario de Ciencias Jurídicas y Sociales, 1)   (3355
   Jones 542a.

-----. Letra de cambio; guía bibliográfica
(con la traducción de las partes pertinentes
al alemán, francés, inglés e italiano)
Buenos Aires, 1940. 420 p. (Guías bibliográficas del Seminario de Ciencias Jurídicas
y Sociales, 2)   (3356
   Classified with indexes of subjects,
authors, reviews, etc.---Jones 542b.

ARGENTINA

BANCO Central de la República Argentina. Buenos Aires. Biblioteca y Museo Numismático.
Bibliografía bancaria argentina (Edicion
provisional). Buenos Aires, 1951. 163 p.
(Serie Bibliografías, 1)
   Cited in Catálogo, Instituto Bibliotecológico, item 551.

ESTEVEZ, Alfredo. La literatura sobre el
Banco Central de la República Argentina,
1935-1946. Prologo por el profesor Dr.
Pedro J. Baiocco. Buenos Aires, Ministerio

ESTEVEZ, Alfredo. La literatura... (Cont.)
de Educación, Universidad de Buenos Aires,
Facultad de Ciencias Económicas, 1954.
223 p.   (3358
   The author announces a second part to
this work under the title: "El Banco Central nacionalizado" (Prólogo, p. 9).

WILLIAMS, John Henry. Argentina international
trade under inconvertible paper money, 1880-
1900. Cambridge, Harvard Univ. Pr., 1920.
282 p. (Harvard economic studies, v.
22)   (3359
   Bibliography: p. 263-71.---Jones 885.

BOLIVIA

MARSH, Margaret Charlotte. The bankers in Bolivia, a study in American foreign invest-
ment. New York, Vanguard Pr., 1928.
233 p.   (3360
   Bibliography: p. 179-98.---Jones 922.

BRAZIL

SOMBRA, Severino. Historia monetária do Brasil colonial; ed. rev. e aum. Rio de Janeiro, Laemmert, 1938. 430 p.   (3361
   Includes a calendar of documents referring
to the subject.---Jones 1202.

CHILE

CHILE. Dirección de Contabilidad. Resumen
de la hacienda pública de Chile. Summary
of the finances of Chile. Desde la independencia hasta 1900. Editado en castellano e inglés por la Dirección Jeneral de Contabilidad, 1901. From the independence to
1900; pub. in Spanish and English by the
Accountant General's Department. [Santia-
go] 1901. 757 p.   (3362
   Prepared for the Pan American Exposition
1901.
   "A Chilean bibliography of the national
finances": 64 p. at end.---Jones 1427.

FETTER, Frank Whitson. Monetary inflation
in Chile. Princeton, Univ. Pr., 1931.
213 p.   (3363
   Bibliography: p. 197-205.---Jones 1480.

MOLINA A., Evaristo. Ensayo bibliografico
chileno sobre la hacienda pública. Santiago, Impr. Nacional, 1901. 64 p.   (3364
   A list of the works on public finance
found in Briseño's Estadística bibliográ-
gráfica, Toro y Melo's Catálogo and the
Anuario de la prensa chilena (Cf. Laval)
---Jones 1550.

WAGEMANN, Ernst Friedrich. Die wirtschaftsver-
fassung der Republik Chile; zur entwicklungs-
geschichte der geldwirtschaft und der papier-
währung. München und Leipzig, Duncker &
Humblot, 1913. 253 p.   (3365
   "Quellen und literatur": p. 238-46.---
Jones 1661.

COLOMBIA

RIPPY, James Fred. The capitalists in Colombia. New York, The Vanguard Pr., 1931.
256 p.   (3366
   Bibliography: p. 235-41.---Jones 1767.

CUBA

CUBA. Congreso. Cámara de Representantes.
Biblioteca. Bibliografía sobre bancos y
crédito, obras que se hallan en la Biblioteca. Edición preliminar. Habana, Impr.
"El Siglo XX," 1921. 59 p.   (3367
   Prepared by Luis Marino Pérez.---Jones
1806.

MEXICO

BANCO de México. Biblioteca. Inversiones
extranjeras, 1940-1961. México, D.F., 1962.
41 p. (Banco de México, Departamento de
Estudios Económicos. Ser. de bibliografías
especiales, no. 4)   (3368

GLONER, Prosper. Les finances des Etats-Unis
Mexicains d'apres les documents officiels.
Berlin, Puttkammer & Mühlbrecht, 1896.
703 p.   (3369
   Bibliographie: p. 683-91.
   Contains a list of Memorias de la Secre-
taría de Hacienda y Crédito Público.---
Jones 2208.

MENDOZA, Salvador. Las finanzas de la nueva
era. México, D.F., "Cultura", 1931.
145 p.   (3370
   Bibliografía: p. 113-24.---Jones 2340.

MEXICO. Ministerio de Hacienda y Crédito Público. Memoria, correspondiente al cuadra-
gésimoquinto año económico. Presentada por
el Secretario de Hacienda al Congreso de la
Unión el 16 de setiembre de 1870. México,
Impr. del Gobierno, 1870. 1075 p.   (3371
   "Catálogo de los volúmenes que se han exa-
minado": p. 1061-75.---Jones 2363.

PAN AMERICAN UNION. Division of Economic
Research. Selected references pertaining
to devaluation of the Mexican peso. [Wash-
ington, D.C., 1948] 2 p.   (3372

NICARAGUA

HILL, Roscoe R. Fiscal intervention in Nicaragua. New York, 1933. 117 p.   (3373
Bibliography: p. 115-17.---Jones 1337.

VENEZUELA

VENEZUELA. Ministerio de Hacienda. Bosquejo
historico de la vida fiscal de Venezuela.

VENEZUELA. Ministerio de Hacienda... (Cont.)
Caracas, Tip. Vargas, 1924. 167 p.   (3374
Bibliografía: p. 67-163 by Manuel S. Sán-
chez.---Jones 2969.

------. ------. Historical sketch of the fis-
cal life of Venezuela. Caracas, Vargas Lit.
& Print. Off., 1925. 168 p.   (3375
Bibliography, 1830-1894: p. 65-163.---
Jones 2970.

FOLKLORE

GENERAL

BOGGS, Ralph Steel. Bibliography of Latin
American folklore. New York, The H. W.
Wilson Co., 1940. 109 p. (Inter-American
Bibliographical and Library Association.
Publications, ser. 1, v. 5)   (3376
A classified list with frequent notes
including bibliographical data, numbered
1 to 643, by author, single numbers often
covering several titles.---Jones 64a.

-----. Folklore bibliography for 1942.
[1943] p. 13-73.   (3377
Reprinted from the Southern folklore
quarterly, v. 7, no. 1, 1943.

CAMPA, Arthur Leon. A bibliography of Spanish folk-lore in New Mexico. Albuquerque,
1930. 28 p. (The University of New Mexico bulletin. Language ser., v. 2,
no. 3)   (3378
Jones 2111.

COLLUCIO, Félix. Folkloristas e institucio-
nes folklóricas del mundo. Buenos Aires,
El Ateneo [1951] 155 p.   (3379
Bio-bibliographical information.

GUICHOT Y SIERRA, Alejandro. Noticia histórica del folklore, orígenes en todos los
países hasta 1890, desarrollo en España
hasta 1921. Sevilla, Hijos de G. Alvarez,
1922. 256 p.   (3380
Jones 181.

LEHMANN NITSCHE, Robert. Adivinanzas rioplatenses. Buenos Aires, Impr. de Coni y Hermanos, 1911. 496 p.   (3381
Jones 749b. "Bibliografía", p. 405.

OCAMPO JIMENEZ, Arturo. Bibliografía sobre
temas de navidad. Medellín, Universidad
de Antioquia, Biblioteca General, 1963.
mimeogr.   (3382
Cited in Peraza Fichas, t. 7, item 619.

PAN AMERICAN UNION. Division of Intellectual
Cooperation. Latin American costumes.
[Washington, D.C., 1941?] 8 p.
mimeogr.   (3383

-----. Latin American costumes; bibliographical
references. Sources of costume dolls and
illustrations. Washington, D.C., 1944. 16 p.
mimeogr.   (3384

-----. -----. Revised ed. 1945. 15 p.
mimeogr.   (3385

SIMMONS, Merle Edwin. A bibliography of the
romance and related forms in Spanish America.
Bloomington, Indiana Univ. Pr., 1963. 396 p.
(Indiana. University. Folklore ser.,
no. 18)   (3386
Contains 2108 entries.

VALLE, Rafael Heliodoro. El folklore en la literatura de Centro América. (Journal of American folklore, New York, v. 36, p. 105-34,
1923)   (3387
Bibliografía del folklore centroamericano:
p. 110-34.---Jones 1260a.

VOLKSKUNDLICHE bibliographie für das jahr 1917- .
Im auftrage des Verbandes deutscher vereine
für volkskunde herausgegeben... Berlin und
Leipzig, W. de Gruyter & Co., 192- .   (3388
Editor: Eduard Hoffmann-Krayer. Volkskundliche bibliographie 1917-1920 supersedes Die
volkskundliche literatur des jahres 1911
(Leipzig, 1913) which, in turn, was published
in continuation of the Volkskundliche zeit-
schriftenschau, 1903-1905 published in Hes-
sische blätter für volkskunde, v. 1-5, 1902-
1906.---Jones 521.

ARGENTINA

BECCO, Horacio Jorge. Bibliografía argentina
actual relacionada con el Congreso Internacional de Folklore, 1958-1960. Buenos Aires,
1960. 4 p. (Congreso Internacional de Folklore, Buenos Aires, 1960, Doc. 171)   (3388a

BECCO, Horacio Jorge. Contribución a la bibliografía folklórica argentina. Buenos Aires, 1960. 11 p. (Congreso Internacional
de Folklore, Buenos Aires, 1960.
Doc. 144)   (3388b

BUENOS AIRES. Universidad. Instituto de Literatura Argentina. Catálogo de la colección de folklore donada por el Consejo Nacional de Educación. Buenos Aires, Impr. de
la Universidad, 1925. 186 p.   (3389
   Includes "volumes by provinces listing ms.
materials sent in to the archive by school
teachers" (Boggs).---Jones 662.

CHERTUDI, Susana. El cuento folklórico y literario regional. Buenos Aires, 1962.
35 p.   (3390
   (Bibliografía argentina de artes y letras;
compilaciones especiales, no. 16)

CORTAZAR, Augusto Raúl, and DELEPIANE CALCENA,
Carlos. Contribución a la bibliografía
folklórica argentina, 1956-1960. Buenos Aires, Dirección General de Cultura [1961]
(Comisión Internacional Permanente de Folklore, no. 3)   (3391
   Cited in Boletín de adquisiciones, Medellín, jul. 1963. Similar title also in
HLAS, 23, item 713.

CORTAZAR, Augusto Raúl. Guía bibliográfica
del folklore argentina; primera contribución. Buenos Aires, Impr. de la Universidad, 1942. 291 p. (Universidad de Buenos
Aires, Facultad de Filosofía y Letras, Instituto de Literatura Argentina; Sección de
bibliografía, t. 1, no. 1)   (3392

BRAZIL

CARNEIRO, Edison. O folclore nacional (1943-
1953). Rio de Janeiro, Edit. Souza, 1954.
73 p. (Ser. bibliografica de estudos brasileiros, 2)   (3393

GORHAM, Rex. The folkways of Brazil; a bib-
liography; edit. by Karl Brown. N. Y., New
York Public Library, 1944. 67 p.   (3394
   Reprinted with additions and corrections
from the Bulletin of the New York Public
Library, Apr., Jul. 1943 and Apr., May 1944.

MAGALHÃES, Basilio de. O folclore no Brasil.
Rio de Janeiro, Livraria Quaresma, 1928.
332 p.   (3395
   Includes bibliographical data.---Jones
1087. Another edition in 1939.

ORICO, Oswaldo. Os mythos amerindios, sobrevi-
vencias na tradição e na literatura brasileira. Rio, São Paulo, Editora Limitada, 1929.
142 p.   (3396
   Bibliographia: p. 137-42.---Jones 1121.

CHILE

PEREIRA SALAS, Eugenio. Guía bibliográfica para el estudio del folklore chileno. [Santia-
go de Chile] Instituto de Investigaciones Musicales, Universidad de Chile [1952]
112 p.   (3397
   Reprinted from Los Archivos del folklore
chileno, Instituto "Ramón A. Laval", Fasc. 4,
1952.

VICUÑA CIFUENTES, Julio. Mitos y supersticio-
nes recogidos de la tradición oral chilena.
Santiago, Impr. Universitaria, 1915. XX,
342 p.   (3398
   Bibliografía: p. XIII-XX.---Jones 1653.

CUBA

TRELLES Y GOVIN, Carlos Manuel. Noticias bibliográficas acerca del folklore cubano.
(Archivos del folklore cubano, La Habana,
t. 1, p. 103-11; t. 2, p. 137-58, 1924-
1926)   (3399
   Lists some 130 works.---Jones 1929.

MEXICO

BOGGS, Ralph Steele. Bibliografía del folklore
mexicano. México, D.F., Instituto Panamericano de Geografía e Historia, 1939.
121 p.   (3400
   Issued as an appendix to Boletín bibliográfico de antropología americana, v. 3, no. 3,
1939. Lists 1,323 items.---Jones 2091.

CISNEROS, María Guadalupe. De la literatura jalisciense; el folklore literario musical; Ar-
cadio Zúñiga y Tejeda; algunos aspectos del
teatro. México, D.F., 1933. 133 p. (3401
   Jones 2131.

ECHANIZ, Guillermo M., Librería, México, D.F.
Clasificación decimal Dewey aplicada a la bibliografía mexicana. México, D.F., Librería
Anticuaria "México en Libros" G. M. Echániz,
1947. v. 1. (unpaged)   (3402
   Vol. 1 contains bibliography of articles
which appeared in Mexican folkways, 1925-1937,
each entry under appropriate Dewey classification numbers.

SPENCE, Lewis. The gods of Mexico. London, T.
F. Unwin, [1922] 388 p.   (3403
   Bibliography: p. 371-81.---Jones 2517.

-----. The myths of Mexico and Peru. New York,
Farrar & Rinehart, 1931. 366 p.   (3404
   Bibliography: p. 335-39.---Jones 2518.

PERU

ANGELES CABALLERO, César Augusto. Bibliografía del folklore peruano. (Primera contribución) Lima, 1952. 23 p.   (3405

-----. -----. Lima [Edit. San Marcos] 1958.
64 p.   (3406
Reprinted from Boletín bibliográfico,
Universidad Mayor de San Marcos, Lima,
v. 28.

ARGUEDAS, José María. Bibliografía del
folklore peruano. México, D.F., 1960.
186 p. (Instituto Panamericano de Geografía e Historia, Publ., no. 230)   (3407
Issued also as publication 92 of the Commission on History and no. 1 of the Committee on Folklore.

VENEZUELA

TAMAYO, Francisco. Introducción y bibliografía del folklore del Estado Lara. Barquisi-
meto, Venezuela, Edit. Continente [1952?]
p. 95-109.   (3408
Reprinted from Guía económica y social del
estado Lara, 1949-1954. Cited in Anuario bibliográfico venezolano, 1949/1954, item
3361.

WEST INDIES

WILLIAMS, Joseph John. Voodoos and obeahs,
phases of West Indian witchcraft. New York,
Dial Pr., 1932. 257 p.   (3409
Bibliography: p. 237-48.---Jones 3015.

GENEALOGY

AMUNATEGUI Y SOLAR, Domingo. La sociedad chilena del siglo XVIII, mayorazgos i títulos
de Castilla; memoria histórica presentada
a la Universidad de Chile. Santiago de Chile, Impr. Barcelona, 1901-1904. 3 v.   (3410
"Se compone de una serie de monografías de
familias chilenas, de todas aquellas que en
nuestra sociedad del siglo XVIII podían os-
tentar un título de Castilla o enorgullecer-
se con la posesión de un mayorazgo en Chile".
---Jones 1389.
Contains copious bibliographical footnotes.

CARVALHO, Mario Teixeira de. Nobiliario sul-
riograndense. Porto Alegre, Barcellos, Bertaso & Cia., 1937. 370 p.   (3411
"Fontes principaes" given for each family.
---Jones 1213.

CUADRA GORMAZ, Guillermo de la. Los de Larraín
en Chile; trabajo publicado en la Revista chilena de historia y geografía. Santiago de
Chile, Impr. Universitaria, 1917.
19 p.   (3412
Jones 1441.
Contains footnote references to sources.

-----. Origen de doscientas familias coloniales de Santiago. Santiago de Chile, Impr.
Universitaria, 1914. 186 p.   (3413
"Publicado en el no. 15-18 de la Revista
chilena de historia y geografía".---Jones
1442. Sources are the Archivo de Escribanos
in the National Library and the works of
Tomás Thayer Ojeda. Citations given in
parentheses in text.

ESPEJO, Juan Luis. Nobiliario de la antigua
capitanía general de Chile. Santiago de Chile, Impr. Universitaria, 1917-1921.

ESPEJO, Juan Luis. Nobiliario de la... (Cont.)
2 v.   (3414
"Ensayo bibliográfico": v. 1, p. 291-96.
Jones 1469.

LORD, Robert Archibald. Contribution toward a
bibliography of the O'Higgins family in America. Durham, N.C., 1932. p. 107-38.   (3415
Reprinted from the Hispanic American historical review, v. 12, no. 1, Feb., 1932.---Jones
265, 1520.

-----. Ensayo de una bibliografía sobre la familia O'Higgins en América. (Boletín de la
Biblioteca Nacional, Santiago de Chile, año 6,
p. 58-63, 74-9, 93-5, 106-11, 123-25,
1935)   (3416
Jones 1521.

MOYA, Salvador de. Bibliografía heráldico-
genealógica; catálogo de autores ibero-ameri-
canos. São Paulo, Edição da Revista Genealógica Brasileira [1955] 224 p. (Biblioteca
genealógica latina, 4)   (3416a
Cited in Boletín bibliográfico, Biblioteca
Nacional, Rio de Janeiro, v. 5, t. 2, p. 297,
1955.

-----. Catalogo de auctores genealogicos.
(Revista do Arquivo Municipal, São Paulo.
v. 38, p. 81-160, 1937)   (3417
Jones 1106.

-----. Diccionario bibliografico de apelidos
luso-brasileiros. (Revista do Arquivo Municipal, São Paulo, v. 60, p. 175-204; v. 61,
p. 53-76; v. 62, p. 263-302, 1939)   (3418
A-C only.---Jones 1106a.

GEOGRAPHY

GENERAL

ANGHIERA, Pietro Martire d'. Mondo nuovo (De
orbe novo), a cura di Temistocle Celotti
libri tradotti e collegati, con introduzione
e note. Milano, Edizioni "Alpes", 1930.
388 p. (Viaggi e scoperte di navigatori ed
esploratori italiani, 16)   (3419
   Bibliografía: p. 371-74.---Jones 15.

BIBLIOGRAPHIE géographique internationale.
25/29- . Bibliographie annuelle, Paris, A.
Colin, 1921- . v. 1- .   (3420
   Bibliographies for the years 1891 to 1913/
1914 were issued with Annales de géographie.
(1891-1892 are included in v. 1-2 of the
Annales. Beginning with 1893 the bibliographies have separate title-pages and paging.
The volumes from 1899-1913/1914 have title:
Bibliographie géographique annuelle.)
   Vols. 25/29 cover years 1915/1919; v. 30/
31 cover years 1920-1921. Beginning with
v. 32 (1922) issued annually.
   Published with collaboration of the American Geographical Society, v. 33- ; of the
Comitato Geografico Nazionale Italiano and
the Royal Geographical Society of London,
v. 34- ; of the Société Royale de Géographie
d'Egypte, v. 36- ; of the Société Belge d'Etudes Géographiques, v. 40- ; and with the
cooperation of the Fédération des Sociétés
Françaises de Sciences Natirelles, v. 33- .
---Jones 58.

CARLSON, Fred Albert. Geography of Latin
America. New York, Prentice-Hall, 1936.
642 p.   (3421
   Includes bibliographies.---Jones 84.

-----. Rev. ed. 1943. xxiii, 566 p. (3422

-----. 3d ed. 1952. 569 p.   (3423

COX, Edward Godfrey. A reference guide to the
literature of travel, including voyages,
geographical descriptions, adventures, ship-
wrecks and expeditions. Vol. 2, The New
World. Seattle, 1938. 591 p. (The University of Washington. Publ. in language and
literature)   (3424
   Includes sections on West Indies, Mexico,
Central America and South America; arrangement is chronological under each section,
according to date of publication.---Jones
116.

HILLS, Theo L. A select annotated bibliography of the humid tropics; une bibliographie
choisie et annotée des régions tropicales
humides. Montréal, Quebec, Geography Department, McGill University, 1960. 238 p. (3425
   Prepared by the Special Commission on the
Humid Tropics of the International Geographi-

HILLS, Theo L. A select ... (Cont.)
cal Union.

MAI, Richard. Auslanddeutsche quellenkunde,
1924-1933. In verbindung mit dem Volksbund
für das deutschtum im ausland herausgegeben
von dr. Emil Clemens Scherer. Berlin, Weid-
mann, 1936. 504 p.   (3426
   Classified under each country, with author
index.---Jones 276.

PAN AMERICAN UNION. Bibliography: Jews in
Latin America. [Washington, D.C.,
1939] 1 p.   (3427
   Caption title.

-----. Columbus Memorial Library. Books and
magazine articles on geography in the
Columbus Memorial Library. Washington, D.C.,
[1934] 72 p. (Bibliographic ser.,
no. 13)   (3428

-----. -----. Libros y artículos sobre geografía existentes en la Biblioteca Colón de
la Unión Panamericana, Washington, D.C.,
[1934] 72 p. (Bibliographic ser., no. 13)
mimeogr.   (3429

REIN, Adolf. Die europäische ausbreitung über
die erde. Wildpark-Potsdam, Akademische
verlagsgesellschaft Athenaion, 1931.
406 p.   (3430
   "Literaturhinweise": p. 394-98.---Jones
391.

RUBIO Y MUÑOZ-BOCANEGRA, Angel. Bibliografía
de geografía urbana de América. Rio de Janeiro, Instituto Panamericano de Geografía
e Historia, Comissão de Geografia, 1961.
229 p. (Coleção Geografía urbana, publ.
no. 1)   (3431
   Issued as Publication no. 220 of the Pan
American Institute of Geography and History.

SCHMIEDER, Oscar. Länderkunde Mittelamerikas,
Westindien, Mexico und Zentralamerika.
Leipzig und Wien, F. Deuticke, 1934. 194 p.
(Enzyklopädie der erdkunde)   (3432
   Literatur: p. 158-71.---Jones 1249.

SIVERS, Jegór von. Ueber Madeira und die
Antillen nach Mittelamerika. Reisedenkwür-
digkeiten und forschungen. Leipzig, C. F.
Fleischer, 1861. 388 p.   (3433
   "Schrften über die Antillen, Mittelamerika
und Neuspanien": p. 310-62.---Jones 448.

TIELE, Pieter Anton. Mémoire bibliographique
sur les journaux des navigateurs néerlandais
réimprimés dans les collections de de Bry et
de Hulsius, et dans les collections hollandaises du XVIIe siècle, et sur les anciennes
éditions hollandaises des journaux de naviga-

TIELE, Pieter Anton. Mémoire ... (Cont.)
teurs étrangers; la plupart en la possession
de Frederik Muller. Avec tables des voyages,
des editions et des matiéres. Amsterdam, F.
Muller, 1867. 372 p.   (3434
Jones 476.

TORRE REVELLO, José. Viajeros, relaciones,
cartas y memorias, siglos XVII, XVIII y primer decenio del XIX. (Academia Nacional de
la Historia. Historia de la nación argentina. Buenos Aires, 1938. t. 4 (primera sección), p. 545-85)   (3435
Jones 867h.

ZAHM, John Augustine. Following the conquistadores. New York and London, D. Appleton
and Co., 1910-1916. 3 v.   (3436
Vol. 1-2, written under the author's pseud.,
H. J. Mozans. Bibliography at end of each
volume.---Jones 548.

ANTARCTIC REGIONS

CHILE. Congreso. Biblioteca. Antártida.
Santiago, 1959. 7 p. (Ser. bibliografías,
no. 8)   (3437

DENUCE, Jean. Bibliographie antarctique.
Bruxelles, Hayex, Imprimeur de l'Académie
Royale de Belgique, 1913. 271 p.   (3437a

HAYTON, Robert D. National interests in Antarctica; an annotated bibliography. Washington, Govt. Print. Off., 1959 [i.e., 1960]
137 p.   (3438

U.S. NAVAL Photographic Interpretation Center.
Antarctic bibliography. Washington, D.C.,
Govt. Print. Off., 1951. 147 p. (Navaer
10-35-391)   (3438a

ARGENTINA

AMARAL INSIARTE, Alfredo. La Plata a través de
los viajeros, 1882-1912. [La Plata, Ministerio de Educación, 1959] 68 p.   (3438b

BESIO MORENO, Nicolás. Buenos Aires, puerto
del río de la Plata, capital de la Argentina;
estudio crítico de su población, 1536-1936.
Buenos Aires, 1939. 500 p.   (3439
"Notas bibliográficas" (p. 435-78) in
chronological order.---Jones 596a.

BILBAO, Manuel. Buenos Aires desde su fundación hasta nuestros días, especialmente el
periodo comprendido en los siglos XVIII y
XIX. Buenos Aires, Impr. de J. A. Alsina,
1902. 664 p.   (3440
Jones 601a.

DENIS, Pierre. La République Argentine; la
mise en valeur du pays. Paris, A. Colin,
1920. 299 p.   (3441
Bibliographie: p. 283-99. An English
translation was issued in London, 1922.---
Jones 681.

IBARGUREN, Carlos. El paisaje y el alma argentina; descripciones, cuentos y leyendas del
terruño; selección de Carlos Ibarguren, Antonio Aita y Pedro Juan Vignale. Buenos Aires, Comisión Argentina de Cooperación Intelectual, 1938. 392 p.   (3442
Bibliografía: p. 381-88.---Jones 727.

KÜHN, Franz Hermann. Argentinien; handbuch
zur physischen landeskunde. Breslau, F.
Hirt, 1927. 2 v.   (3443
Issued also in Spanish. Contains bibliographies.---Jones 734.

-----. Fundamentos de fisiografía argentina.
Buenos Aires, P. Preusche, 1922.
217 p.   (3444
Contains bibliographies.---Jones 735.

-----. Primer ensayo de bibliografía sobre
exploraciones científicas y corográficas en
la provincia de Entre Ríos. (Anales de la
Facultad de Ciencias de la Educación, Paraná,
t. 1, p. 197-208, 1923)   (3445
Jones 736.

LYNCH ARRIBALZAGA, Enrique. Materiales para
una bibliografía del Chaco y Formosa. Resistencia, 1924.   (3446
Jones 921.

-----. -----. [Resistencia, Arg.] Universidad
Nacional del Nordeste, Departamento de Extensión Universitaria y Ampliación de Estudios,
1959. 51 p.   (3446a

MARTIN GRANIZO, León. Aportaciones bibliográficas. Viajeros y viajes de españoles, portugueses e hispanoamericanos. (Revista de
geografía colonial y mercantil, Madrid, t.
20, p. 275-92, 305-26, 369-96; t. 21, p. 5-
25, 81-101, 145-66, 1923-1924)   (3447
Jones 287.

NICHOLS, Madaline Wallis. The gaucho, cattle
hunter, cavalryman, ideal of romance. Durham, N. C., Duke Univ. Pr., 1942.
152 p.   (3448
Includes bibliography, annotated, of 1,431
items, p. 67-144.---Jones 793a.

OUTES, Félix Faustino. La determinación de
las fuentes de la geografía nacional...
Buenos Aires. 1921. 53 p. (Facultad de Fi-
losofía y Letras. Publ. de la Sección de
Geografía, no. 3)   (3449
Jones 804.

OUTES, Félix Faustino. Plan de agrupación sistemática de la bibliografía geográfica argentina. Buenos Aires, Impr. y casa editora "Coni", 1919. 173-200 p. (3450
"Publicado en los Anales de la Sociedad Científica Argentina," t. 88. A schedule of classification of Argentine geographical material.---Jones 806.

PAZ SOLDAN, Mariano Felipe. Diccionario geográfico estadístico nacional argentino. Buenos Aires, F. Lajouane, 1885. 485 p. (3451
"Biblioteca geográfica argentina": p. 457-77.---Jones 811.

ROHMEDER, Wilhelm, and SANTAMARINA, E. B. de. Bibliografía geográfica de Tucumán. [Tucumán, 1946] 126 p. (Tucumán. Universidad Nacional. Facultad de Filosofía y Letras. Instituto de Estudios Geográficos, Monografías, 8) (3452
Cited in Catálogo, Instituto Bibliotecologico, item 763.

ROSA OLMOS, Ramón. Bibliografía catamarqueña. Catamerca [Tall. Tip. del Diario "La Unión"] 1945. 59 p. (3452a

SANTOS GOMEZ, Susana E. Primera contribución para la bibliografía de viajeros a la Argentina. [Buenos Aires, Universidad de Buenos Aires, Instituto de la Producción] n.d. 50 p. (Publicaciones; ser. bibliográficas, 15) mimeogr. (3453
Includes 371 entries, showing locations.

SERRANO, Pedro Benjamín. Guía jeneral de la provincia de Corrientes, correspondiente al año 1910; homenaje al primer centenario de la independencia, 1810-1910. Corrientes, Tip. de T. Heinecke, 1910. 975 p. (3454
Third edition; 1st edition: Corrientes, 1903. "Monografía: breve noticia sobre trabajos escritos de correntinos [por Eudoro Vargas Gómez]": p. 194-207, 369-94.---Jones 842.

URIBURU, José Evaristo. La República Argentina a través de las obras de los escritores ingleses; compilación. Buenos Aires [Tall. Graf. Claridad] 1948. 211 p. (3454a

URIONDO, Oscar Adolfo. Bibliografía geográfica referente a la Republica Argentina; primera contribución. Buenos Aires, [Tall. Graf. "Junior"] 1964. 110 p. (3454b

WIENER, Charles. La République Argentine. Paris, Librairie Cerf, 1899. 677 p. (Ministère des Affaires Etrangères. Missions commerciales) (3455
Bibliographie: p. 641-61. Alphabetical by title with references principally to economic conditions.---Jones 884a.

BOLIVIA

CORTES, José Domingo. Bolivia; apuntes jeográficos, estadísticos, de costumbres, descriptivos e historicos. París, Tip. Lahure, 1875. 172 p. (3456
Bibliography: p. 156-68.---Jones 910.

PAN AMERICAN UNION. Columbus Memorial Library. Catalogue of books, pamphlets, periodicals and maps relating to the Republic of Bolivia in the Columbus Memorial Library. Washington, D.C., Govt. Print. Off., 1905. 23 p. (3457
Jones 927.

UGARTE, Ricardo. Datos para la bibliografía boliviana. La Paz, Impr. de "La Libertad" de E. Arzadum, 1878. 18 p. (3458
Cited in Abecía, Valentín, Adiciones a la Biblioteca Boliviana, no. 128.---Jones 942.

BRAZIL

ANNUARIO de Minas Geraes; chronologia mineira, govêrno civil e ecclesiástico, notas e informações, institutos de ensino ... chorographia ... historia, estatistica, variedades, letras, bibliographia. Bello Horizonte [impr. Official do Estado] 1906- . Anno 1- . (3459
Jones 957. Subtitle varies.

AVEZAC-MACAYA, Armand d'. Considérations géographiques sur l'histoire du Bresil; examen critique d'une nouvelle histoire génerale du Brésil récemment publiée en portugais à Madrid par M. Françõis-Adolphe de Varnhagen ... rapport fait à la Société de Géographie de Paris dans ses séances des 1er mai, 15 mai et 5 juin 1857. Paris, Impr. de L. Martinet, 1857. 271 p. (3460
Extrait du Bulletin de la Société de Géographie, août/oct. 1857. Bibliographie des histoires générales du Brésil: p. 149-56. Bibliographie des relations originales d'Americ Vespuce: p. 165-73. Les Décades de Pierre Martyr, et les collections de Venise, de Vicence, de Milan et de Bâle: p. 218-26. ---Jones 962.

BASSICHES, Bruno. Bibliografia dos livros, folhetos e artigos referentes a história dos judeus no Brasil, incluindo obras sôbre judaismo publicadas no Brasil. Rio de Janeiro, 1961. 70 p. mimeogr. (3461
Cited in Doria Menezes 102.

BERGER, Paulo. Bibliografia do Rio de Janeiro de viajantes e autores estrangeiros, 1531-1900. Rio de Janeiro, Livraria São José, 1964. 322 p. (3461a

BRANDENBURGER, Clemens. Neuerebrasilische
wissenschaftliche literatur. (Mitteilungen
des Deutsch-Südamerikanischen und Iberischen
Instituts in Köln, Suttgart und Berlin, heft
1-2, p. 49-61, 1920)   (3462
    Jones 982.

BRAZIL. Conselho Nacional de Geografia. Do-
cumentário amazônico; relação das contri-
buições bibliográficas, cartográficas e
aereofotográficas, existentes no Conselho
Nacional de Geografia, oferecida à Reunião
Preparatória da criação do "Instituto Internacional da Hiléia Amazônica", à realizar-se
em Belém, de 12 a 18 de agosto de 1947. Rio
de Janeiro, 1947. 79 p. mimeogr.   (3463

-----. -----. Manual bibliográfico da geografia paulista. São Paulo, 1957.
376 p.   (3464

CORNELIUS, Carl Gustav. Die Deutschen im bra-
silianischen wirtschaftsleben. Stuttgart,
Ausland und Heimat Verlags-Aktiengesellschaft,
1929. xii, 88 p.   (3465
    Literatur: p. x-xii.---Jones 1023.

CRULS, Gastão. A Amazonia que eu vi, Obidos-
Tumucumaque; prefacio de Roquette Pinto.
Rio de Janeiro, 1930. 362 p.   (3466
    Bibliographia: p. 343-62.---Jones 1026.

DIAS, Arthur. The Brazil of to-day; a book
of commercial, political and geographical
information on Brazil; impressions of
voyage, descriptive and picturesque data
about the principal cities, prominent men
and leading events of our days. Nivelles,
Lanneau & Desprèt [1907?] 628 p.   (3467
    "Translated from Portuguese into English
by Louis Raposo". Contains biobibliographical chapters: Inventors and men of
science; Thinkers and writers; Musicians,
painters and sculptors: p. 35-131.---
Jones 1027.

DICCIONARIO historico, geographico e ethnographico do Brasil. (Commemorativo do
primeiro centenario da independencia).
Rio de Janeiro, Impr. Nacional, 1922.
2 v.   (3468
    Jones 1029.
    Historia litteraria, v. 1, p. 1297-1550.
    Historia da imprensa, p. 1550-85.

FERREIRA, João Francisco. Elementos para
uma bibliografia sôbre o Rio Grande do
Sul. [Porto Alegre, Faculdade de Filosofia, Universidade do Rio Grande do Sul,
n.d.] 36 p.   (3469
    Reprinted from Fundamentos da cultura Rio-
Grandense primeira série (1954)

FUNDACÃO Getúlio Vargas. Rio de Janeiro. Centro de Estudos Sociais. Bibliografia sôbre o

FUNDAÇÃO Getúlio Vargas ... (Cont.)
estado da Bahia. [Rio de Janeiro, 1953]
50 p. mimeogr.   (3470
    Cited in Richardson, item 7203.

GALVÃO, Sebastião de Vasconcellos. Diccionario
chorographico, historico e estatistico de Pernambuco. Rio de Janeiro, Impr. Nacional,
1908-1910. 3 v.   (3471
    Useful for biographical information.---Jones
1221.
    Works cited in biographies. La Imprensa da
Recife: v. 3, p. 432-88, lists 1601 items.

GARCIA. Rodolpho. Bibliographia geographica
brasileira, organizada ... para ser apresen-
tada ao sexto Congresso de Geographia de Bello
Horizonte. Revista do Instituto Historico e
Geographico Brasileiro, Rio de Janeiro, 1921.
t. 85, v. 139, p. 5-105, 1921)   (3472
    Jones 1047.

GREENLEE, William Brooks. The voyage of Pedro
Alvares Cabral to Brazil and India from contemporary documents and narratives; translated with introduction and notes, by William
Brooks Greenlee. London, Printed for the
Hakluyt Society, 1938. 228 p. (Works issued
by the Hakluyt Society, 2d ser., no.
81)   (3473
    Bibliography: p. 203-12.---Jones 1052.

INSTITUTO Historico e Geographico Brasileiro,
Rio de Janeiro. Boletim; directoria, socios,
resumo historico, a Revista, publicações es-
peciaes. Rio de Janeiro, Impr. Nacional,
1925. 50 p.   (3474
    Jones 1062a.

JACKSON, William Vernon. Library guide for
Brazilian studies. Pittsburgh, Distributed
by the University of Pittsburgh Book Centers,
1964. 197 p.   (3475
    A preliminary version of this study was
submitted as Working paper no. 12 for the
Eighth Seminar on the Acquisition of Latin
American Library Materials, University of
Wisconsin, 1963. under title: American
library resources for Brazilian studies.

KUDER, Manfred. Die deutsch-brasilianische
literatur und das bodenttädigkeiutsgefühl der
deutschen volksgruppe in Brasilien. (Ibero-
Amerikanisches archiv. Berlin und Bonn,
v. 10, p. 394-494, 1937)   (3476
    "The best account thus far written in any
language on the cultural status of the Ger-
mans and their descendants in Brazil as
reflected in their literature." (Handb. Lat-
Am. Stud., 1937, p. 327)---Jones 1072.

MAACK, Reinhard. Die deutsche literatur ueber
die deutsche einwanderung und siedlung in
Suedbrasilien. Cambridge, Mass., Harvard
Univ. Pr., 1939. p. 399-417.   (3477

GEOGRAPHY

MAACK, Reinhard. Die deutsche ... (Cont.)
Jones 1082a. Reprinted from Handbook of
Latin American studies, 1938.

MACEDO, Roberto. Apontamentos para uma biblio-
grafia carioca. Rio de Janeiro, Edição do
Centro Carioca (Departmento Editorial) 1943.
112 p.   (3478
Publication authorized by the Serviço do
Patrimonio Histórico e Artístico Nacional.

MARCHANT, Alexander. Writings in English,
French, Italian and Portuguese concerning
the German colonies in southern Brazil.
Cambridge, Mass., Harvard Univ. Pr., 1939.
p. 418-31.   (3479
Jones 1095a. Reprinted from Handbook of
Latin American studies, 1938.

MORAES, Rubens Borba de, and BERRIEN, William.
Manual bibliográfico de estudos brasileiros.
Rio de Janeiro, Gráfica Editôra Souza, 1949.
xi, 895 p.   (3480

OAKENFULL, J. C. "Brazil", past, present and
future. London, J. Bale, Sons & Danielsson,
1919.   (3481
Bibliography: p. 794-805. First edition
published 1909.---Jones 1113.

OSCULATI, Gaetano. Esplorazione delle regioni
equatoriali lungo il Napo ed il fiume delle
Amazzoni: frammento di un viaggio fatto
nelle due Americhe negli anni 1846-1847-1848;
2. ed. cor. ed accresciuta, con carte topo-
grafiche, e coll' aggiunta di nuove tavole
rappresentanti costumi e vedute tolte dal
vero dallo stesso autore. Milano, Fratelli
Centenari e Comp., 1854. 344 p.   (3482
"Nota bibliografica commentata delle prin-
cipali opere da consultarsi sulle regioni
inaffiate dal rio delle Amazzoni ... per cura
di Ferdinando Denis": p. 321-33.---Jones
1121a.

PHILLIPS, Philip Lee. A list of books, maga-
zine articles, and maps relating to Brazil,
1800-1900. A supplement to the Handbook of
Brazil (1901) comp. by the Bureau of the
American Republics. Washington, D.C., Govt.
Print. Off., 1901. 145 p.   (3483
Jones 1143.

PIAZZA, Walter F. Nota prévia à bibliografia
para estudo do litoral catarinense. Florianópolis, Academia Catarinense de Letras,
1960. 16 p.   (3484
Cited in Revista do livro, 5(19):243, set.
1960.

SCHERRER, Joseph. Historish-geographischer
katalog für Brasilien (1500-1908). (Annaes
da Bibliotheca Nacional Rio de Janeiro,
v. 35, p. 313-418, 1916)   (3485
Includes Sach-register.---Jones 1192.

RIO DE JANEIRO. Universidade do Brasil. Cen-
tro de Pesquisas de Geografia do Brasil.
Bibliografia geográfica do Brasil, 1951.
Rio de Janeiro, 1956. (Ser. bibliográfica,
II: Geografia, publ. no. 1- .)   (3486
Latest received at DPU: Publ. 3, 1953,
published in 1960.

RIO DE JANEIRO e arredores, guia do viajante.
Rio de Janeiro, Guias do Brasil, 1939.
744 p.   (3487
Bibliography: p. 731-44.---Jones 1175a.

SCHAPPELLE, Benjamin Franklin. The German
element in Brazil, colonies and dialect.
Philadelphia, Americana Germanica Pr., 1917.
66 p. (Americana Germanica, no. 26)   (3488
Bibliography: p. 61-6.---Jones 1191.

SCHILLING, Getúlio. Evolução litteraria da
bibliographia Santamariense. [Santa Maria]
1941. 24 p.   (3489
Edição fóra de Commercio.

SOUZA, Bernardino José de. Dicionário da terra
e da gente do Brasil; 4. edição da Onomastica
geral da geografia brasileira. São Paulo,
Editôra Nacional, 1939. 433 p. (Biblioteca
pedagogica brasileira, ser. 5: Brasiliana,
v. 164)   (3490
Includes bibliography.---Jones 1203.

STRATEGIC index of the Americas. Preliminary
bibliography of Amazonia, compiled from the
Strategic index of the Americas. [Wash-
ington, D.C., 1942] 20 p. mimeogr.   (3491
Published in collaboration with the Coordinator of Inter-American affairs.

STUDART, Guilherme, barão de. Estrangeiros e
Ceará. (Revista trimensal do Instituto do
Ceará, Ceará-Fortaleza, t. 32, p. 191-274,
1918)   (3492
"Lista dos auctores e de suas obras tendo
referencia a ao Ceará:" p. 269-74.---Jones
1210.

TRÜBNER, Nicolas. Biblioteca brazilica.
Ancient and modern books relating to the
empire and the neighboring states. London,
1879.   (3493
Jones 1216.

U.S. Department of State. External Research
Division. Brazil: a selected bibliography.
[Washington, D.C.] 1964. 40 p. (External
research paper, 155)   (3494

-----. Operations Mission in Brazil. Amazonia, a selected bibliography on the Amazon
region in Brazil. [Washington, D.C.]
Public and Business Administration Division
[1956] 12 p. mimeogr.   (3495
The bibliography was compiled by Inéa Fonseca, Librarian of the Division of Public and

U.S. Operations Mission ... (Cont.)
Business Administration at the request of the
Mission Director.

BRITISH HONDURAS

BRITISH HONDURAS. Library Service. A bibliography of published material on British Hondu-
rass found in the National Collection, compiled by L. H. Bradley, L. G. Vernon, and A.
A. Dillet. Belize, 1960. 52 p.   (3496
   Cited in Current Carribean bibliography,
1959/1961.

U.S. Library of Congress. Division of bibliography. British Honduras; a bibliographical
list, compiled by Florence S. Hellman.
Washington, D.C., 1940. 21 p. typewritten.   (3497
   Cited in Yang.

CENTRAL AMERICA

INTERNATIONAL Bureau of the American republics.
A list of books, magazine articles, and maps
relating to Central America, including the
republics of Costa Rica, Guatemala, Honduras,
Nicaragua, and Salvador, 1800-1900. Prepared
by P. Lee Phillips. Washington, D.C., Govt.
Print. Off., 1902. 109 p.   (3498
   Jones 1234.

ROTHERY, Agnes. Central America and the Spanish Main. Boston, Houghton, Mifflin Co.,
1929. 221 p.   (3499
   Bibliography: p. 219-22.---Jones 1248.

U.S. Library of Congress. List of references
on Central America and Mexico (with special
reference to political, economic, social and
military conditions) Washington, D.C., 1922.
5 p.   (3500
   Cited in Yang.

CHILE

AUSTRALIA. Legation, Santiago, Chile. A list
of works dealing with Chile written in English. Santiago, 1949. 25 p.   (3501

CORPORACION de Fomento de la Producción (Chile)
Chile, a selected bibliography in English.
New York, 1964. 21 p.   (3502

EDWARDS, Agustín. Mi tierra; panorama, reminis-
cencias, escritores y folklore. Valparaíso,
Soc., Impr. y Lit. Universo, 1928.
393 p.   (3503
   Indice bibliográfico: p. 381-88.---Jones
1461.

EDWARDS, Agustín. My native land; panorama,
reminiscences, writers and folklore. London,
E. Benn, [1928] 430 p.   (3504
   Bibliographical index: p. 417-25.---Jones
1462.

FONDO Histórico y Bibliográfico José Toribio
Medina. Viajes relativos a Chile, traducidos y prologados por José Toribio Medina.
Ordenados y precedidos de unas Notas para
una bibliografía sobre viajeros relativos a
Chile, por Guillermo Feliú Cruz. Santiago
de Chile, 1962. 2 v.   (3505
   The "Notas para una bibliografía ..."
forms nearly half of Vol. 1. Each travel-
lers account in the two volumes, additionally, is introduced by bibliographical
references on the edition used by Medina.

MARTIN, Carl Edward. Landeskunde von Chile.
2. aufl. Hamburg, L. Friedrichsen & Co.,
1923. 786 p.   (3506
   Bibliographie: p. 750-57. First published in 1909.---Jones 1527.

MEDINA, José Toribio. Biblioteca hispanochilena (1523-1817). Santiago de Chile,
Impreso y grabado en casa del autor, 1897-
1899. 3 v.   (3507
   876 titles, arranged chronologically;
transcribed line for line, with references
to authorities and to libraries where copies
are to be found. Copious quotations and
critical and bibliographical notes.---
Jones 1536.

PHILLIPS, Philip Lee. A list of books, mag-
azine articles, and maps relating to Chile.
Comp. for the International Bureau of the
American Republics. Washington, D.C.,
Govt. Print. Off., 1903. 110 p.   (3508
   Jones 1565.

PICON-SALAS, Mariano, and FELIU CRUZ, Guillermo. Imágenes de Chile; vida y costumbres
chilenas en los siglos XVIII y XIX a través
de testimonios contemporáneos. Santiago
de Chile, Edit. Nascimento, 1933.
339 p.   (3509
   "Bibliografía de viajeros; notas para el
conocimiento de la vida chilena e hispano-
americana en los siglos XVIII y XIX":
p. 317-32. A second edition was issued in
1938.---Jones 1566.

RISO PATRON, Luis. Diccionario jeográfico de
Chile. Santiago, Impr. Universitaria, 1924.
xxiv, 958 p.   (3510
   Obras consultadas: p. vii-xii.---Jones
1588.

VEGA E., M. Album de la colonie française au
Chili. Santiago de Chili, Imprimerie Franco-
Chilienne, 1904. 263 p.   (3511
   2. ptie. Profils et biographies; 6. ptie,

VEGA E., M. Album de la colonie ... (Cont.)
Guide général de la colonie française.---
Jones 1650.

COLOMBIA

DOLLERO, Adolfo. Cultura colombiana; apuntaciones sobre el movimiento intelectual de
Colombia, desde la conquista hasta la época
actual. Bogotá, Edit. de Cromos, 1930.
868 p.   (3512
   Obras consultadas: p. 834-36.---Jones
1707.

GIRALDO JARAMILLO, Gabriel. Bibliografía colombiana de viajes. Bogotá, Edit. ABC, 1957.
224 p. (Biblioteca de bibliografía colombiana, 2)   (3513

GREEN, G. H. Books in English about Colombia
and Venezuela; a selected bibliography.
London, Headley Brothers, 1963.
p. 156-62.   (3514
   Reprinted from Library Association record,
v. 65, no. 4, Apr. 1963.

LOPEZ DE MESA, Luis. Introducción a la historia de la cultura en Colombia; sinopsis del
desarrollo cultural de este país e interpretación de sus causas y dificultades. Datos
sobre la orientación filosófica iberoamericana. Nómina de algunas publicaciones colombianas importantes. Ciudadanos extranjeros
que han contribuído notablemente al progreso
de esta república. Bogotá, 1930.
203 p.   (3515
   "Breve extracto de la bibliografía colombiana": p. 187-92.---Jones 1729.

PEREZ ARBELAEZ, Enrique, and GUHL, Ernesto.
Intento de una bibliografía sobre el Chocó,
sobre sus zonas húmedas adyacentes y alguna
sobre los problemas más importantes de esas
regiones, anterior a 1958. [1958] 40 p.
mimeogr.   (3516

STRATEGIC index of the Americas. Preliminary
bibliography of Colombia. Washington, D.C.,
Coordinator of Inter-American Affairs, 1943.
60 p. mimeogr.   (3517

COSTA RICA

BIOLLEY, Pablo. Bibliografía; obras publicadas en el extranjero acerca de la República
de Costa Rica durante el siglo XIX. (Revista
de Costa Rica en el siglo XIX, San José,
t. 1, p. 363-404, 1902)   (3518
   Jones 1262.

JONES, Chester Lloyd. Costa Rica and civilization in the Caribbean. Madison, University
of Wisconsin, 1935. 172 p. (University of

JONES, Chester Lloyd. Costa Rica ... (Cont.)
Wisconsin studies in the social sciences and
history, no. 23)   (3519
   Bibliography: p. 168-72.---Jones 1272.

PALMERLEE, A. E. A bibliography of maps of
the Republic of Costa Rica, its regions,
provinces, and cities. Preliminary ed.
Lawrence, Kans., Dept. of Geography, University of Kansas, 1961. unpaged.   (3520

CUBA

ACEVEDO, Luciano de. La Habana en el siglo
XIX descrita por viajeros extranjeros (en-
sayo de bibliografía crítica). La Habana,
Cuba Contemporánea, 1919. 52 p.   (3521
   Jones 1781.

CUBA. Biblioteca Nacional. Impresos relativos a Cuba editados en los Estados Unidos de
Norteamérica, compilados bajo la dirección
de Lilia Castro de Morales. Prólogo de
Howard F. Cline. Habana, 1956.
370 p.   (3522
   Contribution of the National Library to the
observance of Día del Libro Cubano, June 7,
1956.

DOLLERO, Adolfo. Cultura cubana (Cuban culture)
Habana, Impr. "El Siglo XX", 1916.
480 p.   (3523
   Spanish and English.---Jones 1817. Also
contains notes on the introduction of printing, a listing of the press, the works of
Fernando Ortiz, and a lengthy list of Cuban
names whose works are mentioned in the information.

-----. -----. (La provincia de Matanzas y su
evolución). Habana, Impr. Seoane y Fernández, 1919. 438 p.   (3524
   In continuation of Cultura cubana (Cuban
culture) published in 1916.---Jones 1818.

-----. -----. (La provincia de Pinar del Río
y su evolución); obra histórico-cultural
ilustrada. Habana, Impr. Seoane y Fernández, 1921. 436 p.   (3525
   Contains much biographical and bibliographical information.---Jones 1819.

FORD, Worthington Chauncey. The Isle of Pines,
1668; an essay in bibliography. Boston,
Club of Odd Volumes, 1920. 116 p.   (3526

HUMBOLDT, Alexander, freiherr von. Ensayo político sobre la isla de Cuba. Introducción
por Fernando Ortiz y correcciones, notas y
apéndices por Francisco Arango y Parreño,
J. S. Thrasher y otros. Habana, Cultural,
S. A., 1930. 2 v. (Colección de libros cubanos --- v. 16-17)   (3527
   Includes bibliography.---Jones 1849.

MARQUES, José de Jesús. Diccionario geográfico, biográfico, estadístico, bibliográfico,
histórico, económico y mercantil de la isla
de Cuba. 1875. (Boletín del Archivo Nacional, Habana, v. 24, p. 81-250,
1925)   (3528
    Jones 1870.

-----. -----. Publícalo, arreglado, anotado y
con una introducción Joaquín Llaverías. Habana, Impr. Pérez, Sierra y Co., 1926.
170 p.   (3529

PAN AMERICAN UNION. Columbus Memorial Library.
Catalogue of books, pamphlets, periodicals
and maps, relating to the Republic of Cuba.
Revised to May 31, 1905. Washington, D.C.,
Govt. Print. Off., 1905. [11] p.
fold.   (3530
    Prepublication gallery sheets.

PEREZ, Luis Marino. Apuntes de libros y folletos impresos en España y el extranjero que
tratan expresamente de Cuba desde principios
del siglo XVII hasta 1812 y de las disposi-
ciones de gobierno impresas en La Habana desde 1753 hasta 1800. Habana, C. Martínez y
Compañía, 1907. 62, 16 p.   (3531
    Apendices: Impresos de la Real Sociedad
Patriótica y del Real Consulado de la Habana;
adiciones a la Imprenta en la Habana de José
Toribio Medina; Imprenta de "Cuba y America",
1907.---Jones 1888.

QUESADA, Gonzalo de. Cuba. Washington, D.C.,
Govt. Print. Off., 1905. 541 p.   (3532
    At head of title: International Bureau of
the American Republics. "Books relating to
Cuba, compiled by Mr. A.P.C. Griffin":
p. 315-445. "Maps relating to Cuba, compiled
by P. Lee Phillips": p. 447-512.---Jones
1896.

-----. Isle of Pines. n.d. 9 p.   (3533
    References are to maps and atlases.

TRELLES Y GOVIN, Carlos Manuel. Biblioteca
geográfica cubana. Matanzas, Impr. de J. F.
Oliver, 1920. 340 p.   (3534
    Jones 1920. Now available in microprint.

-----. Suplemento. Habana, Impr. y Papel.
de Rambla, Bouza y Cía., 1925.
63 p.   (3535

TRO PEREZ, Rodolfo. Cuba; viajes y descripciones, 1493-1949. La Habana, 1950. p. 5-188.
(Revista de la Biblioteca Nacional, 2a. ser.,
t. 1, no. 3, mayo 1950)   (3535a

U.S. Library of Congress. List of books relating to Cuba, including references to collected works and periodicals; by A. P. C.
Griffin; with a bibliography of maps by P.Lee
Phillips. Washington, D.C., Govt. Print.

U.S. Library of Congress ... (Cont.)
Off., 1898. 61 p. (U.S.55th. Cong., 2d sess.,
1897-1898. Senate Doc., no. 161)   (3536
    "Appendix: A synoptical catalogue of ma-
nuscripts in the Library of Congress relating
to Cuba. Comp. by Herbert Friedenwald":
p. 58-61.---Jones 1933.

-----. -----. Division of Bibliography. A list
of references on the Isle of Pines. Washington, D.C., 1936. 9 p. typewritten. (3537
    Cited in Yang.

DOMINICAN REPUBLIC

ADVIELLE, Victor. L'Odyssée d'un Normand à
St. Domingue aux dix huitième siècle. Paris,
Challamel, 1901. 292 p.   (3538
    Notes bibliographiques: p. 285-80.---Jones
2977.

HAZARD, Samuel. Santo Domingo, past and present,
with a glance at Hayti. New York, Harper &
Brothers, 1873. xxix, 511 p.   (3539
    Bibliography of Santo Domingo and Hayti:
p. xxi-xxix.---Jones 2995.

INMAN, Samuel Guy. Through Santo Domingo and
Haiti, a cruise with the marines. Report of
a visit to these island republics in the
summer of 1919. New York, Committee on Cooperation in Latin America, 1919.
96 p.   (3540
    Bibliography: p. 91-6.---Jones 3000.

ROTH, Henry Ling. Bibliography and cartography of Hispaniola. (Royal Geographical Society. Supplementary papers. London, 1887.
v. 2, pt. 1, p. 41-97)   (3541
    Jones 3008.

WELLES, Sumner. Naboth's vineyard, the Dominican Republic, 1884-1924. New York, Payson
& Clarke, 1928. 1058 p.   (3542
    Bibliography included.---Jones 3014.

ECUADOR

EMPRESA Editorial "Raza Latina". La provincia
de Tungurahua en 1928. Ambato, 1928.
365 p.   (3543
    Contains biographies and chapters on jour-
nalism, art, education, etc.---Jones 1796.

ENRIQUEZ B., Eliécer. Quito a través de los
siglos; recopilación y notas biobibliográficas. Quito, Impr. Municipal, 1938.
274 p.   (3544
    Jones 1977a.

PAZ Y MIÑO, Luis Telmo. Bibliografía geográfica
ecuatoriana. Quito, Impr. Nacional, 1927.
69 p. (Publ. de la Biblioteca Nacional de

PAZ Y MIÑO, Luis Telmo. Bibliografía...(Cont.)
Quito. Estudios geográficos no. 1) (3545
Jones 2000. In two sections: Autores nacionales; Autores extranjeros. Published
also in Boletín de la Biblioteca Nacional

TERAN V., Rafael Antonio El Ecuador de hoy y
sus problemas. (Anales de la Universidad
Central, Quito, no. 291-292, 1935) (3546
Bibliografía de referencia: p. 431-33.
---Jones 2018.

FALKLAND ISLANDS or ISLAS MALVINAS

TORRE REVELLO, José. Bibliografías de las Islas Malvinas; obras, mapas y documentos; contribución. Buenos Aires, Impr. de la Universidad, 1953. xi, 260 p. (Universidad de
Buenos Aires, Facultad de Filosofía y Letras,
Publ. del Instituto de Investigaciones Historicas, no. 99) (3547
Contains 1,702 entries.

U.S. Library of Congress. General Reference
and Bibliography Division. The Falkland
Islands and its dependencies: a list of recent references, compiled by Helen F. Conover.
Washington, D.C., 1944. 8 p. typewritten. (3548
Cited in Yang.

GUATEMALA

BRIGHAM, William Tufts. Guatemala: the land
of the quetzal. New York, C. Scribner's
Sons, 1887. 453 p. (3549
A list of works relating to Central America: p. 430-42.---Jones 1286.

INSTITUTO Guatemalteco Americano. Books about
Guatemala; a bibliography of books in English
and Spanish. [Guatemala, 1960?]
34 p. (3550

JONES, Chester Lloyd. Guatemala past and present. Minneapolis, The Univ. of Minnesota
Pr., 1940. 420 p. (3551
"Notes" (p. 357-402) and "Bibliography"
(p. 403-10).---Jones 1299a.

REYES M., José Luis. Bibliografia de los estudios geográficos de la República de Guatemala desde 1574 hasta nuestros días. Guatemala [Edit. del Ministerio de Educacion Pública "José de Pineda Ibarra"] 1960.
70 p. (3552

U.S. Embassy. Guatemala. Selected readings on
Guatemala. [Guatemala, 195-]
unpaged. (3553
Cited in Caribbean acquisitions, 1959,
p. 5.

VILLACORTA CALDERON, José Antonio. Ensayo sobre una bibliografía geográfico-histórica de
Guatemala. (Anales de la Sociedad de Geografía e Historia, Guatemala, t. 2, p. 99-111,
1925) (3554
See also the author's Bibliografía e iconografía de la independencia, in the Anales,
t. 14, p. 3-17, 1937.---Jones 1313.

GUIANA

GROOT, Silvia W. de. Principaux ouvrages de
langue néerlandaise, anglaise et allemande
sur les Guyanes. Paris, Leyde,
1958- . (3555
Cited in Caribbean acquisitions, 1963.
item 56.

U.S. Library of Congress. Division of Bibliography. British Guiana: a bibliographical
list compiled by Florence S. Hellman. Washington, D.C., 1937. 39 p. typewritten.(3556
Cited in Yang.

-----. -----. A selected list of references on
the Guianas, compiled by Florence S. Hellman.
Washington, D.C., 1940. 17 p. (3557
Cited in Yang.

HAITI

MALVAL, Joseph Fritz. A bibliography of material published in English in the United
States about Haiti: followed by a survey of
the trade books listed in this bibliography
which are held by the libraries of selected
universities in the United States. Atlanta,
Ga., 1954. 98 p. typewritten. (3558
Thesis for the M. S. degree at Atlanta
University.

TIPPENHAUER, Louis Gentil. Die insel Haiti.
Leipzig, F. A. Brockhaus, 1893. 693 p.(3559
Bibliographie: p. 672-93.---Jones 3011.

HONDURAS

BOBADILLA, Perfecto H. Monografía geográfica
e histórica de San Pedro Sula. IV centenario de su fundación. San Pedro Sula, Honduras, "Compañía Editora de Honduras", 1936.
236 p. (3560
"El periodismo en San Pedro Sula: p. 216-
26.---Jones 1319.

VALLE, Rafael Heliodoro. Bibliografía que in-
teresa a Honduras. (Centro-América, Guatemala, v. 7, p. 530-34, 1915) (3561
Jones 1330.

MEXICO

ALCORTA GUERRERO, Ramón, and PEDRAZA, José
Francisco. Bibliografía histórica y geográfica del estado de San Luis Potosí. Tacubaya, D.F., México [Tall. de la Edit. Stylo]
1941. 655 p. (Instituto Panamericano de
Geografía e Historia, Publ. no. 60) (3562
Contains 1321 entries.

-----. Primeras adiciones. México, Sociedad
Mexicana de Geografía y Estadística, 1947.
91 p.   (3563
Supplement also published in Boletín de la
Sociedad de Geografía y Estadística, v. 63,
1947.

ALESSIO ROBLES, Vito. Bibliografía de Coahuila, histórica y geográfica. México, 1927.
450 p. (Monografías bibliográficas mexicanas, 10)   (3564
Jones 2041.

ANDERSON, Alexander Dwight. Mexico from the
material stand-point. A review of its mineral, agricultural, forest, and marine
wealth, its manufactures, commerce, railways,
isthmian routes, and finances. Washington,
D.C., New York, Brentano Bros., 1884.
156 p.   (3565
"American and English authorities": p. 143-
56.---Jones 2046.

-----. The silver country of the great southwest, a review of the mineral and other
wealth, the attractions and material development of the former kingdom of New Spain.
New York, G. P. Putnam's Sons, 1877.
221 p.   (3566
"The authorities": p. 130-87.---Jones
2047.

AYALA ECHAVARRI, Rafael. Bibliografía histó-
ca y geográfica de Querétaro. Mexico, Secretaría de Relaciones Exteriores, Depto. de
Información para el Extranjero, 1949. 387 p.
(Monografías bibliográficas mexicanas, 2a.
ser., no. 2)   (3567
Includes 1288 titles.

BARRETT, Ellen C. Baja California, 1535-1956;
a bibliography of historical, geographical
and scientific literature relating to the
Península of Baja California and to the adjacent islands. Los Angeles, California,
Bennett & Marshall, 1957. 284 p.   (3568

CARRASCO PUENTE, Rafael. Bibliografía del Ismo
de Tehuantepec; prólogo del Lic. Alfonso
Francisco Ramírez. México, Secretaría de
Relaciones Exteriores, Depto. de Información
para el Extranjero, 1948. 634 p. (Monografías bibliográficas mexicanas, 2a. ser.,
no. 1)   (3569
Contains 2383 titles.

CENTRAL News Company, México, D.F. Selected
list of books on México. [México] Edit.
Cultura, 1935. 48 p.   (3570

CERVANTES DE SALAZAR, Francisco. México en
1554. Tres diálogos latinos ... Los reim-
prime, con traducción castellana y notas,
J. García Icazbalceta. México, Andrade y
Morales, 1875. 344 p.   (3571
Bibliografía: p. 323-44.---Jones 2124a.

CHASE, Stuart. Mexico; a study of two Americas ... in collaboration with Marian Tyler.
New York, The Macmillan Co. , 1931.
338 p.   (3572
Selected bibliography: p. 329-34.---Jones
2126.

FIGUEROA DOMENECH, J. Guía general descriptiva de la República Mexicana; historia,
geografía, estadística, etc., etc., con
triple directorio del comercio y la industria, autoridades, oficinas públicas, abogados, médicos, hacendados, correos, telégrafos y ferrocarriles, etc. México, R.
de S. N. Araluce [1899] 2 v.   (3573
Jones 2169. Contains chapter on the press
and Mexican authors.

GALINDO Y VILLA, Jesús. Apuntes de epigrafía
mexicana. Breve colección de inscripciones
diversas, acompañadas de algunas noticias
históricas, descriptivas, biográficas y bibliográficas. Tomo I. Epigrafía de la ciudad de México; 2a. ed. México, Impr. del
Gobierno Federal, 1892. 466 p.   (3574
"Noticia de las obras y autores que se han
tenido presentes para escribir los apuntes
que encierra este volumen": p. 413-54.
Reprinted from Memorias de la Sociedad Científica "Antonio Alzate", v. 4, p. 193-237;
v. 5, p. 239-357; v. 6, p. 123-50; v. 7,
p. 93-192, 297-459, México, 1890-1893.
Also published in part in Anales del Museo
Nacional de México, t. 4, pt. 4-12, 1890-
1892. No more published.---Jones 2173a.

GARDINER, C. Harvey. Survey, foreign trav-
elers' accounts of Mexico, 1810-1910.
Washington, D.C. [1952] p. 321-51.   (3575
Reprinted from The Americas, v. 8, no. 3,
Jan. 1952.

GRUENING, Ernest Henry. Mexico and its her-
itage. New York and London, The Century
Co., 1928. 728 p.   (3576
Bibliography: p. 667-92.---Jones 2223.

HEREDIA, José G. Bibliografía de Sinaloa histórica y geográfica. México, [Impr. de la
Secretaría de Relaciones Exteriores] 1926.
185 p. (Monografías bibliográficas mexicanas, no. 6)   (3577
Jones 2242.

HERNANDEZ TAPIA, Germán. Bibliografía poblana de geografía e historia del Estado.
[n.p.] 1962. 177 p. (Publ. del Grupo Literario "Bohemia Poblana")   (3578
Refers to Puebla, México.

IGUINIZ, Juan Bautista. Bibliografía de obras
de viajeros mexicanos en el extranjero.
(Memorias y revista de la Sociedad Científica "Antonio Alzate", México, v. 52, p. 17-72,
1932)   (3579
Jones 2253.

MEXICO. Dirección General de Geografía y Meteorología. Bibliografía geográfica de México. Recopilacion y ordenamiento de Angel
Bassols Batalla. México [1955]
652 p.   (3580

-----. Embajada. U. S. A selected bibliography on Mexico. Washington, D.C., 1958.
34 p. mimeogr.   (3581

NEW YORK. Public Library. List of works in
the New York Public Library relating to
Mexico. New York, 1909. 186 p.   (3582
"Reprinted from the Bulletin, October-
December, 1909."---Jones 2378.

O'GORMAN, Edmundo. Breve historia de las divisiones territoriales; aportación a la historia de la geografía de México, D.F. Edit.
Polis, 1937. 261 p. (Trabajos jurídicos
de homenaje de la Escuela Libre de Derecho
en su XXV aniversario, v. 2,
1. pte.)   (3583
"Indice cronológico de leyes": p. 193-219.
"Bibliografía": p. 243-52.---Jones 2383.

PALACIOS, Enrique Juan. Puebla, su territorio
y sus habitantes. México, 1917. (Memorias
y Revista de la Sociedad Científica "Antonio
Alzate". t. 36, 1-2 pte.)   (3584
Contains biographies and "Bibliografía general": pt. 2, p. 719-36.---Jones 2401.

PAN AMERICAN UNION. Columbus Memorial Library.
Mexicans in the United States; a bibliography.
Washington, D.C., 1942. 14 p. (Bibliogra-
phic ser., no. 27)   (3585
Compiler: Robert C. Jones.

PEQUEÑA bibliografía de la Baja California.
(Maestro rural, México, Oct. 1937)   (3586
Jones 2416.

ROMERO DE TERREROS Y VINENT, Manuel. Bibliografía de cronistas de la ciudad de México.
México, 1926. xxvii, 16 p. (Monografías
bibliográficas mexicanas, no. 4)   (3587
Jones 2471.

TEIXIDOR, Felipe. Viajeros mexicanos [siglos
XIX y XX]. México, Ediciones Letras de México, 1939. 297 p.   (3588

TEIXIDOR, Felipe. Viajeros ... (Cont.)
Includes "Bibliografía" for each author.
"Libros de viaje de autores mexicanos que
forman la colección del compilador": 2d-5th.
leaves at end.---Jones 2523a.

U.S. Library of Congress. Brief list of references on the Japanese in Mexico. Washington, D.C., 1947. 1 p.   (3589
Cited in Yang.

-----. -----. Division of Bibliography.
Lower California; a bibliographical list.
Washington, D.C., 1931. 11 p. type-
written.   (3590

-----. -----. Supplementary list. 1938.
9 p. typewritten.   (3591

-----. War Dept. Library. Index of publications, articles and maps relating to Mexico in the War Department Library. Washington, D.C., Govt. Print. Off., 1896.
120 p.   (3592
Jones 2537.

VALLE, Rafel Heliodoro. Judíos en México.
(Revista chilena de historia y geografía,
Santiago de Chile, v. 81, p. 215-36,
1936)   (3593
Includes bibliography.---Jones 2554a.

-----. Mexico in United States and British
periodicals. (The Hispanic American historical review, Durham, N.C., v. 15,
p. 126-42, Feb. 1935)   (3594
Jones 2557. Edition in Spanish in El libro y el pueblo, Mexico, D.F., p. 55-69,
oct. 1935.

VEGA, Crisóforo. Bibliografía analítica de
los trabajos acerca del lago Pátzcuaro.
México, 1940. p. 503-13.   (3595
Cited in Catálogo, Instituto Bibliotecológico, item 846.

WHITAKER, Arthur Preston. Mexico today. Phi-
ladelphia, 1940. 186 p. (The Annals of
the American Academy of Political and Social
Science, v. 208)   (3596
Bibliography on Mexico today: p. 181-86.
References are mostly to works in English.
---Jones 2583.

MIDDLE AMERICA

UNITED FRUIT Company. Middle America Information Bureau. More books about Middle America. A selected bibliography rev. through
April 1948. N.Y., 1948. 9 p.   (3597
Lists 65 books in English. See also item
3598.

WILSON, Charles Morrow. Books about Middle
America; a selected bibliography. N.Y., The
Middle America Information Bureau conducted
by United Fruit Co. [1943?] 23 p. (3598

NICARAGUA

BIBLIOTECA Americana, Managua, Nicaragua. Una
lista de artículos de revistas sobre Nicaragua apareciendo en importantes revistas de
los Estados Unidos desde 1815 hasta 1945 ...
A list of magazine articles about Nicaragua
appearing in leading magazines of the United
States from 1815 to 1945. Managua, 1945.
15 p.   (3599

KALB, Courtenay de. A bibliography of the
Mosquito Coast of Nicaragua. (Journal of
the American Geographical Society, New York,
v. 26, p. 241-48. 1894)   (3600
Jones 1338.

LEVY, Pablo. Notas geográficas y económicas
sobre la República de Nicaragua, y una exposición completa de la cuestión del canal
interoceánico y de la inmigración con una
lista bibliográfica, la más completa hasta
el día, de todos los libros y mapas relativos a la América Central en general y a Nicaragua en particular. París, E. Denné
Schmitz, 1873. 627 p.   (3601
Bibliografía y cartografía: p. 593-613.
---Jones 1339.

PECTOR, Désiré. Exposé sommaire des voyages
et travaux géographiques au Nicaragua dans
le cours de XIX siècle. Paris, Bibliothèque des Annales Economiques, 1891.
8 p.   (3602
Jones 1345.

PANAMA

RUBIO Y MUÑOZ-BOCANEGRA, Angel. Bibliografía
básica de geografía de Panamá, con especial
referencia a la bibliografía sobre recursos
naturales. [Panamá] 1953. 22 p. (Universidad de Panamá. Departamento de Geografía,
publ. no. 1)   (3603

PARAGUAY

AZARA, Félix de. Geografía física y esférica
de las provincias del Paraguay y misiones
guaraníes. Bibliografía, prólogo y anotaciones por Rodolfo R. Schuller. Montevideo,
1904. 478 p. (Anales del Museo Nacional
de Montevideo. Sección histórico-filosófica,
t. 1)   (3604
Jones 2596.

DECOUD, José Segundo. A list of books, magazine
articles and maps relating to Paraguay. Books,
1683-1903. Maps, 1599-1903. A supplement to
the Handbook of Paraguay, pub. in Sept., 1902,
by the International Bureau of the American
Republics. Wshington, D.C., Govt. Print. Off.,
1904. 53 p.   (3605
Jones 2604.

ELLIOTT, Arthur Elwood. Paraguay; its cultural
heritage, social conditions and educational
problems. New York, Teachers College, Columbia University, 1931. 210 p. (Contributions
to education, 473)   (3606
Bibliography: p. 201-10.---Jones 2607.

KEMPSKI, Karl E. Die landwirtschaft im para-
guayischen Chaco. Buenos Aires, Impr. "Mer-
cur," 1931. 148 p,   (3607
Literaturverzeichnis: p. 137-41.---Jones
2612.

STRATEGIC Index of the Americas. Preliminary
bibliography of Paraguay. Washington, D.C.,
Coordinator of Inter-American Affairs, 1943.
32 p. mimeogr.   (3608
Contains 370 entries.

PERU

BEALS, Carleton. Fire on the Andes. Philadel-
phia, J. B. Lippincott, 1934. 482 p.   (3609
"Selected bibliography": p. 449-57.---
Jones 2631a.

PAZ SOLDAN, Mariano Felipe. Diccionario geográfico estadístico del Perú, contiene además la
etimología aymará y quechua de las principales poblaciones, lagos, ríos, cerros, etc.,
etc. Lima, Impr. del Estado, 1877.
1077 p.   (3610
"Biblioteca geográfica del Perú": p. 1055-
77.---Jones 2713.

PAZ SOLDAN, Mateo. Geografía del Perú. Obra
póstuma corr. y aum. por Mariano Felipe Paz
Soldán. París, Didot Hermanos, 1862-1863.
2 v.   (3611
Noticia bibliográfica: v. 1, p. 715-23.---
Jones 2715.

-----. Géographie du Pérou. Traduction fran-
çaise par P. Arsène Mouqueron. Paris, A.
Durand, 1863. 538 p.   (3612
Catalogue bibliographique: p. 475-84.---
Jones 2716.

POLO, José Toribio. Bibliografía geográfica
del Perú. (Boletín de la Sociedad geográfica de Lima, Lima, t. 43, p. 1-40,
1926)   (3613
Jones 2724.

POLO, José Toribio. Bibliografía geográfica
del Perú, siglo XVI. Lima, 1935.
23 p.   (3614
Jones 2725.

PRET, C. A. Bibliographie pérouvienne. Paris,
1903. 69 p.   (3615
Jones 2728.

SCHÜTZ ZU HOLZHAUSEN, Damian, freiherr von.
Der Amazonas. Wanderbilder aus Peru, Bolivia und Nordbrasilien. 2. durchgesehene und
erweiterte aufl., unter besonderer berück-
sichtigung der vom verfasser gegründeten
tirolisch-rheinischen kolonie Pozuzo, hrsg.
von Adam Klassert. Freiburg im Breisgau, St.
Louis, Mo. [etc.] Herder, 1895. 443 p.
(Illustrierte bibliothek der Länder-u völker-
kunde)   (3616
Litteratur: p. 427-38.---Jones 2748.

VELASCO, Juan de. Catálogo de algunos escritores antiguos y modernos del Perú y Quito.
Quito, Impr. del Gobierno, 1885.
6 p.   (3617
Cited in Chaves, p. 12.

ZELA KOORT, Juan Guillermo. Cincuentisiete
años de bibliografía alemana referente al
Perú. Lima, Compañía de Impresiones y Publicidad, 1949. 15 p.   (3618
Reprinted from Boletín bibliográfico, Lima,
año 21, v. 18, no. 3-4, p. 194-208, 1948.

PUERTO RICO

U.S. Library of Congress. Division of Bibliography. Puerto Rico: a selected list of re-
refences. Washington, D.C., 1939. 50 p.
typewritten.   (3619

-----. Puerto Rico: a selected list of recent
references, compiled by Ann Duncan Brown.
Washington, D.C., 1943. 44 p.   (3620
Primarily a supplement to the 1939 list.

SOUTH AMERICA

DALRYMPLE, Alexander. Catalogue of authors
who have written on Rio de la Plata, Paraguay,
and Chaco. London, 1807-1808. 17, 3,
2 p.   (3621
Jones 678.

JONES, Clarence Fielden. South America. New
York, H. Holt & Co., 1930. 798 p.   (3622
Bibliography: p. 725-65.---Jones 231.

KANTER, Helmuth. Der Gran Chaco und seine
randgebiete. Hamburg, Friedrichsen, de
Gruyter & Co., 1936. 376 p. (Hansische

KANTER, Helmuth. Der Gran Chaco ... (Cont.)
Universität. Abhandlungen aus dem gebiet der
auslandskunde, bd. 43)   (3623
Bibliography: p. 370-75.---Jones 733.

OGILVIE, Alan Grant. Geography of the central
Andes. New York, The American Geographical
Society, 1922. 240 p.   (3624
Selected bibliography: p. 211-23.---Jones
341.

SCHMIEDER, Oscar. Länderkunde Südamerikas.
Leipzig und Wien, F. Deuticke, 1932.
252 p.   (3625
Litteratur: p. 209-40.---Jones 438.

SCHUMACHER, Hermann Albert. Südamerikanische
studien; drei lebens - und cultur - bilder:
Mutis, Caldas, Codazzi, 1760-1860. Berlin,
E. S. Mittler & Sohn, 1884. 559 p. (3626
"Anmerkungen": p. 421-559.---Jones 1773.

U.S. Library of Congress. List of references
on South America. Washington, D.C., 1914.
4 p.   (3627
Cited in Yang.

-----. -----. List of references on South
America (with special reference to political,
economic, social and military conditions)
Washington, D.C., 1922. 11 p.   (3628
Cited in Yang.

-----. -----. List of books on South and
Central America (economic and social conditions, resources, etc.). Washington, D.C.,
1920. 10 p.   (3629
Cited in Yang.

UNITED STATES

NELSON, Ernesto. Bibliografía general de las
obras referentes a Estados Unidos. Buenos
Aires, [Tall. Gráf. Olivieri & Domínguez]
1934. 160 p.   (3630

URUGUAY

GIUFFRA, Elzear Santiago. La República del
Uruguay; explicación geográfica del territorio nacional con 232 notas bibliográficas y un vocabulario topográfico con 6,000
nombres. Montevideo, A. Monteverde y Cía.,
1935. 584 p.   (3631
Jones 2840.

URIOSTE, Antero. Ensayo de una bibliografía,
cartografía e iconografía del departamento
de Rocha, 1516-1945. Montevideo, Casa A.
Barreiro y Ramos, 1947. 479 p.   (3632

VENEZUELA

DALTON, Leonard Victor. Venezuela. London,
T. F. Unwin, 1912. 320 p. (The South Amer-
ican series, v. 8)   (3633
    Bibliography of 411 titles: p. 287-313.
A later edition was published in 1916.---
Jones 2900.

DOLLERO, Adolfo. Cultura de Venezuela; apuntaciones sobre la evolución de la cultura
desde la conquista. Excursiones. Caracas,
Tip. Americana, 1933. 2 v.   (3634
    "Algunas de las obras consultadas:" v. 2,
p. 376-79.---Jones 2907.

GANZENMULLER DE BLAY, María Luisa. Contribución a la bibliografía viajera y descriptiva
de Venezuela; colección de 443 fichas. Caracas, 1958. 54 p.   (3635

GRASES, Pedro. Temas de bibliografía y cultura venezolanas. Buenos Aires, Edit. Nova,
1953. 227 p.   (3636

LANDAETA ROSALES, Manuel. Gran recopilación
geográfica, estadística e histórica de Venezuela ... publicada por disposición del
presidente constitucional de la Republica,
doctor Juan Pablo Rojas Paul. Caracas,
Impr. Bolívar, 1889. 2 v.   (3637
    Bibliography: v. 1, p. viii. "Escrito-
res venezolanos": v. 2, p. 141-44. "Obras
de instruccion popular publicadas en Venezuela hasta 1889": v. 2, p. 145-53.---
Jones 2925.

LAVERDE AMAYA, Isidoro. Un viaje a Venezuela.
Bogotá, Impr. "La Nación", 1889.
406 p.   (3638
    "Lista en orden alfabético de autores dra-
máticos venezolanos y de sus obras": p. 379-
92. 38 authors.---Jones 2927.

SPENCE, James Mudie. The land of Bolivar, or
War, peace and adventure in the Republic of
Venezuela. London, S. Low, Marston, Searle
& Rivington, 1878. 2 v.   (3639
    Bibliography: v. 2, p. 271-93.---Jones
2960.

STRATEGIC Index of the Americas. Tentative
list of references on Venezuela. Washington,
D.C., Coordinator of Inter-American Affairs,
1943. 11 p. mimeogr.   (3640
    Contains 113 titles.

WEST INDIES

BLANCHARD, Linn Rudolph. Martinique. Washington, D.C., Library of Congress, 1942.
57 p. mimeogr.   (3641
    References supplementing a list prepared
in 1923.

GAZIN GOSSEL, Jacques. Eléments de bibliographie genérale, méthodique et historique de
la Martinique. Fort de France, Impr. Antillaise, 1926. 348 p.   (3642

HISS, Philip Hanson. A selective guide to the
English literature on the Netherlands West
Indies, with a supplement on British Guiana.
N.Y, The Netherlands Information Bureau,
1943. xiv, 129 p. (Booklets of the Nether-
lands Information Bureau, no. 9)   (3643

INSTITUTE of Jamaica, Kingston. Library.
Bibliographia jamaicensis; a list of Jamaica
books and pamphlets, magazine articles, newspapers and maps, most of which are in the
Library of the Institute of Jamaica, by Frank
Cundall. Kingston, Jamaica [1902]
83 p.   (3643a

-----. -----. Supplement. Kingston, Jamaica,
1908. 38 p.   (3644

-----. Bibliotheca jamaicensis; some account
of the principal works on Jamaica in the
Library of the Institute of Jamaica.
Kingston, 1895. 38 p.   (3645
    Compiled by Frank Cundall. Reprinted from
Handbook of Jamaica, 1895.

JAMAICA Library Service. Jamaica; a select
bibliography, 1900-1963. [Kingston] 1963.
115 p.   (3646
    "Published by the Jamaica Independence
Festival Committee in commemoration of the
first anniversary of the independence of
Jamaica".

JONES, Chester Lloyd. Caribbean backgrounds
and prospects. New York, D. Appleton & Co.,
1931. 354 p.   (3647
    Bibliography: p. 327-47.---Jones 3001.

NEDERLANDSE Stichting voor Culturele Samen-
werking met Suriname en de Nederlandse Antillen. Opgave van litteratuur betreffende
de Nederlandse Antillen. Amsterdam, 1964.
31 p.   (3647a

-----. Opgave von litteratuur betreffende
Suriname. Amsterdam [1961] 59 p.   (3648

-----. -----. Amsterdam, 1963. 91 p.   (3648a

REID, Charles Frederick. Bibliography of the
Virgin Islands of the United States. New
York, H. W. Wilson, 1941. xvi, 225 p.   (3649
    Prepared by the Works Projects Administra-
tion.

REPERTORIUM op de litteratuur betreffende de
Nederlandsche koloniën, voor zoover zij
verspreid is in tijdschriften en mengelwerken.
Gravenhage, M. Nijhoff, 1895. 454 p.   (3649a
    Includes Dutch West Indies. Compiler: A.

REPERTORIUM op de litteratuur ... (Cont.)
Hartmann.

-----. Supplement. Gravenhage, M. Nijhoff,
1901-1934. 8 v.   (3649b

SENIOR, Clarence Ollson, and ROMAN, Josefina
de. A selected bibliography on Puerto Rico
and the Puerto Ricans. [New York, Migration
Division, Depto. of Labor of Puerto Rico,
1951]. 32 p. mimeogr.   (3650

SEWLAL, Enos. Bibliography of Trinidad and
Tobago with a section on the West Indies.
For the use of visiting students. Port of
Spain, Department of Agriculture, 1958.
77 p. mimeogr.   (3651

TRELLES Y GOVIN, Carlos Manuel. Bibliografía
antillana. n.d.   (3652
    Reprinted from Hispanic American historical
review, v. 4, p. 324-30, May 1921.

U.S. Library of Congress. A list of books
(with references to periodicals) on Porto
Rico. By A. P. C. Griffin. Washington, D.C.,
Govt. Print. Off., 1901. 55 p.   (3653
    Jones 2809.

-----. -----. Division of Bibliography.
British possessions in the Caribbean area:
a selected list of references, compiled by
Ann Duncan Brown. Washington, D.C., 1943.
192 p.   (3654

VAN DEUSEN, Richard James. Porto Rico, a
Caribbean isle. New York, H. Holt and Co.,
1931. 342 p.   (3655
    Books consulted: p. 315-24.---Jones 2810.

WEST INDIES (Federation). Federal Information
Service. Reference Library. A select list
of literature on the West Indies Federation
since 1957. Port-of Spain, Trinidad, 1961.
5 p.   (3655a
    Compiled by M. McConnie. Cited in Benewick,
p. 9.

GEOLOGY

GENERAL

INTERNATIONAL Geological Congress, 16th, 1933.
Copper resources of the world. Washington,
D.C., 1935. 2 v.   (3656
    Includes bibliographies.---Jones 216.

MAFFEI, Eugenio, and RUA FIGUEROA, Ramón.
Apuntes para una biblioteca española de libros, folletos y artículos, impresos y manuscritos, relativos al conocimiento y explotación de las riquezas minerales y a las ciencias auxiliares. Comprenden la mineralogía
y geología . . . la hidrigeología; la química analítica docimástica y metalúrgica; la
legislación y estadística mineras . . . concernientes a la península y a nuestras antiguas y actuales posesiones de ultramar.
Acompañados de reseñas biográficas y de un
ligero resumen de la mayor parte de las obras
que se citan. Madrid, J. M. Lapuente, 1871-
1872. 2 v.   (3657
    Jones 273.

MONTESSUS DE BALLORE, Fernand, comte de. Bibliografía general de temblores y terremotos.
Santiago de Chile, Impr. Universitaria, 1915-
1917. pts. 1-7.   (3658
    5. pte.: América, tierras antárticas y
oceános.
    First published in Revista chilena de his-
toria y geografía.---Jones 1551.

NICKLES, John Milton, and MILLER, Robert B.
Bibliography and index of geology exclusive

NICKLES, John Milton, and MILLER, Robert...(Cont)
of North America. Washington, D.C., Geological Society of America, 1934- . v. 1- .
(Bibliographical contributions)   (3659
    Jones 336a.

PAN AMERICAN UNION. Columbus Memorial Library.
Geology of Latin America. List of books and
magazine articles on the geology of the Latin
American republics in the Columbus Memorial
Library. [Washington, D.C., 1917]
13 p.   (3660
    Jones 354a.

-----. -----. -----. [Washington, D.C., 1922]
20 p. mimeogr.   (3661
    Cited in PAU Bibliographies, p. 29.

-----. Division of Economic Research. List
of references and sources of information
pertaining to petroleum in Latin America.
[Washington, D.C., 1948] 3 p.   (3662

SPARN, Enrique. La diferenciación de las ciencias geológicas de acuerdo con el titulo de
sus revistas. Buenos Aires, Coni, 1927.
p. 341-47.   (3663
    Cited in Catálogo, Instituto Bibliotecoló-
gico, item 661.

ARGENTINA

BUENOS AIRES (Province). Comisión de Investigación Científica. Bibliografía geológica y

BUENOS AIRES (Province). Comisión... (Cont.)
cartográfica de la Provincia de Buenos Aires,
recopilada por ARCAM. La Plata, 1961 [i.e.,
1962] 145 p.   (3663a
    Cited in Geoghegan, 1858.

SPARN, Enrique. Bibliografía de la geología,
mineralogía, y paleontología de la República
Argentina hasta el año 1899. Córdoba, 1921.
93 p. (Academia Nacional de Ciencias, Misc.,
no. 3)   (3664

-----. Bibliografía de la geología, mineralogía y paleontología de la República Argentina, años 1900-1914. Córdoba, 1920. 58 p.
(Academia Nacional de Ciencias, Misc.
no. 2)   (3665
    Jones 851.

-----. Bibliografía de la geología, mineralogía y paleontología de la República Argentina, años 1915 a 1921. [Córdoba, 1922?].
50, vii, xvii p. (Academia Nacional de Ciencias, Misc. no. 5)   (3666
    Jones 851a notes that this number of the
series came out as Fasc. III, and has 2
supplements for the years to 1914.

-----. Bibliografía de la geología, mineralogía y paleontología de la República Argentina, fasc. IV; años 1922-1924, con un Suplemento para los años 1915-1921. Córdoba, Academia Nacional de Ciencias, Misc.
no. 11)   (3667
    Jones 851a.

-----. Bibliografía de la geología, mineralogía, paleontología de la República Argentina, años 1925-1927. Córdoba, 1928. 44 p.
(Academia Nacional de Ciencias, Misc.
no. 17)   (3668

-----. Bibliografía de la geología, mineralogía, paleontología de la República Argentina,
pt. VI, 1928-1931. Buenos Aires, T. Palumbo,
1935. 52 p.   (3669
    Jones 852.

-----. Bibliografía de los yacimientos de minerales y rocas de aplicación de la Provincia de Córdoba (Argentina). Córdoba, Impr.
de la Universidad, 1950. 39 p.   (3670

-----. Bibliografía geológica y mineralógica
de la Provincia de Córdoba. Córdoba, 1935.
34 p.   (3670a
    Published in Revista del Museo Provincial
de Ciencias Naturales, Córdoba, año 1, no. 1,
1935. Cited in Geoghegan, 1873.

BOLIVIA

BOLIVIA. Departamento Nacional de Geología.
Bibliografía geológica, mineralógica y pa-

BOLIVIA. Departamento Nacional ... (Cont.)
leontológica de Bolivia. La Paz, 1962.
186 p. (Departamento Nacional de Geología.
Boletín no. 4)   (3671
    Compilers: Jorge Muñoz Reyes, Leonardo
Branisa, Alfonso J. Freile.

BRAZIL

BRANNER, John Casper. A bibliography of the
geology, mineralogy and paleontology of
Brasil. Rio de Janeiro, Impr. Nacional,
1903. 115 p.   (3672
    "Tirado a parte dos Archivos do Museu Na-
cional do Rio de Janeiro, vol. 12." Contains 1203 titles not including abstracts,
notices and reviews.---Jones 983.

-----. -----. New York, Pub. by the Society,
1909. 132 p. (Bulletin of the Geological
Society of America, v. 20, p. 1-132) (3673
    "An incomplete edition of this bibliogra-
phy was published in the Archivos do Museu
Nacional do Rio de Janeiro, v. 12 in 1903.
The great number of titles added, the corrections made, and the growing interest in
the geology of Brazil have encouraged the
Geological Society of America to publish
the present list. Dr. M. A. R. Lisboa has
now begun the publication of an annual
annotated bibliography of the geology of
Brazil in the Annaes da Escola de Minas."
(p. 1, footnote)---Jones 984.

CAMPOS, José Menescal. Notas bibliográficas
sôbre os terrenos Gonduânicos do Brasil.
Rio de Janeiro, 1940. 39 p. (Brazil.
Depto. Nacional da Produção Mineral. Divisão de Geologia e Mineralogia, Boletim
no. 108)   (3674

FIGUEIREDO MURTA, Domício de. Literatura geologica do estado de Minas Gerais. Belo Horizonte, Secretaria da Agricultura, 1946.
2 v.   (3675
    Cited in Bibliografía brasileira, 1946,
p. 117.

FREYBERG, Bruno von. Die bodenschätze des
staates Minas Geraes (Brasilien). Stuttgart,
Schweizerbart, 1934. 453 p.   (3676
    Includes bibliographies.---Jones 1044.

-----. Ergebnisse geologischer forschungen in
Minas Geraes. Stuttgart, Schweizerbart,
1932. 403 p.   (3677
    Die geologische literatur: p. 331-99.---
Jones 1045.

GONÇALVES, Alpheu Diniz. Bibliographia da geologia, mineralogia e paleontologia do Brasil.
Rio de Janeiro, 1928. 205 p. (Brazil. Serviço Geológico e Mineralógico, Boletim
no. 27)   (3678

GONÇALVES, Alpheu Diniz. ... (Cont.)
Jones 1030.

IGLESIAS, Dolores. Bibliografia e índice da geologia do Brasil, 1641-1940. Rio de Janeiro, 1943. 323 p. (Brazil. Depto. Nacional da Produção Mineral. Divisão de Geologia e Mineralogia, Boletim no. 111) (3679

-----. -----. [Rev. ed.] Rio de Janeiro, 1959. 385 [1] p. (Boletim no. 204) (3680

IGLESIAS, Dolores, and MENEGHEZZI, Maria de Lourdes. Bibliografia e índice da geologia do Brasil, 1941-1942. Rio de Janeiro, 1944. 35 p. (Brazil. Depto. Nacional da Produção Mineral. Divisão de Geologia e Mineralogia, Boletim no. 117) (3681

-----. -----. 1943-1945. Rio de Janeiro, 1949. 45, xvii p. (Brazil. Depto. Nacional da Produção Mineral. Divisão de Geologia e Mineralogia, Boletim no. 131) (3682

-----. -----. 1945-1950. Rio de Janeiro, 1957. 128 p. (Brazil. Depto. Nacional da Produção Mineral. Divisão de Geologia e Mineralogia, Boletim no. 164) (3683

-----. -----. 1941-1950. Rio de Janeiro, 1960. 167 p. (Brazil. Depto. Nacional da Produção Mineral. Divisão de Geologia e Mineralogia, Boletim no. 206) (3684

-----. -----. 1951-1955. Rio de Janeiro, 1957. 80 p. (Brazil. Depto. Nacional da Produção Mineral. Divisão dc Geologia e Mineralogia, Boletim no. 177) (3685

-----. -----. 1956-1957. Rio de Janeiro, 1959. 53 p. (Brazil. Depto. Nacional da Produção Mineral. Divisão de Geologia e Mineralogia, Boletim no. 187) (3686

-----. -----. 1958-1959. Rio de Janeiro, 1960. 56 p. (Brazil. Depto. Nacional da Produção Mineral. Divisão de Geologia e Mineralogia, Boletim no. 210) (3687

-----. -----. 1960-1961. Rio de Janeiro, 1964. 71 p. (Brazil. Depto. Nacional da Produção Mineral. Divisão de Geologia e Mineralogia, Boletim no. 220) (3688

-----. Bibliografia e índice do ferro no Brasil. Rio de Janeiro, Ministério das Minas e Energia, Depto. Nacional da Produção Mineral, 1961. 85 p. (Brazil. Divisão de Geologia e Mineralogia, Boletim no. 212) (3689

LISBOA, Miguel Arrojado Ribeiro. Bibliographia mineral e geologica do Brasil, 1903-1906. Ed. do autor. Ouro Preto, Typ. Medeiros, [1907?] p. 201-19, 62 p. (3690

LISBOA, Miguel Arrojado Ribeiro ... (Cont.)
Reprinted from Annaes, Escola de Minas, Ouro Preto, no. 8-9, 1906-1907. Cited in Iglesias (Bol. 111) p. 149.

MENDES, Josué Camargo. Bibliografia geológica, mineralógica, petrográfica e paleontológica do Estado de São Paulo. São Paulo, Secretaria da Agricultura, Indústria e Comércio, 1944. 57 p. (3691
Cited in Bibliografia brasileira, 1942-1945, v. 2, p. 561.

MEZZALIRA, Sergio, and WOHLERS, Armando. Bibliografia da geologia, mineralogia, petrografia e paleontologia do estado de São Paulo. [São Paulo, 1952] 62 p. (São Paulo. Instituto Geográfico e Geológico, Boletim no. 33) (3692

TRINDADE, Nicéa Maggessi. Pesquisas bibliográficas sôbre as minas de carvão do Gondwana inferior do sul do Brasil. Rio de Janeiro, Serviço Gráfico do Instituto Brasileiro de Geografia e Estadística, 1961. 52 p. (Brazil. Divisão de Geologia e Mineralogia, Boletim no. 208) (3693

WASHBURNE, Chester Wesley. Petroleum geology of the state of São Paulo, Brazil. São Paulo, 1930. 282 p. (3694
Bibliography: 251-72. A Portuguese translation by Joviano Pacheco was published in Rio de Janeiro in 1939.---Jones 1225.

CENTRAL AMERICA

MALDONADO KOERDELL, Manuel. Bibliografia geológica de la América Central. México, D.F., 1958. 288 p. (Publ. del Instituto Panamericano de Geografía e Historia, no. 204) (3695
Title also in English: Geological and paleontological bibliography of Central America.

CHILE

BRÜGGEN, Hans. Bibliografía minera i jeológica de Chile. Santiago, Impr. Universo, 1919. 142 p. (3696
Jones 1411.

-----. 2 pte. Santiago, 1927. 66 p. (3697
"Folletos" 4 and 16 of the Ministry of Agriculture and Industry; about 1990 titles included. Also in Boletín minero de la Sociedad Nacional de Minería, t. 31, p. 441-515, 539-607; t. 38, p. 870-89, 1050-57.---Jones 1411.

-----. Grundzüge der geologie und lagerstättenkunde Chiles. Herausgegeben von der ma-

BRÜGGEN, Hans. Grundzüge der ... (Cont.)
thematisch-naturwissenschftlichen klasse der
Heidelberg Akademie der Wissenschaften.
Heidelberg, 1934. 362 p.   (3698
   Literaturverzeichnis: p. 353-60.---Jones
1410.

COLOMBIA

RAMIREZ, Jesús Emilio. Bibliografía de la
Biblioteca del Instituto Geofísico de los
Andes Colombianos sobre geología y geofísi-
ca de Colombia. Bogotá, 1951. 267 p.
(Instituto Geofísico de los Andes Colombia-
nos, Ser. C - Geología, Boletín 2)   (3699

-----. 2a. ed. corr. y aum. Bogotá, Impr.
del Banco de la República, 1957. 521 p.
(Instituto Geofísico de los Andes Colombianos, Ser. C - Geología, Boletín 6)   (3700

ROYO Y GOMES, José. Bibliografía geológico-
geográfica de Colombia. Bogotá, Inst. Colombiano de Petróleos, 1942. 41 p. (Estudio técnico, no. 3)   (3701
   Cited in Giraldo Jaramillo, p. 110.

-----. Bibliografía geológica, geográfica y
minera de Colombia. Bogotá, Edit. Kelly,
1945. 127 p. (Compilación de los estudios
geológicos oficiales de Colombia, t. 6,
anexo 2)   (3702
   Additions and corrections in v. 8, 1950,
p. 313-44. Cited in Giraldo Jaramillo,
p. 111.

COSTA RICA

DENGO, Gabriel. Bibliografía de la geología
de Costa Rica. [San José] 1959. 27 p.
(Costa Rica. Universidad de Costa Rica.
Publicaciones, Ser. Ciencias naturales,
no. 3)   (3703

-----. -----. [San José] 1962. 67 p. (Publ.,
Universidad de Costa Rica. Ser. Ciencias
naturales, no. 3)   (3704
   Contains additions.

CUBA

BERMUDEZ, Pedro J. Bibliografía geológica cubana. Habana, Carasa y Cía., 1938. 86 p.
(Publ. de la revista "Universidad de la Habana")   (3705
   605 titles, alphabetical by author with
subject and author indexes. Current publications may be found in Bibliographie des
sciences géologiques, pub. annually by the
Société Géologique de France.---Jones 1791.

ORTEGA, Pablo, and HUERTA, Santiago de la. El
carbon de piedra, el petróleo, el asfalto,
los betunes y el gas natural de Cuba. Extractado de la Bibliografía geológica y minera de Cuba (en preparacion). La Habana,
Impr. "El Siglo XX", 1919. 23 p. (Cuba.
Secretaría de Agricultura, Comercio y Trabajo. Dirección de Montes y Minas. Boletín
bibliográfico, no. 1)   (3706

DOMINICAN REPUBLIC

DOMINICAN REPUBLIC. Servicio Geológico. Un
reconocimiento geológico de la República Dominicana. Washington, D.C., 1922. 302 p.
(Memorias, t.1)   (3707
   Bibliografía por Wendel Phillips Woodring:
p. 19-26. Also issued in English, 1921.---
Jones 2990.

DUTCH GUIANA

STEENHUIS, Jakob Frederik. De geologische li-
teratuur over of van belang voor Nederlandsch-
Guyana (Suriname) 'S-Gravenhage, N.V. Boeken
Kunstdrukkerij v/h Mouton & co., 1934.
80 p.   (3708

ECUADOR

SHEPPARD, George. Bibliografía de la geología
del Ecuador. (Anales de la Universidad Central, Quito, no. 276, p. 285-98, 1931) (3709
   Jones 2015.

-----, and VAUGHAN, Thomas Wayland. The geolo-
gy of south-western Ecuador. London, T.
Murby & Co., 1937. 275 p.   (3710
   Bibliography: p. 262-69.---Jones 2016.

FALKLAND ISLANDS or ISLAS MALVINAS

SPARN, Enrique. Bibliografía de la geología y
del clima de las Islas Malvinas. [Córdoba]
Dirección General de Publicidad, Universidad
Nacional de Córdoba, 1954. 29 p.   (3710a
   Cited in Geoghegan 1871.

MEXICO

AGUILAR Y SANTILLAN, Rafael. Bibliografía geológica y minera de la República Mexicana.
México, Of. Tip. de la Secretaría de Fomento, 1898. 158 p. (Boletín del Instituto
Geológico, México, no. 10)   (3711

-----. Bibliografía geológica y minera de la
República Mexicana, completada hasta el año
de 1904. México, Impr. de la Secretaria de
Fomento, 1908. 330 p. (Instituto Geológico

AGUILAR Y SANTILLAN, Rafael ... (Cont.)
de México. Boletín, no. 17)   (3712
First edition, listing publications up to
the end of 1896, appeared in 1898 as "Boletín del Instituto Geológico de México, no.
10".---Jones 2035.

-----. Bibliografía geológica y minera de la
República Mexicana. México, Tip. de la Of.
Impresora de la Secretaria de Hacienda, 1918.
97 p.   (3713
Edición del Boletín minero, órgano del De-
partamento de Minas.---Jones 2036.

-----. Bibliografía geológica y minera de la
Republica Mexicana, 1919 a 1930. México,
Tall. Graf. de la Nación, 1936. iv,
83 p.   (3714

-----. Bibliography of Mexican geology and
mining. (Transactions of the American Institute of Mining Engineers, New York, v. 32,
p. 605-80, 1903)   (3715
Jones 2037.

BLASQUEZ LOPEZ, Luis, and LOEHNBERG, Alfredo.
Bibliografía hidrogeológica de la República
Mexicana. México, D.F., 1961. 101 p.
(México. Universidad Nacional. Instituto
de Geología. Anales, t. 17)   (3716

FABREGAT GUINCHARD, Francisco J. Bibliografía
mineralógica de México. México, 1962. 87 p.
(México. Universidad Nacional. Instituto
de Geología. Anales, t. 20)   (3717

MARTINEZ PORTILLO, Jesús. Bibliografía geoló-
gica minera del Estado de Aguascalientes.
México, 1945. 8 p. mimeogr.   (3718
Cited in Publicaciones editadas of the
Instituto de Geología, Universidad Nacional
Autónoma de México, p. 25.

-----. Bibliografía geológica del Estado de
Zacatecas. México, 1946. 53 p.
mimeogr.   (3719
Cited in Publicaciones editadas of the
Instituto de Geología, Universidad Nacional
Autónoma de México, p. 25.

MUIR, John M. Geology of the Tampico region,
Mexico. Tulsa, Okla., The American Association of Petroleum Geologists, 1936.
280 p.   (3720
Mexican oil-fields bibliography: p. 237-
47.---Jones 2372.

MUÑOZ LUMBIER, Manuel. La seismología en México hasta 1917. México, 1918. 102 p. (Boletín del Instituto Geológico de México,
36)   (3721
Bibliography: p. 92-100.---Jones 2373.

SANTILLAN, Manuel. Anuario del Instituto de
Geología, 1932. México, Ed. Cultura, 1933.

SANTILLAN, Manuel. Anuario ... (Cont.)
162 p.   (3722
Includes much bibliographical material.---
Jones 2487. See also subsequent issues of
the Anuario.

ZUBIRIA Y CAMPA, Luis. Bibliografía minera,
geológica y mineralógica del estado de Durango. (Memorias de la Sociedad Científica
"Antonio Alzate", México, t. 38, p. 177-98,
1919)   (3723
Jones 2595.

PERU

BROGGI, Jorge Alberto. Geología, botánica y
zoología del Perú, 1929-1933. (Boletín de
la Sociedad Geológica del Perú, Lima, v. 7,
p. 23-124, 1934?)   (3724
Jones 2640.

-----. Memoria y bibliografía. Lima, 1934.
123 p. (Boletín de la Sociedad Geológica
del Perú. v. 6, fasc. 2)   (3725
Jones 2641.

CASTRO BASTOS, Leonidas. Bibliografía geológica del Perú. Lima, 1960. 317 p.
mimeogr.   (3726

STEINNMANN, Gustav. Geologie von Perú. Heidel-
berg, C. Winter, 1929. 448 p.   (3727
Verzeichnis der schriften: p. 409-32.---
Jones 2755.

TORRES, J. Leopoldo. Guía bibliográfica con-
sultiva; descripción de minas y oficinas me-
talúrgicas en el Perú, clasificadas por departamentos; compilación de estudios generales
y locales, informes de mineralogía, geología,
explotación de minas y metalurgia insertos
en las obras y publicaciones de la biblioteca
de la Escuela de Ingenieros de Lima. Lima,
E. Moreno, 1904. 27 p.   (3728
Jones 2759.

-----. -----. 2. ed. Lima, P. Berrio, 1908.
85 p.   (3729
Jones 2760.

-----. -----. 3. ed. corr. y aum. Lima, Tip.
de "El Lucero", 1914. 97 p.   (3730
Jones 2761.

SOUTH AMERICA

COURTY, Georges. Explorations géologiques
dans l'Amérique du Sud. Paris, Impr. Natio-
nale, 1907. 208 p. (Mission Scientifique
G. de Créqui Montfort et E. Sénechal de la
Grange)   (3731
Bibliographie géologique: p. 169-80.---
Jones 115.

MILLER, Benjamin L., and SINGEWALD, Joseph
Theophilus. The mineral deposits of South
America. New York, McGraw-Hill Book, 1919.
598 p.   (3732
   Includes selective bibliographies.---Jones
316.

SINGEWALD, Joseph Theophilus. Bibliography of
economic geology of South America. New York,
1943. 159 p. (Geological Society of America. Special papers, no. 50)   (3733
   Contains bibliographies published in The
mineral deposits of South America, by B. L.
Miller and J. T. Singewald.

URUGUAY

LAMBERT, Roger. Bibliographie géologique de
la République Orientale de l'Uruguay. Montevideo, Impr. Nacional, 1939. 79 p. (Instituto Geológico del Uruguay. Boletín,
26)   (3734
   Jones 2844a.

MARSTRANDER, Rolf. Bibliografía de la geología, mineralogía y paleontología de la República Oriental del Uruguay. (Pan American
Scientific Congress, 2d. Proceedings. Washington, 1917. v. 8, p. 659-74)   (3735
   A list of 241 items.---Jones 2850a.

WALTER, Karl. Sedimentos geléticos y clasto-
geléticos del cretáceo superior y terciario
uruguayos. Montevideo, Impr. Nacional, 1930.
142 p. (Boletín del Instituto de Geología
y Perforaciones, no. 13)   (3736
   Bibliografía: p. 87-92. See also his
Estudios geomorfológicos y geológicos, (Montevideo, 1942) which includes bibliography,

WALTER, Karl. Sedimentos ... (Cont.)
   p. 304-19.---Jones 2878.

VENEZUELA

HEDBERG, H. D., and HEDBERG, F. Bibliografia
e índice de la geología de Venezuela. Caracas, Lit. del Comercio, 1945. 81 p. (3737
   Taken from Revista de fomento, no. 58-59,
año VII.

JAHN, Alfredo. Embozo de las formaciones geológicas de Venezuela. Caracas, Lit. del Comercio, 1921. 108 p.   (3738
   Bibliografía: p. 14-6.---Jones 2921.

KEHRER, L. Bibliografía geológica de Venezuela. (Boletín de la Sociedad Venezolana de
Ciencias Naturales, Caracas, no. 28, p. 441-
64, 1936)   (3739
   241 titles.---Jones 2922.

WEST INDIES

HOVEY, Edmund Otis. Bibliography of literature
of the West Indian eruptions published in the
United States. (Bulletin of the Geological
Society of America, Rochester, v. 15, p. 562-
66, 1904)   (3740
   Jones 2999.

RUTTEN, Louis Martin Robert. Bibliography of
West Indian geology. Utrecht, Bij N.V.A.
Oosthoek's Uitg. Mij., 1938. 103 p. (Geo-
graphische en geologische meddedeelingen;
pub. uit het Geographisch en uit het Minera-
logisch-Geologisch Instituut der Rijksuniversiteit te Utrecht, Physiographisch-geolo-
gische reeks, no. 16)   (3741
   Jones 3009.

GOVERNMENT PUBLICATIONS

GENERAL

CHILDS, James Bennett. An account of govern-
ment document bibliography in the United
States and elsewhere. Washington, D.C.,
Govt. Print. Off., 1930. 57 p.   (3742
   Jones 99.

-----. Bibliography of official publications
and the administrative systems in Latin
American countries. Washington, D.C.,
Govt. Print. Off., 1938. 44 p.   (3743
   Reprinted from the Proceedings of the
Inter-American Bibliographical and Library
Association, 1st, 1938.

-----. Government document bibliography in
the United States and elsewhere; 3d. ed.
Washington, D.C., Govt. Print. Off., 1942.

CHILDS, James Bennett. Government... (Cont.)
xxiii, 78 p.   (3744
   Includes Latin American countries.

-----. Hispanic American government documents
in the Library of Congress. 1926. p. 134-
41.   (3745
   Reprinted from the Hispanic American historical review, Durham, N.C., v. 6, no. 1-3,
Feb./Aug. 1926.

-----. The memorias of the republics of Central America and of the Antillas. Washington,
D.C., Govt., Print. Off., 1932.
170 p.   (3746

LIST of the serial publications of foreign
governments, 1815-1931, ed. by Winifred
Gregory for the American Council of Learned

LIST of the serial ... (Cont.)
Societies, American Library Association,
National Research Council. New York, H. W.
Wilson, 1932. 720 p.   (3747
   List of cooperating libraries (with abbre-
viations) on end-papers and on verso of 5th.
prelim. leaf. Contents arranged geographi-
cally by country. Includes listing of Latin
American countries.

MEDELLIN. Escuela Interamericana de Bibliotecología. [B-14]: Publicaciones oficiales;
bibliografía. Medellín, [1961] 2 p.
mimeogr.   (3748

MEYRIAT, Jean. A study of current bibliography
of national official publications. Etude des
bibliographies courantes des publications
officielles nationales. [Paris] Unesco
[1958] 260 p. (Unesco bibliographic handbooks, 7)   (3749
   North America and South America, p. 80-132.

PERAZA SARAUSA. Fermín. Bibliografías sobre
publicaciones oficiales de la América Latina.
Submitted for the 8th Seminar on the Acqui-
sition of Latin American Library Materials.
[Madison, Wisc., 1963] 22 p.   (3750
   Working paper no. 11,

U.S. Library of Congress. A guide to the
official publications of the other American
Republics; James B. Childs, general editor.
Washington, D.C., Govt., Print. Off., 1945-
1948. 19 v. (Latin American ser., no. 9-11,
15, 17, 19, 22-25, 27, 29-31, 33-37) (3751
   Contents: I, Argentina, by James B. Childs.-
II, Bolivia, by James B. Childs.- III, Brazil,
by John DeNoia. - IV, Chile, by O. Neuburger.-
V, Colombia, by James B. Childs. - VI, Costa
Rica, by Henry V. Besso. - VII, Cuba, by James
B. Childs. - VIII, Dominican Republic, by John
DeNoia. - IX, Ecuador, by John DeNoia. - X,
El Salvador, by John DeNoia. - XI, Guatemala,
by Henry V. Besso. - XII, Haiti, by Henry V.
Besso. - XIII, Honduras, by Henry V. Besso. -
XIV, Nicaragua, by John DeNoia. - XV, Panama,
by John DeNoia. - XVI, Paraguay, by James B.
Childs. - XVII, Peru, by John DeNoia. - XVIII,
Uruguay, by John DeNoia and Glenda Crevenna.-
XIX, Venezuela, by Otto Neuburger.

U. U. Office of the Coordinator of Inter-American Affairs. Preliminary listing of publications dealing with Latin America issued by
the agencies of the United States Government
during the past five years. Washington, D.C.,
1941. 27 p. mimeogr.   (3752

WILGUS, Alva Curtis. List of government publications concerning Hispanic America. Durham,
N.C., Duke Univ. Pr., p. 132-48.   (3753
   From the Hispanic American historical review,
v. 16, no. 1, Feb. 1936.---Jones 536.

WILGUS, Alva Curtis. List of government publications concerning Hispanic America. (Hispanic American historical review, Durham, N.C.,
v. 18, p. 127-41, 1938)   (3754
   Covers items listed in Monthly catalogue,
U.S. public documents, Apr.-Sept., 1936.---
Jones 537.

ARGENTINA

ARGENTINA. Dirección de Minas, Geología e Hi-
drogeología. Publicaciones. Buenos Aires,
1940. 31 p.   (3755

-----. Dirección Nacional de Geología y Minería. Catálogo de publicaciones, incluyendo
los informes inéditos. Ordenado y clasificado por Antonio Amato. Buenos Aires, 1960.
113 p.   (3756

-----. Instituto de Microbiología Agrícola.
Catálogo de libros, 1946-1950. Buenos Aires,
Ministerio de Agricultura y Ganadería, 1950.
25 p. (Publicación miscelánea, no. 3) (3757
   Cited in Catálogo, Instituto Bibliotecoló-
gico, item 639.

BRAZIL

BRAZIL. Conselho Nacional de Proteção aos Indios. Catalogo geral das publicações da
Comissão Rondon e do Conselho Nacional de
Proteção aos Indios. Rio de Janeiro, Depto.
de Impr. Nacional, 1950. 32 p. (Publ. no.
96)   (3758

-----. Departamento Administrativo do Serviço
Público. Catalogo de publicações do D.A.S.P.,
seguido de uma lista de titulos de obras editadas de 1938 a 1946. Rio de Janeiro, Impr.
Nacional, 1947. 82 p.   (3759

-----. -----. Catalogo das publicações do D.A.
S.P., atualizado até 30/4/1954. [Rio de Ja-
neiro] 1954. 124 p.   (3760
   Contains: 1a. parte, Relação por assuntos.

-----. -----. (atualizado até 31-7-1956) Rio
de Janeiro, 1958. 153 p.   (3761

-----. -----. -----. [Supl.]: "Obras publicadas no período de 1-8-56/31-11-57". Rio de
Janeiro, 1958. 24 p.   (3762

-----. -----. Circulares do D.A.S.P. de 1938
a 1950, acompanhadas de índices cronológico
e remisivo. Rio de Janeiro, Impr. Nacional,
1953. xxxvii, 223 p.   (3763

-----. -----. Memsagem do D.A.S.P. aos prefei-
tos e vereadores do Brasil. Roteiro bibliográfico para estudo da administração municipal. [Rio de Janeiro] Serviço de Documenta-

BRAZIL. Departamento Administrativo...(Cont.)
ção, 1954. 183 p.   (3764
  2. ed. of the work Roteiro bibliográfico
para estudo da administração municipal, by
Araújo Cavalcanti e Francisco Burkinski, rev.
and enl. by Aida Furtado.

-----. -----. Publicações do D.A.S.P., Rio de
Janeiro, Impr. Nacional, 1944. 40 p. (Biblioteca do D.A.S.P., Guía, no. 2)   (3765

-----. Departamento de Imprensa Nacional.
150 anos de tipografia oficial; seleção de
cento e cinqüenta livros e periódicos impressos de 1808 a 1958. Rio de Janeiro,
1958. 153 unnumbered pages.   (3766
  Exhibition in commemoration of the 150th.
year since the establishment of the Departamento de Imprensa Nacional.

-----. -----. Mostra de livros. Rio de Janeiro, 1941- .   (3767
  The first issue was published in commemoration of the 134th. anniversary of the
founding of the Imprensa Nacional. The 1960
issue is the 20th, published in commemoration
of the 153rd anniversary.

-----. Departamento Nacional da Produção Mineral. Catalogo das publicações (até 1945)
Rio de Janeiro, 1946. 80 p.   (3768

-----. Imprensa Nacional. Imprensa Nacional
(officina official) 1808-1908; apontamentos
historicos, por Oliveira Bello. Rio de Janeiro, Impr. Nacional, 1908. 152 p. (3769
  A history of the national printing office,
with a chapter on its publications. See
also Valle Cabral's Annaes da Imprensa Nacional ... de 1808 a 1822.---Jones 994.

-----. Ministério da Fazenda. Circulares do
Ministro da Fazenda Nacional [Rio de Janeiro]
1942. 30 p.   (3770
  Arrangement of circulars is chronological.

-----. Ministério das Relações Exteriores.
Lista de publicações, 1o./2o. sem. 1943.
Rio de Janeiro, Impr. Nacional, 1944.
50 p.   (3771

-----. -----. Lista de publicações: 1826-1950.
Rio de Janeiro, Serviço de Publicações,
n.d.   (3772
  Cited in Doria Menezes 153.

-----. Ministério do Trabalho, Indústria e
Comércio. Publicações do MTIC. Rio de Janeiro, Serviço de Documentação, 1954.
75 p.   (3773
  Cited in Doria Menezes 154. Compiler: Maria Teresa Coelho.

CABRAL, Alfredo do Valle. Annaes da Imprensa
Nacional do Rio de Janeiro de 1808 a 1822.

CABRAL, Alfredo do Valle. Annaes ... (Cont.)
Rio de Janeiro, Typ. Nacional, 1881.
339 p.   (3774
  "Appendice. Obras publicadas em outras
officinas typographicas do Rio de Janeiro em
1821 e 1822": p. 299-323. "Até as proximi-
dades da independencia, a Impressão regia
foi a unica typographia que existiu no Rio
de Janeiro". Carvalho, Genese e progressos
da imp. periodica no Brasil.---Jones 1217.

CENTRO Brasileiro de Pesquisas Educacionais,
Rio de Janeiro. Lista de publicações do
INEP e do CBPE. Rio de Janeiro, 1964.
8 p.   (3775
  Cited in Doria Menezes 151.

-----. Publicações do Ministério da Educação
e Cultura. Rio de Janeiro, Serviço de Bibliografia, 1964. 4 p.   (3776
  Cited in Doria Menezes 152.

MACHADO, Alberto F. Imprensa Nacional. Catalogo por ordem alphabetica das obras existentes na Bibliotheca. Rio de Janeiro, Impr.
Nacional, 1916. 177 p.   (3777
  Cited in Reis, item 295.

SÃO PAULO (State). Departamento Estadual de
Estatística. Indice alfabético das publicações de 1938 a 1943. São Paulo, [1944]
133 p.   (3778a

CHILE

CHILE. Biblioteca Nacional. Las publicaciones de la Biblioteca Nacional, 1854-1963;
informe elevado al Ministerio de Educación
[por] Guillermo Feliú Cruz, director de la
Biblioteca Nacional. [Santiago de Chile]
Dirección de Bibliotecas, Archivos y Museos, 1964. lxxxi p.   (3779

-----. Servicio Sismológico. Publicaciones,
1909-1914. [n.d.] 4 p.   (3780
  Cited in Laval, item 276.

REYES, Ismael G. Bibliografía astronómica.
Publicaciones del Observatorio Astronómico
Nacional. (Revista de bibliografía chilena
y extranjera, Santiago, año 2, p. 153-59,
1914)   (3781
  Jones 1586.

COLOMBIA

CHILDS, James Bennett. Colombian government
publications. Washington, D.C., 1941.
41 p.   (3782
  Jones 1697a. Reprinted from Proceedings
of the Third Convention of the Inter-American
Bibliographical and Library Association,
1940, p. 301-39.

COLOMBIA. Ministerio de Agricultura. División de Investigaciones Agropecuarias. Guía para publicaciones técnicas del D.I.A. Bogotá, 1960. 19 p. (3783
Cited in Florén, Bibliografía bibliotecológica, 1961/1962, item 242.

-----. Ministerio de Educación Nacional. Catálogo de la Biblioteca Popular de Cultura Colombiana y de otros volúmenes editados por la Sección de Publicaciones . Bogotá, 1948. 5 p. (3784
About 120 titles are given. Cited in Giraldo Jaramillo, p. 39.

CONFERENCIA sobre Administración Pública en los Países en Desarrollo, Bogotá, 1963. Publicaciones oficiales, por Vicente Peñalosa y Tarsicio Higuera. Bogotá, Escuela Superior de Administración Pública, 1963. (3785
Cited in Peraza Fichas, 1962/1963, item 620.

INSTITUTO Caro y Cuervo, Bogotá. Catálogo de las publicaciones. Bogotá, Prensas del Ministerio de Educación Nacional, 1949. 12 p. (3786
Cited in Giraldo Jaramillo, p. 70.

MEDELLIN. Escuela Interamericana de Bibliotecología. Bibliografía oficial colombiana. Medellín, 1964. mimeogr. (3787
Cited in Boletín de adquisiciones, Medellín no. 2, p. 11, Feb. 1965.

PERAZA SARAUSA, Fermín, and BOHORQUEZ C., Ignacio. Publicaciones oficiales colombianas. Gainesville, Fla., 1964. 31 p. (Biblioteca del bibliotecario, 69) (3788
Published also as Doc. 35 of the Conferencia sobre Administración Pública en los Países en Desarrollo.

GUATEMALA

GUATEMALA. Tipografía Nacional. Catálogo general de libros, folletos y revistas editadas en la Tipografía Nacional de Guatemala, desde 1892 hasta 1943. Guatemala, 1944. 352 p. (3789
Peraza 65, 1964, item 197, cites continuation 1944-1953.

MEXICO

CASTILLO, Ignacio B. del. Bibliografía de la Imprenta de la Cámara de Diputados, para servir a los historiadores de la época de Madero, Huerta y la Convención, 1912-1915. México, Of. Impresora de Hacienda, 1918. 48 p. (3790
In prize-winning compilation of bibliogra-

CASTILLO, Ignacio B. del. Bibliografía..(Cont.) phies chosen by the National Library in 1915. Includes 277 items. Cited in Jones 2349.

GOMEZ DE OROZCO, Federico. Las publicaciones del extinto Ayuntamiento de México y del Departamento del Distrito Federal; reseña histórica. México, Graf. Panamericana, 1943. 13 p. (Biblioteca de la II Feria del Libro y Exposición Nacional del Periodismo, 1943) (3791

GONZALEZ, Silvino M. Algunas fichas para una bibliografía general de la Secretaría de la Defensa Nacional. México, [Tall. Linotip. "Nigromante" de González, Martínez y Cía.] 1943. 206 p. (Biblioteca de la II Feria del Libro y Exposición Nacional del Periodismo, 1943) (3792

KER, Annita Melville. Mexican government publications, a guide to the more important publications of the national government of México, 1821-1936. Washington, D.C., Govt. Print. Off., 1940. 333 p. (3793
Jones 2271a.

MEXICO. Departamento Agrario. Publicaciones del Departamento. México, D.F., 1943. 8 p. (Biblioteca de la II Feria del Libro y Exposición Nacional del Periodismo, 1943) (3794
Cited in HLAS, 9, item 55.

-----. Departamento de Informaciones Sociales y Estadística. Biblioteca. Feria del Libro y Exposición Nacional del Periodismo, 1943. México [Tall. Gráf. de la Nación] 1943. 32 p. (Biblioteca de la II Feria del Libro y Exposición Nacional del Periodismo, 1943) (3795
Cover title: Bibliografía de la Secretaría del Trabajo y Prevision Social.

-----. Dirección Genral de Educación Higienica. Bibliografía, que el Departamento de Salubridad Pública presenta en la Feria del Libro y Exposición Nacional del Periodismo. México, 1943. 63 p. (3795a

-----. Dirección General de Estadística. Catálogo de publicaciones. México, Tall. Gráf. de la Nación, 1933. 12 p. (3796
Cited in Millares, item 1740a, Adiciones.

-----. Instituto Nacional de Antropología e Historia. El Instituto Nacional de Antropología e Historia; su contribución a la bibliografía nacional. México, D.F., 1962. 342 p. (3797
Compiled by Antonio Pompa y Pompa.

-----. -----. El Instituto Nacional de Antropología e Historia; su contribución editorial, científica y de cultura. México, D.F., Edit. Cultura, 1954. 89 p. (3798

MEXICO. Secretaría de Agricultura y Fomento. Lista de las publicaciones disponibles. México, D.F., Dirección de Tall. Gráf., 1919. 12 p.   (3799
   Cited in Millares, item 1733a, Adiciones.

-----. Secretaría de Comunicaciones y Obras Públicas. Bibliografía, 1891-1943. México, D.F., Tip. La Nacional, 1943. 189 p.   (3800
   Compiled in relation to the II Feria del Libro y Exposición Nacional del Periodismo, 1943. Contains 444 entries.

-----. Secretaría de la Economía Nacional. Publicaciones oficiales (1933-1942). México, [Publicaciones S.E.N. [1943] 62, 7 p. (Biblioteca de la II Feria del Libro y Exposición Nacional del Periodismo, 1943. (3801

-----. Secretaría de Fomento, Colonización e Industria. Catálogo de las principales obras impresas en la Oficina Tipográfica de la Secretaría de Fomento, Colonización e Industria y que se remiten a la Exposición Internacional de Chicago. México, D.F., 1893. 30 p.   (3802
   Jones 2362.

-----. Secretaría de Hacienda y Crédito Público. Bibliografía de la Secretaría de Hacienda y Crédito Público. México, D.F., 1943. 226 p. (Biblioteca de la II Feria del Libros y Exposición Nacional del Periodismo, 1943)   (3803
   Covers period 1821-1942.

-----. Secretaría de Industria, Comercio y Trabajo. Catálogo [no. 1] de publicaciones. México, Poder Ejecutivo Federal, 1919. 16 p.   (3804
   Jones 2365.

-----. -----. Catálogo, no. 2. México, Dirección de Tall. Gráf., 1920. 14 p.   (3805
   Cited in Millares, item 1740c, Adiciones.

-----. Suplemento a su Catálogo no. 2. de publicaciones. México, Tall. Gráf., 1922. 20 p.   (3806
   Cited in Millares, item 1740d, Adiciones.

-----. Secretaría de Relaciones Exteriores. Catálogo de las publicaciones de la Secretaría. México, Impr. de la Secretaría, 1926. 14 p.   (3807
   Jones 2366.

SALDIVAR, Gabriel. Bibliografía de la Secretaría de Relaciones Exteriores. México, 1943. 96 p. (Secretaría de Relaciones Exteriores, Depto. de Información para el Extranjero, Ser. bibliográficas mexicanas, no. 2)   (3808
   At head of title: Biblioteca de la Feria del Libro y Exposición Nacional del Periodismo.

VERACRUZ, México (State) Imprenta del Gobierno. La imprenta del gobierno del estado de Veracruz. [Jalapa] Tall. Gráf. del Estado, 1943. 16 p.   (3809

PANAMA

PANAMA. Biblioteca Nacional. Guía de organismos oficiales y sus publicaciones. Panamá, 1960. 29 p. (Publicaciones) mimeogr.(3810

PERU

PERU. Ministerio de Hacienda y Comercio. Archivo Histórico. Publicaciones. [Lima, 1962]   (3811

-----. Oficina de Reparto, Depósito y Canje Internacional de Publicaciones. Catálogo de las publicaciones que la "Oficina de Reparto, Depósito y Canje Internacional" tiene disponibles para distribuir. Lima, 1905. 10 p.   (3812
   Jones 2722.

VENEZUELA

VENEZUELA. Dirección de Planificación Agropecuaria. Lista de publicaciones efectuadas, 1959. Caracas, 1960. 4 p.   (3813
   Cited in its Catálogo, p. 10.

-----. -----. Catálogo de las publicaciones efectuadas durante el año 1960. Caracas, Ministerio de Agricultura y Cría, 1961. 16 p.   (3814

-----. -----. Catálogo de las publicaciones efectuadas durante el año 1962. Caracas, 1963. 12 p.   (3815

-----. Presidencia. Catálogo de Publicaciones, 1959/1963. Caracas, 1963. 111 p.   (3816

HISTORY

GENERAL

BARROS ARANA, Diego. Estudios histórico-
bibliográficos. Santiago de Chile, Impr.
Cervantes, 1909-1911. 5 v. (In author's
Obras completas, v. 6, 8-11)   (3817

BUENOS AIRES. Universidad. Facultad de Ciencias Económicas. Biblioteca. Guerra y postguerra, bibliografía. Buenos Aires, 1945.
64 p.   (3818

COSTA, Abel Fontoura da. A marinharia dos des-
cobrimentos. Lisboa, Impr. da Armada, 1933.
521 p.   (3819
    "Separata dos Anais do Club Militar Naval.
Apendice: Bibliografia nautica portuguesa
até 1700: Obras impressas até 1700; Obras
impressas depois de 1700, reprodução de ms.
até este ano; Obras manuscritas." Contains
facsimiles of title-pages.---Jones 1041.

FERNANDEZ DE NAVARRETE, Martín. Biblioteca
marítima española, obra postuma. Madrid,
Impr. de la Viuda de Calero, 1851.
2 v.   (3820
    Bibliographical notes of Spanish authors,
explorers, soldiers, etc., arranged alphabetically by forenames. Contains data
referring to Latin America.---Jones 332.

FIGANIERE, Jorge Cesar de. Bibliographia historica portugueza, ou Catalogo methodico dos
auctores portuguezes, e de alguns estrangeiros domiciliarios em Portugal, que tracta-
ram da historia civil, politica e ecclesias-
tica d'estes reinos e seus dominios, e das
nações ultramarinas. Lisboa, Typ. do Panorama, 1850. 349 p.   (3821
    Jones 1038.

GREENLEE, William Brooks. A descriptive bibliography of the history of Portugal. (Hispanic American historical review, Durham,
N.C., v. 20, p. 491-516, 1940)   (3822
    The object: "to give a summary of the
chief sources for the history of Portugal ...
as a background for the needs of the student
of Brazilian history".---Jones 1051b.

A GUIDE to historical literature, edited by
William Henry Allison, Sidney Bradshaw Fay,
Augustus Hunt Shearer, and Henry Robinson
Shipman. New York, The Macmillan Co., 1931.
1222 p.   (3823
    Other editions.---Jones 182.

HAVANA. Museo Julio Lobo. Sección Biblioteca.
Bibliografía sobre Revolución Francesa, Consulado e Imperio. Havana, Impr. Ucar, García,
1958- .   (3824

MEDELLIN. Escuela Interamericana de Bibliotecología. Bibliografía para Historia de la
civilización. [Medellín, n.d.] 5 p.
mimeogr.   (3825

MEDINA, José Toribio. El descubrimiento del
Océano Pacífico; Vasco Núñez de Balboa, Hernando de Magallanes y sus compañeros. Santiago de Chile, Impr. Universitaria, 1913-
1920. 3 v.   (3826
    Vols. 1 and 3 include bibliographies.---
Jones 300a.

PARIS DE ODDONE, María Blanca. Ciencias auxiliares y tecnicas de la historia; guía bibliográfica. Montevideo, 1963. 27 p.
mimeogr.   (3827
    Cited in Musso 146.

PERAZA SARAUSA, Fermín. Bibliografía cubana
de la II Guerra Mundial. Habana, Anuario
Bibliográfico Cubano, 1945. 53 p. (Biblioteca del bibliotecario, 13)   (3828
    "La presente bibliografía fue publicada de
marzo 1943 a julio 1945, en la Revista de la
Habana".

RAGATZ, Lowell Joseph. Colonial studies in
the United States during the twentieth century. London, A. Thomas [1932] 48 p. (3829

-----. A list of books and articles on colonial history and overseas expansion published in the United States in 1931 and 1932.
Washington, D.C., Paul Pearlman [1933]
41 p.   (3830

SCHÄFER, Ernst. El Consejo Real y Supremo de
las Indias; su historia, organización y labor administrativa hasta la terminación de
la casa de Austria. Sevilla, Impr. M. Carmona, 1935- . v. 1- . (Universidad de Sevilla. Publ. del Centro de Estudios de Historia de América)   (3831
    Bibliografía: v. 1., 386-88. A transla-
tion by the author of: Der Königl. Spanische
oberste Indienrat (Hamburg, Ibero-Amerikanisches Institut, 1936- .)---Jones 437.

SOUSA, José Carlos Pinto de. Bibliotheca historica de Portugal, e do ultramar, na qual
se contem varias historias deste reino, e
de seus dominios ultramarinos, manuscriptas,
e impressas, em prosa, e em verso, só e
juntas com as de outros estados, escritas
por authores portuguezes, e estrangeiros,
com hum resumo das suas vidas, e das opi-
niões que ha acerca do que se cre que alguns
escrevêrão: com huma relação no fim de
outras historias tambem manuscriptas, e impressas, compostas porem somente por authores
portuguezes, e unicamente relativas ao tempo,
e ás vidas positivamente escritas de certos

SOUSA, José Carlos Pinto de ... (Cont.)
soberanos de Portugal, e de alguns de seus
serenissimos descendentes. Lisboa, Na Regia
Officina Typ., 1797. 223 p.   (3832
Jones 1146.

-----. Nova ed. Lisboa, Typ. do Arco do Cego,
1801. 408, 100 p.   (3833
Jones 1146.

AMERICA

ALCINA FRANCH, José, and PALOP MARTINEZ, Josefina. América en la época de Carlos V;
aportación a la bibliografía de este período
desde 1900. Madrid [Asociación Hispanoamericana de Historia] 1958. 236 p.   (3834

ANDERSON, Rasmus Björn. America not discovered
by Columbus, 8th. ed. Madison, Wisc., Leif
Erikson Memorial Association, 1930.
176 p.   (3835
Bibliography of the pre-Columbian discov-
eries of America, by Paul Barron Watson:
p. 129-73.---Jones 13.

ASHER, George Michael. A bibliographical and
historical essay on the Dutch West-India
company and to its possessions in Brazil,
Angola, etc., as also on the maps, charts,
etc., of New-Netherland, with facsimiles of
the map of New-Netherland by N.I. Visscher
and of the three existing views of New-
Amsterdam. Comp. from the Dutch public and
private libraries, and from the collection
of Mr. Frederik Muller in Amsterdam. Amsterdam, F. Muller, 1854-1867. 2 pts. in
1 v.   (3836
Pt. 2 has title: A list of the maps and
charts of New-Netherland, and of the views
of New Amsterdam, by G. M. Asher. Being a
supplement to his Bibliographical essay ...
Amsterdam, F. Muller; New York, C. B. Norton,
1855.
Work on the Dutch in Brazil; 369 (12 in appendix) items, classified, with index.
Dutch titles translated into English.---
Jones 961.

BAGINSKY, Paul H. German works relating to
America, 1493-1800, a list compiled from the
collections of the New York Public Library.
(Bulletin of the New York Public Library,
New York, v. 42-4, 1938-1940)   (3838
Jones 38a.

BAYLE, Constantino. El Dorado fantasma; prólogo del excmo. dr. d. José Joaquín Casas.
Madrid, Edit. Razón y Fe [1930]
488 p.   (3839
"Obras principales aprovechadas en el presente libro": p. 481-88.---Jones 46a.

BOURNE, Edward Gaylord. Spain in America,
1450-1580. New York and London, Harper and
Brothers, 1904. 350 p. (The American nation, v. 3)   (3840
"Critical essay on authorities": p. 320-
37.---Jones 71.

BROWN, Vera Lee. Anglo-Spanish relations in
America in the closing years of the colonial
period (1763-1774). (Hispanic American historical review, v. 5, p. 325-483,
1922)   (3841
Bibliography: p. 479-83.---Jones 78.

GOMEZ MOLLEDA, D. Bibliografía histórica española, 1950-1954. Madrid, C.S.I.C., Instituto
Jerónimo Zurita, Instituto Nicolás Antonio,
1955. 491 p.   (3842
History of America: p. 391-432.

HISTORIOGRAFIA y bibliografía americanista,
1954- . Sevilla, 1956- .   (3843
Compiled as Publicaciones of the Escuela
de Estudios Hispanoamericanos in Sevilla, and
issued as a Sección del Anuario de Estudios
Americanos.

LARRABURE Y UNANUE, Eugenio. Monografías histó-
ricoamericanas. Lima, Impr. de Torres Aguirre,
1893. 426 p.   (3844
Contents: - Cristóbal Colón ante los moti-
nistas de a bordo y los rebeldes de la colonia.- Asuntos indígenas. - La poesía entre
los Incas. - Apuntes arqueológicos. - El
marqués Pizarro y su muerte.- Bibliografía.
---Jones 2662.

LEONARD, Irving Albert. Books of the brave;
being an account of books and of men in the
Spanish conquest and settlement of the Sixteenth-Century New World. Cambridge, Mass.,
Harvard Univ. Pr., 1949. 381 p.   (3845

-----. Los libros del conquistador. México,
Fondo de Cultura Económica [1953] 399 p.
(Sección de lengua y estudios litera-
rios)   (3846
Translation of Books of the brave.

LLORENS TORRES, Luis. América (estudios historicos y filológicos) Colección de articulos escritos y ordenados por d. Luis
Lloréns Torres, con una carta-prólogo de d.
Antonio Cortón. Madrid, V. Suárez, 1898.
204 p.   (3847
Reseña bibliográfica: p. 190-96.---Jones
2795.

MEANS, Philip Ainsworth. The Spanish Main,
focus of envy, 1492-1700. New York, C.
Scribner's Sons, 1935. 278 p.   (3848
Bibliography: p. 255-67.---Jones 295.

TAURO, Alberto. Los pequeños grandes libros
de historia americana. Washington, D.C.,

TAURO, Alberto. Los pequeños ... (Cont.)
Pan American Union, 1954. p. 73-80. (3849
   Reprinted from the Revista interamericana
de bibliografía, v. 4, no. 1/2, en./jun.,
1954. Annotated bibliography of the 16
works forming the series edited by Francisco
A. Loayza from 1941-1948.

VALLE, Rafael Heliodoro. Bibliografía de historia de America, 1937. México, D.F., Impr.
Mundial, 1938. 29 p.   (3850
   Reprinted from the Revista de historia de
América. It is a part of the series of articles appearing in no. 1, mar. 1938- no.
10, dic. 1940, of the same journal.---Jones
503.

WINSOR, Justin. Narrative and critical history of America. Boston and New York,
Houghton, Mifflin and Co., 1884-1889.
8 v.   (3851
   Vols. 1-2 Aboriginal America, and Spanish
settlements in America relate more particularly to Hispanic America.---Jones 544.

ZAVALA, Silvio Arturo. La encomienda indiana.
Madrid, Impr. Helénica, 1935. 356 p. (Junta para Ampliación de Estudios e Investigaciones Científicas. Centro de Estudios Históricos. Sección Hispanoamericana,
Publ. 2)   (3852
   Bibliografía: p. 347-51.---Jones 549.

-----. Las instituciones jurídicas en la conquista de America. Madrid, Centro de Estudios Históricos, 1935. 347 p. (Junta para
Ampliación de Estudios e Investigación Científicas, Centro de Estudios Históricos.
Sección Hispano-americana, Publ. 1) (3853
   Bibliografía: p. 335-42.---Jones 550.

ARGENTINA

ANUARIO de historia argentina, año 1939- .
Buenos Aires, D. Viau y Cía., 1940- .(3854
   Issued by the Sociedad de Historia Argen-
tina. Includes a list of books, pamphlets
and articles in reviews and newspapers on
Argentine and American history published in
Argentina during the current year; also spe-
cial bibliographies and book reviews.---
Jones 560a.
   DPU has año 1942 published in 1943.

ARGENTINA. Caja Nacional de Ahorro Postal.
La Revolución de Mayo; material para uso de
educadores y estudiantes existente en la Biblioteca Domingo F. Sarmiento. Buenos Aires,
Sesquicentenario de la Revolución de Mayo,
1960. 24 p.   (3855

BURZIO, Humberto. Impresos navales, 1814-1829.
Buenos Aires, Comisión Nacional de Homenaje
al Almirante Guillermo Brown, 1957. [24] p.,

BURZIO, Humberto. Impresos navales ... (Cont.)
36 facsms.   (3855a

BUENOS AIRES (Province) Instituto Bibliográfico. Bibliografía argentina de historia; obras
y artículos publicados, no. 1-2, 1960-1961.
La Plata [1964] 2 v.   (3856

CAFFESE, María E., and LAFUENTE, Carlos F. Mayo en la bibliografía. [Buenos Aires] Universidad de Buenos Aires, 1962. 278 p. (Instituto de Historia Argentina, Publ.,
102)   (3857

CAILLET-BOIS, Ricardo Rodolfo. Ensayo sobre el
Rio de la Plata y la revolución francesa.
Buenos Aires, Impr. de la Universidad, 1929.
124 p. (Instituto de Investigaciones Históricas, Publ. no. 49)   (3858
   Bibliografía: p. 118-24. The author has
published various bibliographical articles
in the Boletín del Instituto: Andrés A. Figueroa (t. 11, p. 724-29; t. 12, p. 411-17);
Jorge Cabral (t. 17, p. 796-99) and others.
---Jones 643.

CARBIA, Rómulo D. Historia crítica de la historiografía argentina (desde sus orígenes en
el siglo XVI). La Plata, 1939. 483 p. (Biblioteca "Humanidades", v. 22)   (3859
   Contents: - 1. pte. El proceso historio-
gráfico: 1. Los orígenes, 2. La crónica
jesuítica, 3. Gestación y nacimiento de la
historiografía de origen laical, 4. Comienzo
y posterior desarrollo de la escuela erudita,
5. Las dos corrientes vertebrales de la historiografía argentina. - 2. pte. Los conju-
ros genéricos: 1. Los cronistas, 2. Los ensayistas, 3. La historiografía didascálica,
4. El material erudito. - Indice bibliográfico (p. 383-477)---Jones 651.

-----. Historia de la historiografía argentina.
La Plata, 1925. 324 p. (Biblioteca "Humanidades", v. 1, t.2.)   (3860

CELESIA, Ernesto H. Federalismo argentino;
apuntes históricos, 1815-1821; Córdoba.
Buenos Aires, Librería "Cervantes" de J.
Suárez, 1932. 3 v.   (3861
   Bibliografía: v. 1, p. 1-4.---Jones 663.

CHAVES, Julio César. Historia de las relaciones entre Buenos-Ayres y el Paraguay, 1810-
1813. Buenos Aires, J. Menéndez, 1938.
269 p.   (3862
   Bibliografía: p. 259-66.---Jones 666.

CORDERO, Carlos J. Los relatos de los viajeros
extranjeros, posteriores a la Revolución de
Mayo como fuentes de historia argentina; ensayo de sistematización bibliográfica. Buenos Aires, Impr. y Casa Editora "Coni", 1936.
274 p.   (3863
   Jones 673.

FIGUERERO, Manuel V.   Lecciones de historiografía de Corrientes. Buenos Aires, G. Kraft,
1929- . v. 1- .   (3864
   Bibliografía: v. 1, p. XV-XXXI.---Jones
692.

FREGEIRO, Clemente Leoncio. Bibliografía.
(Boletín del Instituto de Investigaciones
Históricas, Buenos Aires, t. 1, p. 228-302,
1923)   (3865
   Jones 697a.

FURLONG CARDIFF, Guillermo, and GEOGHEGAN,
Abel Rodolfo. Bibliografía de la Revolución
de Mayo, 1810-1928. Buenos Aires, Biblioteca del Congreso de la Nación, 1960. xxxix,
704 p.   (3866
   Listing of over 9,000 items.

GANDIA, Enrique de. Buenos Aires, desde sus
orígenes hasta Hernandarias. Buenos Aires,
Impr. de la Universidad, 1937.
216 p.   (3867
   Bibliography at end of each chapter. See
also La historia de la ciudad de Buenos Aires by Gandía and Rómulo Zavala, Buenos Aires, 1936-1937. 2 v.---Jones 701.

GONZALEZ, B. S. Apuntes para una bibliografia
de la historia de Corrientes. Corrientes,
1926. 39 p.   (3868
   Jones 711.

HUALDE DE PEREZ GUILHOU, Margarita. Aporte
para una bibliografía crítica de la Revolución de Mayo. Mendoza, Universidad Nacional
de Cuyo, 1958. p. 117-50.   (3868a
   Separata del Boletín de estudios políticos,
no. 9, 1958. Cited in Geoghegan 2653.

-----. Contribucion a una bibliografia historica de Mendoza. Mendoza [Argentina] Biblioteca Pública "Gral. San Martín", 1962.
73 p.   (3869
   Lists 810 items.

JUNTA de Historia y Numismática Americana.
Historia de la nación argentina (desde los
orígenes hasta la organización definitiva en
1862) escrita en colaboración por autores e
investigadores y publicada por la Junta de
Historia y Numismática Americana bajo la presidencia de Ricardo Levene. Buenos Aires,
Impr. de la Universidad, 1936- .
v. 1- .   (3870
   "Bibliografía principal" at end of each
chapter. In 1938 the Junta de Historia y
Numismática Americana became the Academia
Nacional de la Historia, v. 4- of the Historia being issued under its directions.---
Jones 732.

LEDESMA MEDINA, Luis A. Reseña de la bibliografía histórica de Santiago del Estero.
(Anuario de historia argentina, año 1939.

LEDESMA MEDINA, Luis A. Reseña de la...(Cont.)
Buenos Aires, 1940. p. 727-50)   (3871
   Jones 748a.

LEVENE, Ricardo. A history of Argentina; tr.
and ed. by William Spence Robertson. Chapel
Hill, The University of North Carolina, 1937.
565 p.   (3872
   Bibliography: p. 529-36.---Jones 753.

MITRE, Bartolomé. Ensayos históricos. Buenos
Aires, La Cultura Argentina, 1918.
254 p.   (3873
   "Los orígenes de la imprenta y del periodismo en el Río de la Plata".---Jones 782.

MUZZIO, Julio A. Diccionario histórico y biográfico de la República Argentina. Buenos
Aires, J. Roldán [1920?] 2 v.   (3874
   Articles usually include references to
other sources.---Jones 792.

QUESADA, Vicente Gregorio. La Patagonia y las
tierras australes del continente americano.
Buenos Aires, Mayo, 1875. 787 p.   (3875
   Bibliografia: p. 657-787.---Jones 823.

RAVIGNANI, Emilio. Historia constitucional
de la República Argentina. Buenos Aires,
Tall. Casa Jacobo Peuser, 1926-1927.
3 v.   (3876
   Bibliografia, v. 1. p. 359-62.---Jones
824b.

-----. El virreinato del Río de la Plata, su
formación histórica e institucional, con
apéndice de documentos. Buenos Aires, Impr.
de la Universidad, 1938. 308,
cxlvi p.   (3877
   "Obra capitalísima, en la que se han utilizado fuentes de primera mano" (Torre
Revello).---Jones 824d.

TOMMASINI, Gabriel. La civilización cristia-
na del Chaco (1554-1810). Buenos Aires,
Libr. Santa Catalina [1937] 2 v. (Biblio-
teca de doctrina católica, v. 25-26)   (3878
   Bibliografia: v. 1, p. i-v (3d group)
---Jones 860.

TORRE REVELLO, José. Documentos referentes a
la Argentina en la Biblioteca Nacional y en
el Deposito Hidrografico de Madrid. Buenos
Aires, Impr. de la Universidad, 1929. 67 p.
(Publicaciones del Instituto de Investigaciones Históricas, no. 43)   (3879
   Jones 866.

-----. Documentos referentes a la historia ar-
gentina en la Real Academia de Historia de
Madrid. Buenos Aires, Impr. de la Universi-
dad, 1929. 66 p. (Publ. del Instituto de
Investigaciones Históricas, Universidad de
Buenos Aires, no. 47)   (3879a
   Jones 866a.

TORRE REVELLO, José. El Museo Colonial e Histórico de Luján. (Revista de las Españas, Madrid, año 5, no. 48-9, p. 428-34, 1930) (3880
Jones 867b.

-----. Museo Mitre. (Revista de historia de América. México, D.F., no. 6, p. 97-115, 1939) (3881
Jones 867c.

TORRES, Luis María. La enseñanza de la historia en la Universidad de La Plata. (Revista argentina de ciencias políticas, Buenos Aires, t. 2, p. 698-711, 1911) (3882
Jones 868c.

TRENTI ROCAMORA, José Luis. Repertorio de crónicas anteriores a 1810 sobre los países del antiguo virreinato del Río de La Plata insertas en publicaciones periódicas y cuerpos documentales. Buenos Aires, Universidad de Buenos Aires, Instituto Bibliotecológico, 1948. 126 p. (3883

ZEBALLOS, Estanislao Severo. La conquista de quince mil leguas; estudio sobre la traslación de la frontera sud de la república al Río Negro. Buenos Aires, Impr. de P. E. Coni, 1878. 370 p. (3884
"Noticia bibliográfica y cartográfica": p. 285-320. For a bibliography of Dr. Zeballos, see Boletín del Instituto de Investigaciones Históricas, Buenos Aires, t. 2, p. 437-61, 1924, and Enrique Arana's Doctor Estanislao S. Zeballos, "bibliografía especial", in Boletín de la Biblioteca de la Facultad de Derecho y Ciencias Sociales, Buenos Aires, 1933, no. 7, p. 670-705.---Jones 890.

ZINNY, Antonio. Bibliografía histórica de las Provincias Unidas del Río de la Plata desde el año 1780 hasta el de 1821. Apéndice a la Gaceta de Buenos Aires. Buenos Aires, Impr. Americana, 1875. 476 p. (3885
Jones 891.

BOLIVIA

BALLIVIAN Y ROJAS, Vicente de. Archivo boliviano. Colección de documentos relativos a la historia de Bolivia, durante la época colonial, con un catálogo de obras impresas y de manuscritos, que tratan de esa parte de la América meridional. t. 1. París, A. Franck (F. Vieweg) 1872. 535 p. (3886
"Unico volumen que se publico." (Bibl. peruana, 1896, v. 1, no. 1567).---Jones 900.

RENE-MORENO, Gabriel. Anales de la prensa boliviana; matanzas de Yáñez, 1861-1862. Santiago de Chile, Impr. Cervantes, 1886. 499 p. (3887
Jones 932.

RENE-MORENO, Gabriel. Bolivia y Argentina, notas biográficas y bibliográficas. Santiago de Chile, Impr. Cervantes, 1901. 553 p. (3888
Contents. - Buenos Aires in 1879. - Benjamín Vicuña Mackenna según un libro reciente. - Benjamín Vicuña Mackenna, necrología. - Letras argentinas. - Nicomedes Antelo. - El doctor don Juan José Segovia, 1728-1809. - El doctor don Felipe Antonio de Iriarte. - Don Angel Justiniano Carranza, necrología. - Documentos sobre la revolución alto-peruana de 1809. - Juan Ramón Muñoz Cabrera, o Aventuras de un periodista en cinco repúblicas, 1819-1869.---Jones 936.

-----. Bolivia y Perú; notas históricas y bibliográficas; 2a. ed., aum. Santiago de Chile, Impr., Lit. y Encuad. Barcelona, 1905. 333 p. (3889
First published in Anales de la Universidad de Chile, 1808-1899.
Contents. - Fray Antonio de la Calancha. - Unión americana. - Mariano Ricardo Terrazas. - De La Paz al Pacífico a vapor treinta años atrás. - La Audiencia de Charcas, 1559-1809. ---Jones 937.

-----. Bolivia y Perú; más notas históricas y bibliográficas. Santiago de Chile, Impr., Lit. y Encuad. Barcelona, 1905. 311 p. (3890
Contents. - D. Mariano Alejo Alvarez y el silogismo altoperuano de 1808. - Informaciones verbales sobre los sucesos de 1809 en Chuquisaca. - Notas adicionales a las precedentes Informaciones.---Jones 938.

-----. Bolivia y Perú; nuevas notas históricas y bibliográficas. Santiago de Chile [Soc., Impr. y Lit. Universo] 1907. 676 p. (3891
Jones 939.

BRAZIL

BARROSO, Gustavo. O Brasil em face do Prata. Rio de Janeiro, Impr. Nacional, 1930. 452 p. (3892
Bibliografía: p. 441-48.---Jones 972.

BRAZIL. Comissão de Estudo dos Textos da História do Brasil. Bibliografía de história do Brasil, 1943- , Rio de Janeiro, 1944- . (3893
Last issue received at DPU: 1o./2o. sem. 1953 and 1954 published in 1962 (353 p.)

CABRAL, Oswaldo R. Santa Catharina (historia-evolução) Edição illustrada. São Paulo, Companhia Editôra Nacional, 1937. 445 p. (Bibliotheca pedagogica brasileira, ser. 5: Brasiliana, v. 80) (3894
"Consultas e referencias": p. 439-45.---

CABRAL, Oswaldo R. Santa ... (Cont.)
Jones 1003a.

CALMON, Pedro. A conquista; historia das ban-
deiras bahianas. Rio de Janeiro, Impr. Nacional, 1929. 229 p.   (3895
Bibliographia: p. 221-29.---Jones 1005.

CALOGERAS, João Pandiá. A history of Brazil,
trans. and edit. by Percy Alvin Martin.
Chapel Hill, The Univ. of North Carolina
Pr., 1939. 374 p. (The Inter-American his-
torical series)   (3896
"Bibliographical notes": p. 357-64.---
Jones 1006a.

CAVALCANTI, João Alcides Bezerra. Bibliographia historica do primeiro reinado á maiori-
dade, 1822-1840. Rio de Janeiro, 1930.
133 p.   (3897
"Separata do volume 34 das Publicações do
Archivo Nacional."---Jones 975.

COORNAERT, E. Aperçu de la production historique récente au Brésil. (Revue d'histoire
moderne, Paris, v. 11, p. 44-60,
1936)   (3898
A review of histories, historians, historical institutions and journals.---Jones
1022a.

GARRAUX, Anatole Louis. Bibliographie brésilienne: catalogue des ouvrages français &
latins relatifs au Brésil (1500-1898)
Paris, Chadenat, 1898. 400 p.   (3899
Alphabetical by author, with subject index.---Jones 1048.

-----. -----. Introdução de Francisco de
Assis Barbosa; 2a. ed. Rio de Janeiro, J.
Olympio, 1962. 519 p. (Coleção Documentos
brasileiros, 100)   (3900

HANDELMANN, Heinrich. Geschichte von Brasilien. Berlin, J. Springer, 1860.
989 p.   (3901
Literatur: p. 969-89.---Jones 1054a.

HISTORIA da colonização portuguesa no Brasil.
Edição monumental comemorativa do primeiro
centenario da independencia do Brasil.
Porto, Lit. Nacional, 1921-1924.
3 v.   (3902
Standard work with illustrations, repro-
ductions and bibliography. Edited by Carlos
Malheiro Dias.---Jones 1057a.

INSTITUTO Brasileiro de Bibliografia e Documentação, Rio de Janeiro. Amazônia: bibliografia, 1614-1962. Rio de Janeiro, 1963.
842 p.   (3903

LEITE, Solidonio Atico. Os judeus no Brasil.
Rio de Janeiro, J. Leite & Cia., 1923.
124 p.   (3904

LEITE, Solidonio Atico. Os judeus...(Cont.)
Bibliographical foot-notes.---Jones 1075.

MAGALHÃES, Basilio de. Expansão geographica
do Brasil colonial; 2a, ed., augm. São Paulo, Companhia Editôra Nacional, 1935.
406 p.   (3905
Bibliographia: p. 389-403.---Jones 1086.

MELLO, José Antonio Gonsalves de. Estudos pernambucanos; crítica e problemas de algumas
fontes da história de Pernambuco. Recife,
Universidade do Recife, Impr. Universitária,
1960. 187 p.   (3906
Contents. - Bento Teizeira, autor da Pro--
sopopéia. - A autoria dos Diálogos das gran-
dezas do Brasil. - A História da guerra de
Pernambuco e o Castrioto lusitano. - A No-
biliarquia pernambucana. - Loreto Couto e
os Desagravos do Brasil e glórias de Pernambuco.

NETSCHER, Pieter Marinus. Les Hollandais au
Brésil, notice historique sur les Pays-Bas
et le Brésil au XVIIe. siècle. La Haye,
Belinfante Frères, 1853. xxxii,
209 p.   (3907
"Liste raisonnée des sources": p. xi-xxiv.
---Jones 1108a.

OAKENFULL, J. C. "Brazil", a centenary of in-
dependence, 1822-1922. Freiburg i. B., C.
A. Wagner, 1922. 826 p.   (3908
Bibliographies interspersed.---Jones 1114.

OILIAM, José. Historiografia mineira; esbôço.
Belo Horizonte, Edit. Itatiaia, [1959]
216 p. (Col. Estudos brasileiros, 2)   (3909
Survey of the writings on Minas Gerais history.

PARA. Quarto centenario do descobrimento do
Brazil: o Pará em 1900; publicação commemo-
rativa feita pelo governo do estado. Pará.
Impr. de A. A. Silva, 1900. xiii,
297 p.   (3910
"Bibliographia scientifica sobre o Amazo-
nas": xiii p. "A imprensa no Pará pelo dr.
Paulino de Breto": p. 281-93.---Jones 1128.

PRADO, João Fernando de Almeida. Pernambuco
e as capitanias do norte do Brasil, 1530-
1630. Edição ilustrada. São Paulo, Editora
Nacional, 1939-1941. 3 v. (Biblioteca pedagogica brasileira, ser. 5: Brasiliana,
v. 175)   (3911
Jones 951a.

-----. Primeiros povoadores do Brasil, 1500-
1530. São Paulo, Companhia Editora Nacional, 1935. 302 p. (Bibliotheca pedagogica
brasileira, ser. 5: Brasiliana, v.
37)   (3912
Bibliografia: p. 237-88.---Jones 952.

REIS, José Antônio dos. Relação dos livros,
verbetes datilográficos de coleções inéditas,
fotografias, relações de cartas geográficas
e mapas estatísticos documentos facsimilares
em taboletas de decretos, jornais antigos e
impressos vários relativos á história de São
Paulo do movimento da independência e aos
principais acontecimentos da história política do Brasil no século XIX. Rio de Janeiro,
Companhia Brasileira de Artes Gráficas, 1954.
26 p.   (3913
   Prepared for the Exposição Histórica Comemorativa do IV Centenário da Fundação da Cidade de São Paulo, as a contribution from
the Arquivo Nacional. Cited in HLAS, 19,
item 4025.

RICARD, Robert. Documents des bibliothèques
espagnoles relatifs au Brésil. Coimbra,
1924. 17 p.   (3914
   Jones 1159.

RODRIGUES, José Carlos. O descobrimento do
Brasil; succinta noticia da descripção im-
pressa mais antiga deste acontecimento. Rio
de Janeiro, Typ. de "Journal do commercio,"
1905. 7 p.   (3915
   Jones 1178.

RODRIGUES, José Honorio and RIBEIRO, Joaquim.
Civilização holandesa no Brasil. São Paulo,
Editora Nacional, 1940. 398 p. (Biblioteca
pedagogica brasileira, ser. 5: Brasiliana,
v. 180)   (3916
   Dutch civilization in Brazil, with bibliography.---Jones 1178a.

RODRIGUES, José Honorio. As fontes da historia do Brasil na Europa. [Rio de Janeiro]
Departamento de Imprensa Nacional, 1950.
42 p.   (3917

-----. Historiografia del Brasil, Siglo XVI.
México, D.F., 1957. 102 p. (Publ. del Instituto Panamericano de Geografía e Historia,
no. 190)   (3918
   Issued also as publication of the Comisión
de Historia, no. 82, and as v. 4 in the series, Historiografías.

-----. Historiografia e bibliografia do Domí-
nio Holandês no Brasil. Rio de Janeiro, Departamento de Imprensa Nacional, 1949. 489 p.
(Instituto Nacional do Livro, Coleção B 1;
Bibliografia, 6)   (3919

SANTOS, Francisco Martins dos. Historia de
Santos, 1532-1936. São Paulo, Empreza Graphica da "Revista dos Tribunaes", 1937.
2 v.   (3920
   Includes bibliographies. "Galeria biogra-
phica santista, 1573-1903": v. 2, p. 185-452.
---Jones 1095d

SODRE, Nelson Werneck. O que se deve lêr para
conhecer o Brasil. Rio de Janeiro, Companhia Edit. Leitura, Mundo Espirita, 1945.
262 p.   (3921

-----. -----. [2a. ed. Rio de Janeiro] Centro Brasileiro de Pesquisas Educacionais,
INEP, Ministério da Educação e Cultura
[1960] 388 p. (Centro Brasileiro de Pesquisas Educacionais, Ser. 3: Libros fonte,
v. 3)   (3922

TAUNAY, Affonso de Escragnolle. San Pablo en
el siglo XVI; historia de la villa de Pira-
tininga; trad. de Benjamín de Garay. Buenos
Aires, [Impr. López] 1947. 340 p. (Biblioteca de autores brasileños, traducidos al
castellano, 11)   (3923

-----. S. Paulo no seculo XVI; historia da
villa piratiningana. Tours, E. Arrault &
Cie., 1921. 292 p.   (3924
   Bibliographia: p. 265-71.---Jones 1035.

-----. S. Paulo nos primeiros annos (1554-
1601); ensaio de reconstituição social.
Tours, Impr. de E. Arrault & Cie., 1920.
216 p.   (3925
   Bibliographia: p. 199-206.---Jones 1036.

WÄTJEN, Hermann Julius Eduard. O dominio colonial hollandez no Brasil: um capitulo de
historia colonial do seculo XVII. São Paulo, Edit, Nacional 1938. 559 p. (Bibliotheca pedagogica brasileira, ser. 5: Brasiliana, v. 123)   (3926
   "Fontes e litteratura de referencia, com
apreciações críticas": p. 21-62.---Jones
1225b.

-----. Das holländische kolonialreich in
Brasilien; ein kapitel aus der kolonial-
geschichte des 17. jahrhunderts. Haag, M.
Nijhoff, 1921. 352 p.   (3927
   "Quellen und literaturnachweise mit krit-
schen einleitungen": p. 1-24.---Jones 1225a.

CALIFORNIA

CALIFORNIA. University. Bancroft Library.
A guide to the Mariano Guadalupe Vallejo
documentos para la historia de California,
1780-1875, by Doris Marion Wright. Berkeley, Univ. of Calif. Pr., 1953. 264 p.
(Guides to manuscript collections in the
Bancroft Library, 1)   (3928

COWAN, Robert Ernest. A bibliography of the
history of California and the Pacific west,
1510-1906, together with the text of John
W. Dwinelle's address on the acquisition
of California by the United States of America. San Francisco, The Book Club of California, 1914. 318 p.   (3929

COWAN, Robert Ernest. A bibliography...(Cont.)
    Jones 2136.

-----. -----. San Francisco, J. H. Nash, 1933.
    3 v.   (3930
    Jones 2137.

KINO, Eusebio F. Historical memoir of Pimería
    Alta; contemporary account of the beginnings
    of California, Sonora, and Arizona, 1683-1711,
    pub. for the first time from the original
    manuscript in the Archives of Mexico; trans.
    into English, edited and annotated by Herbert
    Eugene Bolton. Cleveland, The A. H. Clark
    Co., 1919. 2 v.   (3931
    Bibliography (printed works and manu-
    scripts): v.2, p. 277-96.---Jones 2096.

CENTRAL AMERICA

BANCROFT, Hubert Howe. History of Central
    America. San Francisco, A. L. Bancroft &
    Co., 1882-1887. 3 v. (History of the Paci-
    fic States of North America, v.1-3)   (3932
    "Authorities quoted": v.1, p. xxv-lxxii.
    ---Jones 1228.

BATRES JAUREGUI, Antonio. La América Central
    ante la historia. Guatemala, 1915-1949.
    3 v.   (3933
    "Incluye en el primer tomo un amplio aun-
    que poco ordenado comentario bibliográfico
    sobre nuestros cronistas e historiadores, ya
    publicado en la Revista Guatemala literaria,
    año 1, no. 8, ag. 1903" (D. Vela).---Jones
    1283b.

U.S. Library of Congress. List of references
    on the history of Central America and South
    America. Washington, D.C., 1919.
    6 p.   (3934
    Cited in Yang.

VALLE, Rafael Heliodoro. La anexión de Centro
    América a México (documentos y escritos de
    1821). México, Secretaría de Relaciones Ex-
    teriores, 1924-1949. 6 v. (Archivo históri-
    co diplomático mexicano, no. 11, 24, 40; 2a.
    ser., no. 3-4, 7)   (3935
    Bibliografía: v.1, p. lxiii-lxvii.---Jones
    2545.

CHILE

ANRIQUE REYES, Nicolás, and SILVA ARRIAGADA,
    Luis Ignacio. Ensayo de una bibliografía
    histórica y jeográfica de Chile; obra pre-
    miada con medalla de oro en el certamen de
    la Universidad para presentarla al Congreso
    Internacional de Ciencias Históricas y Jeo-
    gráficas de Roma. Santiago, Impr. Barcelo-
    na, 1902. xix, 679 p.   (3936
    2,561 titles with author index.---Jones

ANRIQUE REYES, Nicolás, and SILVA ... (Cont.)
    1396.

CHIAPPA, Víctor M. Noticias bibliográficas so-
    bre la Colección de historiadores de Chile y
    documentos relativos a la historia nacional.
    Santiago, Impr. de E. Blanchard-Chessi, 1905.
    44 p.   (3937
    Jones 1423.

ECHEVERRIA Y REYES, Aníbal. Ensayo bibliográ-
    fico sobre la revolución de 1891. Santiago
    de Chile, G. E. Miranda, 1894. 28 p. (3938
    Jones 1456.

EDWARDS, Agustín. Contribution sur la biblio-
    graphie coloniale chilienne, avant et après
    1900. Paris, 1931. 70 p.   (3939
    Jones 1459.

-----. Gentes de antaño. Valparaíso, Soc.,
    Impr. y Lit. Universo, 1930. 286 p.   (3940
    Indice bibliográfico: p. 287-89.---Jones
    1460.

FELIU CRUZ, Guillermo. Historiografía colonial
    de Chile. Santiago, Fondo Histórico y Biblio-
    gráfico José Toribio Medina, 1958- . v.1
    (xxx, 519 p.)- .   (3941
    Contents: v.1, 1796-1886.

FIGUEROA, Virgilio. Diccionario histórico,
    biográfico y bibliográfico de Chile, 1800-
    1931. Santiago, Establecimientos Gráficos
    "Balcells & Co.", 1925-1931. 5 v.   (3942
    Jones 1486.

RIQUELME, Daniel. Cuentos de la guerra, y
    otras páginas de Daniel Riquelme; Mariano
    Latorre y Miguel Varas Velásquez compila-
    ron este volumen. Santiago, Impr. Univer-
    sitaria, 1931. 541 p. (Biblioteca de es-
    critores de Chile, v.12)   (3943
    Bibliografía de Daniel Riquelme: p.533-38.
    ---Jones 1587.

COLOMBIA

ACOSTA, Joaquín. Compendio histórico del des-
    cubrimiento y colonización de la Nueva Gra-
    nada en el siglo décimo sexto; 2a. ed.
    Bogotá, Camacho Roldán & Tamayo, 1901.
    296 p.   (3944
    "Catálogo de libros y manuscritos que se
    han tenido presentes al escribir este Com-
    pendio": p. 271-91. First edition, Paris,
    1848.---Jones 1667.

CENTRO de Historia de Santander. Homenaje
    que el Centro de Historia de Santander en
    nombre del gobierno y del pueblo santande-
    reano, rinde a los próceres regionales con
    ocasión de celebrarse el primer centenario
    de la muerte del Libertador Simón Bolívar.

CENTRO de Historia de Santander ... (Cont.)
Bucaramanga, Impr. del Departamento, 1930.
202 p.   (3945
    Includes biobibliographical data.---Jones
1697.

GIRALDO JARAMILLO, Gabriel. Bibliografía histórica colombiana, 1954. Bogotá Edit. Pax,
1954. 37 p.   (3946
    Reprint of Boletín de historia y antigüe-
dades, Bogotá, año 42, no. 483-84, p. 40-68,
en./feb. 1955.

IBOT, Antonio. Los trabajadores del Río Magdalena durante el siglo XVI: geografía histórica, economía, legislación del trabajo
según documentos del Archivo General de Indias. Barcelona, Tall. Gráf. " Veritas ",
1933. 253 p.   (3947
    Bibliografía: p. 137-41.---Jones 1720.

ROMERO, Mario Germán, FERNANDEZ DE ALBA, Guillermo, etc. Papeletas bibliográficas para
el estudio de la historia de Colombia. Bogotá, Impr. Banco de la República, 1961.
115 p.   (3948
    Separata no.1 del Boletín cultural y biblio-
gráfico.

CUBA

AUXIER, George Washington. The Cuban question
as reflected in the editorial columns of
middle western newspapers (1895-1898) [Co-
lumbus, O.] 1938. 328 p.   (3949
    Bibliography: p. 322-27. Typewritten.---
Jones 1785a.

BEALS, Carleton. The crime of Cuba. Philadelphia & London, J. B. Lippincott Co., 1933.
441 p.   (3950
    Selected bibliography: p. 409-15.---Jones
1790.

CHAPMAN, Charles Edward. A history of the Cuban republic. New York, The Macmillan Co.,
1927. 685 p.   (3951
    "Essay on authorities": p. 657-75.---Jones
1801.

DELMONTE Y APONTE, Domingo del. Lista cronológica de los libros inéditos e impresos que
se han escrito sobre la isla de Cuba y de
los que hablan de la misma desde su descubrimiento y conquista hasta nuestros días, formado en París en 1846. Habana, Est. Tip. de
la Vda. de Soler, 1882. 50 p.   (3952
    Jones 1876.

GONZALEZ ALCORTA, Leandro. Datos para la his-
toria de Vuelta-Abajo. Pinar del Río, Impr.
"La Constancia", 1902. v.1.   (3953
    1a. pte: Exploraciones bibliográficas.---
Jones 1833.

GUERRA Y SANCHEZ, Ramiro. Manuel de historia
de Cuba. Habana, Cultural, 1938.
676 p.   (3954
    Jones 1836c.

MESA RODRIGUEZ, Manuel Isaías. Algunas fuentes bibliográficas para la historia de Cuba;
discurso leído en la sesión solemne celebrada el día 9 de octubre de 1958. Habana,
Impr. "El Siglo XX", 1958. 50 p. (Publ. de
la Academia de la Historia de Cuba)   (3955

PEREZ, Luis Marino. Bibliografía de la revolución de Yara; folletos y libros impresos
de 1868 a 1908. Historia y política. Biografías. Masonería ... Asuntos administra-
tivos. Literatura patriòtica. Habana,
Impr. Avisador Comercial, 1908. 73p.   (3956
    Jones 1889.

PEREZ CABRERA, José Manuel. Historiografía
de Cuba. México, D.F., 1962. 394 p.
(Publ. del Instituto de Geografía e Historia, no. 262)   (3957
    Issued also as publication of the Comi-
sión de Historia, 106, and as v.7 of the
series, Historiografías.

REASON, Barbara, MUGHISUDDIN, Margaret B.,
etc. Cuba since Castro; a bibliography
of relevant literature. Washington, D.C.,
Research Division, Special Operations
Research Office, American University,
1962. 2⁵ p.   (3958

ROIG DE LEUCHSENRING, Emilio. Bibliografía
histórica cubana. (Libros cubanos, La Habana, v.1, no.3-4/5, 1940-1941)   (3959
    Jones 1904a.

TRELLES Y GOVIN, Carlos Manuel. Bibliografía
de la segunda guerra de independencia cubana y de la hispano-yankee. Publicada en la
revista ilustrada "Cuba y América". Habana,
1902. 49 p.   (3960
    Arranged chronologically, 1895-1900: in-
cludes references to articles in periodicals.---Jones 1917.

-----. Biblioteca histórica cubana. Matanzas, Impr. de J. F. Oliver, 1922-1926.
3 v.   (3961
    Jones 1923. Now available in microprint.

-----. Matanzas en la independencia de Cuba.
La Habana, Impr. "Avisador Comercial",
1928. 193 p.   (3962
    "Bibliografía revolucionaria de Matanzas":
p. 187-92.---Jones 1928.

-----. El sitio de la Habana y la dominación
británica en Cuba; trabajo de ingreso en la
Academia de la Historia (jueves 3 de julio
de 1919). Habana, Impr. "El Siglo XX", 1925.
64 p.   (3963

TRELLES Y GOVIN, Carlos Manuel ... (Cont.)
"Bibliografía del sitio y rendicion de la
Habana": p.50-63.---Jones 1931.

WISAN, Joseph Ezra. The Cuban crisis as re-
flected in the New York press (1895-1898).
New York, Columbia Univ. Pr.; London, P.S.
King & Son, 1934. 477 p. (Studies in his-
tory, economics and public law, ed. by the
Faculty of Political Science of Columbia
University, no. 403)   (3964
"Selective bibliography": p. 461-66.---
Jones 1940.

DOMINICAN REPUBLIC

COISCON HENRIQUEZ, M. Contribución al estudio
de la bibliografía de la historia de Santo
Domingo y particularmente al de la bibliografía de la primera independencia. (Revista
de educación, Santo Domingo, t.7, no. 25,
p.74-82, no. 26, p.90-6; no.27, p.76-83;
no.28, p.47-56; no.29, p.55-62; no.30, p.61-
4, 1935)   (3965
"An index to the transcripts made by a Dominican commission on materials in the Archivo de Indias with a useful index of persons and places." (Handbook of Latin American Studies, 1935). Continued.---Jones
2985.

ECUADOR

BARRERA, Isaac J. Historiografía del Ecuador.
México, D.F., 1956. 124 p. (Publ. del Instituto Panamericano de Geografía e Historia,
no. 189)   (3966
Issued also as publication of the Comisión
de Historia, 81, and as v.3 of the series,
Historiografias.

EL CENTENARIO; homenaje al centenario de la re-
pública, 1830-1930. Guayaquil, Impr. el
Tiempo, 1930. 476 p.   (3967
"Cronología del periodismo ecuatoriano des-
de 1792 hasta 1930": p. 361-431. Edited by
Neptalí Casanova Loor.---Jones 1967.

GUATEMALA

BATRES JAUREGUI, Antonio. Bibliografía historica guatemalteca. Guatemala, Tip. Nacional,
1908. 22 p.   (3968
Jones 1284.

-----. Guatemalan historical bibliography.
Washington, D.C., Pan American Union [1929]
9 p. (Library and bibliography ser.,
no.1)   (3969
Reprinted from the May 1929 issue of the
Bulletin of the Pan American Union.

SALAZAR, Ramon A. Historia del desenvolvimiento intelectual de Guatemala, Tomo 1: La colonia. Guatemala, 1897. 403 p.   (3970
With bibliography.---Jones 1309.

XIMENEZ, Francisco. Historia de la provincia
de San Vicente de Chiapa y Guatemala de la
Orden de Predicadores. Guatemala, 1929-1931.
3v (Biblioteca "Goathemala" de la Sociedad
de Geografía e Historia, v.1-3)   (3971
Source for the history and biography of
the Dominicans in Guatemala.---Jones 1316.

HAITI

BOISSONNADE, Prosper Marie. Saint-Domingue à
la veille de la revolution. Paris, P. Geuth,
1906. 299 p.   (3972
Sources et bibliographie: p. 290-94.---
Jones 2982.

BONNEAU, Alexandre. Haiti, ses progrès, son
avenir; avec un précis historique sur ses
constitutions, le texte de la constitution
actuellement en vigueur, et une bibliographie
d'Haiti. Paris, E. Dentu, 1862. 176p. (3973
Jones 2973.

PRESSOIR, Catts, TROUILLOT, Ernest, etc. His-
toriographie d'Haiti. México, D.F., 1953.
298 p. (Publ. del Instituto Panamericano
de Geografía e Historia, no. 168)   (3974
Issued also as publication of the Comision
de Historia, 66, and as v.1 in the series,
Historiografias.

STODDARD, Theodore Lothrop. The French revolution in San Domingo. Boston and New York,
Houghton Mifflin Co., 1914. 410 p.   (3975
Select annotated bibliography: p. 395-
410.---Jones 3010.

LATIN AMERICA

AITON, A. S., and others. Publication on Latin American history in 1937. Cambridge,
Mass., 1938. p. 256-341.   (3976
Reprinted from Handbook of Latin American
studies, 1937.

ALTAMIRA Y CREVEA, Rafael, and OTS CAPDEQUI,
José María. Bibliographie d'histoire coloniale (1900-1930). Espagne. Paris, Socie-
té de l'Histoire des Colonies Françaises,
1932. 69 p.   (3977
Bibliographie: p. 20-68. Issued also in
Bibliographie d'histoire coloniale (1900-
1930) publiée par les soins de MM. Alfred
Martineau...Roussler...Tramond. Paris,
1932. "L'histoire coloniale en Espagne depuis 1900, par M. Rafael Altamira": p.5-20.
---Jones 9.

HISTORY

ALTAMIRA Y CREVEA, Rafael. Nota bibliografica de orientación para el estudio de la historia de las instituciones políticas y civiles de América. (Comprende tan solo, salvo excepciones raras muy necesarias, obras en idioma español, y, con preferencia, obras de conjunto) Madrid, Edit. Arte y Ciencia, 1926. [16] p. (3978
 Jones 8.

AZNAR, Luis. Colecciones documentales editas relativas a la historia de la América española. (II Congreso Internacional de Historia de América. Buenos Aires, 1938. v.5, p. 40-55) (3979
 Jones 32.

BARBER, Ruth Kerns. Indian labor in Spanish colonies. Albuquerque, The Univ. of New Mexico Pr., [1932] 135 p. (Historical Society of New Mexico. Publ. in history, v.6, Oct. 1932) (3980
 Bibliography of works cited, p. 129-32.--- Jones 40.

BARRASA Y MUÑOZ DE BUSTILLO, José de. El servicio personal de los indios durante la colonización española en America. Madrid, Tip de la Revista de Archivos, Bibliotecas y Museos, 1925. 206 p. (3981
 Bibliografia: p. 191-202. Issued also under title: La colonización española en America; exposición histórica de la organizacion social de los antiguos imperios de México y el Perú. ---Jones 43.

BAYLE, Constantino. España en Indias, nuevos ataques y nuevas defensas. Vitoria, Edit. Illuminare, 1934. 448 p. (Bibliotheca hispana missionum, v. 7) (3982
 Bibliografia: p.11-24.---Jones 47.

BENZO, Eduardo. La libertad de America; prólogo de Luis Jiménez de Asua. Madrid, Compañia Iberoamericana de Publicaciones [1929] 264 p. (3983
 Bibliografía: p. 257-64.---Jones 52.

BIBLIOGRAFIA historica de España e Hispanoamérica, v.1- , 1953/1954- . Barcelona [Centro de Estudios Internacionales, Universidad de Barcelona] (3984
 At head of title-page: Indice historico español.

CARBIA, Rómulo D. La crónica oficial de las Indias Occidentales; estudio histórico y crítico acerca de la historiografía mayor de Hispano-America en los siglos XVI-XVIII. Con una introducción sobre la crónica oficial en Castilla. La Plata, Rep. Arg., 1934. 303 p. (Biblioteca Humanidades, t.14) (3985
 "Indice bibliográfico de las obras utilizadas en la preparación de la monografía": p. 273-88.---Jones 83.

CHAPMAN, Charles Edward. Colonial Hispanic America; a history. New York, The Macmillan Co., 1933. 405 p. (3986
 "Essay on authorities": p. 347-85.---Jones 96.

-----. Republican Hispanic America; a history. New York, The Macmillan Co., 1937. 463 p. (3987
 "Essay on authorities": p. 391-444.---Jones 97.

CONGRESO Internacional de Historia de América [2o.] reunido en Buenos Aires en los dias 5 a 14 de julio de 1937. Buenos Aires, J. Peuser, 1937. 6v. (3988
 Bibliografía y archivos: v.1, p. 267-98.--- Jones 106a.

FINNEY, George J. Books in Latin American history; a study of collections available in colleges and universities of the United States. Chicago, American Library Association, 1942. 51 p. (Studies of the Committee on Library Cooperation with Latin America, no. 3) (3989

FISHER, Lillian Estelle. The intendant system in Spanish America. Berkeley, Univ. of California, 1929. 385 p. (3990
 Bibliography: p. 345-50.---Jones 150.

GARCIA, Genaro. Carácter de la conquista española en America y en México según los textos de los historiadores primitivos. México, D.F., Of. Tip. de la Secretaría de Fomento, 1901. 456 p. (3991
 Bibliography: p. 399-51.---Jones 2180.

GUTIERREZ DEL ARROYO, Isabel, POSADA, Germán, etc. Estudios de historiografía americana. México, D.F., El Colegio de México [1948] 486 p. (Colegio de México. Publ. del Centro de Estudios Históricos) (3992

HANKE, Lewis. Some studies in progress in Spain on Hispanic American colonial history. (Hispanic American historical review, Durham, N.C., v.15, p. 105-13, 1935) (3993
 Jones 186.

HOSKINS, Halford Lancaster. Guide to Latin-American history. New York [etc.] D. C. Heath & Co., 1922. 121 p. (3994
 References to material in English.---Jones 208.

HUMPHREYS, Robert Arthur. Latin American history; a guide to the literature in English. London, Oxford Univ. Pr., 1958. 197 p. (3994a

JAMES, Herman Gerlach, and MARTIN, Percy Alvin. The republics of Latin America; their history, governments and economic conditions. New York and London, Harper & Brothers, 1923.

JAMES, Herman Gerlach, and MARTIN...(Cont.)
533 p.   (3995
    "Selected readings": p. 497-520.---Jones
223.

KENISTON, Hayward. List of works for the study of Hispanic-American history. New York,
Hispanic Society of America, 1920. 451 p.
(Hisoanic notes and monographs, 5) (3996
    Guide for students of Hispanic American
history and bibliography.---Jones 234.

MOORE, David Richard. A history of Latin America. New York, Prentice-Hall, 1938.
826 p.   (3997
    Bibliography: p. 781-811.---Jones 320.

PAN AMERICAN UNION. Columbus Memorial Library.
List of Latin America history and description
in the Columbus Memorial Library. Washington,
D.C., International Bureau of the American
Republics [1907] 98 p.   (3998
    Jones 356.

-----. Supplement no.1, Nov. 1, 1907 to July
8, 1909. Washington, D.C. [Govt. Print. Off.]
1909. 34 p.   (3999

-----. Supplement no.2, July 9, 1909 to June
1, 1914. Washington, D.C. [Gibson Bros.]
1914. 136 p.   (4000
    Jones 356. Title: Books and magazine
articles on Latin American description and
history received.

PIERSON, William Whatley. Hispanic-American
history: a syllabus; rev. and enl. Chapel
Hill, Univ. of North Carolina Pr., 1926.
169 p.   (4001
    Contains selected bibliography, arranged
by topic. First published in 1916.---Jones
373.

RASMUSSEN, Wayne David. Some general histories
of Latin America. [Washington, D.C.] Dept.
of Agriculture [1942] 9 p. (Bureau of Agricultural Economics. Agricultural history
ser., no.1)   (4002

RIPPY, James Fred. Historical evolution of
Hispanic America. New York, F.S. Crofts &
Co., 1932. 580 p.   (4003
    "Reading lists": p. 541-53.---Jones 405.

-----. Another ed. Oxford, B. Blackwell
[1936] 580 p.   (4004
    Jones 405.

ROBERTSON, William Spence. France and Latin
American independence. Baltimore, Johns
Hopkins Pr., 1939. 626 p.   (4005
    Selected bibliography: p. 587-606.---Jones
412.

ROBERTSON, William Spence. History of the
Latin-American nations. New York, D. Appleton and Co., 1922. 617 p.   (4006
    Suggestions for further reading and study:
p. 571-97.---Jones 415.

-----. -----. Rev. ed. New York, D. Appleton
and Co., 1925. 630 p.   (4007
    Suggestions for further reading and study:
p. 581-609. Revised editions issued also in
1928, 1930, 1932 and 1937.---Jones 416.

-----. Rise of the Spanish-American republics
as told in the lives of their liberators.
New York, D. Appleton and Co., 1918.
380 p.   (4008
    Select bibliography: p. 333-61.---Jones
417.

SANCHEZ ALONSO, Benito. Fuentes de la historia
española e hispanoamericana; 2a. ed. rev. y
ampl. Madrid, 1927. 2 v. (Publicaciones
de la Revista de filología española [8](4009
    13,172 items listed.---Jones 432.

-----. -----. Apéndice. Madrid, 1946.
464 p.   (4010

-----. 3a. ed. corr. y puesta al día. Madrid,
1952. 3 v.   (4011
    Contains over 34,000 references. First
edition, 1919, has title: Fuentes de la historia española.

TERAN, Juan Bautista. El nacimiento de la
América española. Tucuman, Arg., 1927.
338 p.   (4012
    Bibliographical notes at end of each
chapter.---Jones 469a.

-----. La naissance de l'Amérique espagnole;
traduction par Xavier de Cardaillac. Paris,
Editions "Le Livre Libre", 1930. 348 p.(4013
    "Appendice" containing bibliographical
notes: p. 273-348.---Jones 470.

VELAZQUEZ CHAVEZ, Maria del Carmen. Guía
bibliográfica para la enseñanza de la historia en Hispano-América. México, D.F.,
1964. 506, [5] p. (Publicación del Instituto Panamericano de Geografía e Historia,
224)   (4014
    Issued also as publication of the Comisión
de Historia, 86, and 2 of Bibliografías.

WILGUS, Alva Curtis. Colonial Hispanic Amer-
ica. Washington, D.C., George Washington
University, 1936. 690 p.   (4015
    Includes bibliographies. Appendices E-L,
Histories and historians of colonial Hispanic
America.---Jones 531.

-----. The development of Hispanic America.
New York, Farrar & Rinehart, 1941.
941 p.   (4016

WILGUS, Alva Curtis. Colonial ... (Cont.)
"References" at end of each chapter.
"Bibliographical essay on leading works
in various languages dealing with Hispanic
America printed since the year 1800": p.
856-911.---Jones 531a.

-----. Histories and historians of Hispanic
America; a bibliographical essay. Washington, D.C., Inter-American Bibliographical
and Library Association, 1936. 113 p. (Inter-American Bibliographical and Library
Association publications ser. 1, v.2) (4017
Based on the author's Histories of Hispanic America (Washington, D.C., Pan American
Union, 1932) and on the appendices, p. 573-
662, in Colonial Hispanic America (see item
4015) "Bibliographical collections and
aids": p. 98-102.---Jones 532.

-----. -----. 2d ed. New York, H. W. Wilson,
1942. xii, 144 p.   (4018
Revised, corrected and augmented.

-----. The histories of Hispanic America, a
bibliographical account. Washington, D.C.,
Pan American Union, 1932. 115 p. (Columbus
Memorial Library. Bibliographic ser. no.
9)   (4019
Jones 533.

-----. A history of Hispanic America; a text-
book handbook for college students. Washington, D.C., Mime-o-Form Service, 1931.
747 p.   (4020
Includes bibliographies and index guide
to maps.---Jones 534.

WILGUS, Alva Curtis, and EÇA, Raul d'. Outline
history of Latin America. New York, Barnes
& Noble, 1939. 376 p. (College outline
series)   (4021
Contains references to literature in
English.---Jones 540.

-----. Rev. and enl. ed. New York, Barnes &
Noble, [1941] 410 p. (College outline
series)   (4022

MEXICO

ALCINA FRANCH, José. Fuentes indígenas de Méjico; ensayo de sistematización bibliográfica. Madrid, 1956. 119 p.   (4023
Publicado en Revista de Indias, año 15,
no. 61-62.

BANCROFT, Hubert Howe. Mexico. San Francisco,
A. L. Bancroft & Co., 1883-1888. 6 v. (His-
tory of the Pacific States of North America,
v. 4-9)   (4024
"Authorities quoted": v. 1, p. XXI-CXII;
The Bancroft collection was acquired by the
University of California. A catalogue was

BANCROFT, Hubert Howe. Mexico ... (Cont.)
issued by the University.---Jones 2066.

BASAVE Y DEL CASTILLO NEGRETE, Carlos. Exploraciones y anotaciones en libros y folletos
que tratan de la revolucion mexicana. México, D.F., Tall. H. Barrales Sucs., 1931.
34 p.   (4025
Cited in González, item 78.

BAYLE, Constantino. Historia de los descubrimientos y colonización de la Baja California
por los padres de la Compañía de Jesús. Bilbao, Edit. "Cultura Misional", 1933. 230 p.
(Bibliotheca hispana missionum, 3)   (4026
"Registro de los principales documentos
consultados para este trabajo": p. 201-30.
---Jones 2070.

BLOM, Frans Ferdinand. The conquest of Yuca-
tan. Boston, New York, Houghton Mifflin
Co., 1936. 237 p.   (4027
Bibliography: p. 213-20.---Jones 2086.

BOBAN, Eugène. Documents pour servir à l'histoire du Mexique; catalogue raisonné de la
colecction de M. E.-Eugène Goupil (ancienne
collection J.-M.-A. Aubin); manuscrits figu-
ratifs, et autres sur papier indigène d'aga-
ve mexicana et sur papier européen antérieurs
et postérieurs à la conquête du Mexique
(XVI siècle), avec une introduction de M.
E.-Eugène Goupil et une lettre-preface de M.
Auguste Génin. Paris, E. Leroux, 1891.
2 v. and atlas of 80 pl.   (4028
Collection formed originally by L. Boturini
Benaduci and acquired by the Bibliothèque
Nationale, Paris. "Biographie du chevalier
Lorenzo Boturini Benaduci, (d'après M. A.
Chavero)": v. 1, p. 31-51.---Jones 2087.

-----. -----. Table analytique générale des
matières contenues dans les deux volumes des
Documents pour servir à l'histoire du Mexique.
Paris, E. Leroux, 1891. 16 p.   (4029
Jones 2088.

BOTURINI BENADUCI, Lorenzo. Idea de una nueva
historia general de la América Septentrional.
Madrid, Impr. de J. de Zúñiga, 1746.
2 v.   (4030
"Catálogo del Museo Histórico Indiano del
cavallero Lorenzo Boturini Benaduci": 96 p.
at end of v. 2.---Jones 2099.

-----. Another ed. México, D.F., I. Paz, 1887.
232 p.   (4031
Jones 2100.

BRADEN, Charles Samuel. Religious aspects of
the conquest of Mexico. Durham, N.C., Duke
Univ. Pr., 1930. 344 p.   (4032
Bibliography: p. 329-38.---Jones 2101.

BROUWER, Johannes. Hernán Cortés en Monteczuma; Spanjaarden en Azteken in het begin van de zestiende eeuw. Zutphen, W. J. Thieme & Cie., 1933. 378 p.   (4033
    Bibliographie: p. 373-78.---Jones 2104.

CARREÑO, Alberto María. Documentos relacionados con la historia de México existentes en la nueva Biblioteca de Nueva York. (Anales del Museo Nacional de Arqueología, Historia y Etnología, México, t. 4, p. 489-504, 1912)   (4034
    Jones 2113.

CASTILLO, Ignacio B. del. Bibliografía de la revolución mexicana. México, D.F., Tall. Gráf. de la Secretaría de Comunicaciones y Obras Públicas, 1918. 92 p.   (4035
    Jones 2349. One of the prize winning bibliographies chosen by the National Library in 1915. Includes 799 annotated titles.

CHAVERO, Alfredo. Apuntes viejos de bibliografía mexicana. México, D.F., Impr. de J. I. Guerrero y Cía., 1903. 89 p.   (4036
    Jones 2127.

-----. Segunda ser., México, D.F., Impr. de J. I. Guerrero y Cía., 1907. 28 p.   (4037
    Cited in Millares, item 1688.

CHAVEZ OROZCO, Luis. Historia de México. México, D.F., Edit. Patria, 1934. 2 v. (4038
    Includes bibliographies.---Jones 2130.

FISHER, Lillian Estelle. The background of the revolution for Mexican independence. Boston, Christopher Publ. House, 1934. 512 p.(4039
    Includes bibliography of manuscripts and printed sources: p. 425-62.---Jones 2170.

GONZALEZ, Pedro. La bibliografía histórica nacional. (Boletín de la Sociedad Mexicana de Geografía y Estadística, México, 5 ép., t. 5, p. 295-98, 1912)   (4040
    Jones 2211.

GONZALEZ Y GONZALEZ, Luis. Fuentes de la historia contemporánea de México. Libros y folletos, I, con la colaboración de Guadalupe Monroy y Susana Uribe. México, D.F., El Colegio de México, 1961. lxxxii, 527p. (4041
    First of 3 volumes planned. Vol. 1 contains 6873 entries.

GUIA bibliográfica de la historia de México. Epoca precortesiana. México, D.F., Ediciones de "El Libro y el Pueblo", 1935. 74p.(4042
    Jones 2226. Millares, item 1056, ascribes authorship to Antonio Acevedo Escobedo.

GUZMAN Y RAZ GUZMAN, Jesús. Bibliografía de la independencia de México. México, D.F., D.A. P.P., 1937-1939, 3 v. (Bibliografías mexicanas, no. 4-6)   (4043

GUZMAN Y RAZ GUZMAN, Jesús. ... (Cont.)
    Jones 2229.

-----. Bibliografía de la reforma, la intervención y el imperio. México, 1930-1931. 2 v. (Monografías bibliográficas mexicanas, no. 17, 19)   (4044
    Limited to the period 1854 to 1872.---Jones 2230.

HAFERKORN, Henry Ernest. The war with Mexico, 1846-1848; a select bibliography on the causes, conduct, and the political aspect of the war, together with a select list of books and other printed material on the resources, economic conditions, politics and government of the republic of Mexico and the characteristics of the Mexican people. With annotations and an index. Washington Barracks, 1914. 93 p. (Supplement no. 1, Professional memoirs, Mar.-Apr. 1914, v. 6, no. 26. Bibliographical contributions. Bull. no. 1)   (4045
    Jones 2232.

HANS, Albert. La guerre du Mexique selon les Mexicains. Paris, Berger-Levrault & Cie., 1899. 66 p.   (4046
    In large part a review of certain Mexican works on the French intervention, 1861-1867. ---Jones 2234.

JONES, Cecil Knight. Bibliography of the Mexican revolution. Baltimore, 1919. p. 311-14.   (4047
    Reprinted from the Hispanic American historical review, v. 2, no. 2, May 1919.---Jones 2271.

LARRAINZAR, Manuel. Algunas ideas sobre la historia y manera de escribir la de México, especialmente la contemporánea desde la declaración de independencia en 1821, hasta nuestros días. México, Impr. de I. Cumplido 1865. 105 p.   (4048
    Catálogo de los principales historiadores de México, y otros autores que han escrito sobre las cosas de América: p. 92-105.---Jones 2276.

LIEBMAN, Seymour B. A guide to Jewish references in Mexican colonial era, 1521-1821. Philadelphia, Univ. of Pennsylvania Pr., 1964. 134 p.   (4049

MAUDSLAY, Alfred Percival. Bibliography of Mexico. (In Díaz del Castillo, Bernal. True history of the conquest of New Spain. London, 1908. p. 309-68)   (4050
    Jones 2323.

MEANS, Philip Ainsworth. History of the Spanish conquest of Yucatan and the Itzas. Cambridge, Mass., The Museum, 1917. 206 p. (Papers of the Peabody Museum of American Archaeology and Ethnology, Harvard University,

MEANS, Philip Ainsworth. History... (Cont.)
v. 7)   (4051
"The maps of Yucatan, 1501-1800": p. 192-
99. Bibliography: p. 202-06.---Jones 2324.
Includes the greater part of Avendaño's
account of his journey to Petén and Cano's
account of a trip to Guatemala.

MENENDEZ, Carlos R. Noventa años de historia
de Yucatán (1821-1910). Relación sintética
y cronológica de los acontecimientos más notables, políticos, sociales, económicos, ar-
tísticos, literarios, científicos, etc. etc.,
ocurridos en la península de Yucatán, (Yucatán y Campeche) desde el año 1821, de la independencia de España, hasta el de 1910, del
inicio de la revolución maderista. Merida,
Compañía Tip. Yucateca, 1937. 581 p.(4052
Bibliografía: p. 545-49.---Jones 2342.

MEXICO. Departamento de Bibliotecas. Guía
bibliográfica de la historia de México. México, D.F., Ediciones de "El Libro y el Pueblo", 1935. v. 1.   (4053
"Nota preliminar" signed: Antonio Acevedo
Escobedo. The first part, Epoca precortesiana, is based on bibliographical references
in Luis Chávez Orozco's Historia de México
(Epoca precortesiana) No more published.---
Jones 2353.

MIGUEL Y VERGES, José María. La independencia
mexicana y la prensa insurgente. México, D.
F., El Colegio de México, 1941.
344 p.   (4054
Cited in HLAS, 7, item 3186, with note
that contents include a list of periodicals,
an anthology, and a bibliography.

PARTIDO Revolucionario Institucional, México.
Selección bibliográfica revolucionaria. [Mé-
xico] 1943. 46 p. (Biblioteca de la Feria
del Libro y Exposición Nacional de Periodismo)   (4055

PEREZ MARTINEZ, Héctor. Catálogo de documentos
para la historia de Yucatán y Campeche que
se hallan en diversos archivos y bibliotecas
de México y del extranjero. Campeche, 1943.
133 p.   (4056

PESQUEIRA, F. R. Bibliografía formada para
servir de estudio y consulta en la composi-
ción de una historia de Sonora. México,
1921. 38 p.   (4057
Jones 2423.

PFERDEKAMP, Wilhelm. Deutsche in frühen Mexiko; herausgegeben von der Deutsch-Mexikani-
schen Humboldt Gesellschaft in Mexiko.
Stuttgart, Berlin, Deutsche Verlags-Anstalt
[1938] 223 p. (Schriftenreihe, des Deutschen
Ausland-Instituts, Stuttgart, neue reihe,
bd. 6)   (4058
Contents. - 1. Buch, Deutsche im frühen Mex-

PFERDEKAMP, Wilhelm. Deutsche in... (Cont.)
iko. - 2. Buch, Einige dokumente zur geschichte der Deutschen in Mexiko in der kolonialzeit.
- Namensregister. - Quellen und literatur, p.
223-24.---Jones 2425.

PRIESTLEY, Herbert Ingram. Mexican literature
on the recent revolution. (Hispanic American
historical review, Baltimore, v. 2, p. 286-
311, 1919)   (4059
Jones 2435.

-----. The Mexican nation; a history. New
York, The Macmillan Co., 1923. 507 p. (4060
Bibliography: p. 457-74.---Jones 2436.

-----. Modern Mexican history. New York, 1920.
36 p. (Institute of International Education.
International Relations Clubs. Syllabus
6)   (4061
Jones 2437.

-----. -----. Supplement. New York, 1925.
9 p.   (4062
Jones 2438.

PRIETO, Carlos. El sueño de Cíbola; los astu-
rianos en la conquista de la Nueva España.
México, D.F., Tall. Tip. "Regis", 1933.
50 p.   (4063
Notas bibliográficas: p. 41-50.---Jones
2439.

RAMOS, Roberto. Bibliografía de la historia
de México. México, D.F., 1956. 772 p.(4064

-----. Bibliografía de la revolución mexicana.
México, D.F., [Impr. de la Secretaría de Relaciones Exteriores] 1931-1940. 3 v. (Monografías bibliográficas mexicanas, no. 21,
30)   (4065
Vol. 3 published as Bibliografías mexicanas, no. 9, by la Secretaría de Educación
Pública.
Jones 2447-48.

-----. -----. 2d. ed. México, D.F., 1959-1960.
3 v. (Biblioteca del Instituto Nacional de
Estudios Históricos de la Revolución Mexicana,
15)   (4065a
The volumes contain 5,067 items numbered
consecutively.

RICARD, Robert. Chronique hispano-mexicaine.
(Bulletin hispanique, Bordeaux, v. 37, p. 80-
102, 1935)   (4066
Annotated bibliography of recent works
largely on colonial history.---Jones 2457.

-----. La période coloniale de l'histoire du
Mexique d'après les publications récentes.
(Revue historique, Paris, v. 169, p. 604-14,
1932)   (4067
Jones 2459.

RYDJORD, John. Foreign interest in the independence of New Spain; an introduction to
the war for independence. Durham, N.C., Duke
Univ. Pr., 1935. 347 p. (Duke University
publications)   (4068
  Bibliography: p. 309-22.---Jones 2479.

SAVILLE, Marshall Howard. The earliest notices
concerning the conquest of Mexico by Cortés
in 1519. [New York, Museum of the American
Indian, 1920] 54 p. (Indian notes and monographs, v. 9, no. 1)   (4069
  Bibliographical notes: p. 39-54.---Jones
2492.

SIERRA, Carlos J. La prensa liberal frente a
la intervencion y el imperio. México, D.F.,
Dirección General de Prensa, Memoria, Biblioteca y Publicaciones, 1962. 205 p.   (4070
  Contains 1633 entries.

SMITH, Justin Harvey. The war with Mexico.
New York, 1919. 2 v.   (4071
  Includes bibliography.---Jones 2503.

TEJA ZABRE, Alfonso. Guide to the history of
Mexico. Mexico, D. F., Ministry of Foreign
Affairs, 1935. 375 p.   (4072
  Bibliography: p. 359-70.---Jones 2524.
Published also in French.

-----. Panorama histórico de la revolución
mexicana. México, Ediciones Botas, 1939.
220 p.   (4073
  Bibliografía: p. 201-12.---Jones 2524a.

VALDES ACOSTA, José María. A través de las
centurias. Mérida de Yucatán, Tall. "Pluma
y Lápiz", 1923-1926. 2 v.   (4074
  Contains much biographical matter. Typewritten.---Jones 2544.
  Libros consultados: t. 1, p. XI-XII. Escritura y bibliografía: t. 1, p. 139-42.

VALLE, Rafael Heliodoro. Relaciones historicas
de México y Centro América. (Boletín de la
Sociedad de Geografía y Estadística, México,
D.F., 5a. ép. t. 12, no. 1-6, p. 209-57,
1928)   (4075
  Notas bibliográficas: p. 254-57.---Jones
2557a.

VETANCURT, Agustín de. Teatro mexicano. Des-
cripcion breve de los sucesos ejempleres, históricos, políticos, militares y religiosos
del Nuevo Mundo occidental de las Indias.
México, D.F., Impr. de I. Escalante y Ca.,
1870-1871. 4 v.   (4076
  Vol. 4: Menologio franciscano de los varones más señalados que con sus vidas ejemplares, perfección religiosa ... ilustraron
la provincia del Santo Evangelio de México.
1st edition, México, 1698.---Jones 2575.

WYLLYS, Rufus Kay. The French in Sonora (1850-
1854). Berkeley, Calif., 1932. 319 p. (University of California publ. in history,
v. 21)   (4077
  Bibliography: p. 232-40.---Jones 2590.

YALE University. Library. The Mexican war,
1846-1848; a collection of contemporary ma-
terials presented to the Yale University
Library by Frederick W. Beinecke. New Haven,
Conn., 1960. p. 93-123.   (4078
  Reprinted from the University Library Ga-
zette, v. 34, no. 3, Jan. 1960. Comp.: Jerry
E. Patterson.

ZERECERO, Anastasio. Memorias para la historia
de las revoluciones en México. México, D.F.,
Impr. del Gobierno, 1869. 608 p.   (4079
  "Indios célebres de la República Mexicana,
o biografías de los más notables que han
florecido desde 1521 hasta nuestros días",
por Antonio Carrión: p. 436-531.---Jones
2594.

ZURITA, Alonso de. Historia de la Nueva España (siglo XVI) Madrid, V. Suárez, 1909.
v. 1. (Colección de libros y documentos referentes a la historia de América,
t. 9)   (4080
  "El 'Catálogo de los autores que an escrip-
to historias de las Indias' es el primer conjunto definido de bibliografía histórica americanista, y ... resulta todavía útil" (Luis
Aznar in Humanidades, t. 28, p. 269)---Jones
2595b.

NORTH AMERICA

BOLTON, Herbert Eugene, and MARSHALL, Thomas
Maitland. The colonization of North America,
1492-1783. New York, The Macmillan Co.,
1920. xvi, 609 p.   (4081
  "Readings" at end of each chapter.---Jones
2098a.

GRIFFIN, Grace Gardner. Writings on American
history, 1906- . A bibliography of books
and articles on United States and Canadian
history, with some memoranda on other portions of America. New York, The Macmillan
Co., 1908- .   (4082
  Issueds 1906-1917 published independently;
1909-1911 reprinted from the Annual Report
of the American Historical Association;
1918-1929 issued as supplements to the
Annual Report; 1930-1931 as v. 2 of the
Annual Report; 1932 as v. 3; 1933-1934 as
the complete report; and 1935- . as v. 2.
Since 1933 Dorothy M. Louraine assisted in
the compilation.
  "With respect to the regions lying south
of the continental United States ... the in-
tention has been to include all writings on
the history of these regions published in

GRIFFIN, Grace Gardner. Writings...(Cont.)
the United States or Europe; but the products (not relating to the United States)
of South America and other southward regions
have been left to their own bibliographers."
(Preface, 1917)---Jones 176.

PRIESTLEY, Herbert Ingram. The coming of the
white man, 1492-1848. New York, The Mac-
millan Co., 1930. 411 p. (A history of
American life, v. 1)   (4083
Critical essay on authorities: p. 351-86.
---Jones 381.

STECK, Francis Borgia. A tentative guide to
historical materials on the Spanish border-
lands. Philadelphia, The Catholic Historical Society of Philadelphia, 1943.
106 p.   (4084

PANAMA

BIBLIOGRAFIA de Coclé con motivo de su centenario, 1855-1955. [Panamá, Universidad de
Panamá, 1955] 107 p.   (4085
Cited in HLAS, 22, item 3082; also Caribbean acquisitions, 1957/1958, p. 4.

GASTEAZORO, Carlos Manuel. Introducción al
estudio de la historia de Panamá; t. 1.
México, D.F., Edit. Azteca, 1956. 214 p.
(Publicaciones Cultural panameña)   (4085a
Vol. 1 contains references to sources
relative to Spanish colonial period.

SCOTT, John. A bibliography of printed documents and books relating to the Darien Company. Rev. by George P. Johnston. Edinburgh, Priv. print., 1903. 54 p.   (4086
Jones 1252.

-----. -----. With additions and corrections
by George P. Johnson. Edinburgh, Priv.
print., 1906. p. 55-75.   (4087
Jones 1252a.

PARAGUAY

BAEZ, Cecilio. Cuadros históricos y descriptivos. Asuncion, Tall. Nacionales de H.
Kraus, 1906. 344 p.   (4088
Contains biographical sketches.---Jones
2597. Indicacion bibliográfica, p. 337-41.

BEVERINA, Juan. La guerra del Paraguay. Buenos Aires, Ferrari Hnos., 1921. t. 1
(442 p.)   (4089
Includes list of official publications and
historical works (48 titles) and of maps
(9 titles).---Jones 2598.

BOX, Pelham Horton. Los orígenes de la guerra
del Paraguay contra la triple alianza. Ver-

BOX, Pelham Horton. Los orígenes ... (Cont.)
sión castellana de Pablo M. Ynsfrán ... y revisada por el prof. J. R. Carey. Asunción,
La Colmena, 1936. 371 p.   (4090
Bibliografía: p. 321-44.---Jones 2602.

-----. The origins of the Paraguayan war.
Urbana, 1929. 2 v. (University of Illinois
studies in the social sciences, v. 15,
no. 34)   (4091
Bibliography: v. 2, p. 300-26.---Jones
2601.

CARDOZO, Efraim. Historiografía paraguaya; I.
Paraguay indígena, español y jesuita. México, D.F., 1959. 610 p. (Publicación del
Instituto Panamericano de Geografía e Historia, no. 221)   (4092
Issued also as publication of the Comisión
de Historia, 83, and 5 of the series, Historiografías.

FRAGOSO, Augusto Tasso. Historia de guerra
entre a triplice aliança e o Paraguai.
Rio de Janeiro, Impr. do Estado-Maior do
Exercito, 1934. 5 v.   (4093
Bibliografía: v. 5, p. 375-89.---Jones
2608.

ZINNY, Antonio. Bibliografía histórica del
Paraguay y de Misiones. (Revista nacional,
Buenos Aires, v. 4, p. 87-96, 179-91, 372-83;
v. 5, p. 82-96, 168-80, 264-88, 364-84;
v. 6, p. 373-83; v. 7, p. 67-94, 185-92;
v. 8, p. 272-88, 369-83; v. 9, p. 342-83;
v. 10, p. 67-93, 1887-1889)   (4094
"Comprende cerca de 600 títulos de obras,
folletos, revistas, artículos, papeles,
etc." (Binayán)---Jones 2622a.

PERU

BASADRE, Jorge. Historia de la República, 1822-
1899. Lima, Gil, 1939. 626 p.   (4095
Bibliografía: p. 581-616.---Jones 2630.

-----. Historia de la República; 2a. ed. rev.
y aum. Chorrillos, Escuela Militar, 1940.
v. 1. (476 p.)   (4096
Jones 2630a. No more published.

-----. 3a. ed. rev. y aum. Lima, Edit. Cultura Antártica, 1946. 2 v.   (4097

-----. 4a. ed. nuevamente rev. y aum. Lima,
Edit. Cultura Antártica, 1949.   (4098

-----. 5a. ed. aum. y corr. Lima, Ediciones
"Historia", 1961-1964. 10 v.   (4099

-----. -----. Bibliografía; versión preliminar.
Lima, Ediciones "Historia", 1962.
232 p.   (4100

BASADRE, Jorge. Report on sources for national history of Perú. Washington, D.C., Library of Congress, 1960. 23 p. (Hispanic Foundation consultant reports)   (4101
   Cited in Revista interamericana de bibliografía, v. 11, p. 91.

-----. -----. Addenda. Washington, D.C., 1960. 21 p. (Hispanic Foundation consultant reports) mimeogr.   (4102
   Caption title: Bibliografías y listas de obras sobre la época Republicana (hasta 1808)

HERRERA, Jenaro Ernesto. La Universidad Mayor de San Marcos y la guerra del Pacífico, 5 de abril de 1789[!]-23 de octubre de 1883; monografía histórica. Lima, Sanmartí y Cía., 1929. 184 p.   (4103
   "Bibliografía de las obras que se han compulsado para escribirla": p. 23-33.---Jones 2658.

JUNTA del Cuarto Centenario de la Fundacion de Trujillo. "La Fundacion de Trujillo". Recopilación de artículos y trabajos históricos sobre dicha Fundacion. Trujillo, Perú, Impr. Comercial, 1935. 232 p.   (4104
   Includes bibliographies.---Jones 2660.

LIMA. Universidad Católica del Perú. Instituto de Investigaciones Históricas. Cuadernos de estudio. Lima, 1939- .
v.1- .   (4105
   Each number contains a bibliographical section.---Jones 2679.

MEANS, Philip Ainsworth. Fall of the Inca empire and the Spanish rule in Peru: 1530-1780. New York, C. Scribner's Sons, 1932. 351 p.   (4106
   Bibliography: p. 301-25.---Jones 2688.

PAZ SOLDAN, Mariano Felipe. Historia del Perú independiente, 1835-1839. Buenos Aires, Impr. del Courrier de la Plata, 1888. 408, xliv p.   (4107
   Catálogo de documentos manuscritos e impresos que han servido para escribir esta obra": xliv p.---Jones 2714.

PIZARRO, Pedro. Relation of the discovery and conquest of the kingdoms of Peru; translated into English and annotated by Philip Ainsworth Means. New York, The Cortes Society, 1921. 2 v. (Documents and narratives concerning the discovery and conquest of Latin America, no. 4)   (4108
   Notes and bibliography: v. 2, p. 491-561.---Jones 2723.

PORRAS BARRENECHEA, Raúl. Fuentes históricas peruanas; apuntes de un curso universitario. Lima, J. Mejía Baca & P. L. Villanueva, 1954. 601 p.   (4108a

PORRAS BARRENECHEA, Raul. Fuentes históricas peruanas; apuntes de un curso universitario. Lima, 1963. 601 p. (Lima. Universidad Mayor de San Marcos. Instituto Raúl Porras Barrenechea, Publicaciones)   (4108b
   Bibliografía regional: p. 535-63.

RIVA AGÜERO, José de la. La historia en el Perú. Lima, Impr. Nacional de F. Barrionuevo, 1910. 558 p.   (4109
   Contents. - Introducción. - Blas Valera. Garcilaso de la Vega. - Cronistas de convento. - Don Pedro Peralta. - El general don Manuel de Mendiburu. Don Mariano Felipe Paz Soldán. - Epílogo.---Jones 2736.

SANCHO, Pedro. An account of the conquest of Peru, written by Pedro Sancho, secretary to Pizarro and scrivener to his army; tr. into English and annotated by Philip Ainsworth Means. New York, The Cortes Society, 1917. 203 p. Documents and narratives concerning the discovery and conquest of Latin America, no.2)   (4110
   Bibliography: p. 199-203.---Jones 2746.

SARMIENTO DE GAMBOA, Pedro. History of the Incas and the execution of the Inca, Tupac Amarú, by Captain Baltasar de Ocampo; tr. and ed. with notes and an introduction by Sir Clements Markham. Cambridge, Printed for the Hakluyt Society, 1907. 395 p. (Works, the Hakluyt Society, 2d ser., no. 22)   (4111
   Bibliography of Peru, 1526-1907: p. 267-358.---Jones 2747.

-----. -----. Supplement; a narrative of the Vice-regal Embassy to Vilcabamba, 1571, and of the execution of the Inca, Tupac Amarú, Dec. 1571, by Gabriel de Oviedo. London, 1908. p. 397-412. (Works, the Hakluyt Society, 2d ser., no. 22, Supplement)   (4112

TAURO, Alberto. Bibliografía peruana de historia, 1940-1953. Lima, 1953. 196 p. (4113

-----. -----. Primer suplemento. Lima, 1958. p. 361-461.   (4114
   Reprinted from Revista histórica, t. 22, 1955-1956.

-----. Guía de estudios historicos. Lima, 1955. 109 p.   (4115
   Reprinted from Boletín bibliográfico, Biblioteca Central, Universidad Mayor de San Marcos, Lima, año 28, v. 25, no. 1-4, dic. 1955.

VARGAS UGARTE, Rubén. Historia del Perú. Fuentes. Lima, 1939. 330 p.   (4116
   "Este manual proporciona más fidedigna información acerca de los materiales disponibles y su consulta resultará muy provechosa a los especialistas" (Revista de historia de

HISTORY

VARGAS UGARTE, Rubén. Historia ... (Cont.)
América, no. 7)---Jones 2767.

-----. -----. 2a. ed. Lima, Gil, 1945.
360 p.   (4117

-----. Manual de estudios peruanistas. Lima,
Tip. Peruana, 1952. 346 p.   (4118

XEREZ, Francisco de, and ESTETE, Miguel de.
Conquista del Perú, y Viaje de Hernando Pizarro desde Caxamarca hasta Jauja (Sevilla,
1534). Edición preparada por Antonio R. Rodríguez Moñino. Badajoz, Arqueros, 1929.
202 p. (Extremadura en América, 1) (4119
First published, Sevilla, 1534, with title:
Verdadera relación de la conquista del Perú.
"Noticia de la vida y escritos de Francisco
de Xerez, por Antonio R. Rodríguez Moñino":
p. 189-202.---Jones 2776.

PUERTO RICO

MILLER, Paul Gerard. Historia de Puerto Rico.
Chicago, Nueva York, Rand, McNally y Co.,
1922. 549 p.   (4120
Bibliografía: p. 539-42. "Catálogo de
gobernadores de Puerto Rico: Apéndice A,
p. 509-22. Reissued in 1939.---Jones 2797.

SOUTH AMERICA

BINGHAM, Hiram. The possibilities of South
American history and politics as a field
for research. (Monthly bulletin of the International Bureau of the American Republics,
Washington, D.C., v. 26, p. 283-300,
1908)   (4121
Bibliographical foot-notes.---Jones 60.

CORBACHO, Jorge M. South American historical
documents relating chiefly to the period of
revolution. Exhibited at the Hispanic Society of America. New York and London, G.
P. Putnam's Sons, 1919. 66 p.   (4122
Jones 109.

HASBROUCK, Alfred. Foreign legionaries in the
liberation of Spanish South America. New
York, 1928. 470 p. (Studies in history,
economics and public law, Columbia University, no. 303)   (4123
Bibliography: p. 435-47.---Jones 196.

ISPIZUA, Segundo de. Bibliografía histórica
sudamericana; ensayo. Bilbao, Eléxpuru,
1915. 19 p.   (4124
Reviewed in Revista de filología española,
t. 2, no. 4, p. 400-01.---Jones 219.

MARKHAM, Clements Robert. Colonial history
of South America, and the wars of independence. (In Winsor, Justin, Narrative and

MARKHAM, Clements Robert. Colonial...(Cont.)
critical history of America. Boston, New
York, 1884-1889. v.8, p. 295-368)   (4125
Contains critical essay on the sources of
information, and editorial notes, including
a note on the bibliography of Brazil.---Jones
284.

MEANS, Philip Ainsworth. Biblioteca andina.
New Haven, Yale Univ. Pr. [1928] 271-525 p.
(Transactions of the Connecticut Academy of
Arts and Sciences, v.29, May 1928)   (4126
This is part 1: The chroniclers, or, the
writers of the 16th and 17th centuries who
treated of the pre-Hispanic history and culture of the Andean countries. A translation
into Spanish may be found in the Revista
universitaria, Cuzco, v. 14, 1930.---Jones
294.

ORNSTEIN, Leopoldo R. La campaña de los Andes
a la luz de las doctrinas de guerra modernas.
Buenos Aires, Tall. Gráf. del Colegio Militar, 1929. 2 v.   (4127
Bibliografía: v.1, p.3-7.---Jones 799.

THE SOUTHWEST

BOLTON, Herbert Eugene. Spanish exploration
in the Southwest, 1542-1706. New York, C.
Scribner's Sons, 1916. 487 p. (Original
narratives of early American history) (4128
The introductions contain reviews of bibliographical sources.---Jones 2097.

-----. Texas in the middle eighteenth century;
studies in Spanish colonial history and administration. Berkeley, Univ. of California
Pr., 1915. 501 p. (University of California publ. in history, v.3)   (4129
Bibliography: p. 447-70.---Jones 2098.

CROIX, Teodoro de. Teodoro de Croix and the
northern frontier of New Spain, 1776-1783,
from the original document in the Archives
of the Indies, Seville, tr. and ed. by
Alfred Barnaby Thomas. Norman, Univ. of
Oklahoma Pr., 1941. 273 p. (American exploration and travel, 5)   (4130
Bibliography, p. 245-68, includes manuscripts and printed material.---Jones 2137a.

DAY, Arthur Grove. Coronado's quest, the discovery of the southwestern states. Berkeley
and Los Angeles, Univ. of Calif. Pr., 1940.
418 p.   (4131
Bibliography: p. 381-98.---Jones 2146a.

MECHAM, John Lloyd. The northern expansion
of New Spain, 1522-1822; a selected descriptive bibliographical list. Durham, 1927.
p. 233-76.   (4132
Jones 2325. Reprinted from the Hispanic
American historical review, v.7, no.2, May
1927.

WAGNER, Henry Raup. Bibliography of printed
   works relating to those portions of the
   United States which formerly belonged to
   Mexico. Santiago de Chile, Impr. Diener,
   1917. 43 p.   (4133
   Jones 2579.

-----. The Spanish Southwest, 1542-1794; an
   annotated bibliography. Berkeley, 1924.
   302 p.   (4134
   Revised and enlarged of the author's
   Bibliography of printed works in Spanish
   relating to those portions of the United
   States which formerly belonged to Mexico.

-----. -----. Another edition. Albuquerque,
   The Quivira Society, 1937. 2 v. (Quivira
   Society, Publ., v.7)   (4135
   Bibliography: p. 501-24.---Jones 522.

URUGUAY

ARAUJO, Orestes. Historia compendiada de la
   civilización uruguaya. Montevideo, Tip. Escuela Nacional de Artes y Oficios, 1907- .
   v. 1- .   (4136
   "Lista alfabética de los autores consultados": v. 1, p. 331-40: v. 2, p. 273-78.
   ---Jones 2813.

BAUZA, Francisco. Historia de la dominación
   española en el Uruguay; 2a. ed. Montevideo,
   A. Barreiro y Ramos, 1895-1897. 3 v. (4137
   Reseña preliminar (v. 1, p. vii-lviii)
   contains: Bibliografía y archivos coloniales. - Primeros cronistas e historiadores
   de Indias. - Escritores y viajeros subsi-
   guientes. - Bibliografía jesuítica. - Com-
   plementación de los trabajos historiales y
   jurídicos. - Azara. - Movimiento bibliográfico de principios del siglo 19. - Bibliografía argentina. - Bibliografía brasileira. -
   Bibliografía uruguaya.---Jones 2820.

ESTRADA, Dardo. Fuentes documentales para la
   historia colonial; conferencia leída el día
   28 de julio de 1917, con un discurso preliminar del doctor Gustavo Gallinal. Montevideo, Impr. y Casa Edit. "Renacimiento," 1918.
   39 p.   (4138
   Jones 2828.

FALCAO ESPALTER, Mario. Formación histórica
   del Uruguay (1810-1852) Madrid, Espasa-Calpe, 1929. 290 p.   (4139
   Notas y referencias bibliográficas: p.
   281-87.---Jones 2831.

PEREIRA PEREZ, Ramón G. El pueblo de Nico Pérez, hoy denominado José Batlle y Ordóñez;
   nacimiento y desarrollo, apuntes históricos.
   Montevideo, Tall. Gráf. El Demócrata, 1932.
   272 p.   (4140
   Bibliografía: p. 262-68.---Jones 2857.

SCARONE, Arturo. Efemérides uruguayas; prólogo de Raúl Montero Bustamante. Montevideo,
   Instituto Histórico y Geográfico del Uruguay,
   1956. 4 v.   (4141
   Vol. 4 is comprised of indexes.

VENEZUELA

FEBRES CORDERO, Tulio. Archivo de historia y
   variedades. Caracas, Parra León Hermanos,
   1930-1931. 2 v.   (4142
   Bibliografía venezolanista, adiciones a la
   obra por M. S. Sánchez: v. 2, p. 96-112, 48
   titles. Vol. 2 includes other papers on the
   history of printing and bibliography. These
   are listed in Sánchez' Bibliografía de índices bibliográficos.---Jones 2911.

GONZALEZ GUINAN, Francisco. Historia contemporánea de Venezuela. Caracas, 1909-1925.
   15 v.   (4143
   Prensa periódica (1822-1889): v. 15, p.
   731-52.---Jones 2915.

GRASES, Pedro. Contribución a la bibliografía
   del 19 de abril de 1810. Caracas, Impr. Nacional, 1960. 56 p. (Publ. de la Sociedad
   Bolivariana de Venezuela)   (4144

-----. Estudios bibliográficos. Prólogo de
   Rafael Caldera. Caracas, 1961. 387 p.(4145

-----. Traducciones de interés político-cul-
   tural en la época de la independencia de Venezuela. Caracas, 1961. 59 p.   (4146

HUMBERT, Jules. Les origines vénézuéliennes;
   essai sur la colonisation espagnole au Véné-
   zuéla (ouvrage accompagné d'une gravure et
   d'une carte géographique) Bordeaux, Feret
   & Fils; [etc.] 1905. xx, 340 p.   (4147
   Bibliographie: p. vii-xvi. Cartographie:
   p. xvii-xx.---Jones 2917.

ROJAS, Arístides. Estudios históricos; ser. 1.
   Caracas, Lit. y Tip. del Comercio, 1926.
   337 p.   (4148
   Compiler: José E. Machado. "La imprenta
   en Venezuela durante la colonia y la revolución": p. 1-58. "Orígenes del teatro en
   Caracas:" p. 310-25.---Jones 2950.

WEST INDIES

DAMPIERRE, Jacques de. Essai sur les sources
   de l'histoire des Antilles Françaises (1492-
   1664) Paris, A. Picard et Fils, 1904. xl,
   238 p. (Mémoires et documents publiés par
   la Société de l'Ecole des Chartes, v.6)(4149
   Principales bibliographies américaines:
   p. xix-xl.---Jones 2988.

GARRETT, Mitchell Bennett. The French colo-
nial question 1789-1791; dealings of the
Constituent assembly with problems arising
from the revolution in the West Indies. Ann
Arbor, Mich., G. Wahr, 1916. 167 p. (4150
Bibliography: p. 135-60.---Jones 2994.

GOVEIA, Elsa V. A study on the historiography
of the British West Indies to the end of the
Nineteenth Century. Mexico, D.F., 1956.
198 p. (Publ. del Instituto Panamericano de
Geografía e Historia, no. 186) (4151
Issued also as publication of the Comisión
de Historia, no. 78, and 2 of the series,
Historiografías.

HARING, Clarence Henry. The buccaneers in the
West Indies in the xvii century. New York,
E. P. Dutton and Co., 1910. 298 p. (4152
"Sources and bibliography": p. 275-87.---
Jones 2994a.

-----. Los bucaneros de las Indias Occidentales en el Siglo XVII. Traducción especial
del inglés para el "Boletín de la Cámara de
Comercio de Caracas". Caracas, 1925.
272 p. (4153
Translated by Leopoldo Landaeta. "Fuentes
y bibliografía": p. 261-72.---Jones 2994b.

PEYTRAUD, Lucien Pierre. L'esclavage aux An
tilles Françaises avant 1789. Paris, Hachette & Cie., 1897. xxii, 472 p. (4154
Notice bibliographique: p. xiii-xxii.---
Jones 3007.

RAGATZ, Lowell Joseph. A check-list of House
of Commons sessional papers relating to the
British West Indies and to the West Indian
slave trade and slavery, 1763-1834. London,
B. Edwards [1923] 42 p. (4155

-----. A guide for the study of British Carib-
bean history, 1763-1834, including the aboli-
tion and emancipation movements. Washington,
D.C., Govt. Print. Off., 1932. viii, 725 p.
(Annual report of the American Historical
Association, 1930. v. 3) (4156
Index compiled by Mary Parker Ragatz.
Issued also separately; published as House
Document no. 818 of the 71st Congress, 3d
Session.

RENNARD, Joseph. Essai bibliographique sur
l'histoire religieuse des Antilles Françaises.
Paris, Secretariat Général [1931]
95 p. (4156a
Cited in Bissainthe, 7703.

HOUSING AND PLANNING

ARGENTINA. Congreso. Biblioteca. "Bibliografía sobre la vivienda". Buenos Aires,
1964. 113 p. (Serie Antecedentes para la
documentación parlamentaria, no. 7) (4157

-----. Locación urbana; legislación de emergencia. Buenos Aires, 1949. 26 h. (Información bibliografica, publ. no. 3)
mimeogr. (4157a

ARRIGONE, Jorge Luis. Compilación bibliográfica; documento de referencia. Seminario
de Técnicos y Funcionarios en Planeamiento
Urbano. Bogotá, Centro Interamericano de
Vivienda, 1958. 59 p. (Ser.: Enseñanza,
9-D) mimeogr. (4158
Cited in Giraldo Jaramillo, p. 151.

BAZZANELLA, Waldemiro. Problemas de urbani-
zação na América latina; fontes bibliográficas. Rio de Janeiro, 1960. 123 p.
(Centro Latinoamericano de Pesquisas em
Ciências Sociais, Publ., 2) (4159

CALIFORNIA. University. Center for Latin
American Studies. Guide to reference
collection of Latin American urban planning research at the University of California. [Oakland] 1963. 31 p. (Council of Planning Librarians. Exchange bib-

CALIFORNIA. University. Center for ... (Cont.)
liography, LA 5) (4160
Prepared by Francisco Violich in collaboration with Holway R. Jones.

CENTRO Interamericano de Vivienda, Bogotá.
Bibliografía de la vivienda de interés social
en Colombia en 1953. Bogotá, 1954. [35] p.
(Bibliografía, no. 1) (4161
Compilation by Lilia María Cortés.

FLOREN LOZANO, Luis. Bibliografía colombiana
de vivienda de interés social, construcción
y planeamiento 1954-1958; 2a. ed. Bogotá,
1959. 109 p. (Centro Interamericano de Vivienda y Planeamiento, Ser. Bibliografía, 3)
mimeogr. (4162
Listing of more than 800 items.

-----. Bibliografía de la vivienda de interés
social en Colombia en 1953. Bogotá, 1954.
34, [1] p. (Centro Interamericano de Vivienda y Planeamiento, Ser. Bibliografía,
no. 1) (4163

GUZMAN, Louis E. An annotated bibliography
on urban Latin America. Chicago, Dept. of
Geography, University of Chicago, 1952.
53 p. (4164

HARDOY, Jorge E. Bibliography on the evolution of cities in Latin America: the cities of pre-Columbian America; the colonial cities; the period following independence. Oakland, Calif., 1962. 32 p. (Council on Planning Librarians. Exchange bibliography, LA 3)   (4165

MANTILLA BAZO, Víctor. Bibliografía preliminar. Vivienda y planeamiento en America Latina. Washington, D.C., Unión Panamericana, 1952. 112 p.   (4166

MEXICO. Departamento de Prensa y Publicidad. Bibliografía sobre casas baratas. México, Tall. Gráf. de la Nación, 1937. 36 p. (Manuales D.A.P.P. Ser. trabajo)   (4167
   Cited in Millares, item 902.

MITCHELL, Mary E., Bibliography and guide to literature on housing in Latin America, with a classified guide to the contents; 2d ed. New York, New York City Housing Authority, 1939. 75 p.   (4168
   Jones 316a.

SABOR, Josefa Emilia. Guía bibliográfica. Bogotá, 1953. 10 p. (Centro Interamericano de Vivienda y Planeamiento, Ser. Bibliografia, no. 1)   (4169
   Erroneously numbered. In Center's listing in Cat. no. 2-3 this issue is no. 1, bis.

SAO PAULO. Universidade. Faculdade de Arquitetura e Urbanismo. Biblioteca. Pre-fabri-

SAO PAULO. Universidade. Faculdade...(Cont.) cação; bibliografia. São Paulo, 1964. 24 p.   (4170
   Cited in Revista interamericana de bibliografía, no. 33, p. 100.

SHILLABER, Caroline. A brief list of reference on housing in South America. [Cambridge] Harvard Univ., 1944. 2 p. mimeogr.   (4171

-----. A selected bibliography on planning in South America. [Cambridge] Harvard Univ., 1944. 6 p. mimeogr.   (4172

URUGUAY. Poder Legislativo. Biblioteca. Viviendas; material sobre el tema existente en esta Biblioteca. Montevideo, 1948. [42] p. (Referencia, 1)   (4173

VIOLICH, Francis. Bibliografía sobre planeamiento urbano en Colombia. Berkeley, University of California, Latin American Urban Planning Research, 1962. 13 p. (Bibliografía, no. 4) mimeogr.   (4174

-----. Bibliography on community development applied to urban areas in Latin America... asisted by John Miller and John McCallum, in the Latin American Urban Planning Research project, Center for Latin American Studies, University of California, Berkeley. [Berkeley] 1963. 20 p. (Council of Planning Librarians. Exchange bibliography, LA 6)   (4175

INDEXES

GENERAL

EL AMERICANISMO en las revistas: antropología, 1- . Madrid, 1961- . (Publ. del Seminario de Antropología Americana, Facultad de Filosofía y Letras, Universidad de Sevilla, v. 2, 4, 6, 8- .)   (4175a
   Coordinadores: José Alcina Franch y M. Ballesteros Gaibrois.

ANUARIO de estudios americanos. Indices del Anuario de estudios americanos, 1944-1963, I-XX. Preparado por Fernando de Armas Medina, Juan Collantes de Terán, Juan Fernández Márquez, María Teresa Garrido, bajo la dirección de Francisco Morales Padrón. [Sevilla] 1964. (Publ. de la Escuela de Estudios Hispano-Americanos de Sevilla, 157)   (4176

COMAS, Juan. Los congresos internacionales de americanistas; síntesis histórica e índice bibliográfico general, 1875-1952. México, Instituto Indigenista Interamericano, 1954. 224 p. (Ediciones especiales)   (4177

COMAS, Juan. Una década de congresos internacionales de americanistas, 1952-1962. México, Universidad Nacional Autónoma de México, 1964. 128 p. (Instituto de Investigaciones Históricas, Publ. no. 93; Cuadernos, ser. antropológica, no. 18)   (4177a

HASSE, Adelaide Rosalie. Index to United States documents relating to foreign affairs, 1828-1861. Washington, D.C., 1914-1921. 3 v. (Carnegie Institution of Washington. Publ. no. 185)   (4178
   Jones 197.

HISPANIC American historical review. Guide to Hispanic American historical review. Durham, N.C., Duke Univ. Pr., 1950-   (4179
   1918-1945 (251 p.,) edited by Ruth Lapham Butler. 1946-1955 (178 p.), edited by Charles Gibson.

INDICE general de publicaciones periódicas latinoamericanas; humanidades y ciencias sociales. Index to Latin American periodicals; humanities

INDEXES

INDICE general de publicaciones ... (Cont.)
and social sciences, v. 1- ., 1961- . Boston,
G. K. Hall, Scarecrow Pr., [1963]- . (4180
Approximately 320 periodicals in the
fields of the humanities and social sciences
are indexed. Compilation of information at
the Columbus Memorial Library, ed. by Jorge
Grossmann. Fourth issue of each year: cumulative volume. Only annual volume appeared of v. 2-3. Publisher, v. 3- , Scarecrow
Press, Inc. See also item 6183.

LEAVITT, Sturgis Elleno. Revistas hispanoamericanas, índice bibliográfico 1843-1935, recopilado por Sturgis E. Leavitt con la colaboración de Madaline W. Nichols y Jefferson
Rea Spell. Santiago de Chile, Fondo Histórico y Bibliográfico José Toribio Medina,
1960. xxiii, 589 p.   (4181

LIMA. Universidad Mayor de San Marcos. Biblioteca. Lista de artículos publicados en
revistas recientes; los que el mundo piensa
sobre los problemas del momento. [Lima]
1931. 31 p.   (4182

MOLINA NAVARRO, Gabriel. Indice para facilitar
el manejo y consulta de los catálogos de Salvá y Heredia. Madrid, G. Molina, 1913.
162 p.   (4183
Jones 318. Now available in microprint.

OWEN, Eugene D. Index to publications and articles on Latin America. Issued by the
United States Bureau of Labor Statistics,
1902-1943. Washington, D.C., Pan American
Union, 1945. 39 p. (Columbus Memorial Library. Bibliographic series, no. 31) (4184

PAN AMERICAN UNION. Columbus Memorial Library.
Documentos oficiales de la Organización de
los Estados Americanos; índice y lista general, v.1- , 1960- , Washington, D.C., 1961-
(OEA/ser. Z I.1; OEA/ser. Z I.2)   (4185
Vol. 1-3 published in 2 parts: 1st semes-
ter list, and annual cumulated list and index. Vol. 4- , published in 3 parts: no. 1-2,
Lista General (semi-annual), and no. 3, Indice Analítico (annual)

-----. -----. Index to Latin American periodical literature, 1929-1960. Compiled in the
Columbus Memorial Library of the Pan American
Union. Boston, G. K. Hall, 1962. 8 v.
(xv, 6030 p.)   (4186

-----. -----. Indice de la Revista Iberoamericana - Memorias del Congreso Internacional de
Catedráticos de la Literatura Iberoamericana.
Washington, D.C., Unión Panamericana, 1954.
vii, 51 p. (Bibliographic ser., no.
42)   (4187

RAGATZ, Lowell Joseph. A bibliography of articles, descriptive, historical and scientific,

RAGATZ, Lowell Joseph. A bibliography...(Cont.)
on colonies and other dependent territories,
appearing in American geographical and kindred
journals through 1934. London, A. Thomas
[1935] 2 v.   (4188
Vol. 1 includes the Americas, and vol. 2,
the U.S. outlying possessions.

-----. -----. Washington, D.C., Educational
Research Bureau, 1951. 2 v.   (4189
Contains: v. 1 (214 p.) information published in 2 v. (1935) through 1934; v. 2
(149 p.), 1935-1950.

SOUSA, José Soares de. Indice alphabetico do
"Diccionario bibliographico português" de
Inocencio Francisco da Silva. São Paulo,
1938. 264 p.   (4190
Jones 1196.

UNITED NATIONS Educational, Scientific and Cultural Organization. Scientific Cooperation
Office for Latin America, Montevideo. List
of scientific papers published in Latin America, 1948- . Montevideo, [1949-]
v. 1- .   (4191
Title in English, Spanish and French.

U.S. Library of Congress. Legislative Reference Service. Latin American abstracts, a
series of abstracts from literature concerned with Latin America, edited by Lottie M.
Manross. Washington, D.C., 1943-1946. (4192

-----. -----. Science and Technology Division.
A guide to the world's abstracting and index-
ing services in science and technology.
Washington, D.C., 1963. 183 p. (National
Federation of Science Abstracting and Index-
ing Services. Report no. 102)   (4193
Index is arranged by country. Latin Amer-
ican countries are included.

WILGUS, Alva Curtis. Index of articles relating to Hispanic America in the National Geographic Magazine, volumes I-LXI inclusive
(1888-1932) 1932.   (4194
Reprinted from the Hispanic American historical review, v. 12, no. 4, p. 493-502,
Nov. 1932.

-----. List of articles relating to Hispanic
America published in the periodicals of the
American Geographical Society, 1852-1933 in-
clusive. Durham, N.C., 1934. p. 113-
30.   (4195
Reprinted from the Hispanic American his-
torical review, v. 14, no. 1, Feb. 1934.---
Jones 535.

WINSHIP, George Parker. Index of titles relating o America in the "Colección de Documentos inéditos para la historia de España."
(Bulletin, Public Library, Boston, v. 13,
p. 250-63, 1894)   (4196

WINSHIP, George Parker.   Index ... (Cont.)
   Jones 543.

ARGENTINA

ARCHIVOS de pedagogía y ciencias afines.   Indice analítico, 1906-1914; Archivos de ciencias de la educación, 1914-1919.   La Plata,
   Arg., Ministerio de Educación, Dirección de
   Enseñanza Superior Media y Vocacional, Instituto Bibliográfico [1961]   99 p.   (4197

LA BIBLIOTECA, Buenos Aires.   Indice general
   de "La Biblioteca", 1896-1898 [por] Ernesto
   J. A. Maeder.   Resistencia, Chaco, Universidad Nacional del Nordeste, Facultad de Humanidades, Departamento de Historia, 1962.
   20 p.   (4198

CORREA LUNA, Carlos.   Indice general de las
   materias contenidas en el Boletín del Instituto Geográfico Argentino, t. 1-16.   (Boletín, Buenos Aires, t. 17, p. 263-91,
   1897)   (4199
      Continued by E. E. A., v. 17-22, in Boletín
   v. 23, p. 299-312, 1919)---Jones 675.

FARINI, Juan Angel.   Gaceta de Buenos Aires,
   1810-1821; índice general.   Buenos Aires,
   Museo Mitre, 1963.   348 p.   (4200
      Cited in Revista interamericana de biblio-
   grafía, no. 32, p. 391.

FINZI, Marcelo.   Indice alfabético por autores
   y materias de los volúmenes 1-10 (1937-1946)
   del Boletín de la Facultad de Derecho y Ciencias Sociales.   Córdoba, 1947.   200 p.   (Boletín, Facultad de Derecho y Ciencias Sociales, año 11, no. 5, p. 585-797, nov./dic.
   1947)   (4201

INDICE de la literatura dental periódica en
   castellano y portugués, 1952- .   Buenos Aires, Asociación Odontológica Argentina,
   1954- .   (4202

MARTINEZ, Alberto Julián.   Indice de los artículos diversos, cartas, discursos y poesías
   con nombre de autor que le han publicado en
   los XXVII primeros tomos de "El Monitor de
   la Educación Común".   Buenos Aires [n.d.]
   20 p.   (4203
      Cited in Binayán, item 150.

MONCAYO DE MONGE, Germania.   Indice general de
   la revista SUR (Argentina) 1931-1954.   Washington, D.C., Unión Panamericana, 1955.   vi,
   259 p.   (Columbus Memorial Library.   Bibliographic ser., no. 46)   (4204

MUSEO Social Argentino, Buenos Aires.   Boletín.
   Indice analítico-alfabético acumulativo (de
   autores y materias) de los años I a XV (1912
   a 1926).   Preparado por Pedro B. Franco.

MUSEO Social Argentino, Buenos Aires ...(Cont.)
   Buenos Aires, 1927.   187 p.   (4205
   Jones 790.

NUEVA revista de Buenos Aires.   Indice general
   alfabético por materias y autores, t. I-XI.
   (Nueva revista de Buenos Aires, t. 10, 12,
   1884)   (4206
      Binayan, item 151, cites the Indice general
   to [t. 1-9]: Buenos Aires, 1884, lii p.; and
   to t. 10-12: in Nueva revista de Buenos Aires,
   t. 12.

OUTES, Félix Faustino.   Indice de los artículos
   contenidos en la Revista del Museo de La Plata, t. 1-12.   (Revista, Buenos Aires, t. 13,
   p. 123-48, 1906)   (4207
   Jones 805.

PENDOLA, Agustín Julián.   Anales del Museo Na-
   cional de Historia Natural de Buenos Aires.
   Indice de los t. 1-20 (1864-1911).   Buenos
   Aires, Estab. Gráf. "Oceana", 1917.
   32 p.   (4208
   Jones 813.

POLLERO SOLA, Juan Víctor.   Desdoblamiento alfabético del material contenido en "Biblioteca del Oficial" y "Revista Militar"; años
   1941-1944.   Buenos Aires, 1945.   217 p.
   (Círculo Militar.   Biblioteca del oficial,
   v. 320 a)   (4208a

REVISTA argentina.   Indice general de la Revista argentina, 1a. época, 1868-1872 [por] Ernesto J. A. Maeder.   Resistencia, Chaco, Universidad Nacional del Cordeste, Escuela de Humanidades, Departamento de Historia, 1960.
   208-31 p.   (4209
      "Separata del Boletín bibliográfico [Uni-
   versidad Nacional del Nordeste, Resistencia]
   no. 10-11-12, 1959."

LA REVISTA de Buenos Aires.   Indice general de
   la Revista de Buenos Aires, 1863-1871 [por]
   Ernesto J. A. Maeder.   Resistencia, Chaco,
   Universidad Nacional del Nordeste, Facultad
   de Humanidades, Departamento de Historia,
   1961.   64 p.   (4210

REVISTA del Paraná, Paraná, Arg.   Indice general de la Revista del Paraná, 1861 [por] Ernesto J. A. Maeder.   Resistencia, Chaco, Universidad Nacional del Nordeste, Facultad de
   Humanidades, Departamento de Historia, 1962.
   9 p.   (4210a

ROIG, Arturo Andrés.   La literatura y el periodismo mendocinos a través de las páginas del
   Diario "El Debate" (1890-1914) Mendoza, Universidad Nacional de Cuyo, 1963.   120 p.
   (Publ. del Departamento de Extension Universitaria, 2)   (4211

SARMIENTO, Domingo Faustino.   Indice general

SARMIENTO, Domingo Faustino ... (Cont.)
(para los 52 volúmenes de las Obras) Buenos Aires, Impr. Borzone, 1903.
326 p.   (4212
    Las anotaciones de los t. 1 a 7 se refie-
ren a la la. edición impresa en Chile.---
Jones 837a.

SOCIEDAD Científica Argentina. Indice general de las materias contenidas en los Anales, t. 1-29, 1876-1889. Buenos Aires,
Impr. de P. E. Coni e Hijos, 1890.
30 p.   (4213
    Jones 844b.

-----. Indice general de los Anales (t. 1-40
inclusive) por el dr. Juan Valentín. Buenos
Aires, Impr. de P. E. Coni e Hijos, 1897.
168 p.   (4214
    Contain reviews of current scientific pu-
blications.---Jones 845.

SPARN, Enrique. Medio siglo de Boletín de la
Academia Nacional de Ciencias; ensayo bibliográfico. Córdoba, Academia Nacional de
Ciencias, 1929. 115 p.   (4215
    Cited in Catalogo, Instituto Bibliotecoló-
gico, item 249.

TUMBURUS, Juan. Revista de la Sociedad Médica Argentina. Indice general de los volumenes 1-20. Buenos Aires, Impr. de Coni Hnos.,
1913. 148 p.   (4216
    Cited in Binayán.---Jones 874.

UNIVERSIDAD, publicación de la Universidad
Nacional del Litoral: indice general, números 1 a 50. Santa Fé [1965]
276 p.   (4217

VELEZ GUTIERREZ, Bernardo. Indice de la compilación de derecho patrio, 1832, y el Correo judicial, reedición facsimilar, 1834.
Buenos Aires, Facultad de Derecho y Ciencias
Sociales, Instituto de Historia del Derecho
Argentino, 1946. liii, 270 p. (Colección
de textos y documentos para la historia del
derecho argentino, 7)   (4218

BRAZIL

ACADEMIA de Medicina do Rio de Janeiro. Indice
alphabetico das materias de que tratam os
escriptos publicados nos tomos I a LV (1831-
1890) das collecções a que pertencem os
Annaes da Academia de Medicina do Rio de Janeiro. [1890?] 122 p.   (4219
    Cited in Reis, item 137.

BIBLIOTECA Almeida Cunha, Recife. Indice da
Revista do patrimônio histórico e artístico
nacional (números 1 a 10, 1937-1946) Refi-
fe, Brasil, 1954. 18 p. (Boletim 1) (4220
    Cited in HLAS, 19, item 6405.

BRAZIL. Museu Nacional. Arquivos; indice, organizado por Bertha M. J. Lutz, v. 1-22, 1876-
1919. (In Archivos, v. 22, p. 275-90) (4221

OS CADERNOS de cultura, Rio de Janeiro. Catalogo e indice dos volumes 1 a 100 (1952-1956)
[Rio de Janeiro] Ministério da Educação e
Cultura, Serviço de Documentação [1959]
79 p. (Os Cadernos de cultura, 100-A) (4222

INDICE tecnológico; lista classificada de artigos sôbre engenharia e tecnologia publicados
em revistas brasileiras, no. 1- , jan./jun,
1953- . Salvador, Escola Politécnica,
1954- .   (4223

INSTITUTO Histórico e Geográfico de São Paulo.
Indice-repertorio dos cinquenta e um primeiros volumes da Revista, organizado por Dácio
Pires Corrêa. São Paulo, 1964. 535 p. (Revista, v. 60)   (4223a
    Adendo ao indice geral, correspondente aos
volumes 51 a 59, p. 521-35.

MAIA, Jorge de Andrade. Indice geral da Revista de medicina, no. 1-55, 1916-1931. [São
Paulo] 1931. 24 p.   (4224
    Cited in Reis, item 426.

REVISTA americana, Rio de Janeiro. Indice alphabetico e chronologico, 1909-1910. Rio de
Janeiro, Impr. Nacional, 1911. 20 p. (4225
    Cited in Reis, item 272.

REVISTA do Arquivo Publico Mineiro, Rio de Janeiro. Indice da "Revista do Arquivo Público Mineiro". Rio de Janeiro, Arquivo Nacional, 1960. 75 p. (Sér. Instrumentos do
trabalho, Publ. 3)   (4227
    Cited in Richardson, item 7255. Index
prepared by Lygia Nazareth Fernandes.

RODRIGUES, José Honorio. Indice anotado da
Revista do Instituto do Ceará (do I tomo ao
LXVIII). Fortaleza, Ceará, Univ. do Ceará,
1951. 391 p.   (4228

-----. Indice anotado da Revista do Instituto
Arqueológico Histórico e Geográfico Pernambucano. Recife, 1961.   (4229
    Reprinted from the Revista of the Institu-
to, v. 44, 1954/1959. Cited in HLAS, 24,
item 4435.

SÃO PAULO, (City) Universidade. Faculdade de Arquitectura e Urbanismo. Biblioteca.
Indice de arquitectura brasileira, 1950-1962.
[São Paulo] 1963. 2 v. (Publicação
10)   (4230

SÃO PAULO, (State) Secretaria da Agricultura. Secção de Bibliografia Agrícola.
Indice de periódicos, 1960- . [São Paulo
Diretoria de Publicidade Agrícola
[1962-]   (4231

SÃO PAULO, (State) Secretaria...(Cont.)
Latest issue at DPU: 1963.

SERVIÇO especial de abstractos para a indústria mecânica brasileira. Rio de Janeiro,
Confederação Nacional da Indústria,
1952- .   (4232
Cited in Doria Menezes 179.

SOCIEDADE de Medicina e Cirurgia, São Paulo.
Boletim; indice geral dos annos de 1922 a
1927. São Paulo, Sociedade Impr. Paulista,
n.d. 40 p.   (4233
Compiler: Ayres Neto. Cited in Reis, item
374.

CHILE

ANALES de la Universidad de Chile. Indice al-
fabético y analítico de los trabajos publi-
cados, 1843-1887. Santiago de Chile, Impr.
Nacional, 1890. 164 p.   (4234
Jones 1390. Compiler: Eduardo Valenzuela
Guzmán.

-----. Indice de los trabajos contenidos en
los "Anales de la Universidad" desde 1888 hasta 1899. Santiago de Chile, Impr. Cervantes,
1900. 50 p.   (4235
Jones 1391.

-----. Indice general de los Anales de la Universidad de Chile, dispuesto por riguroso orden alfabético de materias y apellidos, y com-
prensivo de trece años, esto es, desde 1843
inclusive hasta 1885 también inclusive, compuesto por don Ramón Briseño. Santiago, 1856.
111 p.   (4236
Jones 1392.

-----. Indice general, 1843-1950; índice por
autores. Santiago, Universidad de Chile,
Biblioteca Central, 1954. 283 p.   (4237

BOLETIN de la Sociedad Nacional de Minería, Santiago. Indice general, 15 dic. 1883 al 31 dic.
1919. Santiago de Chile, Sociedad Impr. y Lit.
Universo, 1921. 129 p.   (4238
Cited in Ochsenius, item 190.

CHIAPPA, Víctor M. Colección de historiadores
de Chile y documentos relativos a la historia
nacional; índice bibliográfico. Santiago,
Impr. "La Tracción", 1931. 64 p.   (4239

COOPERACION intelectual, Santiago. Boletín. Indice general de los números 1 al 32 publicados
entre los años 1935 y 1942. Santiago de Chile.
1943. 184 p. (Cooperación intelectual, año
5, no. 36)   (4240

FUENTES DE LA SOTTA, Augusto, Indice por materias
de las principales leyes y decretos publicados
en el Diario Oficial en el primer semestre de

FUENTES DE LA SOTTA, Augusto, Indice...(Cont.)
1946. Santiago, Edit. Gutenberg, 1946.
32 p.   (4241
Cited in HLAS, 12, item 2963.

INSTITUTO de Ingenieros de Chile. Indice de
los autores de artículos y de las materias
contenidas en el Boletín de la Sociedad de
Ingeniería y en los Anales del Instituto
de Ingenieros de Chile (1888-1918). Santiago, Impr. Cervantes, 1920. 110 p.   (4242
Jones 1498.

LASO JARA-QUEMADA, J. R. Indice del Boletín
de la Sociedad Nacional de Agricultura,
1886-1899. Santiago de Chile, Impr. Moderna, 1900. 120 p.   (4243
Jones 1500.

-----. Indice general del Boletín de la Sociedad de Fomento Fabril, 1884-1904. Santiago
de Chile, Impr. Barcelona, 1905.
173 p.   (4244
Jones 1501.

MEDINA, José Toribio. Indice alfabético de los
nombres de los principales personajes que se
encuentran en la Colección de documentos inéditos para la historia de Chile. Santiago de
Chile, Impr. de E. Blanchard-Chessi, 1907.
26 p.   (4245
Jones 1546.

PAN AMERICAN UNION. Columbus Memorial Library.
Indice general de ATENEA; revista mensual de
ciencias, letras y artes publicada por la
Universidad de Concepción (Chile) 1924-1950.
Washington, D.C., Unión Panamericana, 1954.
205 p. (Bibliographic ser., no. 44)   (4246

REVISTA chilena de historia y geografía; índice
general de los primeros L tomos. Santiago de
Chile, Impr. Cervantes, 1922. 138 p.   (4247
Cited in Ochsenius, item 75. Compiler:
René Feliú Cruz. Jones, 1584, cites portion
published in the Revista t. 51-52, including
letters A-F only.

-----. Indice de los cien primeros numeros:
Revista chilena de historia y geografía,
1911-1942. Santiago, Impr. Universitaria,
1943. 128 p.   (4248
Compiler: René Feliú Cruz.

REVISTA chilena de historia y geografía, 1943-
1957; índice de los números 101 a 125. Santiago de Chile, Sociedad Chilena de Historia
y Geografía, 1963. 99 p.   (4249
Compiler: Francisco Santana.

VICUÑA MACKENNA, Carlos Tomás. Indice de la
Historia general de Chile de don Diego Barros Arana. (Revista chilena de historia y
geografía. Santiago, v. 78, p. 154-231,
1935; v. 79, p. 120-58, 1936; v. 81, p. 237-

INDEXES

VICUÑA MACKENNA, Carlos Tomás. Indice...(Cont.)
69, 1936; v, 82, p. 237-81, 1937)   (4250
Jones 1651a.

-----. -----. Santiago, Impr. Universitaria,
1936. 230 p.   (4251
An index of 7,037 personal names mentioned
in Barros Arana's work.---Jones 1659a.

VILLALOBOS R., Sergio. Indice de la Colección
de historiadores y de documentos relativos a
la independencia de Chile. Santiago, Universidad de Chile, Instituto Pedagógico, Seminario de Historia, 1956. 108 p.   (4252
Through v. 37 of the Colección.

COLOMBIA

BANCO de la República, Bogotá. Biblioteca.
Indice analítico, no. 1, mayo 1956. Bogotá,
1956. 22 p. mimeogr.   (4252a
Index to Anales de Economía y estadística
and its successor, Economía y estadística,
1938-1955. Cited in Giraldo Jaramillo, p.
91.

BIBLIOTECA Aldeana de Colombia. Indices. Bogotá, Edit, Minerva, 1937. 456 p.   (4253
Catalog by volumes and by authors of the
100-volume series. Sections are: prosa literaria, cuento y novela, cuadros de costumbres, historia y leyenda, ciencias y educación, ensayos, periodismo, elocuencia, poesía y teatro.---Jones 1680.

BOHORQUEZ, José Ignacio, and BAQUERO MORALES,
Lucrecia. Indice de los principales artícu-
los de las revistas coleccionadas en la Bi-
blioteca de la ESAP hasta julio de 1963.
Bogotá, Escuela Superior de Administración
Pública. n.d.   (4254

BOLETIN de historia y antigüedades, Bogotá.
Indice general, v. 1-38, 1902-1952. Bogotá,
Academia Colombiana de Historia, 1953.
518 p.   (4255
Compiler: Enrique Ortega Ricaurte. Cited
in Anales bibliográficos colombianos, 1951-
1956, p. 6.

CAMARA Colombiana de la Construcción, Medellín.
Indice general de los boletines de Camacol.
Antioquia... Primera etapa de diciembre de
1957 a enero de 1961. Medellín, 1961. 9 p.
mimeogr.   (4256
"Comprende los boletines, no. 1-161".---
Florén, Bibliografía bibliotecológica, 1961-
1962, item 269.

CARO MOLINA, Fernando. Indice del Boletín de
la Academia de Historia del Valle del Cauca,
1932-1952. [Cali, Impr. Vargas, 1953]
28 p.   (4257

CENICAFE, Chinchiná, Col. Indice general de
los vols. 1 a 10, años 1949-1959. Chinchiná,
Centro Nacional de Investigaciones de Café,
1959. 2 v. (Cenicafé, v. 10, dic. 1959,
no. 12)   (4258
Contents: v. 1, autores; v. 2, materias.
Cited in Florén, 1961/1962, item 218.

COLOMBIA. Departamento Administrativo Nacional
de Estadística. Indice bibliográfico del Boletín mensual de estadística correspondiente
a las estadísticas de producción y consumo.
Bogotá, 1963.   (4259
Cited in Boletín de adquisiciones, Medellín,
no. 8, p. 9, ag. 1963.

CORTES, Jesús M. Indice alfabético general de
los Sueños de Luciano Pulgar [Marco Fidel Suárez. Bogotá], Impr. del Banco de la República, 1956. 343 p.   (4260

HOJAS de cultura popular colombiana, Bogotá.
Indice general por autores. Bogotá, 1957.
14 p.   (4261
Index to 79 numbers.

ORTEGA TORRES, José Joaquín. Indice del "Papel
periódico ilustrado" y de "Colombia ilustrada". Estudio preliminar de Héctor H. Orjuela.
Bogotá, 1961. 243 p. (Instituto Caro y Cuervo. Serie bibliográfica, no. 4)   (4262

EL REPERTORIO colombiano, Bogotá. Indice de
"El repertorio colombiano" [por] José J. Ortega Torres. Bogotá, 1961. (Instituto Caro
y Cuervo. Serie bibliográfica, 3)   (4263

REVISTA de ciencias económicas; órgano de la
Facultad de Ciencias Económicas de la Universidad de Antioquia. Indice, 1953-1960. (v.
1-6, núm. 1-17) Medellín, Edit. Universidad
de Antioquia, 1961. 41 p.   (4264
Cited in Peraza, Fichas, t. 3, item 36.
Compiler: Edgar E. Córdoba Mendoza.

REVISTA del Banco de la República: índice de
los principales artículos, 1927-1962. [Bo-
gotá] Tall. Gráf. de la República [1963?]
84 p.   (4265

REVISTA médica; órgano de la Sociedad de Medicina y Ciencias Naturales, Bogotá. Suplemento: índice de las series I a VII. Bogotá, Impr. de Vapor de Zalamea Hnos.,
1883.   (4266

CUBA

CUBA. Laws, statutes, etc. Indice de leyes-
decretos; relación numérica y clasificación
por ministerios, mar. 10, 1952 a feb. 23,
1955. Habana, Cía. Impresora Undoso, 1955.
60 p.   (4267

CUBA. Laws, statutes, etc. Primer índice
anual de la legislación revolucionaria, 1 de
enero a 31 de diciembre de 1959. Habana,
Lex, 1960. 305 p.   (4268
    Compiler: Mariano Sánchez Roca. Cited in
HLAS, 23, item 4504.

CUBA contenporánea, Habana. Indice [1913-1927]
La Habana, Municipio, Depto. de Cultura,
1940. 143 p. (Publ. de la Biblioteca Municipal de La Habana, Ser. D: Indices de revistas cubanas, 3)   (4269
    Compilation by Fermín Peraza Sarausa.

MARTINEZ-FORTUN Y FOYO, José A. El Diario de
La Habana en la mano; índices y sumarios
(años de 1812 a 1848) Habana, 1955. 260 p.
mimeogr.   (4270

PERAZA SARAUSA, Fermín. Conferencias y discursos, 1943-1950. La Habana, 1944-1951. 8 v.
(Biblioteca del bibliotecario, 6, 11, 16, 19,
22, 26, 30, 33) mimeogr.   (4271
    Annual bibliographies of 36 to 82 pages.

-----. Indice analítico de las obras completas de José Martí. La Habana, Cuba, Edit.
Tropico, 1953. 2 v.   (4272
    (Obras completas de Martí, 71-72)

-----. Indice de "El Aviso" (1805-1808). Habana, Edit. Anuario Bibliográfico Cubano,
1944) 76 p. (Biblioteca del bibliotecario,
5)   (4273

-----. Indice del "Aviso de La Habana" (1809-
1810). Habana, 1944. 66 p. (Biblioteca
del bibliotecario, 7)   (4274

-----. Indice de El Fígaro, 1885-1899. Habana, 1945. 2 v. (Biblioteca del bibliotecario, 9-10)   (4275

-----. -----. 1900-1929. La Habana, 1948.
2 v. (Biblioteca del bibliotecario, 23-
24)   (4276

-----. Indice del Boletin del Archivo Nacional.
Habana, Tall. Archivo Nacional, 1946. xxiii,
118 p. (Publ. del Archivo Nacional,
12)   (4277

REVISTA cubana, Habana. Indice [1885-1895] La
Habana, Municipio, Depto. de Cultura, 1939.
79 p. (Publ. de la Biblioteca Municipal de
La Habana, Ser. D: Indices de revistas cuba-
nas, 2)   (4278
    Jones 1886a. Compilation by Fermín Peraza
Sarausa.

REVISTA cubana; índice de la Revista cubana,
1935-1957, compilado por Rubén Alfonso Quintero. La Habana, Instituto Nacional de Cultura, Ministerio de Educación, [1958]
100 p.   (4279

REVISTA cubana; índice de la ... (Cont.)
    Cited in HLAS, 23, item 3406. Covers v.
1-31.

REVISTA de Cuba, La Habana. Indice [1877-1884]
La Habana, Municipio, Depto. de Cultura, 1938.
87 p. (Publ. de la Biblioteca Municipal de
La Habana, Ser. D: Indice de revistas cubanas, 1)   (4280
    Jones 1887.

UNIVERSIDAD de La Habana. Indice general de
la revista Universidad de La Habana, 1934-1956
por Rubén Alfonso Quintero. [Marianao, Cuba]
1959. 109 p. (Publ. de la Biblioteca Municipal)   (4281

VALLE, Adrian del. Indice de las Memorias de
la Sociedad Económica de Amigos del País,
1793-1896. La Habana, Molina y Cía., 1938-
v. 1- . (Recopilación para la historia de
la Sociedad Económica Habanera, por Fernando
Ortiz, 3)   (4282
    Jones 1935.

EL SALVADOR

EL SALVADOR. Departamento de Estudios Económicos. Bibliografía selecta del Diario Oficial,
v. 162. San Salvador, 1954.   (4283
    Cited in HLAS, no. 21, item 1356.

-----. Instituto de Estudios Económicos. Biblioteca. Bibliografía; índice cumulativo,
1950- . San Salvador, Ministerio de Economía
[1950]- . mimeogr.   (4284
    Last on file at DPU: 1956.

GUION literario, San Salvador. Indice alfabético, no. 1 a 100 [1-10, en. 1956-abr. 1964].
San Salvador, Ministerio de Educación, Dirección General de Publicaciones [1964]
40 p.   (4285

GUATEMALA

MENDEZ, Rosendo P. Indice general de la recopilación de leyes vigentes de la República
de Guatemala. [Guatemala, Tip. Nacional]
1925. 102 [3] p.   (4286

REYES M., José Luis. Catálogo razonado de las
leyes de Guatemala. Guatemala, Tip. Nacional,
1945. 179 p.   (4287
    The present volume covers 1856-1871, with
additions prior to 1856 not appearing in previous compilations.

MEXICO

ACADEMIA Nacional de Ciencias Antonio Alzate,
México. Indice general por autores y mate-

ACADEMIA Nacional de Ciencias ... (Cont.)
rias de los tomos 1 a 52 (1887-1931) de las
Memorias y Revista de la Sociedad Científica
Antonio Alzate. México, D.F., 1934.
179 p.   (4288
    Compilation by Rafael Aguilar y Santillán
y Concepción Mendizabal.

BIBLIOGRAFIA de ciencias penales, formada con
los trabajos publicados en la revista Criminalia de los años I al XXIII de septiembre
de 1933 a diciembre de 1957. México, 1958.
361 p. (Cuadernos "Criminalia", no.
20)   (4289
    Cited in Boletín, Biblioteca Nacional, Mé-
xico, jul./sept. 1960, p. 39.

BOLETIN de la Sociedad Mexicana de Geografía e
Historia. Indice general. Comprende desde
el tomo 1 de la primera época hasta el tomo
VII de la quinta época, 32 tomos, 1839-1918.
México, Departamento de Aprovisionamientos
Generales, 1919. 98 p.   (4290
    Compilation under the supervision of Rafael
Aguilar Santillán. Reprinted from Boletín,
t. 8, 5a. ép.
Jones 2039.

COBB, William Montague. Index to the American
Journal of Physical Anthropology. México,
D.F., 1941. 2 v. (Publ. del Instituto Panamericano de Geografía e Historia, no.
45)   (4291
    Contains: v. 1 (330 p.), Index to original
articles, notes and communications. - v. 2
(394 p.), Index to literature.

CUADERNOS americanos. Indices de Cuadernos americanos por Angel Flores, con la cooperación
de Ricardo Eisman; del numero 1 al número 100.
México, D.F., 1959. 275 p.   (4292

DIAZ Y ALEJO, Ana Elena, OCAMPO ALFARO, Aurora
M., y PRADO VELAZQUEZ, Ernesto. Indices de
"El Domingo"; revista literaria mexicana
91817-1873) México, Impr. Universitaria,
1959. 116 p. (México, Universidad Nacional.
Centro de Estudios Literarios, Publ.
5)   (4293

DIAZ ALEJO, Ana Elena, and PRADO VELAZQUEZ, Ernesto. Indices de El Nacional, periódico literario mexicano, 1880-1884. México, Universidad Nacional Autónoma, 1961. 227 p. (Centro de Estudios Literarios, Publ. 8)   (4294

FERNANDEZ, Justino. Dos décadas de trabajo del
Instituto de Investigaciones Estéticas; catálogo de sus publicaciones; índice de sus Anales. México, 1957. 64 p. (Supl. no. 2 de
los Anales del Instituto de Investigaciones
Estéticas, no. 25)   (4295
    Publications cited: 91. Articles indexed
from no. 1-24 of Anales, 472.

GARCIA, Genaro. Indice alfabético de la "Colección de documentos para la historia de la
guerra de independencia de México, de 1808 a
1821", formada por J. E. Hernández Dávalos.
(Anales del Museo Nacional, México, 1907) 2.
ép., t. 4, p. 225-306, 1907)   (4296
Jones 2182.

-----. Indice alfabético de los "Documentos
para la historia de México", publicados en
cuatro series por d. Manuel Orozco y Berra.
(Anales del Museo Nacional, México, 2. ép.,
t. 3, p. 523-40, 1906)   (4297
Jones 2183.

INGENIERIA hidráulica en México. Indice general por materias, títulos y autores, v. 7
al 12 (1953-1958) [México, Secretaria de
Recursos Hidráulicos, 1958?] 8 p.   (4298

INTER-AMERICAN Indian Institute, México, D.F.
Indices de América indígena y Boletín indigenista, v. 1-13, (1941-1953). México, D.F.,
1954. 196 p. (Ediciones especiales
[20])   (4299
    Compiler: Miguel Leon Portillo.

JANVIER, Catharine A. Index to the Bibliografía Mexicana del Siglo XVI, por Joaquín García Icazbalceta. N.Y., 1890. xii p.   (4300
    Millares 803 notes that only 25 copies
were run in this edition.

-----. Indice alfabético de la Bibliografía
mexicana del siglo XVI de don Joaquín García
Icazbalceta. México, Porrúa, 1938.
19 p.   (4301
Jones 2192.

MCLEAN, Malcolm Dallas. El contenido literario de "El Siglo diez y nueve". Tesis presentada como cumplimiento parcial del reglamento para la obtención del grado de Maestro de Artes en español en la Escuela de
Verano de la Universidad Nacional de México.
México, Impr. Mundial, 1938. 78 p.   (4302
    Escritos que aparecieron en dicho diario
mexicano firmados por Manuel Payno, Guillermo Prieto, José María Vigil, Joaquín Téllez,
Luis Gonzaga Ortiz, Pantaleón Tovar, Rafael
de Zayas Enríquez, Luis G. Urbina, Hilarión
Frias y Soto, José González de la Torre.
(R.H.Valle).---Jones 2312a.

-----. -----. Washington, D.C., Inter-American
Bibliographical and Library Association,
1940. 75 p.   (4303
Jones 2312a.

MEXICAN folkways, México, D.F. Bibliografía
completa, clasificada y comentada de los
artículos de Mexican folkways (MF) con índice por Ralph Steel Boggs. México, D.F.,
1945. p. 221-68.   (4304
    Reprinted from Boletín bibliográfico de an-

MEXICAN folkways, México, D.F. ... (Cont.)
tropología americana, v. 6.

MEXICO. Instituto de Investigaciones Forestales y de Caza y Pesca. Bibliografía forestal; síntesis bibliografica de los principales artículos contenidos en la "Revista forestal mexicana", la "Revista forestal" de
la Dirección General de Agricultura y "México forestal" (1909-1937). México, D.F., D.
A.P.P., 1939. 15 p.   (4305
    Jones 2361.

-----. Museo Nacional de Arqueología, Historia y Etnografía. Reseña histórica e índices de los Anales del Museo Nacional correspondientes a las primeras tres épocas de éstos (1877-1913). México, 1923. xiv,
63 p.   (4306
    Cited in González, item 167.

-----. Secretaría de Relaciones Exteriores.
Indice del Boletín de la Secretaría de Relaciones Exteriores. México, D.F., 1924.
96 p.   (4307
    Indexes ép. 1, t. 1-37, 1895-1913; t. 38,
no. 1 through t. 42, no. 4, 1920-1923. Compiler José Roomero. González 168 and Millares 836 give imprint date as 1929.

LA PALABRA y el hombre. Indices 1957-1962;
primera época, seis volúmenes, números 1 al
24. [Xalapa, Universidad Veracruzana, 1962]
101 p.   (4308

PARRA, P., SORIANO, M. S., and RUIZ, Luis E.
Indice alfabetico general, por materias y
por autores, de los veintitrés primeros tomos de la "Gaceta médica de México", 15 de
septiembre 1864 al 15 de diciembre 1888.
México, D.F., 1889. 105 p.   (4309
    Jones 2404a.

EL RENACIMIENTO, periódico literario, 1869.
Indices de El Renacimiento, semanario litera-
rio mexicano, 1869. Estudio preliminar de
Humberto Batis. México, D.F., 1963. 328 p.
(México (City) Universidad Nacional. Centro
de Estudios Literarios. Publ. 9)   (4310

SOCIEDAD Mexicana de Geografía y Estadística.
Indice general del Boletín. Comprende desde
el tomo I de la primera época hasta el tomo
VII de la quinta época, 32 tomos, 1839-1918.
México, D.F., Departamento de Aprovisionamientos Generales, 1919. 98 p.   (4310a
    Jones 2039. Also published in the Boletin,
ép. 5a., v. 8, no. 2, p. 367-462, sept./dic.
1918.

PERU

LIMA. Universidad Mayor de San Marcos. Seminario de Letras. "La Escuela moderna"; órga-

LIMA. Universidad Mayor de... (Cont.)
no de la Escuela normal de varones de Lima
(1911-1915) (Contribución a una bibliografía pedagógica peruana) por los alumnos del
curso de metodología general de la Sección
Pedagógica de la Facultad, año de 1938.
Lima, Impr. Gila, 1938. 46 p.   (4311

PERU indígena. Bibliografía de "Perú indígena" [no. 1-13, sept. 1948-dic. 1954] Lima,
Instituto Indigenista Peruano [1955]
21 p.   (4311a
    Compiled by César A. Angeles Caballero.

RELACION de los folletos contenidos en los primeros 16 volúmenes de "Papeles varios" pertenecientes a Héctor García Ribeyro. Lima,
[Impr. Americana] 1950. 24 p.   (4312
    Abbreviated catalog of Peruvian books and
pamphlets of the 19th and 20th centuries..
Cited in Anuario bibliográfico peruano,
1949-1950, item 1577.

ROMERO, Emilia. Indice de los "Documentos"
de Odriozola. Lima, Compañía de Impresiones y Publicidad, 1946. 193 p.   (4313
    Reprinted from Boletín bibliográfico, Uni-
versidad Mayor de San Marcos, Lima, v. 15,
no. 3-4, dic. 1945; v. 16, no. 1-2, jun.
1946.

TAURO, Alberto. Amauta, contribución a una
bibliografía peruana. (Boletín bibliográfico, Universidad Mayor de San Marcos, Lima,
11(2): 163-84, jul. 1938; 12(1-2): 46-113,
jul. 1939.   (4314
    Jones 2756.

-----. Indice del contenido de la revista
Letras hasta el no. 17 [dic. 1940] Lima,
Libr. e Impr. Gil, 1941. 76 p.   (4315
    Letras began issue in 1929. Cited in
HLAS, 7, item 196.

TUMBA ORTEGA, Alejandro. Bibliografía de
"Nueva Educación", volumenes I-XI, no. 1-61,
(1945-1953). Lima, Edit. San Marcos, 1955.
222 p.   (4316

-----. Bibliografía de "Pedagogía", 1940-
1944. Lima, Tall. Gráf. de la Edit. Lumen,
1950. p. 297-328.   (4317
    Reprinted from Boletín bibliográfico, Uni-
versidad Mayor de San Marcos, Lima, año 23,
v. 20, no. 3-4, dic. 1950.

-----. Cuarenta años del "Boletín bibliográfico" (1923-1962) (Boletin bibliográfico,
Universidad Mayor de San Marcos, Lima, año
36, no. 3-4, p. 215-340, jul./dic.
1963)   (4317a

VALLE, Arnaldo del. Guía analítica del Boletín de la Sociedad Geográfica de Lima, t.
1-58, 1891-1941. Lima, Impr. Edit. "Miner-

VALLE, Arnaldo del. Guía ... (Cont.)
va", 1942. xiv, 173 p.

URUGUAY

SAYAGUES LASO, Enri~
año 1943-1946''
rial legisl
dencial, doc
nido en todas
jurídicas naci
1943-1947. Mon
1948. 4 v.
Cited in Musso

URUGUAY. Biblioteca
cumentación Cientif.
Indice de trabajos p
Economía, 1947-1958;
Política Económica, 19.
Economía, Finanzas y Ad
1960; Selección de temas
ción pública, 1958-1962.
115 p.

-----. Ejército. Estado Mayo.
letín histórico; índice gener.
1929-1963. Montevideo, 1964.

-----. Poder Legislativo. Biblio.
logo de leyes, 1928-1932. Montev.
1934. 4 v.   .321
Index of the Diario oficial, Regi. ro nacional de Leyes, and Diario de sesiones of
the Asamblea General. DPU has: 1929/1930,
1930, 1932.

-----. Universidad. Instituto de Investigaciones Históricas. Indices de hemeroteca,
1958. Montevideo 1958. viii, 188 p. (Manuales auxiliares para la investigación histórica, 2)   (4322

VENEZUELA

ACADEMIA Nacional de la Historia, Caracas. Indice de los boletines, del no. 1 al no. 124,
1912 a 1948. Caracas, Impr. Nacional, 1949.
75 p.   (4323
Cited in HLAS, 16, item 1468.

CASTELLANOS DE GOA, Alida. La Oliva; índices
analíticos. Caracas, 1956. 22 p. (Venezuela. Universidad Central. Escuela de Biblioteconomía y Archivos. Documentos para la historia de la cultura de Venezuela; serie monografías bibliográficas, no. 4)   (4324
La Oliva was published in Caracas, no. 1-22,
en.1-oct. 1, 1836.

CASTRILLO C., Aminta. Revista literaria por
Juan Vicente González; índices analíticos.
Caracas, 1956. 22 p. (Venezuela. Universi-

ta ... (Cont.)
blioteconomía y
a cultura en Ve-
bliográficas,
(4325
lished in Ca-

enezolano;
32 p.
Escuela
mentos
ezuela;
(4326
-

desde noviembre de
ue 1811" (Sánchez, Bibl.
ol., no. 56).---Jones 2922a.

., María. La Guirnalda; índices analíti-
os. Caracas, 1956. 20 p. (Venezuela.
Universidad Central. Escuela de Biblioteconomía y Archivos. Documentos para la historia de la cultura en Venezuela; serie monografías bibliográficas, no. 5)   (4329
La Guirnalda was published in Caracas,
no. 1-10, jul. 18, 1839-30 abr. 1840.

MARTINEZ RIVERO, Alfredo. Indice de decretos
de la Junta Revolucionaria de Gobierno de
los Estados Unidos de Venezuela. Caracas,
Impr. Nacional, 1947. 386 p.   (4330

MAZZEI DE GIORGI, Olga de. Vargasia; índices
analíticos. Caracas, 1956. 20 p. (Venezuela. Universidad Central. Escuela de Biblioteconomía y Archivos. Documentos para
la historia de la cultura en Venezuela;
serie monografías bibliográficas, no.
3)   (4331
Vargasia was published in Caracas, en./mar.
1868-1870.

PEREZ VILA, Manuel. Indice de los documentos
contenidos en las Memorias del General Daniel Florencio O'Leary. Caracas, Ediciones
de la Sociedad Bolivariana de Venezuela,
1957. 2 v. (v. 1: 505 p.; v. 2:
453 p.)   (4332

REVISTA de la Sociedad Bolivariana de Venezuela; índice, 1939-1955, v. 1-15, no. 1-49.
Nota preliminar por Manuel Pérez Vila. Caracas, 1959. xvi, 378 p.   (4332a
Cited in HLAS, 24, item 4187.

Initials
Date
Add to Collection
Fund Code
Reorder
Repair
Withdraw
Solution:
Problem
Librarian

REVISTA nacional de cultura. Indices de los
cincuenta primeros números de la Revista nacional de cultura, preparados por Marietta
Vaamonde. Caracas, Tip. Americana, 1945.
115 p.   (4333
    Cited in Anuario bibliográfico venezolano,
1945, item 528.

-----. Indice de la "Revista nacional de cultura", 1956. Caracas, Venezuela [195?]
173 p. (Catálogo analítico, Biblioteca Nacional de Venezuela, entrega 3)
mimeogr.   (4334

-----. Indice de la "Revista nacional de cultura", 1938-1958 (nums. 1 al 131). Caracas,
1961. 280 p. (Catálogo analítico, Biblioteca Nacional, entrega no. 5, agosto
1959)   (4335

-----. Indice del no. 1 al 150. Caracas,
1962. 336 p.   (4336

SIC; revista venezolana de orientación. Indice de los primeros 25 años, 1938-1962. Caracas, n.d. 96 p.   (4336a

RISQUEZ, Jesús Rafael. Documentos para la historia de la medicina nacional. Indice de
los trabajos venezolanos publicados en la
Gaceta Médica de Caracas de 1893 a 1938, publicado por disposición de la Academia Nacional de Medicina. Caracas, Tip. Americana, 1939. 166 p.   (4337
    Jones 2946b.

VENEZUELA. Biblioteca Nacional. Bibliografía
de trabajos periodísticos que figuran en publicaciones de nuestra hemeroteca. [Caracas,
1959] 178 p. (Catálogo analítico, entrega
no. 4)   (4338
    Compiler: Martín Perea Romero.

-----. -----. Catálogo analítico, no. 1- ,
feb. 1956- . Caracas, 1956- .   (4339
    Latest number received at DPU: no. 5,
1959, published in 1961.

-----. Laws, statutes, etc. Indice alfabético de la ley del trabajo y su reglamento.
Caracas, 1960. 101 p. (Publ. del Colegio
de Abogados del Distrito Federal, no.
15)   (4340
    Compilers: Rafael Ríos Arrieta and Desi-
derio Maldonado.

-----. -----. Indice alfabético de principales
leyes, decretos, reglamentos y resoluciones
vigentes hasta el 31 de diciembre de 1952.
Caracas [Cromotip] 1953. 209 p.   (4341

-----. -----. -----. Supl. 1, año 1953. Caracas, García y González, 1954. 16 p. (4342

VENEZUELA. Laws, statutes, etc. Indice
de decretos de la Junta de Gobierno,
[1945/1946]- . Caracas, Impr.
Nacional.   (4343
    Began issue as Indice de decretos de la
Junta Revolucionaria; and from 1948-1950 as
Indice de decretos de la Junta Militar de
Gobierno.

-----. -----. Indice de decretos de la Junta
Militar de Gobierno. Caracas, Impr. Nacional, 1950. 84 p.   (4344

-----. -----. Indice informativo de leyes vigentes. Caracas, [1915?]- .   (4345
    Issued annually. In 1944 the 27th edition
(24 p.) is cited in Anuario bibliográfico venezolano, 1944, item 557.

-----. -----. Indice de leyes y reglamentos
vigentes, 1949- . Caracas, Creole Petroleum
Corporation, [1951]- .   (4346

-----. Presidencia. Pensamiento político venezolano del siglo XIX v. 15: indices y guía de
la colección. Caracas, ediciones conmemorativas del sesquicentenario de la independencia, 1962. 405 p.   (4347
    Texts and notes prepared by Pedro Grases
and Manuel Pérez-Vila.

-----. Universidad Central. Facultad de Derecho. Revista. Indice de los primeros veinte
números de la Revista de la Facultad de Derecho, compilación y nota preliminar por Arnoldo García Iturbe. Caracas, 1962.
22 p.   (4348

YANEZ, Antonio Rafael. Diez años de la Revista del Ministerio de Justicia, 1952-1962,
no. 1-40. Caracas, Tip. Caja de Trabajo Pe-
nitenciario Cárcel Modelo, 1962.
124 p.   (4349

-----. Indice de la Revista del Colegio de
Abogados del Distrito Federal, no. 1-108,
años 1937-1959. Caracas, 1960.
149 p.   (4350

WEST INDIES

CARIBBEAN technological abstracts, v. 1- , nov.
1954- . Port of Spain, Caribbean Commission.   (4350a

CARMICHAEL, Gertrude. Index to publications
300-1000 of the Historical Society of Trinidad and Tobago. Trinidad, B. W. I., 1951.
lxxviii p.   (4351

INDUSTRY AND TECHNOLOGY

GENERAL

ALBA, S.A., Fábrica de Pinturas, Esmaltes y Barnices, Buenos Aires. Catálogo general de publicaciones técnicas. [Buenos Aires] 1944. 85 p. mimeogr. (4352
   Cited in *Catálogo*, Instituto Bibliotecológico, item 889.

ARGENTINA. Biblioteca Nacional. Lista de las últimas obras sobre industrias ingresadas en la Biblioteca Nacional (con referencia a los catálogos impresos) Buenos Aires, Tall. Gráf. de la Biblioteca Nacional, 1932. 98 p. (4353
   Classified by industries arranged alphabetically, with author index.---Jones 617.

BIBLIOGRAFIA brasileira de química tecnológica, periódicos e publicações, v. 1, no. 1, 1922/53. Rio de Janeiro, Instituto Nacional de Tecnología, 1954. 153 p. (4354

BIBLIOGRAFIA industrial de México, 1952/53- . México, D.F., Banco de México, Of. de Investigaciones Industriales. (4355
   Compiler of the 1952/1953 volume, José Bullejos; of the 1954/1956 volume, Juan Broc B; of the 1962-1964 volumes, Alfonso Ayensa. Other volumes are 1957/1958, 1959/1960, 1961, 1963.

BUENOS AIRES. Universidad. Obras donadas por el gobierno de los Estado Unidos de América. Buenos Aires, 1939. 9 p. mimeogr. (4356
   Classified, with author index.---Jones 629b.

BULLEJOS, José. Indice bibliográfico de obras y estudios especiales. [México] Banco de México, Departamento de Investigaciones Industriales [1955?] 52 p. (4357

CARRASCO PUENTE, Rafael. Bibliografía industrial. Prologo del Ing. Vito Alessio Robles. México, Secretaría del Trabajo y Previsión Social, 1952. v. 1 (483 p.) (4358

COLOMBIA. Ministerio de Agricultura. Biblioteca y Fichero. Boletín bibliográfico sobre industrias menores. Bogotá, 1963. (4359
   Cited in *Boletín de adquisiciones*, Medellín, p. 15, 5 mayo 1963.

GARDINER, Jewel, and SMITH, Jean Gardiner. Industries, products, and transportation in our neighbor republics; an index and bibliography. [Washington, D.C., Govt. Print. Off., 1942] 39 p. (Office of Education. Bulletin, 1942, no. 6) (4360

MORELOS V., Octavio. Fuentes bibliográficas selectas de documentación técnica y científica. México, Sección de Estudios Técnico-Económicos, Instituto Mexicano de Investigaciones Tecnológicas, 1964. 32 p. (Instituto Mexicano de Investigaciones Tecnológicas, Publ. 64-1) (4360a

PAN AMERICAN UNION. Selected references and sources of information pertaining to industialization of Latin America. [Washington, D.C., 1950] 2 p. (4361

-----. Division of Economic Research. Selected references on electricity in Latin America. [Washington, D.C., 1950] 7 p. (4362

-----. Division of Industrial Technology and Productivity. Lista preliminar de obras sobre productividad. México, 1960. 15 p. (Documento Prod. 5) (4363
   At head of title: Reunión Interamericana de Asesores de Productividad, México, 1960.

PEREZ MARTINEZ, Máximo. Bibliografía de los vinagres. Habana, Departamento de Información Técnica, Ministerio de Industrias, 1963. 120 p. (Serie bibliográfica) (4364

ROSARIO, Arg. Universidad Nacional del Litoral. Facultad de Ciencias Matemáticas Físico-Químicas y Naturales aplicadas a la industria. Crónica bibliográfica. Rosario, 1939-1942. 4 v. (Serie universitaria, Publ. no. 19, 22, 27, 35) (4365
   Publication of reviews. Jones 836c.

SCHNEIDER, Alfred. Die nationalindustrien Südamerikas; entwicklung, stand, und importwirtschaftliche bedeutung. Hamburg, Ibero-Amerikanisches Institut, 1935. 88 p. (Ibero-Amerikanische studien, 2) (4366
   Literaturüberblick: p. 80-8.---Jones 439.

U.S. Library of Congress. Science and Technology Division. Directories in science and technology; a provisional checklist. Washington, D.C., [Govt. Print. Off.] 1963. vi, 65 p. (4367
   Items 137-44 only, of 304 items, refer to South America.

-----. Regional Technical Aids Center, México. Spanish language publications catalog. Catálogo de publicaciones en español, 1962-1963. México, D.F., 1962. xxi, 373 p. (4368

-----. -----. Catálogo general de publicaciones, 1964-1965. México, D.F., [1964] 207 p. (4369

-----. -----. Spanish language books in the field of industrial management. [México, D.F.]

U.S. Regional Technical Aids Center, ...(Cont.)
1958. 10 p. (RATC handlist, no. 1) (4370

-----. -----. Spanish-language publications
available from RTAC, revised. México, 1958.
16 p. (4371

ZAHER, Célia Ribeiro. Guia para pesquisas bibliográficas em ciência e tecnologia; para
uso da cadeira de técnica da organização e
da pesquisa bibliográfica do curso de pesquisas bibliográficas em tecnologia. Rio de Janeiro, 1961. 104 p. (4372

PAPER AND PAPER PRODUCTS

BARRETT, Robert South. Brazilian markets for
paper, paper products, and printing machinery.
Washington, D.C., Govt. Print. Off., 1918.
77 p. (Dept. of Commerce. Bureau of Foreign
and Domestic Commerce. Special agents ser.
no. 171) (4373
    Contains list of Brazilian newspapers and
magazines, with subscription price and other
data.
    Reprinted in the Hispanic American histori-
cal review, v. 3, no. 2, May 1920.---Jones
970.

-----. Chilean market for paper, paper products, and printing machinery. Washington,
D.C., Govt. Print. Off., 1917. 72 p. (Dept.
of Commerce, Bureau of Foreign and Domestic
Commerce. Special agents ser., no.
153) (4374
    Contains list of Chilean newspapers and
magazines, with subscription price and other
data.---Jones 1401.

-----. Paper, paper products, and printing machinery in Argentina, Uruguay, and Paraguay.
Washington, D.C., Govt. Print. Off., 1918.
166 p. (Dept. of Commerce. Bureau of Foreign and Domestic Commerce. Special agents
ser., no. 163) (4375
    Contains list of newspapers and magazines
published in these countries, with subscription price and other data. The list of Argentine periodicals is reprinted in the Hispanic
American historical review, v. 2, no. 1,
Feb., 1919.---Jones 594.

BARRETT, Robert South. Paper, paper products,
and printing machinery in Peru, Bolivia, and
Ecuador. Washington, D.C., Govt. Print. Off.,
1917. 77 p. (Dept. of Commerce. Bureau of
Foreign and Domestic Commerce. Special
agents ser., no. 143) (4376
    Contains list of newspapers and magazines
published in these countries.---Jones 2628.

ATOMIC ENERGY

CHILE. Congreso. Biblioteca. Energía atómica. Santiago, 1959. 7 p. (Serie Bibliografías, no. 7) (4377

INTER-AMERICAN Nuclear Energy Commission, 1st
Meeting, Washington, D.C., 1959. Lista de
publicaciones principales de la Comisión Nacional de Energía Atómica de la República Argentina. List of major publications of the
Argentine National Atomic Energy Commission.
[Washington, D.C., Pan American Union] 1959.
9 p. (Documento de referencia 2) (4378

PETROLEUM

ARGENTINA. Congreso. Biblioteca. Petróleo;
bibliografía. Buenos Aires, 1964. 73 p.
(Serie Asuntos económicos, 3) (4379

MEXICO. Departamento de Petróleo. Bibliografía
del petróleo en México. México, 1927. 169 p.
(Monografías bibliográficas mexicanas,
no. 8) (4380
    Jones 2355.

RESUMOS indicativos. Rio de Janeiro, Biblioteca, Centro de Aperfeiçoamento e Pesquisas de
Petróleo, 1960- . (4381
    Cited in Doria 178.

YACIMIENTOS Petrolíferos Fiscales Bolivianos.
Biblioteca. Bibliografía, no. 1. La Paz,
Impr. YPFB, 1961. 106 p. (4382

MINES AND MINERAL RESOURCES

BERTRAND, Alejandro. Bibliografía de la tecnología del salitre. (Caliche, Santiago, año
1, p. 18-23, 1919) (4383
    Jones 1403.

CALOGERAS, João Pandiá. As minas do Brasil e
sua legislação. Rio de Janeiro, Impr. Nacional, 1904-1905. 3 v. (4384
    Bibliography at end of each chapter. A
new edition revised by Djalma Guimarães, was
published in 1938 by Cia. Editôra Nacional,
São Paulo.---Jones 1006b.

GONÇALVES, Alpheu Diniz. O ferro na economia
nacional. Rio de Janeiro, Directoria de Estatistica da Produção, 1937. 152 p. (4385
    "Bibliographia sôbre o ferro no Brasil":
p. 131-52.---Jones 1030a.

-----. Ferro no Brasil [historia, estatistica
e bibliographia] Rio de Janeiro, Ministerio
da Agricultura, 1932. 150 p. (Brazil, Ser-
vico Geológico e Mineralógico, Bol. 61)(4386
    Bibliographia: p. 129-43.---Jones 1031.

HERMITTE, Enrique. Bibliografía minera argentina. (Tercer censo nacional. Buenos Aires,
1917. t. 7, p. 481-94)   (4387
354 titles listed.---Jones 721a.

MORAIS, Adelaide Vieira da. Bibliografía bra-
sileira do sal, 1877-1962. Rio de Janeiro,
Instituto Brasileiro do Sal, 1962. 109 p.
(Coleção Raul Caldas, Cadernos do sal,

MORAIS, Adelaide Vieira de. ... (Cont.)
1)   (4388
Cited in Doria 86. Reprinted from Brasil
salineiro.

VILA, Tomás. Recursos minerales no-metálicos
de Chile. Santiago de Chile, 1936.
435 p.   (4389
Bibliografía: p. 418-27.---Jones 1660.

INSTITUTIONS, MUSEUMS, SOCIETIES, ETC.

MUSEUMS

BUENOS AIRES. Museo Argentino de Ciencias Naturales "Bernardino Rivadavia", e Instituto
Nacional de Investigación de las Ciencias
Naturales. Biblioteca Central. Catálogo de
las series en curso de publicación (1947-
1955) [i.e., 1957] Buenos Aires, Impr. del
Instituto y Museo [1957] 13 p.   (4390
Cited in Catálogo, Instituto Bibliotecológico, item 467.

-----. Universidad. Museo Antropológico y
Etnográfico. Publicaciones. Buenos Aires,
1939. 22 p.   (4391
Includes listing of the former Instituto
de Investigaciones Geográficas.---Jones 635b.

CARTAGENA. Museo Histórico. Catálogo, 1943.
Cartagena, Edit. Bolívar, [1943]
194 p.   (4392

COLEMAN, Laurence Vail. Directory of museums
in South America. Washington, D.C., The A-
merican Association of Museums, 1929.
133 p.   (4393
Jones 106. Museum publications cited.

IGUINIZ, Juan Bautista. Las publicaciones del
Museo Nacional de Arqueología, Historia y Et-
nología. Apuntes histórico-bibliográficos.
México, Impr. del Museo, 1912. 99 p. (4394
Bibliografía: p. 51-95.---Jones 2259.

LA PLATA. Universidad Nacional. Museo. Indice bibliográfico de sus publicaciones, compilado por R. Lehmann-Nitsche. Buenos Aires,
1928. 23 p.   (4395
Jones 741a.

LUJAN. Museo Colonial e Histórico de la Provincia de Buenos Aires. Catálogo del Mvseo
colonial e Histórico de Lvján; escrito e ilustrado por don E. F. Sánchez Zinny, bajo el
control del director honorario del Museo, don
Enrique Udaondo. Edición 1933-1934. La Plata, Tall. de Impresiones Oficiales de la Provincia de Buenos Aires, 1934. 261 p. (4396
Jones 762b.

NEW YORK. Museum of the American Indian. Heye
Foundation. List of publications of the Mu-
seum of the American Indian, Heye Foundation.
New York, 1921. 38 p. (Indian notes and mo-
nographs)   (4397
Jones 329.

-----. 5th. ed. New York, 1925. 87 p. (4398
Jones 330.

PARA, Brazil. (State) Museu Goeldi de Historia
Natural e Etnographia. Relação das publica-
ções scientificas ... o periodo de 1894-1904.
Bern, Buchdr. H. Jent, [1905] 58 p.   (4399
Reis, 212, cites an edition: Rio de Janei-
ro, 1905.

PARANA. Museo de Entre Ríos. Instituto Martiniano Leguizamón. Catálogo de las colecciones históricas, folklóricas, monetario, archivo y muebles. Paraná, Impr. de la Provincia, 1936. 105 p.   (4400
Jones 808c.

SOCIETIES, ETC.

ACADEMIA de la Historia de Cuba. La vida de
la Academia de la Historia (1910-1924); memoria leída por el secretario dr. Juan Miguel
Dihigo y Mestre y Pedro Figueredo, discurso
del académico de número coronel Fernando Figueredo Socarrás, leído por el académico de
número dr. Antonio L. Valverde y Maruri.
Habana, Impr. "El Siglo XX", 1924.
118 p.   (4401
Jones 1780.

ARGENTINA. Instituto Geográfico Militar. Ca-
tálogo de las publicaciones editadas por el
Instituto Geográfico Militar. Buenos Aires.
Tall. Gráf. del Instituto Geográfico Militar.
Buenos Aires, [1939] 41 p.   (4402

-----. Catálogo del material cartográfico.
Buenos Aires, Tall. Gráf. del Instituto Geográfico Militar, 1927. 16 p. 7 pl.   (4403

-----. -----. Buenos Aires, Tall. Gráf. del
Instituto Geográfico Militar, 1943.
64 p.   (4404

HISPANIC Society of America, N. Y. Catalogue
of publications. N. Y., 1907. 69 p. (4405

-----. -----. N. Y., 1943. xiv, 151 p. (Hispanic notes and monographs; essays, studies,
and brief biographies)   (4406

LUFRIU Y ALONSO, René. La vida de la Academia
de la Historia (1929-1930) La Habana, Impr.
"El Siglo XX", 1930. 55 p.   (4407
Jones 1869.

ORTEGA RICAURTE, Enrique. Bibliografía acadé-
mica. Publicación de la Academia Colombiana
de Historia con motivo del cincuentenario de
su fundación, 1902-1952. Bogotá, Edit. Minerva, 1953. 645 p.   (4408

PRUNEDA, Alfonso. Algunos datos y bibliografía de la Academia Nacional de Medicina de
México. México, 1943. 16 p. (Biblioteca
de la Feria del Libro y Exposición Nacional
del Periodismo, 1943)   (4409

SERVICIO Técnico Agrícola Colombiano Americano,
Bogotá. Biblioteca. Catálogo de las publicaciones del STACA. Bogotá, 1962. 6 p.
mimeogr.   (4410
Cited in Florén, Bibliografía bibliotecológica, 1961/1962, item 237.

VEGA, Crisóforo. Bibliografía de los trabajos
del Instituto de Biología, 1930 a 1937. Chapultepec, D.F., Impr. del Instituto, 1939.
64 p.   (4411
Jones 2565.

VELASCO, Carlos de. La Academia de la Historia de Cuba; los académicos de número. (Publ.
en la Revista de la Biblioteca Nacional, 1910.
68 p.   (4412
Jones 1938.

UNIVERSITIES AND COLLEGES

BUENOS AIRES. Universidad. Facultad de Agronomía y Veterinaria. Biblioteca. Publicaciones, 1906-1942. Buenos Aires., 1942.
26 p.   (4413

-----. -----. Facultad de Ciencias Económicas.
Nómina de publicaciones. Buenos Aires, Impr.
de la Universidad, 1939. 12 p.   (4414
Jones 627a.

-----. -----. Facultad de Filosofía y Letras.
Publicaciones. Buenos Aires, Impr. y Casa
Edit. "Coni", 1939. 48 p.   (4415
Jones 635a.

-----. -----. -----. Publicaciones, 1896-1946.
Buenos Aires, Edit. Coni, 1946. 70p. (4416
Cited in HLAS, 12, item 10.

BUENOS AIRES. Universidad. Instituto Bibliotecológico. Catálogo de las publicaciones
de la Universidad de Buenos Aires editadas
durante el período 1945-1950, con motivo de
la Exposición Feria del Libro Argentino que
se celebra en la ciudad de Buenos Aires para
conmemorar el diez y siete de octubre el Año
del Libertador General San Martín 1950. Buenos Aires [1950] 67 p.   (4417

-----. -----. Instituto de filología. Publicaciones. Buenos Aires, 1938. 31 p. (4418
Jones 636a.

-----. -----. Instituto de Literatura Argentina. Publicaciones, 1923-1939. Buenos Aires,
1939. 16 p.   (4419
Jones 636c.

CHAVEZ, Tobías. Notas para la bibliografía de
las obras editadas o patrocinadas por la Universidad Nacional Autónoma de México. Contiene además las notas bibliográficas de las
tesis presentadas por los graduados, durante
los años de 1937 a 1942, y una breve noticia
histórica de la Universidad. México, D.F.,
Impr. Universitaria, 1943. xiv, 260 p. (Biblioteca de la Feria del Libro y Exposición
Nacional del Periodismo, 1943)   (4420

CHILE. Universidad. Facultad de Filosofía y
Educación. Anuario bibliográfico, 1960- .
Santiago, 1962- .   (4421
Compiler: Alberto Villalón Galdames. The
compilation includes citations of books,
pamphlets, and articles published in Chile
and elsewhere by the departments, institutes,
centers, schools, researchers and professors
of the Facultad de Filosofía y Educación.

ESPEJO NUÑEZ, Teófilo. Contribución a la bibliografía peruana; publicaciones de la Dirección de Educación Artística y Extensión Cultural (1944-1951). [Lima, Impr. de la Universidad de San Marcos, 1959] 12 p.   (4422
Reprinted from Boletín bibliográfico, Universidad Mayor de San Marcos, Lima, v. 29,
no. 1-4, dic. 1959.

LA PLATA, Arg. Universidad. Publicaciones de
la Universidad (catálogo). La Plata [Tall.
Graf. "Tomás Palumbo"] 1941. 636 p. (4423

MEDELLIN, Colombia. Universidad de Antioquia.
Catálogo de las publicaciones editadas por
la Imprenta Universitaria hasta 1960. Medellín, Impr. Universidad de ntioquia, 1962.
63 p.   (4424
Lists 418 items, and additionally periodical publications.

MENDOZA, Arg. (City) Universidad Nacional de
Cuyo. Facultad de Filosofía y Letras. Catálogo de publicaciones (1939-1960): precedido
de un ensayo bibliográfico sobre el despert

MENDOZA, Arg. (City) Universidad...(Cont.)
literario de Mendoza (1607-1900), por Arturo Andrés Roig. Mendoza [1963] 119 p.
(Mendoza, Universidad Nacional de Cuyo. Biblioteca Central. Cuadernos de la biblioteca, 3)   (4425

MERIDA, Venezuela. Universidad de los Andes.
Catálogo, no. 1. Mérida, 1962- .   (4426
Cited in Peraza, 65, 1964, item 221.

MEXICO. Universidad Nacional. Publicaciones.
México, D.F., Impr. Universitaria, 1935.
14 p.   (4427
Cited in Millares, item 1747.

-----. -----. Instituto de Geología, México.
Lista de publicaciones. México, D.F., 1931.
xviii p.   (4428
Cited in Millares, item 1727.

-----. -----. -----. Las publicaciones del
Instituto Geológico. México, D.F., Tall.
Linotip. "El Hogar", 1923. 24 p. (Anales
del Instituto Geológico de México, no.
10)   (4429
Compiler: Carlos G. Mijares.

-----. -----. -----. Publicaciones editadas
desde su fundación (1895) hasta el mes de
julio de 1957. México, D.F., 1957.
26 p.   (4430

-----. -----. Instituto de Investigaciones
Sociales. Catálogo de publicaciones. Méxi-
co, D.F., 1961. 52 p.   (4431
Compilers: Oscar Uribe Villegas and José
María Avilés.

-----. Universidad Obrera de México. Catálogo de las publicaciones. México, D.F.,
1938.   (4432
Cited in Millares, item 1748.

ROSARIO, Arg. Universidad Nacional del Litoral. Departamento de Publicaciones. Catálogo de publicaciones. Santa Fe, 1960.
35 p.   (4433
Cited in Catálogo, Instituto Bibliotecológico, item 231.

SÃO PAULO. Universidade. Biblioteca Central.
Catálogo das publicações periódicas da Univer-
sidade de São Paulo. São Paulo, Reitoria,
Biblioteca Central, 1951. 52 p.   (4433a

-----. -----. -----. 2a ed. [São Paulo], 1959.
73 p.   (4434
Compiled by Zenóbia Mele Pereira da Silva.

-----. -----. Catálogo das publicações periódicas das instituções anexas e complementa-
res da Universidade de São Paulo. [São Paulo, 1953] 74 p.   (4435

-----. -----. Indice bibliográfico das publicações da Universidade de São Paulo. São
Paulo, 1951- .   (4436
DPU collection of v. 1: facs. 1: Faculdade
de Direito. -- fasc. 2: Escola Politécnica. -
fasc. 4: Faculdade de Filosofia, Ciências e
Letras. -- fasc. 8: Faculdade de Higiene e
Saude Pública. -- fasc. 9: Faculdade de Ciências Econômicas e Administrativas e Instituto
de Administração.

TUCUMAN. Universidad Nacional. Publicaciones
de la Universidad Nacional de Tucumán. Tucumán, M. Violetto, 1938. 20 p. (Publ. no.
229. Boletín de la Biblioteca, no. 3) (4437
Jones 872.

-----. -----. -----. 1914-1949. Tucuman, 1950.
41 p. (Publ., no. 476; Boletin de la Biblioteca Central no. 4)   (4438

INTERNATIONAL RELATIONS

GENERAL

BEMIS, Samuel Flagg and GRIFFIN, Grace Gardner.
Guide to the diplomatic history of the United
States, 1775-1921. Washington, D.C., Govt.
Print. Off., 1935. 979 p.   (4439
Published by the Library of Congress.---
Jones 51.

CADY, John Frank. Foreign intervention in the
Río de la Plata, 1835-1850. Philadelphia,
Univ, of Pennsylvania Pr., 1929.
296 p.   (4440
Bibliography: p. 272-89.---Jones 642.

CANYES, Manuel S. Treaties, conventions, international acts, protocols, and agreements.

---

* References to works treating the relations of the United States with other countries, bilaterally, are filed under the name
of the country, while references to works

treating the relations between two Latin
American countries are filed with the first
country mentioned in the citation.

CANYES, Manuel S. Treaties, ... (Cont.)
Cambridge, Mass., Harvard Univ. Pr., 1942.
p. 347-63.   (4441
  Reprinted from Handbook of Latin American
studies, 1941.

CARNEGIE Endowment for International Peace.
Library. Intellectual and cultural relations between the United States and Latin
America; select list of books, pamphlets and
periodical articles. Washington, D.C., 1935.
17 p. (Reading list, 35)   (4442
  Compiled by Mary Alice Matthews.---Jones
85.

-----. Economic and cultural relations between
the United States and Latin America. Washington, D.C., 1927. 10 p. (Reading list,
16) mimeogr.   (4443

COOPER, Russell Morgan. American consultation
in world affairs for the preservation of
peace. New York, The Macmillan Co., 1934.
406 p.   (4444
  Includes bibliography of the Chaco conflict
and the Leticia dispute.---Jones 108.

DEUTSCH-SÜDAMERIKANISCHES und Iberisches Institut in Cöln. Mitteilungen, Stuttgart und
Berlin, Verlag der Deutschen Verlags-Anstalt,
1913- . v. 1- .   (4445
  Contains book reviews and list of current
publications, as well as other bibliographical matter.---Jones 122.

GRIFFIN, Charles Carroll. The United States
and the disruption of the Spanish Empire.
1810-1822. A study of the relations of the
United States with Spain and with the rebel
Spanish colonies. New York, Columbia Univ.
Pr., 1937. 315 p.   (4446
  Classified bibliography: p. 289-302.---
Jones 175.

HAYTON, Robert D. National interests in Antarctica, an annotated bibliography. Compiler for
the U.S. Antarctic projects officer. [Wash-
ington, D.C., Govt. Print. Off.] 1959 [i. e.
1960] 137 p.   (4447
  Arranged geographically by country. Includes Latin American countries.

INTER-AMERICAN Conference on Agriculture, 3d,
Caracas, 1945. Delegation from Mexico. Bibliografía sobre inmigración rural y colonización en los países latinoamericanos, con algunas referencias generales sobre aspectos de-
mográficos conexos. [Caracas] 1945.
87 p.   (4448

JONES, Chester Lloyd. Caribbean interests of
the Unites States. New York, D. Appleton and
Co., 1916. 379 p.   (4449
  "A selected list of recent discussions relating to the Caribbean": p. 353-68.---Jones

JONES, Chester Lloyd. Caribbean ... (Cont.)
228.

-----. Pan-American relations. Madison, Univ.
of Wisconsin, 1932. 32 p.   (4450
  References: p. 24-30.---Jones 229.

KOCK-WESER, Volker. Einwirkungen der regierung
der Vereinigten Staaten von Amerika auf die
Zentral-Amerikanischen und West-Indischen
republiken. Berlin, G. Fisher & Co., 1936.
103 p.   (4451
  Schrifttum: p. 97-103.---Jones 240.

LANGER, William Leonard and ARMSTRONG, Hamilton
Fish. Foreign affairs bibliography; a selected and annotated list of books on international relations, 1919-1932. New York, London, Harper & Brothers, 1933. 551 p. (Publ.
of the Council on Foreign Relations)   (4452
  Classified, with author index. A selected
list, with descriptive and critical notes.
---Jones 241.

MAGARIÑO, Santiago, and PUIGDOLLERS, Ramón.
Panhispanismo, su trascendencia histórica,
política y social; obra premiada en el con-
curso hispano antillano de 1925; prólogo de
Rafael Altamira. Barcelona, Edit. Científico-
Médica, 1926. 142 p.   (4453
  Obras consultadas: p. 137-42.---Jones 274.

MARCHANT, Alexander. Boundaries of the Latin
American republics; an annotated list of
documents, 1493-1943. (Tentative version)
Washington, D.C., Govt. Print. Off., 1944.
386 p. (Department of State, Publ. 2082;
Inter-American ser. 24)   (4454

MORENO, Laudelino. Historia de las relaciones
interestatuales de Centroamérica. Madrid,
Compañía Ibero-Americana de Publicaciones,
[1928] 507 p. (Monografías hispano-americanas, 1)   (4455
  Guía bibliografica: p. 477-89.---Jones
1243.

MYERS, Denis Peter. Manual of collections of
treaties and of collections relating to
treaties. Cambridge, Harvard Univ. Pr.,
1922. 685 p. (Harvard bibliographies; Library series, v. 2)   (4456
  Added title-page in French. Includes section on Latin America.---Jones 331.

NATIONAL Committee of the United States of
America on International Intellectual Cooperation. Preliminary survey of inter-American cultural activities in the United
States. New York, 1939. 159 p.
mimeogr.   (4457
  Includes indexes (1) of organizations, (2)
of individuals, and (3) of publications.---
Jones 331a.

PAN AMERICAN UNION. Existing boundary dispu-
tes. [Washington, D.C., 1924] 52 p.
mimeogr.   (4458
     Cited in PAU Bibliographies p. 29.

-----. Columbus Memorial Library. List of
books and magazine articles on inter-American
relations in the Columbus Memorial Library.
[Washington, D.C., 1920] 8 p.
mimeogr.   (4459
     Cited in PAU Bibliographies p. 29.

-----. -----. Recent trends in inter-American
relations a bibliography. Washington, D.C.,
1939. 52 p. (Bibliographic ser., no. 21)
mimeogr.   (4460
     Jones 360.

-----. -----. Selected list of books and magazine articles on hemisphere defense.
Washington, D.C., 1941. 14 p. (Bibliographic ser., no. 24)   (4461

-----. -----. Selected list of books and magazine articles on inter-American relations.
Washington, D.C., 1932. 19 p. (Bibliographic ser., no. 7) mimeogr.   (4462
     Jones 361.

-----. -----. -----. 2d ed., with added page.
Washington, D.C., 1934. 20 p. (Bibliographic ser., no. 7)   (4463

-----. -----. Selected references on the Inter-American Treaty of Reciprocal Assistance, signed at Rio de Janeiro, Brazil, on
September 2, 1947. [Washington, D.C., 194-]
11 p.   (4464

RIPPY, James Fred. The Caribbean danger zone.
New York, G. P. Putnam's Sons, 1940.
296 p.   (4465
     Bibliography: p. 265-83.---Jones 404.

-----. Pan-Hispanic propaganda in Hispanic
America. New York, 1922. p. 389-
414.   (4466
     From Political science quarterly, v. 37,
no. 3, Sept. 1922. Bibliographical footnotes.---Jones 406.

-----, and SANDERS, William. Publications on
Latin American international relations in
1938. Cambridge, Mass., Harvard Univ. Pr.,
1939. p. 285-312.   (4467
     Reprinted from Handbook of Latin American
studies, 1938. Jones, 405a, cites only
p. 286-96.

ROA, Jorge. Los Estados Unidos y Europa en
Hispano América, interpretación política y
economica de la Doctrina Monroe, 1823-1933;
prefacio crítico por el profesor Edwin R. A.
Seligman, por el doctor L. S. Rowe, y por
el doctor James Brown Scott. Habana, Carasa

ROA, Jorge. Los Estados Unidos y ... (Cont.)
y Cía., 1935. xi, 411 p.   (4468
     "Bibliografía del autor": p. iv. "Biblio-
grafía europea, norteamericana, hispano-americana": p. 377-411.---Jones 411.

ROBERTSON, William Spence. Hispanic American
relations with the United States. New York,
Oxford Univ. Pr., 1923. 470 p. (Publications of the Carnegie Endowment for International Peace)   (4469
     Bibliography: p. 429-55.---Jones 414.

RODRIGUEZ LARRETA, Aureliano. Orientación de
la política internacional en America Latina.
Montevideo, Peña & Cía., 1938. 2 v. (Biblioteca de publicaciones oficiales de la Facultad de Derecho y Ciencias Sociales de la
Universidad de Montevideo, Sección 3,
13)   (4470
     "Obras citadas": v. 2, p. 323-32.---Jones
418.

SAN CRISTOVAL, Evaristo. Bibliografía de la
controversia de límites entre el Peru, Ecuador y Colombia. (Rev. universitaria, Lima,
año 21, v. 4, p. 1054-83, 1927)   (4471
     Jones 428.

STOKES, William W. The causes of inter-American misunderstandings; a selected bibliography, prepared by W. W. Stokes and the Committee on Inter-American Studies for Social
Studies 199, an interdepartmental discussion
course at the University of Wisconsin.
[Madison, 1957] 47 p.

STUART, Graham Henry. Latin America and the
United States. New York, The Century Co.,
1922. 404 p.   (4473
     Includes bibliographical foot-notes and
references to supplementary reading. 2d ed.:
1928; 3d ed.: 1938.---Jones 466.

SUAREZ, Constantino. La verdad desnuda (sobre
las relaciones entre España y América). Madrid, Sucesores de Rivadeneyra, 1924.
185 p.   (4474
     Ensayo de bibliografía: p. 177-85.---
Jones 467.

SULLIVAN, Thelma Lois. The interdependence of
the Americas. Indianapolis, Ind., Indiana
State Library, 1941. 10 p. mimeogr. (4475

UGARTE, Manuel. The destiny of a continent;
edited, with an introduction, by J. Fred
Rippy, translated from the Spanish by Cathe-
rine A. Phillips. New York, A. A. Knopf,
1925. 296 p.   (4476
     Bibliography: p. 293-96.---Jones 496.
Original Spanish edition: Madrid, 1923.

U.S. Dept. of State. Office of the Legal Advisor. Agreements in force between the United

U.S. Dept. of State. Office ... (Cont.)
States of America and other American republics; compiled March 1, 1948 by Treaty Affairs, Office of the Legal Advisor, Department of State. [Washington, D.C.] 1948.
70 p. mimeogr.   (4477

-----. -----. Treaties in force; a list of
treaties and other international agreements
of the United States. [Washington, D.C.,
Govt. Print. Off.] 1929- .   (4478
   Latest issue received at DPU: Treaties in
force, January 1, 1965. Includes Latin American countries. References are given to the
series in which treaties and agreements appeared.

-----. Library of Congress. List of references on immigration to South America. Washington, D.C., 1920. 5 p.   (4478a
   Cited in Yang.

-----. -----. Division of Bibliography. List
of references on international arbitration.
Washington, D.C., Govt. Print. Off., 1908.
151 p.   (4479
   Includes references on the collection of
debts of foreign countries, relations of the
United States and France during the French
occupation of Mexico 1861-1867, the Venezuela case and the Santo Domingo question.---
Jones 502.

-----. -----. General Reference and Bibliography Division. Non-self-governing areas
with special emphasis on mandates and trusteeships; a selected list of references,
compiled by Helen F. Conover. Washington,
D.C., 1947. 2 v.   (4480
   Includes references to possessions of countries in the Americas.

URUGUAY. Poder Legislativo. Biblioteca. Catálogo extensivo por materias: Emigración -
Inmigracion. Montevideo, n.d. 39 p. (Referencia no. 12) mimeogr.   (4481

WILLIAMS, Mary Wilhelmine. Anglo-American
Isthmian diplomacy, 1815-1915. [Baltimore,
The Lord Baltimore Pr., 1916] 356 p. (Prize
essays of the American Historical Associa-
tion, 1914)   (4482
   Bibliography: p. 331-45.---Jones 1363.

WOOD, Bryce. International relations since
1830. Cambridge, Mass., Harvard Univ. Pr.,
1942. p. 337-46.   (4483
   Reprinted from Handbook of Latin American
Studies, 1941.

YEPES, Jesús María. La contribution de l'Amerique Latine au développement du droit international public et privé. Paris, Recueil
Sirey, 1931. 109 p.   (4484
   Bibliographie: p. 103-04.---Jones 547.

INTERNATIONAL AND INTER-AMERICAN ORGANIZATIONS
Publications of

CARIBBEAN Commission. A catalogue of Caribbean Commission publications. Catalogue des
publications de la Commission des Caribes.
Port of Spain, 1957. 25 p.   (4485

CENTRO Interamericano de Vivienda, Bogotá.
Catálogo de publicaciones, no. 1-3, 1953-
1961.   (4486
   Other editions of no. 2: 1958 (16 p.);
Edición preliminar, 1959 (26 p.); 2a. ed.
1959 (58 p.).

INTER-AMERICAN Indian Institute. Catálogo general de las ediciones del Instituto Indigenista Interamericano. México, D.F., 1956.
8 p.   (4487

-----. General catalogue of the publications
of the Inter-American Indian Institute. Mexico, D.F., 1957. 8 p.   (4488

INTER-AMERICAN Statistical Institute. Lista
de publicaciones. Washington, D.C., Unión
Panamericana, 1960. 12 p. (4073 Esp-4/27/
60-2100)   (4489
   A new edition, replacing series no. 4073,
was issued in 1961 (15 p.) with series no.
4338 Esp.-12/5/61-500.

PAN AMERICAN Health Organization. Catálogo de
publicaciones. Washington, D.C., 1962.
26 p.   (4490

PAN AMERICAN UNION. [Catalog of] Publications
pf the Pan American Union in English, Spanish,
Portuguese and French. Washington, D.C.,
1950. 51 p.   (4491

-----. -----. 1951. 28 p.   (4492

-----. -----. 1953. vi, 33 p.   (4493

-----. -----. 1954. 36 p.   (4494

-----. -----. 1955/1956- . Washington, D.C.,
[1956]- .   (4495
   Annual publication. Title also given in
Spanish. Since 1958/1959 published with 2
sections: pt [1], reports and studies, and
pt. [2], Official records of the OAS.

-----. List of publications published or distributed by the Pan American Union. [Wash-
ington, D.C.] 1923. 15 p.   (4496

-----. -----. [Washington, D.C., 1940] 4 p.
mimeogr.   (4497

-----. -----. 1941. 5 p. mimeogr.   (4498

-----. Division of Music and Visual Arts.
Index of the publications [of the Inter-Amer-

INTERNATIONAL RELATIONS

PAN AMERICAN UNION. Division ... (Cont.)
ican Institute of Musicology. Washington,
D.C., 1948] 9 p. (4499

UNITED NATIONS. Office of Conference Services.
United Nations publications, 1945-1963; a
reference catalogue. New York, 1964. 71 p.
(United Nations [Document] ST/CS/Ser.
J/3) (4500
Includes publications relative Latin Amer-
ican economy.

Publications about

BOVE, Susan S. Selected bibliography. [Bos-
ton, 1963]. p. 310-20. (4501
Photographic reproduction from International organization, v. 17, no. 1, Winter 1963.

CARNEGIE Endowment for International Peace.
Library. International American conferences.
Washington, D.C., 1928. 20 p. (Reading list,
25) mimeogr. (4502

GIL, Enrique. Evolución del panamericanismo;
el credo de Wilson y el panamericanismo.
Buenos Aires, J. Menéndez, 1933.
490 p. (4503
Indice bibliográfico: p. 461-67.---Jones
163.

GODOY, José Francisco. Las conferencias panamericanas. México, D.F., A. Garduño y Hno.,
1927. 20 p. (4504
Bibliografía: p. 17-9.---Jones 166.

INMAN, Samuel Guy. Problems in Pan Americanism;
2d ed. New York, George H. Doran Co., 1925.
439 p. (4505
First edition published in 1921. Bibliography, p. 427-30.---Jones 214.

INSTITUTO Brasileiro de Educação, Ciência e
Cultura. Secção de São Paulo. Relação das
publicações dos organismos internacionais re-
cebidas pela Biblioteca Central [da Universidade de São Paulo. São Paulo, 1950. 15 p.]
(Bibliografia no. 1) mimeogr. (4506

INTER-AMERICAN Conference, 10th, Caracas, 1954.
Secretary General. Bibliographical referen-
ces on the Congress of Panama (1826) Caracas,
Lit. y Tip. Vargas, 1952. 18 p. (Collection
"Charlas", no. 14) (4507

-----. References bibliographiques relatives
au Congres de Panama (1826) [Carcas, 1952]
20 p. (Collection "Charlas", no.
14) (4508

-----. Referencias bibliográficas relativas al
Congreso de Panamá (1826) Caracas, 1952.
16 p. (Colección "Charlas", no.
14) (4509

INTER-AMERICAN Conference, 10th, Caracas, 1954.
Secretary General. Referencias bibliográficas relativas ao Congresso de Panamá (1826)
[Caracas, 1952] 20 p. (Coleção "Charlas",
no. 14) (4510

INTERNATIONAL congresses and conferences, 1840-
1937; a union list of their publications
available in libraries of the United States
and Canada, edited by Winifred Gregory under
the auspices of the Bibliographical Society
of America. New York, H. W. Wilson, 1938.
229 p. (4511

LOCKEY, Joseph Byrne. Essays in Pan Americanism. Berkeley, Univ. of California Pr.,
1939. 174 p. (4512
In "Notes", p. 163-74, are references to
sources.---Jones 263a.

-----. Pan Americanism; its beginnings. New
York, The Macmillan Co., 1920. 503 p. (4513
Bibliography: p. 468-86. A "versión castellana con anotaciones, dispuesta por la
Cámara de Comercio de Caracas" was published
in Caracas in 1927 (512 p. including the
bibliography, p. 499-512).---Jones 264.

MORENO QUINTANA, Lucio Manuel. El sistema internacional americano. Buenos Aires, Facultad de Derecho y Ciencias Sociales, 1925-
1926. 2 v. (Estudios editados por la Facultad de Derecho y Ciencias Sociales de la
Universidad de Buenos Aires, 12, 14) (4514
Bibliographies at head of chapters.---Jones
321a.

PAN AMERICAN UNION. American League of Nations;
bibliography. [Washington, D.C., 1939]
5 p. (4516
Cited in PAU Bibliographies, p. 29.

SCOTT, James Brown. Conferencias internacionales americanas, 1889-1936; recopilación de
los tratados, convenciones, recomendaciones,
resoluciones y mociones adoptadas por las
siete primeras conferencias internacionales
americanas, la Conferencia Interamericana de
Conciliación y Arbitraje y la Conferencia
Interamericana de Consolidación de la Paz;
con varios documentos relativos a la organización de las referidas conferencias; prefacio por Leo S. Rowe, introducción por James
Brown Scott. Washington, D.C., 1938. lviii,
746 p. (Publ. de la Dotación Carnegie para
la Paz Internacional) (4517
Bibliografía: p. li-lviii.---Jones 443.
Issued also in English, 1889-1928. Supplements in Spanish: 1938-1942 and 1945-1954.
Supplements in English: 1933-1940; 1942-1954.

SOCIEDAD de la Unión Americana de Santiago de
Chile. Colección de ensayos i documentos relativos a la unión y confederación de los
pueblos hispanoamericanos. Publicada a espen-

SOCIEDAD de la Unión Americana...(Cont.)
sas de la "Sociedad de la Unión Americana de
Santiago de Chile", por una comisión de los
señores don José Victorino Lastarria, don
Alvaro Covarrubias, don Domingo Santa María
i don Benjamín Vicuña Mackenna. Santiago,
Impr. Chilena, 1862. 400 p.   (4518
   "Estudios bibliográficos relativos a la
confederación, independencia i planes de monarquía en América española": p. 379-92.---
Jones 450.

THACIK, Margaret, and DANIELS, Marietta. Bibliografía de las Conferencias Interamerica-
nas. Washington, D.C., Unión Panamericana,
1954. x, 277 p. (Columbus Memorial Library.
Bibliographic ser., no. 41)   (4519

UNION of International Associations. Bibliography of proceedings of international meetings. Bibliographie des comptes rendus des
réunions internationales, 1957-1958. Brussels, 1963-1964. 2 v.   (4519a
   Includes meetings of the OAS and other
inter-American bodies.

UNITED NATIONS Educational, Scientific and
Cultural Organization. Education Clearing
House. Teaching about the United Nations
and the specialized agencies: a selected bibliography. [Paris, 1959] 60 p. (Educational studies and documents, 29)   (4520
   Prepared jointly with the Education Section
of the United Nations. Contains 420 references; Latin America: 280-300.

WALCH, John Weston. Complete handbook on
Western Hemisphere union. [Portland, Me.,
Platform News Publ. Co., 1940] 150 p.
mimeogr.   (4521

-----. Supplementary evidence file on Western
Hemisphere union. Portland Me., Platform
News Publ. Co., 1940-1941. 2 v,
mimeogr.   (4522
   Paged continuously (v.1: 1-[39]; v. 2: [40-
52]

MONROE DOCTRINE

BRADLEY, Phillips. A bibliography of the Monroe Doctrine, 1919-1929. Letchworth, Printed
by the Garden City Printing Co. and Published
by the London School of Economics, 1929.
39 p. (Studies in economics and political
science, no. 7 in the series of bibliographies by writers connected with the London
School of Economics and Political Science)   (4523
   Supplements the bibliography published in
1919 by the Library of Congress, compiled
under the supervision of H. H. B. Meyer.

DIEZ DE MEDINA, Raúl. Autopsy of the Monroe
Doctrine. New York, Macmillan, 1934.
357 p.   (4524
   Selected bibliography: p. 325-33.---Jones
129.

GREZ PEREZ, Carlos E. Los intentos de unión
hispano-americana y la guerra de España en
el Pacífico. Santiago de Chile, Impr. Nascimento, 1928. 560 p.   (4525
   Bibliografía: p. 537-60.---Jones 174.

PAN AMERICAN UNION. Columbus Memorial Library.
Bibliography on the Monroe Doctrine. [Wash-
ington, D.C., 1924] 3, 23 p. mimeogr. (4526

TRELLES Y GOVIN, Carlos Manuel. Estudio de la
bibliografia cubana sobre la doctrina de
Monroe. Habana, Impr. "El Siglo XX", 1922.
234 p.   (4527
   Includes also material relating to the
political relations of the United States
with Cuba and other Spanish-American republics. Published also in Revista de derecho
internacional, Habana, 1922, v.1, p. 15-114,
235-354.---Jones 1927.

U.S. Library of Congress. Division of Biblio-
graphy. List of references on the Monroe
Doctrine. Washington, D.C., Govt. Print.
Off., 1919. 122 p.   (4529

ARGENTINA

ALBANELL MacCOLL, Norah. Bibliografía selecta
sobre inmigración en la República Argentina.
Washington, D.C., Union Panamericana, 1953.
27 p. (Columbus Memorial Library. Bibliographic ser., no. 40)   (4530

GRAZIANI, Giovanni. La emigrazione italiana
nella Repubblica Argentina. Torino, Ditta
G. B. Paravia e Comp., 1905. 192 p.   (4531
   "Notizia bibliografica": p. 167-88.---
Jones 715.

BOLIVIA

BOLIVIA. Ministerio de Relaciones Exteriores.
Escalafón del cuerpo diplomático. La Paz,
1930. 133 p.   (4532
   Jones 906. Bibliography given under each
name when applicable.

GONZALEZ BLANCO, Pedro. Los derechos inobje-
tables de Bolivia al Chaco Boreal. Madrid,
Impr. "Sáez Hermanos", 1934. 111 p.   (4533
   "Bibliografía que se ha tenido en cuenta":
p. 107-11.---Jones 914.

PAN AMERICAN UNION. Bolivia's demand for an
outlet to the sea. [Washington, D.C., 1924]
2, 4 p. mimeogr.   (4534
   Cited in PAU Bibliographies, p. 29.

ESPINOZA Y SARAVIA, Luis. Después de la guerra, las relaciones boliviano-chilenas; 2a.
ed. La Paz, Edit. Renacimiento, 1929. 511,
xvi p.   (4535
    Bibliografía: p. xiii-xvi.---Jones 913.

BRAZIL

BOTELHO, A. Roberto de Arruda. Le Brésil et
ses relations extérieures. Paris, Les Editions Mazarines, 1935. 260 p. (Universite
Catholique de Louvain. Collection de l'Ecole des Sciences Politiques et Socia-
les)   (4536
    Bibliographie: p. 237-46.---Jones 960.

HILL, Lawrence Francis. Diplomatic relations
between the United States and Brazil. Durham, Duke Univ. Pr., 1932. 322 p.   (4537
    Bibliography: p. 306-16.---Jones 1057.

MANCHESTER, Alan Krebs. British preeminence
in Brazil, its rise and decline; a study in
European expansion. Chapel Hill, N.C., The
Univ. of North Carolina, 1933. 371 p. (4538
    Bibliography of citations: p. 343-54.---
Jones 1094.

CHILE

SHERMAN, William Roderick. The diplomatic and
commercial relations of the United States
and Chile, 1820-1914. Boston, R. G. Badger,
1926. 224 p.   (4539
    Bibliography: p. 219-24.---Jones 1616.

COLOMBIA

MINER, Dwight Carroll. The fight for the Panama route, the story of the Spooner Act and
the Hay-Herrán treaty. New York, Columbia
Univ. Pr., 1940. 469 p.   (4540
    Bibliography: p. 433-47.---Jones 1354a.

PAN AMERICAN UNION. Columbus Memorial Library. Bibliography; books and magazine articles in the Library of the Pan American Union
on relations between the United States and
Colombia. [Washington, D.C., 1924] 5, 4 p.
mimeogr.   (4541
    Jones 1752. Prepared by Charles E. Bab-
cock.

PARKS, E. Taylor. Colombia and the United
States, 1765-1934. Durham, N.C., Duke Univ.
Pr., 1935. 554 p.   (4542
    Bibliography: p. 492-529.---Jones 1754.

QUIJANO, Arturo. Colombia y México; relaciones seculares, diplomáticas, literarias y
artísticas. Bogotá, Impr. Nacional, 1922.
160 p.   (4543

QUIJANO, Arturo. Colombia y México...(Cont.)
    Bibliografía: p. 152-60.---Jones 1762.

CUBA

FITZGIBBON, Russel Humke. Cuba and the United
States, 1900-1935. Menasha, Wisc., George
Banta Co., 1935. 311 p.   (4544
    Includes bibliography.---Jones 1830.

GUGGENHEIM, Harry Frank. The United States
and Cuba. New York, Macmillan, 1934.
268 p.   (4545
    Selected bibliography: p. 251-60.---Jones
1837.

DOMINICAN REPUBLIC

KNIGHT, Melvin Moses. The Americans in Santo
Domingo. New York, Vanguard Pr., 1928.
189 p.   (4546
    Bibliography: p. 177-89. A Spanish transla-
tion was published in Ciudad Trujillo, 1939.
---Jones 3002.

PAN AMERICAN UNION. Columbus Memorial Library.
Bibliography; books and magazine articles in
the Library of the Pan American Union on relations between the United States and Dominican
Republic. [Washington, D.C., 1924] 3,
6 p.   (4547
    Jones 3005. Compilation by Charles E. Bab-
cock.

RODRIGUEZ DEMORIZI, Emilio. História diplomática dominicana (bibliografía). (Memoria del
Secretario de Relaciones Exteriores de la República Dominicana, 1939. Ciudad Trujillo,
1940. p. 325-417)   (4548
    A classified list with notes.---Jones 3007b.

TANSILL, Charles Callan. The United States and
Santo Domingo, 1798-1873: a chapter on Caribbean diplomacy. Baltimore, John Hopkins Pr.,
1938. 487 p.   (4549
    Contains footnotes referring to souce ma-
terial.---Jones 3010a. Prepared in the Walter Hines Page School of International Relations of John Hopkins University.

ECUADOR

BUSTAMANTE MUÑOZ, Antonio. Lista de los instrumentos internacionales concluidos por el Ecuador. Quito, Edit. Casa de la Cultura Ecuatoriana, 1960. 319 p.   (4550
    References to sources are given.

FLORES, Pastoriza. History of the boundary dispute between Ecuador and Peru. New York, 1921.
89 p.   (4551
    Bibliography: p. 83-9.---Jones 1981.

GUATEMALA

GUATEMALA. Guatemala-Honduras boundary arbitration; the counter case of Guatemala submitted to the Arbitral Tribunal composed of: the Hon. Charles Evans Hughes, Chief Justice of the United States of America; Hon. Luis Castro Ureña, from Costa Rica; Hon. Emilio Bello Codesido, from Chile. Under treaty of July 16, 1930. Washington, D.C., 1932. 2 v.   (4552
   Contains Annexes.---Jones 1291.

VELA, David. Nuestro Belice. Guatemala, Tip. Nacional, 1939. 195 p. (Publ. de la Revista de la Facultad de Ciencias Jurídicas y Sociales)   (4553
   "Recopilación de la serie de artículos editoriales que viera la luz pública en el diario El Imparcial del 25 de mayo al 10 de agosto de 1938". Bibliografía: p. 185-90. ---Jones 1312b.

HAITI

MONTAGUE, Ludwell Lee. Haiti and the United States, 1714-1938. Durham, N.C., Duke Univ. Pr., 1940. 308 p.   (4554
   Bibliography: p. 293-302.---Jones 3003a.

PAN AMERICAN UNION. Columbus Memorial Library. Bibliography; books and magazine articles in the Library of the Pan American Union on relations between the United States and Haiti. [Washington, D.C., 1924] 3, 5 p.   (4555
   Jones 3006. Compilation by Charles E. Babcock.

TREUDLEY, Mary. The United States and Santo Domingo, 1789-1866. Worcester, Mass. [1916] p. 83-145, 220-74.   (4556
   Reprinted from the Journal of race development, v. 7, no. 1, Jul. 1916; no. 2, Oct. 1916. Bibliography: p. 269-74.---Jones 3012. Thesis (Ph.D.) Clark University.

HONDURAS

VALLEJO, Antonio R. Historia documentada de los límites entre la República de Honduras y las de Nicaragua, El Salvador y Guatemala. Tegucigalpa, 1905-1926. 2 v.   (4557
   Contents: -1. Límites entre Honduras y Nicaragua. Bibliografía. - 2. Límites de Honduras con El Salvador.---Jones 1330a.

MEXICO

BOGARDUS, Emory Stephen. The Mexican immigrant, an annotated bibliography. Los Angeles, Council on International Relations, 1929. 21 p.   (4558

BOGARDUS, Emory Stephen. The Mexican...(Cont.) Jones 2089.

-----. The Mexican in the United States. Los Angeles, 1934. 126 p. (University of Southern California, School of Research Studies, no. 5)   (4559
   Literature and research, p. 99-123.---Jones 2090.

CALLAHAN, James Morton. American foreign policy in Mexican relations. New York, Macmillan, 1932. 644 p.   (4560
   References at end of each chapter.---Jones 2106.

CUMBERLAND, Charles C. The United States-Mexican border; a selective guide to the literature of the region. Ithaca, N.Y., 1960. 236 p. (Supplement to Rural Sociology, v. 25, no. 2, June 1960)   (4561

GAMIO, Manuel. Mexican immigration to the United States. Chicago, Univ. of Chicago Pr., 1930. 262 p.   (4562
   Bibliography: p. 249-56.---Jones 2178.

GONZALEZ RAMIREZ, Manuel. Los llamados tratados de Bucareli; México y los Estado Unidos en las convenciones internacionales de 1923. México, D.F., 1939. 441 p.   (4563
   Bibliografía: p. 431-41.---Jones 2219.

GREGG, Robert Danforth. The influence of border troubles on relations between the United States and Mexico, 1876-1910. Baltimore, John Hopkins Pr., 1937. 200 p. (John Hopkins University studies in historical and political science, ser. 55, no. 3)   (4564
   Bibliography: p. 187-93.---Jones 2220.

MacCORKLE, Stuart Alexander. American policy of recognition toward Mexico. Baltimore, Johns Hopkins Pr., 1933. 119 p. (Johns Hopkins University studies in historical and political science, ser. 51, no. 3)   (4565
   Bibliography: p. 109-13.---Jones 2312.

PAN AMERICAN UNION. Columbus Memorial Library. Books and magazine articles in the Library of the Pan American Union on relations between the United States and Mexico. Washington, D.C., 1924. 14 p.   (4566
   Jones 2402. Prepared by Charles E. Babcock.

RIPPY, James Fred. The United States and Mexico; rev. ed. New York, F. S. Crofts, 1931. 423 p.   (4567
   Bibliography: p. 387-96.---Jones 2461.

RÖMER, Hans G. Amerikanische interessen- und prinzipienpolitik in Mexiko, 1910-1914; ein beitrag zur kritik des Wilsonismus. Hamburg, Friedrichsen, de Gruyter & Co., 1929. 149 p.   (4569

RÖMER, Hans G. Amerikanische ... (Cont.)
    Bibliography: p. 140-49.---Jones 2466.

U.S. Library of Congress. Division of Bib-
    liography. United States relations with
    Mexico and Central America, with special
    reference to intervention: a bibliographical
    list. Washington, D.C., 1928. 30 p. (4569
    Cited in Yang.

PANAMA

McCAIN, William David. The United States and
    the Republic of Panama. Durham, N.C., Duke
    Univ. Pr., 1937. 278 p. (Duke University
    publications)   (4570
    Bibliography: p. 255-67.---Jones 1353.

PAN AMERICAN UNION. Columbus Memorial Library.
    Bibliography of books and magazine articles
    in the Library on relations between the

PAN AMERICAN UNION. Columbus ... (Cont.)
    United States and Panama. [Washington, D.C.,
    1924] 2, 2 p. mimeogr.   (4571
    Cited in PAU Bibliographies, p. 28.

PERU

BORCHARD, Edwin Montefiore. Opinion on the con-
    troversy between Peru and Chile known as the
    question of the Pacific. Washington, D.C.,
    1920. 40 p.   (4572
    Bibliography: p. 38-40.---Jones 2639.

DENNIS, William Jefferson. Tacna and Arica.
    New Haven, Yale Univ. Pr., 1931. 332 p.(4573
    Includes bibliography.---Jones 1445.

SAN CRISTOVAL, Evaristo. Bibliografía; la con-
    troversia limítrofe entre el Perú y el Ecua-
    dor. Vol. 1. Lima, Libr. e Impr. Gil, 1937.
    113 p.   (4574

JOURNALISM

GENERAL

ALISKY, Marvin. Latin American journalism
    bibliography. [Mexico] Fondo de Publicidad
    Interamericana [1958] 59 p.   (4575

CHILCOTE, Ronald H. The press in Latin Amer-
    ica, Spain, and Portugal. Stanford, Calif.,
    Stanford Univ., Institute of Hispanic Amer-
    ican and Luso-Brazilian Studies, 1963.
    48 p.   (4575a
    Includes a listing of newspapers and pe-
    riodicals.

HANSEN, N. Die presse Lateinamerikas. (Mit-
    theilungen des Deutsch-Südamerikanischen
    Instituts. Stuttgart und Berlin, p. 10-54,
    1914)   (4576
    Jones 186a.

HENESTROSA, Andrés, and FERNANDEZ DE CASTRO,
    José Antonio. Periodismo y periodistas de
    Hispano-América. México, D.F., Secretaría
    de Educación Pública, 1947. 150 p. (Biblio-
    teca enciclopedia popular, 2a. ép., no.
    150)   (4577

HOLE, M. Cadwalader. The early Latin-American
    press. (Bulletin, Pan American Union,
    Washington, D.C., v. 60, p. 323-52,
    1926)   (4578
    Jones 205.

TORRE REVELLO, José. Los orígenes del perio-
    dismo en la América española. (Boletín,
    Academia Nacional de la Historia, Buenos
    Aires, t. 12, p. 39-75, 1939)   (4579

TORRE REVELLO, José. Los orígenes ... (Cont.)
    "Han sido anotados todos los periódicos que
    aparecieron en América de habla hispana, des-
    de sus orígenes hasta el año 1810". (Torre
    Revello).---Jones 867e.

UNITED NATIONS Educational, Scientific and Cul-
    tural Organization. Dept. of Mass Communica-
    tions. Tentative international bibliography
    of works dealing with press problems, 1900-
    1952. [Paris, 1954] 96 p. (Reports and
    papers on mass communications, no. 13) (4579a
    Includes Latin American countries.

VALLE, Rafael Heliodoro. Bibliografía del pe-
    riodismo de América española. Cambridge,
    Mass., Harvard Univ. Pr., 1942. p. 559-
    91.   (4580
    Reprinted from Handbook of Latin American
    studies, no. 7, 1941.

ARGENTINA

BUENOS AIRES (Province) Dirección General de
    Estadística. El periodismo en la provincia
    de Buenos Aires, año 1907. Pub. bajo la di-
    rección de Carlos P. Salas. La Plata, Tall.
    de Impresiones Oficiales, 1908. 243 p.(4581
    Includes historical and bibliographical
    data with facsimiles.---Jones 638.

DIAZ L., Rogelio. Síntesis histórico-cronoló-
    gica del periodismo de la provincia de San
    Juan, 1825 a 1937. (Anales del Primer Con-
    greso de Historia de Cuyo, Mendoza, v. 2,
    p. 375-401, 1937)   (4582

DIAZ L., Rogelio. Síntesis ... (Cont.)
Jones 683.

GARRO, Juan M. Páginas dispersas; escritos y
discursos. Buenos Aires, J. Weiss y Preusche, 1916. 310 p.   (4583
"Primeros periódicos y primeros periodistas en Córdoba": p.163-72.---Jones 705.

GUTIERREZ, Juan María. La primera sociedad
literaria y la primera revista en el Río de
la Plata. (Revista del Río de la Plata,
Buenos Aires, t. 1, p. 125-37, 1871) (4584
Jones 720a.

LESSER, Juana. Die argentinische presse, ihre
einfluss in der entwicklung und dem fort-
schritt des landes. El periodismo argentino, su influencia en la evolución y en el
progreso del país. Berlin und Leipzig, W.
de Gruyter & Co., 1938. 268 p.   (4585
Jones 752.

MARTINEZ, Benigno Tejeiro. Orígenes del perio-
dismo argentino y español en el Río de la
Plata. (Revista de la Universidad Nacional,
Córdoba, v. 2, p. 49-65, 1919)   (4586
Jones 771.

ORZALI, Ignacio. La prensa argentina. Buenos
Aires, J. Peuser, 1893. 30 [218] p. (4587
Data given in Spanish, French and English;
facsimiles.---Jones 800.

PEREYRA, Miguel Carlos. Acción e influencia
del periodismo argentino en la cultura popular. Rosario de Santa Fe, E. Fenner, 1918.
93 p.   (4588
Jones 814.

QUESADA, Ernesto. El periodismo argentino
(1877-1883) (Nueva revista de Buenos Aires,
Buenos Aires, t. 9, p. 72-101, 425-47,
1883)   (4589
Jones 822.

RE, Dante. Historia del periodismo en Córdoba. (El Monitor de la educación común, Buenos Aires, año 49, no. 682-83, 1929) (4590
Jones 824e.

TOLEDO, Antonio B. La prensa argentina durante la tiranía 1828-1852) (Juegos florales,
veredicto del jurado, discurso del mantene-
dor, trabajos premiados. Tucumán, 1916.
p. 107-227)   (4591
Contains a chronological list, with bibliographical data, of newspapers and periodicals of Buenos Aires and the provinces
during the Rosas regime.---Jones 859.

BOLIVIA

ACOSTA, Nicolás. Apuntes para la bibliografía

ACOSTA, Nicolás. Apuntes ... (Cont.)
periodística de la ciudad de La Paz. La Paz,
1876. 57 p.   (4592
Jones 895.

LOZA, León M. Bosquejo histórico del periodismo boliviano; 2a. ed. La Paz, 1926.
48 p.   (4593
Jones 920.

BRAZIL

CARVALHO, Alfredo de. O jornalismo litterario
em Pernambuco. (Estudos pernambucanos, Recife, p. 63-140, 1907)   (4594
Jones 1016.

CARVALHO, Oswaldo de. Bibliografia de censura
intelectual. São Paulo, 1956. 32 p.
mimeogr.   (4595

FONSECA, Gondim da. Biografia do jornalismo
carioca (1808-1908) Rio de Janeiro, Livraria Quaresma, 1941. 416 p.   (4596
Indice cronológico dos jornais e revistas
cariocas existentes de 1808 a 1908 inclusive:
p. 271-400.

FREITAS, Affonso A. de. A imprensa periodica
de São Paulo. (Revista do Instituto Historico e Geographico de São Paulo, v. 19,
p. 321-1136, 1915)   (4597
A historical and bibliographical account
of the press in São Paulo from the establishment of O Paulista in 1823 to 1901, including 1,496 titles.---Jones 1043.

GASPAR, Cônego Mauricio M. A imprensa em
Montes Claros; desde o seu inicio até o anno
do Centenario, 1884-1922. Montes Claros,
Typ. Pio XI [1922] 3 p.   (4598
Cited in Reis, item 346.

GUIMARÃES, Teófilo. Subsidios para a historia
do jornalismo em Campos. Rio de Janeiro,
1927. 234 p.   (4600
Cited in Reis, item 369.

A IMPRENSA bahiana, 1811-1899. Bahia, 1899.
60 p.   (4601
Cited in Reis, item 177.

A IMPRENSA no Rio Grande do Norte, 1823-1908.
Natal, 1908.   (4602
Cited in Reis, item 251.

INSTITUTO Historico e Geographico Brasileiro.
Annaes da imprensa periodica brazileira.
Rio de Janeiro, Impr. Nacional, 1908. 2 v.
(Revista trimensal; tomo consagrado á Expo-
sição Commemorativa do Primeiro Centenario
da Imprensa periodica no Brasil, 1908) (4603
Contents: - v.1, pt.1, Genese e progressos
da imprensa periodica no Brazil pelo Dr. Al-

INSTITUTO Historico e Geographico...(Cont.)
fredo de Carvalho. - pt.2, Amazonas, 1851-
1908, por João Baptista de Faria e Souza;
Pará, 1822-1908, por Manoel de Mello Cardozo
Barata; Maranhão, 1821-1908, por Augusto
Olympio Viveiros de Castro; Piauhy, 1835-
1908, por Abdias Néves; Ceará, 1824-1908,
pelo barão de Studart; Rio Grande do Norte,
1832-1908, por Luiz Fernandes; Parahyba,
1826-1908, por Diogenes Caldas; Pernambuco,
1821-1908, por Alfredo de Carvalho; Alagoas,
1831-1908, por Joaquim Thomaz Pereira Die-
gues; Sergipe, 1832-1908, por Manual Armindo
Cordeiro Guaraná. Vol. 2 not published.---
Jones 1062.

PASSOS, Alexandre. A imprensa no período colonial. [Rio de Janeiro] Ministério da Educação e Saúde [1952] 72 p. (Os Cadernos de
cultura)   (4604

PESCHKE, Rudolf. Die deutsche presse in Brasilien. (Auslanddeutsche, Stuttgart, heft
12, Jahrg. 1929)   (4605
Jones 1142.

RODRIGUES, Alfredo Ferreira. Notas para a
historia da imprensa no Rio Grande do Sul.
Rio Grande, Off. a Vapor da Livraria Americana, 1899. 38 p.   (4606
Cited in Reis, item 179.

STUDART, Guilherme, barão de. Para a historia
do jornalismo cearense, 1824-1924. Fortaleza, 1924. 228 p.   (4607
Jones 1211.

TOLEDO, Lafayette de. Imprensa paulista. (Revista do Instituto Historico e Geographico
de São Paulo, v. 3, p. 303-521, 1898)   (4608
From 1827-1896, 1,536 periodicals and newspapers were published in the state of São
Paulo.---Jones 1215.

VIOTTI, Manuel. The press of the state of S.
Paulo, Brasil, 1827-1904. São Paulo, Vanor-
den & Comp., 1904. 20 p.   (4609
Prize winning work in the Exposição de S.
Luiz. Cited in Reis, item 210.

CHILE

BULNES, Alfonso. La prensa chilena en la época de Portales. (Anales de la Universidad
de Chile, Santiago, año 92, no. 16, 3a. ser.,
p. 53-73, 1934)   (4610
Jones 1413.

CHACON DEL CAMPO, Julio, and CHACON DEL CAMPO,
Nazario. Reseña histórica de la prensa de
Parral y relación de sus fiestas cincuente-
narias. Parral, Chile, Impr. "La Democra-
cia", 1915. 84 p.   (4611
Jones 1417.

CHILE. Biblioteca Nacional. Semana retrospectiva de la prensa chilena. [Santiago] Prensas de la Universidad de Chile, 1934.
90 p.   (4612
Reprinted from Anales de la Universidad de
Chile. Contents: - Vicuña, A. Palabras iniciales. - Feliú Cruz, G. Camilo Henríquez,
mentor de la revolución. - Melfi, D. La prensa o'higginista. - Donoso, R. Dos periodistas de antaño: Irisarri y Mora. - Bulnes, A.
La prensa chilena en la época de Portales. -
Correa, M. José Miguel Infante y el Valdi-
viano federal.---Jones 1608.

NIETO DEL RIO, Félix. La alta prensa diaria
en Chile. (Cuba contemporánea, Habana, v.
16, p. 303-09, 1918)   (4613
Jones 1556.

PELAEZ Y TAPIA, José. Bosquejo histórico de
la prensa chilena. Valparaíso, Impr. Victoria, 1924. 36 p.   (4614
Jones 1563.

-----. Un siglo de periodismo chileno. His-
toria del diario "El Mercurio". Santiago,
Tall. de "El Mercurio", 1927. 603 p.   (4615
Jones 1564.

COLOMBIA

ARBOLEDA R., Gustavo. Apuntes sobre la imprenta y el periodismo en Popayán, 1813-
1899. Guayaquil, Tall. Poligráficos de El
Grito del Pueblo, 1905. 56 p.   (4615a
Jones 1951.

OTERO MUÑOZ, Gustavo. Historia del periodismo
en Colombia desde la introducción de la imprenta hasta el fin de la reconquista española (1737-1819) Pt. 1. Bogotá, Edit. Minerva, 1925. 218 p.   (4616
Jones 1747.

-----. -----. Another ed. Bogotá, Edit Minerva, 1936. 140 p. (Biblioteca aldeana,
v. 61)   (4617
Contents. - Primeros periódicos colombianos, El Semanario de Caldas. - Periodismo
de la época revolucionaria. - La Gran Colombia. - La Nueva Granada. - Partidos iniciales. - Personalismo y federación. - La rege-
neración. - Satíricos y humoristas. - Periodismo literario.---Jones 1748.

PUERTA, Luis Eduardo. El periodismo en Manizales. (Boletín de historia y antigüedades,
Bogotá, v. 26, p. 863-78, 1939)   (4618
List of periodicals, giving dates of founding, editors, etc.---Jones 1760a.

COSTA RICA

NUÑEZ, Francisco María. La evolución del periodismo en Costa Rica. San José, Impr. "Minerva", 1921. 86 p.   (4619
   Jones 1273.

CUBA

ALCOVER Y BELTRAN, Antonio Miguel. El periodismo en Sagua; sus manifestaciones. (Apuntes para la historia del periodismo cubano) Habana, Tip. "La Australia", 1901. 227 p.   (4620
   A historical account. Lacks an index of periodicals.---Jones 1783.

CONTRIBUCION a la historia de la prensa periódica [de la Habana]. (Boletín de la Academia Nacional, Habana, t.22, p. 6-53, 1923; t. 23, p. 5-25, 1924)   (4621
   Jones 1802.

LLAVERIAS Y MARTINEZ, Joaquín. Contribución a la historia de la prensa periódica. Prefacio por Emeterio S. Santovenia. Habana, 1957-1959. 2 v. (Publ. del Archivo Nacional, 47-48)   (4622

MARTINEZ-MOLES, Manuel. Periodismo y periódicos espirituanos. La Habana, Impr. "El Siglo XX", 1930. 91 p.   (4623
   "Apéndice: Notas de las colecciones de periódicos que existen encuadernadas en la Biblioteca Municipal".---Jones 1872.

DOMINICAN REPUBLIC

AMIAMA, Manuel A. El periodismo en la República Dominicana. Santo Domingo, "La Nación", 1933. 95 p.   (4624
   Jones 2978.

ECUADOR

ANDRADE COELLO, Alejandro. En torno de la prensa nacional. Quito, Impr. "Ecuador", 1937. 143 p.   (4625
   Jones 1945.

ARBOLEDA R., Gustavo. El periodismo en el Ecuador; ed. corr. y aum. Guayaquil, El Grito del Pueblo, 1909. 239 p.   (4627
   Jones 1953.

CERIOLA, Juan B. Compendio de la historia del periodismo en el Ecuador. Guayaquil, Lit. e Impr. Filantrópica del Guayas, 1909. vi, 196 p.   (4628
   Cited in Chaves, p. 14; also in HLAS, no. 7, p. 579.

DESTRUGE, Camilo. Historia de la prensa de Guayaquil. Quito, Tip. y Encuad. Salesianas, 1924-1925. 2 v. (Memorias de la Academia Nacional de Historia, v.2-3)   (4629
   Jones 1971.

GANGOTENA Y JIJON, Cristóbal de. Ensayo de bibliografía del periodismo en el Ecuador. (Boletín, Biblioteca Nacional, Quito, v. 1, p. 46-86, 1925)   (4630
   Jones 1895a.

RODRIGUEZ, Máximo A. El periodismo lojano. Quito, 1948. 117 p. (Publ. de la Casa de la Cultura Ecuatoriana)   (4631

ROLANDO, Carlos A. Crónica del periodismo en el Ecuador. Guayaquil, Tip. de la Sociedad Filantrópica del Guayas, 1947. 145 p. (4632
   Vol. 1, 1792-1849. Cited in Chaves, p. 16.

-----. Cronología del periodismo ecuatoriano. Pseudónimos de la prensa nacional. Guayaquil, Impr. Monteverde y Velarde, 1920. 166 p.   (4633
   Pseudonyms: p. 87-161. Published also in Congreso Internacional de Historia de América, Rio de Janeiro, 1922, v.1, p. 705-94.---Jones 2008.

-----. -----. Guayaquil, Tip. de la Sociedad Filantrópica del Guayas, 1934. 87 p. (4634
   "Nuestra obra anterior impresa en 1920, contiene los datos hasta el 18 de octubre; en la presente vamos a corregir algunos, aumentar otros y continuar, desde noviembre de 1920, hasta la fecha todo lo que hemos recopilado".---Jones 2009.

EL SALVADOR

LARDE Y LARIN, Jorge. Orígenes del periodismo en El Salvador. [San Salvador, Ministerio de Cultura] 1950. 158 p. (Biblioteca del pueblo, 11)   (4635
   Contains checklist of journals, 1824-1850.

LOPEZ VALLECILLOS, Italo. El periodismo en El Salvador, bosquejo histórico-documental, precedido de apuntes sobre la prensa colonial hispanoamericana. San Salvador, Edit. Universitaria [1964] 478 p.   (4635a

HONDURAS

VALLE, Rafael Heliodoro. El periodismo en Honduras, notas para su historia. [México, D.F. 1959] p. 517-600.   (4636
   Reprinted from Revista de historia de América, México, D.F., no. 48, dic. 1959.

MEXICO

AGÜEROS DE LA PORTILLA, Agustín. El periodismo en México durante la dominación española;
notas historicas, biográficas y bibliográficas. (Anales del Museo Nacional de Arqueología, Historia y Etnología, México, t.2, p.
354-465, 1910)   (4637
Jones 2034.

CARRASCO PUENTE, Rafael. La prensa en México;
datos históricos. México, D.F., Universidad
Nacional Autónoma de México, 1962.
300 p.   (4638

CUELLAR ABAROA, Crisanto. Fichas para la his-
toria del periodismo en Tlaxcala. Tlaxcala,
Tall. Gráf. de Tlaxcala, 1952.   (4639
Cited in González, item 162.

HUITRON, Malaquías, MUÑOZ, Lázaro Manuel, etc.
Reseña histórica del periodismo y de la im-
prenta en el Estado de México. Toluca,
[Impr. de la Escuela de Artes y Oficios]
1943. 127 p.   (4640
Covers the period, 1812-1942.

IBARRA DE ANDA, Fortino. El periodismo en México. México, D.F., Impr. Mundial, 1934-
1935. 2 v.   (4641
Jones 2249.

IGUINIZ, Juan Bautista. El periodismo en Gua-
dalajara, 1809-1915. Guadalajara, Ediciones
I. T. G., 1955. 2 v. (324 p.) (Biblioteca
jalisciense, 13-14)   (4642
Jones 2258. Published also in Anales del
Museo Nacional de Arqueología, Historia y
Etnografía, México, D.F., ep. 4, t.7, no.2,
p. 237-406, en./dic. 1932.

LELEVIER, Armando I. Historia del periodismo
y la imprenta en el territorio norte de la
Baja California. México, D.F., Tall. Gráf.
de la Nación, 1943. 29 p.   (4643
Contribution to the II Feria del Libro y
Exposición Nacional del Periodismo. Contains list of periodicals.

LEPIDUS, Henry. Historia del periodismo mexicano. (Anales del Museo de Arqueología, Historia, y Etnografía, México, D.F., 4a. ép.,
t. 5, no.2 (v.22 de la colección) p. 380-
471, en./dic. 1928)   (4644
Jones 2305. Translation by Manuel Romero
de Terreros.

-----. The history of Mexican journalism.
Columbia, Mo., 1928. 87 p. (University of
Missouri bulletin, v. 29, no. 4)   (4645
References: p. 83-7.---Jones 2304.

MEADE, Joaquín. Hemerografía potosina. Historia del periodismo en San Luis Potosí.
San Luis Potosí, Edit. Universitaria, 1956.

MEADE, Joaquín. Hemerografía ... (Cont.)
199 p.   (4646
Cited in González, item 159.

MENENDEZ, Carlos R. La evolución de la prensa
en la península de Yucatán (Yucatán y Campeche) a traves de los últimos cien años. Mérida, Tall. de la Compañía Tip. Yucateca,
1931. 136 p.   (4647
Jones 2341.

MORALES, Ignacio. Breve reseña sobre el periodismo y su influencia moral y económica en el
pueblo de Nayarit. 1943. 26 p.   (4648
Newspapers published in Nayarit since 1884.
Cited in González, item 157.

PEREZ GALAZ, Juan de Dios. Reseña histórica
del periodismo en Campeche. Campeche, Tall.
Linotip. del Gobierno del Estado, 1943.
45 p.   (4649
Published as a contribution to the II Feria
del Libro y Exposición Nacional del Periodismo, 1943.

SANTAMARIA, Francisco Javier. Datos, materiales i apuntes para la historia del periodismo
en Tabasco (1825-1935) Méjico, Ediciones Botas, 1936. 314 p.   (4650
Supplements the list by Serra and Sánchez
Abalos; 460 publications listed in chronological order, with notes. Few with exact bibliographical data.---Jones 2485.

SPELL, Lota M. The Anglo-Saxon press in Mexico, 1846-1848. Austin, Texas, Univ. of Texas, 1932. 12 p.   (4651
Reprinted from American historical review,
v. 38, p. 20-31, Oct. 1932. Cited in Millares 1254.

TORRES, Teodoro. Periodismo. México, D.F.,
Ediciones Botas, 1937. 272 p.   (4652
List of Mexican periodicals, 1730-1934:
p. 213-72.---Jones 2531.

VELASCO VALDES, Miguel. Historia del periodismo mexicano. Apuntes. México, D.F., Manuel
Porrúa, 1955. 258 p. (Biblioteca mexicana,
14)   (4653

WITTICH, E. Die entwicklung des zeitungswe-
sens in Mexiko. (Zeitungswissenschaft,
Berlin, v.10, p. 479-516, 1935)   (4654
Jones 2588.

PERU

CURIE GALLEGOS, Luis. Periodismo en Parinaco-
chas. Lima [Compañía de Impresiones y Pu-
blicidad] 1946. 68 p.   (4655
Includes a description of the publications
issued since the introduction of printing in
the province in 1900. Cited in Anuario bi-

CURIE GALLEGOS, Luis. Periodismo...(Cont.)
bliográfico peruano, 1946, item 701.

ROMERO, Carlos Alberto. Los orígenes del periodismo en el Perú; de la relación al diario, 1594-1790. Lima, Gil, 1940. 71 p.(4657
    Jones 2736a.

SAN CRISTOVAL, Evaristo. Apuntes bibliográficos sobre el periodismo en el Perú. (Boletín bibliográfico, Biblioteca Central,
Universidad Mayor de San Marcos, Lima, v.3,
no. 1, 1927)   (4658
    Jones 2740.

PUERTO RICO

PEDREIRA, Antonio Salvador. El periodismo en
Puerto Rico; bosquejo histórico desde su
iniciación hasta el 1930. La Habana, Impr.
Ucar, García y Cía. [1941] 470 p. (Puerto
Rico. Universidad, Monografías, ser. A: Es-
tudios hispánicos, no. 3)   (4659

URUGUAY

CORBACHO, Julio R. "El Fanal", 1855-1955.
Contribución a la historia del periodismo
uruguayo. Buenos Aires [Colegio León XIII]
1954. 118 p.   (4660
    Cited in Musso 434.

FALCAO ESPALTER, Mario. Bibliografía del periodismo uruguayo. (Humanidades, La Plata,
v.9, p. 271-316, 1924; v.10, p. 127-64; v.
11, p. 397-431, 1925; v.12, p. 286-313,
1926)   (4661
    Jones 2830.

LOCKHART, Washington. Historia del periodismo en Soriano. Mercedes, Revista historica
de Soriano, 1963. 82 p.   (4663

OFICINA de la Prensa, Montevideo. La prensa
del Uruguay. Montevideo [Bertoni] 1912.
35 p.   (4664
    Cited in Musso 364.

OLARREAGA LEGUISAMO, Manuel. El periodismo en
el departamento de Salto. Salto, 1962.
36 p.   (4665

OLARREAGA LEGUISAMO, Manuel ... (Cont.)
    Cited in Musso 366.

PEREZ, Ernesto R. Cuarenta años de periodismo
en Paso de los Toros: "La Idea" en sus XXV
años de actividad. [Paso de los Toros, La
Idea, 1957] 36 p.   (4666
    Cited in Musso 375.

RAMIREZ, Arbelio. Aportes para la historia
del periodismo en el departamento de Soriano, 1857-1940. [Montevideo, L.I.G.U., 1951]
54 p.   (4667
    Cited in Musso 390.

ZINNY, Antonio. Historia de la prensa periódica de la República Oriental del Uruguay, 1807-
1852. Buenos Aires, C. Casavalle, 1883.
504 p.   (4668
    Jones 2879.

VENEZUELA

CHACIN, F. Gustavo. Historia del periodismo en
Zaraza (Estado de Guárico) Caracas, Tip.
Principios, 1952. 14 p.   (4669
    Augmented reprinting of the same work pub-
lished in Elite, Caracas, no. 828, 1941,
p. 14.

GRASES, Pedro. Tres empresas periodísticas de
Andrés Bello. Bibliografía de la Biblioteca
americana y el Repertorio americano. Caracas,
1955. 64 p.   (4670
    The first part of this work was published
in Revista nacional de cultura, Caracas, no.
108, en/feb. 1955.

GUERRA, Rafael Saturno. Apuntes para la historia del periodismo carabobeño. Caracas,
Edit. Universitaria, 1949. 58 p.   (4671

SAER D'HEGUERT, J. Prensa barquisimetana.
Valencia, Impr. Branger, 1933. 52 p. (4672
    Describes 221 periodicals published in Bar-
quisimeto, 1833-1915.---Jones 2952a.

SANCHEZ, Manuel Segundo. La prensa periódica
de la revolucion emancipadora. Caracas,
Tip. Americana, 1939. 9 p.   (4673
    Jones 2957.

LABOR AND LABORING CLASSES

ARGENTINA. Congreso. Biblioteca. Accidentes
del trabajo. Enfermedades profesionales.
Higiene del trabajo. Buenos Aires, 1949.
79 p. (Información bibliográfica, publ. no.
6)   (4674

ARGENTINA. Ministerio del Interior. Dirección
Nacional de Salud Pública. Bibliografía sobre trabajo, higiene industrial y enfermedades profesionales. Buenos Aires, 1945.
61 p. (Publicación no. 2)   (4675

BRAZIL. Ministério do Trabalho, Indústria e Comércio. Serviço de Documentação. Bibliografia de asuntos trabalhistas. Rio de Janeiro, 1958. 277 p. (Coleção Lindolfo Collor) (4676

-----. -----. Bibliografia de asuntos trabalhistas. Rio de Janeiro, 1961. 275 p. (4677
Cited in Revista do livro, 6 (23-24): 235, set./dez. 1961.

CHILE. Universidad. Instituto de Organización y Administración de Empresas. Bibliografia de relaciones laborales en Chile. [Santiago de Chile, 1960] 26 p. mimeogr. (4678

CLARK, Marjorie Ruth. Organized labor in Mexico. Chapel Hill, Univ. of North Carilina, 1934. 315 p. (4679
Bibliography: p. 292-306.---Jones 2132.

FORERO NOGUES, Marian. Lista preliminar de obras sobre relaciones industriales y del trabajo. Bogotá, 1960. x, 59, 10 p. (Documento de la Reunión Interamericana de Expertos en Relaciones Industriales y del Trabajo, Bogotá, 1960, no. 6) (4680
Cited in Caribbean acquisitions, 1961, p. 5.

INTER-AMERICAN Children's Institute, Montevideo. Bibliografia sobre higiene y seguridad industrial y trabajo de mujeres y menores en Argentina, Costa Rica, Chile, México, Perú, Puerto Rico, Uruguay. [Montevideo, 1958?] 18 p. mimeogr. (4681
Cited in Musso 511.

-----. Bibliografia sobre trabajo del menor. Montevideo, 1961. 26 p. (4682

KROLLMANN, Wilhelm J. Die wichtigsten probleme der mexikanischen wirtschaft. Berlin-Charlottenburg, Gebrüder Hoffmann, 1931. 112 p. (4683
Literaturverzeichnis: p. 108-42.---Jones 2274.

LOMBARDO TOLEDANO, Vicente. Bibliografia del trabajo de la previsión social en México. México, D.F., 1928. 216 p. (Monografías bibliográficas mexicanas, 13) (4684

LOMBARDO TOLEDANO, Vicente ... (Cont.) Jones 2309.

MASSA GIL, Beatriz. Bibliografia sobre migración de trabajadores mexicanos a los Estados Unidos [una tentativa para compilar lo publicado en Estados Unidos acerca de este problema durante los años 1950-1958] México, D.F., Departamento de Estudios Económicos, Biblioteca del Banco de México, 1959. 122 p. mimeogr. (4685

MEXICO. Departamento del Trabajo. La obra social del presidente Rodríguez. México, Tall. de la Nación, 1934. 607 p. (4686
"Apuntes para una bibliografia del Departamento del Trabajo": p. 601-07.---Jones 2357.

PAN AMERICAN UNION. Division of Labor and Social Information. Bibliography on labor and social welfare in Latin America. Washington, D.C., 1940. 31 p. mimeogr. (4687

-----. Rev. ed. Washington, D.C., 1944. 76 p. mimeogr. (4688
Compilation by Sylvia Pollack Bernstein.

RAMA, Carlos M. Mouvements ouvriers et socialistes, chronologie et bibliographie: L'Amerique Latine (1492-1936) Paris, Editions Ouvrières [1959]. t. 5 (222 p.) (4689

TISSEMBAUM, Mariano R. La legislación del trabajo y su fuente de investigación. Santa Fé, Arg., [Impr. de la Universidad del Litoral] 1935. 373 p. (4690
Published by the Facultad de Ciencias Juridicas y Sociales of the Universidad Nacional del Litoral on occasion of the Seminario de Derecho Industrial y Obrero.

URUGUAY. Poder Legislativo. Biblioteca. Bolsas de trabajo (Material sobre el tema existente en esta Biblioteca) Montevideo, 1950. 3, 31 p. (Referencia, 13) mimeogr. (4691

VIEIRA, Oldegar Franco. Bibliografia brasileira de direito de trabalho. [Salvador] 1958. 65 p. (Salvador, Brazil. Universidade. Publ. 8: Bibliografia, 1) (4692

ZAVALA, Silvio Arturo, and CASTELO DE ZAVALA, María. Fuentes para la historia del trabajo en Nueva España. México, D.F., Fondo de Cultura Económica, 1939-[1946] 8 v. (4693
Jones 2591.

LANGUAGE

GENERAL

CIBDAD Y SOBRON, Félix. Los idiomas de la
América Latina; estudios biográfico-biblio-
gráficos. Madrid, Impr. a cargo de V. Saiz
[1876] 137 p.   (4694
  Jones 101.

ECHEVERRIA Y REYES, Anibal. Sobre lenguaje;
disquisición bibliográfica. Valparaíso,
Impr. de "La Tribuna", 1897. 23 p.   (4695
  Jones 134. 73 titles are cited.

MARSDEN, William. A catalogue of dictionaries,
vocabularies, grammars, and alphabets. In
two parts: Part I, Alphabetic catalogue of
authors. Part II, Chronological catalogue
of works in each class of language. London,
1796. 154 p.   (4696
  Contains little about American languages.
---Jones 285.

MEILLET, Antoine, and COHEN, Marcel. Les
langues du monde. Paris, E. Champion, 1924.
811 p. (Collection linguistique, publiée
par la Société de Linguistique de Paris,
16)   (4697
  "Langues américaines" by P. Rivet: p. 597-
712 with bibliography.---Jones 309.

OROZ, Rodolfo. Bibliografía filológica chilena (analítico-crítica) (Boletín de la
Academia Chilena, Santiago, t.7, p. 61-168,
1940)   (4698
  Includes works published up to 1938, 417
titles. This, the first section, is devoted
to "Filología románica".---Jones 1558a.

PALFREY, Thomas Rossman, FUCILLA, Joseph Guerin, and HOLBROOK, William Collar. A bibliographical guide to the romance languages
and literatures. Evanston, Ill., 1939.
82 p.   (4699
  Contains some 1500 entries. Parts 4 and
5 cover Portugal, Brazil, Spain and Spanish
America.---Jones 348a.

PERMANENT International Committee of Linguists.
Bibliographie linguistique, 1948- . Utrecht,
Spectrum, 1951-   (4700
  Each annual volume contains a section on
American languages. Last volume received
at DPU: 1962.

TRÜBNER'S catalogue of dictionaries and grammars of the principal languages and dialects
of the world; 2d ed., considerably enl. and
rev., with an alphabetical index. A guide
to students and booksellers. London, Trübner & Co., 1882. 170 p.   (4701
  "Enumerates nearly 3000 titles. The additions to this new ed. are mainly due to
Mr. Hiersemann".---Jones 495.

ENGLISH

GROPP, Arthur E. Bibliography of English language materials found in certain libraries
of Montevideo. [Montevideo, 1945] 12 p.
mimeogr.   (4702

ITALIAN

HALPERIN, Renata Donghi de. Contribución al
estudio del italianismo en la República Argentina. Buenos Aires, 1925.   (4703
  Jones 684a.

PORTUGUESE

CASTRO, Eugenio de. Relação bibliografica de
lingüística americana. Rio de Janeiro,
1937- . 1a. ser., fasc. 1- .   (4704
  The first part (129 p.) is of value for
Brazilian items.---Jones 88.

GORNALL, Pedro. Les langues brésiliennes.
Monographie. Livres les plus intéressants
considérés sous le rapport de la linguisti-
que du Brésil. Buenos Aires, 1882.
31 p.   (4705
  Museo Mitre. Catalogo ... de la Sección
Lenguas Americanas, v.1, p. 29.---Jones 1051.
See also item 4770.

JUCA, Candido. Lingua nacional? As diferen-
ciações entre o português de Portugal e o
do Brasil autorizam a existência de um ramo
dialetal do português peninsular? Rio de
Janeiro [Estabelecimento Gráphico Apollo]
1937. 135 p.   (4706
  "Principais obras citadas": p. 126-30.---
Jones 1070.

PAIVA, Tancredo de Barros. Bibliographia eth-
nico-linguistica brasiliana. Rio de Janeiro,
Impr. Nacional, 1932. p. 331-400.   (4707
  Jones 1125. Reprinted from Annaes do XX
Congresso Internacional de Americanistas,
v. 3.

RAIMUNDO, Jacques. O elemento afro-negro na
lingua portuguesa. Rio de Janeiro, Renas-
cença Editôra, 1933. 191 p.   (4708
  Bibliografia: p. 181-91.---Jones 1151.

SPANISH

ALONSO, Amado, and LIDA, Raimundo. El español
en Chile, trabajos de Rodolfo Lenz, Andrés
Bello y Rodolfo Oroz; traducción, notas y
apéndices. Buenos Aires, 1940. 374 p.
(Biblioteca de dialectología hispanoamericana, v. 6)   (4709

ALONSO, Amado, and LIDA, Raimundo ... (Cont.)
"Bibliografía por Rodolfo Oroz": p. 299-
324.---Jones 1379a.

ARRAZOLA, Antonio María de. Menorándum bibliográfico de gramática española. Bogotá, Impr.
de F. Torres Amaya, 1879. 37 p.   (4710
The first bibliography of this type published in Colombia. Cited in Giraldo Jaramillo, p. 102.

CANFIELD, Delos Lincoln. Spanish literature
in Mexican languages as a source for the
study of Spanish pronunciation. New York,
Instituto de las Españas, 1934.
257 p.   (4711
Bibliography: p. 230-57.---Jones 2112.

CEJADOR Y FRAUCA, Julio. Bibliografía sobre
el castellano en América. (España moderna,
Madrid, año 19, no. 224, p. 1-26,
1907)   (4712
Cf. his Cabos sueltos, Madrid, 1907, p.
367-436, El castellano en América.---Jones
92.

-----. Historia de la lengua y literatura
castellana ... comprendidos los autores hispano-americanos. Madrid, Tip de la Revista
de Archivos, Bibliotecas y Museos, 1915-1922.
14 v.   (4713
Contains bio-bibliographical information
about recent and contemporary Spanish-American authors.---Jones 93.

COSTA ALVAREZ, Arturo. El castellano en la
Argentina. La Plata, Tall. de la Escuela
San Vicente de Paúl, 1928. 350 p.   (4714
Contains bibliographies.---Jones 676.

GRASES, Pedro. Estudios de castellano. Caracas, Edit. Elite, 1940. 43 p.   (4715
On cover: Publicaciones del Grupo "Vier-
nes". At head of t.p.: Bibliografía venezolana. Jones 2915a: Bibliography of linguistic works by Venezuelans, excluding those
of Bello and Baralt: Alvarado, Calcaño Pa-
niza, Guerrero, Lovera, Rivodó, Semprum and
Villalobos.

HALL, Pauline Cook. A bibliography of Spanish
linguistics: articles in serial publications.
Baltimore, Linguistic Society of America
[1957] 162 p. (Language dissertation no.
54)   (4716
Supplement to Language, v. 32, no. 4, pt.
2, Oct.-Dec. 1956. Thesis - State University of Iowa.

HANSSLER, William. A handy bibliographical
guide to the study of the Spanish language
and literature with consideration of the
works of Spanish-American writers. St.
Louis, Mo., C. Witter, 1915. 63 p.   (4717
Jones 187.

HENRIQUEZ UREÑA, Pedro. El español en Méjico,
los Estados Unidos y la América Central;
trabajos de E. C. Hills, F. Semeleder, C.
Carroll Marden, M. G. Revilla, A. R. Nykl,
K. Lentzner, C. Gagini y R. J. Cuervo. Bue-
nos Aires, 1938. 526 p. (Universidad de
Buenos Aires, Facultad de Filosofía y Letras,
Instituto de Filología. Biblioteca de dia-
lectología hispanoamericana, v. 4)   (4718
Contains bibliographies.---Jones 2238.

-----. El español en Santo Domingo. Buenos
Aires, 1940. 304 p. (Universidad de Bue-
nos Aires, Facultad de Filosofía y Letras,
Instituto de Filología. Biblioteca de dia-
lectología hispanoamericana, v. 5)   (4719
Jones 2997a.

MARDEN, Charles Carroll. A bibliography of
American Spanish (1911-1921) Madrid, Impr.
de los Sucesores de Hernando, 1924. p. 589-
605.   (4720
"Del Homenaje a Menéndez Pidal, t.1".
Continues the author's Notes for a bibliography of American Spanish.---Jones 283.

-----. Notes for a bibliography of American
Spanish. (Studies in honor of A. Marshall
Elliot. Baltimore, Johns Hopkins Pr., 1911.
v. 2, p. 267-92)   (4721
Jones 282.

NICHOLS, Madaline Wallis. A bibliographical
guide to materials on American Spanish,
edited for the Committee on Latin American
Studies of the American Council of Learned
Societies. Cambridge, Mass., Harvard Univ.
Pr., 1941. xii, 114 p. (Misc. publ., no.
2)   (4722

QUESADA, Ernesto. La evolución del idioma nacional. Buenos Aires, Impr. Mercatali, 1922.
68 p.   (4723
Contains bibliographies. A review of Costa Alvarez' Nuestra lengua. Published also
in Nosotros, Buenos Aires, no. 164, p. 5-31,
en. 1923; no. 165, p. 175-207, feb. 1923.
---Jones 819.

RODRIGUEZ GARCIA, José Antonio. Bibliografía
de la gramática y lexicografía castellanas
y sus estudios afines. Primera Parte: Gramática. La Habana, 1903-1912. 2v. (v.1:
899 p.; v.2: 722 p.)   (4724

ROHLFS, Gerhard. Manual de filología hispánica; guía bibliográfica, crítica y metódica; trad. castellana del manuscrito alemán,
por Carlos Patiño Rosselli. Bogotá, Instituto Caro y Cuervo, 1957. 377 p. (Publicaciones 12)   (4724a

ROJAS CARRASCO, Guillermo. Filología chilena,
guía bibliográfica y crítica. Santiago de
Chile, Impr. y Lit. Universo, 1940.

ROJAS CARRASCO, Guillermo ... (Cont.)
300 p.   (4725
    Jones 1588b.

SERIS, Homero. Bibliografía de la lingüística
española. Bogotá, 1964. 981 p. (Publ. del
Instituto Caro y Cuervo, 19)   (4726

TORO Y GISBERT, Miguel de. L'évolution de la
langue espagnole en Argentine. Paris,
Larousse [1932?] 199 p.   (4727
    Auteurs et ouvrages cités: p. 181-85.---
Jones 861.

VIÑAZA, Cipriano Muñoz y Manzano, Conde de la.
Biblioteca histórica de la filología castellana. Madrid, M. Tello, 1893.
1112 p.   (4728
    1,750 titles listed.---Jones 517.

WELLMAN, Esther Turner. Language study; a
bibliography for missionaries in Mexico.
n.d. 12 p.   (4729

WOODBRIDGE, Hensley Charles. Central American
Spanish; a bibliography (1940-1953) Washington, D.C., Pan American Union, 1956.
p. 103-15.   (4730
    Reprinted from Revista interamericana de
bibliografía, v.6, no.2, abr./jun. 1956.

SPANISH - Dialects, Provincialisms, etc.

ALONSO, Amado. Problemas de dialectología hispanoamericana. Buenos Aires, Instituto de
Filología, Facultad de Filosofía y Letras,
Universidad de Buenos Aires, 1930.
173 p.   (4731
    Bibliografía: p. 163-73.---Jones 7.

BENVENUTTO MURRIETA, Pedro M. El lenguaje peruano, t.1. Lima, 1936. 228 p.   (4732
    Bibliography: p. 7-17, 217-28.---Jones
2632.

CABEZON, Carlos. Neógrafos kontemporáneos;
tentatiba bibliográfika (Kongreso zientífiko
chileno de 1894) Santiago de Chile, Impr.
Zerbantes, 1896. 21 p.   (4733
    Jones 1414.

CALLAGE, Roque. Vocabulario gaucho. Porto
Alegre, Barcellos, Bertaso y Cia., 1926.
133 p.   (4734
    Bibliography included in preface.---Jones
1004.

ECHEVERRIA Y REYES, Aníbal. Voces usadas en
Chile. Santiago, Impr. Elzeviriana, 1900.
246 p.   (4735
    Bibliografía: p. 1-21.---Jones 135, 1458.

LENZ, Rodolfo. Bibliografía crítica de las
obras sobre americanismos. (The author's

LENZ, Rodolfo. Bibliografía ... (Cont.)
Diccionario etimológico de las voces chilenas derivadas de lenguas indíjenas americanas. Santiago de Chile, 1904. p. 58-
90)   (4736
    Jones 255.

MALARET, Augusto. Diccionario de americanismos; suplemento. (Boletín de la Academia
Argentina de Letras, Buenos Aires, t.8,
p. 7-66, 1940)   (4737
    Bibliografía: p. 10-35.---Jones 277a.
Continued in the Boletín through oct./dic.
1941.

MARDEN, Charles Carroll. The phonology of the
Spanish dialect of Mexico City. Baltimore,
The Modern Language Association of America,
1896. 66 p.   (4738
    Bibliography: p. 5-11.---Jones 2316.

ROMERO, José Guadalupe. Noticia de las personas que han escrito o publicado algunas obras
sobre idiomas que se hablan en la República.
(Boletín de la Sociedad Mexicana de Geografía
y Estadística, México, v.8, p. 874-86,
1860)   (4739
    Jones 2470.

SANTAMARIA, Francisco Javier. El provincialis-
mo tabasqueño; ensayo de un vocabulario del
lenguaje popular; comprobado con citas, comparado con el de mexicanismos y los de otros
países hispano-americanos. México, D.F., A.
Botas e Hijo [1921] v.1 (437 p.:A-B-C)(4740
    Bibliografía: p. 11-24.---Jones 2486.

TORO Y GISBERT, Miguel de. Americanismos.
Paris, P. Ollendorff [1912] 285 p.   (4741
    "Los diccionarios de Americanismos": p.
169-219.---Jones 478.

LANGUAGES (INDIAN) - Individual languages:

ARAUCANA

ECHEVERRIA Y REYES, Aníbal. Disquisiciones:
La lengua araucana. El puente de cal y canto. La batalla de Rancagua. Primeros almanaques publicados en Chile. El cólera. Santiago de Chile, Impr. Nacional, 1889.
100 p.   (4742
    The first, fourth and fifth papers are bib-
liographical studies.---Jones 1455.

-----. La lengua araucana; notas bibliográficas. Santiago de Chile, Impr. Cervantes,
1889. 32 p.   (4743
    Cited in Laval, item 108.

MEDINA, José Toribio. Bibliografía de la lengua araucana. Santiago de Chile, Impr. en
Casa del Autor, en la Impr. Elzeviriana, 1897.
73 p.   (4744

LANGUAGE

MEDINA, José Toribio. Bibliografía...(Cont.)
Reprint of the "Prólogo" of the Nueve Sermones en la lengua de Chile by Luis de Valdivia. Cited in Laval, item 170.

SCHULLER, Rudolph R. El vocabulario araucano
de 1642-1643, con notas críticas i algunas
adiciones a las bibliografías de la lengua
mapuche. Santiago de Chile, Impr. Cervantes,
1907. 286 p. (4745
Jones 1613.

VALDIVIA, Luis de. Nueve sermones en lengua
de Chile reimpresos a plana y renglón del
único ejemplar conocido y precedidos de una
bibliografía de la misma lengua por José Toribio Medina. Santiago de Chile, Impr. Else-
viriana [1897] 76 p. (4746
The "Bibliografía" (p. 17-73) lists 101
titles.---Jones 1648.

ATACAMENIAN

SCHULLER, Rudolph R. Vocabularios y nuevos
materiales para el estudio de la lengua de
los indios Lican - Antai (Atacameños) - Calchaquí. Santiago, F. Becerra [190 ?] 124 p.
(Biblioteca de lingüística americana (Zona
Atacameña - Cunza - Calchaquí) t.2) (4747
"Obras consultadas": p. 117-24.---Jones
1614.

AYMARA

RIVET, Paul, and CREQUI-MONTFORT, Georges de.
Bibliographie des langues aymará et kicua.
Paris, Institut d'Ethnologie [1951]-1956.
4 v. (Université de Paris. Travaux et mémoires de l'Institut d'Ethnologie,
51) (4748
Published jointly with the Centre National
de la Recherche Scientifique, Paris, and the
Viking Fund, New York. Contents: v.1
(502 p.): 1540-1875; v.2 (656 p.): 1876-1915;
v.3 (784 p.): 1916-1940; v.4 (957 p.): 1941-
1955.

GUARANI

AYROSA, Plínio. Apontamentos para a bibliografia da língua Tupi-Guarani. São Paulo,
Universidade de São Paulo, Faculdade de Filosofia, Ciências e Letras, 1943. 333 p.
(Boletim 33; Etnografia e Tupi-Guarani,
4) (4749

-----. -----. 2a. ed. rev. e atualizada. São
Paulo, 1954. 261 p. (Universidade de São
Paulo. Faculdade de Filosofia, Ciências e
Letras, boletim no. 169; Etnografia e Tupi-
Guaraní, no. 28) (4750

CABRAL, Alfredo do Valle. Bibliographia da
lingua tupi ou guarani tambem chamada lingua
geral do Brazil. Rio de Janeiro, Typ. Nacional, 1880. 81 p. (4751
"Extr. do v. 8 dos Annaes da Bibliotheca
Nacional do Rio de Janeiro".---Jones 1218.

MEDINA, José Toribio. Bibliografía de la lengua guaraní. Buenos Aires, J. Peuser, 1930.
94 p. (Publ. del Instituto de Investigaciones Históricas, no. 51) (4752
Jones 776.

MORINIGO, Marcos A. Hispanismos en guaraní.
Buenos Aires, 1931. 433 p. (Universidad
de Buenos Aires, Facultad de Filosofía y
Letras, Instituto de Filología. Colección
de estudios indigenistas, 1) (4753
Bibliography.---Jones 789.

VICTORICA, Ricardo. Errores y omisiones de una
seudo bibliografía guaraní, con tres mapas
fuera de texto. Buenos Aires, 1934.
157 p. (4754
A criticism of Medina's Bibliografía de la
lengua guaraní, followed by a supplementary
list (p. 61-125).---Jones 777.

KECHUA

FARFAN, José M. B. I. El quechua bibliográfico.
II. Una leyenda del mes de agosto en sus versiones quechua, castellana e inglesa. Lima,
Impr. del Museo Nacional, 1943. p. 228-
38. (4755
Reprinted from Revista del Museo Nacional,
t. 12, no. 2, 1943.

JAUREGUI ROSQUELLAS, Alfredo. Bibliografía
del idioma quechua. (Boletín de la Sociedad
Geográfica de Sucre, p. 143-62, feb.
1937) (4756
Jones 919.

MEDINA, José Toribio. Bibliografia de las lenguas quechua y aymará. New York, 1930.
117 p. (Contributions from the Museum of
the American Indian, Heye Foundation, v.7,
no. 7) (4757
Jones 297.

MAYA

CARRILLO Y ANCONA, Crescencio. Disertación so-
bre la historia de la lengua maya o yucateca.
México, D.F., Impr. del Gobierno, 1872. 63,
257-71 p. (4758
Disertación sobre la literatura antigua de
Yucatán: p. 257-71. Also in Boletín de la
Sociedad de Geografía y Estadística de la
República Mexicana, v.4, p. 134-95, 1872.---
Jones 2114.

HAEBLER, Konrad. Die maya-litteratur und der
mayaapparat zu Dresden. (Centralblatt für
bibliothekswesen, Leipzig, v. 17, p. 537-75,
1895) (4759
Jones 2231.

TOZZER, Alfred Marston. A Maya grammar, with
bibliography and appraisement of the works
noted. Cambridge, Mass., 1921. 301 p.
(Papers of the Peabody Museum of American
Archaeology and Ethnology, v.9) (4760
Bibliography: p. 211-79. Listing of over
700 different works, not including second
editions.---Jones 2535.

NAHUATL

ROMERO, José. Contribución a la bibliografía
azteca. (Investigaciones lingüísticas, México, v.1, no. 3/4, p. 312-21, 1933/
1934) (4761
Jones 2468.

UGARTE, Salvador. El vocabulario manual de
las lenguas castellana y mexicana compuesto
por don Pedro de Arenas; nota bibliográfica.
México, D.F., Librería de Porrua Hnos., 1936.
12 p. (4762

TOBA

LEHMANN-NITSCHE, Robert. Vocabulario toba
(rio Pilcomayo y Chaco oriental) con bibliografía. (Boletín de la Academia Nacional de
Ciencias de la República Argentina, Córdoba,
v.28, p. 179-96, 1925) (4763
A bibliography of Lehmann Nitsche by Fernando Márquez will be found in Revista del
Museo de La Plata (nueva serie) Sección Oficial, Buenos Aires, p. 125-33, 1939.---Jones
750.

TOTONAC

GROPP, Arthur Eric. A bibliography of Totonac
linguistic materials. (Hispanic American
historical review, Durham, N.C., v. 18,
p. 114-26, 1938) (4764
Jones 1233.

YUNGA

ALTIERI, Radamés A. La gramática yunga de F.
de la Carrera, estudio bibliográfico, con
todos los modernos vocabularios. Tucumán,
Instituto de Antropología, 1939. 26 p.
(Universidad Nacional de Tucumán, Publ.
257) (4765
The Arte de la lengua yunga was first published in Lima, 1644.---Jones 554a.

ZAPOTEC

PEÑAFIEL, Antonio. Bibliografía de escritores
en lengua zapoteca. (Gramática de la lengua
zapoteca. México, D. F., 1887.
p. v.-lvii) (4766
Jones 2414.

LANGUAGES (INDIAN) - Geographic Areas

AMERICA

AMUNATEGUI, Miguel Luis. Lenguas indíjenas de
la América. (Revista de Santiago, Santiago
de Chile, t.1, p. 117-28, 1848) (4767
A bibliographical study.---Jones 1382.

ARANA, Enrique. Bibliografía de lenguas americanas. Buenos Aires, Impr. de la Universidad,
1931. 13 p. (4768
Jones 26. Reprint from Boletín del Instituto de Investigaciones Históricas, Facultad
de Filosofía y Letras, Buenos Aires, año 10,
t.13, no. 49-50, p. 138-55, jul.-dic. 1931.

BARROS ARANA, Diego, and LENZ, Rodolfo. La
lingüística americana, su historia i su estado actual. Santiago de Chile, Impr. Cervantes, 1893. 49 p. (4769
"Publicado en los Anales de la Universidad".
---Jones 46.

BUENOS AIRES. Museo Mitre. Catálogo razonado
de la sección Lenguas americanas, por Bartolomé Mitre. Con una introduccion de Luis
María Torres. Buenos Aires, Impr. de Coni
Hermanos, 1909-1911. 3 v. (4770
"Bibliografía lingüística americana": v.1,
p. 5-70.---Jones 624.

-----. Lenguas americanas. Catálogo ilustrado
de la sección X de la Biblioteca. Buenos
Aires, Impr. de Coni Hermanos, 1912.
182 p. (4771
With many facsimiles of original title-
pages.---Jones 625.

GARCIA ICAZBALCETA, Joaquín. Apuntes para un
catálogo de escritores en lenguas indígenas
de América. México, D.F., 1866. 157 p.(4772
175 titles.---Jones 159, 1290.

-----. 2a. ed. México, Agüeros, 1898. (Obras
de Joaquín García Icazbalceta, t. 8, Opusculos varios, v.5, p. 1-181) (4773
Published as t.18 of the Biblioteca de autores mexicanos.

LUDEWIG, Hermann Ernst. The literature of
American aboriginal languages. With additions
and corrections by Wm. W. Turner. Ed. by
Nicolas Trübner. London, Trübner and Co.,
1958. 258 p. (Trübner's bibliotheca glottica,
I) (4774

LUDEWIG, Hermann Ernst. ... (Cont.)
See also (item 4781) Conde de Viñaza's
Bibliografía española de lenguas indígenas
de América.---Jones 268.

MITRE, Bartolomé. Lenguas americanas. Estudio bibliográfico-lingüístico de las obras
del P. Luis de Valdivia sobre el araucano y
el allentiak, con un vocabulario razonado
del allentiak. La Plata, Tall. de Publicaciones del Museo, 1894. 153 p.   (4775
"Publicado en la Revista del Museo de la
Plata".---Jones 317.

PENNSYLVANIA. University. Catalogue of the
Berendt linguistic collection, by Daniel
Garrison Brinton. Philadelphia, Dept. of
Archaeology and Paleontology, Univ. of Penn-
sylvania, 1900. 32 p.   (4776
"Reprinted from Bulletin of the Free Mu-
seums of Science and Art, University of
Pennsylvania, v. 2, no. 4".---Jones 367.

PLATZMANN, Julius. Verzeichnis einer auswahl
amerikanischer grammatiken, wörtbücher,
katechismen, u. s. w. Leipzig, K. F. Köh-
ler, 1876. 38 p.   (4777
Jones 375.

RIO DE JANEIRO. Instituto Cairú. Relação
bibliografica de linguística americana,
fasc. 1o., 1 - Ameríndia (1a. ser.) Rio
de Janeiro, Serviço Gráfico do Ministério
de Educação e Saude, 1937. 129 p.   (4778
Signed at end: Eugenio de Castro.

SCHULLER, Rudolph R. Bibliography of American
linguistics, 1926-1928. (International
journal of American linguistics, New York,
v.6, p. 69-75, 1930)   (4779
Jones 441a.

-----. Lingüística americana, notas bibliográficas. Madrid, Tip. de la Revista de archivos, bibliotecas y museos, 1912.
42 p.   (4780
"De la Revista de archivos, bibliotecas y
museos".---Jones 441b.

VIÑAZA, Cipriano Muñoz y Manzano, Conde de la.
Bibliografía española de lenguas indígenas
de América. Madrid, "Sucesores de Rivadeneyra", 1892. 427 p.   (4781
Jones 516.

BRAZIL

LOUKOTKA, Chestmir. Linguas indigenas do Brasil; distribuição e bibliographia. (Revista
do Arquivo Municipal, São Paulo, v.54, p.
147-74, 1939)   (4782
Jones 1082.

CENTRAL AMERICA

LEHMANN, Walter. Zentral-Amerika; 1. teil. Die
sprachen Zentral-Amerikas. Berlin, D. Reimer,
1920. 595 p.   (4783
With extensive bibliographical references.
---Jones 1240.

SCHULLER, Rudolph R. Las lenguas indígenas de
Centro América, con especial atencion a los
idiomas aborígenes de Costa Rica. San José,
C.R., Impr. Nacional, 1928. 132 p.   (4784
Bibliografía: p. 129-32.---Jones 1250.

SQUIER, Ephraim George. Monograph of authors
who have written on the languages of Central
America, and collected vocabularies or composed works in the native dialects of that
country. New York, C. B. Richardson & Co.,
1861. 70 p.   (4785
Published also by Trübner & Co., London,
1861.---Jones 1254.

MEXICO

DENISON, Thomas Stewart. Mexican linguistics:
including Nahuatl or Mexican in Aryan phonology; The primitive Aryans of America; A Mexican-Aryan comparative vocabulary; Morphology
and the Mexican verb; and The Mexican-Aryan
sibilants; with an appendix on comparative
syntax. Chicago, T. S. Denison & Co., 1913.
449 p.   (4786
Contains bibliographies.---Jones 2147.

LEON, Nicolás. Las lenguas indígenas de México en el siglo XIX. Nota bibliográfica y
critica. (Anales del Museo Nacional de México, 2a. ép., t.2, p. 180-91, 1905)   (4788
Jones 2295.

MARINO FLORES, Anselmo. Bibliografía lingüística de la República Mexicana. Prologo de
Manuel Gamio. México, D.F., Instituto Indigenista Interamericano, 1957. 95 p. (Ediciones especiales)   (4789

STARR, Frederick. Recent Mexican study of the
native languages of Mexico. Chicago, The
Univ. of Chicago Pr., 1900. 19 p. (Chicago.
University. Department of Anthropology)(4790
Annotated list of 75 titles.---Jones 2519.

THOMAS, Cyrus. Indian languages of Mexico and
Central America and their geographical dis-
tribution ... assisted by John R. Swanton.
Washington, D.C., Govt. Print. Off., 1911.
108 p. (Bureau of American Ethnology.
Bulletin 44)   (4791
Issued also as House document 416, 61st
Congress, 2d session. Bibliography: p. 97-
100.---Jones 2526.

UGARTE, Salvador. Catálogo de obras escritas en lenguas indígenas de México o que tratan de ellas, de la biblioteca particular de Salvador Ugarte; prólogo de Daniel Kuri Breña. México, D.F., Edit. Jus, 1949. xxix, 221 p.   (4792
    431 publications and manuscripts listed.

-----. 2a. ed. México, D.F., Offset Vilar, 1954 [i.e., 1955] 307 p.   (4793

NORTH AMERICA

PILLING, James Constantine. Proof-sheets of a bibliography of the languages of the North American Indians. Washington, D.C., Govt. Print. Off., 1885. xl, 1135 p.   (4794
    "List of authorities": p. xi-xxxvi.---Jones 2426.

PERU

PRINCE, Carlos. Libros doctrinarios y de enseñanza en idiomas y dialectos índicos peruanos, publicados a fines del siglo XVI y durante los siglos XVII y XVIII. (Anales del Congreso Científico Latino-Americano, Buenos Aires, t.5, p. 299-360,1898) (4795
    Jones 2731.

SOUTH AMERICA

CHAMBERLAIN, Alexander Francis. Linguistic stocks of South American Indians. (American anthropologist, Lancaster, Pa., v.15, p. 236-47, 1913)   (4796
    Contains bibliographical data; see also other articles by Dr. Chamberlain in earlier and later numbers of this journal.---Jones 95.

-----. on the Puelchean and Tsonekan (Tehuelchean), the Atacameñan (Atacaman) and Chouoan, and the Charruan linguistic stocks of South America. (American anthropologist, Lancaster, Pa., n.s., v.13, p. 458-71, 1911)   (4797
    Includes bibliographies.---Jones 1418.

CHAMBERLAIN, Alexander Francis. The present state of our knowledge concerning the three linguistic stocks of the region of Tierra del Fuego, South America. (American anthropologist, Lancaster, Pa., n.s., v. 13, p. 89-98, 1911)   (4798
    "This paper, largely based on Mitre, contains a critical discussion of most of the sources for the study of the Fuegian languages" (Cooper, Bibliography of the tribes of Tierra del Fuego).---Jones 1419.

NORDENSKIÖLD, Erland. Deductions suggested by the geographical distribution of some post-Columbian words used by the Indians of S. America. Göteborg, Elanders Boktryckeri Aktiebolag, 1922. 176 p. (The author's Comparative ethnographical studies, 5) (4799
    Bibliography: p. 153-76.---Jones 338.

SUMMER Institute of Linguistics. Bibliografía de obras generales y especializadas del Instituto Lingüístico de Verano en el Perú, 1946-1959. Lima, Ministerio de Educación Pública [1959] 15 p.   (4800

TOVAR, Antonio. Catálogo de las lenguas de América del Sur; enumeración con indicaciones tipológicas, bibliografía y mapas. Buenos Aires, Edit. Sudamericana [1961] 412 p.   (4800a

VENEZUELA

CARROCERA, Cayetano de. Las lenguas indigenas de Venezuela y su classificación por familias. (Revista de las Españas, Madrid, no. 95-97, p. 316-21, 1935)   (4801
    Contains bibliography.---Jones 2895.

ROJAS, Arístides. Estudios indígenas. Contribuciones a la historia antigua de Venezuela. Caracas, Impr. Nacional, 1878. 217 p. (4802
    "Literatura de las lenguas indígenas de Venezuela": p. 153-88.---Jones 2951.

-----. -----. Caracas, Edit. Cecilio Acosta, 1941. 219 p.   (4803

GENERAL

AMERICAN Foreign Law Association. Bibliographies of foreign law series, no. 1- . New York, 1926- . (4804
 Contents:-1. Colombia, 1926. 2. Scandinavia, 1926. 3. Bolivia, 1926. 4. France, 1927. 5. Porto Rico, 1928. 6. Soviet law, 1933. 7. Dominican Republic, 1933. 8. Haiti, 1933. 9. Uruguay, 1933. 10. Curação, 1934. 11. Central American republics, 1937. ---Jones 10.

ANTOKOLETZ, Daniel. Tratado de derecho internacional público en tiempo de paz. Buenos Aires, J. Roldán y Cía., 1924-1925. 2 v. (4805
 Includes bibliographies.---Jones 17a.

BAYITCH, S. A. Guide to interamerican legal studies; a selective bibliography of works in English. Coral Gables [Fla.] University of Miami Law Library, 1957. 207 p. (4806

-----. Latin-American law, a selective bibliography of works in English for students' use. Coral Gables, 1954. Various pagings. (University of Miami Law Library. Comparative law series) (4807

BENAVIDES BALBIN, Alberto, and GARCIA RAMOS, Dagoberto. Bibliografía de derecho y ciencias políticas (1936-1950) Lima, Compañía de Impresiones y Publicidad, 1950. 111 p. (4808
 Reprinted from Boletín bibliográfico, Lima, 20 (1-2) jul. 1950.

BISHOP, Crawford M. and MARCHANT, Anyda. A guide to the law and legal literature of Cuba, the Dominican Republic, and Haiti. Washington, D.C., Govt. Print. Off., 1944. 276 p. (Library of Congress, Latin American ser. no. 3) (4809

BLEDEL, Rodolfo. Fuentes bibliográficas para el estudio del derecho angloamericano. Buenos Aires, Sección Publicaciones del Seminario de Ciencias Jurídicas y Sociales, 1940. 89 p. (Facultad de Derecho de la Universidad de Buenos Aires. Extractos del "Boletín mensual" del Seminario de Ciencias Jurídicas y Sociales, 23) (4810
 "Extracto del Boletín mensual no. 101."

BORCHARD, Edwin Montefiore. Guide to the law and legal literature of Argentina, Brazil and Chile. Washington, Govt. Print. Off., 1917. 523 p. (4811
 At head of title: Library of Congress. Reviewed by E. S. Zeballos, with bibliographical additions, in Revista de derecho, historia y letras, Buenos Aires, Jan. 1919,

BORCHARD, Edwin Montefiore. Guide...(Cont.) p. 137-141.---Jones 68.

BUENOS AIRES. Universidad. Facultad de Derecho y Ciencias Sociales. Biblioteca. Derecho administrativo. Buenos Aires, 1939. (Ser. bibliográfica, no. 10) mimeogr. (4812

-----. -----. Derecho civil: contratos. Buenos Aires, 1939, 88, 6, 10 p. (Ser. bibliográfica, no. 15) mimeogr. (4813

-----. -----. Derecho civil: derechos reales e intelectuales. Buenos Aires., 1939. 96, 16, 3, 11, 3 p. (Ser. bibliográfica, no. 13) mimeogr. (4814

-----. -----. Derecho civil: familia. Buenos Aires, 1939. 115, 4, 8 p. (Ser. bibliográfica, no. 17) mimeogr. (4815

-----. -----. Derecho civil: obligaciones. Buenos Aires, 1939. 80, 4, 8 p. (Ser. bibliográfica, no. 14) mimeogr. (4816

-----. -----. Derecho civil: parte general. Buenos Aires, 1939. 139, [1], 7, 15 p. (Ser. bibliográfica, no. 12) mimeogr. (4817

-----. -----. Derecho civil: sucesiones. Buenos Aires, 1939. 86, 3, 10 p. (Ser. bibliográfica, no. 16) mimeogr. (4818

-----. -----. Derecho comercial: quiebras. Buenos Aires, 1938. 37, 5, 2 p. (Ser. bibliográfica, no. 2) mimeogr. (4819

-----. -----. Derecho comercial: letra de cambio. Buenos Aires, 1939. 35, 5, 2 p. (Ser. bibliográfica, no. 7) mimeogr. (4820

-----. -----. Derecho comercial: marítimo. Buenos Aires, 1939. 61, 7, 4 p. (Ser. bibliográfica, no. 8) mimeogr. (4821

-----. -----. Derecho comercial: parte general - actos y contratos. Buenos Aires, 1939. 320, 9, 33 p. (Ser. bibliográfica, no. 9) mimeogr. (4822

-----. -----. Derecho de minería. Buenos Aires, 1938. 29, 4, 3, 7 p. (Ser. bibliografica, no. 1) mimeogr. (4823
 At end, 7 p.: Publicaciones editadas por la Facultad de Derecho y Ciencias Sociales de la Universidad de Buenos Aires.

-----. -----. Derecho procesal. Buenos Aires, Impr. de la Universidad, 1943. 304 p. (Ser. bibliográfica, no. 20) mimeogr. (4824

BUENOS AIRES. Universidad. Facultad de Derecho y Ciencias Sociales. Biblioteca. Derecho romano. Buenos Aires, 1938. 111, 4, 10 p. (Ser. bibliográfica, no. 5) mimeogr. (4825

-----. -----. Derecho rural. Buenos Aires, 1938. 58, 10, 3 p. (Ser. bibliográfica, no. 3) mimeogr. (4826

BUIDE LAVERDE, Ramón. Ensayo bibliográfico acerca de la evolución jurídica del foro. Santiago, 1924. 49 p. (4827
Jones 1412.

CARNEGIE ENDOWMENT for International Peace. Library. The International Commission of Jurists (Rio de Janeiro) and the codification of international law. Washington, D.C., 1933. 8 p. (Select bibliographies no.1) (4828
Compiled by Mary Alice Matthews.

CARVALHO, Oswaldo de. Bibliografia de censura intelectual. São Paulo, 1956. 32 p. (4829

-----. Bibliografia de direitos autórais. São Paulo, 1956. 20 p. mimeogr. (4830

CHECA DROUET, Benigno. La doctrina americana del uti possidetis de 1810. Lima, Gil, 1936. 154 p. (4831
Bibliografia: p. 141-46.---Jones 98.

CUBA. Secretaría de Estado. Catálogo de obras de derecho internacional e historia de América que el gobierno cubano pone a disposición, para su consulta, de los señores delegados a la Sexta Conferencia Internacional Americana. Habana, Montalvo y Cárdenas, 1928. 429 p. (4832
Jones 119.

DOMINICAN REPUBLIC. Universidad. Biblioteca. Bibliografía jurídica. [Ciudad Trujillo] n.d. 74, 8 p. (Monografias bibliográficas, no. 1) mimeogr. (4833

ESQUIVEL OBREGON, Toribio. Latin-Américan commercial law; with the collaboration of Edwin M. Borchard. New York, Banks Law Publ. Co., 1921. 972 p. (4834
Contains bibliographies.---Jones 142.

FECHNER, Erich. Publicaciones recientes sobre el derecho natural; trad. directa del alemán por Hertha Schneider. Córdoba, Arg., Impr. de la Universidad, 1950. 43 p. (Universidad Nacional de Córdoba. Facultad de Derecho y Ciencias Sociales. Instituto de Derecho Comparado, Serie B, no. 34) (4835

FUNDAÇÃO Getúlio Vargas, Rio de Janeiro. Bibliografia de direito constitucional, elaborada pelo Núcleo de Direito Público com a

FUNDAÇÃO Getúlio Vargas ... (Cont.) colaboração da Biblioteca da Fundação Getúlio Vargas. Rio de Janeiro [Impr. Nacional] 1949. 63 p. (4836

GARCIA SANTILLAN, Juan Carlos. Legislación sobre indios del Río de la Plata en el siglo XVI. Madrid, Impr. del Asilo de Huérfanos del S. C. de Jesús, 1928. 464 p. (Biblioteca de historia hispano-americana) (4837
"Apéndice de documentos y bibliografía": p. 321-448.---Jones 704.

INTER-AMERICAN Institute of International Legal Studies, Washington, D.C. Material de referencia sobre la enseñanza del derecho internacional y materias afines en Latinoamerica y Canada. Washington, D.C., 1964. 157 p. (4838
Provisional publication. Latin American journals: p. 135-41. Earlier edition, 1963, 148 p.

INTERNATIONAL Labour Office. Library. Bibliography of labour law. Geneva, 1953. 86 p. (Bibliographical contributions, 8) (4839
Arrangement by country. Latin American countries included. Rev. ed.: 1958. 104 p.

LUQUE COLOMBRES, Carlos A. Libros de derecho en bibliotecas particulares cordobesas, 1573-1810. Córdoba, Arg., Impr. de la Universidad, 1945. xvi, 78 p. (Universidad Nacional de Córdoba. Instituto de Estudios Americanistas. Cuaderno de historia, 9) (4841

MALAGON BARCELO, Javier. La literatura jurídica española del Siglo de Oro en la Nueva España; notas para su estudio. Mexico, D. F., Instituto Bibliografico Mexicano, 1959 [i.e. 1960] 173 p. (México. Biblioteca Nacional. Instituto Bibliográfico Mexicano, Publ. 3) (4842

MALUQUER Y SALVADOR, José. El derecho hispano-americano en la bibliografia española. Madrid, Impr. de la Revista de legislación, 1887. 45 p. (4843
Jones 278.

MANIZALES, Col. Universidad de Caldas. Facultad de Derecho. Biblioteca. Bibliografía sobre derecho civil. Manizales, 1963. (Ser. Bibliografias, no. 1) (4844
Cited in Boletín de adquisiciones, Medellin, p. 16, nov. 1963.

OLIVART, Ramón de Dalmau y de Olivart, marqués de. Bibliographie du droit international. Catalogue d'une bibliothèque de droit international et sciences auxiliaires; 2. éd., rev. et mise à jour. Augm. de quatre tables (auteurs, anonimes, matières et états)

OLIVART, Ramón de Dalmau y de Olivart...(Cont.)
Paris, A. Pedone, 1905-1910. 1278 p. (Bibliothèque internationale et diplomatique,
41)   (4845
Jones 343.

PÜTZ, J. Das Arbeits-, Sozial- und Investi-
tionsrecht iberoamerikanischer Länder; eine
auswohl deutscher und ausländischer veröffentlichungen. Hamburg, Ibero-Amerika Haus,
1963. 62 p. (Institut für Iberoamerika-
Kunde; Reihe "Bibliographie und dokumenta-
tion", heft 1)   (4846

PIAZZA, Luis Guillermo. Tendencias actuales
en la literatura jurídica americana. Washington, D.C., 1949. 19 p. (Columbus Memorial Library. Bibliographic ser., no.
32)   (4847
Revised edition from LEA, no. 7, p. 1-19,
1949.

RAUCHHAUPT, Friedrich Wilhelm von. Völkerrecht-
liche eigentümlichkeiten Amerikas, insbeson-
dere Hispano-Amerikas. Berlin, H. Suck,
1924. 63 p.   (4848
Bibliographical footnotes.---Jones 390.

RIO DE JANEIRO, Casa de Rui Barbosa. Centro
de Pesquisas. Textos constitucionais na
Biblioteca de Rui Barbosa. [Rio de Janeiro]
Ministério da Educação e Cultura, 1960.
370 p. (Coleção de estudos jurídicos,
3)   (4849

SCHUSTER, Edward. Guide to law and legal
literature of Central American republics.
New York, 1937. 153 p. (American Foreign
Law Association. Bibliographies of foreign
law series, no. 11)   (4850
Arranged by country, with 14 subdivisions
under each, including bibliography and historical notes.---Jones 1251.

TUCUMAN, Arg. Universidad Nacional. Instituto de Derecho Comercial. Catálogo bibliográfico sistemático-alfabético de la
sección quiebras y derecho marítimo. Tucumán, 1949. 2 v.   (4851
Compiler: Nicolás di Lella.

U.S. Library of Congress. Law Library.
Index to Latin American legislation, 1950-
1960. Boston, G. K. Hall [1961] 2 v.
(1474 p.)   (4852

-----. Legal codes of the Latin American
republics. Washington, D.C., Govt. Print.
Off., 1943. 95 p. (Latin American ser.,
no. 1)   (4853
Prepared under the direction of Crawford
M. Bishop with assistance of Anyda Marchant
and Miguel E. Vega.

VANCE, John Thomas. The background of Hispanic-
American law. Washington, D.C., The Catholic
University of America, 1937. 280 p.   (4854
Includes bibliography.---Jones 509.

-----. Another ed. New York, New Central Book
Co., 1943. vii, 296 p.   (4855

ARGENTINA

ARGENTINA. Congreso. Biblioteca. Bibliografía sobre amnistia. Buenos Aires, Sección
Publicaciones de la Biblioteca del Congreso
de la Nación, 1958. 26 p. mimeogr.   (4856

-----. -----. Derecho constitucional y derecho público provincial. Buenos Aires, 1949.
150 p. (Información bibliográfica, publ.
no. 1)   (4857

-----. -----. -----. Another ed. Buenos Aires, 1957. 113 p. (Información bibliográfica, publ. no. 13)   (4858

-----. -----. Derecho municipal. Buenos Aires, 1951. 28 p. (Información bibliográfica, publ. no. 10)   (4859

-----. -----. Propiedad intelectual. Buenos
Aires, 1951. 31 p. (Información bibliográfica, publ. no. 9)   (4860

-----. Laws, statutes, etc. Diccionario in-
dice de la legislación argentina. Buenos
Aires [1958] 3 v.   (4860a
Director: Carlos Aparicio Bayo.

-----. -----. 2a. ed. actualizada. Buenos Aires, Librería General de Tomás Pardo [1964]
4 v.   (4860b

-----. Ministerio de Justicia. Dirección General de Publicaciones. Biblioteca y Archivo.
Indice de la bibliografía jurídica; movimiento de trienio 1948-1950. Buenos Aires, 1951.
47 p.   (4861
Cited in Catálogo, Instituto Bibliotecológico, item 573.

CARDINI, Eugenio Osvaldo. La teoría de la im-
prevision en el derecho universal comparado,
en el argentino y en el nuevo proyecto de
Código civil argentino. Buenos Aires,
[Tall. Gráf. Sarmiento] 1937. 298 p. (4862
"Bibliografía general": p. 1-11. Bibliographical foot-notes.---Jones 653a.

CERMESONI, Fernando. Contratos comerciales
ante la ley. Buenos Aires, J. Menéndez,
1922. ccxxxix, 496 p.   (4863
Bibliografia: p. v-xiii.---Jones 665.

CLAGETT, Helen L. A guide to the law and
legal literature of Argentina, 1917-1946.
Washington, D.C., Govt. Print. Off., 1948.
180 p. (Library of Congress, Latin American
ser., no. 32)   (4864
    Supplement to the portion on Argentina
which appeared in Guide to the law and legal
literature of Argentina, Brazil and Chile
(1917)

COLEGIO DE ABOGADOS, Buenos Aires. Catálogo
de constituciones, códigos y leyes argentinos y extranjeros. Buenos Aires, 1931.
23 p.   (4865
    Compiled by León Canaveri.---Jones 669.

GOMEZ, Eusebio. Criminología argentina; reseña bibliográfica, precedida de un estudio
sobre el problema penal argentino. Buenos
Aires, M. A. Rosas y Cía., 1912. 286 p.(4866
    Jones 709.

LUGONES, Julio C. Guía del foro y de la bibliografía jurídica. Indice de sucesiones
convocatorias y quiebras. Bibliografía jurídica, nacional y extranjera. Buenos Aires,
1929. 263 p.   (4867
    Jones 762a.

MARTINEZ PAZ, Enrique. Sistema de filosofía
del derecho; 3a. ed. Buenos Aires, "El
Ateneo", 1940. 449 p.   (4868
    "Notas bibliográficas nacionales": p. 171-
82; "Publicaciones periódicas de filosofía
del derecho": p. 411-13; "Ensayo de una bibliografía argentina de filosofía del derecho": p. 415-18. "Referencias bibliográficas": p. 419-34.---Jones 772a.

MONSEGUR, Sylla J. El derecho internacional
privado en la República Argentina; apuntaciones bibliográficas. Ejercicio escrito
para el curso de derecho internacional privado en la Facultad de Derecho y Ciencias
Sociales de la Universidad de Buenos Aires.
Buenos Aires, Impr. de M. Biedma e Hijo,
1898. 136 p.   (4869
    Jones 786.

PAN AMERICAN UNION. Division of Law and
Treaties. Selected bibliography on legal
and related matters affecting business in
Argentina. [Washington, D.C.] 1951.
20 p.   (4870

PLANAS, José María. Ensayo bibliográfico sobre derecho fiscal. Santa Fe, 1950.
71 p.   (4870a
    Reprinted from Boletín del seminario, no.
1, 1950, de la Facultad de Ciencias Jurídicas
y Sociales, Universidad Nacional del Litoral.

RADAELLI, Sigfrido Augusto. Las fuentes de estudio del derecho patrio en las provincias.
Buenos Aires, Impr. de la Universidad, 1947.

RADAELLI, Sigfrido Augusto. ... (Cont.)
42 p. (Universidad de Buenos Aires, Facultad de Derecho y Ciencias Sociales, Instituto de Historia del Derecho Argentino, Conferencias y comunicaciones, 14)   (4871

SALVAT, Raymundo M. Tratado de derecho civil
argentino (parte general) 2a. ed. aum. y
corr. Buenos Aires, J. Menéndez, 1922, xcvi,
1082 p.   (4872
    Indice bibliográfico: p. xi-xvi.---Jones
835.

-----. 3a. ed. aum. y corr. Buenos Aires, J.
Menéndez e Hijo, 1925. civ, 1148 p.   (4873
    Indice bibliográfico: p. xv-xxi.---Jones
836.

VILARDI, Julián A. El ciclo evolutivo de nuestra constitución bibliograficamente expuesto.
Buenos Aires, 1953. [8] p.   (4874

-----. Constitución argentina; historia bibliográfica, 1810-1949. [Buenos Aires, Impr. Chi-
le] 1952. 14 p.   (4875
    Cited in Catálogo, Instituto Bibliotecológi-
co, item 608.

ZAVALIA, Clodomiro. Historia de la Corte Suprema de Justicia de la República Argentina
en relación con su modelo americano. Con
biografías de sus miembros. Buenos Aires,
"Casa J. Peuser", 1920. 415 p.   (4876
    Jones 887.

ZEBALLOS, Estanislao Severo. Bibliographie argentine de droit international privé, par
ordre chronologique. (Bulletin argentin de
droit international privé, Buenos Aires,
v.1-2, 1903-1910)   (4877
    Jones 889.

BOLIVIA

CLAGETT, Helen L. A guide to the law and
legal literature of Bolivia. Washington,
D,C., Govt. Print. Off., 1947. 110 p.
(Library of Congress, Latin American ser.,
no. 12)   (4878

DURAN PADILLA, Manuel. Bibliografía jurídica
boliviana, 1825-1954. Oruro, Edit. Universitaria, 1957. 256 p. (Biblioteca de estudios jurídicos, políticos y sociales,
3)   (4879

BRAZIL

BRAZIL. Laws, statutes, etc. Codigo penal
dos Estados Unidos do Brazil, commentado
pelo Dr. Antonio José da Costa e Silva.
São Paulo, Companhia Editora Nacional,
1930- . v.1- .   (4880

LAW

BRAZIL. Laws, statutes, etc. ... (Cont.)
Bibliographia: v.1, p. 451-81.---Jones
996.

-----. Ministério da Justiça e Negócios Interiores. Serviço de Documentação. Reforma
constitucional. [Rio de Janeiro] 1956.
78 p. (4881
Divided into sections: Bibliografia, Do-
cumentário, Referência legislativa.

OCTAVIO, Rodrigo. Evolução do direito internacional privado no Brasil. Bibliographia
brasileira do direito internacional privado
até maio de 1927. Rio de Janeiro, Impr. Nacional, 1928. 45 p. (4882
Jones 1115. Contains 69 items.

RIO DE JANEIRO. Casa de Rui Barbosa. Centro
de Pesquisas. Bibliografia brasileira de
direito constitucional, primeiras pesquisas.
[Rio de Janeiro] Ministério da Educação e
Cultura, 1956. xv, 136 p. (Coleção de estudos jurídicos, 1) (4883

CHILE

ALMEYDA, Aniceto. Libros de derecho en el
Anuario de la prensa chilena (1877-1885)
Santiago de Chile, Impr. Universitaria, 1954.
63 p. (4884

BERNASCHINA GONZALEZ, Mario. Fuentes para el
estudio de la constitución política promul-
gada el 18 de septiembre de 1925. Santiago,
Universidad de Chile, 1943. 34 p. (Publ.
del Seminario de Derecho Público de la Escuela de Ciencias Jurídicas y Sociales) (4884a

BIBLIOGRAFIA jurídica chilena (1810-1933)
(Revista de bibliografía chilena y extranjera, Santiago, t.2, p. 42-9, 150-53,
1914) (4885
Jones 1405.

CHILE. Laws, statutes, etc. Recopilación de
leyes i decretos supremos sobre colonización, 1810-1896; 2a. ed. Santiago, Impr.
Nacional, 1896. 1464 p. (4886
At head of title: Julio Zenteno Barros.
"Bibliografía de las obras i publicaciones
sobre colonización e inmigración nacional":
p. 1443-64.---Jones 1429.

CLAGETT, Helen L. A guide to the law and
legal literature of Chile. Washington, D.
C., Govt. Print. Off., 1947. 103 p. (Library of Congress, Latin American ser., no.
28) (4887

ECHEVERRIA Y REYES, Aníbal. Bibliografía de
los códigos chilenos. Santiago de Chile,
Impr. Cervantes, 1890. 31 p. (4888

ECHEVERRIA Y REYES, Aníbal. ... (Cont.)
Lists codes and commentaries. First
published in Revista forense chilena, v.6.
Later revised editions issued in the Colec-
ción de códigos de la República, Santiago,
Librería de Miranda, 1891, 1896 and 1903.---
Jones 1454.

-----. Ensayo de una biblioteca chilena de legislación y jurisprudencia. Santiago de Chile, Impr. Nacional, 1891. 155 p. (4889
Jones 1457.

SHAW, Paul Vanorden. The early constitutions
of Chile, 1810-1833. New York, Chile Publ.
Co., 1931. 181 p. (4890
Bibliography: p. 175-81.---Jones 1615.

COLOMBIA

BACKUS, Richard C, and EDER, Phanor J. A guide
to the law and legal literature of Colombia.
Washington, D.C., Govt. Print. Off., 1943.
222 p. (Library of Congress, Latin American
ser., no. 4) (4891

-----. Supplement. 1946. p. 392-410. (4892
Reprinted from Tulane law review, New Orleans, v. 20, Mar. 1946.

QUIJANO, Arturo. Bibliografía histórica del
derecho colombiano desde la publicación de
los "Derechos del hombre" por el Precursor
(1794) hasta el centenario de la muerte del
Libertador (1930) (Boletín de historia y
antigüedades, Bogotá, v.22, p. 334-52, 529-
44, 686-701, 1935) (4893
Jones 1761.

CUBA

REGÜEIFEROS BOUDET, E. Bibliografía penal de
Cuba. 1 de enero de 1901 a 26 de julio de
1926. Habana, Impr. "El Siglo XX", 1926.
64 p. (4894
Jones 1898.

DOMINICAN REPUBLIC

PAN AMERICAN UNION. Division of Law and
Treaties. Selected bibliography on legal
and related matters affecting business in
the Dominican Republic. Washington, D.C.,
1953. 5 p. (4895

ECUADOR

CLAGETT, Helen L. A guide to the law and
legal literature of Ecuador. Washington,
D.C., Govt. Print. Off., 1947. 100 p.
(Library of Congress, Latin American ser.,

CLAGETT, Helen L. A guide ... (Cont.)
no. 18)   (4896

ECUADOR. Laws, statutes, etc. Indice general
y clave de la legislación publicada en el
Registro Oficial, v.1- . Quito, Tall. Gráf.
del Ministerio del Tesoro, 1925- .   (4897
Annual, 1930-1944; semi-annual 1945- .
Compiler: J. Vicente Villota y D.

EL SALVADOR

GOMEZ, Carlos J. Bibliografía selecta del
Diario oficial, abril-junio 1952. Legisla-
ción general, banca... San Salvador, Minis-
terio de Economía, Instituto de Estudios
Económicos, Biblioteca, 1952. 46 p. (4898
Cited in HLAS, 18, item 3294.

GUATEMALA

URRUTIA, Miguel A. Indice de las leyes emiti-
das por el gobierno democrático de la República de Guatemala, desde el 3 de junio de
1871, hasta el 30 de junio de 1881. Guatemala, Tip. "El Progreso", 1882.
102 p.   (4899

MEXICO

CLAGETT, Helen L. A guide to the law and
legal literature of the Mexican states.
Washington, D.C., Govt. Print. Off., 1947.
180 p. (Library of Congress, Latin American ser., no. 13)   (4900

CRUZADO, Manuel. Bibliografía jurídica mexicana. México, D.F., Tip de la Oficina Impresora de Estampillas, 1905. 385 p.   (4901
830 titles.---Jones 2138.

-----. Memoria para la bibliografía jurídica
mexicana. México, D.F., 1894. 141 p.(4902
Jones 2140.

MEXICO. Universidad Nacional. Instituto de
Derecho Comparado. Ensayo bibliográfico de
derecho constitucional mexicano y de garan-
tías y amparo. México, D.F., Impr. Universitaria, 1947. xvii, 173 p.   (4903
Contains 1,851 entries.

ORTEGA SERRALDE, Eulalio M. Proyecto de legislación sobre propiedad artística musical
y su fundamentación. México, D. F., Impr.
Claret, 1933. 211 p.   (4904
Bibliografía: p. 207-11.---Jones 2393.

TORRE, Juan de la. Catálogo de las obras que
pueden consultarse para el estudio del derecho constitucional mexicano. (Biblioteca
jurídica mexicana, México, D.F., v.1, p. 1-8,

TORRE, Juan de la. Catálogo ... (Cont.)
1901)   (4905
Jones 2529.

-----. Guía para el estudio del derecho constitucional mexicano. La constitución de 1857,
sus adiciones, reformas y leyes orgánicas con
notas que indican las fuentes adonde debe
ocurrirse para su estudio. México, D.F., Tip
de J. V. Villada, 1886. xxiv, 392 p. (4906
Bibliografía: p. xiii-xxiv.---Jones 2530.

VANCE, John Thomas, and CLAGETT, Helen L. A
guide to the law and legal literature of Mexico. Washington, D.C., Govt. Print. Off.,
1945. 269 p. (Library of Congress, Latin
American ser., no. 6)   (4907

VILLA, Margarita de la, and ZAMBRANO, José Luis.
Bibliografía sumaria de derecho mexicano.
México, D.F., Universidad Nacional Autónoma,
1957. 200 p. (México. Universidad Nacional.
Instituto de Derecho Comparado, Ser. A: Fuen-
tes; a: Bibliografía, no. 2)   (4908

VILLASEÑOR Y VILLASEÑOR, Ramiro. La constitución en la bibliografía jalisciense. Guadalajara, 1957. 40 p. (Publ. del Gobierno
del Estado)   (4909

PANAMA

PANAMA. Laws, statutes, etc. Indices de las
leyes expedidas por la Asamblea Nacional de
Panamá, no.1 a no. 104 (año 1941) Panamá
Impr. Nacional, 1942. 88 p.   (4910
The Indices are to volumes 1-3 of the Le-
yes expedidas, 1941. Compilation by Juan
Antonio Susto.

PARAGUAY

CLAGETT, Helen L. A guide to the law and
legal literature of Paraguay. Washington,
D.C., Govt. Print. Off., 1947. 59 p. (Library of Congress, Latin American ser.,
no. 14)   (4911

PERU

CLAGETT, Helen L. A guide to the law and
legal literature of Peru. Washington, D.
C., Govt. Print. Off., 1947. 188 p. (Library of Congress, Latin American ser.,
no. 20)   (4913

DAMMERT ELGUERA, Enrique. Contribución a la
bibliografía del derecho administrativo peruano. (Boletín bibliográfico, Universidad
Mayor de San Marcos, Lima, t.3, p. 317-42,
1928)   (4914
Includes: "Lista detallada de los periódi-

DAMMERT ELGUERA, Enrique. ... (Cont.)
cos oficiales publicados en el Perú."---
Jones 2650.

PUERTO RICO

DAVILA LANAUSSE, José Nilo. Bibliotheca legum
portoricensis, colletanea jurídica; biblio-
grafía legal selecta de Puerto Rico, siglos
XIX-XX. [San Juan] Colegio de Abogados de
Puerto Rico [1962] 505 p.   (4915
Thesis presented at the University of
Puerto Rico.

URUGUAY

CLAGETT, Helen L. A guide to the law and
legal literature of Uruguay. Washington,
D.C., Govt. Print. Off., 1947. 123 p.
(Library of Congress, Latin American ser.,
no. 26)   (4916

PALAMARCHUK, Anatolio, and BACCINO PONS, Víctor. Bibliografía jurídica del Uruguay;
prólogo por Eduardo J. Couture. Montevideo
[Bianchi Altuna] 1956-1963. 2 v. (v.1:
497 p.; v.2: 791 p.) (Biblioteca de publicaciones oficiales de la Facultad de Derecho y Ciencias Sociales, Sección III, 85,
123)   (4917

PALAMARCHUK, Anatolio, and BACCINO...(Cont.)
Contains 3,338 items in v.1; 5,056 in v.2.

VENEZUELA

CALDERA RODRIGUEZ, Rafael. Derecho del trabajo; ensayo de una exposición doctrinal de
la materia analizando la situación venezolana y la legislación y jurisprudencia venezolana. Caracas, Tip. La Nación, 1939.
867 p.   (4918
Bibliografía: p. 843-56.---Jones 2893a.

CARACAS. Biblioteca de los Tribunales del Distrito Federal Fundación Rojas Astudillo.
Bibliografía jurídica venezolana, derecho
civil. Caracas, Edit. Sucre, 1958.
132 p.   (4919
Separata del Boletín de la Biblioteca de
los Tribunales del Distrito Federal, no. 8,
en. 1958.

CLAGETT, Helen L. A guide to the law and
legal literature of Venezuela. Washington,
D.C., Govt. Print. Off., 1947. 128 p.
(Library of Congress, Latin American ser.,
no. 16)   (4920

GRASES, Pedro. Contribucion a la bibliografía
venezolana del derecho constitucional. [Ca-
racas, 1961] 44 p. mimeogr.   (4920a

LIBRARIES

FOR THE BLIND

BIBLIOTECA Argentina para Ciegos, Buenos Aires.
Catalogue of books in Spanish Braille in the
Biblioteca Argentina para Ciegos. Buenos
Aires, n.d.   (4920b
In Braille type.

PRIVATE

ABADIANO, Eufemio. Catalogue of a portion of
the remarkable library of Señor Eufemio Abadiano... consisting more particularly of Mexicana, and works relating to Central and
South America...Mexican history, biography
and discovery...Mexican hieroglyphics and
dialects...also: general literature and other
Americana. [New York, D. Taylor, 1888]
42 p.   (4921
Jones 2024.

AGREDA Y SANCHEZ, José María de. Catálogo de
su biblioteca. México, D.F., 1916.
594 p.   (4922
Alberto María Carreño in Semblanzas, v.1,
p.55, says "la mayor parte la adquirió el

AGREDA Y SANCHEZ, José María de ... (Cont.)
distinguido historiador Genaro García."

BABELON, Jean. La bibliothèque française de
Fernand Colomb, ouvrage pub. sous les aus-
pices de la Société Française de Bibliogra-
phie. Paris, E. Champion, 1913. 340 p.
(Revue des bibliothèques. Suppl. X) (4923
Catalogue critique des livres en langue
française de la bibliothèque de Fernand
Colomb; 276 entries.---Jones 447b.

BARLOW, Samuel Latham Mitchill. Catalogue
of the American library of the late S. L.
M. Barlow, prepared by James Osborne Wright.
New York, 1889. 450, 17 p.   (4924
List of prices: 17 p.---Jones 42. Intro-
duction by Henry Harrisse.

BECU, Teodoro. Catálogo de la Biblioteca
Teodoro Becú. Buenos Aires, Tall. Gráf.
Osvaldo Miller, 1950-1951. 2 v.   (4925
Compiled by Raul Rosarivo.

BEECHE, Gregorio Miguel Pascual de. Bibliografía americana. Estudios i catálogo completo
i razonado de la biblioteca americana colec-

BEECHE, Gregorio Miguel Pascual de...(Cont.)
cionada por el Sr. Gregorio Beéche (cónsul
jeneral de la República Arjentina en Chile)
por B. Vicuña Mackenna. Valparaíso, Impr.
del Mercurio, 1879. 802 p.   (4926
    Jones 49.

PERETTA Y CIA. Catálogo de los libros que for-
maron parte de la biblioteca del Dr. R. Saenz
Peña. [Buenos aires,1919..]   (4927

BERLINCK, Cassius. Catalogo da " liotheca de
Francisco Ramos Paz. Rio de Janeiro, Typ.
d'"O Imparcial", 1920. 420, 2 p.   (4928
    Cited in Reis, item 321; Jones 1019a.

-----. Supplemento. Rio de Janeiro, Typ. do
Jornal do Commercio, de Rodrigues & Cia.,
1920. 100 p.   (4929
    Cited in Reis, item 322.

BIBLIOTECA mexicana. Mexlibris. Libros sobre Mexico exclusivamente. México, D.F.,
1930. 86 p.   (4930
    Millares, item 1434, notes that the items
    included in this catalog came from the Nico-
    lás León Library.

BLISS, Porter Cornelius. Catalogue of the library of the late Porter C. Bliss, including
his very rare collection of Spanish Americana and Mexicana, sold July 27th and 28th,
1885. Geo. A. Leavitt & Co., auctioneers.
New York, 1885. 100 p.   (4931
    Jones 2085.

BRAZIL. Biblioteca Nacional. Catalogo da
colleção Salvador de Mendonça. Rio de Janeiro, Off. Typ. da Bibliotheca Nacional,
1906. 126 p. .   (4932
    "Extr. do v. 27 dos Annaes da Bibliotheca
    Nacional".---Jones 1163.

-----. Ministerio das Relações Exteriores.
Catalogo da coleção Visconde do Rio-Branco.
[Rio de Janeiro] Instituto Rio Branco
[1950] 2 v. (v.1: 508 p.; v.2: 508,
lxxxiv p.)   (4933
    Some 5,122 manuscripts are described.

BREVOORT, James Carson. A collection of rare
Americana, including the remainder of the
notable library...to be sold at auction.
New York, Bangs & Co. [1890] 202 p.(4934
    Comprises early books in various langua-
    ges relating to the discovery, voyages and
    travels, etc. Includes Brazil, Mexico,
    Peru, etc.

BRISEÑO, Ramón. Catálogo de la biblioteca
chileno-americana de don Ramón Briseño.
Santiago de Chile, Impr. Gutenberg, 1889.
376 p.   (4935
    Compiler: Luis Montt.---Jones 1406.

BRISEÑO, Ramón. Catálogo razonado de la biblio-
teca chileno-americana de don Ramón Briseño.
Santiago de Chile, Impr. de "La Estrella de
Chile", 1874. 105 p.   (4936
    Jones 1408.

BROWN, John Carter. Bibliographical notices of
rare and curious books relating to America in
the library of the late John Carter Brown...
by John Russell Bartlett. Providence, Printed for private distribution [by H. O. Houghton and Co.; Cambridge] 1875-1882. 2v.(4937
    Jones 74.

-----. Bibliotheca americana. A catalogue of
books relating to North and South America in
the library of John Carter Brown, with notes
by John Russell Bartlett. Providence, 1865-
1871. 3 pt. in 4 v.   (4938
    Jones 75. Now available in microprint: edi-
    tion of 1871-1875.

-----. -----. Providence, 1875-1882.   (4939
    Second edition of part I-II (first publish-
    ed 1865-1866) enlarged.---Jones 76.

BROWN UNIVERSITY. John Carter Brown Library.
Bibliotheca americana; catalogue of the John
Carter Brown library in Brown University.
Providence, Printed by the Library, 1919-1931.
3 v. in 5 v.   (4940
    Jones 77.

BULLRICH, Adolfo. y Cía, Buenos Aires. Catálogo del primer remate de la biblioteca de D.
Antonio Santamarina: diarios, periodicos,
revistas, boletines, almanaques, anuarios,
calendarios y otras publicaciones. Buenos
Aires, 1955. unpaged.   (4941
    Contains 1039 items.

BUSCHIAZZO, Juan A., and BUSCHIAZZO, Juan Carlos. Catálogo; biblioteca de los arquitectos Juan A. y Juan Carlos Buschiazzo.
[Buenos Aires] 1917. 71 p.   (4942
    Cited in Catálogo, Instituto Bibliotecoló-
    gico, item 924.

CASA RAMON EYZAGUIRRE, Santiago. Gran remate
de la notable biblioteca de la Sucesión de
don Miguel Varas Velázquez. Santiago, oct.
y nov. de 1948. 288 p.   (4943

CATALOGO de la biblioteca de Manuel Molina.
Buenos Aires, Impr. Tragant, 1917.
261 p.   (4945
    Cited in Binayán, item 115, who enters
    Molina in the index as "Molina, Manuel J.

CATALOGO de la Biblioteca Varnhagen. Santiago
de Chile, Imprensa, 1904.   (4946
    Includes 4972 items. Cited in Reis, item
    201.

CATALOGO de la sección de historia y geografía de America. Biblioteca de Jorge Pombo. Obras escogidas. Bogotá, Impr. La Idea, 1906. 60 p. (4947
A large part of this collection is now in the John Crerar Library in Chicago. Cited in Giraldo Jaramillo, p. 66.

CATALOGO de libros pertenecientes a la biblioteca particular del señor Antonio Reyes Otero. Bogotá, Tip. Regina, n.d. 70 p. (4948
Cited in Giraldo Jaramillo, p. 66.

CATALOGO dos livros pertencentes a Joaquim Nabuco. Parte primeira: Brasil-America. Rio de Janeiro, Impr. Nacional, 1924. 115 p. (4949
Cited in Reis, item 354.

CATALOGO dos livros que pertenceram ao sabio Doutor Lund. Rio de Janeiro, Typ. de L. Winter, 1886. 7 p. (4950
Cited in Reis, item 121.

CATALOGUE de la Bibliothèque Eduardo Prado. São Paulo, 1916. (4951
Cited in Reis, item 294.

CATALOGUE de la collection préciuse de la bibliothèque de feu Serge Sobolewsky de Moscou. Leipzig, List et Francke, 1873. xviii, 314 p. (4952
Cited in Giraldo Jaramillo, p. 68.

CAVALCANTI, João Alcides Bezerra. Conferencias. Rio de Janeiro? 1929. 173 p. (4953
A bibliotheca de Oliveira Lima.---Jones 976.

CHAUMETTE DES FOSSES, Jean Baptiste Gabriel Amédée. Catalogue des livres imprimés et manuscrits composant la bibliothèque de M. A. Chaumette des Fossés. Paris, 1842. (4954
2,079 titles, chiefly Peruvian.---Jones 2645.

CHILE. Biblioteca Nacional. Catálogo alfabético i por materias de las obras que contiene la Biblioteca Nacional Egaña de Santiago de Chile. Santiago, Impr. de la Sociedad Egaña, 1860. 149 p. (4955
The collection of Mariano Egaña, containing some 9,000 volumes, was acquired by the Biblioteca Nacional en 1846.---Jones 1597.

-----. -----. Catálogo breve de la Biblioteca Americana que obsequia a la Nacional de Santiago J. T. Medina. Santiago, 1930. 104 p. (4056
Compiler: V. M. Chiappa.

-----. -----. Catálogo breve de la Biblioteca Americana que obsequia a la Nacional de

CHILE. Biblioteca Nacional. ... (Cont.) Santiago J. T. Medina - Libros impresos. Santiago, Impr. Universitaria, 1926. 2 v. (4957
Jones 1598. The first volume was compiled by José Toribio Medina and the second with the collaboration of Guillermo Feliú Cruz.

-----. -----. -----. Suplemento. Santiago, Impr. Universitaria, 1953-1954. 2 v. (4957a

-----. -----. Catálogo breve de la Biblioteca Americana que obsequia a la Nacional de Santiago J. T. Medina. - Manuscritos. Santiago de Chile, Impr. Universitaria, 1928-1951. 4 v. (4958
Begins with v. 84 (doc. 1051) of the Medina collection, the text of the other manuscripts having been published previously by Medina (Colección de documentos inéditos para la historia de Chile, 1888-1902. 30 v.) An index to this serving also as an introductory volume to the present catalog was issued by the Library in 1930 under title: Catálogo breve de la Biblioteca Americana, tomo preliminar, compiled by V. M. Chiappa.
Contents: - v.1, Documentos inéditos para la historia de Chile, 1535-1720. - v.2; Documentos inéditos para la historia de Chile, 1720-1827. - v.3, Manuscritos originales. - v.4, Manuscritos inéditos para la historia de Chile, 1501-1900. v.1-2, 4, compiled by G. Feliú Cruz; v.3, by J. T. Medina. Jones item 1599, 1600

-----. -----. Catálogo de la librería legada por Monseñor Eyzaguirre a la Biblioteca Nacional. Santiago, 1876. 111 p. (4959
Cited in Briseño, v.2, p.43.

CHILE. Instituto Nacional. Catálogo preliminar de la sección Biblioteca Pedro Montt, donada en noviembre de 1911 por la señora Sara del Campo, v. de Montt. Santiago de Chile, Impr. "Barcelona", 1912. 298 p. (4960
Jones 1428.

CHURCH, Elihu Dwight. A catalogue of books relating to the discovery and early history of North and South America forming a part of the library of E. D. Church. Compiled and annotated by George Watson Cole. New York, Dodd, Mead and Co., 1907. 5 v. (4961
Jones 100. Now available in microprint.

-----. -----. New York, P. Smith, 1951. 5 v. facsims. (4962
Reprint of the 1907 edition.

CIRCULO Carboneliano, Montevideo. Catalogo de los libros del fundador de la eubiosis J. Fernando Carbonell. Montevideo, Renacimiento, 1924. 42 p. (4963
Cited in Musso 240.

CUBA. Biblioteca Nacional. Donativo Bustamante. Catálogo de derecho internacional.
Vol. I. Habana, Impr. de la Biblioteca Nacional, 1917. 47 p.   (4964
    Jones item 1826. "Advertencia" signed:
D. Figarola-Caneda, director. Reprinted
from the Revista de la Biblioteca Nacional,
t.5, p. 46-55; t.7, p. 124-33, 1911-1912.

-----. Congreso. Cámara de Representantes.
Biblioteca. Catálogo de la Biblioteca del
Dr. Antonio Govín y Torres, donada por sus
herederos a la Biblioteca de la Cámara de
Representantes de la República de Cuba.
Tomo I. Habana, 1924. 322 p.   (4965
    Compiler: L. M. Pérez.---Jones 1807.

-----. -----. Catálogo de la biblioteca del
Dr. Gonzalo de Quesada y Aróstegui, donada
por sus herederos a la Biblioteca de la
Cámara de Representantes de la República
de Cuba. Habana, 1927. 186 p.   (4966
    Jones 1808.

DECOUD, José Segundo. Biblioteca de J. S.
Decoud, estadista del Paraguay. Buenos
Aires, E. Spinelli, 1912. 465 p.   (4967
    Contains some 3,500 titles, of which 400
refer to Paraguay.---Jones 2603.

DOLGE, Rudolf. Borradores preliminares de
los trabajos intitulados: Materiales de
la colección Dolge para la bibliografía
venezolana. Caracas, 1940. 15 v.   (4968
    Typewritten catalog.---Jones 2906a.

-----. Entregas "Colección Dolge", no. 1-
112. [Caracas, 1945] 7 v. mimeogr.   (4969
    In the Anuario bibliográfico venezola-
no, 1949/1954, item 6421, is noted "Listas de los libros adquiridos en compra
por la Biblioteca Nacional".

ECHEVERRIA Y REYES, Aníbal. Doctor d'Alaer.
Bibliotheca Thebusseana. 1789. 30,
5 p.   (4970
    Cited in Laval, item 104.

FIELD, Thomas Warren. An essay towards an
Indian bibliography. Being a catalogue
of books, relating to the history, antiquities, languages, customs, religion,
wars, literature, and origin of the American Indians in the library of Thomas W.
Field. New York, Scribner, Armstrong
and Co., 1873. 430 p.   (4971
    Jones 145.

-----. -----. Facsimile edition. 1951.
430 p.   (4972
    Cited in HLAS 18, item 6. Contains
1,708 entries.

FIGAROLA CANEDA, Domingo. Indice de los títulos contenidos en las diversas coleccio-

FIGAROLA CANEDA, Domingo. Indice... (Cont.)
nes facticias de la biblioteca adquirida por
compra hecha al Sr. Dr. Vidal Morales. Habana, Impr. de la Biblioteca Nacional, 1905.
64 p.   (4973
    Jones 1827.

GOUPIL, E. Eugène. Catalogue de la Bibliothèque américaine du feu M. E. Eugène Goupil.
Livres anciens imprimés au Mexique, ouvrages
ayant trait a l'histoire, a la ethnographie
et a la linguistique de diverses contrées de
l'Amerique. (Avan-propos de E. Boban -
Albert Reville: Antiquités mexicaines. Les
aventures d'une collection) Paris, 1899.
xviii, 114 p.   (4974
    "La bibliothèque américaine de feu M. E.
Eugène Goupil a éte...formée au Mexique par
feu M. J. A. Aubin".

GUERRICO Y WILLIAMS, Publisher. Notable biblioteca del Dr. Clemente Leoncio Fregeiro.
[Lima, Tall. Gráf. A. García y Cía., 1931.
448 p.]   (4975

HEREDIA, Ricardo. Catalogue de la bibliothèque de M. Ricardo Heredia, comte de Benahavis. Paris, E. Paul, L. Huard et Guillemin,
1891-1894. 4 v.   (4976
    8,304 titles; includes the library ori-
ginally collected by Vicente Salvá y Pérez,
purchased by Heredia. Cataloged by Manuel
R. Zarco del Valle and M. Menéndez y Pelayo.---Jones 199.

INSUA, Manuel, and REY TOSAR, Manuel. Catálogo razonado. Libros, folletos y mapas en
su mayoría referentes a Hispano-América,
pertenecientes a la biblioteca de Enrique
Arana. Buenos Aires, 1935. 369 p.   (4977
    Jones 215a.

JUDICIAL de la biblioteca que perteneció a la
Sucesión del Doctor Andrés Lamas. Catálogo
3o., serie 2a., lote O. El remate se efec-
tuará el 5 de noviembre y días hábiles siguientes a las 8 de la noche, 1905. [Bue-
nos Aires, 1905] 143 p.   (4978
    Cited in Binayán, item 116.

KENNETT, White. Bibliothecae americanae primordia, An attempt towards laying the foundation of an American library, in several
books, papers, and writings, humbly given
to the Society for the Propagation of the
Gospel in Foreign Parts... By a menber of
the Propagation of the Gospel in Foreign
Parts... By a member of the said Society.
London, Printed for G. Churchill, 1713.
275 p., 112 1.   (4979
    Jones 236.

-----. Catalogue of the remaining portion of
the famous collection of early Americana,
formed by the Right Rev. White Kennett, D.

KENNETT, White. Catalogue of ... (Cont.)
D. (1660-1728) bishop of Peterborough, and
given by him in 1712 to the Society for the
Propagation of the Gospel in Foreign Parts.
Sold by order of the Society under a scheme
authorised by the Charity Commissioners of
England... Also of certain other books
bequeathed at different times to the Society... Which will be sold by auction by
Messrs. Sotheby, Wilkinson & Hodge auctioneers, the 30th of July, 1917. [London]
Dryden Pr., J. Davy & Sons [1917]
36 p.   (4980
    Jones 237.

-----. The Primordia of Bishop White Kennett,
the first English bibliography on America.
Introductory study by Frederick R. Goff.
Washington, D.C., Pan American Union, 1959
[i.e., 1960] xliv, 275, [224] p.   (4981
    A publication of the Inter-American Com-
mittee on Bibliography.

LEITE, Solidonio Atico. Catalogo annotado
da Bibliotheca de Solidonio Leite. Primeira parte. Classicos do Catalogo da Academia. Rio de Janeiro, Editores J. Leite &
C [1923?] 377, xxxiv p.   (4982
    Cited in Reis, item 350. The Library of
Congress establishes item as an open entry:
1922?-

LEON, Nicolás. Biblioteca mexicana. Catálogo para la venta de la porciòn màs escogida
de la biblioteca del Dr. Nicolás León.
Sección 1a., Filología mexicana, impresos
mexicanos del siglo XVI y libros ejemplares
únicos conocidos. México, D.F., Impr. de
"El Tiempo", 1896. [2] 37 p.   (4983
    Cited in Millares, item 1432.

-----. -----. Catálogo no.2 para la venta a
precios marcados, del resto de la biblioteca del Doctor Nicolás León. México, D.F.,
Impr. "Cuauhtémoc", de Daniel Cabrera,
1897. 40 p.   (4984
    Cited in Millares, item 1433.

LIMA. Universidad Nacional Mayor de San Marcos. Catálogo del donativo Francisco García Calderon. Lima, 1954. 53 p.
mimeogr.   (4984a
    Cited in Anuario bibliográfico peruano,
1957/1959, item 2135.

LOWERY, Woodbury. The Lowery collection. A
descriptive list of maps of the Spanish
possessions within the present limits of
the United States, 1502-1820. Ed. with
notes by Philip Lee Phillips. Washington,
D.C., Govt. Print. Off., 1912. x,
567 p.   (4985
    Mr. Lowery left his collection of maps to
the Library of Congress. "The monograph
describes 750 maps, of which there are 306

LOWERY, Woodbury. The Lowery ... (Cont.)
in the Lowery collection of maps, 206 not in
the collection but in the Map Division of the
Library, and 184 in neither one nor the other"
(p. vi).---Jones 267.

MEDINA, José Toribio. Biblioteca americana.
Catálogo breve de mi colección de libros relativos a la America Latina; con un ensayo
de bibliografía de Chile durante el período
colonial. Santiago, Typis Authoris, 1888.
478 p.   (4986
    Jones 299. 2,928 items listed.

-----. Catálogo de la colección de mapas, planos y vistas relativos a Chile de la biblioteca de J. T. Medina. Santiago de Chile,
Impr. en Casa del Autor, 1889. 254 p. (4987
    Cited in Ochsenius, item 120; also in
Schaible, item 53.

MORENO, José Fernandes. Bibliotecas jurídicas
particulares; 2. tiragem. [São Paulo, Tip.
Rio Branco, 1936. 18 p.]   (4988
    Jones 1103.

MUÑOZ MORENO, Rafael. Catálogo de los libros,
manuscritos, pinturas, museo y muebles que
fueron de la propiedad del extinto escritor
público Sr. D. Agustín Rivera. León de Al-
damas, 1920. 58 p.   (4989
    Cited in González, item 184.

OLIVERA, Ricardo. Biblioteca del Doctor Ricardo Olivera. Obras selectas de literatura,
arte e historia. Buenos Aires, Comp. Impresora Argentina, 1950. 269 p.   (4990
    Listing of 2,395 titles in auction catalog,
prepared by María Olivera de Pocorobba.

PACHECO, Felix. O valor immenso da bibliotheca brasiliense do Dr. J. Carlos Rodrigues
(Collecção Christiano Ottoni, da Bibliotheca
Nacional) porto em relevo pelos ultimos catalogos de venda na Europa. Lisboa, 1930.
101 p.   (4991
    Cited in Reis, item 401.

PARRABERE, Arnaldo Pedro. Bibliografía de las
obras publicadas en libros, folletos, hojas,
revistas, y documentos del Excmo. e Ilmo. Sr.
Dr. Mariano Soler, primer Arzobispo de Montevideo; coleccionados y existentes en la
biblioteca y archivo de Arnaldo Pedro Parrabere. Montevideo, Tall. Gráf. "Sur" [1942]
47 p.   (4992

PEÑAFIEL, Antonio. Bibliothek des Dr. Antonio
Peñafiel, herausgeber der "Monumentos del
arte mexicano antiguo". Berlin, J. A. Stargardt, 1912. 89 p.   (4993
    Jones 2415.

PEREZ DE VELASCO, Francisco. Catálogo de la
Biblioteca peruana. Lima, Gil, 1918.

PEREZ DE VELASCO, Francisco ... (Cont.)
195 p.   (4994
  Jones 2717. This collection now is nearly
all in Duke University Library.

PEREZ VILA, Manuel. La biblioteca del Libertador. Caracas, 1960. 27 p.   (4995

PINEDA, Anselmo. Biblioteca del ex-coronel
Pineda, o colección de publicaciones hechas
en el Virreinato de Santa Fe y en las repúblicas de Colombia y Nueva Granada, desde
1774 a 1850, y de varios manuscritos nacionales, e impresos extranjeros, relacionados
con los negocios de la republica anteriores,
contemporáneos y posteriores a la revolución
de 1810. Bogotá, Impr. de El Tradicionista,
1872-1873. 2 v.   (4997
  Jones 1758.

POMBO, Jorge. Biblioteca de Jorge Pombo.
Catálogo de la Sección Historia y Geografía
de America (obras escogidas) 1906. Bogotá,
Impr. de "La Idea", 1906. 60 p.   (4998
  Jones 378. Winston L. Yang notes that
most of these materials are in the John
Crerar Library, Chicago.

ROBERTSON, James Alexander. The Oliveira Lima collection of hispanoamericana. (Hispanic American historical review, Baltimore,
v.3, p. 78-83, 1920)   (4999
  Jones 1176.

RODRIGUES, José Carlos. Bibliotheca brasiliense; catalogo annotado dos livros sobre
o Brasil e de alguns autographos e manuscriptos pertencentes a J. C. Rodrigues.
Rio de Janeiro, Typ. do "Jornal do Commercio", 1907. v.1, (680 p.)   (5000
  Pte. 1: Descobrimento da America; Brasil
colonial, 1492-1822.---Jones 1177.

SALVA Y PEREZ, Vicente. Catálogo de la biblioteca de Salvá, escrito por d. Pedro
Salvá y Mallén, y enriquecido con la descripción de otras muchas obras, de sus ediciones, etc. Valencia, Impr. de Ferrer de
Orga, 1872. 2 v.   (5001
  The collection (4,070 items) was acquired
by Ricardo Heredia, conde de Benahavis;
much enlarged (8,304 lots) it was sold at
auction 1891-1894. An index to the Salvá
and Heredia catalogs, compiled by G. Molina Navarro, was published in Madrid, 1913.
---Jones 427. Now available in microprint.

SANTOS, José dos. Catalogo da importante e
preciosissima livraria que pertenceu aos
notaveis escritores e bibliofilos condes de
Azevedo e de Samodães...redigido por José
dos Santos, com uma introdução pelo erudito
escritor e bibliofilo sr. Anselmo Braamcamp
Freire. Porto, Empresa Literaria e Tipogra-
fica, 1921. 2 v.   (5002

SANTOS, José dos. Catalogo ... (Cont.)
  Illustrated and annotated author catalogue,
useful for old Portuguese and Brazilian works.
---Jones 1185a.

SANTOS, Manoel dos. Bibliografia geral ou des-
crição bibliografica de livros tanto de autores portugueses como brasileiros e muitos de
outras nacionalidades impressos desde e seculo XV até a actualidade, com a marcação dos
respectivos preços de venda. Dá se igualmen-
te noticia de muitos manuscritos de evidente
interesse para a historia do Brasil e das pos-
sessoes portuguesas, etc. Lisboa, Tip. Mendonça, 1914- . v.1- .   (5003
  Jones 1186.

SOUZA, Manuel Nogueira de. Bibliotheca brasiliense. Selecta. Catalogo de uma preciosa
colecção de livros, gravuras e mappas, referentes ao Brasil, em especial e a America Latina em geral, que pertencem ao ... Dr. Alfredo de Carvalho. Recife, Livr. Economia,
Manoel Nogueira de Souza, 1916. 258 p.(5004
  Cited in Reis, item 297.

SQUIER, Ephraim George. Catalogue of the library of E. G. Squier. Edited by Joseph Sabin. New York, C. C. Shelley, 1876.
277 p.   (5005
  Jones 460.

STETSON, John Batterson. The John B. Stetson
collection of Hispanic and other Americana.
New York, Parke-Bernet Galleries, 1953.
3 pts.   (5006
  Some 1,400 items most of which refer to
Latin America offered for sale at public
auction.

STEVENS, Henry. Bibliotheca historica; or,
A catalogue of 5,000 volumes of books and
manuscripts relating chiefly to the history
and literature of North and South America,
among which is included the larger propor-
tion of the extraordinary library of the
late Henry Stevens. Boston, H. O. Houghton
and Co., 1870. 234 p.   (5007
  2,455 titles.---Jones 461.

-----. Historical nuggets. Bibliotheca Americana; or, A descriptive account of my collection of rare books relating to America.
London, Printed by Whittingham and Wilkins,
1862. 2 v.   (5008
  First printed in 1857 and a few copies circulated.---Jones 463.

-----. -----. By Henry Stevens... and Henry
Newton Stevens. Second series, v.1 (v.3 of
the whole work) London, H. Stevens & Son,
1885. 2 pt. in 1v.   (5009
  Two "Specimen parts" of a new catalog,
planned to be complete in 8 vols., and to
supplement the two volumes which appeared

STEVENS, Henry. Historical... (Cont.)
under the same title in 1862. 3,612 titles
(A-Backus) No more published.---Jones 464.

TARIFFI, Terzo. Los clásicos griegos de Francisco Miranda. Caracas, Tip. Americana,
1950. 26 p.   (5010
Collection now in the Biblioteca Nacional.

VENEZUELA. Ministerio de Instrucción Pública.
Memoria. Caracas, 1935.   (5011
"Libros donados a la Academia Nacional de
la Historia por el Sr. Don Rodolfo Dolge"
(560 titles): p. 442-511.---Jones 2971a.

WARDEN, David Baillie. Bibliotheca Americana,
being a choice collection of books relating
to North and South America and the West
Indies, including voyages to the southern

WARDEN, David Baillie. Bibliotheca... (Cont.)
hemisphere. Paris, 1831. 138 p.   (5012
This collection "Was purchased by the state
of New York. It numbers 1,118 works, beginning with the Translation of Munster by Belle-
forest (ed. of 1570) and, with the exception
of some rare charts, does not contain anything
of special interest to bibliographers."
(Harrisse, B.A.V., p. xxvi).---Jones 523.

-----. Bibliotheca Americana, being a choice
collection of books relating to North and
South America and the West-Indies, including
voyages to the southern hemisphere, maps,
engravings and medals. Paris, 1840.
124 p.   (5013
Second library of Americana collected by
Warden; 1,979 v. Acquired by the New York
State Library in 1845.

LIBRARY SCIENCE

ARAUJO, H. Carlos. Bibliografía sobre bibliotecnia; obras existentes en bibliotecas uruguayas. Montevideo, 1952. 47 p.
mimeogr.   (5015

A BIBLIOGRAPHY of works in Spanish and Portuguese on library science. n.d. [14 p.]
mimeogr.   (5016
With few exceptions items in the bibliography refer to Latin American imprints.

BOGOTA. Universidad Javeriana. Facultad de
Ingeniería Civil. Libros de consulta en la
Biblioteca de la Universidad. Bogotá,
1961.   (5017
Cited in Boletín de adquisiciones, Me-
dellín, no. 10, p. 20, oct. 1963.

BOUILLIN, Celeste. Concepto sobre libro o
folleto; con un apéndice bibliográfico sobre temas bibliotecológicos. [Buenos Aires]
1956. p. 47-55.   (5018
Cited in Catálogo, Instituto Bibliotecológico, item 390.

BRAZIL. Serviço de Intercambio de Catalogação.
Catálogo de fichas bibliográficas impresas,
set. de 1942-set. de 1946. Rio de Janeiro,
1948. 412 p.   (5019

-----. Supl. no.1. Rio de Janeiro, 1953.
257 p.   (5020

-----. Supl. no.2. Rio de Janeiro, 1953.
254 p.   (5021

CARVALHO, Oswaldo de. Bibliografia brasileira
de biblioteconomia. Ed. preliminar. São
Paulo, 1959. ix, 97 p.   (5022

COLOMBIA. Ministerio de Educación Nacional.
Sección de Servicios Bibliotecarios. Bibliografía bibliotecológica fundamental. Bogotá,
1963. (Divulgaciones bibliotecológicas,
no. 8)   (5023
Cited in Boletín de adquisiciones, Medellín,
no. 11, p. 15, nov. 1963.

COMPANHIA de Seguros de Vida "Previdencia do
Sul", Pôrto Alegre. Biblioteca. Bibliografía de obras de biblioteconomía e referencia,
organizada e compilada por Lygia Vianna Barbosa e Juliana Vianna Rosa. Pôrto Alegre,
1958. 25 p. mimeogr.   (5024

DANIELS, Marietta. La biblioteca pública en
América; una bibliografía selecta. Washington, D.C., Unión Panamericana, 1951.
56 p. (Columbus Memorial Library. Bibliographic ser., no. 34)   (5025

-----. Bibliotecas infantiles y escolares;
una bibliografía. Washington, D.C., Unión
Panamericana, 1955. 20 p. (Columbus Memorial Library. Bibliographic ser., no.
45)   (5026

-----. Lista preliminar de obras de bibliotecología en español esenciales para la organización y administración de bibliotecas y
la preparación de bibliotecarios. Washington, D.C., Unión Panamericana, 1961.
19 p. Ditto reproduction.   (5027

FINO, José Federico. Elementos de bibliología.
Buenos Aires, "Coni", 1940. 368 p.   (5028
Bibliografías universales: p. 281-87.
Lista de obras a consultarse: p. 337-48.---
Jones 694a.

FINO, José Federico, and HOURCADE, Luis A.
Tratado de bibliotecología, historia y técnica de producción de los documentos. Santa
Fe, Castellví, [1954] 382 p. (Serie bibliotecológica, 3)   (5029
New edition of the author's Elementos de
bibliología.

FLOREN LOZANO, Luis. Bibliografía bibliotecol-
lógica colombiana. Bogotá, 1954. 4 l.,
10 p. (Centro Interamericano de Vivienda y
Planeamiento, Ser. bibliográfica, no.
2)   (5030

-----. -----. 1953/1955, 1956/1958, hasta
1960, 1961-1962. Bogotá, 1956-1964. 4 v.
(Manuales de bibliografía y documentación
colombiana, 1)   (5031

-----. Bibliografía bibliotecológica dominicana, 1930-mayo 1952. Ciudad Trujillo, Editora Librería Dominicana, 1952. 28 p. (Materiales para el estudio de la cultura dominicana, 8)   (5032

-----. Bibliografía dominicana; obras de referencia. [Santo Domingo, 1954] xv p.
(Anales, Universidad de Santo Domingo, 60/
70, en./jun. 1954)   (5033
Extract.

-----. Obras de referencia y generales de la
bibliografía colombiana; materiales de clase para el curso B-14 bibliografía. Medellín, Escuela Interamericana de Bibliotecol-
logía, 1960. iv, 76 p.   (5034

FONSECA, Edson Nery da. Bibliografia de obras
de referência pernambucanas. Recife, Impr.
Universitaria, 1964. 86 p.   (5035

FORS, Luis Ricardo. Las bibliotecas de Montevideo; examen y reseña de las mismas. La
Plata, Impr. "La Popular", 1903.
43 p.   (5036
Appendix: - 1, Clasificaciones del catálogo metódico decretado por el gobierno oriental para la Biblioteca de Montevideo. - 2,
Secciones del primitivo catálogo formado
por el d. Mascaró para la Biblioteca de Montevideo. - 3, Clasificación del catálogo para la Biblioteca Pública de la Plata, adop-
tada por su director don Clodomiro Quiroga
hasta 1898. - 4, Catálogo sistemático de la
Biblioteca Pública de La Plata.---Jones 2835.

FURLONG CARDIFF, Guillermo. Las bibliotecas
coloniales en el Río de La Plata. (Boletin
de la Academia Nacional de la Historia,
Buenos Aires, v.13, p. 115-48, 1940) (5037
Jones 697b.

GIETZ, Ernesto Gustavo. Bibliografía y referencia; primer-[segundo] curso. Obras y
publicaciones periódicas citadas. Buenos

GIETZ, Ernesto Gustavo. ... (Cont.)
Aires, Museo Social Argentino, Escuela de
Servicio Social, 1956-1957. 2 v.   (5038
Cited in Catálogo, Instituto Bibliotecoló-
gico, item 344.

GONZALEZ OBREGON, Luis. La Biblioteca Nacional de México, 1833-1910; reseña histórica.
México, D.F., 1910. 110 p.   (039
Jones 2213. Also published in English
translated by Alberto M. Carreño.

GROPP, Arthur Eric. Bibliografía sobre las
bibliotecas nacionales de los países latinoamericanos y sus publicaciones. Washington,
D.C., Unión Panamericana, 1960. 58 p.
(Columbus Memorial Library. Bibliographic
ser., no. 50)   (5040

-----. and KER, Anita Melville. Publications
on Latin American libraries in 1938. Cambridge, Mass., Harvard Univ. Pr., 1939.
14 p.   (5041
Jones 179b. Reprinted from Handbook of
Latin American studies, 1938, p. 385-98.
This section of the Handbook was continued
through 1946.

HAVANA. Universidad. Biblioteca. Lista de
obras de bibliotecología y bibliografía
existentes en la Biblioteca General de la
Universidad. Habana, 1948. 19 p.   (5042
Compiled by Jorge Aguayo on the occasion
of receiving a collection of library science books from the International Relations
Office of the American Library Association.

IGUINIZ, Juan Bautista. La Biblioteca Nacional de México. (Revista de historia de América, México, no. 8, p. 57-86, 1940) (5043
Includes biographical sketches of the directors, library publications, notes on the
collections, etc.---Jones 2353a.

INSTITUTO de Intercambio Cultural Argentino-
Norteamericano, Córdoba. La colección bibliotecológica. Córdoba, 1958. 16 p.
mimeogr.   (5043a
Compiler: William Vernon Jackson.

INTER-AMERICAN Children's Institute, Montevi-
deo. Bibliografía: bibliotecas infantiles.
Libros, folletos y articulos de revistas
existentes en la Biblioteca del Instituto.
Montevideo, 1951. 4 p. mimeogr.   (5044
Cited in Musso 34.

-----. Bibliografía sobre bibliotecnia que
puede ser consultada en su Biblioteca.
[Montevideo] n.d. 5 p. mimeogr.   (5045
Cited in Musso 35.

INTER-AMERICAN Institute of Agricultural
Sciences, Turrialba, C.R. Colección de referencia de la Biblioteca Conmemorativa

INTER-AMERICAN Institute of ... (Cont.)
Orton. Turrialba, 1964. 167 p. (Bibliotecología y documentación, no. 1) (5046

-----. Obras de la colección de referencia de
la Biblioteca. Turrialba, C.R., 1962.
88 p. mimeogr. (5047
Cited in Boletín de adquisiciones, Medellín, no. 5, p. 15, mayo 1963.

LATIN AMERICAN libraries: Argentine library
conditions; the National Library of Mexico;
Library experiences in Mexico; Latin Americana collections in the United States. (Library journal, New York, v. 44, no. 4,
1919) (5048
Jones 247.

LEON, Nicolás. Biblioteconomía. Notas de las
lecciones orales del profesor Dr. Nicolás
León en la Escuela Nacional de Bibliotecarios y Archiveros. México, D.F., Antigua
Impr. de Murguía [1920] 167 p. (5049
Jones 2296.

LINARES, Emma. Bibliografía bibliotecológica.
Washington, D.C., Unión Panamericana, 1960.
233 p. (Columbus Memorial Library. Bibliographic ser., no. 49) (5050

LUCERO, Amador L. Nuestras bibliotecas desde
1810. Buenos Aires, Impr. de Coni Hermanos,
1910. 190 p. (5051
Contains bibliography.---Jones 762.

MANUALES de bibliografia y documentacion colombianas, 1- . Bogota, 1956- . (5052
Contents: - 1, Bibliografia bibliotecologica colombiana, 1953/1955, por Luis Florén.

MATIJEVIC, Nicolás. Bibliografía bibliotecológica argentina. Bahía Blanca, Centro de
Documentación Bibliotecologica, Universidad
Nacional del Sur, 1963. vii, 84 p. (5053
Contains 559 references.

MEDELLIN, Col. Universidad de Antioquia. Escuela Interamericana de Bibliotecología.
B- : Bibliotecas populares y escolares: bibliografía. Medellín, 1962. 2 pt.
mimeogr. (5054
Pt. 1, Bibliotecas populares. - pt. 2,
Bibliotecas escolares.

-----. B-12: Catalogación y clasificación:
Fuentes para investigación de obras anonimas y de pseudónimos. [Medellín] n.d. 2 p.
mimeogr. (5055

-----. B-12: Catalogación y clasificación;
bibliografía. Medellín, 1960. 1 p.
mimeogr. (5056

-----. -----. Medellín [1962] 5 p.
mimeogr. (5057

MEDELLIN, Col. Universidad de Antioquia. Escuela Interamericana de Bibliotecología.
B-13: Servicios de consulta; bibliografia.
Medellín, 1960. 1 p. mimeogr. (5058

-----. B-18: Servicios de consulta (2) y
Selección de materiales; obras de consulta
en campos especiales: humanidades (literatura). Medellín, n.d. 3 p. mimeogr. (5059

-----. -----. Biblioteconomía. Medellín,
1961. 3 p. mimeogr. (5060

-----. -----. Ciencias aplicadas. Medellín,
n.d. 2 p. mimeogr. (5061

-----. -----. Ciencias puras. Medellín, n.d.
2 p. mimeogr. (5062

-----. -----. Ciencias sociales. Medellín,
n.d. 2 p. mimeogr. (5063

-----. -----. Historia y materias afines.
Medellín, n.d. 4 p. mimeogr. (5064

-----. -----. Bellas artes. Medellín, n.d.
2 p. mimeogr. (5065

-----. B-25: Problemas en la organización de
materiales; bibliografia. Medellín, 1960.
1 p. mimeogr. (5066

-----. B-25: Problemas de catalogación y clasificación; bibliografia. Medellín, 1962.
1 p. mimeogr. (5067

-----. B-38: Bibliografía especializada (materiales de clase); Algunas publicaciones
en serie, comerciales o no, de la bibliografía colombiana. Medellín, 1964. (5068

-----. -----. Obras de referencia para Colombia (entrega 1a.) Medellín, 1960. 15 p.
mimeogr. (5069

-----. B-46: Bibliotecas universitarias y especializadas; bibliografia. Medellín, 1960.
2 p. mimeogr. (5070

-----. Catálogo de publicaciones, no. 1- ,
oct. 1959- . Medellín, Edit. Universidad de
Antioquia, 1959- . mimeogr. (5071
no. 1, 2 p.; no. 2, 7 p. 1961; no. 3,
30 p., 1963.

MESA DE ESTUDIO sobre la Situación de la Profesión de Bibliotecario en la America Latina,
Medellín, Col., 1964. Plan de tres años para el "Estudio de la Preparación de los Bibliotecarios en la América Latina"; Mesa de
Estudio de la segunda parte, Medellín, 20-31
de agosto de 1964; Recomendaciones, documentos de trabajo. Medellín, Edit. Universidad
de Antioquia, 1964. Various paging. (Publ.
de la Escuela Interamericana de Biblioteco-

MESA DE ESTUDIO sobre la ... (Cont.)
logía; serie: Seminarios, cursos cortos y
reuniones)   (5072
    Contains bibliographies in relation to
recommended library science studies.

MEXICO. Biblioteca Nacional. Concurso de bibliografía y biblioteconomía convocado por
la Biblioteca Nacional; estudios premiados
dados a luz bajo la dirección de Juan B.
Iguíniz. México, Departamento de Aprovisionamientos Generales, 1918. 92, 48, 114,
28 p.   (5073
    Contents: - Bibliografía de la revolución
mexicana de 1910-1916, por Ignacio B. del
Castillo. - Bibliografía de la imprenta de
la Cámara de Diputados por Ignacio B. del
Castillo. - Los historiadores de Jalisco,
por J. B. Iguíniz. - Los grabadores en México, por Manuel Romero de Terreros.---Jones
2349.

-----. Comité Mexicano Correspondiente a la
Conferencia Internacional de Bibliografía.
Libros y bibliotecas de México; la organi-
zación bibliográfica mexicana. Madrid,
Unión Poligrafica 1934? 26 p.   (5074
Jones 2351.

-----. Departamento de Biblioteca. Apuntes
bibliograficos de biblioteconomía. México,
D.F., Secretaría de Educación Pública, 1925.
14 p. (Publ., t.3, no. 13)   (5075
    Cited in Millares, item 1481, also 1553
in which authorship is ascribed to Juana
Manrique de Lara.

MUSSO, Luis Alberto. Bibliografía bibliotecológica del Uruguay. Medellín, Col., Edit.
Universidad de Antioquia, 1964.
199 p.   (5076
    Published under the auspices of the Es-
cuela Interamericana de Bibliotecologia,
Medellin, Colombia.

O'GORMAN, Edmundo. Bibliotecas y librerías
coloniales, 1585-1694. (Boletín del Archivo General de la Nación, México, D.F.,
v. 10, p. 661-1006, 1939)   (5077
    Includes lists of 7,761 titles of books
presented to the Holy Office of the Inqui-
sition, with indexes of authors and of
Mexican authors and manuscripts (HLAS,
1939).---Jones 2382a.

PAN AMERICAN UNION. Columbus Memorial Library. Obras existentes en la Biblioteca
Colón de la Unión Panamericana sobre organización de bibliotecas y sistemas de clasificación. Washington, D.C., 1933. 13 p.
(Bibliographic ser., no. 8)
mimeogr.   (5078

PAN AMERICAN UNION. Columbus Memorial Library.
Obras existentes en la Biblioteca Colón sobre organización de bibliotecas ... 2a.
ed., rev. 1937. 16 p. (Bibliographic ser.,
no. 8)   (5079

PANAMA. Biblioteca Nacional. Bibliografia bibliotecológica panameña desde el 1o. de enero
de 1948 hasta la fecha. Panamá, 1951. 6 p.
mimeogr.   (5080

-----. Capacítese en el manejo científico de
su biblioteca; libros puestos en circulación
por la B. N. para uso de los alumnos del curso de biblioteconomía que se dicta este verano en la Universidad Nacional. Panamá,
1948.   (5081
    Cited in Gropp, Publicaciones, item 1073.

-----. Universidad. Escuela de Bibliotecología. Catálogo de obras de consulta en español que se encuentran en librerías locales.
Por estudiantes del curso de Obras de Consulta, bajo la dirección de Isaura Salazar
de De las Casas. Panamá, Dollander & Salazar, 1961. 38 p.   (5081a
Cited in Geoghegan, 729.

PERALES OJEDA, Alicia. Las obras de consulta;
reseña histórico-crítica. México, D.F., Universidad Nacional Autónoma de México, 1962.
373 p.   (5082

POPA, Tiana. Catalogación 1o. año: bibliografía selectiva. Buenos Aires, Biblioteca Nacional, 1963. 45 p. (Escuela Nacional de
Bibliotecarios, Ser. Didáctica, no. 1)
mimeogr.   (5082a
Cited in Geoghegan, 680.

RIO GRANDE do Sul. Departamento do Serviço Pú-
blico. Bibliografía de obras sôbre o Rio
Grande do Sul, comp. pelos alunos do Curso de
Biblioteconomia do D.S.P. de 1952-1953.
[Pôrto Alegre, 1953] 9 p. mimeogr.   (5083
Cited in Richardson, item 7285.

REUNION TECNICA de Bibliotecarios Agricolas,
Turrialba, Costa Rica. Informe final compilado por Carlos Víctor Penna. Turrialba,
Instituto Interamericano de Ciencias Agrícolas, 1953. 2 v.   (5084
    The following documents presented in the
meeting are bibliographies: no. 2, Facilidades de intercomunicación científica agricola
en América Latina, por Ralph R. Shaw, Armando Samper, Arthur E. Gropp. - no. 4, Bibliotecarios agricolas; una bibliografía tentativa, por Marietta Daniels y Angelina Martínez.
- no. 8, Lista de revistas agrícolas latinoamericanas, por Angelina Martínez y Noël
James. - no. 20, Documentación bibliografica
en el campo de la agronomía y medicina veterinaria por Hans Gravenhorst. - 35, La bibliografía agrícola de la República Dominicana,

REUNION TECNICA de Bibliotecarios... (Cont.)
por Luis Florén Lozano. - no. 38, Tipos de
publicaciones necesarias en una colección
básica agrícola, con referencia especial a
una biblioteca de investigación en América
Latina, por Angelina Martínez.

ROVIRA, Carmen. Bibliografía bibliotecológica;
suplemento 1960-1962. Washington, D.C.,
Unión Panamericana, 1964. 92 p. (Columbus
Memorial Library, Bibliographic ser., no. 49,
Suppl. 1) (5085
  This compilation brings up to date the Bi-
bliografía bibliotecológica compiled by Emma
Linares and published in the same series in
1960.

SABOR, Josefa Emilia. Manual de fuentes de información; obras de referencia: enciclopedias,
diccionarios, bibliografías, biografías, etc.
Buenos Aires, Edit. Kapelusz [1957] 335 p.
(Contribuciones bibliotecológicas, 2) (5086

SÃO PAULO, Brazil (City). Universidade. Biblioteca Central. Bibliografía bibliotecológica brasileira. São Paulo, 1952. 41 p.
(Serie bibliotec1nômica; bibliografia bibliotecológica, v. 1) (5087
  Compiler: Maria Luisa Monteiro da Cunha.

SCARONE, Arturo. La Biblioteca Nacional de
Montevideo; reseña histórica con motivo del
primer centenario de su fundacion, 1816 -
26 mayo - 1916. Montevideo, Tall. Graf.
del Estado, 1916. 157 p. (5088
  Jones 2865.

SEMINARIO Regional sobre el Desarrollo de las
Bibliotecas Universitarias en América Latina,
Mendoza, 1962. Lista seleccionada de publicaciones sobre los temas que se estudiarán
en el Seminario. Paris, 1962. 26 p. (Unes-
co/LBA/Sem. 9/2) mimeogr. (5088a
  Approximately 300 items are listed. Cited
in Geoghegan, 702.

TAVERNA, Francesco. Selección de obras clási-
cas, antiguas y modernas básicas para la for-
macion de una sólida cultura general. Buenos
Aires, Asociación de Bibliotecarios Graduados
de la República Argentina, 1964. (Ser. Difusión bibliográfica, no. 1) (5089

TAVERNA, Francesco. Selección de ... (Cont.)
  Cited in Boletín de adquisiciones, Medellín,
p. 14, jul. 1964.

TAYLOR, Marion R. Guide to Latin American reference materials, a union list for use in
the Atlanta-Athens area. Atlanta, Georgia
Chapter, Special Libraries Assn., 1958.
102 p. (Regional bibliographies, no.1) (5090

TORRE REVELLO, José. La Biblioteca Nacional de
la República Argentina. (Revista de historia
de América, México, D.F., no. 2, p. 69-92.
1938) (5091
  Jones 865a. Also published in Revista de
la Asociación Cultural de Bibliotécnicos, Buenos Aires, p. 9 24, mar. 1943.

TORRE VILLAR, Ernesto de la. La Biblioteca Pa-
lafoxiana; reseña histórica. Bibliografía
histórica de Puebla, formado por Fausto Marín-
Tamayo y Gregorio de Gante. [Puebla, 1957]
50 p. (Centro de Estudios Históricos de Puebla, 4) (5092
  Cited in Boletín de la Biblioteca Nacional,
México, D.F., p. 46, oct./dic. 1957.

URUGUAY. Poder Legislativo. Biblioteca. Bibliografía de la Biblioteca del Poder Legislativo. Montevideo [1955] 9 p. (Referencia, no. 26) mimeogr. (5093
  Cited in Musso 126.

-----. Universidad. Escuela Universitaria de
Bibliotecnia. Catalogación y clasificación,
2o. curso: bibliografía. [Montevideo] 1961.
5 p. mimeogr. (5094
  Professor: Ermelinda Acerenza.

VEREZ DE PERAZA, Elena Luisa, and PERAZA SARAU-
SA, Fermín. Bibliografía bibliotecológica
cubana, 1948-1955. La Habana, 1949-1956.
8 v. (Biblioteca del bibliotecario, 1, 31,
34, 37, 39, 41-42, 46) (5095

VILLALON GALDAMES, Alberto. Bibliografías y
lecturas bibliotécnicas. Santiago de Chile,
1950. 2v. (5096
  Contents: Ser. A, Organización y administración de bibliotecas: t.1, Publicaciones
aparecidas hasta 1947 inclusive. - Ser. B,
Catalogación y clasificación: t.1, Publicaciones aparecidas hasta 1948 inclusive.

LITERATURE

GENERAL

AYALA DUARTE, Crispín. Resumen histórico-
crítico de la literatura hispanoamericana.
Caracas, Parra León Hermanos, 1927.
310 p. (5097
   Jones 31.

BARRERA, Isaac J. Literatura hispanoamericana.
Quito, Impr. de la Universidad Central,
1934. 459 p. (5098

BIBLIOGRAFIA literaria de la America española,
bajo la dirección del Dr. Pedro Henríquez
Ureña. (Boletín del Instituto de Cultura
Latinoamericana, Buenos Aires, año 2 no. 12,
1938) (5099
   Jones 56a.

BLANCO GARCIA, Francisco. La literatura espa-
ñola en el siglo XIX; 2a. ed. Madrid,
Sáenz de Jubera Hermanos, 1894-1903.
3 v. (5100
   La literatura hispano-americana: pt. 3.
---Jones 62.

BLANCO Y SANCHEZ, Rufino. Elementos de literatura española e hispanoamericana; 3a. ed.
notablemente corr. y aum. Madrid, Tip. de
la "Revista de archivos, bibliotecas y museos", 1925. 567 p. (5101
   Notas bibliográficas: p. 484-500.---Jones
64.

COESTER, Alfred Lester. A bibliography of
Spanish-American literature. [New York,
Columbia Univ. Pr., 1912] p. 68-101. (5102
   Reprinted from the Romanic review, v. 3,
no. 1.---Jones 103.

-----. Historia literaria de la América es-
pañola; trad. de Rómulo Tovar. Madrid,
Hernando, 1929. 564 p. (5103
   Bibliography: p. 547-52.---Jones 105.

-----. The literary history of Spanish America. New York, Macmillan, 1916.
495 p. (5104
   Bibliography: p. 477-82.---Jones 104.

-----. -----. 2d ed. New York, Macmillan,
1928. 522 p. (5105
   Jones 104a.

COMETTA MANZONI, Aída. El indio en la poesía
de América española. Buenos Aires, J.
Torres, 1939. 290 p. (5106
   Study with numerous bibliographical footnotes, "Bibliografía general" (p. 287-90)
and index of authors.---Jones 669a.

-----. -----. Buenos Aires, Edit. Futuro
[1960] 101 p. (Colección Eurindia,

COMETTA MANZONI, Aída. El indio... (Cont.)
14) (5107

CORTES, José Domingo. América poética. Poesías selectas americanas, con noticias biográficas de los autores. París, A. Bouret e
Hijo, 1875. 1032 p. (5108
   Jones 111.

CRAIG, George Dundas. The modernist trend in
Spanish-American poetry; a collection of
representative poems...with commentary.
Berkeley, Calif. Univ. Pr., 1934.
347 p. (5109
   Jones 117.

DAIREAUX, Max. Panorama de la littérature
hispano-américaine. Paris, Editions KRA,
1930. 314 p. (5110

DAVILA SILVA, Ricardo. Apuntes para una biblioteca helenoclásica. Santiago de Chile,
Impr., Lit. y Encuad. Barcelona, 1913.
109 p. (5111
   Cited in Laval, item 93.

DELK, Lois Jo, and GREER, James Neal. Spanish
language and literature in the publications
of American universities; a bibliography.
[Austin] Univ. of Texas Pr., 1952. x, 211 p.
(University of Texas Hispanic studies,
v. 4) (5112

DICCIONARIO de la literatura latinoamericana.
Washington, D.C., Unión Panamericana,
1958- . (5113
   Volumes published: Bolivia (n.d. 121 p.)-
Chile (1958. 234 p.) - Colombia (1959.
179 p.) - Argentina (1960-1961. 2v.) - Ecuador (1962. 172 p.) - América Central (1963.
2v.)

ELIAS DE MOLINS, Antonio. Ensayo de una bibliografía literaria de España y América. Noticias de obras y estudios relacionados con la
poesía, teatro, historia, novela, crítica
literaria, etc. Madrid, V. Suárez [1902]
2 v. (5114
   First printed serially in Revista crítica
de historia y literatura españolas, portuguesas, e hispano-americanas", v.5-7, 1900-
1902. Pt. 2, Literatura americana.---Jones
137.

GONZALEZ RUANO, César. Literatura americana;
ensayos de madrigal y de crítica. 1, Poetisas modernas. Madrid, Impr. Artística, 1924.
139 p. (5115
   Jones 173.

GRISMER, Raymond Leonard. A bibliography of
articles and essays on the literatures of
Spain and Spanish-America. Minneapolis,

GRISMER, Raymond Leonard ... (Cont.)
Perine Book Co., 1935. xx, 423 p.
mimeogr. (5116
"This second volume of bibliography is
intended to supplement the Bibliography of
articles on Spanish literature, published
in 1933". "Names of journals and collections
of essays": p., v-xx,---Jones 177.

GRISMER, Raymond Leonard, LEPINE, Joseph E.
and OLMSTED, Richard H. A bibliography of
articles on Spanish literature. Minneapolis,
Burgess Publ. Co., 1933. 294 p. (5117
Spanish-American literature: p. 232-55.---
Jones 179a.

-----. Indice de doce mil autores hispanoamericanos; una guía a la literatura de la America Española. Nueva York, H. W. Wilson,
1939. xiv, 150 p. (Publ. de la Asociación
Inter-Americana Bibliográfica y Bibliotecaria, ser. 3, t.1) (5118

-----. A new bibliography of the literatures
of Spain and Spanish America, including many
studies on anthropology, archaeology, art,
economics, education, geography, history,
law, music, philosophy, and other subjects.
Minneapolis, Perine Book Co., 1941-1944.
v.1-7. (5119
Bayitch cites 7 volumes. Apparently incomplete, since v.5 covered the alphabet
only from Caa-Carc.

-----. A reference index to twelve thousand
Spanish American authors; a guide to the
literature of Spanish America. New York,
H. W. Wilson, 1939. xvi, 150 p. (Inter-
American Bibliographical and Library
Association, Publ. ser. 3, v.1) (5120
"Bibliography of books on Spanish-Amer-
ican literature consulted for this index:"
p. xiii-xvi.---Jones 179.

HENRIQUEZ UREÑA, Camila. Biblioteca americana. México, D.F., Fondo de Cultura Económica, 1946. 44 p. (5121
Cited in HLAS 12, item 2453.

HENRIQUEZ UREÑA, Max. El retorno de los ga-
leones (bocetos hispánicos) Madrid, Renacimiento, 1930. 259 p. (5122
Bibliografía: p. 235-54. Contents: -
Estudio sobre el intercambio de influencias
literarias entre España y América durante
los últimos cincuenta años. - Desarrollo
histórico de la cultura en la América española durante la época colonial.---Jones
197a.

INSTITUTO INTERNACIONAL de Literatura Ibero-
americana. An outline history of Spanish
American literature. E. Herman Hespelt,
chairman and editor. New York, F. S.
Crofts, 1941. 170 p. (5123

INSTITUTO INTERNACIONAL de Literatura Ibero-
americana. An outline history of Spanish
American literature. 2d ed. rev. New York,
F. S. Crofts, 1942. xxii, 192 p. (5124

INTER-AMERICAN Cultural Council. Committee for
Cultural Action, Mexico. Lista de libros
representativos de America. Washington, D.C.,
Unión Panamericana, 1959. 364 p. (Publication, CAC-E-29) (5124a

JAMES, Concha Romero. An annotated bibliography of Latin American literature. Washington, D.C., Pan American Union [1932] 25 p.
mimeogr. (5125
Jones 222.

JAMES, Concha Romero, and AGUILERA, Francisco.
Latin American literature; references to material in English with annotations. Washington, D.C., Pan American Union, 1941. 51 p.
mimeogr. (5126
Contains references to translations.

JONES, Cecil Knight. Suggested readings in
Spanish American prose. (Hispania, Standord
University, v.3, p. 207-12, 1920) (5127
Jones 227.

LEAVITT, Sturgis Elleno. Hispano-American
literature in the United States; a bibliography of translations and criticism. Cambridge, Mass., Harvard Univ. Pr., 1932. x,
54 p. (5128
Includes chronological listing, 1827-1931.
---Jones 252.

-----, 1932-1934, with additional items from
earlier years. Chapel Hill, N.C., Univ. of
North Carolina Pr., 1935. 21 p. (5129

-----, 1935. [1936] (5130
Reprinted from Hispania, v.19, no. 2,
p. 201-10, May 1936.

LEGUIZAMON, Julio A. Bibliografía general de
la literatura hispanoamericana. Buenos Aires, Editoriales Reunidas [1954]
213 p. (5131

LINCOLN, Joseph Newhall. Guide to the bibliography and history of Hispano-American literature. Ann Arbor, Mich., Edwards Letter
Shop, 1939. 43 p. mimeogr. (5132
Lists 349 items.

MATLOWSKY, Bernice D. Antologías del cuento
americano; guia bibliográfica. Washington,
D.C., Unión Panamericana, 1950. 47 p. (División de Filosofía, Letras y Ciencias.
Monografías bibliográficas, 3) (5133

-----. The modernist trend in Spanish-American
poetry. Washington, D.C., Pan American Union,
1952. 26 p. (Columbus Memorial Library.

MATLOWSKY, Bernice D. The modernist... (Cont.)
Bibliographic ser., no. 38)   (5134

MELENDEZ, Concha. La novela indianista en
Hispano-América (1832-1889) México, D.F.,
1932. 218 p.   (5135
Bibliografía: p. 213-18. Typewritten.---
Jones 310.

-----. Another edition. Madrid, Hernando,
1934. 199 p.   (5136
Bibliografía: p. 191-95.---Jones 311.

MENENDEZ Y PELAYO, Marcelino. Historia de la
poesía hispano-americana. Madrid, V. Suárez, 1911-1913. 2 v. (Obras completas,
t. 2-3)   (5137
Jones 313.

NICHOLS, Madaline Wallis, and KINNAIRD, Lucia
Burk. Bibliografía hispánica. Revista
"Nosotros", artículos sobre literatura his-
panoamericana. New York, Instituto de las
Españas, 1937. 80 p.   (5138
Covers the first"época"of the review,
1907-1934.---Jones 335.

-----. A bibliographic list of the historical
articles in Nosotros. (Hispanic American
historical review, Durham, N. C., v. 14,
p. 378-416, 1934)   (5139
Jones 336.

-----. Bibliography of articles in "Nosotros"
in general literary criticism, exclusive of
Hispanic American literature. New York, Columbia University, 1935. 84 p. (Publ. of
the Institute of French Studies)   (5140

NOE, Julio. Curso y antología de literatura
hispano-americana y especialmente argentina.
Buenos Aires, A. Estrada y Cía., 1940.
797 p.   (5141
Jones 793b.

ONIS Y SANCHEZ, Federico de. Antología de la
poesía española e hispano-americana (1882-
1932) Madrid, Junta para Ampliación de Estudios e Investigaciones Históricas, 1934.
1212 p.   (5142
Includes an exhaustive bibliographical
equipment.---Jones 344.

PAN AMERICAN UNION. Latin American literature. [Washington, D.C., n.d.] 7 p.
mimeogr.   (5143
Cited in PAU Bibliographies, p. 29.

PAYRO, Roberto P. Historias de la literatura
americana; guía bibliográfica. Washington,
D.C., Unión Panamericana, 1950. 59, 1 p.
(División de Filosofía, Letras y Ciencias.
Monografías bibliográficas, 2)   (5144

PETROPOLIS. Prefeitura Municipal. Biblioteca.
Romances e livros de literatura ligeira, em
português que podem ser retirados para lei-
tura em domicilio. [Rio de Janeiro] Tip.
Ipiranga, 1941. 36 p.   (5145
Cited in Reis, item 695.

PHELAN, Marion. A bibliography of Latin American fiction in English. Phoenix, Ariz.,
1956. 37 p.   (5146
Unpublished. Copy at DPU. Prepared at
the American Institute of Foreign Trade.

PINILLA, Norberto. Artículos referentes a la
literatura Américo-hispana en la "Revista
Juventud". Ediciones de la "Revista universitaria". Santiago de Chile, 1939.
16 p.   (5147
Jones 373a.

PIROTTO, Armando D. La literatura en América.
El coloniaje. Buenos Aires, Montevideo,
1937. 223 p. (Ediciones de la Sociedad
Amigos del Libro Rioplatense, v.43)   (5148
Jones 374.

PUBLICATIONS on the language and literature of
Spanish America and Brazil in 1937, by Francisco Aguilera, Sturgis E. Leavitt, Irving
A. Leonard, Samuel Putnam, Leavitt O. Wright.
Cambridge, Mass., Harvard Univ. Pr., 1938.
p. 355-424.   (5149
"Reprinted from the Handbook of Latin American studies for 1937. Reprints also issued
for 1938 and 1939.---Jones 382.

REID, Dorcas Worsley. Fiction in English with
a Hispanic-American locale. (Hispania,
Stanford University, v.22, p. 409-30,
1939)   (5150
A "selected list of fiction with a setting
in some part of Hispanic America. Emphasis
has been given to books published since 1927
as the Sturgis bibliography (The Spanish
world in English fiction) ends at that date".
---Jones 390a.

SANCHEZ, Luis Alberto. Góngora en América y
el Lunarejo y Góngora. Lima, 1927.
44 p.   (5151
Bibliografía: p. 39-44.---Jones 431.

-----. Historia de la literatura americana
(desde los orígenes hasta 1936) Santiago,
Ercilla, 1937. 681 p.   (5152

-----. -----. 2a ed. reformada. Santiago de
Chile, Ercilla, 1940. 690 p.   (5153
Bibliografía elemental: p. 647-50.---Jones
431a. Title varies slightly.

-----. -----. 3a. ed. Santiago, Ediciones
Ercilla, 1942. 690 p.   (5154

SANCHEZ, Luis Alberto. Repertorio bibliográfico de la literatura latino-americana.
[Santiago, Universidad de Chile]
1955- .   (5155
    Published to date:- t. 1, fasc. 1-2, 1955-
1957; t. 2, Bolivia-Brasil, Apéndice 2,
1957; t. 3, Chile-Colombia, 1962.

SERRANO DE WILSON, Emilia, Baronesa de Wilson.
El mundo literario americano; escritores
contemporáneos, semblanzas, poesías, apre-
ciaciones, pinceladas. Barcelona [etc.]
Maucci, 1903. 2 v.   (5156
    Jones 446.

SIMON DIAZ, José. Bibliografía de la literatura hispánica. Madrid, Consejo Superior
de Investigaciones Científicas, 1950-1958.
5 v.   (5157

-----. -----. Adiciones a los tomos I-III.
Madrid, 1954. 104 p.   (5158

-----. -----. 2a. ed. Madrid, Instituto
"Miguel de Cervantes", 1960- .
v.1- .   (5159
    Vol. 2 was published in 1962 (330 p.)

STAFFORD, Lorna Isabella Lavery. La literatura de las Américas. The American Republics in fiction and non-fiction; a selective bibliography for members of the Pan
American Round Table of Mexico City. Mexico, D.F., 1944. 12 p. mimeogr. (5160
    List of 35 titles with annotations.

STURGIS, Cony. The Spanish world in English
fiction; a bibliography. Boston, F. W.
Faxon, 1927. 80 p. (Useful reference
ser., no. 34)   (5161
    Includes historical and other fiction
having Spain, Spanish America, or the
Spanish people as a background.

TOPETE, José Manuel. A working bibliography
of Latin American literature. St. Augustine, Fla., W. B. Fraser, 1952. 162 p.
(Inter-American Bibliographical and Library Association, Publ., ser. 1,
v. 12)   (5162

TORRES RIOSECO, Arturo. La novela en América hispana. Berkeley, 1939. p. 159-255.
(University of California, Publ. in modern
philology, v.21, no. 2)   (5163
    Jones 491.

UGARTE, Manuel. La joven literatura hispanoamericana. Antología de prosistas
y poetas; 2a. ed. con un apéndice.
Paris, A. Colin, 1912. 324 p.   (5164
    Contains biobibliographical data.---
Jones 497.

U.S. Library of Congress. Hispanic Foundation. Index of genres and topics to the
readings in Spanish by selected authors from
the Library of Congress Archive of Hispanic
Literature on Tape. Compiled under the
supervision of Francisco Aguilera for the
Office of Education under NDEA contract
OE-Z-14-019. Washington, D.C., 1962.
43 p.   (5165
    The index is to be used with the guide:
Selected authors and their readings (Spanish)
in the Library of Congress Archive of Hispanic
Literature on Tape.

-----. Selected authors and their readings
(Spanish) in the Library of Congress Archive
of Hispanic Literature on Tape, compiled
under the supervision of Francisco Aguilera
for the Office of Education under NDEA
contract OE-Z-14-019. Washington, D.C., 1962.
196 unnumbered leaves.   (5166
    Refers to the readings of 157 authors.

-----. Voces de poetas y latinoamericanos en
el Archivo de Literatura Hispánica en Cinta
Magnética de la Fundación Hispánica. Washington, D.C., 1960. viii, 33 p.   (5167

WAGNER, Max Leopold. Die Spanisch-Amerikanische
literatur. Leipzig, Berlin, B. G. Teubner,
1924. 81 p.   (5168

WEISINGER, Nina Lee. A guide to studies in
Spanish American literature. Boston, New
York [etc.] D. C. Heath, 1940. 120 p. (Heath
modern language series)   (5169
    Includes bibliographies.---Jones 526a.

WILGUS, Alva Curtis. Latin America in fiction;
a bibliography of books in English for adults,
compiled in collaboration with the Inter-American Bibliographical and Library Association.
Washington, D.C., 1941. 35 p. Columbus Memorial Library. Bibliographic series, no.
26)   (5170
    Approximately 440 books are listed.

TRANSLATIONS

ENGLEKIRK, John Eugene. Bibliografía de obras
norteamericanas en traducción española. México, D.F., 1944. 118 p.   (5171
    Reprinted from Revista iberoamericana.

-----. A literatura norteamericana no Brasil.
México, D.F., 1950. 181 p.   (5172

FLETCHER, William H., and LYMAN, William W.
A guide to Spanish-American literature in
translation. Los Angeles, Los Angeles Junior
College, 1936. 115 p.   (5173
    Jones 150a.

FLORES, Angel. Spanish literature in English
translation. New York, H. W. Wilson, 1926.
82 p.   (5174
    Of slight value for Spanish American
authors.---Jones 151.

GJELSNESS, Rudolph Hjalmar. The American book
in Mexico; a bibliography of books by authors of the United States of America published in Mexico, 1952-1955. Ann Arbor,
Mich., Univ. of Michigan, Department of
Library Science, 1957. 92 p. (Studies,
4)   (5175

GRANIER, James Albert. Latin American belles-
lettres in English translation; a selective
and annotated guide. Washington, D.C.,
1942. 31 p. (Library of Congress. Hispanic Foundation bibliographical ser.,
no. 1) mimeogr.   (5176

-----. -----. 2d rev. ed. Washington, D.C.,
1943. 33 p. (Library of Congress. Hispanic Foundation bibliographical ser.,
no.1)   (5177

HULET, Claude L. Latin American prose in
English translation; a bibliography.
Washington, D.C., Pan American Union, 1964.
191 p. (Division of Philosophy and Letters.
Basic bibliographies, 1)   (5178

JAMIESON, Sally Brewster. English translations of Latin American literature. Washington, D.C., Division of Intellectual
Cooperation, Pan American Union [1947]
17 p. mimeogr.   (5179
    Revised through Jan. 1947.

JONES, Willis Knapp. Latin America through
drama in English. Washington, D.C., Pan
American Union, 1950. 12 p. (Division of
Philosophy, Letters and Sciences. Bibliographical monographs, 1)   (5180

-----. Latin American writers in English
translation; a tentative bibliography.
Washington, D.C., Pan American Union,
1944. 141 p. (Columbus Memorial Library.
Bibliographic ser., no. 30)
mimeogr.   (5181

MANCHESTER, Paul Thomas. A bibliography
and critique of the Spanish translations
from the poetry of the United States.
Nashville, 1927. 67 p. (George Peabody
College for Teachers. Contributions to
education, no. 41)   (5182
    Jones 279.

MEDINA, José Toribio. Biblioteca chilena de
traductores. Santiago de Chile, Soc.,
Impr. y Lit. Universo, 1925. 112p. (5183
    Jones 1534.

MEDINA, José Toribio. Biblioteca chilena de
traductores (1820-1924) Santiago de Chile,
Balcells & Co., 1926. 405 p.   (5184
    1,575 titles. From Anales de la Universi-
dad de Chile, 2a ser., año 4, 1926.---Jones
1535.

PAN AMERICAN UNION. Division of Intellectual
Cooperation. English translations of Latin
American fiction. [Washington, D.C., 1939]
2 p. mimeogr.   (5185

-----. -----. -----. [1941] 3 p.
mimeogr.   (5186

-----. -----. Latin American literature in
English translation. [Washington, D.C.,
1943] 5 p. mimeogr.   (5187

PETRICONI, Hellmuth. Spanish-Amerikanische
romane der gegenwart. Hamburg, C. Behre,
1938. 61 p. (Ibero-Amerikanischen Instituts, Hamburg, 11)   (5188
    Abrief study of the modern Spanish-American
novel, with a list of translations in German.
---Jones 371.

SHUR, Leonid Avel'evich. Khudozhestvennaia
literatura latinskoi Ameriki v russkoi pechati, 1765-1959. Moscow, Izd Vsesoiuzn, Knizh-
noi Palaty, 1960. 290 p.   (5189
    Added title-page in Spanish: Literatura la-
tinoamericana en la imprenta rusa; bibliografía de las obras traducidas al ruso y ensayos críticos, 1769-1959. Book is reviewed
by J. Gregory Oswald in Hispanic American
historical review, v. 42, p. 583-85, Nov.
1962.

U.S. Library of Congress. Hispanic Foundation.
A provisional bibliography of United States
books translated into Portuguese. Washington, D.C., 1957. vii, 182 p. (Hispanic
Foundation bibliographical ser., no.
2)   (5190
    Books printed in Brazil are included.

-----. A provisional bibliography of United
States books translated into Spanish.
Washington, D.C., 1957. 471 p. (Hispanic
Foundation bibliographical ser., no.
3)   (5191
    Books printed in Latin American countries
are cited.

-----. Spanish and Portuguese translations of
United States books, 1955-1962; a bibliography. Washington, D.C., 1963. 506 p.
(Hispanic Foundation bibliographical ser.,
no. 8)   (5192

ARGENTINA

AITA, Antonio. La literatura argentina contem-

AITA, Antonio. La literatura ... (Cont.)
poránea, 1900-1930. Buenos Aires, L. J.
Rosso, 1931. 156 p.   (5193
    Bibliografía: p. 127-56.---Jones 551.

ALONSO CRIADO, Emilio. Compendio de la literatura argentina; 3a. ed. Buenos Aires,
Est.-Tip. J. Carbone, 1908. 93 p. (5194
    Jones 554.

AYALA DUARTE, Crispín. Historia de la literatura argentina. Caracas, Parra León Hermanos, 1928. 195 p.   (5195
    A brief review.---Jones 590.

BARREDA, Ernesto Mario. Nuestro parnaso;
colección de poesías argentinas. Buenos
Aires, J. L. Dasso & Cía., 1914.
4 v.   (5196
    Jones 593.

BECCO, Horacio Jorge. Contribución a la bibliografía de la literatura argentina.
[Buenos Aires] Universidad de Buenos Aires,
Departamento Editorial [1959]
50 p.   (5197
    Cited in Catálogo, Instituto Biblioteco-
lógico, item 742.

COESTER, Alfred Lester. A tentative bibliography of the belles-lettres of the Argentine Republic. Cambridge, Mass., Harvard
Univ. Pr., 1933. 94 p. (Bibliographies of
Spanish-American literature)   (5198
    Jones 668a.

ESTRELLA GUTIERREZ, Fermín. Panorama sinté-
tico de la literatura argentina. Santiago
de Chile, Ercilla, 1938. 147 p.   (5199
    Jones 687a.

FRUGONI DE FRITZSCHE, Teresita. Indice de
poetas argentinos. Buenos Aires, Universidad de Buenos Aires, Facultad de Filosofía
y Letras, Instituto de Literatura Argentina,
1963. v.1 (A-Ch) (Guías bibliográficas,
8)   (5200

GONZALEZ CARBALHO, José. Indice de la poesía
contemporánea argentina. Santiago de Chile,
Ercilla, 1937. 420 p.   (5201
    Bibliographical notes.---Jones 713.

IBAÑEZ, Avelina M. Unitarios y federales en
la literatura argentina. Buenos Aires,
Impr. López, 1933. 595 p.   (5202
    Bibliografía: p. 585-90.---Jones 726.

IBARGUREN, Carlos. Las sociedades literarias
y la revolución argentina. Buenos Aires,
Espasa-Calpe Argentina, 1937. 210 p. (5203
    Includes "Lista de suscriptores al Telé-
grafo mercantil".---Jones 727a.

IBARRA, Néstor. La nueva poesía argentina, ensayo crítico sobre el ultraísmo, 1921-1929.
Buenos Aires, 1930. 132 p.   (5204
    Jones 728.

LAGMANOVICH, David. Bibliografía de la página
literaria de La Gaceta, de S. M. de Tucumán
(1956-1961) Buenos Aires, Fondo Nacional de
las Artes [1963] 48 p. (Bibliografía argentina de artes y letras, Compilaciones especiales, no. 15)   (5205
    Contains 675 entries.

LEAVITT, Sturgis Elleno. Argentine literature;
a bibliography of literary criticism, biography, and literary controversy. Chapel
Hill, Univ. of North Carolina Pr., 1924.
92 p. (University of North Carolina studies
in language and literature, no. 1)   (5206
    A useful reference work for the study of
Argentine letters.---Jones 748.

MARTINEZ, Benigno Tejeira. Antología argentina; colección de trozos históricos crítico-
literarios; discursos y poesías patrióticas
de escritores argentinos en prosa y verso,
precedidas de breves rasgos biográficos y
bibliográficos desde la época colonial hasta
nuestros días. Buenos Aires, J. Peuser, 1890-
1891. 2 v.   (5207
    Jones 770.

MAUBE, José Carlos, and CAPDEVIELLE, Adolfo.
Antología de la poesía femenina argentina.
Con referencias biográficas. Buenos Aires,
1930. 509 p.   (5208
    Jones 775.

NOSOTROS; no. aniversario, 1907-1927; un cuarto
de siglo de vida intelectual, año 21, t. 57.
Buenos Aires, 1927. 511 p.   (5209
    A review of literary and cultural activi-
ties, composed of articles by representative
authors.---Jones 796.

OVIEDO, Jesús J. La literatura gauchesca dentro de la literatura argentina. México, D.
F., 1934. xxv, 151 p. mimeogr.   (5210
    Bibliografía: p. i-xxv. Thesis, Univer-
sity of Mexico.---Jones 808.

PIAGGIO, Juan A. Bibliografía literaria.
Buenos Aires, F. Lajouane, 1889.
180 p.   (5211
    Reprinted from La Nación.

PINTO, Juan. Panorama de la literatura argentina contemporánea. Buenos Aires, Edit.
Mundi, 1941. 385 p.   (5212

PUIG, Juan de la C. Antología de poetas argentinos. Buenos Aires, M. Biedma e Hijo,
1910. 10 v.   (5213
    Contains biographies.---Jones 816.

ROIG, Arturo Andrés. Ensayo bibliográfico
sobre el despertar literario de una provincia argentina. Mendoza, Impr. D'Accurzio,
1963. 64 p. (5214
Cited in Bryant 302.

QUESADA, Ernesto. El "criollismo" en la literatura argentina. Buenos Aires, Coni Hermanos, 1902. 131 p. (5215
Contains bibliographical notes.---Jones
818.

ROJAS, Ricardo. La literatura argentina; ensayo filosófico sobre la evolución de la
cultura en el Plata. Buenos Aires, Impr.
de Coni Hermanos, 1917-1922. 4 v. (5216
Bibliographical notes included.---Jones
828.

-----. -----. 2a. ed. Buenos Aires, Librería
"La Facultad", J. Roldán y Cía., 1924-1925.
8 v. (Obras, t. 8-15) (5217
Jones 829.

ROLLA, Matilde. Disegno storico della lettera-
tura argentina. Roma, Editrice Studium,
1932. 251 p. (5218
Bibliografia: p. 245-46.---Jones 830.

BOLIVIA

ALARCON, Abel. La literatura boliviana, 1545-
1916. (Revue hispanique, New York, t. 41,
p. 563-633, 1917) (5219
Jones 896.

ANTOLOGIA boliviana, con prólogo de D. Arturo
Oblitas. Cochabamba, F. Rejas e Hijo, 1915.
v. 1. (5220
At head of title: Escritores cochabambi-
nos. Includes biographical sketches.---
Jones 897.

GUZMAN, Augusto. Historia de la novela boliviana. La Paz, Revista "México", 1938.
216 p. (5221
Jones 917.

LEAVITT, Sturgis Elleno. A tentative biblio-
graphy of Bolivian literature. Cambridge,
Mass., Harvard Univ. Pr., 1933. 23 p.
(Bibliographies of Spanish-American litera-
ture) (5222
Jones 919a.

OTERO, Gustavo Adolfo. Crestomatía boliviana;
3a. ed. corr. y aum. (Con anotaciones bibliográficas) La Paz, Arnó Hermanos, 1928.
185 p. (5223
Jones 925.

VILLALOBOS, Rosendo. Letras bolivianas; los
poetas y sus obras; los prosistas literarios
(datos hasta 1910) La Paz, Edit. Boliviana,

VILLALOBOS, Rosendo. Letras ... (Cont.)
1936. 139 p. (5224
"Ligero resumen bibliográfico": p. 123-40.
---Jones 944.

VACA GUZMAN, Santiago. La literatura bolivia-
na; breve reseña. Escritores en verso. -
Escritores en prosa. - Medios de publicidad.
- Oratoria. - Influencia de las razas en las
letras alto-peruanas; 2a. ed. Buenos Aires,
Impr. de P. E. Coni, 1883. 206 p. (5225
Jones 918.

BRAZIL

ACADEMIA Brasileira de Letras. Anuario. Rio
de Janeiro, 1937- . (5226
Contains biobibliographical sketches of
members.---Jones 946.

ANUARIO brasileiro de literatura, 1937-1942.
Rio de Janeiro, Pongetti, 1937-1942. (5227
Jones 959.

ANUARIO da literatura brasileira, ano 1, no.
1- , 1960- . Rio de Janeiro. (5228
Editors: S. Castro and W. Ribeiro do Val.

AZEVEDO, Cyro de. Conferencias sobre literatura brasileña dadas en el salón de actos públicos de la Universidad de Montevideo.
Montevideo, A. Barreiro y Ramos, 1918. 142p.
(Anales de la Universidad, año 28, no.
98) (5229
Jones 963.

-----. La literatura brasileña. (Revista de
la Universidad de Buenos Aires, año 16, t.
41-42, p. 165-95, 1919) (5230
Jones 964.

BARBOSA, Francisco de Assis. O romance, a no-
vela e õ conto no Brasil. Rio de Janeiro,
MEC, Serviço de Documentação, 1950. (5231
Reprinted from Cultura, no. 3, p. 193-242.
Bibliography: p. 212-42. Cited in Doria Me-
nezes 89.

CAMPOS, Humberto de. Anthologia da Academia
Brasileira de Letras: trinta annos de discursos academicos, 1897-1927. Rio de Janeiro, Leite Ribeiro, 1928. 352 p. (5232
"Occupantes das quarenta cadeiras da Academia... 1897-1928": p. 347-49.---Jones 1008.

-----. O conceito e a imagem na poesia brasileira. Rio de Janeiro, Leite Ribeiro, 1929.
333 p. (5233
Bibliographia: p. 319-26.---Jones 1009.

CARMO, José Arimateia Pinto do. Novelas y novelistas brasileiros; indicações bibliográficas. Rio de Janeiro, Organização Simoes
Editora, 1957. 67 p. (5234

CARPEAUX [i.e.: Karpfeu] Otto Maria, pseud.
Pequena bibliografia critica da literatura
brasileira. Rio de Janeiro, Ministério da
Educação e Cultura, Serviço de Documentação,
1951. 271 p.   (5235

-----. -----. 2a. ed. rev. e aum. [Rio de Ja-
neiro] Ministério da Educação e Cultura, Serviço de Documentação, 1955. 297 p.   (5236

-----. -----. 3a. ed. rev. e aum. Rio de Janeiro, Edit. Letras e Artes, 1964.
335 p.   (5237

CARVALHO, José Lopes Pereira de. Os membros
da Academia Brasileira em 1915 (Traços bio-
bibliographicos) Rio de Janeiro, Off.
Graph. da Liga Maritima Brazileira [1917?]
630 p.   (5238
Jones 1081.

CARVALHO, Ronald de. Pequena historia da literatura brasileira; 2a. ed. rev. e augm.
Rio de Janeiro, F. Briguiet & Comp., 1922.
401 p.   (5239
Jones 1017. 1st ed.: 1919; 4th ed.: 1929.

-----. -----. 5a. ed. rev. e augm. Rio de
Janeiro, F. Briguiet & Cia., 1935.
389 p.   (5240
Jones 1018. 6th ed.: 1937; 8th ed.: 1949.

COELHO, Henrique. Chrestomathia brasileira.
São Paulo, Weiszflog Irmãos, 1920.
254 p.   (5241
Contains biographical sketches.---Jones
1021.

FORD, Jeremiah Denis Matthias, Whittem,
Arthur F, and RAPHAEL, Maxwell I. A tenta-
tive bibliography of Brazilian belles-
lettres. Cambridge, Mass., Harvard Univ.
Pr., 1931. 201 p. (Bibliographies of
Spanish-American literature)   (5242
Periodicals: p. 187-201.---Jones 1042.

FREIRE, Laudelino de Oliveira. Classicos
brasileiros. Breves notas para a historia
da literatura philologica nacional. Rio
de Janeiro, 1923. 262 p.   (5243
Forty three biographies including bibliographies.---Jones 1116.

-----. Pequena edição dos sonetos brasileiros;
105 sonetos, 105 retratos. Rio de Janeiro,
F. Briguiet & Cia., 1914. 222 p.   (5244
Contains short biographies.---Jones 1117.

GOLDBERG, Isaac. Brazilian literature. New
York, A. A. Knopf, 1922. 303 p.   (5245
Jones 1050.

KRUG, Guilhermina, and CARVALHO, Neely Rezende. Letras rio-grandenses. Porto Alegre,
Livraria do Globo, 1935. 333 p.   (5246

KRUG, Guilhermina, and CARVALHO... (Cont.)
Contains selections and biobibliographical
notes.---Jones 1071.

LINS, Edison. Historia e critica da poesia
brasileira. [Rio de Janeiro] Ariel, 1937.
399 p.   (5247
Jones 1079.

MATTOS, José Dias de Verissimo. Estudos de
literatura brazileira. Rio de Janeiro, H.
Garnier, 1901-1907. 6 v.   (5248
Jones 1224.

MORAES, Alexandre José de Mello, filho. Parnaso brazileiro, seculo XVI-XIX. Rio de Janeiro, B. L. Garnier, 1885. 2 v.   (5249
Contains 98 biographical notes.---Jones
1099.

MOTTA, Arthur. Historia da litteratura brasileira. São Paulo, Comp. Ed. Nacional,
1930. 2 v.   (5250
Contains numerous bibliographies.---Jones
1104.

-----. Vultos e livros, Academia Brazileira
de Letras. São Paulo, Monteiro Lobato & C.,
1921. 284 p.   (5251
Jones 1105. 1st series.

MURICY, José Candido de Andrade. A nova litteratura brasileira, critica e antologia. Porto Alegre, 1936. 425 p.   (5252
"Indice bio-bibliografico": p. 403-13.---
Jones 954.

NEGRÃO, Maria José da Trindade. Levantamento
bibliográfico do conto brasileiro. 1957.
24 p. mimeogr.   (5253
Cited in Doria Menezes 96.

ORBAN, Víctor. Littérature brésilienne; pré-
face de M. de Oliveira Lima. Paris, Garnier
Frères, 1910. 370 p.   (5254
Jones 1119.

-----. -----. 2a. éd. rev. et augm. Paris,
Garnier Frères, 1914. 528 p.   (5255
"Supplément biographique et bibliographi-
que": p. 471-82.---Jones 1120.

PAIXÃO, Mucio da. Movimento litterario em Campos. Rio de Janeiro, 1925.   (5256
Jones 1126.

PARANHOS, Haroldo. Historia do romantismo no
Brasil. S. Paulo, Edições Cultura Brasileira, 1937- . v.1- .   (5257
Contents: - v.1, A evolução da literatura
brasileira antes do romanticismo, 1500-1830.
- v.2, Primeira geração romantica, 1830-1850.
---Jones 1132. HLAS, 3, item 3516 and 5,
item 4084, reported two volumes.

PERIE, Eduardo. A litteratura brazileira nos
tempos coloniaes, do seculo XVI ao começo
do XIX; esboço historico seguido de uma bibliographia e trechos dos poetas e prosado-
res d'aquelle periodo que fundaram no Brazil
a cultura da lingua portugueza. Buenos Aires, E. Perie, 1885. 442 p. (Bibliotheca
luzo-brazileira)   (5258
    Jones 1138.

REIS Antônio Simões dos. Bibliografia da
história da literatura brasileira de Sílvio
Romero. Rio de Janeiro, Livraria Editôra
Zélio Valverde, 1944. v.1 (305 p.) (5259

ROMERO, Sylvio. Historia da litteratura brasileira; 2a. ed. melhorada pelo auctor.
Rio de Janeiro, H. Garnier, 1902-1903.
2 v.   (5260
    Jones 1179.

-----. Novos estudos de litteratura contem-
poranea. Rio de Janeiro, Paris, H. Garnier
[1899] 305 p.   (5261
    Jones 1180.

-----, and RIBEIRO, João. Compendio de historia da literatura brasileira; 2a ed. refun-
dida. Rio de Janeiro, F. Alves, 1909.
550 p.   (5262
    Jones 1181.

SANCHEZ-SAEZ, Braulio. Vieja y nueva literatura del Brasil. Santiago de Chile, Edit.
Ercilla, 1935. 242 p. (Biblioteca América,
v. 14)   (5263
    Reseñas bibliográficas: p. 226-42.---
Jones 1184.

SANTOS, José dos. Bibliografia da literatura classica lusobrasilica. Lisbon, Livraria Lusitana, 1916. 256 p.   (5264
    Parts 1-8, Abelha-Almeida, Teodoro de.---
Jones 1185.

SILVA, João Pinto da. Historia literaria do
Rio Grande do Sul. Porto Alegre, Edição
da Livraria do Globo, 1924. 270 p. (5265
    Jones 1144.

TOPETE, José Manuel. A working bibliography
of Brazilian literature. Gainesville,
Univ. of Florida Pr., 1957. 114 p. (5266

WERNECK, Eugenio. Anthologia brasileira;
collectanea em prosa e verso de escriptores nacionaes; 5a. ed. Petropolis, Off.
Graph. das "Vozes de Petropolis", 1914.
625 p.   (5267
    "166 autores: 140 excerptos em prosa;
148 excerptos em versos; 50 retratos".---
Jones 1227.

WOGAN, Daniel S. A Literatura hispano-americana no Brasil: 1877-1944. Baton Rouge,

WOGAN, Daniel S. A literatura ... (Cont.)
La., Louisiana State University Pr. [1948]
98 p.   (5268

CENTRAL AMERICA

BARRIOS, Roberto. La literatura de Centro-
América; su pasado y su presente. (Centro-
América, Guatemala, p. 42-4, 1915)   (5269
    Jones 1230.

DOYLE, Henry Grattan. A tentative bibliography
of the belles-lettres of the republics of
Central America. Cambridge, Mass., Harvard
Univ. Pr., 1935. 136 p. (Bibliographies of
Spanish-American literature)   (5270
    Jones 1232.

MONTALBAN, Leonardo. Historia de la literatura de la América Central. San Salvador,
1929. 160 p.   (5271
    Jones 1241.

-----. -----. Epoca colonial. San Salvador,
Ministerio de Instrucción Pública, 1931.
338 p.   (5272
    Jones 1242.

URIARTE, Ramón. Galería poética centroamericana. Colección de poesías de los mejores poetas de la América del Centro; precedidas de
ligeros apuntes biográficos y breves juicios
críticos. Guatemala, 1883. 3 v.   (5273
    Jones 1257.

-----. -----. 2a. ed. Guatemala, Tip. "La
Unión", 1888. 2 v.   (5274
    Jones 1258.

CHILE

AMUNATEGUI Y SOLAR, Domingo. Bosquejo histórico de la literatura chilena. Santiago de
Chile, Impr. Universitaria, 1915.
669 p.   (5275
    "Publicado en la Revista chilena de histo-
ria y geografía".---Jones 1383.

-----. -----. Período colonial. Santiago de
Chile, Impr. Universitaria, 1918.
106 p.   (5276
    Jones 1384.

-----. Las letras chilenas; 2a ed. Santiago,
Edit. Nascimento, 1934. 379 p.   (5277
    Jones 1388.

AZOCAR, Rubén. La poesía chilena moderna, antología. Santiago de Chile, 1931.
348 p.   (5278
    Includes bibliography.---Jones 1399.

CASTILLO, Homero, and SILVA CASTRO, Raúl. Historia bibliográfica de la novela chilena. México, D.F., Ediciones de Andrea; Charlottesville, Va., Bibliographical Society of the University of Virginia, 1961. 214 p. (Colección Studium, 28)   (5279

CASTILLO, Homero. La literatura chilena en los Estados Unidos. Santiago, Ediciones de la Biblioteca Nacional, 1963. 127 p.   (5280

ESCUDERO, Alfonso María. La actividad literaria chilena en 1924. (Atenea, Concepción, año 2, p. 66-90, 1925)   (5281
Jones 1465.

-----. La actividad literaria chilena en 1931. (Religión y cultura, Madrid, t.18, p. 399-404, 1932)   (5282
Jones 1466.

-----. La literatura en Chile en 1922; apunte bibliografico. (España y América, Madrid, t. 21, p. 46-57, 1923)   (5283
Jones 1464.

GOIC, Cedomil. Bibliografía de la novela chilena del Siglo XX. Santiago de Chile, Edit. Universitaria, 1962. p. 51-168.   (5284
Separata del Boletín de filología, Santiago, t. 14, 1962. Contains 1,232 entries, including cross-references, accompanied by author and title indices.

HUNEEUS Y GANA, Jorge. Cuadro histórico de la producción intelectual de Chile. [Santiago de Chile, 1910?] 880 p. (Biblioteca de escritores de Chile, v.1)   (5285
Jones 1496.

LATCHAM, Ricardo A. El año literario de 1924. (La Revista católica, Santiago, t. 48, p. 186-202, 1925)   (5286
Jones 1502.

LEAVITT, Sturgis Elleno. Chilean literature, a bibliography of literary criticism, biography and literary controversy. Baltimore, Md., 1923. 89 p.   (5287
Reprinted from the Hispanic American historical review, v. 5, Feb.-Nov. 1922.---Jones 1511.

LILLO, Samuel A. Literatura chilena. Santiago de Chile, Casa Edit. "Minerva", 1918. 171 p.   (5288
Jones 1512.

-----. -----. 2a ed. Santiago, Soc., Impr. y Lit. Universo, 1920. 192 p.   (5289
Bibliografía: p. 7-8.---Jones 1513.

-----. -----. con una antología contemporánea; 5a. ed. Santiago, Edit, Nascimento,

LILLO, Samuel A. con una antología... (Cont.) 1930. 592 p.   (5290

MEDINA, José Toribio. Bibliografía de la Araucana. (In Ercilla y Zúñiga, Alonso de. La Araucana; ed. del centenario ... la publica J. T. Medina. Santiago de Chile, 1910-1918. v. 4, p. 1-60)   (5291
Jones 1531.

-----. Historia de la literatura colonial de Chile. Santiago de Chile, Impr. de la Librería del Mercurio, 1878. 3 v.   (5292
"Indice de los libros y autores cuyas vidas y escritos se examinan en esta obra", v. 3, p. 113-46.---Jones 1543.

-----. La literatura femenina en Chile (notas bibliográficas y en parte críticas) Santiago de Chile, Impr. Universitaria, 1923. 334 p.   (5293
642 titles listed.---Jones 1548.

PINO SAAVEDRA, Yolanda. Die zeitgenossische literatur en Chile. (Ibérica, Hamburg, v. 3, p. 86-102, 1925)   (5294
Jones 1567.

ROJAS CARRASCO, Guillermo. Contribución del profesorado a las letras nacionales. Valparaíso, Edit. "Amanecer", 1947. xii, 164 p.   (5295

SILVA ARRIAGADA, Luis Ignacio. La novela en Chile. Santiago de Chile, Impr. "Barcelona", 1910. (Ensayos bibliográficos sobre la literatura chilena)   (5296
Contents. - 1a. pte., Novelas. - 2a. pte., Cuentos y artículos de costumbres. - 3a. pte., Miscelanea literaria, leyendas, tradiciones histórico-literarias, etc. Addenda. Indice alfabético de autores y nombres citados en la obra.---Jones 1618.

SILVA CASTRO, Raúl. Antología de poetas chilenos del siglo XIX. Santiago de Chile, 1937. 438 p. (Biblioteca de escritores de Chile, 14)   (5297
Each group of poems preceded by a biobibliographical sketch of the author.---Jones 1619.

-----. Los cuentistas chilenos. Antología general desde los orígenes hasta nuestros días. Santiago, Edición Zig-Zag, 1938. 530 p. (5298
"Bibliografía general del cuento chileno": p. 87-151. Includes study of the Chilean short story, with biobibliographical notes. ---Jones 1620.

-----. El cuento chileno; bibliografía. (Anales de la Facultad de Filosofía y Educación, Universidad de Chile, Santiago, t. 1, p. 116-73, 1936)   (5299
Jones 1621.

SILVA CASTRO, Raul. Fuentes bibliográficas
para el estudio de la literatura chilena.
Santiago de Chile, Prensas de la Universidad, 1933. 269 p.   (5300
   See also Anales de la Universidad de Chile, ser. 3, año 2, p. 309-457, 1932.---Jones
1624.

TORRES RIOSECO, Arturo. Breve historia de la
literatura chilena. México, D.F., Edición
de Andrea, 1956. 175 p. (Manuales Studium)   (5301

-----, and SILVA CASTRO, Raúl. Ensayo de bibliografía de la literatura chilena.
Cambridge, Mass., Harvard Univ. Pr., 1935.
71 p. (Bibliographies of Spanish-American
literature)   (5302
   Jones 1645.

VICUÑA MACKENNA, Benjamín. Estudios sobre la
literatura chilena del coloniaje (1541-1810)
(Anales de la Universidad de Chile, Santiago, no. 11, p. 5-16, 1933)   (5303
   Jones 1657.

ZANELLI LOPEZ, Luisa. Mujeres chilenas de
letras. Santiago, Impr. Universitaria,
1917. 203 p.   (5304
   Jones 1665.

COLOMBIA

AÑEZ, Julio. Parnaso colombiano; colección
de poesías escogidas. Estudio preliminar
de d. José Rivas Groot. Bogotá, Camacho
Roldán & Tamayo, 1886-1887. 2 v. (5305
   With bibliographical sketches.---Jones
1669.

ANTOLOGIA de periodistas. Bogotá, Edit.
Minerva, 1936. 238 p. (Biblioteca aldeana de Colombia, no. 70)   (5306
   Includes biographical sketches.---Jones
1671.

ARANGO FERRER, Javier. La literatura de Colombia. Buenos Aires, Impr. y Casa Editora "Coni", 1940. 158 p. (Buenos Aires.
Universidad. Instituto de Cultura Latinoamericana. Las literaturas americanas
3)   (5307

ARIAS, Juan de Dios. Historia de la literatura colombiana; para sexto año de bachi-
llerato; 5a. ed. Bogotá, Edit. Iqueima,
1958. 269 p. (Colección La Salle) (5308
   1a. ed.: Bogotá, Tall. Gráf. Mundo al
Día, 1947. 256 p. (Colección La Salle)

BAYONA POSADA, Nicolás. Panorama de la literatura colombiana; 5a. ed. Bogotá, Librería
Colombiana, 1951. 159 p.   (5309

CAPASO, Carlos Arturo. Antología lírica
(60 poemas colombianos) Bogotá, Impr. del
Departamento de Cundinamarca, 1935. 158 p.
(Biblioteca del maestro)   (5310
   "Notas biográficas y bibliográficas: p. 147-
54.---Jones 1695.

CASA, Enrique Carlos de la. La novela antio-
queña. México, D.F., 1942. 99 p. (Publ.
del Instituto Hispánico de los Estados Unidos, Columbia University, N.Y.)   (5311
   Contains: Bibliografía de Obras de Tomás
Carrasquilla: p. 85-6; and Obras citadas y
consultadas, p. 87-99)

CORREA, Ramón C. Historia de la literatura
boyacense. Tunja, Impr. del Departamento,
1951. 165 p.   (5312
   Cited in Giraldo Jaramillo, p. 176.

CURCIO ALTAMAR, Antonio. Evolución de la novela en Colombia. Bogotá, 1957. xxviii,
339 p. (Publ. del Instituto Caro y Cuervo,
11)   (5313

ENGLEKIRK, John Eugene, and, WADE, Gerald E.
Bibliografía de la novela colombiana. México, 1950. 131 p.   (5314
   Reprinted with additions from Revista Iberoamericana, México, D.F., v. 15, no. 30,
p. 309-411. en. 1950.

GARCIA SAMUDIO, Nicolás. Colombian literature.
(Hispanic American historical review, Balti-
more, v. 4, p. 330-47, 1921)   (5315
   Jones 1713.

GOMEZ RESTREPO, Antonio. Bogotá. La litera-
tura colombiana a mediados del siglo XIX.
Dos ensayos. Bogotá, Tall. de Ediciones
Colombia, 1926. 177 p. (Ediciones Colom-
bia, t. 20)   (5316
   Jones 1714.

-----. Critica literaria. Bogotá, Edit. Minerva, 1935. 197 p. (Biblioteca aldeana
de Colombia, no. 8)   (5317
   Jones 1715.

-----. Historia de la literatura colombiana.
Bogotá, Impr. Nacional, 1938-1947.
4 v.   (5318
   Jones, 1715a, 1716, cites first two volumes.

-----. 3a. ed. Bogotá, Edit. Cosmos, 1953-
1954. 4 v. (Biblioteca de autores colombianos, 66-69)   (5319

-----. 4a. ed. Bogotá, Lit. Villegas, 1956-
1957. 4 v. (Biblioteca de autores colombianos, 66-69)   (5320

-----. La literatura colombiana. N.Y., Paris,
1918. 126 p.   (5321

GOMEZ RESTREPO, Antonio. La lit... (Cont.)
     Jones 1717. "Extrait de la Revue hispa-
     nique, tomo XLIII". p. 79-204.

-----. -----. Nueva ed. Bogotá, 1926. 194 p.
     (Ediciones Colombia, t. 15)   (5322

ISAZA, Emiliano. Antologia colombiana. París,
     México, D.F., Vda. de Ch. Bouret, 1895-1896.
     2 v.   (5323
        Literary biobibliography.---Jones 1723.

LAVERDE AMAYA, Isidoro. Apuntes sobre biblio-
     grafía colombiana, con muestras escogidas en
     prosa y en verso. Con un apéndice que con-
     tiene la lista de las escritoras colombianas,
     las piezas dramáticas, novelas, libros de
     historia y de viajes escritos por colombia-
     nos. Bogotá, Impr. de Zalamea Hermanos,
     1882. 240, 252 p.   (5324
        "Seudónimos de colombianos": p. 237-40.---
     Jones 1724.

LEAVIT, Sturgis Elleno, and GARCIA PRADA, Car-
     los. A tentative bibliography of Colombian
     literature. Cambridge, Mass., Harvard Univ.
     Press, 1934. 80 p. (Bibliographies of
     Spanish-American literature)   (5325
     Jones 1726a.

MATOS HURTADO, B. Compendio de la historia de
     la literatura colombiana. Bogotá, Edit.
     Marconi, 1925. 234 p.   (5326
     Jones 1731.

MAYA, Rafael. Consideraciones críticas sobre
     la literatura colombiana. Bogotá, Edit. de
     la Librería Voluntad, 1944. 146 p.   (5327

ORTEGA TORRES, José Joaquín. Historia de la
     literatura colombiana; con prólogos de Anto-
     nio Gómez Restrepo y de Daniel Samper Ortega;
     2a. ed. aum. Contiene 568 trozos escogidos
     de 180 autores. Bogotá, Edit. Cromos, 1935.
     1214 p.   (5328
     First edition, 1934.---Jones 1741.

OTERO MUÑOZ, Gustavo. Historia de la litera-
     tura colombiana. (Boletín de historia y an-
     tigüedades, Bogotá, v. 21, p. 43-59, 306-29,
     1934)   (5329
     Jones 1745.

-----. Historia de la literatura colombiana
     (resumen) Bogotá, Impr. de La Luz, 1935.
     205 p.   (5330
     Jones 1746.

-----. Historia de la literatura colombiana;
     6a ed. Bogotá, Edit. Librería Voluntad,
     1949.   (5331

-----. La literatura colonial de Colombia, se-
     guida de un cancionerillo popular. La Paz,
     1928. 324 p.   (5332

OTERO MUÑOZ, Gustavo. La literatura...(Cont.)
     Jones 1749.

RUANO, Jesús María. Resumen historico-crítico
     de la literatura colombiana. Bogotá, Casa
     Edit. Santafé, 1925. 210 p.   (5333
     Jones 1770.

-----. -----. 2a. ed. 1933. 207 p.   (5334

-----. -----. 3a. ed. 1936.   (5335
     Cited in Giraldo Jaramillo, p. 185.

-----. -----. 4a. ed. 1945.   (5336
     Cited in Ib.

SANIN CANO, Baldomero. Letras colombianas.
     México, D.F., Fondo de Cultura Económica,
     1944. 213 p. (Colección Tierra Firme
     2)   (5337

VERGARA Y VERGARA, José María. Historia de
     la literatura en Nueva Granada. Parte pri-
     mera. Desde la conquista hasta la indepen-
     dencia (1538-1820) Bogotá, Impr. de Eche-
     verría Hermanos, 1867, 532 p.   (5338
     Jones 1776.

-----. -----, 2a. ed. con prólogo y anotacio-
     nes de Antonio Gómez Restrepo. Bogotá, Li-
     brería Americana, 1905. 515 p.   (5339
     Jones 1777.

-----. Obras escogidas de don José María Ver-
     gara y Vergara, publicadas por sus hijos
     Francisco José Vergara, Ana Vergara de Sam-
     per y Mercedes Vergara y Belcázar, en el
     primer centenario de su nacimiento. Bajo
     la direccion de Daniel Samper Ortega. Bo-
     gotá, Edit. Minerva, 1931. 5 v.   (5340
        Contents:-v. 1. Cuadros de costumbres.-
     v. 2, Artículos literarios.- v. 3, Biogra-
     fías, con notas aclaratorias de Guillermo
     Hernández de Alba.- v. 4-5, Historia de
     la literatura en Nueva Granada, desde la
     conquista hasta la independencia (1538-1820)
     3a. ed. con notas de Antonio Gómez Restrepo
     y Gustavo Otero Muñoz.---Jones 1777a.

COSTA RICA

SOTELA, Rogelio. Literatura costarricense;
     antología y biografías. San José. Schu-
     mann (Sauter & Co.) 1927. 197 p.   (5341
     Jones 1279.

-----. -----. 2a ed. San José, Impr. Alsina
     (Sauter, Arias & Co.) 1932. 200 p. (Tex-
     tos nacionales)   (5341a

-----. -----. 3a. ed. San José, C. R., Leh-
     mann & Co., 1938. 182 p.   (5342
     Jones 1280.

SOTELA, Rogelio. Valores literarios de Costa
  Rica. San José, Impr. Alsina, 1920.
  293 p.   (5343
  Jones 1281.

CUBA

AYALA DUARTE, Crispín. Historia de la literatura cubana. (Anales de la Universidad Central de Venezuela, Caracas, v. 24, p. 154-83,
  1935)   (5344
  Jones 1786.

BACHILLER Y MORALES, Antonio. Apuntes para la
  historia de las letras y de la instrucción
  pública de la isla de Cuba. Habana, Impr.
  de P. Massana [etc.] 1859-1861. 3 v.   (5345
    Contents:-t. 1, pte. 1a., De la educación
  primaria. pte. 2a., Educación secundaria y
  facultativa profesional. De la instrucción
  facultativa literaria. Enseñanzas universitarias.- t. 2, pte. 3a., Imprenta en la
  isla. Periódicos. Canciones. Poema lírico
  y dramatico. Historiadores. Renacimiento.
  Publicaciones periódicas: catálogo razonado
  y cronológico hasta 1840 inclusive.- t. 3,
  pte. 4a., Galería de hombres útiles. Adiciones. Catálogo de libros y folletos publicados en Cuba desde la introducción de la
  imprenta hasta 1840. Adiciones. "Suplementos y adiciones a los catálogos de la bibliografía cubana [312 titles]" in Revista
  de Cuba, v. 7, p. 354-64, 491-98; v. 8,
  p. 71-8, 124-35, 240-54, 363-72.---Jones
  1787.

-----. -----, con introducción por Francisco
  González del Valle y biografía del autor por
  Vidal Morales... Habana, Cultural, 1936-1937.
  3 v. (Colección de libros cubanos, v. 34-
  36)   (5346
  Jones 1788.

CARBONELL Y RIVERO, José. Evolución de la
  cultura cubana (1608-1927) La Habana,
  Impr. "El Siglo XX", 1928. 18 v.   (5347
  Jones 1797.

CASAL, Julián del. Selección de poesías.
  Introducción por Juan J. Geada y Fernández.
  Habana, Cultural, 1931. cxvii, 184p. (5348
  Bibliografía: p. cxv-cxvii.---Jones 1798.

CRUZ, Manuel de la. Cromitos cubanos (Bocetos
  de autores hispano-americanos) Habana,
  Est. Tip. La Lucha, 1892. 436 p.   (5349
  "Bibliografía de los cromitos cubanos":
  p. 423-36.---Jones 1804.

FORD, Jeremiah Denis Matthias and RAPHAEL,
  Maxwell. A bibliography of Cuban belles-
  lettres. Cambridge, Mass. Harvard Univ.
  Pr., 1933. 204 p. (Bibliographies of
  Spanish-American literature)   (5350

FORD, Jeremiah Denis Matthias and... (Cont.)
  Reviewed with additions by Edith L. Kelly:
  Hispania, v. 16, p. 357-62.---Jones 1831.

GAY-CALBO, Enrique. Orígenes de la literatura
  cubana, ensayo de interpretación. (Universidad de La Habana, Habana, no. 20-21,
  p. 190-236, 1938)   (5351
  Includes bibliography.---Jones 1832a.
  Also published as a separate.

GONZALEZ CURQUEJO, Antonio. Florilegio de escritoras cubanas. Habana, "La Moderna Poe-
  sía", 1910. 356 p.   (5352
  Contains biographical notices.---Jones
  1834.

GONZALEZ DEL VALLE, Emilio Martín. La poesía
  lírica en Cuba; apuntes para un libro de
  biografía y de crítica. Barcelona, L. Tasso,
  1900. 347 p.   (5353
  Jones 1835a.

GUIRAO, Ramón. Orbita de la poesía afrocuba-
  na, 1928-1937 (antología) Selección, notas
  biografías y vocabulario. La Habana, Ucar,
  García y Cía., 1938. 196 p.   (5354
  Jones 1839.

HENRIQUEZ UREÑA, Max. Antología cubana de
  las escuelas. Santiago de Cuba, 1929- .
  pt. 1- .   (5355
  Contains (pt. 1) selections from 42 au-
  thors, with succinct biobibliographical notices.---Jones 1846.

IBARZABAL, Federico de. Cuentos contemporáneos. La Habana, Edit. Trópico, 1937.
  222 p. (Antologías cubanas, 1)   (5356
  Includes biobibliographical sketches.---
  Jones 1850.

KELLY, Edith L. A bibliography of Cuban
  belles-lettres, prepared by Jeremiah D. M.
  Ford...and Maxwell I. Raphael: a review
  with additions. (Hispania, Stanford Uni-
  versity, v. 16, p. 357-62, 1933)   (5357
  Jones 1852.

LOPEZ PRIETO, Antonio. Parnaso cubano. Colección de poesías selectas de autores cubanos desde Zequeira a nuestros días, precedida de una introducción histórico-crítica
  sobre el desarrollo de la poesía en Cuba,
  con biografías. Habana, M. de Villa, 1881.
  370 p.   (5358
  Jones 1868.

MITJANS, Aurelio. Estudio sobre el movimiento científico y literario de Cuba. Habana,
  Impr. de A. Alvarez y Cía., 1890.
  395 p.   (5359
  Jones 1874.

LITERATURE

MITJANS, Aurelio. Historia de la literatura
cubana. Del Monte, Heredia, Milanés, Saco,
Gertrudis Gómez de Avellaneda, Zenea, etc.
La vida y la obra de Mitjans, por Manuel de
la Cruz. Madrid, Edit. América [1918?]
389 p. (Biblioteca Andrés Bello,
t. 1)   (5360
  Jones 1875.

PERRIER, José Luis. Bibliografía dramática
cubana. New York, The Phos Pr., 1926.
115 p.   (5361
  Jones 1893.

REMOS Y RUBIO, Juan José. Historia de la
literatura cubana. tomo 1. La Habana, J.
Abela, 1925. 403 p.   (5362
  Jones 1899.

-----. -----. Another ed. [Habana] 1945.
3 v.   (5362a
  Bibliografía: v. 3, p. 507-57.

-----. Resumen de historia de la literatura
cubana. Habana, Tipos, Molina y Cía.,
1930. 415 p.   (5363
  Bibliografía: p. 371-89.---Jones 1900.

-----. Tendencias de la narración imagina-
tiva en Cuba. Habana, La Casa Montalvo-
Cárdenas, 1935. 204 p.   (5364
  Bibliografía: p. 209-11.---Jones 1901.

DOMINICAN REPUBLIC

ALFAU DURAN, Vetilio. Apuntes de bibliografía dominicana, en torno a las rectificaciones hechas a la obra del Prof. Waxman.
Ciudad Trujillo, Impr. Libr. Dominicana,
1956. 8 p.   (5365
  Reprinted from Clio, no. 108, jul/dic.
1956.

ARCHAMBAULT, Pedro María. Pinares adentro,
novela criolla, con un prólogo del doctor
Americo Lugo. Barcelona, Maucci, 1929.
254 p.   (5366
  Bibliography of Dominican literature
included in "Prólogo".---Jones 2979.

AYALA DUARTE, Crispín. Tratado antológico-
crítico de la literatura dominicana. (Boletín de la Academia Venezolana, Caracas,
v. 1, p. 66-91, 1934)   (5367
  Jones 2980.

BOGGS, Ralph Steele. Selective bibliography
of Dominican literature. (Bulletin hispanique, Bordeaux, v. 32, p. 404-12,
1930)   (5368
  Jones 2981.

GARCIA GODOY, Federico. Dominican intellectual life. (Inter-America, New York, v. 3,

GARCIA GODOY, Federico. Dominican... (Cont.)
p. 298-303, 1920)   (5369
  First published in Spanish in Nuestra América, Buenos Aires, July, 1919.---Jones 2992.

-----. La literatura dominicana. New York,
París, 1916. 44 p.   (5370
  "Extrait de la Revue hispanique, t. 37."
---Jones 2993.

HENRIQUEZ UREÑA, Pedro. Bibliografía literaria de Santo Domingo. (Repertorio americano, San José, C.R., no. 7, 12, 14,
1929)   (5371
  Jones 2996.

-----. La cultura y las letras coloniales en
Santo Domingo. Buenos Aires, Universidad
de Buenos Aires, 1936. 193 p. (Biblioteca
de dialectología hispanoamericana)   (5372
  Contains biobibliographical comments.---
Jones 2997.

-----. Literatura dominicana. New York, Pa-
rís, 1917. 26 p.   (5373
  "Extrait de la Revue hispanique, t. xl."
Intended to supplement García Godoy's study.
---Jones 2998.

LUGO, Américo. Bibliografía. Santo Domingo,
Impr. La Cuna de América, 1906. 115 p.(5374

MEJIA, Abigail. Historia de la literatura dominicana. Ciudad Trujillo, Edit. "Caribes",
1937. 146 p.   (5375
  Jones 3003.

RODRIGUEZ DEMORIZI, Emilio. Poesía popular
dominicana, v. 1. Ciudad Trujillo. Impr.
de la Nación, 1938. 300 p.   (5376
  Jones 3007c.

WAXMAN, Samuel Montefiore. A bibliography of
the belles-lettres of Santo Domingo. Cambridge, Mass., Harvard Univ. Pr., 1931.
31 p. (Bibliographies of Spanish American
literature)   (5377
  Jones 3013.

ECUADOR

ALBORNOZ, Miguel Angel. Algo sobre el movimiento literario nacional en la primera centuria de independencia, 24 de mayo de 1922.
Quito, Impr. de la Universidad Central, 1922.
38 p.   (5378
  From Revista jurídico-literaria de Quito,
v. 26 p. 53-90.---Jones 1941.

ANDRADE COELLO, Alejandro. El Ecuador intelectual: índice del movimiento literario reciente. Córdoba, B. Cubas, 1919. 27 p.   (5379
  "De la Revista de la Universidad Nacional
de Córdoba, año 6, no. 2 y 3, abr. y mayo de
1919".---Jones 1944.

ANDRADE COELLO, Alejandro. Intellectual
development in Ecuador. (Bulletin of Pan
American Union. Washington, D.C. v. 50,
p. 265-75, 1920)   (5380
English version of an article in Revista
de la Universidad Nacional de Córdoba.---
Jones 1946.

-----. Intellectual Ecuador, an index to the
recent literary movement. (Inter-America,
New York, v. 3, p. 144-56, 1920)   (5381
Jones 1947.

ARIAS ROBALINO, Augusto. El cristal indígena
(Francisco Eugenio Javier de Santa Cruz y
Espejo) Quito, Edit. América, 1934.
209 p.   (5382
Bibliografía: p. 203-09.---Jones 1954.

-----. Panorama de la literatura ecuatoriana. Quito, 1936. 144 p.   (5383
Jones 1955.

-----. -----. Quito, Empresa Editorial "El
Comercio" 1946. 399 p. (Biblioteca ecuatoriana "Ultimas noticias", 3)   (5384

BARRERA, Isaac J. Apuntaciones históricas
sobre la literatura ecuatoriana. (Boletín
de la Biblioteca Nacional, Quito, v. 1,
p. 1-33, 192-232, 1926)   (5385
Jones 1956.

-----. Literatura ecuatoriana; apuntaciones
históricas. (Revista de la Sociedad Jurídico-Literaria de Quito, t. 29, p. 77-195,
1924)   (5386
Jones 1957.

-----. La literatura ecuatoriana. Contribución al libro centenario El Mundo Boliviano. Quito, Impr. de la Universidad Central,
1924.   (5387
Jones 1958.

-----. -----. 2a. ed. Quito, Impr. Nacional,
1926, 152 p.   (5388
Jones 1959.

CUADRA, José de la. 12 siluetas, (Escritores
y artistas ecuatorianos) Quito, Edit. América, 1934. 150 p.   (5389
Jones 1969.

GALLO ALMEIDA, Luis. Sumario de la literatura ecuatoriana para uso de los alumnos de
instrucción secundaria. Quito, Tip. de la
"Prensa Católica", 1921. 256 p.   (5390
Jones 1984.

HERRERA, Pablo. Ensayo sobre la historia de
la literatura ecuatoriana. (Boletín de la
Biblioteca Nacional, Quito, t. 2, p. 37-65,
73-124, 1927)   (5391
Jones 1990.

MERA, Juan León. Antología ecuatoriana. Can-
tares del pueblo ecuatoriano, precedida de
un estudio sobre ellos, ilustrada con notas
acerca del lenguaje del pueblo y seguido de
varias antiguallas curiosas. Ed. hecha por
orden y bajo el auspicio de la Academia
Ecuatoriana. Quito, Impr. de la Universidad
Central del Ecuador, 1892, 504 p.   (5392
Jones 1992.

-----. Ojeada histórico-crítica sobre la poesía ecuatoriana, desde su época más remota
hasta nuestros días. Quito, Impr. de J. P.
Sanz, 1868. 503 p.   (5393
Jones 1993.

-----. -----., 2a. ed. seguida de nuevos apéndices. Barcelona, Impr. de J. Cunil Sala,
1893. 633 p.   (5394
Jones 1994.

RIVERA, Guillermo. A tentative bibliography
of the belles-lettres of Ecuador. Cambridge,
Mass., Harvard Univ. Pr., 1934. 76 p. (Bibliographies of Spanish-American literature)   (5395
Jones 2004a.

ROLANDO, Carlos A. Las bellas letras en el
Ecuador. Guayaquil, Impr. i Tall. Municipales, 1944. 157 p. (Bibliografía de autores nacionales: Literatura)   (5396

RUMAZO GONZALEZ, Alfonso. Siluetas líricas de
poetas ecuatorianos. Quito, Edit. Bolívar,
1932. 203 p. (Biblioteca ecuatoriana. Serie independiente)   (5397
Jones 2013.

VASCONES, Francisco. Historia de la literatu-
ra ecuatoriana. t. 1. Quito, Tip. de la
Prensa Católica, 1919. 285, 195 p.   (5398
Jones 2023.

EL SALVADOR

MAYORGA RIVAS, Román. Guirnalda salvadoreña.
Colección de poesías de los bardos de la República del Salvador, precedidas de apuntes
biográficos y juicios críticos sobre cada
uno de sus autores. Con un prólogo del dr.
don Tomás Ayón. San Salvador, Impr. del
doctor F. Sagrini, 1884-1886. 3 v.   (5399
Jones 1370.

GUATEMALA

ARGÜELLO, Santiago. Modernismo y modernistas.
Guatemala, 1935. 2 v.   (5400
Jones 28.

CIRUTE, Juan. The Guatemalan novel: a critical
bibliography. 1959.   (5401

CIRUTE, Juan. The Guatemalan... (Cont.)
Manuscript., PHD. dissertation, Tulane
University. Cited in Bryant, item 80.

MENCOS FRANCO, Agustín. Literatura guatemal-
teca en el período de la colonia. Guatemala,
Tip. Nacional, 1937. 192 p.   (5402
Jones 1302.

PORTA MENCOS, Humberto. Parnaso guatemalteco
(1750-1928) Con notas biográficas y bibliográficas. Guatemala, 1928. 560 p.   (5403
Jones 1306.

RODRIGUEZ CERNA, José. Panorama de la literatura guatemalteca. (Boletín de la Biblioteca Nacional, Guatemala, v. 1, p. 267-72,
1934)   (5404
Jones 1308.

HONDURAS

CASTRO, Jesús. Antología de poetas hondure-
ños, 1869-1910. Tegucigalpa, Tall. Tip.
Nacionales, 1939. 304 p.   (5405
Includes bibliographical notes.---Jones
1320.

DURON Y GAMERO, Rómulo Ernesto. Honduras literaria; colección de escritos en prosa y
verso, precedidos de apuntes biográficos.
Tegucigalpa, Tip. Nacional, 1896-1899.
2 v.   (5406
Jones 1324.

MEXICO

ALTAMIRANO, Alberto I. Influence de la littérature française sur la littérature mexi-
caine; essai de littérature comparée. México, D.F., Cosmos (1935?) 111 p.   (5407
Bibliographie: p. 103-05.---Jones 2044.

ARREOLA CORTES, Raúl. Letras michoacanas contemporáneas. Morelia, Mich., 1949.
16 p.   (5408

GARCIA CANTU, Rafael. Algunos apuntes acerca
de las letras y la cultura de Nuevo Leon en
la centuria de 1810 a 1910. Monterrey,
1910. 621 p.   (5409
Jones 2187.

GONZALEZ PEÑA, Carlos. Historia de la literatura mexicana. México, D.F., 1929.
550 p.   (5410
Jones 2218.

-----. -----. 2a. ed. corr. y aum. México,
D.F., 1940. 327 p.   (5411
Jones 2218.

HENRIQUEZ UREÑA, Pedro. La literatura mexicana
de la época de la independencia (1800-1821)
(Anales del Museo Nacional de Arqueología,
Historia y Etnografía, México, t. 5, 14 p.
1913.   (5412
Jones 2239.

JIMENEZ RUEDA, Julio. Historia de la literatura mexicana. México, D.F., Edit. "Cultura",
1928. 296 p.   (5413
Bibliografía: p. 233-54.---Jones 2269.

-----. -----. 2a. ed. México, D.F., Botas,
1934. 323 p.   (5414
Bibliografía: p. 251-74.---Jones 2270.

-----. -----. 3a. ed. puesta al día y aum. con
buen número de notas bibliográficas. México,
D.F., Ediciones Botas, 1942. 316 p.   (5415

-----. -----. 4a. ed. México, D.F., Botas,
1946. 347 p.   (5415a

-----. -----. 5a. ed. México, D.F., Botas,
1953. 387 p.   (5415b

LEAL, Luis. Bibliografía del cuento mexicano.
México, D.F., Ediciones de Andrés, 1958.
162 p. (Colección Studium, 21)   (5416

MARTINEZ, José Luis. Literatura mexicana, siglo XX, 1910-1949. México, D.F., Robredo,
1949-1950. 2 pts. (Clásicos y modernos,
creación y crítica literaria, 3-4)   (5417
Part 2: Guías bibliográficas.

MENDOZA, Vicente T. El romance español y el
corrido mexicano; estudio comparativo. México, D.F., Ediciones de la Universidad Nacional Autónoma, 1939. 832 p.   (5418
"Lista de romances impresos en México durante la época colonial": p. 783-85. "Lista de
corridos que no aparecen en esta obra": p.
786-92. Bibliografía: p. 793-99.---Jones
2340a.

MOORE, Ernest Richard. Obras críticas y biográficas referentes a la novela mexicana anterior al siglo XX. (Revista iberoamericana,
México, D.F., v.3, p. 235-64, 1941)   (5419
380 titles.---Jones 2371c.

OLAVARRIA Y FERRARI, Enrique de. El arte literario en México. Noticias biográficas y críticas de sus más notables escritores. Madrid,
187-? 224 p.   (5420
Title from Nicolás León's Bibliografía bibliográfica mexicana.---Jones 2389.

-----. -----. 2a. ed. Madrid, Espinosa y Bautista [1878] 224 p.   (5421
Jones 2390.

ORTIZ DE MONTELLANO, Bernardo. La poesía indígena de México. México, D.F., Tall. Gráf. de

ORTIZ DE MONTELLANO, Bernardo. ... (Cont.)
la Nación, 1935. 93 p. (5422
Jones 2397.

PIMENTEL, Francisco. Historia crítica de la
literatura y de las ciencias en México desde la conquista hasta nuestros días. Poetas. México, D.F., Librería de la Enseñanza, 1885. 736 p. (5423
Includes poets only. No more published.
---Jones 2428.

-----. Historia crítica de la poesía en México; nueva ed. corr. y muy aum. México, D.F.,
Of. Tip. de la Secretaría de Fomento, 1892.
976 p. (5424
Jones 2429.

-----. -----. (In the author's Obras. México, D.F., 1903-1904. t. 4-5) (5425
Cited in Iguíniz, p. 457.

QUIROZ, Alberto. Situacion de la literatura
mexicana. León, Ediciones Guanajuato-Méxi-
co, 1934. 62 p. (5426
Jones 2441.

READ, John Lloyd. The Mexican historical
novel, 1826-1910. New York, Instituto de
las Españas, 1939. 337 p. (5427
Bibliography: p. 320-37.---Jones 2451.

SANCHEZ MARMOL, Emmanuel. National letters.
(In Sierra, Justo. México, its social
evolution. México, D.F., 1900. t. 1, v.2,
p. 603-63) (5428
Published also in Spanish.---Jones 2483.

TAYLOR, Bárbara H. de. La tradición y la
leyenda en la literatura mexicana. México,
D.F., 1936. 80 p. mimeogr. (5429
Bibliografía de obras consultadas: p. 67-
80.---Jones 2521a.

TORRES BODET, Jaime. Perspectiva de la literatura mexicana actual, 1915-1928. México,
D.F., 1928. 43 p. (5430
Bibliografía escogida: p. 34-42.---Jones
2532.

TORRES RIOSECO, Arturo. Bibliografía de la
novela mejicana. Cambridge, Mass., Harvard Univ. Pr., 1933. 58 p. (Bibliographies of Spanish-American literature) (5431
Intended to supplement Iguíniz' Bibliografía de novelistas mexicanos.---Jones
2533.

-----, and WARNER, Ralph Emerson. Bibliogra-
fía de la poesía mexicana. Cambridge, Mass.
Harvard Univ. Pr., 1934. xxxix, 86 p.
(Bibliographies of Spanish-American litera-
ture) (5432
Jones 2534.

URBINA, Luis Gonzaga, HENRIQUEZ UREÑA, Pedro,
and RANGEL, Nicolás. Antología del centenario, estudio documentado de la literatura
mexicana durante el primer siglo de independencia. México, D.F., Impr. de M. León Sánchez, 1910. 2 v. (5433
Pt. 1, 1800-1821. Bibliografía general:
v. 1, p. ccxlvi-cclvi.---Jones 2538.

URIBE-ECHAVARRIA, Juan. La novela de la revolucion mexicana y la novela hispanoamericana actual. (Anales de la Universidad de Chile, Santiago, 4o. trim. 1935, p. 1-95,
1936) (5434
Bibliografía: p. 90-5.---Jones 2539.

PANAMA

DOYLE, Henry Grattan. A tentative bibliography
of the belles-lettres of Panama. Cambridge,
Mass., Harvard Univ. Pr., 1934. 21 p. (Bibliographies of Spanish-American literature) (5435
Jones 1350.

GARCIA S., Ismael. Historia de la literatura
panameña. México, D.F., Universidad Nacional Autónoma de México, 1964. 189 p. (Manuales universitarios. Textos de la Escuela de Verano) (5435a
Bibliography: p. 181-89.

MENDEZ PEREIRA, Octavio. Parnaso panameño, con
prólogo y biografías. Panamá, Tip. El Istmo,
1916. 392 p. (5436
Jones 1354.

MIRO, Rodrigo. Bibliografía poética panameña.
Panama, 1942. 60 p. (5437

PARAGUAY

RAPHAEL, Maxwell Isaac, and FORD, Jeremiah
Denis Matthias. A tentative bibliography
of Paraguayan literature Cambridge, Mass.,
Harvard Univ. Pr., 1934. 25 p. (Bibliogra-
phies of Spanish-American literature) (5438
Jones 2620.

PERU

BASADRE, Jorge. Una bibliografía de la literatura peruana. (Boletín bibliográfico, Biblioteca Central, Universidad Mayor de San
Marcos, Lima, año 9, no. 2, p. 28-38,
1936) (5439
Jones 2629.

BIBLIOTECA de cultura peruana, 1a. ser. Paris,
Desclée de Brouwer, 1938. 12 v. (5440
Editor: Ventura García Calderón. Includes
bibliographies. Contents: - v.1, Literatura

BIBLIOTECA de cultura peruana ... (Cont.)
inca, selección de Jorge Basadre. Introducción general. - v. 2, Los cronistas de la
conquista; selección, prólogo, notas y con-
cordancias de Horacio H. Urteaga. - v.3,
Vega (El Inca) Garcilaso de la. Páginas escogidas. - v.4, Los cronistas de convento;
selección de Pedro M. Benvenutto Murrieta y
Guillermo Lohmann Villena, dirigida por José
de la Riva Agüero. - v. 5, El apogeo de la
literatura colonial: Las poetisas anónimas,
El Lunarejo, Caviedes. - v. 6, Concolorcorvo.
El Lazarillo de ciegos caminantes desde Buenos Aires hasta Lima. - v. 7, Los místicos.
- v. 8, Los románticos. - v. 9, Costumbris-
tas y satíricos. 2v. - v. 10, Paz Soldán y
Unanue, Pedro. Diccionario de peruanismos.
- v. 11, Palma, Ricardo. Tradiciones escogidas. - v. 12, Chocano, J. S. Poesías escogidas.---Jones 2634.

GARCIA CALDERON, Ventura. La literatura peruana (1535-1914) New York, París, 1914.
91 p.   (5441
"Extrait de la Revue hispanique, t. 31".
---Jones 2655.

LEAVITT, Sturgis Elleno. A bibliography of
Peruvian literature (1821-1919)   (5442
Jones 2667. Reprinted from the Romanic
review, v. 13, no.2, p. 151-94, Apr./June
1922.

-----. A tentative bibliography of Peruvian
literature. Cambridge, Mass., Harvard Univ.
Pr., 1932. 37 p. (Bibliographies of Spanish-American literature)   (5443
A list of bibliographies, histories of
literature and biographies consulted: 5th
preliminary leaf. For a review, see Jorge
Basadre's article in the Boletín bibliográfico, Biblioteca Central, Universidad Mayor de San Marcos, año 9, no. 2, p. 28-38.
---Jones 2668.

NUÑEZ, Estuardo. Panorama actual de la poesía peruana. Lima, 1938. 144 p.   (5444
Jones 2705.

PRADO Y UGARTECHE, Javier. El genio de la
lengua y la literatura castellana y sus caracteres en la historia intelectual del Perú.
Lima, 1918. 194 p.   (5445
Jones 2726.

PRINCE, Carlos. I. Bosquejo de la literatura
peruana colonial, causas favorables y adver-
sas a su desarrollo. II. Biblioteca peruana
de la colonia. Lima, Impreso en Casa del
Autor, 1910-1911. 311 p.   (5446
1,378 titles are listed, including manuscripts, "Periódicos de la época colonial impresos en Lima" (no. 1145-1170) Contains
also an alphabetical list of authors arranged
by century, 16th, 17th, 18th and 19th to 1821.

PRINCE, Carlos. I. Bosquejo de la... (Cont.)
---Jones 2730.

-----. Suplemento a la biblioteca peruana colonial. Lima, Impreso en Casa del Autor,
1912. 142 p.   (5447

RIVA AGÜERO, José de la. Carácter de la lite-
ratura del Perú independiente. Lima, E.
Rosay, 1905. 299 p.   (5448
Jones 2735.

SANCHEZ, Luis Alberto. Historia de la litera-
tura peruana. 1. Los poetas de la colonia.
Lima, 1921. 301 p.   (5449
Jones 2741.

-----. Indice de la poesía peruana contempo-
ránea (1900-1937) Santiago de Chile, Edi-
ciones Ercilla, 1938. 359 p. (Colección
Biblioteca América)   (5450
Contains biobibliographical notices.---
Jones 2742.

-----. La literatura del Perú. Buenos Aires,
Impr. de la Universidad, 1939. 189 p. (Instituto de Cultura Latino-Americana. Las literaturas americanas, 1)   (5451
Bibliografía elemental: p. 181-86.---Jones
2743.

-----. La literatura del Perú republicano.
Derrotero para una historia espiritual del
Perú. (Atenea, Concepción, Chile, año 13,
v.33, p. 49-90, 1936)   (5452
Jones 2744.

-----. Literatura peruana. Lima, Casa Edit.
"La Opinión Nacional", 1929. v. 2.   (5453
Jones 2745.

-----. Literatura peruana. Derrotero para
una historia espiritual del Perú. Lima,
Edit. PTCM, 1946. 253 p.   (5454
2a. ed., corresponds to v. 1 of the edition published in 1950-1951 in Buenos Aires.

-----. ------. Buenos Aires, Guaranía, 1950-
1951. 6 v.   (5455

TAURO, Alberto. Bibliografía peruana de lite-
ratura, 1931-1958. Lima, 1959.   (5456
Reprinted from Boletín de la Biblioteca
Nacional, no. 19-20, p. 109-298, 1956-1957.

PUERTO RICO

AYALA DUARTE, Crispín. Historia de la literatura en Puerto Rico. (Boletín de la Academia Venezolana, Caracas, v.1, p. 310-44,
1934)   (5457
Jones 2783.

COLL Y TOSTE, Cayetano. Historia de la poesía en Puerto Rico. (Boletín histórico de
Puerto Rico, San Juan, v.13, p. 140-66,
1926)   (5458
Jones 2787.

FERNANDEZ JUNCOS, Manuel. Antología portorri-
queña, prosa y verso, para lectura escolar.
New York, Hinds, Noble & Eldredge, 1913.
267 p.   (5459
Biographical notices of 28 authors. Other
editions: 1907, 1923.---Jones 2790.

RIVERA, Guillermo. A tentative bibliography
of the belles-lettres of Porto Rico. Cambridge, Mass., Harvard Univ. Pr., 1931.
61 p. (Bibliographies of Spanish-American
literature)   (5460

SOUTH AMERICA

MOSES, Bernard. Spanish colonial literature
in South America. London, New York, Hispanic Society of America, 1922. 661 p. (Hispanic notes and monographs. Hispanic American series, 1)   (5461
Bibliography: p. 585-650.---Jones 322.

U.S. Library of Congress. List of references on South American literature. Washington, D.C., 1916. 4 p.   (5462
Cited in Yang.

-----. Select list of references on the literature and art of South America. Washington, D.C., 1912. 4 p.   (5463
Cited in Yang.

URUGUAY

BARBAGELATA, Hugo D. Una centuria literaria,
1800-1900. (Poetas y prosistas uruguayos)
París, Biblioteca Mundo-Latino, 1924.
486 p.   (5464
Extracts preceded by biobibliographical
sketches of 68 Uruguayan authors.---Jones
2819.

CAILLAVA, Domingo A. La literatura gauchesca en el Uruguay; sinopsis histórica, proe-
mio de Don Mario Falcao Espalter. Montevideo, C. García, 1921. 71 p.   (5465
"Catalogo razonado de las publicaciones
de índole gauchesca, editadas en Montevideo."---Jones 2824.

COESTER, Alfred Lester. A tentative bibliography of the belles-lettres of Uruguay.
Cambridge, Mass., Harvard Univ. Pr., 1931.
22 p. (Bibliographies of Spanish-American
literature)   (5466
Jones 2826.

GARCIA CALDERON, Ventura, and BARBAGELATA, Hugo
D. La literatura uruguaya (1757-1917) (Revue
hispanique, New York [etc.] v.40, p. 415-542,
1917)   (5467
Jones 2839.

LEAVITT, Sturgis Elleno. Uruguayan literature;
a bibliography of literary criticism, bio-
graphy and literary controversy. Stanford
University, 1922. 22 p.   (5468
Reprint from Hispania, v. 5, no. 2-3, Mar-
May, 1922.---Jones 2846.

LUISI, Luisa. A traves de libros y autores.
Buenos Aires, Ediciones de "Nuestra América",
1925. 271 p.   (5469
Contents. - Carlos Reyles, novelista. -
Adolfo Montiel Ballesteros. - Vicente A. Sa-
laverri. - La poesía de Delmira Augustini. -
"El hermano Asno", novela de Eduardo Barrios.
- La poesía de Enrique González Martínez. -
Tres aspectos de la poesía uruguaya contem-
poránea: la gracia, lo pintoresco, la profun-
didad.---Jones 2847.

-----. La literatura del Uruguay en al año de
su centenario (1930) Washington, D.C., Unión
Panamericana [1930] 58 p. (Serie sobre bibliotecas y bibliografía, no. 4)   (5470
Del Boletín de la Unión Panamericana, julio
de 1930.

-----. The literature of Uruguay in the year
of its constitutional centenary. (Bulletin,
Pan American Union, Washington, D.C., v.64,
p. 655-92, 1930)   (5471
Literature of Uruguay in the Library of
the Pan American Union: p. 692-95.---Jones
2848. Also published in the series, Library
and bibliography, no. 4. 41 p.

NUÑEZ REGUEIRO, Manuel. Contemporary Uruguayan literature. (Inter-America, New York,
v.3, p. 306-15, 1920)   (5472
From Nuestra América, Buenos Aires, June
1919.---Jones 2856.

RELA, Walter. Contribución a la bibliografía
de la literatura uruguaya, 1835-1962. Montevideo, Universidad de la Republica, 1963.
76 p. (Publ. del Departamento de Literatura Iberoamericano de la Facultad de Humanidades y Ciencias).   (5473

ROXLO, Carlos. Historia crítica de la litera-
tura uruguaya. Montevideo, A. Barreiro y
Ramos, 1912-1916. 7 v.   (5474
Jones 2861.

ZUM FELDE, Alberto. Crítica de la literatura
uruguaya. Montevideo, M. Barcía, 1921.
356 p. (Colección estudios)   (5475
Jones 2880.

ZUM FELDE, Alberto. La literatura del Uruguay. Buenos Aires, Instituto de Cultura Latino-Americana, 1939. 146 p. (Las literaturas americanas, 2) (5476
Bibliografía: p. 144.---Jones 2881.

-----. Proceso intelectual del Uruguay y crítica de su literatura. Montevideo, Impr. Nacional Colorado, 1930. 3 v. (5477
"Obras consultadas": v.1, p. 314-15.--- Jones 2882.

-----. -----. Montevideo, Edit. Claridad [1941] 639 p. (Biblioteca de escritores uruguayos, v.8) (5478

VENEZUELA

ANGARITA ARVELO, Rafael. Historia y crítica de la novela en Venezuela. Leipzig, Impr. de A. Pries, 1938. 173 p. (5479
Jones 2882a.

ASOCIACION Venezolana de Literatura, Ciencias y Bellas Artes. Primer libro venezolano de literatura, ciencias y bellas artes, ofrenda al Gran Mariscal de Ayacucho. Caracas, Tip. El Cojo (1a. pte.); Tip. Moderna (2a. pte.) 1895. 216 p. (5480
Contents. - 1a.pte., Buenas letras. Ciencias. Bellas Artes. Bibliografía. - 2a. pte., Antología general. Notas biográficas. Ultimas páginas. Indice. Includes Frydensberg's Materiales para la bibliografía nacional of about 2,000 titles.---Jones 2886.

BRICEÑO IRAGORRY, Mario. Lecturas venezolanas. Caracas, Edit. Sur-América, 1930. 319 p. (5481
With biographical notices.---Jones 2891.

CALCAÑO, Julio. Parnaso venezolano; colección de poesías de autores venezolanos desde mediados del siglo XVIII hasta nuestros días precedida de una introducción acerca del origen y progreso de la poesía en Venezuela. Caracas, Tip. de "El Cojo", 1892. 574 p. (5482
Jones 2892.

-----. Reseña histórica de la literatura venezolana. Caracas, Tip de El Cojo, 1888. 29 p. (5483
Jones 2893.

CARBONELL, Diego. Venezuela literaria, científica e industrial. Rio de Janeiro, Pimenta de Mello & C., 1922. 75 p. (5484
Jones 2894.

GARCIA CHUECOS, Héctor. Historia de la cultura intelectual de Venezuela desde su descubrimiento hasta 1810. (Boletín de la Academia Venezolana, Caracas, v.3, p. 76-135,

GARCIA CHUECOS, Héctor. Historia de... (Cont.) 227-81, 1936) (5485
Jones 2913.

GRASES, Pedro. Fuentes generales para el estudio de la literatura venezolana. [Caracas] Dirección de Cultura y Bellas Artes, n.d. 30 p. (5486
Reprinted from Revista nacional de cultura, no. 81, p. 86-99, jul./ag. 1950, with index of authors and of titles added.

-----. Nuevos temas de bibliografía y cultura venezolanas. Maracaibo, Universidad de Zulia, 1960. 379 p. (5487
Guide to cultural and historical bibliography of Venezuela, 1810-1950.

PICON-FEBRES, Gonzalo. La literatura venezolana en el siglo diez y nueve (ensayo de historia crítica) Caracas, "Empresa El Cojo", 1906. 429 p. (5488
Jones 2944.

PICON SALAS, Mariano. Formación y proceso de la literatura venezolana. Caracas, Edit. C. Acosta, 1940. 271 p. (5489
"Bibliografía de la literatura venezolana 1930-1940 por Pascual Venegas Filardo": Appendix: 132 titles.---Jones 2944a.

QUIROS, Luis Ovidio. El Zulia literario del siglo XIX. Caracas, 1933. 40 p. (5490
Jones 2945.

RATCLIFF, Dilwyn Fritschel. Venezuelan prose fiction. New York, Instituto de las Españas, 1933. 286 p. (5491
Bibliography: p. 266-73.---Jones 2946.

ROJAS, José María. Biblioteca de escritores venezolanos contemporáneos, ordenada con noticias biográficas. Caracas, Rojas Hermanos, 1875. 808 p. (5492
Jones 2952.

SOLA, Otto d'. Antología de la moderna poesía venezolana. Caracas, Edit. Impresores Unidos, 1940. 2 v. (5493
Includes biographical notices.---Jones 2959a.

USLAR PIETRI, Arturo, and PADRON, Julián. Antología del cuento moderno venezolano (1895-1935) Caracas, Escuela Técnica Industrial, 1940. 2 v. (Biblioteca venezolana de cultura) (5494
Includes biobibliographical notices.--- Jones 2962a.

VENEZUELA. Universidad Central. Escuela de Letras. Centro Literarios. Bibliografía de la novela venezolana. [Caracas] Facultad de Humanidades y Educación [1963] 69 p. (5495

WAXMAN, Samuel Montefiore. A bibliography of
the belles-lettres of Venezuela. Cambridge,
Mass., Harvard Univ. Pr., 1935. 145 p.
(Bibliographies of Spanish-American litera-
ture)   (5496
Jones 2976.

WEST INDIES

CANTON, E. Berthe. A bibliography of West
Indian literature, 1900-1957; bibliographie

CANTON, E. Berthe. A bibliography ... (Cont.)
de littérature antillaise, 1900-1957. [Port-
of-Spain, Caribbean Commission [1958]
57 p.   (5497
Published as part I of the Current Caribbean
bibliography, v. 7, 1957.

MONA, Jamaica. University College of the West
Indies. Library. West Indian literature; a
select bibliography. Mona, 1964. 32p. (5498
Based on A bibliography of the West Indian
literature, 1900-1957. See previous item.

MAPS

GENERAL

AMERICAN Geographical Society of New York. A
catalogue of maps of Hispanic America, including maps in scientific periodicals and
books, and sheet and atlas maps, with articles on the cartography of the several countries, and maps showing the extent and character of existing surveys. New York,
[1933] 4 v. (Map of Hispanic America, publ.
3)   (5499
Contents: - v.1, Maps of Mexico, Central
America and the West Indies. - v.2, Maps of
South America, Colombia, Ecuador, Peru, and
Bolivia. - v.3, Maps of Venezuela, the Guianas, Brazil and Paraguay. - v.4, Maps of the
Argentine Republic, Chile, and Uruguay. The
work of compiling the catalogue was begun in
1920 under the direction of F. J. Teggart;
the examination of the collection in seven
libraries and the selection and preparation
of map lists was done by Nicolas George.
(Cf. Introd. by Raye R. Platt).---Jones 11.

AMERICAN Scientific Congress, 8th, Washington,
D.C., 1940. Catalogue of an exhibition of
maps...comprising some 400 maps and other
materials related to the programs of Section
III, Geological sciences and Section VIII,
History and Geography, arranged by Lawrence
Martin. Washington, D.C., Govt. Print. Off.,
1940. 14 p.   (5500
122 maps are listed.

ARGENTINA. Biblioteca Nacional. Catálogo de
la mapoteca. Prólogo de M. Selva. Buenos
Aires, Impr. de la Biblioteca Nacional,
1941. 2v.   (5501

BRAVO, Francisco Javier. Atlas de cartas geográficas de los países de la América Meridional, en que estuvieron situadas las más importantes misiones de los Jesuitas; como
también de los territorios sobre cuya posesión versaron allí las principales cuestiones
entre España y Portugal; acompañado de varios documentos sobre estas últimas, y pre-

BRAVO, Francisco Javier. Atlas de... (Cont.)
cedido de una introducción histórica. Madrid, Impr. de M. Rivadeneyra, 1872.
51 p.   (5503
"Catálogo de los documentos relativos a
las cuestiones entre españoles y portugueses
en el Río de la Plata y Amazonas, y que forman parte de mi colección": p. 33-40. "Catalogo de los documentos relativos a los tratados ajustados entre España y Portugal sobre
límites de los territorios que poseían en
América ambas naciones (De mi colección)":
p. 41-51.---Jones 72.

CABRAL, Alfredo do Valle. Relação dos mappas,
chartas, planos, plantas e perspectivas geographicas relativos a America meridional que
se conservam na Secção de Manuscriptos da
Bibliotheca Nacional. (Annaes da Bibliotheca
Nacional, Rio de Janeiro, v.1, p. 321-34,
1876-1877)   (5504
Jones 1219.

CHICAGO, University. Library. Atlases in
libraries of Chicago, a bibliography and
union check list. Chicago, 1936.
244 p.   (5505
Includes the Americas.

LATORRE, Germán. La cartografía colonial ame-
ricana. Sevilla, Estab. Tip. de la Guía
Oficial, 1916. 79 p.   (5506
From the Boletín del Centro de Estudios
Americanistas, 1915-1916. Subtitle: Car-
tas geográficas más antiguas referentes al
Nuevo Mundo, contenidas en el Archivo Ge-
neral de Indias.---Jones 248.

MUÑOZA MALUSCHKA, Dora. Cartografía primitiva americana. (Revista chilena de historia y geografía, Santiago, v. 55, p. 211-
44, 1927)   (5507
Jones 326.

PAN AMERICAN UNION. Division of Intellectual
Cooperation. Maps and charts of Latin America. [Washington, D.C., 1947] 2 p. (5508

PHILLIPS, Philip Lee. A list of works relating to cartography. Washington, D.C., Govt. Print. Off., 1901. 90 p.   (5509
Reprinted from A list of maps of America in the Library of Congress.

SCHULLER, Rudolph R. Primera contribución al estudio de la cartografía americana. Montevideo, A. Barreira y Ramos, 1905. 59 p. (Anales del Museo Nacional de Montevideo. Sección Histórico-Filosófica, t. 2, entrega 1)   (5511
Bibliografía: p. 49-56.---Jones 442.

SPAIN. Ejército. Servicio Geográfico. Archivo de Planos: catálogo de atlas. [Madrid] 1962. 419 p.   (5512

TULANE University of Louisiana, New Orleans. Middle American Reserach Institute. Maps in the Frederick L. Hoffman Collection. New Orleans, 1939. 146 p. (Inventory of the collections of the Middle American Research Institute, no. 3)   (5513
Prepared in cooperation with the Historical Records Survey of the Works Projects Administration.

-----. -----. Maps in the Library of the Middle American Research Institute. New Orleans, 1941. viii, 282 p. (Inventory of the collections of the Middle American Research Institute, no. 4)   (5514
Prepared in cooperation with the Historical Records Survey of the Works Projects Administration.

U.S. Library of Congress. Division of Maps. Catalogue of an exhibition in the Division of Maps comprising some 200 Hispanic-American maps, atlases, geographies, globes, and portraits of historical, diplomatic, and cartographic interest, ranging through four centuries, by Lawrence Martin, Edith Fitton and Clarence G. Johnson upon the occasion of the general assembly of the Pan American Institute of Geography and History at Washington, D.C., Oct. 14-19, 1935. Washington, D.C., Govt. Print. Off., 1935. 20 p. (5515
Jones 285a.

-----. -----. Division of Maps and Charts. A list of maps of America in the Library of Congress, preceded by a list of works relating to cartography, by P. Lee Phillips. Washington, D.C., Govt. Print. Off., 1901. 1137 p.   (5515a
Includes Latin American countries.

VINDEL, Francisco. Mapas de América en los libros españoles de los siglos XVI al XVII (1503-1798) Madrid, 1955. 378 p.   (5516

WILGUS, Alva Curtis. Maps relating to Latin America in books and periodicals. Wash-

WILGUS, Alva Curtis. Maps relating... (Cont.) ington, D.C., Pan American Union, 1933. 103 p. (Columbus Memorial Library. Bibliographic ser. 10)   (5517
Jones 538.

ANTARCTIC REGIONS

U. S. Library of Congress, Map Division. Selected maps and charts of Antarctica; an annotated list of maps of the south polar regions published since 1945. Washington, D.C., 1959. 193 p.   (5517a
Compiler: Richard W. Stephenson.

ARGENTINA

ARGENTINA. Dirección de Hidrografía, Faros y Balizas. Catálogo de cartas y libros para navegación. Buenos Aires, 1926. 15 p.(5518
Jones 576.

-----. Dirección General de Navegación y Comunicaciones. Catálogo de cartas y libros para navegación; 3a. ed., 1930. Buenos Aires, "Las Ciencias", Estab. Tip. Lit. y Casa Edit. de A. G. Buffarini, 1930. 15 p.   (5520
Earlier editions were issued by the Dirección de Hidrografía, Faros y Balizas. "Lista de publicaciones de la Oficina Hidrográfica Internacional": no. 1, 13-15.---Jones 579.

-----. Dirección General de Navegación e Hidrografía. Catálogo de cartas y libros para navegación; 7a. ed. Buenos Aires, Tall. Graf. Garrot, 1944. 13 p.   (5521

-----. -----. -----. 8a. ed. Buenos Aires, Impr. Bedaumine Hnos., 1945. 19 p.   (5522

-----. -----. -----. 9a. ed. Buenos Aires, Tall. Gráf. "Continental", 1945. 19 p.(5523

-----. -----. -----. 10a. ed. Buenos Aires, 1950. 69 p.   (5524
Title varies from other editions: "Catálogo de cartas, libros y otras publicaciones de ayuda a la navegación."

-----. Servicio Hidrográfico. Catálogo de cartas y libros para navegación; 4a. ed., 1934. Buenos Aires, G. Kraft [1934] 13 p.   (5525
Jones 577. The 3d. ed. 1930, was issued by the Dirección General de Navegación y Comunicaciones.

BUENOS AIRES. Museo Mitre. Planos, vistas y cartas geográficas, catálogo de la sección XVI. Buenos Aires, 1913. 230 p.   (5526
Jones 625b.

FURLONG CARDIFF, Guillermo. Cartografía jesuítica del Río de La Plata. Buenos Aires,
Tall. Casa Jacobo Peuser, 1936. 228 p. and
portfolio of 62 pl. (Buenos Aires. Universidad Nacional. Instituto de Investigaciones
Históricas. Publ. no. 7)   (5527
  Bibliografía: p. 137-38.---Jones 698a.

PUSCH, Roberto. Catálogo de mapas, planos y
croquis de la República Argentina y parte
de los países limítrofes, con indicación de
institutos, reparticiones, bibliotecas, etc.,
donde tales elementos pueden consultarse.
Buenos Aires, Tall. Gráf. de la Sección Publicaciones e Informes del Ministerio de
Agricultura de la Nación, 1935. v. 1
(120 p.) (Argentina. Dirección de Minas y
Geología. Publ. no. 108)   (5528
  Contents. - 1a. pte. Provincia de Buenos
Aires y zona limítrofe.---Jones 817.

SORIA, Gaspar. Biblioteca y mapoteca históri-
co-geográfica de la República Argentina.
(Anuario del Instituto Geográfico Militar,
Buenos Aires, v. 2, anexo, p. 85-116; v.3,
anexo, p. 113-32, 1913-1914)   (5529
  Jones 849.

-----. Biblioteca y mapoteca histórico-geográ-
fica de la República Argentina (1810-1828)
(Anuario del Instituto Geográfico Militar,
Buenos Aires, v. 5, p. 245-80, 1922) (5530
  Jones 850.

BRAZIL

ADÔNIAS, Isa. A cartografia da região amazônica; catálogo descritivo: 1500-1961 ...
[com a colaboração da Sra. Maria de Lourdes
Jovita] Rio de Janeiro, Conselho Nacional
de Pesquisas, Instituto Nacional de Pesquisas da Amazônia, 1963- . v. 1
(716 p.)- .   (5531

BIBLIOGRAFIA cartográfica do Brasil, 1951- .
Rio de Janeiro, 1954- . (Faculdade Nacional
de Filosofia, Centro de Pesquisas de Geografia, Universidade do Brasil; Ser. bibliografica, Publ. 1- .)   (5532
  Last received at DPU, Publ. 5 covering
1955.

BRAZIL. Arquivo Nacional. Catálogo dos mapas
existentes na Biblioteca do Arquivo Nacional. Rio de Janeiro, Cia. Brasileira de Artes Gráficas, 1944. 64 p.   (5533
  Prepared on the occasion of the 2nd
Meeting of Consultation on Geodesy Aeronautical Charts and Topographic Maps, Rio de
Janeiro, 1944.

BRAZIL. Biblioteca Nacional. Ensaio de char-

BRAZIL. Biblioteca Nacional ... (Cont.)
tographia brasileira extrahido do Catalogo
da exposição de historia do Brasil. Rio de
Janeiro, 1883. 261 p.   (5534
  Jones 1167.

-----. Directoria de Hidrografia e Navegação.
Catálogo de cartas e outras publicações.
[São Paulo?] 1953. 39 p. (DN 63-4) (5535

-----. Ministério das Relações Exteriores.
Catalogo da mappotheca do Ministro das Relações Exteriores. Rio de Janeiro, Impr. Nacional, 1926-1929. 2 v.   (5536
  Jones 1002.

-----. -----. Catálogo das peças pertencentes
a mapoteca do Ministério das Relações Exteriores, que figuram na Exposição anexa ao
IX Congresso Brasileiro de Geografia. Flori-
anapolis, 1940. 46 p.   (5537
  Cited in Reis, item 600.

-----. -----. Mapoteca. As peças raras da
Mapoteca do Ministério das Relações Exteriores, por Isa Adônias. Rio de Janeiro, 1956.
xii, 68 p. (Museu histórico e Diplomático
do Itamaraty. Publ. no. 3)   (5538

-----. -----. -----. Mapas e planos manuscritos relativos ao Brasil colonial conservados
no Ministério das Relações Exteriores e descritos por Isa Adônias para as comemorações
do quinto centenário da morte Infante Dom
Henrique. Rio de Janeiro, 1960. 2 v.
(xxix, 692 p.)   (5539
  Description of 823 items.

INSTITUTO Histórico e Geographico Brasileiro,
Rio de Janeiro. Catalogo das cartas geographicas, hidrographicas, atlas, planos e vistas existentes na Bibliotheca do Instituto
Historico, Geographico e Ethnographico Brasileiro. Rio de Janeiro, Typ. Perseverança,
1885. 118 p.   (5540
  Organisado por Tristão de Alencar Araripe.
---Jones 1064.

-----. Catalogo dos atlas, cartas, planos
geographicos, hydrographicos, cartas astro-
nomicas, mappas historicos e panoramicos e
vistas photographicas pertencentes a Bibliotheca do Imperador e por elle doados ao
Instituto Historico e Geographico Brasileiro. Rio de Janeiro, Impr. Nacional, 1901.
90 p.   (5541
  Cited in Reis, item 190.

PARA. Bibliotheca Publica. Cartographia;
catalogo dos mappas e cartas geographicas
da Bibliotheca e Archivo Publico. Pará,
Impr. Official, 1910. 128 p.   (5542
  Jones 1129.

CENTRAL AMERICA

BIBLIOGRAFIA y cartografía centro-americanas.
(Centro-América, Guatemala, v. 5, p. 182-96,
1913)   (5543
     Jones 1231.

CHILE

CHILE. Ministerio de Marina. Catálogo de
los planos i cartas hidrográficas i topográ-
ficas que existen en el Ministerio. Santiago de Chile, Impr. Nacional, 1863.
11 p.   (5544
     Jones 1433.

MEDINA, José Toribio. Ensayo acerca de una
mapoteca chilena o sea de una colección de
los títulos de los mapas, planos y vistas
relativos a Chile arreglados cronológicamente, con una introducción histórica acerca
de la geografía y cartografía del país.
Santiago de Chile, Impr. Ercilla, 1889.
254 p.   (5545
     Jones 1541.

-----. -----. Introd. de Elías Almeyda Arroyo. Homenaje del Ejército de Chile a su
autor en el centenario de su nacimiento,
1852-1952. [Santiago de Chile, 1952]
cxxviii, 254 p.   (5546
     Fascimile edition.

-----. Indice de autores y nombres [por]
Carlos Stuardo Ortiz. [Santiago de Chile,
1952] 109 p.   (5547

COLOMBIA

POSADA, Eduardo. Cartografía colombiana.
(Boletín de la Sociedad Geográfica de Colombia, Bogotá, v. 4, p. 206-20; v. 5,
p. 34-52, 147-56, 255-67, 1937-1938)   (5548
     "Bibliographical notes on 16th century
maps". (HLAS, 1938).---Jones 1759a.

URICOECHEA, Ezequiel. Mapoteca colombiana.
Colección de los títulos de todos los mapas, planos, vistas, etc. relativos a la
América española, Brasil e islas adyacentes. Arreglada cronológicamente i precedida de una introducción sobre la historia
cartográfica de América. Londres, Trübner
& Cía., 1860. 215 p.   (5549
     Jones 506.

COSTA RICA

DOBLES SEGREDA, Luis. Lista de mapas de Costa Rica. San José, Lehmann, 1928.
64 p.   (5550
     Jones 1268.

CUBA

FIGAROLA CANEDA, Domingo. Cartografía cubana
del British Museum; catálogo cronológico de
cartas, planos y mapas de los siglos XVI al
XIX; 2a. ed. Habana, Impr. de la Biblioteca Nacional, 1910. 21 p.   (5551
     Lists 128 maps; supplemented by Juan Pérez
de la Riva's: Contribución a una cartografía
cubana del siglo XVIII, in Boletín del Archivo Nacional, t. 35, p. 18-28, 1937, listing
50 items in the British Museum and Public
Record Office.---Jones 1792, 1821.

JAMAICA

INSTITUTE of Jamaica, Kingston. Library. Jamaica cartography; chronological history of
maps of Jamaica in the library, both on separate sheets and in books. Kingston [1897]
15 p.   (5551a
     Compiler: Frank Cundall.

MEXICO

MEXICO. Universidad Nacional. Instituto de
Investigaciones Estéticas. Planos de la ciudad de México. Siglos XVI y XVII. Estudio
histórico, urbanístico y bibliográfico. México, D.F., 1938. 200 p.   (5552
     Prepared by Manuel Toussaint, Federico Gó-
mez de Orozco and Justino Fernández for the
XVI Congreso Internacional de Planificación
y de la Habitación.

MIRABAL LAUSAN, Joaquín. Mapas, códices y
planos existentes en el Departamento de Cartografía de la Sociedad Mexicana de Geografía y Estadística, hasta el 31 de agosto de
1927. (Boletín de la Sociedad Mexicana de
Geografía y Estadística. México, v. 47,
p. 129-231, 1937)   (5553
     Jones 2369a.

OROZCO Y BERRA, Manuel. Materiales para una
cartografía mexicana. Edición de la Sociedad de Geografía y Estadística. México,
D.F., Impr. del Gobierno, 1871. 337p.   (5554
     Jones 2392.

SOCIEDAD Mexicana de Geografía y Estadística.
Cuatro siglos de cartografía tabasqueña.
Guía sumaria de la exposición de mapas y
planos referentes al Estado de Tabasco.
Villahermosa, Impr. del Gobierno, 1951.
30 p.   (5555
     Cited in HLAS 18, item 3285.

TAMAYO, Jorge L., and ALCORTA GUERRERO, Ramón.
Catálogo de la Exposición de Cartografía Mexicana. México, D.F., Edit. Cultura, 1941.
160 p. (Publ. del Instituto Panamericano de
Geografía e Historia, no. 59)   (5556

NICARAGUA

BIBLIOGRAFIA y cartografía de Nicaragua.
(Centro-América, Guatemala, v. 6, p. 548-61,
1914)   (5557
   A short reading list, with notices of 78
maps, 1822-1900.---Jones 1332.

PARAGUAY

MACHUCA MARTINEZ, Marcelino. Mapas históricos
del Paraguay Gigante. Asunción [Tall. Graf.
"El Arte" de Vázquez e Hijo, 1951]
44 p.   (5557a
   Description and comment of 16 maps.

PERU

PERU. Ministerio de Relaciones Exteriores.
Departamento de Archivo y Biblioteca. Catalogo de la mapoteca; del Siglo XVI al Siglo XX. Lima [La Perla, Impr. Colegio Militar Leoncio Prado] 1957. 512 p. Publicaciones, t. 1)   (5558
   Preparada por Carlos Ortiz de Zevallos
Paz-Soldán.

SOUTH AMERICA

PHILLIPS, Philip Lee. Guiana and Venezuelan
cartography. Washington, D.C., Govt. Print.
Off., 1898. p. 681-776.   (5559
   From the Annual report of the American
Historical Association for 1897.---Jones
2943.

RAMOS GIMENEZ, Leopoldo. El Chaco a través
de los siglos en los mapas de la Colección
Rio Branco. Rio de Janeiro, Edit, Alba,
1933. 16 p.   (5560
   Jones 1154.

SULLIVAN, Henry B. A catalogue of geological
maps of South America. New York, American
Geographical Society, 1922. 192 p. (American Geographical Society. Research ser.
no. 9)   (5561
   Jones 469.

VENEZUELA

INSTITUTO Panamericano de Geografía e Historia. Cartografía histórica de Venezuela,
1635-1946. Caracas, 1946. 51 p.   (5561a
   Presented at the IV Assembly of the Pan
American Institute of Geography and History.

MATHEMATICS

BIBLIOGRAFIA brasileira de matemática e física,
v. 1- , no. 1- . 1950/54- . Rio de Janeiro,
Instituto Brasileiro de Bibliografia e Documentação, 1955- .   (5562
   v. 2 covers period 1900-1957; v. 3, 1958-
1960.

BUFFARA, Regina, and CARDOSO, Jayme Machado.
Matemática: bibliografia selecta. Curitiba,
1959. 90 p. (Curitiba, Universidade do Paraná. Conselho de Pesquisas. Serie Bibliografia e documentação, no. 1)   (5563

DASSEN, Claro Cornelio. Las matemáticas en la
Argentina. Buenos Aires, 1924. 140 p.
(Evolución de las ciencias en la República
Argentina, 4)   (5564
   Includes bibliography.---Jones 679.

KARPINSKI, Louis Charles. Bibliography of ma-
thematical works printed in America through
1850, by Louis C. Karpinski, with the cooperation for Washington libraries of Walter F.
Shenton. Ann Arbor, The Univ. of Michigan
Pr.; London H. Milford, Oxford Univ. Pr,
1940. 697 p.   (5565
   "Works consulted": p. 613-18. Includes
works printed in Latin America, with many
facsimiles of title-pages and extensive
comments.---Jones 233a.

PI CALLEJA, Pedro. Sobre orientación biblio-
gráfica en matemática. Buenos Aires, Tall.
Gráf. "T. Palumbo", 1946. 17 p.   (5565a
   Cited in Geoghegan, 1836. Reprinted from
Ciencia y técnica, Buenos Aires, v. 107,
no. 529.

MEDICINE

GENERAL

BIBLIOTECA Artigas-Washington, Montevideo. Bibliografía sobre enfermería y temas relacionados en la Biblioteca Artigas-Washington.

BIBLIOTECA Artigas-Washington ... (Cont.)
[Montevideo, 1952] 4 p. mimeogr.   (5566
   Compiler: Ermelinda Acerenza. Cited in
Musso 187.

MEDICINE

CANTON, Eliseo. Historia de la medicina en el Rio de la Plata desde su descubrimiento hasta nuestros días, 1512 a 1925. Madrid, Impr. G. Hernández y Calo Sáez, 1928. 6 v.   (5567
  Jones 648. Bibliography: v. 6 (5 p. at end)

CHILE. Universidad. Escuela de Medicina. Lista no. 9 de libros, tesis y revistas ofrecidas en canje. Santiago [1962?]   (5568
  Cited in Boletín de adquisiciones, Medellín, Col., no. 9, p. 18, sept. 1963.

GUERRA, Francisco. Estudio crítico y bibliográfico de la medicina colonial hispanoamericana. México, D.F., 1953. 322 p.   (5569
  Thesis. University of Mexico. Published also under title: Historiografía de la medicina colonial hispanoamericana.

-----. Historiografía de la medicina colonial hispanoamericana. México, Abastecedora de Impresos, 1953. 322 p.   (5569a

INDICE de libros y revistas de medicina y ciencias. [Montevideo] n. d. 12 p. (Documento, no. 39)   (5570
  Musso, 175, ascribes authorship to "Francia. Ministerio de Información de la República. Oficina Central para América del Sur".

INTER-AMERICAN Children's Institute, Montevideo. Bibliografía: vacunación contra la poliomielitis; folletos y artículos de revistas existentes en la Biblioteca del Instituto. Montevideo, 1956. 16 p. mimeogr.   (5571
  Cited in Musso 185.

-----. Bibliografía sobre bacilo Calmette Guerin; libros, folletos y artículos existentes en la Biblioteca del Instituto. Montevideo, 1949. 37 p.   (5572
  Cited in Musso 178. In 177, he cites another edition of the same bibliography.

-----. -----. Suplemento 1956. Montevideo, 1956. 18 p. mimeogr.   (5573
  Cited in Musso 179.

JONES, Harold W. Central and South American literature in the Army Medical Library. (Proceedings of the third Convention of the Inter-American Bibliographical and Library Association. New York, H. W. Wilson, 1941. p. 66-82)   (5574
  "It is believed that there are now approximately 5,000 medical books by Mexican, Central American, and South American authors in the Library". "List of books and periodicals printed before 1840 referring to Central and South American medicine" (54 titles): p. 78--82.---Jones 231a.

MEDELLIN, Col. Universidad de Antioquia. Facultad de Medicina. Biblioteca. Lista de duplicados ofrecidos en canje. Medellín, 1962. 3 t. mimeogr.   (5575
  Cited in Peraza, Fichas, v. 4-6, item 546.

PAN AMERICAN Health Organization, Washington, D.C. Bibliografía de oncocercosis. Washington, D.C., 1950. 339 p. (Publ. de la Oficina Sanitaria Panamericana, no. 242)   (5576

-----. Suplemento. Washington, D.C., 1961. 42 p. (Serie publicaciones varias, no. 67)   (5576a

PAN AMERICAN UNION. Columbus Memorial Library. Catalogue of all books and pamphlets on medicine in the Columbus Memorial Library. [Washington, D.C.. 1922] 3, 84 p.   (5577
  Cited in PAU Bibliographies, p. 29.

UNITED NATIONS Educational, Scientific and Cultural Organization. Education Clearing House. Educacion sanitaria; bibliografía selecta. Paris, n.d. 65 p. (Unesco. Departamento de Educación, Centro de Información. Documentos especiales de educación, 11) (5578
  Prepared jointly with the World Health Organization. Includes Latin American countries.

-----. -----. Health education; a selected bibliography. Paris, n.d. 56 p. (Unesco. Education Clearing House. Occasional papers in education, no. 11)   (5579
  Prepared jointly with the world Health Organization. Includes Latin American countries.

U.S. Regional Technical Aids Center, México. Bibliografía médica. Guía de obras médicas en español traducidas del inglés por diversas editoriales. México, D.F., 1963. 40 p.   (5580

VAN PATTEN, Nathan. The medical literature of Mexico and Central America. (Papers of the Bibliographical Society of America, Chicago, v. 24, p. 150-99, 1930)   (5581
  Jones 2562.

ZAHER, Célia Ribeiro, and GOMES, Hagar Espanha. Guia de literatura médica e biológica; súmulas para utilização no Curso de Pesquisas Bibliográficas em Medicina. Rio de Janeiro, 1962. 98, 17 p.   (5582
  Prepared under the auspices of the Instituto Brasileiro de Bibliografia e Documentação of the Conselho Nacional de Pesquisas.

ARGENTINA

AREAS BLANCO, Manuel. Bibliografía médica argentina (correspondiente al año 1916) (Re-

AREAS BLANCO, Manuel. Bibliografía... (Cont.)
vista médica, Rosario, t. 7, no. 4, suplemento, 120 p., 1917)   (5583
Jones 567.

ARGAÑARAZ, Raúl. Apuntes para la historia de
la oftalmología en la República Argentina.
(Boletín de la Sociedad de Oftalmología,
Buenos Aires, t. 4, p. 235-372, 1917) (5584
Bibliography: p. 296-372.---Jones 568.

ARTAZA, Evaristo. Saneamiento urbano en la
República Argentina; provisión de agua y de-
sagües urbanos. La Plata, 1937. 121 p.
(Publ. de la Facultad de Ciencias Físico-
Matemáticas, no. 112)   (5585
Bibliografía: p. 95-121.---Jones 587.

BUENOS AIRES. Universidad. Facultad de Cien-
cias Médicas. Instituto de Fisiología.
Lista de trabajos, 1919-1939. Buenos Aires,
Impr. y Casa Edit. "Coni", 1941.
210 p.   (5585a
Compiler: Enrique A. Aubrun.

HOUSSAY, Bernardo Alberto. La acción fisioló-
gica de los extractos hipofisiarios. Buenos
Aires, Tall. Gráf. A. Flaiban, 1918. 284,
75 p.   (5586
Binayán, item 27, notes that the first 40
pages of the final 75 pages are bibliography
which previously was published in El Canje,
año 2, no. 8-10, 1914.

MOLINARI, José Luis. Primeros impresos médicos bonaerenses, 1780-1810. Buenos Aires
[Tall. Gráf.] S. de Amorrortu e Hijos,
1941. 110 p.   (5586a

RESTANIO, Antonio. Atlas sanitario de la pro-
vincia de Buenos Aires. La Plata, 1923.
378 p.   (5587
At head of title: Ministerio de Obras
Públicas de la provincia de Buenos Aires.
Includes bibliographies.---Jones 392.

TUMBURUS, Juan. Bibliografía de hidatidosis.
Buenos Aires, 1927. 714 p. (II Congreso
Nacional de Medicina. Actas y trabajos,
6)   (5588
Jones 873.

BRAZIL

ACADEMIA Nacional de Medicina, Rio de Janeiro.
Em commemoração do centenário do ensino mé-
dico. Rio de Janeiro, Typ. do "Jornal do
Commercio" de Rodrigues & C., 1908.
749 p.   (5589
The contributions are chiefly bibliogra-
phical, and vary in length, the most exten-
sive being that by José Pereira Rego filho,
Epidemias (estudo bibliographico): p. 73-368.
---Jones 947.

BIBLIOGRAFIA brasileira de medicina, v. 1- ,
1937/1938- . Rio de Janeiro, Instituto Brasileiro de Bibliografia e Documentação,
1939- .   (5590
Title varies: - v. 1-4: Indice catálogo
médico brasileiro, published in São Paulo.
Editor Jorge de Andrade Maia.

GUERRA, Francisco. Bibliografía médica brasileira, periodo colonial, 1808-1821. New
Haven, 1958. 54 p. (Yale University, School
of Medicine, Department of the History of
Medicine, Publ. no. 34)   (5590a

INSTITUTO Brasileiro de Bibliografia e Documentação, Rio de Janeiro. Bouba; bibliografia
brasileira. Rio de Janeiro, 1958.
20 p.   (5591

-----. Curare, bibliografia. Rio de Janeiro,
Conselho Nacional de Pesquisas, 1957.
386 p.   (5592

-----. Doença de Chagas. Rio de Janeiro,
1958. 126 p. (Bibliografias brasileiras
sobre doenças tropicias, 2)   (5593
Doria, 17, cites Supplemento 1963.

-----. Esquistossomose. Rio de Janeiro, 1958.
85 p. (Bibliografias brasileira sôbre doenças tropicais, 3)   (5594
Doria, 18, cites Suplemento, 1963.

-----. Fiebre amarela. Rio de Janeiro, 1958.
88 p. (Bibliografias brasileiras sôbre doenças tropicais, 4)   (5595

-----. Leishmaniose. Rio de Janeiro, 1958.
57 p. (Bibliografias brasileiras sôbre doenças tropicais, 5)   (5596
Doria, 20, cites Suplemento 1962.

-----. Malaria. Rio de Janeiro, 1958.
129 p. (Bibliografias brasileiras sôbre
doenças tropicais, 6)   (5597

MAGALHÃES, Fernando de. A obstetricia no Brasil. Rio de Janeiro, Leite Ribeiro, 1922.
399 p.   (5598
Bibliographia: p. 241-399.---Jones 1089.

MAIA, Jorge de Andrade. Catálogo-diccionario
das theses inauguraes, defendidas perante a
Faculdade de Medicina da Universidade de
São Paulo, 1919-1935. São Paulo, 1935.
vii, 38 p.   (5599

-----. Indice-catalogo médico brasileiro,
1937-1938. São Paulo, [Laboratórios Andrô-
maco] 1939. v. 1 (299 p.)   (5600
Jones 1092. See also Bibliografia brasileira de medicina (item 5590)

-----. Indice-catalogo medico paulista, 1860-
1936. São Paulo, 1938. 640 p.   (5601

MAIA, Jorge de Andrade. Indice- ... (Cont.)
Jones 1093.

PUECH, Rezende. A Sociadade de Medicina e
Cirurgia de São Paulo, indice bibliogra-
phico, 1895-1921, São Paulo, Typ. Casa
Garraux, 1921. p. 39-178. (5602

SÃO PAULO. Universidade. Faculdade de Medicina. Resenha bibliográfica da produção
cientifica, 1952-1960. [São Paulo], 1960.
55 p. mimeogr. (5603
Compilers: Felícia Henriques and Santo
Meneghetti with introduction by Zeferino
Vaz. Cited in Revista do livro, 6(23-24):
235, set./dez. 1961.

SÃO PAULO (State) Departamento de Profilaxia
da Lepra. Biblioteca. Indice bibliografico
de lepra, 1500-1943. São Paulo, 1948.
3 v. (5603a
Compiler: Luisa Keffer. Cited in Bibliografia Brasileira, 1947-1952, v. 2, p. 1142.

CHILE

ECHEVERRIA Y REYES, Aníbal. El colera; ensayo bibliográfico. Folletos publicados en
Chile con motivo de esta epidemia, 1886-
1888. Santiago de Chile, Impr. Nacional,
1888. 14 p. (5604
Cited in Laval, item 105.

FERRER, Pedro Lautaro. Historia general de
la medicina en Chile (documentos inéditos,
biografías y bibliografia) desde el descubrimiento y conquista de Chile, en 1535,
hasta nuestros días. Talca, Impr. Talca,
de J. Martin Garrido C., 1904. v. 1
(485 p.) (5605
t. 1, desde 1535, hasta la inauguración
de la Universidad de Chile en 1843.---
Jones 1579. Bibliographic information:
p. 439-81.

MANN, Wilhelm. Bericht über die schulhy-
gienische literatur Chiles für die jahre
1901 bis 1904. (Internationales archiv
für schulhygiene, Leipzig, p. 313-224,
1906) (5606
Jones 1524. Pagination not verified.

ORREGO LUCO, Augusto. La literatura medica
en Chile. (Revista chilena, Santiago,
t. 13, p. 255-62, 1879) (5607
Jones 1558b.

SUNDT, Roberto. Bibliografía dental chilena. Santiago, Impr. Universitaria,
1918. 66 p. (5608
From Revista de bibliografía chilena y
extranjera, año 6.---Jones 1635.

COLOMBIA

BONILLA NAAR, Alfonso. Historia de la medicina tropical, parasitología e higiene en Colombia; referencias bibliográficas, 1526-1944.
Bogotá, Cooperativa Nacional de Artes Gráficas, 1950. 168 p. (5609
Lists approximately 1,500 items. Cited in
Giraldo Jaramillo, p. 134.

PATIÑO, Alberto. Bibliografia dental colombiana. Bogota, 1910. (5610
Cited in Biblioteca Nacional, Catálogos,
1914, p. 293.---Jones 1755.

CUBA

LEROY Y CASSA, Jorge Eduardo. Consideraciones
sobre la prensa médica en Cuba. Habana, Impr.
"El Siglo XX", 1913. 17 p. (5611
Jones 1858.

TRELLES Y GOVIN, Carlos Manuel. Bibliografia
médico-farmaceutica cubana. (Revista de medicina y cirugía, Habana, t. 11-12, 1906-
1907) (5612
Describes 2,000 books, pamphlets, and articles.---Jones 1921.

-----. -----. Indices. Habana, Impr. Avisador Comercial, 1907. 31 p. (5613
Jones 1921a.

ECUADOR

ROLANDO, Carlos A. Bibliografia médica ecuatoriana. Guayaquil, Tip. de la Benemerita
Sociedad Filantrópica del Guayas, 1953 [i.e.,
1954] 387 p. (5614

GUATEMALA

AGUILAR, Francisco J. Oncocercosis; bibliografia guatemalense. Guatemala, Universidad de San Carlos, Facultad de Ciencias Médicas [1947] 25 p. (5614a

HAITI

LEON, Rulx. Notes bio-bibliográphiques; médec-
cins et naturalistes de l'ancienne colonie
française de Saint Domingo. Port-au-Prince,
1933. 89 p. mimeogr. (5615
Cited in Bissainthe, item 2777; also in
Caribbean acquisitions, 1959. p. 4.

MEXICO

FASTLIGHT, Samuel. Bibliografía odontológica
mexicana. México, D.F., La Prensa Médica Me-

FASTLIGHT, Samuel. Bibliografía ... (Cont.)
xicana, 1954. 220 p.   (5616

FERNANDEZ DEL CASTILLO, Francisco. Historia
bibliográfica del Instituto Médico Nacional
de México (1888-1915), antecesor del Instituto de Biología de la Universidad Nacional
Autónoma de México, por Francisco Fernández
del Castillo con la colaboración técnica de
Luz Ardizana. México, D.F., Impr. Universitaria, 1961. 206, 5 p.   (5617

FOURNIER VILLADA, Raoul. Bibliografía mexicana del abceso hepático. México, D.F., La
Prensa Médica Mexicana, 1956. 112 p. (5618

GUERRA, Francisco. La bibliografía de la historia de la medicina mexicana. México, D.
F., La Prensa Médica Mexicana, 1949.
30 p.   (5619
    Lists approximately 100 titles.

-----. Bibliografía de la materia médica mexicana. Catálogo alfabético. México, D.F.,
La Prensa Médica Mexicana, 1950.
423 p.   (5619a
    Includes 5,357 items, 1552-date.

-----. Iconografía médica mexicana. México,
D.F., Impr. del Diario Español, 1953. xvi,
ccclxxviii.   (5619b

HERNANDEZ MOREJON, Antonio. Historia bibliográfica de la medicina española. Madrid
[Impr. de la Viuda de Jordán e Hijos] 1842-
1850. 7 v.   (5620
    v. 2-7 issued by Manuel F. Hidalgo.---
Jones 202.

IZQUIERDO, José Joaquín. Balance cuatricentenario de la fisiología en México. México,
D.F., Ediciones Ciencia, 1934. 358p. (5621
    Includes biographical and bibliographical
material.---Jones 2263.

LEON, Nicolás. La anquilostomiasis en México.
Notas históricas y bibliográficas. Popotla,
D.F., 1923. 16 p. (México. Departamento
de Salubridad Pública, Monografías del Departamento de Higiene, no. 1, Sección de Estadística)   (5622
    Cited in Millares, item 988.

-----. La obstetricia en México. Notas bibliográficas, étnicas, históricas, documentarias
y críticas. Pte. 1-2. México, D.F., 1910.
67, 743 p.   (5623
    Jones 2297.

MEXICO. Universidad Nacional. Instituto de
Biología. Bibliografía: 1. Rlativa a
onchocercosis en México y Guatemala, por
Eduardo Caballero y C. 2. Relativa a erpe-
tología mexicana, por Cristóforo Vega. Chapultepec, D,F., Impr. del Instituto de Bio-

MEXICO. Universidad Nacional ... (Cont.)
logía, 1931. 10 p.   (5624

SORIANO, Manuel S. Bibliografía médica nacional. (Boletín de la Sociedad Mexicana de
Geografía y Estadística, México, 5a. ép.,
t. 1, no. 12, p. 722-24, 1906; t. 2, no. 1,
p. 22-8, 1907)   (5625

VALLE, Rafael Heliodoro. La cirugía mexicana
del siglo XIX. México, D.F., Tip. Sag,
1942. xcvi, 349 p.   (5626
    The introductory part is a history of the
subject, followed by 237 pages of bibliography. Contains also biographies of Mexican surgeons. Jones 2550b.

PERU

LASTRES, Juan B. Las enfermedades nerviosas
en el coloniaje. Lima, Ed. Rimac, 1938.
173 p.   (5627
    Includes bibliographical foot-notes.---
Jones 2663.

MORTIMER, William Golden. Peru; history of
coca, "The divine plant" of the Incas;
with an introductory account of the Incas,
and of the Andean Indians of to-day. New
York, J.H. Vail & Co., 1901. 576 p.   (5628
    Bibliography: p. 517-44.---Jones 2703.

LA ODONTOLOGIA en el Perú. Lima, Edit. Perú
Moderno, 1935. 160 p.   (5629
    Includes biographies of Peruvian dentists.
---Jones 2707.

SAENZ, Luis N. La coca; estudio médico-social
de la gran toxicomanía peruana. Lima, Impr.
de la Escuela de la Guardia Civil y Policía,
1938. 234 p.   (5630
    "Bibliografía" at end of each chapter.---
Jones 2737a.

VALDIZAN, Hermilio. Apuntes para la bibliografía médica peruana. Lima, Impr. Americana, 1928. 390 p.   (5631
    429 items arranged in chronological order
with notes.---Jones 2767.

URUGUAY

RODRIGUEZ, Elvira R. Bibliografía neurológi-
ca uruguaya, 1927-1954. Montevideo, 1955.
119 p.   (5632
    Working paper presented to the VI Congre-
so Latinoamericano de Neurocirugía.

URUGUAY. Biblioteca Nacional. Centro de Documentación Científica, Técnica y Económica.
Contribución a la bibliografía sobre epide-
miología y epizootología de las zoonosis en
el Uruguay. Montevideo, 1957. 7 p.

URUGUAY. Biblioteca Nacional ... (Cont.)
mimeogr.   (5633
   Presented to Cuarta Reunión Sanitaria Regional, Porto Alegre, Feb. 12-16, 1957.

VIDAUR DE CARNELLI, Elvira, and ORTIZ AGUIAR,
Raquel. Bibliografía nacional de medicina,
tomada de publicaciones periódicas existentes en la Biblioteca, 1960. Montevideo,
[Biblioteca, Facultad de Medicina] 1962.
14 p. mimeogr.   (5634
   Cited in Musso 191.

VENEZUELA

ARCHILA, Ricardo. Bibliografía médica venezolana. Caracas, Edit. Grafolit, 1946.
705 p. (Publ. de la "Fundación Biogen",
no. 4)   (5635
   Cited in Archila, p. 128.

-----. -----. 2a. ed. Colaboradora especial: Sra. María T. de Guerra. Caracas,
Edit. Bellas Artes, 1955. 1041 p. (5635a

-----. -----. 3a. ed. Caracas, Impr. Nacional, 1960. xi, 494 p.   (5635b

-----, and CONDE JAHN, Franz. Bibliografía
otorrinolaringológica venezolana hasta
1950. Caracas, [Edit. Bolivia] 1951.
69 p.   (5636
   Cited in Archila, p. xv.

-----. Contribucion bibliográfica a la geografía médico-sanitaria de Venezuela, en
colaboración con los medicos jefes de uni-
dades sanitarias. Caracas, 1943.
39 p.   (5637
   Contains 532 references. Cited in Archila, p. xv.

CALCAÑO, Julio, and AURRECOECHEA, José María.
Recopilacion bibliográfica nacional (de obstetricia y ginecología) [Caracas, Tip. A.
B.C.] 1952. 135 p.   (5638
   Cited in Anuario bibliográfico venezolano,
1949/1954, item 3282. Published únder auspices de la Sociedad de Obstetricia Ginecología de Venezuela, Caracas.

DEGWITZ CELIS, Guillermo. Bibliografía pe-
diátrica venezolana, 1952. (Publ.
Biogen)   (5640
   Cited in Archila, p. xv.

FERNANDEZ ALBENDIN, Alicia de. Venezuelan me-

FERNANDEZ ALBENDIN, Alicia de ... (Cont.)
dical and related periodicals, libraries and
societies; publicaciones periódicas venezolanas de medicina y ciencias afines, bibliotecas y sociedades. Caracas, 1963.
9 p.   (5641
   Report to the Second International Congress on Medical Librarianship, Washington,
D.C., June 16-22, 1963.

JORNADA Venezolana de Venereología y Dermatología, 1a. Comité Organizador. 40 trabajos
científicos venezolanos de venereología y
dermatología. Caracas, Tip. Americana,
1943. 68 p.   (5642
   Cited in Archila, p. xv.

PARDO, Isaac José. Las pequeñas resecciones
pulmonares en el tratamiento de la tuberculosis. [Caracas, 1953] p. 307-400.   (5643
   Reprint from v. 2 of the Memorias of the
X Congreso Panamericano de la Tuberculosis,
1953. Contains: "Apendice bibliográfico"
by I. J. Pardo, Ladislao Pollak, and Victor
Giménez F.: p. 345-400. Cited in Anuario
bibliográfico venezolano, 1949/1954, item
2639.

PEREZ GALDOS, Ignacio. Resúmen de trabajos
médicos venezolanos, 1943-1944. Caracas,
1944-1947. 2 v. (Publ. de la Fundación
Biogen, no. 2, 6)   (5644
   Cited in Archila, p. xvi.

PRINCIPE MERCHAN, Alejandro. Documentos para
la historia de la fisiología nacional; índice de 370 trabajos venezolanos sobre tuberculosis. Caracas, Edit. Grafolit, 1943.
47 p.   (5645
   Cited in Archila, p. 709.

VELEZ BOZA, Fermín. Bibliografía venezolana
sobre alimentación y nutrición. Caracas,
Edit. "Bolívar," 1950. 155 p. (Publ. del
Instituto Nacional de Nutrición, Cuaderno,
3)   (5646
   Cited in Archila, p. xvi.

-----. -----. 2a. ed., corr. y aum. Caracas,
1961. 452 p. (Venezuela. Instituto Nacional de Nutrición, Cuaderno, 20)   (5646a

-----. Bibliografía venezolana de histología,
embriología y genética. Caracas, Universidad Central de Venezuela, 1961. 259 p.
(Ediciones de la Biblioteca; Colección bibliografías, 1)   (5647

METEOROLOGY

AGUILAR Y SANTILLAN, Rafael. Bibliografía meteorológica mexicana que comprende las publicaciones de meteorología, física del globo y climatología hechas hasta fines de 1889. México, D.F., Edición de la Sociedad "Antonio Alzate", 44 p.　　　　(5648
　From Memorias de la Sociedad Científica "Antonio Alzate", v. 4.---Jones 2038.

ARGENTINA. Servicio Meteorológico Nacional. Selección de reseñas bibliográficas, meteorológicas y geofísicas, año 1951. Buenos Aires, Dirección General del Servicio Meteorológico Nacional, 1952. 129 p. (Publ. ser. G., no. 4)　　　　(5649
　Cited in Catálogo, Instituto Bibliotecológico item 375. Geoghegan, 1884, cites compilation through 1954.

BANCO do Nordeste do Brasil, Fortaleza. Contribução à bibliografia das sêcas. Fortaleza, 1957. 49 p. mimeogr. (Banco do Nordeste do Brasil, Publ. no. 22)　(5650
　Cited in Richardson, item 7200.

INDACOCHEA G., Angel J. Bibliografía climatológica del Perú. Lima [Sanmartí y Compañía] 1946. 81 p. (Instituto Geológico del Perú, Bol. no. 4)　　　　(5651

PAIVA, Tancredo de Barros. Bibliographia do clima brasileiro; notas. Rio de Janeiro, Typ. do Serviço de Informações do Ministério de Agricultura, 1928. 34 p.　　(5653
　Jones 1125.

SPARN, Enrique. Bibliografía del clima de la provincia de Córdoba (Argentina) Córdoba, Impr. de la Universidad, 1952. 37p. (5654
　Cited in Catálogo, Instituto Bibliotecológico, item 658.

-----. Bibliografía meteorológica de la República Argentina. Córdoba, 1923. 72 p. (Academia Nacional de Ciencias. Miscelánea, 7)　　　　(5655
　Jones 854. Contains Apendice: Literatura sobre meteorología y climatología de las regiones antartica y sub-antártica americanas.

SPARN, Enrique. Bibliografía meteorológica y climatológica de la República Argentina y de las regiones antártica y subantártica americanas correspondiente a los años 1924-1931. Córdoba, 1934. 47 p.　　　　(5656
　From Revista de la Universidad Nacional de Córdoba, v. 20, p. 278-319, 1933.---Jones 855.

-----. Segunda contribución al conocimiento de la bibliografía meteorológica y climatológica de la República Argentina. Córdoba, Academia Nacional de Ciencias, 1941. p. 215-67.　　　　(5657
　Cited in Catálogo, Instituto Bibliotecológico, item 659.

-----. Tercera contribución al conocimiento de la bibliografía meteorológica y climatológica de la República Argentina (años 1921-1948) Córdoba, Academia Nacional de Ciencias, 1949. p. 379-414.　　　(5658
　Cited in Catálogo, Instituto Bibliotecológico, item 664.

-----. Tercera contribución al conocimiento de la bibliografía meteorológica y climatológica del quadrante americano de la Antártida y sub-antártica. Córdoba, 1945. p. 332-41.　　　　(5659
　Cited in Catálogo, Instituto Bibliotecológico, item 665.

-----. Cuarta contribución al conocimiento de la bibliografía meteorológica y climatológica del cuadrante americano de la Antártica y sub-antártica. Córdoba, 1951. p. 274-89.　　　　(5660
　Cited in Catálogo, Instituto Bibliotecológico, item 660.

WELCH, M. Bibliography on the climate of South America. (Monthly weather review. Suppl. no. 18. Washington, D.C., 1921. 42 p.)　　　　(5661
　Jones 527.

ZIMMERMAN, Anne, and WANG, Jen-Yu. Bibliography for agrometeorological studies on South America; the first collection, 1960. Madison, Wisc., Univ. of Wisconsin Pr., 1960. 23 p.　　　　(5662

MUSIC

GENERAL

BIBLIOTECA Benjamín Franklin, México. Música, libros y composiciones. México, D.F., 1944. 23 p.　　　　　　　　　　　　(5663

BRAZIL. Biblioteca Nacional. Edições raras de obras musicais. [Rio de Janeiro, 1955] 24 p.　　　　　　　　　　　　　(5664

-----. -----. -----; coleção Teresa Cristina Maria. Rio de Janeiro, 1954. 56 p. (5665

-----. -----. Literatura musical, séculos XVI-XVII-XVIII. [Catálogo. Rio de Janeiro, 1954] 23 p.　　　　　　　　　(5666
　　Cited in Boletín bibliografico, Biblioteca Nacional, v. 4, t. 2, p. 178, 1954.

CHASE, Gilbert. Bibliography of Latin American folk-music. Washington, D.C., 1942. 140 p.　　　　　　　　　　　(5667
　　Contains 1,122 entries, edited by the Music Section of the Library of Congress.

-----. A guide to Latin American music. Washington, D.C., 1943. xiii, 274 p. (Library of Congress, Latin American ser., no. 5)　　　　　　　　　　(5668

CORTIJO ALAHIJA, L. Musicología latinoamericana. La música popular y los músicos célebres de la América Latina. Barcelona, Maucci, 1920. 443 p.　　　　(5669
　　Jones 113.

FIORDA KELLY, Alfredo. Cronología de las óperas, dramas líricos, oratorios, himnos, etc., cantados en Buenos Aires. Buenos Aires, Impr. Riera y Cía., 1934. 83 p.　　　　　　　　　　　(5670
　　Jones 695.

HAGUE, Eleanor. Latin American music, past and present. Santa Ana, Calif., Fine Arts Pr., 1934. 98 p.　　　　　　(5671
　　Bibliography: p. 89-98.---Jones 183.

LABASTILLE, Irma Goebel. A guide to the material on the music of the Caribbean area. (Handbook of Latin American studies, 1936. Cambridge, Mass., 1937. p. 459-72) (5672
　　Jones 1853. Title taken from table of contents. Title on p. 459: The music of Mexico and Central America.

PAN AMERICAN UNION. List of Latin American band and orchestra music available in the United States. [Washington, D.C.] 1932. unpaged.　　　　　　　　　　(5673

PAN AMERICAN UNION. List of Latin American music (vocal, piano, instrumental, orchestral and band) which can be purchased in the United States; 2d. ed., rev. and enl. Washington, D.C., 1933. 60 p.　　　　(5674

-----. Division of Intellectual Cooperation. References on Latin American music, the theatre and the dance. Washington, D.C., 1941. 7 p.　　　　　　　　(5675

-----. -----. 1942. 9 p.　　　　　　(5676

-----. Music Division. Latin American music published in connection with the editorial project of the Music Division of Pan American Union in cooperation with the Music Educators National Conference, and a partial list of other publications of Latin American music and books on Latin American music. [Washington, D.C.] 1942. 7 p.　　(5677

-----. -----. Partial list of Latin American music obtainable in the United States, with a supplementary list of books and a selective list of phonograph records, compiled by Gilbert Chase. Washington, D.C., Pan American Union, 1941. 36 p. (Music ser., no. 1) mimeogr.　　　　　　(5678

-----. -----. -----. Rev. and enl., compiled by Leila Fern Thompson. Washington, D.C., Pan American Union, 1947. 57 p. (Music ser., no. 1)　　　　　　　　(5679

-----. -----. -----. 3d. ed. rev. and enl., compiled by Leila Fern Thompson. Washington, D.C., Pan American Union, 1948. 57, 17 p.　　　　　　　　　　　(5680
　　Contains supplement no. 1 of additional material published since 1947.

-----. Music Section. Latin American orchestral music available in the United States. Washington, D.C., Pan American Union [1956] 79 p.　　　　　　　　　　(5681
　　Supersedes a shorter register of similar character, issued in 1955. "The Edwin A. Fleischer Collection of Orchestral Music in the Free Library of Philadelphia, Pennsylvania": p. [25]-79.

PRAT MARSAL, Domingo. Diccionario biográfico, bibliográfico, histórico y crítico de guitarristas. Buenos Aires, Casa Romero y Fernández, 1934. 468 p.　　　　　(5682
　　Jones 380.

SALAZAR, Adolfo. Música y sociedad en el siglo XX, ensayo de crítica y de estética desde el punto de vista de su función social. México, D.F., Casa de España en México, 1939. 221 p.　　　　　　　　　　　(5683

SALAZAR, Adolfo. Música y sociedad...(Cont.)
Bibliography included in "Notas": p. 187-
221.---Jones 2481a.

THOMPSON, Leila Fern. Selected list of Latin
American song books and references for guidance in planning fiestas; 3d. ed. enl.
with addenda. Washington, D.C., Pan American, 1943. 11 p.   (5684

-----. -----. 3d. ed. with addenda. 1944.
12 p.   (5685

-----. -----. 4th ed., 1945. 13 p.   (5686

-----. -----. 5th. ed. rev. 1946.
11 p.   (5687

-----. -----. 6th ed. rev. 1947.
12 p.   (5688
Title varies: Selected ... for guidance
in planning programs of music and dance.

-----. -----. 7th ed. rev. 1949.
12 p.   (5689
Title same as for previous entry.

-----. Selected references in English on
Latin American music; a reading list.
Washington, D.C., Pan American Union, 1944.
20 p. mimeogr. (Music ser. no. 13) (5690

ARGENTINA

CARRIZO, Juan Alfonso. Cancionero popular
de Salta. Buenos Aires, A. Baiocco y
Cía., 1933. 707, [101] p.   (5691
Autores citados: p. 713-16. See also
the author's Antiguos cantos populares argentinos (Buenos Aires, 1926, 260 p.),
Cancionero popular de Jujuy (Tucumán, 1935,
542 p.), and Cancionero popular de Tucumán
(Buenos Aires, 1937, 2 v.)---Jones 658.

DRAGHI LUCERO, Juan. Cancionero popular cu-
yano. Mendoza, Best Hermanos, 1938.
632 p.   (5692
"Crónicas de Cuyo": p. 445-545. Bibliografía: p. 627-32. "Tiraje aparte del material publicado en el VII volumen de Anales del Primer Congreso de Historia de Cuyo".---Jones 684b.

LUPER, Albert Thomas. The music of Argentina. Washington, D.C., Music Division, Pan
American Union, 1942. 3 p. 1., 30 p. (Music ser., no. 5)   (5693
Bibliography: p. 11-14. "A brief list
of Argentine music obtainable in the United
States": p. 15-27. "A selected list of
recordings of Argentine music": p. 28.
"Guide to music and record sources": p. 29.

-----. -----. 1945. 37 p.   (5694
Fourth printing.

VEGA, Carlos. Danzas y canciones argentinas,
teorías e investigaciones; un ensayo sobre
el tango. Buenos Aires, 1936. 309 p. (5695
Bibliografía: p. 305-07.---Jones 882.

BRAZIL

AZEVEDO, Luís Heitor Correia de. Bibliografia
musical brasileira (1820-1950) Rio de Janeiro, Instituto Nacional do Livro, 1952.
252 p. (Coleção B 1: Bibliografia 9) (5696
Over 1,600 references to the literature of
Brazilian music.

-----. Relação das operas de autores brasileiros. Rio de Janeiro, Ministério de Educação
e Saude, 1938. 116 p. (Coleção brasileira
de teatro; ser. D: Estudos sôbre teatro,
II)   (5697

LUPER, Albert Thomas. The music of Brazil.
Washington, D.C., Music Division, Pan American Union, 1944. 40 p. (Music ser., no.
9)   (5698
Bibliography: p. 13-7; "A partial list of
Brazilian music in the United States", p. 18-
36; "Guide to music and record sources",
p. 37-8.

REIS, Mercedes de Moura. A música militar no
Brasil no século XIX. [Rio de Janeiro] Impr.
Militar, 1952. 97 p.   (5699
At head of title-page: Primeira Exposição
Geral do Exército. Lists 215 items, "Hinos
não identificados", and "Bibliografia sôbre
hinos e canções militares".

CHILE

CHILE. Biblioteca Nacional. Bibliografía musical, composiciones impresas en Chile y
composiciones de autores chilenos publicadas
en el extranjero; 2a. pte., 1886-1896. Santiago, 1898. 89 p.   (5700
The first part covering material prior to
1886 has not been published. See also Música de autores chilenos existentes en la Sección "Lectura a domicilio" de la Biblioteca
Nacional in Revista de bibliografía chilena
y extranjera, t. 4, p. 302-09, 1916, which
lists 445 titles.---Jones 1595.

PEREIRA SALAS, Eugenio. Los orígenes del arte
musical en Chile. Santiago, Impr. Universitaria, 1941. 373 p.   (5701
"Inventario de la producción musical chilena de 1714-1860": p. 304-10. Bibliografía: p. 345-56.---Jones 1564a.

COLOMBIA

MARTINEZ MONTAYA, Andrés. Reseña histórica sobre la música en Colombia desde la época co-

MARTINEZ MONTAYA, Andrés. Reseña... (Cont.)
lonial hasta la fundación de la Academia
Naciooonal de Música. (Anuario de la Academia Colombiana de Bellas Artes. Bogotá,
1932. v. 1, p. 61-76)   (5702
Jones 1730. Bibliografía: p. 76.

CUBA

RAMIREZ, Serafín. La Habana artística. Apuntes históricos. Habana, Impr. del E. M. de
la Capitanía General, 1891. 684p. (5703
"Notas biográficas": p. 359-548. "Estudios
de crítica y literatura musical": 549-654.
"Composiciones musicales": p. 671-87.---
Jones 1897.

MEXICO

HERRERA Y OGAZON, Alba. El arte musical en

HERRERA Y OGAZON, Alba. El arte ... (Cont.)
México; antecedentes - El Conservatorio,
compositores e intérpretes. México, D.F.,
Dirección General de las Bellas Artes, 1917.
227 p.   (5704
Jones 2245.

SALDIVAR, Gabriel. Historia de la música en
México (épocas precortesiana y colonial)
México, Edit. "Cultura", 1934. 324 p. (5705
Bibliografía: p. 311-20.---Jones 2482.

URUGUAY

AYESTARAN, Lauro. Fuentes para el estudio de
la música colonial uruguaya. Montevideo,
Impresora Uruguaya, 1947. 57 p.   (5705a
Reprinted from Revista de la Facultad de
Humanidades y Ciencias, año 1, no. 1.

NATURAL HISTORY

CARTWRIGHT, Paul Russell. The great natura-
lists explore South America. New York,
Macmillan, 1939. 340 p.   (5706
Includes bibliography.---Jones 85a.

IHERING, Hermann von, and IHERING, Rudolph
von. Bibliographia 1902-1904; historia natural e anthropologia do Brasil. S. Paulo,
1904. 76 p.   (5707
From Revista do Museu Paulista, v. 6.---
Jones 1059.

MEDELLIN. Escuela Interamericana de Bibliotecología. Bibliografía; B-7: Introducción
a las ciencias naturales y físicas. [Me-
dellín, n.d.] 2 p. mimeogr.   (5708

PORTER, Carlos Emilio. Ensayo de una bibliografía chilena de historia natural. Valparaíso, Impr. Gillet, 1900. 68 p. (5709
From Revista chilena de historia natural.
---Jones 1576.

-----. Materiales para la historia de las
ciencias naturales; notas bibliográficas,
los estudios sobre ciencias naturales relativos a países extranjeros publicados en
Chile. Santiago, Prensas de la Universidad
de Chile, 1933. 79 p. (Fascículo I: trabajos en la Revista Chilena de Historia Natural)   (5710
Jones 1578. Reprinted from Anales de la
Universidad de Chile, 3. ser., 2 trim.,
p. 540-63, 1932.

-----. Reseña histórica y bibliografía razonada de las ciencias naturales en Chile,

PORTER, Carlos Emilio. Reseña ... (Cont.)
t. 14: Botánica agrícola e industrial. Santiago, Balcells & Co., 1929. 168 p. (5711
Jones 1572, cites publications in Anales
de la Universidad de Chile, año 7, 2a. ser.,
3r. trim., p. 861-917, 1925, and that the
compilation forms a part of the author's
work which he had been compiling since 1898
in the Revista chilena de ciencias naturales.

SAMPAIO, Alberto José de. Biographia dynamica;
a natureza e o homem no Brasil, noções geraes
e estudo especial da "Protecção á natureza
no Brasil." São Paulo, Companhia Edit. Nacional, 1935. 337 p.   (5712
Includes bibliographies.---Jones 1183.

SÃO PAULO. Museu Paulista. Biblioteca. Ache-
gas para a bibliographia das sciencias naturaes, resumo de obras, opusculos e artigos
publicados no estrangeiro e interessando o
Brasil (1917-1921) São Paulo, Off. do "Diario official", 1927. 210 p.   (5713
Abstracts by Affonso de E. Taunay, Adolph
Hempel and F. C. Hoehne of material in the
Library of the Museu Paulista. "Reprinted
from t. 15 da Revista do Museu Paulista."---
Jones 1189.

TAUNAY, Affonso de Escragnolle. Ensaio de bibliographia referente ao Brasil e ás sciencias naturaes. São Pàulo, 1919.
265 p.   (5714
Contents: - 1a. pte., Literatura brasileira. - 2a. pte., Literatura estrangeira.---
Jones 1033.

NUMISMATICS

BURNS, Jack F. A bibliography of Cuban numismatics. [Pittsburgh, 1958] 25 p.   (5715

MEDINA, José Toribio. Bibliografía numismática colonial hispano-americana. Santiago de Chile, Impreso en Casa del Autor, 1912. 198 p.   (5716
   Jones 298.

OLIVEIRA, Alvaro de Salles. Bibliografía numismática brasileira. São Paulo, Tip. Ideal, 1946. 131 p.   (5716a

OLIVEIRA, Alvaro de Salles ... (Cont.)
   Cited in Geoghegan, 2176.

QUESADA, Ernesto. Los numismáticos argentinos. Córdoba, B. Cubas, 1918. 101 p.   (5717
   From Revista de la Universidad de Córdoba, v. 4, p. 464-556, 1917. "Contiene bibliografía de lo aparecido en volumen sobre numismática y lista de las publicaciones de la Junta de Historia y Numismática Americana" (Binayán)---Jones 821.

PERIODICALS

ARCHIVAL PERIODICALS

ARGENTINA

ARCHIVO General de la República Argentina, 1821-1899//. Buenos Aires.   (5718
   Issued as Archivo general de la Provincia de Buenos Aires, 1821-1883; as Revista, 1869-1872. v.1-14, 1894-1899, issued as 2a. época.

REVISTA de la Biblioteca y Archivo Histórico de la Provincia de Santa Fe, 1- , mar. 1941- . Santa Fe.   (5719

REVISTA del Archivo, no. 1-22, 1924-1930//. Santiago del Estero.   (5720
   Cited in Catálogo colectivo, Buenos Aires, p. 602

REVISTA del Archivo Histórico, 1- , 1944- . Córdoba.   (5721

BOLIVIA

BOLETIN y catálogo del Archivo General de la Nación, 1- , 1886- . Sucre.   (5722
   Cited in Hill, p. 16. ULS p. 62, gives beginning date as 1890. Jones 901a.

REVISTA de la Biblioteca y Archivo Nacionales, 1- , 1932 (?)-1943//. Sucre.   (5723
   Jones 902. Hill, p. 16, notes that starting date was 1937. However, DPU collection has no. 3, junio 1936. In this issue the director, p. 24, writes: "Continuamos la publicación del Catálogo ... a partir del último número de este Boletín que se publicó en febrero de 1932". Two issues of the Revista de la Biblioteca Nacional were publblished in 1920, before the Archivo Nacional was merged with the Biblioteca Nacional.

BRAZIL

ANAIS do Arquivo da Marinha, 1- , 1942- . Rio de Janeiro.   (5724

ANAIS do Arquivo Público e Publicações, 1- , 1917- . Salvador, Bahia.   (5725

REVISTA do Arquivo Municipal, 1- , 1934- . São Paulo, Divisão do Arquivo Histórico, Secretaria de Educação e Cultura.   (5726

REVISTA do Arquivo Publico Mineiro, anno 1-24, 1896- 1933//? Ouro Preto; Bello Horizonte.   (5727
   Contains biographical and bibliographical material such as "A imprensa em Bello Horizonte" by J. Nabuco Linhares (v.8, p. 583-614) and "Genealogía de familias mineiras" (v. 12, p. 283-369)---Jones 1155.

REVISTA do Museo e Arquivo Histórico do Rio Grande do Sul, 1-24, 1921-dez. 1930; n.s., v.1- , 1951- . Porto Alegre.   (5728
   Revista do Archivo Público do Rio Grande do Sul, jan. 1921-jun. 1925.

CHILE

REVISTA chilena de historia y geografía, 1- , 1911- . Santiago de Chile, Sociedad Chilena de Historia y Geografía.   (5729
   Hill, p. 45, notes that the Archivo Nacional, since 1926, is in charge of preparing the Revista.

COLOMBIA

REVISTA del Archivo Nacional, 1- , 1936- . Bogotá.   (5730

COSTA RICA

REVISTA de los Archivos Nacionales, año 1- ,
1936- . San José. (5731
Jones 1275.

CUBA

BOLETIN del Archivo Nacional, 1- , 1902- .
La Habana. (5732

DOMINICAN REPUBLIC

BOLETIN del Archivo General de la Nación,
año 1, no. 1- , mar. 1938- . Santo Domingo. (5733

ECUADOR

ANALES del Archivo Nacional de Historia y
Museo Unico, ép. 2a., v.1, 1939. (5734

BOLETIN del Archivo Nacional de Historia,
1- , en./jun. 1950- . Quito, Casa de la
Cultura Ecuatoriana. (5736

TROPICO, año 1, no.1-2, abr.-mayo/jun.
1938//. Quito, Archivo Nacional de Historia y Museo Unico. (5737

GUATEMALA

BOLETIN del Archivo General del Gobierno,
año 1, no.1- , 1935- . Guatemala. (5738
Last issue received at DPU: jun. 1946.

HONDURAS

BOLETIN de la Biblioteca y Archivo Nacionales, no. 1- , en. 1939- . Tegucigalpa. (5739
The last issue received at DPU: jun. 1947.

REVISTA del Archivo y Biblioteca Nacionales,
año 1- , nov. 10, 1904- . Tegucigalpa. (5740
Jones 1327. Suspended publication:
dic. 1909-jun. 1927, feb.-jun. 1938. The
Revista is also organ of the Sociedad de
Geografía e Historia de Honduras.

MEXICO

BOLETIN del Archivo General de la Nación,

BOLETIN del Archivo General de la ... (Cont.)
1- , 1930- . México, D.F. (5741
Jones 2343.

PANAMA

BOLETIN de los Archivos Nacionales, no. 1,
1927//. Panamá. (5742
Hill, p. 132, notes that no more were
published.

PERU

REVISTA del Archivo Histórico, 1- , 1950- .
Cuzco, Universidad Nacional del Cuzco.(5743

Revista de archivos y bibliotecas nacionales,
See under Bibliographical periodicals -
Perú.

REVISTA del Archivo Nacional, 1- , 1920- ,
Lima. (5744
Hill, p. 140, gives beginning date as 1928.

UNITED STATES

BOLETIN informativo, no.1- , abr. 1962- .
Washington, D.C., National Archives for the
Consejo Interamericano Técnico para Archi-
vos. (5745

URUGUAY

REVISTA del Archivo Histórico Administrativo,
1- , 1885-1921. Montevideo. (5746
Hill, p. 145, notes that 4 volumes were
published before 1890 and 7 after 1911.

REVISTA histórica; Archivo y Museo Histórico
Nacional, 1- , 1907- . Montevideo, Casa
de Rivera. (5747
Suspended publication 1926-1940.

VENEZUELA

BOLETIN del Archivo General de la Nación, 1- ,
1923- . Caracas. (5748
Boletín del Archivo Nacional, 1923-1945.

BOLETIN del Archivo Histórico de la Provincia
de Mérida, 1- , 1943- . Mérida, Oficina Principal de Registro Público. (5749

BOLETIN del Archivo Histórico de Miraflores,
1- , jul./ag. 1959- . Caracas. (5750

BIBLIOGRAPHICAL JOURNALS*

ARGENTINA

ANALES de la Sociedad Científica Argentina,
t.1- , 1876- . Buenos Aires.   (5751
Jones 844a.

BIBLIOGRAFIA, no. 1-? , jul. 1945-jul. 1946//.
Buenos Aires, Subsecretaría de Informaciones, Ministerio del Interior.   (5752

BIBLIOGRAFIA argentina de artes y letras,
no. 1- , en./mar. 1959- . Buenos Aires,
Fondo Nacional de las Artes.   (5753

BIBLIOGRAMA; boletín del Instituto Amigos del
Libro Argentino, no.1- , jun./jul. 1953- .
Buenos Aires.   (5754
    Title varies: Boletín del Instituto Amigos
del Libro Argentino, no.1, jun./jul. 1953-
no.14, mayo/jun. 1956.

BIBLIOGRAPHICA; boletín de la Biblioteca, año
1, no.1-año 2, no. 10, oct. 1932-sept.
1934//. Buenos Aires, Facultad de Derecho
y Ciencias Sociales, Universidad de Buenos
Aires.   (5755
    Jones 631a. Boletín de la Biblioteca,
1932-1933.

LA BIBLIOTECA, t.1-8, jun. 1896-1898; 2a. ép.,
t.9, no.1- , 1er. trim. 1957- . Buenos Aires, Biblioteca Nacional.   (5756
    Editor of the first series: Paul Groussac.
For the period, 1936-1951, see Revista de
la Biblioteca Nacional.

BIBLIOTECA; órgano de la Dirección General de
Bibliotecas, no.1- , 1951- . La Plata,
Ministerio de Educación.   (5757

BIBLIOTECARIO, no.1- , abr. 1954- . Buenos
Aires, Asociación de Bibliotecarios de la
Capital Federal.   (5758

BIBLOS, año 1, no.1- , jun. 1941- . Buenos
Aires, Cámara Argentina del Libro.   (5759

BOLETIN bibliografico, año 1, no.1-año 2,
no. 22, mar. 1928-dic. 1929//. Buenos
Aires.   (5760
    Monthly publication, directed by Emilio
Vera y González. Includes a list of books
copyrighted in Argentina.---Jones 604.

BOLETIN bibliográfico, 1- , 1959- . Bahía
Blanca, Biblioteca Central, Universidad
Nacional del Sur.   (5761

BOLETIN bibliográfico. Buenos Aires, Biblioteca y Museo Numismático, Banco Central de
la República Argentina.   (5762
Geoghegan, 1106, cites [no.1]: abr. 1944.

BOLETIN bibliográfico. v.1, no.1-v.3, no. 27,
nov. 1927-dic. 1924//. Buenos Aires, Círculo de la Librería.   (5763

BOLETIN bibliográfico. Buenos Aires, Comisión
Nacional de la Energía Atómica.   (5764
    Cited in Catálogo colectivo, Buenos Aires,
p. 846.

BOLETIN bibliográfico, no.1- , 1906- . Buenos
Aires, Lajouane, Librería v Editorial. (5765
    Lajouane's bibliographical service, 1959- ,
with earlier numbering continued.

BOLETIN bibliográfico, 1- , 1934- . Buenos
Aires, Departamento de Bibliotecas, Ministerio de Agricultura y Ganadería.   (5766
    Jones 580a.

BOLETIN bibliográfico, 1- , 1952- . Buenos
Aires, Biblioteca Sanitaria, Ministerio de
Asistencia Social y Salud Pública.   (5767

BOLETIN bibliográfico. Buenos Aires, Dirección General de Fabricaciones Militares, Ministerio de Defensa Nacional.   (5768
    Cited in Catálogo colectivo, Buenos Aires,
p. 846.

BOLETIN bibliográfico, 1- , 1958- . Buenos
Aires, División Biblioteca, Ministerio de
Economía.   (5769
    Cited in Catálogo colectivo, Buenos Aires,
p. 846.

BOLETIN bibliográfico, año 1, t.1- , 1943/1944- .
Buenos Aires, Bibliotecas de Marina, Servi-
cio de Informaciones Navales, Ministerio de
Marina.   (5770

BOLETIN bibliográfico, 1- , 1945- . Buenos
Aires, Biblioteca, Ministerio de Obras y Servicios Públicos.   (5771
    Cited in Catálogo colectivo, Buenos Aires,
p. 846.

BOLETIN bibliográfico, 1/2- , 1953- . Buenos
Aires, Servicio de Bibliotecas y Publicacio-
nes de Transportes, Ministerio de Obras y
Servicios Públicos.   (5772

BOLETIN bibliográfico, 1- , 1951- . Buenos
Aires, Biblioteca Arquitecto Alejandro
Christophersen, Sociedad Central de Arqui-
tectos.   (5773

---

    * Identical titles within a country group
are filed alphabetically, first by place and
then by the name of the responsible agency.
Exception to this arrangement is made when

te title, Anales, Boletim, Boletín, or Revista, stands alone. In these cases the
name of the agency follows the title and is
considered in the alphabetical arrangement.

BOLETIN bibliográfico. Buenos Aires, Biblioteca, Facultad de Agronomía y Veterinaria, Universidad de Buenos Aires. (5774
The earliest issue cited in the ULS is 1944.

BOLETIN bibliográfico, año 1, no.1-año 6, feb. 1923-1928//. Buenos Aires, Seminario de Economía y Finanzas, Facultad de Ciencias Económicas, Universidad de Buenos Aires. (5775
Jones 631b. Issued as part of the Revista de ciencias económicas, 1923-mayo 1925.

BOLETIN bibliográfico, 1- , 1959- . Buenos Aires, Biblioteca, Facultad de Ciencias Médicas, Universidad de Buenos Aires. (5776

BOLETIN bibliográfico, 1-3, 1951-1953//. Buenos Aires, Biblioteca Central, Facultad de Filosofía y Letras, Universidad de Buenos Aires. (5777
Cited in Catálogo colectivo, Buenos Aires, p. 188.

BOLETIN bibliográfico, 1- , 1953- . Córdoba, División Normas y Documentación, Instituto Aerotécnico. (5778

BOLETIN bibliográfico, año 1, no.1- año 3, no. 5, abr. 1930-1936//. Córdoba, Biblioteca Mayor, Universidad Nacional de Córdoba. (5779
Jones 603a.

BOLETIN bibliográfico. Córdoba, Instituto Interuniversitario de Historia de la Arquitectura. (5779a
No. 3, 1962 cited in HLAS 28, p. 16.

BOLETIN bibliográfico, 1- , [1957?]- . La Plata, Biblioteca Pública Central de la Provincia "Gral. José de San Martín. (5780
In Catálogo colectivo, Buenos Aires, p. 189, Buenos Aires is given as the place of publication.

BOLETIN bibliográfico, 1- , 1936- . La Plata, Biblioteca, Facultad de Agronomía, Universidad Nacional de La Plata. (5781

BOLETIN bibliográfico, 1- , 1937- . La Plata, Cátedra de Saneamientos Urbanos y Rurales, Facultad de Ciencias Físico-Matemáticas, Universidad Nacional de la Plata. (5782
Cited in Catálogo colectivo, Buenos Aires, p. 189.

BOLETIN bibliográfico, año 1, no.1- , en./jul. 1959- . La Plata, Biblioteca, Facultad de Ciencias Jurídicas y Sociales, Universidad Nacional de La Plata. (5783

BOLETIN bibliográfico, año 1, ... (Cont.)
In Catálogo colectivo, Buenos Aires, p. 188, beginning date is given as 1945/1947.

BOLETIN bibliográfico, 1- , 1958- . La Plata, Facultad de Ciencias Naturales y Museo, Universidad Nacional de La Plata. (5784
Cited in Catálogo colectivo, Buenos Aires, p. 189.

BOLETIN bibliográfico, 1, no.1- , oct. 1940- . Mendoza, Biblioteca Central, Universidad Nacional de Cuyo. (5785
Jones 676a.

BOLETIN bibliográfico, 1942-1948//. Mendoza, Sección Lengua y Literatura Alemana, Instituto de Lenguas y Literaturas Modernas, Facultad de Filosofía y Letras, Universidad Nacional de Cuyo. (5786

BOLETIN bibliográfico, no.1- , 1956?- . Paraná, Sección de Biblioteca y Difusión, Subsecretaría de Economía de la Provincia de Entre Ríos. (5787

BOLETIN bibliográfico, año 1, no.1/3- , en./mar. 1959- . Resistencia, Chaco, Arg., Depto. de Extensión Universitaria y Ampliación de Estudios, Universidad Nacional del Nordeste. (5788

BOLETIN bibliográfico, no.1- , en./mar. 1964- . Rosario, Facultad de Ciencias Económicas, Comerciales y Políticas, Universidad Nacional del Litoral. (5789
Cited in HLAS 26, item 23.

BOLETIN bibliográfico, 1- , 1941- , Rosario, Instituto Social de la Universidad Nacional del Litoral. (5790

BOLETIN bibliográfico, no.1-[23] sept./oct. 1940-en./feb. 945//. Rosario, Museo Social, Universidad Nacional del Litoral. (5791

BOLETIN bibliográfico, 1- , 1943-1948//. Tucumán, Ministerio de Asistencia Social y Salud Pública. (5792
Cited in Catálogo colectivo, Buenos Aires, p. 189.

BOLETIN bibliográfico, 1- , en/jun. 1946- . Tucumán, Biblioteca, Facultad de Filosofía y Letras, Universidad Nacional de Tucumán (5793

BOLETIN bibliográfico agrometeorológico, 1- , 1947- . Buenos Aires, Dirección General del Servicio Meteorologico Nacional, Ministerio de Defensa Nacional. (5794
Cited in Catalogo colectivo, Buenos Aires, p. 845.

Boletín bibliográfico argentino, see Boletín bibliográfico nacional.

BOLETIN bibliografico bimensual, mar./abr.
1960- . Santa Fe, Biblioteca, Escuela de
Técnicos para la Sanidad, Universidad Nacional del Litoral   (5795

BOLETIN bibliográfico de ciencias médicas,
t.1- , 1929- . Buenos Aires.   (5796

BOLETIN bibliográfico de servicio social, año
1- , 1964?- . Buenos Aires.   (5797

BOLETIN bibliográfico mensual, año 1, no. 1/2-
año 4, no. 5/12, en./feb. 1915-mayo/dic.
1918//. Buenos Aires, Museo Social Argentino.   (5798
    List of accessions to the Library arrang-
ed by Decimal Classification.---Jones 791.

BOLETIN bibliográfico nacional, no.1- , en./
jun. 1937- . Buenos Aires, Dirección General de Cultura.   (5799
    Jones 605. Boletín bibliográfico argen-
tino, no. 1- 25/26, 1937-1949. Issued by
the Comisión Nacional de Cooperación Intelectual, 1937-1946; the Junta Nacional de
Intelectuales, 1947-1949; the Dirección
General de Cultura, 1952/1953- . Last issue
received at DPU: no. 33, 1955.

BOLETIN bibliográfico sudamericano, 1-2, en.
1870-jul. 1871//. Buenos Aires   (5799a
    Editor: Carlos Casavalle. Cited in Sabor,
p. 149.

BOLETIN de bibliografía botánica, 1- , 1950- .
Buenos Aires, Instituto de Botánica "Darwi-
nion", Academia Nacional de Ciencias Exactas, Físicas y Naturales.   (5800
    Cited in Catálogo colectivo, Buenos Ai-
res, p. 187.

BOLETIN de la Academia Argentina de Letras,
t.1- , en./mar. 1933- . Buenos
Aires.   (5801
    Bibliographies included.---Jones 550a.

BOLETIN de la Academia Nacional de la Histo-
ria, t.1- , mayo 1924- . Buenos
Aires.   (5802
    Prior to 1938, issued as Boletín de la
Junta de Historia y Numismática Americana.
Contains bibliographical articles, biblio-
graphies of members, etc.---Jones 605a.

Boletín de la Biblioteca, Facultad de Derecho
y Ciencias Sociales, Buenos Aires, see
Bibliographica; boletín de la Biblioteca.

BOLETIN de la Biblioteca "América" de la Universidad de Santiago de Compostela (España)
no.1- , 1910- . Buenos Aires.   (5803
    Published by G. Busto in Argentina as a
record of donations from the Spanish-American republics received by him for the Biblioteca "América".---Jones 66. The ULS

BOLETIN de la Biblioteca "América"... (Cont.)
records 13 numbers.

BOLETIN de la Biblioteca del Congreso de la Nación Argentina, v.1- , 1918-1929; [2a. ép.]
v.1-2, 1932-1933; [3a. ép.] no.1- , 1934- .
Buenos Aires.   (5804
    Jones 570a. Suspended publication 1944-
jun. 1946; 1949-oct. 1956.

BOLETIN de la Biblioteca Obrera Juan B. Justo,
1-2, no. 7, jul. 1929-mar. 1931//. Buenos
Aires.   (5805
    Title varies: Boletín bibliográfico, v.1,
no. 1.

BOLETIN de la Biblioteca Pública de la Provincia de Buenos Aires, v.1, no.1-v.3, no. 82,
1899-1905; [n.s.] no.1-7, 1906-1907//. La
Plata.   (5806

BOLETIN de la Comisión Protectora de Bibliotecas Populares, t.1-2 (no.1-5), 1872-1874;
[nueva época] año 1, no.1- , abr./jun. 1933-
Buenos Aires, Ministerio de Justicia e Instrucción Pública.   (5807
    Publication suspended: jul. 1947-mayo 1962.

Boletín de la Junta de Historia y Numismática
Americana, see Boletín de la Academia Nacional de la Historia.

BOLETIN de la Oficina Bibliográfica, año 1,
no.1- , mayo 1931- . Córdoba, Universidad
Nacional.   (5809

BOLETIN de novedades. Buenos Aires, Edit.
Sudamericana.   (5810
    Title varies.

BOLETIN de novedades, mayo 1951- . Buenos Aires, Librería del Colegio.   (5811
    Looseleaf.

Boletín del Instituto Amigos del Libro Argentino, see Bibliograma.

BOLETIN del Instituto de Cultura Latino-Americana, año 1, no. 1-año 11, t.2, no. 61, en.
1937-feb. 1947//. Buenos Aires, Facultad
de Filosofía y Letras, Universidad de Buenos
Aires.   (5812
    Jones 728a.

BOLETIN del Instituto de Investigaciones Históricas, v.1, no.1-v.29, no. 101/104, jul.
1922-jul. 1944/jun. 1945//. Buenos Aires,
Universidad de Buenos Aires.   (5813

BOLETIN informativo, no.1- , mar. 1927- . Ba-
hía Blanca, Biblioteca Rivadavia, Asociación
Bernandino Rivadavia.   (5814
    Title varies: Guía de lector, 1927-1932;
Boletín 1932-1934.

BOLETIN informativo, 1-2, 1938/1939-1941//.
Buenos Aires, Comisión Nacional de Coordina-
ción de Transportes. Ministerio de Obras y
Servicio Públicos. (5815
Previously issued with title: Boletín bi-
biográfico.

BOLETIN informativo, no.1- , sept. 1964- .
Buenos Aires, Instituto Bibliotecológico,
Universidad de Buenos Aires. (5816
No. 1 has title: Nuevas obras incorpora-
das.

BOLETIN informativo, año 1, no.1- , 193 ?- .
Rosario, Biblioteca "Estanislao S. Zeballos",
Facultad de Ciencias Económicas, Comerciales
y Políticas, Universidad Nacional del Litoral. (5817

BOLETIN internacional de bibliografía argentina, no.1-18, nov. 1930-nov./dic. 1932//.
Buenos Aires, Biblioteca y Archivo, Ministerio de Relaciones Exteriores. (5818
Jones 569.

BOLETIN quincenal; síntesis bibliográfica de
publicaciones periódicas, año 1- , en.
1960- . Rosario, Biblioteca, Facultad de
Ciencias Económicas, Comerciales y Políticas, Universidad Nacional del Litoral. (5818a
Cited in Geoghegan 1125.

EL CANJE, boletín, t.1-2, jun. 1912-[mar.]
1914//. Buenos Aires, Biblioteca, Facultad
de Ciencias Médicas. (5819
Cited in Binayán, item 161.

CEDULAS; catalogo bibliográfico, no. 1- , feb.
1916- . La Plata, Sección Argenti-
na. (5820
Cited in Binayán, item 160, noting that the
second issue had been published.

CIRCULAR bibliográfico, no.1- , 195 ?- . Buenos Aires, Departamento de Bibliotecas, Ministerio de Agricultura y Ganadería (5821

CIRCULAR mensual informativo, 1- , 1946- .
Buenos Aires, Centro de Estudios Bibliotecológicos, Museo Social Argentino. (5822

EDICIONES bibliográficas, no. 1-7, oct. 1947-ag.
1951//. Buenos Aires, Instituto Nacional de
Previsión Social, Secretaría de Trabajo y Previsión. (5823

FICCION, no.1- , mayo/jun. 1956- . Buenos Aires, Edit. Goyanarte.

FICHERO; revista bibliográfica, no.1- , jun.
1958- . Buenos Aires. (5825

GACETA del libro, no.1-37/38, mar. 1945-mar./
abr. 1948//. Buenos Aires. (5826

GUIA quincenal de la actividad intelectual y
artístico argentina, 1-4, 1947-1950//. Buenos Aires, Dirección General de Cultura, Comisión Nacional de Cultura. (5827

GUIA temática de los trabajos y colaboraciones
más importantes aparecidos en revistas y publicaciones en general recibidas, 1- , oct.
1950- . Santa Fe, Biblioteca Central, Ministerio de Salud Pública y Bienestar Social. (5828

HORIZONTE bibliotecológico, año 1, no.1- ,
sept. 1954- . Rosario. (5829

INDICE; organo informativo mensual, año 1, no.
1-año 2, no. 10/11, abr./mayo 1935-sept./dic.
1936//. La Plata, Biblioteca Pública, Universidad Nacional de La Plata. (5830

INDICE bibliográfico, no.1- , 1964- . Buenos
Aires, Instituto Argentino del Petro-
leo. (5830a
Cited in Geoghegan 2082.

INDICE de publicaciones periódicas, derecho,
economía y ciencias sociales, t.1, no.1-4,
mar.-dic. 1950//. Buenos Aires, Lajouane,
Librería y Editorial. (5831

INFORMACION bibliográfica, año 1, no.1- , mayo
1948- . Buenos Aires, Biblioteca Domingo
Faustino Sarmiento, Caja Nacional de Ahorro
Postal. (5832

INFORMATIVO, v.1, no.1- , set. 960- . Córdoba, Biblioteca Mayor, Universidad Nacional. (5834
Each issue has section: Ultimas obras incorporadas a la Biblioteca Mayor.

INFORMATIVO bibliográfico, no. 1- , 1961- .
Buenos Aires, Instituto Nacional de Tecno-
logía Industrial. Centro de Investigación
Documentaria. (5834a

INFORMATIVO bibliográfico, no.1-21, 1938-1940;
n.s., v.1, no.1- , 1947- . Buenos Aires,
Biblioteca, Facultad de Ciencias Económicas,
Universidad de Buenos Aires. (5835
Cited in Catálogo colectivo, Buenos Aires,
p. 406. Title: Boletín bibliográfico mensual, 1947-1955. Publication suspended
1956.

INVENTARIO de documentos publicados, no.1- ,
jul./sept. 1924- . Buenos Aires, Instituto
de Investigaciones Históricas, Universidad
de Buenos Aires. (5836
Suplemento of the Boletín del Instituto
de Investigaciones Históricas. DPU has collection through no.5, jul. 1934/mar. 1935.

Lajouane's bibliographical service, see Boletín bibliográfico.

LIBROS de hoy, año 1, no.1-41/42, mayo 1951-
oct./dic. 1955//. Buenos Aires.   (5837

LIBROS y bibliotecas, no.1-2/3, oct.-nov./dic.
1926//. Buenos Aires, Comisión Protectora
de Bibliotecas Populares.   (5838

LIST of acquisitions, 1- , 1950- . Buenos Aires, Biblioteca Lincoln.   (5839

LISTA de las últimas obras argentinas ingresadas, en./jun. 1932-en/dic. 1935//. Buenos
Aires, Biblioteca Nacional.   (5839a
    Cited in Geoghegan, 601.

LISTA de obras. Buenos Aires, Edit. Sopena
Argentina.   (5840

LA LITERATURA argentina; revista bibliográfica, año 1, no.1-año 9, no. 105, sept. 1928-
sept. 1937//. Buenos Aires.   (5841
    Director: Lorenzo J. Rosso. Includes ar-
ticles, book reviews, lists of books copyrighted and supplementary section, "Bibliografía general argentina", A-Echegaray
(no. 1-96)---Jones 756.

LITERATURAS americanas, 1-7, 1939-1948//.
Buenos Aires, Instituto de Literatura Ibe-
roamericana, Facultad de Filosofía y Letras,
Universidad de Buenos Aires.   (5842

LOGOS, año 1, no.1- , 4o. trim. 1941- . Buenos Aires, Facultad de Filosofía y Letras,
Universidad de Buenos Aires.   (5843

MAS LIBROS; boletín informativo, año 1, v.1,
no.1-año 3, no. 10/11, primavera 1944-otoño
1947//. Bernal, Biblioteca Popular "Mariano Moreno".   (5844

NEGRO sobre blanco; boletín literario bibliográfico, mar. 1960- . Buenos Aires, Edit.
Losada.   (5845
    Cited in Peraza, Bibliografías corrien-
tes, 1964, item 48.

NOTICIA bibliográfica, año 1- , 1950- . Buenos Aires, Librería Hachette.   (5846
    DPU registered año 1, no.3, ag. 1950.

NOTICIERO Franklin, no.1- , dic 1964- . Buenos Aires, Fundación Interamericana de Bibliotecología Franklin.   (5847

NOTICIOSO de revistas e informativo bibliográfico, no.1- , 1940- . Buenos Aires, Dirección Nacional de Vialidad, Ministerio de
Obras y Servicios Públicos.   (5848

NOVA; boletín literario y bibliográfico, año
1, no.1- año 2, no. 5, jul. 1945-ag. 1946//.
Buenos Aires, Edit. Nova.   (5849

NOVEDADES de librería, año 1, no.1- , jun.

NOVEDADES de librería ... (Cont.)
1960- . Buenos Aires, Cámara Argentina de
Editoriales Técnicas.   (5850

POLIBIBLON; bibliografía acumulativa argentina
e hispanoamericana, v.1, no.1-6/7, abr.-jul./
ag. 1947//. Buenos Aires.   (5851

REGISTRO bibliográfico de obras y artículos sobre ciencias jurídicas y sociales publicados
en el país, no.1- , ag. 1959- . La Plata,
Biblioteca Pública Joaquín V. González, Facultad de Ciencias Jurídicas y Sociales, Universidad Nacional.   (5852
    First issue covers year 1957.

REVISTA bibliográfica; crítica argentina del
pensamiento americano, año 1, no.1-año 2,
no. 19/20, en. 1944- jul./ag. 1945//. Buenos Aires.   (5853

REVISTA bibliográfica de medicina, 1-5, 1942-
1945//. Buenos Aires.   (5854
    Cited in Catálogo colectivo, Buenos Aires,
p. 609.

REVISTA de ciencias económicas, 1- , jul. 1913- .
Buenos Aires, Centro de Estudiantes de Ciencias Económicas, Colegio de Graduados en
Ciencias Económicas; Facultad de Ciencias
Económicas, Universidad de Buenos Aires.   (5855
    Ser. 1, v.1-8, 1913-1920; ser.2, v.9-35,
1921-1948; ser. 3, v.36-45, 1948-1957; ser.4,
v.46- , 1958- .

REVISTA de derecho, historia y letras, año 1-25,
t.1-76, jul. 1898-dic. 1923//. Buenos Aires,
J. Peuser.   (5856
    Beginning with v.17 includes "Bibliografía
argentina", by E. S. Zeballos, of which
earlier portions were published in Boletín
del Instituto Geográfico Argentino, v.17-19.
"Indice alfabético-analítico de los diez tomos": v. 11, p. 158-60.---Jones 393.

REVISTA de filología hispánica, 1-8, no.1/2,
en./mar. 1939-en./jun. 1946//. Buenos Aires,
Instituto de Filología, Facultad de Filosofía y Letras, Universidad de Buenos Aires;
Instituto de las Españas en los Estados Unidos, New York.   (5857
    Jones, 395a, notes that this title super-
sedes the Revista de filología española.

REVISTA de la Biblioteca Nacional, t.1-25, no.
1-59, en./mar. 1937-jul./sept. 1951//. Buenos Aires.   (5858
    Superseded by La Biblioteca.

REVISTA de la Comisión Protectora de Bibliotecas Populares, año 1, no.1-3a. ép., no.6,
1948-1960//. Buenos Aires.   (5859

SERIE bibliográfica mensual, no.1- , 1941(?)- .

SERIE bibliográfica ... (Cont.)
Buenos Aires, Biblioteca, Congreso de la
Nación.   (5861
    Title varies: Serie bibliográfica, 1941-
1942; serie bibliográfica mensual, 1942- .

ULTIMAS adquisiciones, no.1- , jun. 30, 1962- .
Bahía Blanca, Biblioteca Central, Universidad
Nacional del Sur.   (5862

"VIRTUS"; revista argentina de bibliografía,
año 1, no.1- , 1920- . Buenos Aires. (5863
    Jones 883.

BOLIVIA

REVISTA de la Biblioteca Nacional, año 1, no.
1-2, jun./jul. 1920//. Sucre.   (5864
    Jones 902. Changed title to Revista de
la Biblioteca y Archivo Nacionales. See
note under item 5723.

BRAZIL

AUTORES e livros, anno 1, v.1, no.1- , ag. 10,
1941- . Rio de Janeiro.   (5865
    "Suplemento literario" of A Manha.

BBB; boletim bibliográfico brasileiro, see
    BBB; revista dos editôres.

BBB; revista dos editôres, v.1- , nov. 1952/fev.
1953- . Rio de Janeiro [Sindicato Nacional
das Empresas Editôras de Libros e Publicações
Culturais]   (5866
    Formerly Boletim bibliográfico brasileiro,
v.1-6, nov. 1952/fev. 1953-nov/dez. 1957;
BBB; Boletim bibliográfico brasileiro, v.7-8,
1958-1959.

BIL; bibliografia e informações para leitores,
ano 1- , 1956- . Rio de Janeiro.   (5867
    Cited in HLAS, 4275.

BIBLIOGRAFIA; Centro Latino Americano de Pesquisas em Ciências Sociais, 1962- . Rio de
Janeiro.   (5868
    Cited in Doria, 45.

BIBLIOGRAFIA economico-social, ano 1- , sept.
1950- . Rio de Janeiro, Fundação Getulio
Vargas.   (5869

BIBLIOGRAFIA selecionada de artigos de periódicos recibidos, 1961- . Recife, Instituto
Joaquim Nabuco.   (5870
    Cited in Doria 171.

O BIBLIOGRAPHO, boletim de informações bibliographicas, v.1-3, no.4, dez. 1930-set.
1932//. Rio de Janeiro.   (5871

A BIBLIOTECA, ano 1, no.1- , fev. 1944- . Rio
de Janeiro, Departamento Administrativo do
Serviço Público.   (5872
    Suplemento do Boletim do D.A.S.P.

BOLETIM bibliográfico, ano 1- , jul. 1962- .
Belo Horizonte, Universidade de Minas
Gerais.   (5873
    Cited in Doria, 172.

BOLETIM bibliográfico, no.1- , jan. 1954- .
Campinas, Biblioteca, Instituto Agronômico.   (5874

BOLETIM bibliográfico, 1938- . Pelotas, Rio
Grande do Sul, Biblioteca, Escola de Agro-
nomia Eliseu Maciel.   (5875
    Cited in Peraza, 1964, item 161.

BOLETIM bibliográfico. Pôrto Alegre, Serviço
Social do Comercio, Administração Regional
do Rio Grande do Sul (SESC)   (5876
    DPU issues begin with v.2, no.1, jan./jul.
1959.

BOLETIM bibliográfico. Pôrto Alegre, Instituto Teconológico do Rio Grande do Sul. (5877
    Cited in Catálogo colectivo, Buenos Aires,
p. 838.

BOLETIM bibliográfico. Recife, Serviço Social
Rural. mimeogr.   (5878
    Doria, 173, cites 1961- .

BOLETIM bibliográfico. Mossoró, Rio Grande do
Sul, Biblioteca Pública Municipal e Museu
Municipal.   (5879
    DPU issues begin with ano 2, no. 24, 1950.

BOLETIM bibliográfico, anno 1-4, no. 1/2, 1918-
jan./jun. 1921; n.s., v.1- , 1951- . Rio
de Janeiro, Biblioteca Nacional.   (5880
    Childs, in his official publication of Bra-
zil, indicates issues in 1931. The Bibliografia brasileira, 1938, lists an issue for
1938, and in the first issue 1951, it is
noted that back issues from 1946 would be
published. Issues before 1931 included all
accessions to the Library, and only Brazilian
works beginning with 1931. In the preface
of the first issue 1918, it is noted that the
Boletim bibliographico will continue compilations begun in 1886, referred to by Doria Menezes in her working paper to the Seminar on
the Acquisition of Latin American Library
Materials, 1964, as the Boletim das acquisi-
ções mais importantes, 1886-1888. Doria,
item 3, mentions also publication of the
Boletim bibliográfico for the year 1945.

BOLETIM bibliográfico, v.1- , 1o./2o. trim.
1951- . Rio de Janeiro, Divisão de Obras
Raras e Publicações, Biblioteca Nacional.   (5881

BOLETIM bibliográfico, no.1- , 1948?- . Rio
de Janeiro, Biblioteca, Instituto Brasileiro de Geografia e Estatística.   (5882

BOLETIM bibliográfico, v.1, no.1- , maio 1957-
Rio de Janeiro, Instituto Brasileiro de Geo-
grafia e Estatística, Conselho Nacional de
Estatística.   (5883

BOLETIM bibliografico, no.1-40, 31 maio 1935-
jan. 15, 1937//. Rio de Janeiro, Directoria
de Estatística da Produção, Ministério da
Agricultura. mimeogr.   (5884
    Cited in Reis, item 486.

BOLETIM bibliográfico, 1951?- . Rio de Janeiro, Biblioteca, Ministério do Trabalho, Indústria e Comércio.   (5885

BOLETIM bibliografico, ano 1, v.1- , out./dez.
1943- . São Paulo, Biblioteca Pública Municipal.   (5886

BOLETIM bibliográfico. São Paulo, Instituto
de Direito Social.   (5887
    DPU records no.4 and 6 received in 1951.

BOLETIM bibliográfico, no.1- , out. 1953- .
São Paulo, Secção de Bibliografia Agrícola,
Secretaria da Agricultura.   (5888

Boletim bibliográfico brasileira, see BBB.

BOLETIM bibliográfico dos livros adquiridos,
1955- . Recife, Escola de Belas Artes,
Universidade.   (5889
    Cited in Peraza, 1964, item 79.

BOLETIM bibliográfico e informativo, 1959- .
São Paulo, Instituto Astronômico e Geofísico,
Universidade de São Paulo.   (5890

BOLETIM bibliográfico e informativo, 1- ,
1956- . São Paulo, Instituto de Estudos Portugueses, Universidade de São Paulo.   (5891

BOLETIM bibliographico, 1931/1934-1935. Rio
de Janeiro, Departamento de Diffusão Cultural, Bibliotheca Municipal.   (5892
    Cited in Reis 476, 712.

BOLETIM bibliographico. Rio de Janeiro, J.
Leite e Cia.   (5893
    Jones 980a.

BOLETIM da Academia Brasileira de Letras, v.1-2,
1897- . 1901//. Rio de Janeiro.   (5894
    Jones 946a.

BOLETIM da Biblioteca, no.1- , out. 1949- .
Santos, Instituto Histórico e Geográfico de
Santos.   (5895

BOLETIM da Biblioteca da Câmara dos Deputados,
v.1, no.1- , jan./jun. 1952- . Rio de Janei-

BOLETIM da Biblioteca... (Cont.)
ro.   (5896
    DPU issues begin with v.5, no.1/2, jan./
    jun. 1956.

BOLETIM de notícias bibliográficas. Rio de
Janeiro, Biblioteca do Exército, Ministério
da Guerra.   (5897

BOLETIM informativo, v.1, no.1- , jan./mar.
1959- . Pôrto Alegre, Companhia de Seguros
de Vida "Providência do Sul", Biblioteca.
mimeogr.   (5898

BOLETIM informativo, no. [1]- , maio 1959- .
Pôrto Alegre Instituto de Belas Artes do
Rio Grande do Sul.   (5899

BOLETIM informativo, v.1, no.1- , jan./fev.
1955- . Rio de Janeiro, Instituto Brasileiro de Bibliografia e Documentação
(IBBD)   (5900

BOLETIM informativo, no.1- , set. 1947- .
Rio de Janeiro, Biblioteca do Ministério da
Fazenda.   (5901

BOLETIM informativo, no.1- , jul. 1959- .
São Paulo, Serviço de Documentação, Universidade de São Paulo.   (5902

BOLETIM mensal bibliográfico e noticioso da
Comissão Nacional de Folclore. Rio de Ja-
neiro, Instituto Brasileiro de Educação,
Ciencia e Cultura (IBECC)   (5903
    Doria, 59, gives beginning date as 1948;
    the Unesco Directory of current Latin Amer-
    ican periodicals as 1956.

BOLETIM mensal de informações e de bibliografia. Rio de Janeiro, Real Gabinete Portu-
gûes de Leitura.   (5904

CATALOGO, 1- , 1956- . Rio de Janeiro, Biblioteca, Comissão de Energia Atómica.(5905

CORREIO litterario e bibliographico; publicação mensal da Livraria Laemmert & C., no.1-
12, fev.-dez. 1890; n.s., v.1-8, abr. 1898-
1905//? Rio de Janeiro.   (5906
    Jones 1025.

EDICOES brasileiras, no.1- , jan. 1963- .
Rio de Janeiro, Sindicato Nacional dos Editôres de Livros.   (5907

A ESTANTE; revista brasileira de bibliografia
e cultura, v.1, no.1- , 1952- . Rio de Janeiro.   (5908
    First on file at DPU, v.1, no.2, ag. 1952.

FICHARIO; resenha da bibliografia brasileira,
ano 1, no.1-4, jan./fev.-jul./sept. 1950//.
Rio de Janeiro.   (5909

IBBD, see Boletim informativo.

INDICE de periódicos, 1962- . São Paulo,
Secção de Bibliografia Agrícola, Secretaria da Agricultura. (5910
In ULS beginning date is 1960, issued by
the Diretoria de Publicidade Agrícola.

JUS documentação, boletim informativo mensal,
1- , 1948- . Rio de Janeiro, Serviço de Documentação, Ministério da Justicia e Negócios Interiores. (5911

LEITORES e livros, ano 1, no.1- , jul./sept.
1950- . Rio de Janeiro, Liga Universitária
Católica Femenina, Ação Católica Brasileira. (5912

LEITURA, ano 1, no.1- , dez. 1942- . Rio de
Janeiro. (5913
Suspended between jul. 1946-abr. 1947.
Subtitle varies: crítica e informação bi-
bliográfica; a revista dos melhores escrito-
res; arte e literatura econômica e finan-
ças; arte y literatura política e econômica.
Subtitle omitted after no. 89.

LEITURA de todos. Rio de Janeiro, Instituto
Brasileiro de Educação, Ciencia e Cultura
(IBECC) Commissão Brasileira da Unes-
co. (5914
DPU collection: ano 3, no.7-ano 4, no.8,
jun. 1953-jul. 1956.

LISTA selecionada das publicações recibidas,
no.1- , mar./abr. 1955- . Rio de Janeiro,
Instituto Brasileiro de Bibliografia e Documentação. (5915

LIVROS novos; revista mensal de bibliographia
e litteratura, 1919- . Rio de Janeiro. (5916
Jones 1077.

NOSSOS livros; boletim bibliográfico da
"Agir", ano 1- , jan./fev. 1957- . Rio de
Janeiro, Livr. AGIR Editôra. (5917

NOTICIAS bibliográficas, no.1- , 1947- .
Rio de Janeiro, Serviço de Informação Agrícola, Ministério da Agricultura. (5918

NOTICIAS diversas, v.1, no.1- , jan. 1961- .
Rio de Janeiro, Instituto Brasileiro de Bibliografia e Documentação. (5919

RELAÇÃO bibliográfica. São Paulo, União Cultural Brasil-Estados Unidos. (5920

RELAÇÃO de publicações catalogadas, no.1- ,
jan. 1954- . Campinas, Biblioteca, Divisão de Experimentação e Pesquisas. (5921

REVISTA bibliográfica, ano 1, no.1-3, jan.-
dez. 1941//. São Paulo, Universidade de São

REVISTA bibliográfica ... (Cont.)
Paulo. (5922

REVISTA bibliográfica de medicina e cirugía,
v.1-2, no.11, fev.-dez. 1931//. Rio de Janeiro. (5923

REVISTA bibliográfica "Torres", 1- , 1949- .
São Paulo. (5924

REVISTA brasileira de geografia, 1- , 1939- .
Rio de Janeiro, Instituto Brasileiro de Geo-
grafia e Estatística. (5925
Jones 1154b.

REVISTA do Instituto de Estudos Genealógicos;
Instituto Heráldico-Genealógico, v.1- , jun.
1937- . São Paulo. (5926
Jones 1060. After Feb. 1940 the Instituto
de Estudos Genealógicos became Instituto Heráldico-Genealógico.

REVISTA do Instituto Historico e Geographico,
1- , 1894/1895- . São Paulo. (5927
Among articles are: Imprensa paulista, by
Lafayette de Toledo, v.3, p. 303-521. - A
typographia e a lythographia no Brazil, by
Estevam Leão Bourroul, v.13, p.3-39: A imprensa regia, by Ernesto Senna, p. 41-60. -
Os representantes de São Paulo nos parlamen-
tos do antigo regimen, by Affonso d'Escragnolle Taunay, v.14, p. 347-72. - A imprensa
periodica de S. Paulo, by Affonso A. de Freitas, v.19, p. 321-1136. - Table of contents
to v.1-18 in Freitas, Imprensa...p. 749-68,
entry 656.---Jones 1068.

REVISTA do livro, ano 1, no.1- , jun. 1956- .
Rio de Janeiro, Instituto Nacional do Livro. (5928

REVISTA do livro; resenha mensal bibliográfica, ano 1, no. 1-4, 1939-mar. 1940//. Rio
de Janeiro. (5929
Jones 1155a.

REVISTA trimensal, 1- , 1887- . Fortaleza,
Instituto do Ceará. (5930
Jones 1061. Editor: Barão de Studart.

SINTESE; resumos selecionados de literatura
médica, no.1- , 1953- . Pôrto Alegre, Bureau de Divulgação Científica. (5931

STUDIUM; boletim bibliográfico, ano 1, no.1-ano
7, no. 9, out./dez. 1940-abr./jun. 1949//.
São Paulo, Livr. Academica Saravia &
Cía. (5932

STUDIUM; revista bibliográfica, ano, 1, no.1-3,
out./dez. 1949-abr./jun. 1950//. São Paulo,
Saravia, S.A. (5933

SUMARIOS bibliográficos, 1933- . São Paulo,
Biblioteca, Departamento de Profilaxia da

SUMARIOS bibliográficos ... (Cont.)
Lepra.   (5934

SUMARIOS de energia nuclear, 1959- . Rio de
Janeiro, Instituto Brasileiro de Bibliografia e Documentação.   (5935

CHILE

ARTICULOS de revistas, no.1- , mayo 1952- .
Santiago, Biblioteca de Parasitología, Universidad de Chile.   (5936

BABEL, no.1-60, mayo 1939-oct./dic. 1951//.
Santiago de Chile, Livr. y Edit. Nascimento.   (5937

BIBLIOGRAFICO, no.1- , jun. 1935- . Santiago
de Chile, Libr. y Edit. "Splendor". (5938

BOLETIN bibliográfico, no.1, 1888//. Santiago de Chile, Libr. Americana de Carlos
2o.   (5939
   Cited in Laval, item 148.

BOLETIN bibliográfico, año 1, no.1- ,
[1964?]- . Santiago de Chile, Centro de
Documentación Pedagógica, Superintendencia
de Educación.   (5940
   DPU has on record no.4, nov. 1964.

BOLETIN bibliográfico, no.1- , oct. 1,
1875- // Valparaíso, Libr. de Julio Real
y Prado.   (5941
   Jones 1580. Laval, item 280, cites
issues 1-23, oct. 1, 1875-mar. 1879.

BOLETIN de información científica y biblio-
gráfica, no.1- , en. 1952- . Santiago,
Clínica de Neurología, Universidad de
Chile.   (5942

BOLETIN de la Biblioteca Central y de las bibliotecas especializadas, no.1- , oct./dic.
1953- . Santiago de Chile, Universidad Católica.   (5943
   Title varies slightly.

BOLETIN de la Biblioteca Nacional, no. 1-92,
oct. 31, 1901-dic. 1913; 2a. ép., año 1-8/9,
1929/1931-1937/1938. Santiago de Chile.   (5944
   Suspended publication: 1907, 1914-1928.
   ---Jones 1596. Title varies: Revista; continuación del boletín, 1912.

Chilean bibliographic news services, see Servicio bibliográfico chileno.

FICHERO chileno de medicina. Santiago de Chile, Biblioteca Central, Escuela de Medicina,
Universidad de Chile.   (5945

LECTURAS; revista mensual de información literaria, 2a.ép., no.1-7(?) , jul. 1945-feb.
1948//. Santiago, "Zig-Zag"   (5946
   Formerly Lecturas para toda América.

LECTURAS para toda América. Santiago, "Zig-
Zag".   (5947
   DPU collection: no.9-12, 1939-[n.d.]//

NUEVOS títulos; lista de libros, tésis, etc.,
mar. 1956- . Santiago, Biblioteca Central,
Universidad de Chile.   (5948

NUEVOS títulos, 1- , jun. 1954- . Santiago,
Biblioteca Central, Escuela de Medicina,
Universidad de Chile.   (5949

Revista; continuación del boletín, see Boletín de la Biblioteca Nacional.

REVISTA bibliográfica, v.1, no.1-4, en. 1-abr.
1, 1887//. Santiago de Chile, Libr. Antigua
i Moderna de Roberto Miranda.   (5950

REVISTA bibliográfica chilena, no.1-5, jul./
sept. 1956-jul./sept. 1957//. Santiago de
Chile.   (5951

REVISTA chilena de historia y geografía, año
1, no.1- , 1911- . Santiago de Chile, Sociedad Chilena de Historia y Geografía (5952
Jones 1583.

REVISTA de bibliografía chilena, 1er. trim.
1927-4o. trim. 1929//. Santiago de Chile,
Biblioteca Nacional.   (5953
   Editor: Raúl Silva Castro. Superseded:
Revista de bibliografía chilena y extranje-
ra.

REVISTA de bibliografía chilena y extranjera,
año 1, no.1- , año 6, no. 12, en. 1913-dic.
1918//. Santiago de Chile, Biblioteca Nacional.   (5954
   Jones 1585. Superseded by: Revista de bibliografía chilena.

SERVICIO bibliográfico chileno; Chilean bibliographic news service, no.1- , sept.
1940- . Santiago de Chile, Zamorano y Caperán.   (5955

SERVICIO de información bibliográfica, no.1- ,
1947- . Santiago, Sección Educación Sanitaria, Caja de Seguro Obligatorio.   (5956

COLOMBIA

BIBLIOGRAFIA oficial colombiana, no.1- , 1964- .
Medellín, Escuela Interamericana de Bibliotecología.   (5957

LA BIBLIOTECA Fabricato informa... : un notice-
ro bibliográfico para información de la fa-

PERIODICALS

LA BIBLIOTECA Fabricato ... (Cont.)
milia Fabricato, no.1- , mar. 1962- . Bello,
mimeogr. (5958
Cited in Florén, Bibliografía bibliotecológica, 1961/1962, item 386.

BIBLIOTECAS y libros; órgano de la Biblioteca
del Centenario, año 1, no.1-año 2, no. 23/
24, jul./ag. 1939//. Cali. (5959

BOLETIN analítico mensual, no.1- , mar. 1963- .
Medellín, Biblioteca, Facultad de Agronomía
e Instituto Forestal. (5960

BOLETIN bibliográfico, no.1-7, jul. 1946-oct.
1947//. Bogotá, Biblioteca, Banco de la República. (5961

BOLETIN bibliográfico; publicaciones recibidas, no.1- , 1956- . Bogota, Departamento
de Investigaciones Económicas, Banco de la
República. (5962

BOLETIN bibliográfico, 1- , jul. 1954- .
Bogotá, Biblioteca, Centro Nacional de Investigaciones Agrícolas. "Tibaitatá". (5963

BOLETIN bibliográfico (nuevas adquisiciones)
no.1- , ag. 1962- . Bogotá, Biblioteca,
Departamento Administrativo de Planeacion
y Servicios Técnicos. (5964
Cited in Florén, Bibliografía bibliotecológica, 1961/1962, item 391.

BOLETIN bibliográfico, 1- , 1958- . Bogotá,
División de Información, Publicaciones y
Biblioteca, Departamento Administrativo
Nacional de Estadística. (5965

BOLETIN bibliográfico, no.1- , en. 1961- .
Bogotá, Biblioteca, Instituto de Asuntos
Nucleares. (5966

BOLETIN bibliográfico, no. [1]- , jun. 1961- .
Bogotá, Instituto de Fomento Algodonero
(IFA). (5967
Cited in Florén, Bibliografía bibliote-
cológica, 1961/1962, item 393.

BOLETIN bibliográfico, [1a. entrega]- ,
1961- . Bogota, Biblioteca, Laboratorio
Quimico Nacional. (5968
Cited in Florén, Bibliografía bibliotecológica, 1961/1962, item 388.

BOLETIN bibliográfico, no.1- , en./mayo 1956- .
Bogotá, Servicio Geológico Nacional.(5969

BOLETIN bibliográfico, no.1- , mayo 1964- .
Bogotá, Facultad de Derecho, Universidad
Externado de Colombia. (5970

BOLETIN bibliografico, año 1, no.1- , oct.
1959- . Bogotá, Biblioteca "Antonio García

BOLETIN bibliográfico ... (Cont.)
Banus", Facultad de Quimica e Ingeniería
Química, Universidad Nacional de Colom-
bia. (5971

BOLETIN bibliográfico, no.1- , ag. 1963- .
Medellín, Biblioteca, Asociación Nacional de
Industriales (ANDI) (5972

BOLETIN bibliográfico, no.1- , jul. 1962- .
Medellín, Biblioteca de la Facultad de Ciencias Económicas, Universidad de Antioquia. (5973

BOLETIN bibliográfico (nuevas adquisiciones)
no.1- , en. 1962- . Popayán, Biblioteca, Facultad de Electromecánica y Telecomunicacio-
nes, y Facultad de Ingeniería Civil, Universidad del Cauca. (5974
Cited in Florén, Bibliografía bibliotecológica, 1961/1962, item 392.

BOLETIN bibliográfico, no.1- , jul. 1958- .
Tunja, Biblioteca General, Universidad Pedagógica de Colombia. (5975

BOLETIN bibliográfico agropecuario, no.1- , en.
1962- . Pasto, Biblioteca, Instituto Tecnológico Agrícola, Universidad de Nariño (5976
Florén in Bibliografía bibliotecológica,
1961/1962, item 394, notes title varies: "no.
1 al 6 se llamó Boletín bibliográfico; desde
el no.7 se llama Boletín bibliográfico agropecuario."

Boletín bibliográfico bolivariano, see Bolívar.

BOLETIN cultural y bibliográfico, no.1- , en.
1958- . Bogotá, Biblioteca "Luis Angel Arango", Banco de la República. (5977

BOLETIN de adquisiciones, no.1- , jun. 1962- .
Barranquilla, Biblioteca, Universidad del
Atlántico. (5978
Cited in Florén, Bibliografía bibliotecoló-
gica, 1961/1962, item 395.

BOLETIN de adquisiciones, no.1- , 1962- . Bogotá, Biblioteca, Instituto Colombiano de la
Reforma Agraria. (5979
Cited in Florén, Bibliografía bibliotecológica, 1961/1962, item 397.

BOLETIN de adquisiciones, no.1- , feb. 1961- .
Cali, Biblioteca Central, Universidad del
Valle. (5980
Cited in Florén, Bibliografía bibliotecoló-
gica, 1961/1962, item 396.

BOLETIN de adquisiciones, no.1- , oct. 1959- .
Medellín, Escuela Interamericana de Bibliotecología, Universidad de Antioquia. (5981
Title varies: no. 1, Lista de adquisiciones.

BOLETIN de bibliografía antioquena, no.1- ,
ag./oct. 1963- . Medellín, Biblioteca General, Universidad de Antioquia.   (5981a

BOLETIN de la Biblioteca, Departamento Administrativo Nacional de Estadística, no.1- ,
1958-   Bogotá.   (5982

BOLETIN de la Librería Colombiana. Bogotá,
Camacho Roldán y Tamayo.   (5983
Jones 1692.

BOLETIN historial, año 1, no.1-año 6, no. 77,
mayo 1915-jun. 1935//. Cartagena, Academia
de la Historia de Cartagena de Indias.   (5984
Suspended mayo 1919-dic. 1925; abr. 1926-
dic. 1928; feb.-jun. 1929. "Periódicos
oficiales de Colombia, 1810-1910": año 1,
p. 176-79.---Jones 1693

BOLETIN informativo, v.1, no.1- , abr. 1961-
Bogotá, Centro de Bibliografía y Documentación, Universidad Nacional.   (5985

BOLETIN informativo, no.1- , nov. 1954- .
Manizales, Biblioteca Departamental (5986

BOLETIN informativo y bibliográfico, no.1- ,
jul. 1961- . Medellín, Biblioteca General,
Universidad de Antioquia.   (5987
Cited in Florén, Bibliografía bibliotecológica, 1961/1962, item 398.

BOLETIN informativo y bibliográfico, no.1- ,
abr. 1962- . Pasto, Biblioteca General,
Universidad de Nariño.   (5988

BOLETIN informativo y bibliográfico, no.1- ,
oct. 1962- . Pereira, Biblioteca, Universidad Tecnológica.   (5989
Cited in Florén, Bibliografía bibliotecológica, 1961/1962, item 399.

BOLETIN jurídico-bibliográfico, año 1, no.1- ,
jun. 1945- . Medellín, Biblioteca, Facultad de Derecho, Universidad de Antioquia.   (5990

BOLETIN mensual del material seleccionado
de las publicaciones y artículos recibidas,
no.1-68, 1957-1959//. Bogotá, Sección de
Fichero y Biblioteca, Ministerio de Agricultura.   (5991
Cited in Giraldo Jaramillo, p. 81.

BOLIVAR; órgano de la Biblioteca Central, 1- ,
jul. 1941- . Medellín, Universidad Católica Bolivariana.   (5992
No. 1-18, jul. 1941-abr./jun. 1947, Boletín bibliográfico bolivariano.

LA CARIDAD, v.1-14, 1864-1882//. Bogotá.   (5993
Includes information on Colombian authors.

LA CARIDAD, v.1-14, 1864-1882//... (Cont.)
---Jones 1695a

CUADERNO bibliográfico, no.1- , 1961- . Bogotá, Biblioteca, Departamento de Capacitación, Empresa Nacional de Telecomunica-
ciones.   (5994
Cited in Florén, Bibliografía bibliotecológica 1961/1962, item 389.

CUADERNOS de cultura, año 1, no.1- , jun.
1953- . Cali, Biblioteca "Jorge Garcés
B."   (5995

INDICE cultural; revista mensual de arte, literatura y bibliografía, año 1, no.1-año 5,
no. 21, jun. 1952-jun. 1955//. Bogotá (5996

INDICE económico colombiano, v.1, no.1 - ,
oct. 1962- . Medellín, Biblioteca, Facultad de Ciencias Económicas, Universidad de
Antioquia.   (5997

INDICE médico colombiano, no.1- , jul./sept.
1961- . Medellín, Escuela Interamericana
de Bibliotecología, Universidad de Antioquia.   (5998

INFORMACION mensual, en. 1963- . Bogotá, Biblioteca, Escuela Superior de Administración Pública.   (5999

EL INFORMADOR literario, 1936- . Bogotá, Librería Colombiana.   (6000
Jones 1721.

LIBROS, oct. 1939-feb. 1940(?)//. Cartagena,
Biblioteca Fernández de Madrid.   (6001

LIBROS colombianos, no.1- , mar. 1961- . Bogotá, Cámara Colombiana del Libro.   (6002

Lista de adquisiciones. Medellín, Escuela Interamericana de Bibliotecología, see Boletín de adquisiciones.

LISTA de nuevas adquisiciones, no.1- , jul.
1959- . Bogotá, Biblioteca, Centro de Estudios sobre Desarrollo Económico, Universidad de los Andes.   (6002a

LISTA de nuevas adquisiciones, jun. 1952- .
Bogotá, Servicio de Intercambio Científico,
Centro Interamericano de Vivienda.   (6003
Monthly issues published periodically in
cumulated form.

LISTA de publicaciones recibidas, abr./mayo
1961- . Cali, Biblioteca, Facultad de Ingeniería, Química e Ingeniería Electromecánica.   (6004
Cited in Florén, Bibliografía bibliotecológica, 1961/1962, item 401.

NOTICIAS bibliográficas, no.1- , jun. 1962- .
Bucuramanga, Biblioteca General, Universidad Industrial de Santander.   (6005
Cited in Florén, **Bibliografía bibliotecológica**, 1961/1962, item 402, with title varies note: no.1-3, Boletín de adquisiciones.

LA POLILLA, no.0- , nov. 1963- . Medellín,
Círculo Bibliotecológico, Escuela Interame-
ricana de Bibliotecología, Universidad de
Antioquia.   (6006

NUEVAS adquisiciones, no.1- , ag. 1962- .
Bogotá, Biblioteca, Universidad de los
Andes.   (6007
Cited in Florén, **Bibliografía biblioteco-
lógica**, 1961/1962, item 403.

PAPEL periódico ilustrado, año 1-5, 1881-
1888//. Bogotá.   (6008
Jones 1752a.

REPERTORIO colombiano, v.1-21, no.1, jul.
1878-oct. 1899//. Bogotá.   (6009
Jones 1763a.

REVISTA bibliográfica, 1o. ag. 1878-1879//.
Bogotá, Librería "Torres Caicedo". (6010
Giraldo Jaramillo, p. 76, notes that
39 numbers were published and that no.
25-39 were issued by L. M. Pérez e Hijos.

REVISTA de la Biblioteca Nacional, año 1-3,
no.1-21/22, en. 1923-feb./mar. 1930//.
Bogotá.   (6011
Jones 1690a.

REVISTA de la instrucción pública de Colombia, 1-29, no.2, en. 1893-feb. 1918//.
Bogotá, Ministerio de Instrucción Pública.   (6012
Superseded Anales de la instrucción pública en Colombia, 1880-1892. "Lista de
libros y folletos recibidos en la Biblioteca Nacional": v.2, no. 8-10. ag.-oct.
1893. - "Catálogo de las obras americanas
existentes en la Biblioteca Nacional":
v.3-5, no. 16-22, 24, abr.-oct., dic.
1894; no. 25-27/28, feb.-abr. 1896. - "Catálogo de las obras hispano-americanas
existentes en la Biblioteca Nacional adicional al publicado en 1897": v.10, no.
59-60, 62-64, jun.-jul., sept.-nov. 1899.
---Jones 1703.

[REVISTA del] Colegio de Bibliotecarios Colombianos, v.1, no.1- , dic. 1963- . Medellín.   (6013

REVISTA del Museo del Atlántico, núm preli-
minar- , oct. 1941- . Barranqui-
lla.   (6014
Issue no.1 is dated jun. 1942. Includes
"Sección bibliográfica".

ULTIMAS adquisiciones de la Biblioteca. Medellín, Biblioteca, Facultad de Agronomía,
Universidad Nacional.   (6015

COSTA RICA

BOLETIN de la Biblioteca Nacional, año 1, no.1-
año 6, no. 60, ag. 1898-1924/1927//. San
José.   (6016
Jones 1276. Publication suspended ag.
1900-sept. 1920.

LISTA de nuevas adquisiciones, en./feb. 1958- .
San José, Escuela Superior de Administración
Pública.   (6017

LISTA de publicaciones puestas al servicio de
la Biblioteca [no.1] sept. 1951- . San José,
Dirección General de Estadística y Censos,
Ministerio de Economía y Hacienda.   (6018
Formerly: Lista de publicaciones recibidas,
no. 1-37, sept. 1951- 1o. sem. 1959.

NOTICIAS de la Biblioteca, no.1- , 1959- .
San José, Biblioteca, Universidad.   (6019

NUEVAS adquisiciones. San José, Biblioteca,
Universidad.   (6020

REPERTORIO centroamericano, no.1- , dic. 1964- .
San José, Secretaría Permanente del Consejo
Superior Universitario Centroamericano(6021

REVISTA de Costa Rica en el siglo XIX, t.1,
1902//. San José, Comisión Conmemorativa
de Costa Rica en el Siglo XIX.   (6022
Editors: Francisco M. Iglesias and Juan
F. Ferraz.---Jones 1274.

SERVICIO de materiales de extensión, 1956(?)- .
Turrialba, Instituto Interamericano de Ciencias Agrícolas.   (6023

TURRIALBA; suplemento bibliográfico, v.1, no.
1- , jul. 1950- . Turrialba, Instituto Interamericano de Ciencias Agrícolas.   (6024
Issued in Turrialba, 1950-1953; separately
with v.4-10, en./mar. 1954-1960.

CUBA

ARCHIVOS del folklore cubano, v.1- , 1924- .
La Habana, Impr. "El Siglo XX".   (6025
Published by the Sociedad del Folklore Cubano, Edited by Fernando Ortiz.---Jones
1784.

BIBLIOTECAS, año 1, no.1- , en./feb. 1963- .
La Habana, Dirección General de Bibliotecas.
Consejo Nacional de Cultura.   (6026

BOLETIN de la Biblioteca, Facultad de Tecnología, Universidad de La Habana. La Haba-

BOLETIN de la Biblioteca ... (Cont.)
na.   (6027
   DPU issues begin with año 2, no.2, abr./
jun. 1964.

BOLETIN del Anuario Bibliográfico Cubano, año
1, no.1- , feb./abr. 1938- . La Habana.   (6028
   Imprint varies: 1961- , Medellín, Colombia.

BOLETIN del Comité de Archivos, año 1, no.1- ,
en. 1958- . La Habana, Comisión de Historia,
Instituto Panamericano de Geografía e Historia.   (6029

CERVANTES: revista bibliográfica mensual ilus-
trada, año 1-21, 1925-1946//. La Habana,
Cultural, S.A.; Librería La Moderna Poesía;
Librería Cervantes.   (6030
   Suspended publication: jul.-dic. 1931;
sept.-dic. 1932.

LIBROS cubanos, año 1, no.1-año 2, no.3/4,
mayo/jun. 1940-jul./dic. 1942//. Habana.   (6032
   Jones 1863a.

MAS LUZ; boletín bibliográfico literario, año
1, no.1- año 3, no.1, sept. 1936-mayo 1938//.
Santiago de las Vegas.   (6033

NOTICIAS bibliográficas, v.1, no.1-v.10, no.1,
jul. 1952-en. 1961//. Habana, División de
Bibliotecas, Unesco.   (6034
   Information incorporated in Bulletin on
bibliography documentation and terminology,
Paris, subsequent to v.10, no.1.

REVISTA bibliográfica, no.1-39/40, en./feb.
1954- jul./dic. 1960//? Habana, Libr.
Martí.   (6035

REVISTA bibliográfica cubana, t.1, no.1-t.3,
no. 17/18, en./feb. 1936-sept./dic. 1939//.
Habana.   (6036
   Edited by Lorenzo Rodríguez Fuentes.---
Jones 1902.

REVISTA de la Biblioteca Nacional, año 1-4,
t. 1-6, 1909-1912; 2a. ép., año 1-9, no.1,
abr. 1949-dic. 1958; [3a. ép.] año 1, no.
1/4- , 1959- . Habana.   (6037

REVISTA del Banco Nacional de Cuba, año 1, no.
1- , en. 1955- . La Habana.   (6038
   Includes section "Indice bibliográfico"
prepared in the Library of the Bank.

DOMINICAN REPUBLIC

BIBLION; boletín bibliográfico mensual, no.1,

BIBLION; boletín bibliográfico ... (Cont.)
oct. 1941-2a. ép., no.15/16, nov./dic.
1945//. Ciudad Trujiillo, Biblioteca, Universidad de Santo Domingo.   (6039

BOLETIN bibliográfico, 1a. ép., no.1, 20 feb.
1945//? Ciudad Trujillo, Cámara Oficial de
Comercio, Agricultura e Industria del Distrito de Santo Domingo.   (6040
   Only issue recorded at DPU.

BOLETIN bibliográfico dominicano, año 1, no.
1-2, jul./ag.-sept./dic. 1945//. Ciudad
Trujillo, Oficina de Canje y Difusión Cultural, Archivo General de la Nación.   (6041

BOLETIN de la Biblioteca, año 1, no.1- , mayo/
jun. 1954- . Ciudad Trujillo, Universidad
de Santo Domingo.   (6042

INFORMACION bibliográfica, v.1, no.1- , jul.
1963- . Santo Domingo, Biblioteca, Universidad Autónoma de Santo Domingo.   (6043

ECUADOR

BOLETIN bibliográfico, no.1- , dic. 25, 1945- .
Cuenca, Biblioteca "Juan Bautista Vázquez",
Universidad de Cuenca.   (6044

BOLETIN de bibliografía americana, no.1- ,
en. 1940- . Quito.   (6045
   Directors: Alfredo Martínez and Jorge Pérez Concha.---Jones 65a.

BOLETIN de la Biblioteca Municipal, t.1- ,
1910- . Guayaquil.   (6046
   Jones 1987.

BOLETIN de la Biblioteca Nacional, v.1, no.1,
ag. 1918-v.2, no.9, oct. 1919; n.s., no.1,
oct. 1920-[unnumbered] mayo 24, 1922; n.s.,
no.1-12, dic. 1925-sept./oct. 1927//. Quito.   (6047
   Jones 1973. See also Mensaje de la Biblioteca Nacional.

LETRAS y números; revista literaria, bibliografía, y de cultura social, año 1, no.1-
año 9, no. 85, ag. 1921-en. 1932//. Guayaquil, Libr. e Impr. Gutenberg.   (6048

LIBROS y bibliotecas, año 1, no.1-7, mar.
1939-en. 1947//. Guayaquil, Biblioteca de
Autores Nacionales "Carlos A. Rolando".   (6049

MENSAJE de la Biblioteca Nacional, no. 1-10/
11, feb. 1936-jul. 1940//. Quito.   (6050
   Title of no.1: Revista. The Mensaje has
in caption: 3a. ep.---Jones 1975.

PRESENCIA, año 1- , 1950- . Quito, Libr.
Americana. (6051
DPU registered año 1, no. 2- , dic.
1950- .

Revista de la Biblioteca Nacional, see Mensaje.

EL SALVADOR

ANAQUELES, 5a. ép., no.1- , en./abr. 1951- .
San Salvador, Biblioteca Nacional. (6052
Jones 1373a. Previous titles: Boletín,
no.1-5 [1920-1921]; Revista bibliográfica
científica-literaria, año 1, no.1, 30 jul.
1929-año 3, no. 24, jun. 1931; Boletín,
2a. ép., no.1, mayo 1932-no. 26/28, oct./dic.
1935; 3a. ép., no.1, mar. 1939-no.70/81,
abr./jun 1946; Revista, 4a. ép., v.1, en./
abr. 1948-v.5, mayo/ag. 1949. Latest recorded at DPU: no.6, sept. 1955/dic. 1959.

BIBLIOGRAFIA, no.1- , sept. 1950- . San Salvador, Instituto de Estudios Económicos,
Ministerio de Economía. (6053

BOLETIN bibliográfico, en./feb. 1959- . San-
ta Tecla, Biblioteca, Centro Nacional de
Agronomía. (6054
Cited in Peraza, 1964, item 77.

Boletín de la Biblioteca Nacional, San Salvador, see Anaqueles.

INDICE de artículos en publicaciones periódicos, no.1- , dic. 1950- . San Salvador,
Instituto de Estudios Económicos. (6055
No.6 issued by the Departamento de Estudios Económicos.

LISTA de publicaciones recibidas, jun. 1952(?)-
jun. 1956//. San Salvador, Punto Focal Nacional de Informaciones Estadísticas, Dirección General de Estadística y Censos(6056

NOMINA de adquisiciones durante el mes, en.
1962- . San Salvador, Biblioteca Universitaria "Mauricio Esquivel Salguero", Universidad de El Salvador. (6057
Cited in Peraza, Bibliografías corrientes,
1964, item 57.

PUBLICACIONES catalogadas. San Salvador, Dirección General de Estadística y Censos. (6058

Revista bibliográfica científica-literaria,
see Anaqueles.

Revista de la Biblioteca Nacional, San Salvador, see Anaqueles.

ENGLAND

BRITISH bulletin of publications on Latin America, the West Indies, Portugal and Spain.,
1- , June 1949- . London, Library, Canning
House. (6059
Compiled by A. J. Walford on recommenda-
tion of the Pan American Institute of Geography and History.

INDEX to foreign legal periodicals, v.1- ,
1960- . London, Institute of Advanced Legal
Studies, University of London in co-opera-
tion with the American Association of
Law Libraries. (6060
The Index includes nearly 30 legal journals published in Latin America of about 250
journals included in the index.

GERMANY

IBERICA; zeitschrift für spanische und portu-
giesische auslandskunde, v.1-7, no.3/4, abr.
1924-jul./sept. 1927//. Hamburg. (6061
Jones 210.

IBERO-AMERICANISCHES archiv, Jahrg. 1-18, no.
1/2, Okt. 1924-1944//. Berlin, Ibero-Ameri-
kanisches Institut. (6062
Title varies: v.1-3, Zeitschrift des
Ibero-Americanischen Forschungs-Instituts,
Universität Bonn.

GUATEMALA

Artículos seleccionados de publicaciones periódicas, Biblioteca, Banco de Guatemala,
see Boletín de Biblioteca.

BOLETIN bibliográfico, 1- , 1955- . Guatemala, Biblioteca, Instituto de Fomento de la
Producción. (6063
DPU collection begins: 2a. ép., no.1- ,
en. 1956.

Boletín bibliográfico mensual, Biblioteca, Banco de Guatemala, see Boletín de Biblioteca.

Boletín bibliográfico semestral, Biblioteca,
Banco de Guatemala, see Boletín de Biblioteca.

BOLETIN de Biblioteca [1]- , en./jun. 1953- .
Guatemala, Biblioteca, Banco de Guatemala. (6064
Title varies: Boletín bibliográfico semestral, en./jun. 1953; Boletín bibliográfico
mensual, jun./ag. 1953. Also Artículos seleccionados de publicaciones periódicas nacionales y extranjeras; Libros y folletos
ingresados. DPU records, in 1956, that
publication was suspended.

Boletín de la Biblioteca Nacional, see Revista de la Biblioteca Nacional, Guatemala.

BOLETIN de la Tipografía Nacional, año 1, no.
1- , mar. 1951- . Guatemala.   (6065

Boletín de museos y bibliotecas, see Revista de la Biblioteca Nacional.

INDICE; editorial del pueblo, año 1, no.1-año
2, no. 5, ag. 1946-en./feb. 1947//. Guatemala, Dirección de Educación Extraescolar,
Ministerio de Educación Pública.   (6066

Libros y folletos ingresados, Biblioteca,
Banco de Guatemala, see Boletín de Biblioteca.

REVISTA de la Biblioteca Nacional, año 1, no.
1- , mayo 1932- . Guatemala.   (6067
  Title varies: Boletín, año 1, no.1-año
9, no.4, mayo 1932-en. 1941; Boletín de
museos y bibliotecas, 2a. ép., [año 1]-año
4, no.4, abr. 1941-en. 1945; Boletín, 3a.
ép., año 1, no.1-4, abr.-dic. 1945; Boletín, 4a. ép., año 1, no.1-2, dic. 1948-dic.
1945; Boletín, 4a. ép., año 1, no.1-2, dic.
1948-dic. 1951; Revista, 4a. [i.e., 5a.]
ép., año 1, no.1- , ag. 1962- .

HAITI

BULLETIN du Bureau d'Ethnologie, no.1- , fev.
1942- . Port-au-Prince.   (6068

HONDURAS

BIBLIOTECAS; órgano del Departamento de Bibliotecas y Central de Información Bibliográfica de la Universidad Nacional de Honduras, no.1- , en./mar. 1962- . Tegucigalpa.   (6069

MEXICO

ANUARIO de biblioteconomía y archivonomía,
año 1- , 1961- . México,D.F., Facultad de
Filosofía y Letras, Universidad Nacional
Autónoma de México.   (6070

AVISO de libros, lecturas y reuniones en la
Editorial Séneca, año 1, no.1- , en.
1941- . México, D.F.   (6071

B. B. A. A. ; boletín bibliográfico de antropología americana, v.1, no.1/2- , en./
jun. 1937- . México, D. F., Instituto Panamericano de Geografía e Historia. (6072
  Jones 65. v.1-11, 1937-1948: Boletín
bibliográfico de antropología americana.

B. B. G. O. A. ; Boletín bibliográfico de geofísica y oceanografía americanas; Boletim
bibliografico de geofísica e oceanografia
americanas; Bibliographical bulletin of American geophysics and oceanography; Bulletin
bibliographique de geophysique et oceanogra-
phie americaines, v.1- , 1958- . México, D.
F., Instituto Panamericano de Geografía e
Historia.   (6073
  Published in 2 pts.: Geofísica, v.1- ,
1958- . and Oceanográfica, v.1- , jul. 1958/
jun. 1959- .

LA BIBLIOGRAFIA, 1a. ép., 1 dic. 1904- . México, D.F., Libr. Porrua Hnos.   (6074
  Millares, 1624, notes that the 2a. ép. covers sept. 1908-abr. 1929; 3a. ép., feb.
1931-dic. 1940; 4a. ép., en. 1942- . González notes that in 1942 it merged with Boletín bibliográfico mexicano.

BIBLIOGRAFIA económica de México, v.1- , mar.
1955- . México, D.F., Biblioteca, Banco de
México.   (6075

BIBLIOGRAFIA mexicana, no.[1]-4, sept.-dic.
1930//. Tacubaya, D.F.   (6076
  Director: Rafael Heliodoro Valle.---Jones
2078.

BIBLIOGRAFIA mexicana; órgano de la Asociación
de Libros de México, t.1, no.1/2, jul. 1938-
t.3, no.1, abr. 1940//. México, D.F.   (6077
  Editor: Francisco J. Gamoneda.

BIBLION. México, D.F., Espasa Calpe. No. 90/
92 issued sept./nov. 1935.   (6078

Biblios, see Biblos.

BIBLOS, v.1-4, no. 1-198, en. 18, 1919-nov. 4,
1922; 2a. ép., no.1-9/15, mayo 1925-en./jul.
1926//. México, D.F., Biblioteca Nacional.   (6079
  Title varies: Biblios, no.1-39.

BIBLOS; revista mensual, no.1-3, oct. 1912-ag.
1913//. México, D.F., Libr. General.   (6080
  Cited in Millares 1627.

BOLETIN bibliográfico, v.1, no.1- , en. 1955- .
México, D.F., Biblioteca, Depto. de Estudios
Económicos, Banco de México.   (6081

BOLETIN bibliográfico, no.1- , ag. 1937- . México, D.F., Comisión Nacional de Irriga-
ción.   (6082
  Cited in Pan American Institute of Geography and History, publ. 79, pt.1, p. 66.

BOLETIN bibliográfico, no.1- , feb. 1935- //?
México, D.F., Departamento de Biblioteca y
Archivos Económicos, Dirección General de Es-
tudios Hacendarios.   (6083
  DPU records: "Ceased publication".

BOLETIN bibliográfico, t.1, no.1- , sept./
oct. 1953- . México, D.F., Escuela Nacional de Bibliotecarios y Archivistas. (6084
Title varies: Boletín, t.1, no.1-t.2, no.
3/4, sept./oct. 1953-en./abr. 1954. Suspended publication: ag. 1954-en. 1957.

BOLETIN bibliográfico, t.1- , 1954- . México,
D.F., Libr. Universitaria, Universidad Nacional Autónoma.   (6085

BOLETIN bibliográfico, no.1- , nov. 10, 1954- .
México, D.F., Departamento de Bibliotecas,
Secretaría de Hacienda y Crédito Público.   (6086
ULS gives beginning date as nov. 10, 1954
and frequency: daily, no. 1-26, nov. 20-dic.
1954; semi-monthly, no. 27- , en.15, 1955- ,
Ker, p.233, and the PAIGH catalog (publ. 79)
p. 66, cite an earlier series. Ker records
no.1-8, nov. 1934-nov./dic. 1936, and the
PAIGH catalog, no.9-10, en./feb.-mar./abr.
1942.

BOLETIN bibliográfico, año 1, no.1- , oct./
dic. 1940-jul./dic. 1945//. México, D.F.,
Centro de Estudios Filosóficos, Facultad de
Filosofía y Letras, Universidad Nacional
Autónoma.   (6087

Boletín bibliográfico de antropología americana, see B. B. A. A.

BOLETIN bibliográfico de legislación fiscal.
México, D.F.   (6087a
Kerr, p. 233, cites earliest issue as jul.
1934. DPU registered jul. 1934-ag. 1939.
Jones, 2362a, also gives 1934 as beginning
year.

BOLETIN bibliográfico mexicano, año 1, no.1,
oct. 1939//. México, D.F., Instituto Panamericano de Bibliografía y Documentación.   (6088
Jones 2093. For continuation see next
entry.

BOLETIN bibliográfico mexicano, año 1, no.1- ,
en. 1940- . México, D.F., Libr. Porrúa
Hermanos.   (6089
Monthly publication edited by the Instituto Panamericano de Bibliografía y Documentación.

BOLETIN bibliográfico y escolar, 1-3, 1891-
1893//. Tacubaya, D.F.   (6090
Cited in Millares, 1629, as beginning in
1881, while the ULS gives 1891.

BOLETIN de bibliografía yucateco, no.1-18,
oct. 1938-jul./sept. 1943//. Mérida, Biblioteca Yucateca "Crescencio Carrillo y Ancona",
Museo Arqueológico e Histórico de Yucatán.   (6091
Jones 2094.

BOLETIN de la Asociación de Bibliotecarios Me-
xicanos, t.1, no.1-14, oct. 1924-oct. 1927//.
México, D.F.   (6092
Jones 2964.

BOLETIN de la Biblioteca Ibero-Americana de
Bellas Artes, no.1-7/9, 20 nov. 1938-jun./
ag. 1939//. México, D.F.   (6093
Jones 2079a.

BOLETIN de la Biblioteca Nacional, año 1, no.
1-v.13, no.1, jul. 1904-en./feb. 1929; 2a.
ép., t.1- , en./mar. 1950- . México,
D.F.   (6094
Jones 2344.

BOLETIN de petróleo, v.1-35, no. 4/6, 1916-
abr./jun. 1933//. México, D.F., Departamento de Petróleo.   (6095
Jones 2356. Superseded by Boletín de petróleo y minas, no.1- , 1933- , of the Dirección General de Minas y Petroleo, Secretaría de Economía Nacional.

BOLETIN del Centro de Documentación Científica
y Técnica, v.1-11, no.2, en. 1952-feb.
1962//. México, D.F.   (6096
With v.5, the Boletín was issued in numbered sections, each continuing the volume numbering:- 1, Matemáticas, astronomía y astrofísica, física, geología, geofísica. - 2,
Ingeniería. - 3, Química. - 4, Medicina. -
5, Biología, agricultura, zootecnia e industrias de la alimentación. Superseded by
Indice bibliográfico del Centro de Investigación y de Estudios Avanzados del Instituto Politécnico Nacional de México.

BOLETIN del derecho de autor, no.1- , jul.
1960- . México, D.F., Dirección General
del Derecho de Autor, Secretaría de Educación Pública.   (6097

BOLETIN del Instituto Bibliográfico Mexicano,
v.1-11, 1902-1918//. México, D.F.   (6098
Includes Nicolás León's Bibliografía mexicana del Siglo XVIII, etc.---Jones 2359.

BOLETIN del Instituto Nacional del Libro. México, D.F.   (6099
DPU has on record: no. 6, sept./oct. 1946.

BOLETIN jurídico bibliográfico, año 1, no.1-
año 4, no. 27, jun. 15, 1940-jul./dic. 1943//.
México, D.F., Escuela Libre de Derecho (6100
No issues published, ag. 1942-jun.1943.

BUENS prensa; boletín mensual bibliográfico,
1- , 1938- . México, D.F.   (6101

EL CONSULTOR bibliográfico, 2a. ép., año 1,
no.1- , oct./dic. 1943- . México, D.F (6102
Ceased publication?

356

PERIODICALS

CONTEMPORANEOS; revista mexicana de cultura,
año 1-11, no.1-43, jun. 1928-dic. 1931//.
México, D.F.   (6103
   Jones 2134.

CORREO del libro mexicano. México, D.F., Sociedad de Amigos del Libro Mexica-
no.   (6104
   DPU has on record: año 8, no.1, 4 de feb.
1961, and 2a. ép., no.1- , nov. 1961- .

CRONICA bibliográfica, año 1, no.1- , 1957- .
México, D.F., Biblioteca Central, Instituto Mexicano del Seguro Social.   (6105

ETHNOS, t.1, no.1-2, abr. 1920-nov. 1920/mar.
1921; 2a. ép., t.1, no.1-2, nov. 1922/en.
1923-feb./abr. 1923; 3a. ép., t.1, no.1-5;
en./feb.-mayo 1925//. México, D.F (6106
   Jones 2162a.

FICHAS bio-bibliográficas mexicanas, 2a. ép.,
no.1-4a. ép., no. 8/13, 1938-1941//. México. D.F.   (6107

FICHAS de bibliografía potosina, año 1, no.
1- , jul./ag. 1939- . San Luis Potosí,
Biblioteca, Universidad Autónoma de San
Luis Potosí.   (6108

LA GACETA, año 1, no.1- , 1954- . México,
D.F., Fondo de Cultura Económica. (6109

HORIZONTES; revista bibliográfica, año 1,
no.1- , en./feb. 1958- . México, D.F.,
Libr. Patria.   (6110

INDICE bibliográfico, v.1, no.1/3-v.3, no.
10/12, mar. 1962-oct./dic. 1964//. México D.F., Centro de Investigación y de Estudios Avanzados, Instituto Politécnico
Nacional.   (6112
   Supersedes the Boletín del Centro de Documentacion Científica y Técnica. The Indice bibliográfico was issued in sections:
- 1, Matemáticas, astronomía, y astrofísica,
física, geología, geofísica, geodesia. -
2, Ingeniería y arquitectura. - 3, Química.
- 4, Medicina. - 5, Biología, agricultura,
zootecnia, industrias de la alimentación.

INMEX, año 1, no.1- , mar. 1939- . México,
D.F., Instituto Mexicano de Difusión del
Libro.   (6113

INTER-FOLIA; órgano mensual, oct. 1953- .
Monterrey, Biblioteca Universitaria "Alfonso Reyes".   (6114

INVESTIGACIONES historicas, v.1, no.1-4, oct.
1938-jun. 1939//. México, D.F.   (6115
   Edited by José C. Valadés. Includes, in
installments, Genaro García's Nuevas notas
de bibliografía mexicana.---Jones 2261a.

INVESTIGACIONES lingüisticas, v.1-5, no.2, ag.
1933-mar. 1938//. México, D.F., Instituto
de Investigaciones Lingüisticas.   (6116
   Jones 2262. Supplement to Cuadernos lingüis-
ticos.

LECTURA; revista crítica de ideas y libros, t.1,
no.1- , 1937- . México, D.F.   (6117

LETRAS; bibliografía mexicana, v.1-2, no.1,
1929-ag. 1936//. México, D.F.   (6118

LETRAS; bibliografía mexicana, año 1, no.1- ,
jun. 1936- . México, D.F.   (6119

LETRAS de México; gaceta literaria y artistica,
1- , 1937- . México, D.F.   (6120
   Jones 2305a.

EL LIBRO y el pueblo, v.1, no.1- , mar. 1922- .
México, D.F., Departamento de Bibliotecas,
Secretaría de Educación Pública.   (6121
   Jones 2306. Suspended publication: dic.
1935-mar. 1941; nov. 1941-nov. 1950.

LIBROS, 1930- . México, D.F., Libr. "Cultura".   (6122
   Jones 2307.

LIBROS buenos, 1- , abr.? 1942- . México, D.F.,
Libr. Edit. "San Ignacio".   (6123

LIBROS mexicanos, 1, no.1- , jun. 1957- . México, D.F., Centro Mexicano de Escritores.   (6124

LIBROS selectos; boletín bibliográfico, no.1- ,
1959- . México, D.F.   (6125

LIBROS universitarios; boletín bibliográfico,
v.1- , 1963- . México, D.F., Libr. Universitaria.   (6126
   DPU has on file: v.1, no.2, jul. 22, 1963.

LISTA de adquisiciones, ag. 1956- . México,
D.F., Biblioteca José Toribio Medina, Instituto Panamericano de Geografía e Historia.   (6127

MEMORIAS y revista de la Academia Nacional de
Ciencias Antonio Alzate, t.1- , jul. 1887- .
México, D.F.   (6128
   The Academia was known as the Sociedad
Científica "Antonio Alzate", 1884-1929.
Includes Ensayo bibliográfico mexicano del
siglo XVII, por Vicente de P. Andrade, 1894
(Incomplete: p. 1-96 issued with t.8-12.
Completes work published in 1899 by the Museo Nacional); and Bibliografia meteorológica mexicana que comprende las publicaciones de meteorología, física del globo y climatología hechas hasta fines de 1889, compiled by Rafael Aguilar Santillán, published
in v.4 (reprinted in separate form, continued
for the years 1890-1895 in v.4-9). "Indice

MEMORIAS y revistas de la... (Cont.)
    general de los t. 1-27", in v.27, p. 277-
    380, 1908/1909.---Jones 2028-29. Includes
    section: Revista científica y bibliográfica;
    in later volumes: Revista bibliográfica.

MIRADOR; revista de información bibliográfica,
    año 1, no.1-año 5, no.19, en./mar. 1955-mayo
    1959//. México, D.F.   (6129

EL MUNDO de los libros; boletín bibliográfico,
    no.1- , oct./ dic. 1957- . México, D.F.,
    Organización Edit. Novaro.   (6130

EL NOTICIERO bibliográfico, t.1, no.1-t.4, no.
    27, ag. 1939-1945//. México, D.F., Fondo
    de Cultura Económica.   (6131

RTAC record, Jan. 1964- . México, D.F., Re-
    gional Technical Aids Center.   (6132

RECENT books in Mexico, v.1, no.1- , Nov. 15,
    1954- . México, D.F., Centro Mexicano de
    Escritores.   (6133

REVISTA de historia de América, v.1, no.1- ,
    mar. 1938- . México, D.F., Instituto Pana-
    mericano de Geografía e Historia.   (6134
        Jones 395b, 2455. Editor: Silvio Zavala.

REVISTA iberoamericana, v.1, no.1- , mayo
    1939- . México, D.F., Instituto Internacio-
    nal de Literatura Iberoamericana.   (6135
        Jones 397.

REVISTA mexicana de economía, v.1, no.1-4,
    sept. 1928-jun. 1929//? México, D.F. Ins-
    tituto Mexicano de Investigaciones Econó-
    micas.   (6136
        Jones 2455a.

REVISTA universitaria, t.1, no.1- , feb./abr.
    1943- . Guadalajara, Asociación de Post-
    Graduados y Ex-Alumnos de la Universidad de
    Guadalajara.   (6137

SELECTED list of books received. México, Bi-
    blioteca Benjamín Franklin.   (6138
        In 1959 the List had reached no. '167.

SERVICIO de información bibliográfica, no.1- ,
    en. 1959- . México, D.F., Fondo de Cultura
    Económica.   (6139

STUDIUM; gacetilla bibliográfica cultural me-
    xicana, 1- , en./feb. 1950- . México, D.F.,
    Centro Mexicano de Libros [Libr. Stu-
    dium].   (6140

SUMA bibliográfica, año 1-4, no.1-20, abr.
    1946-jul./sept. 1949//. México, D.F. (6141

NICARAGUA

BOLETIN de la Biblioteca Central, 1- , jun./jul.
    1963- . León, Universidad Nacional de Nicara-
    gua.   (6142

PANAMA

HERALDO; boletín de información literaria y bi-
    bliográfica, año 1, no.1- , nov. 1959- . Pa-
    namá, Libr. Cultural Panameña.   (6143
        HLAS, 22, item 6281.

PERU

BOLETIN bibliográfico, publicación mensual, no.
    1-88, 1 en. 1888-15 jul. 1901//. Lima (6144
        René-Moreno in Ensayo de una bibliografía
    general de los periódicos de Bolivia, items
    1350-52, cites no. 81-88, and states that
    the Boletín bibliográfico is the organ of
    the Imprenta y Librería de Carlos Prince.
    Jones, 2637, cites the collection, 1888-1901.

BOLETIN bibliográfico, no.1- , 1955- . Lima,
    Biblioteca, Banco Central de Reserva. (6145

BOLETIN bibliográfico, año 1, no.1- , [1940?]- .
    Huancayo, Biblioteca Municipal A. Deus-
    tua.   (6146
        HLAS 7, item 5359 reports año 2, no.2,
    jun./jul. 1941.

BOLETIN bibliografico, año 1, no.1- , nov.
    1943- . Lima, Biblioteca, Cámara de Dipu-
    tados.   (6147
        Title varies: Boletín de la Biblioteca,
    jul. 1947- .

BOLETIN bibliográfico, no.1- , mayo 1956- .
    Lima, Biblioteca Central, Ministerio de Tra-
    bajo y Asuntos Indígenas.   (6148

BOLETIN bibliográfico, año 1, no.1- , jul.
    1923- . Lima, Biblioteca, Universidad Ma-
    yor de San Marcos.   (6149
        Jones 2638.

BOLETIN bibliográfico, v.1- , 1945- . Lima,
    Biblioteca, Facultad de Medicina, Universidad
    Mayor de San Marcos.   (6150
        Annual: 1945-1946.

BOLETIN bibliográfico EASO, año 1, no.1- , ma-
    yo 1955- . Lima, Libr. EASO.   (6151
        Cited in Anuario bibliográfico peruano,
    1955/1957, item 2913.

BOLETIN de información bibliográfica, año 1,
    no.1- , 1953(?)- . Lima, Dirección de Edu-
    cación Rural, Ministerio de Educación Pú-
    blica.   (6152

BOLETIN de la Biblioteca del Colegio de Abogados, año 1, no.1- , 1951- . Lima. (6153

BOLETIN de la Biblioteca Municipal, año 1,
no.1- , 1954?- . Lima.   (6154

BOLETIN de la Biblioteca Nacional, t.1, no.
1-t.2, en. 1919-mar. 1920; año 1, no.1- ,
oct. 1943- . Lima.   (6155
Jones 2677.

BOLETIN del Proyecto Bibliográfico, no.1- ,
en./jun. 1958- . Lima, Comité del Plan Regional para el Desarrollo del Sur, Ministerio de Agricultura y Servicio Cooperativo
Interamericano del Plan del Sur.   (6156

BOLETIN "Studium", no.1- , en. 1956- . Lima,
Libr. "Studium".   (6157

CUADERNOS de información bibliografica, año 1,
no.1- , abr. 1957- . Lima, Seminario de Historia, Instituto Riva-Agüero, Universidad
Catolica del Perú.   (6158

FENIX, no.1- , 1er. sem. 1944- . Lima, Biblioteca Nacional.   (6159

GACETA bibliotecaria del Perú, no.1- , en.
1963- . Lima, Biblioteca Nacional.   (6160

GARCILASO; boletín bibliográfico, libros y
ediciones, año 1, no.1- , abr. 1957- . Lima.   (6161

MARIS Aestus, año 1, no.1- , jul. 1962- . Lima, Biblioteca, Ministerio de Relaciones Exteriores.   (6162

REVISTA de archivos y bibliotecas nacionales,
v.1-5, 1898-1900//. Lima.   (6163
"Noticia bibliográfica" por C. A. Romero,
v.1, p. vii-xvii.---Jones 2732.

REVISTA peruana, v.1-5, no.1, en. 1879-jun.
1889//. Lima.   (6164
Founded by Mariano Felipe Paz Soldán.
Editor: Carlos Paz Soldán. Contains bibliographical information. Among the contributions of value for biographical data may be
noted:-Los obispos de Cuzco. - Los obispos
de Trujillo. - Apuntes historicos sobre las
encomiendas del Perú by E. Torres Saldamando. - Las fuentes de la historia eclesiástica, by M. González de la Rosa.---Jones
2733.

REVISTA universitaria, v.1-24, no.2/3, mayo
1906-abr./ag. 1930; 2a. ép., v.1-4, no.9,
jul./sept. 1935-oct./dic. 1938//. Lima,
Universidad Mayor de San Marcos.   (6165
"Catálogo de las obras de la Biblioteca",
v.1, p.639-86, 776-838.---Jones 2734.

PORTUGAL

BOLETIM internacional de bibliografia luso-bra-
sileira, v.1, no.1- , jan/mar. 1960- . Lisboa, Fundação Caluste Gulbenkian.   (6166

PUERTO RICO

SELECTIVE list of recent additions to the Library, v.1, no.1-v.3, no.3/4. 1962-oct./nov.
1964//. Hato Rey, Library, Caribbean Organization.   (6167

SPAIN

ARCHIVO bibliografico hispano-americano, t.1,
no.1- , en. 1909- . Madrid.   (6168

BIBLIOGRAFIA general española e hispanoamericano, v.1-14, no.7, en. 1923-sept. 1936//.
Madrid.   (6169

BOLETIN de bibliotecas y bibliografía, v.1-2,
no.3, jul./sept. 1934-jul./sept. 1935//.
Madrid, Asociación de Bibliotecarios y Bibliógrafos de España.   (6170
Jones 66a.

LA CIUDAD de Dios; revista quincenal religiosa, científica y literaria, v.1-13, en. 1881-
jun. 1887; 2a. ep., v.14-20, jul. 1887-dic.
1889; 3a. ép., v. 21- , en. 1890- . Valladolid, Colegio de Agustinos Filipinos, 1882-
1889; Madrid, Real Monasterio de San Lorenzo
del Escorial, 1890- .   (6171
Includes "Catálogo de escritores agustinos
españoles, portugueses y americanos", por
el p. Bonifacio Moral, issued serially to
v.28.---Jones 102.

EL CONSULTOR bibliográfico, año 1-5, 1925-dic.
1927//? Barcelona.   (6172
Jones 107.

INDICE historico español, v.1, no.1- , en./
mar. 1953- . Barcelona, Centro de Estudios
Históricos Internacionales, Universidad de
Barcelona.   (6173

REVISTA de filología española, 1- , en./mar.
1914- . Madrid, Instituto Antonio de Ne-
brija, Consejo Superior de Investigaciones
Científicas.   (6174
Edited by Ramon Menéndez Pidal. Contains
critical articles and reviews, and a classified bibliography of books and articles
dealing with Spain and Latin America in all
languages.---Jones 395.

REVISTA de libros; boletín mensual de bibliografia española e hispanoamericana, no.1-13,
jun. 1913-mar. 1920//. Madrid.   (6175
Jones 396. Suspended ag.1914-oct.1919.

SWEDEN

LISTA over viktigara nyfoervaerv till Biblioteket,1- , 1955- . Stockholm, Ibero-Ameri-
kanska Biblioteket, Institutet vid Handel-
shögskolan.   (6176

UNITED STATES

ABSTRACTS of New World archaeology, v.1- ,
1959- . Washington, D.C., Society for American Archaeology, 1960- .   (6177
Annual. v.1: 128 p.

ACQUISITIONS/Adquisiciones, no. 64-1- ,
[1964]- . Washington, D.C., Inter-American
Defense College.   (6178

BOLETIN bibliográfico de Ibero-American Books,
v.1, no.1-v.2, no.1, primavera 1960-en./jun.
1961//. New York.   (6179

BOOKS abroad, 1- , 1927- . Norman, Okla.,
University of Oklahoma.   (6180

DOCUMENTS que se pueden consultar, lista no.1-
18; oct. 1959-nov./dic. 1963//. Washington,
D.C., Servicio de Documentación e Información, División de Educación, Unión Panamericana.   (6181

DOORS to Latin America, v.1, no.1- , Jan.
1954- . Gainsville, Fla., Inter-American
Bibliographical and Library Association,
University of Florida Libraries.   (6182

FICHERO bibliográfico hispanoamericano, v.1,
no.0- , oct. 1961- . New York, R. R. Bowker.
Quarterly.   (6182a
Became a monthly with v.4, no.1, oct.
1964, when the Company began issuance from
its Buenos Aires office.

INDEX to Latin American periodicals, v.1, no.
1- , 1st. quarter 1961- . Boston, G. K.
Hall (v.1-2); Metuchen, New Jersey, Scarecrow Pr. (v.3-)   (6183
Editor Jorge Grossmann. Prepared in the
Columbus Memorial Library of the Pan American Union. Includes indexing from some
320 periodicals in the fields of the humanities and the social sciences. The 4th
issue of v.1-2 is a cumulation in a single
alphabet of the indexing for the year,
totalling approximately 8,000 articles.
Beginning with v.3, only the author index is
cumulated into a single alphabet in the
fourth issue of each year. See also 4180.

INDICE bibliográfico. New York, The Latin
American Index, P.O. Box 171, Washington
Bridge Station.   (6183a
On file at DPU: Serie II, Invierno 1959.

Indice general de publicaciones periodicas
latinoamericanas, see Index to Latin
American periodicals.

INFORMATIVO trimestral; lista de los principa-
les documentos ingresados en el Servicio,
no.1- , en./mar. 1964- . Washington, D.C.,
Servicio de Documentación e Información,
Departamento de Asuntos Educacionales, Unión
Panamericana.   (6184

INTER-AMERICAN bibliographical review, v.1,
no.1-v.3, no.4, Spring 1941-1943//. Washington, D.C., Inter-American Bibliographical
and Library Association.   (6185

INTER-AMERICAN review of bibliography, v.1,
no.1- , Jan./Mar. 1951- . Washington, D.C.,
Division of Philosophy and Letters, Pan
American Union.   (6186
Issued with bilingual title: Revista interamericana de bibliografía. English title
varies: 1951, Review of Inter-American Bibliography. First issue prepared by Columbus Memorial Library. Supersedes: LEA.

INTER-AMERICAN library relations, no.1- , Apr/
June 1955- . Washington, D.C., Columbus Memorial Library.   (6187
Issued also in Spanish: Noticiero bibliotecario interamericano.

LATIN America in periodical literature, v.1,
no.1-v.2, no. 6, Jan. 1962-June 1963//.
Los Angeles, University of California, Center of Latin American Studies.   (6188

LEA; librarians, editors, authors. Libros,
editores, autores, no.1-12, Mar. 1949-Feb.
1950//. Washington, D.C., Columbus Memorial
Library, Pan American Union.   (6189

EL LIBRO americano, t.1, no.2-t.7, no.6; abr.
1938-jun. 1944. Washington, D.C., Biblioteca Colón, Unión Panamericana.   (6190
Vol.1, no.1 not published. Merged with
the English edition, The Pan American book-
shelf, Jul. 1944.

LIST of books accessioned and periodical ar-
ticles indexed, Aug. 1950- . Washington,
D.C., Columbus Memorial Library, Pan Amer-
ican Union.   (6191
Title varies: Accessions for the month,
Aug. 1950-Jan. 1951.

LIST of recent additions, no.1- , Mar. 24,
1947- . Washington, D.C., Joint Library,
International Monetary and International
Bank for Reconstruction and Development.   (6192

LIST of recent periodical articles, no.1- ,
Mar. 31, 1947- . Washington, D.C., Joint
Library, International Monetary Fund and In-

LIST of recent additions ... (Cont.)
ternational Bank for Reconstruction and
Development.   (6193

Lista mensual de publicaciones recibidas,   see
Monthly accession list of publications,
Inter-American Statistical Institute.

Lista trimestral de publicaciones en circulación,   see Quarterly list of publications
released, Office of Publications, Pan American Union.

MONTHLY accession list of publications: Lista
mensual de publicaciones recibidas, [1]- ,
Mar. 1944- . Washington, D.C., Inter-American Statistical Institute.   (6194

QUARTERLY list of publications released; Lista trimestral de publicaciones en circulación, v.1, no.1-v.2, no. 1/2, 1962//. Washington, D.C., Office of Publications, Pan
American Union.   (6195

NEW LATIN American books, list 1- , Sept.
1962- . New York, Stechert-Hafner. (6196
An advance checklist of newly published
titles acquired under the Latin American
Cooperative Project(LACAP). Not issued in
numbered series: Books from the Caribbean,
June 1963, and Latin American subscriptions,
Oct. 1963.

NOTICIERO bibliotecario interamericano, no.
31- , en./mar. 1963- . Washington, D.C.,
Columbus Memorial Library, Pan American
Union.   (6197
Issued also in English with title: Inter-
American library relations. Issues prior to
no. 31, were included in the List of books
accessioned and periodical articles indexed,
May 1955-Apr. 1963.

PAN AMERICAN book shelf, v.1, no.1-v.11, no. 12,
Mar. 1938-Dec. 1948//. Washington, D.C.,
Columbus Memorial Library, Pan American
Union.   (6198
Jones 349. Absorbed the Spanish edition,
El Libro americano, Jul. 1944. Superseded
by LEA, Mar. 1949.

PERIODICALS; articles indexed. Publicaciones
periódicas; índice de artículos, P-64-1- ,
[1964]- . Washington, D.C., Inter-American
Defense College.   (6199

RECENT acquisitions; Latin America, list 1- ,
1960- . New York, Stechert-Hafner. (6200

Review of Inter-American bibliography,   see
Inter-American review of bibliography.

REVISTA de estudios hispánicos, v.1-2, 1928//.
New York, Instituto de las Españas en los
Estados Unidos; Departamento de Estudios

REVISTA de estudios hispánicos ... (Cont.)
Hispánicos, Universidad de Puerto Rico (6201
Edited by Federico de Onís. Includes sec-
tion "Bibliografía hispano-americana".---
Jones 394.

REVISTA hispánica moderna, v.1- , oct. 1934- .
New York, Instituto de las Españas en los
Estados Unidos; Buenos Aires, Instituto de
Filosofía y Letras, Universidad de Buenos
Aires.   (6202
Editor: Federico de Onis.---Jones 396a.

Revista interamericana de bibliografía,   see
Inter-American review of bibliography.

STECHERT-HAFNER book news, v.1, no.1- , Nov.
1946- . New York, Stechert-Hafner.   (6203

URUGUAY

ARTICULOS de diarios y periódicos, en. 1948-
mar. 1959//. Montevideo, Biblioteca, Poder
Legislativo.   (6204
Musso, 636, notes that this title ceased
publication.

BVC; boletín de la Biblioteca Popular Villa
Colón, no.1- , 1941- . Montevideo.   (6205
Also issued with title: Boletín de informaciones del Centro Social y Biblioteca Popular "Villa Colón",

BIBLIOGRAFIA; órgano de la Sección Bibliografía de la Colección Abadie-Santos, no.1- ,
1932- . Montevideo.   (6206
Published as Boletín bibliográfico de jurisprudencia (Colección Abadie Santos) no.1-
85.

BIBLIOGRAFIA uruguaya, en./abr. 1962- . Montevideo, Biblioteca, Poder Legislativo (6207
Issued 3 times annually, the 3d issue
being an annual cumulation.

BOLETIN bibliográfico, año 1, no.1-año 2, no.2,
en/ag. 1946-set. 1946/jun. 1947//. Montevideo, Biblioteca y Museo Pedagógicos.   (6208
Cited in Musso 623.

BOLETIN bibliográfico, no.1-23, 1953-en./jun.
1962//. Montevideo, Biblioteca, Consejo Nacional de Enseñanza Secundaria.   (6209
Cited in Musso 613.

BOLETIN bibliográfico, no.1- , jul./dic. 1955-
Montevideo, Biblioteca, Consejo Nacional de
Gobierno.   (6210

BOLETIN bibliográfico, no.1-4, oct./dic. 1942-
1944//. Montevideo, Cooperativa Nacional de
Productores de Leche (C.O.N.A.P.R.O.L.
E.).   (6211
Cited in Musso 624.

BOLETIN bibliográfico, v.1, no.1-v.4, no.1,
mayo 1953-en. 1956//. Montevideo, Biblioteca, Ministerio de Ganadería y Agricultura. (6212
   Cited in Musso 621.

BOLETIN bibliográfico, año 1, no.1- , jun.
1962- . Montevideo, Biblioteca, Ministerio
de Ganadaría y Agricultura. (6212a
   Cited in Musso 622.

BOLETIN bibliográfico, no.1- , 1950- . Montevideo, Biblioteca, Facultad de Arquitectura,
Universidad de Montevideo. (6213

BOLETIN bibliográfico, no.1- , en. 1935- .
Montevideo, Biblioteca, Facultad de Derecho
y Ciencias Sociales, Universidad de Montevideo. (6214

BOLETIN bibliográfico, no.1- , abr./mayo
1950- . Montevideo, Biblioteca, Facultad
de Humanidades y Ciencias, Universidad de
Montevideo. (6215

BOLETIN bibliografico, v.1, no.1-2, mar. 1948-
feb. 1949; jun. 1955-mar. 1956//. Montevideo, Biblioteca, Facultad de Medicina, Universidad de Montevideo. (6216
   Musso, 617-18, gives separate entries for
the two periods of publications. In this
entry it is implied that publication was
suspended mar. 1949-mayo 1955.

BOLETIN bibliografico, no.1- , en./jul. 1963- .
Montevideo, Biblioteca, Facultad de Odonto-
logía, Universidad de Montevideo. (6217
   Cited in Musso 619.

BOLETIN bibliográfico, año 1, no.1-año 11,
no.2, 1952-1962//. Montevideo, Biblioteca,
Facultad de Veterinaria. (6218
   Cited in Musso 620.

BOLETIN bibliográfico "Barreiro", no.1-9, en.
1916-en. 1922//. Montevideo, Libr. Nacional
A. Barreiro y Ramos. (6219
   Cited in Musso 609. Also Jones 2823.

BOLETIN bibliográfico mensual, año 1, no.1-año
2, no. 20, abr. 1905-nov. 1906//. Montevideo,
Libr. Internacional A. Marchetti y
Cía. (6220
   Cited in Musso, no. 625.

BOLETIN bibliográfico uruguayo, año 1, no.1,
en. 30, 1898-año 3, no.1, en. 1901//. Montevideo, Libr. Nacional de Antonio Barreiro
y Ramos. (6221
   Cited in Musso 626.

BOLETIN informativo, no.1-71?, 1953-1961//.
Montevideo, Museo y Biblioteca Pedagógicos. (6222

BOLETIN latino americano de música, t.1-6,
1935-1946//. Montevideo. (6223
   Edited by Francisco Curt Lange; published
by the Instituto de Estudios Superiores de
Montevideo.---Jones 67.

BOLETIN mensual de libros americanos, no.1-33,
jul. 1939-mar. 1944/en. 1947//. Montevideo,
Libr. de la Feria. (6224
   Musso 627 notes that the oct. 1942 Suplemento contains "Bibliografía Artiguista".

CARTA bibliográfica, jul.-ag. 1964//. Montevideo, Biblioteca, Poder Legislativo. (6226
   Cited in Musso 628.

CATALOGO analítico de anales, boletines y revistas, v.1-10, set. 1948-mar. 1957//. Montevideo, Biblioteca, Poder Legislativo (6227
   Cited in Musso 637.

INFORMACION bibliográfica, no.1- , mar. 1963- .
Montevideo, Biblioteca Pedagógica Central. (6228

INFORMATIVO, año 1, no. 1- , en. 1953- . Montevideo, Biblioteca, Facultad de Química y
Farmacia, Universidad de la República. (6229

LIBROS, año 1, no.1-4, abr.-ag./sept. 1948//.
Montevideo. (6230
   Cited in Musso 630.

LIBROS americanos, no.1-21 [1951]-1964//. Montevideo, Libr. Anticuaria Americana. (6231
   Musso, 631, notes that the Librería formerly was the Librería de Salamanca.

LIST of scientific papers published in Latin
America, 1- , 1948- . Montevideo, Centro
de Cooperación Científica para América Latina, UNESCO. (6232
   Title in French: Liste des travaux scientifiques publiés en Amerique Latine; in Spanish: Lista de artículos científicos publicados en América Latina.

LISTA de libros incorporados a la Biblioteca,
en./feb. 1945- . Montevideo, Biblioteca
Artigas-Washington. (6233

LISTA de obras incorporadas, en./jun. 1939-
1964//. Montevideo, Biblioteca, Poder Legislativo. (6234
   Musso in Bibliografía del Poder Legislativo, item 712, notes that the Lista was semi-
annual, 1939-1946; monthly, 1947-1959; annual,
1961-1964; suspended jun. 1959-1960.

PORTADAS; suplemento del Boletín mensual de libros americanos, año 1, no.1-2, dic. 1952-en.
1953//. Montevideo, Feria del Libro. (6235

REVISTA de bibliografía uruguaya y extranjera,
año 1, no.1, dic. 1915//. Montevideo, Bolsa

REVISTA de bibliografía uruguaya...(Cont.)
de los Libros.   (6236

REVISTA histórica, año 1, t.1, no.1- , 1907-
Montevideo, Museo Histórico Nacional(6237
Jones 2874. Suspended publication 1925-
jul. 1941. Issued by the Universidad de la
República, dic. 1907-ag. 1909; by the Archivo y Museo Histórico Nacional, sept. 1909-
1924; by the Museo Histórico Nacional, ag.
1941- . Segunda época: año 35, t.13, no.
37- , ag. 1941- .

REVISTA nacional; literatura, arte, ciencia,
año 1, no.1- , en. 1938- . Montevideo, Ministerio de Instrucción Pública.   (6238
Jones 2858a.

REVISTA uruguaya de bibliografía, año 1, no.
1-13, dic. 1928-dic. 1929//. Montevideo.   (6239
Jones 2859.

VENEZUELA

BIBLIOGRAFIA; boletín de orientación biblio-
gráfica de la Biblioteca Pública "Juan
Bautista Rodríguez", año 1, no.1- , 1940- .
Quíbor, Estado de Lara.   (6240

BIBLIOGRAFIA; la primera revista venezolana
de la especialidad, año 1, no.1- , mayo
1963- . Caracas, Libr. Historia.   (6241
Cited in HLAS 26, item 11.

BIBLIOGRAFIA y documentación, año 1, no.1- ,
feb./mar. 1951- . Caracas, Instituto de
Economía, Facultad de Ciencias Económicas
y Sociales, Universidad Central de Venezuela.   (6242
Title varies: año 1, 1951, Boletín bibliográfico.

BIBLIOS; órgano de la Librería Venezolana.
El Valle; Caracas.   (6243
National Library holdings: no.5, en.
1943; 2a.ép., no. 7-8 cited in Anuario bi-
bliográfico venezolano, 1943, item 704.
Place of publication: no. 7- , Caracas.

BIBLIOTHECA, año 1, no.1-año 3, no. 27, en.
1954-oct./dic. 1956//. Mérida, Universidad de Los Andes.   (6244

BOLETIN bibliográfico. Caracas, Banco Central de Venezuela.   (6245
Geoghegan 1107 cites no.1 as feb. 1947.

BOLETIN bibliográfico, 1- , 1949- . Caracas,
Fundación Biogen.   (6246

BOLETIN bibliográfico mensual, año 1, no.1- ,
ag. 1958- . Caracas, Instituto de Investigaciones Económicas, Facultad de Economía,

BOLETIN bibliográfico mensual ... (Cont.)
Universidad Central de Venezuela.   (6247

BOLETIN bibliográfico, no.1- dic. 1953- . Ma-
racay, Biblioteca, Facultad de Agronomía,
Universidad Central de Venezuela.   (6248

BOLETIN bibliográfico, año 1, no.1- , feb.
1947- . Mérida, Biblioteca Central, Universidad de Los Andes.   (6249

BOLETIN de la Biblioteca de los Tribunales del
Distrito Federal (Fundación Rojas Astudillos,
no.1- , 1951- . Caracas.   (6250

BOLETIN de la Biblioteca General, Universidad
del Zulia, no.1- , jul./dic. 1961- . Maracaibo.   (6251

BOLETIN de la Biblioteca Nacional, no.1-40,
nov. 1, 1923- 1933; 2a. ép., no. 41-43, en.-
mar. 1936; 3a. ép.[no.] 1- , en./feb. 1959-
Caracas.   (6252
Jones 2964.

BOLETIN de publicaciones recibidas. Caracas,
Biblioteca, Facultad de Derecho, Universidad
Central de Venezuela.   (6253
First on file at DPU: no. 6, jun. 1957.

BOLETIN informativo; publicaciones recibidas,
1- , 1950- . Caracas, Biblioteca, Universidad Central de Venezuela.   (6254

BOLETIN trimestral, jul./sept. 1955- . Caracas, Biblioteca, Electricidad de Caracas.   (6255

COLBAV; Colegio de Bibliotecónomos y Archivistas de Venezuela, v.1, no.1- , jun./jul.
1964- . Caracas.   (6256

CATALOGO de obras ingresadas, oct./nov.
1959- . Caracas, Biblioteca, Universidad
Central de Venezuela.   (6257
Title varies: Until nov./dic. 1960, Libros ingresados.

INDICE bibliográfico, no.1- , en./jun. 1956- .
Caracas, Biblioteca Nacional.   (6258

EL LIBRO; órgano mensual, año 1, no.1-12, ag.
1949-jul. 1950//. Mérida, Libr. Venezolana.   (6259

LIBROS y folletos recibidos. Caracas, Departamento de Canje, Biblioteca Nacional.(6260

Lista de publicaciones recibidas, see Boletín bibliográfico, Biblioteca, Facultad de
Agricultura, Universidad Central de Venezuela.

PUBLICACIONES, no.1- , ag. 1943- . Caracas,
Fundación Biogen.   (6261

PUBLICACIONES venezolanas recibidas. Caracas, Biblioteca Nacional.   (6262
  HLAS 6, item 4779, records en./mar.-jun./
sept. 1940.

VIEJO y raro; revista para bibliófilos y co-
leccionistas, no.1- , mar. 1955- . Caracas,
Libr. Viejo y Raro.   (6263

CATALOGS, GUIDES, etc.

GENERAL

BABCOCK, Charles Edwin. Newspaper files in
the Library of the Pan American Union.
Durham, N. C., Duke Univ. Pr., 1926. p. 288-
303.   (6264
  From Hispanic American historical review,
v. 6, no. 4.---Jones 359.

BERLIN. Ibero-Amerikanisches Institut. Liste
der fortlaufend eintreffenden zeitschriften
und zeitungen. Berlin, 1931- . v.1- .
mimeogr.   (6265
  Jones 53.

-----. Universität. Deutsches Institut für
Zeitungskunde. Handbuch der weltpresse, eine
darstellung des zeitungswesens aller länder.
Berlin, C. Duncker, 1931. 362 p.   (6266
  Compiled by Karl Bömer.---Jones 54.

BOEHM, Eric H., and ADOLPHUS, Lalit. Historical periodicals; an annotated world list of
historical and related serial publications.
Santa Barbara, Calif., Clio Pr., 1961. xvii,
618 p. (Clio reference publications) (6267
  Includes section: Latin America and the
West Indies.

CARTER, Boyd George. Las revistas literarias
de hispanoamérica, breve historia y contenido. México, D.F., Ediciones de Andrea, 1959.
282 p. (Colección Studium, v. 24) (6268

CATALOGO dos jornais mais importantes da França,
Belgica. Allemanha e Estados Unidos com os
preços das assignaturas. Rio de Janeiro,
Lombaerts & Filho, 1874. 22 p.   (6269
  Cited in Reis, item 60.

CONNOLLY, Brendan. Political newspapers and
journals of Latin America. [Carbondale, Ill.,
Southern Illinois Univ.] 1961. 133 p. (Seminar on the Acquisition of Latin American Library Materials, 6th, Working paper, no. 3)
mimeogr.   (6269a

DAVIS, Edward P. Periodicals of international
organizations. Washington, D.C., Pan American Union, 1950. 21 p. (Columbus Memorial
Library. Bibliographic ser., no.
33)   (6270
  Contains: pt. 1, The United Nations and

DAVIS, Edward P. Periodicals of ... (Cont.)
specialized agencies.- pt. 2, Inter-American
organizations. Reprinted from LEA, no. 8,
p. 1-9, 1949; no. 12, p. 1-12, 1950.

GARZA, Jeannette M. de la. Alphabetical list
of medical and public health journals of
Latin America. Washington, D.C., Pan American Sanitary Bureau, 1942. 60 p. (Pan
American Sanitary Bureau, Publ., no.
185)   (6271

-----. Classified list of medical and public
health journals of Latin America. Lista clasificada de las revistas de medicina, sanidad
y ciencias aliadas, de la América latina.
Washington, D.C., [1943] 68, 2. (Pan American Sanitary Bureau, Publ. 199)
mimeogr.   (6272

GROPP, Arthur Eric. Union list of Latin American newspapers in libraries in the United
States. Washington, D.C., Pan American
Union, 1953. 235 p. (Columbus Memorial Library, Bibliographic ser., no. 39) (6273

GRUPO de Trabajo para la Selección de Revistas
Científicas Latinoamericanas, Río Piedras, P.
R., 1964. Grupo de Trabajo para la Selección
de Revistas Científicas Latinoamericanas; Río
Piedras, Puerto Rico, 28 abril -1o. mayo 1964.
[Montevideo] Centro de Cooperación Científi-
ca de la Unesco para América Latina [1964]
various pagings.   (6274

HARRIS, Chauncy Dennison, and FELLMANN, Jerome
D. International list of geographical serials.
Chicago, 1960. lix, 194 p. (Chicago. Uni-
versity. Department of Geography, Research
paper, no. 63)   (6275
  Includes some Latin American countries.

HÖCKER, Rudolf. Die literaturzeitschriften
des hispano-amerikanischen kulturkreises.
(Büchern und bibliotheken. Festschrift für
E. Kuhnert. Berlin, p. 132-45, 1928) (6276
  Jones 204.

IBERO AMERICAN red book (press directory).
Anuario de la prensa iberoamericana, 1930.
New York, Pan American News Service, 1930.
167 p.   (6277
  Jones 210a.

INDICE de revistas francesas de filosofía, historia y literatura. [Montevideo, Goes] n.d.
20 p. (Documento 69)   (6278
  Cited in Musso 326.

INTER-CONTINENTAL press guide. Directorio latino-americano de prensa, v. 1- . jul. 1944-
La Habana, R. Rayneri.   (6278a
  A directory of leading newspapers and magazines published in Latin America. Probably
ceased publication in 1959.

INTERNATIONAL Bureau of the American Republics. Newspaper directory of Latin America. Washington, D.C., Govt. Print. Off.,
1892. 38 p.   (6279
   Jones 215c.

INTERNATIONAL Federation for Documentation.
Commission for Latin America. CAPPAL (Catalogo colectivo de publicações periodicas
da America Latina] 1960/1962. Rio de Janeiro, Instituto Brasileiro de Bibliografia e
Documentação, 1962. 2 v.   (6280
   Contains 6,889 entries, contributions of
60 libraries from 7 countries. Brazilian
libraries are not included in this compilation.

KENISTON, Hayward. Periodicals in American
libraries for the study of the Hispanic
languages and literatures. New York, Hispanic Society of America, 1927.
66 p.   (6281
   Jones 235.

LEVI, Nadia. Las publicaciones periódicas.
México, D.F., 1964. 195 p. (México. Universidad Nacional. Facultad de Filosofía
y Letras. Colegio de Biblioteconomía y
Archivonomía, Ser. B, Seminario de Investigaciones Bibliotecológicas, no. 2) (6282

McCABE, Martha R. An annotated list of pe-
riodicals useful in the study of Latin
American countries. Washington, D.C.,
Office of Education, 1943. 11 p.   (6284

MADRID. Hemeroteca Municipal. Relación de
las publicaciones periódicas que se reciben en la Hemeroteca Municipal. Madrid,
Artes Gráficas Municipales, 1933.
84 p.   (6285
   Third edition.---Jones 271.

MARTINEZ, Angelina, and JAMES, C. Noel. Lista de revistas agrícolas latinoamericanas.
Preliminar. Turrialba, C.R., Instituto Interamericano de Ciencias Agrícolas, 1953.
p. 93-115.   (6286

MEDICAL LIBRARY Association. Committee on
Periodicals and Serial Publications. A
selective list of Latin-American serials.
Washington, D.C., Army Medical Library,
1951. 33 p.   (6287

MORGAN, Katherine Leonore. Journals dealing
with the natural, physical and mathemati-
cal sciences published in Latin America, a
tentative directory. Washington, D.C.,
Division of Intellectual Cooperation, Pan
American Union, 1944. 62 p. mimeogr.(6288

-----. Latin American university journals
and serial publications; a tentative directory. Washington, D.C., Division of Intel-

MORGAN, Katherine Leonore ... (Cont.)
lectual Cooperation, Pan American Union,
1944. 74 p. mimeogr.   (6289

NEW YORK. Public Library. Latin-American periodicals current in the reference department. New York, 1920. 7 p.   (6290
   From Bulletin of the New York Public Library, Sept., 1920.---Jones 334.

PAN AMERICAN Health Organization. Medical and
public health journals from Latin America
received by the library of the Pan American
Sanitary Bureau. Washington, D.C., Pan
American Sanitary Bureau [1935] 11 p.
mimeogr.   (6291

-----. -----. Washington, D.C., 1940. 51[4]
p. (Publ. 152)   (6291a
   Jones 349b.

PAN AMERICAN Institute of Geography and History. Lista de publicaciones periódicas
actualmente recibidas en la Biblioteca del
Instituto Panamericano de Geografía e Historia. List of periodicals currently received in the library of the Pan American
Institute of Geography and History, preparada por Lea Salinas y Salvador Galán. México, D.F., 1961. 122 p.   (6292

PAN AMERICAN UNION. Latin American philatelic
magazines. [Washington, D.C., 1941.
3 p.]   (6293

-----. Columbus Memorial Library. Catalogue
of newspapers and magazines in the Columbus
Memorial Library. Washington, D.C., 1931.
112 p. (Bibliographic series no. 6) (6294
   Previously published under title: List of
newspapers and magazines in the Library...
---Jones 352. Revised from the 1929 edition.

-----. -----. Current Latin American periodical relating to economic subjects in the
Library of the Pan American Union. Washington, D.C., 1938. (Bibliographic ser.,
no. 20) mimeogr.   (6295

-----. -----. -----. Supplementary list.
[Washington, D.C., n.d.] 7 p. mimeogr (6296

-----. -----. Current periodicals printed in
English relating exclusively to Latin America received in the Library of the Pan American Union. Washington, D.C., 1939. 12 p.
mimeogr.   (6297

-----. -----. -----. Washington, D.C., 1941.
10 p. mimeogr.   (6298

-----. -----. -----. Washington, D.C., 1942.
9 p. mimeogr.   (6299

PAN AMERICAN UNION. Columbus Memorial Library. Current periodicals relating to education in the Library of the Pan American Union. Washington, D.C., 1936. 7 p. (6300

-----. -----. Guide to Latin American periodicals. Washington, D.C., 1957. 2 v. Typewritten, carbon copy. (6301
Draft copy submitted to Unesco for publication. Published with considerable revision (See item 6308)

-----. -----. Latin American newspapers (other than official) received in the Library of the Pan American Union. Washington, D.C., 1942. 11 p. (6302

-----. -----. List of daily newspaper files in the Columbus Memorial Library. Washington, D.C., [1941] 11 p. mimeogr (6303

-----. -----. A list of literary and cultural magazines received in the Columbus Memorial Library. Washington, D.C., 1940. 27 p. (Bibliographic ser., no. 22) (6304

-----. -----. List of newspapers and magazines in the Library of the Pan American Union. Washington, D.C., 1929. 180 p. (6305
Jones 358.

-----. -----. Magazines and newspapers received currently in the Columbus Memorial Library; revised. [Washington, D.C., 1942] 55 p. (6306

-----. -----. Pan American magazines relating to architecture, art and music. Washington, D.C., 1942. 13 p. mimeogr. (6307

-----. -----. Repertorio de publicaciones periódicas actuales latinoamericanas. Directory of current Latin American periodicals. Répertoire des periodiques en cours publiés en Amérique Latine. Paris, Unesco, 1958. xxv, 266 p. (Manuales bibliográficos de la Unesco [8] (6308
Lists 3,375 titles of periodicals.

-----. -----. A selected list of Latin American periodicals containing laws and legal information. Washington, D.C., 1942. 27 p. (Bibliographic ser., no. 28) (6309

-----. Division of Agricultural Cooperation. List of agricultural periodicals, societies, experiment stations, and schools in Latin America. Washington, D.C., 1941. 58 p. mimeogr. (6310

-----. -----. Sociedades, revistas, estaciones experimentales, organismos de enseñanza y comisiones nacionales de cooperación agrícola de las repúblicas americanas. Listas com-

PAN AMERICAN UNION. Division of ... (Cont.) piladas por la División de Cooperación Agrícola, Unión Panamericana. Washignton, D.C., 1930. 39 p. mimeogr. (6311

-----. -----. Tentative directory of agricultural periodicals, societies, experiment stations, and schools in Latin America. Washington, D.C., 1945. 90 p. (6312

-----. Division of Intellectual Cooperation. Latin American journals dealing with the social sciences and auxiliary disciplines. Washington, D.C., 1941. 74 p. (6313
Compiler: Edmundo Lasalle.

-----. -----. A partial list of Latin American educational journals. Washington, D. C., 1940. 25 p. (6315

-----. -----. A selective list of periodicals of general interest published in Latin America. Washington, D.C., 1940. 28 p. mimeogr. (6316
Jones 362a.

-----. -----. -----. Rev. ed. Washington, D. C., 1944. 20 p. mimeogr. (6317

-----. Division of Labor and Social Affairs. Directorio de periódicos obreros de América Latina con referencias especiales sobre publicaciones de interés para los trabajadores. Washington, D.C., 1951. 20 p. (Serie sobre educación del trabajador, no. 7) (6318

-----. Division of Science Development. Guía de publicaciones periódicas científicas y técnicas de América Latina; una lista anotada. México, Centro de Documentación Científica y Técnica, 1962. 193 p. (6319
Anexo: publicación de revistas científicas y técnicas en América Latina; un análisis estadístico. p. 165-93.

-----. -----. Guide to Latin American scientific and technical periodicals; an annotated list. Prepared by the Division of Science Development of the Pan American Union and the Centro de Documentación Científica y Técnica de México under a grant from the National Science Foundation of the United States of America. Washington, D.C., Pan American Union, 1962. xii, 187 p. (6320

-----. Social Science Section. Directorio de publicaciones periódicas en el campo de las ciencias sociales; primera parte: América latina. Washington, D.C., 1955. 83 p. (Its Directorios, 3) (6321

PLENN, Abel. List of Latin American serials; a survey of exchanges available in U. S. li-

PLENN, Abel. List of Latin ... (Cont.)
braries. Chicago, American Library Association, 1941. 70 p. (Studies of the
A.L.A. Committee on Library Cooperation
with Latin America, no. 1)   (6322

POMA, Cesare. De los periódicos escritos en
lenguas indígenas de América. Memoria leída en el Congreso de Americanistas (Sesión
del 19 de octubre de 1895, México) México,
D.F., Impr. y Lit. de Díaz de León, Sucrs.,
n.d. 4 p.   (6323
    Published also in Actas del Congreso In-
ternacional de Americanistas., México,
1895. 1897. p. 299-303.---Jones 377.

LA PRENSA ibero-americana, 1932. [Buenos Ai-
res] Edición de la Revista Americana de
Buenos Aires [1933]   (6324

-----. 1933; 2a. ed. [Buenos Aires] Edición
de la Revista Americana de Buenos Aires
[1934]   (6325

-----, 1934; 3a. ed. [Buenos Aires] Edición
de la Revista Americana de Buenos Aires
[1935]   (6326
    Jones 261. Appeared in Revista americana,
en./feb. 1934. Compiler Victoriano Lillo
Catalán.

-----, 1936; 4a. ed. Buenos Aires, Edición
de la Revista Americana de Buenos Aires
[1936] 186, 8 p.   (6327
    "La 4a. ed. de la Prensa Ibero-Americana
corresponde a los nos. 141-142, en./feb. de
1936 de la Revista americana de Buenos Aires.

REVISTAS francesas de medicina, veterinaria y
farmacia. [Montevideo, Goes] n.d. 30 p.
(Documento 73]   (6328
    Cited in Musso 327.

SPARN, Enrique. Catálogo universal de revistas de ciencias exactas, físicas y naturales,
con sus correspondientes números de tomos o
años durante las fechas de aparición. Córdoba, Academia Nacional de Ciencias, 1920.
255 p. (Academia Nacional de Ciencias,
misc., 1)   (6329
    Jones 856. Supplements 1-3 issued as
Miscelánea, 6, 1922; 9, 1925; and 20, 1932
of the Academia Nacional de Ciencias.

-----. Cuarto y último suplemento, 1931-1937.
Córdoba, Impr. de la Universidad, 1939.
38 p.   (6329a
    Reprinted from Boletín de la Facultad de
Ingeniería, Universidad Nacional de Córdoba,
año 2, no. 1.

-----. Las más costosas colecciones de revistas científicas. V: Botánica pura. [Valpa-
raíso, 1938] p. 212-16.   (6330
    Cited in Catálogo, Instituto biblioteco-

SPARN, Enrique. Las más costosas... (Cont.)
lógico, item 497.

-----. Las más costosas colecciones de revistas de ciencias químicas en el mundo. Córdoba, Impr. de la Universidad, 1931.
20 p.   (6331
    Cited in Catálogo, Instituto Biblioteco-
lógico, item 498.

-----. Otros trabajos argentinos presentados
al cuarto Congreso Sudamericano de Ferrocarriles (Bogotá) Las más costosas colecciones de revistas científicas. VII: Ciencias geológicas. [Córdoba, Impr. de la Universidad Nacional de Córdoba, 1943]
22 p.   (6332
    Cited in Catálogo Instituto Bibliotecoló-
gico, item 663.

UNITED NATIONS. Dag Hammarskjold Library.
Annotated list of official gazettes in the
United Nations Headquarters Library. [N.
Y.] 1959. 54 p. (UN/Misc. Doc. 17)   (6333
    Arrangement by country. Latin American
countries included.

-----. -----. Government gazettes; an annotated list of gazettes held in the Dag Hammarskjold Library. New York, 1964. 50 p.
(United Nations. [Document] ST/LIB/Ser.
B/10)   (6334

-----. Library, México. Guía analítica de
publicaciones periódicas. México, 1960.
[38] p.   (6335

UNITED NATIONS Educational, Scientific and
Cultural Organization. Educational periodicals; [2d ed. Paris, 163] 260 p. (International directories of education) (6336

-----. Liste mondiale des périodiques spécia-
lisés dans les sciences sociales. World
list of social science periodicals. [Paris,
1953] 161 p. (Documentation in the social
sciences.)   (6337
    Social science journals from Latin America
included. Arrangement is geographical.

-----. -----. 2d. ed. rev. and enl. Prepared by the International Committee for Social Sciences Documentation. [Paris, 1957]
209 p. (Documentation in the social sciences)   (6338
    Social science journals from Latin America
included. Arrangement is geographical.

-----. Education Clearing House. Draft international list of educational periodicals.
[Paris, 1956] 137 p.   (6339

-----. -----. Repertorio internacional de re-
vitas pedagógicas. Paris [1957] 200 p.
(Estudios y documentos de educación, no.

UNITED NATIONS Educational, ... (Cont.)
23)   (6340
    Prepared jointly with the Education Press
Association of America. Includes Latin
American countries.

U.S. Department of Agriculture. Library.
A preliminary list of Latin American periodicals and serials. Washington, D.C., 1943.
195 p. (Library list, 5)   (6341

-----. Library of Congress. Latin American
periodicals currently received in the Li-
brary of Congress and in the Library of the
Department of Agriculture. Washington, D.C.,
Govt. Print. Off., 1944. 249 p. (Latin
American ser. no. 8)   (6342
    Compiler: Charmion Shelby. New edition
of the 1941 compilation prepared by Murray
M. Wise.

-----. -----. Census Library Project. Statistical bulletins; an annotated bibliography of the general statistical bulletins
of major political subdivisions of the world,
prepared by Phyllis G. Carter. Washington,
D.C., 1954. x, 93 p.   (6343
    Companion to Statistical yearbooks, pu-
blished in 1953.

URUGUAY. Biblioteca Nacional. Centro de Documentación Científica, Técnica y Económica.
Revistas latino-americanas de economía.
Montevideo, Biblioteca Nacional, 1959.
12 p.   (6344

WINSHIP, George Parker. Early South American
newspapers. Worcester, The Davis Pr., 1908.
15 p.   (6345
    Reprinted from the Proceedings of the Amer-
ican Antiquarian Society, Oct. 1908.
    "List of news sheets printed at Lima in
Peru, 1621-1767, recorded in J. T. Medina's
La imprenta en Lima, Santiago de Chile,
1904": p. 10-15.---Jones 2775.

WISE, Murry M. Latin American periodicals
currently received in the Library of Con-
gress. Preliminary edition. Washington,
D.C., The Hispanic Foundation, Library of
Congress, 1941. viii, 137, ix-xv p.
mimeogr.   (6346
    "Prepared ... with the assistance of Anyda
Marchant, Virginia Brewer, Joseph V. Butt".
---Jones 544b.

ZIMMERMAN, Irene. A guide to current Latin
American periodical: humanities and social
sciences. Gainesville, Fla., Kallman Publ.
Co., 1961. 357 p.   (6347

-----. Latin American periodicals currently
received in the University of Florida Libraries, as of March 1, 1953. Gainesville,
Fla., Department of Reference and Biblio-

ZIMMERMAN, Irene. Latin American... (Cont.)
graphy, Univ. of Florida Libraries [1953]
19 p. mimeogr.   (6348

ARGENTINA

ANUARIO de la prensa argentina, 1896, Jorge
Navarro Viola, director. Buenos Aires, 1897.
428 p.   (6349
    "La prensa socialista", by R. J. Payró:
p. 51-70.---Jones 561.

ANUARIO prensa argentina y latinoamericana,
1939- . Buenos Aires, 1939- .   (6350
    Title varies: 1st ed.: Anuario prensa
argentina. Subtitle also varies: 1st ed.:
Argent-press guía Solana de publicaciones,
diarios, periódicos y revistas ...; 2d ed.
(1942); 3d ed. (1946): Guía de publicaciones periódicas; 4th. ed. (1955): Guía periodística publicitaria; 5th. ed. (1961):
Guía publicitaria.

ARGENTINA. Biblioteca Nacional. Catálogo de
las revistas y periódicos existentes en la
Biblioteca Nacional (con exclusión de los
diarios políticos) Buenos Aires, Impr. de
la Biblioteca Nacional, 1901. 48 p.   (6351
    Jones 611.

-----. -----. Catálogo de las revistas y periódicos existentes en la Biblioteca Nacional (con exclusión de los diarios políticos)
Buenos Aires, Impr. de la Biblioteca Nacional, 1904. 76 p.   (6352

-----. -----. -----. Buenos Aires, 1923.
94 p.   (6353

-----. -----. Un siglo de periódicos en la
Biblioteca Nacional (políticos); catálogo
por fechas, 1800-1899. Buenos Aires, Impr.
de la Biblioteca Nacional, 1935. 74 p. (6354
    Jones 618.

-----. Consejo Nacional de Investigaciones
Científicas y Técnicas. Guía de publicaciones periódicas científicas y técnicas
que se editan en la República Argentina;
2a. ed. Buenos Aires, 1964. 133, 8 p (6355

ASOCIACION de la Prensa Técnica Argentina.
Primera guía de las publicaciones especializadas y técnicas argentinas. Buenos Aires
[1959] 64 p.   (6356

BUENOS AIRES. Universidad. Facultad de Agronomía y Veterinaria. Biblioteca. Catálogo
de publicaciones periódicas. Buenos Aires
[Tall. Gráf. Ferrari Hnos.] 1937. 28 p (6357
    Cited in Catálogo, Instituto Bibliotecoló-
gico, item 469.

BUENOS AIRES. Universidad. Facultad de
Agronomía y Veterinaria. Biblioteca. Catálogo de publicaciones periodicas; Suplemento no. 1- , dic. 1961- . Buenos Aires,
1961- .   (6358
    Cited in Ib.

-----. -----. Facultad de Ciencias Económicas. Anuario bibliográfico de la sección
revistas y publicaciones oficiales y periódicas. Buenos Aires, 1938. 316 p. (6359
    Contains a list of articles in periodicals
in the library classified by subject, 1906-
1938, and of publications of the League of
Nations, International Labour Office, etc.
---Jones 626.

-----. -----. -----. Catálogo de la sección
revistas, diarios y periodicos. Buenos Aires, Impr. de la Universidad, 1932.
189 p.   (6360
    Jones 627.

-----. -----. Facultad de Ciencias Exactas,
Físicas y Naturales. Biblioteca. Catálogo de las publicaciones periódicas que lle-
gan regularmente a la Biblioteca. Buenos
Aires, 1937. 79 p. mimeogr.   (6361
    Jones 629.

-----. -----. -----. Departamento de Biblioteca y Publicaciones. Catálogo de publicaciones periódicas. Buenos Aires, 1960.
64 p.   (6362
    Cited in Catálogo, Instituto Biblioteco-
lógico, item 918.

-----. -----. -----. Suplemento no. 1- , dic.
1961- . Buenos Aires, 1961- .   (6363
    Cited Ib.

-----. -----. Facultad de Ciencias Médicas.
Catálogo de revistas de la Biblioteca.
Buenos Aires, Impr. Flaibán y Camilloni,
1916. 72 p.   (6364
    Binayán, item 88, notes that a reprint in
8 p. was issued, with title, "Nómina de las
revistas", from the Revista de la Sociedad
Médica Argentina, XI, p. 719-24, 1903.

-----. -----. Facultad de Derecho y Ciencias
Sociales. Catálogo de revistas de la Biblioteca. Buenos Aires, Impr. Flaibán y Camilloni, 1916. 72 p.   (6365
    Jones 632.

-----. -----. Instituto Bibliotecológico.
Biblioteca. Nómina de publicaciones periódicas de bibliotecología y documentacion
existentes en la biblioteca. Buenos Aires,
1958. 20 p. mimeogr.   (6366

CARRASCO, Gabriel. El periodismo en la República Argentina. (Boletín demográfico argentino, publicación de la Oficina Demográfica

CARRASCO, Gabriel. El periodismo... (Cont.)
Nacional, Buenos Aires, año 2, no. 5, p. 1-
33, 1901)   (6367
    A list of periodicals and newspapers pu-
blished in 1899 giving name, place, character, price and other data.---Jones 656.

CORDOBA, Argentina. Universidad Nacional.
Biblioteca Mayor. Catálogo de periódicos.
Córdoba, Bautista Cubas, 1922. (Folleto,
no. 1)   (6367a

-----. -----. -----. Catálogo de revistas;
por orden alfabético y metódico. Córdoba,
B. Cubas, 1923. 112 p. (Publ. de la Biblioteca Mayor. Folleto no. 2)   (6367b
    Cited in Geoghegan, 778.

GANS, Richard. Catálogo de revistas de ciencias exactas, naturales y de ingeniería existentes en bibliotecas argentinas, confeccio-
nado bajo los auspicios de la Sociedad Científica Alemana. Buenos Aires, Compañía Sud-
americana de Billetes de Banco, 1917.
45 p.   (6368
    Jones 702.

GUIA periodística argentina, 1913. Buenos Aires, n.d. 301 p.   (6369

GUIA periodística argentina y de las repúblicas latinoamericanas. Buenos Aires, 1928-
1930, 1930-1931.   (6370
    Arranged by country and place; includes
bibliographical and historical data.---Jones
717.

IBAÑEZ, Avelina M. Sinopsis tabular de las
publicaciones de carácter periodístico aparecidas en Buenos Aires hasta 1830. (II.
Congreso Internacional de Historia de America. Buenos Aires, 1938. v. 5, p. 145-
87)   (6371
    Arranged under the following divisions:
date, title, press, editor, character, dura-
tion and location.---Jones 725.

KEMPNY, José C., LOPEZ MONTOYA, Francisco I.,
etc. Nómina de publicaciones periódicas
que interesan al quimico, con indicación de
las bibliotecas que las reciben. Extracta-
da de la "List of periodicals abstracted
by Chemical Abstracts". Buenos Aires, 1940.
84 p. mimeogr.   (6372

-----. Nómina de publicaciones periódicas argentinas que interesan al quimico, con indicación de las bibliotecas que las reciben.
Buenos Aires, 1940. 10 p. mimeogr.   (6373

LA PLATA. Universidad. Biblioteca. Catálogo
de periódicos sudamericanos existentes en la
Biblioteca Pública de la Universidad (1791-
1861), publicación del cincuentenario de la
Biblioteca Pública de la Universidad y de la

LA PLATA. Universidad. Biblioteca... (Cont.)
ciudad de La Plata. Prólogo de Alberto
Palcos. La Plata, 1934. 231 p.   (6374
Jones 242, 742a.

LAFLEUR, Héctor René, PROVENZANO, Sergio D.,
etc. Las revistas literarias argentinas,
1893-1960. [Buenos Aires] Ediciones Culturales Argentinas, Ministerio de Educación
y Justicia, Dirección General de Cultura
[1962] 282 p. (Biblioteca del sesquicentenario. Serie cuadernos culturales) (6375

LOIS, Ricardo J., and GHISIO, Renato Luis.
Lista de abreviaturas de títulos de revistas agropecuarias. Buenos Aires, Ministerio de Agricultura y Ganadería, Departamento de Bibliotecas, 1956. p. 43-64. (6375a
Reprinted from Boletín bibliográfico, Ministerio de Agricultura y Ganadería, v. 21,
no. 4. Cited in Geoghegan 2117.

MANTILLA, Manuel F. Bibliografía periodísti-
ca de la provincia de Corrientes. Buenos
Aires, Impr. y Libr. de Mayo, 1887.
167 p.   (6376
Contains extensive bibliographical notes.
---Jones 763.

MARTINEZ, Alberto B. Censo de los diarios,
periódicos y revistas de 1895 y de 1914.
(Argentina. Tercer censo nacional. Buenos Aires, 1917. t. 9, p. 271-319)   (6377
Jones 769.

MENDEZ PAZ, Emilio. Periódicos correntinos,
1825-1900. Buenos Aires, 1953. 123p.(6378

MILLAN, Roberto. Catálogo de las publicaciones periódicas de la Argentina sobre agricultura. (Boletín del Ministerio de Agricultura de la Nación, Buenos Aires, v. 30,
p. 227-306, 1931)   (6379
213 periodicals, since 1807.---Jones 780.

PEÑA, Enrique. Estudio de los periódicos y
revistas existentes en la "Biblioteca Enrique Peña". Buenos Aires, Impr. Amorrortu,
1935. 632 p.   (6380
Study with descriptive and bibliographical
notes, facsimiles, etc.---Jones 812.

QUESADA, Ernesto. El movimiento intelectual
argentino: revistas y periódicos. (in the
author's Reseñas y críticas. Buenos Aires,
1893. p. 119-41)   (6381
More detailed information will be found in
"Memorias de la Biblioteca Pública, 1876-1877"
and in "La Biblioteca Pública de Buenos Aires
en la Exposición Universal de París, 1878"
(Cf. p. 132-33).---Jones 820.

ROSARIO, Arg. Dirección General de Estadística
del Municipio. Publicaciones periódicas editadas en el año 1939 en la ciudad de Rosario.

ROSARIO, Arg. Dirección... (Cont.)
[Rosario, 1940] 8 p. mimeogr.   (6382
Lists approximately 130 titles.

SALVADOR, Nélida. Revistas argentinas de van-
guardia (1920-1930). Buenos Aires, Facultad
de Filosofía y Letras, Universidad de Buenos
Aires, [1962] 108 p. (Publ. de la Facultad
de Filosofía y Letras, Instituto de Literatura Argentina "Ricardo Rojas", Crítica, t. 6,
no. 1.   (6383

-----. Revistas literarias argentinas (1893-
1940); aporte para una bibliografía. Buenos
Aires, Fondo Nacional de las Artes
[1962]   (6384
Section 2 of Bibliografía argentina de artes y letras, no. 9, p. 47-116, en./mar. 1961.

SANCHEZ SORONDO, Matías Guillermo. Nómina de
las publicaciones comunistas y de otras ideo-
logías extremistas editadas en el país y en
el extranjero, que circulan por el correo.
(Diario de sesiones de la Cámara de Diputados, Buenos Aires, t. 3, p. 95-121,
1937)   (6385
Radical periodicals for Hispanic America
as follows: Argentina, 127 titles, Brazil,
10; Colombia, 4; Costa Rica, 1; Cuba, 15;
Chile, 14; Ecuador, 5; México, 24; Perú, 3.
---Jones 433.

SOCIEDAD Argentina de Bibliotecarios de Instituciones Sociales, Científicas, Artísticas
y Técnicas, Buenos Aires. Catálogo de publicaciones periódicas científicas y técnicas, recibidas en las bibliotecas de las
instituciones adheridas al Comité. Buenos
Aires, Consejo Nacional de Investigaciones
Científicas y Técnicas, 1942. xx,
342 p.   (6386
Lists 7,387 periodicals with indication
of location in 64 libraries.

-----. 2a. ed. Buenos Aires, 1962.
1726 p.   (6387
Lists 25,129 periodicals with indication
of location in 142 libraries.

SOCIEDAD Rural Argentina, Buenos Aires. Biblioteca. Catálogo de publicaciones periódicas.
Buenos Aires, 1961. 59 p.   (6388

SQUIBB, E. R. and Sons, Buenos Aires. Biblioteca. Catátolo de revistas. [Buenos Aires]
1958. 22 p.   (6389
Cited in Catálogo, Instituto Bibliotecológico, item 499.

UNION Industrial Argentina, Buenos Aires. Biblioteca. Catálogo de las revistas recibidas
en las bibliotecas de la institución y firmas
asociadas, con una tabla geográfica y otra
por materias. Buenos Aires, 1946.
122 p.   (6393

VANOSSI, Reinaldo. Catálogo de las publicaciones periódicas existentes en la biblioteca de la Sociedad Científica Argentina. Buenos Aires, Compañía Impresora Argentina, 1927. 201 p.   (6394
   Jones 881.

ZINNY, Antonio. Efemeridografía argirometropolitana hasta la caída del gobierno de Rosas. Contiene el título, fecha de su aparición y cesación, formato, imprenta, número de que se compone cada colección, nombre de los redactores que se conocen, observaciones y noticias biográficas sobre cada uno de éstos, y la biblioteca pública o particular donde se encuentra el periódico. Buenos Aires, Impr. del Plata, 1869. 545 p.   (6395
   First published in Revista de Buenos Aires, v. 9, 1866- v. 13, 1867, with title: Bibliografía periodística de Buenos Aires hasta la caída del gobierno de Rosas. "Monobibliografía del Dr. d. Gregorio Funes ... seguida de la continuación de su Bosquejo histórico hasta la batalla de Maipú"; p. 413-545.---Jones 892.

-----. Efemeridografía argiroparquiótica o sea de las provincias argentinas. Buenos Aires, Impr. y Libr. de Mayo, 1868. 300 p. (6396
   From Revista de Buenos Aires, v. 16-17, 1868.---Jones 893.

-----. La Gaceta mercantil de Buenos Aires, 1823-1852; resumen de su contenido con relación a la parte americana y con especialidad a la historia de la República Argentina. Buenos Aires, Impr. Americana, 1875. 384 p.   (6397
   1a. entrega, oct. 1823-en. 1831; no more published.---Jones 894.

BOLIVIA

CARDOZO GONZALEZ, Armando. Revistas agrícolas bolivianas; cronología y clasificación. La Paz, Bolivia, Sociedad de Ingenieros Agrónomos de Bolivia, 1962. 69 p. (Sociedad de Ingenieros Agrónomos de Bolivia. Boletín bibliográfico, no. 2)   (6398

GOLDE, Werner. Bibliographie der bolivianischen zeitschriften, 1953-1954. Bibliografía de las revistas bolivianas, 1953-1954. La Paz, Deutsche Schule, Colegio Alemán "Mariscal Braun", 1955. 66 p. mimeogr.   (6399

RENE-MORENO, Gabriel. Ensayo de una bibliografía general de los periódicos de Bolivia, 1825-1905. Santiago de Chile, 1905. 344 p.   (6400
   Includes "Suplemento" (1905-1907), Santiago, 1908. 1,435 periodicals listed with notes of numbers, dates, frequency, etc.---Jones 940.

RENE-MORENO, Gabriel. Ensayo de ... (Cont.) Now available in microprint.

BRAZIL

ANUARIO da imprensa, rádio e televisão, 1941- . Rio de Janeiro, Impr. Nacional, 1942- . (6401
   Began in 1941 with title Anuário da imprensa brasileira. Title varies: -1956/1957, Anuário brasileiro da imprensa.

ASSOCIAÇÃO Brasileira de Química. Relação das publições periodicas sôbre química e assuntos afins. [Rio de Janeiro, 1943?] 180 p. (6401a
   Cited in Geoghegan, 1851.

BELO HORIZONTE. Archivo Publico Mineiro. Relação dos jornaes mineiros pertencentes a collecção. Bello Horizonte, Impr. Off, do Estado de Minas Geraes, 1908. 25 p.   (6402
   Cited in Reis, item 233.

BELLIDO, Remijio de. Catalogo dos jornaes paraenses, 1822-1908. Pará, Impr. Official, 1908. 163 p.   (6403
   1. pte. Catalogo alphabetico e descriptivo. 2. pte. Catalogo chronologico. - 3. pte. Catalogo segundo as localidades.---Jones 974.

BESSA, Alberto. 100 annos de vida, a expansão da imprensa brasileira no primeiro seculo da sua existencia. Lisboa, Gomes de Carvalho, 1929. 313 p.   (6404
   Review of Brazilian periodicals arranged by year, 1808-1905, with descriptive and historical notes.---Jones 974b.

BRAZIL. Departamento da Imprensa e Propaganda. Relação das publicações periodicas brasileiras anotadas na Secretaria do Conselho Nacional de Imprensa até fev. de 1944. Rio de Janeiro, Impr. Nacional, 1945. 257 p.   (6404a

-----. Departamento Nacional de Estatística. Estatística da imprensa periodica no Brasil (1929-1930) Rio de Janeiro, Typ. do Depto. Nacional de Estatística, 1931. 144 p. (6405
   In 2 sections: (1) Periódicos existentes no Brasil: (2) Estatística da imprensa periodica. Arranged by state.---Jones 990.

BRODBECK, Sully. Publicações periódicas na Biblioteca do ITERS [Instituto Tecnológico do Rio Grande do Sul. Porto Alegre] 1953. 53 p. (Boletim no. 24)   (6406

CARVALHO, Alfredo de. Annaes da imprensa periódica Pernambucana (1821-1908) Recife, 1908. 640 p.   (6407
   Jones 1013.

CARVALHO, Oswaldo de. Bibliografia de hemerografias. Sau Paulo, 1956. 56 p. mimeogr.   (6408

CATALOGO geral dos perodicos existentes na
  Biblioteca do Departamento de Profilaxia
  da Lepra do Estado de S. Paulo. São Paulo,
  1942?-1951. 3 v.   (6410
  Doria, 145, notes that IBBD continued
  the publication with v. 4, 1956- .

CUTIN, Noemia Lerner. Periódicos nas bibliotecas universitárias e especializadas. São
  Paulo, 1956. 96 p.   (6411

DIARIO de Pernambuco (1825-1908) Recife,
  1908. 65 p.   (6412
  Cited in Reis, item 240.

FERREIRA, Athos Damasceno. Jornais críticos
  e humorísticos de Pôrto Alegre no século
  XIX. Pôrto Alegre, Livr. do Globo, 1944.
  33 p.   (6413
  The "Jornais" are mentioned by title only
  throughout the text.

GEHSE, Hans. Die deutsche presse in Brasilien
  von 1852 bis zur gegenwart; ein beitrag zur
  geschichte und zum aufgabenkreis ausland-
  deutschen zeitungswesens. Münster in West-
  falen, Aschendorffsche Verlagsbuchhandlung,
  1931. xi, 174 p. (Deutschtum und ausland;
  studien zum auslanddeutschtum und zur aus-
  landkultur, 43, hft.)   (6414
  Literaturverzeichnis: p. vii-xi.---Jones
  1049.

INSTITUTO Brasileiro de Bibliografia e Documentação, Rio de Janeiro. Periódicos de
  agricultura e ciências afins existentes nas
  bibliotecas brasileiras; levantamento apresentado, pelo catálogo coletivo nacional, ao
  Seminario sôbre Bibliotecas Agricolas, Rio
  de Janeiro, 11-13 de novêmbro de 1963. Rio
  de Janeiro, 1963. unpaged.   (6415
  Contains 190 entries of foreign and 121 of
  Brazilian origin.

-----. Serviço de Bibliografia. Periódicos
  brasileiros de cultura. Edição preliminar.
  Rio de Janeiro, 1956. 182 p.   (6416

JORNAES pernambucanos de 1821-1889. Pernambuco, Typ. do Jornal do Recife, 1899.
  42 p.   (6417
  Reprinted from the Revista, Instituto Archeologico e Geographico Pernambuco, no. 52.
  Cited in Reis, item 176.

MARTINS, Alfredo Romairo. Catalogo dos jornaes publicados no Paraná de 1854-1907.
  Curytiba, Typ. e Lith. a Vapor Impr. Paranaense, 1908. 155 p.   (6418
  Cited in Reis, item 254.

OLIVEIRA, João Batista Perdigão de. Catalogo
  dos jornaes, revistas e outras publicações
  periodicas do Ceará, 1824-1904. [Fortaleza]
  Typ. "Guarany" de J.G.D.S., 1905.

OLIVEIRA, João Batista Perdigão de ... (Cont.)
  60 p.   (6419
  Jones 1135.

PERNAMBUCO. Bibliotheca Publica do Estado.
  Centenário do Diario de Pernambuco, 7 de no-
  vembro de 1825. Homenagem da Bibliotheca
  Publica do Estado, 7 de novembro de 1925.
  Recife [Rep. de Publicações Officiais] 1925.
  10 p. (Boletim bibliographico)   (6420

PÔRTO ALEGRE, Brasil. Universidade. Serviço
  Central de Informações Bibliograficas. Catalogo coletivo regional de periódicos, RGS,
  v. 1 (622 p.)- , out. 1961- . Pôrto Alegre,
  1961- .   (6421

SÃO PAULO. Instituto Adolfo Lutz. Biblioteca.
  Relação das publicações periodicas existentes na Biblioteca. São Paulo [1944]
  133 p.   (6422
  Cited in Catálogo, Instituto Bibliotecológico, item 493.

-----. Universidade. Escola Politecnica.
  Instituto de Pesquisas Tecnologicas. Biblioteca. A biblioteca do I.P.T. e sua organização por Lygia Macedo Scaramelli. Relação dos
  periódicos da Biblioteca. São Paulo, 1944.
  48 p.   (6423

-----. -----. Instituto de Administração. Catálogo da Seção de Periódicos da Biblioteca.
  São Paulo, 1954. 124 p. (Publ. no. 151)
  mimeogr.   (6424
  Cited in Richardson, item 7292.

STUDART, Guilherme. Catalogo dos jornaes de
  pequeno e grande formato publicados em Ceará.
  Fortaleza, Typ. Studart, 1896. 32 p. (6424a
  Jones 1208.

-----. -----. Fortaleza, Typ. Studart, 1898.
  47 p.   (6424b
  369 journals are listed. Cited in Reis,
  item 171.

-----. -----. Fortaleza, Typ. Minerva de Assis
  Bezerra, 1904. 93 p.   (6424c
  Reprinted from Revista do Instituto do
  Ceará. Cited in Reis, item 209.

TORRES, João N., and CARVALHO, Alfredo de.
  Annaes da imprensa da Bahia. 1o centenário,
  1811-1911. Catalogo organizado pelos socios
  do Instituto Historico. Bahia, Typ. Bahiana
  de Cincinato Melchiades, 1911. 302 p. (6425
  Cited in Reis, item 279.

CHILE

AHUMADA MATURANA, Rómulo. Revista de revistas.
  (Revista de artes y letras, Santiago, t. 5-6,
  1886)   (6426

AHUMADA MATURANA, Rómulo. Revista... (Cont.)
Study of 26 literary and scientific re-
views published in Chile before 1882.---
Jones 1379.

AMUNATEGUI SOLAR, Domingo. El "Mercurio" de
Chile. Santiago de Chile, Impr. Cervantes,
1896. 29 p.   (6427
Published in Anales de la Universidad de
Chile. Cited in Laval, item 10.

ANRIQUE REYES, Nicolás. Bibliografía de las
principales revistas i periódicos de Chile.
(Anales de la Universidad de Chile, Santiago de Chile, t. 115, p. 121-62,
1904)   (6428
35 periodicals listed with bibliographical
data and notes of contents.---Jones 1393.

CHILE. Biblioteca Nacional. Anuario de publicaciones periódicas chilenas, 1915- ,
Santiago de Chile, 1915- .   (6429
Jones 1607. Lists were included in the
Anuario de la Prensa Chilena, 1886-1915.
Title varies: 1915-1928, Lista de publicaciones periódicas chilenas; 1929: Revistas,
diarios y periódicos chilenos; 1930-1938:
Publicaciones periódicas chilenas. Publication suspended, 1939-1951. Renewed publication under present title in 1952.

-----. -----. Lista de publicaciones periódicas chilenas. Santiago de Chile, Impr. Universitaria, 1915-1928.   (6430
Reprinted from Revista de bibliografía chilena y extranjera: 1915-1918. Cited in Ochsenius, item 21-28, 178-179: years 1915-1918,
1921, 1923, 1925-1927. Jones cites 1923 in
item 1607. See also item 6429.

-----. -----. Publicaciones periódicas chilenas recibidas en 1914. Santiago de Chile,
Impr. Universitaria, 1914. Santiago de Chile,
Impr. Universitaria, 1914. 9 p.   (6431
Lists 390 titles. Reprinted from Revista
de bibliografía chilena y extranjera, año 11,
no. 4. Cited in Laval, item 59. See also
item 6429.

-----. -----. Publicaciones periódicas chile-
nas, anuarios de 1937 y 1938. Santiago,
Impr. y Lit. Universo, 1939. 45 p. (6432
Jones 1607a. See also item 6429.

-----. Universidad. Escuela de Medicina.
Lista alfabética de revistas en la Biblioteca. Santiago de Chile, 1962.   (6433
Cited in Boletín de adquisiciones, Medellín,
no. 9, p. 18, sept. 1963.

-----. -----. -----. Lista de revistas por materia. Santiago de Chile [1962]   (6434
Cited in Boletín de adquisiciones, Medellín
no. 9, p. 18, sept. 1963.

CHILE. Universidad. Escuela de Medicina.
Títulos de revistas incorporadas en 1963.
Santiago, 1963.   (6435
Arrangement by subject. Cited in Boletín
de adquisiciones, Medellín, no. 9, p. 18,
sept. 1963.

-----. -----. -----. Biblioteca Central.
"Union list" de revistas médicas. Santia-
go, 1948. 187 p. mimeogr.   (6435a

CONCEPCION, Chile. Universidad. Catálogo colectivo de publicaciones periódicas de la
Universidad de Concepción, compilado por
Blanca Matas Anguita de acuerdo a las listas
proporcionadas por las bibliotecas participan-
tes. Concepción, Universidad de Concepción,
1963. 167 p. mimeogr.   (6436

DONOSO, Ricardo. Veinte años de la historia de
El Mercurio. Santiago de Chile, Impr. Cervantes, 1927. 199 p.   (6437
La prensa periódica chilena desde "La Aurora" a "El Mercurio". p. 9-40.---Jones 1453.

SANFUENTES Y CORREA, Enrique. Los periódicos
chilenos olvidados. (Revista de bibliografía chilena y extranjera, Santiago, año 2,
p. 383-402, 433-53, 1914; año 3, p. 185-95,
291-302, 1915)   (6438
Jones 1591.

SANTIAGO de Chile. Universidad Católica. Biblioteca Central. Catálogo colectivo de revistas y publicaciones periódicas en economía y materias afines existentes en treinta
y cinco bibliotecas en Santiago. Preparado
conjuntamente por la Biblioteca Central de
la Pontificia Universidad Católica y la Biblioteca del Instituto de Economía de la
Universidad de Chile, Santiago, 1962. 220,
53 p.   (6439

-----. -----. Instituto de Física y Astronomía. Lista de las revistas y publicaciones
periódicas recibidas. [Santiago, 1960]
23 p.   (6440

VILCHES, Roberto. Las revistas literarias chilenas del Siglo XIX. Santiago de Chile,
Impr. Universitaria, 1942. 78 p.   (6441

COLOMBIA

ASOCIACION Nacional de Industriales. Biblioteca. Publicaciones periódicas, Medellín,
1962. 11 p. mimeogr.   (6442
Cited in Florén, Bibliografía bibliotecológica, 1961/1962, item 223.

BOGOTA. Universidad Javariana. Biblioteca
Central. Lista de revistas técnicas que posee la Biblioteca Central. Bogotá, 1961.
18 p.   (6443

BOGOTA. Universidad Javariana ... (Cont.)
Cited in Peraza, Fichas, t. 3, item 147.

BUCARAMANGA. Universidad Industrial de Santander. División de Investigaciones Científicas. Inventario general de las revistas que posee la hemeroteca del Centro de
Documentación e Información. Bucaramanga,
1962. Various pagings. mimeogr.   (6444
Cited in Floren, Bibliografía bibliotecológica, 1961/1962, item 232.

CENTRO Nacional de Investigaciones Agrícolas
"Tibaitatá". Biblioteca. Selección de pu-
blicaciones periódicas recibidas. Bogotá,
1955. 32 p. mimeogr.   (6445
Compiled by Angela Hernández Arango and
Amalia Ramírez.

COLOMBIA. Biblioteca Nacional. Catálogo de
periódicos y libros de la Biblioteca Nacional. Bogotá, Impr. Nacional, 1914.
315 p.   (6446
Jones 1689.

-----. -----. Catálogo de publicaciones periódicas editadas en Colombia, en.-dic.,
1940. [Bogotá, 1941] 25 p.   (6447

-----. -----. Catálogo de todos los periódicos que existen desde su fundación hasta el
año de 1915, inclusive. Bogotá, Impr. Nacional, 1917. 366 p.   (6448
Jones 1684.

-----. -----. -----, hasta el año de 1935, in-
clusive. Edición oficial. Bogotá, Edit.
"El Gráfico", 1936. 2 v.   (6449
Jones 1685.

-----. -----. Catálogos de periódicos y libros de la Biblioteca Nacional de Bogotá.
Bogotá, 1916. 179 p.   (6450

-----. Ministerio de gobierno. Memoria.
Bogotá, Impr. Nacional, 1926. 444 p (6452
"Cuadros ... de periódicos que ven la luz
en el país": p. 399-425.---Jones 1702.

-----. Universidad, Bogotá. Facultad de
Agronomía. Biblioteca. Publicaciones periódicas y seriadas que ofrecemos en canje;
trabajo realizado por Amelia Rodríguez y
Gladys Rivillas. Medellín, 1963.   (6453
Cited in Peraza, Bibliografías corrientes
de la América latina, 1964, item 73.

-----. -----. -----, trabajo elaborado por
Amelia Rodríguez y Jilma Jaramillo. Medellín,
1963.   (6454
Cited in Peraza Ib., 1964, item 74.

-----. -----. Facultad de Medicina. Biblioteca. Inventario de revistas médicas y afines.
Bogotá, 1961. 42 p. mimeogr.   (6455

COLOMBIA. Universidad, Bogotá ... (Cont.)
Cited in Florén, Bibliografía bibliotecológica, 1961/1962, item 302.

HERNANDEZ DE CALDAS, Angela, and RODRIGUEZ,
Amelia. Lista de publicaciones en serie
que recibe la Biblioteca de la Facultad
Nacional de Agronomía de Medellín. Medellín
1954. 50 p. mimeogr.   (6456
Cited in Giraldo Jaramillo, p. 83.

HERNANDEZ DE CALDAS, Angela. Publicaciones
periódicas agropecuarias, botánicas y daso-
nómicas de América latina. Pasto, [1963]
79 p. (Universidad de Nariño. Instituto
Tecnológico Agrícola. Biblioteca. Ser.
bibliográfica, no. 4)   (6457

-----. Publicaciones periódicas y organismos
agropecuarios colombianos 1906-1962. Pasto,
1962. 72 p. (Universidad de Nariño. Instituto Tecnológico Agrícola. Ser. bibliográfica, no. 1)   (6458
Listing of 98 titles.

-----. -----, 1887-1963. Medellín, Edit. Universidad de Antioquia, 1964. 50 p.   (6459

-----, and RAMIREZ, Amalia. Selección de publicaciones periódicas recibidas en el Centro Nacional de Investigaciones Agrícolas
"Tibaitatá". Bogotá, 1955. 32 p.
mimeogr.   (6460

MARIN ARIAS, Stella, and OCAMPO JIMENEZ, Arturo. Catálogo de las revistas colombianas.
Medellín, Colombia, 1962. xvi, 32 p.   (6461
Cited in Florén, Bibliografía bibliotecológica, 1961/1962, item 240.

MARSHALL, Mary Louise. Serial holdings of
the medical school libraries of Colombia,
as of December 1959. Medellín, 1960.
36 p.   (6462
Cited in Revista interamericana de bibliografía, v. 10, p. 432.

MEDELLIN. Universidad de Antioquia. Biblioteca General. Hemeroteca. Catálogo de revistas extranjeras, por Arturo Ocampo Jiménez. Revisado por Stella Marín Arias y Ju-
lialba Hurtado Marulanda. [Medellín,
1963?] vii, 74 p. mimeogr.   (6463

-----. -----. Facultad de Medicina. Lista de
publicaciones periódicas existentes. Medellín, 1963. mimeogr.   (6464
Cited in Peraza Fichas, t. 7, item 536.

-----. -----. -----. Lista de publicaciones
periódicas colombianas de medicina y afines.
[Medellín] 1964. mimeogr.   (6465
Cited in Boletín de adquisiciones, Medellín, no. 10, p. 9, oct. 1964.

OTERO MUÑOZ, Gustavo. Primeros periódicos
colombianos (Senderos, Bogotá, v. 1,
p. 31-6, 1934)   (6466
     Jones 1750.

RODRIGUEZ, Amelia, and JARAMILLO, Jilma.
Lista de las publicaciones seriadas que se
encuentran en la Biblioteca de la Facultad
de Agronomía de Medellín. Medellín, Universidad Nacional de Colombia, 1963. (6467
     Cited in Boletín de adquisiciones, Mede-
llín, no. 10, p. 25, oct. 1963.

SERVICIO Técnico Agrícola Colombiano Americano, Bogotá, [Indice de las publicaciones
periódicas y seriadas que posee la Biblio-
teca] Bogotá, n.d. 25 p.
mimeogr.   (6468
     Cited in Florén, Bibliografía biblioteco-
lógica, 1961/1962, item 238.

VEGA FEBRES-CORDERO, Cecilia. Catalogo de
las publicaciones periódicas universitarias
colombianas. Medellín, Escuela Interamericana de Bibliotecología, 1964.
140 p.   (6469
     Thesis presented at the Escuela Interame-
ricana de Bibliotecología.

VEREZ DE PERAZA, Elena Luisa. Directorio de
revistas y periodicos de Medellín. Medellín, Ediciones Anuario Bibliográfico Cubano, 1962. 21 p. (Biblioteca del bibliotecario, 64) mimeogr.   (6470

COSTA RICA

ASOCIACION Costarricense de Bibliotecarios.
Catálogo colectivo de publicaciones periódicas extranjeras de ciencias sociales,
ciencias puras y ciencias aplicadas existentes en las principales bibliotecas de
Costa Rica, compilado por la Asociación
Costarricense de Bibliotecarios en colaboración con las principales bibliotecas del
país, mediante contrato celebrado con la
Unesco. San José, Departamento de Publicaciones, Universidad de Costa Rica, 1957.
xix, 469 p. mimeogr.   (6471

INTER-AMERICAN Institute of Agricultural
Sciences, Turrialba, Costa Rica. Publicaciones periódicas de la Biblioteca Conmemorativa Orton; una lista descriptiva.
Turrialba, 1964. 83 p. (Bibliotecología
y documentacion, no. 2)   (6472

CUBA

ATENEO de Cienfuegos, Cuba. Periódicos y
revistas de Cienfuegos, 1845-1940. Cienfuegos, Impr. "La Moderna", 1940. 17 p.
(Cuaderno de cultura popular, no.

ATENEO de Cienfuegos, Cuba ... (Cont.)
1)   (6473
     Lists 253 newspapers and magazines.

CUBA. Biblioteca Nacional. Publicaciones periódicas de fechas más recientes que se
hallan a disposición del público en la sala
de lectura. Habana, Impr. de la Biblioteca
Nacional, 1914. 14 p.   (6474

FINA GARCIA, Francisco. Bibliografía de la
prensa del término municipal de las Vegas.
Santiago de las Vegas, Tall. Tip. Miklef,
1941. [4] p.   (6475

HAVANA. Universidad. Escuela de Medicina.
Biblioteca. Catálogo general de revistas,
jun. 1937 y Suplemento no. 1, jul.-dic. 1937.
La Habana, 1937-1938. 2 v.   (6476
     List in three sections: (1) Alphabetical
by title, (2) by country, and (3) by subject.
---Jones 1845.

MOLINER, Israel M. Indice cronológico de la
prensa en Matanzas. Matanzas, 1955.
18 p.   (6477

PERAZA SARAUSA, Fermín. Directorio de revistas y periódicos de Cuba. Edición de 1942.
La Habana, Ed. Anuario Bibliográfico Cubano,
1942. 37 p. mimeogr.   (6478

-----. -----. La Habana, Ediciones Anuario
Bibliográfico Cubano, 1944. 58 p. (Biblioteca del bibliotecario, 3) mimeogr. (6479
     Cited in Anuario bibliográfico cubano,
1944. p. 51.

-----. -----. 1945. 56 p. (Biblioteca del
bibliotecario, 3) mimeogr.   (6480
     Cited in Anuario bibliográfico cubano,
1945, p. 80.

-----. -----. 1950. 54 p. (Biblioteca del
bibliotecario, 3)   (6481

-----. -----. Ed. de 1963. Gainesville, Fla.,
1963. 21 p. (Biblioteca del Bibliotecario,
3)   (6482

-----. -----. Ed. de 1964. Gainesville, Fla.,
1964. 32 p.   (6483

SANCHEZ ROIG, Mario. Bibliografía de la prensa médica cubana, 1840-1885. Habana [Impre-
so por "La Propagandista"] 1939. 25 p.(6484
     Jones 1906a. "Portadas de los periódicos
de medicina"; 1840-1885. Presented to the
VII Congreso de la Prensa Médica

TRELLES Y GOVIN, Carlos Manuel. Bibliografía
de la prensa cubana (de 1704 a 1900) y de
los periódicos publicados por cubanos en el
extranjero. (Revista bibliográfica cubana,
Habana, v. 2, p. 7-40, 81-114, 145-68, 209-

TRELLES Y GOVIN, Carlos Manuel... (Cont.)
68, 1936; v. 3, p. 67-100, 1939) (6485
To be continued. "When finished this will
contain information about 4,000 newspapers
and magazines." (S. E. Leavitt).---Jones
1916.

DOMINICAN REPUBLIC

DOMINICAN REPUBLIC. Universidad. Biblioteca.
Fuentes de información bibliográfica de la
Biblioteca de la Universidad de Santo Domin-
go. Ciudad Trujillo, 1949. 68 p. (Mono-
grafías bibliográficas, no. 3) (6486
Bibliographical journals, p. 1-30.

LUGO LOVATON, Ramón. Periódicos dominicanos
en el Archivo General de la Nación. Ciudad
Trujillo, Editora Montalvo, 1953.
49 p.   (6487

ECUADOR

ANDRADE CHIRIBOGA, Alfonso. Hemeroteca azuaya. Cuenca, El Mercurio, 1950. 2 v. (v.
1: 287 p.; v. 2: 245 p.)   (6488
Information about 128 periodicals published in the Province of Azuay during the
19th century.

ANUARIO de la prensa ecuatoriana, publicado
por la Biblioteca Municipal de Guayaquil,
año 1-3; 1892-1894. Guayaquil, 1893-1895.
3 v.   (6489
"Publicaciones de autores ecuatorianos o
relativas al Ecuador, impresas en el extranjero durante los años 1892 [-1894]": año 2,
1893, p. 81-3; año 3, 1894, p. 106-09.
"Diarios, periodicos y revistas": 1894,
p. 90-105. No more published?---Jones 1949.

ECUADOR. Dirección General de Correos. Nómina de publicaciones periódicas que se editan
en la República al 26 de mayo de 1931. Quito, Tall. Tip. Nacionales, 1931.
11 p.   (6490

JARAMILLO, Miguel Angel. Indice bibliográfico de las revistas de la Biblioteca Jaramillo de Escritos Nacionales. Cuenca, Casa
de la Cultura Ecuatoriana, Núcleo del Azuay,
1953. 180 p.   (6491
Cited in HLAS 19, item 6431. Reprinted
from Revista, Núcleo del Azuay, Casa de la
Cultura Ecuatoriana, t. 5, no. 7, p. 9-152,
1953.

MADERA, Luis F. Periódicos ibarreños. Ibarra,
Tip. El Comercio, 1927. 34 p.   (6492
Cited in Chaves, p. 14.

EL SALVADOR. Universidad. Facultad de Medicina. Biblioteca. Catálogo de revistas
científicas. Suplemento, no. 2. San Salvador, 1963. 36 p.   (6493

GUATEMALA

INSTITUTO de Nutrición de Centro América y Panamá, Guatemala. Lista de publicaciones periódicas técnicas y científicas existentes
en algunas bibliotecas de Centro América y
Panamá, compilada por Raquel Flores. Ed.
preliminar. [Guatemala] 1962. 96 p.
mimeogr.   (6494

-----. -----. Compilada por Raquel Flores y
Adelina Corado. [Guatemala] 1965.
180 p.   (6495

HAITI

HAITI. Archives nationales. Répertoire des
journaux. [n.p., 1958] 21 p.   (6496
Cited in Caribbean acquisitions, 1959,
p. 4. LC entry (1960, v. 2) describes item
as "typescript".

MEXICO

ACEVEDO ESCOBEDO, Antonio. Periódicos socia-
listas de México. (El Libro y el pueblo,
México, t. 13, p. 3-14, 1935)   (6497
Jones 2031.

ANDRADE, Vicente de Paula. Noticia de los
periódicos que se publican dentro y fuera
de la capital. México, 1901. 57 p. (6498
Jones 2056.

BIBLIOTECA Benjamín Franklin, México. Lista
de las revistas y otras publicaciones en
serie que se encuentran en la biblioteca.
México, D.F., 1944. 73 p. mimeogr. (6499

CARRASCO PUENTE, Rafael. Hemerografía de Za-
catezas, 1825-1950; con datos biográficos
de algunos periodistas zacatecanos. Prólogo de José María González de Mendoza.
México, Secretaría de Relaciones Exteriores, Departamento de Información para el
Extranjero, 1951. 203 p. (Monografías
bibliográficas mexicanas, 2a. ser., no.
4)   (6500

CENTRO de Documentación Científica y Técnica,
México. Lista de revistas científicas mexicanas. [México, D.F., 1953] 8 p. (6501

CENTRO de Documentación Científica y Técnica, México. Lista de publicaciones en su hemeroteca. México, D.F., Secretaría de Educación Pública, 1960. 110 p.   (6502

COMAS, Juan. El Boletín bibliográfico de antropología americana en su X aniversario. México, 1948. p. 89-97.   (6503
  Reprinted from Boletín bibliográfico de antropología americana, v. 10.

KER, Annita Melville. A survey of Mexican scientific periodicals, to which are appended some notes on Mexican historical periodicals. Baltimore, Md., Printed at the Waverly Pr., 1931. 105 p. (Publ. of the Harvey Bassler Foundation)   (6504
  Jones 2272.

MENDOZA LOPEZ, Margarita. Catálogo de publicaciones periódicas mexicanas. México, Centro Mexicano de Escritores, 1959. 262 p.   (6505

MERIDA, Yucatán. Biblioteca "Carlos R. Menéndez". Catálogo de las colecciones de periódicos de la Biblioteca ... desde la introducción de la imprenta hasta nuestros días; y de importantes periódicos metropilitanos. Mérida, 1955. 22 p.   (6506
  Cited in Boletín, Biblioteca Nacional, México, p. 57, en./mar. 1956.

MEXICO. Comisión Impulsora y Coordinadora de la Investigación Científica. Catálogo colectivo de publicaciones periódicas existentes en las bibliotecas de la ciudad de México. Sección medicina y ciencias biológicas. Editado por la Comisión Impulsora y Coordinadora de la Investigación Científica y la Biblioteca Benjamín Franklin. Dirigido por Rudolph H. Gjelsness, María Teresa Chávez y Helen M. Ranson. México, 1949. xviii, 494 p.   (6508

-----. Dirección General de Correos. Lista de publicaciones autorizadas como correspondencia de segunda clase, vigentes en todas las administraciones de la República, hasta el día 31 de julio de 1953. México, D.F., 1953. 53 p.   (6509
  Cited in Boletín Biblioteca Nacional, México, p. 60, abr./jun. 1955.

-----. -----. Noticia de las publicaciones registradas como artículos de segunda clase en las oficinas de correos de la República, hasta junio de 1912. México, D.F., "El Siglo XIX", 1912. 26 p.   (6510
  Cited in Gonzalez, item 147.

-----. Dirección General de Correos y Telégrafos. Lista general de publicaciones registradas como artículos de segunda clase, vigente hasta el 30 de noviembre de 1935. Mé-

MEXICO. Dirección General de... (Cont.) xico, D.F., 1936. 49 p.   (6511

-----. -----. -----, hasta el 31 de diciembre de 1938. México, D.F., D.A.P.P., 1939. 40 p.   (6512

-----. -----. -----, hasta el 31 de diciembre de 1940. México, D.F., 1941. 31 p.   (6513

-----. -----. Relación General de publicaciones registradas como artículos de segunda clase, vigentes hasta el 30 de abril de 1933 en todas las administraciones de correos y telégrafos de la República. México, D.F., 1933. 32 p.   (6514
  Cited in González, item 148.

-----. Instituto Nacional de Bellas Artes. Las revistas literarias de México. México, D.F., 1963. 254 p. (Ediciones del Instituto Nacional de Bellas Artes)   (6515

-----. -----. Departamento de Literatura. Las revistas literarias de México, 2a. ser. México, D.F., 1963. 209 p. (Ediciones del Instituto Nacional de Bellas Artes)   (6515a
  Cover date and colophon: 1964.

MEXICO (City) Universidad Nacional. Facultad de Medicina. Departamento de Fisiología. Biblioteca. Catálogo de la hemerobiblioteca. México, D.F., 1958. 206 p.   (6516

-----. Suplemento no. 1. Ciudad Universitaria, D.F., 1961. 35 p.   (6517

NOTICIA de las publicaciones periódicas existentes en los estados, territorios y Distrito federales. (Diario oficial, México, D.F., p. 2-4, 13 de abr., 1891)   (6518
  Jones 2380.

PAN AMERICAN Institute of Geography and History. Lista de publicaciones periódicas actualmente recibidas en la Biblioteca; List of periodicals currently received in the Library. México, D.F., 1961. 122 p.   (6519
  Compilers: Lea Salinas and Salvador Galán.

-----. Lista de publicaciones periódicas de la Biblioteca del Instituto Panamericano de Geografía e Historia. Parte II: títulos no recibidos actualmente. List of periodical publications in the Library of the Pan American Institute of Geography and History. Part II: titles not currently received. Preparada por Lea Salinas y Salvador Galán. México, D.F., 1962. 74 p.   (6520

LA PRENSA médica mexicana. México, D.F., 1963. 64 p.   (6521

SPELL, Jefferson Rea. Mexican literary perio-

SPELL, Jefferson Rea ... (Cont.)
dicals of the 19th century. (Proceedings,
Modern Language Association, v. 52, no. 1,
p. 272-312, Mar. 1937)   (6522
Jones 2515.

UNITED NATIONS Educational, Scientific and
Cultural Organization. Technical Assistance Mission in Mexico. Lista de revistas
científicas mexicanas. México, D.F.,
[1954?] 8 p.   (6523

PERU

LIMA. Universidad Mayor de San Marcos. Biblioteca. Periódicos nacionales del siglo
XIX, que existen en la Biblioteca Central,
por Alejandro Tumba Ortega. Lima, Compañia
de Impresiones y Publicidad, 1945.
146 p.   (6524

ODRIOZOLA, Manuel de. Catálogo de los periódicos nacionales existentes en la Biblioteca Nacional. (Boletín bibliográfico, Biblioteca Central, Universidad Mayor de San Marcos, Lima, t. 1, p. 170-79, 234-65,
1924)   (6525
Jones 2708.

PUERTO RICO

CARIBBEAN Organization, Hato Rey, Puerto Rico.
Library. Periodicals received in the Library of the Central Secretariat. Périodiques
recus à la Bibliotheque du Secrétariat Central. Hato Rey, Puerto Rico, 1963.
34 p.   (6526

URUGUAY

INVENTARIO de la prensa metropolitana, año
1933. (Revista del Instituto Histórico y
Geográfico del Uruguay, Montevideo, t. 10,
p. 529-38, 1933)   (6527
Jones 2843.

PRADERIO, Antonio. Indice cronológico de la
prensa periódica del Uruguay, 1807-1852.
Montevideo, 1962. 126 p. (Uruguay. Universidad. Instituto de Investigaciones
Históricas. Manuales auxiliares para la
investigación histórica, no. 3)   (6528

URUGUAY. Biblioteca Nacional. Catálogo de
publicaciones periódicas de Montevideo,
1950. Montevideo, 1951. 54 p.
mimeogr.   (6529

-----. -----. Catálogo de publicaciones pe-
riódicas; departamentos de interior, 1950.
[Montevideo, n.d.] 19 p. mimeogr. (6530
Compiled by José M. Díaz.

URUGUAY. Biblioteca Nacional. Lista de las
principales publicaciones periódicas del interior de la República O. del Uruguay. [Mon-
tevideo, 1949] 3 p. mimeogr.   (6531

-----. -----. Lista de los principales periódicos del interior. [Montevideo, 1962] 4 p.
mimeogr.   (6532
Cited in Musso 353.

-----. -----. Lista de las principales publicaciones periódicas editadas en Montevideo.
[Montevideo, 1949] 4 p. mimeogr.   (6533

-----. -----. -----. [Montevideo, 1955] 6 p.
mimeogr.   (6534
Cited in Musso 352.

-----. -----. Publicaciones periódicas cesa-
das, año 1948. [Montevideo, 1950] 11 p.
mimeogr.   (6535

-----. -----. Publicaciones periódicas inicia-
das, año 1948-1949. [Montevideo, 1950] 2 v.
(14, 8 p.) mimeogr.   (6536
Cited in Musso, 355-356.

-----. -----. Centro de Documentación Científica, Técnica y Económica. Catálogo de las
revistas científicas, técnicas y económicas
en curso de publicación en el Uruguay. Montevideo, 1961. 21 p. mimeogr.   (6537
A listing of 164 titles.

-----. -----. -----. Catálogo de las revistas
científicas, técnicas y económicas en curso
de publicación en el Uruguay en 1961, con
suplemento hasta 1963. Compilado por Maria
Luisa di Vita. Montevideo, 1963. 30 p.
mimeogr.   (6538

-----. -----. -----. Catálogo de las revistas
científicas, técnicas y económicas publicadas en Uruguay desde 1850. Montevideo, 1954.
29 p.   (6539
Compilers: Zulma Pucurull de Pérez Gomar,
Marta Nogueira Abella, Maria Teresa Carballal, and Elena Araujo, listing 358 titles.

-----. -----. -----. Guía de revistas biblio-
gráficas científicas, técnicas y económicas.
Montevideo, 1963. 19 p. mimeogr.   (6540
Musso 39, also 360.

URUGUAY. Biblioteca Nacional. Centro de Documentación Científica, Técnica y Económica.
Inventario de las revistas científicas, técnicas y económicas existentes en las bibliotecas del Uruguay.   (6541
Contents: Fasc. I, Biblioteca Nacional,
por Zulma Pucurull de Pérez Gomar. - II, Biblioteca Artigas Washington, por Ermelinda
Acerenza. - III, Biblioteca del Instituto de
Investigaciones de Ciencias Biológicas, por
Elsa Trinkle y Eliana Sánchez Rosas. - IV,

URUGUAY. Biblioteca Nacional ... (Cont.)
Biblioteca del Servicio Cooperativo Interamericano de Salud Pública, por Margarita Mon-
tedónico. - V, Biblioteca del Centro de Cooperación Científica de la Unesco para América Latina. - VI, Biblioteca de la Facultad
de Humanidades y Ciencias, por Esther Dosil
de Ramírez, Matilde Servetti de Torrano y
Leonor Pessaj. - VII, Biblioteca de la Dirección de Agronomía, por Sofía Naville de Mo-
rassi; Biblioteca de la Facultad de Agronomía, por Esther Cabarco; Biblioteca del Servicio de Información y Prensa del Ministerio
de Ganadería y Agricuultura, por J. F. Tajes.
- VIII, Asociación Odontológca, por Marta
Nogueira. - IX, Biblioteca de la Facultad de
Veterinaria, por Marta Nogueira. - X, Biblioteca de la Sociedad de Arquitectos del Uruguay, por Z. Pucurull de Pérez Gomar y Marta
Nogueira; Biblioteca de la Facultad de Arquitectura, por María S. de Toledo y Juanita
Blasco Moll de Sarrasqueta. - XI, Biblioteca
de la Asociación de Química y Farmacia, por
María Teresa Castilla; Biblioteca de la Aso-
ciación de Químicos Industriales, por Esther
Cabarco; Biblioteca del Instituto Sudameri-
cano del Petróleo, por Esther Cabarco. - XII,
Biblioteca del Departamento de Bio-física de
la Facultad de Medicina, por Z. Pucurull y
Marta Nogueira; Biblioteca del Centro de Es-
tudios Laríngeos y Biblioteca del Instituto
de Endocrinología, por María Teresa Castilla.
- XIII, Biblioteca de la Sociedad Uruguaya de
Pediatría y Biblioteca del Instituto de Clínica Pediátrica e Higiene Infantil Dr. Luis
Morquio, por S. Scosería; Biblioteca del Hospital Pedro Visca, por Z. Pucurull. - XIV,
Biblioteca del Instituto de Tisiología, por
Z. Pucurull. - XV, Biblioteca de la Facultad
de Odontología, por N. Rezzano y E. Araújo. -
XVI, Biblioteca de la Facultad de Ingeniería,
por N. Zigler de Cabrera. - XVII, Biblioteca
del Instituto de Matemáticas y Estadística,
por [Maria Teresa] Carballal. - XVIII, Biblioteca de la Facultad de Ciencias Económicas, por Z. Pucurull; Biblioteca del Instituto de Estadística, por Z. Pucurull; Biblioteca del Instituto de Teoría y Política Económicas, por Z. Pucurull. - XIX, Biblioteca del
Instituto de Anatomía Normal; Biblioteca del
Instituto de Anatomía Patológica y Parasito-
lógica; Biblioteca del Instituto de Bacteriología; Biblioteca del Instituto de Fisiología; Biblioteca del Instituto de Industria
Animal; Biblioteca del Instituto de Zootécni-
ca; Biblioteca del Contralor de la Leche. -
XX, Biblioteca del Instituto de Higiene, por
Marta Nogueira Abella, Nelly Huertas, y Zulma
Pucurull. Data taken from prospectus.

-----. Consejo Nacional de Enseñanza Primaria
y Normal. Indice de los periódicos y revistas escolares del Uruguay, años 1949-1950.
Montevideo, n.d. 2 p. mimeogr.   (6542
Cited in Musso 411.

URUGUAY. Consejo Nacional de Gobierno. Nómina de las principales publicaciones que se
editan en el país, al 1o. de marzo de 1955.
[Montevideo] n.d. 5 p. mimeogr.   (6543
Cited in Musso 412.

-----. -----. [Montevideo, 1958] 6 p.
mimeogr.   (6444
Cited in Musso 413.

-----. Instituto de Investigaciones de Ciencias Biológicas. Biblioteca. Publicaciones
periódicas: revistas y seriados gratuitos:
162 títulos. [Montevideo] 1963. 17 p.
mimeogr.   (6545
Compiler: Elsa Trinkle.

-----. -----. -----. Publicaciones periódicas
recibidas, indizadas y no indizadas en
"Current Contents". [Montevideo], 1963.
8 p. mimeogr.   (6546
Compilers: Elsa Trinkle and Blanca Ferrey-
ra Modernell.

-----. Poder Legislativo. Biblioteca. Guía
de diarios y periódicos archivados en la Ca-
mareta Salón no. 20: obras reservadas.
Montevideo, n.d. 37 p. (Referencia no.
31)   (6547

-----. -----. -----. Lista de anales, boleti-
nes y revistas que se reciben actualmente.
Montevideo [1938] 37 p.   (6548
Contents: - I, Indice por países y loca-
lidades. - II, Indice por orden alfabético.
---Jones 2850c.

-----. -----. -----. -----. Montevideo, 1939.
32 p.   (6549

-----. -----. -----. -----, 1948/1959. Montevideo, 1949-1959. 2 v. mimeogr.   (6550
1959 issue is Referencia, no. 35.

-----. -----. -----. -----. Montevideo, 1939.
17 p.   (6551
Another issue in 1959 (12 p.) as Referencia
no. 34.

ZORRILLA DE SAN MARTIN, Juan. "El Bien Públi-
co"; diario católico. Montevideo, El Bien
Público, 1878. 30 p.   (6552
Cited in Musso 496.

VENEZUELA

BONFANTI, Celestino, and GOMEZ M., E. Fuentes
periódicas de información bibliográfica. Ma-
racay, 1963. 9 p. mimeogr.   (6553
Basic list of materials available in the
Library of the Facultad de Agronomía, Universidad Central de Venezuela, including also
titles available in the libraries of the Facultad de Ciencias Veterinarias and the Cen-

PERIODICALS

BONFANTI, Celestino, and GOMEZ M., E ...(Cont.)
tro de Investigaciones Agronómicas.

FERNANDEZ, Alicia de. Venezuelan medical and
related periodicals, libraries and societies.
Publicaciones periódicas venezolanas de medicina y ciencias afines; bibliotecas y sociedades. Caracas [1963?] 9 p.   (6554
   Report to the Second International Congress
on Medical Librarianship, Washington, D.C.,
June 16-22, 1963.

FERNANDEZ ALBENDIN, Alicia de. Catálogo de publicaciones periódicas existentes hasta jul.
1961. Caracas, Instituto Nacional de Higiene, 1961.   (6555
   Cited in Boletín de adquisiciones, Medellín, p. 13, jul. 1963.

LOPEZ DE SAGREDO Y BRU, José. Indice de periódicos y periodistas del Estado Zulia,
desde 1823 hasta 1948. [Maracaibo, Tip.
Cervantes] 1948. 142 p.   (6556

MACHADO, José Eustaquio. Lista de algunos periódicos que vieron la luz en Caracas en
1808 a 1900. Caracas, Tip. Vargas, 1929.
74 p.   (6557
   An addition of 16 titles to this list is
included in Febres Cordero's Archivo de historia y variedades (Caracas, 1931, v. 2,
p. 113-15) Machado describes 127 periodicals.---Jones 2928.

VENEZUELA. Ministerio de Fomento. Prensa de
la República. (Gaceta oficial, Caracas,
año 61, núm. extraordinario, p. 1-21, 4 de
feb. 1933)   (6558
   Gives title, year of founding, place,
number of issues, character, and frequency.
---Jones 2068.

-----. Ministerio de Relaciones Exteriores.
Periódicos y revistas de la República.
[Caracas] 1947. 15 p.   (6559
   Cited in Anuario bibliográfico venezolano,
1947/48, item 915.

VENEZUELA. Ministerio de Sanidad y Asistencia
Social. Biblioteca. Catálogo de publicacio-
nes periódicas existentes hasta julio 1961.
Elaborado por: Alicia de Fernández Albendín.
Caracas, Instituto Nacional de Higiene, 1961.
146 p.   (6560

-----. -----. Indice alfabético de las revistas existentes, Caracas, 1948- .   (6561
   Compiler: Alicia de Fernández Albendín.

-----. -----. Nómina de las revistas que existen en la Biblioteca y lista de las que se
reciben en la actualidad. Caracas, 1942.
23 p. mimeogr.   (6562
   Cited in Anuario bibliográfico venezolano, 1942, item 538.

-----. -----. Venezuelan medical and related
periodicals, libraries and societies; report
to the Second International Congress on Medical Librarianship, Washington, D.C., 1963.
Caracas, 1963.   (6563

-----. Universidad Central. Catálogo de revistas científicas. Caracas, 1959.
110 p.   (6564

-----. -----. Facultad de Ingeniería. Biblioteca. Indice alfabético de las revistas existentes hasta diciembre de 1963.
Caracas, 1963.   (6564a
   Boletín de adquisiciones, Medellín, p. 12.
mayo 1966.

-----. -----. Instituto Anatómico. Biblioteca de Ciencias Morfológicas. Catálogo
de libros y revistas. Caracas, 1964. (6564b

-----. -----. Instituto de Medicina Experimental. Biblioteca. Indice alfabético de
las revistas existentes. [Caracas, 1958]
49 p.   (6565

PHILOSOPHY

ARANGO BETANCOUR, Ignacio, and CADAVID ARANGO,
Carlos. Catálogo de los libros de filosofía
existentes en las bibliotecas de la Universidad de Antioquia. Medellín, 1962. 125 p.
mimeogr.   (6566
   Cited in Peraza, Fichas, t. 4-6, item 35.

ARCE, David N. Sobre lo existencial y algunos "ismos". Ensayo de respuesta y amago
bibliográfico; 2a. ed. México, D.F. [Edit.
Jus] 1954. 43 p.   (6567
   Originally published in Boletín, Bibliote-

ARCE, David N. Sobre lo... (Cont.)
ca Nacional, México, D.F., 2a. ép., 5(1):
21-56, en./mar. 1954.

ARGENTINA. Comisión Nacional de Cooperación
Intelectual. Bibliografía argentina de pu-
blicaciones filosóficas, año 1937 a 1943.
Buenos Aires, 1943. 31 p.   (6567a

BRUGGER, Ilse. Filosofía alemana traducida al
español. Repertorio bibliográfico. Buenos
Aires, Universidad de Buenos Aires, Facultad

BRUGGER, Ilse. Filosofía alemana... (Cont.)
de Filosofía y Letras, Instituto de Estudios Germánicos, 1942. vii, 195 p. (6568
    Luis Juan Guerrero and Francisco Romero,
collaborators.

-----. Primer suplemento. Buenos Aires, Coni, 1954. 74 p.   (6568
    Cited in Catálogo, Instituto Biblioteco-
lógico, item 531.

BUENOS AIRES (Province). Instituto Bibliográfico. Bibliografía argentina de filosofía, obras y articulos publicados durante
1960, no. 2, nov. 1961. La Plata, Provincia de Buenos Aires, Ministerio de Educación, Instituto Bibliográfico, [1962]
230 p.   (6570
    No. 1 published under the title: Biblio-
grafía argentina de filosofía y ciencias.
See item 6571.

-----. Instituto Bibliográfico. Bibliografía argentina de filosofía y ciencias de
la educacion; obras y artículos publicados,
1958/1959- , no. 1- , jun. 1960- , La Plata, Ministerio de Educación, Dirección de
Enseñanza Superior Media y Vocacional,
1960- .   (6571
    No. 1 (1959), 133 p.; no. 2 (1961), 230 p.
Beginning with no. 2 title changed to Bi-
biografía argentina de filosofía, and main-
taining the same numbering. The part of education was published separately under title:
Bibliografía argentina de ciencias de la
educación.

CHILE. Universidad. Facultad de Filosofía
y Educacion. Anuario bibliografico.
1960- . Santiago, 1962.   (6572
    Director: 1960- , Alberto Villalón Gal-
dames. Last issue received at DPU: 1962.

ENDARA, Julio. La cultura filosófica en el
Ecuador durante la colonia. (Revista de
filosofía, Buenos Aires, año 6, no. 6, 400-
29, nov. 1920)   (6573
    Jones 1977.

GARCIA RAMOS, Dagoberto, and BENAVIDES BALBIN,
Alberto. Bibliografía de filosofía, 1936-
1948. Lima, Compañía de Impresiones y Publicidad, 1949. 28 p.   (6574
    Reprinted from Boletín bibliográfico,
Universidad Mayor de San Marcos, Lima, año
22, 19(3/4) dic. 1949. Title in Boletín
bibliográfico: "Bibliografía de religión y
filosofía, 1936-1948".

KINNAIRD, Lucia Burk, and NICHOLS, Madeline
W. A bibliography of articles in psychology: Nosotros, v. 1-76. [N.Y.?, 1935?]
p. 237-42.
    Jones 336. Offprinted from Psychological
bulletin, v. 32, no. 3, Mar. 1935. The

KINNAIRD, Lucia Burk, and NICHOLS ... (Cont.)
compilers also published the following bibliographies of articles in Nosotros: on history
in Hispanic American historical review, v. 14,
p. 378-416, 1934; on philology in Philologi-
cal quarterly, Jul. 1934, Oct. 1935; general
literary criticism in Publications of the
Institute of French studies, Columbia University, 1935; on sociology in American journal
of sociology, Jan. 1935; and on education in
Bulletin of bibliography May-Aug., Sept.-
Dec. 1935, Jan.-Apr. and May-Aug. 1936.

LASALLE, Edmundo. Philosophic thought in Latin
America; a partial bibliography. [Washington,
D.C., Division of Intellectual Cooperation,
Pan American Union, 1941] 17 p.   (6576

MARTINEZ GOMEZ, Luis. Bibliografía filosófica
española hiapanoamericana (1940-1958) Barcelona, Juan Flores, 1961. xxv, 500 p. (Pen-
samientos; ser. Difusión, v. 1)   (6577
    Cited in Revista Interamericana de Biblio-
grafía, v. 12, p. 326.

MEDELLIN. Escuela Interamericana de Bibliotecología. Bibliografía B-2: Filosofía, Psicología y Religión. [Medellín, n.d.] 2 p.
mimeogr.   (6578

MONDOLFO, Rodolfo. Guía bibliográfica de la filosofía antigua. Buenos Aires, Losada, 1960.
102 p. (Colección Filosófica)   (6579

PARRA, Caracciolo. Filosofía universitaria venezolana, 1788-1821. Caracas, Parra León Hermanos, 1933. 280 p.   (6580
    Indices, fuentes y bibliografia: p. 243-78.
A second edition was published in 1934.---
Jones 2940.

PINILLA, Norberto. Bibliografía de estética.
Santiago, Chile, Edit. M. Barros Borgoño,
1939. 64 p.   (6580a

SERVETTI DE TORRANO, Matilde. Aportes bibliográficos al tema: existencialismo. Fuentes,
obras, crítica, etc. Montevideo, 1951. 40 p.
(Uruguay. Universidad. Facultad de Humanidades y Ciencias, no. 3) mimeogr.   (6581
    Cited in Musso 97.

VALVERDE TELLEZ, Emeterio. Apuntaciones históricas sobre la filosofia en México. México,
D.F., Herrero Hermanos, 1896. xiv, 477p (6582
    Cited in Iguiniz, p. 458.

-----. Bibliografía filosófica mexicana. México, D.F., Tip. de la Viuda de F. Díaz de
León, 1907. 218 p.   (6583
    Jones 2557.

-----. -----. 2a. ed., notablemente aum. León,
1913. 2 v.   (6584
    Jones 2560

PHILOSOPHY

VALVERDE TELLEZ, Emeterio. Crítica filosófica o estudio bibliográfico y crítico de
las obras de filosofía escritas, traducidas o publicadas en México desde el siglo

VALVERDE TELLEZ, Emeterio. Crítica...(Cont.)
16 hasta nuestros días. México, D.F., 1904.
497 p.   (6585
Jones 2561.

POLITICAL SCIENCE

GENERAL

AMERICAN Committee on Dependent Territories.
Bibliografía selecta sobre territorios dependientes en América y otros asuntos conexos. Washington, D.C., Unión Panamericana,
1949. 83 p.   (6586

ARGENTINA. Congreso. Biblioteca. Gobierno
de facto; validez de decretos-leyes (bibliografía). Buenos Aires, 1963. 39 p. (Serie
Antecedentes para la documentación parlamentaria, no. 7)   (6587

BOWMAN, Isaiah. Possibilities of settlement
in Latin America. (In the author's Limits
of land settlement. New York, Council of
Foreign Relations, 1937. p. 293-
337)   (6588
Bibliography by K. J. Pelzer: p. 339-72
(Latin America: p. 364-72.---Jones 71a.

BROWN, Lyle C. A selected bibliography on
Latin American government and politics,
compiled with the assistance of Sharon
Tolbert and students enrolled in political
science 304. [Waco, Tex.] Baylor University, 1963. iv, 33 p. mimeogr.   (6589

CENTRO Brasileiro de Pesquisas Educacionais.
Bibliografia sôbre educação democrática.
Rio de Janeiro, 1961. 17 p.
mimeogr.   (6590
Cited in Doria 33.

CORNELIUS, Carl Gustav. Die foederalistischen
staatsverfassungen Lateinamerikas. Berlin,
F. Vahlen, 1932. 88 p.   (6591
Quellen-verzeichnis: p. 84-5.---Jones
110.

GLASER, Karl. Erwerb und verlust der staat-
sangehörigkeit in Hispano-Amerika. Leipzig,
R. Noske, 1930. xi, 113 p. (Abhandlungen
des Instituts für Politische Auslandskunde
an der Universität Leipzig, hf. 9)   (6592
Literatur: p. vii-xi.---Jones 165.

INTERNATIONAL bibliography of political scien-
ce, v. 1- , 1953- . [Paris, London]
Unesco.   (6593
Includes Latin American countries.

KANTOR, Harry. Bibliografía para los estudiantes del segundo curso del Instituto de

KANTOR, Harry. Bibliografía ... (Cont.)
Educación Política. San José, Costa Rica,
1961. 69 p.   (6594

LARROYO, Francisco. El mundo de socialismo;
una bibliografía comentada de las publicaciones sobre el socialismo. México, D.F.,
Edit. "Logos", 1937- . v. 1- . (Biblioteca de actualidades - ciencias socia-
les)   (6595
Jones 2278.

LAUERHASS, Ludwig I. Communism in Latin America; a bibliography. The post-war years
(1945-1960) Los Angeles, Center of Latin
American Studies, University of California,
1962. 78 p.   (6596

MUNRO, Dana Gardner. The five republics of
Central America, their political and economic
development and their relations with the
United States; edited by David Kinley. New
York, Oxford Univ. Pr., 1918. 332 p. (Car-
negie Endowment for International Pea-
ce)   (6597
Bibliography: p. 321-26.---Jones 1244.

PAN AMERICAN UNION. Communism, Fascism and
Nazism in Latin America; bibliography.
[Washington, D.C., 1939] 9 p.   (6598
Caption title.

-----. Emancipation of Argentine Republic,
Chile and Peru. [Washington, D.C., 1925]
8 p. mimeogr.   (6599
Cited in PAU Bibliographies, p. 29.

ROSARIO, Arg. Universidad Nacional del Litoral. Instituto de Investigaciones Jurídico-
Políticas. Derecho político; teoría general del estado, ciencia política, historia
de las doctrinas políticas. Santa Fé, 1942.
200 p. (Ser. bibliográfica, 1)   (6600

SLADE, William Franklin. The federation of
Central America. Worcester, Mass. [1917]
p. 79-150, 204-75.   (6601
Selected bibliography: p. 270-75. Reprinted from the Journal of race development,
v. 8.---Jones 1253.

U.S. Library of Congress. Legislative Reference Service. World communism; a selected
annotated bibliography (bibliographic materials through September 1963) Prepared at

U.S. Library of Congress ... (Cont.)
the request of the Subcommittee to Inves-
tigate the Administration of the Internal
Security Act and Other Internal Security
Laws of the Committee on the Judiciary,
United States Senate. Washington, D.C.,
Govt. Print. Off., 1964. 394 p. (88th
Congress, 2d sess. Senate. Document no.
69)   (6602
     Communism in Latin America, p. 304-18,
item 2434-2545.

URUGUAY. Poder legislativo. Biblioteca.
Comunismo; material existente en la Biblioteca. Montevideo, 1949. 15,5,25 p. (Refe-
rencia, 5)   (6603

VICUÑA MACKENNA, Benjamín. Estudios bibliográficos relativos a la confederación, independencia y planes de monarquía en la
América española. (Colección de ensayos y
documentos relativos a la unión y confederación de los pueblos hispano-americanos,
publicada por la Sociedad de la Unión Americana de Santiago de Chile. Santiago, Impr.
Chilena, 1862. p. 379-92.   (6604

WILLIAMS, Mary Wilhelmine. The people and
politics of Latin America. Boston, Ginn
& Co., 1930. 845 p.   (6605
     Bibliography: p. 799-820.---Jones 541.

-----. New ed. Boston, New York, Ginn & Co.,
1938. 888 p.   (6606
     Bibliography: p. 837-61.---Jones 542.

ARGENTINA

ARGENTINA. Congreso. Biblioteca. Régimen
de partidos políticos. Buenos Aires, 1962.
various paging. (Serie: Legislación argen-
tina)   (6606a

-----. Ministerio de Agricultura y Ganadería.
Depto. de Bibliotecas. Catálogo centraliza-
do de la Biblioteca Justicialista. Buenos
Aires, 1955. 186 p. (Circular bibliográ-
fica interna, no. 5)   (6607

BUENOS AIRES. Biblioteca Nacional del Docente y del Estudiante Argentinos. Catalogo
de ciencias políticas y sociales; derecho y
legislación. Buenos Aires, Biblioteca Nacional de Maestros, 1939. 206 p. (6608
     Cited in Catálogo, Instituto Biblioteco-
lógico, item 906.

GIL, Octavio. Autonomía provincial, historia
y concepto constitucional. Buenos Aires,
J. Menéndez, 1928. 198 p.   (6609
     Bibliografía: p. 189-93.---Jones 707.

GOMEZ, Hernán Félix. Los últimos sesenta
años de democracia y gobierno en la provin-

GOMEZ, Hernán Félix. Los últimos... (Cont.)
cia de Corrientes, 1870-1930. Buenos Aires,
L. J. Rosso, 1931. 355 p.   (6610
     Obras del doctor Hernán F. Gómez: p. 347-
55.---Jones 710.

ROSARIO, Arg. Universidad Nacional del Litoral. Instituto de Investigaciones Jurídico-
Políticas. Bibliografía sobre partidos políticos. Santa Fé [1943?] 39 p.
mimeogr.   (6611
     Cited in Catálogo, Instituto Bibliotecoló-
gico, item 548.

UNION Cívica Radical. Comité de la Provincia
de Buenos Aires. Bibliografía para el estudio del radicalismo. Buenos Aires, 1952.
29 p.   (6611a
     Cited in Geoghegan, 1101.

-----. Comité Nacional. Guía de lecturas para conocimiento de la historia y desarrollo
del pensamiento político y de la doctrina
de la Unión Cívica Radical. Buenos Aires,
1954. 37 p.   (6611b
     Cited in Geoghegan, 1102.

BOLIVIA

CACERES BILBAO, Pío. Bolivia, el Senado Nacional (álbum); bosquejo histórico parlamen-
tario, 1825-1925. La Paz, Lit. e Impr. Uni-
das, 1927. 584, 197 p.   (6612
     Jones 908. Contains biographical infor-
mation with citations of works published.

CLEVEN, Nels Andrew. The political organization of Bolivia. Washington, D.C., Carnegie Institution of Washington, 1940.
253 p.   (6613
     Bibliography: p. 230-40.---Jones 909a.

PAZ, Franklin Antezana. Le régime parlemen-
taire en Bolivie. Paris, Les Editions
Domat-Montchrestien, 1933. 169 p.   (6614
     Bibliographie: p. 163-66.---Jones 930.

BRAZIL

BRAZIL. Congresso. Câmara dos Deputados.
Livro do centenario da Camara dos Deputados
(1826-1926) Rio de Janeiro, Empreza Brasil
Editora, 1926. 3 v.   (6615
     Jones 986.

HUNSCHE, Karl Heinrich. Der brasilianische
integralismus, geschichte und wesen der
faschistischen bewegung Brasiliens.
Stuttgart, W. Kohlhammer, 1938. 247p. (6616
     Literatur: p. 243-47.---Jones 1058.

PICCHIA, Paulo Menotti del. Soluções nacionaes: I. A crise de democracia. II. A cri-

PICCHIA, Paulo Menotti del ... (Cont.)
se brasileira. III Soluções nacionaes.
Rio de Janeiro, J. Olympio, 1935. 295 p.
(Problemas políticos contemporaneos, no.
7)   (6617
    Bibliographia: p. 289-95.---Jones 1101.

SÃO PAULO (State). Congresso. Câmara dos De-
putados. - Câmara dos Deputados do estado de
São Paulo, 1919-1924. Organisado por Abilio
Fontes Junior e Antonio C. da Fonseca. S.
Paulo, Esc. Prof. Salesianas do Lyceu C. de
Jesus, 1924. 276 p.   (6618
    Includes biographical sketches.---Jones
1187.

CHILE

URZUA VALENZUELA, Germán. Bibliografía de los
partidos políticos chilenos. [Santiago?]
1961. 55 p. (Colección: Fuentes del pensamiento político chileno, no. 1)   (6619

MEXICO

CALLCOTT, Wilfrid Hardy. Liberalism in Mexico, 1857-1929. Stanford, Calif., Stanford
University, 1931. 410 p.   (6620
    Bibliography: p. 384-401.---Jones 2108.

COSIO VILLEGAS, Daniel. La historiografía política del México moderno. México, D.F.,
1953. 91 p.   (6621
    Reprinted from Memoria del Colegio Nacio-
nal.

ORTIZ DE AYALA, Tadeo. México considerado como
nación independiente y libre, o sean Algunas
indicaciones sobre los deberes más esenciales
de los mexicanos. Burdeos, Impr. de C. La-
walle, sobrino, 1832. 598 p.   (6622
    Chapter 5, De los beneficios del cultivo de
las ciencias y las artes (p. 173-256) contains
a review of authors, artists, etc., from the
15th to the 19th centuries.---Jones 2396.

PANAMA

PANAMA. Secretaría de Gobierno y Justicia.
Memoria, 1926. Panamá, Tip. "La Moderna",
1926. 328 p.   (6623
    Panamá en el Archivo de Indias: p. 301-
28.---Jones 1355.

PARAGUAY

GONZALEZ, Juan Natalicio. Evolución política
y literaria del Paraguay. (Revista americana de Buenos Aires, Buenos Aires, año 11,
p. 5-18, 1935)   (6624
    Jones 2610.

PERU

AYARZA, Víctor E. Reseña histórica del Senado del Perú, 1821-1921. Lima, Impr. T.
Aguirre, 1921. 309, cxliv, 147, xxv,
lxi p.   (6625
    Contains biographical information.---Jones
2626.

DELGADO, Luis Humberto. Historia del Senado
del Perú, 1829-1929, mandada escribir por
la Honorable Cámara. Lima, American Ex-
press, 1929. 223 p.   (6626
    Contains biographical information.---Jones
2652.

KANTOR, Harry. Sources for the study of the
Peruvian Aprista movement. Gainesville,
Fla., Dept. of Reference and Bibliography,
Univ. of Florida Libraries, 1955. 39 p.
(Bibliographic ser., no. 2)   (6627

VIDAURRE, Pedro N. Relación cronológica de
los alcaldes que han presidido el Ayuntamiento de Lima desde su fundación hasta nuestros días. Formada de orden de la Alcaldía,
y en vista de documentos auténticos, que
originales se conservan en el archivo de la
ciudad. Lima, Impr. de J. F. Solís, 1889.
109 p.   (6628
    Jones 2773.

PUERTO RICO

DIFFIE, Bailey Wallys, and DIFFIE, Justine
Whitfield. Porto Rico, a broken pledge.
New York, The Vanguard Pr., 1931.
252 p.   (6628
    Bibliography: p. 221-33.---Jones 2789.

VENEZUELA

GRASES, Pedro. Traducciones de interés po-
lítico-cultural en la época de la independencia de Venezuela. Caracas, 1961.
59 p.   (6630
    "Fue publicado este estudio en el t. 2 de
la serie sobre El movimiento emancipador de
Hispanoamérica preparada y editada por la
Mesa Redonda de la Comisión de Historia del
Instituto Panamericano de Geografía e Historia, Caracas, 1961".

WEST INDIES

CUNDALL, Frank. Political and social distur-
bance in the West Indies. A brief account
and bibliography. Kingston, Pub. for the
Institute of Jamaica by the Educational
Supply Co., London, H. Sotheran & Co., 1906.
35 p.   (6631
    Jones 2987.

INSTITTE of Jamaica, Kingston. West India
Reference Library. A list of books on West
Indian Federation. [Kingston, 1957] 12 p.
mimeogr. (6632
    Compiled by Ursula Raymond.

INSTITUTE of Jamaica, Kingston. A list of
books on West Indian Federation. [2d ed.]
Kingston, West Indian Reference Library,
1962. 47 p. (6633
    Compiled by Anne Benewick.

PRINTING

GENERAL

ALESSIO ROBLES, Vito. La primera imprenta en
las provincias internas de oriente, Texas,
Tamaulipas, Nuevo Leon y Coahuila. México,
Antigua Librería Robredo, de J. Porrúa e
Hijos, 1939. 79 p. (6634
    Jones 2042a.

BROWN. University. John Carter Brown Library. Books printed in South America elsewhere than at Lima before 1801. [Boston,
1908] 1 p. (6635

CANTER, Juan. La imprenta en el Río de la
Plata. Buenos Aires, Impr. de la Universidad, 1938. 73 p. (6636

CASTAÑEDA, Carlos Eduardo. The beginning of
printing in America. (Hispanic American historical review, Durham, N. C., v. 20,
p. 671-85, 1940) (6637
    Jones 87.

FAHEY, Herbert printing in California, from
its beginning in the Mexican territory to
statehood. San Francisco, Book Club of California, 1956. 141 p. (6638

FURLONG CARDIFF, Guillermo. Historia y bibliografía de las primeras imprentas rioplatenses, 1700-1850. Buenos Aires, 1953-1959.
3 v. (6639
    Imprint of v. 1 (596 p.): Edit. Guaranía.
Contains: La imprenta en las reducciones
del Paraguay, 1700-1727; la imprenta en Córdoba, 1765-1767; la imprenta en Buenos Aires,
1780-1784; Imprint of v. 2 (596 p.): Librería del Plata. Contains: La imprenta en
Buenos Aires, 1785-1807. v. 3 contains: La
imprenta en Buenos Aires, 1808-1810; la imprenta en Montevideo, 1807-1810.

-----. Los jesuítas y la imprenta en la América Latina. Buenos Aires, Academia Literaria del Plata, 1940. 58 p. (6640
    Reprinted from Estudios, Buenos Aires,
p. 237-60, mar. 1940; p. 311-36. abr. 1940.

-----. Orígenes de la imprenta en las regiones
del Río de la Plata. Buenos Aires, 1918.
21 p. (6641
    From Estudios, v. 15, p. 96-114, 1918. Cf.
also his Notas y aclaraciones al estudio so-

FURLONG CARDIFF, Guillermo. Orígenes ...(Cont.)
bre "Los orígenes de la imprenta" (Estudios,
v. 17, p. 16-22, 381-84, 1919) Contains the
bibliography of the press of the Jesuit missions. The author has published various bibliographical articles in periodicals: In
Estudios, Buenos Aires: La imprenta jesuítica de Córdoba, 1763-1767 (t. 20, p. 241-
48); Las bibliotecas jesuíticas en las reducciones del Paraguay y del Chaco (t. 28,
p. 469-75); Nuevos datos sobre los orígenes
del arte tipográfico en la Argentina (t. 49,
p. 340-46). In Boletín del Instituto de Investigaciones Históricas: El p. Martín
Dobrizhoffer (t. 6, p. 417-84); El p. Joaquín Camaño Bazán (t. 7, p. 233-85); Impresos varios de la imprenta del Ejército republicano 1826-1828 (t. 10, p. 159-64, 166-75);
Antiguos periódicos argentinos en la Biblioteca Nacional de Montevideo (t. 14, p. 111-
19).---Jones 699.

-----. Orígenes del arte tipográfico en América, especialmente en la República Argentina. Buenos Aires, Edit. Huarpes, 1947.
225 p. (6642

GOMEZ RODELES, Cecilio. Imprenta de los antiguos Jesuítas en Europa, América y Filipinas
durante los siglos XVI al XVIII; 2a. ed.,
corr. y aum. Madrid, Sucesores de Rivadeneyra, 1910. 32 p. (6643
    Articles first published in Razón y fe,
t. 25-27, 1909-1910.---Jones 170.

GRASES, Pedro. La primera editorial inglesa
para Hispanoamérica. Caracas, 1955.
30 p. (6644
    Reprinted from Revista Shell, Caracas, no.
15, jun. 1955.

HARDING, George Laban. A census of California
Spanish imprints, 1833-1845. San Francisco,
1933. 18 p. (6645
    Reprinted from the Quarterly of the Cali-
fornia Historical Society, v. 12, no. 2.---
Jones 2235.

HARRISSE, Henry. Introducción de la imprenta
en América, con una bibliografía de las obras
impresas en aquel hemisferio desde 1540 a
1600. Madrid, Rivadeneyra, 1872. 59p.(6646
    A revised translation, with additions, of
Harrisse's Brief disquisition concerning the

HARRISSE, Henry. Introducción... (Cont.)
early history of printing in America,
drawn from passages in the Biblioteca americana vetustissima.---Jones 190.

McMURTRIE, Douglas C. The first printing in
South America; facsimile of the unique copy
of the "Pragmatice sobre los diez dias del
año", Lima, 1584, preserved in the John Carter Brown Library. Providence, R. I., John
Carter Brown Library, 1926. 8 [4] p. (6648

MEDINA, José Toribio. Historia de la impren-
ta en los antiguos dominios españoles de
América y Oceanía. Prólogo de Guillermo
Feliú Cruz; complemento bibliográfico de
José Zamudio Z. Santiago de Chile, Fondo
Histórico y Bibliográfico José Toribio Medi-
na, 1958. 2 v. (6649

-----. Historia y bibliografía de la imprenta en el antiguo Virreinato del Río de la
Plata. La Plata, Tall. de Publicaciones del
Museo, 1892. 4 pt. in 1 v. (Historia y bibliografía de la imprenta en la América española. [pte. 2]) (6650
    Added half-title: Anales del Museo de La
Plata. Materiales para la historia física
y moral del continente sud-americano. Publicados bajo la dirección de Francisco P. Moreno. Sección de historia americana, III.
Contents: - pte. I, Historia y bibliografía
de la imprenta en el Paraguay (1705-1727) -
pte. 2. En Córdoba (1766) - pte. 3. En Buenos Aires (1780-1810) - pte. 4. En Montevideo (1807-1810).---Jones 778. Now available
in microprint.

-----. La imprenta en America, Virreinato del
Río de La Plata, 1705-1810. Epítome. Santiago de Chile, En casa del Autor, 1890.
51 p. (6651
    Jones 778a.

-----. Introducción de la imprenta en América;
carta que al sr. d. José Gestoso y Pérez di-
rige J. T. Medina. Santiago de Chile, Impr.
Cervantes, 1910. 104 p. (6652
    "Tirada de cincuenta ejemplares numerados
y sólo para la circulación privada."
From the introductory matter to v. 1 of the
author's Imprenta en México (cf. Dedication)
---Jones 305, 2335.

-----. Notas bibliográficas referentes a las
primeras producciones de la imprenta en algunas ciudades de la América española (Ambato, Angostura, Curazao, Guayaquil, Maracaibo,
Nueva Orleans, Nueva Valencia, Panamá, Popayán, Puerto España, Purto Rico, Querétaro,
Santa Marta, Santiago de Cuba, Santo Domingo,
Tunja y otros lugares) (1754-1823) Santiago de Chile, Impr. Elzeviriana, 1904.
116 p. (6653
    Jones 307.

MITRE, Bartolomé. El primer impreso en Sud-
América. (Revista del Río de la Plata,
Buenos Aires, t. 8, p. 176-97, 1873) (6654
    Jones 783a.

NODAR, Carlos Enrique. La imprenta en Salto,
Paysandú y Concordia; algunas primeras edi-
ciones. Notas bibliográficas. [Salto?]
Tall. Gráf. Ondina [1914?] 97 p. (6655
    Cited in Musso 113.

QUESADA, Vicente Gregorio. The history of
printing and early publications in the
Spanish American colonies; tr. by Gustavo
E. Archila. New York, 1938. 113 p.
(Translation into English of foreign social
science monographs, no. 18) (6656
    Translation from: La vida intelectual en
la América española. (Buenos Aires, 1917)

RODRIGUEZ BETETA, Virgilio. La imprenta y los
impresores en Centro América durante la colonia. (El Arte tipográfico, Nueva York, t.
17-18, 1919-1921) (6657
    "Introducción a la historia del periodismo
en el antiguo reino de Guatemala."---Jones
1247.

SILVA ARRIAGADA, Luis Ignacio. La imprenta en
la América Española. Santiago de Chile, Impr.
La Tracción, 1930. 40 p. (6658
    Jones 1617. Reprinted from Boletín de la
Biblioteca Nacional, año 1, no. 10, en./abr.,
no. 11, mayo 1930.

THOMAS, Isaiah. The history on printing in
America, with a biography of printers, and
an account of newspapers; 2d. ed. with the
author's corrections and additions, and a
catalogue of American publications previous
to the revolution of 1776. Albany, N.Y.,
J. Munsell, printer, 1874. 2 v. (Archaeo-
logia americana. Transactions and collections of the American Antiquarian Society,
v. 5-6) (6659
    History of printing in Spanish America,
communicated by John R. Bartlett, with lists
of books printed in Mexico and Peru before
1600. Appendices B-I.---Jones 475.

THOMPSON, Lawrence Sidney. Printing in colonial Spanish America. Hamden, Conn., Archon
Books [1962] 108 p. (6660

TORRE REVELLO, José. Los bibliógrafos y la
bibliografía relativa a la historia de la
imprenta e impresos de la América colonial.
(Síntesis, Buenos Aires, año 2, no. 25,
p. 47-53, 1929) (6661
    Also in Boletín de la Biblioteca Nacional,
Santiago de Chile, año 4, no. 11, p. 183-86,
1933)---Jones 865.

-----. Orígenes de la imprenta en España y su
desarrollo en América española; editado por

TORRE REVELLO, José. Orígenes de... (Cont.)
Institución Cultural Española con motivo
del quinto centenario de la imprenta. Buenos Aires, 1940. 354 p.   (6662

-----. Los orígenes de la imprenta en la América española. Madrid, F. Beltrán, 1927.
39 p.   (6663
    "Epítome bibliográfico": p. 31-8.---
Jones 482.

UGARTECHE, Félix de. Pequeña historia de la
imprenta en América. [Buenos Aires, Impr.
Lopez] 1943. 35 p.   (6664

VALLE, Rafael Heliodoro. The fourth centenary of printing in America. (Bulletin, Pan
American Union, Washington, D.C., v. 73,
p. 688-97, 1939)   (6665
    Jones 508a.

WATKINS, George Thomas. American typographi-
cal bibliography, being a list of brief
titles of books and pamphlets relating to
the history of printing in America. Indianapolis, 1898. 11 p.   (6666
    Jones 524.

-----. Bibliography of printing in America;
books, pamphlets, and some articles in magazines relating to the history of printing
in the New World. Boston, The compiler,
1906. 31 p.   (6667
    Jones 525.

ARGENTINA

CABRERA, Pablo. Imprenta e impresos en nuestro pasado. (Revista de la Universidad Nacional, Córdoba, v. 11, p. 237-62,
1924)   (6669
    Jones 640.

-----. La segunda imprenta de la Universidad
de Córdoba adqvirida por svscripción popular
en 1823 bajo el gobierno del general d. Jvan
Bautista Bustos. Córdoba, Impr. de la Universidad, 1930. (Universidad Nacional de
Córdoba. Dirección de publicidad. [Publi-
caciones] serie I, no. 1)   (6670
    Includes a bibliography of the press,
containing: Los periódicos, insertos a
continuación por orden cronológico y acompañados de la biografía de los redactores. -
Publicaciones mayores de la segunda imprenta.
- Publicaciones menores de la imprenta.---
Jones 641.

CABRERA DOMINGUEZ, Arturo. Contribución al estudio de la primera imprenta argentina, observaciones de circunstancias. Buenos Aires,
1928.   (6671
    Jones 641a.

CESPEDES, Conrado. La prensa de Mendoza, sus
primeros establecimientos tipográficos y primeros órganos de publicidad. (Revista de la
Junta de Estudios Históricos de Mendoza, t. 3,
p. 12-34, 1936)   (6672
    Jones 665a.

COLOMBO; fine printing. Buenos Aires, [1960]
112 p.   (6673
    A history of the press of Colombo, founded
by Francisco A. Colombo. Preface by Joaquín
Neyra.

FIGUERERO, Manuel V. Bibliografía de la Imprenta del Estado en Corrientes desde sus orígenes en 1826 hasta su desaparición en 1865.
Buenos Aires, Impr. y Casa Editora "Coni",
1919. 323 p.   (6674
    Jones 691.

FURLONG CARDIFF, Guillermo. El Colegio de
Montserrat y la primera imprenta rioplatense.
(Estudios, Buenos Aires, t. 58, p. 357-76,
1937)   (6675
    Jones 698.

GUTIERREZ, Juan María. Bibliografía de la primera imprenta de Buenos Aires desde su fundación hasta el año de 1810 inclusive; o Catálogo de las producciones de la Imprenta de
Niños Expósitos, con observaciones y noticias
curiosas, precedida de una biografía del
Virrey don Juan José de Vértiz y de una disertación sobre el orijen del arte de impri-
mir en América y especialmente en el Río de
la Plata. Buenos Aires, Impr. de Mayo, 1866.
43, 34, 246 p.   (6676
    Describes 229 imprints, 1781-1810. Re-
printed from Revista de Buenos Aires, v. 7-
10, 1805-1866. See also Medina's Hist. y
bibl. de la imprenta en el antig. virreinato
del Río de la Plata, Buenos Aires, 1892,
pte. 3, Imprenta de Buenos Aires, 1780-1810,
which describes 851 imprints. Cf. Binayán,
Narciso, Nuevos datos para la bibliografía
de la Imprenta de Niños Expósitos, (Boletín,
Instituto de Investigaciones Históricas, t.
1, p. 78-84, 1922.---Jones 719. Now available in microprint.

HERAS, Carlos. Orígenes de la Imprenta de
Niños Expósitos. Con una introducción sobre Los primeros trabajos de la Imprenta de
Niños Expósitos. La Plata, Tall. de Impresiones Oficiales, 1943. xxii, 363 p. (Documentos del Archivo Histórico de la Provincia de Buenos Aires, t. 10)   (6677
    Lists imprints of the press to 1783.

-----. Los primeros trabajos de la Imprenta
de Niños Expósitos. (Boletín de la Junta
de Historia y Numismática Americana, Buenos
Aires, v. 6, p. 19-34, 1929?)   (6678
    "Valiosa contribución documental" (Torre
Revello)---Jones 721.

LA PLATA. Biblioteca Pública. Indice cronológico de los trabajos ejecutados en la
Imprenta de los Niños Expósitos de Buenos
Aires durante los siglos XVIII y XIX y que
existen en la Biblioteca Pública Provincial de La Plata, por Luis Ricardo Fors.
La Plata, Tall. de Publicaciones, 1904.
74 p.   (6679
  Jones 741.

LEGUIZAMON, Martiniano. El primer libro im-
preso en las Misiones. (Páginas argentinas,
Buenos Aires, p. 227-41, 1911)   (6680
  Jones 749a.

McMURTRIE, Douglas Crawford. A preliminary
check list of published materials relating
to the history of printing in Argentina.
Chicago, 1942. 14 p. mimeogr.   (6681

MEDINA, José Toribio. La imprenta en Buenos
Aires. (El Museo Histórico, Buenos Aires,
t. 2, p. 59-127, 1893)   (6682
  Jones 778b.

-----. The origin of the printing-press in
Buenos Aires. (Inter-America (English)
New York, v. 7, p. 219-22, 1924)   (6683
  From Revista chilena, jul./ag. 1923.---
Jones 779.

MITRE, Bartolomé. Orígenes de la imprenta
argentina. (Argentina. Tercer Censo Nacional. Buenos Aires, 1917. t. 9, p. 243-
61)   (6684

OUTES, Félix Faustino. Datos para la bibliografía de la Imprenta de los Niños Expósitos. Buenos Aires, Impr. de la Revista Nacional, 1900. 7 p.   (6685
  Additions to Medina's Hist. y bibl. de
la imprenta en el antiguo virreinato del
Río de la Plata, Buenos Aires, 1892 (pte.
3, La imprenta en Buenos Aires, 1780-1810)
From Revista nacional, v. 30, p. 139-43,
1900.---Jones 803.

PILLADO, J. A. Papeles viejos (La imprenta
y los diarios antiguos) Buenos Aires,
1912.   (6686
  Includes 98 facsimiles of periodicals
published between 1801 and 1872.---Jones
815a.

QUESADA, Vicente Gregorio. El primer periódico publicado en Buenos Aires (1801)
(Revista de Buenos Aires, t. 1, p. 148-53,
1863)   (6687
  Jones 823a.

SOLA, Miguel. La imprenta en Salta, cien años
de prensa (1824-1924) y bibliografía antigua
de la imprenta salteña. Buenos Aires, Tall.
Gráf. Porter Hnos., 1924. 131 p.   (6688
  The "Imprenta de los Niños Expósitos" was

SOLA, Miguel. La imprenta en... (Cont.)
acquired by General Arenales for the city
of Salta in 1824.---Jones 848.

URGARTECHE, Félix de. La imprenta argentina;
sus orígenes y desarrollo. Buenos Aires,
1929. 911 p.   (6689
  Contents: - 1. La imprenta guaranítica
(1700). - 2. La imprenta de Córdoba (1764).
- 3. La Imprenta de los Niños Expósitos
(1780-1825). - 4. Los primeros impresos por-
teños (1780-1799). - 5. Los impresos de la
primera década del siglo XIX. - 6. Bibliografía histórica de la primera década revolucionaria. - 7. La imprenta argentina en
el siglo XIX. - 8. Tres importantes entida-
des gráficas. - 9. Las artes gráficas a través de los últimos censos y exposiciones. -
10-11. Reseña de establecimientos. - 12.
Los proveedores de las artes gráficas.---
Jones 879.

BRAZIL

BAIA, Alcides, SOUZA, A. Monteiro, etc. A imprensa no Amazonas. Manaos, Typ. da Impr.
Oficial, 1908. 110 p.   (6690
  Covers period 1851-1908. Publication prepared for the 100th Anniversary of the introduction of printing in Brazil. Cited in
Reis, item 234.

BOITEUX, José Artur. A imprensa catharinense
(Conferencia) Rio de Janeiro, Establecimen-
to Lith.-Typ. Alexandre Borges & C., 1911.
23 p.   (6691
  Cited in Reis, item 274.

CARVALHO, Alfredo de. Genese e progressos da
imprensa periodica no Brasil. (Instituto
Historico e Geographico Brasileiro. Revista trimensal, Rio de Janeiro, 1908. Tomo
consagrado á Exposição commemorativa do primeiro centenario da imprensa periodica no
Brasil, 1908, pte. 1, p. 1-89)   (6692
  Jones 1015.

LOPES, Antônio. História da imprensa no Maranhão, 1821-1925. Rio de Janeiro, [D.A.S.
P., Serviço de Documentação] 1959.
130 p.   (6693

McMURTRIE, Douglas Crawford. A preliminary
check list of published materials relating
to the history of printing in Brazil. Chicago, 1942. 7 p. mimeogr.   (6694

PASSOS, Alexandre. A imprensa no período colonial. Rio de Janeiro, Ministério da Educação e Saúde, 1952. 72 p. (Os Cadernos
de cultura)   (6695

SERRA, Joaquim. A imprensa no Maranhão, 1820-
1880. Rio de Janeiro, Edit. Faro & Lima,

SERRA, Joaquim. A imprensa ... (Cont.)
1883. 153 p.   (6696
Cited in Reis, item 103.

SOUSA, Eusébio Néri Alves de. A imprensa do
Ceará, dos seus primeiros dias aos atuais.
[Rio de Janeiro] Typ. Gadelha, 1933.
45 p.   (6697
Reprinted from Annuario do Ministério da
Educação e Saúde Pública. Cited in Reis,
item 465.

STUDART, Guilherme, barão de. Annaes da imprensa Cearense. Catálogo. Rio de Janeiro,
Impr. Nacional, 1908. 101 p.   (6698
Jones 1205. Reprinted from v. 1, part 2
of "Tomo especial", Revista do Instituto
Histórico e Geographico Brazileiro. See
also item 4603.

TAUNAY, Affonso de Escragnolle. De Brasiliae
rebus pluribus. São Paulo, Impr. Official
do Estado, 1936. 150 p.   (6699
"O primeiro livro impresso no Brasil":
p. 7-58.---Jones 1032a. Contains also
"Inéditos de Antônio Vieira".

VEIGA, Jose Pedro Xavier da. A imprensa em
Minas Gerais, 1807-1894. Ouro Preto, Impr.
Official de Minas Gerais, 1894.
72 p.   (6700
Cited in Reis, item 151.

-----. 1807-1897. Ouro Preto, Impr. Official
de Minas Gerais, 1898. 103 p.   (6701
Cited in Reis, item 173.

VIANNA, Helio. Contribuição a história da imprensa brasileira (1812-1869). Rio de Janeiro, Impr. Nacional, 1945. 664 p. (Instituto Nacional do Livro, Coleção B 1; Bibliografia 4)   (6702

CHILE

CATALOGO de los libros y folletos impresos en
Chile desde que se introdujo la imprenta.
(Revista de ciencias y letras, Santiago,
t. 1, p. 739-68, 1858)   (6703
Jones 1415.

CHILE. Biblioteca Nacional. Impresos chilenos, 1776-1818. Santiago, 1963.
2 v.   (6704
Contents. - Bibliografía histórica de la
imprenta en Santiago de Chile. Impresos
chilenos, 1776-1818, textos. Indice cronológico de los impresos que posee la Biblioteca Nacional, 1776-1818. - v. 2. Descripciones bibliográficas de los impresos chilenos, 1776-1818. Textos manuscritos: actas,
bandos, proclamas, órdenes, decretos, pasto-
rales, manifiestos, etc., 1813-1814. Indice
cronológico de los impresos chilenos, 1776-

CHILE. Biblioteca Nacional ... (Cont.)
1818. Indice cronológico de los textos
manuscritos.

FELIU CRUZ, Guillermo. Bibliografía histórica de la imprenta en Santiago de Chile.
Santiago, Tall. de la Edit. Nascimento,
1964. 162 p.   (6705

-----. La imprenta durante el gobierno de
O'Higgins; estudio histórico. Santiago,
Impr. Universitaria, 1952. 70 p.   (6706

HERNANDEZ CORNEJO, Roberto. Los primeros pa-
sos del arte tipográfico en Chile y especialmente en Valparaíso. Camilo Henríquez
y la publicación de la "Aurora en Chile".
Valparaíso, Impr. Victoria, 1930.
45 p.   (6707
Jones 1495.

McMURTRIE, Douglas Crawford. A preliminary
check list of published materials relating
to the history of printing in Chile. Chicago, 1942. 7 p. mimeogr.   (6708

MEDINA, José Toribio. Bibliografía de la imprenta en Santiago de Chile desde sus orígenes hasta febrero de 1817. Santiago, Impreso en Casa del Autor, 1891. 179 p.(6709
Jones 1532. Now available in microprint.

-----. -----. Adiciones y amplificaciones.
Obra póstuma, la publica con una introducción Guillermo Feliú Cruz. Santiago, Universidad de Chile, 1939. 140 p.   (6710
Jones 1532a. Now available in microprint.

-----. -----. Seguida de las adiciones y am-
liaciones del mismo autor. Ed. facsimilar.
Introducción de Guillermo Feliú Cruz. Santiago, Fondo Histórico y Bibliográfico José Toribio Medina, 1961. xxxviii, xli,
179, xiv, 131 p.   (6711

VICUÑA CIFUENTES, Julio. Contribución a la
historia de la imprenta en Chile. Santiago, Impr. Cervantes, 1903. 50 p.   (6712
"Tirada aparte de la Introducción que en-
cabeza la reproducción paleográfica de la
Aurora de Chile publicada en 1903".---Jones
1652.

COLOMBIA

ARBOLEDA R., Gustavo. La imprenta en el Valle y los escritores vallecaucanos. (Boletín histórico del Valle, Cali, entregas
8-9, 1933)   (6713
Jones 1676a.

CURREA RESTREPO, A. La imprenta en Santa Fé
de Bogotá. (Boletín de historia y antigüedades, Bogotá, v. 24, p. 197-231,

CURREA RETREPO, A. La imprenta... (Cont.)
1937)   (6714
Jones 1706.

IBAÑEZ, Pedro Modesto. La imprenta en Bogotá,
desde su introducción hasta 1810. (Revista literaria, Bogotá, no. 7-8,
1890)   (6715
Reprinted in La Gaceta municipal de Guayaquil, Aug. 13 and Oct. 1, 1898.---Jones
1718.

McMURTRIE, Douglas Crawford. A preliminary
check list of published materials relating
to the history of printing in Colombia.
Chicago, 1942. 7 p. mimeogr.   (6716

MEDINA, José Toribio. La imprenta en Bogotá
(1739-1821) Notas bibliograficas. Santiago de Chile, Impr. Elzeviriana, 1904.
101 p.   (6717
Jones 1733. Now available in microprint.

-----. La imprenta en Cartagena de las Indias (1809-1820) Notas bibliográficas.
Santiago de Chile, Impr. Elzeviriana, 1904.
70 p.   (6718
Jones 1734. Now available in microprint.

ORTIZ, Sergio Elias. Noticias sobre la imprenta y las publicaciones del Sur de Colombia durante el siglo XIX. Pasto, Impr.
del Departamento, 1935. 276 p. (Supl. no.
2 del Boletín de estudios históricos, v. 6,
no. 66-67)   (6719
Jones 1710.

POSADA, Eduardo. La imprenta en Santa Fè de
Bogotá, en el siglo XVIII. Madrid, V.
Suárez, 1917. 153 p.   (6720
88 publications are described, 1739-1800.
---Jones 1760.

CUBA

CUESTA JIMENEZ, Valentín Bernardo. Evolución
del papel periódico en Güines; historia de
la imprenta y del periodismo desde 1862 a
1899. Güines, Cuba, 1956. 52 p. (Biblioteca "Ideas").   (6721

MEDINA, Jose Toribio. La imprenta en La Habana (1707-1810) Notas bibliográficas.
Santiago de Chile, Impr. Elzeviriana, 1904.
199 p.   (6722
Jones 1873. Now available in microprint.

PERAZA SARAUSA, Fermín. La imprenta y el estado en Cuba. Matanzas, Impr. "Estrada",
1926. 29 p. (Publicaciones: Amigos de la
cultura cubana, Matanzas, Cuba, 1) (6723
Jones 1886.

PEREZ BEATO, Manuel. La imprenta en La Habana.
(El Curioso americano, Habana, p. 109-12,
152-55, 1908)   (6724
The author published also "Cartografía cubana" in the same periodical in 1910.---Jones
1891.

-----. La imprenta en Santiago de Cuba. (El
Curioso americano, Habana, p. 19-24, 33-8,
107-09, 1908)   (6725
Jones 1892.

DOMINICAN REPUBLIC

McMURTRIE, Douglas Crawford. A preliminary
list of materials relating to the history
of printing in the Dominican Republic. Chicago, 1942. 7 p. mimeogr.   (6728

RODRIGUEZ DEMORIZI, Emilio. La imprenta y los
primeros periódicos de Santo Domingo. Ciudad Trujillo, Impr. San Francisco, 1944.
255 p.   (6729

ECUADOR

CASTILLO, Abel Romeo. La imprenta de Guayaquil independiente, 1821-1822. Guayaquil,
Impr. Casa de la Cultura Ecuatoriana, 1956.
204 p.   (6730
Contains a list of 105 newspapers.

GONZALEZ SUAREZ, Federico. Bibliografía ecuatoriana. La imprenta en el Ecuador durante
el tiempo de la colonia, 1750-1792. Quito,
Impr. de la Universidad, 1892. 36 p. (6731
From Anales de la Universidad, 7, p. 1-36,
jul. 1892.---Jones 1986.

MEDINA, José Toribio. La imprenta en Quito
(1760-1818) Notas bibliográficas. Santiago de Chile, Impr. Elzeviriana, 1904.
86 p.   (6732
Jones 1991. Now available in microprint.

SANCHEZ, Carlos Enrique. La imprenta en el
Ecuador; en conmemoración del IV Centenario
de la fundación de Quito, 1534-1934, y el
primer centenario de la Imprenta Nacional.
Quito, Tall. Gráf. Nacionales, 1935.
214 p.   (6733
Jones 2014.

STOLS, Alexander Alphonse Marius. Historia de
la imprenta en el Ecuador de 1755 a 1830.
Quito, Casa de la Cultura Ecuatoriana, 1953.
261 p.   (6734
Contains: Bibliografía de los impresos
ecuatorianos, 1755-1830; Los periódicos ecuatorianos, 1809-1830; Lista cronológica de los
periódicos ecuatorianos de 1792-1830; Quito,
1809-1830; Guayaquil, 1821-1830; Cuenca, 1828-
1829.

GUATEMALA

DIAZ, Víctor Manuel. Historia de la imprenta en Guatemala desde los tiempos de la colonia hasta la época actual. Guatemala, Tip. Nacional, 1930. 181 p. (6735
Jones 1289.

GONZALEZ R., Mario Alberto. Introducción de la imprenta en Guatemala. Guatemala, Edit. del Ministerio de Educación Pública "José de Pineda Ibarra", 1961. 43 p. (6736

McMURTRIE, Douglas Crawford. A preliminary check list of published materials relating to the history of printing in Guatemala. Chicago, 1942. 7 p. mimeogr. (6737

MEDINA, José Toribio. La imprenta en Guatemala (1660-1821) Santiago de Chile, Impreso en Casa del Autor, 1910. 696 p. (6738
Additions have been made by Gilberto Valenzuela in 1933 (Diario de Centro América) and also in Boletín de la Biblioteca Nacional, año 5, no. 1.---Jones 1301. Now available in microprint.

-----. La imprenta en Guatemala [1660-1821] 2a. ed. [Guatemala] Tip. Nacional, 1960. 2 v. (Colección Tricentenario) (6739

MERIDA, Martín. Origen de la imprenta en Guatemala; su desarrollo hasta la independencia. Guatemala, Biblioteca Nacional, 1956. 66 p. (6740

REYES M., José Luis. Acotaciones para la historia de un libro (El Puntero apuntado con apuntes breves) Guatemala, Edit. del Ministerio de Educación Pública "José de Pineda Ibarra", 1960. 109 p. (Colección del III Centenario de la Introducción de la Imprenta en Centro América) (6741

REYES MORALES, Mario Roberto. La imprenta en Guatemala, Edit. del Ministerio de Educación Pública, "José de Pineda Ibarra" 1960. 78 p. (6742

RODRIGUEZ BETETA, Virgilio. Nuestra bibliografía colonial. (Anales de la Sociedad de Geografía e Historia de Guatemala, Guatemala, t. 2, p. 83-98, 227-38, 1925) (6743
Jones 1307.

STOLS, Alexander Alphonse Marius. La introducción de la imprenta en Guatemala; ensayo publicado en conmemoración del tercer centenario, 1660-1960. México, D.F., Universidad Nacional Autónoma, 1960. 37 p. (6744

VALENZUELA, Gilberto. La imprenta en Guatemala; algunas adiciones a la obra que con este título publicó en Santiago de Chile el ilustre literato don José Toribio Medina. Gua-

VALENZUELA, Gilberto. La imprenta... (Cont.) temala, C.A., 1933. 72 p. (Folletín del "Diario de Centro América") (6745
Arranged chronologically (1676-1821) with "Adiciones" (p. 65-6) and index of persons. ---Jones 1312.

VELA, David. La imprenta en la colonia. Guatemala, Edit. del Ministerio de Educación Pública, "José de Pineda Ibarra", 1960. 49 p. (Colección "José de Pineda Ibarra", 1) (6746

VILLACORTA CALDERON, José Antonio. Epítome de la historia de la imprenta en Guatemala durante la colonia. (Anales de la Sociedad de Geografía e Historia de Guatemala, Guatemala, v. 12, p. 278-87, 1936) (6747
Jones 1314.

HONDURAS

COELLO, Augusto C. La imprenta y el periódico oficial en Honduras; ligeros apuntes. Tegucigalpa, Tip. Nacional, 1929. 7 p. (6748
Jones 1321.

MEXICO

ALESSIO ROBLES, Vito. La primera imprenta en Coahuila. México, D.F., Universidad Nacional de México, 1932. 43 p. (6749
Jones 2042.

ALMADA, Francisco R. La imprenta y el periodismo en Chihuahua. Publicación del gobierno del Estado de Chihuahua. México, D.F., 1943. 49 p. (6750
Contens. - La introducción de la imprenta. - El periodismo en la ciudad de Chihuahua. - El periódico oficial. - El periodismo fuera de la capital.

ANDRADE, Vicente de Paula. Ensayo bibliográfico mexicano del siglo XVII. Ed. de la Sociedad Científica "Antonio Alzate". México, Impr. del Gobierno Federal, 1894. 96 p. (6751
Cited in Millares, item 808.

-----. -----. 2a. ed. México, Impr. del Museo Nacional, 1899. 803 p. (6752
Reprinted, in part, from the Boletín de la Sociedad Antonio Alzate, 1894. Forms, with García Icazbalceta's Bibliografía mexicana del siglo XVI (1886) and Nicolás León's Bibliografía mexicana del siglo XVIII (1902-) a continuous bibliography of Mexican literature, 1539-1800. 1228 titles, transcribed line for line. Arranged chronologically and followed by alphabetical indexes of authors and anonymous works. ---Jones 2055. Now available in microprint.

ANTUNEZ, Francisco. La imprenta en Morelia. Morelia, Impr. de la Escuela Tipo, 1933. 22 p. (6753
Cited in Millares, item 1103.

ASOCIACION de Libreros de México. IV centenario de la imprenta; la primera en América. Conferencias sustentadas en su conmemoración. México, D.F., 1939. 613 p. (6754

AYALA ECHAVARRI, Rafael. Bibliografía de la primera imprenta que se estableció en la ciudad de Querétaro. México, D.F., Artes Graficas del Estado, 1947. (6755
Reprinted from Boletín de la Sociedad Mexicana de Geografía y Estadística, t. 63, no. 1, p. 100-160.

CONGRESO bibliográfico mexicano, 1o. IV centenario de la fundación de la imprenta en México, 1936. Trabajos. México, D.A.P.P., 1937. 230 p. (6756
Includes papers of bibliographic interest: El cuarto centenario de la imprenta en América, por Genaro Estrada; Los escritores mexicanos y la imprenta en México, por A. Arnáiz; Las obras biologicas impresas en México durante los siglos XVI y XVII, por F. Ocaranza; Bibliografía sobre la higiene infantil y puericultura en México, por A. Vergara; Lo que México ha publicado acerca de eugenesia, por A. M. Saavedra; La imprenta en Michoacán, por J. Romero Flores; Bibliografía médico-mexicana del siglo XVI, por O. Rojas Avendaño; La imprenta y sus beneficios en la República Dominicana, por A. de Espradel y R. Mata Díaz; La imprenta en Guatemala, por J. G. Salazar; Cédulas de obras referentes a México, impresas en España en el siglo XVI, por J. Casares; La imprenta en Chile, por M. Bianchi.--- Jones 2133a.

FERNANDEZ DE CORDOBA, Joaquín. Nuevos documentos para la historia de la imprenta en Morelia. Impresores e impresos morelianos del Siglo XIX. México, D.F., Biblioteca Benjamin Franklin, 1943. 62 p. (6757

-----. Verdadero origen de la imprenta en Morelia. Reproducción facsimilar de los primeros impresos vallisoletanos de 1821. México, D.F., Tall. Gráf. de la Nación, 1949. 116 p. (6758
Additions and corrections to the author's Nuevos Documentos para la historia de la imprenta en Morelia. The author in 1946 published a short "edición mimeográfica incompleta y provisional" (12 p.) with the same title.

FERNANDEZ LEDESMA, Enrique. Historia critica de la tipografía en la ciudad de México; impresos del siglo XIX. México, D.F., Ediciones del Palacio de Bellas Artes, 1934-1935.

FERNANDEZ LEDESMA, Enrique. Historia... (Cont.) 185 p. (6759
Jones 2165.

GESTOSO Y PEREZ, José. Documentos para la historia de la primitiva tipografía mexicana. Carta dirigida al sr. d. José Toribio Medina. Sevilla, Tip. de la Andalucía Moderna, 1908. 14 p. (6760
Jones 2207.

GONZALEZ DE COSSIO, Francisco. La imprenta en México, 1594-1820. Cien adiciones a la obra de don José Toribio Medina. Prologo de Agustín Millares Carlo. México, D.F., Antigua Librería Robredo, de J. Porrúa e Hijos, 1947. 205 p. (6761

-----. -----. 510 adiciones a la obra de José Toribio Medina en homenaje al primer centenario de su nacimiento. México, D.F., Universidad Nacional de México, 1952. xvii, 354 p. (6762

IGUINIZ, Juan Bautista. La imprenta en la Nueva España. México, Porrúa Hnos., 1938. 61 p. (Enciclopedia ilustrada mexicana, no. 8) (6763
Jones 2258.

-----. La imprenta en la Nueva Galicia, 1793-1821. Apuntes bibliográficos. México, Impr. del Museo Nacional de Arqueología, Historia y Etnografía, 1911. p. 253-336. (6764
Sobretiro del tomo 3, de los Anales del Museo Nacional de Arqueología, Historia y Etnografía.---Jones 2257.

JIMENEZ DE LA ESPADA, Marcos. La imprenta en México. (Boletín del Instituto Bibliográfico Mexicano, México, no. 6, p. 7-16, 1905) (6765
Jones 2267.

LAMA, José. La imprenta y el periodismo en el estado de Veracruz. Jalapa [Tall. Gráf. del Gobierno de Veracruz] 1943. 41 p. (6766

LEON, Nicolás. La imprenta en México; ensayo histórico y bibliográfico. México, D.F., Tip. de "El Tiempo", 1900. 38 p. (6767
A list of presses in Mexico about 1827 not included in Dr. Osores' Adiciones a la Biblioteca de Beristain (cf. p. 6)---Jones 2294.

-----. -----. [2a. ed. corr. y aum.] (Boletín del Instituto Bibliográfico Mexicano, México, no. 3, p. 27-51, 1902) (6768
Jones 2294.

LIGA de Acción Social, Mérida. Memoria de la sesión solemne celebrada el 17 de noviembre de 1939 para conmemorar el establecimiento de la imprenta en la Nueva España y en la península de Yucatán. Mérida, Impr. Oriente, 1939.

LIGA de Acción Social, Mérida ... (Cont.)
39 p.   (6769
   The Memoria contains articles by Gonzalo
Cámara, Mireya Priego de Arjona, Nicolás
Castellanos A., José Ignacio Rubio Mañé and
Antonio Canto López.

McMURTRIE, Douglas Crawford. A preliminary
check list of published materials relating
to the history of printing in Mexico. Chicago, 1942. 33 p. mimeogr.   (6770

MARTINEZ ALOMIA, Gustavo. Introducción de la
imprenta en Campeche y cien portadas de impresos mexicanos, estudio bibliográfico.
(Boletín del Instituto Bibliográfico Mexicano, México, no. 3, p. 1-25, 1902)   (6771
   Jones 2321.

MAZA, Francisco de la. Enrico Martínez, cos-
mógrafo e impresor de Nueva España. México,
1943. 174 p. (Ediciones de la Sociedad de
Geografía y Estadística: Temas de México,
ser. Historia, 2)   (6772
   Millares, 1192, gives this item as "in
press", containing a list of the imprints
and a catalog of Martínez Library as well
as a list of his writings.

MEDINA, José Toribio. La imprenta en Guadalajara de México (1793-1821) notas bibliográficas. Santiago de Chile, Impr. Elzeviriana, 1904. 104 p.   (6773
   Jones 2327.

-----. La imprenta en Guadalajara, Mérida de
Yucatán, Oaxaca y Veracruz. (Boletín del
Instituto Bibliográfico Mexicano, México,
no. 6, p. 17-32, 1905)   (6774
   Jones 2328.

-----. La imprenta en la Puebla de los Ange-
les (1640-1821) Santiago de Chile, Impr.
Cervantes, 1908. 823 p.   (6775
   Jones 2329.

-----. La imprenta en Mérida de Yucatán
(1813-1821), notas bibliográficas. Santiago de Chile, Impr. Elzeviriana, 1904.
32 p.   (6776
   Jones 2330. Now available in micriprint.

-----. -----. Ed. conmemorativa del centenario del nacimiento del autor, con un prólogo y dos apéndices, por Víctor M. Suárez.
Mérida, Ediciones Suárez, 1956. 102 p.
(Colección "Ventana yucateca", v. 3) (6777

-----. La imprenta en México. Epítome (1539-
1810) Sevilla, Impr. de E. Rasco, 1893.
291 p.   (6778
   2599 titles.---Jones 2331.

-----. -----. Santiago de Chile, Impreso en
Casa del Autor, 1907-1912. 8 v.   (6779

MEDINA, José Toribio. La imprenta...(Cont.)
12,412 entries. "Introducción" contains:
I, Preliminares; II, Los impresores; III,
Los grabadores; IV, Los libreros; V, Los
bibliógrafos; VI, Leyes y privilegios.---
Jones 2332. Now available in microprint.

-----. La imprenta en Oaxaca (1720-1820), no-
tas bibliográficas. Santiago de Chile, Impr.
Elzeviriana, 1904. 29 p.   (6780
   Jones 2333.

-----. La imprenta en Veracruz (1794-1821),
notas bibliográficas. Santiago de Chile,
Impr. Elzeviriana, 1904. 34 p.   (6781
   Jones 2334.

MONTEJANO Y AGUIÑAGA, Rafael. La introducción
de la imprenta y el grabado en San Luis Potosí, 1964. 39 p.   (6782
   Contains list of publications and of engravings from the press of the Infante family.

MUÑOZ-LEDO Y MENA, Manuel. Vida tipográfica
de Querétaro; reseña histórica. Querétaro,
Impr. de M. Muñoz-Ledo y Mena, 1943.
xxiv p.   (6783
   Edición especial para la Feria del Libro.

LEA, Héctor R. La primera imprenta en las provincias de Sonora y Sinaloa. México, 1943.
68 p.   (6784

ORTEGA, Miguel F. La imprenta y el periodismo en el Sur en el Siglo XIX. México, D.F.,
[Pluma y Lápiz de México] 1943. 59 p. (6785

PEREZ GALAZ, Juan de Dios. La introducción de
la imprenta en Campeche. Campeche, Gobierno
del Estado de Campeche, 1942. 79 p.   (6786
   Cited in HLAS, 8, item 72. Contains a
report on periodicals published since 1820.

PEREZ SALAZAR, Francisco. Dos familias de impresores mexicanos del siglo XVII. (Memorias y revista de la Sociedad Científica
"Antonio Alzate", México, D.F., t. 43,
p. 447-511, 1924)   (6787
   Jones 2421.

RODRIGUEZ FRAUSTO, Jesús. Orígenes de la imprenta y del periodismo en Guanajuato. Guanajuato, Archivo Histórico, Universidad de
Guanajuato, 1961. 107 p.   (6788

ROMERO FLORES, Jesús. La imprenta en Michoacán.
México, D.F., 1943. 134 p.   (6789
   Published as a contribution from the State
to the II Feria del Libro y Esposición Nacional del Periodismo, 1943. Includes 571 items.

RUIZ MEZA, Víctor. La primera imprenta en Toluca, 1830-1837. México, 1949. 92 p. (6790
   Lists 47 titles of books and 8 of periodicals.

SPELL, Lota May (Harrigan) Pioneer printer: Samuel Bangs in Mexico and Texas. Austin, Univ. of Texas Pr., [1963] xii, 230 p. (6791
   "Extant specimens of Samuel Bangs' printing, a tentative listing": p. 167-99. Bibliography: p. 201-14.

UGARTE, Salvador. Notas de bibliografía mexicana. México, [Impr. Aldina, Robredo y Rosell] 1943. 107 p. (6792
   Describes 60 items.

UNION Linotipográfica de la República mexicana. 1909-1935. XXVI aniversario. Edición especial en homanaje al primer centenario de la linotipo. México, Tall. Gráf. de la Nación, 1935. 80 p. (6793
   Cited in Millares 1263.

U.S. Library of Congress. Colonial printing in México; catalog of an exhibition held in 1939 commemorating the four hundredth anniversary of printing in the New World. Washington, D.C., Govt. Print. Off., 1939. 60 p. (6794
   Jones 2536. Includes 85 items. Introduction signed: Robert C. Smith.

VALTON, Emilio. Impresos mexicanos del siglo XVI (Incunables americanos en la Biblioteca Nacional de México, el Museo Nacional y el Archivo General de la Nación, estudio bibliográfico precedido de una introducción sobre los orígenes de la imprenta en América. México, D.F., Impr. Universitaria, 1935. 244 p. (6795
   Jones 2558.

-----. El primer libro de alfabetización en America, impreso por Pedro Ocharte en México, 1569. México, D.F., Antigua Libr. Robredo, 1947. 156 p. (6796

VINDEL, F. El primer libro impreso en América fue para el rezo del Santo Rosario (México, 1532-1534) Madrid, 1953. 102 p. (6797

-----. -----. Apendice. Madrid, 1954. 46 p. (6798

WATERS, Williard O. Mexican imprints, 1544-1600, in the Huntington Library. (Library journal, v. 65, p. 50-3, Jan. 1940) (6799
   Exhibition commemorating the 400th anniversary of the introduction of printing into the New World.---Jones 2581.

WINSHIP, George Parker. Early Mexican printers. Cambridge, 1899. 10 p. (6800
   "From the Proceedings of the Massachusetts Historical Society, Jan. 12, 1899".---Jones 2585. Millares, 1282, cites an edition with title: The earliest American imprints, Milwaukee, 1899, and notes that the referen-

WINSHIP, George Parker. Early ... (Cont.) ces included are to Mexico.

PANAMA

CASTILLERO REYES, Ernesto de Jesús. Origen y desarrollo de la imprenta en Panamá, primeros periódicos y libros publicados en el istmo en el siglo diecinueve. Panamá, 1958. 35 p. (6802

PERU

BROWN University, Providence, R.I., John Carter Brown Library. Books printed in Lima, 1585-1800. [Boston, 1908] 4 p. (6803

-----. Books printed in Lima and elsewhere in South America after 1800. Boston, The Merrymount Pr., 1908. 4 p. (6804

McMURTRIE, Douglas Crawford. A preliminary check list of published materials relating to the history of printing in Peru. Chicago, 1942. 8 p. mimeogr. (6805

MEDINA, José Toribio. La imprenta en Arequipa, el Cuzco, Trujillo y otros pueblos del Perú durante las campañas de la independencia (1820-1825); notas bibliográficas. Santiago de Chile, Impr. Elzeviriana, 1904. 71 p. (6806
   Jones 2692. Now available in microprint.

-----. La imprenta en Lima, 1584-1810. Epitome. Santiago de Chile, En Casa del Autor, 1890. 118 p. (6807
   Jones 2694.

-----. -----. 1584-1824. Santiago de Chile, Impreso en Casa del Autor, 1904-1907. 4 v. (6808
   Jones 2693. Now available in microprint.

ZEVALLOS QUIÑONES, Jorge. La imprenta en el Norte del Perú; Trujillo, Piura, Huaraz, Cajamarca, Chachapoyas (1823-1900) Lima, Compañía de Impresiones y Publicidad, 1949. 84 p. (6809
   Bibliography of 111 items.

-----. La imprenta en Lambayeque. Lima, 1947. 79 p. (6810

-----. -----. Adiciones. Lima, Compañía de Impresiones y Publicidad, 1948. 25 p. (6811

URUGUAY

ARREDONDO, Horacio. Bibliografía uruguaya. (Revista del Instituto Histórico y Geográfico del Uruguay, Montevideo, v. 6, p. 433-610,

ARREDONDO, Horacio. Bibliografía... (Cont.)
1929)   (6812
   Intended to supplement Estrada's Historia
y bibliografía de la imprenta en Montevideo.
Arranged chronologically. The introduction
includes a review of the more important bibliographies of the South American countries.
---Jones 2814a. Now available in microprint.

CASTELLANOS, Daniel. "La Estrella del Sur" en
campo de hipótesis. Conferencia pronunciada
en el Instituto Histórico y Geográfico del
Uruguay el 21 de octubre de 1943. [Montevi-
deo] n.d. 29 p.   (6813
   Reprinted from Revista del Instituto Historico y Geográfico del Uruguay, Montevideo,
t. 18, p. 3-28, 1949. Cited in Musso 431.

ESTRADA, Dardo. Historia y bibliografía de la
imprenta en Montevideo, 1810-1865. Montevideo, Libr. Cervantes, 1912. 318 p. (6814
Jones 2829. Now available in microprint.

FERNANDEZ Y MEDINA, Benjamín. La imprenta y
la prensa en el Uruguay desde 1807 a 1900.
Montevideo, Impr. de Dornaleche y Reyes,
1900. 87 p.   (6815
   Reprinted with additions from Orestes
Araujo's Diccionario geográfico del Uruguay,
1900.---Jones 2834.

FURLONG CARDIFF, Guillermo. La "Imprenta de
la Caridad" (1822-1855); historia. Bibliografía por Enrique Arana (h) Montevideo,
Impr. "El Siglo Ilustrado", 1932.
164 p.   (6816
   Reprinted from Revista del Instituto Histórico y Geográfico del Uruguay, t. 9, 1932.
---Jones 2836.

TORRE REVELLO, José. Contribución a la historia y bibliografía de la imprenta en Montevideo. Buenos Aires, 1926. 15 p. (Publ.
del Instituto de Investigaciones Históricas,
no. 31)   (6917
   Jones 2873.

VENEZUELA

ARISMENDI, Santos Erminy. La imprenta y el
periodismo en Carúpano. (Boletín de la Biblioteca Nacional, Caracas, año 2, p. 202-
06, 1925)   (6818
   Jones 2885.

BRICEÑO, Luis F. La imprenta en el Táchira.
Caracas, Impr. Bolívar, 1883. 16 p (6819
   "Noticia cronológica de los periódicos que
desde al año de 1845 hasta el de 1883 se han
publicado en la sección Táchira:" p. 8-16.
---Jones 2889.

DUARTE LEVEL, Lino. La imprenta en Angostura.
(El Cojo ilustrado, Caracas, año 23, no. 529,

DUARTE LEVEL, Lino. La imprenta ... (Cont.)
1914)   (6820
   Jones 2909.

FEBRES CORDERO G., Julio. Tres siglos de imprenta y cultura venezolanas, 1500-1800. Caracas, [Impr. Nacional] 1959. 223 p. (6821

GRASES, Pedro. La fecha de impresión del libro
de Quintana. Caracas, 1956. 8 p.   (6822
   Reprinted from Revista nacional de cultura,
Caracas, no. 115, mar./abr. 1956.

-----. Orígenes de la imprenta en Cumaná. Caracas, 1956. 14 p.   (6823
   Reprinted from Farol, Caracas, no. 164, jun.
1956. Four items are described.

-----. Orígenes de la imprenta en Venezuela y
primicias editoriales de Caracas. Caracas,
El Nacional, 1958. 428 p.   (6824

-----. El primer libro impreso en Venezuela;
edición facsimilar del Calendario manual y
guía universal de forasteros en Venezuela
para el año de 1810. Caracas, Ediciones del
Ministerio de Educación, 1952. 100 p., 64
facsims. (Biblioteca venezolana de cultura,
Colección "Andrés Bello")   (6825

McMURTRIE, Douglas Crawford. A preliminary
check list of published materials relating to
the history of printing in Venezuela. Chicago, 1942. 7 p.   (6826

MEDINA, José Toribio. Contribución a la historia de la imprenta en Venezuela. Presenta-
ción y notas de Pedro Grases. [Caracas] Ediciones del Ministerio de Educación, n.d.
73 p.   (6827
   Edition in commemoration of the 100th anniversary of the birth of Medina.

-----. La imprenta en Caracas (1808-1821);
notas bibliográficas. Santiago de Chile,
Impr. Elzeviriana, 1904. 29 p.   (6828
   Jones 2932. Now available in microprint.

OVALLES, Víctor Manuel. Notas sobre la imprenta
y el periodismo en el oriente del Guárico.
La Pascua, Tip. de "Minerva", 1901.
56 p.   (6829
   47 periodicals, 1881-1901, listed.---Jones
2936.

PEREZ VILA, Manuel. Orígenes de la imprenta en
Maracaibo. Maracaibo, Publicaciones de la
Dirección de Cultura de la Universidad del
Zulia, 1962. 15 p.   (6830
   Reprinted from first number of Boletín de
la Biblioteca General, Universidad del Zulia.

ROJAS, Arístides. La imprenta en Venezuela durante la colonia y la revolución. (Documentos para la historia de la vida púplica

ROJAS, Arístides. La imprenta en...(Cont.)
del Libertador, recopilados por el presbítero José Félix Blanco y Ramón Azpurúa.
Caracas, 1875. t. 2, p. 342-61)   (6831
Jones 2951a.

SANCHEZ, Manuel Segundo. La imprenta de la
expedición libertadora; capítulo de la obra
en preparación: Historia y bibliografía de
la imprenta en Venezuela. Caracas, Lit. del
Comercio, 1916. [12] p.   (6832
Jones 2955.

-----. La imprenta de la expedición pacifica-
dora. Capítulo de la obra en preparación
Historia y Bibliografía de la Imprenta en
Venezuela. Caracas, Lit. del Comercio,
1916. 16 p.   (6833
Reprinted in Cultura venezolana, Caracas,
7(54): 15-23.---Jones 2956.

SILVA MONTAÑES, Ismael. Imprentas y periódicos caroreños. Carora, Tip. Arte, 1933.
34 p.   (6833a
Covers 77 periodicals, 1875-1931.---Jones
2959.

WEST INDIES

CUNDALL, Frank. A history of printing in Jamaica from 1717 to 1834. Kingston, Institute of Jamaica, 1935. 63 p.   (6833b
Reprinted from the Centenary number of
the Gleaner, Sept. 13, 1934.

McMURTRIE, Douglas Crawford. Early printing
on the Island of Antigua; with a facsimile
of a broadside of 1753, preserved in the
Library of Congress. Evanston, Illinois,
1943. 7 p.   (6834

PUBLIC ADMINISTRATION

BOHORQUEZ C., José I., and CALVO DE RIBERO,
Blanca. Bibliografía sobre administración.
Bogotá, Biblioteca de la Escuela Superior
de Administración Pública, 1964.   (6835
Cited in Boletín de adquisiciones, Mede-
llín, p. 19, feb. 1965.

BOHORQUEZ C., José Ignacio. Catálogo de publicaciones sobre las principales materias
existentes en la Biblioteca de la Escuela
Superior de Administración Pública. Bogotá, ESAP, 1962. 179 p.   (6836

BRAZIL. Departamento Administrativo do Serviço Público. Bibliografia sôbre organização. [Rio de Janeiro] Impr. Nacional, 1942.
16 p.   (6837
Cited in Richardson, item 7221.

----- -----. Roteiro bibliográfico para o
estudo da administração municipal; prefacio
de Arizio de Viana. II Congresso Nacional
dos Municípios Brasileiros, São Vicente,
1952. [Rio de Janeiro, Impr. Nacional,
1952] 96 p.   (6838
"Documentação bibliográfica elaborada pelos Drs. Araújo Cavalcanti e Francisco Burkinski.

CONFERENCIA sobre Administración Pública en
los Países en Desarrollo, Bogotá, 1963.
Lista de documentos. Bogotá, Escuela Superior de Administración Pública,
1963.   (6839
Cited in Boletín de adquisiciones, Medellín, no. 8, p. 9, ag. 1963.

ESCUELA Superior de Administración Pública
América Central, San José. Catalogo de pu-
blicaciones, no. 1- . feb. 1959- . San
José, C.R., 1959- .   (6840

FERRAZ, Sonia Sterman. Registro bibliográfico
brasileiro. São Paulo, Instituto de Administração, 1948-1949. 3 v. (São Paulo. Universidade. Instituto de Administração Pública,
v. 49, 77, 79)   (6841
Cited in Indice bibliográfico das publicações, Universidade de São Paulo, v. 1, fasc.
9, item 62-4.

GROSSMANN, Jorge. Bibliography on public administration in Latin America; 2a. ed. Washington, D.C., Pan American Union, 1958. xii,
198 p. (Columbus Memorial Library, Bibliographic ser., no. 43)   (6842
First edition by Rosa Salomão.

MISSÃO Norte-Americana de Cooperação Técnica
no Brasil. Administração pública; bibliografia. Rio de Janeiro, 1956. 8 p.
mimeogr.   (6844
Cited in Richardson, item 7265.

LA PAZ, Bolivia. Universidad Mayor de San
Andrés. Escuela de Administración Pública.
Biblioteca. Indice bibliográfico en administración pública; libros y otras publicaciones en idioma español por Katherine L.
Montague y Marcela Meneses Orosco. La Paz,
1959. xii, 130 p.   (6843
Published in cooperation with the University of Tennessee.

MURATTI, Natalio. Bibliografía concerniente
a la municipalización de los servicios públicos. Rosario [Tall. Gráf. P. Moreno]
1933. 14 p.   (6845
   Published in Revista de la Facultad de
Ciencias Económicas, Comerciales y Políticas, Universidad Nacional del Litoral, 3a.
ser., t. 3, no. 1.

PAN AMERICAN UNION. Columbus Memorial Library. Bibliografía de procedimientos aduaneros y formalidades de puerto, compilada en
la Biblioteca de la Unión Panamericana para
los miembros de la Comisión Panamericana
sobre Procedimientos Aduaneros y Formalidades de Puerto. Washington, D.C., 1929.
12 p.   (6846
   Jones 350.

PERU. Congreso. Cámara de Diputados. Biblioteca. Municipalidades; bibliografía
y guía legislativa. Lima, 1958.
125 p.   (6847

PIMENTEL, Antônio Fonseca. Pequena bibliografia sôbre treinamento. [Rio de Janeiro]
Escola Brasileira de Administração Pública

PIMENTEL, Antônio Fonseca. Pequena...(Cont.)
[1954?] 34 p. (Cadernos de administração,
7)   (6848
   Cited in Richardson, item 7275. In Bibliografia brasileira de ciências sociais, no. 1,
item 2, an edition in 28 p. is cited.

RICHARDSON, Iván L. Bibliografia brasileira
de administração pública e assuntos correla-
tos. Rio de Janeiro, Fundação Getúlio Vargas, 1964. xxii, 840 p.   (6849
   Includes 7,300 entries.

SALOMÃO, Rosa. Bibliography on public administration in Latin America. Washington, D.C.,
Pan American Union, 1954. vii, 115 p. (Columbus Memorial Library, Bibliographic ser.,
no. 43)   (6850
   Second edition by Jorge Grossmann, see
item 6842.

URUGUAY. Universidad. Facultad de Ciencias
Económicas y de Administración. Biblioteca.
Bibliografía sobre administración pública.
Montevideo, 1962. 16 p. mimeogr. (6851
   Cited in Musso 89.

RELIGION

ANALECTA sacra tarraconensia, anuari de la
Biblioteca Balmes. Barcelona,
1925- .   (6852
   Includes section "Bibliografia hispánica
de ciencias histórico-eclesiastiques".---
Jones 12.

ANDRADE, Vicente de Paula. Bibliografía mexicana del Sagrado Corazón de Jesús. México,
1906. 56 p.   (6853
   Jones 2051.

ANGULO, Domingo. Santa Rosa de Santa María;
estudio bibliográfico. Prólogo de Carlos
Alberto Romero. Lima, Sanmartí y Cía.,
1917. 249 p.   (6854
   Jones 2625.

ARANA, Enrique. Bibliografía del patronato
nacional. (Proceedings of the third Convention of the Inter-American Bibliographical
and Library Association. New York, H. W.
Wilson, 1941. p. 98-234)   (6855
   435 titles, arranged chronologically, annotated, with historical introduction.---Jones
565a.

BIBLIOGRAFIA catolica brasileira [1950/1955]-
   Rio de Janeiro.   (6855a
   Cited in Geoghegan 974.

BRAZIL. Biblioteca Nacional. O Catolicismo
no Brasil. [Rio de Janeiro] Ministério da
Educação e Cultura [1955] 24 p.   (6855b

-----. -----. Catalogo por ordem chronologica das biblias, corpos de biblia. Rio de
Janeiro, Typ. Leuzinger, 1895. 337 p (6856
   Reprinted from Annaes da Bibliotheca Nacional, v. 17, 1891-1892. 1895.

CABRERA LEIVA, Guillermo. Bibliografia sobre
el protestantismo en las Antillas españolas.
Washington, D.C., 1954. 11 p.   (6857

CALIFORNIA. State Library. Sutro Branch, San
Francisco. The Sutro Library catalogue of
works on the Catholic Church by Spanish,
Portuguese and Spanish American writers before 1800. Compiled by the Works Progress
Administration. San Francisco, 1941. v. 1-
2 (Occasional papers, bibliographic ser.,
no. 3, pt. 1-2)   (6858
   437 entries from Abad through Curtell.
Charles O'Malley, compiler.

CALLCOTT, Wilfrid Hardy. Church and state in
Mexico, 1822-1857. Durham, N.C., Duke
Univ. Pr., 1926. 357 p.   (6859
   Bibliography: p. 325-40.---Jones 2107.

CATALOGOS de los eclesiásticos de ambos cle-
ros, casas religiosas, iglesias y capillas
del Arzobispado de Santiago de Chile a principios del año 1912. Santiago de Chile,
Impr. de San José, 1912. 147 p.   (6860
Jones 1416.

CORDOBA, Arg. Universidad Nacional. Biblioteca Mayor. Catálogo de la Librería Jesuítica. Córdoba, Impr. de la Universidad Nacional de Córdoba, 1942. 311 p. (Publicaciones de la nueva serie, 4)   (6861
Author list through the letter F, all published before 1767, mostly theology and
philosophy.

CRIVELLI, Camilo. Directorio protestante de
la América Latina. Isola del Liri, A. Macioce & Pisani, 1933. 714 p. (Facultatis
Historiae Ecclesiasticae in Universitate
Gregoriana operum editorum series,
1)   (6863
Includes bibliographies.---Jones 118.

CUEVAS, Mariano. Historia de la iglesia en
México. Tlalpam, D.F., Impr. del Asilo
"Patricio Sanz", 1921-1926 (v. 1-4); El
Paso, Texas, Edit. Revista Católica, 1928
(v. 5) 5 v.   (6864
Includes bibliography.---Jones 2141.

-----. -----. El Paso, Tex., Edit. "Revista
Católica", 1928. 5 v.   (6865
Jones 2142.

DAVILA GARIBI, José Ignacio Paulino. Bibliografía. El magisterio del quinto metropoli-
tano de Guadalajara. Extracto de los documentos expedidos durante su pontificado.
Fascículo primero (1913-1917). Guadalajara,
Impr. C. M. Sáinz, 1926. 88 p.   (6866
Cited in González, item 123.

DOMINGUEZ, Olegario. Bibliografía misional
hispanoamericana, 1948. Burgos, Biblioteca
ID, Instituto Español de Misiones Extranjeras [1949] 24 p. (Cuadernos de cultura misional, no. 1)   (6866a

EYZAGUIRRE, José Ignacio Víctor. Histoire
ecclésiastique, politique et littéraire du
Chili; trad. par L. Poillon. Lille, L.
Lefort, 1855. 3 v.   (6867
"Liste des principaux écrivains consultés",
v. 2, p. 359-61.

-----. Historia eclesiástica, política y literaria de Chile. Valparaíso, Impr. del Comercio, 1850. 3 v.   (6868
Jones 1471.

FERNANDEZ, Alonso. Historia eclesiástica de
nuestros tiempos, qve es compendio de los
excelentes frvtos qve en ellos el estado

FERNANDEZ, Alonso. Historia ... (Cont.)
eclesiástico y sagradas religiones han hecho
y hazen en la conuersión de idólatras y re-
ducción de hereges. Toledo, Viuda de P.
Rodríguez, 1611. 496 p.   (6869
Medina, Bib. hisp. am., no. 571; 2 chapters on authors of the New World.---Jones
144.

GARCIA GUTIERREZ, Jesús. Apuntamientos para
una bibliografía crítica de historiadores
guadalupanos. Zacatecas, México, 1939.
152 p.   (6870
"Se publicaron estos artículos en el Boletín eclesiástico de la dióceses ... Co-
menzó la publicación en la segunda mitad
de 1936".

GARCIA Y MOYEDA, Manuel. Episcopado mexicano
nacional. Pequeña relación por orden cronológico de los illmos. obispos nacidos en
el suelo mexicano. México, D.F., Tip. Barbedillo, 1884.   (6871
Jones 2205 cited an undated León edition
with 87 p.

GONZALEZ DAVILA, Gil. Teatro eclesiástico de
la primitiva iglesia de las Indias Occidentales, vidas de sus arzobispos y obispos y
cosas memorables de sus sedes. Madrid, D.
Díaz de la Carrera, 1649-1655. 2 v. (6872
"La obra es de poco interés, y la edición
poco esmerada". (B. Sánchez Alonso, Fuentes de la historia esp. e hispanoamer.)---
Jones 171.

GRENON, Juan Pedro. Manual bibliográfico de
historia eclesiástica argentina; un primer
ensayo. Córdoba [Impr. Biffignandi] 1943.
20 p.   (6872a
Cited in Geoghegan, 2652.

GUIA eclesiástica de la República Argentina
(publicación oficial) Director: Mons.
Santiago M. Ussher [3a. ed.] Buenos Aires,
Cabaut y Cía., [1915?] 517 p.   (6873
Other editions.---Jones 716. Includes
"Periodismo católico".

KNIGHTS OF COLUMBUS. Texas State Council.
Our Catholic heritage in Texas, 1519-1936.
Paul J. Foik, editor. Austin, von Boeck-
mann-Jones Co., 1936- . v. 1- .   (6874
Contents: - v. 1, The mission era, the
finding of Texas, 1519-1693, by C. E. Castañeda. Bibliography (p. 379-401). - The mission era, the winning of Texas, 1693-1731,
by C. E. Castañeda. Bibliography (p. 349-
68).---Jones 2273.

LEGON, Faustino J. Doctrina y ejercicio del
patronato nacional. Buenos Aires, J. Lajouane & Cía., 1920. 628 p.   (6875
Bibliografía: p. 9-30.---Jones 749.

LEON, Nicolás. Apuntamientos bibliográficos
sobre el Concilio IV Mexicano. Querétaro
1898. x p.   (6876
   Jones 2284. Reprinted from the introduction to the Concilio IV Mexicano, Querétaro,
1898. Published also in Boletín del Instituto Bibliográfico Mexicano, no. 3, p. 71-8,
1902.

MacKAY, John Alexander. That other America.
New York, Friendship Pr., 1935.
214 p.   (6877
   Reading list: p. 204-09.---Jones 270.

MECHAM, John Lloyd. Church and state in Latin
America. Chapel Hill, Univ. of North Caro-
lina Pr., 1934. 550 p.   (6878
   Bibliography: p. 509-32.---Jones 296.

MEDINA, José Toribio. Ensayo de una bibliografía extranjera de santos y venerables
americanos. Santiago de Chile, Impr. Elzeviriana, 1919. 212 p.   (6879
   Jones 303.

MEMORIAL de los conventos, doctrinas y religiosos desta provincia del Santísimo nombre
de Jesús de Guatemala, Honduras y Chiapa de
los frailes menores. (Colección de documentos inéditos para la historia de España.
Madrid, 1891. t. 100, p. 492-502)   (6880
   Jones 2336.

MURRAY, John Lovell. A selected bibliography
of missionary literature. New York, Student
Volunteer Movement, 1920. 58 p.   (6881
   Latin America: p. 33-5. Previously
issued in 1912.---Jones 328.

PITA, Enrique Benigno. Educación cristiana;
bibliografía. Buenos Aires, Señales [1956]
48 p.   (6881a

POMPA Y POMPA, Antonio. Album del IV centenario guadalupano. México, Cultural, 1938.
240 p.   (6882
   Includes bibliography of historical sources.---Jones 2431a.

PRAT DE SABA, Onofre. Vicennalia sacra peruviana, sive De viris peruvianis religione
illustribus hisce viginti annis gloriosa
morte functis. Ferrariae, ex Typ. F. Poma-
telli, 1788. 200 p.   (6883
   Includes biographies of 15 Jesuits of
Peru.---Jones 2727.

RAMIREZ APARICIO, Manuel. Los conventos su-
primidos en Méjico. Estudios biográficos,
históricos y arqueológicos. Méjico, J. M.
Aguilar y Cía., 1861. 525 p.   (6884
   Jones 2445.

RESTREPO OSPINA, Octavio. Bibliografía crítica mariológica colombiana. Bogotá, Edit.

RESTREPO OSPINA, Octavio ... (Cont.)
"Prensa Católica", 1954. 144 p. (Tesis,
no. 61)   (6885
   Cited in Giraldo Jaramillo, p. 149.

RICARD, Robert. La conquête spirituelle du
Méxique. Essai sur l'apostolat et les métho-
des missionnaires des ordres mendiants en
Nouvelle-Espagne de 1523-1524 a 1572. Paris,
Institut d'Ethnologie, 1933. 404 p.   (6886
   "Essai d'inventaire des ouvrages en langues
indigènes ou relatifs aux langues indigènes
écrits par des religieux entre 1524 et 1572":
p. 345-52.---Jones 2458.

-----. Etudes et documents pour l'histoire mis-
sionnaire de l'Espagne et du Portugal. Louvain, 1931. 237 p. (Collection de la Section
Scientifique de l'Aucam, no. 1)   (6887
   Liste des ouvrages et articles cités:
p. 152-54.---Jones 399.

RIPPY, James Fred, and NELSON, Jean Thomas.
Crusaders of the jungle. Chapel Hill, Univ.
of North Carolina Pr., 1936. 401 p.   (6888
   "Notes": p. 371-88.---Jones 407.

ROLANDO, Carlos A. Bibliografía catequística
en la República del Ecuador; contribución al
1er. Congreso catequístico diocesiano, celebrado en Guayaquil. Guayaquil, Impr. Gutenberg de E. A. Uzcátegui, 1941. 31 p.   (6889

ROMMERSKIRCHEN, Giovanni, and DINDINGER, Giovanni. Bibliografia missionaria, Roma, Soc.
Tip. A. Macioce & Pisani, 1936. 191 p.(6890
   Begun in 1935 as an appendix to the Guida
della missioni cattoliche (p. 142-223) Includes a section on Latin America.---Jones
420a.

-----. -----. Bibliografia missionaria... .
Anno 3, 1936. Roma, Soc. Tip. A. Macioce &
Pisani, 1937. 108 p.   (6891
   Cited in Millares, item 93.

-----. -----. Anno 4, 1937. Roma, Soc. Tip.
A. Macioce & Pisani, 1938. 179 p.   (6892
   Latin America: p. 96-107. Cited in Milla-
res, item 94.

RYAN, Edwin. The church in the South American
republics. New York, The Bruce Publ., Co.,
1932. 119 p.   (6893
   Bibliography: p. 111-15.---Jones 424.

SANTIAGO de Chile. Universidad Católica. Biblioteca Central. Bibliografía eclesiástica
chilena. Santiago, Edit. Universidad Católica, 1959. xxx, 358 p.   (6894
   Compilation directed by María Teresa Sanz.

SEPERIZA ZANINOVIC, Lucas. Ensayo histórico
sobre la literatura de la diócesis de La Serena. Santiago, Impr. San José, 1923.

SEPERIZA ZANINOVIC, Lucas.   Ensayo... (Cont.)
52 p.   (6895
Cited in Bibliografía eclesiástica de Chile, p. 323.

SILVA COTAPOS, Carlos. Historia eclesiástica
de Chile. Santiago, Impr. de San José,
1925. viii, 387 p.   (6896
Bibliography: p. iv-viii.---Jones 1627.

SOARES, José Carlos de Macedo. Fontes da his-
tória da Igreja Católica no Brasil. São
Paulo, Tip. Edanee, 1954. 384 p.   (6897
Cited in HLAS, 19, item 4029.

-----. -----. Rio de Janeiro, 1954.
338 p.   (6898
Reprinted from Revista do Instituto Histórico y Geográfico Brasileiro, v. 220,
jul./sept. 1953.

SOSA, Francisco. El episcopado mexicano; galería biográfica ilustrada de los illmos.
señores arzobispos de México desde la época
colonial hasta nuestros días. México, H.
Iriarte y S. Hernández, 1877-1879.
252 p.   (6899
Autores consultados: p. 241-45.---Jones
2508.

STREIT, Robert. Bibliotheca missionum. Münster i. W., Aachen, 1916- . v. 1- . (Veröffentlichungen des Internationalen Instituts
für Missionswissenschaftliche Forschung)   (6900
On t.-p. of v. 6- : Bibliotheca missionum,
begonnen von p. Robert Streit ... fortgeführt
und ergänzt von p. Johannes Dindinger.
"Alphabetisches verzeichnis bibliographischer
hilfsquellen ..." in each volume.
Contents. - 1. bd., Grundlegender und
allgemeiner teil. - 2. bd., Americanische
missionsliteratur, 1493-1699. - 3. bd., Americanische missionsliteratur, 1700-1909. -
4. bd., Asiatische missionsliteratur, 1245-
1599. - 5. bd., Asiatische missionsliteratur,
1600-1699. - 6. bd., Missionsliteratur Indiens, der Philippinen, Japans und Indochi-
nas, 1700-1799. - 7. bd., Chinesische missionsliteratur, 1700-1799. - 8. bd., Missionsliteratur Indiens u. Indonesiens, 1800-
1909. - 9. bd., Missionsliteratur der Philippinen, 1800-1909. - 10. bd., Missionsliteratur Japans und Koreas, 1800-1909.---Jones
465.

TABLANTE GARRIDO, Pedro Nicolás. Apuntes para
un catálogo de versiones castellanas totales
y parciales de la Santa Biblia. Mérida, Venezuela, Biblioteca Bíblica Bereana, 1953.
11, 20 p.   (6901
Cited in Anuario bibliográfico venezolano,
1949/1954, item 3351.

TAMARON Y ROMERAL, Pedro. Demonstración del
vastísimo obispado de la Nueva Vizcaya -
1765; Durango, Sinaloa, Sonora, Arizona,
Nuevo México, Chihuahua y porciones de Texas,
Coahuila y Zacatecas; con una introducción
bibliográfica y anotaciones por Vito Alessio
Robles. México, D.F., Antigua Librería Robredo, 1937. 464 p. (Biblioteca histórica mexicana de obras inéditas, 7)   (6902
Bibliografía: p. 425-34.---Jones 2521.

TOBAR DONOSO, Julio. La iglesia ecuatoriana
en el siglo XIX. Con una introducción por
el dr. Remigio Crespo Toral. Quito, "Edit.
Ecuatoriana", 1934- . v. 1- . (Publ. de la
Academia Ecuatoriana)   (6903
Indice de obras consultadas: v. 1, p.
619-30.---Jones 2019.

VALENZUELA, Pedro Armengol. Los regulares en
la iglesia y en Chile. Roma, Impr. Tiberi-
na, 1900. 512 p.   (6904
Contains bibliographical data regarding
both printed works and manuscripts (Laval,
no. 334).---Jones 1649.

VALVERDE TELLEZ, Emiterio. Bio-bibliografía
eclesiástica, 1821-1943. México, D.F., Jus,
1949-1954. 3 v. (Colección de estudios históricos)   (6905

VERA, Fortino Hipólito. Tesoro guadalupano.
Noticia de los libros, documentos, inscripciones, & c. que tratan de Nuestra Señora
de Guadalupe. Amecameca, Impr. del "Colegio Católico," 1887-1889. 2 v.   (6906
Includes publications from 1531-1731.---
Jones 2573.

WATTERS, Mary. A history of the Church in Venezuela, 1810-1930. Chapel Hill, N.C.,
Univ. of North Carolina Pr., 1934.
260 p.   (6907
Bibliography: p. 238-52.---Jones 2975.

ZEGARRA, Félix Cipriano C. Santa Rosa de Lima
(Isabel Flores y Oliva) Estudio bibliográ-
fico. (Concurso literario en honor de Santa
Rosa de Lima celebrado en el tercer centena-
rio de su nacimiento, 30 de abril de 1886.
Lima, Impr. de Torres Aguirre, 1886. p. 61-
128)   (6907a
Jones 2647.

RELIGIOUS ORDERS*

AGUSTINIANS

ANDRES de San Nicolás. Historia general bio-

_____
* The works on religious orders cited by
Jones are included in this edition, although
many of them are more historical and biographical than bibliographical treatises.

ANDRES de San Nicolás. Historia... (Cont.)
grafica y bibliográfica de los religiosos
descalzos de San Agustín de la Congregación
de España e Indias. Madrid, 1879.   (6908
    Cited in Enciclopedia universal, v. 8, p.
622.---Jones 14.

BASALENQUE, Diego. Historia de la provincia
de San Nicolás de Tolentino, de Michoacán,
del orden de N. P. S., Agustín, Edición de
la "Voz de México." México, D.F., Tip. Barbedillo y Comp., 1886. 3 v.   (6909
    1st edition, México, 1673.---Jones 2067.

CALANCHA, Antonio de la. Corónica moralizada
del Orden de San Avgvstín en el Perú, con
svcesos egenplares vistos en esta monarqvía.
Divídese este primer tomo en qvatro libros;
lleva tablas de capítulos i lugares de la
Sagrada Escritura. Barcelona, P. Lacavalle-
ría, 1639. 922 p.   (6910
    "A second volume of this work was printed
at Lima in 1653 [or 1654] but was never published, owing probably to certain obnoxious
passages contained in it. It is a smaller
volume than the first, and is of very rare
occurrence." (Stevens, Hist. nuggets, v.1,
1862, p. 108) This second volume was
written in part by Bernardo de Torres, whose
Cronica de la provincia pervana del Orden de
los Ermitaños de S. Avgvstín, Lima, 1657,
was also published as supplementary to the
first volume of Calancha's work and included
an epitome of it. (cf. René-Moreno, Bolivia
y Perú; notas hist. y bibl., 1905, p. 1-9;
Bibl. peruana, t. 1, 1896, nos. 404, 412;
Medina, Bibl. hisp-amer., t. 2, 1900, no.
977).---Jones 2644.

ESCOBAR, Matías. Americana Thebaida, Vitae pa-
trum de los religiosos hermitaños de nuestro
padre San Augustín de la provincia de San Nicolás Tolentino de Michoacán. La imprime por
vez primera el doctor Nicolás León. Morelia,
Impr. La Escuela de Artes, 1890. 193 p.
(Biblioteca histórico-filológica michoacana.
Sección 2: Historia, no. 1)   (6911
    "Cap. XVII: De todos los escritores, que
a hauido desta provincia de Mechoacan": p.
109-18. Reissued in Mexico, 1924.---Jones
2157.

-----. México, D.F., Impr. Victoria 1924.
xlvii, 897 p.   (6911a

GRIJALVA, Juan de. Cronica de la Orden de N.
S. P. Augustín en las provincias de la Nueva
España. En cuatro edades desde el año de
1533 hasta el de 1592. México, En el Convento de S. Augustín, y Impr. de I. Ruyz, 1624.
218 l.   (6912
    Jones 2221.

-----. Crónica de la provincia agustiniana
del Santísimo Nombre de Jesús de México,

GRIJALVA, Juan de. Cronica de la... (Cont.)
libro qvinto compuesto por el p. m. fr. Esteban García y pub. por la provincia del
Santisimo Nombre de Jesús de Filipinas en
su Archivo histórico hispano-agustiniano.
Madrid, Impr. de G. López del Horno, 1918.
404 p.   (6913
    Continuation of Juan de Grijalva's Cronica.
---Jones 2222.

-----. México, Impr. Victoria, 1924. 717,
xciii p.   (6914
    Reprint of the 1624 edition, prepared by
Federico Gómez de Orozco.

MALDONADO, Juan Martín. Breve svmma de la
provincia del Perv del Orden de los Ermitaños de San Avgvstín nuestro padre y de los
insignes y memorables coventos, hijos, y
sugetos que tiene en el estado y siglo presente de este año de 1651. Roma, F. Moneta,
1651. 51 p.   (6915
    Jones 2683.

MATURANA, Víctor. Historia de los Agustinos
en Chile. Santiago de Chile, Impr. Valparaíso, de F. T. Lathrop, 1904. 2 v. (6916
    Jones 1529.

MATUTE, Santiago. Los padres candelarios en
Colombia, o Apuntes para la historia. Bogotá, Tip~. de E. Pardo, 1897-1903.
6 v.   (6917
    Jones 1732.

PORTILLO Y AGUILAR, Sebastián. Chrónica espiritual augustiniana. Vidas de santos, bea-
tos, y venerables religiosos y religiosas
del Orden de su gran padre San Agustín.
Madrid, Impr. de A. de Orozco, 1731.
4 v.   (6918
    Medina, Bib. hisp.-am., 2813.---Jones
379.

SANTIAGO VELA, Gregorio de. Ensayo de una bi-
blioteca ibero-americana de la Orden de San
Agustín, por el p. Gregorio de Santiago Vela
de la Provincia del Smo. nombre de Jesús de
Filipinas. Obra basada en el catálogo bio-
bibliográfico agustiniano del p. Bonifacio
Moral. Pub. a expensas de la expresada
Provincia de Filipinas. Madrid, Impr. del
Asilo de Huérfanos de S. C. de Jesús,
1913- . v. 1- .   (6919
    Jones 435, reports v. 8 printed in 1931.

TORRES, Bernardo de. Crónica de la provincia
peruana del Orden de los Ermitaños de S.
Agustín. Lima, Impr. de J. Santos de Saldaña, 1657.   (6920
    The second part is an epitome of Calan-
cha's Crónica (1551-1593); the first part
continues this chronicle from 1594 to 1657
(Medina, Impr. en Lima, no. 381)---Jones
2758.

VALLADOLID. Colegio de agustinos. Biblioteca bibliográfico-agustiniana del Colegio de Valladolid, ordenada por el r. p. Antonio Blanco. Valladolid, Tip. de J. M. de La Cuesta, 1909. 629 p. (6921
    Jones 507.

VERA, Pedro de. Relación fidedigna, hecha en la provincia de Mechoacán de la Nueva España, por mandado del ilustrísimo señor conde de Lemos y de Andrade, en que se refiere el número de conventos que hasta el día de la fecha hay en esta provincia de San Nicolás de Tolentino, de la Orden de Santo Agustino, y los religiosos della, fecha por noviembre del año de 1603. (Colección de documentos inéditos para la historia de España. Madrid, 1891. t. 100, p. 459-76) (6922
    Jones 2574.

CAPUCHINOS

IGNACIO (de Pamplona) Historia de las misiones de los pp. Capuchinos en Chile y Argentina (1849-1911) Santiago de Chile, Impr. "Chile", 1911. 567 p. (6923
    Jones 1497.

REZENDE, Modesto. Os missionarios capuchinhos no Brasil; esboço historico prefaciado pelo dr. Alfonso de E. Taunay. São Paulo, Convento da Immaculada Conceição, 1931. xvi, 603 p. (6924
    "Elenco das ovras que consultamos": p. xi-xiv. "Appendice: Elenco dos missionarios capuchinhos": p. 573-601.---Jones 1156.

CARMELITES

AZEVEDO, Miguel de. Catalogo dos rev. mos priores provinciaes, ill. mos ex. mos srs. arcebispos e bispos, e escriptores na provincia dos carmelitas calçados em os reinos de Portugal, Algarve e seus dominios. Lisboa, 1810. 36 p. (6925
    Of little value.---Jones 965.

HERMANAS Carmelitas Descalzas Misioneras, Medellín. IV Centenario de la Reforma Carmelitana, 1562-1962. Noticia bibliográfica sobre Santa Teresa de Jesús. Medellín, 1963. (6926
    Cited in Peraza, Fichas, 1964, item 533.

DOMINICANS

ANGULO, Domingo. La Orden de Santo Domingo en el Perú; estudio bibliográfico. [Lima, Sanmartí y Ca., 1910] 299 p. (6927
    Jones 2624.

BAZAN, Hernando. Memorial del número de religiosos y de sus cualidades, que hay en esta provincia de Santiago de Méjico y pertenecen a ella, de la Orden de Predicadores, y de sus conventos, colegios y doctrinas de indios. (Colección de documentos inéditos para la historia de España. Madrid, 1891. t. 100, p. 480-91) (6928
    Jones 2071.

BURGOA, Francisco de. Palestra historial de virtudes y exemplares apostólicos. Fundada del zelo de insignes héroes de la sagrada Orden de Predicadores de este Nuevo Mundo. México, D.F., I. Ruyz, 1670. 269 numb. l. (6929
    Medina, Impr. en México, no. 1019.---Jones 2171.

DAVILA PADILLA, Agustín. Historia de la fundación y discurso de la provincia de Santiago de México de la Orden de Predicadores, por las vidas de sus varones insignes, y casos notables de Nueva España. Madrid, En casa de P. Madrigal, 1596. 815 p. (6930
    For continuation see Franco y Ortega and Ojea.---Jones 2145.

-----. -----. Brussels, En Casa de Iván de Meerbeqve, 1675. 654 p. (6931

FRANCO Y ORTEGA, Alonso. Segunda parte de la Historia de la provincia de Santiago de México, Orden de Predicadores en la Nueva España, año de 1645 en México. México, D.F., Impr. del Museo Nacional, 1900. 573 p.(6932
    A continuation of Dávila Padilla's Historia de la provincia de Santiago de México; edited by José María de Agreda y Sánchez. ---Jones 2172.

MARTINEZ VIGIL, Ramón. La Orden de Predicadores, sus glorias en santidad, apostolado, ciencias, artes y gobierno de los pueblos, seguidas del ensayo de una biblioteca de Domínicos españoles. Madrid, G. del Amo, 1884. 430 p. (6933
    Jones 290.

MELENDEZ, Juan. Tesoros verdaderos de las Indias en la historia de la gran Provincia de San Juan Bautista del Perú, de el Orden de Predicadores. Roma, N. A. Tinassio, 1681-1682. 3 v. (6934
    Jones 2696.

MESANZA, Andrés. Bibliografía de la provincia dominicana de Colombia. Caracas, Edit. Sur-América, 1929. 337 p. (6935
    Jones 1737.

-----. Los obispos de la Orden dominicana en América. Einsiedeln, Suiza, Benziger & Co., 1939. 190 p. (6936
    "El autor se ha concretado a hacer un catá-

MESANZA, Andrés. Los obispos de la... (Cont.)
logo con breves noticias biográficas.---Jones
313a.

OJEA, Hernando. Libro tercero de la historia
religiosa de la provincia de México de la
Orden de Sto. Domingo. México, Impreso por
el Museo Nacional, 1897. 73 p.   (6937
   Written as a continuation of Dávila Padilla's Historia de la fundación y discurso de
la provincia de Santiago de México de la Orden de los Predicadores, edited by J. M. de
Agreda y Sánchez.---Jones 2384.

QUETIF, Jacques. Scriptores Ordinis praedica-
torum recensiti, notisque historicis et cri-
ticis illustrati, opis quo singulorum vita,
praeclareque gesta referuntur, chronologia
insuper, seu tempus quo quisque floruit certo
statuitur: fabulae exploduntur: scripta
genuina dubia, supposititia expendutur, re-
centiorum de iis judicium aut probatur, aut
emendatur: codices manuscripti, variaeque e
typis editions, & ubi habeantur, indicantur:
alumni dominicani, quos alieni rapuerant,
vindicantur, dubii, & extranei, falsoque as-
cripti ad eujusque seculi finem rejiciuntur,
& suis restituuntur: praemittitvr in prole-
gomenis notitia ordinis qualis fuit ab initio
ad an. MD. Tum series capitulorum genera-
lium iis annis habitorum, denique index eorum
qui ad ecclesiasticas dignitates promoti fue-
runt, vel in hoc tomo laudatorum, vel alias
ab aliis omissorum. Inchoavit R. P. F. Jacobus Quetif, absolvit R. P. F. Jacobus Echard.
Lutetiae Parisiorum, apud J. -B.-C. Ballard
et N. Simart, 1719-1721. 2 v.   (6938
   "Un verdadero monumento de investigaciones
bio-bibliográficas, cuya consulta es indispensable cuando se trata de autores y libros americanos." (Medina, Bib. hisp.-am., v. 6,
p. cxxviii)---Jones 388.

-----. -----. [Torino, Bottega d'Erasmo, 1961]
2 v.   (6939

RIOS ARCE, Francisco E. de los. Puebla de los
Angeles y la Orden dominicana. Estudio histórico para ilustrar la historia civil, eclesiástica, científica, literaria y artística
de esta ciudad de Los Angeles. Puebla, "El
Escritorio," 1910. 2 v.   (6940
   Jones 2460.

FRANCISCANS

ADAMS, Eleanor Burnham. A bio-bibliography of
Franciscan authors in colonial Central Ameri-
ca. Washington, D.C., Academy of American
Franciscan History, 1953. xxi, 97 p. (Publ.
of the Academy of American Franciscan History.
Bibliographical ser., v. 2)   (6941

BALTASAR (de Lodares). Los franciscanos capuchinos en Venezuela; 2a. ed. Caracas, Empresa Gutenberg, 1929-1931. 3 v.   (6942
   Jones 2887.

CARROCERA, Cayetano de. La orden franciscana
en Venezuela; documentos para la historia
de sus misiones en esta república durante
el siglo XIX. Caracas, Lit. Tip. Mercantil,
1929. 302 p.   (6943
   Jones 2896.

CASTRO, José de. Primera y segunda parte de
El Arbol cronológico de la santa provincia
de Santiago. Salamanca, F. García, 1722-
1727. 2 v.   (6944
   Vol. 2: Santiago, A. Frayz, 1727. Vol.
1 has a bibliography of works of Franciscans
up to 1721. (V. Vindel, Cat. 1, 1924.)---
Jones 89.

COMPTE, Francisco María. Varones ilustres de
la Orden seráfica en el Ecuador, desde la
fundación de Quito hasta nuestros días;
2a. ed., corr. y aum. por el mismo autor.
Quito, Impr. del Clero, 1885. 2 v.   (6945
   Jones 1968.

CORDOBA, Antonio Santa Clara. La orden franciscana en las repúblicas del Plata (sin
tesis histórica), 1536-1934. Buenos Aires,
Impr. López, 1934. 382 p.   (6946
   Jones 836a.

CORDOVA Y SALINAS, Diego de. Corónica de la
religiosíssima Provincia de los doze apóstoles del Perú, de la Orden de N. P. S.
Francisco. Lima, I. López de Herrera,
1651. 214, 690, 679-95 p.   (6947
   cf. Medina, Impr. en Lima, no. 339 and
Streit.---Jones 2646.

EIJAN, Samuel. Franciscanismo iberoamericano
en la historia, la literatura y el arte.
Barcelona, Bib. Franciscana, 1927.
525 p.   (6948
   Jones 136.

ESPINOSA, Isidro Félix de. Chrónica apostólica, y seráphica de todos los colegios de
propaganda fide de esta Nueva-España, de
missioneros franciscanos observantes: eri-
gidos con autoridad pontificia, y regia, para la reformación de los fieles, y conversión de los gentiles. México, Por la Viuda
de J. B. de Hogal, 1746-1792. 2 v.   (6949
   Vol. 2 has title: Crónica seráfica y
apostólica del Colegio de propaganda fide
de la Santa Cruz de Querétaro en la Nueva
España. Escrita por el p. f. Juan Domingo
Arricivita. 2a. parte (México, Por F. de
Zúñiga y Ontiveros, 1792)
   One of the earlist sources for the history
of the Franciscan college at Querétaro. (cf.
Streit).---Jones 2158.

ESPINOSA, Isidro Félix de. Cronica de la
provincia franciscana de los apóstoles San
Pedro y San Pablo de Michoacán; la publica
por vez primera el dr. Nicolás León. México, Impr. "El Tiempo", 1899. 574 p. (6950
Jones 2159.

GEIGER, Maynard. Biographical dictionary of
the Franciscans in Spanish Florida and Cuba
(1528-1841) Paterson, N.J., St. Anthony
Guild Pr., 1940. 140 p. (Franciscan studies, 21) (6951
A list, with brief biographies and references to sources, of more than 700 Franciscan friars.---Jones 1832b.

HERNANDEZ, P. P. Notas de bibliografia franciscana. (Archivo ibero-americano, Madrid,
v. 21, p. 64-95, 1924) (6952
Jones 201.

IZAGUIRRE ISPIZUA, Bernardino. Historia de
las misiones franciscanas y narración de
los progresos de la geografía en el oriente
del Perú; relatos originales y producciones
en lenguas indígenas de varios misioneros,
1619-1921. Lima, Tall. Tip. de la Penitenciaría, 1922-1929. 14 v. (6953
"Fuentes de esta historia": v. 1, p. 41-
60.---Jones 2659.

JUAN DE SAN ANTONIO. Bibliotheca universa
franciscana. Matriti, ex Typ. Causae V.
Matris de Agreda, 1731. 3 v. (6954
Jones 232. Cited also in Giraldo Jaramillo, p. 137. Palau gives 1733 as imprint
date. Giraldo Jaramillo cites, p. 137, a
2 v. work with same title by Fray Juan de
Soto (1732)

-----. Minorum fratrum, origine, domiciliove
descalceatorum, attramento & sanguine scriptorum bibliotheca pro supplemento Wadlingia-
na, incrementoque novae franciscanae bibliothecae authorum omnium sub unico generali
ministro in ordinibus tribus efformabilis.
Salmanticae, ex typ. E. García de Honorato
& S. Miguel, 1728. 32 1., 239, 108 p.,
39 1. (6955
"Libro indispensable al bibliógrafo americano y filipino" (Medina. Bib. hisp. am.,
2706)---Jones 232a.

MARCELLINO (da Civezza). Saggio di bibliografia geografica, storica, etnografica sanfran-
cescana. Prato, R. Guasti, 1879.
698 p. (6956
Notices of 819 writers and their works
(including over 250 mss.) arranged alphabetically by authors; with extracts from and
some reprints of the rarer works, many of
which concern early explorations of Spanish
America.---Jones 280.

MARCELLINO (da Civezza) Storia universale
delle missioni francescane, Roma, Tip. Tibe-
rina, 1857-1895. 9 v. (6957
"Appendice bibliografica alla prima parte
del vii. libro della Storia Universale delle
missioni francescane" (87 p.) bound with
v. 7, pt. 1.---Jones 281.

MEDINA, Baltasar de. Chrónica de la Santa
Provincia de San Diego de México, de religiosos descalços de N. S. P. S. Francisco
en la Nueva España. Vida de ilvstres y venerables varones, que la han edificado con
excelentes virtudes. México, J. de Ribera,
1682. 259 numb. 1. (6958
Jones 2326.

OCARANZA, Fernando. Capítulos de la historia
franciscana. (Primera - segunda serie),
México, 1933-1934. 2 v. (6959
"Nómina de los ministros generales de la
Orden de San Francisco de Asís desde su fundación, en el año de 1210, hasta el de 1869":
v. 2, p. 29-40. "Principales obras que escribieron los frailes franciscanos en Nueva
España, durante los siglos XVI y XVII, según
fr. Agustín de Vetancourt": v. 2, p. 67-78.
"Acerca de algunos libros escritos por franciscanos en el siglo XIX": v. 1, p. 517-20;
v. 2, p. 323.---Jones 2382.

REA, Alonso de la. Crónica de la Orden de N.
seráfico P. S. Francisco, provincia de San
Pedro y San Pablo de Michoacán en la Nueva
España. México, D.F., 1882. 488 p. (6960
Reprint of the rare edition of 1634.---
Jones 2450.

TELLO, Antonio. Libro segundo de la Crónica
miscelánea, en que se trata de la conquista
espiritual y temporal de la Santo Provincia
de Xalisco en el Nuevo Reino de la Galicia
y Nueva Vizcaya y descubrimiento del Nuevo
México. Guadalajara, Impr. de "La República Literaria" 1891. 886 p. (6962
"Introducción bibliográfica" by José López Portillo y Rojas.---Jones 2525. Another
edition was published in Guadalajara, 1890-
1891 but with some chapters omitted.

UDAONDO, Enrique. Crónica histórica de la ve-
nerable Orden tercera de San Francisco en
la República Argentina. Buenos Aires, S.
de Amorrortu, 1920. 454 p. (6963
Jones 876.

VAZQUEZ, Francisco. Crónica de la provincia
del Santísimo nombre de Jesús de Guatemala
de la Orden de N. seráfico padre San Francisco en el reino de Nueva España; 2a. ed.
Guatemala, Tip. Nacional, 1937-1944. 4 v.
(Biblioteca "Guathemala", v. 14-17) (6965
Jones 1312. "Prólogo, notas e índices"
in v.4 by Lázaro Lamadrid.

ZULAICA GARATE, Román. Los franciscanos y
la imprenta en México en el siglo XVI. México, Edit. Pedro Robredo, 1939.
373 p.   (6966
    A bibliographical study of the relation
of the Franciscans to the development of
printing in Mexico, with descriptions of
the books published by Franciscans.---
Jones 2595a.

JESUITS

ALEGRE, Francisco Javier. Historia de la Compañía de JesÚS EN Nueva España que estaba
escribiendo el p. Francisco Javier Alegre
al tiempo de su expulsión. Publicala Carlos
María Bustamante. México, Impresa por J.
M. Lara, 1841-1842. 3 v.   (6967
    For a continuation see Dávila y Arrillaga.
---Jones 2040.

AMUNATEGUI Y SOLAR, Domingo. Jesuitas, gobernantes, militares y escritores. Santiago
de Chile, 1934. 224 p. (Biblioteca América, 2)   (6968
    Jones 1386.

ARGENTINA. Biblioteca nacional. Catalogo
de documentos referentes a jesuitas (1581-
1805) Director: Gustavo Martínez Zuviría.
Prologo de Manuel Selva. Buenos Aires,
Impr. de la Biblioteca Nacional, 1940.
79 p.   (6969

ASTRAIN, Antonio. Historia de la Compañía
de Jesús en la asistencia de España. Madrid, Sucesores de Rivadeneyra, 1902-1925.
7 v.   (6970
    Jones 30.

BACKER, Augustin de, and BACKER, Aloys de.
Bibliothèque de la Compagnie de Jésus.
1. ptie: Histoire par le père Auguste Carayon. Nouv. éd. par Carlos Sommervogel,
publ. par la Province de Belgique. Bruxelles, O. Schepens; Paris, A. Picard,
1890- . v. 1- .   (6971
    1. ptie. (v. 1-10, 1890-1909) includes
Anonymes. Pseudonymes. Index geographique
des auteurs et des domiciles and Tables de
la Première partie par P. Bliard.---Jones
37.

-----. -----. Corrections et additions à la
Bibliothèque de la Compagnie de Jésus.
Supplément au "De Backer-Sommervogel," par
Ernest M. Rivière. Toulouse, L'Auteur,
1911-1917. pts. 1-4.   (6972
    Jones 38.

-----. Bibliothèque des écrivains de la Compagnie de Jésus ou, Notices bibliographiques:
1o., de tous les ouvrages publiés par les
membres de la Compagnie de Jésus, depuis la

BACKER, Augustin de, and BACKER, ...(Cont.)
fondation de l'ordre jusqu'à nos jours: 2o.,
des apologies, des critique littéraires, et
scientifiques suscitée à leur sujet. Liège,
L. Grandmont-Donders, 1853-1961. 7 v.(6973
    Jones 36.

BORDA, José Joaquín. Historia de la Compañia
de Jesús en la Nueva Granada. Poissy, S.
Lejay et Cie., 1872. 2 v.   (6974
    Jones 1694.

CABALLERO, Raimundo Diosdado. Bibliotheca
scriptorum Societatis Jesu supplementum
primum [et alterum] Romae, 1814-1816.
2 v.   (6975
    "A Estudiar la vida y obras de esos Je-
suítas expulsados de España y América y que
se establecieron en Italia están destinados
los dos suplementos." (Medina, Bib. hisp-am.
v. 6, cxxvii.)---Jones 409.

CARAYON, Auguste. Bibliographie historique
de la Compagnie de Jésus; ou Catalogue des
ouvrages rélatifs à l'histoire des Jésuites,
depuis leur origine jusqu'à nos jours.
Paris, A. Durand [etc.] 1864. 612 p. (6976
    Pt. III, chap. 4 deals with missions in
America, citing briefly some 200 titles.---
Jones 82.

CASSANI, Jose. Historia de la provincia de la
Compañía de Jesús del Nuevo Reyno de Granada
en la América, descripción y relación exacta
de sus gloriosas missiones en el reyno, lla-
nos, Meta, y río Orinoco, almas y terreno
que han conquistado sus misioneros para dios.
Madrid, Impr. M. Fernández, 1741. 2 v.(6977
    Jones 1696a.

CATALOGUS personarum et officiorum Provinciae
Mexicanae Societatis Jesu, in Indiys, 1764.
(Reprinted in León, Nicolas. Bibliografía
mexicana del siglo XVIII. México, 1906.
Sección 1, 3. pte., p. 76-118)   (6978
    Index alphabeticus cognomium sociorum in
Provincia Mexicana (with dates of birth):
p. 101-18.---Jones 2122.

COLAZO, Manuel. Catalogus Provinciae Mexicanae Societatis Jesu, in quo singulorum no-
men, cognomen, patria, aetas atque ingres-
sus in eanden continetur. Mexici, ex Re-
galis & Antiquioris Divi Ildefonsi Collegii
Typis, 1758. 13 1.   (6979
    2a. ed., first published in 1751.---Jones
2133.

DAVILA Y ARRILLAGA, Jose Mariano. Continuación de la historia de la Compañía de Jesús en Nueva España del p. Francisco Javier
Alegre. Puebla, Impr. del Colegio Pío de
Artes y Oficios, 1888-1889. 2 v.   (6980
    Jones 2146.

ENRICH, Francisco. Historia de la Compañía de Jesús en Chile. Barcelona, Rosal, 1891. 2 v. (6981
Jones 1463.

FURLONG CARDIFF, Guillermo. Los Jesuítas y la cultura rioplatense; exploradores, colonizadores, geógrafos. Montevideo, Urta y Curbelo, 1933. 161 p. (6982
Jones 698c.

GARSCH, Bruno. Der einfluss der Jesuitenmissionen auf den wandel der naturlandschaft zur kulturlandschaft im stromgebiet des Paraguay-Paraná. Breslau, D. Borgmeyer, 1934. 150 p. (6983
Bibliography: p. 144-50.---Jones 2609.

GOMEZ RODELES, Cecilio. La Compañía de Jesús catequista. Madrid, Impr. G. L. Horno, 1913. 415 p. (6984
Jones 169.

HEREDIA, Carlos M. Los Jesuítas de la Nueva España, catequistas. (Razón y fe, Madrid, t. 38, p. 462-74, 1914) (6985
Jones 2241.

HERNANDEZ, Pablo. Reseña histórica de la misión de Chile-Paraguay de la Compañía de Jesus desde su origen en 1836 hasta el centenario de la restauración de la Compañía en 1914. Barcelona, Edit. Iberica, 1914. 319 p. (6986
"Principales libros que se han publicado": p. 258-61.---Jones 200.

IGUINIZ, Juan Bautista. Bibliografía de los escritores de la provincia mexicana de la Compañía de Jesus desde su restauración en 1816 hasta nuestros días. México, D.F., Edit, Buena Prensa, [1945] 526 [36] p. (6987

JACOBSEN, Jerome Vincent. Educational foundation of the Jesuits in sixteenth-century New Spain. Berkeley, Univ. of California Pr., 1938. 292 p. (6988
Bibliography: p. 241-49.---Jones 2264.

LEAL, Antônio Henriques. Apontamentos para a historia dos Jesuitas no Brasil. Maranhão, 1874. 2 v. (6989
Jones 1055.

LEITE, Serafim. Historia da Companhia de Jesus no Brasil. Lisboa, Livraria portugalia; Rio de Janeiro, Civilização Brasileira, 1938-1950. 10 v. (6990
"Introdução bibliográfica": v. 1, p. xix-xxxii; v. 2, p. ix-xv.---Jones 1074. "Indice Geral": v. 10.

LEONHARDT, Carlos. Papeles de los antiguos Jesuítas de Buenos Aires y Chile. Buenos Aires,

LEONHARDT, Carlos. Papeles de los... (Cont.) 1926. 48 p. (6991
Jones 751b.

MEDINA, José Toribio. Noticias bio-bibliográficas de los Jesuítas expulsos de América en 1767. Santiago de Chile, Impr. Elzeviriana, 1914. 327 p. (6992
Jones 308.

NIEREMBERG, Juan Eusebio, and ANDRADE, Alonso de. Varones ilustres de la Compañía de Jesús; 2a. ed., t. 4. Misiones del Perú, Nueva Granada, Quito, Paraguay, Chile. Bilbao, Administración de "El Mensajero del Corazón de Jesús", 1889. 642 p. (6993
Jones 510.

PASTELLS, Pablo. Historia de la Compañía de Jesús en la provincia del Paraguay (Argentina, Paraguay, Uruguay, Perú, Bolivia y Brasil) según los documentos originales del Archivo General de Indias, extractados y anotados por el r. p. Pablo Pastells. Madrid, V. Suárez, 1912-1948. 8 v. (6994
Jones 365.

PERAMAS, José Manuel. De vita et moribus sex sacerdotum paraguaycorum. Faventiae, ex Typ. Archii, 1791. 299 p. (6995
Contains biographical sketches of Emmanuel de Vergara, Emmanuel Querini, Petrus Joannes Andreu, Joannes Escandon, Vincentius Sans and Sigismundus Griera.---Jones 2617.

-----. De vita et moribus tredecim virorum paraguaycorum. Faventiae, ex. Typ. Archii, 1793. 462 p. (6996
Includes biographical sketches of Ignatius Morro, Joannes Mesner, Joannes Suarez, Ignatius Chome, Franciscus Ruiz de Villegas, Joannes Angelus Amilaga, Antonius del Castillo, Stephanus Pallozius, Clemens Baigorri, Franciscus Urrejola, Joachimus Iribarren, Cosmas Agullo and Martinus Schmid. ---Jones 2618.

PEREZ, Rafael. La Compañía de Jesús en Colombia y Centro-América después de su restauración. Valladolid, L. N. de Gaviria, 1896-1898. 3 v. (6997
Jones 1757.

PEREZ DE RIBAS, Andrés. Crónica y historia religiosa de la Provincia de la Compañía de Jesús de México en Nueva España. México, D.F., Impr. del Sagrado Corazón de Jesús, 1896. 2 v. (6998
Jones 2418.

RIVADENEIRA, Pedro de. Bibliotheca scriptorum Societatis Iesv opvs inchoatvm a Pedro Ribadeneira, anno salutis 1602. Continvatvm a Philippo Alegambe, vsque ad annum

RIVADENEIRA, Pedro de. Bibliotheca...(Cont.)
1642. Recognitum & productum ad annum Ju-
bilaei M. DC. LXXV a Nathanaele Sotvello.
Romae, ex Typ. de L. Varesii, 1676.
984 p.   (6999
   Caballero's Bibliotheca scriptorum Societatis Jesu forms a supplement to this work.
Jones 408.

SHIELS, William Eugene. Gonzalo de Tapia
(1561-1594) founder of the first permanent
Jeuit Mission in North America. New York,
1934. 198 p. (United States Catholic Historical Society. Monograph series,
14)   (7000
   Bibliography: p. 180-95.---Jones 2501.

TECHO, Nicolás del. Historia provinciae Para-
guariae Societatis Jesv. Leodii, ex Officina Typ. J. M. Hovii, 1673. 390 p. (7001
Jones 2621.

TORRES SALDAMANDO, Enrique. Los antiguos
Jesuítas del Perú; biografías y apuntes
para su historia. Lima, Impr. Liberal,
1882. 400 p.   (7002
   Contains bibliographical notices of 157
16-17th century authors.---Jones 2763.

URIARTE, José Eugenio de, and LECINA, Mariano.
Biblioteca de escritores de la Compañía de
Jesús pertenecientes a la antigua asisten-
cia de España desde sus orígenes hasta el
año de 1773. Madrid, Impr. de la Viuda de
López del Horno, 1925- . v. 1- .   (7002a
Jones 504.

URIARTE, José Eugenio de. Catálogo razonado
de obras anónimas y seudónimos de autores
de la Compañía de Jesús pertenecientes a la
antigua asistencia española: con un apéndice de otras de los mismos, dignas de especial estudio bibliográfico (28 sept. 1540-
16 ag. 1773) Madrid, Estab. Tip. "Sucesores
de Rivadeneyra," 1904-1916. 5 v.   (7003
   A monumental and indispensable work for
Jesuit bibliography.---Jones 503.

VALLE, Rafael Heliodoro. El Convento de Te-
potzotlán. México, Museo de Arqueología,
Historia y Etnografía, 1924. 130 p (7004
   Includes bibliography.---Jones 2553.

VARGAS UGARTE, Rubén. Jesuítas peruanos des-
terrados a Italia. (Revista histórica, órgano del Instituto Histórico del Perú, Lima,
t. 8, p. 209-42, 1928)   (7005
Jones 2769.

-----. -----. Lima, 1934. 232 p.   (7006
Jones 2770.

XARQUE, Francisco. Insignes misioneros de la
Compañía de Jesús en la provincia del Paraguay. Estado presente de sus misiones en

XARQUE, Francisco. Insignes ... (Cont.)
Tucumán, Paraguay, y Río de la Plata, que
comprehende su distrito. Pamplona, J. Micón,
1687. 432 p.   (7007
Jones 2622.

ZAMBRANO, Francisco. Diccionario bio-bibliográfico de la Compañía de Jesús en México.
México, D.F., Edit. Jus, 1961- .
v. 1- .   (7007a
   v. 1-2: Siglo XVI (1566-1600)

ZELIS, Rafael de. Catálogo de los sugetos de
la Compañía de Jesús que formaban la provincia de México, 25 de junio de 1767. Contiene: los sugetos por orden alfabético, por
orden de edad, por orden de grado: los colegios, las misiones y los difuntos. México,
Impr. de J. Escalante y Ca., 1871.
202 p.   (7008
   "Après la mort du p. de Zelis, le p. Pierre
Márquez completa la liste des défunts. Ce
volume a été publié par le p. André Artola."
(Backer-Sommervogel.)---Jones 2592a.

MERCEDARIANS

DELGADO, Ricardo. Estudio histórico de los
Mercedarios de Chile. (Revista mercedaria
chilena, no. extraord., 1918)   (7009
   Contains a chapter, "Escritores mercedarios y sus publicaciones."---Jones 1444.

GARI Y SIUMELL, José Antonio. Biblioteca mercedaria o sea Escritores de la celeste, real
y militar Orden de la Merced, redención de
cautivos, con indicación de sus obras, tanto
impresas como manuscritas, su patria, títulos, dignidades, hechos memorables, época y
provincia en que florecieron y murieron, y
dos copiosos índices, uno de escritores y
otro de las obras y escritos. Barcelona,
Impr. de los Herederos de la Viuda Plá,
1875. 395 p.   (7010
Jones 160.

GAZULLA, Policarpo. Los primeros Mercedarios
en Chile, 1535-1600. [Santiago de Chile,
Impr. la Ilustración, 1918?] 491 p. (7011
Jones 1489.

PAREJA, Francisco de. Crónica de la provincia
de la visitación de Ntra. Sra. de la Merced,
redención de cautivos de la Nueva España.
Escrita en 1688. México, Impr. de J. R.
Barbedillo, 1882-1883. 2 v.   (7012
Jones 2403.

PEREZ, Pedro Nolasco. Los obispos de la Orden
de la Merced en America (1601-1926); documentos del Archivo General de Indias. Santiago de Chile, Impr. Chile, 1927.
581 p.   (7013
Jones 368.

PEREZ, Pedro Nolasco. Religiosos de la Merced que pasaron a la América española. Sevilla, 1923. 2 v. (Publ. del Centro Oficial de Estudios Americanistas, t. 9
y 12)   (7014
   Jones 369.

RIOS MEZA, Miguel L. Mercedarios chilenos en
la Universidad y en las letras. Santiago,

RIOS MEZA, Miguel L. Mercedario... (Cont.)
   Impr. "Rapid", 1936. 210 p.   (7015

TRINITARIANS

MUÑOZ OLAVE, Reinaldo. Las monjas trinitarias
de Concepción, 1570-1822; relato histórico;
2a. ed. corr. y aum. Santiago de Chile,
Impr. de San José, 1926. 321 p.   (7016
   First edition, 1918.---Jones 1553.

SCIENCE

BARABINO, Santiago E. Bibliografía. Buenos
Aires. Coni, 1919. 32 p.   (7017
   Published in Anales de la Sociedad Cientí-
fica Argentina, t. 86, p. 361 and following.
All reviews written by the author.

CASTELLANOS, Alfredo, and PASOTTI, Pierina.
Crónica bibliográfica: mineralogía y minería, petrografía, geología, geografía, paleontología. Rosario, Impr. de la Universidad, 1939-1958. (Publ. del Instituto de
Fisiología y Geología, A-1939, B-1940, C-
1941, D-1942, E-1943, F-1944, G-1945, H-
1946, I-1947, J-1958)   (7018
   Co-author of A-1939: Cortés Plá. Reviews
of specialized literature. Each issue 47
to 163 pages.

LARREA, Carlos Manuel. Bibliografía científica del Ecuador. Quito, Edit. Casa de la
Cultura Ecuatoriana, 1948-1953.
5 v.   (7020

-----. Bibliografía científica del Ecuador.
Madrid, Ediciones Cultura Hispánica, 1952.
492 p.   (7021

LISBOA, Miguel Arrojada Ribeiro. Um caso de
critica scientifica (artigos publicados
n' "O Commercio de São Paulo" 17 a 25 de junio de 1902) São Paulo, Typ. e Papelaria
de Vanarden & Cia., 1902. 65 p.   (7022
   Cited in Reis, item 198.

NELSON, Edward W. Lower California and its
natural resources. Washington, Govt. Print.
Off., 1921. 194 p. (Memoirs of the National
Academy of Sciences, v. 16, 1st
memoir)   (7023

NELSON, Edward W. Lower... (Cont.)
   Bibliography: p. 147-71.---Jones 2377.

OLAGUIBEL, Manuel de, and IGLESIAS, Enrique.
Bibliografía científica del estado de Mé-
xico. Toluca, Of. Tip. del Gobierno en la
Escuela de Artes, 1899. 30 p.   (7024
   Jones 2385.

PICATOSTE Y RODRIGUEZ, Felipe. Apuntes para
una biblioteca científica española del siglo
XVI; estudios biográficos y bibliográficos
de ciencias exactas, físicas y naturales.
Madrid, Impr. de M. Tello, 1891.
416 p.   (7025
   Jones 372.

RAMIREZ, Arbelio. Dos etapas de la bibliografía científica de la Banda Oriental. [Mon-
tevideo, 1958] 19 p.   (7026
   Reprinted from Revista de geografía e historia Estuario, Montevideo, no. 2-3, nov.
1958. Cited in Musso, 120.

TRELLES Y GOVIN, Carlos Manuel. Biblioteca
científica cubana. Matanzas, Impr. de J.
F. Oliver, 1918-1919. 2 v.   (7027
   Contents. - t. 1. Matemáticas, astronomía,
Ciencias militares, físicas y naturales,
Biología, Antropología, Agricultura. - t. 2.
Ciencias médicas, Ingeniería.---Jones 1922.
Now available in microprint.

TUCUMAN, Arg. Universidad Nacional. Catálogo de astronomía, matemáticas, física, química, bibliografía de obras alemanas, últimas adquisiciones, donación Ing. O. Lederer.
Tucumán, 1937. 90 p. (Boletín de la Biblioteca, no. 2)   (7028
   Jones 871a.

BEHRENDT, Richard F. W. Modern Latin America in social science literature. [Hamilton? N.Y., 1949] 152 p.   (7029
    Bibliography of books, pamphlets and periodicals in English in the fields of economics, politics and sociology of Latin America.

-----. Suplemento a una obra bibliográfica sobre América Latina, 1- . Washington, D.C., Pan American Union, 1950- .   (7030
    Supplement 1, reprinted from Ciencias Sociales, 1(5): 83-95, sept. 1950. Supplement 2, in Ciencias sociales, 1(6): 107-22, nov. 1950.

-----. Selected bibliography of books, pamphlets, and periodicals in English in the field of economics, politics, and sociology of Latin America. Albuquerque, New Mex., School of Inter-American Affairs, Univ. of New Mexico, 1943. 31 p. (Inter-American series, miscellanea) mimeogr.   (7031

DIEZ MIERES, Alfonso. Ensayo sobre una bibliografía sociológica. Buenos Aires, 1953. 19 p.   (7032
    Cited in Catálogo, Inst. Bibliotecológico, item 144.

DOHERTY, Donald K. Preliminary bibliography of colonization and settlement in Latin and Anglo-America. Ottawa, Geographical Branch, Dept. of Mines and Technical Surveys, 1952. 70 p.   (7033

HAMBURG. Welt-Wirtschafts-Archiv. Bibliothek. Ecuador, Peru, Bolivien. Hamburg, 1958. 119 p. (Auslandskunde, Literaturnachweis über die Gebiete Wirtschaft und Politik, Recht und Tecknik. Länder-abteilung, no. 14)   (7034

-----. -----. -----. Lateinamerika. Hamburg, 1954-1955. 2 v. (Auslandskunde. Literaturnachweis die Gebiete Wirtschaft und Politik, Recht und Technik. Länder-abteilung, no. 8-9)   (7035

-----. -----. -----. Mittelamerika und Karibischer Raum. Hamburg, 1956. 114 p. (Auslandskunde; Literaturnachweis über die Gebiete Wirschaft und Politik, Recht und Technik. Länder-abteilung, no. 10)   (7036

-----. -----. -----. Paraguay-Uruguay. Hamburg, 1959. 88 p. (Auslandskunde. Literaturnachweis über die Gebiete Wirtschaft und Politik, Recht und Technik. Länder-abteilung no. 18)   (7037

INTERNATIONAL bibliography of sociology, v. 1- . 1951- . [Paris, London]   (7038
    Includes references to Latin American periodicals. DPU collection begins with no. 2/3, 1955- .

JONES VARGAS, Fernando. Estudio bibliográfico sobre la sociología rural en Centroamérica. Ciudad Universitaria "Rodrigo Facio", Costa Rica, 1964. 40 p.   (7039

KEPNER, Charles David. Social aspects of the banana industry. New York, 1936. 230 p. (Studies in history, economics and public law, ed. by the faculty of political science of Columbia University, no. 414)   (7040
    Bibliography: p. 219-23.---Jones 1237.

MEDELLIN. Escuela Interamericana de Bibliotecología. B-14, Bibliografía: bibliografía de ciencias sociales. [Medellín] 1956? 7 p. mimeogr.   (7041

-----. -----. B-6, Bibliografía clasificada: Introducción a las ciencias sociales. [Medellín, n.d.] 2 p. mimeogr.   (7042

MIR, M. R. Bibliografía sobre cooperativismo. Montevideo, Inspección General de Hacienda, 1963. 20 p.   (7043
    Cited in Tajes, 1962/1963, item 32.

NELSON, Linda. Selected bibliography; sources of information about how families live in Latin America. Turrialba, C.R., 1964. 11 p. mimeogr.   (7044

NICHOLS, Madaline Wallis, and KINNAIRD, Lucia Burk. A bibliography of Spanish sociological articles: Nosotros, v. 1-76, [N.Y., 1935]   (7045
    Reprinted for private circulation from the American journal of sociology, v. 40, no. 4, p. 508-13, Jan. 1935.

PAN AMERICAN UNION. Division of Intellectual Cooperation. Life and customs in Latin America [bibliography] Washington, D.C., [1938] 8 p. mimeogr.   (7046

-----. [1941] 13 p. mimeogr.   (7047

POBLETE TRONCOSO, Moisés. Ensayo de bibliografía social de los países hispano americanos. Santiago de Chile, Edit. Cultura, 1936. 210 p.   (7048
    In 2 parts: pt. 1, arranged alphabetically under each country; pt. 2, classified by subject. "La primera parte de esta obra fue publicada por nosotros en la Revista internacional del trabajo (edición española), órgano de la Oficina Internacional del Trabajo de la Sociedad de Naciones".

PROGRAMA Interamericano de Información Popular. Three preliminary bibliographies of works related to the social sciences in Latin America. Tres bibliografías preliminares de obras relacionadas con las ciencias sociales en América Latina. San José, Costa Rica, 1962. 144 p.   (7049
   Compilers: Juan Díaz Bordenave and Antonio M. Arce. The bibliographies are product of a collaborative program in research between the Department of Communication, Michigan State University and the Programa Interamericano de Información Popular.

RESENHA de periódicos. Rio de Janeiro, Instituto de Ciências Sociais, Universidade do Brasil, 1963- .   (7051
   Cited in Doria 177a.

SPARN, Enrique. Repertorio de libros de derecho y ciencias sociales traducidos a la lengua castellana. (Revista de la Universidad Nacional, Córdoba, v. 24. p. 778-830, 1937)   (7052
   Jones 857. Also reprinted edition: Córdoba, 1938. 110 p.

TAVARES, Regina Helena, and LISBOA, Hadjine. Influências africanas en la América Latina; bibliografía preliminar, contribución al Coloquio sobre Relaciones entre Africa y América Latina. Rio de Janeiro, Centro Latino Americano de Investigaciones en Ciencias Sociales, 1963. 88 p.   (7052a
   Cited in Doria 49.

THOMPSON, Edgar Tristram. Bibliografía de las plantaciones. Washington, D.C., Unión Panamericana, 1957. 93 p. (Estudios monográficos, 4)   (7053
   Contains 1,347 items.

-----. Bibliografía de las plantaciones. Washington, D.C., Unión Panamericana, 1964. vii, 105 p. (Estudios y monografías, 12)   (7054
   A reprinting of the 1957 edition.

-----. The plantation; a bibliography. Washington, D.C., Pan American Union, 1957. 93 p. (Social science monograph, 4) (7055
   Contains 1,347 items.

UNITED NATIONS Educational, Scientific and Cultural Organization. Education Clearing House. Education for community development. Prepared by Unesco and United Nations. [Paris] 1954. 49 p. (Educational studies and documents, 7)   (7056
   Includes Latin American countries.

URUGUAY. Poder Legislativo. Biblioteca. Alcoholismo. Montevideo [1948] various pagings. (Referencia no. 4)   (7057
   Cited in Musso 527.

URUGUAY. Poder Legislativo. Biblioteca. Seguros sociales, artículos de anales, boletines y revistas. Montevideo. n.d. 5, 14 p. (Referencia no. 6)   (7058

ARGENTINA

BOREA, Domingo. La mutualidad y el cooperativismo en la República Argentina. Buenos Aires, Tall. Gráf. de L. J. Rosso y Cía., 1917. 271 p.   (7060
   "La bibliografía cooperativista argentina", p. 85-96.---Jones 608.

CENTRO Latino-americano de Pesquisas em Ciências Sociais. Estratificación y movilidad social en argentina; fuentes bibliográficas (1880-1958) Rio de Janeiro, 1959. 46 p. (Publicação no. 6)   (7061
   Compiler: Sergio Bagu.

HAMBURG. Welt-Wirtschafts-Archiv. Bibliothek Argentinien. Hamburg, 1956. 84 p. (Auslandskunde. Literaturnachweis über die Gebiete Wirtschaft und Politik, Recht und Technik. Länder-abteilung, no. 13)   (7063

KIELER Schriftumskunden zu Wirtschaft und Gesellschaft. Argentinien; teil 1. Kiel, 1961-1962. (Wirtschaftliche Landeskunde, Lieferung 1-3)   (7064
   Cited in Paulus, p. 3.

BRAZIL

BAZZANELLA, Waldemiro. Estratificação e mobilidade social no Brasil, fontes bibliográficas. Rio de Janeiro, Centro Brasileiro de Pesquisas Educacionais, 1956. 116 p. (7065

BIBLIOGRAFIA brasileira de ciências sociais, v. 1, no. 1- , 1954- . Rio de Janeiro, Instituto Brasileiro de Bibliografia e Documentação [1955-]   (7066
   Continues Bibliografia econômico-social edited from Sept. 1950 to May 1954 by the Fundação Getúlio Vargas. Last issue received in DPU: no. 7, 1960.

BRAZIL. Ministério da Fazenda. Biblioteca. Bibliografia. [Rio de Janeiro, 1950-1952] mimeogr.   (7067
   Lists published separately. In DPU collection: Sindicalismo. 1950. 6 p. - Emigração e colonização. 1951. [3] p. - Economia do Brasil. 1951. 3 p. - História econômica do Brasil. 1951. 4 p. - Direito civil. n.d. 23 p.; Supl., jan. 1952. 10 p. - Finanças públicas, n.d. 78 p. - Administração municipal. n.d. 5 p. - Comercio, comunicações. n.d. 38 p. - Direito comercial; Supl. jan. 1952. 7 p. - Direito; Supl. jan. 1952. 8 p. - Direito público e direito in-

BRAZIL. Ministério da Fazenda ... (Cont.)
ternacional público; Supl. jan. 1952. 4 p.
Direito penal; Supl. jan. 1952. 4 p.

-----. Ministério do Trabalho, Indústria e
Commércio. Serviço de Documentação. Biblioteca. Trabalho, previdência social, indústria e commércio, imigração; bibliografia,
ano 1, no. 1- ano 2, no. 2, 1951-1952. Rio
de Janeiro.   (7068
  DPU has the first 6 issues. Reprinted
  from Boletim do M.T.I.C.

CALMON, Pedro. Historia social do Brasil. São
Paulo, Edit, Nacional, 1935-1939. 3 v.
(Biblioteca pedagogica brasileira, ser. 5:
Brasiliana, v. 40, 83, 173)   (7069
  Includes bibliography.---Jones 1006.

FREYRE, Gilberto de Mello. Casa-grande e sen-
zala; formação da familia brasileira sob o
regimen de economia patriarchal. Rio de Janeiro, Maia & Schmidt, 1933. 517 p. (7070
  Work on Brazilian society, studying the
  formation of the family during slavery, with
  an exhaustive bibliography on the subject.
  ---Jones 1045a.

-----. Sobrados e mucambos; decadencia do pa-
triarchado rural no Brasil. São Paulo, Companhia Editôra Nacional, 1936. 405 p. (Bibliotheca pedagogica brasileira, ser. 5;
Brasiliana, v. 64)   (7071
  Bibliographia: p. 393-405.---Jones 1046.

FURTADO, Dilma Ribeiro. Bibliografia afro-
asiática. Rio de Janeiro, Ministério da Educação e Cultura, 1962. 74 p.   (7072

LEÃO, Antonio Carneiro. A sociedade rural,
seus problemas e sua educação. Rio de Janeiro, Edit. A Noite [1939] 368 p.   (7073
  Bibliografia: p. 337-59.---Jones 1012a.

MIGRAÇOES internas no Brasil; bibliografia le-
vantada pelo Instituto Nacional de Imigração
e Centro Latino Americano de Pesquisas em
Ciências Sociais. Rio de Janeiro, [1963?]
27 p. mimeogr.   (7074
  Cited in Doria 48.

MOURA, Valdiki. Bibliografia brasileira do
cooperativismo, pequeno ensaio de sistemati-
zação. Rio de Janeiro, Livr.-Edit. da Casa
do Estudante do Brasil [1951] 132 p. (Coleção Que é o Brasil, 4)   (7075

PIERSON, Donald. Survey of the literature on
Brazil of sociological significance published
up to 1940; edited for the Joint Committee
on Latin American Studies of the National
Research Council, The American Council of
Learned Societies and the Social Science
Research Council. Cambridge, Mass., Harvard

PIERSON, Donald. Survey of the... (Cont.)
Univ. Pr., 1945. xvi, 60 p. (Miscellaneous
publ. no. 4)   (7076
  Contains 585 titles.

RAMOS, Alberto Guerreiro, and GARCIA, Evaldo
da Silva. Notícia sôbre as pesquisas e os
estudos sociológicos no Brasil (1940-1949).
Com especial referência a migrações, conta-
tos de raça, colonização e assuntos correla-
tos. [Rio de Janeiro] Conselho de Imigração e Colonização. Presidência. n.d.
55 p.   (7077

RAMOS, Arthur. The Negro in Brazil, translated from the Portuguese by Richard Pattee.
Washington, D.C., Associated Publishers,
1939. 203 p.   (7078
  Scientific studies on the Negro in Brazil;
  bibliography: p. 177-89.---Jones 1153.

CHILE

BEHRENDT, Richard F. W. A bibliography of national minorities in Chile. [Washington, D.
C., Coordinator of Inter-American Affairs,
1944?] 58 p. mimeogr.   (7079
  Contains 381 entries.

HAMBURG. Welt-Wirtschafts-Archiv. Bibliothek.
Chile. Hamburg, 1959. 99 p. (Auslandskunde
Literaturnachweis über die Gebiete Wirtschaft
und Politik, Recht und Technik. Länder-abteilung, no. 17)   (7080

LOMBARDO TOLEDANO, Vicente. Bibliografía so-
bre cuestiones sociales y económicas de la
República de Chile. (Universidad de México,
México, D.F., t. 6, p. 202-21, 1933) (7081
Jones 1518.

OVIEDO MARTINEZ, Benjamín. Biblioteca masóni-
ca chilena. Santiago de Chile, Impr. "La
Tracción", 1930. 24 p.   (7082
Jones 1561.

RUIZ URBINA, Antonio, ZORBAS D., Alejandro,
etc. Estratificación y movilidad sociales
en Chile; fuentes bibliográficas desde los
orígenes históricos hasta 1960. Rio de Janeiro, 1961. 157 p. (Centro Latino-Americano de Pesquisas em Ciências Sociais.
Publ. no. 17)   (7083

COLOMBIA

CAJA de Crédito Agrario, Industrial y Minero,
Bogotá. Biblioteca. Bibliografía socio-
económica. Bogotá, 1964-1965. 2 pts.
mimeogr.   (7084
  Each part: approximately 40 pages.

HAMBURG. Welt-Wirtschafts-Archiv. Biblio-
thek. Kolumbien. Hamburg, 1958. 61 p.
(Auslandskunde Literaturnachweis über die
Gebiete Wirtschaft und Politik, Recht und
Technik. Länder-abteilung, no. 15) (7085

CUBA

CARABALLO Y SOTOLONGO, Francisco. Mujeres, a
las urnas y al hogar! Habana, Libr. "Cervantes", 1918. 283 p. (7086
    Labor literaria y científica de la mujer
cubana "La prensa femenina": p. 141-68.---
Jones 1794.

RAGGI Y AGEO, Carlos M. Bibliografía político-
social cubana, La Habana, 1940.
24 p. (7086a

TRELLES Y GOVIN, Carlos Manuel. El Primer
Congreso Internacional de Economía Social,
celebrado en Buenos Aires oct. 26 a nov. 4
de 1924. Informe. del delegado de Cuba.
Habana, Impr. de "El Fígaro", 1925.
109 p. (7087
    "Bibliografía social cubana": p. 50-106.
---Jones 1930.

MEXICO

HAMBURG. Welt-Wirtschafts-Archiv. Bibliothek.
México, Hamburg, 1956. 90 p. (Auslandskunde
Literaturnachweis über die Gebiete Wirtschaft
und Politik, Recht und Technik. Länder-
abteilung, no. 11) (7088

SOTO, Jesús S. Aspectos de la nueva ideología
mexicana. México, Tall. Gráf. de la Nación,
1929. 78 p. (Publ. de la Secretaría de Educación Pública, t. 21, no. 12) (7089
    Bibliografía: p. 65-78.---Jones 2510.

PUERTO RICO

BIRD, Augusto. Bibliografía puertorriqueña de

BIRD, Augusto. Bibliografía... (Cont.)
fuentes de investigaciones sociales, 1930-
1945. Ed. provicional. [Rio Piedras] Centro
de Investigaciones Sociales, Universidad de
Puerto Rico, 1946-1947. 2 v. (7090
    Presented as a supplement to the Bibliogra-
fía puertorriqueña, 1493-1930, compiled by
Antonio S. Pedreira.

URUGUAY

CENTRO Latino-Americano de Pesquisas em Ciências Sociais. Estratificación y movilidad
social en el Uruguay; fuentes bibliográficas
(1880-1958) Rio de Janeiro, 1959. 60 p.
(Publicação no. 5) (7091
    Compiler: Isaac Ganón.

MOVIMIENTO Nacional Gustavo Volpe, Montevideo.
Guía bibliográfica. n.d. 6, 1 p. (7092
    Reading list. Cited in Musso 157.

VENEZUELA

HAMBURG. Welt-Wirtschafts-Archiv. Biblio-
thek. Venezuela. Hamburg, 1958. 78 p.
(Auslandskunde. Literaturnachweis über die
Gebiete Wirtschaft und Politik, Recht und
Technik. Länder-abteilung, no. 16) (7093

WEST INDIES

HAMBURG. Welt-Wirtschafts-Archiv. Biblio-
thek. Karibische inseln, Westindien einschl.
der Europ. und US-Amerikan. Gabiete und
Guayana. Hamburg, 1957. 3 v. in 2 v.
(Auslandskunde. Literaturnachweis über die
Gebiete Wirtschaft und Politik, Recht und
Technik. Länder-abteilung, no. 12) (7094
    Published: - v. 1: Cuba, Haiti, Dominik
Republic. - v. 2, pt. 1: Das Gebiet im
ganzen Britischer besitz. - v. 2, pt. 2:
Französischer und Nederländischer besitz,
Puerto Rico und Amerik. Jungfern-Inseln.

SOCIAL WELFARE

ARGENTINA. Instituto Nacional de Previsión Social. Biblioteca. Ediciones bibliográficas
no. 8. Buenos Aires, 1952. 7 p. (7095
    DPU collection has only no. 8 of this se-
ries.

BRAZIL. Serviço de Informação Agrícola. Biblioteca. Bibliografia sôbre assuntos de
bem-estar rural. Rio de Janeiro, 1953.
33 p. mimeogr. (7096

CHERONI SAN ROMAN, Rogelio. Bibliografía de
la seguridad social. Montevideo, 1949.
9 p. mimeogr. (7097
    Cited in Musso 499, noting that 209 titles
are listed.

CHILE. Congreso. Biblioteca. Reconstrucción
de zonas devastadas [bibliografía] Santiago, 1960. 8 p. (Serie Bibliografías,
10) (7098

INTER-AMERICAN Children's Institute, Montevideo. Accidentes en la infancia. [Montevideo, 1961] 3 p. mimeogr.   (7099
   Cited in Musso 504.

-----. Bibliografía; servicio social. Montevideo, L.I.G.U., 1948. 76 p.   (7100
   Reprinted from Boletín del Instituto Internacional Americano de Protección a la Infancia, Montevideo, t. 22, no. 1-3, 1948.

-----. -----. Montevideo, Impresora L.I.G.U., 1957. 52 p.   (7101
   Reprinted from Boletín del Instituto Internacional Americano de Protección a la Infancia, no. 121, p. 212-61, jun. 1957)
   Compilation by Emma Guastavino.

-----. -----. [Montevideo, 1961] 7 p. mimeogr.   (7102
   Cited in Musso 523.

-----. Bibliografía sobre abandono y temas afines. Montevideo, 1959. 104 p.   (7103

-----. Bibliografía sobre alimentación y temas afines; libros, folletos y artículos de revistas existentes en la Biblioteca del Instituto. Montevideo, 1948. 87 p. mimeogr.   (7104
   "Contribución a la Conferencia Latino Americana de Nutrición organizada por la F.A.O. en Montevideo, julio 18 al 28 de 1948"

-----. Bibliografía sobre la conducta antisocial del menor en America. Montevideo, 1963. 56 p.   (7105
   Compiler: Elsa Müller.

-----. Bibliografía sobre menores de conducta antisocial, abandonados y temas afines. Libros, folletos y artículos de revistas

INTER-AMERICAN Children's ... (Cont.)
existentes en la Biblioteca del Instituto. Montevideo, 1948. 37 p. mimeogr.   (7106
   Cited in Musso 514.

-----. -----. Montevideo, 1948. 57 p. mimeogr.   (7107

-----. -----. -----. Suplemento diciembre 1954. Montevideo, 1954. 57 p. mimeogr.   (7108
   Cited in Musso 516.

-----. -----. -----. Suplemento julio 1955. [Montevideo] n.d. 3 p. mimeogr.   (7109
   Cited in Musso 517.

-----. Bibliografía sobre morbilidad y mortalidad perinatales con temas afines. Montevideo, 1960. 35 p.   (7110

-----. Bibliografía sobre pre-escolares. [Montevideo, 1956?] 31 p. mimeogr. (7111
   Cited in Musso 202.

FONSECA, Arnoldo Medeiros da. Investigação de paternidada. Rio de Janeiro, Freitas Bastos, 1940. 369 p.   (7112
   Bibliografía: p. 5-16.---Jones 1096b.

MONCORVO, Arthur, filho. Historico da protecção á infancia no Brazil, 1500-1922. Rio de Janeiro, Paulo Pongetti & C., 1926. xxxi, 383 p.   (7113
   Trabalhos originaes publicados pelo dr. Arthur Moncorvo: p. i-xxii.---Jones 1102.

VELASCO CEBALLOS, Rómulo. Fichas bibliográficas sobre asistencia pública en México. México, D.F., 1943. 86 p. (II Feria del libro y exposición nacional del periodismo, 1943)   (7114
   Covers primarily publications of the Secretaría de Asistencia Pública.

SPORTS

FINO, José Federico. Andinismo en la Argentina. Fuentes de información. Bariloche, Club Andino Bariloche, 1949. [14] p.   (7115

-----. Elementos para una bibliografía andina. Buenos Aires, 1939-1945. 6 pts.   (7116

FINO, José Federico. Elementos... (Cont.)
Jones, item 149a. Imprint varies: pt. 1., Bariloche, Anuario del Club Andino.

PAN AMERICAN UNION. Division of Intellectual Cooperation. References on sports in Latin America. [Washington, D.C. 1946] 4 p. (7117

STATISTICS

GENERAL

INTER-AMERICAN Statistical Institute. Bibliography of selected statistical sources of
the American nations, Bibliografía de fuentes estadísticas escogidas de las naciones
americanas. A guide to the principal statistical materials of the 22 American nations,
including data, analyses, methodology and
laws and organization of statistical agencies. Una guía de los principales materiales estadísticos de las 22 naciones americanas, incluyendo datos, análisis, metodología
y leyes y organización de los organismos de
estadística. Washington, D.C., 1947.
689 p.   (7118

-----. Bibliography of statistical textbooks
and other teaching material. Bibliografía
de tratados y demás material de enseñanza de
estadística. 2d. ed. Washington, D.C., Pan
American Union, 1960. 120 p.   (7119
   "IASI doc. 5074ab-5/2/60-3000 (Class 33,
Training and teaching in general. Clase 33,
Adiestramiento y enseñanza en general)"
   1st ed., 1952, is supplement 2 of Estadística, no. 36, p. 623-69, Sept. 1952.

-----. International statistical standards;
an annotated bibliography of the statistical
recommendations of international conferences,
meetings, and agencies; prelim. ed. Washington, D.C., Pan American Union, 1954. vi,
121 p.   (7120
   "Prepared by Phyllis G. Carter, chief,
Census Library Project, Library of Congress,
under a special contract between the Library
of Congress and the Inter-American Statistical Institute.

-----. -----. [rev. ed.] Washington, D.C.,
Pan American Union, 1955 [i.e. 1956] ii,
144 p.   (7121
   "Prepared by Phyllis G. Carter, Library of
Congress, under a special contract between
the Library of Congress and the Inter-American Statistical Institute."

KULENKAMPFF-SCHENCK, E. Die volksdichte von
Mittelamerika. Bonn und Leipzig, L. Schroe-
der, 1923. xii, 67 p. (Veröffentlichungen
des Romanischen Auslandsinstituts der Rhei-
nischen Friedrich-Wilhelms Universität, Bonn,
band 4)   (7122
   Literatur-verzeichnis: p. ix-xii.---Jones
1239.

MEXICO. Dirección General de Estadística. Bibliografía del método estadístico y sus aplicaciones. México, D.A.P.P., 1938.
167 p.   (7123
   Jones 267a. Classified, with author index.

MEXICO. Dirección General... (Cont.)
Includes works published, 1920 and after.
Mexican authors excluded. Compiler: Gilber-
to Loyo.

U.S. Library of Congress. Census Library
Project. General census and vital statistics
in the Americas; an annotated bibliography
of the historical censuses and current vital
statistics of the 21 American republics...
Prepared under the supervision of Irene B.
Taeuber.   (7124

-----. -----. Statistical yearbooks; an annotated bibliography of the general statistical yearbooks of major political subdivisions of the world. Prepared by Phyllis G.
Carter. Washington, D.C., 1953. viii,
123 p.   (7125

ZELINSKY, Wilbur. A bibliographic guide to
population geography. Chicago, 1962.
257 p. (University of Chicago. Department
of Geography. Research paper, no. 80) (7126
   Arrangement is by geographic regions of the
world.

BRAZIL

BRAZIL. Conselho Nacional de Estatística. Bibliografia geográfico-estatística brasileira.
Rio de Janeiro, 1956. v. 1(xlv,
362 p.)   (7127
   Covers the period 1936-1950.

-----. Departamento Nacional de Estatística.
Estatística intellectual do Brasil (1929).
Rio de Janeiro, Typ. de Dep. Nacional de Estatística, 1931-1932. 2 v.   (7128
   Includes statistics for 1929, and lists of
educational establishments, libraries, learned institutions and societies, periodicals,
publishers and theatres in Brazil in 1930.
---Jones 991.

POMERANZ, Lenina, and SINGER, Paul Israel.
Os números-índices na estatística econômica
brasileira. [São Paulo] Instituto de Administração, 1960. 109 p. (Publicações
avulsas do Instituto de Administração da
Universidade de São Paulo, 191)   (7129

CHILE

CHILE. Oficina de Estadística del Trabajo.
La estadística del trabajo, por Simón B.
Rodríguez. Santiago, Impr. Cervantes, 1908-
1909. 2 v.   (7130
   Parte bibliográfica: v. 2, apéndice (14 p.)
---Jones 1435.

COLOMBIA

COLOMBIA. Departamento Administrativo Nacional de Estadística. Trayectoria bibliográfica del Departamento Administrativo Nacional de Estadística, 1952-1962. Publicación
preparada por Armando Moreno Mattos, jefe de
la División de Información, en colaboración
con el personal de biblioteca. Bogotá,
1963. 7 p. (Boletín no. 7) mimeogr. (7131

CUBA

LE ROY Y CASSA, Jorge Eduardo. Bibliografía
de la estadística en Cuba durante el siglo
XX. (La Reforma social, Habana, t. 9,
p. 134-50, 1917)   (7133
    Jones 1856.

EL SALVADOR

EL SALVADOR. Dirección General de Estadística y Censos. Métodos y procedimientos re-
gistrados, 1952-1954. San Salvador, 1954.

EL SALVADOR. Dirección General... (Cont.)
    12 p. mimeogr.   (7134

MEXICO

BOJORQUEZ, Juan de Dios. Orientaciones de la
estadística en México. México, 1929.
101 p.   (7135
    Apuntes para una bibliografía estadística:
p. 26-101.---Jones 2092.

MEXICO. Dirección General de Estadística.
Bibliografía mexicana de estadística. México, [Tall. Gráf. de la Nación, 1941-1942]
2 v. (v. 1: 696 p; v. 2: 772 p.)   (7136

-----. -----. Catálogo general de las estadísticas nacionales. México, 1960.
127 p.   (7137

-----. -----. México en cifras. México, D.F.,
Tall. Gráf. de la Nación, 1939.   (7138
    30 statistical tables with descriptive
text. Includes a short bibliography on Mexican economics and social development.---
Jones 2357a.

THEATER

GENERAL

GILDER, Rosamond, and FREEDLEY, George. Theatre collections in libraries and museums, an
international handbook. (Published under
the auspices of the New York Public Library
and the National Theatre Conference, with
the cooperation of the American Library Association) New York, Theatre Arts Inc.,
1936. 182 p.   (7139
    Bibliography: p. 160-65. The United
States, Canada, Mexico, and South America,
by Rosamond Gilder.---Jones 164.

TORRE REVELLO, José. Orígenes del teatro en
Hispano América. (Instituto Nacional de Estudios de Teatro. Cuadernos de cultura teatral, Buenos Aires, no. 8, p. 37-64,
1937)   (7140
    Notas de la Conferencia: p. 58-64.

TRENTI ROCAMORA, José Luis. El repertorio de
la dramática colonial hispanoamericana. Buenos Aires [Tall. Gráf. ALEA] 1950.
110 p.   (7140a
    Bibliographical references, p. 89-106.

ARGENTINA

ANUARIO teatral argentino: enciclopedia prác-
tica de la escena argentina; crónicas, historia, biografías. Buenos Aires,

ANUARIO teatral argentino ... (Cont.)
1925- .   (7141
    Contains biographical dictionaries of
authors, actors, singers, critics, composers,
etc., and general information concerning
theatrical productions.---Jones 563.

BOSCH, Mariano G. Historia de la ópera en
Buenos Aires; origen del canto i la música;
las primeras compañías i los primeros can-
tantes. Buenos Aires, Impr. El Comercio,
1905. 256 p.   (7142
    Jones 608a.

-----. Historia de los orígenes del teatro
nacional argentino y la época de Carlos Po-
destá. Buenos Aires, Tall. Gráf. Argentinos L. J. Rosso, 1929. 348 p.   (7143
    Jones 608b.

-----. Historia del teatro en Buenos Aires.
Buenos Aires, Est. Tip. El Comercio, 1910.
518 p.   (7144
    Jones 608c.

-----. Teatro antiguo de Buenos Aires, piezas
del siglo XVIII; su influencia en la educación popular. Buenos Aires, Impr. El Comercio, 1904. 219 p.   (7145
    Jones 608d.

DREIDEMIE, Oscar J. Los orígenes del teatro
en las regiones del Río de la Plata. Obra

DREIDEMIE, Oscar J. Los orígenes... (Cont.)
de los Jesuítas de la Provincia del Paraguay. (Estudios, Buenos Aires, t. 57,
p. 61-80, 1937) (7146
Bibliografía: p. 78-80.---Jones 685.

ECHAGÜE, Juan Pablo. Una época del teatro argentino (1904-1918) 2a. ed. Buenos Aires,
Edit. América Unida [1926] 322 p. (Biblioteca de estudios críticos, v. 1) (7147
A historical sketch followed by reviews of
plays presented.---Jones 685a.

-----. Un teatro en formación. Buenos Aires,
Impr. Tragant, 1919. 404 p. (7148
Jones 685b.

INSTITUTO Nacional de Estudios de Teatro.
Cuadernos de cultura teatral. Buenos Aires,
Comisión Nacional de Cultura,
1936- . (7149
The Cuadernos contain papers on the history of dramatic productions in Latin America,
with special reference to Argentina.---Jones
729.

TAULLARD, Alfredo. Historia de nuestros viejos teatros. Buenos Aires, Impr. López,
1932. 500 p. (7150
"Desde la época colonial a la apertura
del nuevo Colón, esto es, hasta 1908."---
Jones 858.

BRAZIL

BOCCANERA, Silio. Theatro nacional: autores
e actores dramaticos bahianos, em especial
biographias. Bahia, Impr. Off. do Estado,
1923. 488 p. (7151
Jones 980.

PAIXÃO, Mucio da. O theatro no Brasil. Rio
de Janeiro, Editôra Moderna, 1936?
606 p. (7152
Jones 1127.

SILVA, Lafayette. Historia do teatro brasi-
leiro. Rio de Janeiro, Serviço Grafico do
Ministério da Educação e Saúde, 1938.
489 p. (Coleção brasileira de teatro; ser.
D: Estudos sôbre teatro) (7153
Jones 1197.

SOUSA, José Galante de. O teatro no Brasil.
Rio de Janeiro, Instituto Nacional do Livro,
1960. 2 v. (7153a
Contents: v. 1, Evolução do teatro no
Brasil. - v. 2, Subsidios para uma biblio-
grafia do teatro no Brasil.

CHILE

AMUNATEGUI, Miguel Luis. La introducción de
las representaciones teatrales en Chile.

AMUNATEGUI, Miguel Luis. ... (Cont.)
(Revista de Santiago, Santiago de Chile,
t. 1, p. 433- , 1873) (7154
Jones 1381.

ANRIQUE REYES, Nicolás. Ensayo de una bibliografía dramática chilena. Santiago, Impr.
Cervantes, 1899. 184 p. (7155
Published in Anales de la Universidad: 1,
Teatro estranjero relativo a Chile (1612-
1886). - 2, Teatro nacional (1692-1899)
449 titles listed with historical introduction and bibliographical data.---Jones
1395.

DURAN CERDA, Julio. Repertorio del teatro
chileno, bibliografía, obras inéditas y
estrenadas. Santiago, 1962. 247 p. (Chile. Universidad. Instituto de Literatura
Chilena. Publicaciones; Serie C: Bibliografías y registros, no. 1) (7156
1710 items are cited. Estudios fundamentales, p. 169-82.

RELA, Walter. Contribución a la bibliografía
del teatro chileno, 1804-1960. Noticia
preliminar de Ricardo A. Latcham. Montevideo, Universidad de la República, 1960.
51 p. (Departamento de Literatura Ibero-
americana. Publicaciones) (7157

YAÑEZ SILVA, N. Veinte años de teatro chileno. (Atenea, Concepción, t. 21, p. 207-28,
1932) (7158
Jones 1663.

COLOMBIA

ORTEGA RICAURTE, José Vicente. Historia crítica del teatro en Bogotá. Bogotá, Ediciones Colombia, 1927. 318 p. (7159
Jones 1740.

CUBA

GONZALEZ, Jorge Antonio. Repertorio teatral
cubano. La Habana, 1951. p. 69-184. (Revista de la Biblioteca Nacional, 2a. ser.,
t. 2, no. 4, oct./dic. 1951) (7159a

HAVANA. Censor Principal de Teatros. Indice
de las piezas dramáticas permitidas sin ata-
jos ni correcciones, de las permitidas con
ellos y de las absolutamente prohibidas,
presentado al gobierno superior civil de la
isla por el Censor Principal de Teatros de
esta capital. Habana, Impr. del Gobierno
y Capitanía General por S. M., 1852.
58 p. (7160
Jones 1843.

RIVERO MUÑIZ, José. Bibliografía del teatro
cubano. Prólogo de Lilia Castro de Morales.

RIVERO MUÑIZ, José. Bibliografía... (Cont.)
Habana, Biblioteca Nacional, 1957. 120 p.
(Biblioteca Nacional. Publicaciones) (7161
    Prepared as a contribution of the National
Library in celebration of the Día del Libro
Cubano.

MEXICO

LAMB, Ruth Stanton. Bibliografía del teatro
mexicano del siglo XX. México, D.F., Ediciones de Andrea, 1962. 143 p. (Colección
Studium, 33)   (7162

MAÑON, Manuel. Historia del teatro Principal
de México. México, D.F., "Cultura", 1932.
464 p.   (7163
    Jones 2315.

MONTERDE GARCIA ICAZBALCETA, Francisco. Bibliografía del teatro en México. México,
Impr. de la Secretaría de Relaciones Exteriores, 1933 (i.e. 1934) 649 p. (Monografías bibliográficas mexicanas, no.
28)   (7164
    The introduction by Rodolfo Usigli (see
item 7167) gives an historical account of
the Mexican theater. Contains dramas by
Mexican authors, translations of foreign
dramas, works relating to the Mexican drama,
a list of operas, etc.---Jones 2370.

OLAVARRIA Y FERRARI, Enrique de. Reseña histórica del teatro en México; 2a. ed. México, Impr. "La Europea," 1895. 4 v.   (7165

OLAVARRIA Y FERRARI, Enrique de ... (Cont.)
Jones 2391.

ROJAS GARCIDUEÑAS, José J. El teatro de Nueva España en el siglo XVI. México, Impr. de
L. Alvarez, 1935. 221 p.   (7166
    Bibliografía: p. 223-26.---Jones 2467.

USIGLI, Rodolfo. México en el teatro. México, Impr. Mundial, 1932. 220 p.   (7167
    Guía de acotaciones y bibliografía:
p. 179-84.---Jones 2540.

PERU

LOHMANN VILLENA, Guillermo. El teatro en
Lima en el siglo XVI, las primeras representaciones. (Instituto de Investigaciones Históricas de la Universidad Católica
del Perú. Cuadernos de estudio, Lima,
t. 1, p. 44-74, 1939)   (7168
    Jones 2682.

MONCLOA Y COVARRUBIAS, Manuel. Diccionario
teatral del Perú. Lima, Badiola y Berrio,
1905. 198 p.   (7169
    Jones 2701. Bibliografía: p. 197.

VENEZUELA

CHURION, Juan José. El teatro en Caracas.
Caracas, Tip. Vargas, 1924. 230 p.   (7170
    Bibliografía, obras y autores, actores no-
tables: p. 199-225.---Jones 2899.

TOURISM

PAN AMERICAN UNION. Travel Division. A selected bibliography on the tourist industry.
Washington, D.C., 1948. 15 p.   (7171

PAN AMERICAN UNION. Travel... (Cont.)
    Includes also references to countries
other than the American republics.

TRANSPORTATION

BIBLIOGRAFIA de los ferrocarriles de Yucatán,
1861-1937. Mérida, 1940. 16 p. (Boletín
de bibliografía yucateca, no. 12, 1o. de agosto 1940)   (7172
    Jones 2077a. Millares, item 920, ascribes
authorship to Mireya Priego Arjona.

CANAL ZONE. Library-Museum. Balboa Heights.
Subject catalog of the special Panama collection of the Canal Zone Library-Museum; the
history of the Isthmus of Panama as it
applies to interoceanic transportation.
Boston, G. K. Hall, 1964. 341 p.   (7173
    Photo-offset copy of selected titles from

CANAL ZONE. Library-Museum ... (Cont.)
the card catalog.

DIAZ ARQUER, Graciano. Historia bibliográfica e iconográfica de la aeronáutica en
España, Portugal, países hispano-americanos y Filipinas desde los orígenes hasta
1900. Madrid, P. Vindel, 1930.
78 p.   (7174
    Jones 125.

EMPRESA Nacional de Transportes, Buenos Aires.
Servicio de Bibliotecas y Publicaciones de
Transportes. Bibliografía ferroviaria.

EMPRESA Nacional de Transportes ... (Cont.)
Buenos Aires, 1955. 131 p. mimeogr. (7174a
Cited in Geoghegan 1357.

GORDILLO, P. N., and CARRANZA FERRAN, I. Contribución a la bibliografía sobre caminos y
ferrocarriles. (Revista de la Universidad
Nacional de Córdoba, v. 20, no. 9-10,
p. 347-64, 1933; v. 21, no. 3-4, p. 207-17,
1934)   (7175
Jones 714. Author notes that bibliography
is to be continued.

GURRIA LACROIX, Jorge. Bibliografía mexicana
de ferrocarriles. [México, D.F.] Ferrocarriles Nacionales [1956] 499 p. (Biblioteca técnica ferrocarrilera, 50)   (7175a
Cited in Geoghegan, 1358.

MEXICO. Secretaría de Comunicaciones y Transportes. Catálogo de expedientes históricos
seleccionados. Rama: Ferrocarriles. México, D.F., 1959. 158 p.   (7176

NEW YORK. Public Library. American inter-
oceanic canals; a list of references in the
New York Public Library. Compiled by John
C. Frank. New York, 1916. 90 p.   (7177
Reprinted from the Bulletin of the New
York Public Library, Jan. 1916.---Jones 1245.

NUÑEZ OLAECHEA, Samuel. Los ferrocarriles del
estado. 1. Reseña histórica. 2. Esplota-
ción. 3. Diccionario biográfico. Santiago
de Chile, Impr. Chile, 1910. 328 p.   (7178
Jones 1557.

PAN AMERICAN Highway Confederation. Bibliography of the Pan American Highway. Washington, D.C., 1943. 5 p. mimeogr.   (7179

PAN AMERICAN UNION. Department of Economic
Affairs. Transportation Unit. A guide to
institutions in the Washington, D.C.-New
York area containing bibliographical referen-
ces on transportation in Latin America.
Washington, D.C., 1961. 108 p.   (7180

RIVERSIDE, Calif. Public Library. Panama canal;
an old way to California made new. Riverside, 1912. 16 p.   (7181
Jones 1356.

U.S. Library of Congress. Aeronautic Americana; a bibliography of books and pamphlets on
aeronautics published in America before 1900.
N. Y., The Sherman Fairchild Publication
Fund, Institute of the Aeronautical Sciences,
1943. 40 p.   (7182
Compiled by N. H. Randers-Pehrson and A. G.

U.S. Library of Congress ... (Cont.)
Renstrom. Latin America: p. 35-38.

-----. -----. List of books and of articles in
periodicals relating to interoceanic canal
and railway routes. By Hugh A. Morrison.
Washington, D.C., Govt. Print. Off., 1900.
174 p. (56th Congress, 1st session. Senate doc. 59)   (7183
Jones 1360.

-----. -----. List of references on the Panama Canal and the Panama Canal Zone. Washington, D.C., Govt. Print. Off., 1919.
21 p.   (7184
Jones 1361.

-----. -----. Division of Bibliography. The
Panama Canal and the Panama Canal Zone; a
selected list of references, compiled by
Ann Duncan Brown. Washington, D.C., 1943.
57 p.   (7185
Supplement to the 1919 compilation,

-----. Superintendent of Documents. Bibliography of United States public documents
relating to interoceanic communications
across Nicaragua, Isthmus of Panama, Isthmus
of Tehuantepec, etc. Washington, D.C.,
Govt. Print. Off., 1899. 29 p.   (7186
Jones 1256.

-----. -----. Panama Canal and the Canal Zone.
Public documents for sale by the Superintendent of documents, Washington, D.C. [Wash-
ington, D.C., Govt. Print. Off.] 1914.
18 p.   (7187

-----. -----. -----. [2d ed.] 1915.
20 p.   (7187a

-----. -----. Panama canal and the Canal Zone;
including government publications relating
to Suez Canal, Nicaragua route, and treaty
with Colombia, for sale by the Superintendent of Documents. [3d ed. Washington,
D.C.] 1916. 16 p.   (7188

-----. -----. -----. [4th ed.] 1917.
14 p.   (7189
Title varies slightly.

-----. -----. -----. [5th ed.] 1920.
7 p.   (7190

-----. -----. Panama Canal, Canal Zone, Republic of Panama, Colombia treaty, Nicaragua. [6th ed. Washington, D.C., Govt.
Print. Off.] 1921. 7 p.   (7191

VETERINARY MEDICINE

BUFF, Virginia. Bruceloses; contribução bibliográfica. São Paulo [Tip. Brasil, 1945] p. 275-95. (7192
Cited in Catálogo, Instituto Bibliotecológico, item 686.

PERU. Universidad Mayor de San Marcos. Facultad de Medicina y Veterinaria. Contribución a la bibliografía veterinaria americana [recopilada por Ramón Ponce Paz] Lima, Perú [Editora Médica Peruana] 1951. 47 p. mimeogr. (7193
Prepared on the occasion of the Primer Congreso Panamericano de Medicina Veterinaria.

ROVEDA, Rodolfo J. Bibliografía zooparasito-

ROVEDA, Rodolfo J. Bibliografía...(Cont.) lógica veterinaria argentina. Buenos Aires, Impr. de la Universidad, 1954. 67 p. (Buenos Aires. Universidad. Facultad de Agronomía y Veterinaria, Boletín no. 32) (7194
Cited in Catálogo, Instituto Bibliotecológico, item 693.

VERGANI, Franco, and DIAZ UNIGRIA, Carlos. Bibliografía veterinaria venezolana; fichero venezolano de bibliografía veterinaria y ganadería. Caracas, Instituto de Investigaciones Veterinarias, 1963. (Boletín del Instituto de Investigaciones Veterinarias, v. 5, no. 21) (7195
Cited in Boletín de adquisiciones, Medellín, p. 13, dic. 1963.

ZOOLOGY

ARGENTINA

LIZER, Carlos. Apuntaciones para la bibliografía entomológica argentina. (Physis, Buenos Aires, v. 8, p. 505-35, 1927) (7196
Jones 757.

-----. Primer ensayo bibliográfico de entomología argentina. Buenos Aires, "Coni", 1919. 380 p. (7197
"De la Primera Reunión de la Sociedad Argentina de Ciencias Naturales, Tucumán, 1916".---Jones 758.

MARELLI, Carlos A. Bibliografía eurística de los mamíferos de caza y caza marítima. Contribuciones al estudio de la fauna argentina. La Plata, 1936. 189 p. (7198
From Memorias del Jardín Zoológico de La Plata, v. 3, part 2. Includes indexes of genera, families and subfamilies, orders, common names and geological terms.---Jones 765.

-----. Bibliografía relativa a la ornitología (argentina) (Memorias del Jardín Zoológico de La Plata, t. 5, p. 37-106, 1934) (7199
Jones 766.

BRAZIL

BIBLIOGRAFIA brasileira de zoologia. v. 1, 1950/1955- . Rio de Janeiro [1956]- (7200
Issued by the Instituto Brasileiro de Bibliografia e Documentação. Vol. 1: 346 p. 1950/1955; vol. 2: 192 p., 1956/1958.

LIMA, Angelo Moreira de Costa. Terceiro catalogo dos insectos que vivem nas plantas do Brasil. Rio de Janeiro, Directoria de Estatistica da Producção, Secção de Publicidade, 1936. 460 p. (7201
First-second published in Archivos da Escola Superior de Agricultura e Medicina Veterinaria, v. 6, no. 1-2, p. 107-276, Dec. 1922, and v. 8, no. 1-2, p. 69-301, Dec. 1927 under title: Catalogo systematico dos insectos que vivem nas plantas do Brasil e ensaio de bibliographia entomologica brasileira. Supplement to 2d. published in O Campo, v. 1, no. 7, p. 38-48 and no. 12, p. 41-6, July, Dec. 1930. "Bibliographia entomologica (trabalhos publicados no Brazil)": p. 3-104.---Jones 1025a.

CHILE

DELFIN, Federico T. Catálogo de los peces de Chile. (Revista chilena de historia natural, Valparaíso, t. 3-4, 1899-1900) (7202
Contains bibliography.---Jones 1443.

HELLMAYR, Carl Eduard. The birds of Chile. Chicago, 1932. 472 p. (Field Museum of Natural History. Publications 308) (7203
Ornithological bibliography of Chile: p. 429-58.---Jones 1494.

PORTER, Carlos Emilio. Bibliografía ornitológica de Chile. Santiago de Chile, 1912. 14 p. (7204
Reprinted from Boletín del Museo Nacional, t. 4, p. 197-206. abr./dic. 1912.---Jones 1573

SILVA FIGUEROA, Carlos. Reseña histórica y
    bibliográfica de la entomología chilena.
    (Boletín del Museo Nacional de Chile, San-
    tiago, t. 7, p. 166-93, 1914)   (7205
    Jones 1629.

MEXICO

BLASQUEZ LOPEZ, Luis, and LØEHNBERG, Alfredo.
    Bibliografía hidrogeológica de la República
    mexicana. México, 1961. 101 p. (México
    (City) Universidad Nacional. Instituto de
    Geología. Anales, t. 17)   (7206

DATA para la bibliografía zoológica mexicana.
    (El Libro y el pueblo, México, v. 3, p. 198-
    208, 1924)   (7207
    Jones 2143.

SOUTH AMERICA

MURPHY, Robert Cushman. Oceanic birds of
    South America. New York, The American Mu-
    seum of Natural History, 1936.

MURPHY, Robert Cushman. Oceanic... (Cont.)
    2 v.   (7208
    Bibliography: v. 2, p. 1179-1210.---
    Jones 327.

VENEZUELA

RÜHL, Eduardo. Apuntes para la historia y la
    bibliografía de la ornitología venezolana.
    (Boletín de la Sociedad Venezolana de Cien-
    cias Naturales, Caracas, no. 6, p. 201-48,
    1932)   (7209
    Noted are 152 works.---Jones 2949.

WEST INDIES

CORY, Charles Barney. Catalogue of West In-
    dian birds. Boston, The Author, 1892.
    163 p.   (7210
    Ornithological publications relating to the
    West Indies geographically arranged (p. 21-
    60); chronologically arranged (p. 61-80).
    ---Jones 2985a.

INDEX

Entries in index, prefixed by an Asterisk (*) refer to main headings in the bibliography.

426

Argentina
  Centro Nacional de Documentación, 3197
  Church history, 6872a
  Círculo de Aeronáutica
    Biblioteca Nacional de Aeronáutica, 2449
  Climate, 5574-75
  Comisión Nacional de Cooperación Intelectual,
    3442, 5799, 6567a
  Comisión Nacional de Coordinación de Trans-
    portes, 5815
  Comisión Nacional de Cultura, 1223, 5827
  Comision Nacional de Energía Atómica, 4378,
    5764
  Comisión Nacional de Homenaje al Almirante
    Guillermo Brown, 3855a
  Comisión Nacional Ejecutiva del 150o Aniver-
    sario de la Revolución de Mayo, 479a, 3193b
  Comisión Protectora de Biblioteca Populares,
    2854, 2860, 5707-08, 5838, 5859
  Commerce, 3359
  Congreso
    Biblioteca, 19, 683-84, 2004, 2450-54,
      2929, 2981, 4157-57a, 4379, 4674,
      4856-60, 5804, 5861, 6787, 6606a
  Consejo Nacional de Educación, 3389
  Consejo Nacional de Investigaciones Cientí-
    ficas y Técnicas, 6355
  Constitucional history, 3876
  Constitution, 4874-75
  Constitutional law, 4876
  Description and travel, 3441-44, 3451,
    4402-04, 5528-30, 7018
  Diplomatic and consular service, 482
  Dirección de Hidrografía, Faros y Balisas,
    5518
  Dirección de Meteorologia, Geofísica e Hidro-
    logía, 2455
  Dirección de Minas, Geología e Hidrología,
    3755, 5528
  Dirección General de Correos
    Biblioteca, 2457
  Dirección General de Correos y Teléfonos,
    2456
  Dirección General de Cultura, 3199, 5799,
    6375
  Dirección Nacional de Geología y Minería,
    3756
  Dirección General de Navegación
    Biblioteca y Archivo, 2458
  Direccion General de Navegación y Comunica-
    ciones, 5520
  Dirección General de Navegación e Hidrogra-
    fía, 5521-24
  Dirección General del Servicio Meteorológico
    Nacional, 5794
  Economic conditions, 2984-87, 3441, 3455,
    7061, 7063
  Economic policy, 2982
  Ejército
    Estado Mayor, 2459-60
  Embajada, San José, C.R., 3266
  Emigration and immigration, 4530-31
  Escuela Naval Militar, 2461
  Foreign relations, 4440
    Paraguay, 3862

Argentina
  Foreign relations
    United States, 778
  History, 467, 469-72, 475, 483-84, 597, 681,
    683-85, 778, 1224, 1230, 1535-1617, 1947,
    1973, 2295, 3435, 3853-85, 3891, 4396,
    4591, 4837, 5203, 6396
    English Invasions, 494
    Naval, 3855a
    Periodicals, 5718-21
    Wars of independence, 494, 3857, 3862,
      3866, 6395
  Industries, 2985, 4353
  Instituto de Microbiología Agrícola, 3757
  Instituto de Sanidad Vegetal
    Laboratorio Central de Fitopatología
      Biblioteca, 2462, 2530
  Instituto Geográfico Militar, 4402-04
  Instituto Nacional de Prevision Social
    Biblioteca, 7095
  Instituto Nacional de Tecnología Industrial,
    5834a
  Instituto Nacional del Tabaco, 275a-c
  Intellectual life, 5203, 5209, 6381
  Junta Nacional de Intelectuales, 5799
  Ministerio de Agricultura y Ganadería,
    286-87
    Departamento de Biblioteca, 280, 3194,
      5766, 5821, 6607
  Ministerio de Asistencia Social y Salud Pú-
    blica
    Biblioteca Sanitaria, 5767
  Ministerio de Defensa Nacional
    Dirección General de Fabricaciones Mili-
      tares, 5768
  Ministerio de Economía
    División de Biblioteca, 5769
  Ministerio de Justicia
    Dirección General de Publicaciones Biblio-
      teca y Archivo, 4861
  Ministerio de Justicia e Instrucción Pública,
    952, 3195
  Ministerio de Marina, 5770
    Biblioteca, 2463-67
  Ministerio de Obras y Servicios Públicos
    Biblioteca, 5771
    Dirección Nacional de Vialidad, 5848
    Servicio de Biblioteca y Publicaciones de
      Transporte, 5772
  Ministerio de Relacciones Exteriores y Culto,
    681, 685
    Biblioteca, 480-82, 5818
  Ministerio del Interior
    Dirección Nacional de Salud Pública, 4675
    Subsecretaría de Informaciones, 5752
  Museo Histórico Nacional, 483
  Politics and government, 2092, 3876, 5202,
    6607, 6609
  Relations (general) with France, 3858
  Sanitary Affairs, 5585
  Secretaría de Trabajo y Previsión
    Instituto Nacional de Previsión Social,
      5823
  Servicio Hidrográfico, 5525
  Servicio Meteorológico Nacional, 5649

430

Barra, Eduardo de la, 1209
Barra, Felipe de la, 661, 2922
Barra, Fidel, 552
Barranquilla
  Universidad del Atlántico
    Biblioteca, 5978
Barrasa y Muñoz de Bustillo, José de, 3981
Barrau-Dihigo, Louis, 89
Barreda, Ernesto Mario, 5196
Barreda y Laos, Felipe, 3102-02
Barreiro y Ramos, Antonio, 2380, 2382
Barrenechea, Enrique, 970
Barrera, Isaac J., 3966, 5098, 5385, 5386-88
Barrera, Jaime, 380
Barret, P., 22, 200
Barrett, Robert South, 4373-76
Barrial Domínguez, José, 1870
Barriga, Víctor M., 1468a
Barringer, George A., 181
Barrios, Eduardo, 1215, 5469
Barrios, Justo Rufino, 1469
Barrios, Roberto, 5269
Barros Arana, Diego, 23-4, 1186, 1470-71,
    1924, 3252, 3817, 4250-51, 4769
Barroso, Gustavo, 311, 3892
Barry, Mary Elizabeth, 2148
Bartlett, John Russell, 2189, 4937-39, 6659
Basadre, Jorge, 1132, 4095-4102, 5439-40
Basalenque, Diego, 6909
Basave y del Castillo Negrete, Carlos, 4025
Basque language, 4713
Bassiches, Bruno, 3461
Bassols Batalla, Angel, 3580
Batallas, Leónicas, 2090
Batis, Humberto, 4310
Batista, Nair, 1244
Batres Jáuregui, Antonio, 3933, 3968-69
Batrés Montúfar, J., 1315
Baudin, Louis, 380
Bauzá, Francisco, 1472, 4137
Bayitch, S.A., 25, 4806-07
Bayle, Constantino, 3023, 3839, 3982, 4026
Bayona Posada, Nicolás, 5309
Bazán, Hernando, 6928
Bazán de Segura, Consuelo, 303
Bazzonella, Waldemiro, 4159, 7065
Bealer, Lewis W., 1442
Beals, Carleton, 3609, 3950
Beauvois, Eugène, 335
Becco, Horacio Jorge, 1440a, 1623, 1684-85,
    1719, 1786, 1795, 1984, 3388a-b, 5197
Becerra de Leon, Berta, 1525
Bécquer, Gustavo Adolfo, 1473
Becú, Teodoro, 876, 3195, 4925
Beeche, Gregorio Miguel Pascual de, 4926
Behar, David, 2296
Behar, Raúl, 2296
Behavior science bibliographies, 3189
Behrendt, Richard, F. W., 7029-31, 7079
Beinecke, Frederick W., 4078
Belaúnde, Rafael, 2850
Belaúnde, Víctor Andrés, 1486
Belgium
  Periodicals, 6269
Bell, Herbert Clifford, 813

Bellido, Remijio de, 1429, 6403
Bello, Andrés, 4670, 4709
Bello family, 1478
Belo Horizonte
  Archivo Publico Mineiro, 6402
  Facultade Livre de Direito, 2576
  Universidade de Minas Gerais, 5873
Beltrán, Francisco, 26
Bemis, Samuel Flagg, 4439
Benavides, Alonso de, 1480
Benavides Balbín, Alberto, 4808, 6574
Bendfeldt Rojas, Lourdes, 55, 1748, 3124
Benewick, Anne, 6633
Benítez, Rubén, 1473
Bennett, Ellen C., 3568
Bennett, Wendell C., 357, 414
Benson, Nettie Lee, 3325
Benvenuto Murrieta, Pedro M., 4732, 5440
Benzo, Eduardo, 3983
Berendt, Karl Hermann, 2232, 2234, 4776
Beretta y Cía., Buenos Aires, 4927
Berg, Carlos, 1481, 1510
Berger, Paulo, 3461a
Beristain de Souza, José Mariano, 27-31, 1316,
    1482
Berlin
  K. Museen, 4783
  Staatliche Museum
    Museum für Völkerkunde
      Ethnologisches Forschungs u. Lehrinstitut,
        408-410
  Universität
    Deutsches Institut für Zeitungskunde, 6266
Berlinck, Cassius, 4928-29
Berliner, J.J. & Staff, N.Y., 32
Bermejo, Vladimiro, 1358
Bermuda, 51-2
Bermúdez, J.A., 1187
Bermúdez, Pedro J., 3705
Bermúdez de Castro, Diego Antonio, 1322
Bermúdez Plata, Cristóbal, 716-16a
Bernal, Ignacio, 386
Bernal, Argentina
  Biblioteca Popular "Mariano Moreno", 5844
Bernardez, Francisco Luis, 1482a
Bernasconi, I., 2122
Bernstein, Sylvia Pollack, 4688
Berrien, William, 3480
Berroa, Josefina, 1077, 3024
Berruete Ramón, Fernando, 1323
Bertoni, Moisés Santiago, 302
Bertran, Luis, 2381
Bertrand, Alejandro, 4383
Besio Moreno, Nicolás, 3439
Besnes, Irigoyen, J.M., 1376
Bessa, Alberto, 6404
Besso, Henry V., 3751
Best books, 193, 956, 3823
  Cuba, 1031
Besterman, Theodore, 893
Beust, Nora Ernestine, 2149
Beverina, Juan, 4089
Bevilaqua, Clovis, 2643
Beyer, Hermann, 387
Beyhaut, Gustavo, 33

Bunge, Carlos Octavio, 1509
Buonocore, Domingo, 2125
Burdon, John Adler, 815
Bureau of International Research of Harvard
    University and Radcliffe College, 346
Burgin, Miron, 97
Burgoa, Francisco de, 6929
Burkinski, Francisco, 6838
Burland, Cottie Arthur, 453
Burmeister, Carlos Germán Conrado, 1510
Burns, Jack F., 5715
Burzio, Blas F. A., 1430
Burzio, Humberto, 3855a
Busaniche, José Luis, 3198
Buschiazzo, Juan A., 4942
Buschiazzo, Juan Carlos, 4942
Buschiazzo, Mario José, 825
Buse de la Guerra, Hermann, 1584
Bushong, Allen David, 3139
Business
    Periodicals, 5817, 5876, 5885
Bustamante, Carlos María de, 344, 6967
Bustamante, Ricardo José, 1239
Bustamante Muñoz, Antonio, 4550
Bustamante y Hernandez, Luis J., 3270
Bustamante y Sirvén, Antonio Sánchez de,
    4964
Bustamante y Urrutia, José María, 2728
Busto, Gumersindo, 2429a, 5803
Butler, Ruth Lapham, 753, 4179
Butt, Joseph V., 6346
Buxareo Oribe, Félix, 2442
Byrd, Cecil K., 3322
Byrne, Bonifacio, 1511

Caballero, Raimundo Diosdado, 6975
Caballero y Caballero, Eduardo, 5624
Caballero y Rodríguez, José Agustín, 1512
Cabarco, Esther, 6541
Cabello de Balboa, Miguel, 1188
Cabezón, Carlos, 4733
Cabot, Acislo M., 955
Cabral, Alfredo do Valle, 48, 1513, 3220,
    3774, 4751, 5504
Cabral, Jorge, 1188
Cabral, Oswaldo R., 3894
Cabral, Pedro Alvares, 3473
Cabrera, Luis, 1514
Cabrera, Pablo, 6669-70
Cabrera Domínguez, Arturo, 6671
Cabrera Leiva, Guillermo, 6857
Cabrilho, João Rodrigues, 128
Cabrita, F., 2669
Cacao, 251-55
Cadavid Arango, Carlos, 297, 6566
Os Cadernos de cultura, Rio de Janeiro, 6695
    Indexes, 4222
Cady, John Frank, 4440
Caeté, Francisco Barreto, 1559
Caffese, María E., 3857
Caicedo Rojas, José, 5317
Caillava, Domingo A., 5465
Caillet Bois, Ricardo Rodolfo, 1576, 3858
Caixa Económica Federal, São Paulo
    Biblioteca, 2617

Caja de Crédito Agrario, Industrial y Minero,
    Bogotá, 7084
Caja de Seguro Obligatorio, Santiago de Chile
    Sección Educación Sanitaria, 5956
Caja Nacional de Ahorro Postal, Buenos Aires
    Biblioteca Domingo Faustino Sarmiento, 5832
Cajamarca, Peru, 6809
Cakchiquel Indians, 333
Calancha, Antonio de la, 6910
Calangha, Antonio de la, 3889
Calbuco, Chile, 546
Calcagno, Francisco, 1292
Calcaño, Julio, 5482-83, 5638
Caldas, Diogenes, 4603
Caldas y Tenorio, Francisco José de, 3626
Caldera Rodriguez, Rafael, 4145, 4918
Calderón, Alba Rosa, 55, 3124
Calderón Quijano, José Antonio, 590
Calendar, Mexican, 344, 388
Cali, Colombia
    Biblioteca "Jorge Garcés B.", 1000, 5995
    Universidad del Valle
        Biblioteca Central, 5980
        Facultad de Ingeniería, Química e Ingenie-
            ría Electromecánica, 6004
California, 6638, 6645
    History, 689, 3928-31, 4026
    State Library
        Sutro Branch, 1615-17, 2410-13, 6858
    University, 686, 1640-41, 3172, 4077, 4129,
        5163
        Bancroft Library, 104, 756, 2414-16, 3318,
            3928
        Center for Latin American Studies, 4160,
            4165, 4174-75, 6188, 6596
        Library, 2416
California, Baja, 762, 1083, 3499, 3568, 3586,
    3590-91
    Description and travel, 3931
    Economic conditions, 7023
Callage, Roque, 4734
Callahan, James Morton, 4560
Callcott, Wilfrid Hardy, 2017, 6620, 6859
Calle, Manuel J., 1303
Callegari, Guido Valeriano, 1515
Calmon, Pedro, 3895, 7069
Calogeras, João Pandiá, 3896, 4384
Calogeras, Miguel, 610
Calvo, Julian, 1201, 1908
Calvo de Ribeiro, Blanca, 6835
Cámara, Gonzalo, 6769
Cámara Argentina de Editoriales Técnicas,
    Buenos Aires, 959, 5850
Cámara Argentina del Libro, Buenos Aires, 962,
    5759
Cámara Colombiana de Construcción, Medellín,
    4256
Cámara Colombiana del Libro, Bogotá, 6002
Cámara Española de Comercio de la República Ar-
    gentina, Buenos Aires, 3199
Cámara Mexicana del Libro, México, D.F., 3307
Cámara Oficial de Comercio, Agricultura e In-
    dustria del Distrito de Santo Domingo, San-
    to Domingo, 6040
Cámara Oficial del Libro, Barcelona, 56-7

442

Chile
  Dirección de Contabilidad, 3362
  Economic conditions, 2993-94, 3365-66, 7081
  Emigration and immigration, 4886
  Foreign relations
    Bolivia, 4535
    Peru, 4573
    United States, 4539
  Genealogy, 3413-14
  History, 542-45, 550, 594, 602, 1268, 1276-
    77, 1896, 2921, 3505, 3936-43, 4958,
    6867-68, 6968
    Periodicals, 5732
      Indexes, 4239, 4245, 4247, 4248-52
    Societies, 1830
    War of independence, 4127, 4252
    War with Peru, 3943, 4103
    War with Spain, 4525
  Industries, 2993, 4678
  Instituto Nacional, 2722, 4960
  Intellectual life, 5285, 5304
  Ministerio de Colonización, 4886
  Ministerio de Instrucción Pública, 3255
  Ministerio de Marina, 5544
  Ministerio del Interior
    Archivo, 550
  Navy, 2921
  Observatorio Astronómico Nacional, 3781
  Officials and employees, 1268
  Oficina de Estadística del Trabajo, 7130
  Politics and government, 1753, 4890, 6867-
    68
  R. Audiencia, 544
  Relations (general) with Peru, 4572
  Servicio Sismológico, 3780
  Social conditions, 2970, 7081, 7083
  Superintendencia de Educación
    Centro de Documentación, 5940
  Universidad, 1426, 1762, 1852, 2098, 2101,
    2105, 2993, 3087, 4234-37, 4725
    Biblioteca Central, 5948
    Biblioteca de Parasitología, 5936
    Clínica de Neurología, 5942
    Escuela de Medicina, 2723, 5568, 6433-35
      Biblioteca Central, 5945, 5949, 6435a
    Facultad de Ciencias Jurídicas y Socia-
      les, 2724, 4884a
    Facultad de Filosofía y Educación, 1709,
      3252, 4421, 6572
    Instituto de Ciencias Políticas y Admi-
      nistración, 6619
    Instituto de Economía
      Biblioteca, 6439
    Instituto de Investigaciones Musicales,
      3397
    Instituto de Literatura Chilena, 7156
    Instituto de Organización y Administra-
      ción de Empresas, 4678
    Instituto Pedagógico
      Seminario de Historia, 4252
  Social life and customs, 3509
Chillán, Chile - Biography, 1263
Chiloé, Chile, 326, 546
China poblana, 1532

Chiquito Indians, 505
  Languages, 465
Chiriguano Indians, 3186
Chiriquí, Panamá
  Antiquities, 406
Chocano, José Santos, 1192, 5440
Chocó, Colombia, 3516
Chocolate, 251
Cholera, 5604
  Chile, 4742
Chonos, 3181
Choroto Indians, 3187
Chouaca, 4797
Christian, William Florian, 2960
Christmas, 3382
Chronology, Maya, 383
Chuquisaca, Bolivia, 507, 3890-91
  History, 507
Church, Elihu Dwight, 4961-62
Church and state
  Argentina, 6855, 6875
  Latin America, 6878
  Mexico, 6859
Church history, 6869
  Argentina, 6855
Churches
  Mexico, 419, 6853
Churión, Juan José, 7170
Cibbad y Sobrón, Félix, 4694
Cienfuegos, Cuba, 3270
Cieza de León, Pedro de, 1539
Cincinnati
  Public Library
    Rare Book Department, 2195
Cinematography, 2874
Cipriano de Utrera (Fray), 1540
Círculo Carboneliano, Montevideo, 4963
Círculo Cultural Tolosano, Tolosa, Argentina,
  3200
Círculo de Aeronáutica, Buenos Aires, 5860
Círculo de la Librería, Buenos Aires, 5763
Círculo Militar, Buenos Aires
  Biblioteca Nacional Militar, 2922a-23
Cirute, Juan, 5401
Cisneros, Luis Benjamín, 1209
Cisneros, María Guadalupe, 3401
Cities and towns, 19, 421, 436, 2486a, 3431,
  4164-65
Citizenship
  Latin America, 6592
City planning, 19, 4157a-59, 4165
  Argentina, 4157a
  Colombia, 4174
  Latin America, 4160, 4166
  Panama, 886
Civilization
  American, 315
  Hispanic, 103-05, 112
    Catalogs, 2420
Clagett, Helen L., 4864, 4878, 4887, 4896,
  4900, 4907, 4911, 4913, 4916, 4920
Claremont Colleges, Claremont, California, 61
  Library, 2430
Clark, Marjorie Ruth, 4679

458

Goff, Frederick R., 4981
Goiânia, Brazil
  Gabinete Literaria Goyano, 2628
Goic, Cedomil, 5284
Gold, 3363
Gold mines and mining - Brazil, 2988
Goldberg, Isaac, 5245
Golde, Werner, 6399
Goldsmith, Peter H., 93
Gomes, Celuta Moreira, 2028
Gomes, Feliciano de Azevedo, 2659
Gomes, Hagar Espanha, 293, 5582
Gomes de Brito, José Joaquim, 208
Gómez, Eusebio, 4866
Gómez, Hernán Félix, 6610
Gómez, I., 1315
Gómez, Juan Carlos, 1191
Gómez Canedo, Lino, 103, 425, 678
Gómez Carrillo, José, 1192
Gómez de Avellaneda, Gertrudis, 1659-62, 5360
Gómez de Orozco, Federico, 441, 1087, 1658,
    1889, 3791, 5552, 6754, 6914
Gómez de Vidaurre, Felipe, 1275
Gómez M., E., 6553
Gómez Molleda, D., 3842
Gómez Ramírez, José Joaquín, 688
Gómez Ramos, Virginia, 1690
Gómez Restrepo, Antonio, 1663, 5316, 5318-22,
    5328, 5339-40
Gómez Rodeles, Cecilio, 6643, 6984
Gómez Ugarte, Elena, 1097
Gómez Ugarte, José, 1332
Gómez y Báez, Máximo, 1664
Gonçalves, Alpheu Diniz, 3678, 4385-86
Gondra, Manuel, 782
Gonduana, 3674
Góngora y Argote, Luis de, 5151
Gonzaga, Thomaz Antonio, 1665-66
González, Ariosto Domingo, 1384-85, 1976
González, B.S., 3868
González, Héctor, 1098
González, Joaquín Víctor, 1667-68
González, Jorge Antonio, 7159a
González, Juan Natalicio, 6624
Gonzalez, Juan Vicente, 4325
González, Julio César, 1447
González, Luis Felipe, 3093
Gonzalez, Manuel Pedro, 1452, 1801
González, Pedro, 4040
González, Silvino M., 2924-25, 3792
González Alcorta, Leandro, 1669, 3953
Gonzalez Blanco, Pedro, 4533
Gonzalez Carbalho, José, 5201
González Curquejo, Antonio, 5352
González Dávila, Gil., 1202, 6872
González de Cossío, Francisco, 6761-62
González de la Rosa, Manuel Toribio, 2064, 6164
González de Mendoza, José María, 6500
González de Santa Cruz, Roque, 1670
Gonzalez del Valle, Emilio Martín, 5353
González del Valle y Ramírez, Francisco, 1512,
    1671-71a, 1701, 1843
González Galván, Manuel, 1344
González Guinán, Francisco, 4143
González Iglesias, Manuel, 2777

González Martínez, Enrique, 1332, 1861, 5469
González Obregón, Luis, 30, 1076, 1334-35,
    1543, 1618-20, 1591, 1672, 1949-50, 5039
González Ortega, José, 3588
González Peña, Carlos, 1532, 3588, 5410-11
González Prada, Alfredo, 1673
González Prada, Manuel, 1192, 1672a-73
González R., Mario Alberto, 6736
González Ramírez, Manuel, 4563
González Ruano, César, 5115
González Suárez, Federico, 1303, 1674-75, 6731
González Vigil, Francisco de, 1676
González y González, Luis, 4041
González Zeledón, Manuel, 1676a
Goodwin, Albert, 50
Gordillo, P. N., 7175
Gorham, Rex, 3394
Gornall, Pedro, 4705
Gorokhoff, Cecilia J., 152
Gorostiza, Manuel Eduardo de, 1677
Gorriti, Juana Manuela, 1209
Gotschlich, Bernardo, 1923
Goupil, E. Eugène, 607, 4028, 4974
Goveia, Elsa V., 4151
*Government publications, 868, 2454, 3742-3816
  Argentina, 3751, 3755-57
  Barbados, 206
  Bolivia, 3751
  Brazil, 3751, 3758-78a
  Central America, 3746
  Chihuahua, Mexico, 6750
  Chile, 3751, 3779-81
  Colombia, 3751, 3782-88, 5984
  Costa Rica, 3751
  Cuba, 868, 3746, 3751
  Dominican Republic, 3746, 3751
  Ecuador, 3751
  El Salvador, 3751
  Great Britain, 614, 4155
  Guatemala, 3751, 3789
  Haiti, 3746
  Honduras, 3751, 6748
  Latin America, 934, 3743, 3745, 3750-51,
    6333-34
  Mexico, 3790-3809
  Nicaragua, 3751
  Panama, 886, 3746, 3751, 3810
  Paraguay, 3751
  Peru, 3751, 3811-12, 4914
  United States, 3742, 3744, 3752-54, 7186-91
    Indexes, 4178
  Uruguay, 3751
  Venezuela, 3751, 3813-16
  Vera Cruz, Mexico (State), 3809
Governors - Rio de Janeiro, 518, 521
Govín y Torres, Antonio, 4965
Goya y Lucientes, Francisco José de, 1678
Graham, Robert Cunningham, 1678a
Grain, 2985
Granier, James Albert, 924, 5176-77
Grases, Pedro, 308, 890-92, 948a, 1160, 1463-64,
    1476, 1679-80, 1722, 1977, 2012, 2204, 3338,
    3344, 3636, 4144-46, 4347, 4670, 4715,
    4920a, 5486-87, 6822-25, 6827
Grasses, 284

464

Institut de France, 1414
Institut Franco Brésilien de Haute Culture,
  Rio de Janeiro, 45-6
Institut für Iberoamerika-Kunde, Hamburg, 4846
Institute of International Education, 4061
Institute of Jamaica, Kingston, 6631
  Library, 2806a-c, 3643a-45, 5551a, 6632-33
*Institutions, societies, museums, etc., 4390-
  4438
Instituto Aerotécnico, Córdoba
  División Normas y Documentación, 5778
Instituto Agronômico, Campinas, Brazil, 258-
  60, 5874
Instituto Amigos del Libro Argentino, Buenos
  Aires, 5754
Instituto Archeológico e Geographico Alagoano,
  Maceió, Brazil, 532
Instituto Archeológico e Geographico Pernambu-
  cano, see Instituto Arqueológico e Geográ-
  fico Pernambucano, Recife
Instituto Argentino de Artes Gráficas
  Buenos Aires, 1212
Instituto Argentino del Petroleo, 5830a
Instituto Arqueológico, Histórico e Geográfico
  Pernambucano, Recife, 533-34, 4229
Instituto Bibliográfico Mexicano, Mexico, 435,
  1103, 6098
Instituto Bonaerense de Numismática y Antigüe-
  dades, Buenos Aires, 3202
Instituto Brasileiro de Bibliografía e Documen-
  tação, Rio de Janeiro, 290, 877, 1164,
  2383, 2389, 2629, 2899, 3243, 3903, 4372,
  5562, 5590, 5591-97, 5900, 5915, 5919,
  5935, 6415-16, 7066, 7200
Instituto Brasileiro de Cultura Japonesa, 2630
Instituto Brasileiro de Educação, Ciência e
  Cultura (IBECC), Rio de Janeiro, 5903,
  5914
  Secção de São Paulo, 4506
Instituto Brasileiro de Estudos Afro-Asiáticos,
  Rio de Janeiro, 7072
Instituto Brasileiro de Geografía e Estadística,
  Rio de Janeiro, 5882-83, 5925
Instituto Caro y Cuervo, Bogotá, 916, 1001,
  1563, 3786, 4724a
Instituto Centroamericano de Investigación y
  Tecnología Industrial, Guatemala, 261
Instituto Científico y Literario del Estado,
  San Luis Potosí, 2811
Instituto Colombiano de la Reforma Agraria, Bo-
  gotá, 5979
Instituto Colombiano de Petróleos, 3701
Instituto Cristóforo Colombo, 3015
Instituto Cultural Argentino-Norteamericano,
  Buenos Aires, 3630
Instituto Cultural Argentino-Uruguayo, Buenos
  Aires, 3203
Instituto Cultural Colombo Británico, Medellín,
  2766
Instituto Cultural Venezolano-Británico, Cara-
  cas, 3345-46
Instituto da Ordem dos Advogados Brasileiros,
  3239, 3245
Instituto de Anatomía Normal, Montevideo
  Biblioteca, 6541

Instituto de Anatomía Patológica y Parasito-
  lógica, Montevideo
  Biblioteca, 6541
Instituto de Asuntos Nucleares, Bogotá
  Biblioteca, 5966
Instituto de Bacteriología, Montevideo
  Biblioteca, 6541
Instituto de Belas Artes do Rio Grande do
  Sul, Pôrto Alegre, 2631, 5899
Instituto de Biología, Mexico, 4411
Instituto de Clínica Pediátrica e Higiene
  Infantil Dr. Luis Morquio, Montevideo,
  6541
Instituto de Cultura Italo-Peruano, Lima,
  3305
Instituto de Derecho Comparado Hispano-
  Portugués-Americano, 2972
Instituto de Direito Social, São Paulo,
  5887
Instituto de Educación Política, San José,
  C.R., 6594
Instituto de Endocrinología, Montevideo
  Biblioteca, 6541
Instituto de Estadística, Montevideo
  Biblioteca, 6541
Instituto de Estudos Genealógicos, São Paulo,
  5926
Instituto de Fisiología, Montevideo
  Biblioteca, 6541
Instituto de Fomento Algodonero (IFA), Bogotá,
  5967
Instituto de Higiene, Montevideo
  Biblioteca, 6541
Instituto de Industria Animal, Montevideo
  Biblioteca, 6541
Instituto de Ingenieros de Chile, 4242
Instituto de Intercambio Cultural Argentino-
  Norteamericano, Córdoba, 5043a
Instituto de Investigaciones Veterinarias,
  Caracas, 7195
Instituto de las Españas en los Estados Unidos,
  see Hispanic Institute in the United
  States, New York
Instituto de Matemáticas y Estadística, Monte-
  video
  Biblioteca, 6541
Instituto de Nutrición de Centro América y
  Panamá, Guatemala, 6494-95
Instituto de Teoría y Política Económicas,
  Montevideo, 4320, 6541
Instituto de Tisiología, Montevideo, 6541
Instituto de Zootécnia, Montevideo
  Biblioteca, 6541
Instituto del Cemento Portland Argentino, Bue-
  nos Aires
  Biblioteca, 2516-18
Instituto do Ceará, Fortaleza, Brazil, 4228,
  5930
Instituto dos Bachareis em Lettras
  Bibliotheca, 2582
Instituto Etnológico del Magdalena, Santa Mar-
  ta, Colombia, 3165
Instituto Geofísico de los Andes Colombianos,
  3699-700

466

Inter-American Indian Institute, 351, 629,
4177, 4299, 4487-88, 4789
Inter-American Institute of Agricultural
Sciences, Turrialba, Costa Rica, 235, 245,
254, 265-68, 279, 284, 871, 1173-74, 1178,
3127-28, 5046-47, 5084, 6023-24, 6286,
7044
Library, 252-253, 270-71, 6472
Inter-American Institute of International
Legal Studies, Washington, D.C., 4838
Inter-American Seminar on Elementary Education,
Montevideo, 3047
Inter-American Seminar on Vocational Education,
College Park, Md., (1952), 3045-46
Inter-American Statistical Institute, 4489,
6194, 7118-21
Inter-American system, 4185, 4484, 4514-15,
4519, 4521-22
Inter-American Treaty of Reciprocal Assistance,
4464
International American History Congress, Buenos
Aires, 1769
International and Inter-American agencies
Publications about, 2758, 4501-22, 6270
Publications of, 4485-4500
International Bank for Reconstruction and De-
velopment, 2757, 6192-93
International Bureau of Education, Geneva, 3064
International Bureau of the American Republics,
Washington, D.C., 3483, 3498, 3508, 3532,
3605, 4121, 6279
International business enterprises, 3354
International Commission of Jurists, Rio de Ja-
neiro, 1927, 4828
International Committee for Social Science Docu-
mentation, 2939, 6338
International Congress of Americanists, 34, 189,
355a, 386, 6323
Proceedings
Indexes, 4177-77a
International Congress of Medical Librarianship,
Washington, D.C., (1963), 6563
International cooperation, 2953-54, 4444, 4457,
4521-22
International Economic Association, 2939
International Federation for Documentation
Commission for Latin America, 6280
International Federation for Housing and
Planning, Mexico, 1938, 5552
International Geographical Union
Special Commission on the Humid Tropics, 3425
International Geological Congress, 3656
International Labour Office, 4839, 6359
International Monetary Fund, 6192-93
*International relations, 2608, 4439-4574
Argentina, 4530-31
Bolivia, 4532-35
Brazil, 4536-38
Chile, 4539
Colombia, 4540-43
Cuba, 4544-45
Dominican Republic, 4546-49
Ecuador, 4550-51

International relations
Guatemala, 4552-53
Haiti, 4554-56
Honduras, 4557
Mexico, 4558-69
Panama, 4570-71
Peru, 4572-74
International Social Economy Congress, Buenos
Aires, (1924), 7087
International trusteeships, 4480
International Union of American Republics, see
Pan American Union
Intervention, 4514, 4451
Investments
Foreign, 3354
Colombia, 3366
Latin America, 3352-53
Mexico, 3368
United States, 3360, 4449
Iowa - University, 2089
Iriarte, Felipe Antonio de, 3888
Iribarren, Alfredo A., 490b
Irigoyen, Ulises, 3588
Irisarri, Antonio José de, 1727-31, 4612
Iron industry and trade - Brazil, 3689
Iron mines and mining - Brazil, 4385-86
Iron ores, 3689
Irrigation - Mexico, 6082
Irvine, Marie Hunter, 767
Isaacs, Jorge, 1209, 1732
Isaza, Emiliano, 5323
Isla de Pinos, 3526, 3533, 3537
Isola, Mario, 354
Ispizúa, Segundo de, 4124
Itaguahi, Brazil
Biblioteca Municipal, 2634
Italians in Argentina, 4531, 4703
Italy, 3305
Commerce - Venezuela, 3020
Iturbide, Agustín de, 1733
Itza Indians, 4051
Izaguirre Ispizúa, Bernardino, 6953
Izikowitz, Karl Gustav, 3183
Izquierdo, José Joaquín, 5621

Jackson, James, 901
Jackson, William Vernon, 3475, 5043a
Jacob, Ernest Gerhard, 112
Jacobsen, Jerome Vincent, 6988
Jacquet, Constant H. 113
Jaén, Ana María, 886
Jahn, Alfredo, 1926, 3738
Jalapa, Mexico
Universidad Veracruzana
Instituto de Antropología, 389
Jalisco, México, 1122-22a, 1339
Biography, 1339, 5073
Constitution, 4909
History, 6962
Jamaica, 817, 2409, 2806a-c, 3643a-46
Library Service, 3646
James, C. Noel, 252-53, 265-67, 271, 279, 871,
5084, 6286

468

472

478

482

Montevideo, 6812, 6814, 6816-17
  History, 4138
  Instituto de Estudios Superiores, 6223
  Intendencia Municipal
    Sección Biblioteca, 139
  Museo Nacional, 5511
  Museo y Biblioteca Pedagógicos, 6208, 6222,
    6228
Montiel Ballesteros, Adolfo, 5469
Montignani, John Brommer, 2427
Montoro y Valdés, Rafael, 1870, 5360
Montt, Luis, 994, 1507, 2024, 4935
Montt, Pedro, 4960
Montt, Sara del Campo, Viuda de, 4960
Moore, David Richard, 3997
Moore, Ernest Richard, 1271, 1345, 1439, 1453,
    1578, 1644, 1987-88, 5419
Mora, José Antonio, 1854
Moraes, Alexandre José de Mello, filho, 1253,
    5249
Moraes, E. Vilhena de, 509
Moraes, Manuel de, 1260
Moraes, Rubens Borba de, 2216, 3480
Morais, Adelaide Vieira da, 4388
Moral, Bonifacio, 6171, 6919
Morales, Ignacio, 4648
Morales Cabrera, Pablo, 350
Morales Ferrer, Abelardo, 1145
Morales Guiñazú, Fernando, 496
Morales Hernandez, Florentino, 3270
Morales Padrón, Francisco, 696, 3843, 4176
Morales y Morales, Vidal, 574, 4973
Moreira, Júio Estrella, 982-83
Morel-Fatio, Alfred, 604
Morelia, Mexico, 6753, 6757-58
Morelos V., Octavio, 4360a
Morelos, México, 1084
Moreno, Francisco Pascasio, 1871, 6650
Moreno, José Fernandes, 4988
Moreno, José María, 1230
Moreno, Juan, 476
Moreno, Laudelino, 4455
Moreno, Mariano, 1872
Moreno Fraginals, Manuel, 599
Moreno Mattos, Armando, 7131-32
Moreno Quintana, Lucio Manuel, 4514
Moreno Toscano, Alejandra, 2057
Morey Otero, Sebastián, 2861
Morgan, Katherine Leonore, 6288-89
Mori, Mario, 3015
Moríñigo, Marcos A., 4753
Morley, Sylvanus Griswold, 383
Morphology, 351
Morquio, Luis, 1873, 6541
Morrison, Hugh Alexander, 7183
Mortheiru Salgado, Pedro, 2019
Mosaics, 402
Moscow
  Akademiia Nauk SSSR., 140-42
  Usesoiuznaia Gosudar-Stvennaia
    Biblioteka Inostrannoi Literatury, 5189
Moses, Bernard, 5461
Mosquera, Manuel José, 3263
Mosquito Coast, Nicaragua, 3600
Mosquito Indians, 3157

Mosquitoes - Extermination, 1626
Mossoró, Rio Grande do Sul
  Biblioteca Pública Municipal e Museu Munici-
    pal, 5879
Mostajo, Francisco, 1361
Motolinia, Toribio, 1874
Motta, Arthur, 5250-51
Mountaineering, 7115-16
Moura, Valdiki, 7075
Movimiento Nacional Gustavo Volpe, Montevideo,
    7092
Moxo Indians, 505
Moya, Salvador de, 3416a-18
Moya de Perera, Ana M., 3047
Moyssen Echeverría, Xavier, 1344
Mozans, H.J., see Zahm, John Augustine
Mueller, Wolf, 255
Mugglestone, Ethel Annie, 143
Mughisuddin, Margaret B., 3958
Mugridge, Donald Henry, 1550
Muir, John M., 3720
Müller, Elsa, 7105
Muller, Frederik, 2271-73, 3434, 3836-37
Müller, Lauro Severiano, 1874a
Munden, Kenneth, 770-72
Mundy, E. Evangeline, 1594
Muñecas, Ildefonso de las, 1239
Municipal cooperations, 4859, 6847
Municipal government, 436, 6838, 7067
  Brazil, 3764
  Latin America, 433-34
  Peru, 6847
Municipal ownership - Argentina, 6845
Muniz, Antônio Ferrão, 2562
Muñoz, Bonifacio, 2346, 2793
Muñoz, Juan Bautista, 1875
Muñoz, Lázaro Manuel, 4640
Muñoz, Leonardo J., 1043
Muñoz Cabrera, José Ramón, 1239, 3888
Muñoz-Ledo y Mena, Manuel, 6783
Muñoz Lumbier, Manuel, 3721
Muñoz Marín, Luis, 1369
Muñoz Moreno, Rafael, 4989
Muñoz Olave, Reinaldo, 7016
Muñoz Reyes, Jorge, 3671
Muñoz Sañudo, Lisardo, 1297
Muñoza Maluschka, Dora, 5507
Munro, Dana Gardner, 6597
Mural painting and decoration, 1329
Muratori, Ludovico Antonio, 1875a
Muratti, Natalio, 6845
Muricy, José Candido de Andrade, 5252
Murillo, Pedro Domingo, 1239
Muro Arias, Luis Felipe, 665
Muro Orejón, Antonio, 1875
Murphey, Elizabeth, 2987
Murphy, Robert Cushman, 7208
Murray, John Lovell, 6881
Murúa, Martín de, 1188
Museo del Atlántico, Barranquilla, 6014
Museo Social Argentino, Buenos Aires, 4205,
    5798
Museo Social Argentino, Buenos Aires
  Centro de Estudios Bibliotecológicos, 5822

484

Neiva, Arthur, 2390
Nelson, Edward W., 7023
Nelson, Ernesto, 3630
Nelson, Jean Thomas, 6888
Nelson, Linda, 7044
Nemésio, Jorge, 1921
Nemirovsky, Lázaro, 288
Neruda, Pablo, 1882-83
Nerval, Gastón, pseud., see Diez de Medina,
    Raúl
Nervo, Amado, 1884-85, 3588, 5400
Nervous system, 5627, 5632
Nery, Fernando, 1465
Nery, Sant'Anna, 3910
Netherlands
    Algemeen Rijksarchief, 819
    Colonies, 3649a-b
        Brazil, 3907
Netherlands Information Bureau, 3643
Netscher, Pieter Marinus, 3907
Neves, Abdias, 4603
Neves, Alvaro, 208
New England Institute of Inter-American
        Affairs, Boston, 147
New Jersey
    State College, Trenton
        Library, 148
New Mexico
    Antiquities, 359-60
    History, 786, 1899, 6962
    Historical Society, 3980
    University, 3378
New Orleans, 6653
New World studies, 707
New York
    Missionary Research Library, 113
    Museum of the American Indian
        Heye Foundation, 384, 399-403, 4069,
            4397-98
        Public Library, 20, 149-50, 847, 2429, 3394,
            3582, 4034, 6290, 7139, 7177
New York (State) - History, 3836-37
Newberger, Otto, 3751
Newberry Library, Chicago
    Edward E. Ayer Collection, 753, 2428
Newspapers, 6264, 6266, 6305-06, 6367a
    EERICA? ''[(
    Argentina, 4581, 4787-89, 4591, 6349-50,
        6354, 6377, 6381, 6395-96, 6686-87
    Bahia, 6425
    Bolivia, 4593, 6400
    Brazil, 1927, 6401, 6404a, 6408
    Caracas, 6557
    Carora, Venezuela, 6833a
    Ceará, Brazil, 6419, 6424a-c
    Chile, 4611-15, 4619, 6429-32
    Cienfuegos, Cuba, 6473
    Colombia, 6452, 6466
    Corrientes (Prov.) Arg., 6376, 6378
    Costa Rica, 3092
    Cuba, 1804, 4620, 4622, 6473, 6477-83, 6485
        Indexes, 4270
    Dominican Republic, 6729, 6487
    Ecuador, 6489, 6730
    El Salvador, 4635a

Newspapers
    German
        Brazil, 6414
    Haiti, 6496
    Havana, 4621
    Ibarra, Ecuador, 6492
    Latin America, 2143, 3284, 4579, 6269a, 6277,
        6278a, 6279, 6294, 6302-03, 6324-27, 6350
        Union lists, 6273
    Loja, Ecuador, 4631
    Medellín, Col., 6470
    Mendoza, Argentina, 4211
    Mexico, 4638, 4640, 4643-54, 6498, 6509-14,
        6518
        Indexes, 4302-03
    Middle America, 868
    Montevideo, 6552
    Paraná, 6418
    Pernambuco, 6407, 6420
    Peru, 3306, 4657, 6345, 6524-25
    Puerto Rico, 4659
    Rio de Janeiro, 4596
    Rio Grande do Sul, 4606
    Sancti Spiritus, Cuba, 4623
    São Paulo (State), 4608-09
    Spain, 6324-27
    Táchira, Venezuela, 6819
    Union lists, 6421
    U.S., 3949
    Uruguay, 2859, 4664, 4668, 6527-28
        Indexes, 4322
    Venezuela, 4671, 6559, 6819
        Indexes, 4338
    Yucatan, 6506
    Zacatecas, Mexico, 6500
Newton, Helen K., 271c
Neyra, Joaquín, 6673
Nicaragua, 1124, 3498, 3599, 3601, 7191
    Antiquities, 361
    Archivo Nacional, 655
    Archivo Histórico, 654
    Biblioteca Nacional, 2833-34
    Boundaries
        Honduras, 4557
    Description and travel, 3602
    Economic conditions, 3601
    Emigration and immigration, 3601
    Foreign relations
        United States, 3373
    History, 598, 654
    Universidad Nacional
        Biblioteca Central, 6142
Nicaragua Canal, 3601, 7186-90
Nichols, Madeline Wallis, 3048, 3448, 4181,
    4722, 5138-40, 6575, 7045
Nickles, John Milton, 3659
Nico Perez, Uruguay, see José Batlle y Ordó-
    ñez, Uruguay
Nieremberg, Juan Eusebio, 6993
Nieto Caballero, Luis Eduardo, 1009-11
Nieto del Río, Félix, 4613
Nitrates - Chile, 4383
Nodar, Carlos Enrique, 6655
Noé, Julio, 5141
Nogueira Abella, Marta, 6439, 6541

490

494

500

Uruguay
  Universidad
    Facultad de Humanidades y Ciencias
      Biblioteca, 1810, 2088, 6215, 6541
    Facultad de Ingeniería y Agrimensura,
      3145
    Facultad de Ingeniería y Ramos Anexos,
      2875
      Biblioteca, 6541
      Instituto de Electrotécnica, 2876
    Facultad de Medicina, 3113, 3334, 5634
      Biblioteca, 6216
      Departamento de Biología
        Biblioteca, 6541
    Facultad de Odontología
      Biblioteca, 6217, 6541
    Facultad de Química y Farmacia
      Biblioteca, 6229
    Facultad de Veterinaria, 6541
      Biblioteca, 6218
    Instituto de Investigaciones Históricas,
      2223, 4322, 6528
    Instituto de Teoría y Política Económicas,
      3019
Urzua Valenzuela, Germán, 6619
Usigli, Rodolfo, 7164, 7167
Uslar Pietri, Arturo, 5494
Utrecht
  Rijksuniversiteit
    Bibliotheek, 116a, 229-30
    Spaans, Portugees en Iber-Amerikaans Ins-
      tituut, 231
Uxmal, Yucatán, 400
Uzielli, Gustavo, 2064

Vaamonde, Marietta, 4333
Vaca Guzmán, Santiago, 5225
Vail, Robert William G., 201-01a
Vaillant, George Clapp, 345, 365, 382
Vaïsse, Emilio, 912, 998, 1478
Val, Waldir Ribeiro de, 5228
Valades, José C., 1089, 1406, 6115
Valcárcel, Luis Eduardo, 1142
Valcárcel Esparza, Carlos Daniel, 669, 771,
  2069
Valderrama, Lucila, 670
Valdés, Gabriel de la Concepción, 2070
Valdés Acosta, José María, 4074
Valdés Domínguez, Eusebio, 1035
Valdivia, Luis de, 4744, 4746, 4775
Valdivia, Pedro de, 2071
Valdivia, Chile, 546
Valdizán, Hermilio, 5631
Valencia M., Lucía, 3125-25a
Valentín, Juan, 4213-14
Valenzuela, Gilberto, 1059-62, 6745
Valenzuela, M., 1280
Valenzuela, Pedro Armengol, 6904
Valenzuela Reyna, Gilberto, 1063-65
Valenzuela y Guzmán, Eduardo, 4234
Valera, Blas, 4109
Valladares, José, 831-33
Valladolid - Colegio de Agustinos, 6921
Valle, Adrián del, 4282
Valle, Arnaldo del, 4318

Valle, José Cecilio del, 2072
Valle, Rafael Heliodoro, 320, 868, 885, 997,
  1073, 1116-20, 1217, 1299, 1398, 1411,
  1494, 1537, 1557, 1610-11, 1496, 1733,
  1749, 1854, 1861, 1904, 2041-42, 2072,
  3387, 3561, 3593-94, 3850, 3935, 4075,
  4580, 4636, 5626, 6076, 6665, 6754, 7004
Valle Arizpe, Artemio de, 1332
Valle Goicochea, Luis, 1468a
El Valle, Colombia, 6713
Vallejo, Antonio R., 4557
Vallejo, César, 2073
Vallejo, Mariano Guadalupe, 3928
Valles, Roberto, 1770-72
Valparaíso, Chile
  Escuela de Derecho
    Biblioteca, 2729
  History, 553
  Municipalidad, 552-53
Valtón, Emilio, 6754, 6795-96
Valverde, Vicente de, 1188
Valverde Tellez, Emeterio, 6582-85, 6905
Valverde y Maruri, Antonio L., 1440, 4401
Van Deusen, Richard James, 3655
Van Patten, Nathan, 5581
Vance, John Thomas, 4854-55, 4907
Vanossi, Reinaldo, 6394
Varas Velásquez, Miguel, 3943, 4943
Varela, Héctor F., 1191
Varela, J. A., 1376
Vargas, José María, 603
Vargas Gómez, Eudoro, 3454
Vargas Lugo, Elisa, 1344
Vargas Salas, José E., 1398
Vargas Ugarte, Rubén, 439-40, 507, 1143,
  2074, 2109, 4116-18, 7005-06
Vargasia, Caracas
  Indexes, 4331
Varnhagen, Francisco Adolpho de, 614a, 2075-78,
  3460, 4946
Varona, Enrique José, 2080-84, 2161
Vasconcelos, José, 1332, 2085, 3588
Vascones, Francisco, 5398
Vásquez de Coronado, Francisco, 4131
Vatican - Biblioteca Vaticana, 1183
Vaughan, Thomas Wayland, 3710
Vaz, Zeferino, 5603
Vaz Ferreira, Carlos, 2087-88
Vázquez, Francisco, 6965
Vázquez, Honorato, 2086
Vázquez, S., 1376
Vázquez Segreda, Carlos, 2123
Vega, Carlos, 5695
Vega, Crisóforo, 1894, 3595, 4411, 5624
Vega, Garcilaso de la (El Inca), 5440
Vega, Miguel E., 4853
Vega Carpio, Lope Félix de, 1198, 2089
Vega E., M., 3511
Vega Febres-Cordero, Cecilia, 6469
Vegalara, Humberto, 2996
Vegetables, 276-279
Veiga, José Pedro Xavier da, 6700-01
Vela, David, 922, 4553, 6746
Vela, Juan B., 1303
Vela V., Vicente, 695